T0214924

Lecture Notes in Computer Science　8694

Commenced Publication in 1973
Founding and Former Series Editors:
Gerhard Goos, Juris Hartmanis, and Jan van Leeuwen

David Fleet   Tomas Pajdla   Bernt Schiele
Tinne Tuytelaars (Eds.)

Computer Vision – ECCV 2014

13th European Conference
Zurich, Switzerland, September 6-12, 2014
Proceedings, Part VI

 Springer

Volume Editors

David Fleet
University of Toronto, Department of Computer Science
6 King's College Road, Toronto, ON M5H 3S5, Canada
E-mail: fleet@cs.toronto.edu

Tomas Pajdla
Czech Technical University in Prague, Department of Cybernetics
Technicka 2, 166 27 Prague 6, Czech Republic
E-mail: pajdla@cmp.felk.cvut.cz

Bernt Schiele
Max-Planck-Institut für Informatik
Campus E1 4, 66123 Saarbrücken, Germany
E-mail: schiele@mpi-inf.mpg.de

Tinne Tuytelaars
KU Leuven, ESAT - PSI, iMinds
Kasteelpark Arenberg 10, Bus 2441, 3001 Leuven, Belgium
E-mail: tinne.tuytelaars@esat.kuleuven.be

Videos to this book can be accessed at
http://www.springerimages.com/videos/978-3-319-10598-7

ISSN 0302-9743   e-ISSN 1611-3349
ISBN 978-3-319-10598-7   e-ISBN 978-3-319-10599-4
DOI 10.1007/978-3-319-10599-4
Springer Cham Heidelberg New York Dordrecht London

Library of Congress Control Number: 2014946360

LNCS Sublibrary: SL 6 – Image Processing, Computer Vision, Pattern Recognition, and Graphics

Typesetting: Camera-ready by author, data conversion by Scientific Publishing Services, Chennai, India

Printed on acid-free paper

Springer is part of Springer Science+Business Media (www.springer.com)

Foreword

The European Conference on Computer Vision is one of the top conferences in computer vision. It was first held in 1990 in Antibes (France) with subsequent conferences in Santa Margherita Ligure (Italy) in 1992, Stockholm (Sweden) in 1994, Cambridge (UK) in 1996, Freiburg (Germany) in 1998, Dublin (Ireland) in 2000, Copenhagen (Denmark) in 2002, Prague (Czech Republic) in 2004, Graz (Austria) in 2006, Marseille (France) in 2008, Heraklion (Greece) in 2010, and Florence (Italy) in 2012. Many people have worked hard to turn the 2014 edition into as great a success. We hope you will find this a mission accomplished.

The chairs decided to adhere to the classic single-track scheme. In terms of the time ordering, we decided to largely follow the Florence example (typically starting with poster sessions, followed by oral sessions), which offers a lot of flexibility to network and is more forgiving for the not-so-early-birds and hard-core gourmets.

A large conference like ECCV requires the help of many. They made sure there was a full program including the main conference, tutorials, workshops, exhibits, demos, proceedings, video streaming/archive, and Web descriptions. We want to cordially thank all those volunteers! Please have a look at the conference website to see their names (http://eccv2014.org/people/). We also thank our generous sponsors. Their support was vital for keeping prices low and enriching the program. And it is good to see such a level of industrial interest in what our community is doing!

We hope you will enjoy the proceedings ECCV 2014.

Also, willkommen in Zürich!

September 2014

Marc Pollefeys
Luc Van Gool
General Chairs

Preface

Welcome to the proceedings of the 2014 European Conference on Computer Vision (ECCV 2014) that was in Zurich, Switzerland. We are delighted to present this volume reflecting a strong and exciting program, the result of an extensive review process. In total, we received 1,444 paper submissions. Of these, 85 violated the ECCV submission guidelines and were rejected without review. Of the remainder, 363 were accepted (26,7%): 325 as posters (23,9%) and 38 as oral presentations (2,8%). This selection process was a combined effort of four program co-chairs (PCs), 53 area chairs (ACs), 803 Program Committee members and 247 additional reviewers.

As PCs we were primarily responsible for the design and execution of the review process. Beyond administrative rejections, we were not directly involved in acceptance decisions. Because the general co-chairs were permitted to submit papers, they played no role in the review process and were treated as any other author.

Acceptance decisions were made by the AC Committee. There were 53 ACs in total, selected by the PCs to provide sufficient technical expertise, geographical diversity (21 from Europe, 7 from Asia, and 25 from North America) and a mix of AC experience (7 had no previous AC experience, 18 had served as AC of a major international vision conference once since 2010, 8 had served twice, 13 had served three times, and 7 had served 4 times).

ACs were aided by 803 Program Committee members to whom papers were assigned for reviewing. There were 247 additional reviewers, each supervised by a Program Committee member. The Program Committee was based on suggestions from ACs, and committees from previous conferences. Google Scholar profiles were collected for all candidate Program Committee members and vetted by PCs. Having a large pool of Program Committee members for reviewing allowed us to match expertise while bounding reviewer loads. No more than nine papers were assigned to any one Program Committee member, with a maximum of six to graduate students.

The ECCV 2014 review process was double blind. Authors did not know the reviewers' identities, nor the ACs handling their paper(s). We did our utmost to ensure that ACs and reviewers did not know authors' identities, even though anonymity becomes difficult to maintain as more and more submissions appear concurrently on arXiv.org.

Particular attention was paid to minimizing potential conflicts of interest. Conflicts of interest between ACs, Program Committee members, and papers were based on authorship of ECCV 2014 submissions, on their home institutions, and on previous collaborations. To find institutional conflicts, all authors,

Program Committee members, and ACs were asked to list the Internet domains of their current institutions. To find collaborators, the DBLP (www.dblp.org) database was used to find any co-authored papers in the period 2010–2014.

We initially assigned approximately 100 papers to each AC, based on affinity scores from the Toronto Paper Matching System and authors' AC suggestions. ACs then bid on these, indicating their level of expertise. Based on these bids, and conflicts of interest, approximately 27 papers were assigned to each AC, for which they would act as the primary AC. The primary AC then suggested seven reviewers from the pool of Program Committee members (in rank order) for each paper, from which three were chosen per paper, taking load balancing and conflicts of interest into account.

Many papers were also assigned a secondary AC, either directly by the PCs, or as a consequence of the primary AC requesting the aid of an AC with complementary expertise. Secondary ACs could be assigned at any stage in the process, but in most cases this occurred about two weeks before the final AC meeting. Hence, in addition to their initial load of approximately 27 papers, each AC was asked to handle three to five more papers as a secondary AC; they were expected to read and write a short assessment of such papers. In addition, two of the 53 ACs were not directly assigned papers. Rather, they were available throughout the process to aid other ACs at any stage (e.g., with decisions, evaluating technical issues, additional reviews, etc.).

The initial reviewing period was three weeks long, after which reviewers provided reviews with preliminary recommendations. Three weeks is somewhat shorter than normal, but this did not seem to cause any unusual problems. With the generous help of several last-minute reviewers, each paper received three reviews.

Authors were then given the opportunity to rebut the reviews, primarily to identify any factual errors. Following this, reviewers and ACs discussed papers at length, after which reviewers finalized their reviews and gave a final recommendation to the ACs. Many ACs requested help from secondary ACs at this time.

Papers, for which rejection was clear and certain, based on the reviews and the AC's assessment, were identified by their primary ACs and vetted by a shadow AC prior to rejection. (These shadow ACs were assigned by the PCs.) All papers with any chance of acceptance were further discussed at the AC meeting. Those deemed "strong" by primary ACs (about 140 in total) were also assigned a secondary AC.

The AC meeting, with all but two of the primary ACs present, took place in Zurich. ACs were divided into 17 triplets for each morning, and a different set of triplets for each afternoon. Given the content of the three (or more) reviews along with reviewer recommendations, rebuttals, online discussions among reviewers and primary ACs, written input from and discussions with secondary ACs, the

AC triplets then worked together to resolve questions, calibrate assessments, and make acceptance decisions.

To select oral presentations, all strong papers, along with any others put forward by triplets (about 155 in total), were then discussed in four panels, each comprising four or five triplets. Each panel ranked these oral candidates, using four categories. Papers in the two top categories provided the final set of 38 oral presentations.

We want to thank everyone involved in making the ECCV 2014 Program possible. First and foremost, the success of ECCV 2014 depended on the quality of papers submitted by authors, and on the very hard work of the reviewers, the Program Committee members and the ACs. We are particularly grateful to Kyros Kutulakos for his enormous software support before and during the AC meeting, to Laurent Charlin for the use of the Toronto Paper Matching System, and Chaohui Wang for help optimizing the assignment of papers to ACs. We also owe a debt of gratitude for the great support of Zurich local organizers, especially Susanne Keller and her team.

September 2014

David Fleet
Tomas Pajdla
Bernt Schiele
Tinne Tuytelaars

Organization

General Chairs

Luc Van Gool	ETH Zurich, Switzerland
Marc Pollefeys	ETH Zurich, Switzerland

Program Chairs

Tinne Tuytelaars	KU Leuven, Belgium
Bernt Schiele	MPI Informatics, Saarbrücken, Germany
Tomas Pajdla	CTU Prague, Czech Republic
David Fleet	University of Toronto, Canada

Local Arrangements Chairs

Konrad Schindler	ETH Zurich, Switzerland
Vittorio Ferrari	University of Edinburgh, UK

Workshop Chairs

Lourdes Agapito	University College London, UK
Carsten Rother	TU Dresden, Germany
Michael Bronstein	University of Lugano, Switzerland

Tutorial Chairs

Bastian Leibe	RWTH Aachen, Germany
Paolo Favaro	University of Bern, Switzerland
Christoph Lampert	IST Austria

Poster Chair

Helmut Grabner	ETH Zurich, Switzerland

Publication Chairs

Mario Fritz	MPI Informatics, Saarbrücken, Germany
Michael Stark	MPI Informatics, Saarbrücken, Germany

Demo Chairs

Davide Scaramuzza   University of Zurich, Switzerland
Jan-Michael Frahm   University of North Carolina at Chapel Hill,
                                    USA

Exhibition Chair

Tamar Tolcachier   University of Zurich, Switzerland

Industrial Liaison Chairs

Alexander Sorkine-Hornung   Disney Research Zurich, Switzerland
Fatih Porikli   ANU, Australia

Student Grant Chair

Seon Joo Kim   Yonsei University, Korea

Air Shelters Accommodation Chair

Maros Blaha   ETH Zurich, Switzerland

Website Chairs

Lorenz Meier   ETH Zurich, Switzerland
Bastien Jacquet   ETH Zurich, Switzerland

Internet Chair

Thorsten Steenbock   ETH Zurich, Switzerland

Student Volunteer Chairs

Andrea Cohen   ETH Zurich, Switzerland
Ralf Dragon   ETH Zurich, Switzerland
Laura Leal-Taixé   ETH Zurich, Switzerland

Finance Chair

Amael Delaunoy   ETH Zurich, Switzerland

Conference Coordinator

Susanne H. Keller   ETH Zurich, Switzerland

Area Chairs

Lourdes Agapito	University College London, UK
Sameer Agarwal	Google Research, USA
Shai Avidan	Tel Aviv University, Israel
Alex Berg	UNC Chapel Hill, USA
Yuri Boykov	University of Western Ontario, Canada
Thomas Brox	University of Freiburg, Germany
Jason Corso	SUNY at Buffalo, USA
Trevor Darrell	UC Berkeley, USA
Fernando de la Torre	Carnegie Mellon University, USA
Frank Dellaert	Georgia Tech, USA
Alexei Efros	UC Berkeley, USA
Vittorio Ferrari	University of Edinburgh, UK
Andrew Fitzgibbon	Microsoft Research, Cambridge, UK
JanMichael Frahm	UNC Chapel Hill, USA
Bill Freeman	Massachusetts Institute of Technology, USA
Peter Gehler	Max Planck Institute for Intelligent Systems, Germany
Kristen Graumann	University of Texas at Austin, USA
Wolfgang Heidrich	University of British Columbia, Canada
Herve Jegou	Inria Rennes, France
Fredrik Kahl	Lund University, Sweden
Kyros Kutulakos	University of Toronto, Canada
Christoph Lampert	IST Austria
Ivan Laptev	Inria Paris, France
Kyuong Mu Lee	Seoul National University, South Korea
Bastian Leibe	RWTH Aachen, Germany
Vincent Lepetit	TU Graz, Austria
Hongdong Li	Australian National University
David Lowe	University of British Columbia, Canada
Greg Mori	Simon Fraser University, Canada
Srinivas Narasimhan	Carnegie Mellon University, PA, USA
Nassir Navab	TU Munich, Germany
Ko Nishino	Drexel University, USA
Maja Pantic	Imperial College London, UK
Patrick Perez	Technicolor Research, Rennes, France
Pietro Perona	California Institute of Technology, USA
Ian Reid	University of Adelaide, Australia
Stefan Roth	TU Darmstadt, Germany
Carsten Rother	TU Dresden, Germany
Sudeep Sarkar	University of South Florida, USA
Silvio Savarese	Stanford University, USA
Christoph Schnoerr	Heidelberg University, Germany
Jamie Shotton	Microsoft Research, Cambridge, UK

Kaleem Siddiqi   McGill, Canada
Leonid Sigal   Disney Research, Pittsburgh, PA, USA
Noah Snavely   Cornell, USA
Raquel Urtasun   University of Toronto, Canada
Andrea Vedaldi   University of Oxford, UK
Jakob Verbeek   Inria Rhone-Alpes, France
Xiaogang Wang   Chinese University of Hong Kong, SAR China
Ming-Hsuan Yang   UC Merced, CA, USA
Lihi Zelnik-Manor   Technion, Israel
Song-Chun Zhu   UCLA, USA
Todd Zickler   Harvard, USA

Program Committee

Gaurav Aggarwal	Joao Barreto	Kristin Branson
Amit Agrawal	Jonathan Barron	Steven Branson
Haizhou Ai	Adrien Bartoli	Francois Bremond
Ijaz Akhter	Arslan Basharat	Michael Bronstein
Karteek Alahari	Dhruv Batra	Gabriel Brostow
Alexandre Alahi	Luis Baumela	Michael Brown
Andrea Albarelli	Maximilian Baust	Matthew Brown
Saad Ali	Jean-Charles Bazin	Marcus Brubaker
Jose M. Alvarez	Loris Bazzani	Andres Bruhn
Juan Andrade-Cetto	Chris Beall	Joan Bruna
Bjoern Andres	Vasileios Belagiannis	Aurelie Bugeau
Mykhaylo Andriluka	Csaba Beleznai	Darius Burschka
Elli Angelopoulou	Moshe Ben-ezra	Ricardo Cabral
Roland Angst	Ohad Ben-Shahar	Jian-Feng Cai
Relja Arandjelovic	Ismail Ben Ayed	Neill D.F. Campbell
Ognjen Arandjelovic	Rodrigo Benenson	Yong Cao
Helder Araujo	Ryad Benosman	Barbara Caputo
Pablo Arbelez	Tamara Berg	Joao Carreira
Vasileios Argyriou	Margrit Betke	Jan Cech
Antonis Argyros	Ross Beveridge	Jinxiang Chai
Kalle Astroem	Bir Bhanu	Ayan Chakrabarti
Vassilis Athitsos	Horst Bischof	Tat-Jen Cham
Yannis Avrithis	Arijit Biswas	Antoni Chan
Yusuf Aytar	Andrew Blake	Manmohan Chandraker
Xiang Bai	Aaron Bobick	Vijay Chandrasekhar
Luca Ballan	Piotr Bojanowski	Hong Chang
Yingze Bao	Ali Borji	Ming-Ching Chang
Richard Baraniuk	Terrance Boult	Rama Chellappa
Adrian Barbu	Lubomir Bourdev	Chao-Yeh Chen
Kobus Barnard	Patrick Bouthemy	David Chen
Connelly Barnes	Edmond Boyer	Hwann-Tzong Chen

Tsuhan Chen
Xilin Chen
Chao Chen
Longbin Chen
Minhua Chen
Anoop Cherian
Liang-Tien Chia
Tat-Jun Chin
Sunghyun Cho
Minsu Cho
Nam Ik Cho
Wongun Choi
Mario Christoudias
Wen-Sheng Chu
Yung-Yu Chuang
Ondrej Chum
James Clark
Brian Clipp
Isaac Cohen
John Collomosse
Bob Collins
Tim Cootes
David Crandall
Antonio Criminisi
Naresh Cuntoor
Qieyun Dai
Jifeng Dai
Kristin Dana
Kostas Daniilidis
Larry Davis
Andrew Davison
Goksel Dedeoglu
Koichiro Deguchi
Alberto Del Bimbo
Alessio Del Bue
Hervé Delingette
Andrew Delong
Stefanie Demirci
David Demirdjian
Jia Deng
Joachim Denzler
Konstantinos Derpanis
Thomas Deselaers
Frederic Devernay
Michel Dhome

Anthony Dick
Ajay Divakaran
Santosh Kumar Divvala
Minh Do
Carl Doersch
Piotr Dollar
Bin Dong
Weisheng Dong
Michael Donoser
Gianfranco Doretto
Matthijs Douze
Bruce Draper
Mark Drew
Bertram Drost
Lixin Duan
Jean-Luc Dugelay
Enrique Dunn
Pinar Duygulu
Jan-Olof Eklundh
James H. Elder
Ian Endres
Olof Enqvist
Markus Enzweiler
Aykut Erdem
Anders Eriksson
Ali Eslami
Irfan Essa
Francisco Estrada
Bin Fan
Quanfu Fan
Jialue Fan
Sean Fanello
Ali Farhadi
Giovanni Farinella
Ryan Farrell
Alireza Fathi
Paolo Favaro
Michael Felsberg
Pedro Felzenszwalb
Rob Fergus
Basura Fernando
Frank Ferrie
Sanja Fidler
Boris Flach
Francois Fleuret

David Fofi
Wolfgang Foerstner
David Forsyth
Katerina Fragkiadaki
Jean-Sebastien Franco
Friedrich Fraundorfer
Mario Fritz
Yun Fu
Pascal Fua
Hironobu Fujiyoshi
Yasutaka Furukawa
Ryo Furukawa
Andrea Fusiello
Fabio Galasso
Juergen Gall
Andrew Gallagher
David Gallup
Arvind Ganesh
Dashan Gao
Shenghua Gao
James Gee
Andreas Geiger
Yakup Genc
Bogdan Georgescu
Guido Gerig
David Geronimo
Theo Gevers
Bernard Ghanem
Andrew Gilbert
Ross Girshick
Martin Godec
Guy Godin
Roland Goecke
Michael Goesele
Alvina Goh
Bastian Goldluecke
Boqing Gong
Yunchao Gong
Raghuraman Gopalan
Albert Gordo
Lena Gorelick
Paulo Gotardo
Stephen Gould
Venu Madhav Govindu
Helmut Grabner

Roger Grosse
Matthias Grundmann
Chunhui Gu
Xianfeng Gu
Jinwei Gu
Sergio Guadarrama
Matthieu Guillaumin
Jean-Yves Guillemaut
Hatice Gunes
Ruiqi Guo
Guodong Guo
Abhinav Gupta
Abner Guzman Rivera
Gregory Hager
Ghassan Hamarneh
Bohyung Han
Tony Han
Jari Hannuksela
Tatsuya Harada
Mehrtash Harandi
Bharath Hariharan
Stefan Harmeling
Tal Hassner
Daniel Hauagge
Søren Hauberg
Michal Havlena
James Hays
Kaiming He
Xuming He
Martial Hebert
Felix Heide
Jared Heinly
Hagit Hel-Or
Lionel Heng
Philipp Hennig
Carlos Hernandez
Aaron Hertzmann
Adrian Hilton
David Hogg
Derek Hoiem
Byung-Woo Hong
Anthony Hoogs
Joachim Hornegger
Timothy Hospedales
Wenze Hu

Zhe Hu
Gang Hua
Xian-Sheng Hua
Dong Huang
Gary Huang
Heng Huang
Sung Ju Hwang
Wonjun Hwang
Ivo Ihrke
Nazli Ikizler-Cinbis
Slobodan Ilic
Horace Ip
Michal Irani
Hiroshi Ishikawa
Laurent Itti
Nathan Jacobs
Max Jaderberg
Omar Javed
C.V. Jawahar
Bruno Jedynak
Hueihan Jhuang
Qiang Ji
Hui Ji
Kui Jia
Yangqing Jia
Jiaya Jia
Hao Jiang
Zhuolin Jiang
Sam Johnson
Neel Joshi
Armand Joulin
Frederic Jurie
Ioannis Kakadiaris
Zdenek Kalal
Amit Kale
Joni-Kristian
    Kamarainen
George Kamberov
Kenichi Kanatani
Sing Bing Kang
Vadim Kantorov
Jörg Hendrik Kappes
Leonid Karlinsky
Zoltan Kato
Hiroshi Kawasaki

Verena Kaynig
Cem Keskin
Margret Keuper
Daniel Keysers
Sameh Khamis
Fahad Khan
Saad Khan
Aditya Khosla
Martin Kiefel
Gunhee Kim
Jaechul Kim
Seon Joo Kim
Tae-Kyun Kim
Byungsoo Kim
Benjamin Kimia
Kris Kitani
Hedvig Kjellstrom
Laurent Kneip
Reinhard Koch
Kevin Koeser
Ullrich Koethe
Effrosyni Kokiopoulou
Iasonas Kokkinos
Kalin Kolev
Vladimir Kolmogorov
Vladlen Koltun
Nikos Komodakis
Piotr Koniusz
Peter Kontschieder
Ender Konukoglu
Sanjeev Koppal
Hema Koppula
Andreas Koschan
Jana Kosecka
Adriana Kovashka
Adarsh Kowdle
Josip Krapac
Dilip Krishnan
Zuzana Kukelova
Brian Kulis
Neeraj Kumar
M. Pawan Kumar
Cheng-Hao Kuo
In So Kweon
Junghyun Kwon

Junseok Kwon
Simon Lacoste-Julien
Shang-Hong Lai
Jean-François Lalonde
Tian Lan
Michael Langer
Doug Lanman
Diane Larlus
Longin Jan Latecki
Svetlana Lazebnik
Laura Leal-Taixé
Erik Learned-Miller
Honglak Lee
Yong Jae Lee
Ido Leichter
Victor Lempitsky
Frank Lenzen
Marius Leordeanu
Thomas Leung
Maxime Lhuillier
Chunming Li
Fei-Fei Li
Fuxin Li
Rui Li
Li-Jia Li
Chia-Kai Liang
Shengcai Liao
Joerg Liebelt
Jongwoo Lim
Joseph Lim
Ruei-Sung Lin
Yen-Yu Lin
Zhouchen Lin
Liang Lin
Haibin Ling
James Little
Baiyang Liu
Ce Liu
Feng Liu
Guangcan Liu
Jingen Liu
Wei Liu
Zicheng Liu
Zongyi Liu
Tyng-Luh Liu

Xiaoming Liu
Xiaobai Liu
Ming-Yu Liu
Marcus Liwicki
Stephen Lombardi
Roberto Lopez-Sastre
Manolis Lourakis
Brian Lovell
Chen Change Loy
Jiangbo Lu
Jiwen Lu
Simon Lucey
Jiebo Luo
Ping Luo
Marcus Magnor
Vijay Mahadevan
Julien Mairal
Michael Maire
Subhransu Maji
Atsuto Maki
Yasushi Makihara
Roberto Manduchi
Luca Marchesotti
Aleix Martinez
Bogdan Matei
Diana Mateus
Stefan Mathe
Yasuyuki Matsushita
Iain Matthews
Kevin Matzen
Bruce Maxwell
Stephen Maybank
Walterio Mayol-Cuevas
David McAllester
Gerard Medioni
Christopher Mei
Paulo Mendonca
Thomas Mensink
Domingo Mery
Ajmal Mian
Branislav Micusik
Ondrej Miksik
Anton Milan
Majid Mirmehdi
Anurag Mittal

Hossein Mobahi
Pranab Mohanty
Pascal Monasse
Vlad Morariu
Philippos Mordohai
Francesc Moreno-Noguer
Luce Morin
Nigel Morris
Bryan Morse
Eric Mortensen
Yasuhiro Mukaigawa
Lopamudra Mukherjee
Vittorio Murino
David Murray
Sobhan Naderi Parizi
Hajime Nagahara
Laurent Najman
Karthik Nandakumar
Fabian Nater
Jan Neumann
Lukas Neumann
Ram Nevatia
Richard Newcombe
Minh Hoai Nguyen
Bingbing Ni
Feiping Nie
Juan Carlos Niebles
Marc Niethammer
Claudia Nieuwenhuis
Mark Nixon
Mohammad Norouzi
Sebastian Nowozin
Matthew O'Toole
Peter Ochs
Jean-Marc Odobez
Francesca Odone
Eyal Ofek
Sangmin Oh
Takahiro Okabe
Takayuki Okatani
Aude Oliva
Carl Olsson
Bjorn Ommer
Magnus Oskarsson
Wanli Ouyang

Geoffrey Oxholm
Mustafa Ozuysal
Nicolas Padoy
Caroline Pantofaru
Nicolas Papadakis
George Papandreou
Nikolaos
    Papanikolopoulos
Nikos Paragios
Devi Parikh
Dennis Park
Vishal Patel
Ioannis Patras
Vladimir Pavlovic
Kim Pedersen
Marco Pedersoli
Shmuel Peleg
Marcello Pelillo
Tingying Peng
A.G. Amitha Perera
Alessandro Perina
Federico Pernici
Florent Perronnin
Vladimir Petrovic
Tomas Pfister
Jonathon Phillips
Justus Piater
Massimo Piccardi
Hamed Pirsiavash
Leonid Pishchulin
Robert Pless
Thomas Pock
Jean Ponce
Gerard Pons-Moll
Ronald Poppe
Andrea Prati
Victor Prisacariu
Kari Pulli
Yu Qiao
Lei Qin
Novi Quadrianto
Rahul Raguram
Varun Ramakrishna
Srikumar Ramalingam
Narayanan Ramanathan

Konstantinos
    Rapantzikos
Michalis Raptis
Nalini Ratha
Avinash Ravichandran
Michael Reale
Dikpal Reddy
James Rehg
Jan Reininghaus
Xiaofeng Ren
Jerome Revaud
Morteza Rezanejad
Hayko Riemenschneider
Tammy Riklin Raviv
Antonio Robles-Kelly
Erik Rodner
Emanuele Rodola
Mikel Rodriguez
Marcus Rohrbach
Javier Romero
Charles Rosenberg
Bodo Rosenhahn
Arun Ross
Samuel Rota Bul
Peter Roth
Volker Roth
Anastasios Roussos
Sebastien Roy
Michael Rubinstein
Olga Russakovsky
Bryan Russell
Michael S. Ryoo
Mohammad Amin
    Sadeghi
Kate Saenko
Albert Ali Salah
Imran Saleemi
Mathieu Salzmann
Conrad Sanderson
Aswin
    Sankaranarayanan
Benjamin Sapp
Radim Sara
Scott Satkin
Imari Sato

Yoichi Sato
Bogdan Savchynskyy
Hanno Scharr
Daniel Scharstein
Yoav Y. Schechner
Walter Scheirer
Kevin Schelten
Frank Schmidt
Uwe Schmidt
Julia Schnabel
Alexander Schwing
Nicu Sebe
Shishir Shah
Mubarak Shah
Shiguang Shan
Qi Shan
Ling Shao
Abhishek Sharma
Viktoriia Sharmanska
Eli Shechtman
Yaser Sheikh
Alexander Shekhovtsov
Chunhua Shen
Li Shen
Yonggang Shi
Qinfeng Shi
Ilan Shimshoni
Takaaki Shiratori
Abhinav Shrivastava
Behjat Siddiquie
Nathan Silberman
Karen Simonyan
Richa Singh
Vikas Singh
Sudipta Sinha
Josef Sivic
Dirk Smeets
Arnold Smeulders
William Smith
Cees Snoek
Eric Sommerlade
Alexander
    Sorkine-Hornung
Alvaro Soto
Richard Souvenir

Anuj Srivastava
Ioannis Stamos
Michael Stark
Chris Stauffer
Bjorn Stenger
Charles Stewart
Rainer Stiefelhagen
Juergen Sturm
Yusuke Sugano
Josephine Sullivan
Deqing Sun
Min Sun
Hari Sundar
Ganesh Sundaramoorthi
Kalyan Sunkavalli
Sabine Süsstrunk
David Suter
Tomas Svoboda
Rahul Swaminathan
Tanveer
   Syeda-Mahmood
Rick Szeliski
Raphael Sznitman
Yuichi Taguchi
Yu-Wing Tai
Jun Takamatsu
Hugues Talbot
Ping Tan
Robby Tan
Kevin Tang
Huixuan Tang
Danhang Tang
Marshall Tappen
Jean-Philippe Tarel
Danny Tarlow
Gabriel Taubin
Camillo Taylor
Demetri Terzopoulos
Christian Theobalt
Yuandong Tian
Joseph Tighe
Radu Timofte
Massimo Tistarelli
George Toderici
Sinisa Todorovic

Giorgos Tolias
Federico Tombari
Tatiana Tommasi
Yan Tong
Akihiko Torii
Antonio Torralba
Lorenzo Torresani
Andrea Torsello
Tali Treibitz
Rudolph Triebel
Bill Triggs
Roberto Tron
Tomasz Trzcinski
Ivor Tsang
Yanghai Tsin
Zhuowen Tu
Tony Tung
Pavan Turaga
Engin Türetken
Oncel Tuzel
Georgios Tzimiropoulos
Norimichi Ukita
Martin Urschler
Arash Vahdat
Julien Valentin
Michel Valstar
Koen van de Sande
Joost van de Weijer
Anton van den Hengel
Jan van Gemert
Daniel Vaquero
Kiran Varanasi
Mayank Vatsa
Ashok Veeraraghavan
Olga Veksler
Alexander Vezhnevets
Rene Vidal
Sudheendra
   Vijayanarasimhan
Jordi Vitria
Christian Vogler
Carl Vondrick
Sven Wachsmuth
Stefan Walk
Chaohui Wang

Jingdong Wang
Jue Wang
Ruiping Wang
Kai Wang
Liang Wang
Xinggang Wang
Xin-Jing Wang
Yang Wang
Heng Wang
Yu-Chiang Frank Wang
Simon Warfield
Yichen Wei
Yair Weiss
Gordon Wetzstein
Oliver Whyte
Richard Wildes
Christopher Williams
Lior Wolf
Kwan-Yee Kenneth
   Wong
Oliver Woodford
John Wright
Changchang Wu
Xinxiao Wu
Ying Wu
Tianfu Wu
Yang Wu
Yingnian Wu
Jonas Wulff
Yu Xiang
Tao Xiang
Jianxiong Xiao
Dong Xu
Li Xu
Yong Xu
Kota Yamaguchi
Takayoshi Yamashita
Shuicheng Yan
Jie Yang
Qingxiong Yang
Ruigang Yang
Meng Yang
Yi Yang
Chih-Yuan Yang
Jimei Yang

Bangpeng Yao
Angela Yao
Dit-Yan Yeung
Alper Yilmaz
Lijun Yin
Xianghua Ying
Kuk-Jin Yoon
Shiqi Yu
Stella Yu
Jingyi Yu
Junsong Yuan
Lu Yuan
Alan Yuille
Ramin Zabih
Christopher Zach

Stefanos Zafeiriou
Hongbin Zha
Lei Zhang
Junping Zhang
Shaoting Zhang
Xiaoqin Zhang
Guofeng Zhang
Tianzhu Zhang
Ning Zhang
Lei Zhang
Li Zhang
Bin Zhao
Guoying Zhao
Ming Zhao
Yibiao Zhao

Weishi Zheng
Bo Zheng
Changyin Zhou
Huiyu Zhou
Kevin Zhou
Bolei Zhou
Feng Zhou
Jun Zhu
Xiangxin Zhu
Henning Zimmer
Karel Zimmermann
Andrew Zisserman
Larry Zitnick
Daniel Zoran

Additional Reviewers

Austin Abrams
Hanno Ackermann
Daniel Adler
Muhammed Zeshan
   Afzal
Pulkit Agrawal
Edilson de Aguiar
Unaiza Ahsan
Amit Aides
Zeynep Akata
Jon Almazan
David Altamar
Marina Alterman
Mohamed Rabie Amer
Manuel Amthor
Shawn Andrews
Oisin Mac Aodha
Federica Arrigoni
Yuval Bahat
Luis Barrios
John Bastian
Florian Becker
C. Fabian
   Benitez-Quiroz
Vinay Bettadapura
Brian G. Booth

Lukas Bossard
Katie Bouman
Hilton Bristow
Daniel Canelhas
Olivier Canevet
Spencer Cappallo
Ivan Huerta Casado
Daniel Castro
Ishani Chakraborty
Chenyi Chen
Sheng Chen
Xinlei Chen
Wei-Chen Chiu
Hang Chu
Yang Cong
Sam Corbett-Davies
Zhen Cui
Maria A. Davila
Oliver Demetz
Meltem Demirkus
Chaitanya Desai
Pengfei Dou
Ralf Dragon
Liang Du
David Eigen
Jakob Engel

Victor Escorcia
Sandro Esquivel
Nicola Fioraio
Michael Firman
Alex Fix
Oliver Fleischmann
Marco Fornoni
David Fouhey
Vojtech Franc
Jorge Martinez G.
Silvano Galliani
Pablo Garrido
Efstratios Gavves
Timnit Gebru
Georgios Giannoulis
Clement Godard
Ankur Gupta
Saurabh Gupta
Amirhossein Habibian
David Hafner
Tom S.F. Haines
Vladimir Haltakov
Christopher Ham
Xufeng Han
Stefan Heber
Yacov Hel-Or

David Held
Benjamin Hell
Jan Heller
Anton van den Hengel
Robert Henschel
Steven Hickson
Michael Hirsch
Jan Hosang
Shell Hu
Zhiwu Huang
Daniel Huber
Ahmad Humayun
Corneliu Ilisescu
Zahra Iman
Thanapong Intharah
Phillip Isola
Hamid Izadinia
Edward Johns
Justin Johnson
Andreas Jordt
Anne Jordt
Cijo Jose
Daniel Jung
Meina Kan
Ben Kandel
Vasiliy Karasev
Andrej Karpathy
Jan Kautz
Changil Kim
Hyeongwoo Kim
Rolf Koehler
Daniel Kohlsdorf
Svetlana Kordumova
Jonathan Krause
Till Kroeger
Malte Kuhlmann
Ilja Kuzborskij
Alina Kuznetsova
Sam Kwak
Peihua Li
Michael Lam
Maksim Lapin
Gil Levi
Aviad Levis
Yan Li

Wenbin Li
Yin Li
Zhenyang Li
Pengpeng Liang
Jinna Lie
Qiguang Liu
Tianliang Liu
Alexander Loktyushin
Steven Lovegrove
Feng Lu
Jake Lussier
Xutao Lv
Luca Magri
Behrooz Mahasseni
Aravindh Mahendran
Siddharth Mahendran
Francesco Malapelle
Mateusz Malinowski
Santiago Manen
Timo von Marcard
Ricardo Martin-Brualla
Iacopo Masi
Roberto Mecca
Tomer Michaeli
Hengameh Mirzaalian
Kylia Miskell
Ishan Misra
Javier Montoya
Roozbeh Mottaghi
Panagiotis Moutafis
Oliver Mueller
Daniel Munoz
Rajitha Navarathna
James Newling
Mohamed Omran
Vicente Ordonez
Sobhan Naderi Parizi
Omkar Parkhi
Novi Patricia
Kuan-Chuan Peng
Bojan Pepikj
Federico Perazzi
Loic Peter
Alioscia Petrelli
Sebastian Polsterl

Alison Pouch
Vittal Premanchandran
James Pritts
Luis Puig
Julian Quiroga
Vignesh Ramanathan
Rene Ranftl
Mohammad Rastegari
S. Hussain Raza
Michael Reale
Malcolm Reynolds
Alimoor Reza
Christian Richardt
Marko Ristin
Beatrice Rossi
Rasmus Rothe
Nasa Rouf
Anirban Roy
Fereshteh Sadeghi
Zahra Sadeghipoor
Faraz Saedaar
Tanner Schmidt
Anna Senina
Lee Seversky
Yachna Sharma
Chen Shen
Javen Shi
Tomas Simon
Gautam Singh
Brandon M. Smith
Shuran Song
Mohamed Souiai
Srinath Sridhar
Abhilash Srikantha
Michael Stoll
Aparna Taneja
Lisa Tang
Moria Tau
J. Rafael Tena
Roberto Toldo
Manolis Tsakiris
Dimitrios Tzionas
Vladyslav Usenko
Danny Veikherman
Fabio Viola

Table of Contents

Context and 3D Scenes

Poster Session 7

All-In-Focus Synthetic Aperture Imaging

Tao Yang[1], Yanning Zhang[1], Jingyi Yu[2], Jing Li[3], Wenguang Ma[1],
Xiaomin Tong[1], Rui Yu[4], and Lingyan Ran[1]

[1] SAIIP, School of Computer Science, Northwestern Polytechnical University, China
[2] Deptartment of CIS, University of Delaware, USA
[3] School of Telecommunications Engineering, Xidian University, China
[4] Deptartment of Computer Science, University College London, UK
yangtaonwpu@163.com, ynzhangnwpu@gmail.com, yu@eecis.udel.edu

Abstract. Heavy occlusions in cluttered scenes impose significant challenges to many computer vision applications. Recent light field imaging systems provide new see-through capabilities through synthetic aperture imaging (SAI) to overcome the occlusion problem. Existing synthetic aperture imaging methods, however, emulate focusing at a specific depth layer but is incapable of producing an all-in-focus see-through image. Alternative in-painting algorithms can generate visually plausible results but can not guarantee the correctness of the result. In this paper, we present a novel depth free all-in-focus SAI technique based on light-field visibility analysis. Specifically, we partition the scene into multiple visibility layers to directly deal with layer-wise occlusion and apply an optimization framework to propagate the visibility information between multiple layers. On each layer, visibility and optimal focus depth estimation is formulated as a multiple label energy minimization problem. The energy integrates the visibility mask from previous layers, multi-view intensity consistency, and depth smoothness constraint. We compare our method with the state-of-the-art solutions. Extensive experimental results with qualitative and quantitative analysis demonstrate the effectiveness and superiority of our approach.

Keywords: occluded object imaging, all-in-focus synthetic aperture imaging, multiple layer visibility propagation.

1 Introduction

The capability of seeing through occlusions in heavily cluttered scenes is beneficial to many computer vision practical application fields, ranging from hidden object imaging to detection, tracking and recognition in surveillance. Since traditional imaging methods use a simple camera to acquire the 2D projection of the 3D world from a single viewpoint, they are unable to directly resolve the occlusion problem.

A fundamental solution to the problem is to exploit new imaging procedures. For example, emerging computational photography techniques based on generalized optics provide plausible solutions to capture additional visual information.

D. Fleet et al. (Eds.): ECCV 2014, Part VI, LNCS 8694, pp. 1–15, 2014.

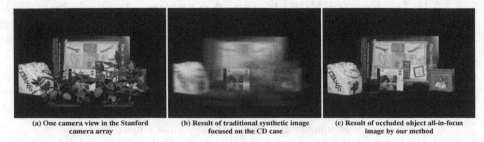

(a) One camera view in the Stanford camera array

(b) Result of traditional synthetic image focused on the CD case

(c) Result of occluded object all-in-focus image by our method

Fig. 1. Comparison results of occluded object synthetic aperture imaging methods

In particular, Synthetic Aperture Imaging or SAI [1–15] provides a unique capability of seeing-through occlusions. SAI warps and integrates the multiple view images to simulate a virtual camera with an ultra-large convex lens and it can focus on different frontal-parallel [1] or oblique [2] planes with a narrow depth of field. As a result, objects lying on the virtual focus plane, even being occluded in reality, would be clearly imaged. A downside of traditional SAI, however, is that objects off the virtual focus plane would appear blurry even though they are not occluded. The see-through results, hence, depend on the depth of the virtual focus plane.

The objective of this work is to develop a novel algorithm to generate a depth-free all-in-focus image(as shown in Fig.1(c)). Here, the all-in-focus image would contain not only objects on the virtual focus plane of camera array, but also all objects observed inside the input scene at various depths. Depth free refers to that given a certain depth, the algorithm can see through all occluders in front of this depth and generate a clear and complete all-in-focus image of the scene contents behind it.

Different to in-painting algorithms [16, 17] which can generate visually plausible results but not guarantee the correctness of the result, our technique is based on the light field visibility analysis. For every 3D point, we trace all rays passing through it back to the camera array, and then construct a visibility layer in which the 3D point is visible in all active cameras. To recover the all-focus image behind a specific depth layer, we partition the scene into multiple visibility layers to directly deal with layer-wise occlusion, and apply an optimization framework to propagate the visibility information between multiple layers. On each layer, visibility and optimal focus depth estimation is formulated as a multiple label energy minimization problem. The energy integrates the visibility mask from previous layers, multi-view intensity consistency, and depth smoothness constraint. We compare our method with the state-of-the-art solutions on publica available Stanford and UCSD light field dataset, and a dataset captured by ourselves with multiple occluders. Extensive experimental results with qualitative and quantitative analysis demonstrate the superiority of our approach.

The organization of this paper is as follows. Section 2 introduces several related works. Section 3 presents the visibility layer propagation based imaging model. Section 4 details the visibility optimization algorithm. Section 5 describes the dataset, implementation details and the experimental results. We conclude the paper and point out the future work in Section 6.

2 Related Work

Tremendous efforts have been made on developing light field imaging systems and post-processing algorithms. On the hardware front, light field camera arrays with different number of cameras, resolution, effective aperture size have been built, e.g., Stanford [3], CMU [4], UCSD [5], Alberta [6], Delaware [7], NPU [8], PiCam [15], etc., and the camera array synthetic aperture imaging technique has been proved to be a powerful way to see object through occlusion. Similar camera array technique has been adopted in producing movie special effects. For instance, in the 1999 movie The Matrix, a 1D camera array is used to create an impressive bullet dodging scene that freezes time but changes viewpoint towards the character.

On the algorithm front, one of the most important technique is synthetic aperture imaging (SAI). By integrating appropriate rays in the camera array, SAI can generate view that would be captured by a virtual camera having a large aperture. In addition, through shearing or warping the camera array images before performing this integration, SAI can focus on different planes in the scene. For example, the Stanford LF camera array by Levoy et al. [3] consists of 128 Firewire cameras, and for the first time align multiple cameras to a focus plane to approximate a camera with a very large aperture. The constructed synthetic aperture image has a shallow depth of field, so that objects off the focus plane disappear due to significant blur. This unique characteristic makes the synthetic aperture imaging a powerful tool for occluded object imaging.

Taking advantages of the geometry constraints of the dense camera array, Vaish et al.[11] present a convenient plane + parallax method for synthetic aperture imaging. A downside of their work, however, is that all rays from the camera array are directly integrated without further analysis. Thus, the clarity and contrast of their imaging result would be reduced by rays from the foreground occluders.

Visibility analysis through occlusion is a difficult but promising way to improve the occluded object imaging quality, and many algorithms have been developed in this way. Vaish et al.[12] study four cost functions, including color medians, entropy, focus and stereo for reconstructing occluded surface using synthetic apertures. Their method achieves encouraging result under slight occlusion; however the cost functions may fail under severe occlusion. Joshi et al.[10] propose a natural video matting algorithm using a camera array. Their method uses high frequencies present in natural scenes to compute mattes by creating a synthetic aperture image that is focused on the foreground object. Their result is inspiring and it has potential to be used for visibility analysis. However, this algorithm may fail in case of textureless background, and cannot deal with occluded object matting. Pei et al.[13] propose a background subtraction method for segmenting and removing foreground occluder before synthetic aperture imaging.

Their result is encouraging in simple static background, however since this approach is built on background subtraction, it cannot handle static occluder. In addition, their performance is very sensitive to cluttered background, and may fail under crowded scene.

Our method is perhaps closest to the work of Pei et al. [6] which solves the foreground segmentation problem through binary labelling via graph cuts. Instead of labelling the visibility and focusing depth, they label whether a point is on focus in a particular depth, and aggregate these focus labels in a given depth range to get a visibility mask for occluded object imaging. Although the result is encouraging,this method can only deal with front occluder(whose depth range need to be provided as a prior) labeling problem, and may fail if the occluder has severe self occlusion or there are multiple occluded objects due to lack of visibility propagation. In addition, the result of method [6] can only focus on particular depth of the scene instead of all-in-focus imaging, and the performance will be decreased in textureless background.

3   Visibility Layer Propagation Based Imaging Model

In this section we will introduce our multiple layer propagation based synthetic aperture imaging method. Instead of segmenting the observed scene into various depth layers, our approach segments the entire scene into multiple visibility layers. The **visibility layer** is defined on each layer as all the rays which are not occluded in any cameras, and computed by energy minimization. Points on each visibility layer do not necessarily need to correspond to the same object or surface.

By modelling the scene as visibility layers and propagating visibility information through layers, we can obtain the focussing depth and corresponded cameras for all the objects in the scene, including the occlusion object and occluded objects. So each visibility layer consists of pixels that are visible in all **active** cameras. The word active refers to the fact that the pixel position of the camera has not been labelled as occluded, e.g. not occupied by previous layers. Extraction of each visibility layer is based on the information of previous visibility layers. More precisely, according to occlusion mask information of previous layers, we firstly obtain the current visibility layer, then estimate the depth map of this layer, and finally update the occlusion mask.

For better understanding of the proposed method, we provide an example workflow with the Stanford Light Field data in Figure 2.

There are mainly two reasons why we introduce the concept of visibility layer. First, taking advantage of introduced visibility layer,occlusion problem can be tackled more directly. The visibility information is propagated from layer to layer, and in each layer occlusion mask needs to be updated only once. Second, segmenting the scene into visibility layers instead of depth layers is more beneficial as neighbouring pixels in the same layer tend to belong to the same object and depth smoothness constraint can be enforced when estimating the depth map.

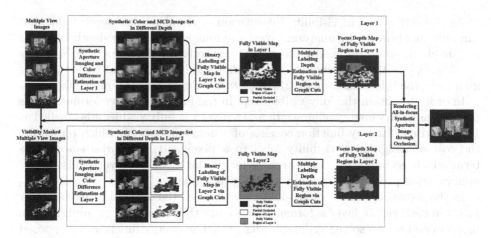

Fig. 2. Flowchart of the multiple layer visibility propagation based synthetic aperture imaging algorithm

Let L denotes the number of visibility layers in the scene. For each layer, we need to find a labelling function $f : \Omega \to \mathcal{L}$, where Ω refers to the set of all unmasked pixels in all images and $\mathcal{L} = \{0, d_1, d_2, \ldots, d_m\}$ denotes the set of possible labels of these pixels. d_i $(i = 1, 2, \ldots, m) > 0$ represents the depth range of our scene. For a pixel $\mathbf{x}$, if $f(\mathbf{x}) > 0$, then $\mathbf{x}$ is fully visible in all active camera views. Otherwise if $f(\mathbf{x}) = 0$, then $\mathbf{x}$ is partially occluded.

Considering the labelling redundancy of camera array(the labels in different cameras are highly related), the problem can be further simplified. Instead of labelling all the unmasked pixels of all the cameras, we label **all the pixels** of the reference camera equivalently(not only the unmasked pixels, as a masked pixel of the reference camera may still be fully visible in all the other active cameras). This means if there are N cameras in camera array, we only label all pixels of the reference camera view instead of labelling all the unmasked pixels of all cameras. Specifically, instead of finding above labelling function, we seek a more succinct labelling, $g : I_{ref} \to \mathcal{L}$, where I_{ref} refers to the whole image area of the reference camera. In our implementation, visibility and depth map is calculated first on the reference image, then the visibility and depth maps of all the other cameras are derived based on the calibration information of the camera array.

Therefore, for each layer ℓ , the problem of estimating fully visible pixels and corresponded depths can be formulated as a following energy minimization problem:

$$E(g; V_1, V_2, \ldots, V_{\ell-1}) = E_d(g) + E_s(g) \tag{1}$$

where the data term E_d is the sum of data cost of each pixel, and the smooth term E_s is a regularizer that encourages neighboring pixels to share the same label, while the visibility information $V_k(k = 1, 2, \ldots, \ell-1)$ from previous layers is used to encode and block the occluded rays.

As the estimation of visibility information is coupled with depth value and can only be obtained by analyzing synthetic images of different depth layers, it is difficult to minimize energy function (1) directly. In this paper, we solve for $g = \{V_\ell, D_\ell\}$ by the following two optimization modules:1) optimize the visibility map V_ℓ in the reference camera, 2) calculate the depth map D_ℓ of visible pixels.

In order to obtain the fully visible map, in the first module we formulate this problem as binary energy minimization. If a pixel $\mathbf{x}$ is fully visible, it is labelled as 1, otherwise 0. Energy function consists of a unary data term which represents the cost of assigning a visibility label to a pixel and a pairwise smoothness term which accounts for smoothness prior of the visibility layer. This energy minimization problem is then optimized by graph cuts [18].

In the second optimization module, estimation of the optimal focus depth for pixels in each visible layer is formulated as a multiple label energy minimization problem and is also solved via graph cuts [18]. The energy function is composed of a unary data term which indicates the cost of assigning a depth label to a pixel, and a pairwise smoothness term which accounts for smoothness constraint of the depth map.

4   Multiple Layer Visibility Optimization

Since our method propagates the binary visibility map between multiple layers, for a certain layer $\ell \in \{1, 2, \ldots, L\}$, occluders in front of this layer have been labelled and can be easily removed in the images of all cameras. To make the notation uncluttered, we do not write previous visibility layers $V_k(k = 1, 2, \ldots, \ell - 1)$ explicitly unless necessary. As a result, the visibility energy function can be written as follows:

$$E(V_\ell) = E_d(V_\ell) + E_s(V_\ell) \qquad (2)$$

Data Term: If a pixel is fully visible in current layer, it should be in focus for some depth value, and at the same time corresponding pixels that form the synthetic aperture image should be related by the same point of an object (except those occluded by previous layers). Since if a scene point is in focus, its corresponding pixel in the synthetic aperture image will have a good clarity and contrast,which can be measured by state-of-the-art focusing metrics. In addition, the corresponding pixels that form the synthetic aperture image should have a similar intensity value, which can be measured by various intensity constance metrics. In this paper, focusing metrics and intensity constance metrics are all referred to focusing metrics. We define the cost of labelling a pixel as fully visible based on its corresponding curve of focusing metrics in synthetic images of different depth layers.

The ideal curve of a fully visible pixel (Figure 3, point A) should satisfy the following two constraints: (1)it is unimodal throughout the focus depth scope, and (2) the curve reaches a global minimal, if and only if all visible rays intersect at the same point on an object in the scene. In contrast, a partially occluded pixel or a free point without focus should always have a large value through the entire focus depth scope (Figure 3, point C). That's because these points

Fig. 3. Typical focusing curve of different kinds of points. Point A:fully visible texture region. Point B: Fully visible region with pure color. Point C: partial occluded region or free point. Point D: textureless region.

are only visible in some of the cameras, thus for unfocused depth and even for focused depth the cost of those points is high. A textureless object pixel should have a small value in a small range of depths around the focusing depth (Figure 3, point B),while a textureless background pixel should have a small value over a broad focus range due to its similarity with the neighborhood pixels (Figure 3, Point D). Besides, in Figure 3, Point D gives a sharp peak near the origin. That's caused by the position of focusing depth plane, when it's too close to the camera, the out of focus trouble results in an unexpected value.

Reasonably, we cannot estimate the depth of the textureless background pixels. Thus, according to the width of low value depth range we remove the textureless background region before our binary visibility optimization.

Based on the above analysis, we have compared different kinds of metrics to obtain the desired ideal curve. Part of the comparison result is shown in Figure 4.Figure 4(a) gives the input images of different cameras, while Figure 4(b), (c) and (d) display the synthetic aperture imaging result, variance image, and maximal color difference(MCD) image in different depths. Comparing Figure 4(c) and (d), we can see that our MCD Image could describe the minimal color difference more accurately than the viriance Image. Thus, the MCD measurement is more suitable for visibility analysis.

Figure 4(e) shows the corresponded curves of points A, B and C marked in Figure 4(a). The focus measures evaluated include DCT energy ratio (DCTR) [19], diagonal Laplacian (LAPD) [20], steerable filters (SFIL) [21], variance and MCD. For the first three focus measures,we compute the focus metric using a 5x5 pixel block on one hundred sampled focus planes. All the results are normalized and mapped to [0 1], where low value represents a good focus. The result indicates that for a point in textured region without occlusion, all focus measures can successfully find the focus point(point A in Figure 4(e)). However, when the textured point is occluded in some cameras(point B in Figure 4(e)), the curves of DCTR, LAPD, SFIL and variance measures are multimodal with multiple local minima. In contrast, MCD metric is more stable and more insensitive to occlusion. In the low texture region (Figure 4(e), point C), the first three measures contain many noises. In contrast, both the variance and MCD measure reach the global minimum around the ground truth. In addition, the MCD curve is more sharp than variance and more close to the ideal curve.

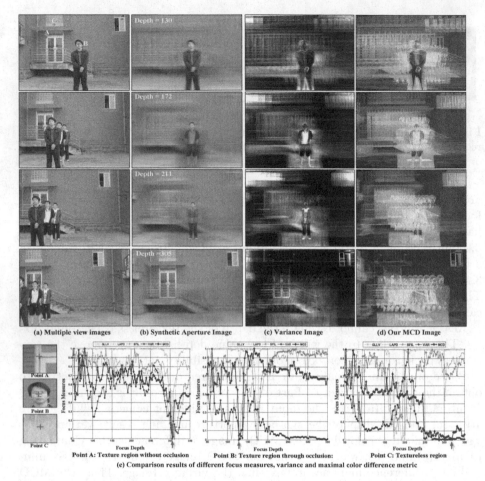

(a) Multiple view images   (b) Synthetic Aperture Image   (c) Variance Image   (d) Our MCD Image

Point A: Texture region without occlusion   Point B: Texture region through occlusion: Point C: Textureless region

(e) Comparison results of different focus measures, variance and maximal color difference metric

Fig. 4. Comparison results of focus measures for different kinds of points, the manually labeled ground truth focus depth is marked with the red arrow

Based on the analysis above, we select MCD measure to define the data cost $E_d\,(V_\ell)$ for each pixel $\mathbf{x}$ in the reference camera:

$$E_d\,(V_\ell) = \sum_{\mathbf{x} \in I_{ref}} \left(V_\ell\,(\mathbf{x}) - (1 - \min_{d \in \mathcal{D}}(MCD^d(\mathbf{x}))) \right) \tag{3}$$

where $\mathcal{D} = \{d_1, d_2, \ldots, d_m\}$ is the depth range of the scene, $MCD^d(\mathbf{x})(d \in \mathcal{D})$ is the MCD focus measure value of the pixel $\mathbf{x}$ in depth d:

$$MCD^d(\mathbf{x}) = \max_{\forall i \neq j} \left(|I_i^d(\mathbf{x}) - I_j^d(\mathbf{x})| \cdot B_i^\ell(\mathbf{x}) \cdot B_j^\ell(\mathbf{x}) \right) / 255 \tag{4}$$

$$B_i^\ell(\mathbf{x}) = \begin{cases} 0 \ if \ \sum_{\ell_0=1}^{\ell-1} V_{\ell_0}^i(\mathbf{x}) > 0 \\ 1 \qquad otherwise \end{cases} \tag{5}$$

$I_i^d(\mathbf{x})$ represents the value of pixel $\mathbf{x}$ on the warped image of camera i in depth d. $B_i^\ell(\mathbf{x})$ is a binary map of camera i to mask fully visible pixels of previous layers. $V_{\ell_0}^i$ is the visibility layer ℓ_0 of camera i, and can be obtained easily from V_{ℓ_0} of the reference camera. If $B_i^\ell(\mathbf{x}) = 0$, $\mathbf{x}$ is occupied by previous layers, otherwise $B_i^\ell(\mathbf{x}) = 1$.

A good energy function should reach good solution when the energy is low. In order to achieve this, we design the data term of the visibility optimization model as Equation (3), which is introduced to classify all the pixels as visible or invisible. When min(MCD) is small, or data term is small, the probability that the point is occluded is low, thus the cost of assigning as a visible point is low. In addition, according to the definition of MCD, even if one of the camera view is occluded, the min(MCD) appears to be a large value, and the cost of assigning this point as a visible point is high by Equation (3). Thus for visibility labelling, it is straightforward to see that our data term should achieve its minimum when it is correctly assigned, and achieve a large value for occluded point, which is a perfect data term that we want.

Smoothness Term: The smoothness term $E_s(V_\ell)$ at layer ℓ is a prior regularizer that encourages overall labelling is smooth. The prior is that two neighbouring pixels have a higher probability to belong to the same object and should be both visible or occluded in the reference camera at the same time. Here we adopt the standard four-connected neighbourhood system, and penalize the fact if labels of two neighbouring pixels are different:

$$E_s(V_\ell) = \sum_{\substack{\mathbf{p} \in I_{ref} \\ \mathbf{q} \in \mathcal{N}\mathbf{p}}} S_{\mathbf{p},\mathbf{q}}(V_\ell(\mathbf{p}), V_\ell(\mathbf{q})) \tag{6}$$

$$S_{\mathbf{p},\mathbf{q}}(V_\ell(\mathbf{p}), V_\ell(\mathbf{q})) = \min(\tau_v, \beta(\mathbf{p},\mathbf{q}) \cdot |V_\ell(\mathbf{p}) - V_\ell(\mathbf{q})|) \tag{7}$$

$$\beta(\mathbf{p},\mathbf{q}) = h(|\min_{d \in \mathcal{D}}(MCD^d(\mathbf{p})) - \min_{d \in \mathcal{D}}(MCD^d(\mathbf{q}))|) \tag{8}$$

where τ_v and $\beta(\mathbf{p},\mathbf{q})$ denote the maximum and weight of smoothness term respectively. h is a decreasing weighting function that takes into account the MCD measure similarity between neighbouring pixels. The more similar MCD measure is, the weight will be higher and the smoothness constraint between pixels will be stronger.

In this paper, the parameters are given by experiment and we choose he inverse proportional function as $h(.)$. With the above data term and smoothness term, our energy function can be minimized via graph cuts [18].

After obtain V_ℓ, we formulate the optimal focus depth estimation inside the visible layer as a multiple label optimization problem, which is also solved via graph cuts in this work.

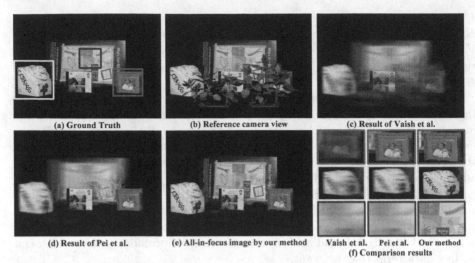

(a) Ground Truth   (b) Reference camera view   (c) Result of Vaish et al.

(d) Result of Pei et al.   (e) All-in-focus image by our method   Vaish et al.   Pei et al.   Our method
(f) Comparison results

Fig. 5. Comparison result of different methods on CD case behind plants from Stanford

5   Experimental Results

We have compared the performance of our method with the synthetic aperture imaging methods of Vaish et al.[11] and Pei et al. [6] on four datasets, including the CD case behind plants from Stanford, the crowd surveillance scene from UCSD, and two dataset captured by ourselves. In addition, to illustrate that our method can be successfully applied when there are multiple visibility layers, we have captured another two datasets where there are multiple occluders.

To avoid explicit imaging for all the objects far away in the scene, we limit our search to a range of depths around the objects that our concern. For the CD case behind plants from Stanford and our own dataset, the accuracy of each method is compared with the ground truth separately. More implementation details are given below.

• Experiment 1: CD case behind plants

This dataset contains 105 views on a 21x5 grids (synthetic aperture size 60cm by 10cm) and the image resolution is 650x515. The scene contains some plants occluding two CD cases. Our goal is to estimate the depths for all the objects in the scene and image the scene behind the plants.

Figure 5 shows the comparison result of Vaish et al. [11], Pei et al. [6] and our method. We can see that all the three methods could see the occluded CD through the plants, as shown in Figure 5(c), (d) and (e). Pei et al. [6] is better than Vaish et al. [11] in imaging of the two CD cases. However, the objects away from the focus plane are blurring, including the CD on the right, who is just near the focus plane. All-in-focus image in Figure 5(e) shows much better clarity of our method and is closer to the ground truth in Figure 5(a).

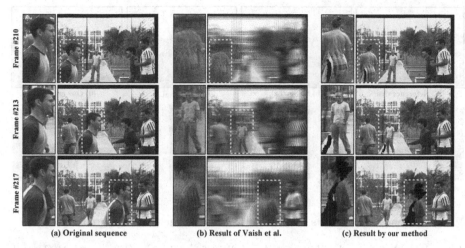

| (a) Original sequence | (b) Result of Vaish et al. | (c) Result by our method |

Fig. 6. Comparison results on crowd surveillance data from UCSD light field data

Figure 5(f) gives the comparison of imaging for several local regions. It can seen that our method can give all-in-focus image for all the three objects of different depths, while the method of Vaish et al. [11], Pei et al. [6] can only focus on given depth plane.

Besides, we use the peak signal-to-noise ratio (PSNR) assessment to compare these methods quantitively (see Table 1). Calculation of PSNR is given in equation (13) and (14). The PSNR of our all-in-focus synthetic aperture image achieves 31.1088, which is much higher than 20.8774 of Pei et al. [6]and 18.1225 of Vanish et al [11].

$$PSNR = 10\log_{10}(I_{max}^2/MSE) \tag{9}$$

$$MSE = \frac{1}{w \cdot h} \sum_{\mathbf{x} \in \mathcal{X}} (I(\mathbf{x}) - I'(\mathbf{x}))^2 \tag{10}$$

where w and h denote the image width and height, $\mathcal{X}$ is the image region, $I(\mathbf{x})$ is the pixel intensity value at $\mathbf{x}$ in the ground truth image and I' denotes the image to be assessed. $I_{max} = 255$ is the maximal intensity value.

• **Experiment 2: Crowd surveillance scene**

The "Crowd" dataset is captured by UCSD with 8 synchronous views on an 8x1 grid. There are 276 frames and the image resolution is 640x480. The scene contains five people moving in the scene and they are frequently occluded by each other. Our goal is to see through the occluder in the front and image for all others continuously.

Figure 6 shows the comparison result of our method and Vaish et al [11]. In frame#210, the man in saffron cloth is occluded. In Vaish's result(Figure 6(b)), the occluded man is blurred by shadows from the occluder. In addition, people out of the focus plane are all blurred. In contrast, our approach could see

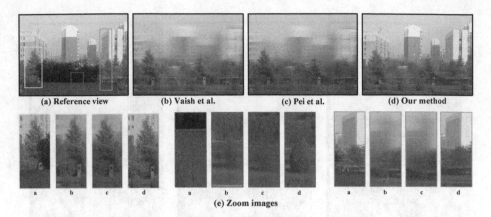

(a) Reference view   (b) Vaish et al.   (c) Pei et al.   (d) Our method

a   b   c   d   a   b   c   d   a   b   c   d

(e) Zoom images

Fig. 7. Comparison results of different methods in the challenging outdoor scene

through occlusion and achieve a clear all-in-focus image (Figure 6(c)). Details of local region results are shown in Figure 6(d). Our method also shows better performance in frame#213 and #217 than Vanish's method.

The success of our work comes from the idea that for every synthetic aperture imaging result on each frame, the scene can be regarded as static and there are no moving objects. It's quite reasonable as no object would make obvious movements considering the high frequency that camera works. Figure 6 shows the result of several subsequent frames.

The limitation of our approach is that a scene point needs to be visible at least in two camera views, otherwise the black hole will appear in the all-in-focus image(Figure 6(c)).

• **Experiment 3: Complex outdoor scene**

To further test our method on severe occlusion cases, we have done another experiment with complex outdoor scene. As shown in Figure 7,the street ,trees and distant buildings are all occluded by nearby flowers. Our aim is to see the behind scene through the occlusion of front flowers. Comparison results of Vaish's method [11], Pei's method [6] and our method are shown in Figure 7(b) and Figure 7(c) and Figure 7(d). As Vaish's method only focus on a given depth plane and cannot eliminate front occluders completely, it cannot provide an all-in-focus image of the behind scene. And although Pei's method can remove some foreground occluder through foreground occluder segmentation and get a more clear result of target, the targets out of focus plane is still very blurring, for example the building shown in Figure 7(e). In comparison, our method could provide a depth free view point and all-in-focus image for any given depth range. For instance, Figure 7(d) shows the all-in-focus image of scene behind the flowers. Please note that although the depth change and occlusion in this scene is extremely complex, our method accurately gives the desired all-in-focus result.

• **Experiment 4: Seeing through multiple occluded objects**

Our method can be applied to the scene where there are multiple occluded objects. Due to visibility propagation between different layers, we can remove

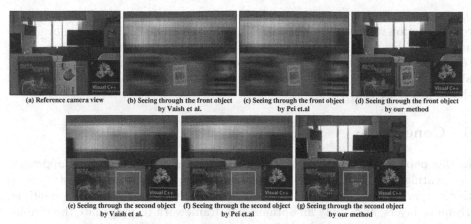

Fig. 8. Comparison results of synthetic aperture imaging through multiple objects

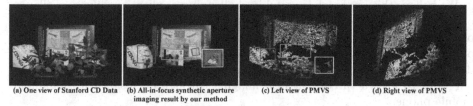

Fig. 9. Comparison with multi-view 3D reconstruction on CD case behind plants dataset

multiple occluders, focus on the occluded object and obtain an all-in-focus image of the occluded scene. Figure 8 shows the result of our synthetic aperture imaging method when there are multiple occluders. Figure 8(a)is the input image of the reference camera, it can be seen that the red book is occluded by the playing card, which is further occluded by front yellow box. The standard synthetic aperture imaging result of the playing card and red book is shown in Figure 8(b) and Figure 8(e)respectively. It can be seen that due to severe occlusion, Vanish's method[11] can only get a blurred image of the occluded object. The state-of-art synthetic aperture imaging result of playing card and red book is shown in Figure 8(c) and Figure 8(f) respectively. It can be seen that in the case of severe occlusion, Pei's method[6] can only get a blurred image of the occluded object due to the inaccuracy of the estimated foreground label. In comparison, our method can remove front occluders completely and provide an all-in-focus image of the scene behind the yellow box(Figure 8(d)) and even the playing card(Figure 8(g)).

• **Experiment 5: Comparison with multi-view 3D reconstruction**

Because it may be possible to apply stereo matching for producing see-through images, in this experiment we compare our approach with one of the state-of-the-art 3D reconstruction methods PMVS [22] on the public Stanford CD dataset. Two views of reconstruction result of the scene by PMVS are given in Figure

9(c) and (d). Due to the severe occlusion of foreground leaves and flowers, the reconstruction results of background CD contain many holes (as shown by green and yellow boxes). Our approach performs as an image-based depth peeling technique, it sequentially removes the front-most visible layers and generates an all-in-focus image of the observed scene through visibility layer prorogation(as shown in Figure 9(b)).

6 Conclusions

In this paper, we have presented a novel synthetic aperture imaging approach for creating all-in-focus images through occlusion. Different from existing synthetic aperture imaging algorithms, we have segment the scene into multiple visibility layers, and apply an optimization framework to propagate the visibility information between multiple layers to produce all-in-focus image even under occlusion.

We believe this approach is useful in challenging applications like surveillance of occluded people in crowded areas where seeing the people's appearance maybe of primary interest, or reconstructing hidden objects through severe occlusion, or even rendering a depth free viewpoint image. In the future, we would like to design more robust cost functions for the focus depth estimation, and extend our work to unstructured light field imaging through occlusion with handhold mobile phone.

Acknowledgements. We thank the anonymous reviewers for their valuable comments and detailed suggestions. This work is supported by the National Natural Science Foundation of China (No.61272288,No.61231016), NSF grants IIS-CAREER-0845268 and IIS-1218156, Foundation of China Scholarship Council (No.201206965020, No.201303070083), Foundation of NPU New Soaring Star, NPU New People and Direction (No.13GH014604), Graduate Starting Seed Fund of NPU,and NPU Soaring Star (No.12GH0311).

References

1. Isaksen, A., McMillan, L., Gortler, S.J.: Dynamically reparameterrized light fields. In: SIGGRAPH, pp. 297–306 (2000)
2. Vaish, V., Garg, G., Talvala, E., Antunez, E., Wilburn, B., Horowitz, M., Levoy, M.: Synthetic aperture focusing using a shear-warp factorization of the viewing transform. In: CVPR, pp. 129–134 (2005)
3. Wilburn, B., Joshi, N., Vaish, V., Talvala, V.E., Antunez, E., Barth, A., Adam, A., Horowitz, M., Levoy, M.: High performance imaging using large camera arrays. ACM T GRAPHIC 24(3), 765–776 (2005)
4. Zhang, C., Chen, T.: A self-reconfigurable camera array. In: SIGGRAPH (2004)
5. Joshi, N., Avidan, S., Matusik, W., Kriegman, D.J.: Synthetic aperture tracking: tracking through occlusions. In: ICCV, pp. 1–8 (2007)
6. Pei, Z., Zhang, Y.N., Chen, X., Yang, Y.H.: Synthetic aperture imaging using pixel labelling via energy minimization. Pattern Recognition 46(1), 174–187 (2013)

7. Ding, Y.Y., Li, F., Ji, Y., Yu, J.Y.: Synthetic aperture tracking: tracking through occlusions. In: ICCV, pp. 1–8 (2007)
8. Yang, T., Zhang, Y.N., Tong, X.M., Zhang, X.Q., Yu, R.: A new hybrid synthetic aperture imaging model for tracking and seeing people through occlusion. IEEE TCSVT 23(9), 1461–1475 (2013)
9. Basha, T., Avidan, S., Hornung, A., Matusik, W.: Structure and motion from scene registration. In: CVPR, pp. 1426–1433 (2012)
10. Joshi, N., Matusik, W., Avidan, S.: Structure and motion from scene registration. In: SIGGRAPH, pp. 779–786 (2006)
11. Vaish, V., Wilburn, B., Joshi, N., Levoy, M.: Using plane + parallax for calibrating dense camera arrays. In: CVPR, pp. 2–9 (2004)
12. Vaish, V., Szeliski, R., Zitnick, C.L., Kang, S.B., Levoy, M.: Reconstructing occluded surfaces using synthetic apertures: stereo, focus and robust methods. In: CVPR, pp. 2331–2338 (2006)
13. Pei, Z., Zhang, Y.N., Yang, T., Zhang, X.W., Yang, Y.H.: A novel multi-object detection method in complex scene using synthetic aperture imaging. Pattern Recognition 45(4), 1637–1658 (2011)
14. Davis, A., Levoy, M., Durand, F.: Unstructured light fields. EUROGRAPHICS 31(2), 2331–2338 (2012)
15. Venkataraman, K., Lelescu, D., Duparr, J., McMahon, A., Molina, G., Chatterjee, P., Mullis, R.: Picam: An ultra-thin high performance monolithic camera array. ACM T. Graphics 32(5), 1–13 (2013)
16. Bertalmio, M., Sapiro, G., Caselles, V., Ballester, C.: Image inpainting. In: SIGGRAPH, pp. 417–424 (2000)
17. Tauber, Z., Li, Z.N., Drew, M.S.: Review and preview: disocclusion by inpainting for image-based rendering. IEEE TSMC 37(4), 527–540 (2007)
18. Boykov, Y., Kolmogorov, V.: An experimental comparison of min-cut/max-flow algorithms for energy minimization in vision. TPAMI 26(9), 1124–1137 (2004)
19. Lee, S.Y., Yoo, J.T., Kumar, Y., Kim, S.W.: Reduced energy-ratio measure for robust autofocusing in digital camera. Signal Processing Letters 16(2), 133–136 (2009)
20. Thelen, A., Frey, S., Hirsch, S., Hering, P.: Interpolation improvements in shape-from-focus for holographic reconstructions with regard to focus operators, neighborhood-size, and height value interpolation. TIP 18(1), 151–157 (2009)
21. Minhas, R., Mohammed, A.A., Wu, Q.M.J., Sid-Ahmed, M.A.: 3D shape from focus and depth map computation using steerable filters. In: Kamel, M., Campilho, A. (eds.) ICIAR 2009. LNCS, vol. 5627, pp. 573–583. Springer, Heidelberg (2009)
22. Furukawa, Y., Ponce, J.: Accurate, dense, and robust multi-view stereopsis. TPAMI 32(8), 1362–1376 (2010)

Photo Uncrop

Qi Shan[1], Brian Curless[1], Yasutaka Furukawa[2],
Carlos Hernandez[3], and Steven M. Seitz[1,3]

[1] University of Washington, Seattle, WA, USA
[2] Washington University in St. Louis, St. Louis, MO, USA
[3] Google Inc., Mountain View, CA, USA

Abstract. We address the problem of extending the field of view of a photo—an operation we call *uncrop*. Given a reference photograph to be uncropped, our approach selects, reprojects, and composites a subset of Internet imagery taken near the reference into a larger image around the reference using the underlying scene geometry. The proposed Markov Random Field based approach is capable of handling large Internet photo collections with arbitrary viewpoints, dramatic appearance variation, and complicated scene layout. We show results that are visually compelling on a wide range of real-world landmarks.

Keywords: Computational photography, image based rendering.

1 Introduction

Travel photos often fail to create the experience of re-visiting the scene, as most consumer cameras have limited field of view (FOV). Indeed, mobile phone cameras (which far outnumber any other photography device) typically have a FOV around 50-65 degrees, significantly narrower than the human eye [4]. Capturing large scenes is therefore tricky. Modern cell phones are equipped with camera apps providing a panorama mode, which allows you to take multiple pictures and stitch them into a bigger image. However, the process is often tedious. Furthermore, you cannot operate on your past photos. As a result, your photos are often more tightly *cropped* than desired (See Fig. 1).

We address the problem of extending the FOV of a photo—an operation we call *uncrop*. The goal is to produce a larger FOV image of the scene captured in your photo, leveraging other photos of the same scene from the Internet (captured at different times by other people). We make an important distinction between producing a *plausible* extended image using a technique such as texture synthesis [19], vs. producing an extended rendering of the *true scene* which is intended to be accurate. The latter case is more challenging and potentially more useful, as it gives you information about the real world, allowing you to *zoom out* of any photo to get better spatial context.

For almost any photo you take at a tourist site, there exist many other photos from nearby viewpoints, collectively capturing the scene across a potentially large FOV. Our approach is to automatically select, reproject, and composite a subset of this imagery into a large image screen centered on your photo. This problem is challenging for several reasons. First, the photos are not captured from the same optical center, resulting in too much parallax for existing state-of-the-art panorama stitchers (which produce severe

D. Fleet et al. (Eds.): ECCV 2014, Part VI, LNCS 8694, pp. 16–31, 2014.

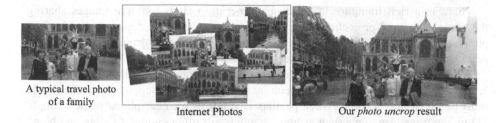

A typical travel photo
of a family

Internet Photos   Our *photo uncrop* result

Fig. 1. Capturing family photos with the desired background in the image frame can be tricky. Our approach expands the FOV of a user photo thus enables better spatial context. Landmark: Stravinsky Fountain in Paris.

artifacts as we will show). Second, the appearance (color, exposure, and illumination) varies dramatically between photos, making it difficult to produce a coherent composite. And finally, the presence of people, cars, trees, windows, and other transitory or hard-to-match objects make the alignment problem especially challenging.

This problem represents a compelling application that sits between traditional panorama stitching, which requires capturing many images and is thus labor intensive, and full 3D scene reconstruction, which has too many failure modes. Indeed, our experiments with state-of-the-art 3D reconstruction techniques [9,14,22] rarely produce hole-free geometry, omitting ground, people, trees, windows, and many other salient scene aspects. Our approach therefore assumes *incomplete* geometry in the form of depth maps, and leverages a novel Markov Random Field (MRF) based compositing technique to generate compelling full-scene composites complete with people, trees, etc. The method automatically generates results for multiple FOV expansions; the user can then choose the desired FOV and crop as desired to discard image boundaries with significant artifacts.

Our contributions are two-fold: (i) the first system to produce compelling uncropping results with dramatic boundary expansion from Internet photos; (ii) a novel MRF-based formulation adapted to handle significant geometry errors.

We show convincing results on a wide range scenes, each covered by 100s to 1000s of Internet images. Like existing panorama stitchers, our results are not entirely free of artifacts, and stitching seams and misregistration artifacts are occasionally noticable. However, we argue that for the intended application (giving you spatial context for your photo), small artifacts are quite tolerable. I.e., it's less important that every pixel is right than being able to zoom out and see that the building behind you is the Uffizi, or that you're standing in the middle of a large town square.

2 Related Work

Many texture synthesis techniques support image interpolation and extrapolation [19,28,13,5]; perhaps most related are those that leverage Internet imagery [24,11,15]. While these methods can produce extremely realistic results, they generally depict extrapolated scenes that don't actually exist; none of the extrapolation approaches attempt to capture the appearance of the real underlying scene.

There is a rich literature in panorama generation from multiple images sharing the same center of projection [23] with widespread popular deployment on smart phones [17]. There also exist large scale panorama creation projects, generating giga-pixel [16], and more recently tera-pixel [7] images.

When input images do not share the same center of projection, the alignment problem becomes significantly more difficult, as parallax, which depends on scene depth, must be taken into account. When parallax is small or for near-planar scenes, simple 2D image transformations such as homographies are often enough to align and blend images without artifacts [2,18,10].

In more general configurations, proper estimation of scene depths is essential for producing artifact-free images. Panorama stitching with scene depth estimation has been demonstrated for certain specialized camera motion cases including circles [23,26,21] and linear motion [20]. The addition of depth information enables new applications in these systems, such as the generation of depth of focus effects and 3D stereo images [21]. However, these techniques require continuous and often restricted camera paths and do not operate on community photo collections (e.g., Flickr) or other unstructured imagery. In this work, our goal is to extend the FOV of an input photograph by harnessing online community photo collections, via careful geometric analysis and blending techniques.

Most recently, and most similar to our own work, Zhang et al. [27] propose to expand the boundary of a personal photo (among other applications) using online collections. However, their method requires all images to overlap with the reference, limiting the effective expansion range. Further, they adopt a relatively simple, median-based averaging process for blending, which produces heavily blurred/ghosted composites on our examples.

An alternative approach would be to fully model geometry and reflectance of the scene, enabling (in principle) photorealistic scene rendering from any desired viewpoint. Despite exciting recent progress, however, state-of-the-art techniques rarely produce complete, high resolution reconstructions, and fail to model trees, people, windows, thin objects, and other very salient scene elements [22].

3   Input Data

We download images from Flickr (http://www.flickr.com) for a variety of sites, and use existing structure from motion (SfM) software [25] to compute camera poses. Uncropping is performed on images selected from the SfM model to show the capability of our system, though it would be straightforward to apply our system to an arbitrary new photograph by simply adding it to the relevant image set and performing incremental SfM. Publicly available multi-view stereo software is used to reconstruct per-view depthmaps [8]. Then, we warp each image by reprojecting its depth map and colors to the viewpoint of the image to be uncropped. More details on these preprocessing steps are found in Section 5.

4   Uncrop Algorithm

We propose an MRF-based compositing algorithm to construct a wide FOV target image around a reference image. We assign a label l to each source image, such that $l \in \{-1, 0, 1, \cdots, N - 1\}$, where N is the number of images that survived the view selection process (including the reference image itself), and -1 is the null label. After re-projecting each source image, we have a set of partial, warped images $C_l(p)$ that each cover parts of the target image. We seek to solve for the label map $l(p)$ over target pixels p that will yield a high quality composite when copying warped image colors to the target image. We include the null label $l = -1$ to allow for a small number of pixels not covered by any of the images. After computing the composite, we perform a Poisson blend to give the final result.

We formulate the MRF problem as the sum of a unary term, a binary term, and a label cost term:

$$E(l) = \sum_p E_{\text{unary}}(p, l(p)) + \sum_{\{p,q\} \in \mathcal{N}(p,q)} E_{\text{binary}}(p, l(p), q, l(q)) + E_{\text{label}}(l). \quad (1)$$

where $\mathcal{N}(p, q)$ denotes pairs of neighboring pixels in a standard 4-connected neighborhood. With abuse of notation, l here denotes the set of all the labels in the image. What is novel is the actual formulation of the unary and binary terms. We first describe their principles, where detailed formulation will be discussed in the following sections.

4.1   Principles

E_{unary}: It is nearly impossible to reconstruct perfect geometry for a complicated scene like ours, and a warped image may not be exactly aligned with the reference image. Therefore, the unary term incorporates the confidence of estimated depth information. Appearance mismatch is another source of artifacts. For example, compositing a daytime photo with a nighttime shot is challenging. We assign each image a score that measures the appearance similarity to the reference. Furthermore, appearance variation within an image due to shadows, over-saturation, and flash photography can result in spatially varying pixel quality. Thus, we assign lower cost to high contrast pixels.

E_{binary}: Traditional image stitching uses E_{binary} to minimize seams by looking for cuts on image edges. We follow a similar path, but also introduce a new measure to encourage any given reconstructed patch in the composite to resemble at least one warped source image at the same location. This helps to avoid making abrupt transitions in the composite that can arise from geometric misalignments, because noticeable artifacts at such transitions do not resemble corresponding regions in any of the input images.

E_{label}: Building a composite out of many images can lead to a quiltwork of stitched patches that can stray from the desired result. It is natural instead to encourage the stitcher to take pixel examples from a sparse set of warped views. In our approach, we achieve this by assigning a constant cost to each unique label used in the compositing.

4.2 Unary Term

We construct the unary term from several components:

$$E_{\text{unary}}(p,l) = E_{\text{geometry}}(p,l) + \alpha_1 E_{\text{appearance}}(l) + \alpha_2 E_{\text{contrast}}(p,l) + \alpha_3 E_{\text{reference}}(p,l), \quad (2)$$

where $\alpha_1 = 10$, $\alpha_2 = 5$, $\alpha_3 = 1$ are used in all of our experiments. Note that each warped source image $C_l(p)$ only partially covers the target image; if warped image l does not have a color at pixel p, the unary term is automatically set to infinity.

Geometry: We define the geometry term $E_{\text{geometry}}(p,l)$ as the possible error in the position of a reprojected pixel. It is determined by two factors: the accuracy of the original depth value and the baseline between the reference view and the source view. First, we model the accuracy using the range of depths in a local neighborhood in the source image l. More concretely, let u denote a source pixel in image l, and U to be the corresponding 3D point on the depthmap, which is re-projected to p in the reference. We look at a local neighborhood of size 11×11 pixels centered at u, and compute the minimum and the maximum depth values in the window. We have assumed a 1% depth error, and subtracts from the minimum and add to the maximum depth values by $0.01 D_u$, where D_u is the depth value at u. We take the 3D point U and shift its location to the minimum and the maximum depth locations, and project it to the reference image. Let us call the two projected location $p_{\text{near}}(p,l)$ and $p_{\text{far}}(p,l)$, respectively. Then, the geometry term is defined as follows:

$$E_{\text{geometry}}(p,l) = \max(|p - p_{\text{near}}(p,l)|, |p - p_{\text{far}}(p,l)|). \quad (3)$$

By minimizing this term, the optimization will favor pixels from images that have a smaller baseline relative to the reference view (less room for parallax errors) and images that sample surface regions more densely in close-ups and thus are more likely to cover a smaller range of depths. It is possible that multiple pixels u may warp to pixel p (see Section 5), in which case, we simply take the average projected location.

Appearance: Internet photos exhibit a wide range of illumination conditions. It is important to encourage the use of images with similar appearance. To do this, we assign an appearance cost to each source image. Specifically, we take the color histogram of each image, and score it by its KL divergence from the histogram of the reference image. Then the images are sorted in ascending order. Let k_l be the index of image l in this sorted list. We now define the overall image appearance cost as:

$$E_{\text{appearance}}(l) = k_l / N, \quad (4)$$

where N is the number of images in the set. Smaller cost in this case means less divergent from (more similar to) the reference image. Note that this unary term is constant for image l, regardless of which target pixel is being considered.

Contrast: Undesirable appearance variations such as shadows and over-saturation can be penalized based on the contrast. We address this by defining a local contrast cost. Let (G_x^l, G_y^l) be the finite difference gradient of image l after mapping image l to grayscale (intensity values $\in [0,1]$). We use the following formula to measure the lack of contrast over 11×11 window Ω centered at u in image l, which corresponds to p after the warping:

$$E_{\text{contrast}}(p, l) = \frac{1}{|\Omega|} \sum_{v \in \Omega} \sqrt{(1 - |G_x^l(v)|)^2 + (1 - |G_y^l(v)|)^2}. \tag{5}$$

If multiple pixels from source image l map to p after warping, we again simply take the average of their scores.

Reference: Finally, it is important to respect the reference image. Let us define the core region of the image Ω_{core} to be a set of pixels inside the reference image and more than 11 pixels in distance from its boundary. The reference cost is defined by applying the following four rules from top to bottom:

$$E_{\text{reference}}(p, l) = \begin{cases} 0, & l = l_{\text{ref}} \\ 10000, & l = -1 \\ 100, & p \notin \Omega_{\text{core}} \\ \infty, & p \in \Omega_{\text{core}} \end{cases} \tag{6}$$

where l_{ref} is the label of the reference image. It is possible that some of the pixels in the target image are not covered by any of the images, thus we allow the $l = -1$ label, with high cost.

4.3   Binary Term

Similar to previous work [3], we encourage label switches in regions with edges, where seams will be less noticeable. Further, we use a novel compatibility term to encourage constructing regions in the target image that resemble warped source image regions. Our binary term can then be written:

$$E_{\text{binary}} = E_{\text{edge}} + \beta E_{\text{compatibility}}. \tag{7}$$

where β trades off the relative contribution of the compatibility term. (We set $\beta = 10$ in all of our experiments.)

Edge: We first define a Sobel filter cost for a single pixel u and in (unwarped) source image l:

$$E_S(u, l) = \left(6 - \frac{\|S(u, l)\|_1}{4}\right)^2. \tag{8}$$

$S(u, l)$ is the concatenation of the Sobel filter responses in the x and y directions for each of the r, g, and b color channels, where we take the L_1 norm of this 6-dimensional vector. Now, for neighboring target pixels p and q with labels l and m, respectively, the binary edge cost is:

$$E_{\text{edge}}(p, l, q, m) = \begin{cases} 0, & l = m \\ E_S(u, l) + E_S(u, m), & l \neq m. \end{cases} \tag{9}$$

If multiple pixels correspond to p after warping, we take their average over u.

Compatibility: To encourage regions in the target image to resemble regions in the source image, we introduce a novel label compatibility term. Consider a pixel p and one of its neighbors q in the target image, and an image l. We define an 11×11 window around the two pixels and collect the pixels of $C_l(p)$ (corresponding to the warped version of image l) in the overlap into a vector $W_{p,q}(l)$. If there will be a transition between labels l and m in going from p to q, respectively, then the resulting window in the final result will likely resemble the average of the windows $W_{p,q}(l)$ and $W_{p,q}(m)$. This average in turn should resemble at least one of the (warped) source images. Thus, we define the following compatibility cost:

$$E_{\text{compatibility}}(p, l, q, m) = 1 - \max_n \text{NCC}\left[\frac{1}{2}\left(W_{p,q}(l) + W_{p,q}(m)\right), W_{p,q}(n)\right] \quad (10)$$

where $NCC[\cdot, \cdot] \in [-1, 1]$ is the normalized cross-correlation between two vectors, and n ranges over all of the labels. Note that, by this definition, this term becomes 0 when $l = m$. In addition, we set the term to ∞ if either $W_{p,q}(l)$ or $W_{p,q}(m)$ includes pixels where $C_l(p)$ or $C_m(p)$ are undefined.

4.4 Label Cost

We encourage the image stitcher to take color from a small number of images by assigning a constant cost for each additional label. If K is the number of unique labels in the composite, we set $E_{\text{label}}(l) = 500000 \cdot K$.

4.5 Optimizations and Accelerations

The energy definition in Eq. (1) falls naturally in the category of multi-label optimization with label cost. We optimize it with an iterative alpha-expansion solver [6].

Directly solving the problem is impractical due to the image resolution (millions of pixels) and the large label space (thousands of labels). Therefore, we apply (i) a simple up-sampling scheme and (2) a pre-filtering process to limit the solution space. The computational time varies from 10 seconds to a few minutes for solving the graph cut problem with a single thread on a 3.4Hz CPU.

Up-Sampling a Lower Resolution Label Map: The iterative alpha-expansion solver is performed on a target image that is $1/8$ the resolution (in each dimension) of the desired result. After optimization, the label values are upsampled as follows. Each pixel in the original high resolution target image has four possible label candidates at the 4 nearest pixels in the low-resolution label image. We simply pick the label with the lowest appearance penalty (Eq. 4).

Pre-filtering: First, we reduce the label set by discarding input images that are far from the COP of the reference view or cover only a small portion of the target image (see Section 5 for more details of this process). Next, we observe that the optimization process tends to reject pixels that (i) have large geometry cost, (ii) have poor patch compatibilities, or (iii) are too dark or over-saturated (essentially, pixels in solid black or white regions). Removing some obviously low quality pixels before performing the

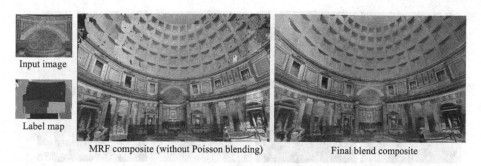

Input image

Label map

MRF composite (without Poisson blending)   Final blend composite

Fig. 2. Landmark: Pantheon in Rome. Typically 10-20 unique labels are present in the label map after the graph-cut optimization. It is used to create an MRF composite.

optimization limits the solution space and can thus greatly improve the computational efficiency. Specifically, we remove a label l at pixel p from the solution space, that is, assigning infinity cost, when (i) $E_{geometry}(p, l) > 20$, $E_{compatibility}(p, l, p, l) > 0.6$, or $E_{contrast}(p, l) > \sqrt{2} - 0.01$.

4.6 Poisson Image Blending

The final, blended composite is computed from the MRF composite by solving a Poisson equation (Fig 2). We first compute the x, y gradient from the MRF composite, and set the values to be 0 at places where the label changes or where the label is -1. The blended composite should keep the color from the reference images; thus, we set a large weight (1000) to penalize differences from the reference image colors at the locations where reference pixels are available.

5   Implementation Details

Depth Map Reconstruction: We use publicly available multi-view stereo software [8] to reconstruct per-view depth maps, then apply cross bilateral filtering [12] for smoothing, as noise and high frequency geometric details often cause artifacts during image warping. The local window radius is 50 and the regularization parameter is 0.16 (suggested by the code of [12]). Note that we use the corresponding color image as the reference for the bilateral filtering. This process also helps in filling in missing depth values, where kernel weights are simply set to 0 for holes in an initial depth map. Finally, we compute a normal per pixel based on the depths.

Image Selection and Warping: Given a reference photograph and the SfM reconstruction, we first remove each source image with an optical center that is more than a distance τ_{COP} from the reference; we set $\tau_{COP} = 50^1$ in our experiments.

---

[1] The length of 1 unit in our 3D models is the distance between the first pair of images selected by VisualSfM. The pair is selected to have a large number of features in common while having a sufficiently large triangulation angle (greater than 4 degrees between their optical axes).

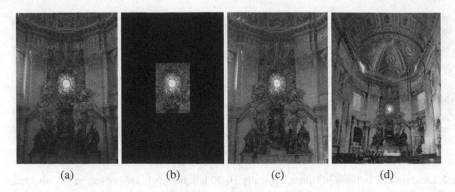

(a)   (b)   (c)   (d)

Fig. 3. Ground truth experiment (San Peter Cathedral). (a) The ground truth image. (b) We only keep 1/9 of the image in the center, which is the input to our system. (c) Uncropped to the ground truth image size. The ground truth image in (a) was not used in creating this composite. (d) Uncropped to even wider FOV than the original.

Next, we forward-warp the remaining source images into the target image using splatting and a soft Z-buffer algorithm. We project each source image pixel into the target view, eliminating source pixels that are backfacing to the target view. In general, re-projected source pixels land between target pixels; furthermore, due to occlusions, foreshortening, and differences in image resolution, it is possible for multiple source pixels to land between the same set of target pixels. We associate each source pixel with the four nearest target pixels, storing at each target pixel p a sample $\{u, l, C, w, d\}$ comprised of the position u, image identifier l, color C, bilinear weight w, and re-projected depth d of the source pixel. We project all source images in this manner, storing a list of samples at each pixel. We then eliminate all samples that are behind the reference viewer ($d < 0$) or occluded by other samples based on a soft Z-buffer; i.e., for each target pixel p, we find the closest positive depth d_{closest} and consider a given sample with depth d at p to be occluded if $d > d_{\text{closest}} + \tau_{\text{depth}}$. (We set $\tau_{\text{depth}} = 20$ in our experiments.) For each target pixel p, we then collect all the samples from the same image l, compute a weighted average color $C_l(p)$ and a source pixel list $U_l(p)$, which will be used in computing label costs in the MRF formulation. Note that $C_l(p)$ only covers part of the target image and is "invalid" elsewhere; further, it is possible for source samples to land apart from each other due to grazing angle surfaces or if the source image is low resolution, leaving gaps between the projected samples.

Finally, we perform one last image selection step: for each image l, if the valid portion of $C_l(p)$ which lies outside of the reference image region covers less than 5% of the target image, then image l is eliminated from further consideration. This step tends to remove images that are: not looking in the direction of the scene of interest, are much lower resolution than the target image, or are close-ups of only a small portion of the scene of interest.

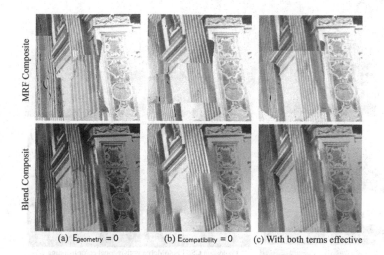

Fig. 4. Evaluating the effectiveness of $E_{geometry}$ and $E_{binary\ compatibility}$ (San Peter Cathedral). We show close-up views of the image mosaic and the Poisson blended results for better visualization. (a) $E_{geometry}$ is turned off. (b) $E_{binary\ compatibility}$ is turned off. (c) Both terms are turned on.

6 Results and Evaluations

We evaluated our system on 10 datasets from the city of Rome and Paris. The number of images in each dataset (i.e., SfM model) ranges from 262 (Stravinsky Fountain) to 2397 (Piazza Navona), where the largest two datasets contain more than 2000 images. We do not have enough space to show results on all the datasets, and refer the reader to the supplementary material[2] for more comprehensive results and evaluations. For each example, we generated results for several target image sizes and kept the largest image that looked plausible after manually cropping to discard image boundaries with significant artifacts. Automatically selecting the target image sizes and cropping is an area for future work.

6.1 Ground Truth Experiment

Figure 3 illustartes an experiment which allows us to compare our result againt the ground truth. We take a relatively wide FOV image (one from San Peter Cathedral dataset), crop to $1/9$ of the image in the center, then run our system to uncrop. Note that the ground truth image is not used for stitching. Despite minor intensity differences, our result faithfully reconstructs the original image using other photographs. In fact, our result has better contrast and reveals more details, in particular, in the bottom half of the image. To take this one step further, we can expand the FOV even more than the original image and generate a convincing composite with much wider field of view than the input.

---

[2] Please visit the project webpage at http://grail.cs.washington.edu/projects/sq_photo_uncrop/ for more information.

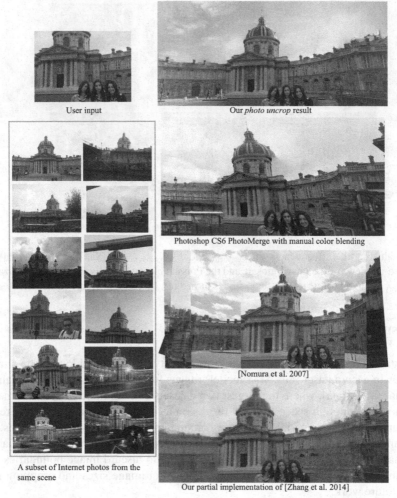

User input

Our *photo uncrop* result

Photoshop CS6 PhotoMerge with manual color blending

[Nomura et al. 2007]

A subset of Internet photos from the same scene

Our partial implementation of [Zhang et al. 2014]

Fig. 5. Institut de France in Paris. We don't show the color blend result of [Nomura et al. 2007] since it is not straight forward from the output of their released executable.

6.2 Evaluation of the Geometry and Compatibility Terms

Here we evaluate the effectiveness of two novel components of our MRF formulation: E_{geometry} and $E_{\text{compatibility}}$. The E_{geometry} term prefers source pixels from smaller baseline views with more accurate depth estimates. These views typically produce fewer distortions. Fig. 4(a) shows the MRF composite and its Poisson blend when E_{geometry} is set to 0. The optimizer picks a patch with large geometry distortion, causing misalignment artifacts. On the other hand, $E_{\text{compatibility}}$ is designed to discourage switching labels to a misaligned image. We show the result of setting $E_{\text{compatibility}} = 0$ in Fig. 4(b). Severe misalignment is visible at the boundaries between image patches in the MRF composite. By incorporating both terms (Fig. 4(c)), the optimizer creates a better composite with fewer visible artifacts.

Fig. 6. Two datasets from Piazza del Popolo. Notice the geometry misalignment in results from PhotoMerge and [Nomura et al. 2007], as well as the blurred composites from [Zhang et al. 2014].

User input   Photo uncrop results

Fig. 7. More results

6.3   Comparitive Evaluation against Baseline Methods

To the best of our knowledge, there does not exist a system that can achieve unlimited FOV expansions on the same uncropping problem by chaining together overlapping community photos. The closest ones are the Photoshop CS6 PhotoMerge tool [1], Scene Collage [18] (with executables released), and the boundary expansion method in [27]. Here we treat the first two as baseline methods. Neither of them is capable of handling the large amount of images in our datasets (processes crash with our 64-bit Windows machine with 48 GB memory). To favor the baseline methods, we provide them with the set of images, which pass the pre-filtering process described in Sec. 5, where the number of remaining images is typically around 100. The source code for the third method [27] (which assumes that all images overlap the input) was not available and was not straightforward to reproduce: it involves many steps including depth-based warping in some areas, homography warping in others, texture synthesis in other parts, and seam carving for still other parts, and the description of the method is fairly brief and high-level. Instead, we used own warping method, which allows wider FOV expansion, and just applied the median-based blending step described in [27] to evaluate the compositing part of their pipeline.

A common problem of the baseline methods is the inability to handle non-planar geometry and reason about visibility, as shown in Fig. 5. Both PhotoMerge and Scene Collage copy pixels from a bridge that is *behind* the camera. The baseline methods usually prefer wider FOV source images, thus tend to use images containing occluders, the bridge and the bus in this case, in the composite.

The presence of large parallax is also a challenge for the baseline methods. Most 2D image transformations used for image stitching, such as a planar homography, are not sufficient to correctly warp images, unless the underlying geometry is near planar. This problem is well illustrated at the top portion of Institut de France in Fig. 5. Results in Fig. 6 show similar misalignment artifacts with the baseline methods, where our composites are significantly better.

Finally, for our examples, the simple median-based blending approach used in [27] produced heavily blurred/ghosted composites (Fig. 5, 6).

More experimental results are provided in Fig. 7, which clearly illustrates that the uncropped images with extended FOV provides better spatial context of the scenes.

7   Conclusion

This paper presents the first work on utilizing Internet imagery to extend the field of view of a user photo. We employ multi-view stereo to warp images into a target, wide FOV image and propose a novel MRF-based formulation designed to handle inevitable geometric inaccuracies. It creates results with image content that resembles the *real scene*. The evaluations on a wide range of real world datasets demonstrate the effectiveness of our approach. The results, while not perfect, are convincing and provide real spatial and visual context not available in the original user photo.

Our approach does have limitations. First, it only works for photos taken at sites where a sufficient number of Internet photos are available (e.g., tourist sites with 100s to 1000s of images in our examples) and would fail to reconstruct regions where there is no coverage. The ground is often a problem area, as people seldom photograph the ground (examples in Fig. 7). As with most panorama stitchers, transient objects in the source images – e.g., people and cars – can be problematic, and seams through them may occur. Recognition and segmentation algorithms could help address this problem. If the user photo itself contains transient objects that are not entirely in frame, then they will remain clipped in the final composite if the new field of view extends beyond them; automatically and realistically extending such objects (people, cars, etc.) out of frame would be interesting if quite challenging.

Acknowledgments. This work was supported by funding from National Science Foundation grant IIS-0963657, Google, Intel, Microsoft, and the UW Animation Research Labs.

References

1. Adobe: PhotoShop CS6 PhotoMerge, http://helpx.adobe.com/en/photoshop/using/create-panoramic-images-photomerge.html
2. Agarwala, A., Agrawala, M., Cohen, M., Salesin, D., Szeliski, R.: Photographing long scenes with multi-viewpoint panoramas. SIGGRAPH (2006)
3. Agarwala, A., Dontcheva, M., Agrawala, M., Drucker, S., Colburn, A., Curless, B., Salesin, D., Cohen, M.: Interactive digital photomontage. SIGGRAPH (2011)
4. Apple: iPhone 5 Specifications, http://support.apple.com/kb/sp655
5. Barnes, C., Shechtman, E., Finkelstein, A., Goldman, D.B.: PatchMatch: A randomized correspondence algorithm for structural image editing. SIGGRAPH 28(3) (2009)
6. Delong, A., Osokin, A., Isack, H.N., Boykov, Y.: Fast approximate energy minimization with label costs. IJCV 96(1), 1–27 (2012)
7. Fay, D., Fay, J., Hoppe, H., Poulain, C.: Terapixel, http://research.microsoft.com/en-us/projects/terapixel/
8. Fuhrmann, S., Goesele, M.: Fusion of depth maps with multiple scales. SIGGRAPH Asia (2011)
9. Furukawa, Y., Curless, B., Seitz, S.M., Szeliski, R.: Towards internet-scale multi-view stereo. In: CVPR (2010)
10. Garg, R., Seitz, S.M.: Dynamic mosaics. 3DimPVT (2012)
11. Hays, J., Efros, A.A.: Scene completion using millions of photographs. SIGGRAPH 26(3) (2007)
12. He, K., Sun, J., Tang, X.: Guided image filtering. In: Daniilidis, K., Maragos, P., Paragios, N. (eds.) ECCV 2010, Part I. LNCS, vol. 6311, pp. 1–14. Springer, Heidelberg (2010)
13. Hertzmann, A., Jacobs, C.E., Oliver, N., Curless, B., Salesin, D.H.: Image analogies. SIGGRAPH (2001)
14. Jancosek, M., Pajdla, T.: Multi-view reconstruction preserving weakly-supported surfaces. In: CVPR (2011)
15. Kaneva, B., Sivic, J., Torralba, A., Avidan, S., Freeman, W.T.: Infinite images: Creating and exploring a large photorealistic virtual space. In: Proceedings of the IEEE (2010)
16. Kopf, J., Uyttendaele, M., Deussen, O., Cohen, M.F.: Capturing and viewing gigapixel images. SIGGRAPH 26(43) (2007)
17. Microsoft: Photosynth, http://photosynth.net/preview
18. Nomura, Y., Zhang, L., Nayar, S.: Scene collages and flexible camera arrays. In: Eurographics Symposium on Rendering (2007)

19. Pritch, Y., Kav-Venaki, E., Peleg, S.: Shift-map image editing. In: ICCV (2009)
20. Rav-Acha, A., Engel, G., Peleg, S.: Minimal aspect distortion (MAD) mosaicing of long scenes. IJCV 78(2-3), 187–206 (2008)
21. Richardt, C., Pritch, Y., Zimmer, H., Sorkine-Hornung, A.: Megastereo: Constructing high resolution stereo panoramas. In: CVPR (2013)
22. Shan, Q., Adams, R., Curless, B., Furukawa, Y., Seitz, S.M.: The visual Turing test for scene reconstruction. In: Joint 3DIM/3DPVT Conference (3DV) (2013)
23. Shum, H.Y., Szeliski, R.: Stereo reconstruction from multiperspective panoramas. In: ICCV (1999)
24. Whyte, O., Sivic, J., Zisserman, A.: Get out of my picture! internet-based inpainting. In: Proceedings of the 20th British Machine Vision Conference, London (2009)
25. Wu, C.: VisualSFM: A visual structure from motion system, http://ccwu.me/vsfm/
26. Zelnik-Manor, L., Peters, G., Perona, P.: Squaring the circle in panoramas. In: ICCV (2005)
27. Zhang, C., Gao, J., Wang, O., Georgel, P., Yang, R., Davis, J., Frahm, J.M., Pollefeys, M.: Personal photo enhancement using internet photo collections. TVCG (2014)
28. Zhang, Y., Xiao, J., Hays, J., Tan, P.: Framebreak: Dramatic image extrapolation by guided shift-maps. In: CVPR (2013)

Solving Square Jigsaw Puzzles with Loop Constraints

Kilho Son, James Hays, and David B. Cooper

Brown University

Abstract. We present a novel algorithm based on "loop constraints" for assembling non-overlapping square-piece jigsaw puzzles where the rotation and the position of each piece are unknown. Our algorithm finds small loops of puzzle pieces which form consistent cycles. These small loops are in turn aggregated into higher order "loops of loops" in a bottom-up fashion. In contrast to previous puzzle solvers which avoid or ignore puzzle cycles, we specifically seek out and exploit these loops as a form of outlier rejection. Our algorithm significantly outperforms state-of-the-art algorithms in puzzle reconstruction accuracy. For the most challenging type of image puzzles with unknown piece rotation we reduce the reconstruction error by up to 70%. We determine an upper bound on reconstruction accuracy for various data sets and show that, in some cases, our algorithm nearly matches the upper bound.

Keywords: Square Jigsaw Puzzles, Loop Constraints.

1 Introduction

Puzzle assembly problems have aroused people's intellectual interests for centuries and are also vital tasks in fields such as archeology [18]. The most significant physical remnants of numerous past societies are the pots they leave behind, but sometimes meaningful historical information is only accessible when the original complete shape is reconstructed from scattered pieces. Computational puzzle solvers assist researchers with not only configuring pots from their fragments [16] but also reconstructing shredded documents or photographs [21,11]. Puzzle solvers may also prove useful in computer forensics, where deleted block-based image data (e.g. JPEG) is difficult to recognize and organize [9]. Puzzle solvers are also used in image synthesis and manipulation by allowing scenes to be seamlessly rearranged while preserving the original content [3].

This paper proposes a computational puzzle solver for non-overlapping square-piece jigsaw puzzles. Many prior puzzle assembly algorithms [4,13,19,6,15] assume that the orientation of each puzzle piece is known and only the location of each piece is unknown. These are called "Type 1" puzzles. More difficult are "Type 2" puzzles where the orientation of each piece is also unknown [8]. Our algorithm assembles both Type 1 and Type 2 puzzles with no anchor points and no information about the dimensions of the puzzles. Our system is also capable of simultaneously reconstructing multiple puzzles whose pieces are mixed together [18].

The most challenging aspect of puzzle reconstruction is the number of successive local matching decisions that must be correct to achieve an accurate reconstruction. For example, given a puzzle with 432 pieces, an algorithm needs to return 431 true positive

D. Fleet et al. (Eds.): ECCV 2014, Part VI, LNCS 8694, pp. 32–46, 2014.

matches with no false positive matches. Even if the pairwise matches can be found with 0.99 precision (rate of true matches in positive matches), the likelihood that a naive algorithm will chain together 431 true matches is only 0.013. Our method focuses not on a dissimilarity metric between pairs of pieces but on a strategy to recover the complete shape from fragments given a dissimilarity metric. Thus, our method can be extended to the various types of puzzle problems without significant modification. The key idea in our puzzle solver, which stands in contrast to previous strategies, is to explicitly find all small loops or cycles of pieces and in turn group these small loops into higher order "loops of loops" in a bottom-up fashion. Our method uses these puzzle loops, specifically 4-cycles, as a form of outlier rejection whereas previous methods, e.g. Gallagher [8], treat cycles as a nuisance and avoid them by constructing cycle-free trees of puzzle pieces. During the bottom-up assembly, some of the small loops discovered may be spurious. Our algorithm then proceeds top-down to merge unused loop assemblies onto the dominant structures if there is no geometric conflict. Otherwise, the loop assemblies are broken into sub-loops and the merging is attempted again with smaller loops. If the loops of 4 pieces still geometrically conflict with the dominant structures, we remove them as an another form of outlier rejection. We test our method with various Type 1 and Type 2 puzzle datasets to verify that our solver outperforms state-of-the-art methods [4,13,19,6,8,15]. Our contributions are summarized below:

- We propose a conceptually simple bottom-up assembly strategy which operates on top of any existing metric for piece similarity. Our method requires no random field formulations with complex inference procedures, no learning, and no tree construction over a graph of puzzle pieces.
- The proposed square puzzle solver approaches precision 1 (perfect reconstructions) given dissimilarity metrics used in prior literature. We empirically show that the precision of pair matches is likely to increase as pieces (or small loops of pieces) are assembled into higher order loops and reaches 1. Specifically, when our solver is able to construct loop assemblies of puzzle pieces above a *dimension*[1] of 4 or 5, the configurations are always correct – piece pair matches in the assemblies are all true positives. Details are discussed in Section 3.
- Our solver significantly outperforms state-of-the-art methods [4,13,19,6,8,15] with the standard data sets [4,12,13]. For the more challenging Type 2 puzzle setup, we reduce the error rate by up to 70% from the most accurate prior work [8]. In fact, we show that our algorithm is approaching the theoretical upper bound in reconstruction accuracy on the data set from Cho *et al.* [4].
- We evaluate the robustness of Type 2 puzzle solving strategies to image noise (iid Gaussian noise). At high noise levels, the performance gap between our work and previous methods [8] is even more pronounced.

1.1 Related Work

Initiated by Freeman and Gardner [7], the puzzle solving problem has been addressed numerous times in the literature. An overview of puzzle tasks and strategies is well described in [8]. Our puzzle solver is in a line with recent works [2,4,13,19,6,8,15] which

---

[1] For example, a loop assembly of dimension (order) 2 is a block of 2 by 2 pieces.

solve non-overlapping square-piece jigsaw puzzles. Even though Demaine *et al.* [5] discover that puzzle assembly is an NP-hard problem if the dissimilarity metric is unreliable, the literature has seen empirical performance increases in Type 1 puzzles by using better compatibility metrics and proposing novel assembly strategies such as greedy methods [13], particle filtering [19], genetic algorithms [15], and Markov Random Field formulations solved by belief propagation [4]. The most closely related prior work from Gallagher [8] defines and solves a new type (Type 2) of non-overlapping square-piece jigsaw puzzle with unknown dimension, unknown piece rotation, and unknown piece position. Gallagher [8] also proposes a new piece dissimilarity metric based on the Mahalanobis distance between RGB gradients on the shared edge. They pose the puzzle problem as minimum spanning tree problem constrained by geometric consistency such as a non-overlap between pieces and solve it by modifying Kruskal's Algorithm [10]. Even though we argue for a puzzle assembly strategy which is effectively opposite to Gallagher [8], because we try to leverage puzzle cycles early and they try to avoid them, their proposed distance metric is a huge improvement on the previous works and their method performs well.

Possibly related to our work at a high level are the "Loop Constraints" widely used to estimate extrinsic parameters of cameras [17,20]. With prior knowledge that the pose of cameras forms a loop, these constraints increase accuracy of camera pose estimation by reducing accumulated error around the loop. Multiple 3D scenes are registered by optimizing over the graph of neighboring views [14]. They optimize the global cost function by decomposing the graph into a set of cycle which can be solved in closed form. The "Best Buddies" strategy [13] that prefers pair matches when each piece in the pair independently believes that the other is its most likely match can be considered as a type of loop. Our loop constraints are different from Pomeranz *et al.* [13] because we exploit a higher-order fundamental unit of 4 pieces that agree on 4 boundaries rather than 2 pieces that agree on 1 boundary. This higher ratio of boundaries to pieces gives us more information to constrain our matching decisions. Our algorithm also proceeds from coarse to fine, so that higher-order loops can reject spurious smaller loops.

2   Square Jigsaw Puzzle Solver with Loop Constraints

We explain our puzzle assembly strategy in the case of Type 2 puzzles – non-overlapping square pieces with unknown rotation, position, and unknown puzzle dimensions. Later we will also quantify performance for the simpler Type 1 case with known piece rotation in Section 4.

The main contribution of our work is a novel, loop-based strategy to reconstruct puzzles from the local matching candidates. Using small loops (4-cycles) as the fundamental unit for reconstruction is advantageous over alternative methods in which candidates are chained together without considering cycles (or explicitly avoiding cycles) because the loop constraint is a form of outlier rejection. A loop of potential matches indicates a consensus among the pairwise distances. While it is easy to find 4 pieces that chain together across 3 of their edges with low error, it is unlikely that the fourth edge completing the cycle would also be among the candidate matches by coincidence. In fact, to build a small loop which is not made of true positive matches, *at least* two of the

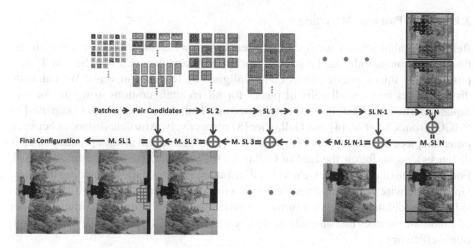

Fig. 1. We discover small loops of increasing dimension from a collection of pieces. The first small loops, made from four pieces, are of dimension 2 (SL 2). We then iteratively build higher-order, larger dimension loops from the lower order loops, e.g. 4 SL 2s are assembled into SL 3s, and so on. We continue assembling loops of loops in a bottom-up fashion until the algorithm finds some maximum sized small loop(s) (SL N). The algorithm then proceeds top-down to merge unused loop assemblies onto the dominant structures (Details are in Section 2.2). This top-down merging is more permissive than the bottom-up assembly and has no "loop" constraint. As long as two small loops share at least two pieces in consistent position they are merged. At a particular level, remaining loops are considered for merging in order of priority, where priority is determined by the mean dissimilarity value of all pair matches in that loop. After all possible merges are done for loops of a particular dimension, the unused loops are broken into their sub-loops and the merging is attempted again with smaller loops. If the reconstruction is not rectangular, trimming and filling steps are required.

edge matches must be wrong. While some small loops will contain incorrect matches that none-the-less lead to a consistent loop, the likelihood of this decreases as higher-order loops are assembled. A small loop of dimension 3, built from 4 small loops of dimension 2, reflects the consensus among many pairwise distance measurements. This is also analyzed further in Section 3.

We use the term "small loop" to emphasize that our method focuses on the shortest possible cycles of pieces at each stage – loops of length 4. Longer loops could be considered, but in this study we use only small loops because (1) longer loops are less likely to be made of entirely true positive pairwise matches and (2) the space of possible cycles increases exponentially with the length of the cycle. While it is possible for us to enumerate all 4-cycles built from candidate pairwise matches in a puzzle, this becomes intractable with longer cycles. (3) Our algorithm is coarse-to-fine, so larger scale cycles are already discovered by finding higher order assemblies of small loops.

2.1 Local, Pairwise Matching

Before assembling loops we must consider the pairwise similarity metric which defines piece compatibility and a strategy for finding candidate pair matches. In Type 2 puzzles, two square puzzle pieces can be aligned in 16 different ways. We calculate dissimilarities between all pairs of pieces for all 16 configurations using the Sum of Squared Distances (SSD) in LAB color space and Mahalanobis Gradient Compatibility (MGC) from Cho *et al.* [4] and Gallagher [8] respectively. Absolute distances between potential piece matches are not comparable (e.g. sky pieces will always produce smaller distances), so we follow the lead of Gallagher [8] and use *dissimilarity ratios* instead. For each edge of each piece, we divide all distances by the smallest matching distance. Unless otherwise stated, edge matches with a dissimilarity ratio less than 1.07 are considered "candidate" matches for further consideration.[2] We limit the maximum number of candidate matches that one side of a piece can have to ζ (typically 10) for computational efficiency.

2.2 Puzzle Assembly with Loop Constraints

We introduce our representation of Type 2 puzzles and operations. We formulate the two major steps of our puzzle assembly: bottom-up recovery of multi-order (i.e. arbitrarily large) small loops in the puzzle and top-down merging of groups of pieces. A visual overview of the assembly process is described in Figure 1.

Formal Representation of Puzzle and Puzzle Operations. Pieces are represented by complex numbers where real and imaginary parts are IDs of pieces and their rotation, respectively. The real parts of the complex numbers range from 1 to the total number of pieces and have unique numbers. The imaginary parts of the complex numbers are $\{0, 1, 2, 3\}$ and represent the counter-clockwise number of rotations, each of 90 degree for the pieces (For Type 1 puzzles, the pieces have no imaginary component to their representation). We pose the puzzle problem as arranging 2D sets of complex numbers. The final result of the puzzle solver is 2D complex-valued matrix. To generally represent configurations in matrices, we also allow 'NaN' which means that no piece occupies the position. We define a rotational transformation function $Rot_n(.)$ where an input is a 2D complex-valued matrix. The function $Rot_n(.)$ geometrically turns the input matrix n times in a counter-clockwise direction. In other words, the individual pieces are rotated by $90 \times n$ degrees in a counter-clockwise direction and the entire matrix turns counter-clockwise (See Figure 2).

Relational symbols are defined given complex-valued matrices U and V. If matrices U and V share at least two of the same ID pieces, they are aligned by one of the shared pieces. If there is no a geometric conflict, such as a overlap with different complex

---

[2] Using dissimilarity ratios makes edge distances more comparable but it has the downside that the first-nearest-neighbor distance is exactly 1 for every edge and thus they are no longer comparable. To alleviate this, the smallest dissimilarity ratio is substituted with the reciprocal of the second smallest dissimilarity ratio. This is only relevant for experiments where the candidate threshold is lowered below 1.

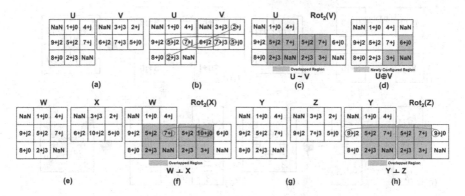

Fig. 2. An example representation of groups of pieces using complex-valued matrices and their relational operations. The top row shows two matrices U and V which are compatible for a merge, and the bottom row shows variations of matrices which are instead incompatible. (a) Given complex-valued matrices U and V, (b) which share multiple pieces with the same IDs (real parts of the complex numbers), (c) we rotate matrix V ($Rot_2(V)$) to align the shared pieces. (d) If the shared region is consistent to each matrix, we merge the two matrices. (e) Given complex-valued matrices W and X, (f) we align them by shared pieces. However, the matrices W and X are in conflict because the overlapped region includes different complex numbers (different IDs or rotations). (g,h) The matrices Y and Z also conflict because the non-overlapped regions include the same ID pieces (real parts of the complex numbers) in both matrices.

numbers (ID or rotation) or an existence of same IDs (real part of a complex number) in a non-shared region, the matrices U and V are geometrically consistent, represented by $U \sim V$. Otherwise, geometric inconsistency is represented by $U \perp V$. If the matrices U and V are geometrically consistent, we can merge the two matrices $U \oplus V$ (See Figure 2). If less than two of the same ID pieces are in both matrices, we assume that they are not related with each other $U \| V$.[3]

Recovering Small Loops of Arbitrary Order in the Puzzle. In this step we discover small loops with candidate pair matches given by the local matching algorithm described in Section 2.1. In the first iteration, small loops of width 2 (SL 2) are formed from four candidate matches. Once all consistent loops are discovered, these loops (e.g. SL 2) are assembled into higher-order 4 cycles (e.g. SL 3) if piece locations are geometrically consistent (piece index and rotation are the same) among all 4 lower-order loops. The algorithm iteratively recovers SL i loops by assembling SL i-1 elements. The procedure continues until no higher-order loops can be built and some maximum size small loop is found (SL N).

---

[3] A single piece correspondence is enough to establish the geometric relationship between two groups of pieces, but we choose not merge on the basis of singe piece correspondences. Such correspondences are more likely to be spurious. However, if they are true correspondences it is likely that as the pieces grow they will eventually have two or more shared pieces and thus become merge-able by our criteria.

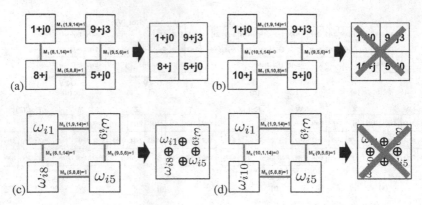

Fig. 3. *Recovering small loops of arbitrary order.* The match candidates from the local, pairwise matching step (Section 2.1) are represented in a sparse 3D binary matrix M_1 of size $K_1 \times K_1 \times 16$. (a) If M_1 indicates that all the pairs (1-9, 9-5, 5-8 and 8-1) are match candidates, the four pieces form a small loop. We make a new matrix (2×2) with the small loop and save it as an element of the 2nd-order set Ω_2. (b) If one or more pairs are not match candidates (in this case, 10-1), the four pieces do not form a small loop. (c) For the ith-order set Ω_i, matrix M_i indicates the match candidates between elements of Ω_i. M_i is size $K_i \times K_i \times 16$. If M_i indicates that all the pairs ($\omega_{i1} - \omega_{i9}, \omega_{i9} - \omega_{i5}, \omega_{i5} - \omega_{i8}$ and $\omega_{i8} - \omega_{i1}$) are match candidates the four groups of pieces form a ith-order small loop. We make a new matrix (($i + 1) \times (i + 1)$) by merging the four groups of pieces and save it as an element of the $(i + 1)$th-order set Ω_{i+1}. (d) If one or more pairs are not match candidates (in this case, $\omega_{i10} - \omega_{i1}$), the four groups of pieces do not form the ith-order small loop.

More formally, the input puzzle is represented by a set of complex numbers $\Omega_1 = \{\omega_{11}, \omega_{12}, \ldots \omega_{1K_1}\}$ where K_1 is a total number of pieces. Match candidates from the local, pairwise matching step (Section 2.1) are stored in a 3D binary matrix M_1 of size $K_1 \times K_1 \times 16$. If $M_1(x, y, z)$ is 1, the piece ID x and the piece ID y are a match candidate with the configuration z. The piece ID y turns $\lfloor \frac{z-1}{4} \rfloor + 1$ times counter-clockwise and places above, to the right, below or to the left of the piece ID x according to $(z - 1) \bmod 4 + 1$.

In the same way, we search for all small loops with combinations of 4 pairs of match candidates given Ω_1 and the binary match candidate matrix M_1 (See Figure 3). All the small loops are saved as elements of the 2nd-order set Ω_2.

Iteratively, given the i th-order set $\Omega_i = \{\omega_{i1}, \omega_{i2}, \ldots \omega_{iK_i}\}$ where the size of the each element (ω_{ix}) is $i \times i$, we generate a 3D binary matrix M_i of size $K_i \times K_i \times 16$. M_i stores match candidates between the elements in the i th-order set Ω_i. If the size of the overlap between the elements ω_{ix} and ω_{iy} is $i \times (i - 1)$ or $(i - 1) \times i$ and there is no geometric conflict ($\omega_{ix} \sim \omega_{iy}$), we set $M_i(x, y, z)$ as 1, otherwise it is 0 where the number z encodes the relative rotation and position of the two matrices. Iteratively, we find small loops of dimension i+1 from elements in the Ω_i with the matrix M_i and save them as elements of the (i+1) th-order set Ω_{i+1} (See Figure 3 (b)). We find a maximum-order of set (Ω_N) until the set is not a null set.

Algorithm 1: Merge matrices in the set Ω_N

Data: Ω_N
Result: Λ_N

$\Lambda_N = \Omega_N$
while *Two or more elements are overlapped between two matrices in the set Λ_N* **do**
  ω_{Nj} and ω_{Nk} are the overlapped pairs with the highest priority among them.
  $\Lambda_N = \Lambda_N \setminus \{\omega_{Nj}, \omega_{Nk}\}; \Lambda_N = \Lambda_N \cup f_m(\omega_{Nj}, \omega_{Nk});$
end
return Λ_N

Merging Groups of Pieces. At this point the algorithm proceeds in a top-down fashion and merges successively smaller remaining small loops without enforcing loop constraints. Merges are performed when two piece assemblies overlap by two or more pieces in geometrically consistent configuration. If a small loop conflicts geometrically with a larger assembly, the small loop is broken into its constituent lower order loops. If two small loops of the same dimension conflict, the loop with the smaller mean value of dissimilarity among its edge matches is used. If the assembly of pieces is not a rectangular shape, the algorithm estimates the dimension of the configuration given the number of pieces and the current configuration. Based on the estimated dimension, the method configures the final shape of the puzzle by trimming (so as to break minimum dimension of small loops in the biggest configuration) and filling.

More formally, we define a merge function given two matrices ω_x, ω_y below

$$
f_m(\omega_x, \omega_y) = \begin{cases}
\omega_x \oplus \omega_y, & \text{if } \omega_x \sim \omega_y \\
\omega_x, & \text{if } \omega_x \perp \omega_y \wedge f_p(\omega_x) \geq f_p(\omega_y) \\
\omega_y, & \text{if } \omega_x \perp \omega_y \wedge f_p(\omega_x) < f_p(\omega_y) \\
\omega_x, \omega_y, & \text{if } \omega_x \| \omega_y
\end{cases}
\tag{1}
$$

where the priority function $f_p(\omega_x, \omega_y)$ is defined below

$$
\begin{cases}
f_p(\omega_x) \geq f_p(\omega_y), & \text{if } \#(\omega_x) > \#(\omega_y) \\
f_p(\omega_x) \geq f_p(\omega_y), & \text{if } \#(\omega_x) = \#(\omega_y) \wedge \bar{\omega}_x < \bar{\omega}_y \\
f_p(\omega_x) < f_p(\omega_y), & \text{Otherwise}
\end{cases}
\tag{2}
$$

where $\#(.)$ is a number of elements in the matrix (except NaN) and $\bar{\omega}_x$ is a mean value of the dissimilarity metrics of all pairs in the group ω_x.

Given the sets of sets $\{\Omega_1, \Omega_2, \Omega_3, \ldots \Omega_N\}$ from the previous step, the method begins with performing the Algorithm 1 to generate a new set Λ_N from the Ω_N. The Λ_N is a set of matrices which are results of merging the matrices in the Ω_N. We performs the Algorithm 2 iteratively to generate a Λ_{i-1} from the Λ_i and Ω_{i-1} until we generate a Λ_2. The Λ_{i-1} is a set of output matrices by merging the matrices in the Λ_i and Ω_{i-1}. We generate Λ_1 by merging remaining pair matching candidates to the set Λ_2.

Elements of a set (Λ_1) of 2D matrices are either a complex number or NaN. The 2D matrices in a set Λ_1 are final configurations by loop constraints. Λ_1 normally contains

Algorithm 2: Merge matrices in the sets Λ_i and Ω_{i-1}

Data: Λ_i and Ω_{i-1}

Result: Λ_{i-1}

$\Lambda_{i-1} = \{\Lambda_i \cup \Omega_{i-1}\} = \{s_1, s_2, \ldots\}$

while *Two or more elements are overlapped between two matrices in the set* Λ_{i-1} **do**

    s_j and s_k are the overlapped pairs with the highest priority among them.

    $\Lambda_{i-1} = \Lambda_{i-1} \backslash \{s_j, s_k\}; \Lambda_{i-1} = \Lambda_{i-1} \cup f_m(s_j, s_k);$

end

return Λ_{i-1}

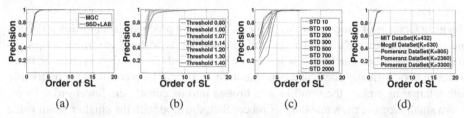

Fig. 4. The average precision of pair matches changes as a function of small loop dimension (order of small loops) (a) for different distance metrics (with the MIT dataset), (b) at different local matching thresholds (with the MIT dataset), (c) at different noise levels (with the MIT dataset), and (d) with different datasets (with the MGC metric). The leftmost point, SL1, represents the performance of the local matching by itself with no loop constraints. The noise levels in (c) are high magnitude because the input images are 16 bit. The patch size is $P = 28$ for all the experiments.

a single 2D large matrix, which is a main configuration from the puzzle. If Λ_1 contains multiple matrices, we consider a matrix that contains complex numbers maximally as a main configuration and break the other configurations into pieces[4]. If the main matrix (configuration) contains NaN it means that the final configuration of the puzzle is not rectangular. In this case we estimate most probable dimension of the puzzle given the current main configuration and the total number of pieces. With the estimated dimension of the puzzle, the method trims the main configuration so that it cuts minimum order of small loops in the main configuration. This is because higher order of small loops are more reliable than smaller one. We fill the NaN with the remaining pieces in the order of minimum total dissimilarity score across all neighbors.

3 Empirical Verification of Small Loop Strategy

We observe in Figure 4 that as higher-order small loops are built from smaller dimension loops the precision of pair matches increases significantly even in the presence of noise with dataset from Cho *et al.* [4] (MIT dataset). In figure 4 (a), for the MGC and SSD+LAB distance metrics, the precisions are 0.627 and 0.5 for local, pairwise edge

---

[4] If we search multiple configurations from mixed puzzles, we consider all matrices in Λ_1 as main configurations.

matches (see order 1 of SL) and jumps dramatically to 0.947 and 0.929 (see order 2 of SL) with our method with the lowest dimension small loop. The precision keeps increasing as order of small loops grows eventually reaching 1 for both metrics (although the recall has dropped considerably by this point). This tendency of the precision to reach 1 as higher order small loops are assembled persists even when the threshold for candidate matches is varied (Figure 4 (b)) and when noise (pixel-wise Gaussian) is added to the puzzle pieces (Figure 4 (c)). With the various datasets, the precision also reaches to 1 as the order of small loops increases (Figure 4 (d)). For most of the experiments, precision approaches 1 when the order of small loops is above 4 or 5. Notably, although the precision of pair matches is below 15% under severe noise (2000 STD), it increases significantly and reaches to 1 as order of small loops grows.

4   Experiments

We verify our square jigsaw puzzle assembly algorithm with sets of images from Cho *et al.* [4] (MIT dataset), Olmos *et al.* [12] (Mcgill dataset) and Pomeranz *et al.* [13]. Each paper provides a set of 20 images and Pomeranz *et al.* [13] additionally presents 2 sets of 3 large images. All the data sets are widely used as a benchmark to measure the performance of square jigsaw puzzle solvers. For some images, the camera is perfectly aligned with the horizon line and image edges (e.g. building boundaries) align exactly with puzzle edges. Some patches contain insufficient information (homogeneous region such as sky, water and snow) and others present repetitive texture (man-made textures and windows). As a result, the pairwise dissimilarity metrics return many false positives and false negatives on these data sets.

We measure performance using metrics from Cho *et al.* [4] and Gallagher [8]. "**Direct Comparison**" measures a percentage of pieces that are positioned absolutely correctly. "**Neighbor Comparison**" is a percentage of correct neighbor pairs and "**Largest Component**" is a percentage of image area occupied by the largest group of correctly configured pieces. "**Perfect Reconstruction**" is a binary indicator of whether or not all pieces are correctly positioned with correct rotation.

For many experiments we also report an "upper bound" on performance. Particular puzzles may be impossible to unambiguously reconstruct because certain pieces are identical, as a result of camera saturation. The upper bound we report is the accuracy achieved by correctly placing every piece that is not completely saturated.

Type 1 Puzzles (known orientation and unknown position): We test on 20 puzzles of 432 pieces each ($K = 432$) with the piece size of 28×28 pixels (P=28) from the MIT dataset. We use MGC as a dissimilarity metric for solving Type 1 puzzles. Table 1 reports our performance for solving Type 1 puzzles. The proposed algorithm outperforms prior works [4,19,13,6,8,15]. Our improvement is especially noteworthy because our algorithm recovers the dimension of the puzzles rather than requiring it as an input as in [4,19,13,6,15]. Our performance is very near the upper bound of the MIT dataset for Type 1 puzzles.

We also test our method with 20 puzzles ($K = 540, P = 28$) from the Mcgill dataset and 26 puzzles (20 ($K = 805, P = 28$), 3 ($K = 2360, P = 28$) and 3 ($K = 3300, P = 28$)) from Pomeranz *et al.* [13] (See Table 2). Notably, for the puzzles

Table 1. Reconstruction performance on Type 1 puzzles from the MIT dataset, The number of pieces is $K = 432$ and the size of each piece is $P = 28$ pixels

	Direct	Nei.	Comp.	Perfect
Cho et al. [4]	10%	55%	-	0
Yang et al. [19]	69.2%	86.2%	-	-
Pomeranz et al. [13]	94%	95%	-	13
Andalo et al. [6]	91.7%	94.3%	-	-
Gallagher et al. [8]	95.3%	95.1%	95.3%	12
Sholomon et al. [15]	80.6%	95.2%	-	-
Proposed	**95.6%**	**95.5%**	**95.5%**	**13**
Upper Bound	96.7%	96.4%	96.6%	15

Table 2. Reconstruction performance on Type 1 puzzles from Olmos et al. [12] and Pomeranz et al. [13]. The size of each piece is $P = 28$ pixels.

	540Pieces [12]		805Pieces [13]		2360Pieces [13]		3300Pieces [13]	
	Direct	Nei.	Direct	Nei.	Direct	Nei.	Direct	Nei.
Pomeranz [13]	83%	91%	80%	90%	33.4%	84.7%	80.7%	85.0%
Andalo [6]	90.6%	**95.3%**	82.5%	93.4%	-	-	-	-
Sholomon [15]	90.6%	94.7%	92.8%	**95.4%**	82.7%	87.5%	65.4%	91.9%
Proposed	**92.2%**	95.2%	**93.1%**	94.9%	**94.4%**	**96.4%**	**92.0%**	**96.4%**

with large numbers of pieces ($K = 2360$, $K = 3300$), our method improves the reconstruction performance significantly (more than 10%) under both Direct and Neighbor Comparison. As the number of puzzle pieces increases, our algorithm has the opportunity to discover even higher order loops of pieces which tend to be high precision.

Type 2 Puzzles (unknown orientation and position): Type 2 puzzles are a challenging extension of Type 1 puzzles. With K pieces, Type 2 puzzles have 4^K times as many possible configurations as Type 1 puzzles. For small puzzles with $K = 432$ this means that Type 2 puzzles have $4^{432} \approx 1.23 \times 10^{26}$ times as many solutions. Due to this increased complexity, there is still room for improvement in Type 2 puzzles solving accuracy whereas performance on Type 1 puzzles is nearly saturated by our algorithm and previous methods.

With Type 2 puzzles ($K = 432, P = 28$) from the MIT dataset, we examine our proposed method with the sum of squared distance (SSD) in LAB color space and MGC as metrics and compare with Gallagher [8] (Table 3). Given the same dissimilarity metric, our method increases the performance by 12% under the Direct Comparison, thus reducing the error rate by up to 70%. Because both methods use the same local distance metric, this difference is entirely due to loop assembly strategy versus the tree-based algorithm in Gallagher [8] (See visual comparisons of results in Figure 5).

We compare our method with Gallagher [8] with different piece sizes (P=14 and 28) and numbers of pieces ($K = 221, 432$ and 1064) on puzzles from the MIT dataset. We use MGC as a dissimilarity metric from now on unless otherwise stated. In all cases, our

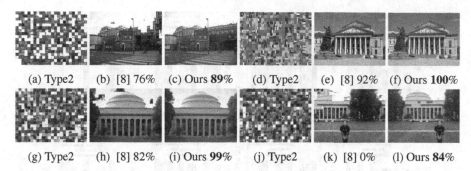

(a) Type2   (b) [8] 76%   (c) Ours **89%**   (d) Type2   (e) [8] 92%   (f) Ours **100%**

(g) Type2   (h) [8] 82%   (i) Ours **99%**   (j) Type2   (k) [8] 0%   (l) Ours **84%**

Fig. 5. Visual comparisons of the results on Type 2 puzzles ($P = 28, K = 432$). The percentage numbers indicate Direct Comparisons.

Table 3. Reconstruction performance on Type 2 puzzles ($P = 28, K = 432$) from the MIT dataset

	Direct	Nei.	Comp.	Perfect
Tree-based+L.SSD [8]	42.3%	68.2%	63.6%	1
S.L.+L.SSD (Proposed)	54.3%	79.7%	66.3%	2
Tree-based+MGC [8]	82.2%	90.4%	88.9%	9
S.L.+MGC (Proposed)	**94.7%**	**94.9%**	**94.6%**	**12**
Upper Bound	96.7%	96.4%	96.6%	15

method outperforms Gallagher's algorithm [8] (See Figure 6 (a) and (b)). Notably, we almost achieve the upper bound of the performance in the case $K = 1064, P = 28$. Our method is verified with more puzzles ($K = 550, 805, 2260$ and 3300) from the Mcgill dataset and Pomeranz *et al.* [13] (Figure 6 (c)). Our puzzle solver distinctively outperforms Gallagher [8] when the number of puzzle pieces increases ($K = 2260, 3300$).

Noise Analysis on Type 2 Puzzles: We further analyze the robustness of our puzzle solver by adding pixel-wise Gaussian noise to the MIT dataset. Experiments are conducted 5 times ($P = 28, K = 432$) and the performance values are averaged. Figure 7 shows that our method tends to outperform Gallagher [8] as noise increases (26% improvement in 2000 STD Gaussian noise under Neighbor Comparison). As pixel-wise Gaussian noise increases in the pieces, the dissimilarity metrics are no longer reliable. The constrained Kruskal's algorithm in [8] has a strong implicit belief in dissimilarity metrics so performance decreases considerably as noise increases. Our method, however, is more robust to spurious pairwise comparisons because loops require consensus between many dissimilarity measurements and thus avoid many false pairwise matches.

Extra Type 2 Puzzles: As opposed to prior works [4,19,13,6,15], our method does not require the dimension of resulting puzzles as an input. This allows us to solve puzzles from multiple images with no information except the pieces themselves. Our solver perfectly assembles 1900 mixed Type 2 puzzle pieces from [1] (See Figure 8).

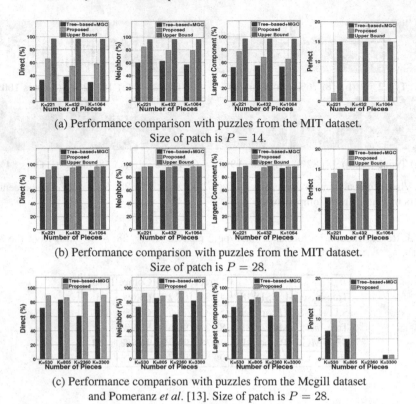

(a) Performance comparison with puzzles from the MIT dataset.
Size of patch is $P = 14$.

(b) Performance comparison with puzzles from the MIT dataset.
Size of patch is $P = 28$.

(c) Performance comparison with puzzles from the Mcgill dataset
and Pomeranz *et al.* [13]. Size of patch is $P = 28$.

Fig. 6. Performance comparison between ours and Tree-based MGC [8] on Type 2 with various cases. A table is presented in a supplemental material.

As observed in the previous experiments, our solver significantly outperforms prior works especially as a number of puzzle pieces increases in both Type 1 and Type 2 puzzles. This is because the opportunity to recover high order small loops (above 4 or 5 orders) increases. (the precision approaches to 1 if the order of small loops is above 4 or 5.) Big images from [1] are used for more intensive experiments with large numbers of puzzle pieces. Our solver configures 9801 and 4108 piece Type 2 puzzles perfectly (See Figure 8). We believe that these are the largest puzzles to date that are perfectly reconstructed with unknown orientation and position (Type 2).

The complexity for searching all small loops (4-cycles) is $O(\zeta^3 * N_p)$, where ζ is the maximum number of positive pair matches that one side of a piece can have and N_p is a number of pair matching candidates. ζ is normally from 1 to 3 and maximally 10 in our experiments and each operation is just an indexation of a binary matrix. The average time for finding all small loops is 0.308 second with the MIT dataset (432-piece Type 2 puzzles) in Matlab. Most of the time is spent in pairwise matching, unoptimized merging, trimming and filling steps. Using MGC, our algorithm spends 140 seconds for 432 pieces and 25.6 hours for 9801 pieces (Type 2) on a modern PC.

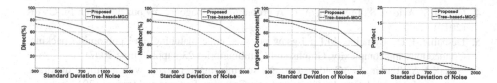

Fig. 7. Performance comparison in the presence of noise. Experiments are conducted 5 times ($P = 28, K = 432$) and the performance values are averaged. Our method outperforms Gallagher [8], especially as noise increases.

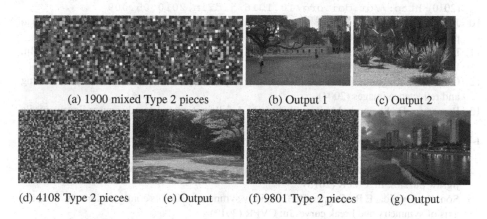

(a) 1900 mixed Type 2 pieces   (b) Output 1   (c) Output 2

(d) 4108 Type 2 pieces   (e) Output   (f) 9801 Type 2 pieces   (g) Output

Fig. 8. Reconstructions on mixed Type 2 puzzles and very large Type 2 puzzles (P = 28)

5 Conclusion

We propose a non-overlapping square-piece jigsaw puzzle solver based on loop constraints. Our algorithm seeks out and exploits loops as a form of outlier rejection. The proposed square-piece jigsaw puzzle solver approaches precision 1 given existing dissimilarity metrics. As a result, our method outperforms the state of the art on standard benchmarks. The performance is even better when the number of puzzle pieces increases. We perfectly reconstruct what we believe to be the largest Type 2 puzzles to date (9801 pieces). Our algorithm outperforms prior work even in the presence of considerable image noise.

Acknowledgments. This work was partially supported by NSF Grant # 0808718 to Kilho Son and David B. Cooper, and NSF CAREER award 1149853 to James Hays.

References

1. http://cdb.paradice-insight.us/
2. Alajlan, N.: Solving square jigsaw puzzles using dynamic programming and the hungarian procedure. American Journal of Applied Science 5(11), 1941–1947 (2009)
3. Cho, T.S., Avidan, S., Freeman, W.T.: The patch transform. PAMI (2010)

4. Cho, T.S., Avidan, S., Freeman, W.T.: A probabilistic image jigsaw puzzle solver. In: CVPR (2010)
5. Demaine, E.D., Demaine, M.L.: Jigsaw puzzles, edge matching, and polyomino packing: Connections and complexity. Graphs and Combinatorics 23(suppl.) (June 2007)
6. Andal, F.A., Taubin, G., Goldenstein, S.: Solving image puzzles with a simple quadratic programming formulation. In: Conference on Graphics, Patterns and Images (2012)
7. Freeman, H., Garder, L.: Apictorial jigsaw puzzles: the computer solution of a problem in pattern recognition. Electronic Computers 13, 118–127 (1964)
8. Gallagher, A.C.: Jigsaw puzzles with pieces of unknown orientation. In: CVPR (2012)
9. Garfinkel, S.L.: Digital forensics research: The next 10 years. Digit. Investig. 7, S64–S73 (2010), http://dx.doi.org/10.1016/j.diin.2010.05.009
10. Joseph, B., Kruskal, J.: On the shortest spanning subtree of a graph and the traveling salesman problem. American Mathematical Society (1956)
11. Liu, H., Cao, S., Yan, S.: Automated assembly of shredded pieces from multiple photos. In: ICME (2010)
12. Olmos, A., Kingdom, F.A.A.: A biologically inspired algorithm for the recovery of shading and reflectance images (2004)
13. Pomeranz, D., Shemesh, M., Ben-Shahar, O.: A fully automated greedy square jigsaw puzzle solver. In: CVPR (2011)
14. Sharp, G.C., Lee, S.W., Wehe, D.K.: Multiview registration of 3D scenes by minimizing error between coordinate frames. PAMI 26(8), 1037–1050 (2004)
15. Sholomon, D., David, O., Netanyahu, N.: A genetic algorithm-based solver for very large jigsaw puzzles. In: CVPR (2013)
16. Son, K., Almeida, E.B., Cooper, D.B.: Axially symmetric 3D pots configuration system using axis of symmetry and break curve. In: CVPR (2013)
17. Williams, B., Cummins, M., Neira, J., Newman, P., Reid, I., Tardós, J.: A comparison of loop closing techniques in monocular slam. Robotics and Autonomous Systems (2009)
18. Willis, A., Cooper, D.B.: Computational reconstruction of ancient artifacts. IEEE Signal Processing Magazine, 65–83 (2008)
19. Yang, X., Adluru, N., Latecki, L.J.: Particle filter with state permutations for solving image jigsaw puzzles. In: CVPR (2011)
20. Zach, C., Klopschitz, M., Pollefeys, M.: Disambiguating visual relations using loop constraints. In: CVPR (2010)
21. Zhu, L., Zhou, Z., Hu, D.: Globally consistent reconstruction of ripped-up documents. PAMI 30(1), 1–13 (2008)

Geometric Calibration of Micro-Lens-Based Light-Field Cameras Using Line Features

Yunsu Bok, Hae-Gon Jeon, and In So Kweon

KAIST, Korea

Abstract. We present a novel method of geometric calibration of micro-lens-based light-field cameras. Accurate geometric calibration is a basis of various applications. Instead of using sub-aperture images, we utilize raw images directly for calibration. We select proper regions in raw images and extract line features from micro-lens images in those regions. For the whole process, we formulate a new projection model of micro-lens-based light-field cameras. It is transformed into a linear form using line features. We compute an initial solution of both intrinsic and extrinsic parameters by a linear computation, and refine it via a non-linear optimization. Experimental results show the accuracy of the correspondences between rays and pixels in raw images, estimated by the proposed method.

Keywords: Calibration, plenoptic, light-field cameras.

1 Introduction

A light-field or plenoptic camera captures angular and spatial information on the distribution of light rays in space, which obtains a multi-view of a scene in a single photographic exposure. The concept of a light-field camera was proposed by Adelson and Wang [1], and light-field photography has been an emerging technology in recent years.

For light-field acquisition, Wilburn et al. [17] presented a bulky camera array. The system can obtain a light-field image with high spatial and angular resolution, but is very expensive. Liang et al. [9] encoded angular information of light rays using programmable aperture patterns. Veeraraghavan et al. [15] presented a simple light-field acquisition technique based on a transparent mask attached at the front of a camera's sensor. Taguchi et al. [12] used hemispherical mirrors for light-field rendering with a wide field of view. However, these approaches have some impediments to commercialization due to manufacturing cost or low quality of the light-field image.

Ng [10] proposed a hand-held light field camera using a micro-lens array. Ng augmented a camera sensor by placing a micro-lens array in front of it. Each micro-lens plays a role in a tiny sharp image of the lens aperture, estimating the directional distribution of incoming rays through it. Georgiev and Lumsdaine [7] presented a modified version of Ng's model that interprets the micro-lens array as an imaging system focused on the focal plane of the main camera lens. Their system is able to capture a light-field image with higher spatial resolution

D. Fleet et al. (Eds.): ECCV 2014, Part VI, LNCS 8694, pp. 47–61, 2014.

than Ng's model, but its angular resolution is decreased. Based on these approaches using a micro-lens array, commercial light-field cameras such as Lytro and Raytrix have been released.

In the computer vision and graphics field, research on applications using hand-held light-field cameras has garnered interest. A representative application of light-field cameras is refocusing [10], which changes the in-focus region of an image after capturing it. A major drawback of such hand-held systems is low spatial resolution. In order to overcome this limitation, several light-field super-resolution methods have been developed [3,11]. Light-field panorama [2] and disparity estimation [13,16] are also interesting applications. In the robotics field, light-field cameras composed of a camera array have shown their usefulness for visual odometry and visual SLAM [6,4]. As is widely known, the performance of these applications can be enhanced if the geometric information of hand-held light-field cameras is available. However, there has been few works on the geometric calibration of hand-held light-field cameras.

An earlier work [14] dealing with a camera array system is based on combining plane and parallax methods. Johannsen et al. [8] present a metric calibration method using a dot pattern with a known grid size and a depth distortion correction for focused light-field cameras [7]. The most similar previous works to the present study is that of Dansereau et al. [5], who proposed a geometry calibration approach for commercial light-field cameras. They modeled pixel-to-ray correspondences of commercial light-field cameras in 3D space, and presented a 4D intrinsic matrix from a conventional pinhole and thin-lens model. However, it has remaining issues such as estimating the initial values of the cameras physical parameters.

In this paper, we present a novel geometric calibration method for micro-lens-based light-field cameras. Instead of using sub-aperture images, we utilize raw images of light-field cameras directly. Since conventional methods of generating sub-aperture images are based on assumptions on light-field cameras, they must be generated 'after' geometric calibration of raw images. We present a new formulation of the projection model of micro-lens-based light-field cameras. We extract line features from raw images and compute an initial solution of both intrinsic parameters and extrinsic parameters of light-field cameras by a linear method. The initial solution is then refined via a non-linear optimization.

2   Line Features from Raw Image

The most important data for calibration of any sensor are correspondences between known environments and sensor measurements. For example, we usually detect corners of a checkerboard with known size for conventional camera calibration. Figure 1 shows examples of raw images captured by Lytro, a popular micro-lens-based camera. It is difficult to extract precise locations of checkerboard corners in small micro-lens images. We have observed that border lines of black and white regions are more visible than corners in micro-lens images. In this paper, we extract line features from raw images and utilize them to calibrate micro-lens-based light-field cameras.

Fig. 1. Examples of raw images captured by Lytro. It is difficult to extract precise locations of checkerboard corners from raw images. However, lines are relatively visible in small micro-lens images.

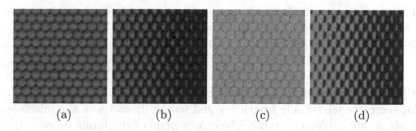

(a)	(b)	(c)	(d)

Fig. 2. Vignetting effect of micro lenses. Left two figures (a, b) and right two figures (c, d) are examples of raw images with vignetting and without vignetting, respectively. Raw images are divided by white-plane images to remove the vignetting effect. Checkerboard images without vignetting (d) are better than those with vignetting (b) for line feature extraction.

Extraction of line features consists of two steps: (1) selection of micro-lenses to extract lines and (2) computation of line parameters for every micro-lens. We assume that the centers of micro-lenses are already known by any means, such as using data given by manufacturers or computing centers from white-plane images. White-plane images with vignetting are used for two purposes: estimating micro-lens centers and removing the vignetting effect from raw images. As shown in Fig. 2(b), the vignetting effect of micro-lenses makes it difficult to estimate the accurate location of line features. We simply divide raw images by white-plane images to generate images without vignetting. In this paper, we use raw images from which the vignetting effect of micro lenses is removed (see Fig. 2(d)).

2.1   Line Feature Extraction

Micro-lens images are usually too small (10×10 pixels for Lytro) to be applied to conventional line fitting techniques. In this paper, we propose an indirect line fitting method. Instead of extracting lines directly from micro-lens images, we generate a number of samples with known line parameters and compare them to actual micro-lens images.

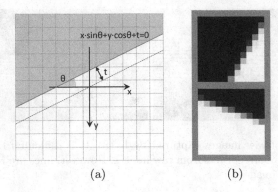

(a)   (b)

Fig. 3. Template generation for line feature extraction. (a) Line equation is determined by an angle θ and a translation t. (b) Example of template. Top: $\theta = 60$(deg), $t = -2.5$(pixel), bottom: $\theta = -20$(deg), $t = 1.7$(pixel).

Let (u_c, v_c) be the center of a micro-lens image. First we prepare a small rectangular template whose side length is equal to the diameter of the micro-lenses (11 pixels in our implementation). The center pixel of the template corresponds to the pixel of the micro-lens image closest to its actual center. Let (u_r, v_r) be the round-off result of (u_c, v_c), and (u'_r, v'_r) the center pixel of the template ($u'_r = v'_r = 6$ in our implementation). The micro-lens center (u'_c, v'_c) in the template is defined as

$$\begin{bmatrix} u'_c \\ v'_c \end{bmatrix} = \begin{bmatrix} u'_r \\ v'_r \end{bmatrix} + \left(\begin{bmatrix} u_c \\ v_c \end{bmatrix} - \begin{bmatrix} u_r \\ v_r \end{bmatrix} \right). \tag{1}$$

Templates are generated by varying the rotation angle θ and translation t of a line (see Fig. 3(a)). Setting the center pixel of the template as $(0,0)$, a line equation is defined as

$$x \cdot \sin \theta + y \cdot \cos \theta + t = 0. \tag{2}$$

Examples of template are shown in Fig. 3(b).

We generate templates with varying parameters $-90 \leq \theta \leq 90$(deg) and $-$(radius)$\leq t \leq$ (radius) (radius=5(pixels) in our implementation using Lytro). They are compared to micro-lens images via normalized cross-correlation (NCC). We compute the 'absolute value' of 'weighted' NCC using Gaussian weight to consider inverted templates and ignore the outside region of micro-lens images. After selecting a template with the maximum NCC value, we adjust the constant term of its line equation to set the actual micro-lens center in the template (1) as the origin:

$$\begin{aligned} (x + (u_c - u_r)) \cdot \sin \theta + (y + (v_c - v_r)) \cdot \cos \theta + t \\ = x \cdot \sin \theta + y \cdot \cos \theta + t + (u_c - u_r) \sin \theta + (v_c - v_r) \cos \theta \qquad (3) \\ = x \cdot \sin \theta + y \cdot \cos \theta + t'. \end{aligned}$$

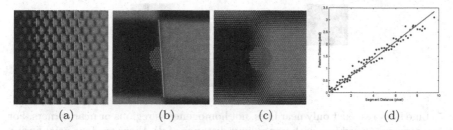

(a)   (b)   (c)   (d)

Fig. 4. Upper-limit distance estimation of line segment. (a) 'Feature distance' refers to the distance between the micro-lens center (red dot) and the line feature (green line) in the raw image. (b) 'Segment distance' is the distance between the micro-lens center (red dot) and line segment (green line) connecting two adjacent corners in the sub-aperture image. (c) An example of N nearest micro-lens centers from the center of a line segment. (d) Relation between feature distance (vertical axis) and segment distance (horizontal axis) is estimated via line fitting.

2.2   Micro Lens Selection

In a raw image of a checkerboard, micro-lenses are classified into three categories: corner, line, and homogeneous. We extract line features from only micro-lens images that contain border lines of black and white regions, not corners or homogeneous regions. In order to identify the class of each micro-lens, we utilize a sub-aperture image at the center (i.e., a collection of center pixels of micro-lens images). This is based on the conventional assumption on micro-lens-based light-field cameras, but is sufficient to provide useful information for the selection.

The distance of a line feature from the micro-lens center in a raw image (feature distance, see Fig. 4(a)) is nearly proportional to that of a line segment from the micro-lens center in a sub-aperture image (segment distance, see Fig. 4(b)). For each line segment connecting adjacent corners of checkerboard, we measure the upper limit of the segment distance that guarantees the existence of a line feature in the micro-lens. This must be measured for each line segment because it depends on the distance from the camera to the checkerboard in the real world.

We compute the center of a line segment in a sub-aperture image, and then select N nearest micro-lens centers from it (see Fig. 4(c)). A line feature is extracted from each micro-lens center. We compute the feature distance and estimate the relation between the feature distance and the segment distance (see Fig. 4(d)). We consider a segment distance corresponding to a user-defined feature distance as the upper limit of the segment distance of a line segment.

Each line segment in a sub-aperture image has a small region where line features exist in the raw image. This is shown in Fig. 5. For each line segment, there are at most four neighboring line segments perpendicular to it. Each perpendicular line has its own upper-limit distance. We classify regions near perpendicular segments within their upper-limit distances multiplied by a user-defined constant

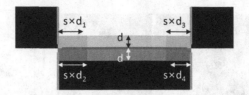

Fig. 5. Line features exist only near lines, not homogeneous regions or near corners. For each line segment (a red line with upper-limit distance of d), there are four neighboring line segments (orange lines with upper-limit distances of $d_1 \sim d_4$) perpendicular to it. Blue regions near perpendicular segments within their upper-limit distances multiplied by s are classified as 'corner regions'. The remaining region (green region) near the line segment within its upper-limit distance is classified as a 'line region'. We extract line features from only micro-lenses whose centers are in line regions of a sub-aperture image.

s as 'corner regions'. Since the upper-limit distances of neighboring perpendicular lines may be different ($d_1 \neq d_2$, $d_3 \neq d_4$ in Fig. 5), we choose a larger one between two distances. The region near each line segment within its upper-limit distance except corner regions is classified as a 'line region'. We extract line features from micro-lenses whose centers are in line regions of the sub-aperture image.

3   Projection Model of Micro-Lens-Based Light-Field Cameras

Micro-lens-based light-field cameras contains two layers of lenses: the main lens and a micro-lens array. We apply the 'thin lens model' to the main lens and the 'pinhole model' to the micro-lenses, similar to [5].

Let F be the focal length of a thin lens. All rays from an arbitrary point with distance a from a lens pass through it and head to a common point called an 'image (see Fig. 6). That is why we may consider the location of an image as that of a point. The word 'image' refers to 'a common point of rays' only in this section while it refers to 'data captured by a camera' in the other sections.

The image, point, and lens center are collinear because a ray passing through them (red line in Fig. 6) is not refracted by the lens. If the lens center is set as the origin, the coordinates of the image can therefore be computed using those of the point and a distance ratio b/a. The distance b of the image from the lens is computed using a and F as follows:

$$\frac{1}{a} + \frac{1}{b} = \frac{1}{F} \tag{4}$$

$$b = \frac{aF}{a - F} = \frac{F}{a - F} \cdot a. \tag{5}$$

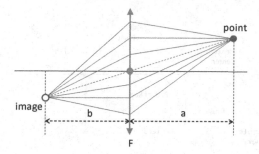

Fig. 6. Thin lens model. All rays from an arbitrary point pass through a common point called an 'image'. Observing a point through a lens, we may treat the location of an image as that of the point. If the lens center is set as the origin, the coordinates of the image are computed using those of the point and a distance ratio b/a because a ray (dotted red line) passing through them and the lens center is not refracted by the lens.

Figure 7 shows the projection model of micro-lens-based light-field cameras. The projected location of an arbitrary point is the intersection of the CCD array and a ray that passes through an image of the point and a micro-lens center (see Fig. 7(a)). The actual path of the ray is indicated by a red line, but we do not have to be concerned with this because we consider the location of the image as that of the point.

Since there are many micro-lenses, a point is projected onto multiple locations (one location for each micro-lens). In Fig. 7(b), the left part of the main lens in Fig. 7(a) is rotated 180 degrees. Without loss of generality, we set the center and optical axis of the main lens as the origin and the z-axis of the camera coordinate system, respectively. The relation between the coordinates of point (X_c, Y_c, Z_c) and image (X, Y, Z) is described as

$$\begin{bmatrix} X \\ Y \\ Z \end{bmatrix} = \frac{F}{Z_c - F} \begin{bmatrix} X_c \\ Y_c \\ Z_c \end{bmatrix}. \tag{6}$$

The ratio among elements is not changed because both of them lie on a line that passes through the origin of the camera coordinate system.

Let L and l be the distances from the micro-lens array to the main lens and the CCD array, respectively. The physical center of the micro-lens is computed using its projected location (x_c, y_c):

$$\text{(physical center of micro lens)} = L \begin{bmatrix} x_c \\ y_c \\ 1 \end{bmatrix}. \tag{7}$$

Note that projected locations are expressed in a normalized coordinate system $(z = 1)$.

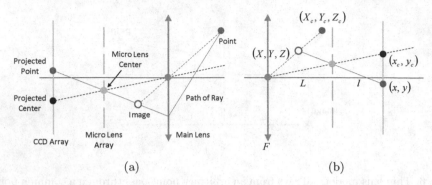

(a)   (b)

Fig. 7. Projection model of micro-lens-based light-field cameras. (a) All rays from an arbitrary point pass through the image of the point. For each micro-lens, a ray from the image passes through its center and meets with the CCD array. (b) The left part of the main lens is rotated 180 degrees to make further computation easier, similar to the conventional pinhole model.

The projected location (x, y) of an image is computed by extending the line connecting the image and the micro-lens center as follows:

$$(L+l)\begin{bmatrix} x \\ y \\ 1 \end{bmatrix} = \begin{bmatrix} X \\ Y \\ Z \end{bmatrix} + \frac{L+l-Z}{L-Z}\left(L\begin{bmatrix} x_c \\ y_c \\ 1 \end{bmatrix} - \begin{bmatrix} X \\ Y \\ Z \end{bmatrix} \right) \tag{8}$$

$$\begin{bmatrix} x \\ y \end{bmatrix} = -\frac{l}{(L-Z)(L+l)}\begin{bmatrix} X \\ Y \end{bmatrix} + \frac{L(L+l-Z)}{(L-Z)(L+l)}\begin{bmatrix} x_c \\ y_c \end{bmatrix}. \tag{9}$$

Equation (9) is simplified by subtracting the projected micro-lens center (x_c, y_c) from it:

$$\begin{bmatrix} x - x_c \\ y - y_c \end{bmatrix} = \frac{l}{(L-Z)(L+l)}\left(-\begin{bmatrix} X \\ Y \end{bmatrix} + Z\begin{bmatrix} x_c \\ y_c \end{bmatrix} \right). \tag{10}$$

Substituting (6) into (10),

$$\begin{bmatrix} x - x_c \\ y - y_c \end{bmatrix} = \frac{l}{(L - \frac{F}{Z_c-F}Z_c)(L+l)}\left(-\frac{F}{Z_c-F}\begin{bmatrix} X_c \\ Y_c \end{bmatrix} + \frac{F}{Z_c-F}Z_c\begin{bmatrix} x_c \\ y_c \end{bmatrix} \right)$$

$$= \frac{1}{K_2(K_1 Z_c - 1)}\left(-\begin{bmatrix} X_c \\ Y_c \end{bmatrix} + Z_c\begin{bmatrix} x_c \\ y_c \end{bmatrix} \right), \tag{11}$$

where $K_1 \equiv 1/F - 1/L$ and $K_2 \equiv L(L/l + 1)$.

4   Calibration of Micro-Lens-Based Light-Field Cameras

The projection model of (11) contains normalized coordinates of projected points. They can be computed if and only if we know the transformation between the normalized coordinates and the image coordinates. In the case of conventional pinhole cameras, the transformation is defined by a 3×3 matrix called an intrinsic parameter. We simplify it by assuming zero skew, single focal length, and zero center (coordinate of image center is set to $(0,0)$). The image coordinates (u, v) are then computed simply by scaling the normalized coordinates(x, y):

$$\begin{bmatrix} u \\ v \end{bmatrix} = f \begin{bmatrix} x \\ y \end{bmatrix}, \tag{12}$$

where f is the focal length of intrinsic parameters. Actually f indicates the number of pixels in one measurement unit (millimeter in this paper). Adopting (12) to the projection model (11),

$$\begin{bmatrix} u - u_c \\ v - v_c \end{bmatrix} = \frac{1}{K_2(K_1 Z_c - 1)} \left(-f \begin{bmatrix} X_c \\ Y_c \end{bmatrix} + Z_c \begin{bmatrix} u_c \\ v_c \end{bmatrix} \right). \tag{13}$$

The simplified model (12) will be restored to a 3×3 upper triangular matrix in Sect. 5.

We apply (13) to line features extracted from raw images of a checkerboard pattern. Unfortunately, projections of two adjacent corners do not lie exactly on their corresponding line feature because of nonlinear terms such as the left multiplier term $1/K_2(K_1 Z_c - 1)$ of (13) and radial distortion of the main lens. We do not know which part of a line segment is projected onto micro-lens images and extracted as line features. However, projections of corners are close enough to corresponding line features to use an approximation that they lie on the features. Let (a, b, c) be the parameters of a line feature:

$$a(u - u_c) + b(v - v_c) + c = 0 \quad (a^2 + b^2 = 1). \tag{14}$$

Substituting corner projections (13), the line equation (14) becomes

$$a(-f X_c + Z_c u_c) + b(-f Y_c + Z_c v_c) + c K_2(K_1 Z_c - 1) = 0. \tag{15}$$

Let (X_w, Y_w, Z_w) be one of two corners that define a line segment in the world coordinate system (i.e., the checkerboard coordinate system). It must be transformed into the camera coordinate system by an unknown transformation matrix with a 3×3 rotation matrix $\mathbf{R}$ and a 3×1 translation vector $\mathbf{t}$

$$\begin{bmatrix} X_c \\ Y_c \\ Z_c \end{bmatrix} = \mathbf{R} \begin{bmatrix} X_w \\ Y_w \\ Z_w \end{bmatrix} + \mathbf{t} = \begin{bmatrix} r_{11} X_w + r_{12} Y_w + t_1 \\ r_{21} X_w + r_{22} Y_w + t_2 \\ r_{31} X_w + r_{32} Y_w + t_3 \end{bmatrix}, \tag{16}$$

where r_{ij} and t_i are the elements of $\mathbf{R}$ and $\mathbf{t}$ at the i-th row and the j-th column, respectively. Without loss of generality, the z-coordinate of the checkerboard pattern is set to zero ($Z_w = 0$ for all corners). Substituting (X_c, Y_c, Z_c) by (16), (15) becomes an $\mathbf{Ax} = \mathbf{0}$ form:

$$
\begin{bmatrix}
-aX_w \\
-aY_w \\
-a \\
-bX_w \\
-bY_w \\
-b \\
(au_c + bv_c)X_w \\
(au_c + bv_c)Y_w \\
(au_c + bv_c) \\
cX_w \\
cY_w \\
c
\end{bmatrix}^{\top}
\begin{bmatrix}
fr_{11} \\
fr_{12} \\
ft_1 \\
fr_{21} \\
fr_{22} \\
ft_2 \\
r_{31} \\
r_{32} \\
t_3 \\
K_1 K_2 r_{31} \\
K_1 K_2 r_{32} \\
K_2(K_1 t_3 - 1)
\end{bmatrix} = 0. \tag{17}
$$

For each micro-lens whose center is in line regions shown in Fig. 5, two equations are derived from two corners that define a line segment corresponding to a line feature in the lens. Stacking all line features to the matrix $\mathbf{A}$, its right singular vector $\mathbf{v}$ corresponding to its smallest singular value is selected as an initial solution multiplied by an unknown scale λ ($\mathbf{v} = \lambda \mathbf{x}$). Let v_n be the n-th element of $\mathbf{v}$. Initial values of unknown parameters are computed using $\mathbf{v}$ as follows:

$$
f = \sqrt{\frac{-v_1 v_2 - v_4 v_5}{v_7 v_8}} \quad (\because r_{11}r_{12} + r_{21}r_{22} + r_{31}r_{32} = 0), \tag{18}
$$

$$
\lambda = \sqrt{(v_1/f)^2 + (v_4/f)^2 + v_7^2} \quad (\because r_{11}^2 + r_{21}^2 + r_{31}^2 = 1), \tag{19}
$$

$$
\mathbf{r}_1 = \frac{1}{\lambda f}\begin{bmatrix} v_1 & v_4 & fv_7 \end{bmatrix}^{\top}, \quad \mathbf{r}_3 = \frac{\mathbf{r}_1 \times \begin{bmatrix} v_2 & v_5 & fv_8 \end{bmatrix}^{\top}}{\left\| \mathbf{r}_1 \times \begin{bmatrix} v_2 & v_5 & fv_8 \end{bmatrix}^{\top} \right\|}, \quad \mathbf{r}_2 = \mathbf{r}_3 \times \mathbf{r}_1, \tag{20}
$$

$$
\mathbf{t} = \frac{1}{\lambda f}\begin{bmatrix} v_3 & v_6 & fv_9 \end{bmatrix}^{\top}, \tag{21}
$$

$$
K_2 = \frac{1}{\lambda}\left(\frac{(v_{10} + v_{11})t_3}{r_{31} + r_{32}} - v_{12} \right), \quad K_1 = \frac{v_{10} + v_{11}}{\lambda K_2(r_{31} + r_{32})}, \tag{22}
$$

where $\mathbf{r}_n$ is the n-th column of $\mathbf{R}$. The scale λ is always positive in (19); however, it can be negative in real cases. We determine its sign by checking that of the third term of $\mathbf{t}$ (v_9/λ) because it must be positive (i.e., the planar pattern must be in front of the camera). If it is negative, we change the signs of $\mathbf{r}_1$, $\mathbf{r}_2$, $\mathbf{t}$, K_1 and K_2.

5   Non-linear Optimization

The initial solution computed in Sect. 4 is refined via a non-linear optimization. We have mentioned that checkerboard corners do not lie exactly on corresponding line features. Let (u, v) and (u', v') be projections of two adjacent corners (X_w, Y_w) and (X'_w, Y'_w), respectively, onto a micro-lens image whose center is at (u_c, v_c). We compute a point on the line connecting (u, v) and (u', v') that is closest to (u_c, v_c) by computing a constant k'. In the optimization process, we project $(X_w, Y_w) + k'(X'_w - X_w, Y'_w - Y_w)$ onto the micro-lens image and compute the distance between the projected location and corresponding line feature as follows:

$$k' = \operatorname*{argmin}_{k} \left\| \begin{bmatrix} u \\ v \end{bmatrix} + k \left(\begin{bmatrix} u' \\ v' \end{bmatrix} - \begin{bmatrix} u \\ v \end{bmatrix} \right) - \begin{bmatrix} u_c \\ v_c \end{bmatrix} \right\|^2. \tag{23}$$

In Sect. 4, we simplified the transformation between normalized coordinates and image coordinates as (12) and (13). However, the simplified transformation is not suitable for real cameras. We restore it to a generalized model with zero skew as follows:

$$\begin{bmatrix} u \\ v \\ 1 \end{bmatrix} = \begin{bmatrix} f_x & 0 & c_x \\ 0 & f_y & c_y \\ 0 & 0 & 1 \end{bmatrix} \begin{bmatrix} x \\ y \\ 1 \end{bmatrix} \tag{24}$$

$$\begin{bmatrix} u - u_c \\ v - v_c \end{bmatrix} = \frac{1}{K_2(K_1 Z_c - 1)} \left(- \begin{bmatrix} f_x X_c \\ f_y Y_c \end{bmatrix} + Z_c \begin{bmatrix} u_c - c_x \\ v_c - c_y \end{bmatrix} \right). \tag{25}$$

Initial values of f_x and f_y are set to that of f, and those of c_x and c_y are set to the coordinates of the center pixel of raw images.

Moreover, we also consider radial distortion of the main lens. An arbitrary point (X_c, Y_c, Z_c) in the camera coordinate system is distorted using a popular model,

$$\begin{bmatrix} \hat{X}_c \\ \hat{Y}_c \\ \hat{Z}_c \end{bmatrix} = \begin{bmatrix} (1 + k_1 r^2 + k_2 r^4) X_c \\ (1 + k_1 r^2 + k_2 r^4) Y_c \\ Z_c \end{bmatrix} \quad \left(r^2 = (X_c/Z_c)^2 + (Y_c/Z_c)^2 \right), \tag{26}$$

mentioned in Zhang's work on camera calibration [18]. The camera coordinate (X_c, Y_c, Z_c) in (25) is substituted by $(\hat{X}_c, \hat{Y}_c, \hat{Z}_c)$.

The final version of the cost function of the non-linear optimization is

$$\begin{aligned} & g(K_1, K_2, \mathbf{R}, \mathbf{t}, f_x, f_y, c_x, c_y, k_1, k_2) \\ & = \sum \| a \cdot (u + k'(u' - u) - u_c) + b \cdot (v + k'(v' - v) - v_c) + c \|^2, \end{aligned} \tag{27}$$

which is a combination of the equations mentioned above. First we transform adjacent corners of a checkerboard into the camera coordinate system using (16). They are distorted by (26) and then projected onto micro-lens images using (25). The cost function g is a squared sum of distances between the closest points computed by (23) and corresponding line features (14). Note that just one distance is computed for each line feature, instead of two.

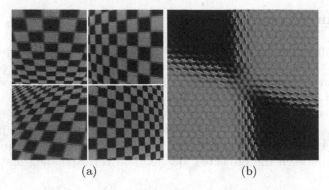

(a)   (b)

Fig. 8. (a) A part of raw images used for calibration. (b) Example of line features extracted from raw images. Red dots and green lines indicate micro-lens centers and line features, respectively. No line features are extracted from corner regions.

The proposed algorithm can be applied to a single raw image of a checkerboard. In the case of using multiple frames, we compute an average value of f first and compute initial values of the other parameters using it. Since a small number of frames may provide an imaginary value for f due to noise and mathematical error, we ignore those values and compute the average of only real values. Values of K_1 and K_2 are also averaged to make the final solution converge faster.

6 Experimental Results

We captured a dataset of checkerboard images using a Lytro camera. The size of raw images are 3280×3280 pixels, and the grid size of a checkerboard is 10 mm. Line parameters (θ, t) in Sect. 2.1 are selected among $\theta = 0 : 0.5 : 180$(deg, MATLAB expression) and $t = -4 : 0.05 : 4$(pixels) via a coarse-to-fine search. For the line fitting described in Fig. 4(d), we selected $N = 100$ nearest micro-lens centers from each line segment and discarded the centers whose feature distance is larger than 3 pixels. The upper limit of the segment distance in Sect. 2.2 is set to the value corresponding to the user-defined feature distance of 2 pixels. The value of s is set to 2.5 because the radius of micro-lens images is 5 pixels in the case of using Lytro. We extracted 155,474 line features from 9 raw images shown in Fig. 8(a). Examples of line features extracted from raw images are displayed in Fig. 8(b). Since we did not extract corners, we projected them onto corner regions of raw images to verify the accuracy of the results. Figure 9 shows an example of a corner projected onto a raw image. Our dataset and executables are available online[1].

After calibrating the camera using raw images, we generated a number of sub-aperture images based on the calibration result. Since the average distance between adjacent micro-lens centers is near 10 pixels, the size of the sub-aperture images is set to 328×328 (1/10 of raw images). We extracted corner features from

---

[1] https://sites.google.com/site/yunsubok/lf_geo_calib

Fig. 9. Corners are projected onto raw images to verify the accuracy of line features extracted from raw images. The right image is a magnified view of the region denoted by a red rectangle in the left image. Red circles and green dots indicate micro-lenses and projected corners, respectively. The projected location in each micro-lens image is very close to its actual location.

Table 1. Projection error of sub-aperture images (unit: pixel)

Distance from center	-3	-2	-1	0	1	2	3
-3	0.9944	0.5913	0.5301	0.5152	0.5253	0.5766	0.7563
-2	0.5587	0.4634	0.4508	0.4451	0.4487	0.4578	0.5357
-1	0.4795	0.4308	0.4163	0.3759	0.3917	0.4285	0.4625
0	0.4451	0.4127	0.3859	0.3368	0.3526	0.4036	0.4253
1	0.4332	0.3944	0.3937	0.3589	0.3675	0.3885	0.4137
2	0.4344	0.3825	0.3615	0.3623	0.3684	0.3830	0.4229
3	0.5331	0.4055	0.3945	0.3885	0.3896	0.3968	0.5079

sub-aperture images independently and computed the RMS value of projection errors. Extrinsic parameters of the calibration result are the transformation from the checkerboard coordinate system to the camera coordinate system of the raw images. Transformation from the camera coordinate system to each sub-aperture coordinate system is computed using the calibration result. Projection errors of sub-aperture images are summarized in Table 1. Although extrinsic parameters of sub-aperture images are not estimated independently but 'predicted' using the calibration result, the projection errors are very small. Details of generating sub-aperture images are described in our supplementary material.

For direct comparison of the proposed method with [5], we also measured ray re-projection errors in millimeters using the same datasets[2]. The results are shown in Table 2. Although our RMS ray re-projection errors are almost the same as those of [5], our method has two advantages. The first is that we have obtained similar results using a smaller number of parameters (6 parameters) than [5] (12 parameters). This is verified by reducing the number of images used for calibration, as shown in Table 2. In addition, our sub-aperture images are geometrically closer to images captured by a parallel multi-camera array than those of [5].

---

[2] http://marine.acfr.usyd.edu.au/research/plenoptic-imaging

Table 2. RMS ray re-projection error of sub-aperture images (unit: mm). The numbers (N) of the proposed method indicate the number of images used for calibration among 18 images for each dataset.

Method	Previous [5]	Proposed	Proposed
Dataset B (grid 3.61)	0.0628	(9) 0.0717	(5) 0.0700
Dataset E (grid 35.1)	0.363	(14) 0.365	(5) 0.331

(a)   (b)   (c)   (d)

Fig. 10. (a) Sub-aperture image using the method in [5]. (b) Disparity map estimated using (a). (c) Sub-aperture image using the proposed method. (d) Disparity map estimated using (c).

High accuracy of geometric calibration is essential for good results in various applications. In order to verify the geometric accuracy of the proposed method, we estimated disparity maps using a state-of-the-art disparity labeling method [16] as an example application. It uses a structure tensor to find correspondences between sub-aperture images and it provides accurate results if corresponding points in sub-aperture images are aligned well. We fixed user-defined parameters for a fair comparison. Sub-aperture images from [5] in Fig. 10(a) lead to outliers while those from the proposed method in Fig. 10(c) provide reliable results.

7   Conclusion

We presented a novel method of geometric calibration of micro-lens-based light-field cameras. Instead of using sub-aperture images, line features are extracted from raw images directly. We formulated a projection model based on the thin-lens model and the pinhole model and applied it to line features. An initial solution of both intrinsic and extrinsic parameters are estimated using a linear computation, and it is refined via a non-linear optimization. Since the correspondences between rays and pixels in raw images are estimated accurately using the proposed method, geometrically well-aligned sub-aperture images provide small projection errors and a disparity map with less noise. Future work will include improving the accuracy of line features, overcoming limitations of thin-lens and pinhole models, and modeling the lens distortion of outer sub-aperture images.

Acknowledgement. This research is supported by the Study on Imaging Systems for the next generation cameras funded by the Samsung Electronics Co., Ltd (DMC R&D center) (IO130806-00717-02).

References

1. Adelson, E.H., Wang, J.Y.A.: Single lens stereo with a plenoptic camera. IEEE Transactions on Pattern Analysis and Machine Intelligence 14(2), 99–106 (1992)
2. Birklbauer, C., Opelt, S., Bimber, O.: Rendering gigaray light fields. Computer Graphics Forum 32(2), 469–478 (2013)
3. Bishop, T.E., Zanetti, S., Favaro, P.: Light field superresolution. In: International Conference on Computational Photography, pp. 1–9 (2009)
4. Dansereau, D.G., Mahon, I., Pizarro, O., Williams, S.B.: Plenoptic flow: Closed-form visual odometry for light field cameras. In: IEEE/RSJ International Conference on Intelligent Robots and Systems, pp. 4455–4462 (2011)
5. Dansereau, D.G., Pizarro, O., Williams, S.B.: Decoding, calibration and rectification for lenselet-based plenoptic cameras. In: IEEE Conference on Computer Vision and Pattern Recognition, pp. 1027–1034 (2013)
6. Dong, F., Ieng, S.H., Savatier, X., Etienne-Cummings, R., Benosman, R.: Plenoptic cameras in real-time robotics. The International Journal of Robotics Research 32(2), 206–217 (2013)
7. Georgiev, T., Lumsdaine, A.: Reducing plenoptic camera artifacts. Computer Graphics Forum 29(6), 1955–1968 (2010)
8. Johannsen, O., Heinze, C., Goldluecke, B., Perwaß, C.: On the calibration of focused plenoptic cameras. In: Grzegorzek, M., Theobalt, C., Koch, R., Kolb, A. (eds.) Time-of-Flight and Depth Imaging. LNCS, vol. 8200, pp. 302–317. Springer, Heidelberg (2013)
9. Liang, C.K., Lin, T.H., Wong, B.Y., Liu, C., Chen, H.H.: Programmable aperture photography: multiplexed light field acquisition. ACM Transactions on Graphics 27(3), Article 55 (2008)
10. Ng, R., Levoy, M., Brédif, M., Duval, G., Horowitz, M., Hanrahan, P.: Light field photography with a hand-held plenoptic camera. Stanford University Computer Science Technical Report CSTR 2(11) (2005)
11. Perez Nava, F., Luke, J.: Simultaneous estimation of super-resolved depth and all-in-focus images from a plenoptic camera. In: 3DTV Conference: The True Vision-Capture, Transmission and Display of 3D Video, 2009, pp. 1–4 (2009)
12. Taguchi, Y., Agrawal, A., Veeraraghavan, A., Ramalingam, S., Raskar, R.: Axial-cones: modeling spherical catadioptric cameras for wide-angle light field rendering. ACM Transactions on Graphics 29(6), Article 172 (2010)
13. Tao, M.W., Hadap, S., Malik, J., Ramamoorthi, R.: Depth from combining defocus and correspondence using light-field cameras. In: IEEE International Conference on Computer Vision, pp. 673–680 (2013)
14. Vaish, V., Wilburn, B., Joshi, N., Levoy, M.: Using plane+parallax for calibrating dense camera arrays. In: IEEE Conference on Computer Vision and Pattern Recognition, pp. I-2-I-9 (2004)
15. Veeraraghavan, A., Raskar, R., Agrawal, A., Mohan, A., Tumblin, J.: Dappled photography: Mask enhanced cameras for heterodyned light fields and coded aperture refocusing. ACM Transactions on Graphics 26(3), Article 69 (2007)
16. Wanner, S., Goldluecke, B.: Globally consistent depth labeling of 4d lightfields. In: IEEE Conference on Computer Vision and Pattern Recognition, pp. 41–48 (2012)
17. Wilburn, B., Joshi, N., Vaish, V., Talvala, E.V., Antunez, E., Barth, A., Adams, A., Horowitz, M., Levoy, M.: High performance imaging using large camera arrays. ACM Transactions on Graphics 24(3), 765–776 (2005)
18. Zhang, Z.: Flexible camera calibration by viewing a plane from unknown orientations. In: IEEE International Conference on Computer Vision, pp. 666–673 (1999)

Spatio-temporal Matching
for Human Detection in Video

Feng Zhou and Fernando De la Torre

Robotics Institute,
Carnegie Mellon University,
Pittsburgh, PA, 15213, USA

Abstract. Detection and tracking humans in videos have been long-standing problems in computer vision. Most successful approaches (*e.g.*, deformable parts models) heavily rely on discriminative models to build appearance detectors for body joints and generative models to constrain possible body configurations (*e.g.*, trees). While these 2D models have been successfully applied to images (and with less success to videos), a major challenge is to generalize these models to cope with camera views. In order to achieve view-invariance, these 2D models typically require a large amount of training data across views that is difficult to gather and time-consuming to label. Unlike existing 2D models, this paper formulates the problem of human detection in videos as spatio-temporal matching (STM) between a 3D motion capture model and trajectories in videos. Our algorithm estimates the camera view and selects a subset of tracked trajectories that matches the motion of the 3D model. The STM is efficiently solved with linear programming, and it is robust to tracking mismatches, occlusions and outliers. To the best of our knowledge this is the first paper that solves the correspondence between video and 3D motion capture data for human pose detection. Experiments on the Human3.6M and Berkeley MHAD databases illustrate the benefits of our method over state-of-the-art approaches.

1   Introduction

Human pose detection and tracking in videos have received significant attention in the last few years due to the success of Kinect cameras and applications in human computer interaction (*e.g.*, [1]), surveillance (*e.g.*, [2]) and marker-less motion capture (*e.g.*, [3]). While there have been successful methods that estimate 2D body pose from a single image [4–8], detecting and tracking body configurations in unconstrained video is still a challenging problem. The main challenges stem from the large variability of people's clothes, articulated motions, occlusions, outliers and changes in illumination. More importantly, existing extensions of 2D methods [4, 5] cannot cope with large pose changes due to camera view change. A common strategy to make these 2D models view-invariant is to gather and label human poses across all possible viewpoints. However, this is impractical, time consuming, and it is unclear how the space of 3D poses can

D. Fleet et al. (Eds.): ECCV 2014, Part VI, LNCS 8694, pp. 62–77, 2014.

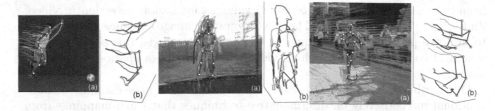

Fig. 1. Detection and tracking of humans in three videos using spatio-temporal matching (STM). STM extracts trajectories in video (gray lines) and selects a subset of trajectories (a) that match with the 3D motion capture model (b) learned from the CMU motion capture data set. Better viewed in color.

be uniformly sampled. To address these issues, this paper proposes to formulate the problem of human body detection and tracking as one of spatio-temporal matching (STM) between 3D models and video. Our method solves for the correspondence between a 3D motion capture model and trajectories in video. The main idea of our approach is illustrated in Fig. 1.

Our STM algorithm has two main components: (1) a spatio-temporal motion capture model that can model the configuration of several 3D joints for a variety of actions, and (2) an efficient algorithm that solves the correspondence between image trajectories and the 3D spatio-temporal motion capture model. Fig. 1 illustrates examples of how we can rotate our motion capture data model to match the trajectories of humans in video across several views. Moreover, our method selects a subset of trajectories that corresponds to 3D joints in the motion capture data model (about $2 - 4\%$ of the trajectories are selected). As we will illustrate with the Human3.6M database [9] and the Berkeley MHAD database [10], the main advantage of our approach is that it is able to cope with large variations in viewpoint and speed of the action. This property stems from the fact that we use 3D models.

2   Related Work

Early methods for detecting articulated human body in video sequences built upon on simple appearance models with kinematic constraints [11]. State-of-the-art methods for pose detection and body tracking make use of deformable part models (*e.g.* [4, 12, 5, 6]) or regressors [7]. Andriluka*et al.* [13] combined the initial estimate of the human pose across frames in a tracking-by-detection framework. Sapp *et al.* [14] coupled locations of body joints within and across frames from an ensemble of tractable sub-models. Burgos *et al.* [15] merged multiple independent pose estimates across space and time using a non-maximum suppression. More recently, Tian *et al.* [16] explored the generalization of deformable part models [4] from 2D images to 3D spatio-temporal volumes for action detection in video. Zuffi *et al.* [17] exploited optical flow by integrating image evidence across frames to improve pose inference. Compared to previous methods, this paper enforces temporal consistency by matching video trajectories to a spatio-temporal 3D model.

Our method is also related to the work on 3D human pose estimation. Conventional methods rely on discriminative techniques that learn mappings from image features (*e.g.*, silhouettes [18]) to 3D pose with different priors [19, 20]. However, many of them require an accurate image segmentation to extract shape features or precise initialization to achieve good performance in the optimization. Inspired by recent advances in 2D human pose estimation, current works focus on retrieving 3D poses from 2D body part positions estimated by the off-the-shelf detectors [4, 12, 5]. For instance, Sigal and Black [21] learned a mixture of experts model to infer 3D poses conditioned on 2D poses. Simo-Serra *et al.* [22] retrieved 3D poses from the output of 2D body part detectors by a robust sampling strategy. Ionescu *et al.* [7] reconstructed 3D human pose by inferring over multiple human localization hypotheses on images. Inspired by [23], Yu *et al.* [24] recently combined human action detection and a deformable part model to estimate 3D poses. Compared to our approach, however, these methods typically require large training sets to model the large variability of appearance of different people and viewpoints.

3   Spatio-temporal Matching

This section describes the proposed STM algorithm. The STM algorithm has three main components: (1) In training, STM learns a bilinear spatio-temporal 3D model from motion capture data, (2) Given an input video, STM extracts 2D feature trajectories and evaluates the pseudo-likelihood of each pixel belonging to different body parts; (3) During testing STM finds a subset of trajectories that correspond to 3D joints in the spatio-temporal model, and compute the extrinsic camera parameters.

3.1   Trajectory-Based Video Representation

In order to generate candidate positions for human body parts, we used a trajectory-based representation of the input video. To be robust to large camera motion and viewpoint changes, we extracted trajectories from short video segments. The input video is temporally split into overlapped video segments of length n frames (*e.g.*, $n = 15$ in all our experiments).

For each video segment, we used [25] to extract trajectories by densely sampling feature points in the first frame and track them using a dense optical flow algorithm [26]. The output of the tracker for each video segment is a set of m_p trajectories (see notation[1]),

$$\mathbf{P} = \begin{bmatrix} \mathbf{p}_1^1 & \cdots & \mathbf{p}_{m_p}^1 \\ \vdots & \ddots & \vdots \\ \mathbf{p}_1^n & \cdots & \mathbf{p}_{m_p}^n \end{bmatrix} \in \mathbb{R}^{2n \times m_p},$$

where each $\mathbf{p}_j^i \in \mathbb{R}^2$ denotes the 2D coordinates of the jth trajectory in the ith frame. Notice that the number of trajectories (m_p) can be different between segments. Fig. 2b illustrates a video segment with densely extracted feature trajectories. Compared to the sparser KLT-based trackers [27, 28], densely tracking the feature points guarantees a good coverage of foreground motion and improves the quality of the trajectories in the presence of fast irregular motions.

To evaluate a pseudo-likelihood of each trajectory belonging to a 3D joint, we applied a state-of-the-art body part detector [5] independently on each frame. We selected a subset of $m_q = 14$ body joints (Fig. 2a) that are common across several datasets including the PARSE human body model [5], CMU [29], Berkeley MHAD [10] and Human3.6M [9] motion capture datasets.

For each joint $c = 1 \cdots m_q$ in the ith frame, we computed the SVM score a_{cj}^i for each trajectory $j = 1 \cdots m_p$ by performing an efficient two-pass dynamic programming inference [30]. Fig. 2c shows the response maps associated with four different joints. The head can be easily detected, while other joints are more ambiguous. Given a video segment containing m_p trajectories, we then computed a trajectory response matrix, $\mathbf{A} \in \mathbb{R}^{m_q \times m_p}$, whose element $a_{cj} = \sum_{i=1}^n a_{cj}^i$ encodes the cumulative cost of assigning the jth trajectory to the cth joint over the n frames.

3.2 Learning Spatio-temporal Bilinear Bases

There exists a large body of work that addresses the representation of time-varying spatial data in several computer vision problems (*e.g.*, non-rigid structure from motion, face animation), see [31]. Common models include learning linear basis vectors independently for each frame [32] or discrete cosine transform bases independently for each joint trajectory [33]. Despite its simplicity, using a shape basis or a trajectory basis independently fails to exploit spatio-temporal regularities. To have a low-dimensional model that exploits correlations in space and time, we parameterize the 3D joints in motion capture data using a bilinear spatio-temporal model [34].

---

[1] Bold capital letters denote a matrix $\mathbf{X}$, bold lower-case letters a column vector $\mathbf{x}$. All non-bold letters represent scalars. $\mathbf{x}_i$ represents the ith column of the matrix $\mathbf{X}$. x_{ij} denotes the scalar in the ith row and j^{th} column of the matrix $\mathbf{X}$. $[\mathbf{X}_1; \cdots ; \mathbf{X}_n]$ and $[\diagdown_i \mathbf{X}_i]$ denote vertical and diagonal concatenation of sub-matrices $\mathbf{X}_i$ respectively. $\mathbf{1}_{m \times n}, \mathbf{0}_{m \times n} \in \mathbb{R}^{m \times n}$ are matrices of ones and zeros. $\mathbf{I}_n \in \mathbb{R}^{n \times n}$ is an identity matrix. $\|\mathbf{X}\|_p = \sqrt[p]{\sum |x_{ij}|^p}$ and $\|\mathbf{X}\|_F = \sqrt{\text{tr}(\mathbf{X}^T \mathbf{X})}$ designate the p-norm and Frobenius norm of $\mathbf{X}$ respectively. $\mathbf{X}^\dagger$ denotes the Moore-Penrose pseudo-inverse.

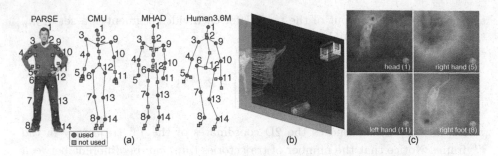

Fig. 2. Example of feature trajectories and their responses. (a) Geometrical configuration of 14 body joints shared across 3D datasets. (b) Dense trajectories extracted from a video segment. (c) Feature response maps for 4 joints (see bottom-right corner).

Given a set of 3D motion capture sequences of different lengths, we randomly select a large number (> 200) of temporal segments of the same length, where each segment denoted by $\mathbf{Q}$,

$$\mathbf{Q} = \begin{bmatrix} \mathbf{q}_1^1 & \cdots & \mathbf{q}_{m_q}^1 \\ \vdots & \ddots & \vdots \\ \mathbf{q}_1^n & \cdots & \mathbf{q}_{m_q}^n \end{bmatrix} \in \mathbb{R}^{3n \times m_q},$$

contains n frames and m_q joints. For instance, Fig. 3a shows a set of motion capture segments randomly selected from several kicking sequences.

To align the segments, we apply Procrustes analysis to remove the 3D rigid transformations. In order to build local models, we cluster all segments into k groups using spectral clustering [35]. The affinity between each pair of segments is computed as,

$$\kappa(\mathbf{Q}_i, \mathbf{Q}_j) = \exp\left(-\frac{1}{\sigma^2}(\|\mathbf{Q}_i - \tau_{ij}(\mathbf{Q}_j)\|_F^2 + \|\mathbf{Q}_j - \tau_{ji}(\mathbf{Q}_i)\|_F^2)\right),$$

where τ_{ij} denotes the similarity transformation found by Procrustes analysis when aligning $\mathbf{Q}_j$ towards $\mathbf{Q}_i$. The kernel bandwidth σ is set to be the average distance from the 50% closest neighbors for all $\mathbf{Q}_i$ and $\mathbf{Q}_j$ pairs. As shown in the experiments, this clustering step improves the generalization of the learned shape models. For instance, each of the 4 segment clusters shown in Fig. 3b corresponds to a different temporal stage of kicking a ball. Please refer Fig. 4 for examples of temporal clusters.

Given a set of l segments[2], $\{\mathbf{Q}_i\}_{i=1}^{l}$, belonging to each cluster, we learn a bilinear model [34] such that each segment $\mathbf{Q}_i$ can be reconstructed using a set of weights $\mathbf{W}_i \in \mathbb{R}^{k_t \times k_s}$ minimizing,

$$\min_{\mathbf{T}, \mathbf{S}, \{\mathbf{W}_i\}_i} \sum_{i=1}^{l} \|\mathcal{Q}(\mathbf{T}\mathbf{W}_i\mathbf{S}^T) - \mathbf{Q}_i\|_F^2, \tag{1}$$

---

[2] To simplify the notation, we do not explicitly specify the cluster membership of the motion capture segment ($\mathbf{Q}_i$) and the bilinear bases ($\mathbf{T}$ and $\mathbf{S}$).

where the columns of $\mathbf{T} \in \mathbb{R}^{n \times k_t}$ and $\mathbf{S} \in \mathbb{R}^{3m_q \times k_s}$ contain k_t trajectories and k_s shape bases respectively. In the experiment, we found $k_t = 10$ and $k_s = 15$ produced consistently good results. $\mathcal{Q}(\cdot)$ is a linear operator that reshapes any n-by-$3m_q$ matrix to a $3n$-by-m_q one, $i.e.$,

$$\mathcal{Q}\left(\begin{bmatrix} \mathbf{q}_1^{1T} & \cdots & \mathbf{q}_{m_q}^{1T} \\ \vdots & \ddots & \vdots \\ \mathbf{q}_1^{nT} & \cdots & \mathbf{q}_{m_q}^{nT} \end{bmatrix} \right) = \begin{bmatrix} \mathbf{q}_1^1 & \cdots & \mathbf{q}_{m_q}^1 \\ \vdots & \ddots & \vdots \\ \mathbf{q}_1^n & \cdots & \mathbf{q}_{m_q}^n \end{bmatrix}, \forall\, \mathbf{q}_j^i \in \mathbb{R}^3.$$

Unfortunately, optimizing Eq. 1 jointly over the bilinear bases $\mathbf{T}$, $\mathbf{S}$ and their weights $\{\mathbf{W}_i\}_i$ is a non-convex problem. To reduce the complexity and make the problem more trackable, we fix $\mathbf{T}$ to be the discrete cosine transform (DCT) bases (Top of Fig. 3c). Following [34], the shape bases $\mathbf{S}$ can then be computed in closed-form using the SVD as,

$$[\mathbf{T}\mathbf{T}^\dagger \mathcal{Q}^{-1}(\mathbf{Q}_1); \cdots ; \mathbf{T}\mathbf{T}^\dagger \mathcal{Q}^{-1}(\mathbf{Q}_l)] = \mathbf{U}\mathbf{\Sigma}\mathbf{S}^T. \tag{2}$$

For example, the left part of Fig. 3c plots the first two shape bases $\mathbf{s}_i$ learned from the 3rd cluster of segments shown in Fig. 3b, which mainly capture the deformation of the movements of the arms and legs.

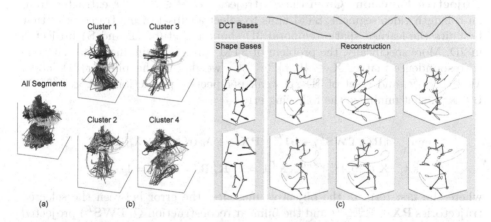

Fig. 3. Spatio-temporal bilinear model learned from the CMU motion capture dataset. (a) All the motion capture segments randomly selected from a set of kicking sequences. (b) Clustering motion capture segments into 4 temporal clusters. (c) The bilinear bases estimated from the 3rd cluster. Left: top-2 shape bases ($\mathbf{s}_i$) where the shape deformation is visualized by black arrows. Top: top-3 DCT trajectory bases ($\mathbf{t}_j$). Bottom-right: bilinear reconstruction by combining each pair of shape and DCT bases ($\mathbf{t}_j \mathbf{s}_i^T$).

3.3   STM Optimization

This section describes the objective function and the optimization strategy for the STM algorithm.

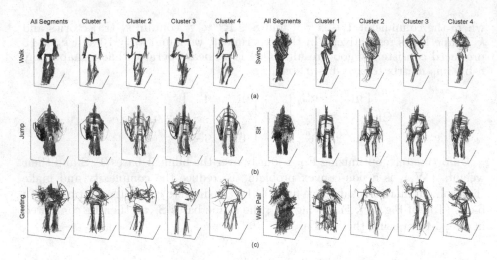

Fig. 4. Clustering motion capture segments into four clusters for different datasets. (a) CMU motion capture dataset [29]. (b) Berkeley MHAD dataset [10]. (c) Human3.6M dataset [9].

Objective Function. Given the m_p trajectories $\mathbf{P} \in \mathbb{R}^{2n \times m_p}$ extracted from an n-length video segment, STM aims to select a subset of m_q trajectories that best fits the learned spatio-temporal 3D shape structure ($\mathbf{T}$ and $\mathbf{S}$) projected in 2D. More specifically, the problem of STM consists in finding a many-to-one correspondence matrix $\mathbf{X} \in \{0,1\}^{m_p \times m_q}$, weights of the bilinear 3D model $\mathbf{W} \in \mathbb{R}^{k_t \times k_s}$, and a set of 3D-2D weak perspective projections[3] $\mathbf{R} \in \mathbb{R}^{2n \times 3n}$, $\mathbf{b} \in \mathbb{R}^{2n}$, that minimize the following error

$$\min_{\mathbf{X},\mathbf{W},\mathbf{R},\mathbf{b}} \quad \|\mathbf{R}\mathcal{Q}(\mathbf{TWS}^T) + \mathbf{b}\mathbf{1}^T - \mathbf{PX}\|_1 + \lambda_a \operatorname{tr}(\mathbf{AX}) + \lambda_s \|\mathbf{TW\Sigma}^{-1}\|_1, \qquad (3)$$

$$\text{s.t.} \quad \mathbf{X} \in \{0,1\}^{m_p \times m_q}, \ \mathbf{X}^T\mathbf{1} = \mathbf{1}, \ \mathbf{R}_i^T\mathbf{R}_i = \mathbf{I}_2 \ \forall \ i = 1 \cdots n,$$

where the first term in the objective measures the error between the selected trajectories $\mathbf{PX} \in \mathbb{R}^{2n \times m_q}$ and the bilinear reconstruction $\mathcal{Q}(\mathbf{TWS}^T)$ projected in 2D using $\mathbf{R}$ and $\mathbf{b}$. The error is computed using the l_1 norm instead of the Frobenious norm, because of its efficiency and robustness. Given the trajectory response $\mathbf{A} \in \mathbb{R}^{m_q \times m_p}$, the second term measures the appearance cost of the trajectories selected by $\mathbf{X}$ and weighted by λ_a. The third term weighted by λ_s penalizes large weights $\mathbf{TW} \in \mathbb{R}^{n \times k_s}$ of the shape bases, where the singular value $\mathbf{\Sigma} \in \mathbb{R}^{k_s \times k_s}$ computed in Eq. 2 is used to normalize the contribution of each basis. In our experiment, the regularization weights λ_a and λ_s are estimated using cross-validation.

---

[3] $\mathbf{R} = [\searrow_i \theta_i \mathbf{R}_i] \in \mathbb{R}^{2n \times 3n}$ is a block-diagonal matrix, where each block contains the rotation $\mathbf{R}_i \in \mathbb{R}^{2 \times 3}$ and scaling θ_i for each frame. Similarly, $\mathbf{b} = [\mathbf{b}_1; \cdots ; \mathbf{b}_n] \in \mathbb{R}^{2n}$ is a concatenation of the translation $\mathbf{b}_i \in \mathbb{R}^2$ for each frame.

Optimizing Eq. 3 is a challenging problem, in the following sections we describe an efficient coordinate-descent algorithm that alternates between solving $\mathbf{X}, \mathbf{W}$ and $\mathbf{R}, \mathbf{b}$ until convergence. The algorithm is initialized by computing $\mathbf{X}$ that minimizes the appearance cost $\text{tr}(\mathbf{AX})$ in Eq. 3 and setting $\mathcal{Q}(\mathbf{TWS}^T)$ to be the mean of the motion capture segments.

Optimizing STM over $\mathbf{X}$ and $\mathbf{W}$. Due to the combinatorial constraint on $\mathbf{X}$, optimizing Eq. 3 over $\mathbf{X}$ and $\mathbf{W}$ given $\mathbf{R}$ and $\mathbf{b}$ is a NP-hard mixed-integer problem. To approximate the problem, we relax the binary $\mathbf{X}$ to be a continuous one and reformulate the problem using the LP trick [36] as,

$$\min_{\mathbf{X}, \mathbf{W}, \mathbf{U}, \mathbf{V}, \mathbf{U}_s, \mathbf{V}_s} \mathbf{1}^T(\mathbf{U} + \mathbf{V})\mathbf{1} + \lambda_a \, \text{tr}(\mathbf{AX}) + \lambda_s \mathbf{1}^T(\mathbf{U}_s + \mathbf{V}_s)\mathbf{1}, \tag{4}$$

$$\text{s.t.} \quad \mathbf{X} \in [0,1]^{m_p \times m_q}, \mathbf{X}^T\mathbf{1} = \mathbf{1},$$
$$\mathbf{R}\mathcal{Q}(\mathbf{TWS}^T) + \mathbf{b1}^T - \mathbf{PX} = \mathbf{U} - \mathbf{V}, \mathbf{U} \geq 0, \mathbf{V} \geq 0,$$
$$\mathbf{TW\Sigma}^{-1} = \mathbf{U}_s - \mathbf{V}_s, \mathbf{U}_s \geq 0, \mathbf{V}_s \geq 0,$$

where $\mathbf{U}, \mathbf{V} \in \mathbb{R}^{2n \times m_q}$ and $\mathbf{U}_s, \mathbf{V}_s \in \mathbb{R}^{n \times k_s}$ are four auxiliary variables used to formulate the l_1 problem as linear programming. The term $\mathbf{R}\mathcal{Q}(\mathbf{TWS}^T)$ is linear in $\mathbf{W}$ and we can conveniently re-write this expression using the following equality as:

$$\text{vec}\left(\mathbf{R}\mathcal{Q}(\mathbf{TWS}^T)\right) = (\mathbf{I}_{m_q} \otimes \mathbf{R}) \, \text{vec}\left(\mathcal{Q}(\mathbf{TWS}^T)\right)$$
$$= (\mathbf{I}_{m_q} \otimes \mathbf{R})\mathbf{\Pi}_{\mathcal{Q}} \, \text{vec}(\mathbf{TWS}^T) = \underbrace{(\mathbf{I}_{m_q} \otimes \mathbf{R})\mathbf{\Pi}_{\mathcal{Q}}(\mathbf{S} \otimes \mathbf{T})}_{\text{Constant}} \text{vec}(\mathbf{W}),$$

where $\mathbf{\Pi}_{\mathcal{Q}} \in \{0,1\}^{3nm_q \times 3nm_q}$ is a permutation matrix that re-orders the elements of a $3nm_q$-D vector as,

$$\mathbf{\Pi}_{\mathcal{Q}} \text{vec}\left(\begin{bmatrix} \mathbf{q}_1^1 & \cdots & \mathbf{q}_{m_q}^1 \\ \vdots & \ddots & \vdots \\ \mathbf{q}_1^n & \cdots & \mathbf{q}_{m_q}^n \end{bmatrix}\right) = \text{vec}\left(\begin{bmatrix} \mathbf{q}_1^{1T} & \cdots & \mathbf{q}_{m_q}^{1T} \\ \vdots & \ddots & \vdots \\ \mathbf{q}_1^{nT} & \cdots & \mathbf{q}_{m_q}^{nT} \end{bmatrix}\right), \forall \, \mathbf{q}_j^i \in \mathbb{R}^3. \tag{5}$$

After solving the linear program, we gradually discretize $\mathbf{X}$ by taking successive refinements based on trust-region shrinking [36].

Optimizing STM over $\mathbf{R}$ and $\mathbf{b}$. If $\mathbf{X}$ and $\mathbf{W}$ are fixed, optimizing Eq. 3 with respect to $\mathbf{R}$ and $\mathbf{b}$ becomes an l_1 Procrustes problem [37],

$$\min_{\mathbf{R}, \mathbf{b}} \|\mathbf{RQ} + \mathbf{b1}^T - \mathbf{PX}\|_1, \quad \text{s.t.} \quad \mathbf{R}_i^T\mathbf{R}_i = \mathbf{I}_2 \, \forall \, i = 1 \cdots n, \tag{6}$$

where $\mathbf{Q} = \mathcal{Q}(\mathbf{TWS}^T)$. Inspired by the recent advances in compressed sensing, we approximate Eq. 6 using the augmented Lagrange multipliers method [38] that minimizes the following augmented Lagrange function:

$$\min_{\mathbf{L}, \mathbf{E}, \mu, \mathbf{R}, \mathbf{b}} \|\mathbf{E} - \mathbf{PX}\|_1 + \text{tr}\left(\mathbf{L}^T(\mathbf{RQ} + \mathbf{b1}^T - \mathbf{E})\right) + \frac{\mu}{2}\|\mathbf{RQ} + \mathbf{b1}^T - \mathbf{E}\|_F^2, \tag{7}$$

$$\text{s.t.} \quad \mathbf{R}_i^T\mathbf{R}_i = \mathbf{I}_2 \, \forall \, i = 1 \cdots n,$$

where $\mathbf{L}$ is the Lagrange multiplier, $\mathbf{E}$ is an auxiliary variable, and μ is the penalty parameter. Eq. 7 can be efficiently approximated in a coordinate-descent manner. First, optimizing Eq. 7 with respect to $\mathbf{R}$ and $\mathbf{b}$ is a standard orthogonal Procrustes problem,

$$\min_{\mathbf{R},\mathbf{b}} \quad \|\mathbf{RQ} + \mathbf{b1}^T - (\mathbf{E} - \frac{\mathbf{L}}{\mu})\|_F^2, \quad \text{s.t. } \mathbf{R}_i^T\mathbf{R}_i = \mathbf{I}_2 \; \forall \; i = 1\cdots n,$$

which has a close-form solution using the SVD. Second, optimizing Eq. 7 with respect to $\mathbf{E}$ can be efficiently found using absolute value shrinkage [38] as,

$$\mathbf{E} := \mathbf{PX} - \mathcal{S}_{\frac{1}{\mu}}(\mathbf{PX} - \mathbf{RQ} - \mathbf{b1}^T - \frac{\mathbf{L}}{\mu}),$$

where $\mathcal{S}_\sigma(p) = \max(|p| - \sigma, 0)\operatorname{sign}(p)$ is a soft-thresholding operator [38]. Third, we gradually update $\mathbf{L} \leftarrow \mathbf{L} + \mu(\mathbf{RQ} + \mathbf{b1}^T - \mathbf{E})$ and $\mu \leftarrow \rho\mu$, where we set the incremental ratio to $\rho = 1.05$ in all our experiments.

3.4 Fusion

Given a video containing an arbitrary number of frames, we solved STM independently for each segment of n frames ($n = 15$ in our experiments). Recall that we learned k bilinear models ($\mathbf{T}$ and $\mathbf{S}$) from different clusters of motion capture segments (e.g., Fig. 3b) in the training step. To find the best model for each segment, we optimize Eq. 3 using each model and select the one with the smallest error. After solving STM for each segment, the final joint position $\bar{\mathbf{P}}_i \in \mathbb{R}^{2 \times m_q}$ at frame i is the average coordinates of the selected trajectories $\{\mathbf{P}_c\mathbf{X}_c\}_c$ from all the l_c segments overlapped at i, i.e., $\bar{\mathbf{P}}_i = \frac{1}{l_c}\sum_c \mathbf{P}_c^{i_c}\mathbf{X}_c$, where $\mathbf{P}_c^{i_c} \in \mathbb{R}^{2 \times m_p}$ encodes the trajectory coordinates at the i_c^{th} frame within the cth segment and i_c the local index of the ith frame in the original video.

4   Experiments

This section compares STM against several state-of-the-art algorithms for body part detection in synthetic experiments on the CMU motion capture dataset [29], and real experiments on the MHAD [10] and the Human3.6M [9] datasets.

For each dataset, the 3D motion capture model was trained from its associated motion capture sequences. The 3D motion capture training data is person-independent, and it does not contains samples of the testing subject. Notice that the annotation scheme is different across datasets (Fig. 2a). We investigated four different types of 3D models for STM: (1) Generic models: **STM-G1** and **STM-G4** were trained using all sequences of different actions with $k = 1$ and $k = 4$ clusters respectively. (2) Action-specific models: **STM-A1** and **STM-A4** were trained independently for each action from each dataset. In testing, we assumed we know what action the subject was performing. As before, **STM-A1** and **STM-A4** were trained with $k = 1$ and $k = 4$ clusters respectively.

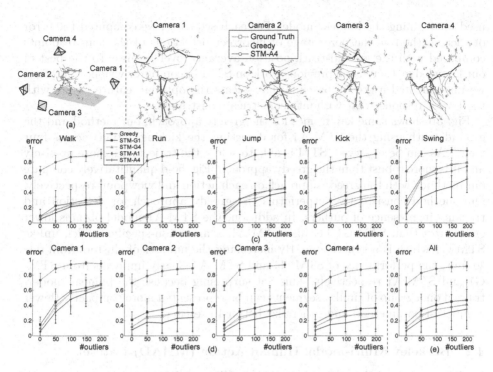

Fig. 5. Comparison of human pose estimation on the CMU motion capture dataset. (a) Original motion capture key-frames in 3D with 50 outliers that were synthetically generated. (b) Results of the greedy approach and our method on four 2D projections. (c) Mean error and std. for each method and action as a function of the number of outliers. (d) Mean error and std. for each camera view. (e) Mean error and std. for all actions and cameras.

4.1   CMU Motion Capture Dataset

The first experiment validated our approach on the CMU motion capture dataset [29], from which we selected 5 actions including walking, running, jumping, kicking, golf swing. For each action, we picked 8 sequences performed by different subjects. For each sequence, we synthetically generated $0 \sim 200$ random trajectories as outliers in 3D. Then we projected each sequence (with outliers included) onto 4 different 2D views. See Fig. 5a for examples of the 3D sequences as well as the camera positions. To reproduce the response of a body part detector at each frame, we synthetically generate a constant-value response region centered at the ground-truth location with the radius being the maximum limb length over the sequence. The response value of the jth feature trajectory for the cth body part at i^{th} frame is considered to be $a^i_{cj} = -1$ if it falls in the region or 0 otherwise. Our goal is to detect the original trajectories and recover the body structure.

We quantitatively evaluated our method with a leave-one-out scheme, *i.e.*, each testing sequence was taken out for testing, and the remaining data was used for training the bilinear model. For each sequence, we computed the error of each method as the percentage of incorrect detections of the feature points compared with the ground-truth position averaged over frames. To the best of our knowledge, there is no previous work on STM in computer vision. Therefore, we implemented a greedy baseline that selects the optimal feature points with the lowest response cost without geometrical constraints.

Fig. 5b shows some key-frames for the greedy approach, our method and the ground truth using the STM-A4 for detecting the kicking actions across four views. As can be observed, STM is able to select the trajectories more precisely and it is more robust than the greedy approach. Fig. 5c-d quantitatively compare our methods with the greedy approach on each action and viewpoint respectively. Our method consistently outperforms the greedy approach for detection and tracking in presence of outliers. In addition, the STM-A1 model obtains lower error rates than STM-G1 because STM-A1 is an action-specific model, unlike STM-G1 which is a generic one. By increasing the number of clusters from one to four, the performance of STM-G4 and STM-A4 clearly improves from STM-G1 and STM-A1 respectively. This not surprising because the bilinear models trained on a group of similar segments can be represented more compactly (fewer number of parameters) and generalize better in testing.

4.2   Berkeley Multi-modal Human Action (MHAD) Dataset

In the second experiment, we tested the ability of STM to detect humans on the Berkeley multi-modal human action database (MHAD) [10]. The MHAD database contains 11 actions performed by 12 subjects. For each sequence, we took the videos captured by 2 different cameras as shown in Fig. 6a. To extract the trajectories from each video, we used [25] in sliding-window manner to extract dense trajectories from each 15 frames segment. The response for each trajectory was computed using the SVM detector score [5]. The bilinear models were trained from the motion capture data associated with this dataset.

To quantitatively evaluate the performance, we compared our method with two baselines: the state-of-the-art image-based pose estimation method proposed by Yang and Ramanan [5], and the recent video-based method designed by Burgos *et al.* [15] that merges multiple independent pose estimates across frames. We evaluated all methods with a leave-one-out scheme. The error for each method is computed as the pixel distance between the estimated and ground-truth part locations. Notice that a portion of the error is due to the inconsistency in labeling protocol between the PARSE model [5] and the MHAD dataset.

Fig. 6b-d compare the error to localize body parts of our method againts [5] and [15]. Our method largely improves the image-based baseline [5] for all actions and viewpoints. Compared to the video-based method [15], STM achieves lower errors for most actions except for "jump jacking", "bending", "one-hand waving" and "two-hand waving", where the fast movement of the body joints cause much larger error in tracking feature trajectories over time. Among the four STM models, STM-A4 performs the best because the clustering step improves the generalization of the bilinear model. As shown in Fig. 6d, the hands are the most difficult to accurately detect because of their fast movements and frequent occlusions.

Fig. 6e-g investigate the three main parameters of our system, segment length (n), number of bases (k_s and k_t) and the regularization weights (λ_a and λ_s). According to Fig. 6e, a smaller segment length is beneficial for "jump jacking" because the performance of the tracker [25] is less stable for fast-speed action. In contrast, using a larger window improves the temporal consistency in actions such as "throwing" and "standing up". Fig. 6f shows the detection error of STM using different number of shape (k_s) and trajectories (k_t) bases for the first subject. Overall, we found the performance of STM is not very sensitive to small change in the number of shape bases because the contribution of each shape basis in STM (Eq. 3) is normalized by their energies (Σ). In addition, using a small number (*e.g.*, 5) of trajectory bases can lower the performance of STM. This result demonstrates the effectiveness of using dynamic models over the static ones (*e.g.*, a PCA-based model can be considered as a special case of the bilinear model when $k_t = 1$). Fig. 6g plots the cross-validation error for the first subject, from which we pick the optimal λ_a and λ_s.

Our system was implemented in Matlab on a PC with 2GHz Intel CPU and 8GB memory. The codes of [5, 15] were downloaded from authors' webpages. The linear programming in Eq. 4 was optimized using the Mosek LP solver [39]. Fig. 6f analyzes the computational cost (in seconds) for tracking the human pose in a sequence containing 126 frames. The most computationally intensive part of the method is calculating the response for each joint and each frame using [5]. Despite a large number of candidate trajectories ($m_p \approx 700$) per segment, STM can be computing in about 8 minutes.

4.3   Human3.6M Dataset

In the last experiment, we selected 11 actions performed by 5 subjects from the Human3.6M dataset [9]. Compared to the Berkeley MHAD dataset, the motions in Human3.6M were performed by professional actors, that wear regular clothing to maintain as much realism as possible. See Fig. 7a for example frames.

As in the previous experiment, our methods were compared with two baselines [5, 15] in a leave-one-out scheme. The bilinear models were trained from the motion capture data associated with this dataset. Fig. 6b-c show the performance of each method on localizing body part for each action and viewpoint respectively. Due to the larger appearance variation and more complex motion performance, the overall error of each method is larger than the one achieved on the previous Berkeley MHAD dataset. However, STM still outperforms both the baselines [5, 15] for most actions and viewpoints. If the action label is known a priori, training action-specific models (STM-A1 and STM-A4) achieves better performance than the ones trained on all actions (STM-G1 and STM-G4).

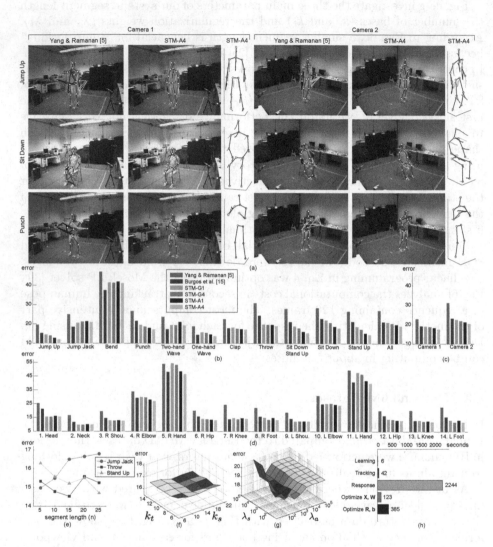

Fig. 6. Comparison of human pose estimation on the Berkeley MHAD dataset. (a) Result of [5] and our method on three actions of two views, where the 3D reconstruction estimated by our method is plotted on the right. (b) Errors for each action. (c) Errors for each camera view. (d) Errors of each joint. (e) Errors with respect to the segment length (n). (f) Errors with respect to the bases number (k_s and k_t). (g) Errors with respect to the regularization weights (λ_a and λ_s). (h) Time cost of each step.

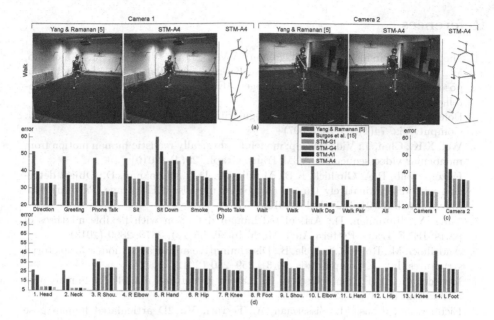

Fig. 7. Comparison of human pose estimation on the Human 3.6M dataset. (a) Result of [5] and our method on three actions of two views, where the 3D reconstruction estimated by our method is plotted on the right. (b) Errors for each action. (c) Errors for each camera view. (d) Errors of each joint.

5   Conclusion

This paper presents STM, a robust method for detection and tracking human poses in videos by matching video trajectories to a 3D motion capture model. STM matches trajectories to a 3D model, and hence it provides intrinsic view-invariance. The main novelty of the work resides in computing the correspondence between video and motion capture data. Although it might seem computationally expensive and difficult to optimize at first, using an l_1-formulation to solve for correspondence results in an algorithm that is efficient and robust to outliers, missing data and mismatches. We showed how STM outperforms state-of-the-art approaches to object detection based on deformable parts models in the (MHAD) [10] and the Human3.6M dataset [9].

A major limitation of our current approach is the high computational cost for calculating the joint response, which is computed independently for each frame. In future work, we plan to incorporate richer temporal features [25] to improve the speed and accuracy of the trajectory response. Also, we are solving STM independently for each segment (sub-sequence), which might result in some discontinuity in the estimation of the pose; a straight-forward improvement could be made by imposing consistency between overlapping segments.

References

1. Shotton, J., Girshick, R.B., Fitzgibbon, A.W., Sharp, T., Cook, M., Finocchio, M., Moore, R., Kohli, P., Criminisi, A., Kipman, A., Blake, A.: Efficient human pose estimation from single depth images. IEEE Trans. Pattern Anal. Mach. Intell. 35(12), 2821–2840 (2013)
2. Boiman, O., Irani, M.: Detecting irregularities in images and in video. Int. J. Comput. Vis. 74(1), 17–31 (2007)
3. Wei, X.K., Chai, J.: VideoMocap: modeling physically realistic human motion from monocular video sequences. ACM Trans. Graph. 29(4) (2010)
4. Felzenszwalb, P.F., Girshick, R.B., McAllester, D.A., Ramanan, D.: Object detection with discriminatively trained part-based models. IEEE Trans. Pattern Anal. Mach. Intell. 32(9), 1627–1645 (2010)
5. Yang, Y., Ramanan, D.: Articulated human detection with flexible mixtures of parts. IEEE Trans. Pattern Anal. Mach. Intell. 35(12), 2878–2890 (2013)
6. Andriluka, M., Roth, S., Schiele, B.: Discriminative appearance models for pictorial structures. Int. J. Comput. Vis. 99(3), 259–280 (2012)
7. Ionescu, C., Li, F., Sminchisescu, C.: Latent structured models for human pose estimation. In: ICCV (2011)
8. Eichner, M., Jesús, M., Zisserman, A., Ferrari, V.: 2D articulated human pose estimation and retrieval in (almost) unconstrained still images. Int. J. Comput. Vis. 99(2), 190–214 (2012)
9. Ionescu, C., Papava, D., Olaru, V., Sminchisescu, C.: Human3.6M: Large scale datasets and predictive methods for 3D human sensing in natural environments. IEEE Trans. Pattern Anal. Mach. Intell. (2014)
10. Ofli, F., Chaudhry, R., Kurillo, G., Vidal, R., Bajcsy, R.: Berkeley MHAD: A comprehensive multimodal human action database. In: IEEE Workshop on Applications on Computer Vision (WACV), pp. 53–60 (2013)
11. Poppe, R.: Vision-based human motion analysis: An overview. Comput. Vis. Image Underst. 108(1-2), 4–18 (2007)
12. Sapp, B., Toshev, A., Taskar, B.: Cascaded models for articulated pose estimation. In: Daniilidis, K., Maragos, P., Paragios, N. (eds.) ECCV 2010, Part II. LNCS, vol. 6312, pp. 406–420. Springer, Heidelberg (2010)
13. Andriluka, M., Roth, S., Schiele, B.: Monocular 3D pose estimation and tracking by detection. In: CVPR (2010)
14. Sapp, B., Weiss, D., Taskar, B.: Parsing human motion with stretchable models. In: CVPR (2011)
15. Burgos, X., Hall, D., Perona, P., Dollár, P.: Merging pose estimates across space and time. In: BMVC (2013)
16. Tian, Y., Sukthankar, R., Shah, M.: Spatiotemporal deformable part models for action detection. In: CVPR (2013)
17. Zuffi, S., Romero, J., Schmid, C., Black, M.J.: Estimating human pose with flowing puppets. In: ICCV (2013)
18. Agarwal, A., Triggs, B.: Recovering 3D human pose from monocular images. IEEE Trans. Pattern Anal. Mach. Intell. 28(1), 44–58 (2006)
19. Elgammal, A.M., Lee, C.S.: Inferring 3D body pose from silhouettes using activity manifold learning. In: CVPR (2004)
20. Urtasun, R., Fleet, D.J., Fua, P.: 3D people tracking with Gaussian process dynamical models. In: CVPR (2006)

21. Sigal, L., Black, M.J.: Predicting 3D people from 2D pictures. In: Perales, F.J., Fisher, R.B. (eds.) AMDO 2006. LNCS, vol. 4069, pp. 185–195. Springer, Heidelberg (2006)
22. Simo-Serra, E., Ramisa, A., Alenyà, G., Torras, C., Moreno-Noguer, F.: Single image 3D human pose estimation from noisy observations. In: CVPR (2012)
23. Yao, A., Gall, J., Gool, L.J.V.: Coupled action recognition and pose estimation from multiple views. Int. J. Comput. Vis. 100(1), 16–37 (2012)
24. Yu, T.H., Kim, T.K., Cipolla, R.: Unconstrained monocular 3D human pose estimation by action detection and cross-modality regression forest. In: CVPR (2013)
25. Wang, H., Kläser, A., Schmid, C., Liu, C.L.: Dense trajectories and motion boundary descriptors for action recognition. Int. J. Comput. Vis. 103(1), 60–79 (2013)
26. Farnebäck, G.: Two-frame motion estimation based on polynomial expansion. In: Bigun, J., Gustavsson, T. (eds.) SCIA 2003. LNCS, vol. 2749, pp. 363–370. Springer, Heidelberg (2003)
27. Messing, R., Pal, C.J., Kautz, H.A.: Activity recognition using the velocity histories of tracked keypoints. In: ICCV (2009)
28. Matikainen, P., Hebert, M., Sukthankar, R.: Trajectons: Action recognition through the motion analysis of tracked features. In: ICCVW (2009)
29. Carnegie Mellon University Motion Capture Database, http://mocap.cs.cmu.edu
30. Park, D., Ramanan, D.: N-best maximal decoders for part models. In: ICCV (2011)
31. Bronstein, A.M., Bronstein, M.M., Kimmel, R.: Numerical geometry of non-rigid shapes. Springer (2008)
32. Bregler, C., Hertzmann, A., Biermann, H.: Recovering non-rigid 3D shape from image streams. In: CVPR (2000)
33. Akhter, I., Sheikh, Y., Khan, S., Kanade, T.: Trajectory space: A dual representation for nonrigid structure from motion. IEEE Trans. Pattern Anal. Mach. Intell. 33(7), 1442–1456 (2011)
34. Akhter, I., Simon, T., Khan, S., Matthews, I., Sheikh, Y.: Bilinear spatiotemporal basis models. ACM Trans. Graph. 31(2), 17 (2012)
35. Ng, A.Y., Jordan, M.I., Weiss, Y.: On spectral clustering: analysis and an algorithm. In: NIPS, pp. 849–856 (2001)
36. Jiang, H., Drew, M.S., Li, Z.N.: Matching by linear programming and successive convexification. IEEE Trans. Pattern Anal. Mach. Intell. 29(6), 959–975 (2007)
37. Trendafilov, N.: On the l_1 Procrustes problem. Future Generation Computer Systems 19(7), 1177–1186 (2004)
38. Lin, Z., Chen, M., Ma, Y.: The augmented Lagrange multiplier method for exact recovery of corrupted low-rank matrices. arXiv preprint arXiv:1009.5055 (2010)
39. Mosek, http://www.mosek.com/

Collaborative Facial Landmark Localization
for Transferring Annotations Across Datasets

Brandon M. Smith and Li Zhang

University of Wisconsin – Madison
http://www.cs.wisc.edu/~lizhang/projects/collab-face-landmarks/

Abstract. In this paper we make the first effort, to the best of our knowledge, to combine multiple face landmark datasets with different landmark definitions into a super dataset, with a union of all landmark types computed in each image as output. Our approach is flexible, and our system can optionally use known landmarks in the target dataset to constrain the localization. Our novel pipeline is built upon variants of state-of-the-art facial landmark localization methods. Specifically, we propose to label images in the target dataset jointly rather than independently and exploit exemplars from both the source datasets and the target dataset. This approach integrates nonparametric appearance and shape modeling and graph matching together to achieve our goal.

1 Introduction

Facial landmark localization is a popular and extensively studied area in computer vision. Many approaches have been proposed over the years, from classic methods like Active Shape Models (ASMs) [4], Active Appearance Models (AAMs) [3], and Constrained Local Models (CLMs) [6] to more recent exemplar-based [2], voting-based [26], and supervised descend-based methods [25]. Many datasets have also been proposed to evaluate these methods, from early datasets collected in the lab like CMU PIE [21], Multi-PIE [7], AR [14], and XM2VTSDB [15], to more recent in-the-wild datasets like LFPW [2], AFLW [10], AFW [30], Helen [11], and IBUG [17].

On one hand, new datasets pose new challenges to the research community and foster new ideas. On the other hand, as researchers, we must choose specific datasets for evaluation to publish our work, which becomes increasingly difficult because different datasets have different landmark definitions (for example, AFLW uses a 21-landmark markup, while Helen uses 194 contour points). As a result, models trained on one dataset often cannot be evaluated on other datasets. Furthermore, inconsistencies between datasets make it difficult to train robust landmark localization models that combine many different datasets.

Ideally, it would be desirable to have a common and unified definition of landmarks and collect datasets following the same definition. However, this goal is challenging in practice because the speed of collecting labels will always lag the speed of collecting face data. Furthermore, it is difficult to predict which landmark definitions (*e.g.*, ears) new applications will find useful.

D. Fleet et al. (Eds.): ECCV 2014, Part VI, LNCS 8694, pp. 78–93, 2014.

In this paper we make the first effort, to the best of our knowledge, to combine multiple face landmark datasets with different landmark definitions into a super dataset, with a union of all landmark types computed in each image as output. Specifically, we present a novel pipeline built upon variants of state-of-the-art facial landmark localization methods that transfers landmarks from multiple datasets to a target dataset. Our system labels images in the target dataset jointly rather than independently and exploits exemplars from both the source datasets and the target dataset. This approach allows us to integrate nonparametric appearance and shape modeling and graph matching together to transfer annotations across datasets. Toward this goal, our paper makes the following contributions:

1. A pipeline that transfers landmark annotations from multiple source datasets to never-before-labeled datasets.
2. An algorithm that takes multiple source datasets as input and labels a partially labeled target dataset using a union of landmarks defined in the source datasets. Our system can optionally use known landmarks in the target dataset as constraints.
3. 64 supplementary landmarks for faces in the AFLW database [10], for a total of 85 landmarks. AFLW is significant in that, to the best of our knowledge, it is currently the largest publicly available in-the-wild face dataset with 25,000 annotated faces.

2   Related Work

We are aware of no other works that explicitly address the problem of *automatically* combining multiple datasets that have different landmark annotations. However, components of our system are inspired by and/or are built upon existing methods in the literature, which we summarize below.

Like Smith *et al.* [22] and Shen *et al.* [20], we use a Hough voting approach to generate landmark response maps in Stage 2 of our system. Yang and Patras [26] also rely on a Hough voting scheme for facial feature detection; they use several 'sieves' to filter out votes that are not relevant. In our approach, we adjust the weight of each vote by considering how well it agrees with other votes from matched features in other images.

Our landmark detection algorithm optionally uses known landmarks in the target image as constraints. Cootes and Taylor [5] proposed a constrained AAM that utilizes some known landmarks in the target image; AAMs are parametric models, while our approach is nonparametric and exemplar-based. Sagonas *et al.* [18] proposed a semi-automatic method for creating facial landmark annotations using person-specific models. Their process is iterative: users label results as 'good' or 'bad', and good results are used in later iterations as training data. Sagonas *et al.* used this approach to re-annotate several facial landmark datasets according to a consistent set of landmark definitions for the 300 Faces in-the-Wild Challenge (300-W) [17]. However, because their procedure is semi-automatic, it does not scale well to very large datasets like AFLW [10]. Further, their procedure requires a consistent training dataset and ignores existing landmarks in the target datasets, *i.e.*, it completely overwrites them. In contrast, our method is fully automatic (our system has the ability to take user input, but we do not consider it in our experiments) and our pipeline transfers all existing landmarks across different datasets so that previous annotation efforts are utilized rather than wasted.

Exemplar-based approaches have been popular since Belhumeur *et al.*'s pioneering work [2]. Zhao *et al.* [28] use grayscale pixel values and HOG features to select k-nearest neighbor training faces, from which they construct a target-specific AAM at runtime. Smith *et al.* [22] and Shen *et al.* [20] perform Hough voting using k-NN exemplar faces; we use the same basic approach in our system. Finally, Zhou *et al.* [29] combine an exemplar-based approach with graph matching for robust facial landmark localization. We extend Zhou *et al.*'s approach to integrate different landmarks from multiple source datasets.

3   Our Approach

In this section we first give a brief overview of our system followed by a more detailed explanation of each stage in subsequent sections.

3.1   Overview

The input to our system is one or more *source* face datasets, and one *target* face dataset. We assume that each source dataset consists of a set of face images, in which each image is labeled with a set of facial landmarks, *e.g.*, eye centers, mouth corners, nose tip. Importantly, we do not require the landmark definitions to be consistent between source datasets. Optionally, each target image can have known landmarks, which our system uses as additional constraints. The output of our system is a combined set of landmark estimates (*i.e.*, the union set of landmark types from all source datasets) for each target face.

Stage 0: Preprocessing. We first rotate and scale all faces such that the eyes are level and the size is approximately the same across all face instances.[1] We then extract dense SIFT [13] features across each face at multiple scales. Following the approach in [20], we quantize each SIFT descriptor using fast approximate k-means [16], which efficiently maps each descriptor to a visual word.

Stage 1: Selection of Top Source Faces. For each target face, retrieve a separate subset of top k similar faces from each source dataset. The goal is to retrieve source faces that are similar to the target face in appearance, shape, expression, and pose so that features in the source images will produce accurate landmark votes in the target image.

---

[1] Eyes are easier to locate than other parts of the face, and so we assume they can be located accurately beforehand to rectify the face, *i.e.*, using an eye detector as in [28]. However, our method is not that sensitive to eye localization accuracy.

Stage 2: Weighted Landmark Voting. For each target face, independently compute a separate voting map for each landmark type from each source dataset using a generalized Hough transform [12]. Each feature from the top k source faces casts a vote for a possible landmark locations in the target image.

Stage 3: Shape Regularization. For each target face, compute a separate set of landmark estimates from each source dataset. Due to local ambiguities, occlusions, *etc.* each voting map may contain multiple peaks. We employ a robust nonparametric shape regularization technique [2] that avoids false peaks and estimates a globally optimized set of landmarks from each source dataset.

Stage 4: Final Landmark Estimation and Integration. For each target face, retrieve the top m most similar faces from the *target* dataset. The goal is to exploit the correlation between landmark estimates from Stage 3 among similar target faces to consistently label all target images. We combine estimates for landmarks common to multiple source datasets, and we optionally use known landmarks in each target image to constrain the optimization. We extend the graph matching technique in [29] for landmark integration from multiple source datasets. The final output for each target face is a full set of landmark estimates; by 'full' we mean the union of landmark types from all source datasets.

Input: One or more source face datasets, and one target dataset

Output: A combined set of landmark estimates for each target face

Stage 0: Preprocessing
for all target faces **do**
    | **Stage 1**: Selection of Top Source Faces
    | **Stage 2**: Weighted Landmark Voting
    | **Stage 3**: Shape Regularization
end
for all target faces **do**
    | **Stage 4**: Final Landmark Estimation and Integration
end

Fig. 1. Overview of our pipeline. Stage 4 is in a separate loop because it uses all the target face results from Stage 3 to help constrain and consistently estimate the final landmark results.

3.2 Stage 1: Selection of Top Source Faces

To transfer landmarks from each source dataset to the target image, the shape and appearance of the source faces and the target face should be similar. For example, a frontal face has much different appearance and shape than a profile face; there are few geometric feature-landmark correlations between the two. We therefore select a top subset of source faces for further processing.

Many strategies exist for retrieving similar face images from a database. In our system, we use a generalized Hough transform framework to score each source face. Specifically, we use the features on the target face to vote for the center of the face in each source image. The final score for each source face is the height of the maximum peak in the voting map associated with each source image. The intuition is that source faces with many shared features in similar geometric layouts with the target image will produce many consistent votes for the center of the face. We sort the scores and select the top $k = 200$. Shen *et al.* [20] adopt a similar strategy for retrieving exemplar faces in the validation step of their face detection algorithm.

3.3   Stage 2: Weighted Landmark Voting

For efficiency, rather than exhaustively sliding each source landmark region over the target image, we use quantized features and employ an inverted index file to efficiently retrieve matched features (*i.e.*, features in the same quantization bin) from the top k source images. When a feature in the target image is matched to a feature in a source image, the feature-to-landmark offset in the source image is transferred to the target image. The offset vector extends from the feature in the target image toward a potential landmark location and produces a vote. After many such votes, a voting map is formed, where the votes tend to cluster at landmark locations.

In practice, due to errors in the feature quantization step, image noise, occlusions, locally ambiguous image regions, *etc.*, many of the votes are incorrect, which can significantly impact overall voting accuracy. Yang and Patras [26] eliminate bad votes via a cascade of 'sieves.' Shen *et al.* [20] attempt to downweight potentially bad votes using a heuristic from object retrieval: $\frac{\mathrm{idf}^2(k)}{\mathrm{tf}_Q(k)\mathrm{tf}_D(k)}$, where $\mathrm{idf}^2(k)$ is the squared inverse document frequency of visual word k, and $\mathrm{tf}_Q(k)$ and $\mathrm{tf}_D(k)$ are the term frequencies of k in the query image and the database image, respectively.

We instead compute a weight for each vote online as follows. For a given feature in the target image, retrieve all features in the top k source images that share the same quantization bin. For each of these features, compute their offset from landmark l. After rejecting outlier votes (*i.e.*, by measuring the distribution and rejecting vote offsets outside the inter-quartile range), we compute the variance σ_v^2 of the remaining offsets. We then cast a "fuzzy" vote from each offset using a 2D Gaussian $\mathcal{N}(v; \sigma^2)$ centered on the vote location v. Intuitively, this rewards matched features that produce consistent voting offsets and suppresses features that disagree. Our weighting scheme is similar to [22] and is less heuristic than [20]. Because our weights are computed online, we can easily add additional faces to the source dataset. In contrast, [22] and [26] require retraining when the training dataset changes.

We note that the Hough voting strategy is sensitive to scale and rotation differences between source and target faces. Shen *et al.* [20] address this problem by performing Hough voting over multiple scales. We instead normalize the scale and orientation of each face in Stage 0, which eliminates the need to search for scale and rotation parameters.

3.4 Stage 3: Shape Regularization

There are many strategies for enforcing shape constraints, *e.g.*, [2,19,25,29,30]. However, in our case, we use an exemplar-based approach to shape regularization [2], which fits nicely with our exemplar-based Hough voting strategy for generating landmark response maps.

Belhumeur *et al.* [2] use SVM-based landmark detectors to establish an initial set of landmark location hypotheses, which forms the input to their final shape optimization algorithm. Each SVM attempts to capture all the local appearance variation around each landmark within a single model. This works well on faces with limited head pose variation. In contrast, our Hough voting strategy creates a nonparametric appearance model for each landmark, specific to each target face, which works well on faces with extreme head pose variation. Also, by aggregating the votes from many features, our method takes advantage of the larger appearance context around each landmark, which provides much more robustness to local noise, occlusions, *etc.* We therefore use our landmark voting maps in place of the local detector response maps used in [2].

Additionally, rather than using the entire set of exemplar face shapes as input, which is the approach taken in [2], we use only the top k source faces retrieved in Stage 1 of our pipeline. The top k source faces tend to be better tailored to the target face than the general set of faces, which further aids the optimization.

3.5 Stage 4: Final Landmark Estimation and Integration

The goal of this stage is to combine the individual landmark estimates from each source dataset into a single result for each target image. We incorporate several constraints into the optimization:

1. We model each landmark location as a linear combination of the other landmarks, which provides an affine-invariant shape constraint [29].
2. If available, known landmarks in the target image are fixed and help steer nearby landmark estimates to their correct locations.
3. Only one estimate is allowed for each landmark type irrespective of the number of source datasets contributing estimates for each type.

We address the shape constraint first. Let $\mathbf{P} = [\mathbf{p}_1, \ldots, \mathbf{p}_{N_P}]$ be a face shape composed of N_P landmarks. Following [29], we assume that the c-th landmark location $\mathbf{p}_c$ can be reconstructed by a linear combination of neighboring landmarks: $\mathbf{p}_c = \mathbf{P}\mathbf{w}_c$, where $\mathbf{w}_c \in \mathbb{R}^{N_P}$ is a vector of weights for the other $N_P - 1$ landmarks (the c-th entry of $\mathbf{w}_c$ is fixed to zero).

Suppose we have N_S source datasets and therefore N_S {target image t, source dataset s} pairs. Each pair has a union set of landmark types, $L_{ts} = \{L_t \cup L_s\}$, composed of landmark types L_t defined in the target image[2] or landmark types L_s defined in the source dataset. Each L_{ts} contains all landmark types either known *a priori* in target image t, or estimated from source s or both. We aim to compute an optimal $\mathbf{w}_{tsc}$ for $c \in L_{ts}$ for each {target image t, source dataset s} pair (we subsequently omit t and s subscripts in $\mathbf{w}_{tsc}$ for simplicity).

To accomplish this task we need a set of example shapes that include all landmark types in L_{ts}. Given a target image t, we retrieve the m most similar face shapes among the target face images; the face shapes for the target images come from the regularized landmark localization results from Stage 3. As a distance metric, we simply use the mean Euclidean error between shapes after similarity transformation alignment. Using [29], we compute the $\mathbf{w}_c$ for image t that minimizes the sum of reconstruction errors among the top m most similar shape results from Stage 3:

$$\min_{\mathbf{w}_c} = \sum_j^m ||\mathbf{P}^j \mathbf{w}_c - \mathbf{p}_c^j||_2^2 + \eta ||\mathbf{w}_c||_2^2 \tag{1}$$

$$\text{s.t. } \mathbf{w}_c^{\mathsf{T}} \mathbf{1}_{N_P} = 1, \quad w_{cc} = 0, \quad w_{cr} = 0 \ \forall r \notin L_{ts},$$

where $\mathbf{P}^j$ is the j-th most similar face shape relative to t among other results from Stage 3; the constraint $w_{cr} = 0 \ \forall r \notin L_{ts}$ means that we force weights to zero if the r-th landmark is undefined in L_{ts}; and $\eta ||\mathbf{w}_c||_2^2$ is a regularization term that penalizes the sparsity of the weight vector, *i.e.*, it promotes more uniformity in the weights, which means that non-local landmarks can also carry importance in determining the c-th landmark location. Eq. (1) is a small convex quadratic problem, which we solve independently for each $\mathbf{w}_c$. The formulation of Eq. (1) is the same as [29] except for our added third constraint.

We compose the joint weight matrix as $\mathbf{W}_s = [\mathbf{w}_1, \ldots, \mathbf{w}_{N_P}]$, and we repeat the process for each source dataset s to create a set of N_S joint weight matrices $\mathbf{W}_1, \ldots, \mathbf{W}_{N_S}$ specific to target image t. Note that undefined columns in each $\mathbf{W}_s$ (corresponding to landmarks not defined in L_{ts}) are set to zero.

Following [29], let us now define a global coordinate matrix $\mathbf{Q} = [\mathbf{Q}_1, \ldots, \mathbf{Q}_{N_P}] \in \mathbb{R}^{2 \times N}$, where $\mathbf{Q}_c \in \mathbb{R}^{2 \times N_c}$ denotes candidate locations for the c-th landmark and $N = \sum_c N_c$. Let $\mathbf{G} \in \{0, 1\}^{N_P \times N}$ be a binary association matrix, where $g_{ci} = 1$ if the i-th point belongs to the c-th landmark. Note that the candidate locations are the locations of the local peaks in the landmark response maps in Stage 3. When a landmark is common in multiple source datasets, we average the response maps from different source datasets before finding the local peaks. Let $\mathbf{A} \in \mathbb{R}^{N_P \times N}$ denote the assignment cost matrix, *i.e.*, $a_{ci} = -\log(R_c(\mathbf{q}_i))$, where $R_c(\mathbf{q}_i)$ is the height value in the c-th voting map at $\mathbf{q}_i$ after the voting map is normalized to sum to 1.

Given the candidates $\mathbf{Q}$, $\mathbf{G}$, $\mathbf{A}$ and the shape constraints $\mathbf{W}_1, \ldots, \mathbf{W}_{N_S}$, the problem consists of finding the optimal correspondence $\mathbf{X}$ that minimized the following error:

---

[2] L_t can be empty, in which case the target dataset has no known landmarks.

$$\min_{\mathbf{X}} \quad \lambda \mathrm{tr}(\mathbf{A}\mathbf{X}^\mathsf{T}) + \sum_{s}^{N_S} \|\mathbf{Q}\mathbf{X}^\mathsf{T}(\mathbf{I}_s - \mathbf{W}_s)\|_1 \tag{2}$$

$$\text{s.t.} \quad \mathbf{X}\mathbf{1}_N = \mathbf{1}_{N_P}, \quad \mathbf{X} \in [0,1]^{N_P \times N}, \quad x_{ci} = 0, \quad [c,i] \in \{[c,i]|g_{ci} = 0\},$$

where $\mathbf{I}_s$ is an $N_P \times N_P$ identity matrix except that we set $\mathbf{I}_s(r,r) = 0 \; \forall r \notin L_{ts}$ (*i.e.*, the r-th diagonal element is set to zero if landmark r is not defined in the target image or in dataset s). Eq. (2) is inspired from [29] except here we sum over multiple shape constraint terms instead of just one. Due to the integer constraint on $\mathbf{X}$, optimizing Eq. (2) is NP-hard. Like [29], we solve Eq. (2) by relaxing the integer constraint with a continuous one, and by reformulating the problem to incorporate two auxiliary variables that replace the non-smooth ℓ_1 norm with a smooth term and a linear constraint. Please see [29] for more details.

Incorporating known landmarks in the target image as constraints in Eq. (2) is straightforward. We simply provide a single candidate location for each of the known landmarks via the matrices $\mathbf{Q}$ and $\mathbf{G}$.

Because we use the same correspondence matrix $\mathbf{X}$ for all terms in Eq. (2), we obtain only one estimate for each landmark type, regardless of how many source datasets contribute to the estimate.

3.6   Implementation Details and Runtime

For quantizing SIFT features we use fast approximate k-means [16] with $k = 10^5$ clusters. For efficiency, we quantize the spatial variance σ_v^2 measurement of each vote cluster in Section 3.3 and convolve each voting map after all voting is complete using a set of precomputed Gaussian kernels. We also threshold σ_v to prevent erroneous spikes in the voting maps: we do not allow σ_v to fall below 3 pixels. In Stage 4, we set $\eta = 1000$, $\lambda = 100$, and we use about 200 candidates for each landmark.

Because our system operates on face datasets, we consider our pipeline to be entirely 'offline.' However, it is not prohibitively slow despite the number of steps involved. All tests were conducted on an Intel Xeon E5-2670 workstation. For each 480×480 image in our evaluation set, feature extraction and quantization takes less than a second. For each {target image, source dataset} pair, top exemplar selection (Stage 1) takes approximately 2.5 seconds, landmark voting (Stage 2) across 84 landmarks takes approximately 15 seconds, and shape regularization (Stage 3) takes approximately 10 seconds using our MATLAB implementation. The final stage is the most expensive (approximately 30 seconds per image) in part because MATLAB's linear program solver is relatively slow with many landmarks and candidate locations. We remark that most parts of our pipeline can be easily parallelized.

4   Results and Discussion

In this section we present two groups of experiments to evaluate the accuracy of our approach. First, we compare our accuracy with recent facial landmark

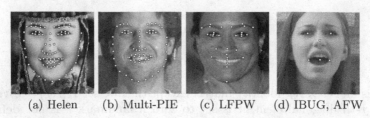

(a) Helen   (b) Multi-PIE   (c) LFPW   (d) IBUG, AFW

Fig. 2. Experimental datasets. When each dataset is acting as source, we use the landmark annotations shown above. There are 85 landmark types across all datasets.

localization methods [1, 2, 23, 25, 27–30]. For fair comparison, we assume that no landmarks are known in the target images, and we measure accuracy over a common subset of landmarks computed across all methods. We show that our algorithm generally outperforms recent methods on especially challenging in-the-wild faces. Second, we measure the accuracy of our algorithm using different numbers of known landmarks in the target dataset to show that our method exploits additional known landmarks as constraints to further significantly improve accuracy. For all experiments we use multiple source datasets, each with a different set of landmark definitions.

4.1   Experimental Datasets

We used five face datasets for our quantitative evaluation: Multi-PIE [7], Helen [11], LFPW [2], AFW [30], and IBUG [17]. In the literature, there are two versions of landmark annotations for Helen, LFPW, and AFW: (1) the annotations provided when the datasets were originally released, which we refer to as 'original' hereafter; and (2) the recent annotations provided as part of the 300 Faces in-the-wild Challenge (300-W) [17], which we refer to as '300-W' hereafter. We use both versions of the landmarks; details are described in the context of individual experiments.

As in [23, 27, 30], we measure the size of the face as the average of the height and width of the rectangular hull around the ground truth landmarks. We favor this size measurement over inter-ocular distance (IOD) because it is more robust to yaw head rotation. Prior to evaluating all algorithms, we rescaled all test faces to a canonical size (200 pixels) and rotated them to make the eyes level.

4.2   Comparisons with Recent Works

In this section we quantitatively compare our algorithm with recent works [1, 2, 23, 25, 27–30]. The source datasets for training consist of Multi-PIE, Helen, and LFPW. For our algorithm, we used the ground truth landmark annotations shown in Figure 2 for Multi-PIE, Helen, and LFPW as training. The ground truth landmarks come from both the original annotations and the 300-W annotations (300-W annotations are favored in cases of redundant definitions). We note that there are 85 unique landmark types across all datasets.

Our target datasets for testing are AFW [30] and IBUG [17]. We use these two datasets for evaluation because they are particularly challenging, *e.g.*, they

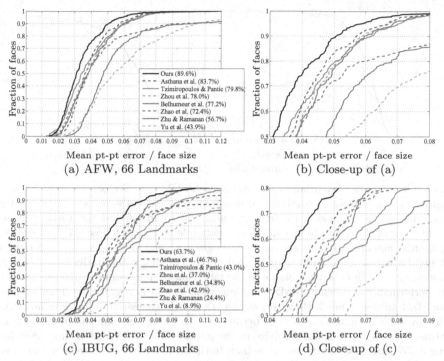

Fig. 3. Two sets of cumulative error distribution (CED) curves on AFW and IBUG face datasets. In all cases, the average localization error is normalized by the face size as defined in [30]. The numbers in parantheses are the fraction of faces at 0.05 error. Here we compare the accuracy of our approach with several recent works: Asthana *et al.* [1], Tzimiropoulos and Pantic [23], Zhou *et al.* [29], Belhumeur *et al.* [2], Zhao *et al.* [28], Zhu and Ramanan [30], and Yu *et al.* [27]. We see that our approach generally produces significantly more accurate results among those evaluated above. **Best viewed in color.**

include a large percentage of faces with extreme facial expression and/or head pose. In contrast, other popular datasets like BioID [9], Helen [11], LFW [8], and LFPW [2] contain faces with less challenging variations, which are consequently well addressed by current methods.

We made every effort to implement Belhumeur *et al.* [2] and Zhou *et al.* [29] algorithms faithfully; we trained them on the source dataset (Multi-PIE, Helen, and LFPW) using only 300-W annotations. For all other algorithms, we used the original authors' implementations. We used the off-the-shelf models provided with each implementation, with the exception of Zhao *et al.* [28]. Zhao *et al.* compute target face-specific models online from a given training database; for their algorithm, like Belhumeur *et al.* [2] and Zhou *et al.* [29], we provided Multi-PIE, Helen, and LFPW faces as training data using only 300-W annotations.

Initialization. For Belhumeur *et al.* [2] and Zhou *et al.* [29] we initialized the position of each landmark detector using a mean face shape aligned to the face. The diameter of each detector window was set to the larger of 33% of the face

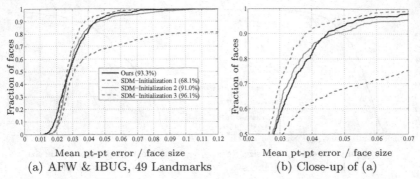

(a) AFW & IBUG, 49 Landmarks   (b) Close-up of (a)

Fig. 4. CED curves comparing our accuracy with SDM [25]. We observe that SDM is sensitive to initialization, especially for non-frontal faces, and so we evaluate it using three different initialization strategies. Initialization 1 and 3 follow the authors' strategy: fit a mean shape to the face detection rectangle. For 1 we follow [17] and use the rectangular hull around all 68 ground truth landmarks, and for 3 we use a much tighter rectangular hull around the interior 49 ground truth landmarks. Initialization 2 follows the strategy of [28]: fit a mean shape to the target face using ground truth eye centers. Our performance is similar to SDM–Initialization 2, and is slightly lower on average than SDM–Initialization 3. However, we remark that Initialization 3 provides an artificially favorable initialization to SDM because it is much tighter than Initialization 1. In contrast, our approach is not sensitive to the initialization: we initialize our algorithm using a 25% larger bounding rectangle than Initialization 1 (the least reliable but most realistic initialization here), and we do not rely on an initial shape. Unlike SDM, our full pipeline can use known landmarks in the target image as constraints to further significantly improve accuracy, as shown in Figure 6. **Best viewed in color.**

size or large enough to overlap the true landmark location. Zhao *et al.*'s implementation [28] is initialized via eye detectors; we provided their algorithm with ground truth eye centers. Tzimiropoulos and Pantic's [23] algorithm requires a face bounding box for initialization; for this we provided the ground truth bounding boxes as defined by [17].

Zhu and Ramanan's [30] algorithm is tied to their detection algorithm, and so we do not provide it with an initialization. We set their detection threshold to $-\infty$ to avoid missing faces. For each ground truth face annotation, we select the output face with the largest bounding box overlap (the area of intersection divided by the area of union), and we ignore all false positives. Zhu and Ramanan provide three models with their implementation. We used their *Independent-1050* model for all of our experiments since it generally performs best.

Asthana *et al.* [1] and Yu *et al.* [27] each rely on a version of [30] for initialization, and so we do not provide one separately. However, since Yu *et al.*'s implementation only returns landmark estimates for the highest scoring face in each image, we isolated the true face by cropped it out (the crop window was centered on the true face and set to approximately twice the face height/width).

Xiong and De la Torre's Supervised Descent Method (SDM) [25] is considered the current state of the art. The authors use the Viola-Jones face detector [24] for initialization. Unfortunately, Viola-Jones fails to detect 10% and 26% of

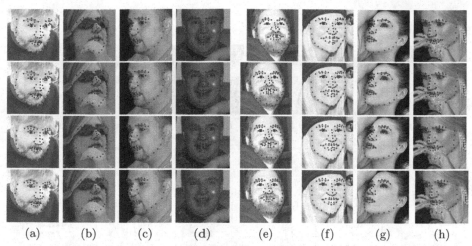

(a)   (b)   (c)   (d)   (e)   (f)   (g)   (h)

Fig. 5. Qualitative results on AFW faces (a)-(f) and IBUG faces (g)-(h) with varying numbers of known landmarks in the target images. Green points are estimated landmark locations, and red points are known landmark locations. From the top row to the bottom row, results were computed with 32, 21, 6, and 0 known landmarks. We see that errors are corrected with additional known landmarks, *e.g.*, the eyebrows in (a) and (f), and the lips in (d) and (g). Even with no known landmarks (bottom row), our algorithm performs well on challenging faces, including those with significant head pitch rotation (a, e, g, and h), head yaw rotation (b, c, g, and h), occlusion (b and h), and facial hair (a and e). Figure 3 shows quantitative results with no known landmarks in the target images. **Best viewed electronically in color.**

AFW and IBUG faces, respectively, despite our pre-rectification step. We instead initialized SDM using three different strategies, described in Figure 4.

Quantitative Results. Figure 3 shows two sets of cumulative error distribution (CED) curves, which compare the accuracy of our approach with others. Using Multi-PIE, Helen, and LFPW as source datasets, our algorithm produces 84 landmark estimates (a union of both 300-W and original annotations from the three source datasets).[3] We evaluated the accuracy of 66 landmarks in Figure 3 because [1] estimates 66 landmarks. Errors are computed relative to the 300-W ground truth landmarks as the mean point-to-point error normalized by the face size. We compare with SDM [25] separately in Figure 4 because the authors' implementation estimates 49 landmarks instead of 66. We see that our approach generally outperforms recent methods on AFW and IBUG faces.

---

[3] We supplemented the 300-W annotations on Helen with 10 landmarks from the original annotations (three on each eyebrow, four on the nose). When we use LFPW as a source dataset, we use only the 29 landmarks from the 300-W annotations that coincide with the original annotations. When we use AFW and IBUG as source datasets, we use only the six 300-W annotations that coincide with the original AFW annotation. Figure 2 shows the layout of landmarks for each source dataset.

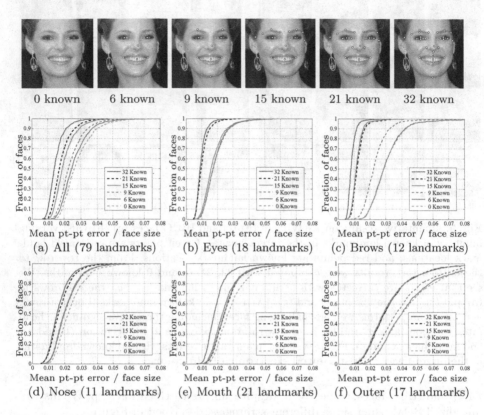

0 known   6 known   9 known   15 known   21 known   32 known

(a) All (79 landmarks)   (b) Eyes (18 landmarks)   (c) Brows (12 landmarks)

(d) Nose (11 landmarks)   (e) Mouth (21 landmarks)   (f) Outer (17 landmarks)

Fig. 6. Quantitative evaluation of our full pipeline with six different trials, each assuming a different number of known landmarks. The top row shows the arrangement of known landmarks for each trial. "6 known" corresponds to the original AFW layout; "21 known" corresponds to AFLW; and "32 known" closely resembles the original LFPW annotations. In (a) we see the overall mean accuracy is high with 0 known landmarks (96.5% at 0.05), and the accuracy continues to improve significantly as additional landmarks become known. For reference, Belhumeur *et al.* [2] showed that their algorithm surpasses the average accuracy of human labelers on most landmarks, and our algorithm further improves Belhumeur *et al.*'s localization accuracy (see Figure 3) even with 0 known landmarks. We note that inherent ambiguities exist on the face, especially on longer contours such as the lips and the outer face contour. For example, a landmark estimate on the outer contour may be qualitatively correct, but in disagreement with "ground truth" in terms of its location along the contour. This phenomenon partly explains the lower CED curves in (c), (e), and (f). In general, we see that our approach correctly estimates landmarks on a large majority of faces, especially with 21 or 32 known landmarks. This suggests that our approach is well-suited for automatically supplementing the landmarks in large, sparsely annotated datasets like AFLW. **Best viewed in color.**

4.3   Evaluation with Known Target Landmarks

We have quantitatively evaluated our full pipeline using 1035 images from LFPW as the target dataset, and using Multi-PIE, Helen, AFW, and IBUG as source datasets. The union of the different annotation definitions results in a total of 85 landmarks. We performed six different trials, with each trial assuming a different number of known landmarks in the target dataset: 0, 6, 9, 15, 21, and 32. Among these different numbers, we chose 6 because it corresponds to the original AFW annotations; we chose 21 because it corresponds to annotations provided in the AFLW dataset [10]; and we chose 32 because it closely resembles the original annotations in LFPW. The top of Figure 6 shows the arrangement of known landmarks for each trial. For each face, we measure the accuracy of 79 landmarks (out of 85 estimated) relative to ground truth annotations from 300-W and the original LFPW dataset; the ground truth of the remaining 6 landmarks are not available for LFPW.

The CED curves in Figure 6 show the accuracy of our algorithm on each of these trials across 79 landmarks. We see that the accuracy of our algorithm is high with 0 known landmarks (96.5% at 0.05 average overall), and the accuracy continues to improve with additional known landmarks.

A prime target dataset for our approach is AFLW [10], which contains 25,000 in-the-wild face images from Flickr, each manually annotated with up to 21 sparse landmarks. Our approach is well-suited to automatically supplementing AFLW with additional landmarks from source datasets like Multi-PIE [7] and Helen [11]. Our supplementary AFLW landmarks are available at our project website: http://www.cs.wisc.edu/~lizhang/projects/collab-face-landmarks/.

5   Conclusions

Our quantitative comparison shows that our approach generally significantly outperforms recent methods, and achieves accuracy comparable to the current state of the art on challenging in-the-wild faces, even with zero known landmarks in the target dataset. Our evaluation using different numbers of known landmarks in the target dataset show that our approach is well-suited to automatically supplementing an existing dataset with additional landmarks from other source datasets. However, our algorithm is not perfect and occasionally makes mistakes. For infrequent problem cases, our system naturally allows the user to provide a few additional landmarks as constraints. For these reasons, we want to build upon our system to include humans in the loop as part of a crowdsourcing platform for efficiently adding landmarks to large face datasets.

Acknowledgements. This work is supported by NSF IIS-0845916, NSF IIS-0916441, a Sloan Research Fellowship, and a Packard Fellowship for Science and Engineering.

References

1. Asthana, A., Zafeiriou, S., Cheng, S., Pantic, M.: Robust discriminative response map fitting with constrained local models. In: IEEE Conference on Computer Vision and Pattern Recognition (2013)
2. Belhumeur, P.N., Jacobs, D.W., Kriegman, D.J., Kumar, N.: Localizing parts of faces using a consensus of exemplars. In: IEEE Conference on Computer Vision and Pattern Recognition (2011)
3. Cootes, T.F., Edwards, G.J., Taylor, C.J.: Active appearance models. In: Burkhardt, H., Neumann, B. (eds.) ECCV 1998. LNCS, vol. 1407, pp. 484–498. Springer, Heidelberg (1998)
4. Cootes, T.F., Taylor, C.J.: Active shape models – 'smart snakes'. In: British Machine Vision Conference (1992)
5. Cootes, T.F., Taylor, C.J.: Constrained active appearance models. In: IEEE International Conference on Computer Vision (2001)
6. Cristinacce, D., Cootes, T.F.: Feature detection and tracking with constrained local models. In: British Machine Vision Conference, pp. 929–938 (2006)
7. Gross, R., Matthews, I., Cohn, J.F., Kanade, T., Baker, S.: Multi-PIE. Image and Vision Computing 28(5), 807–813 (2010)
8. Huang, G.B., Ramesh, M., Berg, T., Learned-Miller, E.: Labeled faces in the wild: A database for studying face recognition in unconstrained environments. Tech. Rep. 07-49, University of Massachusetts, Amherst (October 2007)
9. Jesorsky, O., Kirchberg, K.J., Frischholz, R.W.: Robust face detection using the hausdorff distance. In: Bigun, J., Smeraldi, F. (eds.) AVBPA 2001. LNCS, vol. 2091, p. 90. Springer, Heidelberg (2001)
10. Koestinger, M., Wohlhart, P., Roth, P.M., Bischof, H.: Annotated facial landmarks in the wild: A large-scale, real-world database for facial landmark localization. In: First IEEE International Workshop on Benchmarking Facial Image Analysis Technologies (2011)
11. Le, V., Brandt, J., Lin, Z., Bourdev, L., Huang, T.S.: Interactive facial feature localization. In: Fitzgibbon, A., Lazebnik, S., Perona, P., Sato, Y., Schmid, C. (eds.) ECCV 2012, Part III. LNCS, vol. 7574, pp. 679–692. Springer, Heidelberg (2012)
12. Leibe, B., Leonardis, A., Schiele, B.: Combined object categorization and segmentation with an implicit shape model. In: European Conference on Computer Vision Workshop on Statistical Learning in Computer Vision (2004)
13. Lowe, D.G.: Distinctive image features from scale-invariant keypoints. International Journal of Computer Vision 60(2), 91–110 (2004)
14. Martinez, A., Benavente, R.: The AR Face Database. Tech. Rep. 24, CVC (1998)
15. Messer, K., Matas, J., Kittler, J., Luettin, J., Maitre, G.: XM2VTSDB: The extended m2vts database. In: 2nd International Conference on Audio and Video-Based Biometric Person Authentication (1999)
16. Muja, M., Lowe, D.G.: Fast approximate nearest neighbors with automatic algorithm configuration. In: VISAPP International Conference on Computer Vision Theory and Applications (2009)
17. Sagonas, C., Tzimiropoulos, G., Zafeiriou, S., Pantic, M.: 300 faces in-the-wild challenge: The first facial landmark localization challenge. In: IEEE International Conference on Computer Vision (ICCV-W 2013), 300 Faces in-the-Wild Challenge (300-W) (2013)

18. Sagonas, C., Tzimiropoulos, G., Zafeiriou, S., Pantic, M.: A semi-automatic methodology for facial landmark annotation. In: IEEE Conference on Computer Vision and Pattern Recognition Workshop (2013)
19. Saragih, J.M., Lucey, S., Cohn, J.F.: Face alignment through subspace constrained mean-shifts. In: IEEE International Conference on Computer Vision (2009)
20. Shen, X., Lin, Z., Brandt, J., Wu, Y.: Detecting and aligning faces by image retrieval. In: IEEE Conference on Computer Vision and Pattern Recognition (2013)
21. Sim, T., Baker, S., Bsat, M.: The CMU pose, illumination, and expression database. IEEE Transactions on Pattern Analysis and Machine Intelligence 25(12), 1615–1618 (2003)
22. Smith, B.M., Brandt, J., Lin, Z., Zhang, L.: Nonparametric context modeling of local appearance for pose- and expression-robust facial landmark localization. In: IEEE Conference on Computer Vision and Pattern Recognition (2014)
23. Tzimiropoulos, G., Pantic, M.: Optimization problems for fast AAM fitting in-the-wild. In: IEEE International Conference on Computer Vision (2013)
24. Viola, P., Jones, M.J.: Robust real-time face detection. International Journal of Computer Vision 57(2), 137–154 (2004)
25. Xiong, X., De la Torre, F.: Supervised descent method and its applications to face alignment. In: IEEE Conference on Computer Vision and Pattern Recognition (2013)
26. Yang, H., Patras, I.: Sieving regression forest votes for facial feature detection in the wild. In: IEEE International Conference on Computer Vision (2013)
27. Yu, X., Huang, J., Zhang, S., Yan, W., Metaxas, D.N.: Pose-free facial landmark fitting via optimized part mixtures and cascaded deformable shape model. In: IEEE International Conference on Computer Vision (2013)
28. Zhao, X., Shan, S., Chai, X., Chen, X.: Locality-constrained active appearance model. In: Lee, K.M., Matsushita, Y., Rehg, J.M., Hu, Z. (eds.) ACCV 2012, Part I. LNCS, vol. 7724, pp. 636–647. Springer, Heidelberg (2013)
29. Zhou, F., Brandt, J., Lin, Z.: Exemplar-based graph matching for robust facial landmark localization. In: IEEE International Conference on Computer Vision (2013)
30. Zhu, X., Ramanan, D.: Face detection, pose estimation, and landmark localization in the wild. In: IEEE Conference on Computer Vision and Pattern Recognition (2012)

Facial Landmark Detection
by Deep Multi-task Learning

Zhanpeng Zhang, Ping Luo, Chen Change Loy, and Xiaoou Tang

Dept. of Information Engineering, The Chinese University of Hong Kong,
Hong Kong, China

Abstract. Facial landmark detection has long been impeded by the problems of occlusion and pose variation. Instead of treating the detection task as a single and independent problem, we investigate the possibility of improving detection robustness through multi-task learning. Specifically, we wish to optimize facial landmark detection together with heterogeneous but subtly correlated tasks, e.g. head pose estimation and facial attribute inference. This is non-trivial since different tasks have different learning difficulties and convergence rates. To address this problem, we formulate a novel tasks-constrained deep model, with task-wise early stopping to facilitate learning convergence. Extensive evaluations show that the proposed task-constrained learning (i) outperforms existing methods, especially in dealing with faces with severe occlusion and pose variation, and (ii) reduces model complexity drastically compared to the state-of-the-art method based on cascaded deep model [21].

1 Introduction

Facial landmark detection is a fundamental component in many face analysis tasks, such as facial attribute inference [17], face verification [15, 22, 23, 35], and face recognition [33, 34]. Though great strides have been made in this field [8, 9, 10, 16], robust facial landmark detection remains a formidable challenge in the presence of partial occlusion and large head pose variations (Figure 1).

Facial landmark detection is traditionally approached as a single and independent problem. Popular approaches include template fitting approaches [8, 32, 27] and regression-based methods [3, 4, 9, 26, 31]. For example, Sun et al. [21] propose to detect facial landmarks by coarse-to-fine regression using a cascade of deep convolutional neural networks (CNN). This method shows superior accuracy compared to previous methods [2, 4] and existing commercial systems. Nevertheless, the method requires a complex and unwieldy cascade architecture of deep model.

We believe that facial landmark detection is not a standalone problem, but its estimation can be influenced by a number of heterogeneous and subtly correlated factors. For instance, when a kid is smiling, his mouth is widely opened (second image in Figure 1). Effectively discovering and exploiting such an intrinsically correlated facial attribute would help in detecting the mouth corners more accurately. Also, the inter-ocular distance is smaller in faces with large yaw

D. Fleet et al. (Eds.): ECCV 2014, Part VI, LNCS 8694, pp. 94–108, 2014.

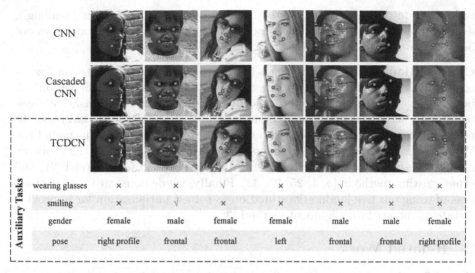

Fig. 1. Examples of facial landmark detection by a single conventional CNN, the cascaded CNN [21], and the proposed Tasks-Constrained Deep Convolutional Network (TCDCN). More accurate detection can be achieved by optimizing the detection task jointly with related/auxiliary tasks.

rotation (the last image in Figure 1). Such pose information can be leveraged as additional source of information to constrain the solution space of landmark estimation. Given the rich set of plausible related tasks, treating facial landmark detection in isolation is counterproductive.

This study aims to investigate the possibility of *optimizing facial landmark detection (the main task) with related/auxiliary tasks*, which include head pose estimation, gender classification, age estimation [6], facial expression recognition, or facial attribute inference [17]. There are several unique challenges. First, despite all the tasks share facial images as their common input, their output spaces and decision boundaries are different. Importantly, different tasks are inherently different in learning difficulties. For instance, learning to identify 'wearing glasses' attribute is easier than determining if one is smiling. In addition, we rarely have related task with similar number of positive/negative cases. Hence, different tasks have different convergence rates. Certain tasks are likely to be over-fitting earlier than the others when learning simultaneously, which could jeopardises the learning convergence of the whole model.

To this end, we propose a *Tasks-Constrained Deep Convolutional Network* (TCDCN) to jointly optimize facial landmark detection with a set of related tasks. Specifically, we formulate a task-constrained loss function to allow the errors of related tasks to be back-propagated jointly to improve the generalization of landmark detection. To accommodate related tasks with different learning difficulties and convergence rates, we devise a task-wise early stopping criterion to facilitate learning convergence. To show the usefulness of the proposed model, we select a diverse set of related tasks deliberately, as depicted in Figure 1. These tasks include appearance attribute ('wearing glasses'), expression ('smiling'), demographic ('gender'), and head pose. Note that the proposed model does not limit the number of related tasks.

Contribution: Multi-task learning is not new (see Section 2), but to our knowledge, this is the first attempt to investigate how facial landmark detection can be optimized together with heterogeneous but subtly correlated tasks. We systematically show that multiple tasks share and learn common deep layers, so the representations learned from related tasks facilitate the learning of the main task. We further show that tasks relatedness are captured implicitly by the proposed model. The proposed approach outperforms the cascaded CNN model [21] and other existing methods [3, 4, 25, 27, 32]. Finally, we demonstrate the effectiveness of using our five-landmark estimation as robust initialization for improving a state-of-the-art face alignment method [3].

2   Related Work

Facial Landmark Detection: Conventional facial landmark detection methods can be divided into two categories, namely regression-based method and template fitting method. A regression-based method estimates landmark locations explicitly by regression using image features. For example, Valstar et al.[24] predict landmark location from local image patch with support vector regression. Cao et al. [4] and Burgos-Artizzu et al. [3] employ cascaded fern regression with pixel-difference features. A number of studies [9, 10, 26] use random regression forest to cast votes for landmark location based on local image patch with Haar-like features. Most of these methods refine an initial guess of the landmark location iteratively, the first guess/initialization is thus critical. By contrast, our deep model takes raw pixels as input without the need of any facial landmark initialization. Importantly, our method differs in that we exploit related tasks to facilitate landmark detection learning.

A template fitting method builds face templates to fit input images [8, 14]. Part-based model has recently been used for face fitting [1, 27, 32]. Zhu and Ramanan [32] show that face detection, facial landmark detection, and pose estimation can be jointly addressed. Our method differs in that we do not limit the learning of specific tasks, i.e. the TCDCN is readily expandable to be trained with additional related tasks. Specifically, apart from pose, we show that facial attribute, gender, and expression, can be useful for learning a robust landmark detector. Another difference to [32] is that we learn feature representation from raw pixels rather than pre-defined HOG as face descriptor.

Landmark Detection by CNN: The closest method to our approach is the cascaded CNN by Sun et al. [21]. The cascaded CNN requires a pre-partition of faces into different parts, each of which are processed by separate deep CNNs. The resulting outputs are subsequently averaged and channeled to separate cascaded layers to process each facial landmark individually. Our model requires neither pre-partition of faces nor cascaded layers, leading to drastic reduction in model complexity, whilst still achieving comparable or even better accuracy.

Multi-task Learning: The proposed approach falls under the big umbrella of multi-task learning. Multi-task learning has proven effective in many computer vision problems [28, 29]. Deep model is well suited for multi-task learning since the features learned from a task may be useful for other task. Existing multi-task deep models [7] are not suitable to solve our problem because they assume similar learning difficulties and convergence rates across all tasks. Specifically, the iterative learning on all tasks are performed without early stopping. Applying this assumption on our problem leads to difficulty in learning convergence, as shown in Section 4. We mitigate this shortcoming through task-wise early stopping. Early stopping is not uncommon in vision learning problems [13, 19]. Neural network methods [20] have also extensively used it to prevent over-fitting by halting the training process of a single task before a minimum error is achieved on the training set. Our early stopping scheme is inspired by Caruana [5], but his study is limited to shallow multilayer perceptrons. We show that early stopping is equally important for multi-task deep convolutional network.

3   Tasks-Constrained Facial Landmark Detection

3.1   Problem Formulation

The traditional multi-task learning (MTL) seeks to improve the generalization performance of multiple related tasks by learning them jointly. Suppose we have a total of T tasks and the training data for the t-th task are denoted as $(\mathbf{x}_i^t, y_i^t)$, where $t = \{1, \ldots, T\}$, $i = \{1, \ldots, N\}$, with $\mathbf{x}_i^t \in \mathbb{R}^d$ and $y_i^t \in \mathbb{R}$ being the feature vector and label, respectively[1]. The goal of the MTL is to minimize

$$\operatorname*{argmin}_{\{\mathbf{w}^t\}_{t=1}^T} \sum_{t=1}^T \sum_{i=1}^N \ell(y_i^t, f(\mathbf{x}_i^t; \mathbf{w}^t)) + \Phi(\mathbf{w}^t), \tag{1}$$

where $f(\mathbf{x}^t; \mathbf{w}^t)$ is a function of $\mathbf{x}^t$ and parameterized by a weight vector $\mathbf{w}^t$. The loss function is denoted by $\ell(\cdot)$. A typical choice is the least square for regression and the hinge loss for classification. The $\Phi(\mathbf{w}^t)$ is the regularization term that penalizes the complexity of weights.

In contrast to conventional MTL that maximizes the performance of all tasks, our aim is to optimize the main task r, which is facial landmark detection, with the assistances of arbitrary number of related/auxiliary tasks $a \in A$. Examples or related tasks include facial pose estimation and attribute inference. To this end, our problem can be formulated as

$$\operatorname*{argmin}_{\mathbf{W}^r, \{\mathbf{W}^a\}_{a \in A}} \sum_{i=1}^N \ell^r(y_i^r, f(\mathbf{x}_i; \mathbf{W}^r)) + \sum_{i=1}^N \sum_{a \in A} \lambda^a \ell^a(y_i^a, f(\mathbf{x}_i; \mathbf{W}^a)), \tag{2}$$

---

[1] In this paper, scalar, vector, and matrix are denoted by lowercase, bold lowercase, and bold capital letter, respectively.

where λ^a denotes the importance coefficient of a-th task's error and the regularization terms are omitted for simplification. Beside the aforementioned difference, Eq.(1) and Eq.(2) are distinct in two aspects. First, different types of loss functions can be optimized together by Eq.(2), e.g. regression and classification can be combined, while existing methods [30] that employ Eq.(1) assume implicitly that the loss functions across all tasks are identical. Second, Eq.(1) allows data $\mathbf{x}_i^t$ in different tasks to have different input representations, while Eq.(2) focuses on a shared input representation $\mathbf{x}_i$. The latter is more suitable for our problem, since all tasks share similar facial representation.

In the following, we formulate our facial landmark detection model based on Eq.(2). Suppose we have a set of feature vectors in a shared feature space across tasks $\{\mathbf{x}_i\}_{i=1}^N$ and their corresponding labels $\{\mathbf{y}_i^r, y_i^p, y_i^g, y_i^w, y_i^s\}_{i=1}^N$, where $\mathbf{y}_i^r$ is the target of landmark detection and the remaining are the targets of auxiliary tasks, including inferences of 'pose', 'gender', 'wear glasses', and 'smiling'. More specifically, $\mathbf{y}_i^r \in \mathbb{R}^{10}$ is the 2D coordinates of the five landmarks (centers of the eyes, nose, corners of the mouth), $y_i^p \in \{0, 1, .., 4\}$ indicates five different poses $(0°, \pm30°, \pm60°)$, and $y_i^g, y_i^w, y_i^s \in \{0, 1\}$ are binary attributes. It is reasonable to employ the least square and cross-entropy as the loss functions for the main task (regression) and the auxiliary tasks (classification), respectively. Therefore, the objective function can be rewritten as

$$\underset{\mathbf{W}^r, \{\mathbf{W}^a\}}{\operatorname{argmin}} \frac{1}{2} \sum_{i=1}^N \|\mathbf{y}_i^r - f(\mathbf{x}_i; \mathbf{W}^r)\|^2 - \sum_{i=1}^N \sum_{a \in A} \lambda^a y_i^a \log(p(y_i^a | \mathbf{x}_i; \mathbf{W}^a)) + \sum_{t=1}^T \|\mathbf{W}\|_2^2,$$
(3)

where $f(\mathbf{x}_i; \mathbf{W}^r) = (\mathbf{W}^r)^\mathsf{T} \mathbf{x}_i$ in the first term is a linear function. The second term is a softmax function $p(y_i = m | \mathbf{x}_i) = \frac{\exp\{(\mathbf{W}_m^a)^\mathsf{T} \mathbf{x}_i\}}{\sum_j \exp\{(\mathbf{W}_j^a)^\mathsf{T} \mathbf{x}_i\}}$, which models the class posterior probability ($\mathbf{W}_j^a$ denotes the jth column of the matrix), and the third term penalizes large weights ($W = \{\mathbf{W}^r, \{\mathbf{W}^a\}\}$). In this work, we adopt the deep convolutional network (DCN) to jointly learn the share feature space $\mathbf{x}$, since the unique structure of DCN allows for multitask and shared representation.

In particular, given a face image $\mathbf{x}^0$, the DCN projects it to higher level representation gradually by learning a sequence of non-linear mappings

$$\mathbf{x}^0 \xrightarrow{\sigma((\mathbf{W}^{s_1})^\mathsf{T} \mathbf{x}^0)} \mathbf{x}^1 \xrightarrow{\sigma((\mathbf{W}^{s_2})^\mathsf{T} \mathbf{x}^1)} \ldots \xrightarrow{\sigma((\mathbf{W}^{s_l})^\mathsf{T} \mathbf{x}^{l-1})} \mathbf{x}^l.$$
(4)

Here, $\sigma(\cdot)$ and $\mathbf{W}^{s_l}$ indicate the non-linear activation function and the filters needed to be learned in the layer l of DCN. For instance, $\mathbf{x}^l = \sigma\left((\mathbf{W}^{s_l})^\mathsf{T} \mathbf{x}^{l-1}\right)$. Note that $\mathbf{x}^l$ is the shared representation between the main task r, and related tasks A. Eq.(4) and Eq.(3) can be trained jointly. The former learns the shared space and the latter optimizes the tasks with respect to this space, and then the errors of the tasks can be propagated back to refine the space. We iterate this learning procedure until convergence. We call the learned model as Tasks-Constrained Deep Convolutional Network (TCDCN).

Fig. 2. The TCDCN extracts shared features for facial landmark detection and related tasks. The first row shows the face images and the second row shows the corresponding features in the shared feature space, where the face images with similar poses and attributes are close with each other. This reveals that the learned feature space is robust to pose, expression ('smiling'), and occlusion ('wearing glasses').

The TCDCN has four convolutional layers and a fully connected layer on the top. Each convolutional layer is followed by a max pooling layer. It is worth noting that in comparison to the cascaded CNN approach [21] that deploys 23 CNNs, our formulation constructs only one single CNN, of which complexity is similar to that of a CNN in the first-level cascade of [21]. We compare the complexity of these two approaches in Section 4.3. Further details of the network architecture is provided in Section 4 to facilitate re-implementation of the proposed model. Several pairs of face images and their features of the shared space of TCDCN are visualized in Figure 2, which shows that the learned features are robust to large poses and expressions. For example, the features of smiling faces or faces have similar poses exhibit similar patterns.

3.2   Learning Tasks-Constrained Deep Convolutional Network

A straightforward way to learn the proposed network is by stochastic gradient descent, whose effectiveness has been proven when a single task is present [12]. However, it is non-trivial to optimize multiple tasks simultaneously using the same method. The reason is that different tasks have different loss functions and learning difficulties, and thus with different convergence rates. Existing methods [30] solve this problem by exploring the relationship of tasks, e.g. through learning a covariance matrix of the weights of all tasks. Nevertheless, such methods can only be applied if the loss functions of all tasks are identical. This assumption is not valid when we wish to perform joint learning on heterogeneous tasks. Moreover, it is computationally impractical in dealing with weight vectors in high dimension.

Task-Wise Early Stopping: We propose an efficient yet effective approach to "early stop" the auxiliary tasks, before they begin to over-fit the training set and thus harm the main task. The intuition behind is that at the beginning of the training process, the TCDCN is constrained by all tasks to avoid being trapped at a bad local minima. As training proceeds, certain auxiliary tasks are no longer beneficial to the main task after they reach their peak performance, their learning process thus should be halted. Note that the regularization offered by early stopping is different from weight regularization in Eq.(3). The latter globally helps to prevent over-fitting in each task through penalizing certain parameter configurations. In Section 4.2, we show that task-wise early stopping is critical for multi-task learning convergence even with weight regularization.

Now we introduce a criterion to automatically determine when to stop learning an auxiliary task. Let E_{val}^a and E_{tr}^a be the values of the loss function of task a on the validation set and training set, respectively. We stop the task if its measure exceeds a threshold ϵ as below

$$\frac{k \cdot \text{med}_{j=t-k}^{t} E_{tr}^a(j)}{\sum_{j=t-k}^{t} E_{tr}^a(j) - k \cdot \text{med}_{j=t-k}^{t} E_{tr}^a(j)} \cdot \frac{E_{val}^a(t) - \min_{j=1..t} E_{tr}^a(j)}{\lambda^a \cdot \min_{j=1..t} E_{tr}^a(j)} > \epsilon, \qquad (5)$$

where t denotes the current iteration and k controls a training strip of length k. The 'med' denotes the function for calculating median value. The first term in Eq.(5) represents the tendency of the training error. If the training error drops rapidly within a period of length k, the value of the first term is small, indicating that training can be continued as the task is still valuable; otherwise, the first term is large, then the task is more likely to be stopped. The second term measures the generalization error compared to the training error. The λ^a is the importance coefficient of a-th task's error, which can be learned through gradient descent. Its magnitude reveals that more important task tends to have longer impact. This strategy achieves satisfactory results for learning deep convolution network given multiple tasks. Its superior performance is demonstrated in Section 4.2.

Learning Procedure: We have discussed when and how to switch off an auxiliary task during training before it over-fits. For each iteration, we perform stochastic gradient descent to update the weights of the tasks and filters of the network. For example, the weight matrix of the main task is updated by $\Delta \mathbf{W}^r = -\eta \frac{\partial E^r}{\partial \mathbf{W}^r}$ with η being the learning rate ($\eta = 0.003$ in our implementation), and $\frac{\partial E^r}{\partial \mathbf{W}^r} = (\mathbf{y}_i^r - (\mathbf{W}^r)^\mathsf{T} \mathbf{x}_i) \mathbf{x}_i^\mathsf{T}$. Also, the derivative of the auxiliary task's weights can be calculated in a similar manner as $\frac{\partial E^a}{\partial \mathbf{W}^a} = (p(y_i^a | \mathbf{x}_i; \mathbf{W}^a) - y_i^a) \mathbf{x}_i$. For the filters in the lower layer, we compute the gradients by propagating the loss error back following the back-propagation strategy as

$$\varepsilon^1 \xleftarrow{(\mathbf{W}^{s2})^\mathsf{T} \varepsilon^2 \frac{\partial \sigma(u^1)}{\partial u^1}} \varepsilon^2 \xleftarrow{(\mathbf{W}^{s3})^\mathsf{T} \varepsilon^3 \frac{\partial \sigma(u^2)}{\partial u^2}} \dots \xleftarrow{(\mathbf{W}^{sl})^\mathsf{T} \varepsilon^l \frac{\partial \sigma(u^{l-1})}{\partial u^{l-1}}} \varepsilon^l, \qquad (6)$$

where ε^l is the error at the shared representation layer and $\varepsilon^l = (\mathbf{W}^r)^\mathsf{T} [\mathbf{y}_i^r - (\mathbf{W}^r)^\mathsf{T} \mathbf{x}_i] + \sum_{a \in A} (p(y_i^a | \mathbf{x}_i; \mathbf{W}^a) - y_i^a) \mathbf{W}^a$, which is the integration of all tasks' derivatives. The errors of the lower layers are computed following Eq.(6). For instance, $\varepsilon^{l-1} = (\mathbf{W}^{sl})^\mathsf{T} \varepsilon^l \frac{\partial \sigma(u^{l-1})}{\partial u^{l-1}}$, where $\frac{\partial \sigma(u)}{\partial u}$ is the gradient of the activation function. Then, the gradient of the filter is obtained by $\frac{\partial E}{\partial \mathbf{W}^{sl}} = \varepsilon^l \mathbf{x}_\Omega^{l-1}$, where Ω represents the receptive field of the filter.

Prediction: First, a test face image $\mathbf{x}^0$ is projected to the shared space to obtain $\mathbf{x}^l$. Second, we predict the landmark positions by $(\mathbf{W}^r)^\mathsf{T}\mathbf{x}^l$ and the results of the auxiliary tasks by $p(y^a|\mathbf{x}^l;\mathbf{W}^a)$. This process is efficient and its complexity is discussed in Section 4.3.

4 Implementation and Experiments

Network Structure: Figure 3 shows the network structure of TCDCN. The input of the network is 40×40 gray-scale face image. The feature extraction stage contains four convolutional layers, three pooling layers, and one fully connected layer. Each convolutional layer contains a filter bank producing multiple feature maps. The filter weights are not spatially shared, that means a different set of filters is applied at every location in the input map. The absolute tangent function is selected as the activation function. For the pooling layers, we conduct max-pooling on non-overlap regions of the feature map. The fully connected layer following the fourth convolutional layer produces a feature vector which is shared by the multiple tasks in the estimation stage.

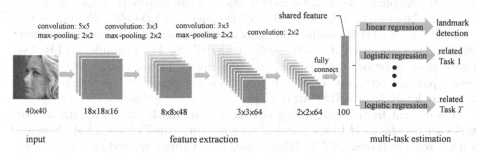

Fig. 3. Structure specification for TCDCN

Model Training: The training dataset we use is identical to [21], consisting of 10,000 outdoor face images from the web. Each image is annotated with bounding box and five landmarks, i.e. centers of the eyes, nose, corners of the mouth, as depicted in Figure 1. We augmented the training samples by small jittering, including translation, in-plane rotation, and zooming. The ground truths of the related tasks are labeled manually. This dataset, known as Multi-Task Facial Landmark (MTFL) dataset, and the landmark detector will be released for research usage[2].

Evaluation Metrics: In all cases, we report our results on two popular metrics [3, 4, 10, 21], including mean error and failure rate. The mean error is measured by the distances between estimated landmarks and the ground truths, normalizing with respect to the inter-ocular distance. Mean error larger than 10% is reported as a failure.

---

[2] http://mmlab.ie.cuhk.edu.hk/projects/TCDCN.html

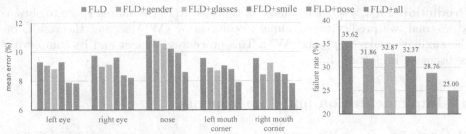

Fig. 4. Comparison of different model variants of TCDCN: the mean error over different landmarks, and the overall failure rate

4.1   Evaluating the Effectiveness of Learning with Related Task

To examine the influence of related tasks, we evaluate five variants of the proposed model. In particular, the first variant is trained only on facial landmark detection. We train another four model variants on facial landmark detection along with the auxiliary task of recognizing 'pose', 'gender', 'wearing glasses', and 'smiling', respectively. The full model is trained using all the four related tasks. For simplicity, we name each variants by facial landmark detection (FLD) and the related task, such as "FLD", "FLD+pose", "FLD+all". We employ the popular AFLW [11] for evaluation. This dataset is selected because it is more challenging than other datasets, such as LFPW [2]. For example, AFLW has larger pose variations (39% of faces are non-frontal in our testing images) and severe partial occlusions. Figure 10 provides some examples. We selected 3,000 faces randomly from AFLW for testing.

It is evident from Figure 4 that optimizing landmark detection with related tasks are beneficial. In particular, FLD+all outperforms FLD by a large margin, with a reduction over 10% in failure rate. When single related task is present, FLD+pose performs the best. This is not surprising since pose variation affects locations of all landmarks globally and directly. The other related tasks such as 'smiling' and 'wearing glasses' are observed to have comparatively smaller influence to the final performance, since they mainly capture local information of the face, such as mouth and eyes. We examine two specific cases below.

FLD vs. FLD+smile: As shown in Figure 5, landmark detection benefits from smiling attribute inference, mainly at the nose and corners of mouth. This observation is intuitive since smiling drives the lower part of the faces, involving Zygomaticus and levator labii superioris muscles, more than the upper facial region. The learning of smile attributes develops a shared representation that describes lower facial region, which in turn facilitates the localization of nose and corners of mouth.

We use a crude method to investigate the relationship between tasks. Specifically, we study the Pearson's correlation of the learned weight vectors of the last fully-connected layer, between the tasks of facial landmark detection and 'smiling' prediction, as shown in Figure 5(b). The correlational relationship is indicative to the performance improvement depicted in Figure 5(a). For instance, the

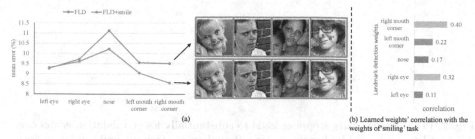

(a)

(b) Learned weights' correlation with the weights of 'smiling' task

Fig. 5. FLD vs. FLD+smile. The smiling attribute helps detection more on the nose and corners of mouth, than the centers of eyes, since 'smiling' mainly affects the lower part of a face.

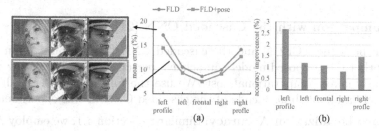

Fig. 6. FLD vs. FLD+pose. (a) Mean error in different poses, and (b) Accuracy improvement by the FLD+pose in different poses.

weight vectors, which are learned to predict the positions of the mouth's corners have high correlation with the weights of 'smiling' inference. This demonstrates that TCDCN implicitly learns relationship between tasks.

FLD vs. FLD+pose: As observed in Figure 6(a), detection errors of FLD increase along with the degree of head pose deviation from the frontal view to profiles, while these errors can be partially recovered by FLD+pose as depicted in Figure 6(b).

4.2   The Benefits of Task-Wise Early Stopping

To verify the effectiveness of the task-wise early stopping, we train the proposed TCDCN with and without this technique and compare the landmark detection rates in Figure 7(a), which shows that without task-wise early stopping, the accuracy is much lower. Figure 7(b) plots the main task's loss errors of the training set and the validation set within 2,600 iterations. Without early stopping, the training error converges slowly and exhibits substantial oscillations. However, convergence rates of both the training and validation sets are fast and stable when using the proposed early stopping scheme. In Figure 7(b), we also point out when and which task has been halted during the training procedure. For example, 'wearing glasses' and 'gender' are stopped at the 250th and 350th iterations, and 'pose' lasts to the 750th iteration, which matches our expectation that 'pose' has the largest benefit to landmark detection, compared to the other related tasks.

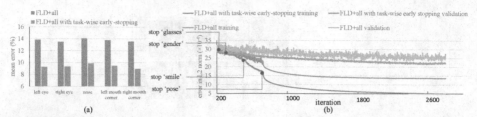

Fig. 7. (a) Task-wise early stopping leads to substantially lower validation errors over different landmarks. (b) Its benefit is also reflected on the training and validation error convergence rate. The error is measured in L2-norm with respect to the ground truth of the 10 coordinates values (normalized to [0,1]) for the 5 landmarks.

4.3 Comparison with the Cascaded CNN [21]

Although both the TCDCN and the cascaded CNN [21] are built upon CNN, we show that the proposed model can achieve better detection accuracy with a significantly lower computational cost. We use the full model "FLD+all", and the publicly available binary code of the cascaded CNN in this experiment.

Landmark Localization Accuracy: Similar to Section 4.1, we employ AFLW images for evaluation due to its challenging pose variations and occlusion. Note that we use the same 10,000 training faces as in the cascaded CNN method. Thus the only difference is that we exploit a multi-task learning approach. It is observed from Figure 8 that our method performs better in four out of five landmarks, and the overall accuracy is superior to that of cascaded CNN.

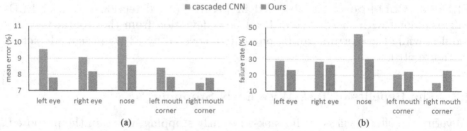

Fig. 8. The proposed TCDCN vs. cascaded CNN [21]: (a) mean error over different landmarks and (b) the overall failure rate

Computational Efficiency: Suppose the computation time of a 2D-convolution operation is τ, the total time cost for a CNN with L layers can be approximated by $\sum_{l=1}^{L} s_l^2 q_l q_{l-1} \tau$, where s^2 is the 2D size of the input feature map for l-th layer, and q is the number of filters. The algorithm complexity of a CNN is thus $O(s^2 q^2)$, directly related to the input image size and number of filters. Note that the input face size and network structure for TCDCN is similar to cascaded CNN. The proposed method only has one CNN, whereas the cascaded CNN [21] deploys multiple CNNs in different cascaded layers (23 CNNs in its implementation). Hence, TCDCN has much lower computational cost. The cascaded CNN

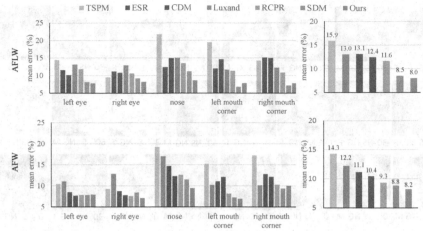

Fig. 9. Comparison with RCPR [3], TSPM [32], CDM [27], Luxand [18], and SDM [25] on AFLW [11] (the first row) and AFW [32] (the second row) datasets. The left subfigures show the mean errors on different landmarks, while the right subfigures show the overall errors.

requires 0.12s to process an image on an Intel Core i5 CPU, whilst TCDCN only takes 17ms, which is *7 times faster*. The TCDCN costs 1.5ms on a NVIDIA GTX760 GPU.

4.4 Comparison with Other State-of-the-Art Methods

We compare against: (1) Robust Cascaded Pose Regression (RCPR) [3] using the publicly available implementation and parameter settings; (2) Tree Structured Part Model (TSPM) [32], which jointly estimates the head pose and facial landmarks; (3) A commercial software, Luxand face SDK [18]; (4) Explicit Shape Regression (ESR) [4]; (5) A Cascaded Deformable Model (CDM) [27]; (6) Supervised Descent Method (SDM) [25]. For the methods which include their own face detector (TSPM [32] and CDM [27]), we avoid detection errors by cropping the image around the face.

Evaluation on AFLW [11]: Figure 9 shows that TCDCN outperforms all the state-of-the-art methods. Figure 10(a) shows several examples of TCDCN's detection, with additional tags generated from related tasks. We observe that the proposed method is robust to faces with large pose variation, lighting, and severe occlusion. It is worth pointing out that the input images of our model is 40×40, which means that the model can cope with low-resolution images.

Evaluation on AFW [32]: In addition to AFLW, we also tested on AFW. We observe similar trend as in the AFLW dataset. Figure 9 demonstrates the superiority of our method. Figure 10(b) presents some detection examples using our model.

(a) Results on AFLW: Faces with occlusion (row 1), pose variation (row 2), different lighting conditions (column 1-2 in row 3), low image quality (column 3 in row 3), different expressions (column 4-5 in row 3), three inaccurate cases are shown in column 6-8 in row 3.

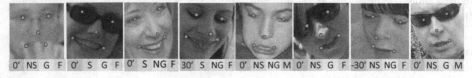

(b) Results on AFW

Fig. 10. Example detections by the proposed model on AFLW [11] and AFW [32] images. The labels below each image denote the tagging results for the related tasks: $(0°, \pm30°, \pm60°)$ for pose; S/NS = smiling/not-smiling; G/NG = with-glasses/without-glasses; M/F = male/female. Red rectangles indicate wrong tagging.

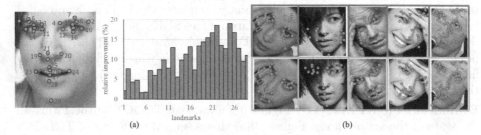

Fig. 11. Initialization with our five-landmark estimation for RCPR [3] on COFW dataset [3]. (a) shows the relative improvement on each landmark (relative improvement $= \frac{\text{reduced error}}{\text{original error}}$). (b) visualizes the improvement. The upper row depicts the results of RCPR [3], while the lower row shows the improved results by our initialization.

4.5 TCDCN for Robust Initialization

This section shows that the TCDCN can be used to generate a good initialization to improve the state-of-the-art method, owing to its accuracy and efficiency. We take RCPR [3] as an example. Instead of drawing training samples randomly as initialization as did in [3], we initialize RCPR by first applying TCDCN on the test image to estimate the five landmarks. We compare the results of RCPR with and without TCDCN as initialization on the COFW dataset [3], which includes 507 test faces that are annotated with 29 landmarks. Figure 11(a) shows the relative improvement for each landmark on the COFW dataset and Figure 11(b) visualizes several examples. It is demonstrated that with our robust initialization, the algorithm can obtain improvement in difficult cases with rotation and occlusion.

5 Conclusions

Instead of learning facial landmark detection in isolation, we have shown that more robust landmark detection can be achieved through joint learning with heterogeneous but subtly correlated tasks, such as appearance attribute, expression, demographic, and head pose. The proposed Tasks-Constrained DCN allows errors of related tasks to be back-propagated in deep hidden layers for constructing a shared representation to be relevant to the main task. We have shown that task-wise early stopping scheme is critical to ensure convergence of the model. Thanks to multi-task learning, the proposed model is more robust to faces with severe occlusions and large pose variations compared to existing methods. We have observed that a deep model needs not be cascaded [21] to achieve the better performance. The lighter-weight CNN allows real-time performance without the usage of GPU or parallel computing techniques. Future work will explore deep multi-task learning for dense landmark detection and other vision domains.

References

1. Asthana, A., Zafeiriou, S., Cheng, S., Pantic, M.: Robust discriminative response map fitting with constrained local models. In: CVPR, pp. 3444–3451 (2013)
2. Belhumeur, P.N., Jacobs, D.W., Kriegman, D.J., Kumar, N.: Localizing parts of faces using a consensus of exemplars. In: CVPR, pp. 545–552 (2011)
3. Burgos-Artizzu, X.P., Perona, P., Dollar, P.: Robust face landmark estimation under occlusion. In: ICCV, pp. 1513–1520 (2013)
4. Cao, X., Wei, Y., Wen, F., Sun, J.: Face alignment by explicit shape regression. In: CVPR, pp. 2887–2894 (2012)
5. Caruana, R.: Multitask learning. Machine Learning 28(1), 41–75 (1997)
6. Chen, K., Gong, S., Xiang, T., Loy, C.C.: Cumulative attribute space for age and crowd density estimation. In: CVPR, pp. 2467–2474 (2013)
7. Collobert, R., Weston, J.: A unified architecture for natural language processing: Deep neural networks with multitask learning. In: ICML, pp. 160–167 (2008)
8. Cootes, T.F., Edwards, G.J., Taylor, C.J.: Active appearance models. PAMI 23(6), 681–685 (2001)
9. Cootes, T.F., Ionita, M.C., Lindner, C., Sauer, P.: Robust and accurate shape model fitting using random forest regression voting. In: Fitzgibbon, A., Lazebnik, S., Perona, P., Sato, Y., Schmid, C. (eds.) ECCV 2012, Part VII. LNCS, vol. 7578, pp. 278–291. Springer, Heidelberg (2012)

10. Dantone, M., Gall, J., Fanelli, G., Van Gool, L.: Real-time facial feature detection using conditional regression forests. In: CVPR, pp. 2578–2585 (2012)
11. Kostinger, M., Wohlhart, P., Roth, P.M., Bischof, H.: Annotated facial landmarks in the wild: A large-scale, real-world database for facial landmark localization. In: ICCV Workshops, pp. 2144–2151 (2011)
12. Krizhevsky, A., Sutskever, I., Hinton, G.E.: Imagenet classification with deep convolutional neural networks. In: NIPS (2012)
13. Li, H., Shen, C., Shi, Q.: Real-time visual tracking using compressive sensing. In: CVPR, pp. 1305–1312 (2011)
14. Liu, X.: Generic face alignment using boosted appearance model. In: CVPR (2007)
15. Lu, C., Tang, X.: Surpassing human-level face verification performance on LFW with GaussianFace. Tech. rep., arXiv:1404.3840 (2014)
16. Luo, P., Wang, X., Tang, X.: Hierarchical face parsing via deep learning. In: CVPR, pp. 2480–2487 (2012)
17. Luo, P., Wang, X., Tang, X.: A deep sum-product architecture for robust facial attributes analysis. In: CVPR, pp. 2864–2871 (2013)
18. Luxand Incorporated: Luxand face SDK, http://www.luxand.com/
19. Nair, V., Hinton, G.E.: Rectified linear units improve restricted boltzmann machines. In: ICML, pp. 807–814 (2010)
20. Prechelt, L.: Automatic early stopping using cross validation: quantifying the criteria. Neural Networks 11(4), 761–767 (1998)
21. Sun, Y., Wang, X., Tang, X.: Deep convolutional network cascade for facial point detection. In: CVPR, pp. 3476–3483 (2013)
22. Sun, Y., Wang, X., Tang, X.: Deep learning face representation by joint identification-verification. Tech. rep., arXiv:1406.4773 (2014)
23. Sun, Y., Wang, X., Tang, X.: Deep learning face representation from predicting 10,000 classes. In: CVPR (2014)
24. Valstar, M., Martinez, B., Binefa, X., Pantic, M.: Facial point detection using boosted regression and graph models. In: CVPR, pp. 2729–2736 (2010)
25. Xiong, X., De La Torre, F.: Supervised descent method and its applications to face alignment. In: CVPR, pp. 532–539 (2013)
26. Yang, H., Patras, I.: Sieving regression forest votes for facial feature detection in the wild. In: ICCV, pp. 1936–1943 (2013)
27. Yu, X., Huang, J., Zhang, S., Yan, W., Metaxas, D.N.: Pose-free facial landmark fitting via optimized part mixtures and cascaded deformable shape model. In: ICCV, pp. 1944–1951 (2013)
28. Yuan, X.T., Liu, X., Yan, S.: Visual classification with multitask joint sparse representation. TIP 21(10), 4349–4360 (2012)
29. Zhang, T., Ghanem, B., Liu, S., Ahuja, N.: Robust visual tracking via structured multi-task sparse learning. IJCV 101(2), 367–383 (2013)
30. Zhang, Y., Yeung, D.Y.: A convex formulation for learning task relationships in multi-task learning. In: UAI (2011)
31. Zhang, Z., Zhang, W., Liu, J., Tang, X.: Facial landmark localization based on hierarchical pose regression with cascaded random ferns. In: ACM Multimedia, pp. 561–564 (2013)
32. Zhu, X., Ramanan, D.: Face detection, pose estimation, and landmark localization in the wild. In: CVPR, pp. 2879–2886 (2012)
33. Zhu, Z., Luo, P., Wang, X., Tang, X.: Deep learning identity-preserving face space. In: ICCV, pp. 113–120 (2013)
34. Zhu, Z., Luo, P., Wang, X., Tang, X.: Deep learning multi-view representation for face recognition. Tech. rep., arXiv:1406.6947 (2014)
35. Zhu, Z., Luo, P., Wang, X., Tang, X.: Recover canonical-view faces in the wild with deep neural networks. Tech. rep., arXiv:1404.3543 (2014)

Joint Cascade Face Detection and Alignment

Dong Chen[1], Shaoqing Ren[1], Yichen Wei[2], Xudong Cao[2], and Jian Sun[2]

[1] University of Science and Technology of China
{chendong,sqren}@mail.ustc.edu.cn
[2] Microsoft Research
{yichenw,xudongca,jiansun}@microsoft.com

Abstract. We present a new state-of-the-art approach for face detection. The key idea is to combine face alignment with detection, observing that aligned face shapes provide better features for face classification. To make this combination more effective, our approach learns the two tasks jointly in the same cascade framework, by exploiting recent advances in face alignment. Such joint learning greatly enhances the capability of cascade detection and still retains its realtime performance. Extensive experiments show that our approach achieves the best accuracy on challenging datasets, where all existing solutions are either inaccurate or too slow.

1 Introduction

Face detection is one of the mostly studied problems in vision [31]. The seminal work of Viola and Jones [26] has established the two foundation principles for practical solutions: 1) boosted cascade structure; 2) simple features. Most (if not all) realtime face detectors in academia and industry nowadays are based on the two principles. Such detectors work well for near-frontal faces under normal conditions but become less effective for faces non-frontal or under more wild conditions (lighting, expression, occlusion), because the simple features like Harr in the cascade training are insufficient to capture the more complex face variations.

Many works are on multi-view face detection [10,17,27,7]. They adopt a similar divide and conquer strategy: different face detectors are trained separately under different viewpoints or head poses, which are roughly quantized and estimated simultaneously. Because the viewpoint estimation problem is difficult as well and quantization also introduces inaccuracy, such training is more difficult and resulting detectors are usually slower or not accurate enough.

Recently, several new approaches that do not use boosted cascade have been proposed. Zhu et al. [32] used a mixture of deformable part models to capture large face variations under different viewpoints and expressions. The model is comprehensive and allows to estimate the head pose and facial points at the same time in addition to detection. Shen et al. [24] proposed the first exemplar-based face detector and exploited advanced image retrieval techniques to avoid the expensive sliding window search. Both methods are better than Viola-Jones style detectors on wild and challenging datasets [32,9]. However, those accurate

D. Fleet et al. (Eds.): ECCV 2014, Part VI, LNCS 8694, pp. 109–122, 2014.
© Springer International Publishing Switzerland 2014

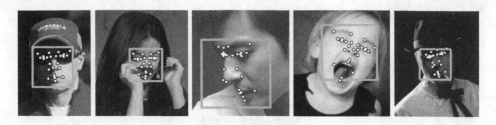

Fig. 1. Face detection and alignment results on challenging examples

detectors, as well as the state-of-the-art commercial face detector in Google Picasa, are all quite slow due to their high complexity. Detection in an image takes a few seconds and this makes such detectors unpractical for many scenarios.

In this work, we present a face detector that establishes the new state-of-the-art in terms of both accuracy and speed. It follows the "boosted cascade structure + simple features" principles. We use simple pixel differences as feature which bring advantages on the efficiency. Our detector takes only 28.6 milliseconds for a VGA image, more than 1000 times faster than [32]. It also achieves the best accuracy on the challenging datasets [32,9,22], significantly outperforms all existing academia solutions including [32,24], and is on bar with the commercial system in Google Picasa. Figure 1 shows our example detection results under large viewpoints, occlusion and poor lighting.

Our work is motivated by the observation that accurate face alignment (location of facial points) is helpful to distinguish faces/non-faces. In Section 2, we experimentally verified that a simple SVM classifier using facial point based features in the post processing can significantly improve the accuracy of a Viola-Jones detector. This finding is not surprising because face alignment finds corresponding parts between faces, makes them directly comparable, and simplifies the face/non-face classification problem. Similar observations have also been made in [32,14]. While the observation is clearly useful, the real problem is how to use it effectively. Previous methods [32,14] are too slow. Our post classification is also insufficient, because when high recall is expected, a cascade detector would return too many false positives and the SVM classifier would be slow too.

Our approach benefits from the recent advances in cascade face alignment [19,4,28,29,21]. In such works, the face shape is progressively updated via boosted regression. The regression learning in each stage not only depends on the image, but also depends on the estimated shape from the previous stage. Features learnt this way are called *shape indexed features*. Such features present more invariance to the geometric variations in the face shapes and they are crucial for high alignment accuracy and speed. As the cascade structure has been proven effective in detection and alignment, we propose to combine the two to benefit each other. In Section 3, we present a general cascade framework that unifies the two tasks. The detection learning is made more effective with embedded alignment information, and alignment is achieved simultaneously without performing it separately. In Section 4, we extend the recent state-of-the-art alignment method [21] under the new framework. We show how to use the same simple shape indexed features

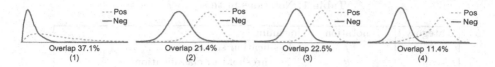

Overlap 37.1%   Overlap 21.4%   Overlap 22.5%   Overlap 11.4%
(1)   (2)   (3)   (4)

Fig. 2. The distribution of classification scores. (1): original cascade detector; (2)(3)(4) post SVM classifiers using three types of features, as described in Section 2.

also for detection so both are efficient. This results in new training and testing algorithms for joint cascade detection and alignment. In summary, we present the first joint cascade face detection and alignment method. We firstly show that simple shape indexed features are effective for detection as well. Extensive experiment results in Section 5 verify the superior performance of our approach in both accuracy and speed.

2 Alignment Helps Detection: A Post Classifier

We illustrates the effectiveness of using face alignment for detection on the challenging FDDB dataset [9]. We use the Viola-Jones detector in OpenCV with a low threshold to ensure a high recall. The detector outputs a lot of image windows, of which many are false positives. We split all the images into two parts, use the positive and negative output windows in the first part to train a linear SVM classifier, and test all the output windows in the second part. We call it a *post classifier* as it operates on the output of a cascade detector. All windows are resized into 96*96 pixels. We compare three types of features, without and with alignment.

1. we divide the window into 6*6 non-overlapping cells and extract a SIFT descriptor in each cell.
2. we use a fixed mean face shape with 27 facial points and extract a SIFT descriptor centered on each point.
3. we align the 27 facial points using the alignment algorithm in [21] and extract a SIFT descriptor centered on each point.

In the three cases, all the SIFT descriptors are concatenated as the final feature vector for the SVM. We plot different classification score distributions over the testing windows in Figure 2: (1) classification scores from original cascade detector; (2)(3)(4) SVM classification score of three types of features described above. It clearly shows that features at the aligned facial points are much more effective to separate those difficult windows.

While effective, the face alignment based post classifier is brute force and too slow for a standard cascade detector when a high recall is desired. In our experiment, a low threshold is set to achieve 99% recall of the OpenCV detector and each image outputs 3000 windows on average. Applying the post classifier for those windows takes a few seconds.

Table 1. Notations in this paper

category	notation	meaning
scalars	f	classification score;
	θ	bias threshold in classification;
	$y \in \{1, -1\}$	classification label;
vectors	$\mathbf{x}$	image window;
	$\mathbf{S}(\Delta\mathbf{S})$	face shape (increment);
functions	$\mathcal{C}$	a general weak classifier;
	$\mathcal{R}$	regression tree in [21];
	$\mathcal{CR}$	classification/regression tree in this work;
parameters and values	$L = 27$	# facial points;
	$T = 5$	# stages of cascade alignment;
	$N = 5400$	# total weak classifiers of cascade detection;
	$K = N/T = 1080$	# weak classifier/regressor in each stage;

3   A Unified Framework for Cascade Face Detection and Alignment

To better exploit the alignment information, we propose a unified framework for cascade face detection and alignment. We explain the notations when they are firstly used. They are also summarized in Table 1 for clarity and reference.

Cascade Detection. Without loss of generality, the classification score in the cascade detection can be written as

$$f^N = \sum_{i=1}^{N} \mathcal{C}^i(\mathbf{x}). \tag{1}$$

Each $\mathcal{C}^i$ is a weak classifier. To test an image window $\mathbf{x}$, the weak classifiers are sequentially evaluated and the window is rejected immediately whenever $f^n < \theta^n$ for any $n = 1, 2, ..., N$, where θ^n is the bias threshold. Therefore, the cascade detection is very fast because most negative image windows are rejected after evaluating only a few weak classifiers.

Cascade Alignment. Recent work [19] proposes a pose regression framework that combines pose indexed features with boosted regression. The framework has been shown highly effective for face alignment [4,28,29,21].

Let a face shape $\mathbf{S}$ be a $2L$ dimensional vector for L facial points. In the cascade regression, it is progressively updated through T stages as

$$\mathbf{S}^t = \mathbf{S}^{t-1} + \mathcal{R}^t(\mathbf{x}, \mathbf{S}^{t-1}), t = 1, ..., T. \tag{2}$$

Algorithm 1. The general testing algorithm for cascade face detection and alignment for an image window **x**.

1: initialize the face shape **S** as the mean shape in window of **x**
2: initialize the detection score $f = 0$
3: **for** $t = 1$ to T **do**
4:    **for** $k = 1$ to K **do**
5:        $f = f + \mathcal{C}_k^t(\mathbf{x}, \mathbf{S})$
6:        **if** $f < \theta_k^t$ **then**
7:            return "not a face"
8:        **end if**
9:    **end for**
10:    $\Delta\mathbf{S} = \mathcal{R}^t(\mathbf{x}, \mathbf{S})$
11:    $\mathbf{S} = \mathbf{S} + \Delta\mathbf{S}$
12: **end for**
13: return "is a face with shape **S**"

Each $\mathcal{R}^t$ is a regression function. It adds an increment to the estimated shape from the previous stage $\mathbf{S}^{t-1}$. It is learnt to minimize the shape residual error between the ground truth shape $\hat{\mathbf{S}}$ and estimated shape in the current stage, as

$$\mathcal{R}^t = \arg\min_{\mathcal{R}} \sum_i \|\hat{\mathbf{S}}_i - (\mathbf{S}_i^{t-1} + \mathcal{R}(\mathbf{x}_i, \mathbf{S}_i^{t-1}))\|^2, \tag{3}$$

where index i iterates over all the training samples.

A Unified Framework. A key innovation in the cascade alignment framework is that each regressor $\mathcal{R}^t$ depends on the previous shape $\mathbf{S}^{t-1}$. During learning, the features are defined relative to $\mathbf{S}^{t-1}$, so called *pose/shape indexed features* [19,4]. Such features present better geometric invariance to the shape variations and they are crucial for the cascade framework.

We propose to apply such features in detection as well, by making the learning of weak classifier $\mathcal{C}^i(\mathbf{x})$ in Eq. (1) also dependent on the face shape. Note that the number of weak classifiers N in detection is usually hundreds or thousands. It is much larger than the number of stages T in alignment, which is usually less than 10^1. To unify the learning of two tasks, we divide the N weak classifiers into the T stages. Each stage has $K = N/T$ weak classifiers and they depend on the face shape from the previous stage. The classification score in Eq. (1) is rewritten as

$$f = \sum_{t=1}^{T} \sum_{k=1}^{K} \mathcal{C}_k^t(\mathbf{x}, \mathbf{S}^{t-1}). \tag{4}$$

In principle, the regression and classification functions in the same stage t do not have to be learnt and applied simultaneously. Algorithm 1 illustrates a

---

[1] Using a large number of stages would cause the shape indexed features unstable and lead to poorer performance [4].

Stage 1   Stage 3   Stage 5

Fig. 3. Illustration of our cascade face detection and alignment

general testing algorithm for cascade detection and alignment, where the two parts are separate. However, in practice, we would expect that the two parts are related or even share the same features, because this is more efficient for both training and testing. Figure 3 illustrates the testing algorithm of our cascade face detection and alignment. The negative image windows are gradually rejected and the facial points of positive windows are gradually aligned stage by stage. In the next section, we present an effective joint learning approach.

4   Our Approach

As shown in Section 3, any cascade shape indexed face alignment method [4,28,29,21] can actually be used for cascade detection. We adopt the most recent and state-of-the-art approach [21], because it is most accurate, fastest, and easy to integrate the weak classifier learning for detection. Notably, it is significantly faster (dozens of times) than the previous best methods [4,28] and runs in thousands of frames per second to align dozens of facial points. Such high speed is crucial for a real time face detector as well.

We briefly review the work in [21] in Section 4.1 and describe how to extend it for joint alignment and detection in Section 4.2.

4.1   Review of Face Alignment in [21]

Its regression function $\mathcal{R}^t$ is simply the sum of K tree based regressors,

$$\mathcal{R}^t(\mathbf{x}, \mathbf{S}^{t-1}) = \sum_{k=1}^{K} \mathcal{R}_k^t(\mathbf{x}, \mathbf{S}^{t-1}). \tag{5}$$

Each $\mathcal{R}_k^t$ is a decision tree that stores a shape increment in every leaf. For the face window $\mathbf{x}$, it outputs the increment of the leaf into which $\mathbf{x}$ falls.

Learning of all $\mathcal{R}_k^t$ consists of two steps:

1. *Local learning of the tree structure*: for each of the L facial point, a standard regression forest [2] is learnt to estimate the increment of this point, using the shape indexed pixel difference features [4].
2. *Global learning of the tree output*: the point increments in the leaves are discarded. Instead, each leaf stores a shape increment and all such shape increments are optimized simultaneously by solving Eq. (3). Note that this is simply a global linear regression problem.

Algorithm 2. Our testing algorithm for cascade face detection and alignment for an image window $\mathbf{x}$. The model consists of all weak learners $\{\mathcal{CR}_k^t\}$ and classification thresholds $\{\theta_k^t\}$.

1: initialize the face shape $\mathbf{S}$ as the mean shape in window of $\mathbf{x}$
2: initialize the detection score $f = 0$
3: **for** $t = 1$ to T **do**
4:     $\Delta\mathbf{S} = \mathbf{0}$
5:     **for** $k = 1$ to K **do**
6:         $(f', \Delta\mathbf{S}') = \mathcal{CR}_k^t(\mathbf{x}, \mathbf{S})$
7:         $f = f + f'$
8:         **if** $f < \theta_k^t$ **then**
9:             return "not a face"
10:        **end if**
11:        $\Delta\mathbf{S} = \Delta\mathbf{S} + \Delta\mathbf{S}'$
12:    **end for**
13:    $\mathbf{S} = \mathbf{S} + \Delta\mathbf{S}$
14: **end for**
15: return "is a face with shape $\mathbf{S}$"

The strength of this approach lies in the two step learning. The local learning focuses on an easier problem (one point regression in a local patch) and is more resistant to the noises in the simple pixel features, compared to [4]. Its learnt pixel features are more effective than the hand crafted SIFT features as in [28]. The global step enforces the dependence between individual facial points and reduces the local estimation errors. Given the fixed tree structures, this step achieves the global optimal solution. Therefore, the two step learning achieves a very strong local optimal solution in terms of Eq. (3).

4.2   Joint Learning of Detection and Alignment

Noticing that both the weak classifiers in Eq. (4) and tree regressors in Eq. (5) share a similar additive form, we propose to learn both classification and regression in a single decision tree. That is, each regression tree $\mathcal{R}_k^t$ in Eq. (5) is upgraded to a mixed tree $\mathcal{CR}_k^t$ that also outputs a classification score, in addition to its shape increment. Consequently, during testing, the classification and regression parts are evaluated simultaneously, as illustrated in Algorithm 2. As $\mathcal{CR}_k^t$ uses the same features for both classification and regression, such testing is faster than the general testing in Algorithm 1.

To learn a mixed classification/regression decision tree, we use a similar strategy as in hough forest [6]: in the split test of each internal node, we randomly choose to either minimize the binary entropy for classification (with probability ρ) or the variance of the facial point increments for regression (with probability $1 - \rho$). Intuitively, the parameter ρ should be larger in earlier stages to favor classification learning and reject easy negative samples more quickly. It should be smaller in later stages to favor regression learning and improve the alignment

Algorithm 3. Training of cascade and joint face detection and alignment.

1: **Input:** all training samples $\{\mathbf{x}_i\}$, class labels $\{y_i\}$
2: **Input:** ground truth shapes $\hat{\mathbf{S}}_i$ for positive samples, $y_i = 1$
3: **Output:** all weak learners $\{\mathcal{CR}_k^t\}$, classification thresholds $\{\theta_k^t\}$
4: set the initial face shapes $\mathbf{S}_i^0$ as random perturbations of the mean shapes in windows of $\mathbf{x}_i$
5: set all initial classification scores $f_i = 0$
6: **for** $t = 1$ to T **do**
7:    **for** $k = 1$ to K **do**
8:       **for** each training sample i **do**
9:          compute its weight w_i according to Eq. (6)
10:      **end for**
11:      select a point ($k \bmod L$) for regression /*local learning in Section 4.1*/
12:      learn the structure of classification/regression tree $\mathcal{CR}_k^t$ as in Section 4.2
13:      **for** each tree leaf **do**
14:         set its classification score according to Eq. (7)
15:      **end for**
16:      **for** each training sample i **do**
17:         update its classification score as $f_i = f_i + \mathcal{CR}_k^t(\mathbf{x}_i, \mathbf{S}_i^{t-1})$
18:      **end for**
19:      use all $\{f_i\}$ to set the bias θ_k^t, according to a preset precision-recall condition

20:      remove samples whose $f_i < \theta_k^t$ from training set
21:      perform hard negative sample mining if negative samples are insufficient
22:   **end for**
23:   learn the shape increments of all leaves /* global learning in Section 4.1 */
24:   compute $\mathbf{S}_i^t$ for all samples according to Eq. (2) and (5)
25: **end for**

accuracy. We empirically make this parameter linearly decreasing with respect to the regression stage number t, that is, $\rho(t) = 1 - 0.1t, t = 1, ..., T$.

During split test for an internal node, we extend the shape indexed pixel difference features in [4] to multi-scale. Specifically, we generate three scales of images by down sampling the input image to half and one fourth. To generate a feature, we randomly choose an image scale, pick up two random facial points in the current shape, generate two random offsets with respect to the points and take the difference of the two offsetted pixels as the feature. We found the multi-scale pixel difference feature is more robust to noises and necessary for detection learning.

We use the RealBoost algorithm for the cascade classification learning. Before learning a decision tree, each sample i is associated with a weight w_i as

$$w_i = e^{-y_i f_i}, \tag{6}$$

where $y_i \in \{-1, 1\}$ is the face/non-face label and f_i is the current classification score. Such weights are used to compute a weighted binary entropy during the split test of internal node, as mentioned earlier.

In each tree leaf node, the classification score is computed as

$$\frac{1}{2} \ln \left(\frac{\sum_{\{i \in leaf \cap y_i = 1\}} w_i}{\sum_{\{i \in leaf \cap y_i = -1\}} w_i} \right), \tag{7}$$

where the enumerator and denominator are the sum of positive and negative samples' weight in the leaf node, respectively.

The complete training algorithm of our cascade face detection and alignment is summarized in Algorithm 3. Note that all face shapes are normalized with respect to the windows containing them.

5   Experiments

We collected about 20,000 face images and 20,000 natural scene images without faces from web. All faces are manually labeled with 27 facial points. We use these images and their flipped versions for training. Only grayscale images are used. Most training parameters are listed in Table 1. For each classification/regression tree, the tree depth is set to 4 and number of split tests for each internal node is 2000. The training takes three days on a 16-core machine. Afterwards, we also train an alignment based SVM post classifier using the output windows in the training images, as described in Section 2. In detection we use standard sliding window search. Each window returned by the detector is then passed to the post classifier. All passing windows go through a non-maximum suppression process: the window rectangles are clustered and one window is selected in each cluster as the final detection.

For evaluation we use three challenging public datasets: FDDB [9], AFW [32] and CMU-MIT [22]. They do not include our training images. FDDB and AFW datasets are collected under wild conditions. They are widely used to evaluate the face detection methods [32,14,24]. CMU-MIT dataset is slightly out-of-date but its faces are low quality and quite different from those in FDDB, AFW and our training images. Thus, it is also challenging. We use it to test the generalization capability of our detector.

5.1   Effect of Alignment for Cascade Detection

The effect of alignment is verified by comparing our detector with a baseline detector without the alignment part. The baseline detector is trained in almost exactly the same way as ours. The only difference is that, line 24 in Algorithm 3 is ignored and the face shapes always remain as the initial mean shapes. It is essentially a standard Viola-Jones style cascade detector.

We compared the two detectors on FDDB dataset. We adjust the thresholds so that both have the same recalls and they can be fairly compared. Note that the post classifier is not used in this comparison. We firstly compare the false positive rates with respect to the number of tested weak classifiers. The left result of Figure 4 shows that our detector has much lower false positive rate

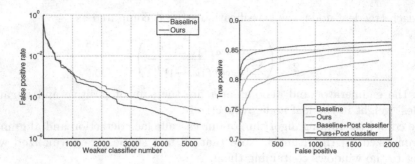

Fig. 4. Comparison of our detector and a baseline detector without alignment. Left: false positive rates all over the detection cascades. Right: recall versus number of false positives, with and without a post classifier.

all over the cascades and is more accurate. On average, each negative window requires 35.4 weak classifiers to reject it in the baseline detector, and this number in our detector is 26.1, indicating that our detector is also much faster. It demonstrates that the shape indexed features are more effective to distinguish negative samples, especially those hard ones in late stages.

The number of positive detection windows of the two detectors are close (22.2 for baseline and 21.5 for ours). However, the negative detections of the baseline is about 6 times larger than ours (82.1 and 13.3). Those hard negative samples cannot be easily removed by the post classifier. The comparison in the right of Figure 4 shows that although using a post classifier can significantly improve both detectors, the baseline detector is always worse than ours.

5.2   Comparison with the State-of-the-Art

In this part, our detector is comprehensively compared to the state-of-the-art. On FDDB dataset, we compare with all the published results in the platform [26,32,24,14,23,12,16,8,25,18,30,13,15]. It has two evaluation protocols: discrete and continuous. In the discrete setting, a detection window is considered correct if its "intersection-over-union" ratio with respect to an annotated face region is larger than 0.5. This criteria is commonly used in object detection evaluation. In the continuous setting, the overlapping ratio is used as a weight for every detection window. This criteria is much more strict. Figure 5 and 6 compare our approach with previous academia solutions and commercial systems, respectively. Our result outperforms all previous results by a large margin, under both protocols. Figure 9 shows our example detection results under various challenging conditions. Particularly, it is worth noting that that our detector already achieves a high recall (80.07%) when there are only 4 false positives, which are actually faces, as shown in Figure 9.

In AFW dataset, we use the precision-recall curves and the 50% overlapping criteria for evaluation, as in previous work [32,24]. We compare with the

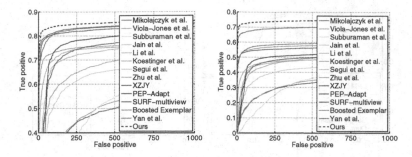

Fig. 5. Comparison with academia methods on FDDB dataset, under the discrete (left) and continuous (right) protocols

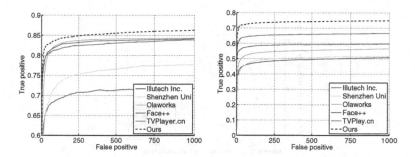

Fig. 6. Comparison with commercial systems on FDDB dataset, under the discrete (left) and continuous (right) protocols

following methods[2]: (1) OpenCV multi-view Viola-Jones; (2) Boosted multi-view face detector of [11]; (3) Deformable part model (DPM) [5]; (4) Mixture of trees [32]; (5) Face detection by retrieval [24]; (6) face.com's face detector; (7) Google Picasa's face detector. The results in the left of Figure 7 show that our detector is much better than previous academia methods and on bar with the best commercial face detector in Google Picasa.

In CMU-MIT dataset, we compare with following methods[3]: (1) Viola and Jones detector; (2) polygon-feature detector [20]; (3) recycling-cascade detector [3]; (4) soft cascade detector [1]; (5) SURF cascade [16]; (6) Google Picasa. The comparison results on CMU-MIT dataset is shown in the right of Figure 7. Our method is still the best. Note that the images in this dataset are quite different from others. Google Picasa only achieves 74% recall on this dataset.

5.3 Evaluation of Face Alignment

Our detector also outputs aligned face shapes as a by product. We evaluate the alignment accuracy on AFW dataset using the same settings in [32]. We compare

---

[2] The results of the other methods are provided by the author of [32,24].

[3] The results of the other methods are from [16].

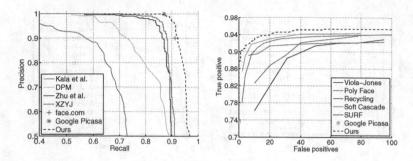

Fig. 7. Comparison with previous state-of-the-art methods on AFW (Left) and CMU-MIT (Right) dataset

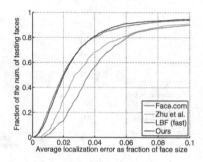

Fig. 8. Compare face alignment result with state-of-the-art methods

with the following methods: 1) face.com alignment system; 2) Zhu et al. [32]; 3) method in [21]. The results of first two methods are from [32]. The last is the state-of-the-art face alignment method. We implemented this method and used our detected faces as its input. Figure 8 shows that our face alignment accuracy is comparable to that in [21], not surprisingly, and is better than the first two.

5.4 Efficiency

Our detector is more efficient in terms of computation time and memory. We compare our detector with OpenCV detector and Zhu et al [32]. For all methods, we detect faces larger than 80×80 in a VGA image. Our detector takes 28.6 milliseconds using single thread on a 2.93 GHz CPU. This performance is more than 1000 times faster than Zhu et al. [32], which takes 33.8 seconds on the same image. Our detector approximates the speed of Viola-Jones detector in OpenCV, which is 23.0 milliseconds.

In the runtime, our detector needs only 15MB memory. Comparing with other methods, Li et al. [13] requires around 150MB memory and Shen et al. [24] requires 866MB memory[4], our detector is more practical for real scenarios such as mobile applications or on embedded devices.

---

[4] The results of the other methods are from [13].

Fig. 9. The top two rows are our example detection results on FDDB dataset. Note that the last four images in the second row contain the four false positives in green rectangles, as described in the text. They are actually faces missed in the annotation. The last two rows are our example detection results on AFW and CMU-MIT datasets.

References

1. Bourdev, L.D., Brandt, J.: Robust Object Detection via Soft Cascade. In: Computer Vision and Pattern Recognition, vol. 2, pp. 236–243 (2005)
2. Breiman, L.: Random Forests. Machine Learning 45, 5–32 (2001)
3. Brubaker, S.C., Wu, J., Sun, J., Mullin, M.D., Rehg, J.M.: On the Design of Cascades of Boosted Ensembles for Face Detection. IJCV 77, 65–86 (2008)
4. Cao, X., Wei, Y., Wen, F., Sun, J.: Face Alignment by Explicit Shape Regression. In: Computer Vision and Pattern Recognition (2012)
5. Felzenszwalb, P.F., Girshick, R.B., McAllester, D.A., Ramanan, D.: Object Detection with Discriminatively Trained Part-Based Models. IEEE Transactions on Pattern Analysis and Machine Intelligence 32, 1627–1645 (2010)
6. Gall, J., Lempitsky, V.S.: Class-specific Hough forests for object detection. In: Computer Vision and Pattern Recognition, pp. 1022–1029 (2009)
7. Huang, C., Ai, H., Li, Y., Lao, S.: High-Performance Rotation Invariant Multiview Face Detection. IEEE Transactions on PAMI 29, 671–686 (2007)

8. Jain, V., Learned-Miller, E.: Online domain adaptation of a pre-trained cascade of classifiers. In: CVPR (2011)
9. Jain, V., Learned-Miller, E.: Fddb: A benchmark for face detection in unconstrained settings. Tech. Rep. UM-CS-2010-009, University of Massachusetts, Amherst (2010)
10. Jones, M.J., Viola, P.: Fast Multi-view Face Detection. In: CVPR (2003)
11. Kalal, Z., Matas, J., Mikolajczyk, K.: Weighted Sampling for Large-Scale Boosting. In: British Machine Vision Conference (2008)
12. Koestinger, M., Wohlhart, P., Roth, P.M., Bischof, H.: Robust face detection by simple means. In: DAGM 2012 CVAW Workshop
13. Li, H., Lin, Z., Brandt, J., Shen, X., Hua, G.: Efficient boosted exemplar-based face detection. In: CVPR (2014)
14. Li, H., Hua, G., Lin, Z., Brandt, J., Yang, J.: Probabilistic Elastic Part Model for Unsupervised Face Detector Adaptation. In: ICCV (2013)
15. Li, J., Zhang, Y.: Learning surf cascade for fast and accurate object detection. In: CVPR (2013)
16. Li, J., Wang, T., Zhang, Y.: Face detection using SURF cascade. In: International Conference on Computer Vision (2011)
17. Li, S.Z., Zhu, L., Zhang, Z., Blake, A., Zhang, H., Shum, H.: Statistical Learning of Multi-view Face Detection. In: Heyden, A., Sparr, G., Nielsen, M., Johansen, P. (eds.) ECCV 2002, Part IV. LNCS, vol. 2353, pp. 67–81. Springer, Heidelberg (2002)
18. Mikolajczyk, K., Schmid, C., Zisserman, A.: Human detection based on a probabilistic assembly of robust part detectors. In: Pajdla, T., Matas, J(G.) (eds.) ECCV 2004. LNCS, vol. 3021, pp. 69–82. Springer, Heidelberg (2004)
19. Dollar, P., Welinder, P., Perona, P.: Cascaded pose regression. In: CVPR (2010)
20. Pham, M.T., Gao, Y., Hoang, V.D.D., Cham, T.J.: Fast polygonal integration and its application in extending haar-like features to improve object detection. In: Computer Vision and Pattern Recognition, pp. 942–949 (2010)
21. Ren, S., Cao, X., Wei, Y., Sun, J.: Face Alignment at 3000 FPS via Regressing Local Binary Features. In: Computer Vision and Pattern Recognition (2014)
22. Schneiderman, H., Kanade, T.: Probabilistic Modeling of Local Appearance and Spatial Relationships for Object Recognition. In: CVPR, pp. 45–51 (1998)
23. Segui, S., Drozdzal, M., Radeva, P., Vitri, J.: An integrated approach to contextual face detection. In: ICPRAM (2012)
24. Shen, X., Lin, Z., Brandt, J., Wu, Y.: Detecting and Aligning Faces by Image Retrieval. In: Computer Vision and Pattern Recognition (2013)
25. Venkatesh, B.S., Marcel, S.: Fast bounding box estimation based face detection. In: ECCV Workshop on Face Detection (2010)
26. Viola, P.A., Jones, M.J.: Rapid Object Detection using a Boosted Cascade of Simple Features. In: Computer Vision and Pattern Recognition, pp. 511–518 (2001)
27. Wu, B., Ai, H., Huang, C., Lao, S.: Fast Rotation Invariant Multi-View Face Detection Based on Real Adaboost. In: ICAFGR, pp. 79–84 (2004)
28. Xiong, X., DelaTorre, F.: Supervised Descent Method and its Applications to Face Alignment. In: Computer Vision and Pattern Recognition (2013)
29. Sun, Y., Wang, X., Tang, X.: Deep convolutional network cascade for facial point detection. In: Computer Vision and Pattern Recognition (2013)
30. Yan, J., Lei, Z., Wen, L., Li, S.Z.: The fastest deformable part model for object detection. In: CVPR (2014)
31. Zhang, C., Zhang, Z.: A Survey of Recent Advances in Face Detection (2010)
32. Zhu, X., Ramanan, D.: Face detection, pose estimation and landmark localization in the wild. In: Computer Vision and Pattern Recognition (2012)

Weighted Block-Sparse Low Rank Representation for Face Clustering in Videos

Shijie Xiao[1], Mingkui Tan[2], and Dong Xu[1]

[1] School of Computer Engineering, Nanyang Technological University, Singapore
[2] School of Computer Science, University of Adelaide, Australia

Abstract. In this paper, we study the problem of face clustering in videos. Specifically, given automatically extracted faces from videos and two kinds of prior knowledge (the face track that each face belongs to, and the pairs of faces that appear in the same frame), the task is to partition the faces into a given number of disjoint groups, such that each group is associated with one subject. To deal with this problem, we propose a new method called weighted block-sparse low rank representation (WBSLRR) which considers the available prior knowledge while learning a low rank data representation, and also develop a simple but effective approach to obtain the clustering result of faces. Moreover, after using several acceleration techniques, our proposed method is suitable for solving large-scale problems. The experimental results on two benchmark datasets demonstrate the effectiveness of our approach.

Keywords: low rank representation, block-sparsity, subspace clustering, face clustering.

1 Introduction

Face clustering in videos [7, 28] is an important but challenging problem in computer vision. Specifically, given the faces automatically extracted from a piece of video (*e.g.* a movie or an episode of TV series), the task is to partition these faces into a given number of clusters, such that the faces assigned to each cluster belong to the same subject. Face clustering is important for many related applications, such as video organization, video segmentation and content based video retrieval. However, the video face clustering problem is challenging because the faces are generally captured in uncontrolled environments and thus the faces are with large variations in poses, illuminations and facial expressions. Moreover, the faces may be occluded by hands, glasses or other objects.

Instead of treating each face individually, existing works [7, 28] (see Section 2 for more details) often consider the information based on face tracks (where each face track is a sequence of faces) when performing the face clustering in videos. Thus, the following two kinds of relationships among faces can be directly explored:

1. The *inner-track* relation: any two faces in the same face track should belong to the same subject.

D. Fleet et al. (Eds.): ECCV 2014, Part VI, LNCS 8694, pp. 123–138, 2014.

2. The *inter-track* relation: if any two faces appear in the same frame of the video, the corresponding two face tracks should belong to different subjects.

It is worth mentioning that, with such prior knowledge, the face clustering problem can be considered as "self-supervised" [7].

On the other hand, the subspace clustering problem [1, 10, 17] is studied in many recent works such as [20, 10, 17, 21, 27]. Specifically, given the data sampled from a union of (linear) subspaces, the goal of subspace clustering is to partition the data into several clusters, so that each cluster corresponds to one subspace. Among the subspace clustering methods, the compressed sensing based approaches [10, 17] assume that the data is self-expressible (*i.e.*, each data point in its subspace can be represented as a linear combination of the data points from the same subspace). Particularly, the low rank representation based methods [17], which encourage the data representation to be low-rank, have been successfully used in various applications. For example, the result of subspace clustering can be obtained based on the learnt data representation. Unfortunately, these unsupervised methods cannot effectively utilize the possible supervision (such as the prior knowledge) in our problem.

Motivated by the above two aspects, in this paper, we propose a low-rank representation based approach for face clustering in videos, by effectively exploiting the available prior knowledge (*i.e.* the inner-track and inter-track relations). Specifically, we design a weighted block-sparse regularizer on the data representation to incorporate both kinds of prior knowledge, so that the resultant data representation should be more discriminative. Ideally, the faces in any face track are linearly represented only by the tracks of faces from the same subject/subspace, because we encourage the sparsity of the blocks (which correspond to the face tracks) in the data representation. Moreover, if any faces from two face tracks appear in the same frame, the corresponding representation coefficients are penalized. Accordingly, we name the proposed method as weighted block-sparse low rank representation (WBSLRR). We adopt the alternating direction method (ADM) [4, 17] to solve the optimization problem and we further use several acceleration techniques to make the algorithm scalable to large-scale dataset. Moreover, we also propose an efficient method to obtain the face clustering result based on the learnt data representation.

In summary, the contributions of this work include:

- By considering both inner-track and inter-track relations of faces in videos, we develop a new method named WBSLRR to learn a more discriminative low rank representation of faces. We also propose an efficient method to obtain the face clustering result based on the learnt data representation.
- Several acceleration techniques are used to make the proposed method scalable to large-scale datasets.
- Experiments on two benchmark face datasets demonstrate the effectiveness of our WBSLRR approach for face clustering in videos.

2 Related Work

There are several existing works [7, 28] for face clustering in videos. Specifically, based on the information of face tracks, the unsupervised logistic discrinative metric learning (ULDML) method [7] learns a distance metric, so that faces in the same track are pulled closer, while faces in any face track are pushed away from the ones in another face track with the inter-track relation. More recently, based on the Hidden Markov Random Fields (HMRF) model, a probabilistic constrained clustering method called HMRF-com [28] is proposed for face clustering in videos. By exploiting the prior knowledge in the neighborhood system of HMRF, HMRF-com has shown competitive clustering performance. Besides, the problem of face clustering in videos can be treated as a constrained clustering problem, as studied in the works such as Penalized Probabilistic Clustering (PPC) [23], COP-KMeans [24] and HMRF-KMeans [2].

The subspace clustering methods [20, 10, 17, 21, 27] have been applied for face clustering. However, these methods do not exploit the valuable prior knowledge in our problem. Moreover, the face images studied in these works are usually captured under controlled environment, and may be further contaminated by artificial noises [17], while the face images in our problem are in-the-wild faces automatically detected from videos, which makes the clustering task more realistic and challenging.

The problem studied in this work is related to several other learning tasks, e.g., the traditional face verification task [9], the image set based classification task [26, 6, 25, 22] and the weakly supervised learning task [12, 33, 14–16, 30]. In the traditional face verification (resp., the image set based classification) problem, each training/test example is a pair of faces (resp., a set of faces from one subject). In contrast, our problem is basically a clustering problem, where labeled data (i.e., the faces with groundtruth names) are not available. In the weakly supervised learning problem, the weak supervision information usually comes from the captions of news images [12, 33] or the tags of web images [14–16, 30]. For example, in [12, 33], given a set of images, where each image contains several faces and is associated with a few names in the corresponding captions, the goal of caption-based face naming is to infer the correct name of each face. Different from such weak supervision, the prior knowledge in our task is the inner-track and inter-track relations based on the information of faces tracks.

3 Our Proposed Approach

3.1 Problem Statement

In the remainder of this paper, we use the lowercase/uppercase letter in boldface to denote a vector/matrix (e.g. , $\mathbf{a}$ denotes a vector and $\mathbf{A}$ denotes a matrix). The corresponding non-bold letter with a subscript denotes the entry in a vector/matrix (e.g. , a_i denotes the i-th entry of the vector $\mathbf{a}$, and $A_{i,j}$ denotes an entry at the i-th row and j-th column of the matrix $\mathbf{A}$). The superscript $'$

denotes the transpose of a vector or a matrix. Moreover, $\|\mathbf{A}\|_*$ denotes the nuclear norm of $\mathbf{A}$, $\text{tr}(\mathbf{A})$ denotes the trace of $\mathbf{A}$ (*i.e.*, $\text{tr}(\mathbf{A}) = \sum_i A_{i,i}$), $\|\mathbf{A}\|_F$ denotes the Frobenius norm of $\mathbf{A}$ (*i.e.*, $\|\mathbf{A}\|_F = (\sum_{i,j} A_{i,j}^2)^{1/2}$) and $rank(\mathbf{A})$ denotes the rank of $\mathbf{A}$. $\langle \mathbf{A}, \mathbf{B} \rangle$ denotes the inner product of two matrices (*i.e.*, $\langle \mathbf{A}, \mathbf{B} \rangle = \text{tr}(\mathbf{A}'\mathbf{B})$). $\mathbf{I}_n$ denotes a $n \times n$ identity matrix, and we omit the subscript when the size is obvious. $\mathbf{e}_i$ denotes the i-th column of $\mathbf{I}_n$. $diag(\mathbf{a})$ denotes a diagonal matrix where the diagonal elements are in the vector $\mathbf{a}$.

For the problem of face clustering in videos, let $\{\mathbf{X}^i\}_{i=1}^m$ denote the face tracks, where $\mathbf{X}^i \in \mathbb{R}^{d \times n_i}$ is the feature matrix corresponding to the i-th face track containing n_i faces, m is the total number of face tracks and d is the feature dimension. Besides, let $\mathbf{X} = [\mathbf{X}^1, \ldots, \mathbf{X}^m] \in \mathbb{R}^{d \times n}$ denote the feature matrix of all faces, where $n = \sum_{i=1}^m n_i$ is the total number of faces. Moreover, let us define a matrix $\mathbf{H} \in \{0,1\}^{m \times m}$, where $H_{i,j} = 1$ if there is a face from the face track $\mathbf{X}^i$ and a face from the face track $\mathbf{X}^j$ that appear in one frame, and $H_{i,j} = 0$ otherwise, $\forall i,j = 1, \ldots, m$. The goal of our task is to cluster the n faces into l groups, where each group contains the faces from one subject.

3.2 Weighted Block-Sparse Low Rank Representation

Let us assume that the given data are drawn from a union of l independent linear subspaces, where each linear subspace corresponds to one subject [20, 17]. Following [10], we also assume that there are enough data sampled from each subspace, and data matrix is *self-expressive*, so we have $\mathbf{X} = \mathbf{X}\mathbf{Z}$, where $\mathbf{Z} \in \mathbb{R}^{n \times n}$ is the data representation matrix. Similarly as in [10, 17], we propose to obtain the final clustering results of faces based on the data representation matrix $\mathbf{Z}$, which describes the relationship between faces. To achieve promising clustering result, we expect that the data representation $\mathbf{Z}$ has the following *ideal property* [10, 17]: $Z_{i,j} \neq 0$ (only) if the i-th face and the j-th face are from the same subject/subspace, and $Z_{i,j} = 0$ otherwise. In other words, any face from a subject should be linearly represented only by the faces from this subject.

As shown in [17], if $\mathbf{X}$ is a collection of samples *strictly* drawn from multiple independent linear subspaces (*i.e.*, $\mathbf{X}$ is *noise-free*), the optimal solution to the following problem satisfies the above mentioned ideal property:

$$\min_{\mathbf{Z}} \|\mathbf{Z}\|_* \quad s.t. \quad \mathbf{X} = \mathbf{X}\mathbf{Z}, \tag{1}$$

where $\|\mathbf{Z}\|_*$ is a convex approximation of $rank(\mathbf{Z})$ [17, 32]. The resultant data representation matrix after solving (1), which is called the shape intersection matrix (SIM) [8], has been widely used for subspace segmentation [17]. Note that the formulation in (1) essentially deals with an unsupervised learning problem, without considering the prior knowledge in our face clustering problem. Therefore, to learn a more discriminative data representation, we propose to further exploit the prior knowledge. Specifically, we additionally introduce a regularizer $\Omega(\mathbf{Z})$ to incorporate the prior knowledge, and formulate our learning problem as follows:

$$\min_{\mathbf{Z}} \|\mathbf{Z}\|_* + \gamma \Omega(\mathbf{Z}), \quad s.t. \quad \mathbf{X} = \mathbf{X}\mathbf{Z}, \tag{2}$$

where γ is a tradeoff parameter. Now, the remaining problem is how to design the regularizer $\Omega(\mathbf{Z})$ to model the prior knowledge. In this work, we propose a new regularizer that exploits both kinds of prior knowledge, which will be introduced below in details.

Recall that $\mathbf{X} = [\mathbf{X}^1, \ldots, \mathbf{X}^m]$, where each $\mathbf{X}^i$ corresponds to a face track. Accordingly, we can divide $\mathbf{Z}$ into $m \times m$ blocks as follows:

$$
\mathbf{Z} = \begin{bmatrix} \mathbf{Z}^{(1,1)} & \cdots & \mathbf{Z}^{(1,m)} \\ \vdots & \ddots & \vdots \\ \mathbf{Z}^{(m,1)} & \cdots & \mathbf{Z}^{(m,m)} \end{bmatrix} \tag{3}
$$

where each sub-matrix $\mathbf{Z}^{(i,j)} \in \mathbb{R}^{n_i \times n_j}$ contains the coefficients for representing the faces in the face track $\mathbf{X}^j$ using the ones in the face track $\mathbf{X}^i$, as shown in Figure 1.

Considering the inner-track relation, we extend the previously mentioned ideal property of the data representation $\mathbf{Z}$ to the following *block-wise ideal property*: The elements in $\mathbf{Z}^{(i,j)}$ are non-zeros (only) if the i-th face track and the j-th face track are from the same subject, otherwise the elements in $\mathbf{Z}^{(i,j)}$ should be zeros. As a result, the elements in each $\mathbf{Z}^{(i,j)}$ of such ideal representation matrix should be either large or zeros, namely the ideal $\mathbf{Z}$ should be *block-sparse*, as illustrated in Fig 1.

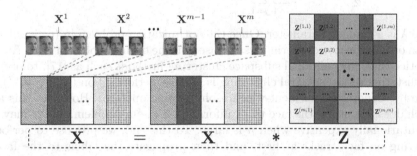

Fig. 1. Illustration of the block-sparse property of $\mathbf{Z}$, as well as the relationship between $\mathbf{X}$ and $\mathbf{Z}$ in the *noise-free* case. The different colors in $\mathbf{X}$ denote different face tracks.

Inspired by the minimization of the $\ell_{2,1}$ norm [17] which promotes the column sparsity of a matrix, we encourage the above mentioned *block-sparse* property by minimizing $\Omega_0(\mathbf{Z}) = \sum_{i=1}^{m} \sum_{j=1}^{m} \frac{1}{\sqrt{n_i n_j}} \|\mathbf{Z}^{(i,j)}\|_F$, where we use $\frac{1}{\sqrt{n_i n_j}}$ to normalize the Frobenius norms of $\{\mathbf{Z}^{(i,j)}\}_{i,j=1}^{m}$ due to different sizes of the sub-matrices.

Now, let us further consider the *inter-track* relation. Intuitively, when two faces respectively from $\mathbf{X}^i$ and $\mathbf{X}^j$ appear in the same frame, these two face tracks should be from different subjects. As a result, the elements in the corresponding two sub-matrices $\mathbf{Z}^{(i,j)}$ and $\mathbf{Z}^{(j,i)}$ are zeros in the ideal case. To this end, we propose a new regularization term $\Omega(\mathbf{Z})$ based on $\Omega_0(\mathbf{Z})$ as follows:

$$\Omega(\mathbf{Z}) = \sum_{i=1}^{m} \sum_{j=1}^{m} Q_{i,j} \|\mathbf{Z}^{(i,j)}\|_F, \tag{4}$$

where $Q_{i,j} = \frac{1}{\sqrt{n_i n_j}} + \mu H_{i,j}$, with μ being a large scalar (which is empirically set to 1000 in our experiments). Compared with $\Omega_0(\mathbf{Z})$, if the i-th face track and the j-th face track are with the inter-track relation, the weight w.r.t. $\|\mathbf{Z}^{(i,j)}\|_F$ will be enlarged from $1/\sqrt{n_i n_j}$ to $Q_{i,j}$, so the elements in the resultant $\mathbf{Z}^{(i,j)}$ and $\mathbf{Z}^{(j,i)}$ will tend to be closer to zeros. With $\Omega(\mathbf{Z})$ defined in (4), we detail the optimization problem in (2) as follows:

$$\min_{\mathbf{Z}} \|\mathbf{Z}\|_* + \gamma \sum_{i=1}^{m} \sum_{j=1}^{m} Q_{i,j} \|\mathbf{Z}^{(i,j)}\|_F \quad s.t. \quad \mathbf{X} = \mathbf{XZ}. \tag{5}$$

Recall that, for the in-the-wild faces in our problem, the data $\mathbf{X}$ is often contaminated by noise, so the equality constraint in (5) may not be perfectly satisfied. Following [10], we assume that the data $\mathbf{X}$ is corrupted by the Gaussian noise, so the squared Frobenius norm [29] is used to regularize the representation error (*i.e.*, $\mathbf{X} - \mathbf{XZ}$). Accordingly, we arrive at the *weighted block-sparse low rank representation* (WBSLRR) problem as follows:

$$\min_{\mathbf{Z}} \|\mathbf{Z}\|_* + \gamma \sum_{i=1}^{m} \sum_{j=1}^{m} Q_{i,j} \|\mathbf{Z}^{(i,j)}\|_F + \frac{\lambda}{2} \|\mathbf{X} - \mathbf{XZ}\|_F^2, \tag{6}$$

where λ is a tradeoff parameter. Once the optimization problem in (6) is solved, we can obtain the face clustering result based on the optimal solution $\mathbf{Z}^* \in \mathbb{R}^{n \times n}$.

Notice that, in traditional subspace clustering methods such as [17], to obtain the clustering result, spectral clustering is usually performed on $(|\mathbf{Z}^*| + |\mathbf{Z}^*|')/2$, where $|\cdot|$ denotes the element-wise absolute value operator. However, this approach does not utilize the face track information in our problem, and it may be computationally expensive when n is large. To this end, we propose to perform clustering on face tracks at first, and then propagate the labels to the faces, instead of performing clustering on the faces directly. Specifically, we convert $\mathbf{Z}^*$ into an affinity matrix $\mathbf{A} \in \mathbb{R}^{m \times m}$, where each element $A_{i,j} = \|\mathbf{Z}^{*(i,j)}\|_F / \sqrt{n_i n_j}$ describes the affinity between the corresponding pair of face tracks. Afterwards, we follow [17] to post-process this affinity matrix $\mathbf{A}$, and use the spectral clustering method [10, 20, 27] on the post-processed affinity matrix to perform clustering on the face tracks. Finally, the clustering result of faces can be directly obtained by propagating the label from each face track to the corresponding faces within this face track.

4   Optimization

There are two major challenges when solving the optimization problem in (6). Firstly, it contains a nuclear norm regularization on $\mathbf{Z}$, which is non-differentiable.

Secondly, for the face clustering problem in vedios, it is possible that a lot of faces are automatically detected, and the corresponding data matrix $\mathbf{X}$ can be very large (e.g., we have 17337 faces in the BF0502 dataset, see Section 5 for more details).

To tackle the first challenge, we use the alternating direction method (ADM) [4, 17], which has been widely used in the nuclear norm related optimization problems such as [18, 17]. To address the second challenge, inspired by a recent work [18], we decompose the representation matrix $\mathbf{Z}$ as $\mathbf{Z} = \mathbf{GW}$, in which $\mathbf{G} \in \mathbb{R}^{n \times r}$ is a column-wise orthonormal matrix with r being a scalar smaller than n (r is empirically set to 1000 in our experiments), and $\mathbf{W} \in \mathbb{R}^{r \times n}$. For the convenience of optimization, we further introduce two variables $\mathbf{P} = \mathbf{I} - \mathbf{GW} \in \mathbb{R}^{n \times n}$ and $\mathbf{J} = \mathbf{P} \in \mathbb{R}^{n \times n}$, and reformulate our optimization problem as follows,

$$\min_{\mathbf{G}'\mathbf{G}=\mathbf{I}, \mathbf{W}, \mathbf{P}, \mathbf{J}} \quad \|\mathbf{W}\|_* + \gamma \Omega(\mathbf{I} - \mathbf{J}) + \frac{\lambda}{2}\|\mathbf{XP}\|_F^2 \tag{7}$$
$$s.t. \quad \mathbf{I} - \mathbf{GW} = \mathbf{P}, \ \mathbf{J} = \mathbf{P}.$$

To solve the optimization problem in (7) using ADM [4, 17], we operate on the following augmented Lagrangian function:

$$\mathcal{L}(\mathbf{G}, \mathbf{W}, \mathbf{J}, \mathbf{P}, \mathbf{L}, \mathbf{\Lambda}, \rho) = \|\mathbf{W}\|_* + \gamma \Omega(\mathbf{I} - \mathbf{J}) + \frac{\lambda}{2}\|\mathbf{XP}\|_F^2 + \langle \mathbf{I} - \mathbf{GW} - \mathbf{P}, \mathbf{L}\rangle$$
$$+ \langle \mathbf{J} - \mathbf{P}, \mathbf{\Lambda}\rangle + \frac{\rho}{2}\left(\|\mathbf{I} - \mathbf{GW} - \mathbf{P}\|_F^2 + \|\mathbf{J} - \mathbf{P}\|_F^2\right),$$

where $\mathbf{L} \in \mathbb{R}^{n \times n}$ and $\mathbf{\Lambda} \in \mathbb{R}^{n \times n}$ are the Lagrange multipliers and ρ is the penalty parameter. The optimization problem can be solved by iteratively updating the variables $\{\mathbf{G}, \mathbf{W}, \mathbf{J}, \mathbf{P}\}$, the Lagrange multipliers $\{\mathbf{L}, \mathbf{\Lambda}\}$ and the penalty parameter ρ until convergence. We introduce the detailed updating steps at the t-th iteration as follows:

Updating G: $\mathbf{G}_{t+1}$ is calculated as $\mathrm{argmin}_\mathbf{G}\mathcal{L}(\mathbf{G}, \mathbf{W}_t, \mathbf{J}_t, \mathbf{P}_t, \mathbf{L}_t, \mathbf{\Lambda}_t, \rho_t)$, i.e., the optimal solution to the following subproblem:

$$\min_{\mathbf{G}'\mathbf{G}=\mathbf{I}} \|(\mathbf{I} - \mathbf{P}_t + \frac{\mathbf{L}_t}{\rho_t}) - \mathbf{GW}_t\|_F^2.$$

This problem is known as the matrix procrustes problem [18]. Based on [18], the optimal solution of the above problem is given by $\mathbf{G}_{t+1} = \mathbf{U}_G\mathbf{V}'_G$, where $\mathbf{U}_G$ and $\mathbf{V}_G$ are two orthogonal matrices obtained by using singular value decomposition (SVD) of $(\mathbf{I} - \mathbf{P}_t + \frac{\mathbf{L}_t}{\rho_t})\mathbf{W}'_t$, i.e., $\mathbf{U}_G\mathbf{\Sigma}_G\mathbf{V}'_G = (\mathbf{I} - \mathbf{P}_t + \frac{\mathbf{L}_t}{\rho_t})\mathbf{W}'_t$.

Updating W: $\mathbf{W}_{t+1}$ is calculated as $\mathrm{argmin}_\mathbf{W}\mathcal{L}(\mathbf{G}_{t+1}, \mathbf{W}, \mathbf{J}_t, \mathbf{P}_t, \mathbf{L}_t, \mathbf{\Lambda}_t, \rho_t)$, i.e., the optimal solution to the following subproblem:

$$\min_{\mathbf{W}} \|\mathbf{W}\|_* + \frac{\rho_t}{2}\left\|\mathbf{W} - \mathbf{G}'_{t+1}\left(\mathbf{I} - \mathbf{P}_t + \frac{\mathbf{L}_t}{\rho_t}\right)\right\|_F^2, \tag{8}$$

which can also be solved in closed form by using the Singular Value Thresholding (SVT) [5] method.

Updating J: $\mathbf{J}_{t+1}$ is calculated as $\text{argmin}_\mathbf{J}\mathcal{L}(\mathbf{G}_{t+1}, \mathbf{W}_{t+1}, \mathbf{J}, \mathbf{P}_t, \mathbf{L}_t, \mathbf{\Lambda}_t, \rho_t)$, *i.e.*, the optimal solution to the following subproblem:

$$\min_\mathbf{J} \ \Omega(\mathbf{I} - \mathbf{J}) + \frac{\rho_t}{2\gamma}\left\|\mathbf{J} - \mathbf{P}_t + \frac{\mathbf{\Lambda}_t}{\rho_t}\right\|_F^2. \tag{9}$$

For convenience, let us define $\hat{\mathbf{J}} = \mathbf{I} - \mathbf{J}_{t+1}$ and $\mathbf{R} = \mathbf{I} - \mathbf{P}_t + \frac{\mathbf{\Lambda}_t}{\rho_t}$, the above problem can be rewritten as:

$$\min_{\hat{\mathbf{J}}} \ \Omega(\hat{\mathbf{J}}) + \frac{\rho_t}{2\gamma}\left\|\hat{\mathbf{J}} - \mathbf{R}\right\|_F^2.$$

Similarly as in (3), we also decompose $\hat{\mathbf{J}}$ and $\mathbf{R}$ into $m \times m$ blocks. Let us denote $\hat{\mathbf{J}}^{(i,j)}$ (*resp.*, $\mathbf{R}^{(i,j)}$) as the (i,j)-th block of $\hat{\mathbf{J}}$ (*resp.*, $\mathbf{R}$), then the above problem can be equivalently rewritten as

$$\min_{\{\hat{\mathbf{J}}^{(i,j)}\}_{i,j=1}^m} \ \sum_{i=1}^m\sum_{j=1}^m Q_{i,j}\|\hat{\mathbf{J}}^{(i,j)}\|_F + \frac{\rho_t}{2\gamma}\sum_{i=1}^m\sum_{j=1}^m\left\|\hat{\mathbf{J}}^{(i,j)} - \mathbf{R}^{(i,j)}\right\|_F^2,$$

which can be divided into the following m^2 subproblems:

$$\min_{\hat{\mathbf{J}}^{(i,j)}} \ \tau_{i,j}\|\hat{\mathbf{J}}^{(i,j)}\|_F + \frac{1}{2}\left\|\hat{\mathbf{J}}^{(i,j)} - \mathbf{R}^{(i,j)}\right\|_F^2, \quad i,j = 1,\ldots,m, \tag{10}$$

where $\tau_{i,j} = \gamma Q_{i,j}/\rho_t$. Based on Lemma 3.3 in [31], the closed form solution of the problem in (10) can be obtained as $\hat{\mathbf{J}}^{*(i,j)} = \max\left(1 - \frac{\tau_{i,j}}{\|\mathbf{R}^{(i,j)}\|_F}, 0\right)\mathbf{R}^{(i,j)}$. With $\{\hat{\mathbf{J}}^{*(i,j)}\}_{i,j=1}^m$ obtained after solving the m^2 subproblems in (10), $\mathbf{J}_{t+1}$ can be recovered by $\mathbf{J}_{t+1} = \mathbf{I} - \hat{\mathbf{J}}^*$. In this way, the optimization problem in (9) can be solved.

Updating P: $\mathbf{P}_{t+1}$ is calculated as $\text{argmin}_\mathbf{P}\mathcal{L}(\mathbf{G}_{t+1}, \mathbf{W}_{t+1}, \mathbf{J}_{t+1}, \mathbf{P}, \mathbf{L}_t, \mathbf{\Lambda}_t, \rho_t)$, *i.e.*, the optimal solution to the following subproblem:

$$\min_\mathbf{P} \ \frac{\lambda}{2}\|\mathbf{X}\mathbf{P}\|_F^2 + \rho_t\|\mathbf{P} - \mathbf{C}_{t+1}\|_F^2. \tag{11}$$

where $\mathbf{C}_{t+1} = \frac{1}{2}(\mathbf{I} - \mathbf{G}_{t+1}\mathbf{W}_{t+1} + \mathbf{J}_{t+1} + \frac{1}{\rho_t}\mathbf{L}_t + \frac{1}{\rho_t}\mathbf{\Lambda}_t)$. Note that, the gradient of the above objective function *w.r.t.* $\mathbf{P}$ is $\lambda\mathbf{X}'\mathbf{X}\mathbf{P} + 2\rho_t(\mathbf{P} - \mathbf{C}_{t+1})$. By setting the gradient to zeros, we obtain the optimal solution for (11) as

$$\mathbf{P}_{t+1} = \left(\frac{\lambda}{2\rho_t}\mathbf{X}'\mathbf{X} + \mathbf{I}\right)^{-1}\mathbf{C}_{t+1}. \tag{12}$$

We now discuss how to calculate $\mathbf{P}_{t+1}$ in (12) more efficiently without using matrix inversion. Let $\mathbf{V}_X diag([\sigma_1,\ldots,\sigma_{rx},0,\ldots,0]')\mathbf{V}_X' = \mathbf{X}'\mathbf{X}$ denote the SVD of $\mathbf{X}'\mathbf{X}$, where $\mathbf{V}_X \in \mathbb{R}^{n \times n}$ is an orthogonal matrix and $\{\sigma_i\}_{i=1}^{rx}$ are *positive*

Algorithm 1. The algorithm for solving WBSLRR.

Input: $\mathbf{X} = [\mathbf{X}^1, \ldots, \mathbf{X}^m] \in \mathbb{R}^{d \times n}$, $\mathbf{H} \in \{0,1\}^{m \times m}$, λ and γ.

Initialize $\mathbf{P}_0$, $\mathbf{G}_0$, $\mathbf{W}_0$, $\mathbf{J}_0$, $\mathbf{L}_0$, $\boldsymbol{\Lambda}_0$ as zero matrices and set $t = 0$.

while not converge **do**

    1. Calculate $\mathbf{G}_{t+1}$ by using $\mathbf{G}_{t+1} = \mathbf{U}_G \mathbf{V}'_G$, where $\mathbf{U}_G \boldsymbol{\Sigma}_G \mathbf{V}'_G = (\mathbf{I} - \mathbf{P}_t + \frac{\mathbf{L}_t}{\rho_t}) \mathbf{W}'_t$.

    2. Calculate $\mathbf{W}_{t+1}$ by solving (8) using the SVT method [5].

    3. Calculate $\mathbf{J}_{t+1}$ by using $\mathbf{J}_{t+1} = \mathbf{I} - \hat{\mathbf{J}}^*$, with $\hat{\mathbf{J}}^*$ obtained by solving (10) for $\{\hat{\mathbf{J}}^{*(i,j)}\}_{i,j=1}^m$.

    4. Calculate $\mathbf{P}_{t+1}$ as in (13).

    5. Calculate $\mathbf{L}_{t+1}$ as $\mathbf{L}_{t+1} = \mathbf{L}_t + \rho_t(\mathbf{I} - \mathbf{G}_{t+1}\mathbf{W}_{t+1} - \mathbf{P}_{t+1})$, and compute $\boldsymbol{\Lambda}_{t+1}$ as $\boldsymbol{\Lambda}_{t+1} = \boldsymbol{\Lambda}_t + \rho_t(\mathbf{J}_{t+1} - \mathbf{P}_{t+1})$.

    6. Calculate ρ_{t+1} as $\rho_{t+1} = \min(\rho_t(1 + \Delta\rho), \rho_{max})$.

    7. Check the following convergence conditions: $\|\mathbf{I} - \mathbf{G}_{t+1}\mathbf{W}_{t+1} - \mathbf{P}_{t+1}\|_\infty \le \epsilon$ and $\|\mathbf{J}_{t+1} - \mathbf{P}_{t+1}\|_\infty \le \epsilon$.

    8. $t \leftarrow t + 1$.

end while

Output: the data representation $\mathbf{Z}^* = \mathbf{G}_t \mathbf{W}_t$.

---

singular values sorted in descending order, with $r_X = rank(\mathbf{X}) = rank(\mathbf{X}'\mathbf{X})$. As a result, we have $\frac{\lambda}{2\rho_t}\mathbf{X}'\mathbf{X} + \mathbf{I} = \mathbf{V}_X diag([1+\omega\sigma_1, \ldots, 1+\omega\sigma_{r_X}, 1, \ldots, 1]')\mathbf{V}'_X$ and $(\frac{\lambda}{2\rho_t}\mathbf{X}'\mathbf{X} + \mathbf{I})^{-1} = \mathbf{V}_X diag([\frac{1}{1+\omega\sigma_1}, \ldots, \frac{1}{1+\omega\sigma_{r_X}}, 1, \ldots, 1]')\mathbf{V}'_X$, where $\omega = \frac{\lambda}{2\rho_t}$. For convenience, we define $\mathbf{V}_{r_X} \in \mathbb{R}^{n \times r_X}$ which contains the first r_X columns of $\mathbf{V}_X$, and we define $\boldsymbol{\Lambda} \in \mathbb{R}^{r_X \times r_X}$ as $\boldsymbol{\Lambda} = diag([\frac{\omega\sigma_1}{1+\omega\sigma_1}, \ldots, \frac{\omega\sigma_{r_X}}{1+\omega\sigma_{r_X}}]')$. Accordingly, we obtain $(\frac{\lambda}{2\rho_t}\mathbf{X}'\mathbf{X} + \mathbf{I})^{-1} = \mathbf{I} - \mathbf{V}_{r_X}\boldsymbol{\Lambda}\mathbf{V}'_{r_X}$, so $\mathbf{P}_{t+1}$ in (12) can be equivalently calculated as

$$\mathbf{P}_{t+1} = \mathbf{C}_{t+1} - \mathbf{V}_{r_X}\boldsymbol{\Lambda}\mathbf{V}'_{r_X}\mathbf{C}_{t+1}, \tag{13}$$

for which the computational cost is $O(r_X n^2)$.

Other details, including updating the Lagrange multipliers and the penalty parameter, as well as the details of the convergence conditions, are summarized in Algorithm 1, where $\{\rho_0, \Delta\rho, \rho_{max}, \epsilon\}$ is set similarly as in [17].

Time Complexity and Convergence Analysis. The computational complexities of the main steps for updating the variables $\{\mathbf{G}, \mathbf{W}, \mathbf{J}, \mathbf{P}\}$ in each iteration are $O(rn^2)$, $O(rn^2)$, $O(n^2)$ and $O(r_X n^2)$, respectively. Therefore, the overall computational complexity for each iteration in Algorithm 1 is $O((r + r_X)n^2)$, and the step 3 for updating $\mathbf{J}$ can be efficiently performed in parallel.

The theoretical convergence of ADM with more than two blocks is still an open issue [17]. However, it has been widely used in many applications because it empirically converges well in general [17]. In the following experiments, we also show the empirical convergence of Algorithm 1 (see Section 5 for more details). Alternatively, the optimization problem in (6) can be addressed by using a recently proposed algorithm LADMPSAP [19] with convergence guarantees in theory, which will be studied in our future work.

5   Experiments

5.1   Datasets

We evaluate the performances of the proposed method and the baseline methods on two benchmark face datasets (*i.e.*, the Notting-Hill dataset [28] and the BF0502 dataset [11]) used in [28]. On both datasets, we strictly follow the experimental setting in [28]. The Notting-Hilldataset contains 4460 faces in 76 tracks detected from the movie "Notting Hill", and the faces are corresponding to 5 main casts. Following [28], we use the pixel intensities as the feature, so that each face is represented as a 18000 dimensional feature vector. The BF0502 dataset contains faces detected from the TV series "Buffy the Vampire Slayer". In our experiments, we use the 17337 faces in 229 tracks corresponding to 6 main casts. To represent each face, we use the 1937-dimensional descriptor [11] extracted from 13 facial points (*e.g.* the left and right corners of each eye).

We define the distinguishability value to as the criterion to evaluate how difficult the clustering problem is on each dataset. Specifically, based on the groundtruth labels, let us call a pair of face tracks as "same-subject pair" if these two tracks are from the same subject, otherwise we call it aa "different-subject pair". For each pair of face tracks, we calculate the mean of the squared Euclidean distance between the faces in one track and the faces in the other track. Then, we define the distinguishability value as the ratio between the average distance corresponding over same-subject pairs and the average distance over different-subject pairs. Generally speaking, a larger distinguishability value indicates that the corresponding clustering problem on this dataset is easier.

A brief summary of the information of the two datasets can be found in Table 1. According to this table, the BF0502 dataset, with more faces and face tracks and a smaller distinguishability value, should be more challenging than the Notting-Hill dataset.

5.2   Baselines and Evaluation Criterion

We compare our proposed method with the most recent work HMRF-com [28], as well as the baselines mentioned in [28]. Specifically, the following methods are used as the baselines:

- *the traditional clustering method*: Kmeans [3] is used in two ways as the baselines in [28]. Specifically, "Kmeans-1" is directly performed on the whole dataset after using PCA, and "Kmeans-2" denotes the Algorithm 2 in [28], in which Kmeans is used in Stage 2. Note that neither of these two approaches utilize the prior knowledge.
- *the constrained clustering method*: The Penalized Probabilistic Clustering (PPC) method [23] used the Gaussian mixture models, with the prior knowledge in our problem considered as pairwise constraints.
- *the metric learning based method*: The unsupervised logistic discriminant metric learning (ULDML) method [7] proposed for the face track clustering in

videos. In [28], two methods (called "ULDML-cl" and "ULDML-km") are proposed based on the learnt metric. Specifically, for ULDML-cl, a complete-link hierarchical clustering method is employed on the corresponding distance matrix between the face tracks [7]. For ULDML-km, Kmeans is performed based on the learnt metric.

– *the hidden markov random fields based method*: HMRF-com [28] is a probablistic constrained clustering approach based on HMRF. Note that the prior knowlege is considered in the combined neighborhood system.

To further study our proposed method, we also compare our WBSLRR with the following five compressed sensing based subspace clustering methods on both datasets: Least Squares Regression (LSR) [20] , Sparse Subspace Clustering (SSC) [10], Low Rank Representation (LRR) [17], Correlation Adaptive Subspace Segmentation (CASS) [21] and Low Rank Sparse Subspace Clustering (LRSSC) [27]. For fair comparison, we apply our acceleration techniques in our implementation of LRSSC [27], and we use the LRR method with the squared Frobenius norm regularization on the representation error. Basically, both WBSLRR and these subspace clustering methods seek for a desired data representation $\mathbf{Z}$, based on which clustering can be performed. The major difference between these approaches is the regularizations on $\mathbf{Z}$ in their objective functions, which are briefly summarized in Table 3. Based on Table 3, we can observe that LRR is a special case of our WBSLRR if we drop $\Omega(\mathbf{Z})$ in (6), while LRSSC can be treated as a special case of our WBSLRR by replacing $\Omega(\mathbf{Z})$ with $\|\mathbf{Z}\|_1$ (*i.e.*, LRSSC encourages the general sparsity without considering of the information of the face tracks). For fair comparison, for all these subspace clustering methods (*i.e.*, LSR, SSC, LRR, CASS and LRSSC), the clustering is also performed based on the affinity matrix $\mathbf{A} \in \mathbb{R}^{m \times m}$ (as we introduced in Section 3.2), so that the information of face tracks is also utilized.

Following [28], we use *accuracy* (based on the confusion matrix) for performance evaluation, which is defined as the number of correctly clustered faces over the total number of faces. The confusion matrix is derived from the best 1-to-1 match between the partition of all faces and the groundtruth labels, which is obtained by using the Hungarian method [13]. As suggested in [28], each algorithm is repeated for 30 times, and the mean accuracy and standard deviation are reported. Due to the page limitation, we omit the parameter settings of these baselines, which can be found in [28]. The results of the state-of-the-art baselines listed in Table 2 are from the tables in [28]. For fair comparision, we manually tune the parameters and report the best results of our method and the subspace clustering methods as suggested in [28].

5.3 Experimental Results

In this section, we verify the effectiveness of our proposed method with two experiments. In the first experiment, we compare the results of our proposed method with the state-of-the-art results in [28] on the two datasets. In the second experiment, we compare our method with several subspace clustering approaches.

Table 1. A brief summary of information about the two datasets. "#" means "the number of", and "dim" stands for the feature dimension.

Dataset	m(#tracks)	n(#faces)	d(dim)	l(#subjects)	distinguishability value
BF0502	229	17337	1937	5	1.09
Notting-Hill	76	4660	18000	6	1.46

Table 2. The clustering accuracies (mean±standard deviation%) of the state-of-the-art methods and our proposed method on two datasets under two settings. The results of the baseline methods are from [28]. The best accuracies are highlighted in boldface.

Methods	BF0502		Notting-Hill	
	Setting 1	Setting 2	Setting 1	Setting 2
Kmeans-1	39.31 ± 4.51	39.31 ± 4.51	69.16 ± 3.22	69.16 ± 3.22
Kmeans-2	42.05 ± 5.45	42.05 ± 5.45	73.43 ± 8.12	73.43 ± 8.12
PPC	43.64 ± 4.61	42.54 ± 3.98	79.71 ± 2.14	78.88 ± 5.15
ULDML-km	29.05 ± 2.84	41.62 ± 0.00	72.66 ± 12.78	73.18 ± 8.66
ULDML-cl	39.01 ± 0.00	49.29 ± 0.00	51.72 ± 0.00	36.87 ± 0.00
HMRF-com	47.77 ± 3.31	50.30 ± 2.73	81.33 ± 0.43	84.39 ± 1.47
WBSLRR (ours)	$\mathbf{59.55 \pm 0.51}$	$\mathbf{62.76 \pm 1.10}$	$\mathbf{95.24 \pm 0.00}$	$\mathbf{96.29 \pm 0.00}$

Comparison with the State-of-the-Art Methods. In this experiment, we evaluate all the methods under the following two settings:

- Setting 1: we only utilize the inner-track relation in all the methods,
- Setting 2: both inter-track and inter-track relations are available to all the methods.

For our WBSLRR method, we solve the optimization problem in (6) with the second term, namely $\Omega(\mathbf{Z})$, replaced with $\Omega_0(\mathbf{Z})$, in order to exclude the consideration of inter-track relation under setting 1. and directly solve the optimization problem implement (6) under setting 2. For each method, the clustering accuracies on two datasets are shown in Table 2. According to Table 2, we have the following observations:

Firstly, our proposed method WBSLRR outperforms all the baseline methods (on both datasets) under both settings. Comparing WBSLRR with the second best method (*i.e.* the HMRF-com method) on the two datasets, the relative improvement is about 20% (resp., 15%) on the BF0502 dataset (resp., the Notting-Hill dataset). The results clearly demonstrate that WBSLRR can make better use of the prior knowledge (*i.e.* the inner-track and inter-track relation) for the face clustering problems in videos .

On both datasets, the performances of WBSLRR under setting 2 are better when compared with those under setting 1, which demonstrates that it is beneficial to additionally consider the inter-track relation in (6). For HMRF-com, we have similar observations, *i.e.*, the results under setting 2 are better than those under setting 1 on both datasets.

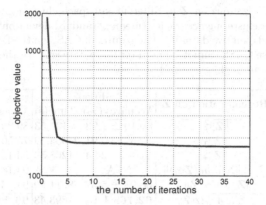

Fig. 2. The objective values of our optimization problem in (6) with respect to the number of iterations, on the Notting-Hill dataset

For almost all the methods, the performances on the Notting-Hill dataset are generally better than those on the BF0502 dataset. One possible explanation is that, the BF0502 dataset contains more faces and face tracks and it is also with smaller distinguishability value, which indicates that the face clustering task on the BF0502 dataset is more challenging.

Last but not least, we take the Notting-Hill dataset as an example to show the objective values of the optimization problem in (6) with respect to different iteration numbers in Figure 2. We can observe that our optimization algorithm empirically converges well.

Comparison with the Subspace Clustering Methods. The mean accuracies and the standard deviations as well as the running times of five existing subspace clustering methods and our WBSLRR on both datasets are reported in Table 3. All the algorithms are executed on a desktop with Intel Xeon CPU (3.2Ghz) and 16GB memory).

From Table 3, we observe that our WBSLRR achieves the best accuracies on both datasets and it is also reasonably fast compared with other methods. Note that the difference between our WBSLRR and LRR is that we additionally use the regularizer $\Omega(\mathbf{Z})$ to encourage the block-sparsity of the representation matrix $\mathbf{Z}$. WBSLRR outperforms LRR, which clearly demonstrates the effectiveness of the proposed regularizer $\Omega(\mathbf{Z})$ for exploiting the available prior knowledge in our task.

Moreover, we observe that both WBSLRR and LRSSC outperform LRR in terms of the clustering accuracy, which indicates that more robust results can be achieved by further encouraging the sparsity of $\mathbf{Z}$. Our WBSLRR achieves better results than LRSSC, which demonstrates it is more beneficial to encourage the weighted block-sparsity on the data representation according to the prior knowledge in our WBSLRR, rather than promoting the general sparsity by using the ℓ_1 norm regularization as in LRSSC.

Table 3. The regularizations on $\mathbf{Z}$ in different subspace clustering methods and our WBSLRR, and their clustering accuracies (mean±standard deviation%) as well as running times (in seconds) on two datasets. The results of CASS on the BF0502 dataset are not available because CASS cannot be used on large datasets like the BF0502 dataset. The best accuracies are highlighted in boldface.

Methods	Regualrization on $\mathbf{Z}$	BF0502		Notting-Hill	
		Accuarcy(%)	Time(s)	Accuarcy(%)	Time(s)
LSR	$\|\mathbf{Z}\|_F^2$	50.19 ± 1.93	131.53	89.89 ± 0.00	7.36
SSC	$\|\mathbf{Z}\|_1$	36.52 ± 0.91	24554.59	75.50 ± 7.90	2931.00
LRR	$\|\mathbf{Z}\|_*$	51.17 ± 2.94	1208.53	93.11 ± 0.00	31.92
CASS	$\sum_{i=1}^n \|\mathbf{X} \, diag(\mathbf{Z}\mathbf{e}_i)\|_*$	N/A	N/A	93.18 ± 0.00	29610.15
LRSSC	$\|\mathbf{Z}\|_* + \gamma\|\mathbf{Z}\|_1$	58.08 ± 5.37	8211.20	94.03 ± 0.00	545.93
WBSLRR (ours)	$\|\mathbf{Z}\|_* + \gamma\Omega(\mathbf{Z})$	$\mathbf{62.76\pm1.10}$	693.43	$\mathbf{96.29\pm0.00}$	194.14

LRR outperforms LSR and SSC on both datasets. One possible explanation is that by using the nuclear norm regularizer on $\mathbf{Z}$, LRR can better grasp the global structure [17] of the given data. While CASS achieves relatively better results than LRR, LSR and SSC on the Notting-Hill dataset, it is slow and thus cannot be applied on the large dataset BF0502.

Finally, the five subspace clustering methods generally achieve better results than the baseline methods in Table 2. One possible explanation is that, the self-expressiveness assumption of the data is generally satisfied and the prior knowledge is also considered in the post-processing procedures of these subspace clustering methods.

6   Conclusions

To effectively solve the face clustering problem in videos, in this paper, we have proposed the WBSLRR method, which exploits the two kinds of prior knowledge (*i.e.* the inner-track and inter-track relations) while learning a low rank representation of the given data. We also propose a post-processing approach to efficiently obtain the clustering result of faces based on the resultant data representation. After using several acceleration techniques in our algorithm, the proposed method is scalable for solving large scale problems. The experimental results have demonstrated the effectiveness of our approach when compared with several state-of-the-art baselines and subspace clustering methods.

Acknowledgement. This work is supported by the Singapore MoE Tier 2 Grant (ARC42/13).

References

1. Agrawal, R., Gehrke, J., Gunopulos, D., Raghavan, P.: Automatic subspace clustering of high dimensional data for data mining applications. In: SIGMOD (1998)

2. Basu, S., Bilenko, M., Banerjee, A., Mooney, R.J.: Probabilistic semi-supervised clustering with constraints. In: Semi-Supervised Learning. MIT Press (2006)
3. Bishop, C.M.: Pattern recognition and machine learning. Springer (2006)
4. Boyd, S., Parikh, N., Chu, E., Peleato, B., Eckstein, J.: Distributed optimization and statistical learning via the alternating direction method of multipliers. Foundations and Trends in Machine Learning 3(1), 1–122 (2011)
5. Cai, J., Emmanuel, C., Shen, Z.: A singular value thresholding algorithm for matrix completion. SIAM Journal on Optimization 20(4), 1956–1982 (2010)
6. Cevikalp, H., Triggs, B.: Face recognition based on image sets. In: CVPR, pp. 2567–2573 (2010)
7. Cinbis, R.G., Verbeek, J.J., Schmid, C.: Unsupervised metric learning for face identification in TV video. In: ICCV, pp. 1559–1566 (2011)
8. Costeira, J.P., Kanade, T.: A multibody factorization method for independently moving objects. International Journal of Computer Vision 29(3), 159–179 (1998)
9. Cui, Z., Li, W., Xu, D., Shan, S., Chen, X.: Fusing robust face region descriptors via multiple metric learning for face recognition in the wild. In: CVPR, pp. 3554–3561 (2013)
10. Elhamifar, E., Vidal, R.: Sparse subspace clustering. In: CVPR, pp. 2790–2797 (2009)
11. Everingham, M., Sivic, J., Zisserman, A.: Hello! my name is... Buffy – automatic naming of characters in TV video. In: BMVC, pp. 899–908 (2006)
12. Guillaumin, M., Mensink, T., Verbeek, J., Schmid, C.: Automatic face naming with caption-based supervision. In: CVPR, pp. 1–8 (2008)
13. Kuhn, H.W.: The hungarian method for the assignment problem. Naval Research Logistics Quarterly 2(1-2), 83–97 (1955)
14. Li, W., Duan, L., Tsang, I.W., Xu, D.: Batch mode adaptive multiple instance learning for computer vision tasks. In: CVPR, pp. 2368–2375 (2012)
15. Li, W., Duan, L., Tsang, I.W., Xu, D.: Co-labeling: A new multi-view learning approach for ambiguous problems. In: ICDM, pp. 419–428 (2012)
16. Li, W., Duan, L., Xu, D., Tsang, I.W.: Text-based image retrieval using progressive multi-instance learning. In: ICCV, pp. 2049–2055 (2011)
17. Liu, G., Lin, Z., Yan, S., Sun, J., Yu, Y., Ma, Y.: Robust recovery of subspace structures by low-rank representation. TPAMI 35(1), 171–184 (2013)
18. Liu, G., Yan, S.: Active subspace: Toward scalable low-rank learning. Neural Computation 24(12), 3371–3394 (2012)
19. Liu, R., Lin, Z., Su, Z.: Linearized alternating direction method with parallel splitting and adaptive penalty for separable convex programs in machine learning. In: ACML, pp. 116–132 (2013)
20. Lu, C.Y., Min, H., Zhao, Z.Q., Zhu, L., Huang, D.S., Yan, S.: Robust and efficient subspace segmentation via least squares regression. In: Fitzgibbon, A., Lazebnik, S., Perona, P., Sato, Y., Schmid, C. (eds.) ECCV 2012, Part VII. LNCS, vol. 7578, pp. 347–360. Springer, Heidelberg (2012)
21. Lu, C., Feng, J., Lin, Z., Yan, S.: Correlation adaptive subspace segmentation by trace Lasso. In: ICCV, pp. 1345–1352 (2013)
22. Lu, J., Wang, G., Moulin, P.: Image set classification using holistic multiple order statistics features and localized multi-kernel metric learning. In: ICCV, pp. 329–336 (2013)
23. Lu, Z., Leen, T.K.: Penalized probabilistic clustering. Neural Computation 19(6), 1528–1567 (2007)
24. Wagstaff, K., Cardie, C., Rogers, S., Schrödl, S., et al.: Constrained k-means clustering with background knowledge. In: ICML, pp. 577–584 (2001)

25. Wang, R., Guo, H., Davis, L.S., Dai, Q.: Covariance discriminative learning: A natural and efficient approach to image set classification. In: CVPR, pp. 2496–2503 (2012)
26. Wang, R., Shan, S., Chen, X., Gao, W.: Manifold-manifold distance with application to face recognition based on image set. In: CVPR, pp. 1–8 (2008)
27. Wang, Y.X., Xu, H., Leng, C.: Provable subspace clustering: When LRR meets SSC. In: NIPS, pp. 64–72 (2013)
28. Wu, B., Zhang, Y., Hu, B.G., Ji, Q.: Constrained clustering and its application to face clustering in videos. In: CVPR, pp. 3507–3514. IEEE (2013)
29. Xu, D., Huang, Y., Zeng, Z., Xu, X.: Human gait recognition using patch distribution feature and locality-constrained group sparse representation. IEEE Transactions on Image Processing 21(1), 316–326 (2012)
30. Xu, X., Tsang, I.W., Xu, D.: Handling ambiguity via input-output kernel learning. In: ICDM, pp. 725–734 (2012)
31. Yang, J., Yin, W., Zhang, Y., Wang, Y.: A fast algorithm for edge-preserving variational multichannel image restoration. SIAM Journal on Imaging Sciences 2(2), 569–592 (2009)
32. Zeng, Z., Chan, T.H., Jia, K., Xu, D.: Finding correspondence from multiple images via sparse and low-rank decomposition. In: Fitzgibbon, A., Lazebnik, S., Perona, P., Sato, Y., Schmid, C. (eds.) ECCV 2012, Part V. LNCS, vol. 7576, pp. 325–339. Springer, Heidelberg (2012)
33. Zeng, Z., Xiao, S., Jia, K., Chan, T.H., Gao, S., Xu, D., Ma, Y.: Learning by associating ambiguously labeled images. In: CVPR, pp. 708–715 (2013)

Crowd Tracking with Dynamic Evolution of Group Structures

Feng Zhu[1], Xiaogang Wang[2,3], and Nenghai Yu[1]

[1] Department of Electronic Engineering and Information Science,
University of Science and Technology of China, Hefei, China
[2] Department of Electronic Engineering, The Chinese University of Hong Kong,
Hong Kong, China
[3] Shenzhen Institutes of Advanced Technology, Chinese Academy of Sciences,
Shenzhen, China

Abstract. Crowd tracking generates trajectories of a set of particles for further analysis of crowd motion patterns. In this paper, we try to answer the following questions: what are the particles appropriate for crowd tracking and how to track them robustly through crowd. Different than existing approaches of computing optical flows, tracking keypoints or pedestrians, we propose to discover distinctive and stable mid-level patches and track them jointly with dynamic evolution of group structures. This is achieved through the integration of low-level keypoint tracking, mid-level patch tracking, and high-level group evolution. Keypoint tracking guides the generation of patches with stable internal motions, and also organizes patches into hierarchical groups with collective motions. Patches are tracked together through occlusions with spatial constraints imposed by hierarchical tree structures within groups. Coherent groups are dynamically updated through merge and split events guided by keypoint tracking. The dynamically structured patches not only substantially improve the tracking for themselves, but also can assist the tracking of any other target in the crowd. The effectiveness of the proposed approach is shown through experiments and comparison with state-of-the-art trackers.

1 Introduction

Crowd motion analysis has recently drawn many attentions because of its important applications in crowd video surveillance including recognizing different crowd events and traffic modes [29, 34–36, 11], detecting abnormal crowd behaviours [29, 15], and predicting crowd behaviours [35]. Different than many conventional surveillance approaches which focus on tracking individuals and analysing their behaviours, crowd surveillance treats the whole crowd as a union at the macroscopic level. It does not require extracted motions exactly corresponding to individual objects, as long as they reflect the motion patterns of the whole crowd. On the other hand, the learned motion patterns can assist tracking a particular target of interest through the crowd [2, 13, 21, 23]. Existing works learn crowd motion patterns through computing optical flows [2, 13, 21, 23], tracking keypoints [34–36] or pedestrians [1, 22, 26].

D. Fleet et al. (Eds.): ECCV 2014, Part VI, LNCS 8694, pp. 139–154, 2014.

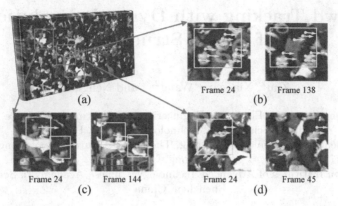

Fig. 1. (a) Crowd video. (b) A good mid-level patch for tracking with coherent internal motions. Since the motions of keypoints and the patch are consistent, tracking the patch well reflects local motions of the crowd. The patch covers three persons whose relative positions are stable over time. They form unique visual pattern for tracking. (c) Multi-scale patches. The red patch covers two small yellow patches. They have coherent motions. The red patch can assist tracking the yellow patches by adding spatial constraint at a larger scale. (d) A patch with incoherent internal motions. It is not suitable for tracking as it cannot keep stable visual pattern. Since its motion differs from those of keypoints inside, it cannot accurately reflect local motion of the crowd.

We can treat crowd tracking as generating trajectories of different length from a set of particles (i.e., pixels, keypoints, patches or pedestrians) at different scale levels. The major challenges of crowd tracking lie in three aspects: (1) partial or full occlusions caused by frequent interactions among objects; (2) a large number of individuals with similar appearance; and (3) significant appearance variation due to the perspective distortion of camera views. Different types of crowd tracking provide different amount of information for further motion analysis, and they also need to balance the risk of tracking errors.

Optical flows are computed at all pixels but their tracking only lasts for one frame. Keypoint tracking only selects good feature points to track. Those keypoints can be considered as the smallest patches. If they are well tracked over multiple frames, keypoint tracking can provide accurate information for crowd motion analysis. However, keypoint tracking is very sensitive to even small occlusions, since a feature point does not contain appearance information from a large area. Therefore, only short tracklets can be obtained. Tracking with pedestrian detection is very difficult because of heavy occlusions especially in very dense crowd and large changes of viewpoints. So far there is no pedestrian detector working robustly in all kinds of crowd scenes.

The above observations motivate us to find good mid-level patches to track, which cover larger areas than keypoints and are more robust to occlusions. Patch tracking can provide us longer trajectories which are useful for crowd motion analysis. We can even track patches with different sizes (Fig. 1 (c)). Large patches are more robust and take less risk of drifting. However, motions captured by them are less accurate, since they are not sensitive to local movements. Then the key question is what are good patches for tracking. Different from other tracking problems, one patch may be placed on multiple objects in crowd as shown in Fig. 1 (b). Such a patch may not be bad for tracking, as long as the two objects move coherently with stable relative positions. Moreover, study [18] has shown that neighbouring pedestrians may form unique visual patterns which make the patch distinctive for tracking. Since keypoint tracking provides accurate motions within short periods, it can help to find patches with stable internal structures and distinctive visual patterns [6, 20, 27]. It is important to detect patches with coherent internal motions, because such patches keep stable appearance and can accurately reflect the motions of the crowd as shown in Fig. 1 (b) and (d).

Scientific studies [14, 16] have shown that when a person is placed in crowd, he or she tends to form collective behaviours with others instead of moving freely. Thus crowd tends to form groups with coherent motions [34]. The relative positions of individuals within a group are more stable. Moreover, the collectiveness of crowd increases as it becomes denser [33]. Therefore, patches within the same coherent group should be tracked together by modeling their spatial structures. It will significantly improve the robustness when tracking through occlusions.

We target on automatically detecting distinctive and stable mid-level patches and jointly tracking them with dynamically evolved group structures. Keypoint tracking, patch tracking and group evolution are integrated at three different levels. It is motivated by our insights on the strength and weakness of the three aspects in crowd tracking. While patch tracking is more robust to partial occlusion and appearance change, keypoint tracking provides more accurate motion information in short periods. Keypoint tracking can help to detect patches with stable internal structures, and organize patches into groups with coherent motions and stable structures. Patches are tracked with a new dynamic hierarchical tree structure. It models the spatial relationships between patches at different scales and the evolution of group structures. Since crowd motions change dynamically, group structures are updated through merge and split over time.

2   Related Work

Some works [2, 13, 21, 23] have been done on tracking targets through crowd by learning models of scene structures and long-term motion patterns from optical flows or trajectories of keypoints. Ali and Shah [2] proposed multiple floor fields to assist tracking targets through crowd. These floor fields characterize forces from dominant paths, preferred exit regions, and boundaries of scene structures. Rodriguez et al. [21] employed the Correlated Topic Model [5] to learn a mixture of motion patterns for a specific scene and used it as prior to guide tracking. In [23], they extended this approach such that the learned priors of crowd behaviors can be transferred across scenes. Kratz and Nishino [13] captured the crowd motion at each spatio-temporal location with 3D Gaussian distributions and HMM, and used it as prior to guide tracking. All these models of scene structures and crowd motion patterns are learned from optical flows with off-line training.

None of them jointly track multiple targets together. Their focus is on *tracking a particular particle through the crowd* instead of *tracking the whole crowd with a set of particles* as we do. Our online-tracking approach does not require a training process to obtain priors of scene structures or motion patterns.

Recently, the social force model [9] has been used to track multiple pedestrians by modeling their interactions, the influence of destinations and scene structures with a physical model [19, 24]. This approach requires a lot of prior knowledge on scene structures and only suitable to top-down views. The parameters of the physical models need to be manually set or trained for each scene specifically. The initialization of tracking must rely on a pedestrian detector on "all" the individuals rather than keypoint or patch detectors (since the social force model is based on the psychological and physiological interactions of individuals) which generally does not work well in crowded scene. Manual initialization was used in [19, 24]. It is not suitable for general crowd tracking.

Many model-free trackers [13, 3, 8, 30] are proposed to track general objects including patches. They track each target separately without modeling the spatial constraints among targets. Idrees, Warner and Shah [10] tracked the crowd using neighbourhood motion concurrence. The work most relevant to ours is the structure preserving multi-object tracking proposed by Zhang and Maaten [31]. It jointly tracks multiple objects by modeling their spatial constraints. This work has several major differences with ours. Its patches are manually initialized and considered as one group during the whole tracking process (i.e. its group structure and the number of edges connecting patches are fixed), while we automatically detect patches and dynamic update group structures through merge and split operations. In [31], all the patches are placed on coherently moving objects with stable relative positions. However, in crowd tracking, patches may be on groups moving in different directions, and adding spatial constraints on them may bias the tracking. In [31], the spatial constraints of patches are modeled at a single scale, while a hierarchical tree structure at multiple scales is used by us.

3 Our Method

Our crowd tracking framework is shown in Fig. 2. It integrates low-level keypoint tracking, mid-level patch detection and tracking, and high-level group evolution. Keypoints are tracked with the KLT tracker [28]. Whenever ambiguity arises due to occlusions or other factors, keypoint tracking stops. Therefore, keypoint tracking can provide accurate information on crowd motions within short periods. Keypoint tracking results are used to detect mid-level patches suitable for tracking (Section 3.1), and update group structures over time (Section 3.2). Patches are tracked together with the spatial constraints added by the dynamic hierarchical tree structures (Section 3.3).

3.1 Patch Detection

Patches good for tracking should satisfy two requirements: (1) the appearance is distinctive; and (2) points inside the patch have coherent motions. In [25],

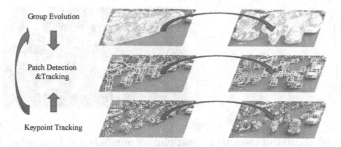

Fig. 2. Our crowd tracking framework integrates low-level keypoint tracking, mid-level patch detection and tracking, and high-level group evolution. Both group evolution and patch detection are guided by keypoint tracking. Group structures, which are used to assist patch tracking, are updated during high-level group evolution.

feature points good for tracking are selected as "Shi-Tomasi Corners" which are distinctive in local areas. We assume that patches with high density of such corner points are easy to track as they contain more distinctive textures. In order to find such patch candidates, we adopt the clustering method proposed in [32] to find dense clusters of keypoints. In [32], a K-NN graph is built from keypoints and graph indegrees well reflect the boundaries of keypoint distributions with different density levels. Outliers with low indegrees are removed and dense clusters with high indegrees are detected through agglomerative clustering. These dense clusters help to generate patch candidates.

Instead of clustering keypoints directly on K-NN graph, we first measure motion coherence [34] between neighbouring keypoints. If a keypoint moves coherently with others, its neighbour set should keep invariant over time and its motion correlation with neighbours should be high. To achieve this, starting at frame t, the invariant neighbours of keypoint i in the successive $d+1$ frames are found as $\mathcal{M}_{t\to d}^i = \bigcap_{\tau=t}^{t+d} \mathcal{N}_\tau^i$, where $\mathcal{N}_\tau^i$ is the K-NN set of keypoint i in frame τ. The motion correlation between i and its invariant neighbour j is measured by

$$C_{i,j} = \begin{cases} \dfrac{1}{d+1} \sum_{\tau=t}^{t+d} \dfrac{\mathbf{v}_\tau^i \cdot \mathbf{v}_\tau^j}{\|\mathbf{v}_\tau^i\| \cdot \|\mathbf{v}_\tau^j\|}, & \text{if } j \in \mathcal{M}_{t\to d}^i, \\ 0, & \text{otherwise}, \end{cases} \quad (1)$$

where $\mathbf{v}_\tau^i$ is the velocity of i in frame τ and $C_{i,j}$ is the (i,j) entry of motion correlation matrix $\mathbf{C}$. Given motion coherence, a graph is built among keypoints and it is represented with matrix $\mathbf{G}$ which is derived from $\mathbf{C}$ with entries

$$G_{i,j} = \begin{cases} 1, & \text{if } C_{i,j} > C_h \ \& \ C_{j,i} > C_h, \\ 0, & \text{otherwise}, \end{cases} \quad (2)$$

C_h is a predefined threshold set as 0.8 in all our experiments. $G_{i,j} = 1$ stands for an edge between i and j. Edges are only assigned to pairs which are both in the invariant neighbour set of each other and have high motion correlation.

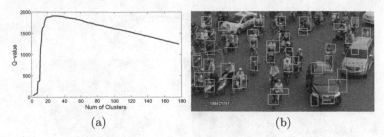

(a)   (b)

Fig. 3. (a) A typical curve of Q-value against cluster numbers. (b) Examples of detected patches, red boxes are layer-2 patches mentioned in Section 3.3.

We cluster these keypoints based on a weighted version $\mathbf{G}^w$ of graph $\mathbf{G}$ by integrating accurate spatial information

$$G_{i,j}^w = \begin{cases} \exp(-\dfrac{dist(i,j)^2}{\sigma^2}), & \text{if } G_{i,j} = 1, \\ 0, & \text{otherwise,} \end{cases} \qquad (3)$$

where $dist(i,j)$ is the Euclidean distance between i and j, and $\sigma^2 = \sum_{i,j} (dist(i,j)^2 \cdot G_{i,j}) / \sum_{i,j} G_{i,j}$. We apply the graph-based bottom-up clustering algorithm in [32] to find dense keypoint clusters and determine the number of clusters using "Q-value" [17]. A typical curve of Q-value against cluster numbers is in Fig. 3(a). We choose the cluster number with the maximum Q-value.

Patches are estimated from the detected keypoint clusters as follows: $x = \frac{1}{N} \sum_{i=1}^{N} x_i$, $y = \frac{1}{N} \sum_{i=1}^{N} y_i$, $w = 2\sigma_x$, $h = 2\sigma_y$, where (x, y) is the patch center, w and h are width and height respectively, (x_i, y_i) is the coordinate of the ith keypoint, σ_x and σ_y are the standard deviation of x_i and y_i, and N is the number of keypoints in the cluster.

Some examples of patches detected in videos are shown in Fig. 3(b). Static keypoints on the background are filtered out by motion correlation in Eq.(1), so patches locate on moving targets. Since the graph is built with K-NN, the sizes of clusters/patches increase with K. In the extreme case, a fully connected graph becomes one cluster. In Section 3.3, patches are generated with two different scales by choosing $K = 10$ and $K = 20$.

3.2   Group Evolution

Pedestrians in crowd interact with each other and form groups with coherent motions. The relative positions of individuals in the same group are more stable. So it is profitable to identify groups and track targets in the same group jointly. However, crowd group structures are also changeable and affected by pedestrian destinations and scene structures, and therefore need to be updated dynamically.

We derive groups of patches from the results of keypoint tracking, since they provide more accurate motion information. Within a short period Δ, the whole crowd is segmented into several coherent motion patterns with the Collective

Fig. 4. Group evolution and dynamic structures, both group merge and split occurs

Merging algorithm [33]. It results in several groups of keypoints, such that each group exhibits one collective motion pattern. Grouping information from the keypoint-level guides the organization of mid-level patches. We assign keypoint k a unique label y_k indicating which collective motion it belongs to and determine the label for patch i by majority vote of the keypoints covered by i.

Final groups for patches are generated by temporal smoothing. Let l_t^i be the label of patch i at frame t, then connectivity matrix $\mathbf{L}_t$ is defined as

$$L_t(i,j) = \begin{cases} 1, & \text{if } l_t^i = l_t^j, \\ 0, & \text{otherwise,} \end{cases} \tag{4}$$

where $L_t(i,j)$ is the (i,j) entry of $\mathbf{L}_t$. We sum up connectivity matrices over time by $\mathbf{L}_{sum} = \sum_{k=0}^{k_c-1} \mathbf{L}_{t-k\Delta}$, where k_c is the length of temporal buffer ($k_c = 10$ in all our experiments), and Δ is a short time period for calculating each $\mathbf{L}_t$ ($\Delta = 3$ in all our experiments). Then entry (i,j) of $\mathbf{L}_{sum}$ is set to 1 if $L_{sum}(i,j) \geq \kappa k_c$ and otherwise 0. The connected components in $\mathbf{L}_{sum}$ are extracted to be final groups at frame t. κ controls the value of threshold and is set as $\kappa = 0.7$ in all of our experiments. The buffer window makes the group structures change smoothly and robust to errors of detected collective motions.

By regularly detecting collective motions and grouping patches, we dynamically adjust group structures through merge and split events with the evolution of crowd (Fig. 4).

3.3   Dynamic Hierarchical Tree Structure

Because of frequent occlusions and neighbours with similar appearance, trackers that only utilize appearance features of targets are likely to drift in crowd scenes. We propose a dynamic hierarchical tree structure which imposes spatial constraints on patches in a hierarchical manner and update structures dynamically according to the evolution of groups.

As illustrated in Fig. 5, each group of patches constitute a hierarchical structure which could model more spatial relationships and appearance features than a single tree structure. Since patches selected in Section 3.1 suggest coherent internal motions, we generate patches for the second layer using the same method but with a larger K than the first layer. Then, cross-layer constraints are added

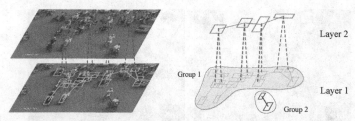

Fig. 5. Dynamic hierarchical tree structure. Patches of different color in the first layer indicates different groups which are generated dynamically. Lines connecting patches stand for spatial relationships.

straightforwardly between layer-2 patches and overlapping layer-1 ones. For each group, the structure at each layer are initialized as a minimum spanning tree with respect to spatial locations, so constraints tend to be added between neighbouring patches. When merge or split occurs, the structures will be merged or split accordingly as shown in Fig. 4. We also re-initialize structures in each group regularly to make sure that constrains are always imposed on adjacent patches.

For each group, we represent the set of patches at layer m by $P^m = \{\, p_i^m \mid p_i^m = (\mathbf{x}_i^m, w_i^m, h_i^m)\,, i = 1, \ldots N_m \}$, where $(\mathbf{x}_i^m, w_i^m, h_i^m)$ defines a bounding box for patch p_i^m with location $\mathbf{x}_i^m$, width w_i^m and height h_i^m. Edges within each layer are denoted as E^m, and E_c stand for cross-layer edges. In coming new frames, each group of patches are tracked by maximizing

$$S(\mathcal{C}; \mathbf{I}) = \sum_m \sum_{P^m} D(\mathbf{I}, p_i^m) - \sum_m \sum_{E^m} L(p_i^m, p_j^m) - \sum_{E_c} L_c(p_i^1, p_j^2), \qquad (5)$$

where $\mathcal{C}$ is the locations of all patches to be optimized given the new frame $\mathbf{I}$. The first term $D(\mathbf{I}, p_i^m)$ is a unary term that measures appearance similarity between p_i^m and the corresponding appearance model. $L(p_i^m, p_j^m)$ and $L_c(p_i^1, p_j^2)$ are pairwise terms that encode spatial constraints between patches. $L(p_i^m, p_j^m)$ stands for intra-layer constraints and $L_c(p_i^1, p_j^2)$ are inter-layer ones.

The appearance score is measured as

$$D(\mathbf{I}, p_i^m) = \mathcal{L}(\mathbf{w}_i^m \cdot f(\mathbf{I}, p_i^m)), \qquad (6)$$

where $f(\mathbf{I}, p_i^m)$ is the HOG feature vector extracted in p_i^m, $\mathbf{w}_i^m$ is the linear weights on HOG features trained for patch p_i^m using linear SVM. $\mathcal{L}$ stand for logistic function that regularize filter responses to $[0, 1]$. $\mathbf{w}_i^m$ is updated using a passive-aggressive algorithm similarly to [31].

Spatial constraint is defined as

$$L(p_i^m, p_j^m) = \lambda_{ij}^m \|(\mathbf{x}_i^m - \mathbf{x}_j^m) - \mathbf{e}_{ij}^m\|^2, \qquad (7)$$

where $\mathbf{e}_{ij}^m$ is the expected relative position between target i and j, parameter λ_{ij}^m ($\lambda_{ij}^m = 0.001$ in all of our experiments) controls the deformation cost in the final score $S(\mathcal{C}; \mathbf{I})$. Spatial constraint $\mathbf{e}_{ij}$ between patch i and j is initialized as

$\mathbf{e}_{ij} = \mathbf{x}_i - \mathbf{x}_j$, and updated by $\mathbf{e}_{ij}^{new} = 0.5(\mathbf{x}_i^{new} - \mathbf{x}_j^{new}) + 0.5\mathbf{e}_{ij}^{old}$. Inter-layer constraints $L_c(p_i^1, p_j^2)$ are formulated similarly to $L(p_i^m, p_j^m)$.

Though it is hard to perform exact inference on loopy graphs, Eq.(5) can be maximized efficiently with an iterative approach. First, the optimal configuration of patches in the first layer regardless of inter-layer constraints is found by

$$\hat{P}^1 = \max_{P^1} \sum_{P^1} D(\mathbf{I}, p_i^1) - \sum_{E^1} L(p_i^1, p_j^1), \tag{8}$$

where $\hat{P}^1 = \{\hat{p}_i^1 \mid i = 1, \dots, N_1\}$ represents the optimal solution. Since the first layer is tree-structured, exact inference can be performed in Eq.(8) via dynamic programming. Then, patches in the second layer are located by integrating $\hat{P}^1$ as known

$$\hat{P}^2 = \max_{P^2} \sum_{P^2} D(\mathbf{I}, p_i^2) - \sum_{E^2} L(p_i^2, p_j^2) - \sum_{E_c} L_c(\hat{p}_i^1, p_j^2), \tag{9}$$

where the first two terms are similar to Eq.(8), and $L_c(\hat{p}_i^1, p_j^2)$ turns into a unary term since $\hat{p}_i^1$ is fixed. So Eq.(9) can also be solved efficiently by dynamic programming. Then, $\hat{P}^1$ can be refined by adding inter-layer term $L_c(p_i^1, \hat{p}_j^2)$ with fixed $\hat{p}_j^2$ to Eq.(8) and optimize it again. After several iterations, the overall score $S(\mathcal{C}; \mathbf{I})$ will converge to a stable value, and we stop iterations at the condition that $|S_{new}(\mathcal{C}_{new}; \mathbf{I}) - S_{old}(\mathcal{C}_{old}; \mathbf{I})| < \epsilon$, where ϵ is a small constant which we set as $\epsilon = 10^{-4}$ in our work. It usually takes 2~4 iterations before convergence.

4   Experiments

We conduct two sets of experiments for evaluation and comparison. In both experiments, our tracker automatically detects mid-level patches regularly and tracks them together with the selected target (which is manually initialized, since all the other trackers in comparison require manual initialization) by adding spatial constraints. Automatically detected patches act as "assistant patches". Targets and assistant patches are tracked together as described in Section 3.2 and 3.3. Assistant patches in layer 1 are treated equally with targets, while ones in layer-2 are discarded if their appearance scores defined in Eq.(6) are lower than a threshold (0.3 in our experiments). Newly detected patches are assigned to current groups and those leaving the field of view are discarded during tracking.

The task of the first experiment is to track a single target through crowd videos. In comparison, several state-of-the-art model-free trackers are also used to track the target. We will show that tracking the crowd as a whole can effectively improve the tracking of any single target in the crowd. In the second experiment, we compare with the structure preserving multi-object tracking (SPOT) approach [31] by jointly tracking multiple targets manually initialized. SPOT also models the spatial constraints among targets during tracking. We will show the advantage of our dynamic hierarchical tree structures during multi-object tracking compared with keeping static structures unchanged in SPOT.

Fig. 6. Tracking single target together with assistant patches. Bounding boxes stand for tracked areas (yellow: the selected target; cyan: layer-1 assistant patches; red: layer-2 assistant patches) and lines connecting these boxes are spatial constraints (cyan: constraints in layer 1; red : constraints in layer 2 and cross-layer constrains).

The dataset[1] used in our experiments contains six videos of crowd scenes as shown in Fig. 7. Three of them (i.e., "Traffic", "Crowds" and "Marathon") are downloaded from the Web. The other three (i.e., "Split", "Merge", "Cross") are captured by us and they exhibit three types of group evolution. The resolutions of these videos are in the range of 480×360 to 768×568.

Due to frequent occlusions, KLT tracker is very unstable and produces highly fragmented tracklets. The average length of its tracks is 10.03 pixels on this dataset, while ours is 94.33. We did not compare with crowd tracking methods relying on priors of "repeated" motion patterns and scene structures [2, 13, 21, 23], since they need offline training to obtain priors. Our videos such as "Split", "Merge" and "Cross" do not have such motion priors since events only happen once. We only compare with model-free trackers as our tracker does not rely on priors of scene structures or repeated motion patterns. Social force models [19, 24] are not compared, since they require human detection on "all" the individuals as initialization. It is impractical in crowd tracking. See details in Sec. 2.

We set $K = 10$ and 20 for detecting patches in layer 1 and 2 respectively. 4×4 cells are used for HOG feature extraction. Other parameter settings are explained in Section 3. Experiments on all the videos share the same settings of parameters. The tracking speed depends on video resolutions and scene crowdness. With an unoptimized matlab implementation, our tracking speed is in the range of 7 fps to 14 fps on this dataset by using Intel Core 2 Duo of CPU 3.0GHz.

4.1   Experiment I: Single-Object Tracking

In this experiment, we manually annotate the tracks of 10 targets through each video (60 targets in total) to evaluate the tracking performance. Only one target is tracked in each time with manual initialization. Experiments run for 10 times on each video. Performance of trackers is evaluated by two metrics: (1) **Error**: average distance between the center of hypothesis returned by trackers and that of the ground truth; and (2) **Recall**: percentage of successfully tracked frames (in which the overlap of hypothesis and ground truth is larger than 50%).

Four state-of-the-art model-free trackers are compared: OAB [8], MIL [3], TLD [12] and CXT [7]. The first 3 trackers concentrate on modeling appearance of tracked targets while the CXT tracker explores context (supporters and distracters) from background to help tracking.

---

[1] Available from http://home.ustc.edu.cn/~zhufengx/crowdTracking/

Table 1. Error and Recall of Experiment I. Bold font indicates best performance.

	Ours		TLD [12]		MIL [3]		OAB [8]		CXT [7]	
	Error	Recall	Error	Recall	Error	Recall	Error	Recall	Error	Recall
Traffic	**3.29**	**97%**	85.85	46%	49.86	50%	46.1	67%	47.5	73%
Crowds	**4.37**	**96%**	16.52	67%	10.69	71%	9.87	76%	70.4	55%
Marathon	**5.57**	**87%**	7.35	41%	26.85	31%	15.75	53%	129.5	20%
Split	**3.93**	**91%**	23.91	57%	9.06	64%	21.48	58%	46.8	67%
Merge	**5.67**	**89%**	34.36	47%	14.98	58%	15.31	65%	94.9	40%
Cross	**4.10**	**90%**	22.33	54%	30.09	37%	37.05	50%	97.6	47%

Fig. 6 shows the selected target, assistant patches and spatial constrains in our approach. Tracking result frames shown in Fig. 7 and quantitative comparisons reported in Table 1 indicate that our tracker significantly outperforms others in comparison with large margins. It benefits from the assistance of auxiliary patches used in crowd tracking and also the fact that our approach can successfully detect and track these patches. In "Traffic" and "Crowds" videos, occlusions between objects occur frequently. OAB, MIL and TLD do not work well on such videos as they only model the appearance of targets being tracked without using the motion information from nearby objects. Therefore, these trackers tend to drift when the target is occluded. By tracking the target jointly with automatically detected mid-level patches, selected targets can be tracked well through occlusions. In the "Marathon" video, the targets for tracking are small and less distinctive as the video is captured from bird-view and humans in the scene wear similar clothes. By tracking targets jointly with spatial constraints from neighbouring individuals, targets are less likely to drift among similar objects. In "Split", "Merge" and "Cross" videos, pedestrian heads are selected for tracking. Targets in these videos have large scale variations due to perspective distortion and all heads are very similar in appearance. Our tracker has drawn promising results in such videos. Though CXT tracker has also utilized context information around the target, it can not handle frequent occlusions and too many similar objects in crowd scenes. In our experiment, CXT tracker tend to drift when occlusion happens or jump among analogous neighbours, which lead to the worst performance in all compared trackers.

4.2   Experiment II: Multi-Object Tracking

In this experiment, we compare with the SPOT tracker [31] which has also utilized spatial constraints for multi-target tracking. While in SPOT, tree structures at a single scale are initialized in the first frame and remain unchanged (though relative positions between nodes can be updated) during tracking. We also compare with the NMC [10] tracker which utilizes neighbourhood motion concurrence to predict positions of targets in Experiment II.

More targets are annotated to evaluate multi-object tracking performance, such that the manually initialized and annotated targets can cover the whole crowd. The number of annotated targets for the "Traffic", "Crowds", "Marathon",

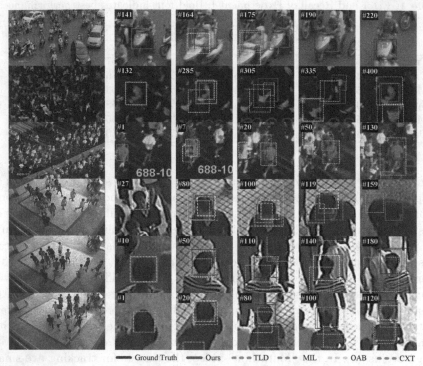

Fig. 7. Snapshots of test videos and some tracking results in Experiment I. From top to bottom: "Traffic", "Crowds", "Marathon", "Split", "Merge", "Cross".

"Split", "Merge", and "Cross" videos are 31, 18, 17, 19, 22, and 19. We also compare with ourselves by removing some functional parts of our tracker. The trackers for evaluation are summarized as (1) DHT+AP: manually selected targets and multi-scale assistant patches (AP) are jointly tracked with our dynamic hierarchical tree structure (DHT); (2) DHT: targets are tracked with only layer-2 assistant patches compared to DHT+AP; (3) TREE: single tree structure connecting all targets which are initialized in the first frame and stays unchanged during tracking (our implementation of SPOT); (4) SPOT; (5) NMC.

Results are presented in Table 2 and 3. Table 2 shows Errors and Recalls which are defined as before, and CLEAR MOT metrics [4] for multi-object tracking are reported in Table 3. In CLEAR MOT metrics, we make correspondence between object and hypothesis if their overlap is larger than 0, so for both MotP (multi-object tracking precision) and MotA (multi-object tracking accuracy), larger value indicates better performance. DHT+AP and DHT outperform other trackers in both Error/Recall and CLEAR MOT metrics. The NMC tracker predicts positions of targets using motions of neighbouring individuals without identifying different groups in crowd, which makes tracking performance drop significantly in scenes with complex motions (e.g. Traffic, Cross). TREE and SPOT are similar in algorithm, but differ in some implementation details (e.g., we perform exact

Table 2. Error and Recall of Experiment II. Bold font indicates best performance.

	DHT+AP		DHT		TREE		SPOT [31]		NMC [10]	
	Error	Recall	Error	Recall	Error	Recall	Error	Recall	Error	Recall
Traffic	**3.03**	**99%**	3.27	97%	8.93	92%	17.37	81%	35.89	74%
Crowds	8.17	**90%**	8.94	83%	19.78	71%	15.10	64%	**6.64**	81%
Marathon	4.57	88%	**4.26**	**92%**	11.44	77%	112.68	2%	5.97	70%
Split	5.02	86%	**4.50**	**86%**	24.09	59%	68.47	25%	9.77	70%
Merge	8.27	82%	8.41	**85%**	27.23	62%	48.87	57%	11.57	77%
Cross	5.82	89%	**4.61**	**89%**	48.00	51%	90.96	27%	20.62	69%

Table 3. CLEAR MOT metrics of Experiment II. Bold font indicates best performance.

	DHT+AP		DHT		TREE		SPOT [31]		NMC [10]	
	MotP	MotA	MotP	MotA	MotP	MotA	MotP	MotA	MotP	MotA
Traffic	0.81	**99%**	**0.82**	98%	0.81	84%	0.68	52%	0.72	59%
Crowds	**0.72**	90%	0.70	87%	0.68	72%	0.61	77%	0.66	**99%**
Marathon	0.70	91%	**0.72**	91%	0.69	72%	0.22	-74%	0.62	**94%**
Split	**0.68**	86%	**0.68**	**92%**	0.60	49%	0.45	-6%	0.65	65%
Merge	0.68	84%	**0.71**	81%	0.64	50%	0.62	44%	0.69	69%
Cross	**0.72**	90%	0.71	**93%**	0.63	18%	0.49	-10%	0.65	74%

inference on tree structures instead of transforming them into star-structured ones first as in the released code of SPOT). Although performance is improved by better implementation compared to SPOT, static structures used in TREE still do not work well in crowd scenes. Spatial constraints could indeed help track targets which have stable relative positions in crowd, but they may bias tracking if constraints are imposed between targets moving in different directions. Comparisons between DHT and TREE show that our dynamic structure is more suitable for tracking in crowd scenes than the static structure. There seems to be no significant difference in performance between DHT+AP and DHT because we have manually selected sufficient targets for tracking, so finding more mid-level patches does not help more. In "Split", "Merge" and "Cross" videos, group motions change drastically, so that a "good" spatial constraint may turn into a "bad" one as the group evolves. Our approach can identify these changes, and adjust group structures through merge and split (Fig. 8(a)). The proposed DHT tracker even outperforms TREE in videos with stable group structures, e.g. the "Marathon" sequence shown in Fig. 8(b). Layer-2 patches and hierarchical tree structure used in DHT model more appearance features and spatial constrains than the single tree structure, which can help prevent targets from drifting (in Fig. 8(b), target 15 in the second column, target 17 in the third column, target 10 and 15 in the fourth column).

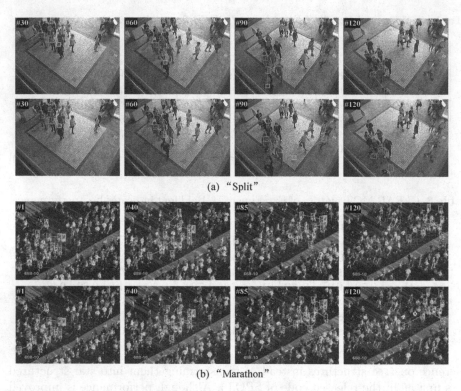

(a) "Split"

(b) "Marathon"

Fig. 8. Some tracking results in Experiment II. Red dots: centers of ground truth; cyan boxes: manually selected targets for tracking; dashed red boxes: automatically detected layer-2 patches in DHT tracker. Row 1 and 3: tracking results of DHT tracker (layer-2 patches are hidden in row 1 for better visualization); Row 2 and 4: tracking results of TREE tracker. (a): dynamic structure outperforms static structure in crowd scenes; (b): hierarchical structure could help prevent targets from drifting.

5   Conclusions

We have proposed to detect distinctive and stable patches, and jointly track them using dynamic hierarchical tree structures in order to capture crowd motions. We integrate low-level keypoint tracking, mid-level patch tracking and high-level group evolution into one united framework, in which keypoint tracking provide accurate motion information in short periods, patch tracking is more robust to partial occlusion or appearance changes, and group evolution guide the update of group structures. Experimental results show that our tracker can track targets more accurately than traditional trackers in crowd videos. The proposed dynamic hierarchical tree structure outperforms static single-tree structure.

Acknowledgement. This work is supported by the National Science Foundation of China (No.61371192, No.61103134), the General Research Fund sponsored by the Research Grants Council of Hong Kong (Project Nos. 417110, 417011, 419412), and Shenzhen Basic Research Program (JCYJ20130402113127496).

References

1. Ali, I., Dailey, M.N.: Multiple human tracking in high-density crowds. Image and Vision Computing 30(12), 966–977 (2012)
2. Ali, S., Shah, M.: Floor fields for tracking in high density crowd scenes. In: Forsyth, D., Torr, P., Zisserman, A. (eds.) ECCV 2008, Part II. LNCS, vol. 5303, pp. 1–14. Springer, Heidelberg (2008)
3. Babenko, B., Yang, M.H., Belongie, S.: Robust object tracking with online multiple instance learning. PAMI 33(8), 1619–1632 (2011)
4. Bernardin, K., Stiefelhagen, R.: Evaluating multiple object tracking performance: the clear mot metrics. EURASIP Journal on Image and Video Processing 2008 (2008)
5. Blei, D.M., Lafferty, J.D.: A correlated topic model of science. Annals of Applied Statistics 1(1), 17–35 (2007)
6. Brostow, G.J., Cipolla, R.: Unsupervised Bayesian detection of independent motion in crowds. In: CVPR (2006)
7. Dinh, T.B., Vo, N., Medioni, G.: Context tracker: Exploring supporters and distracters in unconstrained environments. In: CVPR (2011)
8. Grabner, H., Grabner, M., Bischof, H.: Real-time tracking via on-line boosting. In: BMVC (2006)
9. Helbing, D., Molnar, P.: Social force model for pedestrian dynamics. Physics Review 51(5), 4282–4286 (1995)
10. Idrees, H., Warner, N., Shah, M.: Tracking in dense crowds using prominence and neighborhood motion concurrence. Image and Vision Computing 32(1), 14–26 (2014)
11. Jing, S., Loy, C.C., Wang, X.: Scene-independent group profiling in crowd. In: CVPR (2014)
12. Kalal, Z., Mikolajczyk, K., Matas, J.: Tracking-learning-detection. PAMI 34(7), 1409–1422 (2012)
13. Kratz, L., Nishino, K.: Tracking pedestrians using local spatio-temporal motion patterns in extremely crowded scenes. PAMI 34(5), 987–1002 (2012)
14. Le Bon, G.: The crowd: A study of the popular mind. The Macmillan Co. New York (1897)
15. Mahadevan, V., Li, W., Bhalodia, V., Vasconcelos, N.: Anomaly detection in crowded scenes. In: CVPR (2010)
16. Moussaid, M., Garnier, S., Theraulaz, G., Helbing, D.: Collective information processing and pattern formation in swarms, flocks, and crowds. Topics in Cognitive Science 1(3), 469–497 (2009)
17. Newman, M.E.: Finding community structure in networks using the eigenvectors of matrices. Physical Review E 74(3), 036104 (2006)
18. Ouyang, W., Wang, X.: Single-pedestrian detection aided by multi-pedestrian detection. In: CVPR (2013)
19. Pellegrini, S., Ess, A., Schindler, K., van Gool, L.: You'll never walk alone: Modeling social behavior for multi-target tracking. In: ICCV (2009)

20. Rabaud, V., Belongie, S.: Counting crowded moving objects. In: CVPR (2006)
21. Rodriguez, M., Ali, S., Kanade, T.: Tracking in unstructured crowded scenes. In: ICCV (2009)
22. Rodriguez, M., Laptev, I., Sivic, J., Audibert, J.Y.: Density-aware person detection and tracking in crowds. In: ICCV (2011)
23. Rodriguez, M., Sivic, J., Laptev, I., Audibert, J.Y.: Data-driven crowd analysis in videos. In: ICCV (2011)
24. Scovanner, P., Tappen, M.F.: Learning pedestrian dynamics from the real world. In: ICCV (2009)
25. Shi, J., Tomasi, C.: Good features to track. In: CVPR (1994)
26. Shu, G., Dehghan, A., Oreifej, O., Hand, E., Shah, M.: Part-based multiple-person tracking with partial occlusion handling. In: CVPR (2012)
27. Sugimura, D., Kitani, K.M., Okabe, T., Sato, Y., Sugimoto, A.: Using individuality to track individuals: clustering individual trajectories in crowds using local appearance and frequency trait. In: CVPR (2009)
28. Tomasi, C., Kanade, T.: Detection and tracking of point features, Technical report, CMU-CS-91-132 (1991)
29. Wang, X., Ma, X., Grimson, E.: Unsupervised activity perception in crowded and complicated scenes using hierarchical bayesian models. PAMI 31(3), 539–555 (2009)
30. Yao, R., Shi, Q., Shen, C., Zhang, Y., van den Hengel, A.: Part-based visual tracking with online latent structural learning. In: CVPR (2013)
31. Zhang, L., van der Maaten, L.: Structure preserving object tracking. In: CVPR (2013)
32. Zhang, W., Wang, X., Zhao, D., Tang, X.: Graph degree linkage: Agglomerative clustering on a directed graph. In: Fitzgibbon, A., Lazebnik, S., Perona, P., Sato, Y., Schmid, C. (eds.) ECCV 2012, Part I. LNCS, vol. 7572, pp. 428–441. Springer, Heidelberg (2012)
33. Zhou, B., Tang, X., Wang, X.: Measuring crowd collectiveness. In: CVPR (2013)
34. Zhou, B., Tang, X., Wang, X.: Coherent filtering: Detecting coherent motions from crowd clutters. In: Fitzgibbon, A., Lazebnik, S., Perona, P., Sato, Y., Schmid, C. (eds.) ECCV 2012, Part II. LNCS, vol. 7573, pp. 857–871. Springer, Heidelberg (2012)
35. Zhou, B., Tang, X., Wang, X.: Understanding collective crowd behaviors: Learning a mixture model of dynamic pedestrian-agents. In: CVPR (2012)
36. Zhou, B., Wang, X., Tang, X.: Random field topic model for semantic region analysis in crowded scenes from tracklets. In: CVPR (2011)

Tracking Using Multilevel Quantizations

Zhibin Hong[1], Chaohui Wang[2], Xue Mei[3],
Danil Prokhorov[3], and Dacheng Tao[1]

[1] Centre for Quantum Computation and Intelligent Systems,
Faculty of Engineering and Information Technology,
University of Technology, Sydney, NSW, Australia
[2] Max Planck Institute for Intelligent Systems, Tübingen, Germany
[3] Toyota Research Institute, North America, Ann Arbor, MI, USA

Abstract. Most object tracking methods only exploit a single quantization of an image space: pixels, superpixels, or bounding boxes, each of which has advantages and disadvantages. It is highly unlikely that a common optimal quantization level, suitable for tracking all objects in all environments, exists. We therefore propose a hierarchical appearance representation model for tracking, based on a graphical model that exploits shared information across multiple quantization levels. The tracker aims to find the most possible position of the target by jointly classifying the pixels and superpixels and obtaining the best configuration across all levels. The motion of the bounding box is taken into consideration, while Online Random Forests are used to provide pixel- and superpixel-level quantizations and progressively updated on-the-fly. By appropriately considering the multilevel quantizations, our tracker exhibits not only excellent performance in non-rigid object deformation handling, but also its robustness to occlusions. A quantitative evaluation is conducted on two benchmark datasets: a non-rigid object tracking dataset (11 sequences) and the CVPR2013 tracking benchmark (50 sequences). Experimental results show that our tracker overcomes various tracking challenges and is superior to a number of other popular tracking methods.

Keywords: Tracking, Multilevel Quantizations, Online Random Forests, Non-rigid Object Tracking, Conditional Random Fields.

1 Introduction

Online object tracking is a classic topic in computer vision and is used in many practical applications, such as video surveillance and autonomous driving. Given the position of the target in one frame, a tracker should be able to track the target in subsequent frames and be able to overcome various challenges, such as appearance variations, occlusions and illumination changes. Building an effective tracker is therefore extremely difficult, especially without prior knowledge of the appearance of the object to be tracked. However, a number of trackers have been proposed and show promising results [39,54,55].

D. Fleet et al. (Eds.): ECCV 2014, Part VI, LNCS 8694, pp. 155–171, 2014.

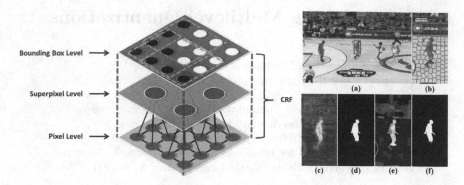

Fig. 1. Illustration of the structure of the proposed hierarchical appearance representation model (left) and a practical example (right). In the proposed framework, a node in the Conditional Random Field (CRF) models each pixel, superpixel, and bounding box. At the pixel level, each pixel receives a measurement from a Random Forest and connects to the corresponding superpixel at the middle level. At the superpixel level, each superpixel also obtains a probability output by another Random Forest and suggests the pixels within the same superpixel to share the same label. At the bounding box level, different candidate bounding boxes (green) are considered, and the best position (red) with the best configuration is found. (a) shows the tracking result (in red bounding box) at Frame #226 in the *Basketball* sequence. (b) displays the superpixelization of the image. (c) and (d) are the output of the pixel-level RF and final labeling result, respectively, while (e) and (f) are the output of the superpixel-level RF and final labeling result.

Many tracking methods operate by making a single quantization choice in an image space, i.e., using pixels [14], superpixels [52], or bounding boxes [46], each of which has its pros and cons. For example, a tracker built on pixel-level quantization may be able to capture and thus better handle non-rigid deformation, but performs relatively poorly in scenarios where there is excessive background clutter due to the lack of holistic appearance of the target. In contrast, trackers that utilize higher-level quantization, such as bounding box-based matching, are robust to occlusions but tend to fail when the target undergoes non-rigid deformation. Therefore, a single optimal quantization level suitable for all objects in all environments is unlikely to exist.

Motivated by the above observation, in this paper, we propose a novel hierarchical appearance representation formulation of object tracking based on Conditional Random Fields (CRFs), which unifies multiple disparate quantizations of the image space. Based on the information derived from different quantization levels (pixel, superpixel, bounding box), we integrate them into a principled framework to optimize the decision-making. At the lowest level, an Online Random Forest (ORF) [48] equipped with color-texture features is employed to provide a soft label of each pixel, which indicates the probability that the pixel belongs to the target. At the middle level, superpixels are generated by considering various cues such as the spatial relationship and feature similarity between pixels, which suggests a consistent pixel labeling within each superpixel. Besides, another ORF based on normalized histogram features of superpixels is also trained on the mid-level quantization. At the highest level, a bounding box-level regularization term is introduced, which enables to flexibly incorporate other information of a given bounding box, such as shape and motion, or even the measurement given by other trackers. The model bridges the hierarchical appearance representations by fusing multilevel quantization information and efficiently solves the optimization with the use of dynamic graph cuts [27]. However, the contribution of this paper is not limited to the application of the novel hierarchical appearance representation framework to object tracking. We also address appearance variations by exploiting color-texture features and powerful, yet efficient, ORFs. These ORFs are strategically updated in the framework to capture appearance changes due to deformation or illumination over time. The proposed method is illustrated in Fig. 1.

2   Related Work

There has been recent progress in visual object tracking research, with several ideas that focus on various challenges being proposed; these are extensively discussed in elsewhere [39,55]. In addition, standard benchmark datasets and quantitative evaluation metrics have been developed [15,54] to facilitate research in this area.

Some existing approaches use the pixel level of the image space to explore low-level cues for tracking. For instance, Avidan [4] proposed an ensemble tracker to track the object based on the result of the pixel-level classification. Although the discriminative setting enables the tracker to distinguish foreground from background, the pixel-based representation still limits robustness to a cluttered background and heavy occlusion [52]. More recently, Duffner and Garcia proposed the PixelTrack [14], which also addresses tracking at the pixel-level. The tracker works by combining a Hough voting-based detector with a soft segmentation approach similar to [3]. Although an efficient implementation is achieved, the tracker appears to be sensitive to the initialization and is prone to fail in grayscale sequences due to the dependence on the segmentation performance and the lack of global information.

Compared to pixel-level representations, mid-level visual cues provide more information about the local structure of images, while retaining the flexibility to model non-rigid deformation [2,11,28,52]. In particular, Adam *et al.* [2] employed an appearance model and used local patches to handle partial occlusion. Superpixel tracking [52] aims to explore the mid-level cues and use the superpixel as the object representation. The normalized color histogram of each superpixel is extracted, and a confidence map is obtained by the superpixel-level, rather than pixel-level, classification [4]. In [11], the target is represented by a set of different regions. The regions are modeled by a Gaussian mixture model in a joint feature-spatial space, and the motion of the target is modeled by the level set evolution.

Many trackers are built to exploit high-level visual information using holistic appearance models [5,19,41,46]. In [46], Ross *et al.* presented a tracking method that incrementally learns a low-dimensional subspace representation of the target. The L1 tracker, proposed by Mei *et al.* [41], and its variations [21,38,42,56] appear to be robust to the illumination changes and occlusions but sensitive to non-rigid deformation. Babenko *et al.* [5] employ Multiple Instance Learning (MIL) to overcome the label ambiguity problem, in which the training samples are collected as bag of image patches. Random Forests (RFs) [9] have become increasingly popular in computer vision due to their attractive properties, and have been used in tracking [25,48,49]. Specifically, Saffari *et. al* [48] proposed an online version of RFs, which grows extremely randomized trees online, rather than offline. The Online RFs (ORFs) are then adopted for tracking by utilizing the features captured at the bounding box level, and this method has demonstrated better performance over the online boosting [16].

Multilevel data fusing has been exploited for image segmentation and labeling using Conditional Random Fields (CRFs) or Markov Random Fields (MRFs) [18,22,31,50,53]. In [31], a single optimization framework is presented in which a hierarchical random field model allows integration of features computed at different levels of the quantization hierarchy. In [18], labeling information from local image statistics, regional label features, and global label features are combined in order to label images with a predefined set of class labels. In [22], a hierarchical two-stage CRF model is used to combine parametric and nonparametric image labeling methods. In [32,53], integration of object detection and pixel-wise scene labeling boosts the performance of both tasks, since they are mutually beneficial. Also, previous works have addressed tracking problems by combining multilevel information [26,51,57]. For example, in [57], a collaborative model is proposed to combine a Sparsity-based Discriminative Classifier (SDC) with Sparsity based Generative Model (SGM), which collaboratively considers holistic object templates and local image patches for target representations. Motivated by these advances, here we propose the Multilevel Quantization Tracker (MQT), which explores the quantization hierarchy from coarse to fine and unifies the information derived from multiple quantization levels in a coherent CRF framework. In this way, each quantization level benefits from other levels and, as a consequence, the overall performance of each individual level is enhanced.

3   Tracking with Multilevel Quantizations

The proposed tracker combines multilevel quantizations as a single graphical model to produce an efficient and robust solution to online object tracking. We first introduce the general multilevel quantization model and then describe other important components of the tracker, including feature extraction, online color-texture forests, ORF training, and occlusion handling.

3.1   Multilevel Quantizations Model

The whole model is built on multiple quantizations from three hierarchical appearance representation levels, namely pixels, superpixels and bounding boxes. We first extract information at each level before fusing them using a graphical model so as to perform inference.

Pixel is the finest quantization level in an image, and is the most obvious choice for quantization. Let each pixel $i \in \mathcal{P}$ ($\mathcal{P}$ denotes the set of pixels) be represented as a d-dimensional feature vector $\mathbf{f}_i \in \mathbb{R}^d$ that consists of some local information, and associated with a unique binary label $x_i \in \{0$ (background), 1 (foreground/object)$\}$. The pixel-level unary energy function is defined as:

$$\phi_i^{\mathrm{p}}(x_i) = -\log p(x_i; \mathbf{H}^{\mathrm{P}}), \tag{1}$$

where $p(x_i; \mathbf{H}^{\mathrm{P}})$ denotes the probability that pixel i is labeled as class x_i, output by an ORF with parameters $\mathbf{H}^{\mathrm{P}}$, which are updated online (Section 3.3). An example of $p(x_i; \mathbf{H}^{\mathrm{P}})$ output by an ORF is shown in Fig. 1(c).

Superpixels provide very useful mid-level support for image understanding tasks (e.g., [1,37]). In order to exploit mid-level information, we employ the SLIC (Simple Linear Iterative Clustering) algorithm [1] to cluster the pixels and generate superpixels as shown in Fig. 1(b). For each superpixel $k \in \mathcal{S}$ ($\mathcal{S}$ denotes the set of superpixels), we also assign a binary label $y_k \in \{0, 1\}$, which is similar to x_i at pixel level. Again, an ORF is trained to output the probability that the superpixel belongs to the foreground or background, using the features extracted from each superpixel (Fig. 1(e)). Similarly, superpixel-level energy function is defined as:

$$\phi_k^{\mathrm{s}}(y_k) = -\log p(y_k; \mathbf{H}^{\mathrm{s}}), \tag{2}$$

where the symbols are analogous to those in (1).

At the highest level, like many existing online trackers [46,17], we use a bounding box to delimit the object of interest. Let $\mathbf{B}(z)$ denote the bounding box with pose parameters z and energy function $\varphi(\mathbf{B}(z))$ encode the occurrence likelihood of the target in bounding box $\mathbf{B}(z)$. In contrast to other online trackers (e.g., [19,41,46]) which optimize merely $\varphi(\mathbf{B}(z))$ to get the tracking solution, we unify $\varphi(\mathbf{B}(z))$ with information from the other quantization levels, as explained above. The choice of $\varphi(\mathbf{B}(z))$ is modular and it can vary from simple matching techniques [10] to sophisticated classification models [17].

In our experiments, we use the Median Flow Tracker (MFT) [24] for the bounding box level quantization. MFT uses the feature matching to estimate the motion of target. Moreover, it measures the discrepancies of the forward and backward tracking in consecutive frames and reports failure when the target is lost [25]. We assign 0 to the tracking result z^M if failure is detected. The bounding box energy function $\varphi(\mathbf{B}(z))$ is defined as:

$$\varphi(\mathbf{B}(z)) = \begin{cases} 0 & , z^M = 0 \\ D^2(\mathbf{B}(z), \mathbf{B}(z^M)), & \text{otherwise} \end{cases} \tag{3}$$

where $D(\mathbf{B}(z), \mathbf{B}(z^M))$ is the distance between the centers of two bounding boxes $\mathbf{B}(z)$ and $\mathbf{B}(z^M)$ (the results of MFT) in the image.

Given the above three levels, we adopt a Conditional Random Field (CRF) model to fuse the information from different levels. Each unit (pixel, superpixel, bounding box) at different levels is represented by a node in the graph, and use corresponding unary potential functions to encode those terms in (1), (2), and (3). Then we capture the interactions between these nodes via connecting them using CRF's edges with appropriate potential functions.

Firstly, we associate an edge between a pair of neighboring pixel nodes (4-neighborhood system is considered in the experiment) and the following potential function to encode the interaction between the labeling of the pixels:

$$\psi_{i,j}(x_i, x_j) = \begin{cases} \exp(-\frac{\|\mathbf{f}_i - \mathbf{f}_j\|^2}{\sigma^2}), & \text{if } x_i \neq x_j \\ 0 & \text{, otherwise} \end{cases} \tag{4}$$

where $\|\mathbf{f}_i - \mathbf{f}_j\|$ is the distance between x_i and x_j in the feature space, and σ is a parameter controlling the shape of the monotonically decreasing function, which is similar to [7]. We use $\mathcal{E}^{\mathrm{PP}}$ to denote all such edges between neighboring pixels.

One important fact regarding the pixel- and superpixel-level quantizations is that the pixels in the same superpixel tend to share the same superpixel label. Hence, for each pixel i in superpixel k, we associate an edge using the Potts model as its potential function:

$$\xi_{i,k}(x_i, y_k) = \begin{cases} 1, & \text{if } x_i \neq y_k \\ 0, & \text{otherwise} \end{cases} \tag{5}$$

which penalizes the inconsistency in labeling between superpixels and pixels. We use $\mathcal{E}^{\mathrm{sp}}$ to denote all such edges.

We also connect all pixel nodes with the bounding box node. The pairwise potential function $w_i(z, x_i)$ is used to encourage consistency between pixel labeling and the pose of the bounding box:

$$w_i(z, x_i) = \begin{cases} d(z, i), & \text{if } (x_i = 1, i \in \mathcal{P}_{\mathbf{B}(z)}^{\mathrm{Out}}) \text{ or } (x_i = 0, i \in \mathcal{P}_{\mathbf{B}(z)}^{\mathrm{In}}) \\ 0 & \text{, otherwise} \end{cases} \tag{6}$$

where $d(z, i)$ represents the minimum normalized distance (which considers the size of bounding box and is detailed in Section 4.1) between the pixel i to the boundary of the bounding box $\mathbf{B}(z)$; $\mathcal{P}_{\mathbf{B}(z)}^{\mathrm{in}}$ and $\mathcal{P}_{\mathbf{B}(z)}^{\mathrm{Out}}$ denote the set of pixels inside and outside the bounding boxes, respectively. The choice of function is based on the observation that the pixels inside the bounding box tend to belong to the object, while the pixels outside the bounding box tend to belong to the background. Moreover, the closer the pixel is to the boundary, the more ambiguous the pixel label is. The pixel is penalized for having different label from what is expected, using a cost that is proportional to the distance between the pixel and the boundary of the bounding box, which is similar to the idea in [51].

Finally, given an image I, the joint probability of the realization $(z, \mathbf{x}, \mathbf{y}) = (z, \mathbf{x} = (x_i)_{i \in \mathcal{P}}, \mathbf{y} = (y_k)_{k \in \mathcal{S}})$ of all random variables in the CRF model is formulated as a Gibbs distribution $P(z, \mathbf{x}, \mathbf{y}|I) = e^{-E(z,\mathbf{x},\mathbf{y})}$. The corresponding

Gibbs energy $E(z, \mathbf{x}, \mathbf{y})$ is defined as the sum of the above unary potentials and pairwise potentials:

$$
\begin{aligned}
E(z, \mathbf{x}, \mathbf{y}) = & \mu\varphi(\mathbf{B}(z)) + \sum_{i \in \mathcal{P}} \phi_i^{\mathrm{p}}(x_i) + \alpha \sum_{k \in \mathcal{S}} \phi_k^{\mathrm{s}}(y_k) + \lambda \sum_{i \in \mathcal{P}} \omega_i(x_i, z) \\
& + \beta \sum_{\{i,k\} \in \mathcal{E}^{\mathrm{sp}}} \xi_{i,k}(x_i, y_k) + \gamma \sum_{\{i,j\} \in \mathcal{E}^{\mathrm{pp}}} \psi_{i,j}(x_i, x_j),
\end{aligned}
\tag{7}
$$

where μ, α, λ, β, γ are the weight coefficients which balance the importance of each potential term.

In the tracking problem, we aim to determine the optimal pose parameters z for the bounding box. Since the minimization of $E(z, \mathbf{x}, \mathbf{y})$ with respect to $\mathbf{x}$ and $\mathbf{y}$ can be efficiently solved using the well-known graph cuts [8] for each possible z, we define an auxiliary function $\hat{E}(z)$ and search for the optimal z^* for $\hat{E}(z)$ using any off-the-shelf optimization algorithm:

$$
z^* = \operatorname*{argmin}_z \{\hat{E}(z) = \min_{\mathbf{x} \in \{0,1\}^{|\mathcal{P}|}, \mathbf{y} \in \{0,1\}^{|\mathcal{S}|}} E(z, \mathbf{x}, \mathbf{y})\}.
\tag{8}
$$

For example, one can use the local dense sampling search as done in [5,17]. In this paper, we simply adopt the Nelder-Mead Simplex Method [33] to directly search for the solution. Note that during the search of z in the problem (8), the update of z only causes small change[1] in ω_i, which motivates the use of dynamic MRF algorithms [26] (e.g., dynamic graph cuts [27]) to efficiently obtain the value of $\hat{E}(z)$ and significantly accelerate the optimization.

3.2   Online Color-Texture Forests

The selection of features and an appropriate online learning process has been shown to be very important for tracker performance [4,20,46,48]. In this section, we elaborate online color-texture forests, which are used to obtain pixel- and superpixel-level potentials in (1) and (2).

The color feature is one of the most widely used visual features in tracking. The most important advantages of color feature are power of representing visual content of images, simplicity in extracting color information of images and high efficiency, independent of image size and orientation. However, only using color feature is difficult to tackle many real-world tracking scenarios, such as distractive background clutter and drastic illumination change. We combine texture with color as a complementary feature for tracking to better represent object appearance. For each pixel, we extract RGB (3-dim), CIELAB (3-dim) and texture features (48-dim) as the pixel-level representation with 54 dimensions. The texture feature is generated by the Leung-Malik (LM) Filter Bank [36], which consists of the first and second derivatives of Gaussians at 6 orientations and 3 scales, 8 Laplacian of Gaussian (LOG) filters, and 4 Gaussian filters. With respect to the superpixel level, we utilize normalized histogram-based features to

---

[1] $\mu\varphi(\mathbf{B}(z))$ would change but would not affect the optimum of $E(z, \mathbf{x}, \mathbf{y})$ with respect to $\mathbf{x}$ and $\mathbf{y}$.

capture the photometric properties of each superpixel, similar to [52].We extract a 64-bin normalized histogram in the HSV color space and a 10-bin normalized histogram based on uniform rotation-invariant local binary patterns (LBPs) [43], to form a 74 dimensional color-texture feature for each superpixel.

Random forests consist of a set of randomized decision trees. In each decision tree, an internal node corresponds to a random test on an input feature, which determines to which child node the feature should go. Therefore, a feature vector is presented to the root of a tree and it follows a specific path to a leaf node, which stores a histogram (occurrence frequency of each class) obtained during the training phase. Given a test sample $\mathbf{f}$, the probability is estimated by averaging the probabilities of all the trees:

$$p(\text{class} = c|\mathbf{f}) = \frac{1}{N} \sum_{n=1}^{N} p_n(\text{class} = c|\mathbf{f}),$$

where N denotes the number of the trees, and $p_n(\text{class} = c|\mathbf{f})$ is the probability that the feature belongs to class c output by the tree n.

RFs have demonstrated great promise in various computer vision tasks including object recognition [35] and image classification [6]. We adopt the Online Random Forests [48] to incorporate the high-dimensional color-texture feature for our online tracking. The resulting online color-texture forest turns out to provide very discriminative classification results for our potential functions.

3.3   ORF Training and Occlusion Handling

To train the two RFs for pixels and superpixels, a key issue is how to get positive and negative samples for training. In the first frame, given the target bounding box, Grabcut [47] is adopted to automatically determine the pixels corresponding to the object which are then used as positive examples for training the RF for pixels. This generally improves the accuracy compared to treating all pixel inside the bounding box as foreground, since the object may not occupy the whole bounding box due to its shape. To deal with cases that object is not well segmented by Grabcut, we check the percentage of pixels with foreground labels in the bounding box. If it is greater than 70%, the result of Grabcut is accepted, otherwise it is rejected and all the pixels inside the bounding box are used as the positive samples. On the other hand, all the pixels outside the bounding box are used as negative samples. For superpixels, they are labeled using a voting scheme, i.e., the label of the superpixel is decided by the majority of the pixels inside it.

During the tracking, the ORFs are progressively updated to handle the appearance changes. Since pixels and superpixels are labeled in the whole formulation by jointly exploiting the information from multiple levels during the tracking, we only treat the pixels and superpixels as candidate positive samples if they are inside the target bounding box $\mathbf{B}(z^*)$ and labeled as positive by our tracker using (8). The pixels and superpixels outside the bounding box are treated as candidate negative samples. Moreover, only the candidate samples

---

Algorithm 1. Tracking with Multilevel Quantizations

Input: The target bounding box $\mathbf{B}(z_1^*)$ in the first frame; T frames to track.
Output: Estimated target position $\mathbf{B}(z_t^*)$, where $t = 2, 3..., T$ is the frame index.
 1: /*Initialization*/
 2: Apply Grabcut[47] to find the positive and negative samples.
 3: Train pixel- and superpixel-level RFs using the collected samples.
 4: /*Start to track*/
 5: **for** $t = 2$ to T **do**
 6:     /*Pixel level*/
 7:     Extract features for each pixel i and obtain the pixel-level measurement $p(x_i; \mathbf{H}^P)$.
 8:     /*Superpixel level*/
 9:     Apply SLIC [1] to generate superpixels.
10:     Extract features for each superpixel k and obtain the superpixel-level measurement $p(y_k; \mathbf{H}^s)$.
11:     /*Bounding box level and combine multilevel quantizations*/
12:     Estimate the motion of target using MFT [24] and obtain $\mathbf{B}(z_t^M)$.
13:     Find the target $\mathbf{B}(z_t^*)$ by solving (8) using [33] with dynamic graph cuts [27].
14:     **if** *not occluded* **then**
15:         Update $\mathbf{H}^P$ of the pixel-level RF using $\mathcal{X}_p^+$, $\mathcal{X}_p^-$.
16:         Update $\mathbf{H}^s$ of the superpixel-level RF using $\mathcal{X}_{sp}^+$, $\mathcal{X}_{sp}^-$.
17:     **end if**
18: **end for**

---

that are not classified with a high confidence or incorrectly classified by their respective RFs are assigned to RFs for updates. A similar strategy is employed in [25]. More specifically, the final positive sample set $\mathcal{X}_p^+$ and negative sample set $\mathcal{X}_p^-$ for the pixel-level RF update are respectively determined as:

$$\mathcal{X}_p^+ = \{i | x_i = 1, p(x_i = 1; \mathbf{H}^P) < \varepsilon_p^+, i \in \mathcal{P}_{\mathbf{B}(z^*)}^{In}\}, \tag{9}$$

$$\mathcal{X}_p^- = \{i | p(x_i = 1; \mathbf{H}^P) > \varepsilon_p^-, i \in \mathcal{P}_{\mathbf{B}(z^*)}^{Out}\}, \tag{10}$$

where ε_p^+, ε_p^- (and ε_{sp}^+, ε_{sp}^- below) are the predefined thresholds. For the superpixel-level RF, the positive sample set $\mathcal{X}_{sp}^+$ and negative sample set $\mathcal{X}_{sp}^-$ are similarly determined as

$$\mathcal{X}_{sp}^+ = \{k | y_k = 1, p(y_k = 1; \mathbf{H}^s) < \varepsilon_{sp}^+, k \in \mathcal{S}_{\mathbf{B}(z^*)}^{In}\}, \tag{11}$$

$$\mathcal{X}_{sp}^- = \{k | p(y_k = 1; \mathbf{H}^s) > \varepsilon_{sp}^-, k \in \mathcal{S}_{\mathbf{B}(z^*)}^{Out}\}, \tag{12}$$

where $\mathcal{S}_{\mathbf{B}(z^*)}^{in}$ and $\mathcal{S}_{\mathbf{B}(z^*)}^{Out}$ denote the set of superpixels inside and outside the bounding box $\mathbf{B}(z^*)$, respectively. Noted that in (11) and (12), the voting scheme previously presented is still used to determine whether a superpixel is inside or outside the bounding box.

Fig. 2. Occlusion handling on the *Jogging* sequence. The index is specified in the top-left of each frame, and the two figures between each frame are the corresponding outputs of the pixel-level RFs and labels x_i, respectively. The occlusion is detected from the Frame #049, from which point the RFs stop updating until the target moves out of occlusion.

As discussed in previous works [4,52], it is also important to take occlusions into account during updates, especially when the target is temporarily out-of-view. The pixel labeling provided by our approach also can be used to handle occlusions: a flag of occlusion is trigged if the percentage of foreground pixels inside the found bounding box is less than a predefined threshold θ (0.3). In this case, the RFs are kept unchanged without update. An example of the occlusion handling is shown in Fig. 2. Finally, a systematic view of the whole algorithm is summarized in Algorithm 1.

4   Experiments

In this section, we first present implementation details about important aspects of MQT, including the parameter setting for evaluation. We then present a set of qualitative experimental results as well as quantitative comparison with several state-of-the-art trackers on two benchmarks.

4.1   Implementation Details

Similar to [4,52], the optimal tracking result at each frame is achieved by searching in a region centered around the target bounding box determined from the previous frame, as illustrated in Fig. 1(b). As in [5,17,19], we use a bounding box with a fixed size during the tracking in the current implementation. In order to track objects with different resolutions using the same parameters, we resize the image and let the short side of the target bounding box in the first frame to have a length of 35 pixels. After tracking, the results of MQT are projected back to the original image for fair comparison. To obtain meaningful superpixels of appropriate size, the regularized size of SLIC [1] is set to 17. Regarding the parameters of the proposed model in (7), we set $\sigma = 0.1$, $\alpha = 5$, $\beta = 0.3$, $\lambda = 2$, $\gamma = 0.1$, and $\mu = \frac{w \times h}{100^2}$, where w and h are the width and the height of the target bounding box, respectively. The minimum normalized distance $d(z, i)$ in (6) is computed by measuring minimum distance between the pixel i and the boundary of bounding box $\mathbf{B}(z)$ in a resized coordinate system, in which the size of target bounding box becomes $w' = h' = 1$. The number of trees T is set to 15 for

Table 1. Non-rigid object tracking: percentage of correctly tracked frames

	HT [15]	TLD [25]	PixelTrack [14]	SPT[52]	MQT	P	S	B	P&S	P&B	S&B
Cliff-dive 1	100.00	69.12	100.00	100.00	100.00	100.00	97.06	100.00	100.00	100.00	100.00
Motocross 1	100.00	15.38	57.69	29.49	43.59	30.13	30.13	40.38	44.87	66.67	35.26
Skiing	100.00	6.85	100.00	17.28	100.00	100.00	7.41	9.88	98.77	98.77	9.88
Mountain-bike	100.00	81.36	94.55	100.00	100.00	100.00	4.39	39.04	100.00	100.00	18.86
Cliff-dive 2	100.00	8.20	32.79	100.00	100.00	100.00	78.69	50.82	100.00	100.00	62.30
Volleyball	45.12	42.28	100.00	46.55	100.00	100.00	28.46	25.00	60.16	100.00	28.66
Motocross 2	100.00	100.00	100.00	100.00	100.00	100.00	100.00	100.00	100.00	100.00	100.00
Transformer	38.71	33.06	94.35	100.00	100.00	100.00	100.00	100.00	100.00	100.00	100.00
Diving	21.21	24.68	88.74	41.56	**97.84**	13.42	35.06	24.24	96.54	13.85	55.84
High Jump	77.87	35.25	94.26	19.67	**98.36**	84.43	8.20	8.20	90.16	91.80	41.80
Gymnastics	98.87	84.75	99.09	21.90	100.00	96.87	95.57	29.47	98.17	97.13	59.06
Average	80.16	45.54	87.41	61.50	**94.53**	84.08	53.18	47.91	89.88	88.02	55.60

Note: The left panel shows the comparison between different trackers. Right panel summaries the results of baseline performance, where P, S, B are the trackers using single quantization of pixel (RF), superpixel (RF), and bounding box (MFT), respectively, and P&S the tracker using the two quantizations from pixel and superpixel, etc.

both pixel- and superpixel-level RFs. Other parameters specific to the sample selection in ORF model training are $\epsilon_p^+ = 0.8$, $\epsilon_p^- = 0.3$, $\epsilon_{sp}^+ = 0.5$, $\epsilon_{sp}^- = 0.5$. It should be noted that we strictly follow the protocols proposed in [14,54] and fix all parameters for all video sequences in the following evaluations. We use the initial bounding box given by the dataset as the starting point for our tracker.

The tracker was implemented using Matlab & C++ without intensive program optimization. The average time cost for all testing sequences is 1.1s per frame on a cluster node (3.4GHz, 8 Cores, 32GB RAM, less than 19% CPU used), consisting of: feature extraction (0.13s), SLIC (0.10s), RF prediction (0.18s), RF update (0.38s), and dynamic graph cuts (0.30s). It should be noted that parallel programming can be easily adopted for some key components (e.g., feature extraction, graph cuts, and ORF) to significantly reduce the run-time.

4.2   Tracking Non-rigid Objects

We first evaluate the performance of our tacker on the non-rigid object tracking dataset, which was first collected by [15] and was recently used to test a state-of-the-art tracking method [14]. This dataset consists of 11 sequences, where significant non-rigid deformation of objects is present. Quantitative results on a set of representative frames are shown in Fig. 3. For quantitative comparison, we compare MQT with a set of state-of-the-art methods[2], including PixelTrack [14], Hough Tracker (HT) [15], TLD [25], and the Superpixel Tracker (SPT) [52], by computing the success rate, defined as the percentage of frames in which the object is successfully tracked. In each frame, the overlap measure (i.e., half of the DICE coefficient) $S_o = \frac{|R_t \cap R_g|}{|R_t \cup R_g|}$ is computed, where R_t is the bounding box output by a tracker and R_g is the ground truth bounding box. The tracking is considered successful is S_o is larger than a given threshold t_o. For a fair comparison, we use the same protocol as in [14] by setting t_o to 0.1. The quantitative results of the comparative trackers are summarized in the left panel of Tab. 1.

---

[2] The performance of SPT is evaluated by using the code released by Wang *et al.* [52], and the data for the other three competitors' is from [14].

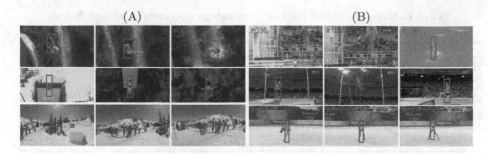

Fig. 3. Tracking results of MQT in the non-rigid object tracking dataset. Frame numbers are shown in the top left of each figure. Each column contains results of three sequences: (A) Cliff-dive 1, Cliff-dive 2, Mountain-bike; (B) Diving, High Jump, Gym.

As pointed out in [14], one of the most difficult videos for the PixelTrack is *Motocross 1*, where the motor-bike does a complete flip, changes its size rapidly, and the background is very cluttered. The rapid size change poses great challenge to our tracker given a fixed size bounding box we adopt. The quantitative evaluation shows that our tracker successfully tracks objects in almost all of the sequences in this dataset, and significantly outperforms the other four methods. Our tracker is demonstrated to be a promising method for tracking non-rigid objects, possessing the advantage of multilevel appearance representation incorporated in a graphical model, compared to the methods (e.g., PixelTrack, SPT, TLD) based on only a single level representation.

Moreover, to better understand the importance of different components in the proposed framework, we also conducted the baseline experiments to evaluate performance on parts of our tracker by switching off some components and summarized the average performance in the right panel of Tab. 1.

4.3   Evaluation on Comprehensive Benchmark

The second experiment is conducted on the CVPR2013 tracking benchmark [54], which is an up-to-date comprehensive benchmark specifically designed for evaluation of tracking performance. The whole dataset consists of 50 fully annotated sequences. Each sequence is tagged with a number of attributes indicating to the presence of different challenges, e.g. Occlusion (OCC), Deformation (DEF). To evaluate the strength and weakness of different methods, the sequences are categorized according to those attributes and 11 challenge subsets are therefore created. In [54], the evaluation is based on two different metrics: the precision plot and success plot. The precision plot shows the percentage of frames on which the Center Location Error (CLE) of a tracker is within a given threshold r, where CLE is defined as the center distance between R_t and R_g, and a representative precision score ($r = 20$) is used for ranking. Another metric is to compute the bounding box overlap S_o introduced in the previous experiment (Section 4.2), and the success plot shows the ratios of successful frames at a given threshold

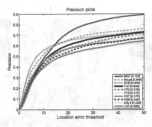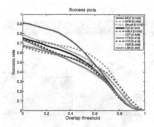

Fig. 4. Quantitative comparison in CVPR2013 benchmark. The performance score for each tracker is shown in the legend. For each figure, only the top 10 trackers are presented. The trackers appearing in the legend are as follows: MQT (ours), Struck [17], SCM [57], TLD [25], VTD [29], VTS [30], CXT [13], CSK [19], ASLA [23], LOT [44], LSK [40].

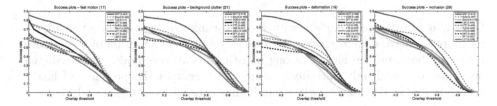

Fig. 5. Success plots for some challenge subsets of CVPR2013 tracking benchmark. The performance score for each tracker is shown in the legend. The value appears in the title is the number of sequences in that subset. Only the top 10 trackers are presented. The trackers appearing in the legend are as follows: OAB [16], TM-V [12], DFT [34], CPF [45], MIL [5].

t_o varied from 0 to 1. In success plot, the ranking is based on the area under curve (AUC) instead of using a specific threshold. For the comparative trackers, it currently includes 29 popular tracking algorithms, and most of them operated on a single choice of quantization. For more details about the benchmark, we refer readers to the original paper [54].

We run the One-Pass Evaluation (OPE) [54] on the benchmark using the proposed MQT. For comparison, we use the online available[3] tracking results and the unified tool provided by [54] to compute the evaluation plots. In this experiment, the proposed MQT achieves overall the best performance using both the metrics, which is shown in Fig. 4. MQT also ranks in the top ten from all 30 trackers over all challenge subsets using either the measurement of precision plots or success plots and takes the first places in the nine out of the eleven challenge subsets when using the success plots as measurement. According to the results, MQT is more robust to background clutter, deformation, occlusion challenges comparing to the other 29 trackers. We show the success plots of the some challenge subsets in Fig. 5, but omit other figures due to the space limits.

---

[3] http://visual-tracking.net/

Fig. 6. Tracking results in the CVPR2013 benchmark. Only top five trackers on success plots are presented. Frame numbers are shown in the top left of each figure. Each column contains results of two sequences: (A) Basketball, David3; (B) David, Tiger1.

Finally, qualitative comparison with the top-rank trackers is shown in Fig. 6 for more intuitive demonstration. Note that, due to the adoption of a fixed-size bounding box and the lack of strong holistic-appearance model, the predicted bounding box will only partially capture the target in the presence of heavy occlusion and scale changes, which can be interpreted from Fig. 4 and Fig. 5.

5   Conclusions and Future Work

In this paper, we propose a tracking method based on a hierarchical appearance representation using multilevel quantization. The different levels of the representation are incorporated into a Conditional Random Field model using a coherent framework. By exploiting all the quantization levels, the method utilizes and integrates the information contained at each representation level by explicitly modeling the interactions and constraints between them; this results in significantly improved performance compared to other state-of-the-art tracking methods based on a single quantization. Moreover, Online Random Forests are used to update the appearance model in different levels of the tracker, in order to capture changes in object appearance over time. The experimental results demonstrate that the proposed method is capable of taking advantage of multilevel information and significantly boosting tracking performance. In the future, we will improve our tracker by considering the scale change of the target and extend it by taking more sophisticated high-level information into consideration.

Acknowledgment. This project is supported by Australian Research Council Discovery Projects number FT-130101457 and DP-120103730, and it is also supported by Toyota Research Institute NA collaborative project 2013001793.

References

1. Achanta, R., Shaji, A., Smith, K., Lucchi, A., Fua, P., Susstrunk, S.: SLIC super-pixels compared to state-of-the-art superpixel methods. TPAMI 34(11), 2274–2282 (2012)
2. Adam, A., Rivlin, E., Shimshoni, I.: Robust fragments-based tracking using the integral histogram. In: CVPR, pp. 798–805 (2006)
3. Aeschliman, C., Park, J., Kak, A.C.: A probabilistic framework for joint segmentation and tracking. In: CVPR, pp. 1371–1378 (2010)
4. Avidan, S.: Ensemble tracking. TPAMI 29(2), 261–271 (2007)
5. Babenko, B., Yang, M., Belongie, S.: Robust object tracking with online multiple instance learning. TPAMI 33(8), 1619–1632 (2011)
6. Bosch, A., Zisserman, A., Muoz, X.: Image classification using random forests and ferns. In: ICCV, pp. 1–8 (2007)
7. Boykov, Y., Funka-Lea, G.: Graph cuts and efficient nd image segmentation. IJCV 70(2), 109–131 (2006)
8. Boykov, Y., Kolmogorov, V.: An experimental comparison of min-cut/max-flow algorithms for energy minimization in vision. TPAMI 26(9), 1124–1137 (2004)
9. Breiman, L.: Random forests. Machine Learning 45(1), 5–32 (2001)
10. Brunelli, R.: Template matching techniques in computer vision: theory and practice. John Wiley & Sons (2009)
11. Chockalingam, P., Pradeep, N., Birchfield, S.: Adaptive fragments-based tracking of non-rigid objects using level sets. In: ICCV, pp. 1530–1537 (2009)
12. Collins, R., Liu, Y., Leordeanu, M.: Online selection of discriminative tracking features. TPAMI 27(10), 1631–1643 (2005)
13. Dinh, T.B., Vo, N., Medioni, G.: Context tracker: Exploring supporters and distracters in unconstrained environments. In: CVPR, pp. 1177–1184 (2011)
14. Duffner, S., Garcia, C.: Pixeltrack: a fast adaptive algorithm for tracking non-rigid objects. In: ICCV, pp. 2480–2487 (2013)
15. Godec, M., Roth, P.M., Bischof, H.: Hough-based tracking of non-rigid objects. In: ICCV, pp. 81–88 (2011)
16. Grabner, H., Bischof, H.: On-line boosting and vision. In: CVPR, pp. 260–267 (2006)
17. Hare, S., Saffari, A., Torr, P.H.: Struck: Structured output tracking with kernels. In: ICCV, pp. 263–270 (2011)
18. He, X., Zemel, R.S., Carreira-Perpiñán, M.Á.: Multiscale conditional random fields for image labeling. In: CVPR, pp. 695–702 (2004)
19. Henriques, J.F., Caseiro, R., Martins, P., Batista, J.: Exploiting the circulant structure of tracking-by-detection with kernels. In: Fitzgibbon, A., Lazebnik, S., Perona, P., Sato, Y., Schmid, C. (eds.) ECCV 2012, Part IV. LNCS, vol. 7575, pp. 702–715. Springer, Heidelberg (2012)
20. Hong, Z., Mei, X., Prokhorov, D., Tao, D.: Tracking via robust multi-task multi-view joint sparse representation. In: ICCV, pp. 649–656 (2013)
21. Hong, Z., Mei, X., Tao, D.: Dual-force metric learning for robust distracter-resistant tracker. In: Fitzgibbon, A., Lazebnik, S., Perona, P., Sato, Y., Schmid, C. (eds.) ECCV 2012, Part I. LNCS, vol. 7572, pp. 513–527. Springer, Heidelberg (2012)
22. Huang, Q., Han, M., Wu, B., Ioffe, S.: A hierarchical conditional random field model for labeling and segmenting images of street scenes. In: CVPR, pp. 1953–1960 (2011)

23. Jia, X., Lu, H., Yang, M.H.: Visual tracking via adaptive structural local sparse appearance model. In: CVPR, pp. 1822–1829 (2012)
24. Kalal, Z., Mikolajczyk, K., Matas, J.: Forward-backward error: Automatic detection of tracking failures. In: ICPR, pp. 2756–2759 (2010)
25. Kalal, Z., Mikolajczyk, K., Matas, J.: Tracking-learning-detection. TPAMI 34(7), 1409–1422 (2012)
26. Kohli, P., Rihan, J., Bray, M., Torr, P.H.: Simultaneous segmentation and pose estimation of humans using dynamic graph cuts. IJCV 79(3), 285–298 (2008)
27. Kohli, P., Torr, P.H.: Dynamic graph cuts for efficient inference in markov random fields. TPAMI 29(12), 2079–2088 (2007)
28. Kwon, J., Lee, K.M.: Tracking of a non-rigid object via patch-based dynamic appearance modeling and adaptive basin hopping monte carlo sampling. In: CVPR, pp. 1208–1215 (2009)
29. Kwon, J., Lee, K.M.: Visual tracking decomposition. In: CVPR, pp. 1269–1276 (2010)
30. Kwon, J., Lee, K.M.: Tracking by sampling trackers. In: ICCV, pp. 1195–1202 (2011)
31. Ladicky, L., Russell, C., Kohli, P., Torr, P.H.: Associative hierarchical crfs for object class image segmentation. In: ICCV, pp. 739–746 (2009)
32. Ladický, L., Sturgess, P., Alahari, K., Russell, C., Torr, P.H.S.: What, where and how many? Combining object detectors and CRFs. In: Daniilidis, K., Maragos, P., Paragios, N. (eds.) ECCV 2010, Part IV. LNCS, vol. 6314, pp. 424–437. Springer, Heidelberg (2010)
33. Lagarias, J.C., Reeds, J.A., Wright, M.H., Wright, P.E.: Convergence properties of the nelder–mead simplex method in low dimensions. SIAM Journal on Optimization 9(1), 112–147 (1998)
34. Learned-Miller, E., Sevilla-Lara, L.: Distribution fields for tracking. In: CVPR, pp. 1910–1917 (2012)
35. Lepetit, V., Fua, P.: Keypoint recognition using randomized trees. TPAMI 28(9), 1465–1479 (2006)
36. Leung, T., Malik, J.: Representing and recognizing the visual appearance of materials using three-dimensional textons. IJCV 43(1), 29–44 (2001)
37. Levinshtein, A., Sminchisescu, C., Dickinson, S.: Optimal contour closure by superpixel grouping. In: Daniilidis, K., Maragos, P., Paragios, N. (eds.) ECCV 2010, Part II. LNCS, vol. 6312, pp. 480–493. Springer, Heidelberg (2010)
38. Li, H., Shen, C., Shi, Q.: Real-time visual tracking using compressive sensing. In: CVPR, pp. 1305–1312 (2011)
39. Li, X., Hu, W., Shen, C., Zhang, Z., Dick, A., Hengel, A.V.D.: A survey of appearance models in visual object tracking. ACM Transactions on Intelligent Systems and Technology (TIST) 4(4) (2013)
40. Liu, B., Huang, J., Yang, L., Kulikowsk, C.: Robust tracking using local sparse appearance model and k-selection. In: CVPR, pp. 1313–1320 (2011)
41. Mei, X., Ling, H.: Robust visual tracking and vehicle classification via sparse representation. TPAMI 33(11), 2259–2272 (2011)
42. Mei, X., Ling, H., Wu, Y., Blasch, E., Bai, L.: Efficient minimum error bounded particle resampling L1 tracker with occlusion detection. TIP 22(7), 2661–2675 (2013)
43. Ojala, T., Pietikainen, M., Maenpaa, T.: Multiresolution gray-scale and rotation invariant texture classification with local binary patterns. TPAMI 24(7), 971–987 (2002)
44. Oron, S., Bar-Hillel, A., Levi, D., Avidan, S.: Locally orderless tracking. In: CVPR, pp. 1940–1947 (2012)

45. Pérez, P., Hue, C., Vermaak, J., Gangnet, M.: Color-based probabilistic tracking. In: Heyden, A., Sparr, G., Nielsen, M., Johansen, P. (eds.) ECCV 2002, Part I. LNCS, vol. 2350, pp. 661–675. Springer, Heidelberg (2002)
46. Ross, D., Lim, J., Lin, R., Yang, M.: Incremental learning for robust visual tracking. IJCV 77(1), 125–141 (2008)
47. Rother, C., Kolmogorov, V., Blake, A.: Grabcut: Interactive foreground extraction using iterated graph cuts. ACM Transactions on Graphics (TOG) 23(3), 309–314 (2004)
48. Saffari, A., Leistner, C., Santner, J., Godec, M., Bischof, H.: On-line random forests. In: ICCV Workshops, pp. 1393–1400 (2009)
49. Santner, J., Leistner, C., Saffari, A., Pock, T., Bischof, H.: Prost: Parallel robust online simple tracking. In: CVPR, pp. 723–730 (2010)
50. Wang, C., Komodakis, N., Paragios, N.: Markov random field modeling, inference & learning in computer vision & image understanding: A survey. CVIU 117(11), 1610–1627 (2013)
51. Wang, C., de La Gorce, M., Paragios, N.: Segmentation, ordering and multi-object tracking using graphical models. In: ICCV, pp. 747–754 (2009)
52. Wang, S., Lu, H., Yang, F., Yang, M.H.: Superpixel tracking. In: ICCV, pp. 1323–1330 (2011)
53. Wojek, C., Schiele, B.: A dynamic conditional random field model for joint labeling of object and scene classes. In: Forsyth, D., Torr, P., Zisserman, A. (eds.) ECCV 2008, Part IV. LNCS, vol. 5305, pp. 733–747. Springer, Heidelberg (2008)
54. Wu, Y., Lim, J., Yang, M.H.: Online object tracking: A benchmark. In: CVPR, pp. 2411–2418 (2013)
55. Yang, H., Shao, L., Zheng, F., Wang, L., Song, Z.: Recent advances and trends in visual tracking: A review. Neurocomputing 74(18), 3823–3831 (2011)
56. Zhang, T., Ghanem, B., Liu, S., Ahuja, N.: Robust visual tracking via multi-task sparse learning. In: CVPR, pp. 2042–2049 (2012)
57. Zhong, W., Lu, H., Yang, M.H.: Robust object tracking via sparsity-based collaborative model. In: CVPR, pp. 1838–1845 (2012)

Occlusion and Motion Reasoning for Long-Term Tracking

Yang Hua, Karteek Alahari, and Cordelia Schmid

Inria*

Abstract. Object tracking is a reoccurring problem in computer vision. Tracking-by-detection approaches, in particular Struck [20], have shown to be competitive in recent evaluations. However, such approaches fail in the presence of long-term occlusions as well as severe viewpoint changes of the object. In this paper we propose a principled way to combine occlusion and motion reasoning with a tracking-by-detection approach. Occlusion and motion reasoning is based on state-of-the-art long-term trajectories which are labeled as object or background tracks with an energy-based formulation. The overlap between labeled tracks and detected regions allows to identify occlusions. The motion changes of the object between consecutive frames can be estimated robustly from the geometric relation between object trajectories. If this geometric change is significant, an additional detector is trained. Experimental results show that our tracker obtains state-of-the-art results and handles occlusion and viewpoints changes better than competing tracking methods.

1   Introduction

Although tracking objects is a well-established problem in computer vision [11,22,23,46,48,49], it still remains a challenging task. Many of the previous works have approached this problem from the perspective of either a motion tracker or an object detector. In recent years, tracking-by-detection, i.e., approaches that treat the tracking problem as a task of detecting the object over time [2,3,18,20,24,27,40,46,47], has become an increasingly popular method for object tracking. In fact, the latest evaluation papers [36,42,48] have shown such an approach, namely Struck [20], to be the best-performer on a diverse set of examples. One of the critical steps in these methods is to update and improve the object model over time. Consider the example in Figure 1. It shows a scenario where the object of interest—a car—is occluded when it goes under a bridge. If the model is updated in every frame, this results in the well-known issue of drift [32]. In other words, a part of the bridge might be tracked instead of the car in the latter frames in the sequence. In this paper we present an algorithm which can handle such occlusions as well as significant viewpoint changes in a principled way, based on state-of-the-art quasi-dense long-term trajectories [35,45].

---

* LEAR team, Inria Grenoble Rhône-Alpes, Laboratoire Jean Kuntzmann, CNRS, Univ. Grenoble Alpes, France.

D. Fleet et al. (Eds.): ECCV 2014, Part VI, LNCS 8694, pp. 172–187, 2014.

These trajectories rely on dense optical flow [8] in combination with a forward-backward matching criterion. Sundaram et al. [45] showed that they significantly outperform the Kanade-Lucas-Tomasi (KLT) tracker [30], often used in tracking approaches [14,24]. Our main contribution is to use these long-term trajectories in combination with graph-cut based track labelling to identify the state of the object, e.g., partial or full occlusion, as well as change in viewpoint, and to choose and adapt positive object samples accordingly to improve the model.

The goal of this paper is to track the object, given a bounding box initialization in the first frame. Our approach begins by learning an initial appearance model from the annotation in the first frame, similar to [20,24,46], and uses it to propose candidate object locations in the latter frames. We incorporate motion cues to refine the candidate region search space and avoid incorrect object proposals (Section 2). In order to determine whether a candidate location in a frame contains the object, we compute long-term motion tracks in the video [45], and use them to predict the state of the object, i.e., the transformation it has undergone with respect to the previous frames (Section 3). More specifically, we estimate states such as, partial or full occlusion, change in appearance of the object. This is achieved with an energy-based formulation, where the task is to assign each track an object or background label. When a significant part of the tracks within a candidate region belong to the background, the object is identified to be occluded. We will show that other types of change in state, such as a significant change in viewpoint, can also be estimated with our formulation. With this additional cue in hand, we build a temporally-evolving object model which deals with these state changes by updating the initially learned detector accordingly (Section 3.2). In essence, our tracker proposes a new way to interleave the motion-based and tracking-by-detection paradigms. Its performance is evaluated on sequences from a recent benchmark dataset [48] and videos used in [3,20,24,46] (Section 5).

1.1 Related Work

The two key components of a tracking algorithm are the object representation (appearance model) and the inference method used to localize it in each frame. Examples of object representations include colour histograms [11] as well as appearance representations learned with generative [26,29,33,41] and discriminative [2,10,20,46] models. Our work builds on these discriminative models by using the estimated state of the object to update the model. The inference methods range from Kalman filtering techniques, to those that use multiple cues [4,5,13,34,37,38,43,44] and fuse their results with methods like particle filtering [22], error analysis [44], and Markov chain Monte Carlo schemes [37]. These inference methods have shown promising results, but tend to suffer from drift. Furthermore, it is unclear if they can recover from the object leaving or re-entering the field of view.

Given the significant advances in algorithms for object detection [12,15], the tracking-by-detection approach [2,27,40,47] has gained popularity. A variant of these approaches, known as adaptive tracking-by-detection, updates the object

Fig. 1. Three sample frames from the Carchase sequence in the TLD dataset [24]. Each image also shows the result of our method (in green) and Struck [20] (in red). As the car starts to move to a severely occluded state, updating the appearance model with the prediction result leads to model drift, as shown by the Struck result. Our proposed method estimates such states, and does not update the model in such cases. (Best viewed in pdf.)

model over time [3,18,20,24,46]. It typically consists of two phases: (i) tracking, where the detector is used to predict the object location in each frame; and (ii) learning, where the estimated object locations (in the form of bounding boxes) are used to generate training examples to improve the learned object model. Observing that many of the adaptive methods lack a principled way of generating the training samples, a joint structured output formulation (Struck) was proposed in [20]. This work learns a function to predict the object location in a frame based on its location in the previous frame and a predefined search space. The prediction function is a dot product of a weight vector and a joint kernel map. This weight vector is learned and updated with an online structured output framework. Our approach is based on a similar philosophy, in that, we learn and update a prediction function. However, we use state-of-the-art long-term motion tracks [45] to determine the state of the object and produce an effective set of training exemplars for the update step. In the example shown in Figure 1, we predict that the object is severely occluded in the middle frame and thus do not update our detector. Note that Struck (result shown in red in Figure 1) drifts onto a part of the bridge in this example.

Our method is also closely related to two other recent approaches [24,46]. The TLD algorithm [24] aims to combine the benefits of tracker- and detector-based approaches. It decomposes the tracking task into specialized components for tracking, learning and detection, which are run simultaneously. The result of this algorithm is a combination of the predictions from the frame-to-frame tracking based on median optical flow and a detection component. The two components mutually update each other. Specifically, the results of the tracker provide training data to update the detector, and the detector re-initializes the tracker when it fails, for example, when the object leaves the field-of-view. While this is an interesting approach, it is somewhat restrictive as the object model is a set of fixed-size template patches, i.e., TLD cannot handle severe changes in object size, such as the scenario shown in Figure 2. Furthermore, the motion information is limited to frame-to-frame constraints.

Fig. 2. Three frames from the CarScale sequence in [48] are shown to highlight the severe change in object size over time in some of the videos

Supancic and Ramanan [46] presented a tracking-by-detection method, where the detector is updated using a pre-fixed number of frames, i.e., the top-k frames chosen according to an SVM objective function, irrespective of the state of the object. This does not handle long-term occlusions. In contrast, our algorithm updates the model with only the frames that show a significant presence of the object, as it relies on the long-term motion cues to choose the training exemplars, unlike [46] which uses only the detector.

We experimentally compare with these related works [20,24,46], and show the benefits of our approach in Section 5.

2   Overview

In line with the tracking-by-detection approach, our tracker comprises three stages. First, a detector is learned from a given training set of positive and negative exemplars. Second, we track with this learned detector. Third, we update the object model with a carefully selected subset of frames. We now present an overview of these stages and then provide more details in Sections 3 and 4.

Initial Detector and Tracking. An initial object detector is required to set off our tracker. It is learned with a training set, where the positive example is the ground truth annotation in the first frame of the sequence, and the negative samples are harvested from the frame, similar to [46]. The initial model is then learned with HOG features [12,17] extracted from the bounding boxes and a linear SVM.

The detector is used to predict candidate locations of the object in other frames. In each frame, we find the most likely location of the object by evaluating the detector in a region estimated from motion cues (optical flow computed from the previous frame), and then choosing the bounding box with the best detection score, as shown in Figure 3. The motion-refined search is not only computationally efficient, but also avoids incorrect detections due to background clutter. Note that the bounding box obtained from this step is not labelled as the object yet.

We compute and analyze the motion cues to make the object label assignment in each frame. To this end, we extract long-term point tracks which extend over many frames in the video [45], see Figure 3-*Left*. At this stage, we discard tracks less than 5 frames long, which are typically less reliable. We then propose an energy-based formulation to label the remaining tracks as object or background.

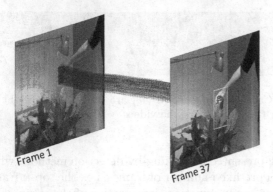

Fig. 3. Left: Long-term tracks beginning in frame 1 of the Coke sequence [48]. The yellow box shows the search region used to compute the bounding box most likely to contain the object (green box). We use the tracks to estimate the object state. Right: Close-up of the track labels in frame 37. Here, less than 60% of the tracks within the predicted bounding box are assigned to the object (blue), and the remaining are labelled as background (red). Thus, the object is predicted to be in an occluded state. (Best viewed in pdf.)

This is related to the labelling framework used in [28] for motion-clustering tracks. The tracks within the bounding box in the first frame, i.e., the ground truth annotation, are initialized with the object label, and those that lie outside are given the background label. With these initial assignments and pairwise energy terms (which measure track similarity), we optimize the energy function and label all the new tracks, i.e., tracks that begin in the second or latter frames, see Figure 3-*Right*.

Occlusion. If a significant part (40% or more) of the tracks within the bounding box take the background label (as in Figure 3), we consider the object to be in an occluded state. In this case, the object model is not updated with the detection result. We continue to track the object with the non-updated detector as long as there are object tracks and a detection response. This step avoids model drift [32,46]. For example, in the sequence in Figure 1, the model is not updated with the frame shown in the middle to avoid the tracker drifting onto a part of the bridge, which occludes the car. To handle cases where the object re-appears after a full occlusion (e.g., the frame on the right in Figure 1), the detector is evaluated over the entire image in subsequent frames.

Temporally-Evolving Detector. When the object is not occluded in a frame, the long-term tracks are used to measure geometric transformations that the object may have undergone, such as change in scale, rotation (see Figures 2 and 4). In this work, we approximate these transformations with a similarity matrix [21],[1] and estimate it with track-point correspondences between consecutive frames. The bounding box is then refined with the estimated transformation

---

[1] Other transformations, such as homography, can also be used here.

and is assigned the object label. This is illustrated on an example in Figure 4. Based on the severity of the transformation, we either: (i) update the existing detector; or (ii) learn a new detector. In summary, our detector model evolves temporally to account for changes in object appearance by updating, i.e., learning, with new positive instances.

3   Motion Cues in the Tracker

Motion cues serve two purposes in our algorithm: (1) to determine the search region for evaluating the detector; and (2) to estimate the state of the object. We use dense optical flow computed between two frames for the first task, and cues extracted from long-term tracks for the second.

Given the bounding box labelled as the object in a frame, we compute optical flow [8] for all the pixels within the box, and obtain the median flow. With this flow estimate, the bounding box is translated onto the following frame, and the area surrounding it (an enlarged box) is considered as the search region for the detector. In other words, we restrict the search space for the object detector when finding the most likely location of the object in a new frame. An example is illustrated in Figure 3. This useful cue is inspired by many of the traditional motion-based trackers, but is limited to providing only local motion information. We argue that these local cues are insufficient to reliably estimate (e.g., when the optical flow measurements are poor) whether the new bounding box contains the object or not. Our work integrates richer cues computed from long-term tracks into the framework to make a robust estimation of the state of the object. We achieve this with an energy-based formulation involving the long-term tracks.

Each track is represented with a random variable X_i and takes a label $x_i \in \{0, 1\}$, where 0 denotes the background and 1 is the object. Let n denote the number of tracks, and $\mathbf{X} = \{X_1, X_2, \ldots, X_n\}$ be the set of random variables. A labelling $\mathbf{x}$ refers to any possible assignment of labels to the random variables, and takes values from the set $\{0, 1\}^n$. The cost of a label assignment $E(\mathbf{X} = \mathbf{x})$, or $E(\mathbf{x})$ in short, is defined as:

$$E(\mathbf{x}) = \sum_{i=1}^{n} \phi_i(x_i) + \lambda \sum_{(i,j) \in \mathcal{E}} \phi_{ij}(x_i, x_j), \tag{1}$$

where $\phi_i(x_i)$ is the unary term to measure how likely it is for the track i to take label x_i. The function $\phi_{ij}(x_i, x_j)$ is a smoothness term to encourage similar tracks to take the same label. The set of pairs of interacting tracks is denoted by $\mathcal{E}$, and λ is a parameter to regulate the relative strength of the unary and the pairwise terms. The energy function (1) is minimized exactly to obtain the globally optimal labels for the tracks.

The pairwise smoothness term takes the form of a generalized Potts model [6] and is given by:

$$\phi_{ij}(x_i, x_j) = \begin{cases} \exp(-\lambda_d d(i,j)) & \text{if } x_i \neq x_j, \\ 0 & \text{otherwise,} \end{cases} \tag{2}$$

where $d(i, j)$ measures the dissimilarity between the two tracks i and j and λ_d is a parameter set to 0.1. This term is defined between pairs of neighbouring tracks, and it assigns a low cost for two dissimilar tracks to take different labels. We use the popular dissimilarity measure [7] computed as the maximum distance between time-corresponding spatial coordinates $\mathbf{p}_t^i, \mathbf{p}_t^j$ and velocity values $\mathbf{v}_t^i, \mathbf{v}_t^j$ as: $d(i, j) = \max_t \ \|\mathbf{p}_t^i - \mathbf{p}_t^j\|_2^2 \frac{\|\mathbf{v}_t^i - \mathbf{v}_t^j\|_2^2}{5\sigma_t^2}$. This maximum is computed over points in time where the two tracks overlap. The first term, $\|\mathbf{p}_t^i - \mathbf{p}_t^j\|_2^2$, measures the spatial Euclidean distance, and the second term is the vector difference of the velocities estimated over 5 frames, i.e., $\mathbf{v}_t^i = \mathbf{p}_i^{t+5} - \mathbf{p}_i^t$.

For the unary terms, all the tracks that begin within the ground truth annotation in the first frame are assigned a very high cost to take the background label. This prevents them from changing their label in the latter frames, and is essentially a hard assignment of the object label. Inversely, tracks that lie outside the annotation in the first frame are given a very high cost to take the foreground label. The hard label assignment within the ground truth annotation can be refined, for example, by assigning a subset of the tracks with the object label using Grabcut-like segmentation techniques [9]. We found this refinement step to be non-essential in our case, since the track labels are used in combination with other cues, and not directly to determine the object location. The unary term for any new tracks starting in the second frame and beyond is defined as:

$$\phi_i(x_i = 1) = \begin{cases} 1 - \frac{1}{1+\exp(-(\alpha_t d_t + \beta_t))} & \text{if track } i \in \text{box}_t, \\ 0.5 & \text{otherwise,} \end{cases} \tag{3}$$

and $\phi_i(x_i = 0) = 1 - \phi_i(x_i = 1)$. Here, d_t is the SVM detection score for box$_t$, the bounding box estimate in frame t. The scalars α_t and β_t map this score into a probabilistic output, and are computed using Platt's method [39]. The intuition behind this unary term is that new tracks within a strong detection are likely to belong to the object. For tracks that lie outside the detection box, we allow the pairwise similarity terms to decide on their labels by giving an equal unary cost for assigning object or background labels.

In order to minimize the energy function (1) we apply the mincut/maxflow algorithm [19,25] on a corresponding graph, where each track is represented as a node. All the tracks within the search region in frame t (shown as a yellow box in Figure 3) are added as nodes. Additionally, tracks labelled in the previous frames which continue to exist in the frame are added. The unary and pairwise costs, computed as described earlier, are added as weights on the edges in the graph. We then perform st-mincut on the graph to get the optimal labels for all the nodes. Building the graph and performing inference on it in every frame allows us to update the labels of existing tracks based on new evidence from neighbouring tracks. An illustration of track labels is shown in Figure 3.

3.1   Predicting the State

With the track labels in hand, we determine whether the object has been occluded or a change in viewpoint has occurred. If more than 40% of the tracks

(a) Frame 1	(b) Frame 4

Fig. 4. Sample frames from the MotorRolling sequence [48], where the object undergoes a significant transformation (rotates counter clockwise). (a) Frame 1 showing the bounding box in the first frame. (b) The result of our tracker is shown is green. We show the bounding box transformed with the estimated similarity in yellow. (Best viewed in pdf.)

within box$_t$ belong to the background, it is marked as a partial occlusion. We identify a full occlusion of the object if more than 80% of the tracks are assigned the background label. In other cases where a majority of the tracks continue to belong to the object, we verify if there have been any other transformations, see Figures 2 and 4 for two such examples. We model these transformations with a similarity matrix. It is estimated with a RANSAC approach [21], using points on the tracks (inside the box$_{t-1}$) in frames $t-1$ and t as correspondences. Since it is feasible to obtain more reliable point correspondences between consecutive frames, we compute frame-to-frame similarity matrices, and then accumulate them over a set of frames. For example, the transformation S_3^1, from frame 1 to 3, is computed as the product of the transformations S_3^2 and S_2^1. When a similarity matrix shows a significant change in scale or rotation, fixed empirically as 15% and 10° respectively in all the experiments, we mark the state as change in viewpoint.

To sum up, the candidate region box$_t$ is labelled as occluded when a full occlusion state if predicted. When a change in viewpoint is estimated, box$_t$ is transformed with the similarity matrix S_t^1 to obtain box$_t^S$, which is then assigned the object label. In other cases, i.e., neither occlusion nor change in viewpoint, box$_t$ takes the object label.

3.2 Re-training the Model

Re-training (or updating) the model is crucial to the success of a tracking algorithm to handle situations where the object may change in some form over time. We use the predicted state of the object to precisely define the update step as follows.

Case 1: No change in state. The model update is straightforward, if the object is neither occluded, nor has undergone any of the other transformations. The new bounding box, box$_t$, is treated as a positive exemplar, and is used to update the SVM classifier.

Case 2: Occlusion. When the object is in a (partial or fully) occluded state, the classifier is not updated.

Case 3: Change in viewpoint. The detection result box$_t$ in this case is transformed with the estimated similarity matrix to box$_t^S$. We then fit an image-axes-aligned box that encloses box$_t^S$, as illustrated in the example in Figure 4. This transformation changes either the scale or the aspect ratio of the bounding box containing the object. Recall that our initial detector is trained from a single positive example at one scale, and adding other samples with different scales (or aspect ratios) will deteriorate it. We choose to train a new detector with the new bounding box in frame t, and maintain a set of detectors which capture various scales and aspect ratios of the object, as it changes over time. This idea of maintaining multiple detectors for an object category is similar in spirit to exemplar SVMs [31].

A summary of our method is given in Algorithm 1. Note that in the case of a full occlusion, the best detection is obtained by running the detector over the entire image. The state is estimated based on the strength of the detection, and is set either to occlusion or no change in state, in which case a new track is started.

4   Implementation Details

Detector. We chose a linear SVM and HOG features to learn the object detector in this work, following a recent approach [46] which showed its efficacy on the tracking problem. The regularization parameter in the SVM is fixed to 0.1 for all our experiments. The SVM objective function is minimized with LIBLINEAR [16]. The initial detector is learned with one positive sample in the first frame and many negative examples harvested from bounding boxes (sampled from the entire image) that do not overlap with the true positive by more than 10%. We also perform 5 iterations of hard negative mining, similar to [46]. The learned detector is run at its original scale in the motion-predicted search region. Recall that we handle severe changes in object state (change in scale, rotation) by building a set of detectors (Section 2). For all the experiments, we fixed the maximum size of this set to 4, and replaced the worst performing detector (i.e., the detector with the lowest score when evaluated on the new exemplar), whenever necessary. We found this approach to work better in practice compared to one where a single multiscale detector is used. To update the detector efficiently with new samples, we use the standard warm-start strategy [16,46].

State Prediction. The parameter λ in the energy function (1), which controls the strength of the unary and pairwise terms is set to 1 in all our experiments. Pairwise terms are added between pairs of tracks that are less than a distance of 5 pixels in a frame. We minimize (1) with the graph cut algorithm [19,25].

Algorithm 1. Our approach for tracking an object and estimating its state

---

Data: Image frames $1 \ldots n$, Object location box_1 in frame 1
Result: Object location box_t and state_t in frames $t = 2 \ldots n$
Learn initial detector in frame 1 (Section 2)
Compute long-term tracks (Section 2)
for $t = 2 \ldots n$ **do**
    $\text{box}_t \leftarrow$ Best detection in frame t
    Compute track labels (Section 3)
    $\text{state}_t \leftarrow$ Estimate object state in frame t (Section 3.1)
    switch $\textit{state}_t$ **do**
        case *Full occlusion*
            $\text{box}_t \leftarrow \emptyset$
            No detector update
        end
        case *Partial occlusion*
            No detector update
        end
        case *Change in viewpoint*
            $S_t^1 \leftarrow$ Estimate the transformation
            $\text{box}_t^S \leftarrow \text{Transform}(\text{box}_t, S_t^1)$ (Section 3.2)
            $\text{box}_t \leftarrow \text{box}_t^S$
            Learn new detector model (Section 3.2)
        end
        case *Other*
            Update detector model (Section 3.2)
        end
    endsw
end

The thresholds for determining a partial or full occlusion are empirically fixed to 40% and 80% respectively in all our experiments.

5   Experimental Analysis

We now present a selection of results from experiments on benchmark datasets. Code, additional results and videos are available on the project website [1].

5.1   Datasets

To compare with the most relevant tracking-by-detection approaches, we use the test videos and ground truth annotations from [20,24,46]. We show a sample set of frames from these videos in Figure 5. In particular, we evaluate on the following sequences from the TLD dataset [24]: Carchase, Pedestrian2, Pedestrian3, which contain challenging scenarios with pose, scale and illumination changes, full or partial occlusion, and all the videos used in [20,48,46], many of which contain motion blur, fast motion, rotation, background clutter. We will highlight some of the most interesting cases from these datasets in the paper, and present further analysis on the project website. We note that the sequences in the tracking benchmark dataset [48], do not annotate occlusion states. For example, frames in the Coke sequence where the Coke can is completely occluded by a leaf are still annotated with a bounding box. This inconsistency in evaluation when occlusion happens was also noted by [42]. As a result, our method is evaluated unfairly, in cases where we estimate an occlusion and do not output a bounding box.

5.2   Evaluation Measures

Some of the previous works in tracking have used mean displacement error in pixels to evaluate the accuracy quantitatively. As argued in [46], this measure is not scale-invariant and is not precise for cases when a method loses track of the object. We follow [24,46] and treat an estimated object location as correct if its sufficiently overlaps with the ground truth annotation. Then we compute precision, recall and the F_1 score. In the results shown in Table 1, we use 50% as the overlap threshold.

5.3   Results

In this section we compare our approach with the state-of-the-art methods, namely TLD (2012) [24], SPLTT (2013) [46], and the winner of 2013 benchmark evaluations [48]—Struck [20]. We used the original implementation provided by the respective authors. For TLD, we set the size of the initial object bounding box as 15, since it did not run with the default value of 24 for some of the sequences.

When evaluated on all the 50 sequences from [48], our approach results in 0.657 mean F_1 score (with 50% overlap threshold), whereas Struck [20], SPLTT [46] and TLD [24] achieve 0.565, 0.661 and 0.513 respectively. We illustrate a selection of these sequences in Table 1 and Figure 5.

Our method shows a significant improvement on some of the sequences (rows 1-3 in Table 1). For the Football1 sequence (row 1, Table 1), our F_1 score is 1.000 compared to 0.554 (SPLTT). In Figure 5(a), we see that Struck (columns 2, 3: red box) tends to drift because the model is not selectively updated. SPLTT also performs poorly (column 2: yellow box, column 3: loses track) as it only relies on frame-to-frame optical flow between candidate detections computed in each frame. If either the optical flow or the detection is weak, SPLTT loses track. TLD (column 3: loses track) also uses frame-to-frame optical flow tracking and is prone to drift. In contrast, our method uses long-term tracks and updates the model selectively, which results in better performance.

For the Trellis sequence, our method shows nearly 10% improvement over Struck (0.919 vs 0.821, see row 2, Table 1). Sample frames are shown in Figure 5(b). Here, TLD is confused by the illumination changes, drifts (blue box in column 1) onto a part of the object (the face), and eventually loses track (columns 2 and 3: no blue box). This is potentially due to the weaker object model. The partial occlusions (column 2) and change in viewpoint (column 3)

Table 1. Comparison of our approach with the state-of-the-art methods using the F_1 measure (higher is better). Our approach *plain* and *occ.+vpoint* refers to variants without and with using the object state respectively.

No.	Sequence	Struck	TLD	SPLTT	Our approach	
					plain	*occ.+vpoint*
1	Football1	0.378	0.351	0.554	1.000	1.000
2	Trellis	0.821	0.455	0.701	0.838	0.919
3	Walking	0.585	0.379	0.541	0.476	0.922
4	Car4	0.404	0.003	0.314	0.401	0.398
5	Jumping	0.859	0.843	0.997	0.994	1.000
6	Suv	0.587	0.913	0.904	0.531	0.907
7	Woman	0.936	0.829	0.891	0.935	0.920
8	Coke	0.948	0.694	0.804	0.801	0.880
9	David	0.240	0.773	0.546	0.635	0.679
10	Deer	1.000	0.817	0.986	1.000	1.000
11	MotorRolling	0.146	0.110	0.128	0.134	0.512
12	MountainBike	0.908	0.355	0.908	1.000	1.000
13	Pedestrian2	0.175	0.500	0.950	0.107	0.979
14	Pedestrian3	0.353	0.886	0.989	0.424	1.000
15	Carchase	0.036	0.340	0.290	0.098	0.312

lead to incorrect model updates, and thus poorer results for SPLTT (yellow box) and Struck (red box). Our method (green box) estimates the state of the object (occlusion or change in viewpoint) and performs a correct update step. For the Walking sequence, we achieve an F_1 score of 0.922 compared to 0.585 from Struck (row 3, Table 1), since our tracks adapt to changes in object size (with the help of long-term tracks).

The performance of our method is comparable on some sequences (rows 4-6 in Table 1). For example, an F_1 score of 0.398 compared to 0.404 (Struck) for the Car4 sequence (see row 4, Table 1). In a few cases, our method performs worse than the trackers we compare with. For example, on the Freeman4 sequence, our method fails to track the object (0.004 F_1 score). Struck, TLD and SPLTT perform better than this (0.177, 0.134 and 0.145 respectively), but are still significantly inferior to their average performance on the entire benchmark dataset. As shown in Figure 5(c), none of the methods show a noteworthy performance, and drift or miss the object often. We observed that the minimum size of our detector was not ideal to find the object in this sequence, which is only 15×16 pixels large. All the trackers also perform poorly on the Soccer sequence—0.166 is the best performance, which is comparable to our score, 0.143. In Figure 5(d) we see that the player's face in this sequence is tracked initially, but due to severe motion blur, fails in the latter frames.

In Figure 5(e) we show sample frames from the Woman sequence, where our method identifies that the object is occluded (column 2). Due to the lack of occlusion labelling in the ground truth annotation, our method is penalized for

Fig. 5. Tracking results on (a) Football1, (b) Trellis, (c) Freeman4, (d) Soccer, (e) Woman sequences from the benchmark dataset [48], and (f) Pedestrian2, (g) Carchase sequences from the TLD dataset [24]. Green: Our result, Red: Struck, Yellow: SPLTT, Blue: TLD. See text for details. (Best viewed in pdf.)

frames where we estimate occlusion, and hence our result is slightly worse (0.920 vs 0.936 (Struck), shown in row 7, Table 1). The Coke sequence (row 8, Table 1) is another such case, where our method (0.87) performs significantly better than TLD (0.69) and SPLTT (0.80), but is inferior to Struck (0.95). Results on the Pedestrian2 and Carchase long-term sequences, in Figures 5(f) and 5(g), show that Struck cannot handle cases where the object re-enters the field of view after occlusion, unlike our method.

Discussion. Table 1 also shows a component-level evaluation of our method. Estimating the state of the object improves the performance in most cases (e.g., row 3). In some cases we observe a slight decrease in performance over the plain vanilla method (e.g., row 7) due to lack of occlusion labelling in the ground truth annotation (see text for Figure 5(e) above).

Note that long-term tracks are used as an additional information in our work. If there are insufficient point tracks within the bounding box (< 10), we do not estimate the state, and continue in a tracking-by-detection mode. For estimating the object state, we observed two cases. (1) Object and camera motion: In this case, tracks from [45] do not suffer from significant drift as they tend to be relatively short in length. For example, on the Deer sequence (71 frames), the average length of the track is 10.1, and less than 10% of tracks drift. This does not affect our state estimation. (2) Object or camera motion only: Here, tracks can drift, and then result in incorrect occlusion estimates (e.g., Crossing sequence: 120 frames; average track length 77, 50% drift). In the worst case, our tracker predicts full occlusion and misses the object for a few frames, but recovers when the detector is run over the entire image to overcome this occlusion state. In essence, failures in long-term tracks have a limited impact on our system overall. However, a limiting case of our approach is when an object undergoes occlusion, and re-appears in a viewpoint which has not been seen before the occlusion (i.e., no template is learned).

Computation time of our method depends on the image size and the number of tracks in the sequence. For sequences in Table 1, it takes 6.7s/frame on average, with our unoptimized Matlab code (which does not include time to precompute optical flow – 3.4s/frame on GPU).

Acknowledgements. This work was supported in part by the MSR-Inria joint project, the European integrated project AXES and the ERC advanced grant ALLEGRO.

References

1. http://lear.inrialpes.fr/research/tracking
2. Avidan, S.: Ensemble tracking. PAMI 29(2), 261–271 (2007)
3. Babenko, B., Yang, M.H., Belongie, S.: Robust object tracking with online multiple instance learning. PAMI 33(8), 1619–1632 (2011)
4. Badrinarayanan, V., Pérez, P., Le Clerc, F., Oisel, L.: Probabilistic color and adaptive multi-feature tracking with dynamically switched priority between cues. In: ICCV (2007)

5. Birchfield, S.: Elliptical head tracking using intensity gradients and color histograms. In: CVPR (1998)
6. Boykov, Y., Jolly., M.P.: Interactive graph cuts for optimal boundary & region segmentation of objects in n-d images. In: ICCV (2001)
7. Brox, T., Malik, J.: Object segmentation by long term analysis of point trajectories. In: Daniilidis, K., Maragos, P., Paragios, N. (eds.) ECCV 2010, Part V. LNCS, vol. 6315, pp. 282–295. Springer, Heidelberg (2010)
8. Brox, T., Malik, J.: Large displacement optical flow: Descriptor matching in variational motion estimation. PAMI 33(3), 510–513 (2011)
9. Rother, C., Kolmogorov, V., Blake, A.: Grabcut: Interactive foreground extraction using iterated graph cuts. ACM Trans. Graphics (2004)
10. Collins, R.T., Liu, Y., Leordeanu, M.: Online selection of discriminative tracking features. PAMI 27(10), 1631–1643 (2005)
11. Comaniciu, D., Ramesh, V., Meer, P.: Kernel-based object tracking. PAMI 25(5), 564–577 (2003)
12. Dalal, N., Triggs, B.: Histograms of oriented gradients for human detection. In: CVPR (2005)
13. Du, W., Piater, J.: A probabilistic approach to integrating multiple cues in visual tracking. In: Forsyth, D., Torr, P., Zisserman, A. (eds.) ECCV 2008, Part II. LNCS, vol. 5303, pp. 225–238. Springer, Heidelberg (2008)
14. Everingham, M., Sivic, J., Zisserman, A.: Taking the bite out of automatic naming of characters in TV video. Image and Vision Computing 27(5) (2009)
15. Everingham, M., Van Gool, L., Williams, C.K.I., Winn, J., Zisserman, A.: The Pascal Visual Object Classes (VOC) Challenge. IJCV 88(2), 303–338 (2010)
16. Fan, R.E., Chang, K.W., Hsieh, C.J., Wang, X.R., Lin, C.J.: LIBLINEAR: A library for large linear classification. JMLR 9, 1871–1874 (2008)
17. Felzenszwalb, P.F., Girshick, R.B., McAllester, D., Ramanan, D.: Object detection with discriminatively trained part based models. PAMI 32(9), 1627–1645 (2010)
18. Grabner, H., Leistner, C., Bischof, H.: Semi-supervised on-line boosting for robust tracking. In: Forsyth, D., Torr, P., Zisserman, A. (eds.) ECCV 2008, Part I. LNCS, vol. 5302, pp. 234–247. Springer, Heidelberg (2008)
19. Hammer, P.L.: Some network flow problems solved with pseudo-boolean programming. Operations Research 13, 388–399 (1965)
20. Hare, S., Saffari, A., Torr, P.H.S.: Struck: Structured output tracking with kernels. In: ICCV (2011)
21. Hartley, R.I., Zisserman, A.: Multiple View Geometry in Computer Vision, 2nd edn. Cambridge University Press (2004)
22. Isard, M., Blake, A.: ICONDENSATION: Unifying low-level and high-level tracking in a stochastic framework. In: Burkhardt, H.-J., Neumann, B. (eds.) ECCV 1998. LNCS, vol. 1406, pp. 893–908. Springer, Heidelberg (1998)
23. Jepson, A.D., Fleet, D.J., Maraghi, T.F.E.: Robust online appearance models for visual tracking. PAMI 25(10), 1296–1311 (2003)
24. Kalal, Z., Mikolajczyk, K., Matas, J.: Tracking-learning-detection. PAMI 34(7), 1409–1422 (2012)
25. Kolmogorov, V., Zabih, R.: What energy functions can be minimized via graph cuts? PAMI 26(2), 147–159 (2004)
26. Lee, K., Ho, J., Yang, M., Kriegman, D.: Visual tracking and recognition using probabilistic appearance manifolds. CVIU 99(3), 303–331 (2005)
27. Leibe, B., Schindler, K., Cornelis, N., van Gool, L.: Coupled object detection and tracking from static cameras and moving vehicles. PAMI 30(10), 1683–1698 (2008)

28. Lezama, J., Alahari, K., Sivic, J., Laptev, I.: Track to the future: Spatio-temporal video segmentation with long-range motion cues. In: CVPR (2011)
29. Liu, B., Huang, J., Kulikowski, C., Yang, L.: Robust visual tracking using local sparse appearance model and k-selection. PAMI 35(12), 2968–2981 (2013)
30. Lucas, B., Kanade, T.: An iterative image registration technique with an application to stereo vision. In: IJCAI (1981)
31. Malisiewicz, T., Gupta, A., Efros, A.: Ensemble of exemplar-svms for object detection and beyond. In: ICCV (2011)
32. Matthews, I., Ishikawa, T., Baker, S.: The template update problem. PAMI 26(6), 810–815 (2004)
33. Mei, X., Ling, H.: Robust visual tracking and vehicle classification via sparse representation. PAMI 33(11), 2259–2272 (2011)
34. Moreno-Noguer, F., Sanfeliu, A., Samaras, D.: Dependent multiple cue integration for robust tracking. PAMI 30(4), 670–685 (2008)
35. Ochs, P., Malik, J., Brox, T.: Segmentation of moving objects by long term video analysis. PAMI 36(6), 1187–1200 (2014)
36. Pang, Y., Ling, H.: Finding the best from the second bests - inhibiting subjective bias in evaluation of visual tracking algorithms. In: ICCV (2013)
37. Park, D.W., Kwon, J., Lee, K.M.: Robust visual tracking using autoregressive hidden Markov model. In: CVPR (2012)
38. Pérez, P., Vermaak, J., Blake, A.: Data fusion for visual tracking with particles. Proc. IEEE 92(3), 495–513 (2004)
39. Platt, J.C.: Probabilistic outputs for support vector machines and comparisons to regularized likelihood methods. In: NIPS (1999)
40. Ramanan, D., Forsyth, D., Zisserman, A.: Tracking people by learning their appearance. PAMI 29(1), 65–81 (2007)
41. Ross, D.A., Lim, J., Lin, R., Yang, M.: Incremental learning for robust visual tracking. IJCV 77(1), 125–141 (2008)
42. Song, S., Xiao, J.: Tracking revisited using RGBD camera: Unified benchmark and baselines. In: ICCV (2013)
43. Spengler, M., Schiele, B.: Towards robust multi-cue integration for visual tracking. Machine Vis. App. 14, 50–58 (2003)
44. Stenger, B., Woodley, T., Cipolla, R.: Learning to track with multiple observers. In: CVPR (2009)
45. Sundaram, N., Brox, T., Keutzer, K.: Dense point trajectories by GPU-accelerated large displacement optical flow. In: Daniilidis, K., Maragos, P., Paragios, N. (eds.) ECCV 2010, Part I. LNCS, vol. 6311, pp. 438–451. Springer, Heidelberg (2010)
46. Supancic, J.S., Ramanan, D.: Self-paced learning for long-term tracking. In: CVPR (2013)
47. Wu, B., Nevatia, R.: Detection and tracking of multiple, partially occluded humans by Bayesian combination of edgelet based part detectors. IJCV (2007)
48. Wu, Y., Lim, J., Yang, M.H.: Online object tracking: A benchmark. In: CVPR (2013)
49. Yilmaz, A., Javed, O., Shah, M.: Object tracking: A survey. ACM Comput. Surv. 38(4) (2006)

MEEM: Robust Tracking via Multiple Experts Using Entropy Minimization

Jianming Zhang, Shugao Ma, and Stan Sclaroff

Department of Computer Science, Boston University, USA
{jmzhang,shugaoma,sclaroff}@bu.edu

Abstract. We propose a multi-expert restoration scheme to address the model drift problem in online tracking. In the proposed scheme, a tracker and its historical snapshots constitute an expert ensemble, where the best expert is selected to restore the current tracker when needed based on a minimum entropy criterion, so as to correct undesirable model updates. The base tracker in our formulation exploits an online SVM on a budget algorithm and an explicit feature mapping method for efficient model update and inference. In experiments, our tracking method achieves substantially better overall performance than 32 trackers on a benchmark dataset of 50 video sequences under various evaluation settings. In addition, in experiments with a newly collected dataset of challenging sequences, we show that the proposed multi-expert restoration scheme significantly improves the robustness of our base tracker, especially in scenarios with frequent occlusions and repetitive appearance variations.

1 Introduction

In this paper, we focus on the problem of model-free online tracking of an object, given only the object's initial position and previous observations, within a tracking-by-detection framework. In many online trackers, an object model is maintained via online updates, which are intended to account for appearance changes of the target. However, the process of updating the model also brings the model drift problem, which is a key challenge in online visual tracking.

Model drift occurs because factors like tracking failure, occlusions and misalignment of training samples can lead to bad model updates. One remedy is to incorporate the first frame template or prior knowledge in the online model update procedure [20,15]. However, relying on a fixed model prior tends to restrict the tracker's ability to handle large object appearance changes. Other trackers [22,32,14] use a "censorship mechanism" where an update is prevented when certain criteria are met (or not met). The detection of good or bad updates usually relies upon smoothness assumptions for motion and appearance changes, which are often violated in challenging scenarios. And once the censorship mechanism fails, these trackers will either miss the chance to evolve or get trapped in a background region, due to the fact that the model can only evolve forward, without a mechanism to correct for past mistakes.

Instead of trying to prevent bad updates from happening, we propose a formulation that can correct the effects of bad updates *after* they happen. For this purpose, we introduce a multi-expert tracking framework, where a discriminative tracker and its former

D. Fleet et al. (Eds.): ECCV 2014, Part VI, LNCS 8694, pp. 188–203, 2014.
© Springer International Publishing Switzerland 2014

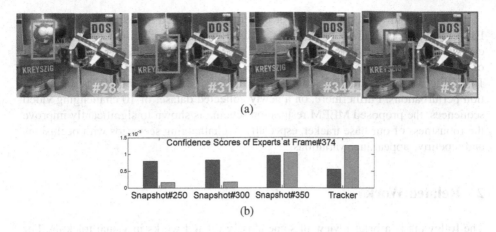

Fig. 1. In (a), green rectangles show the results of our base tracker. After a period severe occlusion, some tracker snapshots give a different prediction in red at frame #374. The chart in (b) shows the confidence scores of the tracker and its three recent snapshots for the two different predictions at frame #374 in corresponding colors. Our multi-expert mechanism favors the snapshot at frame #250, which is less ambiguous when selecting between the red and green hypotheses, even though the current tracker gives the highest confidence score for the green prediction.

snapshots constitute an expert ensemble, and the best expert is selected based on a minimum loss criterion to restore a tracker when a disagreement among the experts occurs. Traditional loss functions, which measure the discrepancy between the prediction and the true label, are only applicable in supervised settings. To get around this, we propose a novel formulation of the tracking-by-detection problem, so as to naturally introduce an entropy-regularized optimization function [10] as our expert selection criterion.

The key observation motivating our approach is that bad model updates usually contaminate a tracker's appearance model with inconsistent training samples, thus leading to ambiguous inference. An example is shown in Fig. 1. During a period of severe occlusion, the tracker's online updates incorporate the wrong foreground image patch. After the target reappears, although the tracker is still responsive to the true target in red, it starts to over-fit the wrong patch in green, yielding an incorrect prediction. In contrast, our formulation maintains a set of tracker snapshots throughout the tracking process. A past snapshot can be identified to localize the target with less ambiguity. This "low ambiguity" model prior is formulated as an entropy term in our expert selection criterion, which can be used to identify (and correct for) model drift.

To implement the base tracker in our multi-expert framework, we adopt an online SVM algorithm [26] that approximates the offline version by employing compact prototype sets, which summarize the effects of all previous training samples near the decision boundary and thereby avoids hard pruning of training samples, as needed in [31,21,11]. However, in [26] the algorithm is not evaluated in the tracking problem, so we carefully reformulated it to account for specific characteristics of the tracking problem. Furthermore, we use a linear kernel and the feature mapping technique of [19] to efficiently find nonlinear decision boundaries in the original feature space.

The main contribution of this paper is a tracking method based on a novel Multi-Expert Entropy Minimization (MEEM) restoration scheme, which allows a tracker to evolve backwards to undo undesirable model updates. On a standard benchmark dataset of 50 videos [27], our method improves over previous leading methods by more than 15% under various evaluation settings, *e.g.* with random spatial or temporal initialization perturbations. Furthermore, on a newly collected dataset of 10 challenging video sequences, the proposed MEEM restoration scheme is shown to significantly improve the robustness of our base tracker, especially in challenging scenarios with occlusions and repetitive appearance variations.

2   Related Work

The following is a brief review of some closely related works in visual tracking. For more comprehensive literature reviews, readers are directed to [18,28].

Tracking-by-Detection. Many discriminative trackers have been proposed. Avidan [1] utilizes an off-line trained SVM classifier in an optical flow based tracker. In [2,7], weak classifiers are combined and updated by a boosting algorithm for model-free tracking. The formulation of [4] combines weak SVM classifiers via randomized weighting vectors. In [3], multiple instance learning is used to avoid the error-prone, hard-labeling process. Structured SVM is proposed by [11] for tracking. While many previous works focus on designing a robust learning mechanism, our method tries to correct the past mistakes of online learning by allowing the tracker to evolve backward.

Hybrid Multi-Tracker Methods. Some tracking methods maintain a tracker ensemble, so the failure of a single tracker can be compensated by other trackers. For example, hybrid generative-discriminative methods are used in [29,32]. In [24] two SVM classifiers are employed in a co-training framework. Kwon *et al.* [16] integrate decorrelated trackers via an MCMC framework. In [17], multiple trackers from a tracker space are sampled and combined to handle challenging scenarios. Our multi-expert scheme differs in that our expert ensemble is made of a single tracker and its previous snapshots, and only one tracker needs to be updated in our system.

Training Sample Management. When memorizing training samples is needed, some trackers keep a fixed set of recent training samples [24,16], and others dynamically maintain a subset of the previous training samples using heuristics. In [11], support vectors that have the least influence on the current decision plane are discarded. In [31,21], templates with the least importance will be replaced when they cannot well represent the target appearance. In [13], older templates are replaced less frequently, assuming that they can be more accurate. Instead of using such heuristics, our tracker maintains a compact prototype set to summarize the effects of all previous training samples, and thereby avoids hard pruning of training samples.

Drift Prevention. Some approaches are designed to detect tracking failures and occlusions, to avert bad updates [4,22,32]. Others employ machine learning methods that are robust to sample labeling errors [3,8]. TLD [14] utilizes two experts to generate positive and negative samples, one based on spatial constraints and the other based on temporal constraints, to alleviate drift. In [23], a self-paced learning framework is proposed for long-term tracking, in which the training set is carefully augmented by iteratively revisiting previous frames. Some other methods address the drift problem by incorporating the original template in the updates [20], or by leveraging additional knowledge about the target [15,9]. Our method differs from these past works in either of the following two respects: first, it does not constrain the model update with fixed prior knowledge; second, it is possible for our tracker to undo negative effects after the bad updates that inevitably happen.

3   Multi-Expert Tracking Using Entropy Minimization

In this section, we introduce the multi-expert tracking framework using the minimum entropy criterion. This tracking framework is general and independent of the implementation of the base tracker.

3.1   Expert Selection for Tracking Using Entropy Minimization

We assume that a binary classifier, *i.e.* a discriminative tracker $\mathcal{T}$ is given, and it keeps updating with incoming training samples. We do not differentiate between a discriminative tracker and a binary classifier in this paper, assuming that other status information of a tracker, *e.g.* predictions, is not retained by the tracker.

$\mathcal{S}_t$ denotes a snapshot of the classifier $\mathcal{T}$ at time t. Then $\mathbf{E} := \{\mathcal{T}, \mathcal{S}_{t_1}, \mathcal{S}_{t_2}, \ldots\}$ is an expert ensemble. Let E denote an expert in the ensemble. Each expert E is assigned a loss $\mathcal{L}_E^t$ at each step t, and the best expert is determined by its cumulative loss within a recent temporal window:

$$E^* = \arg \min_{E \in \mathbf{E}} \sum_{k \in [t-\Delta, t]} \mathcal{L}_E^k, \tag{1}$$

where Δ is the size of the temporal window.

It is a key task to derive a proper loss function in our multi-expert framework. One straightforward option, which is in the same spirit of many ensemble based tracking methods [16,7,4], is to base the loss function (or weighting function) on the likelihood of the experts, in other words, how well the experts fit the labeled training samples. However, for online model-free tracking, training samples are labeled by the tracker. Therefore, the current tracker always tend to be more confident about its own predictions, and when model drift happens, the high confidence score about the wrong predictions will become completely misleading for the expert selection.

To derive a proper loss function that avoids the aforementioned problem, we employ a formulation that was originally developed for the semi-supervised partial-label learning (PLL) problem [10]. In the PLL problem, learning is based on partially labeled training samples $\mathcal{L} = \{(\mathbf{x}_i, \mathbf{z}_i)\}$, where $\mathbf{z}_i$ represents a possible label set that contains the true label $\mathbf{y}_i$ of instance $\mathbf{x}_i$.

In [10], the PLL is solved within a MAP framework that maximizes the log posterior probability of the model parameterized by θ,

$$\mathcal{C}(\theta, \lambda; \mathcal{L}) = L(\theta; \mathcal{L}) - \lambda H_{emp}(Y|X, Z; \mathcal{L}, \theta), \tag{2}$$

where $L(\theta; \mathcal{L})$ is the log likelihood of the model parameters θ, and $H_{emp}(Y|X, Z; \mathcal{L}, \theta)$ is the empirical conditional entropy of class labels conditioned on the training data and the possible label sets, $i.e.$ an empirical approximation of the logarithm of the prior probability of θ. The scalar λ controls the tradeoff between the likelihood and the prior. Readers are referred to [10] for more details. The entropy regularization term favors models with low ambiguity with respect to the partial label sets. For example, when a label set contains two possible labels, then a model giving equally high confidence scores to both labels is less favored than a model giving a high confidence score to one label and a low confidence score to the other.

To use the above minimum entropy criterion in a completely different context, $i.e.$ expert selection for tracking, we propose a novel formulation of the tracking-by-detection problem in a multiple instance PLL setting. At each frame, the expert ensemble $\mathbf{E}$ proposes a bag of instances $\mathbf{x} = \{x^1, \ldots, x^n\}$. Each x^i is a candidate image patch cropped from the frame, which is labeled by $y^i = (\omega^i, l^i)$, where $\omega^i \in \{-, +\}$ denotes the foreground-background label and $l^i \in \mathbb{Z}^2$ denotes the pixel-quantized 2D location of the candidate image patch x^i. Without loss of generality, we can now think of the bag $\mathbf{x}$ as a hyper-instance, whose ground truth label $\mathbf{y} = (y^1, \ldots, y^n)$ lies in a high dimensional label space $\mathcal{Y} = (\{-, +\} \times \mathbb{Z}^2)^n$.

We assume that the instance bag $\mathbf{x}$ contains the target, and the candidate image patches do not substantially overlap each other[1]. Thus, only one image patch in the bag can be the true target. Since the location l^i of a candidate image patch x^i is known, the ground truth label $\mathbf{y}$ must be contained in a small possible label set $\mathbf{z} = \{\mathbf{y}_1, \ldots, \mathbf{y}_n\}$, where for each $\mathbf{y}_j = ((\omega_j^1, l_j^1), \ldots, (\omega_j^n, l_j^n))$, l_j^i equals l^i, and ω_j^i is labeled as positive only when $i = j$.

Now for each frame, we have an instance bag $\mathbf{x}$ that encodes the appearance of the candidate image patches, and a possible label set $\mathbf{z}$ that encodes the specific constraints of the tracking problem. Therefore, according to Eq. 2, we have the following loss function for our expert selection problem (Eq. 1),

$$\mathfrak{L}_E(\mathbf{x}, \mathbf{z}) = -L(\theta_E; \mathbf{x}, \mathbf{z}) + \lambda H(\mathbf{y}|\mathbf{x}, \mathbf{z}; \theta_E), \tag{3}$$

where we define the log likelihood as

$$L(\theta_E; \mathbf{x}, \mathbf{z}) = \max_{\mathbf{y} \in \mathbf{z}} \log P(\mathbf{y}|\mathbf{x}; \theta_E), \tag{4}$$

and the entropy term is computed by

$$H(\mathbf{y}|\mathbf{x}, \mathbf{z}; \theta_E) = \sum_{\mathbf{y} \in \mathcal{Y}} P(\mathbf{y}|\mathbf{x}, \mathbf{z}; \theta_E) \log P(\mathbf{y}|\mathbf{x}, \mathbf{z}; \theta_E). \tag{5}$$

---

[1] Note that in our algorithm, the instance bag is constructed in a way that candidate image patches do not substantially overlap (see Section 5). This is different from the multiple instance formulation in the MIL tracker [3], where multiple significantly overlapping image patches are sampled purposely so that the true target may align well with multiple patches.

To compute $P(\mathbf{y}|\mathbf{x}; \theta_E)$, we assume that each sub-label $y^i = (\omega^i, l^i)$ only depends on x^i. We further assume $P(l^i|\omega^i, x^i) = P(l^i|\omega^i)$, which means their graphical model can be represented by $x^i \rightarrow \omega^i \rightarrow l^i$, $i.e.$ the image patch's appearance x^i provides information about its location l^i only through the appearance based posterior $P(\omega^i|x^i; \theta_E)$ and the spatial prior $P(l^i|\omega^i)$. Then we can have the following decomposition:

$$P(\mathbf{y}|\mathbf{x}; \theta_E) = \prod_i P(\omega^i, l^i|x^i; \theta_E)$$

$$= \prod_i P(l^i|\omega^i)P(\omega^i|x^i; \theta_E), \qquad (6)$$

where the spatial prior $P(l_i|\omega_i = +)$ can be used to encode the motion model. It follows that

$$P(\mathbf{y}|\mathbf{x}, \mathbf{z}; \theta_E) = \frac{\delta_\mathbf{z}(\mathbf{y})P(\mathbf{y}|\mathbf{x}; \theta_E)}{\sum_{\mathbf{y}' \in \mathcal{Y}} \delta_\mathbf{z}(\mathbf{y}')P(\mathbf{y}'|\mathbf{x}; \theta_E)}, \qquad (7)$$

which is the Kullback-Leibler projection of $P(\mathbf{y}|\mathbf{x}; \theta_E)$. The function $\delta_\mathbf{z}(\mathbf{y})$ takes 1 if $\mathbf{y} \in \mathbf{z}$ and 0 otherwise. This concludes all the required computations for Eq. 1.

3.2 Tracking Using Multiple Experts

Given the above formulation, the main loop of the multi-expert tracking framework is composed of the following steps. First, to update the expert ensemble, a snapshot of the tracker is saved every φ frames. The oldest snapshots will be discarded if the number of experts exceeds $\tilde{N}$. Then the expert ensemble proposes an instance bag, which will be detailed in Sec. 5. Given the instance bag and the possible label set described in Section 3.1, the loss function is evaluated for each expert using Eq. 3-7. After that, if a disagreement among the experts is detected, the best expert according to Eq. 1 will be assigned to the current tracker. Note that if the current tracker is the best one, then no restoration occurs. Finally, the tracker outputs the prediction, based on which the tracker is updated. A summary of our multi-expert tracking framework is given in Alg. 1.

4 Online Linear SVM Tracker

The base tracker for our multi-expert framework is inspired by the online SVM algorithm of [26], which makes use of prototype sets to gain an improved approximation to the offline SVM. For our base tracker, the algorithm of [26] is reformulated to better suit the tracking problem. Note that the following formulation is for a stand-alone tracker, which is independent of the multi-expert framework.

The SVM tracker $\mathcal{T}$ contains a compact prototype set $Q = \{\zeta_i = (\phi(q_i), \omega_i, s_i)\}_1^B$ to summarize the previous training data, where $\phi(q_i)$ is the feature vector of an image patch q_i, ω_i is a binary label, and s_i is a counting number that indicates how many support vectors are represented by this instance. We re-train the SVM classifier at each frame using the prototype set and the new data $\mathcal{L} = \{(x_i, y_i)\}_1^J$ by minimizing

$$\min_{\mathbf{w},b} \frac{1}{2}\|\mathbf{w}\|^2 + C\{\sum_{i=1}^B \frac{s_i}{N_{\omega_i}}L_h(\omega_i, q_i; \mathbf{w}) + \sum_{i=1}^J \frac{1}{N_{y_i}}L_h(y_i, x_i; \mathbf{w})\}, \qquad (8)$$

Alg. 1. MEEM-TRACK

input : frames $\{I_t\}_0^T$, initial bounding box $\mathbf{b}_0$
output: bounding box predictions$\{\mathbf{b}_t\}_1^T$

initialize tracker $\mathcal{T}$ using I_0 and $\mathbf{b}_0$
$\mathbf{E} \leftarrow \{\mathcal{T}\}$
for $t = 1 : T$ **do**
$\quad$ **if** $\mathrm{mod}\,(t, \varphi) = 0$ **then**
$\quad\quad$ $\mathbf{E} \leftarrow \mathbf{E} \cup \{\mathcal{S}_t \leftarrow \mathcal{T}\}$, discard the oldest expert when $|\mathbf{E}| > \widehat{N}$
$\quad$ get the instance bag and the label set $(\mathbf{x}, \mathbf{z})$ from $\mathbf{E}$
$\quad$ **foreach** $E \in \mathbf{E}$ **do** compute $\mathfrak{L}_E^t$ by Eq. 3-7 **if** *a disagreement among the experts is detected*
$\quad$ **then**
$\quad\quad$ $\mathcal{T} \leftarrow E^*$ by expert selection using Eq. 1
$\quad$ predict $\mathbf{b}_t$ by $\mathcal{T}$
$\quad$ re-train $\mathcal{T}$ using I_t and $\mathbf{b}_t$

Alg. 2. SVM-UPDATE

input : Tracker $\mathcal{T} = (\mathbf{w}, b, Q)$, training samples $\mathcal{L} = \{(x_i, y_i)\}$
output: Updated tracker $\mathcal{T}$

compute $(\mathbf{w}, b)$ using $\mathcal{L}$ and Q, given in Eq. 8 and Eq. 9
$Q \leftarrow Q \cup \{(\phi(x_{i_k}), y_{i_k}, 1) : (x_{i_k}, y_{i_k}) \in \mathcal{L}$ is a support vector$\}$
while $|Q| > \widehat{B}$ **do**
$\quad$ **if** $|Q^+| > \widehat{B}^+$ **then**
$\quad\quad$ $(i_1, i_2) \leftarrow \arg\min_{\{(i_1, i_2) : \omega_{i1} = \omega_{i2}\}} \|\phi(q_{i1}) - \phi(q_{i2})\|$
$\quad$ **else** $(i_1, i_2) \leftarrow \arg\min_{\{(i_1, i_2) : \omega_{i1} = \omega_{i2} = -\}} \|\phi(q_{i1}) - \phi(q_{i2})\|$ $\zeta^* \leftarrow \mathrm{MERGE}\,(\zeta_{i_1}, \zeta_{i_2})$ by
$\quad$ Eq. 10
$\quad$ delete $\{\zeta_{i_1}, \zeta_{i_2}\}$ from Q, and add ζ^* to Q

---

where L_h is the hinge loss, and

$$N_+ = \sum_{\omega_i = +} s_i + \sum_{y_i = +} 1, \quad N_- = \sum_{\omega_i = -} s_i + \sum_{y_i = -} 1 \qquad (9)$$

are used to equalize the total weight of the positive samples and that of the negative samples. This is to account for the imbalance of training samples, which is not considered in [26]. From Eq. 8, it can be seen that prototype instances with larger counting numbers have greater influence on training.

After training, support vectors from the new training data are added to the prototype set with counting number 1. When the size of the prototype set is larger than a predefined budget B, the pair of prototype instances of the same label with the minimal distance in the feature space are merged into $\zeta^* = (\phi(q^*), \omega^*, s^*)$, where

$$\phi(q^*) = \frac{s_{i_1}\phi(q_{i_1}) + s_{i_2}\phi(q_{i_2})}{s_{i_1} + s_{i_2}}, \quad \omega^* = \omega_{i_1}, \quad s^* = s_{i_1} + s_{i_2}. \qquad (10)$$

Since positive samples usually have much lower diversity than negative ones in the tracking problem, the algorithm of [26] tends to make the positive prototype instances collapse into a single instance. To avoid this for our SVM tracker, positive prototype instances are not merged until their number $|Q^+|$ reaches a predefined bound $\widehat{B}^+$. The complete online SVM algorithm is described in Alg. 2. In our implementation, we use $C = 100$, $\widehat{B} = 80$ and $\widehat{B}^+ = 10$. We have found that, in practice, the performance of our tracker tends to be insensitive to these settings.

To obtain nonlinear decision boundaries with linear SVM, we use the feature mapping technique proposed in [19] to approximate the min kernel SVM. Suppose that each component a of a feature vector $\mathbf{v} = [a_i]$ is in the range $[0, 1]$, and we discretize $[0, 1]$ into K levels. Then the mapping is defined as

$$\phi(a) = \mathcal{U}(\mathcal{R}(Ka)), \tag{11}$$

where $\mathcal{R}(.)$ is a rounding function and $\mathcal{U}(.)$ is a unary representation transformation. For example, when $K = 5$, $\phi(0.6) = \mathcal{U}(3) = [1, 1, 1, 0, 0]$. Then $\phi(\mathbf{v}) = [\phi(a_i)]$ is fed to the SVM classifier for training and inference.

5 Implementation Details

Base Tracker. In the implementation of the SVM tracker, only translation is considered for efficiency. Search for the target is conducted on a Cartesian grid of unit step ϵ_{step} within a radius of $\sqrt{wh}$ of the previous prediction, where (w, h) is the template size. The predicted position gives the positive sample, and the local image patches that do not significantly overlap the prediction (IOU < 0.5) are the negative ones.

Images are transformed into CIE Lab color space. To provide robustness to drastic illumination variations, a non-parametric local rank transform [30] is applied on the L channel of the image. This transform produces a feature map that is invariant to any monotonically increasing transformations of pixel intensities. This feature map and the Lab channels constitute a 4-channel source image, where the appearance of an image patch is represented by its spatially down-sampled version using a sample step that equals ϵ_{step}. This down-sampled 4-channel image patch is reshaped into a vector, which is to be transformed by the feature mapping technique with the quantization number $K = 4$ for our base tracker. The sample step ϵ_{step} is automatically set at runtime, so that the final feature dimension of an image patch is approximately 2000. Training involves about 200 training samples, which takes less than 0.1s in our Matlab implementation.

Multi-Expert Framework. To get the candidate instance bag $\mathbf{x} = \{x^1, \ldots, x^n\}$ for a frame, each expert E outputs a confidence map $\mathcal{F}_E$ for the search region by computing

$$\mathcal{F}_E^{ij} = P(l^{ij}|+)P(+|\phi^{ij}; \theta_E) \tag{12}$$

on the search grid (i, j). l^{ij} and ϕ^{ij} are the location and the feature respectively. For $P(+|\phi^{ij}; \theta_E)$, the SVM scores are transformed to the probability form by a Gaussian cumulative distribution with mean of 0 and STD of 1, and thereby $P(-|\phi^{ij}; \theta_E) = 1 - P(+|\phi^{ij}; \theta_E)$. The spatial prior $P(l^{ij}|+)$ is a 2D Gaussian distribution centered at the previously predicted location with STD σ, and $P(l^{ij}|-)$ is a uniform distribution. Both the spatial prior density functions are normalized for the search grid so that

$\sum_{ij} P(l^{ij}|+) = \sum_{ij} P(l^{ij}|-) = 1$. Each confidence map $\mathcal{F}_E$ is then shifted and scaled to range from 0 to 1.

After non-maxima suppression of $\mathcal{F}_E$ with an $r \times r$ kernel, image patches corresponding to the local maxima with confidence value greater than ψ are added to the candidate instance bag $\mathbf{x}$. If the center distance of two candidate image patches proposed by different experts is smaller than r, we merge the pair to the image patch at their mean position, so that the candidate patches do not substantially overlap.

The global maximum on each confidence map $\mathcal{F}_E$ serves as the prediction of E. If any of the predictions of the experts deviates from their mean position by a distance more than r, a disagreement of the experts is detected. Then the expert selected via Eq. 1 will be assigned to the current tracker.

In our experiments, we use $\sigma = 15$, $r = 5$, both in grid units, and $\psi = 0.9$. We set $\Delta = 5$ in Eq. 1 and $\lambda = 10$ in Eq. 3. These parameters are set via grid search on a small training set. The maximum number of experts $\widehat{N}$ and the time interval for saving a snapshot φ are set to 4 and 50 respectively. We find that increasing $\widehat{N}$ only slightly improves the performance in practice, but more computation would be needed to evaluate the experts at each time step.

Our algorithms are implemented in Matlab and C. It on average runs at roughly 10fps on a 2.93GHz CPU with 8GB memory. Source code is available on our website[2]. All parameters of our tracker are fixed throughout the experiments.

6   Experiment I: General Comparison

In this section, we report an extensive evaluation of the proposed tracking method, denoted as MEEM, in comparison with other state-of-the-art trackers. Testing a tracker on a small number of sequences can sometimes cause biased evaluation because of the peculiarities of the selected sequences. To avoid this problem, we use the benchmark dataset of 50 sequences proposed by [27]. This dataset contains many sequences used in the previous literature, and covers a variety of challenging scenarios for visual tracking.

Evaluation Setting and Metrics. Three experiments are performed as in [27]: one pass evaluation (OPE), temporal robustness evaluation (TRE) and spatial robustness evaluation (SRE). TRE randomizes the starting frame and runs a tracker through the rest of the sequences, and SRE randomizes the initial bounding boxes by shifting and scaling. We use the same spatial and temporal randomization as in [27], and refer readers to [27] for more details. As pointed out by [27], traditional one-pass evaluation cannot fully reflect the robustness of a tracker, and sometimes even a small perturbation can cause very different tracking results.

Following [27], two evaluation methods are used: precision plot and success plot. Both plots show the percentage of successfully tracked frames vs. the threshold. The precision plot thresholds the center location error (in pixels) and the success plot thresholds the intersection over union (IOU) metric. As discussed in [27,3], the precision plot and the success plot are more informative than some widely used metrics, *e.g.* the success rate and the average center location error. To rank the trackers, two types of ranking

---

[2] http://www.cs.bu.edu/groups/ivc/software/MEEM/

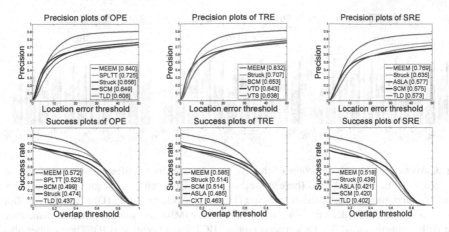

Fig. 2. Average precision plots (top row) and success plots (bottom row) for OPE, SRE and TRE (best viewed in color). The top five trackers with respect to the ranking scores are shown in each plot. The numbers in the square brackets are the ranking scores of the trackers, averaged over all 50 test sequences. Note that the line style of a curve is determined by the ranking of the corresponding tracker in the plot, not by the name of the tracker.

metrics are used as in [27]: the representative precision score at threshold $= 20$ for the precision plot, and the Area Under the Curve (AUC) metric for the success plot. Plots and ranking metrics are computed using the software and annotations provided by [27].

Compared Algorithms. Results of 29 trackers on this benchmark dataset are reported in [27]. For a more complete comparison, we also include three more recent trackers in this experiment: LSHT [12], LSST [25] and SPLTT [23]. SPLTT is only evaluated for OPE due to limited computational resources. We also note that SPLTT employs batch processing for all previous frames on each model update; thus, it is not directly comparable with the other trackers that assume a constant memory budget.

Results. Precision and success plots are shown in Fig. 2. A tracker's curve on a plot is computed by averaging its curves on all 50 test sequences. Due to limited space, only the results of the top five trackers are reported in each plot (SPLTT [23], Struck [11], SCM [32], TLD [14], VTD [16], VTS [17], ASLA [13] and CXT [6]). For results of other trackers, we refer the readers to our supplementary materials. Note that the rankings of the trackers vary on different plots.

From Fig. 2, it can be seen that MEEM attains the best overall performance by a significant margin in all evaluation settings. For example, in the precision plots, the ranking score of MEEM outperforms the second best score by over 0.11 in OPE, TRE and SRE, which is a performance gain of over 15%. Trackers usually give higher ranking scores in TRE and lower ones in SRE than in OPE. This is because in TRE, a tracker is tested by multiple runs starting at different time positions of a sequence, and thus a tracker may skip the challenging parts of a sequence. In contrast, SRE is more challenging due to the misalignment of the initial bounding box.

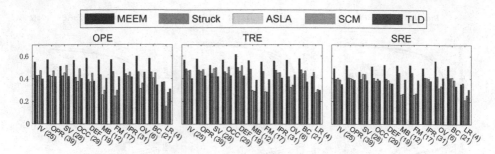

Fig. 3. Average AUC ranking scores of the five leading trackers on different subsets of test sequences in OPE, TRE and SRE (best viewed in color). Each subset of sequences corresponds to an attribute, such as illumination variation (IV), out-of-plane rotation (OPR), scale variation (SV), occlusion (OCC), deformation (DEF), motion blur (MB), fast motion (FM), in-plane rotation (IPR), out-of-view (OV), background clutter (BC), low resolution (LR). The number after each attribute name is the number of sequences that have this attribute. Trackers displayed here are selected based on their AUC ranking scores in SRE.

Each of the 50 benchmark videos is also annotated with attributes that indicate what kinds of challenging factors occur within it. Fig. 3 shows the AUC ranking scores of the leading trackers on different groups of sequences, where each group corresponds to a different attribute. For example, the group of "deformation" (DEF) contains all the sequences in which the target undergoes non-rigid deformation. See [27] for detailed definitions of the annotations. Note that a single video may include multiple attributes.

From Fig. 3, it can be seen that in all evaluation settings, MEEM substantially outperforms the other state-of-the-art trackers on such attribute groups as "deformation" (DEF), "out-of-plane rotation" (OPR), "in-plane rotation (IPR)", "out-of-view (OV)" and "occlusion" (OCC). The ranking scores of precision plots of MEEM show a similar trend, and they are provided as supplementary materials. To be more specific, MEEM tends to better handle those sequences like "basketball", "bolt", "david3", "ironman", "lemming", "liquor", "matrix", and "soccer", which feature either severe occlusions or large appearance variations. This observation is consistent with the overall formulation of our tracking method. Our base tracker, based on an online SVM algorithm with prototype set maintenance and the explicit feature mapping [19], can efficiently find the nonlinear decision boundary through online training. Moreover, when model drift is inevitable, the proposed multi-expert restoration scheme can also help to correct that drift. We also note that even though our tracking method does not account for scale changes, it still compares favorably with the state-of-the-art trackers on sequences with substantial scale variations (SV), as shown in Fig. 3.

To gain further insight into the performance of MEEM, we also compare it with several baselines: (1) MEEM-lkh, a version of MEEM using only the likelihood term for expert selection, i.e. $\lambda = 0$ in Eqn. 3; (2) SVM-avg, the model average of the experts; (3) SVM-base, our base tracker. The results of this comparison are summarized in Table 1 and detailed tables are provided as supplementary material. MEEM outperforms its baselines in all evaluation settings. MEEM gives significantly better performance

Table 1. Average ranking scores of MEEM and SVM-base

	Precision			Success		
	OPE	TRE	SRE	OPE	TRE	SRE
MEEM	0.840	0.832	0.769	0.572	0.585	0.518
MEEM-lkh	0.815	0.819	0.748	0.561	0.578	0.504
SVM-avg	0.804	0.817	0.746	0.559	0.574	0.503
SVM-base	0.804	0.817	0.747	0.559	0.574	0.503

than its baselines on a few of the sequences, such as "david3", "lemming", "jogging-1" and "jogging-2", where factors like occlusions and out-of-plane rotations could lead to model drift. This indicates the proposed entropy-regularized restoration scheme is especially useful in those scenarios. We give further analysis of the our tracking method on more sequences with such challenging factors in the next section.

7 Experiment II: Analysis of MEEM

We now further analyze and illustrate the benefit of the proposed MEEM framework on a newly collected video dataset that better reflects the real world scenarios of frequent occlusions and repetitive appearance variations.

Dataset. To control factors irrelevant to our analysis, *e.g.* large scale changes and highly non-rigid motions, we gathered a new dataset of ten sequences with moderate scale variations, where the target object can be approximately represented by a rigid rectangular template. Most sequences are from Youtube, except "ped1" and "ped2", which are from [5]. These sequences feature severe occlusions ("dance", "boxing1", "boxing2", "ped1", "ped2"), abrupt illumination changes ("carRace", "billieJean"), low contrast ("ball", "ped2", "rocky", "billieJean"), and large repetitive appearance variations ("latin", 'ball", "carRace", "dance", "billieJean"). The total number of frames in this dataset is more than 7500. These sequences tend to cause the drift problem and tracking failure for many state-of-the-art trackers. Sample frames from these sequences are shown in Fig. 4. Test sequences and annotations are available on our website.

Evaluation Setting and Metrics. We use both OPE and SRE for evaluation, so that our analysis will not be sensitive to the perturbation of initialization. Note that TRE is less

Fig. 4. Example frames from the test sequences (best viewed in color)

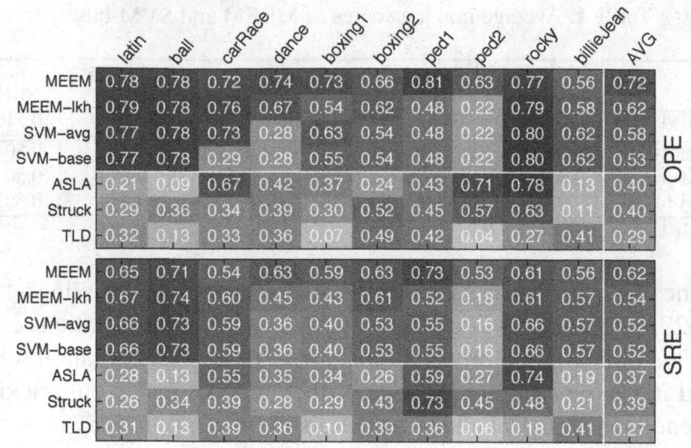

	latin	ball	carRace	dance	boxing1	boxing2	ped1	ped2	rocky	billieJean	AVG	
MEEM	0.78	0.78	0.72	0.74	0.73	0.66	0.81	0.63	0.77	0.56	0.72	OPE
MEEM–lkh	0.79	0.78	0.76	0.67	0.54	0.62	0.48	0.22	0.79	0.58	0.62	
SVM–avg	0.77	0.78	0.73	0.28	0.63	0.54	0.48	0.22	0.80	0.62	0.58	
SVM–base	0.77	0.78	0.29	0.28	0.55	0.54	0.48	0.22	0.80	0.62	0.53	
ASLA	0.21	0.09	0.67	0.42	0.37	0.24	0.43	0.71	0.78	0.13	0.40	
Struck	0.29	0.36	0.34	0.39	0.30	0.52	0.45	0.57	0.63	0.11	0.40	
TLD	0.32	0.13	0.33	0.36	0.07	0.49	0.42	0.04	0.27	0.41	0.29	
MEEM	0.65	0.71	0.54	0.63	0.59	0.63	0.73	0.53	0.61	0.56	0.62	SRE
MEEM–lkh	0.67	0.74	0.60	0.45	0.43	0.61	0.52	0.18	0.61	0.57	0.54	
SVM–avg	0.66	0.73	0.59	0.36	0.40	0.53	0.55	0.16	0.66	0.57	0.52	
SVM–base	0.66	0.73	0.59	0.36	0.40	0.53	0.55	0.16	0.66	0.57	0.52	
ASLA	0.28	0.13	0.55	0.35	0.34	0.26	0.59	0.27	0.74	0.19	0.37	
Struck	0.26	0.34	0.39	0.28	0.29	0.43	0.73	0.45	0.48	0.21	0.39	
TLD	0.31	0.13	0.39	0.36	0.10	0.39	0.36	0.06	0.18	0.41	0.27	

Fig. 5. AUC ranking scores of MEEM, its baselines, and other state-of-the-art trackers for each sequence. Darker cells indicate higher scores. The last column shows the average AUC scores.

suitable for our purposes, since it can make the drift problem less obvious by skipping some parts of a sequence. The same evaluation metrics, precision plot and success plot, are used as in Sec. 6.

Compared Algorithms. We focus on the comparison of MEEM and its baselines, MEEM-lkh, SVM-avg and SVM-base (see Section 6). Scores of some state-of-the-art trackers, ASLA [13], Struck [11] and TLD [14], are also reported, to give a sense of the difficulty levels of the test sequences.

Results. Fig. 5 reports the AUC ranking scores of MEEM, its baselines, and other trackers on each test sequence. On average, MEEM outperforms its baselines and other compared trackers by at least 15% in terms of the AUC ranking score in both OPE and SRE. SVM-avg gives similar overall performance as SVM-base, and MEEM-lkh is slightly better than SVM-avg and SVM-base. This indicates that the the proposed restoration scheme can better alleviate the drift problem than model averaging on the test sequences. In general, model averaging will sacrifice the adaptivity of a tracker, which is not favorable when the target undergoes large appearance changes. The substantial improvement of MEEM over MEEM-lkh verifies the advantage of the entropy regularization term in our expert selection function. On all the test sequences, MEEM is comparable with, if not better than, its best baseline. Significant performance improvement of MEEM over at least one of its baselines is observed on "carRace" (OPE), "dance" (OPE, SRE), "boxing1" (OPE, SRE), "boxing2" (OPE, SRE), "ped1" (OPE, SRE) and "ped2" (OPE, SRE).

In "carRace", the appearance of the car often changes abruptly due to illumination variation and out-of-plane rotation. In "dance", "boxing1", "boxing2", "ped1" and "ped2", the tracked person undergoes different levels of occlusion, non-rigid motion and out-of-plane rotation. These challenging factors often cause the baselines and the other compared trackers to drift on those sequences. In contrast, when the appearance of the

Fig. 6. Example frames where the tracker restoration occurs. (a)-(c) are from "dance" , where the target is the girl; (d)-(f) are from "boxing1", where the target is the boxer in blue; (g)-(h) are from "boxing2", where the target is the boxer in blue. The dashed green rectangles are the predictions of the current tracker before restoration, and the red ones are its predictions after restoration.

target becomes consistent with some previous snapshots again, our entropy-regularized multi-expert scheme can often detect the model drift and restore the tracker.

Fig. 6 shows examples of tracker restoration. In many cases, model drift is corrected by the restoration, resulting in a better localization of the target. It can also happen that the restored tracker gives the same prediction as the original one (*e.g.* Fig. 6(d)(i)), but restoration removes the effects of some recent model updates, which may have made the current tracker more ambiguous. Sometimes a restoration may lead to worse predictions (*e.g.* Fig. 6(e)). However, mistakes made in expert selection do not affect the snapshots already saved, but only the current tracker. Therefore, the effects of an undesirable tracker restoration may also be undone later on, when the target's appearance becomes consistent with some previous snapshots again.

8 Conclusions

In this paper, we propose a multi-expert tracking framework, where the base tracker can evolve backwards to correct undesirable effects of bad model updates using an entropy-regularized restoration scheme. Our base tracker exploits an online linear SVM algorithm, which uses a prototype set to manage the training samples, and an explicit feature mapping technique for efficient model update. The experimental results demonstrated the superior performance of our method, and the utility of the multi-expert scheme for drift correction.

Acknowledgments. This work was supported in part through grants from the US National Science Foundation #1029430 and #0910908.

References

1. Avidan, S.: Support vector tracking. PAMI 26(8), 1064–1072 (2004)
2. Avidan, S.: Ensemble tracking. PAMI 29(2), 261–271 (2007)
3. Babenko, B., Yang, M.H., Belongie, S.: Robust object tracking with online multiple instance learning. PAMI 33(8), 1619–1632 (2011)
4. Bai, Q., Wu, Z., Sclaroff, S., Betke, M., Monnier, C.: Randomized ensemble tracking. In: ICCV (2013)
5. Chu, D.M., Smeulders, A.W.: Thirteen hard cases in visual tracking. In: AVSS (2010)
6. Dinh, T.B., Vo, N., Medioni, G.: Context tracker: Exploring supporters and distracters in unconstrained environments. In: CVPR (2011)
7. Grabner, H., Grabner, M., Bischof, H.: Real-time tracking via on-line boosting. In: BMVC (2006)
8. Grabner, H., Leistner, C., Bischof, H.: Semi-supervised on-line boosting for robust tracking. In: Forsyth, D., Torr, P., Zisserman, A. (eds.) ECCV 2008, Part I. LNCS, vol. 5302, pp. 234–247. Springer, Heidelberg (2008)
9. Grabner, M., Grabner, H., Bischof, H.: Learning features for tracking. In: CVPR (2007)
10. Grandvalet, Y., Bengio, Y.: Semi-supervised learning by entropy minimization. In: NIPS (2005)
11. Hare, S., Saffari, A., Torr, P.H.: Struck: Structured output tracking with kernels. In: ICCV (2011)
12. He, S., Yang, Q., Lau, R.W., Wang, J., Yang, M.H.: Visual tracking via locality sensitive histograms. In: CVPR (2013)
13. Jia, X., Lu, H., Yang, M.H.: Visual tracking via adaptive structural local sparse appearance model. In: CVPR (2012)
14. Kalal, Z., Matas, J., Mikolajczyk, K.: Pn learning: Bootstrapping binary classifiers by structural constraints. In: CVPR (2010)
15. Kim, M., Kumar, S., Pavlovic, V., Rowley, H.: Face tracking and recognition with visual constraints in real-world videos. In: CVPR (2008)
16. Kwon, J., Lee, K.M.: Visual tracking decomposition. In: CVPR (2010)
17. Kwon, J., Lee, K.M.: Tracking by sampling trackers. In: ICCV (2011)
18. Li, X., Hu, W., Shen, C., Zhang, Z., Dick, A., van den Hengel, A.: A survey of appearance models in visual object tracking. arXiv preprint arXiv:1303.4803 (2013)
19. Maji, S., Berg, A.C.: Max-margin additive classifiers for detection. In: CVPR (2009)
20. Matthews, L., Ishikawa, T., Baker, S.: The template update problem. PAMI 26(6), 810–815 (2004)
21. Mei, X., Ling, H.: Robust visual tracking and vehicle classification via sparse representation. PAMI 33(11), 2259–2272 (2011)
22. Mei, X., Ling, H., Wu, Y., Blasch, E., Bai, L.: Minimum error bounded efficient l1 tracker with occlusion detection. In: CVPR (2011)
23. Supancic III, J.S., Ramanan, D.: Self-paced learning for long-term tracking. In: CVPR (2013)
24. Tang, F., Brennan, S., Zhao, Q., Tao, H.: Co-tracking using semi-supervised support vector machines. In: ICCV (2007)
25. Wang, D., Lu, H., Yang, M.H.: Least soft-thresold squares tracking. In: CVPR (2013)
26. Wang, Z., Vucetic, S.: Online training on a budget of support vector machines using twin prototypes. Statistical Analysis and Data Mining 3(3), 149–169 (2010)

27. Wu, Y., Lim, J., Yang, M.H.: Online object tracking: A benchmark. In: CVPR (2013)
28. Yilmaz, A., Javed, O., Shah, M.: Object tracking: A survey. ACM Computing Surveys (CSUR) 38(4), 13 (2006)
29. Yu, Q., Dinh, T.B., Medioni, G.: Online tracking and reacquisition using co-trained generative and discriminative trackers. In: Forsyth, D., Torr, P., Zisserman, A. (eds.) ECCV 2008, Part II. LNCS, vol. 5303, pp. 678–691. Springer, Heidelberg (2008)
30. Zabih, R., Woodfill, J.: Non-parametric local transforms for computing visual correspondence. In: Eklundh, J.-O. (ed.) ECCV 1994. LNCS, vol. 801, Springer, Heidelberg (1994)
31. Zhang, T., Ghanem, B., Liu, S., Ahuja, N.: Low-rank sparse learning for robust visual tracking. In: Fitzgibbon, A., Lazebnik, S., Perona, P., Sato, Y., Schmid, C. (eds.) ECCV 2012, Part VI. LNCS, vol. 7577, pp. 470–484. Springer, Heidelberg (2012)
32. Zhong, W., Lu, H., Yang, M.H.: Robust object tracking via sparsity-based collaborative model. In: CVPR (2012)

Robust Motion Segmentation with Unknown Correspondences

Pan Ji[1], Hongdong Li[1], Mathieu Salzmann[1,2], and Yuchao Dai[1]

[1] Australian National University, Canberra
[2] NICTA, Canberra

Abstract. Motion segmentation can be addressed as a subspace clustering problem, assuming that the trajectories of interest points are known. However, establishing point correspondences is in itself a challenging task. Most existing approaches tackle the correspondence estimation and motion segmentation problems separately. In this paper, we introduce an approach to performing motion segmentation without any prior knowledge of point correspondences. We formulate this problem in terms of Partial Permutation Matrices (PPMs) and aim to match feature descriptors while simultaneously encouraging point trajectories to satisfy subspace constraints. This lets us handle outliers in both point locations and feature appearance. The resulting optimization problem can be solved via the Alternating Direction Method of Multipliers (ADMM), where each subproblem has an efficient solution. Our experimental evaluation on synthetic and real sequences clearly evidences the benefits of our formulation over the traditional sequential approach that first estimates correspondences and then performs motion segmentation.

Keywords: Motion segmentation, point correspondence, subspace clustering, partial permutation matrix.

1 Introduction

Motion segmentation is a challenging problem whose outcome can positively impact many scene understanding techniques. It is well known that, under an affine camera model, the trajectories of independent motions lie in different linear (or affine) subspaces [26]. Thus, given the trajectories of points belonging to multiple moving objects, motion segmentation can be addressed as a subspace clustering problem.

Recently, there has been a surge of subspace clustering algorithms [8,13,30,15,9] reporting highly accurate results on benchmark datasets (e.g., [29]). However, motion segmentation is still far from being a solved problem. Indeed, most existing methods assume that complete point trajectories are available as input. For example, in the Hopkins155 dataset [29], perfect trajectories were obtained by manually labeling the points throughout the sequences. Such manual intervention is, of course, impractical in many realistic scenarios. While some methods are robust to small amounts of outliers (e.g., [8,13,9]), their performance quickly degrades

D. Fleet et al. (Eds.): ECCV 2014, Part VI, LNCS 8694, pp. 204–219, 2014.

as the number of mismatches increases. In practice, interest point detection and correspondence estimation are challenging tasks. Inevitable outliers and missing data make the problem even harder.

While research in the area of point correspondence estimation has also been progressing [19,33,10], existing methods are not being considered in the context of motion segmentation. Therefore, they cannot benefit from constraints associated with the problem. In particular, when observing multiple motions, the underlying point trajectories should lie in a union of subspaces.

In this paper, we introduce an approach to performing motion segmentation with unknown correspondences. In contrast to existing techniques that proceed in two stages (i.e., first correspondence estimation and then motion segmentation), this allows us to (i) benefit from the motion segmentation constraints throughout the entire process; and (ii) not require any pre-processing stage to clean up the trajectories used for motion segmentation, and thus be robust to outliers and missing observations. This, we believe, is a crucial step towards making motion segmentation applicable to more realistic scenarios.

More specifically, given interest points extracted independently in all the frames of a video sequence comprising both inliers and outliers, we exploit the constraint that data lying in the union of subspaces should be self-expressive. In other words, a trajectory lying in a subspace can be expressed as a linear combination of the other trajectories in the same subspace. We therefore search for Partial Permutation Matrices (PPMs) and combination coefficients that automatically select and reorder the inlier points so as to make them self-expressive. Furthermore, we make use of the fact that matched feature descriptors have a similar appearance across the frames and thus, when correctly arranged, should form a low-rank matrix. To obtain a solution to the resulting optimization problem, we employ the Alternating Direction Method of Multipliers (ADMM), and show that each subproblem can be solved efficiently. Given the combination coefficients, we can then separate the different motions by normalized cuts [21] or spectral clustering, as in [8,13,30,15,9].

We demonstrate the robustness and effectiveness of our method on several real sequences. Our experimental evaluation evidences the benefits of our formulation over sequentially solving correspondence estimation and motion segmentation, as is done by existing approaches. Importantly, on Hopkins155, our formulation with unknown correspondences achieves competitive results with the state-of-the-art motion segmentation methods that exploit perfect trajectories as input.

2   Related Work

Over the years, many techniques [1,5,12,25,24,18,8,13,15,9] have been proposed to tackle the problem of motion segmentation. These techniques can be roughly categorized into those working with dense observations, and those tackling the sparse points case.

In the dense scenario, the use of optical flow has been investigated to separate the motion of different objects observed in two frames [5,1], or in very short sequences [25,24]. Dense point trajectories were also employed for motion segmentation in longer videos [18].

Our work is more directly related to methods that perform motion segmentation of sparse trajectories [26,32,31]. In particular, our approach draws inspiration from the recent subspace clustering literature [8,13,15,9]. Subspace clustering approaches exploit the fact that the trajectories of points belonging to multiple independent motions lie in a union of subspaces. As such, the data can be thought of as self-expressive in the sense that each trajectory can be represented as a linear combination of the other trajectories that lie in the same subspace. The motion segmentation problem is then typically recast as that of finding the coefficients of this linear combinations. Different penalty functions have been proposed to regularize these coefficients, such as sparsity in Sparse Subspace Clustering (SSC) [8], low-rank in Low Rank Representation (LRR) [13], or density in [15,9] of the coefficient matrix. The resulting coefficients are then used to build an affinity matrix, from which motion segmentation is achieved via spectral clustering or normalized cuts.

Whether dense or sparse, trajectory-based methods all assume that the correspondence problem has been solved beforehand, and that the trajectories are thus given as input. While some advances have been made towards handling outliers [8,13,9] and incomplete point tracks [23,4], the resulting techniques still require relatively clean data to yield good accuracy.

Ultimately, motion segmentation methods strongly rely on the accuracy of point correspondences. These correspondences can typically be obtained by independently matching local feature descriptors [14,16], or by making use of the temporal nature of the data to track sparse [22] or dense [2] image points. Rather than treating each point independently, several methods have been proposed to jointly find nonrigid correspondences between two sets of points [11,28,7]. In [27], this is achieved by combining point location and appearance.

In the case of a single rigid motion, it was shown that correspondence estimation can be expressed as a rank-minimization problem in terms of PPMs [19]. Indeed, when correctly organized, the trajectories of rigidly moving points form a rank 4 matrix. While, in [19], this was achieved by incrementally incorporating one frame at a time, which is subject to error propagation, this idea was pursued for Robust Object Matching using Low-rank and sparse constraints (ROML) [33,10], where a whole sequence was treated at once. Furthermore, in [33,10], this framework was extended to minimizing the rank of a matrix built from feature descriptors, thus making the approach applicable to more general correspondence problems.

However, while attractive, general solutions to the correspondence problem, such as [27,33,10] do not permit taking into account the specific constraints of the task at hand. Here, in contrast, we introduce an approach that jointly performs correspondence estimation and motion segmentation, and can thus incorporate the subspace constraints in motion segmentation throughout the whole process. As a result, not only does it yield high segmentation accuracy, but it also improves correspondence estimation.

3   Problem Formulation

We now present our approach to robust motion segmentation with unknown correspondences. Intuitively, we seek to select the inlier input points and reorder them such that they satisfy the subspace constraints (i.e., the point trajectories lie in a union of subspaces) and appearance constraints (i.e., the matched feature points have similar appearance across the images).

More specifically, let $\mathbf{w}_{fi} \in \mathbb{R}^{2 \times 1}$ be the 2D location of point i detected in frame f of an F-frame sequence depicting multiple motions. Furthermore, let $\mathbf{t}_{fi} \in \mathbb{R}^{d \times 1}$ be the appearance descriptor of the same point in the same frame. The locations of all points in frame f can be concatenated in a $2 \times N_f$ position matrix $\mathbf{W}_f = [\mathbf{w}_{f1}, \cdots, \mathbf{w}_{fN_f}]$. Similarly, we can group all feature descriptors in frame f in a $d \times N_f$ matrix $\mathbf{T}_f = [\mathbf{t}_{f1}, \cdots, \mathbf{t}_{fN_f}]$.

In the absence of point correspondence across the frames, and even if we assume $N_f = N$, $\forall f$, simply stacking up of all the position matrices $\{\mathbf{W}_f\}_{f=1}^{F}$ does not yield valid point trajectories. However, there exists a reordering of the columns of the position matrix in each frame that yields coherent point trajectories[1]. Furthermore, when applied to the descriptor matrices $\{\mathbf{T}_f\}_{f=1}^{F}$, this ordering should also make the appearance of corresponding features coherent across the frames. In the presence of outliers, i.e., $N_f \neq N_{f'}$, $f \neq f'$, this process should not only reorder the points, but also select the inliers.

Following [19,4,33], we utilize Partial Permutation Matrices (PPMs) to model this reordering. Let $\mathbf{P}_f \in \{0,1\}^{N_f \times N}$ denote the PPM that selects and reorders the N inlier point coordinates in frame f. Given the F PPMs $\{\mathbf{P}_f\}_{f=1}^{F}$, we define the trajectory matrix as

$$\mathbf{D}_c = [(\mathbf{W}_1\mathbf{P}_1)^T | \cdots | (\mathbf{W}_F\mathbf{P}_F)^T]^T .\tag{1}$$

In an ideal, noise-free scenario, there exist PPMs such that the trajectory matrix $\mathbf{D}_c$ satisfies the subspace constraints. In practice, to account for noise of measurements, we decompose $\mathbf{D}_c$ into a clean measurement matrix $\mathbf{L}_c$ and a noise matrix $\mathbf{E}_c$. This can be written as

$$\mathbf{D}_c = \mathbf{L}_c + \mathbf{E}_c .\tag{2}$$

As was shown in [8,13], the fact that trajectories lie in a union of subspaces can equivalently be formulated in terms of self-expressiveness of the data. Note, however, that self-expressiveness only holds in the noise-free case. In our formulation, we therefore make use of the clean measurement matrix $\mathbf{L}_c$ to encode self-expressiveness. This yields

$$\mathbf{L}_c = \mathbf{L}_c\mathbf{C} ,\tag{3}$$

---

[1] Note that this global reordering is subject to an ambiguity, since the order of the trajectories themselves is irrelevant. This, however, can easily be solved by fixing the order in the first frame of the sequence.

where each clean trajectory is represented as a linear combination of the other trajectories, with $\mathbf{C}$ storing the (unknown) combination coefficients. In the presence of affine subspaces, an additional constraint of the form $\mathbf{1}_N^T \mathbf{C} = \mathbf{1}_N^T$, where $\mathbf{1}_N$ is a column vector of 1s, can be further imposed.

For feature appearance, we define the $Nd \times F$ descriptor matrix obtained from the PPMs $\{\mathbf{P}_f\}_{f=1}^F$ as

$$\mathbf{D}_d = [\text{vec}(\mathbf{T}_1\mathbf{P}_1)|\cdots|\text{vec}(\mathbf{T}_F\mathbf{P}_F)] , \tag{4}$$

where $\text{vec}(\cdot)$ vectorizes its matrix argument in a columnwise manner.

Since, in a noise-free scenario, each specific feature point should have the same appearance in all the frames, $\mathbf{D}_d$ should have low rank (ideally rank one). To tackle the more realistic case of noisy measurements, however, we decompose $\mathbf{D}_d$ into a clean low rank component $\mathbf{L}_d$ and a noise component $\mathbf{E}_d$. Therefore, we have

$$\mathbf{D}_d = \mathbf{L}_d + \mathbf{E}_d. \tag{5}$$

In this formalism, our goal is to propose a formulation to motion segmentation with unknown correspondences, which satisfies the following requirements:

1. The matrix of clean inlier point trajectories $\mathbf{L}_c$ should be self-expressive.
2. The matrix of clean inlier feature descriptors $\mathbf{L}_d$ should have low-rank.
3. Noise and outliers in both point locations and feature descriptors must be accounted for.

While Point 1 is partially accounted for by the constraint in Eq. 3, it is crucial to prevent non-zero coefficients in $\mathbf{C}$ for any two trajectories belonging to different motions. Indeed, to perform motion segmentation, $\mathbf{C}$ needs to reflect the membership of the trajectories to their respective subspace. As was shown in [9], this can be achieved with any p-norm regularizer on $\mathbf{C}$. Here, in particular, we make use of the Frobenius norm, which is convex and easy to minimize. To address Point 2 in our requirements, we propose to search for the $\mathbf{L}_d$ with minimum rank. To this end, we employ a nuclear norm regularizer on $\mathbf{L}_d$, which is a convex surrogate to the rank function. Finally, Point 3 is addressed in two different ways. First, outliers in the point locations are accounted for by the PPMs. Second, to model further noise in the locations and in the descriptors, which we expect to be sparse, we make use of ℓ_1 regularizers on $\mathbf{E}_c$ and $\mathbf{E}_d$ as convex surrogates to the ℓ_0 norm.

Integrating all these constraints, we express motion segmentation with unknown correspondences as the optimization problem

$$\min_{\{\mathbf{P}_f\}_{f=1}^F, \mathbf{C}, \mathbf{L}_{c,d}, \mathbf{E}_{c,d}} \frac{1}{2}\|\mathbf{C}\|_F^2 + \lambda_1\|\mathbf{L}_d\|_* + \lambda_2\|\mathbf{E}_c\|_1 + \lambda_3\|\mathbf{E}_d\|_1$$

$$\text{s.t.} \quad \mathbf{L}_c = \mathbf{L}_c\mathbf{C} , \ \left(\mathbf{1}_N^T\mathbf{C} = \mathbf{1}_N^T\right) , \tag{6}$$

$$\mathbf{D}_c = \mathbf{L}_c + \mathbf{E}_c, \ \mathbf{D}_d = \mathbf{L}_d + \mathbf{E}_d ,$$

$$\mathbf{1}_{N_f}^T\mathbf{P}_f = \mathbf{1}_N^T, \ \mathbf{P}_f\mathbf{1}_N \leq \mathbf{1}_{N_f}, \ \mathbf{P}_f \in \{0,1\}^{N_f \times N} ,$$

where λ_1, λ_2, and λ_3 balance the different terms in the objective function, and where the constraints on $\{\mathbf{P}_f\}_{f=1}^F$ enforce these matrices to be PPMs. Note that these PPMs appear in (6) via the matrices $\mathbf{D}_c$ and $\mathbf{D}_d$ as can be seen from their definitions in Eqs. 1 and 4, respectively.

Note that, for motion segmentation with *known* correspondences, the use of the nuclear norm on the coefficients $\mathbf{C}$ has been advocated in the past [13]. This was motivated by the fact that a low-rank $\mathbf{C}$ would inherently incur a low-rank $\mathbf{L}$, thus reflecting the fact that the trajectories of K motion form a rank $4K$ matrix. However, as was shown in [9], under the self-expressiveness constraint $\mathbf{L} = \mathbf{LC}$, $\min_{\mathbf{C}} \frac{1}{2}\|\mathbf{C}\|_F^2$ and $\min_{\mathbf{C}} \|\mathbf{C}\|_*$ are equivalent. With this observation, the Frobenius norm comes as a natural choice over the nuclear norm in (6) due to its computational simplicity.

Importantly, note that, in (6), the trajectory matrix $\mathbf{D}_c$ and the descriptor matrix $\mathbf{D}_d$ share the same PPMs $\{\mathbf{P}_f\}_{f=1}^F$. This induces a connection between motion segmentation and point correspondence, and thus makes the two problems work in a cooperative manner and help each other during the optimization procedure. As will be shown in our experiments, this collaboration not only yields accurate motion segmentation, but also improves the point correspondence results over methods dedicated to this task only.

3.1   Solving (6)

Due to the discrete nature of PPMs, (6) is non-convex. Here, we propose to solve it via the ADMM, which has proven effective for many non-convex problems such as matrix separation [20], non-negative matrix factorization [34], and correspondence estimation [33]. The ADMM works by decomposing the original optimization problem into several smaller subproblems, each of which can be solved efficiently.

We therefore seek to decompose (6) into several subproblems. With the ADMM, this is achieved by first deriving the augmented Lagrangian of (6), which can be expressed as

$$
\begin{aligned}
\mathcal{L}_\rho(\{\mathbf{P}_f\}_{f=1}^F, \mathbf{C}, \mathbf{L}_{c,d}, \mathbf{E}_{c,d}, \{\mathbf{Y}_i\}_{i=1}^4) = & \frac{1}{2}\|\mathbf{C}\|_F^2 + \lambda_1\|\mathbf{L}_d\|_* + \lambda_2\|\mathbf{E}_c\|_1 + \lambda_3\|\mathbf{E}_d\|_1 \\
& + \mathrm{tr}\left(\mathbf{Y}_1^T(\mathbf{L}_c - \mathbf{L}_c\mathbf{C})\right) + \mathrm{tr}\left(\mathbf{Y}_2^T(\mathbf{1}^T\mathbf{C} - \mathbf{1}^T)\right) \\
& + \mathrm{tr}\left(\mathbf{Y}_3^T(\mathbf{D}_c - \mathbf{L}_c - \mathbf{E}_c)\right) + \mathrm{tr}\left(\mathbf{Y}_4^T(\mathbf{D}_d - \mathbf{L}_d - \mathbf{E}_d)\right) \\
& + \frac{\rho}{2}(\|\mathbf{D}_c - \mathbf{L}_c - \mathbf{E}_c\|_F^2 + \|\mathbf{L}_c - \mathbf{L}_c\mathbf{C}\|_F^2 + \|\mathbf{D}_d - \mathbf{L}_d - \mathbf{E}_d\|_F^2 + \|\mathbf{1}^T\mathbf{C} - \mathbf{1}^T\|_2^2) ,
\end{aligned}
$$

$$(7)$$

where $\{\mathbf{Y}_i\}_{i=1}^4$ are the matrices of Lagrange multipliers corresponding to the four constraints in (6), and ρ is the penalty parameter[2]. Note that, although not explicitly written here, the constraints on the PPMs are maintained.

---

[2] Note that, for ease of notation, we have omitted explicitly writing the dimension of the vectors of all 1s, now all denoted by $\mathbf{1}$.

The ADMM then consists of iteratively updating the individual variables so as to minimize $\mathcal{L}_\rho$ while the other variables are fixed. In the following, we derive the update for each of our variables. We denote by a superscript t the current value of the variables and by a superscript $t+1$ the new values.

From Eq. 7, it can be seen that $\mathbf{L}_c$ only appears in linear and least-squares terms. Therefore, its update can easily be obtained in closed-form. More specifically, it is given by

$$\mathbf{L}_c^{t+1} = \left[\left(\mathbf{Y}_3^t + \mathbf{Y}_1^t(\mathbf{C}^{t\,T} - \mathbf{I})\right)/\rho^t + \mathbf{D}_c^t - \mathbf{E}_c^t\right]\left[\mathbf{I} + (\mathbf{I} - \mathbf{C}^t)(\mathbf{I} - \mathbf{C}^{t\,T})\right]^{-1}. \quad (8)$$

Similarly, all the terms involving $\mathbf{C}$ are simple linear and quadratic terms. This yields the closed-form update

$$\mathbf{C}^{t+1} = \left[\mathbf{I} + \rho^t(\mathbf{L}_c^{t+1\,T}\mathbf{L}_c^{t+1} + \mathbf{1}\mathbf{1}^T)\right]^{-1}\left(\mathbf{L}_c^{t+1\,T}\mathbf{Y}_1^t - \mathbf{1}\mathbf{Y}_2^t + \rho^t(\mathbf{L}_c^{t+1\,T}\mathbf{L}_c^{t+1} + \mathbf{1}\mathbf{1}^T)\right). \quad (9)$$

Although not as straightforward, the updates for $\mathbf{L}_d$, $\mathbf{E}_c$ and $\mathbf{E}_d$ can still be computed efficiently. To this end, we note that these updates correspond to the solutions of the following optimization problems:

$$\mathbf{L}_d^{t+1} = \underset{\mathbf{L}_d}{\operatorname{argmin}}\, \lambda_1/\rho^t\|\mathbf{L}_d\|_* + 1/2\|\mathbf{L}_d - (\mathbf{D}_d^t - \mathbf{E}_d^t + \mathbf{Y}_4^t/\rho^t)\|_F^2, \quad (10)$$

$$\mathbf{E}_c^{t+1} = \underset{\mathbf{E}_c}{\operatorname{argmin}}\, \lambda_2/\rho^t\|\mathbf{E}_c\|_1 + 1/2\|\mathbf{E}_c - (\mathbf{D}_c^t - \mathbf{L}_c^{t+1} + \mathbf{Y}_3^t/\rho^t)\|_F^2, \quad (11)$$

$$\mathbf{E}_d^{t+1} = \underset{\mathbf{E}_d}{\operatorname{argmin}}\, \lambda_3/\rho^t\|\mathbf{E}_d\|_1 + 1/2\|\mathbf{E}_d - (\mathbf{D}_d^t - \mathbf{L}_d^{t+1} + \mathbf{Y}_4^t/\rho^t)\|_F^2. \quad (12)$$

Problems (10), (11) and (12) are convex programs whose solutions can be obtained in closed-form. To this end, let us define the soft-thresholding operator [3] $\mathcal{T}_\tau[x] = \operatorname{sign}(x)\cdot\max(|x| - \tau, 0)$, which operates elementwise on scalars or matrices. The optimal solution to (10) can then be obtained as

$$\mathbf{L}_d^{t+1} = \mathbf{U}\mathcal{T}_{\lambda_1/\rho^t}(\mathbf{\Sigma})\mathbf{V}^T, \quad (13)$$

where $[\mathbf{U}, \mathbf{\Sigma}, \mathbf{V}] = \operatorname{svd}(\mathbf{D}_d^t - \mathbf{E}_d^t + \mathbf{Y}_4^t/\rho^t)$. The updates for $\mathbf{E}_c$ and $\mathbf{E}_d$ can be written as

$$\mathbf{E}_c^{t+1} = \mathcal{T}_{\lambda_2/\rho^t}(\mathbf{D}_c^t - \mathbf{L}_c^{t+1} + \mathbf{Y}_3^t/\rho^t). \quad (14)$$

$$\mathbf{E}_d^{t+1} = \mathcal{T}_{\lambda_3/\rho^t}(\mathbf{D}_d^t - \mathbf{L}_d^{t+1} + \mathbf{Y}_4^t/\rho^t). \quad (15)$$

The PPMs $\{\mathbf{P}_f\}_{f=1}^F$ are binary matrices, and thus updating them is non-trivial. Recall that, in Eq. 7, the PPMs appear via $\mathbf{D}_c$ and $\mathbf{D}_d$ only. Therefore, $\{\mathbf{P}_f\}_{f=1}^F$ can be updated by solving the problem

$$\min_{\{\mathbf{P}_f\}_{f=1}^F} \|\mathbf{D}_c - (\mathbf{L}_c^{t+1} + \mathbf{E}_c^{t+1} - \mathbf{Y}_3^t/\rho^t)\|_F^2 + \|\mathbf{D}_d - (\mathbf{L}_d^{t+1} + \mathbf{E}_d^{t+1} - \mathbf{Y}_4^t/\rho^t)\|_F^2$$

$$\text{s.t. } \mathbf{1}^T\mathbf{P}_f = \mathbf{1},\ \mathbf{P}_f\mathbf{1} \le \mathbf{1},\ \mathbf{P}_f \in \{0,1\}^{N_f \times N}, \quad (16)$$

where $\mathbf{D}_c = [(\mathbf{W}_1\mathbf{P}_1)^T|\cdots|(\mathbf{W}_F\mathbf{P}_F)^T]^T$, $\mathbf{D}_d = [\text{vec}(\mathbf{T}_1\mathbf{P}_1)|\cdots|\text{vec}(\mathbf{T}_F\mathbf{P}_F)]$ (as defined in Eqs. 1 and 4, respectively).

Problem (16) can then be decomposed into F independent subproblems, each of which only involves one PPM. The subproblem for frame f can be written as

$$\min_{\mathbf{P}_f} \|\mathbf{W}_f\mathbf{P}_f - \alpha_f^T(\mathbf{L}_c^{t+1} + \mathbf{E}_c^{t+1} - \mathbf{Y}_3^t/\rho^t)\|_F^2$$

$$+\|\text{vec}(\mathbf{T}_f\mathbf{P}_f) - (\mathbf{L}_d^{t+1} + \mathbf{E}_d^{t+1} - \mathbf{Y}_4^t/\rho^t)\mathbf{e}_f\|_2^2 \qquad (17)$$

$$\text{s.t. } \mathbf{1}^T\mathbf{P}_f = \mathbf{1}, \ \mathbf{P}_f\mathbf{1} \leq \mathbf{1}, \ \mathbf{P}_f \in \{0,1\}^{N_f \times N} \ ,$$

where $\mathbf{e}_f$ is a binary column vector with only the fth element set to 1, and $\alpha_f = [\mathbf{e}_{2f-1}|\mathbf{e}_{2f}]$. Problem (17) turns out to be a binary assignment problem, which can be solved by the Hungarian algorithm in polynomial time [17]. The details of the solution of Problem (17) via the Hungarian algorithm are given in appendix. Once we have computed the updates $\{\mathbf{P}_f^{t+1}\}_{f=1}^F$, $\mathbf{D}_c$ and $\mathbf{D}_d$ can be updated accordingly.

Finally, the Lagrange multipliers $\{\mathbf{Y}_i\}_{i=1}^4$ and ρ can be updated as

$$\mathbf{Y}_1^{t+1} = \mathbf{Y}_1^t + \rho(\mathbf{L}_c - \mathbf{L}_c\mathbf{C}) \ , \qquad (18)$$

$$\mathbf{Y}_2^{t+1} = \mathbf{Y}_2^t + \rho(\mathbf{1}^T\mathbf{C} - \mathbf{1}^T) \ , \qquad (19)$$

$$\mathbf{Y}_3^{t+1} = \mathbf{Y}_3^t + \rho(\mathbf{D}_c - \mathbf{L}_c - \mathbf{E}_c) \ , \qquad (20)$$

$$\mathbf{Y}_4^{t+1} = \mathbf{Y}_4^t + \rho(\mathbf{D}_d - \mathbf{L}_d - \mathbf{E}_d) \ . \qquad (21)$$

$$\rho^{t+1} = \min(\eta\rho^t, \rho_m) \ , \qquad (22)$$

where $\eta > 1$ and ρ_m is the predefined maximum for ρ.

The process of iteratively updating all the variables is repeated until convergence, or until a maximum number of iterations is reached. Note that, while the ADMM does not have theoretical guarantee of global convergence for nonconvex problems, in our simulation we find it always converges to the correct solution for our problem. The empirical convergence of our algorithm will be discussed in Section 4. Our algorithm for motion segmentation with unknown correspondences is summarized in Algorithm 1.

4   Experimental Evaluation

To evaluate the effectiveness of our approach for motion segmentation with unknown point correspondences, we conducted extensive experiments on both synthetic data and real images. In total, we performed four different sets of experiments, which we discuss below. To measure/compare the performances of different algorithms, we use the following criteria: (i) Accuracy in motion segmentation, expressed as

$$\text{ACC}_{\text{ms}} = \frac{\text{total number of correctly segmented trajectories}}{\text{total number of trajectories}} \ ,$$

Algorithm 1. Motion segmentation without correspondences via the ADMM

Input:
Position matrices $\{\mathbf{W}_f\}_{f=1}^F$, descriptor matrices $\{\mathbf{T}_f\}_{f=1}^F$,
$\lambda_1, \lambda_2, \lambda_3, \eta > 1, \rho_m, \epsilon$;

Initialize: $\mathbf{C}^0, \{\mathbf{P}_f^0\}_{f=1}^F, \mathbf{E}_c^0 = 0, \mathbf{E}_d^0 = 0, \{\mathbf{Y}_i^0\}_{i=1}^4 = 0, \rho^0$;

    while not converged **do**
        1. Update $(\mathbf{L}_c, \mathbf{C}, \mathbf{L}_d, \mathbf{E}_c, \mathbf{E}_d)$ by Eq. (8), Eq. (9), Eq. (13), Eq. (14) and Eq. (15);
        2. Update $\{\mathbf{P}_f\}_{f=1}^F$ by solving F binary assignment problems (17) using the Hungarian algorithm, and then update $\mathbf{D}_c$ and $\mathbf{D}_d$ accordingly;
        3. Update $\{\mathbf{Y}_i\}_{i=1}^4$ and ρ by Eq. (18)-Eq. (22);
        4. Check the convergence conditions $\|\mathbf{L}_c - \mathbf{L}_c\mathbf{C}\|_\infty \le \epsilon$, $\|\mathbf{1}^T\mathbf{C} - \mathbf{1}^T\|_\infty \le \epsilon$, $\|\mathbf{D}_c - \mathbf{L}_c - \mathbf{E}_c\|_\infty \le \epsilon$ and $\|\mathbf{D}_d - \mathbf{L}_d - \mathbf{E}_d\|_\infty \le \epsilon$;
    end while

Output: Coefficient matrix $\mathbf{C}$, PPMs $\{\mathbf{P}_f\}_{f=1}^F$.

---

and (ii) Accuracy in point correspondences, computed as

$$\text{ACC}_{\text{pc}} = \frac{1}{FN^2} \sum_{f=1}^F \|\mathbf{P}_f \circ \mathbf{P}_f^*\|_0 \,,$$

where $\{\mathbf{P}_f^*\}_{f=1}^F$ are the ground truth correspondences (in PPM matrix), $\circ$ denotes the element-wise (Hadamard) product, and $\|\cdot\|_0$ is the ℓ_0 norm which counts the number of non-zeros entries.

4.1 Experiment-1: Synthetic Data, Noise-Free Case

In this first set of experiments, we aim to study the convergence of our algorithm. In other words, we want to understand, with perfectly controlled inputs, whether or not the proposed algorithm converges; and if so, whether it converges to the correct solution.

To this end, we synthesized two motion matrices $\mathbf{M}_1, \mathbf{M}_2 \in \mathbb{R}^{2F \times 4}$ by simulating F random rotation and translations, and two independently moving objects with shape matrices $\mathbf{S}_1, \mathbf{S}_2 \in \mathbb{R}^{4 \times N/2}$. This yields a total of N 3D points in motion. Under an affine camera model, the measurement matrix of the synthesized sequence can be computed as $\mathbf{X} = [\mathbf{M}_1\mathbf{S}_1 | \mathbf{M}_2\mathbf{S}_2] \in \mathbb{R}^{2F \times N}$. We chose $F = 25$ and $N = 40$ in all our synthetic experiments. In addition to $\mathbf{X}$, which contains point locations, we synthesized a 128-dimensional appearance vector (i.e., feature descriptor) for each feature point. The choice of 128D is only to conform to the convention of SIFT feature descriptors which will be used in all our real image experiments. We randomly generated 128-dimensional random vectors and required that the same feature point across multiple images has identical descriptors. Given this synthesized sequence, we randomly permuted the points, so that all the correspondence information is lost.

With this data, we tested our algorithm starting from two different initialization conditions (V1 and V2): (V1) Initialize the unknown permutation matrices $\{\mathbf{P}_f\}_{f=1}^F$ as the identity matrices (generally only 0-2% accuracy); (V2) Initialize the unknown permutation matrices $\{\mathbf{P}_f\}_{f=1}^F$ by a set of random permutations, under the constraint that 60% of the point correspondences are correct. The parameter of our method were set to (V1) $\rho_0 = 10^{-6}$, $\eta = 1.01$; (V2) $\rho_0 = 10^{-2}$, $\eta = 1.01$, which reflects the better initialization of (V2).

Fig. 1(a) depicts typical convergence curves (observed over 10 random trials) corresponding to the two initialization cases. We report the objective function value ($\frac{1}{2}\|\mathbf{C}\|_F^2 + \lambda_1\|\mathbf{L}_d\|_* + \lambda_2\|\mathbf{E}_c\|_1 + \lambda_3\|\mathbf{E}_d\|_1$) and the primal residuals[3] ($\|\mathbf{D}_c - \mathbf{L}_c - \mathbf{E}_c\|_F, \|\mathbf{L}_c - \mathbf{L}_c\mathbf{C}\|_F, \|\mathbf{D}_d - \mathbf{L}_d - \mathbf{E}_d\|_F, \|\mathbf{1}^T\mathbf{C} - \mathbf{1}^T\|_F$). Note that our algorithm converges to the same objective function value independently of initialization. Note also that better initialization leads to faster convergence. Here, the number of iterations reduces from 1800 to about 700. In terms of wall-clock time, this corresponds to a reduction from about 2 minutes to 46 seconds on a regular Core-i7 PC with 8GB of memory. In this experiment, the average ACC_{ms} and ACC_{pc} over the ten random tests were all 100% for both initializations. This shows that, starting from virtually no point correspondence information, our algorithm successfully recovers both the correct point matches (with 100% accuracy) and the correct motion segmentation results.

4.2 Experiment-2: Synthetic Data, with Noise and Outliers

We then investigated the robustness of our algorithm to different amounts of outliers and noise, using synthetic data. In the same manner as above, we generated a 25-frame sequence of 40 points sampled from two independent motions, and drew feature vectors from i.i.d. Gaussian distributions. We then randomly permuted the point correspondences. We incrementally increased the number of outliers from 0 to 20 by adding gross errors to both the point coordinates and the feature descriptors. In addition to outliers, we also added fixed zero-mean Gaussian noise with standard deviation σ to the inliers.

Fig. 1(b) depicts the performance (averaged over 5 random trials) of our algorithm under different amounts of outliers and at fixed inlier noise level. In particular, we show the motion segmentation accuracy as a function of the number of outliers for 3 different levels of Gaussian noise. Note that the performance of our algorithm degrades gracefully as the amount of noise and outliers increases. Overall, our algorithm is rather robust to these adverse yet realistic conditions. For example, when the amount of measurement noise is moderate (i.e., σ from 0 to 0.1), our algorithm can almost achieve perfect motion segmentation results even for large number of outliers.

4.3 Experiment-3: Real Images, Hopkins155 Dataset

The Hopkins155 multibody dataset is a popular dataset for benchmarking motion segmentation methods. It contains 155 video sequences, which are however

---

[3] Here we plot the maximum value of the four primal residuals.

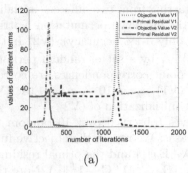 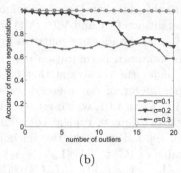

(a)   (b)

Fig. 1. (a) Convergence curves for the objective function value and the primal residuals. Blue curves: initialization (V1); red curves: initialization (V2). (b) Accuracy of motion segmentation by adding different amounts of outliers and Gaussian noise.

all generated from 49 source video sequences. Among the 49 sequences, 28 are indoor scenes containing some checkerboard patterns, and the remaining 21 are outdoor natural scenes with no checkerboard pattern. While having a checkerboard pattern simplifies manual feature point matching, the repetitive pattern can actually confuse an appearance-based automatic feature matching algorithm. For example, SIFT descriptors computed at different corner points in a checkerboard are very similar. Since our algorithm makes use of appearance information (i.e., SIFT), we tested it on the 21 outdoor sequences first. More importantly, these 21 sequences are also much more realistic than the checkerboard ones. By dividing some of the sequences with three motions (g1g2g3) into subsequences with two motions(g1g2, g1g3, and g2g3), we obtained 27 sequences which cover most of the outdoor scenes in Hopkins155. The objective for this set of experiments on the real images of Hopkins155 is to verify the practical usefulness of our algorithm.

To create appearance observations, we computed a 128D SIFT descriptor at each one of the feature point locations provided with the Hopkins155 dataset. We then deliberately threw away all feature correspondence information. Given this input, our goal is to recover the missing point correspondences, and at the same time, to segment (cluster) all the feature points into correct motion groups.

Conventionally, when no point correspondences are given, motion segmentation is performed in a two-stage approach: (i) Point correspondences are estimated by, e.g., matching feature appearance or SIFT descriptors, and (ii) Subspace segmentation methods such as SSC [8] or LRR [13] are applied to the estimated point correspondences. Therefore, we employed the following methods as baselines: (1) SIFT matching followed by SSC, denoted by SIFT+SSC; (2) SIFT matching followed by LRR, denoted by SIFT+LRR; (3) ROML matching using embedded features [27,10] followed by SSC, denoted by RE+SSC; (4) ROML matching using embedded features [27,10] followed by LRR, denoted by RE+LRR; (5) ROML matching using SIFT feature [10,33] followed by SSC, denoted by RS+SSC; (6) ROML matching using SIFT feature followed by LRR, denoted by RS+LRR. Note that the embedded features combine the SIFT

(a)   (b)   (c)   (d)

Fig. 2. Motion segmentation results of different algorithms for the cars2_07_g12 sequence. Points marked with the same color and marker ($\circ$ or $\times$) are from the same motion: (a) SIFT + SSC; (b) RE + SSC (RE: ROML with embedded feature); (c) RS + SSC (RS: ROML with SIFT feature); (d) Our algorithm. Best viewed in color.

features and the point coordinates by manifold learning [27], and were used for ROML in [10].

For ROML-based methods ((3)–(6)) and our algorithm, we initialized $\{\mathbf{P}_f\}_{f=1}^F$ with the PPMs recovered from SIFT matching, and set $\rho_0 = 10^{-2}, \eta = 1.01$. We tuned the respective parameters of baselines to achieve the best results, and empirically set $\lambda_1 = 1, \lambda_2 = 0.05, \lambda_3 = 5/\sqrt{N}$ in our algorithm.

In Table 1, we summarize the results in terms of ACC_{ms} and ACC_{pc}. From Table 1(a), we can see that our algorithm outperforms the baselines in terms of both correspondence and motion segmentation accuracies. Moreover, when given 100% complete trajectories, SSC and LRR achieve ACC_{ms} of 99.31% and 97.16%, respectively. This means that our algorithm, while not requiring any point correspondence as input, achieves motion segmentation results comparable to SSC and better than LRR.

Furthermore, when looking at the sequences whose ACC_{pc} of SIFT matching is less than 75% (see Table 1(b)), we find that our algorithm outperforms the baselines significantly in terms of both motion segmentation and point correspondence. For visual comparison, in Fig 2 we show the motion segmentation results of different algorithms on one sequence of Hopkins155.

Out of curiosity, we also performed experiments on the Hopkins155 checkerboard sequences. Due to the algorithmic complexity of ROML and of our method (mainly in the step solving the binary assignment problems), we selected the sequences with at most 200 trajectories. From the results in Table 2, we can see that our approach also outperforms the baselines on the checkerboard sequences. This shows that jointly solving motion segmentation and feature correspondence indeed helps compensating for the lack of discriminative appearance.

4.4   Experiment-4: Real Images, Other Real Sequences

Here, we show that our algorithm can be applied to perform motion segmentation in more realistic scenarios, where neither interest points nor point correspondences are provided.

Given video sequences with multiple motions, we first ran a SIFT detector over the frames to get the locations and descriptors of the detected interest points. Note that these interest points contain both inliers and outliers. The

Table 1. Average motion segmentation and point correspondence accuracies (%) on the Hopkins155 27 non-checkerboard sequences

Methods	SIFT+SSC	SIFT+LRR	RE+SSC	RE+LRR	RS+SSC	RS+LRR	Ours
(a) All 27 non-checkerboard sequences							
ACC$_{ms}$	84.83	80.10	88.47	88.47	93.03	91.30	**97.29**
ACC$_{pc}$	84.86	84.86	87.86	87.86	95.46	95.46	**98.03**
(b) The 6 sequences whose ACC$_{PC}$ of SIFT matching is less than 75%							
ACC$_{ms}$	75.01	75.57	82.35	79.47	91.60	84.34	**99.59**
ACC$_{pc}$	64.09	64.09	75.73	75.73	86.70	86.70	**95.35**

Table 2. Average motion segmentation and point correspondence accuracies (%) on the Hopkins155 checkerboard sequences with at most 200 trajectories

Methods	SIFT+SSC	SIFT+LRR	RE+SSC	RE+LRR	RS+SSC	RS+LRR	Ours
ACC$_{ms}$	60.86	60.25	75.68	63.14	78.68	66.07	**83.24**
ACC$_{pc}$	32.27	32.37	46.85	46.85	53.76	53.76	**65.02**

number of inlier points can be empirically approximated as $N = N_{sift} - 10$, where N_{sift} is the minimum number of SIFT matches from the first frame to any other frame. We then ran our algorithm to automatically select the inlier points, establish correspondences between them, and segment the trajectories into their respective motions.

We tested our algorithm on the airport sequence taken from the airport motion segmentation dataset [6]. Fig. 3 shows the results on three frames sampled from the 40-frame sequence. The inlier points are marked differently and each type of marker corresponds to one motion. Note that in each frame, 75-125 interest points were automatically extracted by the SIFT detector, and only 21 points are set as inliers, i.e., the number of outliers is 2-4 times as large as that of inliers. Moreover, the measurements of coordinates and descriptors are contaminated by noise due to the illumination variations across the sequence. As challenging as this sequence is for the task of motion segmentation, after manually labeling

Fig. 3. Motion segmentation results of the airport sequence: Points marked with the same color and marker (∘ or ×) are from the same motion. Best viewed in color.

the ground-truth correspondences for evaluation purpose, we found that our algorithm yields $\text{ACC}_{\text{ms}} = 96.43\%$ and $\text{ACC}_{\text{pc}} = 94.17\%$.

5   Conclusions

In this paper, we have proposed a unified framework to solve the problem of motion segmentation with unknown point correspondences. Our problem formulation is based on two important constraints: First, the recovered inlier point trajectories should satisfy the subspace constraints; Second, the matching feature descriptors should be low-rank, ideally rank one. With these two constraints, we have formulated our problem in terms of PPMs, which simultaneously select and reorder the inlier points. We have shown that our problem formulation can be solved via the ADMM. We have verified the effectiveness and robustness of our algorithm on both synthetic and real-world data and showed that it outperforms the existing two steps methods in terms of both motion segmentation and point correspondence accuracies. Our future work will focus on developing more efficient algorithms to solve the binary assignment problem using the inherent spatial constraints of motion segmentation.

Appendix

Solving (17) via the Hungarian Algorithm

From Problem (17), it is not straightforward to get the cost matrix for the Hungarian algorithm. Note, however, that we have $\text{vec}(\mathbf{W}_f \mathbf{P}_f) = (\mathbf{I} \otimes \mathbf{W}_f)\text{vec}(\mathbf{P}_f)$, $\text{vec}(\mathbf{T}_f \mathbf{P}_f) = (\mathbf{I} \otimes \mathbf{T}_f)\text{vec}(\mathbf{P}_f)$, where $\otimes$ is the Kronecker product. Let us define $\mathbf{G}_f = \mathbf{I} \otimes \mathbf{W}_f$, $\mathbf{a}_f = \text{vec}[\alpha_f^T(\mathbf{L}^{t+1} + \mathbf{E}_1^{t+1} - \mathbf{Y}_1^t/\rho^t)]$, $\mathbf{J}_f = \mathbf{I} \otimes \mathbf{T}_f$, and $\mathbf{b}_f = (\mathbf{M}^{t+1} + \mathbf{E}_2^{t+1} - \mathbf{Y}_3^t/\rho^t)\mathbf{e}_f$. Then Problem (17) becomes

$$\min_{\mathbf{P}_f} \|\mathbf{G}_f \text{vec}(\mathbf{P}_f) - \mathbf{a}_f\|_2^2 + \|\mathbf{J}_f \text{vec}(\mathbf{P}_f) - \mathbf{b}_f\|_2^2$$
$$\text{s.t. } \mathbf{1}^T \mathbf{P}_f = 1, \ \mathbf{P}_f \mathbf{1} \leq 1, \ \mathbf{P}_f \in \{0,1\}^{N_f \times N}. \tag{23}$$

Therefore the assignment cost $\mathbf{Q}_f^1$ (or $\mathbf{Q}_f^2$) corresponding to the first (or second) term in (23) is the squared Euclidean distance between each column of $\mathbf{G}_f$ (or $\mathbf{J}_f$) and $\mathbf{a}_f$ (or $\mathbf{b}_f$). The total assignment cost is then $\mathbf{Q}_f = \mathbf{Q}_f^1 + \mathbf{Q}_f^2$. With this assignment cost, Problem (17) becomes solvable via the Hungarian algorithm.

Acknowledgements. NICTA is funded by the Australian Government through the Department of Communications and the Australian Research Council through the ICT Centre of Excellence Program. The research is funded in part by ARC: DP120103896, DP130104567, LP100100588, DE140100180, CE140100016.

References

1. Amiaz, T., Kiryati, N.: Piecewise-smooth dense optical flow via level sets. IJCV 68(2), 111–124 (2006)
2. Brox, T., Malik, J.: Large displacement optical flow: Descriptor matching in variational motion estimation. IEEE TPAMI 33(3), 500–513 (2011)
3. Cai, J., Candes, E.J., Shen, Z.: A singular value thresholding algorithm for matrix completion. SIAM J. Optimization 20(4), 1956–1982 (2010)
4. Cheriyadat, A.M., Radke, R.J.: Non-negative matrix factorization of partial track data for motion segmentation. In: IEEE ICCV, pp. 865–872 (2009)
5. Cremers, D., Soatto, S.: Motion competition: A variational approach to piecewise parametric motion segmentation. IJCV 62(3), 249–265 (2005)
6. Dragon, R., Ostermann, J., Van Gool, L.: Robust realtime motion-split-and-merge for motion segmentation. In: Weickert, J., Hein, M., Schiele, B. (eds.) GCPR 2013. LNCS, vol. 8142, pp. 425–434. Springer, Heidelberg (2013)
7. Duchenne, O., Bach, F., Kweon, I., Ponce, J.: A tensor-based algorithm for high-order graph matching. In: IEEE CVPR, pp. 1980–1987 (2009)
8. Elhamifar, E., Vidal, R.: Sparse subspace clustering: Algorithm, theory, and applications. IEEE TPAMI 35(11), 2765–2781 (2013)
9. Ji, P., Salzmann, M., Li, H.: Efficient dense subspace clustering. In: IEEE WACV, pp. 461–468 (2014)
10. Jia, K., Chan, T.H., Zeng, Z., Ma, Y.: ROML: A robust feature correspondence approach for matching objects in a set of images. arXiv:1403.7877 (2014)
11. Leordeanu, M., Hebert, M.: A spectral technique for correspondence problems using pairwise constraints. In: IEEE ICCV, pp. 1–8 (2005)
12. Li, H.: Two-view motion segmentation from linear programming relaxation. In: IEEE CVPR, pp. 1–8 (2007)
13. Liu, G., Lin, Z., Yan, S., Sun, J., Yu, Y., Ma, Y.: Robust recovery of subspace structures by low-rank representation. IEEE TPAMI 35(1), 171–184 (2013)
14. Lowe, D.: Distinctive image features from scale-invariant keypoints. IJCV 60(2), 91–110 (2004)
15. Lu, C.-Y., Min, H., Zhao, Z.-Q., Zhu, L., Huang, D.-S., Yan, S.: Robust and efficient subspace segmentation via least squares regression. In: Fitzgibbon, A., Lazebnik, S., Perona, P., Sato, Y., Schmid, C. (eds.) ECCV 2012, Part VII. LNCS, vol. 7578, pp. 347–360. Springer, Heidelberg (2012)
16. Mikolajczyk, K., Schmid, C.: Scale and affine invariant interest point detectors. IJCV 60(1), 63–86 (2004)
17. Munkres, J.: Algorithms for the assignment and transportation problems. Journal of SIAM 5(1), 32–38 (1957)
18. Ochs, P., Malik, J., Brox, T.: Segmentation of moving objects by long term video analysis. IEEE TPAMI 36(6), 1187–1200 (2014)
19. Oliveira, R., Costeira, J., Xavier, J.: Optimal point correspondence through the use of rank constraints. In: IEEE CVPR, pp. 1–6 (2005)
20. Shen, Y., Wen, Z., Zhang, Y.: Augmented lagrangian alternating direction method for matrix separation based on low-rank factorization. Optimization Methods and Software 29(2), 239–263 (2014)
21. Shi, J., Malik, J.: Normalized cuts and image segmentation. IEEE TPAMI 22(8), 888–905 (2000)
22. Shi, J., Tomasi, C.: Good features to track. In: IEEE CVPR, pp. 593–600 (1994)

23. Sivic, J., Schaffalitzky, F., Zisserman, A.: Object level grouping for video shots. IJCV 67(2), 189–210 (2006)
24. Sun, D., Sudderth, E.B., Black, M.J.: Layered segmentation and optical flow estimation over time. In: IEEE CVPR, pp. 1768–1775 (2012)
25. Volz, S., Bruhn, A., Valgaerts, L., Zimmer, H.: Modeling temporal coherence for optical flow. In: IEEE ICCV, pp. 1116–1123 (2011)
26. Tomasi, C., Kanade, T.: Shape and motion from image streams under orthography: a factorization method. IJCV 9(2), 137–154 (1992)
27. Torki, M., Elgammal, A.: One-shot multi-set non-rigid feature-spatial matching. In: IEEE CVPR, pp. 3058–3065 (2010)
28. Torresani, L., Kolmogorov, V., Rother, C.: Feature correspondence via graph matching: Models and global optimization. In: Forsyth, D., Torr, P., Zisserman, A. (eds.) ECCV 2008, Part II. LNCS, vol. 5303, pp. 596–609. Springer, Heidelberg (2008)
29. Tron, R., Vidal, R.: A benchmark for the comparison of 3-d motion segmentation algorithms. In: IEEE CVPR, pp. 1–8 (2007)
30. Vidal, R., Favaro, P.: Low rank subspace clustering (LRSC). Pattern Recognition Letters 43, 47–61 (2014)
31. Yan, J., Pollefeys, M.: A general framework for motion segmentation: Independent, articulated, rigid, non-rigid, degenerate and non-degenerate. In: Leonardis, A., Bischof, H., Pinz, A. (eds.) ECCV 2006. LNCS, vol. 3954, pp. 94–106. Springer, Heidelberg (2006)
32. Zelnik-Manor, L., Irani, M.: Degeneracies, dependencies and their implications in multi-body and multi-sequence factorizations. In: IEEE CVPR (2003)
33. Zeng, Z., Chan, T.H., Jia, K., Xu, D.: Finding correspondence from multiple images via sparse and low-rank decomposition. In: Fitzgibbon, A., Lazebnik, S., Perona, P., Sato, Y., Schmid, C. (eds.) ECCV 2012, Part V. LNCS, vol. 7576, pp. 325–339. Springer, Heidelberg (2012)
34. Zhang, Y.: An alternating direction algorithm for nonnegative matrix factorization. Tech. rep., Rice University (2010)

Monocular Multiview Object Tracking with 3D Aspect Parts

Yu Xiang[1,2,*], Changkyu Song[2,*], Roozbeh Mottaghi[1], and Silvio Savarese[1]

[1] Computer Science Department, Stanford University, Palo Alto, USA
{yuxiang,roozbeh}@cs.stanford.edu, ssilvio@stanford.edu
[2] Department of EECS, University of Michigan at Ann Arbor, Ann Arbor, USA
changkyu@umich.edu

Abstract. In this work, we focus on the problem of tracking objects under significant viewpoint variations, which poses a big challenge to traditional object tracking methods. We propose a novel method to track an object and estimate its continuous pose and part locations under severe viewpoint change. In order to handle the change in topological appearance introduced by viewpoint transformations, we represent objects with 3D aspect parts and model the relationship between viewpoint and 3D aspect parts in a part-based particle filtering framework. Moreover, we show that instance-level online-learned part appearance can be incorporated into our model, which makes it more robust in difficult scenarios with occlusions. Experiments are conducted on a new dataset of challenging YouTube videos and a subset of the KITTI dataset [14] that include significant viewpoint variations, as well as a standard sequence for car tracking. We demonstrate that our method is able to track the 3D aspect parts and the viewpoint of objects accurately despite significant changes in viewpoint.

Keywords: multiview object tracking, 3D aspect part representation.

1 Introduction

Traditional object tracking methods focus on accurately identifying the 2D location of objects in the image and associating those locations across frames. While this capability is a critical ingredient in many application scenarios, it is often not sufficient. There are numerous situations (e.g., in autonomous driving) where not only does one need to track the location of an object (e.g., a car) but also infer its 3D pose in time – for instance, if one needs to predict a potential collision, estimating other cars' pose and angular velocities is crucial. Moreover, there are situations (e.g., in robotics or augmented reality) where one needs to identify portions of the object such as its aspects or affordance. For instance, this is critical when an autonomous agent needs to interact with, say, a car and wants to figure out where a door or a window is.

---

* Indicates equal contribution.

D. Fleet et al. (Eds.): ECCV 2014, Part VI, LNCS 8694, pp. 220–235, 2014.

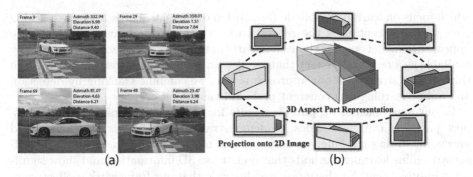

(a)   (b)

Fig. 1. (a) An example output of our tracking framework. Our multiview tracker provides the estimates for continuous pose and 3D aspect parts of the object. (b) An example of the 3D aspect part representation of a 3D object (car) and the projections of the object from different viewpoints.

Unfortunately, most of the existing tracking methods are not capable of (or at least not designed for) estimating the 3D object pose nor tracking portions of the target. In this paper, we seek to address this limitation and propose a new tracking framework that not only tracks the object in 2D, as most the state-of-the-art methods do, but also returns, as part of a joint inference problem, a continuous estimation of the viewpoint in time. Moreover, it is also able to identify and track portions of the object such as its aspects, in time (see Fig. 1(a)).

Our proposed tracker follows and generalizes the philosophy of "tracking by detection" (whereby a track is inferred by using detection hypotheses as observations) and leverages existing 3D (multiview) object representations [39,36,25,37,43,31,13,26] for detecting and estimating the 3D pose of object categories. Unlike traditional tracking by detection methods, however, that just focus on tracking the 2D or 3D location of the object, our approach also "tracks" the 3D pose and parts of the target. We leverage the 3D aspect part representation (see Fig. 1(b)) and use it in a novel particle filtering framework for multiview tracking, where combining viewpoint estimation and the 3D aspect parts enables us to predict the visibility and shape of each 3D aspect part. In particular, we leverage two state-of-the-art object detectors to train the category-level part templates in our multiview tracking framework: Deformable Part Model (DPM) [12] and Aspect Layout Model (ALM) [43]. We believe these are reasonable choices in that: i) DPM achieves state-of-the-art object detection performance and it is suitable for "tracking by detection" implementation as shown in [7,33] ii) ALM achieves state-of-the-art pose estimation results and provides a good platform for injecting 3D information to the 3D pose tracking problem; iii) ALM can recover the object layout in term of the distribution of object aspects in 3D.

Moreover, in order to increase the robustness of our tracker to viewpoint changes as well as occlusions, we propose to inject to our tracker the ability to learn the appearance of the object in an online learning fashion, similar to [2,15,20,3,38,45]. Unlike traditional online learning tracking methods, however, which focus on learning a holistic description of the entire object as the tracking goes by (an exception is the recent work by [45]), we propose to update the appearance model only for the *visible* parts of the object. Part visibility is readily available as a result of the fact that we also estimate the 3D pose of the object in time. A key strength of our approach is that we combine tracking by detection and online learning in a coherent probabilistic framework.

In our experiments, we provide results for viewpoint estimation and 3D aspect part localization. Besides, to demonstrate the usefulness of 3D pose and viewpoint during tracking, we compare our method with some of the state-of-the-art online learning methods that do not use 3D information and show significant improvement. Furthermore, we illustrate that our framework is effective in leveraging temporal information to provide continuous estimates for the object pose with and without online learning. Finally, we show that in the presence of occlusions, online learning helps increase the robustness and accuracy.

Since the current benchmark datasets for online object tracking [41] are not designed to test the ability of the trackers on handling topological appearance changes and do not show significant viewpoint variations, we collected a new challenging dataset with 9 multiview car video sequences from YouTube for experiments. We also test our method on a subset of the KITTI dataset [14] which comprises videos with significant viewpoint changes. Furthermore, we evaluate our method on a standard sequence for car tracking without viewpoint variations [20]. We demonstrate the ability of our method to accurately track viewpoints and 3D aspect parts in videos. Fig. 1(a) shows the tracking results of our method.

Contributions. 1) We propose a multiview tracker to handle the topological appearance change of rigid objects during tracking, which estimates continuous 3D viewpoint in a monocular setting. 2) Our multiview tracker is able to track the 3D aspect parts of an object. 3) We combine category-level pre-trained 3D object detectors and instance-level online-learned part appearance models in a principled way. 4) We contribute a new dataset with 9 car video sequences for multiview object tracking, and show promising tracking results on it.

2   Related Work

Tracking by Detection. Our approach falls in the category of tracking by detection methods [4,5,7,33,44], where category-level detectors are utilized to track the target of interest. However, in contrast to these methods, our focus is on tracking continuous 3D pose and 3D aspect parts.

Online Object Tracking. Online trackers focus on constructing appearance models which adapt to appearance changes during tracking [2,15,20,3,45,38]. By leveraging online learning techniques, such as online multiple instance learning [2], online structural learning [45] and self-paced learning [38], these methods have achieved robust tracking results on benchmark datasets [41]. Since they are able to track generic objects, they are referred to as model-free trackers. However, as shown in our experiments, they cannot handle the topological appearance change of objects caused by severe viewpoint transformations. An exception is the recent work by [29] which extends the Lucas-Kanade algorithm [28] with pixel object/background likelihoods. It shows competitive performance on a vehicle tracking dataset with severe viewpoint changes.

Multiview Object Recognition. Our tracker builds upon the idea of multiview recognition. The goal of multiview object recognition is to recognize objects from arbitrary viewpoints, which dates back to the early works in computer vision (e.g., [27,9]). Recent works in multiview object recognition either represent objects as collections of parts or features which are connected across views [39,36,37], or utilize explicit 3D models with associated visual features to represent objects [25,43,31,13,26]. Our method benefits from the 3D aspect part representation introduced in [43]. While [43] focuses on object detection and pose estimation from single images in a discretized viewpoint space, we show that the 3D aspect part representation can be utilized to estimate continuous object pose and 3D aspect part locations in multiview object tracking.

3D Model-Based Tracking. Multiview object recognition methods have been extended and applied to 3D tracking [35,10,24,6,34,30]. Most of the previous works aim at tracking the 3D pose of an object *instance* using its 3D CAD model, e.g., [10,6,34]. In contrast, we focus on 3D tracking of object *categories* with a 3D object category representation, which is able to handle the intra-class variability among object instances in the same category.

Monocular vs. Multi-Camera Multiview Object Tracking. An alternative way to achieve multiview object tracking is to utilize multi-camera settings, where the target is observed from multiple cameras simultaneously [21,23,17]. Tasks such as occlusion reasoning [21] and 3D reconstruction [17] which are challenging in monocular settings can be solved efficiently in multi-camera environments. Since multiple cameras are only available in specific scenarios, we focus on monocular multiview tracking in this work.

3D Tracking and Reconstruction In contrast to methods that track targets in 3D (e.g., [19,11,32]), we have access only to videos and do not use other sensor modalities such as range data. Compared with methods that perform joint 3D reconstruction and tracking (e.g., [16,18]), we are interested mainly in estimating the 3D pose and shape extent of the target in terms of its part layout.

3   Multiview Tracking Framework

The primary goal of multiview object tracking is to estimate the posterior distribution of the target's state $P(X_t, V_t | Z_{1:t})$ at the current time step t given all observations $Z_{1:t}$ up to that time step, where X_t and V_t denote the location and viewpoint of the target at time t respectively. Instead of tracking the object as a whole, which cannot handle the topological appearance change of object, we propose to track the 3D aspect parts of the object and its viewpoint jointly while modeling the relationship between these parts. By using a 3D aspect part representation of the object (Fig. 1(b)), we can predict the visibility and shape of the parts in arbitrary viewpoints. In this way, the tracking framework is able to handle the appearance change introduced by viewpoint transitions, especially in cases when a part disappears or reappears due to self-occlusion. Consequently, the location of the object at time t is determined by the locations of the 3D aspect parts, i.e., $X_t = \{X_{it}\}_{i=1}^n$, where n is the number of parts and X_{it} denotes the location of part i at time t. The viewpoint V_t is represented by the azimuth a_t, elevation e_t and distance d_t of the camera position in 3D with respect to the object, i.e., $V_t = (a_t, e_t, d_t)$ as shown in Fig. 2(a).

By applying Bayes rule, the posterior distribution can be decomposed as

$$P(X_t, V_t|Z_{1:t}) \propto \tag{1}$$

$$\underbrace{P(Z_t|X_t, V_t)}_{\text{likelihood}} \int \underbrace{P(X_t, V_t|X_{t-1}, V_{t-1})}_{\text{motion prior}} \underbrace{P(X_{t-1}, V_{t-1}|Z_{1:t-1})}_{\text{posterior at time t-1}} dX_{t-1} dV_{t-1},$$

where the likelihood $P(Z_t|X_t, V_t)$ measures the probability of observing measurement Z_t given the state of the target (X_t, V_t) at time t, the motion prior $P(X_t, V_t|X_{t-1}, V_{t-1})$ predicts the state of the target at time t given its previous state, and $P(X_{t-1}, V_{t-1}|Z_{1:t-1})$ is the posterior at time $t - 1$.

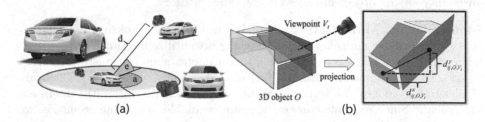

Fig. 2. (a) The viewpoint of the object is represented by the azimuth, elevation, and distance of the camera pose in 3D, $V = (a, e, d)$. (b) Illustration of the relative distance between two parts by projecting the 3D object onto a 2D image.

3.1   Likelihood

The likelihood $P(Z_t|X_t, V_t)$ measures the compatibility between the state of the target (X_t, V_t) with the observation Z_t at time t. Since we track an object by its 3D aspect parts, the likelihood of the object is decomposed as the product of the likelihoods of the 3D aspect parts:

$$P(Z_t|X_t, V_t) = \prod_{i=1}^n P(Z_t|X_{it}, V_t), \tag{2}$$

where $P(Z_t|X_{it}, V_t)$ denotes the appearance likelihood of part i. The likelihood is measured based on category-level pre-trained part appearance models. To make the likelihood more robust in some difficult scenarios (e.g., occlusion), we also use instance-level online-learned part appearance models in computing the likelihoods for 3D aspect parts. In traditional online object tracking, the likelihood of a part is computed using the appearance model of that part learned online, where the assumption is that the part is always visible during tracking. However, this is not necessarily true when the viewpoint changes. When parts with learned appearance models disappear and unseen parts become visible, the tracker loses the target. In our case, when new parts appear, if no online appearance models have been learned for them before, we resort to the category-level part templates to compute the likelihood. Subsequently, the online appearance models for the new parts are initialized according to the tracking output and updated afterwards. The online appearance model is updated according to the 3D pose, i.e., we only update the model for the visible parts. Specifically, we define the likelihood as:

$$P(Z_t|X_{it}, V_t) \propto \exp\left(\Lambda_{\text{category}}(Z_t, X_{it}, V_t) + \Lambda_{\text{online}}(Z_t, X_{it}, V_t)\right), \quad (3)$$

where $\Lambda_{\text{category}}(Z_t, X_{it}, V_t)$ is the potential from the category-level part template for part i, and $\Lambda_{\text{online}}(Z_t, X_{it}, V_t)$ is the potential from the online appearance model for part i.

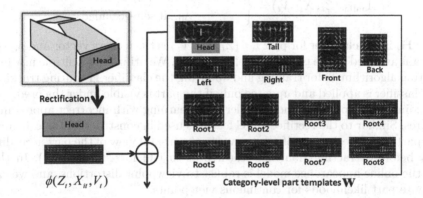

Fig. 3. Illustration of the category-level part templates and the computation of the potential for the Head part, where rectified HOG features are used

A category-level part template is trained with various instances in the same category, which captures the general shape of the part. We define the potential from the category-level part template as

$$\Lambda_{\text{category}}(Z_t, X_{it}, V_t) = \begin{cases} \mathbf{w}_i^T \phi(Z_t, X_{it}, V_t), & \text{if visible} \\ \alpha_i, & \text{if self-occluded}, \end{cases} \quad (4)$$

where $(\mathbf{w}_i, \alpha_i)$ denotes the weights of the part template, and $\phi(Z_t, X_{it}, V_t)$ is the feature vector. The part template $\mathbf{w}_i$ is applied only if the part is visible.

Otherwise, an occlusion weight α_i is assigned to the part. We use rectified HOG features as $\phi(Z_t, X_{it}, V_t)$, where HOG features [8] are extracted after rectifying the image into the frontal view of the part according to the viewpoint V_t. Therefore, the part template $(\mathbf{w}_i, \alpha_i)$ corresponds to the frontal view of the part. This property is critical for continuous viewpoint estimation. In learning the part template from training images, the viewpoint space is discretized. During tracking, we can always first rectify the image into the frontal view of the part from arbitrary continuous viewpoint, and then apply the learned template. In this way, we are able to compute the likelihoods for continuous viewpoints during the Bayesian filtering tracking. All the part templates for 3D aspect parts are jointly learned from training images using a Structural SVM optimization as in [43]. Fig. 3 illustrates the learned category-level part templates and the rectified HOG features. Note that, besides training part templates for 3D aspect parts, we also introduce root templates which correspond to the whole object in different view sections and are obtained from DPM [12].

The online appearance models capture instance-level characteristics of part appearance, which are specialized to the current target. Moreover, the models are updated during tracking to accommodate appearance change. The potential of the online appearance model in Eq. (3) is defined as

$$\Lambda_{\text{online}}(Z_t, X_{it}, V_t) = \begin{cases} \mathbf{H}_i(\psi(Z_t, X_{it}, V_t)), & \text{if visible} \\ \lambda_0, & \text{if self-occluded,} \end{cases} \tag{5}$$

where $\mathbf{H}_i$ is the classifier for part i, $\psi(Z_t, X_{it}, V_t)$ is the feature vector and λ_0 is a constant assigned to the part if it is self-occluded. We utilize the multiple instance boosting algorithm [2] for training and updating the classifier $\mathbf{H}_i$ during tracking. The classifier is applied and updated only if the part is visible under the predicted viewpoint, which prevents the classifier from learning with incorrect appearance features. Similar to the rectified HOG features used in constructing the category-level part templates, we rectify the image to the frontal view of the part according to V_t before extracting Haar-like features as in [40] for $\psi(Z_t, X_{it}, V_t)$. In this way, the online appearance model is robust to viewpoint distortions, and we can compute part likelihoods for continuous viewpoints.

3.2   Motion Prior

The motion prior $P(X_t, V_t | X_{t-1}, V_{t-1})$ predicts the current state of the target based on its previous state. We decompose the motion prior according to part location and viewpoint:

$$\begin{aligned} & P(X_t, V_t | X_{t-1}, V_{t-1}) \\ &= P(X_t | X_{t-1}, V_{t-1}, V_t) P(V_t | X_{t-1}, V_{t-1}) \\ &= P(X_t | X_{t-1}, V_t) P(V_t | V_{t-1}), \end{aligned} \tag{6}$$

where $P(X_t | X_{t-1}, V_t)$ models the change in location, and $P(V_t | V_{t-1})$ is the viewpoint motion. Note that in Eq. (6), two assumptions of conditional independence are imposed to simplify the motion prior. Inspired by [22] which uses a Markov Random Field (MRF) motion prior to capture the interaction between targets, we model the change in location using an MRF that is able to capture the relationships between parts:

$$P(X_t|X_{t-1}, V_t) \propto \prod_{i=1}^{n} P(X_{it}|X_{i(t-1)}) \prod_{(i,j)} \Lambda(X_{it}, X_{jt}, V_t), \tag{7}$$

where $P(X_{it}|X_{i(t-1)})$ is the motion model for part i and $\Lambda(X_{it}, X_{jt}, V_t)$ is the pairwise potential which constrains the relative location of two parts according to the 3D aspect part representation and the viewpoint.

In order to handle abrupt location and viewpoint changes or occlusion, we do not impose a strong motion prior such as the constant velocity motion prior in our multiview tracker. The location motion of a part in Eq. (7) and the viewpoint motion in Eq. (6) are both modeled with Gaussian distributions centered on the previous location and the previous viewpoint respectively:

$$P(X_{it}|X_{i(t-1)}) \sim \mathcal{N}(X_{i(t-1)}, \sigma_x^2, \sigma_y^2) \tag{8}$$

$$P(V_t|V_{t-1}) \sim \mathcal{N}(V_{t-1}, \sigma_a^2, \sigma_e^2, \sigma_d^2), \tag{9}$$

where σ_x^2, σ_y^2, σ_a^2, σ_e^2 and σ_d^2 are the variances of the Gaussian distributions for 2D part center coordinates, azimuth, elevation and distance respectively.

To define the pairwise potential between part locations in Eq. (7), we utilize the 3D aspect part representation (Fig. 1(b)). Let O denote the 3D object representation. Given the viewpoint V_t at time t, we can project the 3D object onto the image according to V_t. Then we obtain the ideal relative distance d_{ij,O,V_t} between part i and part j as shown in Fig. 2(b). We define the pairwise potential to penalize large deviations between the observed relative part locations from the ideal ones with Gaussian priors:

$$\Lambda(X_{it}, X_{jt}, V_t) = P(\Delta_t(x_i, x_j)|V_t)P(\Delta_t(y_i, y_i)|V_t),$$
$$P(\Delta_t(x_i, x_j)|V_t) \sim \mathcal{N}(d_{ij,O,V_t}^x, \sigma_{dx}^2),$$
$$P(\Delta_t(y_i, y_j)|V_t) \sim \mathcal{N}(d_{ij,O,V_t}^y, \sigma_{dy}^2), \tag{10}$$

where $X_{it} = (x_{it}, y_{it})$ and $X_{jt} = (x_{jt}, y_{jt})$ denote the 2D center coordinates of the two parts, $\Delta_t(x_i, x_j) = |x_{it} - x_{jt}|$, $\Delta_t(y_i, y_j) = |y_{it} - y_{jt}|$, d_{ij,O,V_t}^x and d_{ij,O,V_t}^y are the ideal relative distances between the two parts in the x and y directions respectively (Fig. 2(b)), and σ_{dx}^2 and σ_{dy}^2 are the variances of the Gaussian distributions for 2D relative distances, which are set proportionally to the size of the part in the image. The pairwise potential (10) allows the 3D shape of the target to deviate from the 3D object model with some deformation cost. Note that we use a general 3D aspect part representation for an object category and apply it to different instances of that category.

3.3   Particle Filtering Tracking

In order to track the continuous pose of the target, we employ the particle filtering technique to infer the posterior distribution in Eq. (1). We use Markov Chain

Monte Carlo (MCMC) sampling, where the posterior $P(X_{t-1}, V_{t-1}|Z_{1:t-1})$ at time $t-1$ is represented as a set of N unweighted samples $P(X_{t-1}, V_{t-1}|Z_{1:t-1}) \approx (X_{t-1}^{(r)}, V_{t-1}^{(r)})_{r=1}^N$. So we obtain the following Monte Carlo approximation to the Bayesian filtering distribution:

$$P(X_t, V_t|Z_{1:t}) \propto P(Z_t|X_t, V_t) \sum_{r=1}^N P(X_t, V_t|X_{t-1}^{(r)}, V_{t-1}^{(r)}), \tag{11}$$

where $P(Z_t|X_t, V_t)$ is the likelihood and $P(X_t, V_t|X_{t-1}^{(r)}, V_{t-1}^{(r)})$ is given by the motion prior. At time t, we obtain a set of new samples by sampling from Gaussian proposal distributions on both part locations and viewpoint centered on samples at time $t-1$. Then the state of the target at time t, i.e., 3D aspect part locations and viewpoint, is predicted as the MAP of the posterior at time t, which is given by the sample with the largest posterior probability in Eq. (11). By sampling new viewpoints, we are able to predict the topological appearance change of the target, so as to apply and update the part templates accordingly. To initialize the tracker, we use the ground truth viewpoint in the first frame of the video, and aspect parts are initialized automatically by projecting the 3D aspect part model according to the viewpoint. Algorithm 1 summarizes our multiview tracking method using Bayesian particle filtering.

---

input : A video sequence $Z_{1:T}$, initial 3D aspect parts and viewpoint (X_1, V_1)
output: 3D aspect parts and viewpoints for the target in the video $(X_t, V_t)_{t=1}^T$

1   *Initialize samples $(X_1^{(r)}, V_1^{(r)})_{r=1}^N$ for the first frame by sampling viewpoints and part locations according to the motion prior (6) based on (X_1, V_1);*

2   **for** $t \leftarrow 2$ **to** T **do**

3   *Initialize the MCMC sampler: randomly select a sample $(X_{t-1}^{(r)}, V_{t-1}^{(r)})$ as the initial state of the (X_t, V_t) Markov chain;*

4   **repeat**

5   *Sample a new viewpoint from the Gaussian proposal density $Q(V_t'; V_t)$;*

6   *Compute the visibility of 3D aspect parts under viewpoint V_t';*

7   **foreach** *part i visible in both V_t' and V_t* **do**

8   *Sample its location from the Gaussian proposal density $Q(X_{it}'; X_{it})$;*

9   **end**

10   **foreach** *part i visible in V_t' but not in V_t* **do**

11   *Compute its location X_{it}' using the mean distance with respect to other visible parts according to the pairwise distributions (10);*

12   **end**

13   *Compute the acceptance ratio*

$$a = \min\left(1, \frac{P(X_t', V_t'|Z_{1:t})Q(X_t; X_t')Q(V_t; V_t')}{P(X_t, V_t|Z_{1:t})Q(X_t'; X_t)Q(V_t'; V_t)}\right); \tag{12}$$

14   *Accept the sample (X_t', V_t') with probability a. If accepted, $(X_t, V_t) \leftarrow (X_t', V_t')$. Otherwise, leave (X_t, V_t) unchanged;*

15   **until** *N samples are accepted;*

16   *Obtain the new sample set $(X_t^{(r)}, V_t^{(r)})_{r=1}^N$, and find the MAP among it as the tracking output for frame t;*

17 **end**

Algorithm 1. Multiview particle filtering object tracking

4   Experiments

We evaluate the performance of our multiview tracker on car tracking, since the ability to track cars is critical for various real world applications and it represents an informative case study in handling topological appearance change.

4.1   Datasets

The current benchmarks for evaluating trackers that handle appearance changes (e.g., [41]) are not built to emphasize the 'topological' appearance change of the target. So they are not suitable for evaluating our method whose main goal is to handle the topological appearance changes. Hence, we collected a new car tracking dataset of 9 video sequences that contain significant viewpoint change from YouTube. Each video contains one car to be tracked. To provide ground truth annotations for viewpoints and 3D aspect parts, we use the pose annotation tool proposed in [42], which computes accurate viewpoints and 3D aspect part locations of the targets using correspondences between 2D image points and 3D anchor points of CAD models. In order to test our multiview tracker in challenging real world scenarios, we also selected 11 sequences from the KITTI dataset [14] that contain significant viewpoint change. There can be multiple cars in each sequence, but we specify one car to track. In some sequences, the target is occluded temporarily which makes these sequences challenging. Finally, we evaluate our method on a standard sequence for car tracking from [20]. Unfortunately, this sequence does not contain significant viewpoint variations. Refer to the technical report in [1] for details of the annotation process and the statistics for the YouTube and the KITTI sequences.

4.2   Evaluation Measures

Our multiview tracker outputs not only the 2D bounding box of the target, but also its 3D pose and the 2D locations of the 3D aspect parts. So we evaluate the performance of our tracker on these three tasks and compare it with corresponding baselines. For 2D tracking, we report the Pascal VOC overlap ratio, which is defined as $R = Area(B_T \cap B_{GT})/Area(B_T \cup B_{GT})$, where B_T is the predicted bounding box of the target and B_{GT} is the ground truth bounding box.

For viewpoint estimation, we report two metrics. The first metric is the viewpoint accuracy, where an estimated viewpoint is considered to be correct if the deviation between the estimated azimuth and the ground truth azimuth is within $15°$. The second metric is the absolute difference in azimuth between the ground truth viewpoint and the estimated viewpoint. Since the elevation change is small in the sequences in our experiments, we do not present detailed evaluation in elevation estimation.

For 3D aspect part localization, we also use the Pascal VOC overlap ratio, where the intersection over union is computed between the predicted part shape and the ground truth part shape. If a visible part is predicted as self-occluded, the overlap ratio is zero. So we penalize incorrect aspect estimation of the target.

We measure the viewpoint and part locations for the target in one frame only if the target is correctly tracked in the frame, i.e., its overlap ratio with ground truth bounding box is larger than 0.5.

4.3   Experimental Settings

The following parameters have been set experimentally and remain fixed for all of the experiments with different sequences. In the motion prior, the standard deviations of part center coordinates in Eq. (8) are set to $\sigma_x = 4 \cdot w$ and $\sigma_y = 4 \cdot h$, where w and h denote the width and height of the part respectively. The standard deviations of viewpoint in Eq. (9) are set to $\sigma_a = 135°$, $\sigma_e = 5°$ and $\sigma_d = 10$. We use large standard deviations for both part location and viewpoint in order to recover from tracking failures due to occlusions or noisy responses from part templates. In the pairwise potential, both the standard deviations in Eq. (10) are set to $\sigma_{dx} = \sigma_{dy} = h/4$. In Eq. (5), the constant λ_0 can be arbitrary since we only compare the common visible parts of two samples when selecting the MAP sample (Algorithm 1). We compute 40 (viewpoints) × 200K (part locations) samples per frame since the joint space of viewpoint and all parts is huge. To train the templates for 3D aspect parts, we use the 3DObject dataset [36]. For the templates in DPM, we use the car model pre-trained on PASCAL'07 [12].

4.4   Results

2D Object Tracking. Tab. 1 shows the 2D object tracking results in terms of average bounding box overlap ratio on our new car tracking dataset, the KITTI sequences and the 06_car sequence from [20], where we compare our multiview tracker with several baselines. First, four state-of-the-art online tracking methods, MIL [2], L1 [3], TLD [20] and Struct [15], perform poorly on our new dataset and the KITTI sequences. Their mean overlap ratios are below 0.5. This is mainly because these online tracking methods cannot handle the topological appearance change of the cars. When the viewpoint changes, the online trackers keep tracking just a single portion of the object or even lose the target (Fig. 4).

It is evident that the category-level part templates contribute significantly in the multiview tracking setting. In Tab. 1, "Category Model" column shows the case that we use only the category-level part templates in our particle filtering framework without using online learning (refer to Eq. (3)). We can see that "Category Model" improves over the best online tracker by 30% on the new dataset and 19% on the KITTI sequences in terms of mean overlap ratio. By leveraging the 3D aspect part representation and estimating the viewpoint, our "Category Model" is able to predict the aspect change of the target and track the target in different views.

Our full model takes advantages of both category-level part templates and online-learned part appearance models, and it achieves the best mean overlap ratio on the YouTube dataset and the KITTI sequences. The highest improvement is for Race5 and KITTI03, where "Category Model" fails to track the car due to occlusion by smoke and another car, respectively. By combining online

Table 1. 2D object tracking performance using average bounding box overlap ratio

Video	MIL [2]	L1 [3]	TLD [20]	Struct [15]	DPM [12]+PF	Category Model	Full Model
Race1	0.34	0.39	0.20	0.36	0.68	0.68	**0.69**
Race2	0.49	0.49	0.28	0.50	**0.74**	**0.74**	0.73
Race3	0.36	0.26	0.25	0.44	0.74	0.74	**0.77**
Race4	0.53	0.56	0.47	0.63	**0.76**	**0.76**	0.76
Race5	0.29	0.54	0.28	0.26	0.63	0.63	**0.68**
Race6	0.27	0.53	0.48	0.29	0.76	0.76	**0.77**
SUV1	0.58	**0.81**	0.56	0.60	0.78	0.78	0.78
SUV2	0.18	0.12	0.53	0.24	**0.77**	**0.77**	**0.77**
Sedan	0.26	0.23	0.33	0.30	**0.78**	**0.78**	**0.78**
Mean	0.37	0.44	0.38	0.40	0.74	0.74	**0.75**
KITTI01	0.20	0.40	0.44	0.33	0.65	0.64	**0.69**
KITTI02	0.28	0.18	0.20	0.12	0.26	0.26	**0.32**
KITTI03	0.37	**0.59**	0.42	0.36	0.20	0.19	0.50
KITTI04	0.31	0.12	**0.36**	0.34	0.67	0.33	0.33
KITTI05	0.40	0.32	0.51	0.41	0.54	**0.73**	0.72
KITTI06	0.64	0.21	0.54	**0.65**	**0.65**	**0.65**	0.56
KITTI07	0.12	0.33	0.03	0.28	**0.66**	0.65	**0.66**
KITTI08	0.58	0.13	0	0.66	**0.74**	**0.74**	0.72
KITTI09	0.18	0.15	0	0.17	0.18	0.51	**0.52**
KITTI10	0.33	0.46	0.41	0.35	**0.68**	**0.68**	**0.68**
KITTI11	0.28	0.23	0.24	0.28	**0.71**	**0.71**	0.68
Mean	0.34	0.28	0.29	0.36	0.54	0.55	**0.58**
06_car [20]	0.19	0.52	**0.85**	0.48	0.70	0.67	0.70

appearance models, the full model can recover from occlusion and track the car by adapting its appearance models. Fig. 4 shows some tracking outputs from our multiview tracker on SUV1 and Race1. Fig. 5 displays some tracking results on KITTI03, where our full Model recovers from occlusion, but the "Category Model" switches to the occluder.

We also compare our method with a tracking-by-detection baseline, which applies particle filtering to the output of a detector (DPM [12]). Our result is on par with this baseline for 2D object localization in the YouTube and 06_car sequences, and we provide 4% improvement on the KITTI dataset. However, note that this baseline and the online trackers baselines are not able to provide the estimates for the viewpoint and aspect part locations.

The results on the 06_car sequence from [20] demonstrate that our multiview tracker can handle the degenerate case where the viewpoint of the target does not change. MIL, L1 and Struct drift due to occlusion by trees, while TLD is well designed to recover from occlusion and achieves the best performance on this sequence. Our method also recovers from occlusion but obtains lower average overlap ratio than TLD. One main reason is that the elevation angle of the car in this sequence is totally different from that of the instances we used for training the category-level part templates (see [1] for tracking videos on these datasets).

Continuous Viewpoint Estimation. The left half of Tab. 2 shows the viewpoint accuracy and the mean absolute difference in azimuth for viewpoint estimation on our new car dataset and the KITTI sequences. We compare our "Full Model" and "Category Model" with the state-of-the-art object pose estimator ALM [43]. Since ALM does not output tracks of targets, we compare the three models on the commonly tracked frames between the "Full Model" and the

Table 2. Viewpoint accuracy/mean absolute difference in azimuth and average overlap ratio of 3D aspect part on our new car dataset and the KITTI sequences

Video	Viewpoint Estimation			3D Aspect Part Localization		
	Full Model	Category Model	ALM [43]	Full Model	Category Model	ALM [43]
Race1	**0.67/18.73°**	0.59/22.88°	0.52/42.62°	**0.40**	0.39	0.35
Race2	**0.77/10.83°**	0.60/12.65°	0.53/44.30°	**0.45**	0.38	0.34
Race3	**0.83/9.28°**	**0.83/7.79°**	0.64/46.08°	0.45	**0.48**	0.31
Race4	0.69/15.83°	0.68/14.67°	**0.79/13.37°**	**0.48**	0.47	0.42
Race5	0.71/10.75°	**0.74/11.78°**	0.54/57.79°	**0.44**	0.42	0.28
Race6	**0.43/18.47°**	0.40/21.34°	0.31/37.08°	**0.35**	**0.35**	0.29
SUV1	**0.82/7.81°**	0.75/8.52°	0.47/78.38°	**0.42**	0.40	0.24
SUV2	**0.57/19.56°**	0.45/56.33°	0.39/63.41°	**0.30**	0.23	0.18
Sedan	0.76/9.87°	0.78/**9.50°**	**0.79**/20.84°	0.44	**0.45**	0.43
Mean	**0.69/13.46°**	0.65/18.38°	0.54/47.24°	**0.41**	0.40	0.30
KITTI01	**0.95/6.54°**	0.74/8.53°	0.57/44.46°	**0.49**	0.41	0.37
KITTI02	**1.00/5.40°**	0.20/30.06°	0.33/119.54°	**0.60**	0.15	0.13
KITTI03	**0.42/15.64°**	**0.42/15.14°**	0.50/15.99°	0.33	**0.33**	0.24
KITTI04	0.22/27.05°	**0.25/26.03°**	0.17/58.42°	**0.22**	**0.22**	0.14
KITTI05	0.36/23.59°	0.40/**22.17°**	**0.64**/23.65°	0.23	**0.25**	**0.25**
KITTI06	0.31/21.63°	0.29/21.58°	**0.59/20.29°**	0.21	0.21	**0.23**
KITTI07	**0.96/6.86°**	0.89/7.92°	0.70/24.50°	**0.48**	**0.48**	0.39
KITTI08	0.57/**15.61°**	0.48/23.84°	**0.67**/23.26°	**0.37**	0.29	0.26
KITTI09	**0.50**/21.63°	0.42/78.67°	**0.50/17.60°**	**0.28**	0.16	0.23
KITTI10	**0.81/7.99°**	0.79/9.44°	0.44/56.78°	**0.39**	**0.39**	0.21
KITTI11	**0.88/9.33°**	0.78/11.80°	0.68/12.29°	0.39	0.40	**0.41**
Mean	**0.63/14.66°**	0.51/23.20°	0.53/37.89°	**0.36**	0.30	0.26

"Category Model", where we use the most confident detection with overlap ratio larger than 0.5 from ALM as its output. It is clear that "Category Model" outperforms ALM in viewpoint estimation significantly. By utilizing the temporal information from videos, our multiview tracker estimates continuous viewpoints in the particle filtering framework and smoothes the viewpoint estimation via the motion prior. ALM discretizes the viewpoint space into 24 azimuth angles (i.e., 15° interval) and it does not use the temporal information. By combining online appearance models for 3D aspect parts, our full model improves over the "Category Model" by 4%/5° and 12%/9°, and over ALM by 15%/34° and 10%/23° in terms of mean accuracy/mean absolute difference in azimuth on the two datasets respectively. Online appearance models help 2D localization of 3D aspect parts, which in turn benefits viewpoint estimation. Our full model achieves 4.6° mean absolute difference in elevation on the YouTube sequences. Fig. 4 also shows some viewpoint estimation results from our multiview tracker and ALM.

3D Aspect Part Localization. The right half of Tab. 2 shows the 3D aspect part localization performance in terms of PASCAL VOC overlap ratio on our new car dataset and the KITTI sequences. Compared with ALM [43], "Category Model" achieves much better mean overlap ratio. Since part locations and viewpoint are jointly optimized in our multiview tracking framework, the category-level part templates and the motion prior result in accurate viewpoint and 2D part locations. Consequently, the 2D part shapes can be estimated more accurately. By introducing online appearance learning, our full model further improves the 3D aspect part localization, where it outperforms or is on par with the "Category Model" in 7 of the 9 YouTube sequences and in 9 of the 11 KITTI

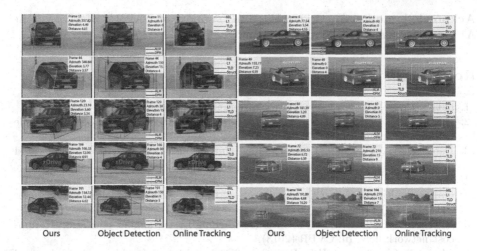

Ours   Object Detection Online Tracking   Ours   Object Detection Online Tracking

Fig. 4. Tracking/Detection outputs from different methods on SUV1 and Race1. "Ours" are the tracking outputs from our multiview tracker. "Object Detection" shows the detection results from DPM [12] and ALM [43]. "Online Tracking" shows the tracking results of four state-of-the-art online tracking methods: MIL [2], L1 [3], TLD [20] and Struct [15].

Fig. 5. The tracking results on KITTI03. "Category Model" fails to track the target and switches to the occluder, while our full model is able to recover from occlusion and track the correct target.

sequences. In Fig. 4, we can see that the 3D aspect parts from our tracker are more accurate than those obtained by ALM.

5   Conclusion

We proposed a novel multiview rigid object tracking framework to handle the topological appearance change of objects caused by viewpoint transitions. Our multiview tracker is able to predict the aspect change of the target, and track the continuous pose and the 3D aspect parts of the target. We conducted experiments on a new challenging car dataset and a set of KITTI sequences with large viewpoint variations, as well as on a standard sequence for car tracking. We demonstrated that our method is effective in tracking continuous 3D pose and aspect part locations, and it is able to handle the changes in viewpoint robustly.

Acknowledgments. We acknowledge the support of DARPA UPSIDE grant A13-0895-S002 and NSF CAREER grant N.1054127.

References

1. http://cvgl.stanford.edu/projects/multiview_tracking
2. Babenko, B., Yang, M.H., Belongie, S.: Robust object tracking with online multiple instance learning. TPAMI 33(8), 1619–1632 (2011)
3. Bao, C., Wu, Y., Ling, H., Ji, H.: Real time robust l1 tracker using accelerated proximal gradient approach. In: CVPR (2012)
4. Breitenstein, M.D., Reichlin, F., Leibe, B., Koller-Meier, E., Van Gool, L.: Online multiperson tracking-by-detection from a single, uncalibrated camera. TPAMI 33(9), 1820–1833 (2011)
5. Butt, A.A., Collins, R.T.: Multi-target tracking by lagrangian relaxation to min-cost network flow. In: CVPR (2013)
6. Choi, C., Christensen, H.I.: Real-time 3D model-based tracking using edge and keypoint features for robotic manipulation. In: ICRA, pp. 4048–4055 (2010)
7. Choi, W., Pantofaru, C., Savarese, S.: A general framework for tracking multiple people from a moving camera. TPAMI (2012)
8. Dalal, N., Triggs, B.: Histograms of oriented gradients for human detection. In: CVPR (2005)
9. Dickinson, S.J., Pentland, A.P., Rosenfeld, A.: From volumes to views: An approach to 3-d object recognition. CVGIP: Image Understanding 55(2), 130–154 (1992)
10. Drummond, T., Cipolla, R.: Real-time visual tracking of complex structures. TPAMI 24(7), 932–946 (2002)
11. Feldman, A., Hybinette, M., Balch, T.: The multi-iterative closest point tracker: An online algorithm for tracking multiple interacting targets. Journal of Field Robotics (2012)
12. Felzenszwalb, P.F., Girshick, R.B., McAllester, D., Ramanan, D.: Object detection with discriminatively trained part-based models. TPAMI (2010)
13. Fidler, S., Dickinson, S., Urtasun, R.: 3D object detection and viewpoint estimation with a deformable 3D cuboid model. In: NIPS (2012)
14. Geiger, A., Lenz, P., Urtasun, R.: Are we ready for autonomous driving? the kitti vision benchmark suite. In: CVPR (2012)
15. Hare, S., Saffari, A., Torr, P.H.: Struck: Structured output tracking with kernels. In: ICCV (2011)
16. Held, D., Levinson, J., Thrun, S.: Precision tracking with sparse 3D and dense color 2D data. In: ICRA (2013)
17. Hofmann, M., Wolf, D., Rigoll, G.: Hypergraphs for joint multi-view reconstruction and multi-object tracking. In: CVPR (2012)
18. Huang, Q.X., Adams, B., Wand, M.: Bayesian surface reconstruction via iterative scan alignment to an optimized prototype. In: Eurographics Symposium on Geometry Processing (2007)
19. Kaestner, R., Maye, J., Pilat, Y., Siegwart, R.: Generative object detection and tracking in 3D range data. In: ICRA (2012)
20. Kalal, Z., Mikolajczyk, K., Matas, J.: Tracking-learning-detection. TPAMI 34(7), 1409–1422 (2012)
21. Khan, S.M., Shah, M.: Tracking multiple occluding people by localizing on multiple scene planes. TPAMI 31(3), 505–519 (2009)

22. Khan, Z., Balch, T., Dellaert, F.: Mcmc-based particle filtering for tracking a variable number of interacting targets. TPAMI 27(11), 1805–1819 (2005)
23. Leal-Taixé, L., Pons-Moll, G., Rosenhahn, B.: Branch-and-price global optimization for multi-view multi-target tracking. In: CVPR (2012)
24. Lepetit, V., Fua, P.: Monocular model-based 3d tracking of rigid objects: A survey. Foundations and Trends in Computer Graphics and Vision 1(1), 1–89 (2005)
25. Liebelt, J., Schmid, C., Schertler, K.: Viewpoint-independent object class detection using 3D feature maps. In: CVPR (2008)
26. Lim, J.J., Pirsiavash, H., Torralba, A.: Parsing ikea objects: Fine pose estimation. In: ICCV (2013)
27. Lowe, D.G.: Three-dimensional object recognition from single two-dimensional images. Artificial Intelligence 31(3), 355–395 (1987)
28. Lucas, B.D., Kanade, T.: An iterative image registration technique with an application to stereo vision. In: Proceedings of Imaging Understanding Workshop (1981)
29. Oron, S., Bar-Hillel, A., Avidan, S.: Extended lucas kanade tracking. In: ECCV (2014)
30. Pauwels, K., Rubio, L., Diaz, J., Ros, E.: Real-time model-based rigid object pose estimation and tracking combining dense and sparse visual cues. In: CVPR, pp. 2347–2354 (2013)
31. Pepik, B., Stark, M., Gehler, P., Schiele, B.: Teaching 3D geometry to deformable part models. In: CVPR (2012)
32. Petrovskaya, A., Thrun, S.: Model based vehicle tracking for autonomous driving in urban environments. In: RSS (2008)
33. Pirsiavash, H., Ramanan, D., Fowlkes, C.C.: Globally-optimal greedy algorithms for tracking a variable number of objects. In: CVPR (2011)
34. Prisacariu, V.A., Reid, I.D.: Pwp3D: Real-time segmentation and tracking of 3D objects. IJCV 98(3), 335–354 (2012)
35. Roller, D., Daniilidis, K., Nagel, H.H.: Model-based object tracking in monocular image sequences of road traffic scenes. IJCV 10(3), 257–281 (1993)
36. Savarese, S., Fei-Fei, L.: 3D generic object categorization, localization and pose estimation. In: ICCV (2007)
37. Su, H., Sun, M., Fei-Fei, L., Savarese, S.: Learning a dense multi-view representation for detection, viewpoint classification and synthesis of object categories. In: ICCV (2009)
38. Supancic III, J.S., Ramanan, D.: Self-paced learning for long-term tracking. In: CVPR (2013)
39. Thomas, A., Ferrari, V., Leibe, B., Tuytelaars, T., Schiele, B., Van Gool, L.: Towards multi-view object class detection. In: CVPR (2006)
40. Viola, P., Jones, M.: Rapid object detection using a boosted cascade of simple features. In: CVPR (2001)
41. Wu, Y., Lim, J., Yang, M.H.: Online object tracking: A benchmark. In: CVPR (2013)
42. Xiang, Y., Mottaghi, R., Savarese, S.: Beyond pascal: A benchmark for 3D object detection in the wild. In: WACV (2014)
43. Xiang, Y., Savarese, S.: Estimating the aspect layout of object categories. In: CVPR (2012)
44. Yang, B., Nevatia, R.: An online learned crf model for multi-target tracking. In: CVPR (2012)
45. Yao, R., Shi, Q., Shen, C., Zhang, Y., van den Hengel, A.: Part-based visual tracking with online latent structural learning. In: CVPR (2013)

Modeling Blurred Video with Layers

Jonas Wulff and Michael Julian Black

Max Planck Institute for Intelligent Systems, Tübingen, Germany
{jonas.wulff,black}@tue.mpg.de

Abstract. Videos contain complex spatially-varying motion blur due to the combination of object motion, camera motion, and depth variation with finite shutter speeds. Existing methods to estimate optical flow, deblur the images, and segment the scene fail in such cases. In particular, boundaries between differently moving objects cause problems, because here the blurred images are a combination of the blurred appearances of multiple surfaces. We address this with a novel layered model of scenes in motion. From a motion-blurred video sequence, we jointly estimate the layer segmentation and each layer's appearance and motion. Since the blur is a function of the layer motion and segmentation, it is completely determined by our generative model. Given a video, we formulate the optimization problem as minimizing the pixel error between the blurred frames and images synthesized from the model, and solve it using gradient descent. We demonstrate our approach on synthetic and real sequences.

Keywords: Optical Flow, Layers, Object Boundaries, Motion Blur.

1   Introduction

Common goals in the analysis of video include the estimation of optical flow, the localization of motion boundaries, and the segmentation of images into regions corresponding to objects. These are all hard problems that become even harder when the frames contain motion blur. However, when a dynamic scene is captured by a camera with finite shutter speed, this will always be the case. In such a setting, traditional assumptions of brightness constancy are violated, particularly at motion boundaries where the pixel values combine information from multiple surfaces blurring into each other.

To address these problems, we propose a novel layered model of images that explicitly models the motion of the layers, the blur induced by this motion, and the un-blurred appearance of each layer (Fig. 1). A key observation is that both the motion blur and the displacement of a surface are results of the same process in the world: the motion of the surface relative to the camera. Hence, the motion blur of a surface is completely determined by the motion of that surface – *estimating the optical flow gives us the blur kernel*. Unlike previous work we formulate this as a generative model and jointly solve for all unknowns. This produces an accurate layer segmentation and precise motion boundaries from a motion-blurred image sequence (Fig. 1(c) and (e)). To this end, layers

D. Fleet et al. (Eds.): ECCV 2014, Part VI, LNCS 8694, pp. 236–252, 2014.

provide a natural framework because they directly model surface interaction at occlusion boundaries. Here we focus on parametric motion within layers and use a two-layer model, as is common in recent approaches [36]. While being limited in terms of motion complexity, we nevertheless find that this model is able to analyze real scenes with different foreground and background motion.

Much of the work on motion blur focuses on the problem of *deblurring*, particularly in single images where the blur is caused by camera shake [13]. These approaches either assume homogeneous blur across the whole image or restrict the blur kernels to those caused by common camera motion paths. On the other hand, existing work on deblurring in the case of object motion is restricted to the case of static backgrounds [2]. We do not address single-image deblurring, but focus on optical flow estimation in sequences with motion blur and motion of both the foreground and the background. In particular, we deal with spatially-varying blur kernels that are determined by the layer motions.

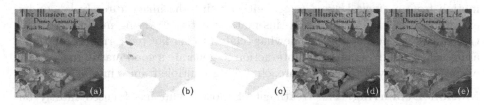

Fig. 1. When computing optical flow from motion blurred video (a), existing methods [44] fail at object boundaries ((b) and (e), red). Our method is able to accurately estimate optical flow (c), deblurred frames (d), and object boundaries ((e), green).

Figure 2 illustrates how a scene is generated as a composition of layers, each of which is *individually* warped and blurred by its motion. This compositing from layers that are independently blurred captures what happens at boundaries while simplifying optimization compared with previous work. We explicitly model the blur as a function of the estimated motion, resulting in an elegant formulation of the problem. Thus, given the estimated motion, the blur within each layer is known, and the latent, sharp, appearance of each layer can be reconstructed. As a result we can reconstruct accurate motion at the boundaries, as well as deblurred estimates for both layers.

To summarize, the main contribution of this work is to estimate optical flow in video sequences in the presence of multiple motions and motion blur. We treat motion blur in a layered framework, allowing us to simultaneously infer the sharp layer segmentation, the object motion, the corresponding motion blur, and the latent (deblurred) object appearances. Our formulation is the first fully generative model of blurred video sequences using a layered framework. We demonstrate the effectiveness of the approach using synthetic and real sequences containing multiple motions. In addition to improving optical flow accuracy, we can deblur sequences that previous methods cannot handle, and show accurate estimation of layer boundaries despite heavy motion blur. We show how it is robust to noise by modeling a degraded sequence of the assassination of John F. Kennedy.

2   Previous Work

Motion Estimation with Motion Blur. Accurate optical flow estimation in the presence of motion blur has been rarely studied so far. One way to integrate motion blur into the optical flow computation is to include an additional regularization term for the motion, minimizing the difference between a latent, sharp image and the observed, blurry one [27]. Alternatively, the motion blur can be integrated directly into the data term, modulating the brightness constancy constraint [30]. This approach has also been used in sparse tracking [20], where the motion is used to modify the expected appearance change of features. However, these methods usually assume a smooth flow field and, unlike our layered model, fail at object boundaries. Additional previous work has focused on computing motion from a *single blurred image*, either using the image directly [6], or by extracting a matte [12,35]. From this matte, spatially varying motion information can be extracted. While somewhat related to our layered formulation, these approaches usually require user interaction to generate a good matte. In contrast we present a fully automatic approach, taking multiple frames into account.

Motion Deblurring. The treatment of motion blur has focused mostly on removing blur from single images captured in low-light scenarios. The scene is usually assumed to be static, and the blur is caused by camera shake. The blur process is modeled either as a complex but spatially-invariant blur kernel [7,13] or as a spatially-varying kernel generated by possible camera motions in 3D [43]. Single-image deblurring is beyond our scope, as are methods relying on special hardware for multiple exposures [34].

In the case of multiple frames, an alternative strategy first estimates motion from the blurred sequence using sparse feature tracking [17], shapes [3], or optical flow [23,46]. The estimated motion is then used to synthesize the blur kernel and deblur the input images non-blindly. These methods fail in the case of strong blur where accurate tracking becomes infeasible [27]. Our approach solves this by explicitly modeling the blur as a function of the motion being estimated. Like us, Li et al. [25] formulate a joint energy function between latent images and motion parameters and optimize it using gradient descent. However, they assume a single motion and cannot handle independently moving objects.

Methods that take object motion into account usually assume purely translational motion [2,4,24] or require user input to generate a matte [11,26]. In these cases the background is generally assumed to be static, or even known, and only foreground motion is modeled. This eliminates the challenge of estimating overlapping motions at object boundaries, making the problem considerably easier. In contrast, we model motion of both the background and the foreground, and assume neither to be known a priori.

Model-free methods for multi-frame deblurring remove motion blur using deconvolution in a coarsely up-sampled spatio-temporal volume [38] or patch-based synthesis methods [8]. While such methods give good deblurring results even in the presence of independently moving objects, they yield neither motion information nor scene segmentation.

Layered Motion Models. Layered models of optical flow describe a scene as a set of overlapping moving regions. This effectively separates motion estimation from segmentation, allows the use of simple models for the motion within a layer [41], and provides an explicit model of the occlusion process [36]. Layered motion models also facilitate temporal reasoning because the structure of most scenes changes slowly over time [36]. Thus, layers are useful for motion segmentation [10,21] and the computation of optical flow [19,36,39,42]. None of these approaches deal with motion blur.

One of the early motivations for layered models, however, was to address blur [40]. The idea was to first compute motion using a layered model and then, given the layer segmentation, model the blur process. Paramanand and Rajagopalan [28] follow this approach and use a layered scene representation to capture different blurs. However, they only consider a static scene with camera shake, model the motion as a similarity transform, and do not explicitly model layer interactions at the object boundaries.

Beyond motion estimation, several authors have used layered models to extract persistent image appearance ("sprites," mosaics, etc.) [15,18,21,31,32,45,47]. This estimation of appearance is a key part of our method but these previous approaches do not model motion blur. For example in [32] the super-resolved layer appearance is estimated using a hand-set blur kernel. This blur only represents lens blur and not spatially varying motion blur. Rav-Acha et al. [31] rely on feature tracking and point out that motion blur causes problems for their method. Chunhe et al. [9] use a layered formulation for single image deblurring. Their work considers non-overlapping layers, more akin to a segmentation, and adapt the spatial prior accordingly. Our notion of layers, in contrast, handles overlapping layers and occlusions.

Closest to ours is the work of Kumar et al. [29] in which the authors segment the video into layers, estimate the appearance of layers and model motion blur in the estimation of flow. Our method differs in several important ways. First, they estimate the appearance of a layer as the mean of the aligned image pixels within the layer. This process *does not model how the appearance is blurred by motion* and consequently cannot deblur the appearance. Second, they *model the blur of each layer independently*. This ignores the critical effect of blur at layer boundaries where the appearance of two elements of the scene are combined. This further means that information about motion blur is not properly incorporated into the segmentation of the layers. Third, their method for estimating flow relies on normalized cross correlation while our method is fully generative, modeling the full appearance of each image from the model. Fourth, they do not directly parameterize the blur kernel based on the motion. In contrast, our explicit parameterization of blur facilitates a simpler unified formulation and optimization scheme.

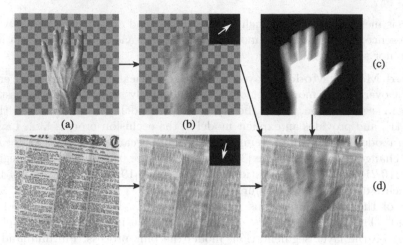

Fig. 2. Generative Model. The sharp layers (a) are blurred (b) using the motion indicated in the top right corners. Together with the blurred layer segmentation (c), an image (d) with complex spatially-varying motion blur is generated. The checkerboard-pattern indicates transparency. Image inspired by [41].

3   A Layered Representation of Motion-Blurred Video

Notation. A superscript denotes a layer l, $0 \leq l \leq L - 1$, where larger l's are closer to the observer. Here we use a simplified model with $L = 2$ layers. A subscript denotes the image frame at time t, $1 \leq t \leq T$, for a sequence with T frames. $I_t \in \mathbb{R}^{m \times n \times 3}$ is an observed color image, $A^l \in \mathbb{R}^{m \times n \times 3}$ is the unblurred color "appearance" of layer l. $G^l \in \mathbb{R}^{m \times n \times 3}$ is the segmentation mask for l; for $l = 0$ (i.e. the background) the mask is assumed to be uniformly one. While G^l does not necessarily have to be binary, here we only consider opaque layers. Note that while G^l does have three color channels, we enforce all three to be the same for a given pixel. A^l and G^l are assumed to be constant across the sequence. For longer sequences, this limitation could either be relaxed, or the sequence could be split into smaller sub-sequences, each exhibiting approximately constant layer shape and layer appearance. For readability, we use the column-vectorized forms of I_t, A^l, G^l; i.e. $\mathbf{i}_t \in \mathbb{R}^{3mn \times 1}$, $\mathbf{a}^l \in \mathbb{R}^{3mn \times 1}$, and $\mathbf{g}^l \in \mathbb{R}^{3mn \times 1}$, respectively.

θ_t^l are the transformation (i.e. motion) parameters for layer l at frame t. The complexity of θ_t^l depends on the motion model, and can range from a single (u, v) value pair in case of purely translational motion to displacement values for every pixel in the case of dense optical flow. Here we focus on affine motion, which is the most common for layered flow. It provides a good middle ground by capturing the most common frame-to-frame transformations, still being a linear transformation. While more complicated motion models such as a full homography are possible to include in our model, perspective effects from frame to frame in a video are often negligible, making affine motion a good approximation.

To cope with object areas leaving the visible frame, $m \times n$ is set to be larger than the observation data by padding in all directions. With this simple approach, we are able to reconstruct objects leaving the frame; i.e. panoramas.

A Single Layer with Motion Blur. To fix ideas, first consider the simplest case of motion blur, in which a single layer undergoes an arbitrary transformation during the period of open shutter. A pixel in the blurred image can then be approximated as a linear combination of pixels of the unblurred layer [33]. Thus, we can model the blur as a blur matrix $\mathbf{H}\left(\theta_t, \theta_{t-1}, s\right) \in \mathbb{R}^{3mn \times 3mn}$, and write the blurred image as

$$\mathbf{i}_{singlelayer} = \mathbf{H}\left(\theta_t, \theta_{t-1}, s\right)\mathbf{a}. \tag{1}$$

$\mathbf{H}$ depends on the affine parameters of the current and the previous frame, as well as the shutter speed s. In this work, we assume the shutter speed to be known and constant; this is a reasonable assumption for digital video cameras and even archival film footage as we show in the experiments. $\mathbf{H}$ is set to influence different color channels equally.[1]

Two Layers without Motion Blur. Without motion blur, an image that is composed of two different layers with appearances $\mathbf{a}^0$ and $\mathbf{a}^1$, can be written as

$$\mathbf{i}_{noblur} = \left(1 - \mathbf{g}^1\right) \odot \mathbf{a}^0 + \mathbf{a}^1. \tag{2}$$

Here, $\odot$ denotes element-wise multiplication. Similar to [2], we enforce $\mathbf{a}^1$ to be zero everywhere where its segmentation is zero.

Two Layers with Foreground Motion and Blur. For readability, we abbreviate $\mathbf{H}_{t,t-1}^l = \mathbf{H}\left(\theta_t^l, \theta_{t-1}^l, s\right)$. Assuming a static background, we get

$$\mathbf{i}_{fg-blur} = \left(1 - \mathbf{H}_{t,t-1}^1\mathbf{g}^1\right) \odot \mathbf{a}^0 + \mathbf{H}_{t,t-1}^1\mathbf{a}^1. \tag{3}$$

Now considering multiple points t in time, Eq. (3) becomes

$$\mathbf{i}_{fg-blur,t} = \left(1 - \mathbf{H}_{t,t-1}^1\mathbf{T}_t^1\mathbf{g}^1\right) \odot \mathbf{a}^0 + \mathbf{H}_{t,t-1}^1\mathbf{T}_t^1\mathbf{a}^1. \tag{4}$$

In addition to the blur matrices $\mathbf{H}_{t,t-1}^l$, we use the transformation matrices $\mathbf{T}_t^l \in \mathbb{R}^{3mn \times 3mn}$ to transform a vectorized image according to the transformation parameters θ_t^l.

Since any blur and transformation can be expressed as linear (re-)combination of pixels in the image, this formulation is very flexible, allowing complex motion models such as homographies or dense optical flow [33].

A Two-Layer Model. While algorithms dealing with spatially-varying blur commonly assume a static background [2,4], this assumption is often invalid in practice; eg. in the presence of camera motion in addition to object motion. Incorporating background motion and its corresponding blur into Eq. (4) yields an estimated image

$$\hat{\mathbf{i}}_t = \left(1 - \mathbf{H}_{t,t-1}^1\mathbf{T}_t^1\mathbf{g}^1\right) \odot \mathbf{H}_{t,t-1}^0\mathbf{T}_t^0\mathbf{a}^0 + \mathbf{H}_{t,t-1}^1\mathbf{T}_t^1\mathbf{a}^1. \tag{5}$$

---

[1] To perform super resolution, A would be larger than I and we would multiply by another matrix to decimate the blurred A in generating I.

Likelihood. The image $\hat{\mathbf{i}}_t$ generated by our model should match the observed image $\mathbf{i}_t$. Hence to estimate the model parameters we minimize

$$E_D\left(\mathcal{I}, \mathcal{G}, \mathcal{A}, \Theta\right) = \sum_t \mathbf{w}^\top \rho\left(\mathbf{i}_t - \hat{\mathbf{i}}_t\right) \tag{6}$$

summed over all pixels, where $\rho(x) = \sqrt{x^2 + \varepsilon^2}$ is a robust Charbonnier function [5]. Here, $\mathbf{w} \in \mathbb{R}^{3mn \times 1}$ contains zeros in the outside padded area, and ones in the inside, restricting the summation to the visible part of the image. The input is the image sequence $\mathcal{I} = \{\mathbf{i}_1, \cdots, \mathbf{i}_T\}$. The estimated parameters are the set of segmentations (excluding the background), $\mathcal{G} = \{\mathbf{g}^1\}$, the set of appearances, $\mathcal{A} = \{\mathbf{a}^0, \mathbf{a}^1\}$, and the set of transformation parameters, $\Theta = \{\theta_0^0, \theta_0^1, \cdots, \theta_T^0, \theta_T^1\}$. For each layer, we obtain $T+1$ values for θ, since each frame $\mathbf{i}_t$, including the first, depends on θ_t and θ_{t-1}.

Regularization. To make Eq. (6) better behaved in weakly structured regions, we impose a number of regularization terms on both the appearance maps $A^{\{0,1\}}$ and the segmentation G^1.

Spatial Smoothness. We regularize both the appearance images $A^{\{0,1\}}$ and the segmentation maps G. Like standard deblurring methods we model the fact that the spatial derivatives of natural images exhibit a heavy-tail distribution [24]. This can be captured using a sparse prior:

$$E_{sparse}(Y, \alpha) = \sum_{x,y} |\nabla_x Y(x,y)|^\alpha + |\nabla_y Y(x,y)|^\alpha. \tag{7}$$

Consistent with natural image statistics, we use $\alpha_A = 0.8$ for the appearance maps.

For a binary segmentation mask G, we use the L1 total variation prior, given by Eq. (7) by setting $\alpha_G = 1$. This prior prefers smooth contours, and has been successfully used in similar tasks before [2].

We approximate the non-differentiable absolute $|\cdot|$ in Eq. (7) with a Charbonnier function [5] with $\epsilon = 10^{-3}$.

Background Preference. We assume the background to generally cover more pixels than the foreground layer. Thus, we impose a slight penalty for pixels that are assigned to the foreground.

$$E_{bg}(Y) = \sum_{x,y} Y(x,y)^2. \tag{8}$$

Objective. The final objective function is

$$E\left(\mathcal{I}, \mathcal{G}, \mathcal{A}, \Theta\right) = E_D\left(\mathcal{I}, \mathcal{G}, \mathcal{A}, \Theta\right) + E_{Reg}\left(\mathcal{G}, \mathcal{A}\right), \tag{9}$$

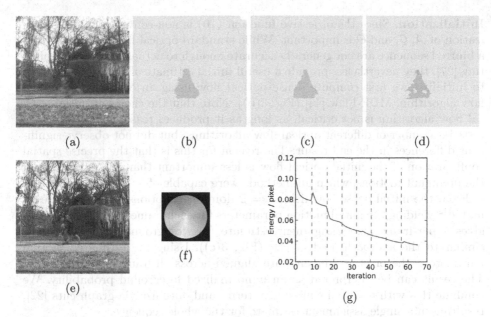

Fig. 3. Illustration of different steps in the algorithm. (a) One of the 5 input frames in the sequence. (b) Initial flow, computed using [44]. (c) Motion initialization from optical flow. (d) Final motion estimate. (e) Deblurred image produced by the generative model. (f) Color key used for optical flow. (g) Normalized energy vs. number of iterations. Red lines show transitions between the pyramid levels. See text for details.

with

$$E_{Reg}(\mathcal{G}, \mathcal{A}) =$$
$$+ \lambda_{sparse,A}\left(E_{sparse}\left(A^0, \alpha_A\right) + E_{sparse}\left(A^1, \alpha_A\right)\right)$$
$$+ \lambda_{sparse,G}E_{sparse}\left(G^1, \alpha_G\right)$$
$$+ \lambda_{bg}E_{bg}\left(G^1\right) . \tag{10}$$

We set the parameters to $\lambda_{bg} = 0.05$, $\lambda_{sparse,A} = 0.001$, $\lambda_{sparse,G} = 0.05$. For the effects of the individual regularizations, please see the **Sup. Mat.**

4   Optimization

We assume that the shutter speed is known and that there are only two moving layers. Our algorithm computes the latent (unblurred) appearance of both the background and the foreground, the motion parameters of both, and the segmentation mask for the foreground. Figure 3 shows an input image, and how the solution changes after each step described here. Note that it is usually possible to reconstruct the parts of the background that are visible in at least one frame of the sequence.

Initialization. Since the objective function (10) is non-convex, a good initialization of $\mathcal{A}$, $\mathcal{G}$, and Θ is important. While standard optical flow estimates from a blurred sequence are not generally accurate enough to actually perform deblurring [27], they nevertheless provide a useful initial estimate of the motion. Thus, to initialize, we first compute dense optical flow using an off-the-shelf optical flow algorithm, MDP-Flow [44] (Fig. 3(b)). Note that the choice of initial optical flow algorithm is not critical, as long as it produces reasonable results. We tested a number of different optical flow algorithms, but did not observe significant differences in the end result. The reason for this is that the precise spatial configuration of the initial optical flow is less important than the extraction of the dominant motions, which all methods were capable of.

From the initial dense flow field, $L = 2$ dominant motions are robustly estimated,[2] yielding the initial motion parameters for each frame. Additionally, this gives a per-frame pixel assignment estimate (i.e. foreground or background), similar to the approach used in [41] (Fig. 3(c)). Using the estimated motion parameters, the pixel assignments are aligned across all frames and added up. The result can be interpreted as an unnormalized foreground probability. We combine this with a spatial consistency term, and optimize via graph cuts [22], resulting in a single assignment estimate for the whole sequence.

Given this segmentation and the estimated motion for each layer, we separate both layers by masking, and use a simple non-blind deblurring method [14] on each layer to obtain initial deblurred estimates. While this initial deblurring causes ringing artifacts and is not strictly necessary, it speeds up convergence by providing a reasonable initialization.

Coordinate Descent. Starting with our initial estimate, we use an iterative, alternating optimization method. We optimize one variable at a time using gradient descent, but terminate the optimization after 3 iterations to avoid reaching local optima, and switch to the next variable. One optimization cycle over all variables makes up a single iteration. We iterate for at most 50 iterations, or until the relative change in energy falls below 1 percent.

For optimization purposes, we relax the binary-valued $\mathbf{g}^1$ and use an element-wise shifted heavy-side function $u(x) = 0.5 + \frac{1}{\pi} \arctan \left(\frac{x-0.5}{\sigma_u} \right)$. We approximate $\mathbf{g}^1 \approx u\left(\tilde{\mathbf{g}}^1\right)$, and optimize the continuous-valued $\tilde{\mathbf{g}}^1$ instead. Empirically, we set $\sigma_u = 0.05$.

To deal with large motions, we use a standard multi-scale approach with a Gaussian pyramid with P levels. We found $P = 7$ and a scaling factor of 1.5 to work well. The initialization is done at the highest resolution, and the estimated starting values are rescaled to the highest pyramid level. The complete optimization schedule is then performed at each pyramid level, and the results form the input of the next level. See **Sup. Mat.** for pseudocode. Figure 3(g) shows the energy per pixel vs. number of iterations. The red dashed lines show the transition points between pyramid levels. While the gradient descent scheme

---

[2] For translational motion, we use the median; for affine, RANSAC.

we use is not guaranteed to reach the global optimum, we nevertheless observe a well-behaved falloff.

We have experimented with different optimizers for the single variables, but found this simple gradient descent algorithm to work best. For the detailed derivatives of the objective function, please see **Sup. Mat.**

After the optimization has converged, we obtain the final mask by smoothing and thresholding $\tilde{g}^1$, and multiply the binary mask element-wise with A^1 to compute the final foreground appearance estimate. Figure 3(d) shows the final estimated flow. Note that the segmentation is significantly improved, with even the shape of the person and rims of the bicycle being evident. A full composite with blur removed is shown in Fig. 3(e).

Using unoptimized Python code, our algorithm takes less than 40min per frame with a resolution of $m = n = 640$ pixels.

5 Evaluation

We evaluate the algorithm in terms of motion accuracy and deblurring performance. Furthermore, we compare the results of our algorithm with and without the blur model. We use both synthetic and real sequences, containing translational and affine motion. The length of the sequences varies from 5 to 10 frames. Two of our 8 test sequences contain static backgrounds (eg. in Fig. 1, or the middle column of Fig. 4), while the remaining 6 contain moving foreground and background. Three of the test sequences contain significant affine motions including scale change and rotation. Here we present an overview of the results; a complete list is given in the **Sup. Mat.**

Motion Estimation Accuracy. We compare our motion estimation accuracy with different methods from the optical flow literature: Sun et al. [36] use a layered optical flow model; Portz et al. [30] incorporate motion blur into an algorithm for optical flow computation, but do not take layers into account; Xu and Jia [44] are representative of a non-layered, but accurate optical flow method. The implementations were either obtained from the author's websites, or provided upon request. In all cases, we used the default parameters. The only exception was [30], for which we were unable to compute reasonable results using the included initialization optical flow method. Therefore, we use the same initialization [44] as for our method.

To quantitatively compare the results, we use two metrics on the synthetic sequences. First, we compare the full dense flow fields of all methods using the average endpoint error ("Error frame" in Table 1). Second, we fit two parametric motions to all flow fields, as described in Sec. 4, and compare those ("Error fitted" in Table 1). Figure 5 shows an example, and Table 1 shows the average errors over all sequences. Flow accuracy with our method improves significantly over the other techniques. As can be seen in Fig. 5, our method is able to extract even very fine details, however, in the absence of texture in the sky, the segmentation of foreground and background is ambiguous.

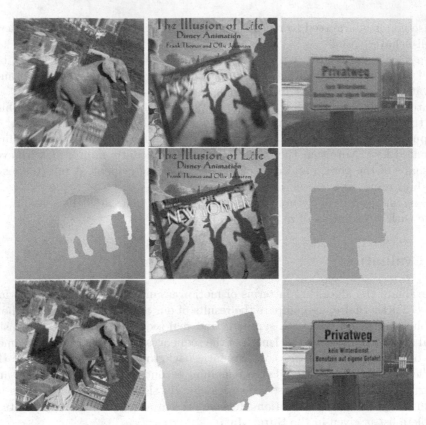

Fig. 4. Example results. The top row shows a frame of the input sequence, the middle row the estimated motion and segmentation, the bottom row the output of our generative image model (i.e. a deblurred image).

To investigate the effect of our explicit motion blur model, we compare the motion estimation accuracy for our method with and without the motion blur modeling enabled. Disabling the motion blur is equivalent to setting the shutter speed to be infinitely short. Without modeling blur, the accuracy of our method is comparable to the other methods. The results in Table 1 clearly show the critical role that the blur model plays in motion estimation accuracy.

Note that compared to other optical flow methods, our method computes good segmentations, as implicitly shown in the optical flow maps. More explicitly, consider Fig. 1(e). Here, the object boundaries extracted from the standard optical flow (as described in Sec. 4) are shown in red, while the layer boundaries extracted from our method are shown in green. While the standard flow method [44] fails to capture the fine details between the fingers due to the motion blur, our method is capable of recovering those details. A similar effect can be observed in Fig. 3(d), and Fig. 5(e).

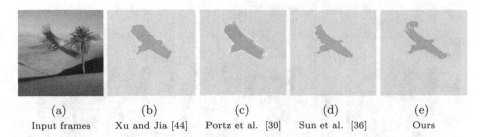

(a)	(b)	(c)	(d)	(e)
Input frames	Xu and Jia [44]	Portz et al. [30]	Sun et al. [36]	Ours

Fig. 5. Conventional optical flow estimation methods fail at object boundaries in the presence of motion blur, since the motion in those areas is a combination of two motion-blurred image regions. (e) shows our result.

Table 1. Optical flow accuracies (average endpoint error)

	Error frame	Error fitted
MDP-Flow [44]	3.58	3.28
Blurflow [30]	4.59	4.92
Layerflow [36]	3.27	4.15
Ours-noblur	3.06	3.42
Ours	**0.73**	**1.25**

Deblurring Accuracy. We compare the results of our approach with those of [7] for deblurring. Figure 6(a) shows an input from a scene in which both layers only undergo translational motion. Within each layer, the blur kernel is therefore spatially invariant. Note that [7] is designed for spatially invariant blur caused by camera shake. To apply it to these images with multiple motions, we use the approach described in Sec. 4 to obtain a rough estimate of background and foreground segmentations. Both segments are then separately deblurred, and the result is composed again. Figure 6 shows a visual comparison of deblurring results. On average, this modified version of [7] achieves a PSNR of 18.34 dB, while our generative model has a PSNR of 29.31 dB. Since [7] was not intended to be used in a spatially-discontinuous setting, this is not an entirely fair comparison. However, by the same token it is not our goal to present a perfect deblurring method. Rather, we show that our generative model of layered motions effectively deblurs the layers resulting in better deblurred images.

Historical Challenge. Figure 7 demonstrates the method for an extremely challenging archival video with large blur, film grain, and extreme noise – the famous Zapruder film of the John F. Kennedy assassination. Using 7 frames, our method removes the motion blur in the scene, both in the rightward driving car and in the background. The non-rigid motions of the people in the scene (e.g. the child's legs) produce some artifacts and require a more flexible motion model. However, even without this our method performs surprisingly well.

| (a) | (b) | (c) |
| One input frame | [7], segmented | Our result |

Fig. 6. Deblurring example (one frame from sequence). Note that there is different foreground and background blur. Conventional deblurring methods suffer from discontinuously varying motion blur at object boundaries.

(a) One original frame and magnification   (b) Deblurred frame, magnification, and computed
motion and layer segmentation

Fig. 7. Kennedy Assassination. Our method is robust to severely degraded input images. *Zapruder Film* ©*1967 (Renewed 1995) The Sixth Floor Museum At Dealey Plaza.*

6   Assumptions, Limitations, and Future Work

To demonstrate our approach, we assume parametric models of the layer motion, which currently restricts our method to scenes with suitable motion. Our model formulation however is general and just as valid for smoothly varying flow within a layer. Future work will address this more general formulation (e.g. [36,42]). The model also assumes a two-layer scene. While such a model is frequently used in comparable work [28,37], it is again somewhat restrictive. Future work will extend our current model to more layers, and allow more varied motion within a given layer. For a preliminary experiment on the effects of gradually increasing perspective motion, please see the **Sup. Mat.**

Our model assumes constant layer appearance over the sequence. Figure 8 shows a case in which reflections in the windshield of the car cause a change in appearance over time. This leads to ringing artifacts in the segmentation and foreground layer estimation. Future work should allow gradual changes in the appearance, or split the sequences into smaller subsets, for which the appearance constancy assumption approximately holds.

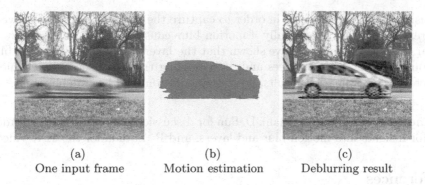

| (a) | (b) | (c) |
| One input frame | Motion estimation | Deblurring result |

Fig. 8. Failure case. A reflection in the windshield causes a changing appearance of the foreground layer, leading to an incorrect segmentation.

The limitations mentioned above should be considered in the light of our claims. We do not claim that we have developed either a full motion estimation or a full deblurring system. Instead we propose a new layered generative model of blurred video and show its feasibility for motion estimation and deblurring. Recent work on layered flow has addressed the estimation of the number of layers, their depth order, and the use of static image cues to improve layer segmentation [36]. Our framework is consistent with these techniques and could be incorporated into them. Future work should include optimizing the code and learning the regularization terms from training data, using more layers, and allowing the layer appearances, $\mathcal{A}$, and segmentation, $\mathcal{G}$, to vary over time. Additionally, future work will include improving the optimization with respect to $\mathcal{A}$ by using a dedicated, state-of-the-art deblurring method, instead of the coordinate descent method employed here.

Here we have considered a classical shutter, but low-cost sensors today, using CMOS technology, have rolling shutters. Modeling such shutters is possible in our framework but remains future work (cf. [16]). Beyond motion blur, images contain further artifacts such as focal blur, discretization, and camera noise. These have been modeled before and could be incorporated into our model, enabling joint motion estimation, denoising, and super-resolution (cf. [1]).

7   Conclusion

We have developed a principled formulation of motion blur in layers, have shown how it can be used to jointly estimate parametric motion, deblurred appearance, and scene segmentation, and have demonstrated the effectiveness of this approach using synthetic and real video sequences with appropriate motion. The results point to the value of incorporating a model of motion blur into the formulation of optical flow. A key insight is that, given the optical flow and the shutter speed, the blur is completely determined. This simplifies the modeling and estimation problem. Additionally, we argue that the scene structure, resulting in occlusion, has to be modeled in order to capture the complex interplay between different depth layers, especially if motion blur causes different depth layers to smear into each other. We have shown that the layered model captures the blur at boundaries between surfaces and, by modeling the blur process, we achieve better motion estimation results, layer segmentation, and layer deblurring.

Acknowledgements. We thank D. Sun for discussions on optical flow, T. Adelson for insights into motion blur and layers, and R. Zavada for the JFK video.

References

1. Baker, S., Kanade, T.: Super-resolution optical flow. Tech. Rep. CMU-RI-TR-99-36, Carnegie Mellon University, The Robotics Institute (1999)
2. Bar, L., Berkels, B., Rumpf, M., Sapiro, G.: A variational framework for simultaneous motion estimation and restoration of motion-blurred video. In: IEEE Int. Conf. on Computer Vision (ICCV), pp. 1–8 (2007)
3. Bascle, B., Blake, A., Zisserman, A.: Motion deblurring and super-resolution from an image sequence. In: Buxton, B.F., Cipolla, R. (eds.) ECCV 1996. LNCS, vol. 1065, pp. 573–582. Springer, Heidelberg (1996), http://dl.acm.org/citation.cfm?id=645310.649034
4. Chakrabarti, A., Zickler, T., Freeman, W.: Analyzing spatially-varying blur. In: IEEE Conf. on Computer Vision and Pattern Recognition (CVPR), pp. 2512–2519 (June 2010)
5. Charbonnier, P., Blanc-Feraud, L., Aubert, G., Barlaud, M.: Two deterministic half-quadratic regularization algorithms for computed imaging. In: IEEE Int. Conf. Image Proc. (ICIP), vol. 2, pp. 168–172 (1994)
6. Chen, W.G., Nandhakumar, N., Martin, W.: Image motion estimation from motion smear-a new computational model. IEEE Trans. on Pattern Analysis and Machine Intelligence (PAMI) 18(4), 412–425 (1996)
7. Cho, S., Lee, S.: Fast motion deblurring. In: ACM Trans. Graphics (TOG) – Proc. SIGGRAPH Asia, pp. 145:1–145:8. ACM, New York (2009), http://doi.acm.org/10.1145/1661412.1618491
8. Cho, S., Wang, J., Lee, S.: Video deblurring for hand-held cameras using patch-based synthesis. ACM Trans. Graph. 31(4), 64:1–64:9 (2012), http://doi.acm.org/10.1145/2185520.2185560
9. Chunhe, S., Hai, Z., Wei, J.: Motion deblurring from a single image using multi-layer statistics priors. In: 2011 IEEE International Conference on Consumer Electronics (ICCE), pp. 481–482 (January 2011)
10. Cremers, D., Soatto, S.: Variational space-time motion segmentation. In: Triggs, B., Zisserman, A. (eds.) Int. Conf. on Computer Vision (ICCV), Nice, vol. 2, pp. 886–892 (October 2003)
11. Dai, S., Wu, Y.: Removing partial blur in a single image. In: IEEE Conf. on Computer Vision and Pattern Recognition (CVPR), pp. 2544–2551 (2009)
12. Dai, S., Wu, Y.: Motion from blur. In: IEEE Conf. on Computer Vision and Pattern Recognition (CVPR), pp. 1–8 (June 2008)
13. Fergus, R., Singh, B., Hertzmann, A., Roweis, S.T., Freeman, W.T.: Removing camera shake from a single photograph. ACM Trans. Graphics (TOG) – Proc. SIGGRAPH 25(3), 787–794 (2006), http://doi.acm.org/10.1145/1141911.1141956

14. Fish, D.A., Brinicombe, A.M., Pike, E.R., Walker, J.G.: Blind deconvolution by means of the richardson–lucy algorithm. J. Opt. Soc. Am. A 12(1), 58–65 (1995), http://josaa.osa.org/abstract.cfm?URI=josaa-12-1-58

15. Frey, B., Jojic, N., Kannan, A.: Learning appearance and transparency manifolds of occluded objects in layers. In: IEEE Conf. on Computer Vision and Pattern Recognition (CVPR), pp. 45–52 (2003)

16. Grundmann, M., Kwatra, V., Castro, D., Essa, I.: Calibration-free rolling shutter removal. In: IEEE International Conference Computational Photography (ICCP), pp. 1–8 (2012)

17. He, X., Luo, T., Yuk, S.C., Chow, K., Wong, K., Chung, R.H.Y.: Motion estimation method for blurred videos and application of deblurring with spatially varying blur kernels. In: Int. Conf. on Computer Sciences and Convergence Information Technology (ICCIT), pp. 355–359 (2010)

18. Jackson, J., Yezzi, A., Soatto, S.: Dynamic shape and apperance modeling via moving and deforming layers. International Journal of Computer Vision (IJCV) 79(1), 71–84 (2008)

19. Jepson, A.D., Fleet, D.J., Black, M.J.: A layered motion representation with occlusion and compact spatial support. In: Heyden, A., Sparr, G., Nielsen, M., Johansen, P. (eds.) ECCV 2002, Part I. LNCS, vol. 2350, pp. 692–706. Springer, Heidelberg (2002), http://dx.doi.org/10.1007/3-540-47969-4_46

20. Jin, H., Favaro, P., Cipolla, R.: Visual tracking in the presence of motion blur. In: IEEE Computer Society Conference on Computer Vision and Pattern Recognition, CVPR 2005, vol. 2, pp. 18–25 (2005)

21. Jojic, N., Frey, B.: Learning flexible sprites in video layers. In: IEEE Conf. on Computer Vision and Pattern Recognition (CVPR), vol. 1, pp. I-199–I-206 (2001)

22. Kolmogorov, V., Zabin, R.: What energy functions can be minimized via graph cuts? IEEE Trans. Pattern Analysis and Machine Intelligence (PAMI) 26(2), 147–159 (2004)

23. Lee, S.H., Moon, N.S., Lee, C.W.: Recovery of blurred video signals using iterative image restoration combined with motion estimation. In: Int. Conf. on Image Processing (ICIP), vol. 1, pp. 755–758 (1997)

24. Levin, A.: Blind motion deblurring using image statistics. In: Schölkopf, B., Platt, J., Hoffman, T. (eds.) Advances in Neural Information Processing Systems, vol. 19, pp. 841–848. MIT Press, Cambridge (2007)

25. Li, Y., Kang, S.B., Joshi, N., Seitz, S., Huttenlocher, D.: Generating sharp panoramas from motion-blurred videos. In: IEEE Conf. on Computer Vision and Pattern Recognition (CVPR), pp. 2424–2431 (2010)

26. Lin, H.T., Tai, Y.W., Brown, M.: Motion regularization for matting motion blurred objects. IEEE Trans. Pattern Analysis and Machine Intelligence (PAMI) 33(11), 2329–2336 (2011)

27. Nir, T., Kimel, R., Bruckstein, A.: Variational approach for joint optic-flow computation and video restoration. Tech. Rep. CIS-2005-03, Technion Israel Institute of Technology (2005)

28. Paramanand, C., Rajagopalan, A.: Non-uniform motion deblurring for bilayer scenes. In: IEEE Conf. on Computer Vision and Pattern Recognition (CVPR), pp. 1115–1122 (2013)

29. Pawan Kumar, M., Torr, P., Zisserman, A.: Learning layered motion segmentations of video. International Journal of Computer Vision (IJCV) 76(3), 301–319 (2008), http://dx.doi.org/10.1007/s11263-007-0064-x

30. Portz, T., Zhang, L., Jiang, H.: Optical flow in the presence of spatially-varying motion blur. In: IEEE Conf. on Computer Vision and Pattern Recognition (CVPR), pp. 1752–1759 (2012)
31. Rav-Acha, A., Kohli, P., Rother, C., Fitzgibbon, A.: Unwrap mosaics: A new representation for video editing. ACM Transactions on Graphics (TOG) - Proc. SIGGRAPH 27(3), 17:1–17:11 (2008)
32. Schoenemann, T., Cremers, D.: A coding cost framework for super-resolution motion layer decomposition. IEEE Trans. Im. Proc. 23(3), 1097–1110 (2012)
33. Seitz, S., Baker, S.: Filter flow. In: 2009 IEEE 12th International Conference on Computer Vision, pp. 143–150 (2009)
34. Sellent, A., Eisemann, M., Goldlucke, B., Cremers, D., Magnor, M.: Motion field estimation from alternate exposure images. IEEE Trans. Pattern Analysis and Machine Intelligence (PAMI) 33(8), 1577–1589 (2011)
35. Shan, Q., Xiong, W., Jia, J.: Rotational motion deblurring of a rigid object from a single image. In: IEEE Conf. on Computer Vision and Pattern Recognition (CVPR), pp. 1–8 (2007)
36. Sun, D., Sudderth, E., Black, M.J.: Layered segmentation and optical flow estimation over time. In: IEEE Conf. on Computer Vision and Pattern Recognition (CVPR), pp. 1768–1775 (2012)
37. Sun, D., Wulff, J., Sudderth, E., Pfister, H., Black, M.: A fully-connected layered model of foreground and background flow. In: IEEE Conf. on Computer Vision and Pattern Recognition (CVPR), Portland, OR, pp. 2451–2458 (June 2013)
38. Takeda, H., Milanfar, P.: Removing motion blur with space-time processing. IEEE Transactions on Image Processing 20(10), 2990–3000 (2011)
39. Torr, P.H.S., Szeliski, R., Anandan, P.: An integrated bayesian approach to layer extraction from image sequences. In: IEEE Int. Conf. on Computer Vision (ICCV), vol. 2, pp. 983–990 (1999)
40. Wang, J.Y.A., Adelson, E.H.: System for encoding image data into multiple layers representing regions of coherent motion and associated motion parameters. US Pat. 5557684 (1996)
41. Wang, J., Adelson, E.: Representing moving images with layers. IEEE Trans. Image Processing 3(5), 625–638 (1994)
42. Weiss, Y.: Smoothness in layers: Motion segmentation using nonparametric mixture estimation. In: IEEE Conf. on Computer Vision and Pattern Recognition (CVPR), Washington, DC, USA, pp. 520–526 (1997),
    http://dl.acm.org/citation.cfm?id=794189.794437
43. Whyte, O., Sivic, J., Zisserman, A., Ponce, J.: Non-uniform deblurring for shaken images. International Journal of Computer Vision (IJCV) 98(2), 168–186 (2012)
44. Xu, L., Jia, J., Matsushita, Y.: Motion detail preserving optical flow estimation. IEEE Trans. Pattern Analysis and Machine Intelligence (PAMI) 34(9), 1744–1757 (2012)
45. Yalcin, H., Black, M.J., Fablet, R.: The dense estimation of motion and appearance in layers. In: IEEE Workshop on Image and Video Registration (June 2004)
46. Yamaguchi, T., Fukuda, H., Furukawa, R., Kawasaki, H., Sturm, P.: Video deblurring and super-resolution technique for multiple moving objects. In: Kimmel, R., Klette, R., Sugimoto, A. (eds.) ACCV 2010, Part IV. LNCS, vol. 6495, pp. 127–140. Springer, Heidelberg (2011),
    http://dl.acm.org/citation.cfm?id=1966111.1966123
47. Zhou, Y., Tao, H.: A background layer model for object tracking through occlusion. In: IEEE Int. Conf. on Computer Vision (CVPR), vol. 2, pp. 1079–1085 (2003)

Efficient Image and Video Co-localization with Frank-Wolfe Algorithm

Armand Joulin*, Kevin Tang*, and Li Fei-Fei

Computer Science Department, Stanford University

Abstract. In this paper, we tackle the problem of performing efficient co-localization in images and videos. Co-localization is the problem of simultaneously localizing (with bounding boxes) objects of the same class across a set of distinct images or videos. Building upon recent state-of-the-art methods, we show how we are able to naturally incorporate temporal terms and constraints for video co-localization into a quadratic programming framework. Furthermore, by leveraging the Frank-Wolfe algorithm (or conditional gradient), we show how our optimization formulations for both images and videos can be reduced to solving a succession of simple integer programs, leading to increased efficiency in both memory and speed. To validate our method, we present experimental results on the PASCAL VOC 2007 dataset for images and the YouTube-Objects dataset for videos, as well as a joint combination of the two.

1 Introduction

With the rising popularity of Internet photo and video sharing sites like Flickr and YouTube, there is a large amount of visual data uploaded to the Internet. In addition to pixels, these images and videos are often tagged with the visual concepts they contain, leading to a natural source of weakly labeled data. Recent research has studied ways of leveraging this data, such as weakly supervised localization [14], co-segmentation [21, 23, 38], and co-localization [37, 44].

In this paper, we address the problem of co-localization in images and videos. Co-localization is the problem of localizing (with bounding boxes) the common object in a set of images or videos. Recent work has studied co-localization in images with potentially noisy labels [44], and co-localization in videos [37] for learning object detectors. Building upon the success of a recent state-of-the-art method [44], we propose a formulation for co-localization in videos that can take advantage of temporal consistency with temporal terms and constraints, while still maintaining a standard quadratic programming formulation. We also show how we can combine both models to perform joint image-video co-localization, the logical way of utilizing all of the weakly supervised data we have available.

To efficiently perform co-localization in both images and videos, we show how our optimization problems can be reduced to a succession of simple integer problems using the Frank-Wolfe algorithm (also known as conditional gradient) [17].

---

* Indicates equal contribution.

D. Fleet et al. (Eds.): ECCV 2014, Part VI, LNCS 8694, pp. 253–268, 2014.
© Springer International Publishing Switzerland 2014

Image Co-localization   Video Co-localization

Fig. 1. In the co-localization problem, our goal is to simultaneously localize the common object of the same class in a set of images or videos. In videos, we have additional temporal consistency information we can leverage to make the problem easier.

For image co-localization, this results in simply taking the maximum of a set of values. For video co-localization, this results in the shortest path algorithm, which can be efficiently solved using dynamic programming.

To re-iterate, we make two key contributions in this paper.

- **Formulation for video co-localization.** We present a novel formulation for video co-localization, extending [44] with temporal terms and constraints.
- **Frank-Wolfe algorithm for efficient optimization.** We show how the Frank-Wolfe algorithm [17] can be used to efficiently solve our optimization problems by solving a succession of simple integer problems.

We present convincing experiments on two difficult datasets: PASCAL VOC 2007 for images [16], YouTube-Objects for videos [37]. We also show results for joint image-video co-localization by combining our models.

2   Related Work

The co-localization problem is similar to co-segmentation [21–24, 38, 39, 47] and weakly supervised localization [14, 31, 32, 43, 46]. Compared to co-segmentation, we seek to localize objects with bounding boxes rather than segmentations, which allows us to greatly decrease the number of variables in our problem. Compared to weakly supervised localization, we are more flexible because we do require any negative images for which we know do not contain our object.

Our work builds upon the formulation introduced in [44] for co-localization in images, which defines an optimization objective that draws inspiration from works in image segmentation [42] and discriminative clustering [3, 21, 49, 51]. Extending their work, we introduce a formulation for co-localization in videos that incorporates constraints and terms that capture temporal consistency, a key property in videos. We also show how the formulation in [44], as well as our video extension, are able to be efficiently solved using the Frank-Wolfe algorithm [17, 26]. Also similar is [14], which generates candidate bounding boxes and tries to select the correct box within each image. However, while they utilize a conditional random field, we adopt a quadratic programming formulation that can be relaxed and efficiently solved. Similar discrete optimization approaches have been shown to work well in various computer vision applications [6, 12, 13].

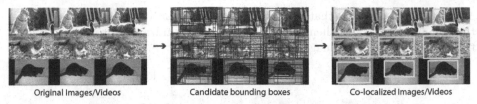

Original Images/Videos   Candidate bounding boxes   Co-localized Images/Videos

Fig. 2. Our co-localization approach starts by generating candidate bounding boxes for each image/video frame. We then jointly select the correct box in each image/video frame that contains the common object.

Our work is also closely related to Chari et al. [9] where they efficiently solve a quadratic program for multi-object tracking using the Frank-Wolfe algorithm.

For video co-localization, most similar is [37], which also tackles the problem of co-localization in videos by proposing candidate regions and selecting the correct one from each video. In [37], the authors try to leverage temporal information by proposing candidate tubes, which suffers from poor performance even with an optimal learning algorithm. In our formulation, we consider the temporal information directly in our model. Co-localization in video also shares similarities to co-segmentation in video, which has recently been studied in [10].

3   Our Approach

We start by briefly describing the co-localization model we use for images [44], and then show how it can be extended to videos. In both models, we take the approach of generating a set of candidate bounding boxes in each image/frame, and then formulating an optimization problem to jointly select the box from each image/frame that contains the common object, as shown in Figure 2.

3.1   Image Model

Given a set of n images $\mathcal{I} = \{I_1, I_2, \ldots, I_n\}$, our goal is to localize the common object in each image. Using objectness [1], we generate m candidate boxes for each image that could potentially contain an object, resulting in a set of boxes $\mathcal{B}_j$ for each image $I_j \in \mathcal{I}$. Our goal then is to jointly select the box from each image that contains the common object. To simplify notation, we define the set of all boxes as $\mathcal{B} = \mathcal{B}_1 \cup \mathcal{B}_2 \ldots \cup \mathcal{B}_n$ and $n_b = nm$ the total number of boxes.

Feature Representation. For each box $b_k \in \mathcal{B}$, we compute a feature representation of the box as $x_k \in \mathbb{R}^d$, and stack the feature vectors to form a feature matrix $X \in \mathbb{R}^{n_b \times d}$. We densely extract SIFT features [29] at every pixel and vector quantize each descriptor into a 1,000 word codebook. For each box, we pool the SIFT features within the box using 1×1 and 3×3 SPM pooling regions [28] to generate a $d = 10,000$ dimensional feature descriptor for each box.

Model Formulation. We associate with each box $b_{j,k} \in \mathcal{B}_j$ a binary label variable $z_{j,k}$, which is equal to 1 if $b_{j,k}$ contains the common object and 0 otherwise. We denote by z the n_b dimensional vector obtained by stacking the $z_{j,k}$.

Making the assumption that in each image there is only one box that contains the common object, we then solve the following optimization problem to select the best box from each image:

$$\underset{z}{\text{minimize}} \qquad z^T(L + \mu A)z - z^T \lambda \log(m)$$

$$\text{subject to} \qquad z \in \{0,1\}, \forall I_j \in \mathcal{I} : \sum_{k=1}^{m} z_{j,k} = 1. \qquad (1)$$

The parameter μ controls the tradeoff between the quadratic terms, while the parameter λ controls the tradeoff between the linear and quadratic terms. The constraints enforce that only a single box is selected in each image. We briefly describe the terms in the objective below, but more details can be found in [44].

Box Prior. The vector m is a prior for each box computed from a saliency map [35] that represents our belief that a box contains the common object given only information within the image.

Box Similarity. The matrix $L = I - D^{-\frac{1}{2}} S D^{-\frac{1}{2}}$ is the normalized Laplacian matrix [42], where D is the diagonal matrix composed of the row sums of S, the $n_b \times n_b$ pairwise χ^2-similarity matrix computed from X. We set the similarity between boxes from the same image/video to 0. This matrix encourages boxes with similar appearances from different images/videos to have the same label.

Box Discriminability. The matrix $A = \frac{1}{n_b}(\Pi_{n_b}(I_{n_b} - X_{box}(X_{box}^T \Pi_{n_b} X_{box} + n_b \kappa I)^{-1} X_{box}^T)\Pi_{n_b})$ is the discriminative clustering term [3, 49], where $\Pi_{n_b} = I_{n_b} - \frac{1}{n_b} 1_{n_b} 1_{n_b}^T$ is the centering projection matrix. This term allows us to utilize a discriminative objective function to penalize the selection of boxes whose features are not easily linearly separable from other boxes. Note that since the matrices L and A are each positive semi-definite, the objective function is convex.

3.2   Video Model

Given a set of n videos $\mathcal{V} = \{V_1, V_2, \ldots, V_n\}$, our goal is to localize the common object in each frame of each video. We approach this problem by considering each video V_i as a collection of temporally ordered frames $\mathcal{I}_i = \{I_{i1}, I_{i2}, \ldots, I_{il_i}\}$, where l_i is the length of video V_i and I_{ij} corresponds to frame j of video V_i. Similar to the image model, we generate a set of m candidate boxes $\mathcal{B}_{ij}$ for each frame of each video using objectness [1]. Our goal then is to select the box from each frame that contains the common object. Similar to the image model, we associate with each box $b_{i,j,k} \in \mathcal{B}_{i,j}$ a binary label variable $z_{i,j,k}$, and stack the variables to obtain z, the $n_b = \sum_{i=1}^{n} l_i m$ dimensional vector.

Defining $\mathcal{I} = \{\mathcal{I}_1, \mathcal{I}_2, \ldots, \mathcal{I}_n\}$ as the set of all frames, we can apply the same objective function and constraints from the image model to $\mathcal{I}$. The image model constraints enforce selecting a single box in each frame, and the image model objective function captures the box prior, similarity, and discriminability within and across different videos.

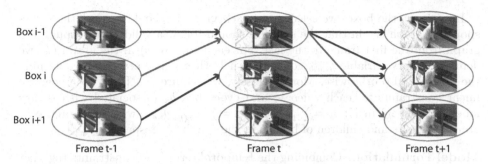

Box i-1

Box i

Box i+1

Frame t-1   Frame t   Frame t+1

Fig. 3. Given consecutive frames of video, we build a graph between adjacent frames. Each node in the graph (blue circle) represents a candidate bounding box, and the directed edges between boxes are defined by a temporal similarity metric that measures how well the boxes agree in size and position. Note that some edges are removed, effectively limiting the possible paths through the graph from first to last frame. The magenta edges represent the optimal path through the frames.

Incorporating Temporal Consistency. In video data, temporal consistency tells us that between consecutive frames, it is unlikely for objects to undergo drastic changes in qualities such as appearance, position, and size. This is a powerful prior that is often leveraged in video tasks such as tracking [2, 4, 19, 33, 36, 45, 50]. In our framework, if two boxes from consecutive frames differ greatly in their size and position, it should be unlikely that they will be selected together. Using this intuition, we can define a simple temporal similarity measure between two boxes b_i and b_j from consecutive frames as follows:

$$s_{\text{temporal}}(b_i, b_j) = \exp\left(-\|b_i^{center} - b_j^{center}\|_2 - \left\|\frac{|b_i^{area} - b_j^{area}|}{\max(b_i^{area}, b_j^{area})}\right\|_2\right), \quad (2)$$

where b_i^{area} is the pixel area of box b_i and b_i^{center} are the center coordinates of box b_i, normalized by the width and height of the frame.

With this similarity metric for all pairs of boxes between adjacent frames, we obtain a weighted graph G_i for each video V_i that connects the boxes within the video based on temporal similarity, as shown in Figure 3. We threshold small values of similarity so that dissimilar edges have a weight of 0 and are thus disconnected. Note that as long as we can obtain a weighted graph, any similarity metric between two boxes from adjacent frames can be used. This makes our temporal framework extremely flexible, and allows us to potentially leverage state-of-the-art methods in object tracking [2, 4, 19, 33, 36, 50].

We collect all the pairwise similarities s_{temporal} between boxes in adjacent frames into a similarity matrix S_t, where $S_t(i, j) = s_{\text{temporal}}(b_i, b_j)$ if b_i and b_j are boxes in adjacent frames, and $S_t(i, j) = 0$ otherwise. With this matrix, we can compute the normalized Laplacian $U = I - D^{-\frac{1}{2}} S_t D^{-\frac{1}{2}}$, where D is the diagonal matrix composed of the row sums of S_t. This matrix encourages us to select boxes that are similar based on the temporal similarity metric.

Intuitively, the boxes we select from each video V_i should respect the corresponding graph G_i, in that the solution should follow a valid path through the graph from the first frame to the last. For each edge (a, b) in the graph G_i, we define a binary variable $y_{i,a,b}$ equal to 1 if both a and b are boxes containing the object and 0 otherwise. More precisely, we require $y \in \{0, 1\}$ to follow the linear constraints for each video V_i and every box b_k (associated with binary label variable z_k) in V_i: $z_k = \sum_{l \in p(k)} y_{i,l,k} = \sum_{l \in c(k)} y_{i,k,l}$, where $p(k)$ and $c(k)$ are the parents and children of box b_k in the graph G_i, respectively.

Model Formulation. Combining the temporal terms and constraints together with the original image model, we obtain the following optimization problem to select the box containing the common object from each frame of video:

$$\underset{z,y}{\text{minimize}} \qquad z^T(L + \mu A + \mu_t U)z - z^T \lambda \log(m) \qquad (3)$$

$$\text{subject to} \qquad z \in \{0, 1\}, \ y \in \{0, 1\},$$

$$\forall I_j \in \mathcal{I} : \sum_{k=1}^{m} z_{j,k} = 1,$$

$$\forall V_i \in \mathcal{V}, \ \forall k \in V_i, \ z_k = \sum_{l \in p(k)} y_{i,l,k} = \sum_{l \in c(k)} y_{i,k,l},$$

where z_i are the binary label variables associated with the boxes in video V_i, and μ_t weights the temporal Laplacian matrix. The additional constraint forces us to choose solutions that respect the edges defined by the underlying graphs for each video, and the additional Laplacian term in the objective function weights these edges. Note that the additional constraint is required to constrain our solutions, as the terms in the objective from the image model can still lead us to select invalid paths if we only had the temporal Laplacian matrix. This formulation allows us to incorporate temporal consistency into the image model. In the rest of this paper, we denote by $\mathcal{P}$ the set of constraints defined in Eq. (3).

In the next section, we present a tight convex relaxation which can be efficiently optimized using the Frank-Wolfe algorithm [17].

4   Optimization

A standard way of dealing with quadratic programs such as Eq. 3 is to relax the discrete non-convex set $\mathcal{P}$ to its convex hull, conv($\mathcal{P}$). Standard algorithms such as interior point methods can be applied but leads to a complexity of $O(N^3)$ which cannot deal with hundreds of videos. We show how it is possible to design an efficient algorithm by using the specificities of our problem.

A key observation towards designing an efficient algorithm for our problem is that the constraints defining the set $\mathcal{P}$ are separable in each video and are equivalent, for each video, to the constraints used in the shortest-path algorithm. This means that if our cost function was linear, we could solve our problem efficiently using dynamic programming.

4.1   Frank-Wolfe Algorithm

Given a convex cost function f and a convex set $\mathcal{D}$, the Frank-Wolfe algorithm [17] finds the global minimum of f over $\mathcal{D}$ by solving a succession of linear problems [15, 20]. More precisely, at each iteration k it solves:

$$\underset{y}{\text{minimize}} \quad y^T \nabla f(z_{k-1})$$

$$\text{subject to} \quad y \in \mathcal{D}. \tag{4}$$

The solution y_k is then used in Frank-Wolfe updates given by:

$$z_k = z_{k-1} + \lambda(y_k - z_{k-1}), \tag{5}$$

where $\lambda > 0$ is found using a line search (see Algorithm 1 for details). Essentially, the Frank-Wolfe algorithm considers a linear approximation of the objective function at each iteration. Although not appropriate for all convex optimization problems, Frank-Wolfe applied to our optimization formulations results in very simple linearizations with integer solutions that are easily solved.

Frank-Wolfe Algorithm on Convex Hull. This algorithm does not need an explicit form for $\mathcal{D}$ as long as it is possible to find the solution of a linear program over $\mathcal{D}$. This is particularly interesting when $\mathcal{D}$ is the convex hull of a set of points $\mathcal{C}$ on which it is possible to solve an integer program. Solving a linear program on $\mathcal{D}$ is then equivalent to solving an integer program over $\mathcal{C}$. This is a particularity of the Frank-Wolfe algorithm that we will exploit in our video setting.

Video Model. For the video model, the Frank-Wolfe algorithm solves the following problem at each iteration:

$$\underset{y}{\text{minimize}} \quad y^T H z_{k-1} \tag{6}$$

$$\text{subject to} \quad y \in \text{conv}(\mathcal{P}).$$

where $H = L + \mu A + \mu_t U$. The cost function and constraints are separable for each video, and optimizing Eq. (6) results in the standard shortest path problem (see supplementary material for details) for each video, which can be solved efficiently using dynamic programming.

Image Model. For the image model, the linearized cost function is separable for each image, and we can efficiently find the best integer solution for this problem by computing the score for each box, $(L + \mu A)z_{k-1}$, and then simply selecting the argmin. Note that there is a trade-off between this algorithm and projected gradient descent in the case of images. While projected gradient descent requires less iterations to converge, each iteration requires a projection over the simplex, which is $O(N \log N)$ whereas each of our updates is only $O(N)$ (or folded into the gradient computation with almost no running time cost).

Since the Frank-Wolfe algorithm for images utilizes the same framework as for videos, an additional advantage is that we can easily learn a shared image/video model with a single algorithm.

Data: $y_0 \in \mathcal{D}$, $\varepsilon > 0$
Result: y^*
Initialization: $k = 0$, $z = y_0$, $\mathcal{S}_0 = \{y_0\}$, $\alpha^0 = \{1\}$;
while $duality\_gap(z) \geq \varepsilon$ **do**

> $k \leftarrow k + 1$;
> $y_k \leftarrow \operatorname{argmin}_{y \in \mathcal{D}} \langle y, \nabla f(z) \rangle$ (FW direction);
> $x_k \leftarrow \operatorname{argmax}_{y \in \mathcal{S}_{k-1}} \langle y, \nabla f(z) \rangle$ (away direction);
> **if** $\langle y_k - z, \nabla f(z) \rangle \leq \langle z - x_k, \nabla f(z) \rangle$ **then**
>> $d_k = y_k - z$;
>> $\gamma_{max} = 1$;
>
> **else**
>> $d_k = z - x_k$;
>> $\gamma_{max} = \alpha_k(x_k)$;
>
> **end**
> Line search: $\gamma_k = \min_{\gamma \in [0, \gamma_{max}]} f(z + \gamma d_k)$;
> $\mathcal{S}_k$, $\alpha_k \leftarrow update\_active\_set(d_k, \gamma_k)$;
> Update $z \leftarrow z + \gamma_k d_k$;
> **if** $f(y_k) < f(y^*)$ **then**
>> $y^* \leftarrow y_k$ (rounding 1);
>
> **end**

end
$y_r \leftarrow \operatorname{argmax}_{y \in \mathcal{D}} \langle y, z \rangle$ (rounding 2);
if $f(y_r) < f(y^*)$ **then**
> $y^* \leftarrow y_r$ (combining rounding);

end

Algorithm 1. Frank-Wolfe algorithm with away step and rounding

4.2   Implementation Details

In this section, we present some details on our implementation of the Frank-Wolfe algorithm.

Away Step. We use an accelerated version termed Frank-Wolfe with away step [48]. The details of this algorithm are given in Algorithm 1. The algorithm keeps a set of previously seen integer solutions (called active corners) $\mathcal{S}_k$ at each iteration such that the current update z is the sum of the corners in $\mathcal{S}_k$ reweighted by α_k. The set $\mathcal{S}_k$ is used to find potentially better directions by moving "away" from an active corner (away step). This version of Frank-Wolfe has been shown to have better convergence rates [18, 25]. The definition of the function $update\_active\_set$ from Algorithm 1 is given in the supplementary material.

Line Seach and Duality Gap. In the case of a quadratic function, both the line search and the duality gap are in closed form (see supplementary material), which significantly improves the speed of our algorithm [26].

Parallel Computation. Our constraints are separable for each image and video, allowing efficient parallel computation of the update. Note that this is a property of any first-order method, including the Frank-Wolfe algorithm. In practice, this allows us to be extremely memory efficient, as we can consider subproblems for each image or video separately.

Rounding. A typical concern with methods based on convex relaxations is obtaining a solution from the relaxed problem that satisfies the non-convex constraints from the original problem. In our case, the rounded solution must belong to the set $\mathcal{P}$. The most natural way of rounding a solution z is to find the closest element in $\mathcal{P}$ given some distance. For the ℓ_2 distance, this means solving $\min_{y\in\mathcal{P}} \|y - z\|_2^2$ which is not possible in general. However, in our case, since the ℓ_2 norm is constant on $\mathcal{P}$ (and equal to the total number of frames/images in the dataset), this projection is equivalent to:

$$\underset{y\in\mathcal{P}}{\text{maximize}} \quad \langle y, z \rangle, \tag{7}$$

which can be solved efficiently using the shortest-path algorithm for the video model, and simply taking the argmax in each image for the image model.

Additionally, the particular form of the Frank-Wolfe updates offers another very natural and inexpensive way of rounding our solution. We can keep track of the solution to the linear problem defined in Eq. (6) that minimizes the cost function defined in Eq. (3). Since this solution is in the original set $\mathcal{P}$, it automatically satisfies the constraints.

In practice, we use both rounding methods and keep the one that results in the lowest value of our cost function, as shown in Algorithm 1.

5   Results

We perform experiments on two challenging datasets, the PASCAL VOC 2007 dataset [16] and the YouTube-Objects dataset [37]. We also combine the two and present results for joint image-video co-localization. Following previous works in weakly supervised localization [14] and co-localization [44], we use the CorLoc evaluation metric, defined as the percentage of images correctly localized according to the PASCAL-criterion: $\frac{area(B_p \cap B_{gt})}{area(B_p \cup B_{gt})} > 0.5$, where B_p is the predicted box and B_{gt} is the ground-truth box. All CorLoc results are given in percentages.

Implementation Details. We set the parameters of our method by optimizing over a small set of images/videos. For the image model, we set $\mu = 0.4$ and for the video model, we set $\mu = 0.6$ and $\mu_t = 1.8$. For both models, we found $\lambda = 0.1$ to perform best. Unless otherwise stated, we extracted 20 objectness boxes from each image. For the video model, we sampled each video every 10 frames, since there is typically little change in such a short amount of time.

5.1   Running Time and Rounding Experiments

In this section, we evaluate the running time of our algorithm. Our implementation is coded in MATLAB and we compare to two standard Quadratic Programming (QP) solvers, Mosek and Gurobi, which are coded in C++. All experiments are done on a single core 2.66GHz Intel CPU with 6GB of RAM.

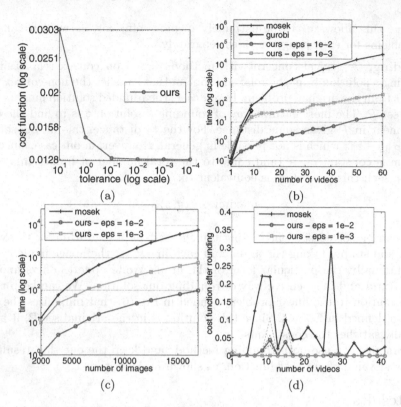

Fig. 4. (a) Value of the cost function for 11 videos as a function of the relative duality gap (log scale). Time comparison between our algorithm and standard QP solvers (time in log scale of second) for (b) video co-localization and (c) image co-localization. (d) Comparison of the value of the cost function obtained with our algorithm and a standard QP solver.

Stopping Criterion. Our stopping criterion is based on the relative duality gap defined as $d = (f - g)/g$, where f is our cost function and g is its dual (see supplementary material for more details). We stop when d is less than some $\varepsilon > 0$. We consider two values for ε, 10^{-2} and 10^{-3}. The choice of these values for ε is motivated by the empirical observation that our cost function remains almost constant for $d < 10^{-2}$, as show in 4(a).

Running Time Analysis. In 4(b)(c), we show how our algorithm scales in the number of videos and images compared to standard QP solvers. For fair running time comparison, we present the time for both standard QP solvers to reach a duality gap less than $\varepsilon = 10^{-2}$. When $\varepsilon = 10^{-3}$, our algorithm runs 100 times faster than standard solvers for more than 20 videos. For $\varepsilon = 10^{-2}$, this factor increases to more than 1000. Typically, for $\varepsilon = 10^{-3}$, solving our problem with 50 videos takes 3 minutes, and 80 videos takes 7 minutes. The gain in speed is mostly due to efficiently computed iterations based on a shortest path algorithm/argmin.

Table 1. Average CorLoc results and upper bound on PASCAL07

Number of objectness boxes [1]	5	10	15	20
Our method	23.96	24.23	24.28	**24.59**
Upper bound	51.04	62.22	67.99	**71.58**

Table 2. CorLoc results on PASCAL07-all compared to previous methods

Method	[40](w/ viewpoint)	[11](w/ viewpoint)	[14](w/ viewpoint)	Our method(w/o viewpoint)
Average CorLoc	14	19	23	22

Rounding Quality. In 4(d), we also compare the quality of the solution obtained after rounding in terms of the original cost function. We compare the relative value of the cost function, $(f - f^*)/f^*$, where f^* is the minimum observed value of the cost function. We round the solutions by solving Eq. (7). For fairness of comparison, we use the solution given by the QP solver for a tolerance of $\varepsilon = 10^{-10}$. Compared to the standard QP solver, our algorithm obtains a significantly better rounded solution in terms of value of the cost function.

Despite numerous advantages of our solver for our specific problem, a limitation of the Frank-Wolfe algorithm with away step in the case of an exponential number of corner points (as is the case in our problem) is that it converges with no guarantee of a linear convergence rate.

5.2   Image Co-localization: PASCAL VOC 2007

In [44], the authors show improved co-localization performance on PASCAL07-6x2, a small subset of PASCAL VOC 2007 divided into specific viewpoints. To illustrate the benefits of the Frank-Wolfe algorithm, which allows us to efficiently consider many more images and boxes per image, we co-localize all images not labeled as difficult for all classes in the PASCAL VOC 2007 dataset [16], which we denote as PASCAL07. This makes the problem much more difficult as we now have to co-localize differing viewpoints together and a much larger set of images. To emphasize the difference in size, the "bicycle-right" class in the PASCAL07-6x2 dataset has the largest number of images at 50, whereas the "person" class in the PASCAL07 dataset has 2,008 images. In all experiments performed in [44], the authors only co-localize a maximum of 100 images at a time due to efficiency concerns. Results for our method varying the number of extracted candidate boxes are given in Table 1, and visualizations are shown in Figure 5. We also show the upper bound on the performance that can be achieved with the candidate boxes, computed by selecting the box in each image with the highest CorLoc.

Number of Candidate Boxes. As we can see, the performance of our model increases when we increase the number of candidate boxes. We can also see that the upper bound becomes much better due to the better recall obtained with more boxes. This helps to validate the importance of efficient methods for co-localization, as they allow us to take advantage of more data in our model.

Fig. 5. Example co-localization results on PASCAL07. From left-right, every two images belong to the same class. Note that we can see a wide variety of viewpoints because we consider all images jointly.

Table 3. CorLoc results for video co-localization on the YouTube-Objects dataset

Method	aeroplane	bird	boat	car	cat	cow	dog	horse	motorbike	train	Average
[37]	**51.7**	17.5	**34.4**	34.7	22.3	17.9	13.5	26.7	**41.2**	25.0	28.5
Our method (image)	18.36	19.35	28.57	32.97	32.77	25.68	38.26	30.14	15.38	21.43	26.29
Our method (image) w/ smoothing	21.26	21.51	30.95	36.26	35.29	25.68	38.26	35.62	15.38	23.21	28.34
Our method (video)	25.12	**31.18**	27.78	**38.46**	**41.18**	**28.38**	33.91	35.62	23.08	25.00	**30.97**
[37] - Upper bound	53.9	19.6	38.2	37.8	32.2	21.8	27.0	34.7	45.4	37.5	34.8
Our method - Upper bound	**95.17**	**70.97**	**91.27**	**93.41**	**73.11**	**89.19**	**80.00**	**64.38**	**83.52**	**76.79**	**81.78**

Comparisons to Previous Methods. We also show results compared to state-of-the-art co-localization methods in Table 2 for the PASCAL07-all dataset [14], which does not consider the "bird", "car", "cat", "cow", "dog", and "sheep" classes. Note that all previous methods utilize additional viewpoint annotations by dividing the images for each class into separate viewpoints, and co-localizing each viewpoint separately with viewpoint-specific priors. On the other hand, our method is run on all of the viewpoints simultaneously, which is a much more difficult problem. Even in this more difficult scenario, we are able to obtain comparable results to previous methods.

5.3   Video Co-localization: YouTube-Objects

The YouTube-Objects dataset [37] consists of YouTube videos collected for 10 classes from PASCAL [16]: "aeroplane", "bird", "boat", "car", "cat", "cow", "dog", "horse", "motorbike", "train". For each class, bounding box annotations for the object are annotated in one frame per shot for 100-290 different shots. We perform video co-localization on all shots with annotations. Results are given in Table 3, where we compare to the co-localization method of [37], our image model with and without smoothing, as well as the upper bounds that can be

Fig. 6. Example co-localization results on YouTube-Objects for our video model (green boxes) and our image model (red boxes). Each column corresponds to a different class, and consists of frame samples from a single video.

obtained using both our methods for candidate box generation. Note that better results are obtained in [34] using unsupervised motion segmentation, which works particularly well for this dataset where objects of interest are moving. In contrast, our method focuses on trying to leverage appearance information across different videos in conjunction with temporal consistency. Thus, we believe that our approaches are orthogonal but complementary, and will likely result in even better performance if combined.

Comparisons to [37]. From our results, we see that we outperform the previous method of [37] for most classes. In addition, we see that the upper bound we can achieve with objectness boxes compared to the candidate tube generation of [7, 37] is much better for all classes. This is likely because object proposals in the image domain have received a great deal of attention and study [1, 8, 30, 41] compared to video [5, 7]. For the "aeroplane" and "motorbike" classes however, we perform much worse. This is likely because the candidate tube extraction algorithm used in [37] is able to effectively track simple and non-deformable objects. However, note that our method is actually agnostic to the underlying candidate region generation algorithm, and we could easily replace our objectness boxes with candidate tubes.

Comparisons to Image Model. Our video model outperforms the image model, which illustrates the importance of leveraging temporal consistency. From the visualizations in Figure 6, we see that the image model often jumps around throughout a single video. For the "dog" class however, our image model actually performs much better than our video model. This is likely due to large amounts of sporadic movement in the "dog" videos caused by both camera movement and object movement. The simple similarity metric we use for temporal consistency may not be invariant to such difficult types of motion, and thus the image model is able to perform better in this case. As noted previously, we can substitute any similarity metric into our framework, and thus potentially take advantage of methods in object tracking [2, 4, 19, 33, 36, 50] to further improve performance.

Table 4. CorLoc results for joint image-video co-localization on YouTube-Objects

Method	aeroplane	bird	boat	car	cat	cow	dog	horse	motorbike	train	Average
Video only	25.12	31.18	27.78	**38.46**	41.18	28.38	33.91	35.62	**23.08**	25.00	30.97
Joint Image+Video	**27.54**	**33.33**	27.78	34.07	**42.02**	28.38	**35.65**	35.62	21.98	25.00	**31.14**

5.4   Joint Image-Video Co-localization

Since the classes in the YouTube-Objects dataset are a subset of the PASCAL07 classes, we can combine the images from the corresponding classes in PASCAL07 with the videos in YouTube-Objects to perform joint image-video co-localization. Results for CorLoc performance on the YouTube-Objects dataset are given in Table 4. We can see that our performance increases slightly for several classes, such as "aeroplane", "bird", "cat" and "dog". It is not unexpected that performance becomes worse for several classes, as there is an inherent domain adaptation problem between images and videos [37, 45]. However, our preliminary results show that with efficient algorithms for image and video co-localization, the problem of jointly considering the two domains is viable, and may present an effective way of taking advantage of all the weakly labeled data available.

6   Conclusions

In this paper, we introduce a formulation for video co-localization that is able to naturally incorporate temporal consistency in a quadratic programming framework. In addition, we show how the image and video co-localization models that are presented can be efficiently optimized using the Frank-Wolfe algorithm. Our experiments on the PASCAL07 and YouTube-Objects datasets illustrate the benefits of our approach for image, video, and joint image-video co-localization.

For future work, we would like to consider jointly performing domain adaption to address the joint image-video co-localization problem with dimensionality reduction techniques [27]. It would also be interesting to consider ways of handling multiple objects per image/frame, multiple object classes, and occlusions.

Acknowledgments. We especially thank Simon Lacoste-Julien for his helpful comments on many technical aspects of this paper. We also thank Vignesh Ramanathan for helpful comments and suggestions. This research is partially supported by an ONR MURI grant, the DARPA Mind's Eye grant, and a NSF GRFP under grant no. DGE-114747 (to K.T.).

References

1. Alexe, B., Deselaers, T., Ferrari, V.: Measuring the objectness of image windows. IEEE T-PAMI 34(11), 2189–2202 (2012)
2. Babenko, B., Yang, M.H., Belongie, S.: Robust object tracking with online multiple instance learning. IEEE T-PAMI 33(8), 1619–1632 (2011)
3. Bach, F., Harchaoui, Z.: Diffrac: a discriminative and flexible framework for clustering. In: NIPS (2007)

4. Berclaz, J., Fleuret, F., Türetken, E., Fua, P.: Multiple object tracking using k-shortest paths optimization. IEEE T-PAMI 33(9), 1806–1819 (2011)
5. Bergh, M.V.D., Roig, G., Boix, X., Manen, S., Gool, L.V.: Online video seeds for temporal window objectness. In: ICCV (2013)
6. Boykov, Y., Veksler, O., Zabih, R.: Fast approximate energy minimization via graph cuts. IEEE T-PAMI 23(11), 1222–1239 (2001)
7. Brox, T., Malik, J.: Object segmentation by long term analysis of point trajectories. In: Daniilidis, K., Maragos, P., Paragios, N. (eds.) ECCV 2010, Part V. LNCS, vol. 6315, pp. 282–295. Springer, Heidelberg (2010)
8. Carreira, J., Sminchisescu, C.: Constrained parametric min-cuts for automatic object segmentation. In: CVPR (2010)
9. Chari, V., Lacoste-Julien, S., Sivic, J., Laptev, I.: On pairwise cost for multi-object network flow tracking. Tech. rep., arXiv (2014)
10. Chiu, W.C., Fritz, M.: Multi-class video co-segmentation with a generative multi-video model. In: CVPR (2013)
11. Chum, O., Zisserman, A.: An exemplar model for learning object classes. In: CVPR (2007)
12. Delong, A., Gorelick, L., Veksler, O., Boykov, Y.: Minimizing energies with hierarchical costs. IJCV 100(1), 38–58 (2012)
13. Delong, A., Osokin, A., Isack, H.N., Boykov, Y.: Fast approximate energy minimization with label costs. IJCV 96(1), 1–27 (2012)
14. Deselaers, T., Alexe, B., Ferrari, V.: Weakly supervised localization and learning with generic knowledge. IJCV 100(3), 275–293 (2012)
15. Dunn, J.C.: Convergence rates for conditional gradient sequences generated by implicit step length rules. SIAM Journal on Control and Optimization 18(5), 473–487 (1980)
16. Everingham, M., Van Gool, L., Williams, C.K.I., Winn, J., Zisserman, A.: The PASCAL Visual Object Classes Challenge 2007 (VOC 2007) Results (2007)
17. Frank, M., Wolfe, P.: An algorithm for quadratic programming. Naval Research Logistics Quarterly 3(1-2), 95–110 (1956)
18. Guelat, J., Marcotte, P.: Some comments on wolfe's away step. Mathematical Programming 35(1), 110–119 (1986)
19. Hare, S., Saffari, A., Torr, P.H.S.: Struck: Structured output tracking with kernels. In: ICCV (2011)
20. Jaggi, M.: Revisiting frank-wolfe: Projection-free sparse convex optimization. In: ICML, pp. 427–435 (2013)
21. Joulin, A., Bach, F., Ponce, J.: Discriminative clustering for image co-segmentation. In: CVPR (2010)
22. Joulin, A., Bach, F., Ponce, J.: Multi-class cosegmentation. In: CVPR (2012)
23. Kim, G., Xing, E.P., Fei-Fei, L., Kanade, T.: Distributed cosegmentation via submodular optimization on anisotropic diffusion. In: ICCV (2011)
24. Kuettel, D., Guillaumin, M., Ferrari, V.: Segmentation propagation in imagenet. In: Fitzgibbon, A., Lazebnik, S., Perona, P., Sato, Y., Schmid, C. (eds.) ECCV 2012, Part VII. LNCS, vol. 7578, pp. 459–473. Springer, Heidelberg (2012)
25. Lacoste-Julien, S., Jaggi, M.: An affine invariant linear convergence analysis for frank-wolfe algorithms. arXiv preprint arXiv:1312.7864 (2013)
26. Lacoste-Julien, S., Jaggi, M., Schmidt, M., Pletscher, P.: Block-coordinate frank-wolfe optimization for structural svms. In: ICML, vol. 28, pp. 1438–1444 (2012)
27. Lampert, C.H., Krömer, O.: Weakly-paired maximum covariance analysis for multimodal dimensionality reduction and transfer learning. In: Daniilidis, K., Maragos, P., Paragios, N. (eds.) ECCV 2010, Part II. LNCS, vol. 6312, pp. 566–579. Springer, Heidelberg (2010)

28. Lazebnik, S., Schmid, C., Ponce, J.: Beyond bags of features: Spatial pyramid matching for recognizing natural scene categories. In: CVPR (2006)
29. Lowe, D.G.: Distinctive image features from scale-invariant keypoints. IJCV 60(2), 91–110 (2004)
30. Manén, S., Guillaumin, M., Van Gool, L.: Prime Object Proposals with Randomized Prim's Algorithm. In: ICCV (2013)
31. Nguyen, M.H., Torresani, L., de la Torre, F., Rother, C.: Weakly supervised discriminative localization and classification: a joint learning process. In: ICCV (2009)
32. Pandey, M., Lazebnik, S.: Scene recognition and weakly supervised object localization with deformable part-based models. In: ICCV (2011)
33. Pang, Y., Ling, H.: Finding the best from the second bests - inhibiting subjective bias in evaluation of visual tracking algorithms. In: ICCV (2013)
34. Papazoglou, A., Ferrari, V.: Fast object segmentation in unconstrained video. In: ICCV (2013)
35. Perazzi, F., Krähenbühl, P., Pritch, Y., Hornung, A.: Saliency filters: Contrast based filtering for salient region detection. In: CVPR (2012)
36. Pérez, P., Hue, C., Vermaak, J., Gangnet, M.: Color-based probabilistic tracking. In: Heyden, A., Sparr, G., Nielsen, M., Johansen, P. (eds.) ECCV 2002, Part I. LNCS, vol. 2350, pp. 661–675. Springer, Heidelberg (2002)
37. Prest, A., Leistner, C., Civera, J., Schmid, C., Ferrari, V.: Learning object class detectors from weakly annotated video. In: CVPR (2012)
38. Rubinstein, M., Joulin, A., Kopf, J., Liu, C.: Unsupervised joint object discovery and segmentation in internet images. In: CVPR (2013)
39. Rubio, J.C., Serrat, J., López, A.: Video co-segmentation. In: Lee, K.M., Matsushita, Y., Rehg, J.M., Hu, Z. (eds.) ACCV 2012, Part II. LNCS, vol. 7725, pp. 13–24. Springer, Heidelberg (2013)
40. Russell, B.C., Efros, A.A., Sivic, J., Freeman, W.T., Zisserman, A.: Using multiple segmentations to discover objects and their extent in image collections. In: CVPR (2006)
41. van de Sande, K.E.A., Uijlings, J.R.R., Gevers, T., Smeulders, A.W.M.: Segmentation as selective search for object recognition. In: ICCV (2011)
42. Shi, J., Malik, J.: Normalized cuts and image segmentation. IEEE T-PAMI 22(8), 888–905 (2000)
43. Siva, P., Russell, C., Xiang, T., de Agapito, L.: Looking beyond the image: Unsupervised learning for object saliency and detection. In: CVPR (2013)
44. Tang, K., Joulin, A., Li, L.J., Fei-Fei, L.: Co-localization in real-world images. In: CVPR (2014)
45. Tang, K., Ramanathan, V., Fei-Fei, L., Koller, D.: Shifting weights: Adapting object detectors from image to video. In: NIPS (2012)
46. Tang, K., Sukthankar, R., Yagnik, J., Fei-Fei, L.: Discriminative segment annotation in weakly labeled video. In: CVPR (2013)
47. Vicente, S., Rother, C., Kolmogorov, V.: Object cosegmentation. In: CVPR (2011)
48. Wolfe, P.: Convergence theory in nonlinear programming. In: Integer and Nonlinear Programming, pp. 1–36 (1970)
49. Xu, L., Neufeld, J., Larson, B., Schuurmans, D.: Maximum margin clustering. In: NIPS (2004)
50. Yilmaz, A., Javed, O., Shah, M.: Object tracking: A survey. ACM Comput. Surv. 38(4) (2006)
51. Zhou, G.T., Lan, T., Vahdat, A., Mori, G.: Latent maximum margin clustering. In: NIPS (2013)

Non-parametric Higher-Order Random Fields for Image Segmentation

Pablo Márquez-Neila[1], Pushmeet Kohli[2], Carsten Rother[3], and Luis Baumela[1]

[1] Universidad Politécnica de Madrid, Spain
[2] Microsoft Research Cambridge, UK
[3] Technische Universität Dresden, Germany
{p.mneila,lbaumela}@upm.es, pkohli@microsoft.com,
carsten.rother@tu-dresden.de

Abstract. Models defined using higher-order potentials are becoming increasingly popular in computer vision. However, the exact representation of a general higher-order potential defined over many variables is computationally unfeasible. This has led prior works to adopt parametric potentials that can be compactly represented. This paper proposes a non-parametric higher-order model for image labeling problems that uses a patch-based representation of its potentials. We use the transformation scheme of [11, 25] to convert the higher-order potentials to a pair-wise form that can be handled using traditional inference algorithms. This representation is able to capture structure, geometrical and topological information of labels from training data and to provide more precise segmentations. Other tasks such as image denoising and reconstruction are also possible. We evaluate our method on denoising and segmentation problems with synthetic and real images.

Keywords: random fields, biomedical image analysis, higher-order models, image denoising, image segmentation, structured prediction.

1 Introduction

Conditional and Markov random fields (CRF/MRF) are popular models for representing regularized solutions to many computer vision problems, such as object segmentation, optical flow and disparity estimation [28]. One variant of these models, the *pairwise random field*, has been extensively used in computer vision because it allows efficient inference of its Maximum a Posterior (MAP) solution. However, the pairwise random fields only allow the incorporation of statistical relationships between pairs of random variables and are unable to enforce the high-level structural dependencies between pixels that have been shown to be extremely useful for a variety of computer vision problems. Some approaches try to overcome the limitations of pairwise terms with dense, fully-connected CRFs [16].

The last few years have seen the successful application of higher-order CRFs and MRFs to some low-level vision problems such as image restoration, disparity

D. Fleet et al. (Eds.): ECCV 2014, Part VI, LNCS 8694, pp. 269–284, 2014.

estimation and object segmentation [6, 10, 17, 18, 23, 24, 29]. These models are composed of higher-order potentials, i.e., potentials defined over multiple variables, which have higher modeling power. In general, it is computationally unfeasible to exactly represent a higher-order potential function defined over many variables. Representation of a general m order potential function of k-state discrete variables requires k^m parameter values. This has led researchers to propose a number of parametric families of higher order potentials that can be compactly represented [4, 8–12, 14, 17, 21, 24–26].

In this paper, we propose a non-parametric pattern-based higher-order random field. The higher-order potentials used in our model are defined using a data driven approach. We use a pattern based representation [11, 14, 25] to encode the structure and shape of the labels. This allows us to use the transformation scheme of [11, 25] to convert the higher-order potentials to a general pairwise form that can be handled using traditional inference algorithms such as belief propagation (BP) [23] and tree-reweighted message passing (TRW) [13]. We evaluate the performance of our method in synthetic images, medical images and the MSRCv2 dataset, and compare our results with conventional pairwise energy regularization, a higher-order method [25] and structured random forests [15].

Although we adopt the transformation scheme in [25], the resulting algorithm is more general. The approach in [25] uses higher-order potentials to define a prior for binary texture denoising. These potentials are defined over each patch in the image, encouraging the pixels in the patch to take a joint labeling from a pre-defined global set of patterns. To make the problem computationally tractable, the size of the global set of patterns is limited to a small number. This makes this approach inadequate for tasks such as segmentation. In contrast, the potentials in our model are conditioned on the data. This means that every potential can choose the most suitable joint labeling from a local set of patterns selected according to the observations. Since this local set can be different for every potential, the global set of patterns that our model considers can be as large as required by the application. Hence, the expressive power of our model is much greater than the one in [25], at the same computational cost.

A number of methods in the literature have also adopted a data-driven philosophy to solve image labeling problems. These methods generally work by finding, for the image patch under consideration, the closest matches in the training dataset [3, 5, 6, 19]. Instead, our approach uses the labeling candidates from the matching patches to define a higher order energy whose minimization performs the label aggregation to obtain a consistent solution.

Higher-order potentials have also been used for curvature regularization. In [22] each potential considers an exhaustive enumeration of possible joint labelings for its pixels. Since the labeling enumeration is exponential in the size of the patches, patches must be small and the potentials can only impose a weak regularization. In our work, however, possible joint labelings are learned from data and are, in consequence, sparser than exhaustive enumeration. This permits larger patches and more expressive potentials.

Our higher order potential can be seen as encoding a higher order likelihood [7] function that takes into account all patches in the training set.

2 Non-parametric Higher-order Random Field (NHRF)

The energy of the pattern-based model for texture denoising is [25]

$$E(\mathbf{y}) = \sum_{i \in \mathcal{V}} \phi_i(\mathbf{y}_i | \mathbf{x}) + \sum_{c \in \mathcal{P}} \phi(\mathbf{y}_c), \tag{1}$$

where $\mathcal{V}$ is the set of pixels of the image, $\mathbf{x}$ is the observed image data, $\mathbf{y}$ is the vector of labels and $\mathcal{P} \subset 2^{\mathcal{V}}$ represents a set of cliques in the pixels of the image. In this model there are two kinds of potentials: unary potentials ϕ_i defined over individual pixels and higher-order potentials ϕ defined over many pixels. The expressions $\mathbf{x}_c$ and $\mathbf{y}_c$ represent the elements of the image $\mathbf{x}$ and the labeling $\mathbf{y}$ that correspond to the clique c. Notice that only the unary potentials ϕ_i, and not the higher-order potentials, are dependent on the data $\mathbf{x}$.

In our model, however, the higher order potentials defined over a set of variables directly depend on the pixel observations. The energy of our model is a sum of higher order potentials ϕ_c,

$$E(\mathbf{y}) = \sum_{c \in \mathcal{P}} \phi(\mathbf{y}_c \mid \mathbf{x}_c) = \sum_{c \in \mathcal{P}} \phi_c(\mathbf{y}_c). \tag{2}$$

The cliques in $\mathcal{P}$ can overlap, have different sizes and shapes and be centered on any pixel. For simplicity we work with square, fixed sized and overlapping cliques centered on a grid of pixels with a given separation among them, that we call *stride*. This layout has proven to be powerful enough for all our experiments. The size of the $m \times m$ clique and the stride of the grid s are hyper-parameters of the model. It is required that $s < m$, or otherwise there would be pixels not affected by any clique. The order of the energy is the number of pixels of every clique in $\mathcal{P}$, i.e., m^2. Figure 1(a) shows the factor graph of our model.

The key idea for our higher-order potentials ϕ_c is that they have a data-driven, non parametric representation based on a set of $m \times m$ patterns $\mathcal{Y} = \{\mathbf{Y}^{(1)}, \mathbf{Y}^{(2)}, \ldots, \mathbf{Y}^{(t)}\}$. As a first approach, the potential $\phi_c(\mathbf{y}_c)$ is defined so that $\mathbf{y}_c$ can only be equal to one of the patterns in $\mathcal{Y}$. Otherwise, if the value of $\mathbf{y}_c$ is not in $\mathcal{Y}$, $\phi_c(\mathbf{y}_c)$ will be infinity. To encode the fact that not all patterns equally suit the observations $\mathbf{x}_c$ of each patch, we use a set of costs $\{\theta_1^c, \ldots, \theta_t^c\}$ associated to each pattern. The cost θ_q^c will be small when the pattern q provides a good explanation for the observations $\mathbf{x}_c$.

Given these considerations, we could define the potential ϕ_c as

$$\phi_c(\mathbf{y}_c) = \begin{cases} \theta_q^c & \text{if } y_i = Y_i^{(q)} \quad \forall i \in c \\ \infty & \text{otherwise} \end{cases}. \tag{3}$$

Hence, the variables of every patch can only have values that perfectly match one of the patterns in $\mathcal{Y}$, which we will call the *active pattern* of the patch. This model is constrained to use the patterns in $\mathcal{Y}$, something very restrictive in practice. To alleviate this restriction we will also allow deviations from patterns $\mathcal{Y}$, but we will penalize those deviations using a set of *deviation cost* functions $d_1^c, \ldots, d_t^c :$ $\mathcal{L}^{|c|} \to \mathbb{R}$. Since their input is discrete, they can be defined as:

$$d_q^c(\mathbf{y}_c) = \sum_{i \in c, l \in \mathcal{L}} w_{qil}^c \delta(y_i = l), \qquad (4)$$

where w_{qil}^c is the cost of assigning the label l to the variable y_i of the clique c when that clique is considered to be associated to the pattern $\mathbf{Y}_q^c$. When a variable has no deviation from the active pattern, the corresponding deviation cost is 0.

With the deviation functions we can define our potentials as

$$\phi_c(\mathbf{y}_c) = \min_{q \in \{1, \ldots, t\}} \theta_q^c + d_q^c(\mathbf{y}_c), \qquad (5)$$

where θ_q^c and d_q^c depend on observation $\mathbf{x}_c$. Thus, given a labeling $\mathbf{y}_c$, the potential $\phi_c(\mathbf{y}_c)$ will be the cost of the best pattern for the labeling plus the costs of the deviations from that pattern.

Since the patches overlap, a pixel i can be included in multiple patches, and it may occur that the labelings for those patches do not agree. The energy minimization solves these disagreements by assigning to y_i the label that minimizes the sum of deviations of the potentials that share the pixel.

The higher-order random field defined in this section does not specify the structure model of the problem. Instead, the structure itself, and not only a set of parameters, is learned from data. Thus, this is a *non-parametric higher-order random field* (NHRF).

2.1 Transformation to a Pair-Wise Form

The energy (2) cannot be minimized directly. Instead, we use the sparse nature of the potentials to transform the higher-order energy into a pairwise one by introducing a pattern selection variable $z_c \in \{1, \ldots, t\}$ for every patch c. This variable selects the active pattern in that patch. This allows the transformation of potentials to the equivalent form

$$\phi_c(\mathbf{y}_c) = \min_{z_c} h_c(z_c) + \sum_{i \in c} g_c(z_c, y_i), \qquad (6)$$

that has only unary and pairwise terms. The unary term $h_c(z) = \theta_z^c$ encodes the cost of choosing the pattern z, and the pairwise terms $g_c(z, y_i) = w_{ziy_i}^c$ encode the deviation costs. Figure 1 depicts how this transformation changes the appearance of the factor graph.

The global energy function (2) becomes

$$E(\mathbf{y}) = \min_{\mathbf{z}} \sum_{c \in \mathcal{P}} h_c(z_c) + \sum_{i \in c} g_c(z_c, y_i), \qquad (7)$$

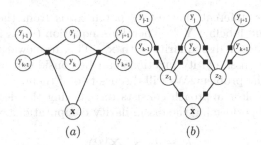

Fig. 1. (a) Factor graph of a simple higher-order random field. (b) Transformation of the higher-order random field to a pairwise random field.

and computing the MAP estimation $\mathbf{y}^* = \operatorname{argmin}_{\mathbf{y}} E(\mathbf{y})$ is just a minimization of a pairwise energy over the labels $\mathbf{y}$ and the selection variables $\mathbf{z}$. We resort to the standard inference algorithms tree-reweighted (TRW) message passing and belief propagation (BP) to minimize it.

3   Training Non-parametric Higher-order Random Fields

Just like other structured prediction methods, our model requires pairs $(\mathbf{x}, \mathbf{y})$ of images and their corresponding segmentations for training. The learning consists on inferring the pattern set $\mathcal{Y}$ from data, as well as a method for estimating the costs of the patterns for an observation of a patch $\mathbf{x}_c$. We could also learn the deviation costs w_{qil}^c from data, but the huge amount of parameters needed would complicate both the model and the learning algorithm. We have seen in our experiments that a single cost α for all deviations,

$$w_{qil}^c = \begin{cases} 0 & \text{if } l = Y_i^{(q)} \\ \alpha & \text{otherwise} \end{cases}, \tag{8}$$

suffices for all practical cases. The deviation cost α is a hyper-parameter of our model. It could be learned by cross-validation, but we have verified in our experiments that large changes in α affect little or nothing the results. Therefore, an arbitrary value such as $\alpha = 1$ is typically used.

The training data consists of a set of images $\mathcal{M} = \{\mathbf{x}^{(1)}, \dots, \mathbf{x}^{(p)}\}$ and their labelings $\mathcal{N} = \{\mathbf{y}^{(1)}, \dots, \mathbf{y}^{(p)}\}$. From training data, we extract many pairs of $m \times m$ image and label patches. We consider all overlapping patches centered on a grid of pixels with a given stride. We will call $\mathcal{X} = \{\mathbf{X}^{(1)}, \dots, \mathbf{X}^{(t)}\}$ to the set of patches extracted from training images, and the corresponding set of patches extracted from labelings is the set of patterns $\mathcal{Y}$ described in previous section.

The patches in $\mathcal{X}$ and $\mathcal{Y}$ are used to estimate the costs when a new patch $\mathbf{x}_c$ from a testing image arrives. The costs θ_q^c are computed by a dissimilarity function

$$\theta_q^c = d(\mathbf{x}_c, \mathbf{X}^{(q)}, \mathbf{Y}^{(q)}) \tag{9}$$

that measures how different the testing patch $\mathbf{x}_c$ is from the training patch with image $\mathbf{X}^{(q)}$ and labeling $\mathbf{Y}^{(q)}$. Therefore, equation (9) assigns higher costs to patterns with higher dissimilarity with $\mathbf{x}_c$. This framework is very flexible and many different dissimilarity functions can be considered depending on the characteristics of the problem. We will discuss two of them.

Perhaps the simplest approach consists on ignoring the dependence on the labeling patch and performing the dissimilarity computations only in the space of image patches:

$$\theta_q^c = d_X(\mathbf{x}_c, \mathbf{X}^{(q)}). \tag{10}$$

The function d_X is in this case just a metric in the space of image patches. This metric could be the standard Euclidean distance but, unless the relationship between images and labels is simple, more involved alternatives such as learned metrics are required. An interesting advantage of using d_X as the dissimilarity function is that, as a metric, it permits using a kd-tree for fast search of patches.

A second, more interesting approach is dropping the dependence on the image patch and computing the dissimilarity directly with the labeling patch that will be used for defining the corresponding higher-order potential:

$$\theta_q^c = d_Y(\mathbf{x}_c, \mathbf{Y}^{(q)}). \tag{11}$$

Since d_Y is not a metric, we need a way to relate the image observations from patch $\mathbf{x}_c$ to the labels in $\mathbf{Y}^{(q)}$. We model this relationship with a probability function $P(\mathbf{Y}^{(q)} \mid \mathbf{x}_c)$, that estimates the probability that the pattern $\mathbf{Y}^{(q)}$ explains the observation $\mathbf{x}_c$, and define

$$d_Y(\mathbf{x}_c, \mathbf{Y}^{(q)}) = -\log P(\mathbf{Y}^{(q)}|\mathbf{x}_c). \tag{12}$$

To deal with the number of parameters needed by this probability function, we assume independence between variables, what leads to the factorization:

$$P(\mathbf{Y}^{(q)} \mid \mathbf{x}_c) = \prod_i P(y_i^{(q)} \mid \mathbf{x}_c). \tag{13}$$

This may seem a very strong assumption, since the labels in a pattern are strongly correlated. However, label dependencies are already implicitly encoded in the set of possible patterns $\mathcal{Y}$ and we do not need to learn them again in the joint probability.

Every factor $P(y_i^{(q)} \mid \mathbf{x}_c)$ is just the probability of a label in a single pixel given the observations. A pixel-wise classifier is responsible of learning this probability. In our experiments, we have used a variety of pixel-wise classifiers ranging from simple Gaussian classifiers to random forests.

A very convenient consequence of dropping the dependence on $\mathbf{X}^{(q)}$ from the dissimilarity function is that the cardinality of the pattern set $\mathcal{Y}$ can be greatly reduced. Indeed, it is not necessary to store the image patches from $\mathcal{X}$ to compute the costs with d_Y. Also, the set $\mathcal{Y}$ has lots of very similar or repeated elements. Therefore, a clustering on $\mathcal{Y}$ is able to reduce the number of patterns by removing duplicates and similar patterns.

Inference. Given a new testing image $\mathbf{x}$, first the set of cliques $\mathcal{P}$ must be defined. Then, for every patch $\mathbf{x}_c$ corresponding to a clique c in the testing image, we should compute the costs, d (9), of all patches extracted in the training step and build the higher-order potentials of the random field with them. However, such an amount of data per potential function is prohibitive in terms of memory.

In practice, we do not keep all t costs and patterns in every higher-order potential ϕ_c, but only a subset of the t' patterns with the lowest costs, with $t' \ll t$. The subset of t' patterns with lowest costs for a clique c of the testing image will be called the set of *local patterns*, or *candidates*, of that clique. The rest of patterns in $\mathcal{Y}$ with larger costs are simply ignored, assuming than their costs are too large to be considered. For reference, t' is in the order of tens or, at most, hundreds.

The NHRF is defined once every potential ϕ_c has been fully determined with its candidates and their associated costs. Then, it is converted to pair-wise form as defined in Section 2.1 and inference is performed via energy minimization with TRW or BP.

To clarify previous discussion, Figure 2 shows an example of the training of a NHRF and Figure 3 shows some details of a NHRF built for a testing image.

4 Experiments

By using patterns previously seen in training data, the NHRFs implicitly integrate high-order geometric and topological information. We have conducted several experiments with both synthetic and real images to assess the power of the NHRFs in image denoising and segmentation, respectively.

4.1 Occluded Squares

In this experiment we analyze the performance of NHRFs and compare it with other approaches using synthetic images. These images feature occlusions and a high level of noise. We use a dataset of 150×150 images with 50×50 squares in several orientations. The images are highly perturbed with noise and circular holes that *occlude* the squares. Figure 4(a,b) shows some images of the testing dataset and the corresponding labelings.

We use 500 images with their labelings for training. We extract all possible 21×21 patches with a stride of 2 pixels. We end up with more than 2 million image and label patches. Since we will use the Euclidean distance in the space of image patches (i.e., d_X) as our dissimilarity function, we build a kd-tree with the image patches.

For a new image, we define our set of cliques $\mathcal{P}$ as all the 21×21 squared cliques with a stride $s = 2$ pixels. For every clique, we look for the nearest $t' = 15$ candidates in the space of image patches.

Figure 4(d) shows the segmentation obtained for a test image. The accuracy of the method is 99.7%, and the average Jaccard index is 97.28%. The NHRF model is able to discover that circular structures are not part of the objects of interest, while straight lines and corners are.

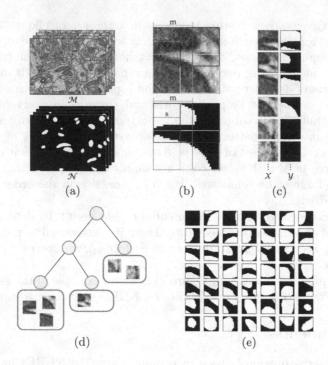

Fig. 2. Training of a NHRF. Given the training data (a), we extract all $m \times m$ patches with stride s as shown in (b). For clarity, (b) shows only a small 40×40 fragment from training data. In this example, $m = 24$ and $s = 16$ pixels. The patches extracted from images and labelings form the sets $\mathcal{X}$ and $\mathcal{Y}$, respectively. (c) shows some elements of these sets. When costs are estimated with dissimilarity d_X, a kd-tree with elements of $\mathcal{X}$ is built (d). When d_Y is used instead, clustering over $\mathcal{Y}$ is performed to obtain a reduced set of patterns without repeated elements. (e) shows some patterns obtained after clustering.

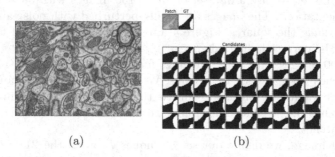

Fig. 3. Example of a higher-order potential in a NHRF. Given a testing image (a), $m \times m$ cliques are configured in a grid with stride s in a similar way to Figure 2(b). For every clique, we look for the t' patterns with lowest costs. These are the candidates for those cliques. (b) shows the candidates found for the the clique marked in (a).

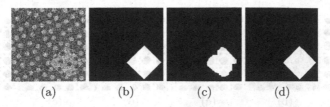

(a)   (b)   (c)   (d)

Fig. 4. Results for the square dataset. (a) Testing images. (b) Ground-truth. (c) Results with a random forest pixel-wise classifier with pairwise regularization. (d) NHRF.

We have also segmented these images using a pixel-wise random forest classifier trained with the same training dataset. The results of the classifier are then regularized minimizing a 4-connected pair-wise energy via graph-cuts [2]. The capacities of the edges are equal across the grid and set via cross-validation. The accuracy reached with pair-wise regularization is 98.45% and the Jaccard index is 86.89%. Figure 4(c) shows the results obtained. Despite the good quantitative results, this figure proves that pixel-wise classifiers and pair-wise regularization are not powerful enough to regularize the segmentation of objects where high-level shape information is present. Instead, the NHRF method exploits that kind of information to obtain better labelings with straight lines and sharp corners. Moreover NHRFs do not present the undesirable effect of the *shrinking bias* and *metrication errors* present in pair-wise regularization (see Figure 4(c)).

4.2   Binary Image Reconstruction and Denoising

In this experiment we examine the performance in image reconstruction and denoising. We use the Brodatz D101 texture shown in Figure 5. A fragment of that texture is used both as the training image $\mathcal{M} = \{\mathbf{x}^{(1)}\}$ and as labeling image $\mathcal{N} = \{\mathbf{y}^{(1)}\}$ (Figure 5(a)). A different fragment is selected as ground-truth (Figure 5(c)). The ground-truth is perturbed with 30% of noise, (Figure 5(b)) and used as input. The patch size is $m = 10$ pixels, and the stride between consecutive patches is $s = 1$ pixel. The costs of the patterns θ_q^c are computed using the dissimilarity d_X. The deviation cost is set to an arbitrarily large number $\alpha = 1000$. The resulting energy is finally minimized using TRW. Figure 5(f) shows the result of the minimization.

We also reconstructed the input image in Figure 5(b) using, first, a standard pair-wise regularization approach with 4-connected pixels, submodular terms and equal capacities for all edges and, second, the global patterns algorithm introduced in [25]. Figure 5(e,f) shows the results obtained with these methods.

Quantitative pixel error of the reconstruction for the NHRF is 5.96%. The error of pair-wise regularization and global patterns are respectively 9.68% and 9.32%.

Qualitatively, the results show that pair-wise regularization does not maintain the overall image structure. The global pattern method of [25] partially maintains the image structure, although it makes some small holes disappear. Moreover,

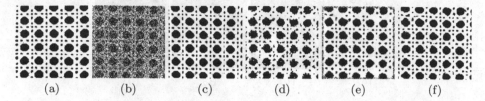

(a)   (b)   (c)   (d)   (e)   (f)

Fig. 5. Example of binary image reconstruction. The training is done with image (a) and the testing with image (b), whose ground-truth is (c). (d) Results with pair-wise regularization, (e) global patterns [25], (f) NHRF. The size of all images is 200 × 200 pixels.

the reconstruction also keeps part of the noise, specially visible in the jagged image boundaries, due to the unary terms. The reconstruction obtained with the NHRF is superior to the others both in terms of maintenance of image structure and noise removal.

This experiment is a good example of the limitations of the global patterns [25]. As discussed in Section 1, the number of global patterns is restricted by practical considerations. In this experiment the chosen number of global patterns, 50, cannot model the variety of shapes and structures that occur in the simple repetitive texture under consideration. In the segmentation of real world images this limitation is expected to be even more pronounced. However, for the NHRF, 50 local patterns for every potential chosen according to the observations, are more than adequate for this problem.

4.3 Mitochondria Segmentation

The segmentation of electron microscopy (EM) imaging of the brain is one of the areas where the NHRFs can provide better results. In the first place, brain structures such as mitochondria have a very characteristic shape and topology: they are simply connected structures with no holes and tubular-like shapes. The NHRFs capacity for learning shape and topology makes them a suitable tool for this application.

We will use the EM dataset from [20]. This dataset is a labeled sample of the rat hippocampus (see Figure 2(a)). The dataset is divided in two stacks of the same size for training and testing. Each stack consists of 165 slices with size 384 × 512 pixels.

We use the the dissimilarity function d_Y to estimate the costs of candidates. From the labeling slices of the training stack we extract all $m \times m$ patches with a stride of s pixels. We have performed experiments with several patch sizes. For reference, in the case of $m = 24$ pixels this gives about 2 million patches. After clustering, the number of patterns drops to 12261. Some of them are shown in Figure 2(e). For our pixel-wise classifier, we use boosted context cues [1], a set of features that has proved to perform specially well for the segmentation of synaptic junctions and other brain structures.

We compare the NHRF method with the performance of the pixel-wise classifier with and without pair-wise regularization. We also include the *structured random forest* (SRF) method from [15] in our comparison. The SRF is an extension to the standard random forest that aims to integrate structural label information of the images to segment. Table 1(left) presents results for some combinations of patch size m and deviation cost α.

As expected, the NHRF model improves the results obtained by the pixel-wise classifier alone and with pair-wise regularization. These results are, to the best of our knowledge, the state-of-the-art in this dataset.

The performance of the SRF is poor in this dataset. This could be attributed to the fact that SRFs are good learning the relative position and relations among the labels, but they do not learn the shapes and topological features of each label, as the NHRFs do.

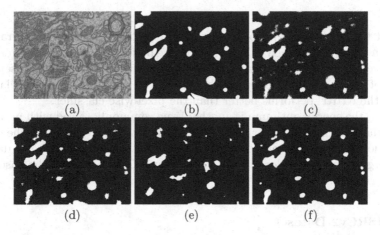

(a)   (b)   (c)

(d)   (e)   (f)

Fig. 6. Results for the hippocampus dataset. (a) Testing image. (b) Ground-truth. (c) Pixel-wise classifier. (d) Pair-wise regularization. (e) Structured random forest [15], (f) NHRF ($m = 24$ pixels, $\alpha = 1$).

Although the quantitative results prove the good performance of the NHRFs, the qualitative results give complementary insights. In Figure 6 the effects of the higher-order regularization are very noticeable. The regions obtained with pair-wise regularization do not resemble the appearance of real mitochondria. The boundaries are ragged and background regions with arbitrary shapes are still present. The NHRF leads to much more realistic looking results. Most regions have smooth, rounded boundaries like real mitochondria. With the SRF the shapes of the regions look less alike real mitochondria.

The running time depends on the size of the patch. For the best size $m = 24$, the inference takes around 10 minutes per image using the TRW implementation from [13]. For $m = 15$ this time falls to 4 minutes.

Figure 7 clarifies some aspects of our method. The patch size m noticeably affects to the results of the segmentation (see Table 1(a)). However, the method

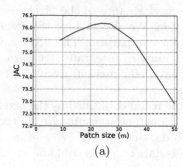
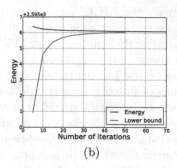

(a)   (b)

Fig. 7. (a) Jaccard score vs. patch size m. The horizontal dashed line marks the performance of the pixel-wise classifier. (b) Energy and lower bound evolution during the inference procedure of a slice. Both plots are for the mitochondria dataset.

is robust to the choice of m, providing similar performance in a broad range of values ($m \in [10, 30]$) as seen in Figure 7(a). The performance falls for larger patch sizes since the available training data is insufficient to provide a representative sample of the space of labeling patches. However, even for patches as large as $m = 50$ the NHRF performs better than the pixel-wise classifier.

Missing the energy optimum is another issue commonly raised with minimization methods such as TRW or BP. Figure 7(b) plots the evolution of the energy and the lower bound computed by TRW for a slice of the mitochondria dataset. The energy comes very close to the lower bound. This has been the case in all our experiments.

4.4 MSRCv2 Dataset

The MSRCv2 dataset [27] consists of 591 images annotated with 21 classes. The annotations are coarse and incomplete, with areas marked as *void* where none of the classes is valid. The 591 images are split into 315 training and 276 testing images (roughly 55%-45%).

From the training images we extract all patches centered at pixels of a grid with a stride of 5 pixels. We repeat this procedure with two different values for the patch size m: 11 and 21 pixels. This leads to approximately 800K patches extracted for $m = 11$ pixels and 750K for $m = 21$ pixels. As in the previous experiment, we use the dissimilarity d_Y to compute costs. After clustering, we obtain $t = 8417$ patterns for the patch of size $m = 11$ pixels and $t = 19549$ patterns for the patch of size $m = 21$ pixels.

From the training data we also train a random forest classifier with HOG, texture and color features. The HOG features are extracted with 6×6 pixels per cell and 4×4 cells per patch, with 9 bins for each histogram. For every cell we also include 4 texture descriptors and 2 color values (the a and b channels of the CIELAB color space), leading to a total of $(9 + 4 + 2) \times 16 = 240$ dimensions of the feature vector.

We perform segmentation and regularization of the testing images with NHRFs for the mentioned patches size, and for different values of the deviation costs. Table 1(right) summarizes the results and compares the performance with other algorithms. In this table we report the global accuracy (the percentage of pixels that were correctly classified) and the average Jaccard index over all classes. As in [15], we ignore the pixels annotated as *void* in the ground-truth from the estimation of all validation metrics.

Table 1. Quantitative results for hippocampus (left) and MSRCv2 (right) datasets. Numbers in parentheses indicate parameters (m, α) of the NHRF.

Hippocampus			MSRCv2		
Method	JAC	ACC	Method	Avg. JAC	ACC
Boost context cues (BCC)	72.50	98.20	Random forest (RF)	23.6	56.6
BCC+pw regularization	73.62	98.31	RF+pw regularization	24.6	58.4
BCC+NHRF (24, 1)	**76.20**	**98.51**	RF+NHRF (11, 1)	24.5	58.6
BCC+NHRF (24,100)	75.94	98.49	RF+NHRF (21, 1)	25.7	**59.9**
BCC+NHRF (50, 1)	72.92	98.32	RF+NHRF (21, 10)	25.7	59.9
SRF [15]	31.68	94.27	SRF [15]	**27.0**	57.6

We also compare our results with the SRF [15]. We use the same training parameters given in [15]: feature patch size of 24×24, 10 trees and 500 iterations per node stopping when less than 5 samples per leaf were available. The results obtained with this method are better for this dataset than for the hippocampus. This is reasonable, since this dataset relies on the relative positions of the classes much more than on the shapes of the classes. In fact, the shapes and geometry of the classes are rather unimportant in this dataset due to the coarse labeling of the training data. This affects negatively the performance of the NHRF method, which is very dependent on shapes. Nevertheless, the NHRF results are still compelling. This proves that they are also able to learn and make use of the relative positions of the classes in a similar way as the structured random forests do. Moreover, the MSRCv2 dataset has been manually segmented in a coarse way, with loose boundaries and imprecise shapes. The Jaccard index is very sensitive to differences in the segmentation of boundaries with respect to the ground-truth, so this affects its reliability in this particular dataset. Hence, the performance differences related to this index are not very informative.

Figure 8 shows a qualitative comparison of the segmentations obtained with different methods for several images. The NHRFs get good results in many images of the dataset. Thanks to the learned shapes and relative positions of labels, they are able to overcome the noisy segmentations produced by the random forests, and in many cases their results are better than the ones obtained with the SRFs.

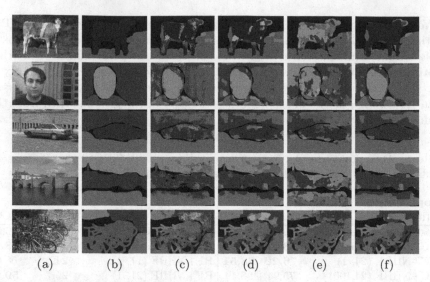

(a)   (b)   (c)   (d)   (e)   (f)

Fig. 8. Qualitative results. (a) Test images. (b) Ground-truth. (c) Random forests. (d) Pair-wise regularization. (e) Structured random forests [15]. (f) NHRF with $m = 21$ pixels and $\alpha = 1$. The last row presents a difficult case where the NHRF fails.

5   Conclusions

Higher-order potentials are required to capture structural, geometric and topological information that weaker pair-wise potentials are unable to exploit. However, parameterizing higher-order potentials is hard. In this paper we propose to use a soft and sparse representation of higher-order potentials based on a set of patterns extracted from training data. Our higher-order potentials are directly conditioned on data and no unary terms are required. This allows us to define a set of local patterns for every higher-order potential, making our method more expressive than approaches with global patterns.

A NHRF is defined as the sum of these higher-order potentials. The inference procedure in a NHRF is constrained to use the patterns of its potentials with small deviations to build the resulting labeling.

Our experiments prove, both in synthetic and real datasets, that NHRFs provide better results than pixel-wise classifiers alone and with pair-wise regularization. Moreover, our results are comparable or better than those of the SRF, that was designed to learn labeling structure, but not shape or topology. The NHRFs have also applications in areas other than segmentation, such as image denoising and reconstruction, where they get appealing results.

Acknowledgments. This research was funded by the *Cajal Blue Brain Project*. The authors thank Carlos Becker for the Boosted Context Cues code, Peter Kontschieder for the Structured Random Forests code and Graham Knott for providing the mitochondria dataset.

References

1. Becker, C.J., Ali, K., Knott, G., Fua, P.: Learning Context Cues for Synapse Segmentation. IEEE Transactions on Medical Imaging 32(10), 1864–1877 (2013)
2. Boykov, Y., Kolmogorov, V.: An experimental comparison of min-cut/max-flow algorithms for energy minimization in vision. IEEE Transactions on Pattern Analysis and Machine Intelligence (PAMI) 26 (2004)
3. Buades, A., Coll, B., Morel, J.M.: A non-local algorithm for image denoising. In: Proc. International Conference on Computer Vision and Pattern Recognition (CVPR), pp. 60–65 (2005)
4. Delong, A., Osokin, A., Isack, H.N., Boykov, Y.: Fast approximate energy minimization with label costs. In: Proc. International Conference on Computer Vision and Pattern Recognition (CVPR), pp. 2173–2180 (2010)
5. Efros, A.A., Freeman, W.T.: Image quilting for texture synthesis and transfer. In: SIGGRAPH, pp. 341–346 (2001)
6. Fitzgibbon, A., Wexler, Y., Zisserman, A.: Image-based rendering using image-based priors. In: Proc. International Conference on Computer Vision (ICCV), pp. 1176–1183 (2003)
7. Glocker, B., Heibel, T.H., Navab, N., Kohli, P., Rother, C.: TriangleFlow: Optical flow with triangulation-based higher-order likelihoods. In: Daniilidis, K., Maragos, P., Paragios, N. (eds.) ECCV 2010, Part III. LNCS, vol. 6313, pp. 272–285. Springer, Heidelberg (2010)
8. Hinton, G.E.: Training products of experts by minimizing contrastive divergence. Neural Computation 14(8), 1771–1800 (2002)
9. Hoiem, D., Rother, C., Winn, J.M.: 3D layoutCRF for multi-view object class recognition and segmentation. In: Proc. International Conference on Computer Vision and Pattern Recognition (CVPR) (2007)
10. Kohli, P., Kumar, M., Torr, P.: P^3 and beyond: Solving energies with higher order cliques. In: Proc. International Conference on Computer Vision and Pattern Recognition (CVPR) (2007)
11. Kohli, P., Kumar, M.P.: Energy minimization for linear envelope MRFs. In: Proc. International Conference on Computer Vision and Pattern Recognition (CVPR), pp. 1863–1870 (2010)
12. Kohli, P., Ladicky, L., Torr, P.H.S.: Robust higher order potentials for enforcing label consistency. International Journal of Computer Vision (IJCV) 82(3), 302–324 (2009)
13. Kolmogorov, V.: Convergent tree-reweighted message passing for energy minimization. IEEE Transactions on Pattern Analysis and Machine Intelligence (PAMI) 28(10), 1568–1583 (2006)
14. Komodakis, N., Paragios, N.: Beyond pairwise energies: Efficient optimization for higher-order MRFs. In: Proc. International Conference on Computer Vision and Pattern Recognition (CVPR), pp. 2985–2992 (2009)
15. Kontschieder, P., Bulo, S., Bischof, H., Pelillo, M.: Structured class-labels in random forests for semantic image labelling. In: Proc. International Conference on Computer Vision (ICCV), pp. 2190–2197 (November 2011)
16. Krahenbuhl, P., Koltun, V.: Efficient inference in fully connected crfs with gaussian edge potentials. In: Shawe-Taylor, J., Zemel, R., Bartlett, P., Pereira, F., Weinberger, K. (eds.) Advances in Neural Information Processing Systems, vol. 24, pp. 109–117 (2011),
http://papers.nips.cc/paper/4296-efficient-inference-in-fully-connected-crfs-with-gaussian-edge-potentials.pdf

17. Ladicky, L., Russell, C., Kohli, P., Torr, P.H.S.: Graph cut based inference with co-occurrence statistics. In: Daniilidis, K., Maragos, P., Paragios, N. (eds.) ECCV 2010, Part V. LNCS, vol. 6315, pp. 239–253. Springer, Heidelberg (2010)
18. Lan, X., Roth, S., Huttenlocher, D., Black, M.: Efficient belief propagation with learned higher-order markov random fields. In: Leonardis, A., Bischof, H., Pinz, A. (eds.) ECCV 2006. LNCS, vol. 3952, pp. 269–282. Springer, Heidelberg (2006)
19. Liu, C., Yuen, J., Torralba, A.: Nonparametric scene parsing via label transfer. IEEE Transactions on Pattern Analysis and Machine Intelligence (PAMI) 33(12), 2368–2382 (2011)
20. Lucchi, A., Li, Y., Fua, P.: Learning for Structured Prediction Using Approximate Subgradient Descent with Working Sets. In: Proc. International Conference on Computer Vision and Pattern Recognition (CVPR) (2013)
21. Nowozin, S., Rother, C., Bagon, S., Sharp, T., Yao, B., Kohli, P.: Decision tree fields. In: Proc. International Conference on Computer Vision (ICCV), pp. 1668–1675 (2011)
22. Olsson, C., Ulen, J., Boykov, Y., Kolmogorov, V.: Partial enumeration and curvature regularization. In: Proc. International Conference on Computer Vision (ICCV), pp. 2936–2943 (December 2013)
23. Potetz, B.: Efficient belief propagation for vision using linear constraint nodes. In: Proc. International Conference on Computer Vision and Pattern Recognition (CVPR) (2007)
24. Roth, S., Black, M.: Fields of experts: A framework for learning image priors. In: Proc. International Conference on Computer Vision and Pattern Recognition (CVPR), pp. 860–867 (2005)
25. Rother, C., Kohli, P., Feng, W., Jia, J.: Minimizing sparse higher order energy functions of discrete variables. In: Proc. International Conference on Computer Vision and Pattern Recognition (CVPR), pp. 1382–1389 (2009)
26. Sharp, T., Rother, C., Nowozin, S., Jancsary, J.: Regression tree fields – an efficient, non-parametric approach to image labeling problems. In: Proc. International Conference on Computer Vision and Pattern Recognition (CVPR), pp. 2376–2383 (2011)
27. Shotton, J., Winn, J., Rother, C., Criminisi, A.: *textonBoost*: Joint appearance, shape and context modeling for multi-class object recognition and segmentation. In: Leonardis, A., Bischof, H., Pinz, A. (eds.) ECCV 2006, Part I. LNCS, vol. 3951, pp. 1–15. Springer, Heidelberg (2006)
28. Szeliski, R., Zabih, R., Scharstein, D., Veksler, O., Kolmogorov, V., Agarwala, A., Tappen, M., Rother, C.: A comparative study of energy minimization methods for Markov random fields. In: Leonardis, A., Bischof, H., Pinz, A. (eds.) ECCV 2006. LNCS, vol. 3952, pp. 16–29. Springer, Heidelberg (2006)
29. Woodford, O., Torr, P., Reid, I., Fitzgibbon, A.: Global stereo reconstruction under second order smoothness priors. In: Proc. International Conference on Computer Vision and Pattern Recognition (CVPR), pp. 1–8 (2008)

Co-Sparse Textural Similarity for Interactive Segmentation[*]

Claudia Nieuwenhuis[1], Simon Hawe[2],
Martin Kleinsteuber[2], and Daniel Cremers[2]

[1] UC Berkeley, USA
[2] Technische Universität München, Germany

Abstract. We propose an algorithm for segmenting natural images based on texture and color information, which leverages the co-sparse analysis model for image segmentation. As a key ingredient of this method, we introduce a novel textural similarity measure, which builds upon the co-sparse representation of image patches. We propose a statistical MAP inference approach to merge textural similarity with information about color and location. Combined with recently developed convex multilabel optimization methods this leads to an efficient algorithm for interactive segmentation, which is easily parallelized on graphics hardware. The provided approach outperforms state-of-the-art interactive segmentation methods on the Graz Benchmark.

1 Introduction

The segmentation of natural images is a fundamental problem in computer vision. It forms the basis of many high-level algorithms such as object recognition, image annotation, semantic scene analysis, motion estimation, and 3D object reconstruction.

Despite its importance, the task of unsupervised segmentation is highly ill-posed and admittedly hard to evaluate. Therefore, we focus on *supervised segmentation* where ambiguities are solved by additional user input (scribbles or bounding boxes) and a clearly defined ground truth for performance evaluation is available. One can compute data likelihoods from a given set of scribbles using color texture or location. The simplest way is to compute the color distance of each pixel to the mean color value for each label [17]. More sophisticated approaches use density estimators, e.g. histograms [1,30], mixtures of Gaussians [25,28], or Parzen kernel density estimators [19]. Texture features were integrated in interactive segmentation by learning classifiers [27,26], filter banks [31] or SIFT features [29]. The integration of spatial information [2,19] also improved the performance. While all features carry relevant information, for natural images texture features are particularly relevant, but harder to capture due to

---

[*] This work was supported by the German Academic Exchange Service (DAAD) and the ERC Starting Grant 'Convex Vision'.

D. Fleet et al. (Eds.): ECCV 2014, Part VI, LNCS 8694, pp. 285–301, 2014.
© Springer International Publishing Switzerland 2014

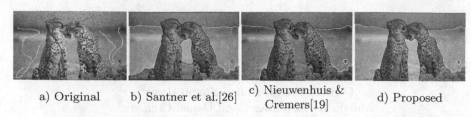

a) Original   b) Santner et al.[26]   c) Nieuwenhuis &   d) Proposed
                                                Cremers[19]

Fig. 1. Leveraging the co-sparse analysis operator for image segmentation yields a simple texture descriptor that ultimately leads to state-of-the-art results on the Graz interactive segmentation database. We compare against b) the texture-based approach by Santner et al. [26], who train a random forest classifier on texture features and c) spatially adaptive color models by Nieuwenhuis and Cremers [19], which locally approximate texture. d) The proposed method based on co-sparsity.

their diversity and spatial extent. To extract textural information from images, methods based on sparse representations are quite successful [13].

Commonly, sparsity is exploited via the synthesis model, aka sparse coding. It assumes that every image patch can be approximated as a linear combination of a few predefined atoms, which form the columns of a dictionary. With this, the textural information is encoded in the set of active dictionary atoms, i.e. the support of the sparse code. Finding this set for a given dictionary, however, requires to solve a costly optimization problem.

In this paper, we propose a more efficient way to obtain textural information by employing the *co-sparse analysis model* [7,18]. In this model, the sparse image representation is determined efficiently by a simple matrix vector product. We derive a novel textural similarity measure for image patches and demonstrate that it can be successfully introduced into image segmentation approaches. To the best of our knowledge, there has not yet been an attempt that employs the co-sparse analysis model for extracting textural information. So far, the model has only been successfully applied to regularize inverse problems such as super-resolution, denoising or depth estimation [5,11]. We refer to [10,24,32] for learning a co-sparse analysis model for natural images. The model has potential impact also for segmentation tasks in other imaging methods, where structure plays a prominent role, e.g. in medical imaging. Figure 1 shows that the proposed measure combined with an efficient convex multilabel approach generates convincing results for supervised segmentation problems, which outperform previous interactive state-of-the-art approaches [26,19].

Contributions

In this paper we present a novel approach for the task of supervised segmentation of natural images, which yields state-of-the-art results on the Graz benchmark for interactive segmentation. In particular, we make the following contributions.

- The co-sparse analysis model is leveraged for image segmentation through a novel texture similarity measure. Until today, this model has only been employed for regularizing inverse problems, such as inpainting or denoising. Showing that it is also useful for analyzing structural similarity (via the proposed novel distance measure) is the main contribution of this paper.

- The proposed algorithm combines the co-sparse analysis model and recent convex relaxation techniques within a single convex optimization problem.
- The method explicitly models the dependence between texture, color and location leading to a space-dependent color and texture model. This accounts for non-iid samples in scribble based probability density estimation.
- We merely require the four images in Figure 2 (which are not part of the benchmark) to train the co-sparse analysis operator for texture recognition and thus avoid over-fitting to specific benchmarks.
- The approach can be efficiently parallelized on graphics hardware with average runtimes of two seconds per image.

The paper is organized as follows. In Section 2, we derive a texture similarity measure from co-sparse analysis. In Section 3, we integrate this likelihood into a variational segmentation scheme, for which we give a convex relaxation and minimization method in Section 4. In Section 5, we present experimental results.

2 Co-Sparse Textural Similarity

The co-sparse analysis model [7,18] is based on the assumption that if $\mathbf{s} \in \mathbb{R}^N$ denotes a vectorized image patch, there exists an analysis operator $\mathbf{O} \in \mathbb{R}^{k \times N}$ with $k > N$ such that $\mathbf{a} := \mathbf{Os}$ is sparse. We refer to $\mathbf{a} \in \mathbb{R}^k$ as the *analyzed version of* $\mathbf{s}$. Notice that the rows of $\mathbf{O}$ can be interpreted as filters and the analyzed version of $\mathbf{s}$ as the corresponding filter responses. The two major differences to the more commonly known synthesis model are: (i) the sparse code is found via a simple matrix vector multiplication and (ii) the *zero* entries of $\mathbf{a}$ are the informative coefficients describing the underlying signal. Concretely, the textural structure of $\mathbf{s}$ is encoded in its co-support

$$\mathrm{Co}(\mathbf{a}) := \{j \mid a_j = 0\}, \tag{1}$$

where a_j denotes the j-th entry of $\mathbf{a}$. Geometrically, $\mathbf{s}$ is orthogonal to all rows that determine the co-support and thus lies in the intersection of the respective hyperplanes. Thus the co-sparsity of a vector $\mathbf{s}$ increases with the cardinality of

Fig. 2. The four training images used for learning the analysis operator

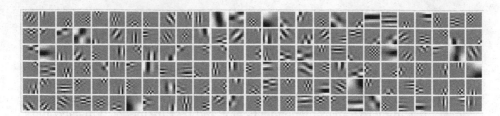

Fig. 3. Sample filters from the co-sparse analysis operator O, which was learned from natural images for 9x9 patches. The samples show that the operator includes low, intermediate and high frequency signals as well as spatially global and local signals.

its co-support $|\text{Co}(\mathbf{a})|$, i.e. with the sparsity of its analyzed version $\mathbf{a}$. A subset of the signals learned by our operator is shown in Figure 3.

A prominent example for an analysis operator is the finite difference operator in image processing. However, the advantage of the low computational complexity of such an analytically given transformation comes at the cost of a poor adaptation to specific signal classes of interest. It is now well-known that for a particular class, sparser signal representations and thus better reconstruction accuracies can be achieved if the analysis operator $\mathbf{O}$ is learned from a representative training set. Here, we employ an analysis operator learned according to the geometric optimization procedure proposed in [10] from patches extracted from natural images. As we only want to gather textural information independent of varying illumination conditions, we follow the simple bias and gain model and use patches $\mathbf{s}$ from a training set $\mathcal{S}$ that have been normalized to zero-mean and unit-norm, i.e. $\sum_i s_i = 0$ and $\|\mathbf{s}\|_2 = 1$. Given the smooth sparsity measure

$$g(\mathbf{a}) := \sum_j \log(1 + \nu a_j^2),\tag{2}$$

where $\nu > 0$ is some constant, the optimal analysis operator aims at minimizing the expected *squared* sparsity

$$\mathbf{O} \in \arg\min_{\hat{\mathbf{O}}} \tfrac{1}{|\mathcal{S}|} \sum_{\mathbf{s} \in \mathcal{S}} g(\hat{\mathbf{O}}\mathbf{s})^2.\tag{3}$$

This can be interpreted as a balanced minimization of expectation and variance of the samples' co-sparsity. For regularizing the set of feasible solutions, the Euclidean norm of the rows of $\mathbf{O}$ is restricted to one, and the so-called coherence property and the rank are controlled via two penalty functions. The optimization problem is then tackled using a conjugate gradient method on an appropriate manifold, cf. [10]. We initialize randomly, which - despite the non-convex nature of the optimization problem - in practice leads to an optimal solution [10].

Since our ultimate goal is to discriminate between distinctive textures in natural images,a measure of textural similarity should better distinguish between representative patches, i.e. patches that fit the co-sparse analysis model of natural image patches, while discriminating moderately for "outlier"-patches, i.e.

patches that seldom occur in natural images. This motivates us to measure the textural similarity between two patches via

$$TSM_{\mathbf{O}}(\mathbf{s}_1, \mathbf{s}_2) := \sum_{j=1}^{k} |\mathbb{1}_{\mathrm{Co}(\mathbf{Os}_1)}(j) - \mathbb{1}_{\mathrm{Co}(\mathbf{Os}_2)}(j)|, \tag{4}$$

where $\mathbb{1}_A$ is the indicator function of a set, i.e. $\mathbb{1}_A(j) = 1$ if $j \in A$ and zero otherwise. This measure has two desired properties: 1) it distinguishes sensibly between patches that fit the model well, i.e. patches with a large co-support, 2) it does not heavily discriminate between patches that fit the model less.

To identify an "average" textural structure from a set of m patches $\mathcal{S} = \{\mathbf{s}_1, \ldots, \mathbf{s}_m\}$ that serves as their textural representative, we provide the following definition. A patch $\mathbf{r} \in \mathbb{R}^N$ is called a *textural representative of $\mathcal{S}$* if

$$\mathbf{r} \in \arg\min_{\mathbf{z}} \sum_{i=1}^{m} TSM_{\mathbf{O}}(\mathbf{s}_i, \mathbf{z}). \tag{5}$$

So far, we considered truly co-sparse image patches, i.e. patches whose analyzed versions contain many coefficients that are exactly zero. However, this is an idealized assumption and in practice those patches are not truly co-sparse but rather contain many coefficients that are close to zero. To account for this, we introduce the mapping $\iota_\sigma \colon \mathbb{R}^k \to \mathbb{R}^k$ as a smooth approximation of the indicator function of the co-support, which is defined component-wise with a free parameter $\sigma > 0$ as

$$(\iota_\sigma(\mathbf{a}))_j = \exp(-a_j^2/\sigma). \tag{6}$$

In fact, it is easily seen that $\mathbb{1}_{\mathrm{Co}(\mathbf{a})}(j) = \lim_{\sigma \to 0}(\iota_\sigma(\mathbf{a}))_j$ and $\lim_{a_j \to 0}(\iota_\sigma(\mathbf{a}))_j = 1$.

With this approximation of the co-support, the textural similarity measure in (4) of two patches $\mathbf{s}_1$ and $\mathbf{s}_2$ associated with the analysis operator $\mathbf{O}$ and σ is approximated by

$$TSM_{\mathbf{O},\sigma}(\mathbf{s}_1, \mathbf{s}_2) = \|\iota_\sigma(\mathbf{Os}_1) - \iota_\sigma(\mathbf{Os}_2)\|_1, \tag{7}$$

with $\|\cdot\|_1$ denoting the ℓ_1-norm. According to Eq. (5), a structural representative $\mathbf{r} \in \mathbb{R}^N$ of a set $\mathcal{S} = \{\mathbf{s}_1, \ldots, \mathbf{s}_m\}$ with respect to $TSM_{\mathbf{O},\sigma}$ is

$$\mathbf{r} \in \arg\min_{\mathbf{z}} \sum_{i=1}^{m} TSM_{\mathbf{O},\sigma}(\mathbf{s}_i, \mathbf{z}). \tag{8}$$

Using the well-known fact that the centroid of a cluster with respect to the ℓ_1-distance is the median of all corresponding cluster points, the approximated co-support of the analyzed version of a structural representative fulfills

$$\iota_\sigma(\mathbf{Or}) = \mathrm{median}(\{\iota_\sigma(\mathbf{Os}_j)\}_{j=1}^{m}). \tag{9}$$

3   Variational Co-sparse Image Segmentation

In this section, we derive a statistical MAP inference formulation for supervised image segmentation based on the novel proposed textural similarity measure. We explicitly model the dependence of texture and color on the scribble location in the image to account for texture variations within regions, e.g. a sky which is partially covered by clouds. At the same time this model alleviates the issue of spatially non-iid distributed scribble samples for density estimation.

3.1   A Space Variant Texture and Color Distribution

For an image domain $\Omega \subset \mathbb{R}^2$, let $I : \Omega \to \mathbb{R}^d$ denote the input color (or gray scale) image.

The segmentation problem can be solved by computing a labeling $l : \Omega \to \{1, .., n\}$ that indicates, which of the n regions each pixel belongs to, i.e. $\Omega_i := \{x \mid l(x) = i\}$. In a statistical MAP framework the labeling l can be computed by maximizing the conditional probability

$$\arg \max_l \mathcal{P}(l \mid I) = \arg \max_l \mathcal{P}(I \mid l) \, \mathcal{P}(l). \tag{10}$$

In the following, we will model the dependence of color and texture on the image location. We use the image for two sources of information, color and structure. Structure is obtained by computing the gray value image by eliminating the hue and saturation and only keeping the luminance channel. Let $\mathbf{s}_x$ denote a small gray value texture patch centered at pixel x. With the assumption that a pixel color jointly depends on the local structure $\mathbf{s}_x$ given a location x and a label $l(x)$, but is independent of the label of other pixels we obtain

$$\mathcal{P}(I \mid l) = \prod_{i=1}^{n} \prod_{x \in \Omega} \mathcal{P}(I(x), \mathbf{s}_x \mid l(x) = i, x). \tag{11}$$

In the following, we derive the probability $\mathcal{P}(I(x), \mathbf{s}_x \mid l(x) = i, x)$ that a pixel at location x belonging to segment i has color $I(x)$ and texture patch $\mathbf{s}_x$. Assuming independence, we can compute the likelihood of a pixel for belonging to region i as

$$\mathcal{P}(I(x), \mathbf{s}_x, \mid l(x) = i, x) = \mathcal{P}(I(x) \mid l(x) = i, x) \mathcal{P}(\mathbf{s}_x \mid l(x) = i, x). \tag{12}$$

Given the set of scribble samples consisting of location, color, and texture patches for each segment i, i.e.

$$S_i := \left\{ (x_{ij}, I_{ij}, \mathbf{s}_{x_{ij}}), \; j = 1, .., m_i \right\} \tag{13}$$

we can estimate the joint distribution from sample data. We use Parzen density estimators [21], since they come with the advantage that they can represent arbitrary kinds of probability densities and provably converge to the true density for infinitely many samples. However, they require independent and identically distributed samples. This assumption may be acceptable for color, but for texture

Fig. 4. Estimation of the variance $\rho_{bg}(x)$ of the spatial kernel in (14) for the background region from the red scribbles. The spatial variance is proportional to the distance of each pixel to the closest background scribble point. The larger the minimum distance to the scribbles the larger the uncertainty in the density estimation and the more samples will be taken into consideration.

and location it is clearly violated since patches and scribbles are by no means spatially independent and identically distributed.

As a remedy, in [19] we proposed a spatially varying color distribution using the following Parzen density

$$\mathcal{P}(I(x) \mid l(x){=}i, x) = \frac{1}{m_i} \sum_{j=1}^{m_i} k_{\rho_i(x)}(x - x_{ij}) k_\mu (I - I_{ij}). \tag{14}$$

Here k denotes a kernel function with variance indicated as subscript. The idea behind the spatial dependence of $\rho_i(x)$ on x is that each color kernel is weighted by a spatial kernel with location dependent variance in order to account for non-iid samples. An intuitive explanation is that for pixels close to a scribble we only want to use few samples in the direct vicinity of the pixel (and thus a small spatial kernel variance) to estimate the color distribution since we are quite certain what the color should be at that pixel. In contrast, if we are far from all scribbles we use a large number of scribble points (and thus a larger kernel variance) since we are uncertain about the color at the current pixel.

The variance of the spatial kernel $\rho_i(x)$ is therefore adapted to the distance of the current pixel x from the nearest user scribble of this label:

$$\rho_i(x) = \alpha |x - x_{v_i}|_2 \tag{15}$$

where x_{v_i} is the closest scribble location of all pixels in segment i and α a scaling factor, which we set to 1.3. Figure 4 shows the function $\rho_i(x)$ for the spider image and the background region. Thus, the spatial dependence of $\rho_i(x)$ accounts for spatially non-iid samples and at the same time for the level of uncertainty in the estimator.

After the spatially varying color distribution we will now formulate the spatially varying texture distribution $\mathcal{P}(\mathbf{s}_x | l(x){=}i, x)$ - see (12). Using a Parzen density estimator in a similar way as in (14) to obtain a texture distribution is only possible for very small patches due to the high dimensionality of the distribution, which would require a prohibitively large amount of samples not

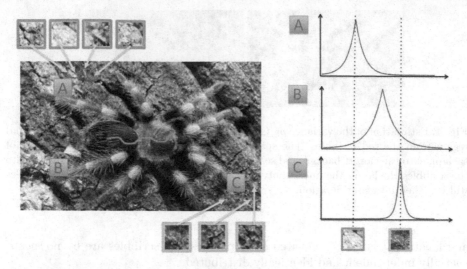

Fig. 5. We exemplarily estimate the spatially varying texture distribution for the background region (red scribbles) at three different locations in the image (A, B and C). The results are shown on the right. The horizontal axis represents the (high-dimensional) texture space with two representative patches below, the vertical axis the corresponding estimated probability. The three distributions are different since we only use sample patches from scribbles, which are close to the current location. If we are close to a scribble (A and C) we only use neighboring background scribble points, but if the closest scribble is far away (B) we use all background scribble samples to estimate the distribution. This results in three different estimated medians in (18) and thus three different peaks in the distribution. This procedure accounts for the spatially non-iid distributed scribble samples.

provided by the user scribbles. For this reason we will formulate a spatially varying texture distribution based on the co-support in equation (1).

As our goal is to extract local textural information in the vicinity of a pixel x, we multiply each patch element-wise with a Gaussian mask to assign more weight to the central pixels prior to normalization to zero-mean and unit-norm according to Section 2. From these patches, we compute the approximated co-support of a textural representative of each set of scribble points according to equation (9), i.e.

$$\mathbf{c}_i = \mathrm{median}(\{\iota_\sigma(\mathbf{Os}_{x_{ij}})\}_{j=1}^{m_i}). \tag{16}$$

Based on this we assign to each pixel x the a posteriori probability of belonging to class i depending on the corresponding patch as

$$\mathcal{P}(\mathbf{s}_x|l(x)=i, x) = \frac{\exp(-\frac{1}{\beta}\|\mathbf{c}_i - \iota_\sigma(\mathbf{Os}_x)\|_1)}{\sum_{j=1}^n \exp(-\frac{1}{\beta}\|\mathbf{c}_j - \iota_\sigma(\mathbf{Os}_x)\|_1)}. \tag{17}$$

The parameter $\beta > 0$ controls the variance of the labeling l. It can be interpreted as a measure of how well we trust the similarity measure for deciding to which class x belongs. Large values of β assign a pixel to each of the classes with approximately equal probability, whereas small values of β assign x to the most similar class with very high probability.

We now introduce the spatial variation (i.e. the dependence on scribble location) into the distribution in (17) in order to obtain a spatially varying texture distribution. Avoiding the Parzen density due to prohibitive dimensionality we compute a spatially varying median based on the spatial kernel variance $\rho_i(x)$ in (15). The idea is that we only use the texture samples which are close to the current pixel x with respect to $\rho_i(x)$ to estimate the median:

$$\mathbf{c}_i(x) = \operatorname*{median}_{|x-x_{ij}|_2 \leq \rho_i(x)} (\{\iota_\sigma(\mathbf{Os}_{x_{ij}})\}_{j=1}^{m_i}). \tag{18}$$

This yields a spatially varying median of co-sparse analyzed texture patches, which we can now introduce into the posterior probability distribution in (17). Figure 5 shows how the spatially varying texture distribution locally adapts to the closer scribble points.

Based on (12) in combination with (14) and (17) we can now compute the joined spatially varying distribution over color and texture, which alleviates the problem of non-iid samples and accounts for variable estimator certainty with respect to the scribble distance.

3.2   Variational Formulation

Based on the segment probabilities $\mathcal{P}\big(I(x), \mathbf{s}_x \mid l(x){=}i, x\big)$ given in (12), (14) and (17) we now define an energy optimization problem for the task of segmentation. We specify the prior $\mathcal{P}(l)$ in (10) to favor regions of shorter boundary

$$\mathcal{P}(l) \propto \exp\big(-\tfrac{1}{2}\sum_{i=1}^{n}\operatorname{Per}_g(\Omega_i)\big), \tag{19}$$

where $\operatorname{Per}_g(\Omega_i)$ denotes the perimeter of each region Ω_i, i.e. the boundary length, measured in the metric $g : \Omega \to \mathbb{R}^+$ (see (24)).

Instead of maximizing the a posteriori distribution (11), we minimize its negative logarithm, i.e. the energy

$$\mathcal{E} = \sum_{i=1}^{n} \tfrac{\lambda}{2}\operatorname{Per}_g(\Omega_i) - \int_{\Omega_i} \log\big(\mathcal{P}\big(I(x), \mathbf{s}_x \mid l(x){=}i, x\big)\big)\ dx. \tag{20}$$

The weighting parameter $\lambda \in [0, \infty]$ balances the impact of the data term and the boundary length.

4   Minimization via Convex Relaxation

Problem (20) is the continuous equivalent to the Potts model, whose solution is known to be NP-hard. However, a computationally tractable convex relaxation of this functional has been proposed in [3,4,12,22,34]. For more information and implementation details see [20]. Due to the convexity of the problem the resulting solutions have the following properties: Firstly, the segmentation is independent of the initialization. Secondly, we obtain globally optimal segmentations for the case of two regions and near-optimal – in practice often globally optimal – solutions for the multi-region case. In addition, the algorithm can be parallelized and run on GPUs.

4.1   Conversion to a Convex Differentiable Problem

To apply convex relaxation techniques, we first represent the n regions Ω_i by the indicator function $u \in BV(\Omega, \{0, 1\})^n$, where

$$u_i(x) = \begin{cases} 1, & \text{if } x \in \Omega_i \\ 0, & \text{otherwise} \end{cases} \quad i \in \{1, .., n\}. \tag{21}$$

Here BV denotes the functions of bounded variation, i.e. functions with a finite total variation. For a valid segmentation we require that the sum of all indicator functions at each location $x \in \Omega$ amounts to one, so each pixel is assigned to exactly one label. Hence,

$$\mathcal{B} = \left\{ u \in BV(\Omega, \{0, 1\})^n \mid \sum_{i=1}^n u_i(x) = 1 \ \forall x \in \Omega \right\}. \tag{22}$$

denotes the set of valid segmentations. To rewrite energy (20) in terms of the indicator functions u_i, we have to rewrite the boundary length prior in (19). The boundary of the set indicated by u_i can be written by means of the total variation. Let $\xi_i \in C_c^1(\Omega, \mathbb{R}^2)$ denote the dual variables and C_c^1 the space of smooth functions with compact support.

Then, following the coarea formula [8] the weighted perimeter of Ω_i is equivalent to the weighted total variation

$$\frac{\lambda}{2}\mathrm{Per}_g(\Omega_i) = \frac{\lambda}{2}\int_\Omega g(x)\,|D\,u_i\,| = \sup_{\xi_i \in \mathcal{K}_g}\int_\Omega \xi_i\,D\,u_i = \sup_{\xi_i \in \mathcal{K}_g} -\int_\Omega u_i\,\mathrm{div}\,\xi_i\,dx \tag{23}$$

with $\mathcal{K}_g = \left\{ \xi \in C_c^1(\Omega, \mathbb{R}^2) \mid |\xi(x)| \leq \frac{\lambda g(x)}{2} \ \forall x \in \Omega \right\}$, see [34,20]. $D\,u_i$ denotes the distributional derivative of u_i (which is $D\,u_i = \nabla u_i\,dx$ for differentiable u_i). The final transformation in (23) follows from integration by parts and the compact support of the dual variables ξ_i. A commonly used choice for the metric g

$$g(x) = \tfrac{1}{2\gamma}\exp\left(-\tfrac{|\nabla I(x)|}{\gamma}\right), \quad \gamma = \tfrac{1}{|\Omega|}\int_\Omega |\nabla I(x)|\,dx, \tag{24}$$

favors boundaries coinciding with strong intensity gradients $|\nabla I(x)|$ and, thus, prevents oversmoothed boundaries. Relaxing the set $\mathcal{B}$ to the convex set $\tilde{\mathcal{B}} = \{u \in BV(\Omega, [0, 1])^n \mid \sum_{i=1}^n u_i(x) = 1 \ \forall x \in \Omega\}$ we finally obtain the convex problem

$$\min_{u \in \tilde{\mathcal{B}}} \sup_{\xi \in \mathcal{K}_g^n} \sum_{i=1}^n \int_\Omega -\log\left(\mathcal{P}(I(x), \mathbf{s}_x \mid l(x) = i, x)\right) u_i\,dx - \int_\Omega u_i\,\mathrm{div}\,\xi_i\,dx. \tag{25}$$

4.2 Implementation

To solve the relaxed convex optimization problem, we employ a primal- dual algorithm proposed in [22]. Essentially, it consists of alternating a projected gradient descent in the primal variables u_i with projected gradient ascent in the dual variables ξ_i. An over-relaxation step in the primal variables gives rise to auxiliary variables $\bar{u}_i$:

$$\xi_i^{t+1} = \Pi_{\mathcal{K}_g}\left(\xi_i^t + \tau_\xi \nabla \bar{u}_i^t\right)$$

$$u_i^{t+1} = \Pi_{\tilde{\mathcal{B}}}\left(u_i^t - \tau_u(-\operatorname{div}\xi_i^{t+1} + f_i)\right) \tag{26}$$

$$\bar{u}_i^{t+1} = u_i^{t+1} + (u_i^{t+1} - u_i^t) = 2u_i^{t+1} - u_i^t$$

where $f_i(x) := -\log\left(\mathcal{P}(I(x), \mathbf{s}_x \mid l(x)=i, x)\right)$, Π denotes the projections onto the respective convex sets and the different τ denote step sizes for primal and dual variables. These are optimized based on [23]. The projections onto $\mathcal{K}_g$ are straightforward, the projection onto the simplex $\tilde{\mathcal{B}}$ is given in [14]. As shown in [22], the update scheme in (26) provably converges to a minimizer of the relaxed problem.

Due to the relaxation we may end up with non-binary solutions $u_i \in \tilde{\mathcal{B}}$. To obtain binary solutions in the set $\mathcal{B}$, we assign each pixel to the label with maximum value u_i, i.e. $l(x) = \arg\max_i u_i(x)$. This operation is known to preserve optimality in case of two regions [4]. In the multi-region case optimality bounds can be computed from the energy difference between the minimizer of the relaxed problem and its reprojected version. Typically the projected solution deviates less than 1% from the optimal energy, i.e. the results are very close to global optimality [20].

5 Experiments and Results

To evaluate the proposed algorithm we apply it to the interactive Graz benchmark [26] for supervised segmentation and compare against state-of-the-art segmentation algorithms. For all experiments we use a patch size of 9×9, and a two times over complete analysis operator, i.e. $k = 2*81$, which we have learned from 50 000 randomly extracted patches from the images shown in Figure 2.

Note, that we do not require any training of the operator on the Graz benchmark set but use it as is, avoiding overfitting to specific benchmarks. The parameter σ in (6) required to measure the textural similarity was set to $\sigma = 0.01$.

5.1 Results on the Graz Benchmark

The Graz benchmark consists of 262 scribble-ground truth pairs from 158 natural images containing between 2 and 13 user labeled segments. We used a brush size of 13 pixels in diameter for scribbling as done by Santner et al. [26] and Nieuwenhuis and Cremers [19], set $\lambda = 2000$ and the color kernel variance in

(14) to $\mu = 1.3$ for all experiments. To rank our method, we compare our results with state-of-the-art interactive segmentation algorithms. The Random Walker algorithm by Grady [9] for each pixel computes the probability that a random walker starting from any scribble seed reaches it first based on color and texture edges. In [27,26] Santner et al. train a random forest classifier based on CIELab color as well as Haralick and Local Binary Pattern (LPB) texture features.

Finally, the approach by Nieuwenhuis and Cremers [19] uses spatially varying color distributions which locally represent the texture in the image. Table 1 shows the average Dice-score [6] for all methods. This score compares the overlap of each region Ω_i with its ground truth $\bar{\Omega}_i$

$$dice(\Omega_1, ..\Omega_n) = \frac{1}{n} \sum_{i=1}^{n} \frac{2|\bar{\Omega}_i \cap \Omega_i|}{|\bar{\Omega}_i| + |\Omega_i|}. \tag{27}$$

The results show that our proposed approach outperforms all of the previous approaches. Especially for images, where texture is important to obtain the correct segmentation due to strongly overlapping color distributions in foreground and background, the proposed method shows significant improvements. We show several of these images in Figure 6. For example for the cats, the scorpion, the leopard and the bears image the texture of the animals is the main distinction criterion with respect to the background. The airplane image contains many different textures with similar colors, which are hard to distinguish, and the sign on the wall can only be distinguished from the background by its texture. The ground beneath the walking men changes color due to lighting and can only be recognized by texture as well. For images, where color is sufficient to distinguish between the objects the improvements were minor, which explains the moderate increase of the overall average benchmark score despite substantial improvements for texture based images.

Table 1. Comparison of the average Dice-score (27) to state-of-the-art supervised segmentation approaches by Grady [9], Santner et al. [26] and Nieuwenhuis and Cremers [19] on the Graz benchmark.

Method	Score
Santner et al. [26], Grayscale images, no texture	0.728
Grady [9], Random Walker	0.855
Santner et al. [26], RGB, no texture	0.877
Nieuwenhuis & Cremers [19], space-constant, no texture	0.889
Santner [26], CIELab plus texture	0.927
Nieuwenhuis & Cremers [19], space-varying color (texture approximation)	0.931
Proposed, space-varying color and co-sparse texture	**0.937**

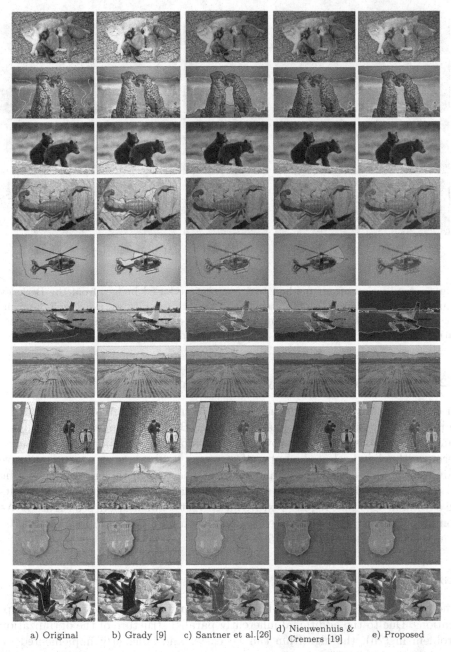

a) Original   b) Grady [9]   c) Santner et al.[26]   d) Nieuwenhuis & Cremers [19]   e) Proposed

Fig. 6. Comparison of supervised segmentation results based on the proposed co-sparse analysis model to the approaches by Grady [9], Santner et al. [26] and Nieuwenhuis and Cremers [19] on the Graz interactive segmentation benchmark. Note that our model obtains strong improvements especially for those images, where color is insufficient and texture is required to distinguish between objects.

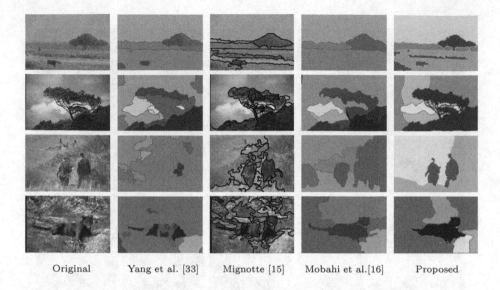

Original   Yang et al. [33]   Mignotte [15]   Mobahi et al.[16]   Proposed

Fig. 7. Application of our method to a few texture based images from the Berkeley segmentation database. To obtain color and texture samples we use simple k-means clustering with a hand-selected number of labels. We compare against texture segmentation methods by Yang et al. [33], Mignotte [15] and Mobahi et al. [16]

5.2   Results on the Berkeley Segmentation Database

In order to compare against other texture segmentation approaches we finally apply our method to a set of images from the Berkeley segmentation database. Since this database does not provide user scribbles we use simple k-means clustering with a hand-selected number of segments to obtain a set of representative samples for each class in color and texture space. Even though this clustering method yields highly suboptimal scribble information we still obtain good results on several images that require texture for correct segmentation, see Figure 7. We compare against the texture based segmentation methods by Mobahi et al. [16], Yang et al. [33] and Mignotte [15].

5.3   Runtimes

The textural similarity analysis is based only on highly parallelizable filter operations. Due to the additional inherently parallel structure of the optimization problem in (26), the algorithm can be easily and efficiently implemented on graphics hardware. The experiments were carried out on an Intel Core i7-3770 3.4 GHz CPU with an NVIDIA Geforce GTX 580 GPU. The average computation time on the Graz Benchmark is 2 seconds, which is along the lines of Santner et al. [26] with 2 seconds and Nieuwenhuis and Cremers [19] with 1.5 seconds.

6 Conclusion

In this paper we introduced co-sparse operator learning for texture recognition into interactive image segmentation. The rows of the learned operator can be interpreted as filters that are trained to deliver sparse filter responses for natural image patches. In contrast to segmentation approaches that use filter banks, we thus do not rely on the typically employed locally windowed filter histograms, but can use an easy-to-implement measure to determine local structural similarity. From this measure, a data likelihood is derived and integrated in a statistical maximum a posteriori estimation scheme in order to combine color, texture, and location information within a spatially varying joint probability distribution. The arising cost functional is minimized by means of convex relaxation techniques. With our efficient GPU implementation of the convex relaxation, the overall algorithm for multiregion segmentation converges within about two seconds. The approach outperforms state-of-the-art methods on the Graz segmentation benchmark.

References

1. Boykov, Y., Jolly, M.: Interactive graph cuts for optimal boundary and region segmentation of objects in n-d images. In: IEEE Int. Conf. on Computer Vision (2001)
2. Brox, T., Cremers, D.: On local region models and a statistical interpretation of the piecewise smooth mumford-shah functional. Int. J. of Computer Vision 84, 184–193 (2009)
3. Chambolle, A., Cremers, D., Pock, T.: A convex approach for computing minimal partitions. Tech. rep., TR-2008-05, University of Bonn, Germany (2008)
4. Chan, T., Esedoḡlu, S., Nikolova, M.: Algorithms for finding global minimizers of image segmentation and denoising models. SIAM Journal on Applied Mathematics 66(5), 1632–1648 (2006)
5. Chen, Y., Ranftl, R., Pock, T.: Insights into analysis operator learning: From patch-based sparse models to higher order MRFs. IEEE Trans. on Image Processing 23, 1060–1072 (2014)
6. Dice, L.: Measures of the amount of ecologic association between species. Ecology 26, 297–302 (1945)
7. Elad, M., Milanfar, P., Rubinstein, R.: Analysis versus synthesis in signal priors. Inverse Problems 3(3), 947–968 (2007)
8. Federer, H.: Geometric Measure Theory. Springer (1996)
9. Grady, L.: Random walks for image segmentation. IEEE Trans. on Pattern Analysis and Machine Intelligence 28(11), 1768–1783 (2006)
10. Hawe, S., Kleinsteuber, M., Diepold, K.: Analysis Operator Learning and Its Application to Image Reconstruction. IEEE Trans. on Image Processing 22(6), 2138–2150 (2013)
11. Kiechle, M., Hawe, S., Kleinsteuber, M.: A joint intensity and depth co-sparse analysis model for depth map super-resolution. In: IEEE Int. Conf. on Computer Vision (2013)
12. Lellmann, J., Kappes, J., Yuan, J., Becker, F., Schnörr, C.: Convex multiclass image labeling by simplex-constrained total variation. Tech. rep., HCI, IWR, University of Heidelberg (2008)

13. Mairal, J., Bach, F., Ponce, J., Sapiro, G., Zisserman, A.: Discriminative learned dictionaries for local image analysis. In: Int. Conf. on Computer Vision and Pattern Recognition, pp. 1–8 (2008)
14. Michelot, C.: A finite algorithm for finding the projection of a point onto the canonical simplex of R^n. Journal of Optimization Theory and Applications 50(1), 195–200 (1986)
15. Mignotte, M.: MDS-based segmentation model for the fusion of contour and texture cues in natural images. Computer Vision and Image Understanding (2012)
16. Mobahi, H., Rao, S., Yang, A., Sastry, S., Ma, Y.: Segmentation of natural images by texture and boundary compression. Int. J. of Computer Vision 95 (2011)
17. Mumford, D., Shah, J.: Optimal approximations by piecewise smooth functions and associated variational problems. Communications on Pure and Applied Mathematics 42, 577–685 (1989)
18. Nam, S., Davies, M.E., Elad, M., Gribonval, R.: The Cosparse Analysis Model and Algorithms. Applied and Computational Harmonic Analysis 34(1), 30–56 (2013)
19. Nieuwenhuis, C., Cremers, D.: Spatially varying color distributions for interactive multi-label segmentation. IEEE Trans. on Patt. Anal. and Mach. Intell. 35(5), 1234–1247 (2013)
20. Nieuwenhuis, C., Toeppe, E., Cremers, D.: A survey and comparison of discrete and continuous multi-label optimization approaches for the Potts Model. Int. J. of Computer Vision 104(3), 223–240 (2013)
21. Parzen, E.: On the estimation of a probability density function and the mode. Annals of Mathematical Statistics (1962)
22. Pock, T., Cremers, D., Bischof, H., Chambolle, A.: An algorithm for minimizing the piecewise smooth Mumford-Shah functional. In: IEEE Int. Conf. on Computer Vision (2009)
23. Pock, T., Chambolle, A.: Diagonal preconditioning for first order primal-dual algorithms in convex optimization. In: IEEE Int. Conf. on Computer Vision, pp. 1762–1769 (2011)
24. Ravishankar, S., Bresler, Y.: Learning Sparsifying Transforms. IEEE Transactions on Signal Processing 61(5), 1072–1086 (2013)
25. Rother, C., Kolmogorov, V., Blake, A.: GrabCut: interactive foreground extraction using iterated graph cuts. ACM Transactions on Graphics (Proc. SIGGRAPH) 23(3), 309–314 (2004)
26. Santner, J., Pock, T., Bischof, H.: Interactive multi-label segmentation. In: Kimmel, R., Klette, R., Sugimoto, A. (eds.) ACCV 2010, Part I. LNCS, vol. 6492, pp. 397–410. Springer, Heidelberg (2011)
27. Santner, J., Unger, M., Pock, T., Leistner, C., Saffari, A., Bischof, H.: Interactive texture segmentation using random forests and total variation. In: British Machine Vision Conference (2009)
28. Tai, Y., Jia, J., Tang, C.: Soft color segmentation and its applications. IEEE Trans. on Patt. Anal. and Mach. Intell. 29(9), 1520–1537 (2007)
29. Tran, T.: Combining color and texture for a robust interactive segmentation algorithm. In: IEEE Int. Conf. Comp. and Comm. Techn., Research, Innov. and Vision for the Future (2010)
30. Unger, M., Pock, T., Cremers, D., Bischof, H.: TVSeg - interactive total variation based image segmentation. In: British Machine Vision Conference (2008)
31. Xiang, S., Nie, F., Zhang, C.: Texture image segmentation: An interactive framework based on adaptive features and transductive learning. In: Narayanan, P.J., Nayar, S.K., Shum, H.-Y. (eds.) ACCV 2006. LNCS, vol. 3851, pp. 216–225. Springer, Heidelberg (2006)

32. Yaghoobi, M., Nam, S., Gribonval, R., Davies, M.E.: Constrained Overcomplete Analysis Operator Learning for Cosparse Signal Modelling. IEEE Transactions on Signal Processing 61(9), 2341–2355 (2013)
33. Yang, A., Wright, J., Ma, Y., Sastry, S.: Unsupervised segmentation of natural images via lossy data compression. Computer Vision and Image Understanding (2008)
34. Zach, C., Gallup, D., Frahm, J.M., Niethammer, M.: Fast global labeling for real-time stereo using multiple plane sweeps. In: Vision, Modeling and Visualization Workshop (VMV) (2008)

A Convergent Incoherent Dictionary Learning Algorithm for Sparse Coding

Chenglong Bao, Yuhui Quan, and Hui Ji

Department of Mathematics
National University of Singapore

Abstract. Recently, sparse coding has been widely used in many applications ranging from image recovery to pattern recognition. The low mutual coherence of a dictionary is an important property that ensures the optimality of the sparse code generated from this dictionary. Indeed, most existing dictionary learning methods for sparse coding either implicitly or explicitly tried to learn an incoherent dictionary, which requires solving a very challenging non-convex optimization problem. In this paper, we proposed a hybrid alternating proximal algorithm for incoherent dictionary learning, and established its global convergence property. Such a convergent incoherent dictionary learning method is not only of theoretical interest, but also might benefit many sparse coding based applications.

Keywords: mutual coherence, dictionary learning, sparse coding.

1 Introduction

Recently, sparse coding has been one important tool in many applications ([24]) including image recovery, machine learning, recognition and etc. Given a set of input patterns, most existing sparse coding models aim at finding a small number of *atoms* (representative patterns) whose linear combinations approximate those input patterns well. More specifically, given a set of vectors $\{y_1, y_2, \ldots, y_p\} \subset \mathbb{R}^n$, sparse coding is about determining a *dictionary* (the set of atoms)

$$\{d_1, d_2, \ldots, d_m\} \subset \mathbb{R}^n,$$

together with a set of coefficient vectors $\{c_1, \ldots, c_p\} \subset \mathbb{R}^m$ with most elements close to zero, so that each input vector y_j can be approximated by the linear combination $y_j \approx \sum_{\ell=1}^{m} c_j(\ell) d_\ell$. The typical sparse coding method, e.g. K-SVD [1], determines the dictionary $\{d_1, d_2, \ldots, d_m\}$ via solving an optimization problem with sparsity-prompting functional on the coefficients:

$$\min_{D, \{c_i\}_{i=1}^p} \sum_{i=1}^{p} (\|y_i - Dc_i\|_2^2 + \lambda \|c_i\|_0), \quad \text{subject to } \|d_j\|_2 = 1, \ 1 \le j \le m, \quad (1)$$

where $\| \cdot \|_0$ counts the number of non-zero entries and $D = \{d_1, \ldots, d_m\}$ is the dictionary for sparse coding. It is well known that the above minimization

D. Fleet et al. (Eds.): ECCV 2014, Part VI, LNCS 8694, pp. 302–316, 2014.

(1) is an NP-hard problem and only sub-optimal solution can be obtained in polynomial time. Most existing methods use an alternating iteration scheme to solve (1).

Despite the success of sparse coding in many applications, the sequence generated by most existing numerical solvers for solving the non-convex problem (1) can only guarantee that the functional value of (1) is decreasing at each iteration, which can not guarantee the generated sequence is convergent. Indeed, the sequence generated by the K-SVD method is not convergent; see Fig. 1 for an illustration. Moreover, as it has been mentioned in the literature, good performance of sparse coding in various recognition tasks requires imposing some additional constraints of the dictionary. One of such essential dictionary properties is the so-called *mutual coherence*:

$$\mu(D) = \max_{i \neq j} |\langle d_i, d_j \rangle|, \tag{2}$$

which further increases the technical difficulty of designing an effective numerical method with theoretical soundness. Although there is no such term in (1), the existing implementation of the K-SVD method implicitly tries to avoid learning a dictionary with high mutual coherence by discarding the learned atom which has large mutual coherence with the existing ones in each iteration.

In this paper, we consider the problem of sparse coding that explicitly imposes additional regularization on the mutual coherence of the dictionary, which can be formulated as the following minimization problem:

$$\min_{D, \{c_i\}_{i=1}^p} \sum_i (\frac{1}{2} \|y_i - Dc_i\|_F^2 + \lambda \|c_i\|_0) + \frac{\alpha}{2} \|D^\top D - I\|_F^2,$$
$$s.t. \quad \|d_j\|_2 = 1, \ 1 \leq j \leq m. \tag{3}$$

The minimization models similar to (3) have been used in several sparse coding based systems; see e.g. [21,16,7]. As a more general optimization problem which contains the K-SVD model (1) by setting $\alpha = 0$, the optimization problem (3) is a even harder problem to solve.

This paper aims at developing a fast alternating iteration scheme specifically designed for solving (3). As shown in the experiments, compared to the generic dictionary generated by the K-SVD method, the dictionary generated by the proposed method has much lower mutual coherence and it provides better performance in several sparse coding based recognition tasks. Moreover, in contrast to the existing numerical solvers for (3), we provided the rigorous analysis on the convergence of the proposed method. It is mathematically proved that the whole sequence generated by the proposed method converges to a stationary point of the problem, while the existing analysis of all other solvers only shows that the functional values of the sequence is decreasing or equivalently only a sub-sequence is convergent. The whole sequence convergence of an iteration scheme is not only of theoretical interest, but also important for applications, e.g. the number of iterations does not need to be empirically chosen for obtaining stability.

1.1   Motivation and Main Contributions

The main motivation of this paper is two-fold: one is the need for learning an incoherent dictionary for sparse coding in many applications, and the other is the need of a numerical solver for solving (3) with proved convergence property.

Motivation. *The need of an incoherent dictionary for sparse coding.* Once a dictionary is learned, the sparse code for each input is then computed via some pursuit methods, e.g. *orthogonal matching pursuit* [25], *basis pursuit* [10]. The success of these methods for finding the optimal sparse code depends on the incoherence property of the dictionary. In [25], Tropp showed that that the OMP can recover the exact support of the coefficients whenever mutual coherence μ is less that $1/(2S-1)$ where S is the number of nonzero entries of the correct coefficients. It is further proved in [23] that the similar requirement on the mutual coherence is also needed for ensuring the correctness of the thresholding-based sparse coding algorithms. In practice, it is also observed that a dictionary with high mutual coherence will impact the performance of sparse coding based methods; see e.g [21,26,8].

The need of a variational model that explicitly regularizes mutual coherence. In a quick glance, the widely used K-SVD method [1] for sparse coding considered a variational model which has no explicit functional on minimizing the mutual coherence of the result, i.e., it considered a special case of (3) with $\alpha = 0$. However, the implementation of the K-SVD method implicitly controlled the mutual coherence of the dictionary by discarding the "bad" atom which is highly correlated to the ones already in the dictionary. Such an ad-hoc approach certainly is not optimal for lowering the overall mutual coherence of the dictionary. In practice, the K-SVD method may still give a dictionary that contains highly correlated atoms, which will lead to poor performance in sparse approximation, see [11] for more details.

The need of a convergent algorithm. The minimization problem (3) is a challenging non-convex problem. Most existing methods that used the model (3) or its extensions, e.g. [15,28,18], simply call some generic non-linear optimization solvers such as the *projected gradient* method. Such a scheme is slow and not stable in practice. Furthermore, all these methods at most can be proved that the functional value is decreasing at each iteration. The sequence itself may not be convergent. From the theoretical perspective, a non-convergent algorithm certainly is not satisfactory. From the application perspective, the divergence of the algorithm also leads to troublesome issues such as when to stop the numerical solver, which often requires manual tune-up.

Main Contributions. In this paper, we proposed a hybrid alternating proximal scheme for solving (3). Compared to the K-SVD method that controls the mutual coherence of the dictionary in an ad-hoc manner, the proposed method is optimized for learning an incoherent dictionary for sparse coding. Compared to the generic numerical scheme for solving (3) adopted in the existing applications, the convergence property of the proposed method is rigorously established in the paper. We showed that the whole sequence generated by the proposed method converges to a stationary point. As a comparison, only sub-sequence convergence can be proved for existing numerical methods. The whole sequence convergence of an iteration scheme is not only of theoretical interest, but also important for applications as the number of iterations does not need to be empirically chosen to keep the output stable.

1.2 Related Work

In this section, we gives a brief review on most related generic dictionary learning methods and incoherent dictionary learning methods for sparse coding.

Generic Dictionary Learning Methods. Among many existing dictionary learning methods, the so-called K-SVD method [1] is the most widely used one. The K-SVD method solves the problem (3) with $\alpha = 0$ by alternatively iterating between sparse code C and the dictionary D. The sparse code C is estimated by using the OMP method [25]: at each step, one atom is selected such that it is most correlated with the current residuals and finally the observation is projected onto the linear space spanned by the chosen atoms. In the dictionary update stage for estimating D, the atoms are updated sequentially by using the rank-1 approximation to current residuals which can be exactly solved by the SVD decomposition. Most other existing dictionary learning methods (e.g. [18,17,2,14]) are also based on the similar alternating scheme between the dictionary update and sparse code estimation. In [17,14], the atoms in the dictionary are updated sequentially with closed form solutions. The projection gradient descent method is used in [18] to update the whole dictionary. For the ℓ_0 norm related minimization problem in the stage of sparse code estimation, many relaxation methods have been proposed and the ℓ_1 norm based relaxation is the most popular one; see e.g. [18,17,14,27]. Among these methods, the convergence analysis is provided in [27] for its proximal method. Recently, an proximal alternating linearized method is presented in [6] to directly solve the ℓ_0 norm based optimization problem for dictionary learning. The method proposed in [6] is mathematically proven to be globally convergent.

Incoherent Dictionary Learning Methods. There are two types of approaches to learn an incoherent dictionary for sparse coding. The first one is to add an additional process in the existing generic dictionary learning method to lower the mutual coherence, e.g. [16,7]. Both [16] and [7] added the decorrelation step after the dictionary update stage in K-SVD method. In [16], the de-correlation is done via minimizing the distance between the learned dictionary generated by the K-SVD method and the space spanned by the dictionaries with certain mutual coherence level. However, this projection step doesn't consider the approximation error and may significantly increase the whole minimization functional value. Thus, in [7], the iterative projection method is introduced to lower the mutual coherence of the dictionary, together with an additional dictionary rotation step to improve the approximation error of the de-correlated dictionary. The other way to learn the incoherent dictionary is directly solving a minimization model that contains the functional related the mutual coherence of the dictionary, e.g. [21,5]. In [21], an additional regularization term on mutual coherence is added to (1) when being applied in image classification and clustering. The approach presented in [7] used the OMP method in sparse code estimation and method of optimal coherence-constrained direction for dictionary update. In [5], the orthogonality constraints on the dictionary atoms are explicitly added in the variational model for dictionary learning such that its mutual coherence is always 0. With the performance comparable to the K-SVD method in image recovery, the orthogonal dictionary based method [5] is significantly faster than the K-SVD method. Such advantages on computational efficiency comes from the fact that both sparse code estimation and dictionary update have closed-form solutions in [5].

2   Incoherent Dictionary Learning Algorithm

We first give an introduction to the definitions and notations used in this section. We define Y be a matrix, y_j be the j-th column of Y and y_{ij} be the (i, j)-th element of Y. Given the matrix Y, the Frobenius norm of Y is defined by $\|Y\|_F = (\sum_{i,j} y_{ij}^2)^{1/2}$, its ℓ_0 norm $\|Y\|_0$ is defined as the number of nonzero entries of Y and the infinity norm of $\|Y\|_\infty = \max_{i,j}\{|y_{ij}|\}$. Define the *hard thresholding operator* $T_\lambda(D)[i,j] = d_{ij}$ if $|d_{ij}| > \lambda$ and $T_\lambda(D)[i,j] = 0$ otherwise.

2.1   Problem Formulation

Given the training samples $Y = (y_1, \ldots, y_p) \in \mathbb{R}^{n \times p}$, we consider the sparse approximation of Y by the redundant dictionary $D \in \mathbb{R}^{n \times m}$. Same as [21], we can introduce the regularization $\|D^\top D - I\|_F^2$ to the variational model to minimize the mutual coherence. The variational model of incoherent dictionary learning model is given as follows,

$$\min_{D,C} \frac{1}{2}\|Y - DC\|_F^2 + \lambda\|C\|_0 + \frac{\alpha}{2}\|D^\top D - I\|_F^2,$$

$$s.t. \quad \|d_j\|_2 = 1,\ 1 \le j \le m; \|c_i\|_\infty \le M,\ 1 \le i \le m,$$

(4)

where $D = (d_1, \ldots, d_m) \in \mathbb{R}^{n \times m}$, $C = (c_1^\top, \ldots, c_m^\top)^\top \in \mathbb{R}^{m \times p}$ and M is the predefined upper bound for the elements in C. It is noted that the predefined upper bound M is mainly for the stability of the algorithm, which is allowed to be set arbitrarily large. For the simplicity of discussion, define $\mathcal{D} = \{D = (d_1, \ldots, d_m) \in \mathbb{R}^{n \times m} : \|d_j\|_2 = 1,\ 1 \le j \le m\}$ and $\mathcal{C} = \{C = (c_1^\top, \ldots, c_m^\top)^\top \in \mathbb{R}^{m \times p}, \|c_i\|_\infty \le M,\ 1 \le i \le m\}$. Then the model (4) can be reformulated as

$$\min_{D,C} \frac{1}{2}\|Y - DC\|_F^2 + \lambda\|C\|_0 + \frac{\alpha}{2}\|D^\top D - I\|_F^2,\ \text{s.t. } D \in \mathcal{D},\ C \in \mathcal{C}. \quad (5)$$

In the next, we will propose the hybrid alternating proximal algorithm for solving (5) with the whole sequence convergence property.

2.2   A Hybrid Alternating Proximal Algorithm

The algorithm for solving (4) is based on a hybrid scheme that combines the alternating proximal method [3] and the alternating proximal linearized method [9], which are about tackling the non-convex minimization problem of the form:

$$\min_{z:=(x,y)} H(x,y) = F(x) + Q(z) + G(y), \tag{6}$$

where F, G are proper lower semi-continuous functions and Q is the smooth function with Lipschitz derivatives on any bounded set, that is, for the bounded set $\mathcal{Z}$, there exists a constant $L > 0$, such that $\|\nabla Q(z_1) - \nabla Q(z_2)\|_F \leq L\|z_1 - z_2\|_F, z_1, z_2 \in \mathcal{Z}$.

The alternating proximal method [3] updates the (x, y) via as follows,

$$\begin{cases} x_{k+1} \in \arg\min_x F(x) + Q(x, y_k) + G(y_k) + \frac{\mu^k}{2}\|x - x_k\|_F^2; \\ y_{k+1} \in \arg\min_x F(x_{k+1}) + Q(x_{k+1}, y) + G(y) + \frac{\lambda^k}{2}\|y - y_k\|_F^2, \end{cases} \tag{7}$$

where μ^k, λ^k are suitable step sizes. In general, the scheme (7) requires solving the non-smooth and non-convex minimization problems in each step which often has no closed form solutions. This motivates a linearized version of alternating proximal algorithm [9] such that each subproblem has a closed form solution. Instead of solving the subproblems as (7), the alternating proximal linearized algorithm replaces the smooth term Q in (7) by its first order linear approximation:

$$\begin{cases} x_{k+1} \in \arg\min_x F(x) + \hat{Q}_{(x_k,y_k)}(x) + G(y_k) + \frac{\mu^k}{2}\|x - x_k\|_F^2; \\ y_{k+1} \in \arg\min_y F(x_{k+1}) + \hat{Q}_{(x_{k+1},y_k)}(y) + G(y) + \frac{\lambda^k}{2}\|y - y_k\|_F^2. \end{cases} \tag{8}$$

where $\hat{Q}_{(x_k,y_k)}(x) = Q(x_k, y_k) + \langle \nabla_x Q(x_k, y_k), x - x_k \rangle$, $\hat{Q}_{(x_k,y_k)}(y) = Q(x_k, y_k) + \langle \nabla_y Q(x_k, y_k), y - y_k \rangle$, and μ^k, λ^k are carefully chosen step sizes.

Although the proximal linearized method has closed form solutions for all subproblems, it requires more iterations to converge than the proximal method as it only provides approximated solutions to two-subproblems in (7). The problem (5) we are solving is different from the generic model considered in the proximal method, as the first sub-problem for sparse code estimation in (7) has a closed-form solution while the second one does not. Motivated by this observation, we proposed a hybrid iteration scheme which uses the formulation of the proximal method for sparse code estimation and uses the formulation of the proximal linearized method for dictionary update. In other words, it is a hybrid version that combines both the proximal method and the proximal linearized method. As a result, the proposed one also has the closed form solutions for all sub-problems at each iteration, but converges faster than the proximal linearized method.

Remark 1. Although both (7) and (8) are the alternating schemes between two variables, they can be extended to the case of the alternating iteration among a finite number of blocks [9,4].

The iterations (7) and (8) can be re-written by using the *proximal operator* [22]:

$$\text{Prox}_t^F(x) := \arg\min_u F(u) + \frac{t}{2}\|u - x\|_F^2.$$

Then, the minimization (7) can be re-written as

$$\begin{cases} x_{k+1} \in \text{Prox}_{\mu^k}^{F+Q(\cdot, y_k)}(x_k), \\ y_{k+1} \in \text{Prox}_{\lambda^k}^{G+Q(x_{k+1}, \cdot)}(y_k), \end{cases} \qquad (9)$$

and the minimization (8) can be re-written as

$$\begin{cases} x_{k+1} \in \text{Prox}_{\mu^k}^F(x_k - \frac{1}{\mu^k}\nabla_x Q(x_k, y_k)), \\ y_{k+1} \in \text{Prox}_{\lambda^k}^G(y_k - \frac{1}{\lambda^k}\nabla_y Q(x_{k+1}, y_k)). \end{cases} \qquad (10)$$

Remark 2. It is shown in [9] that the proximal operator defined in (9), (10) are well defined, i.e., the solution sets of (7) and (8) are nonempty and compact.

The minimization (4) can be expressed in the form (6) by setting

$$\begin{cases} F(C) = \lambda\|C\|_0 + \delta_{\mathcal{C}}(C), \\ Q(C, D) = \frac{1}{2}\|Y - DC\|_F^2 + \frac{\alpha}{2}\|D^\top D - I\|_F^2, \\ G(D) = \delta_{\mathcal{D}}(D), \end{cases} \qquad (11)$$

where $\delta_{\mathcal{C}}(C)$ and $\delta_{\mathcal{D}}(D)$ are indicator functions, that is $\delta_{\mathcal{X}}(x) = 0$ if $x \in \mathcal{X}$ and $\delta_{\mathcal{X}}(x) = +\infty$ if $x \notin \mathcal{X}$. We propose the following alternating scheme to solve (4).

Sparse Code Estimator. given the dictionary $d^{(k)}$, we update the sparse code $c^{(k)} = \{c_j^\top\}_{j=1}^m$ row by row as follows:

$$c_j^{(k)} \in \text{Prox}_{\mu_j^k}^{F(U_j^k) + Q(U_j^k, D^{(k)})}(c_j^{(k-1)}), \quad 1 \le j \le m, \qquad (12)$$

where $U_j^k = (c_1^{(k)\top}, \ldots, c_{j-1}^{(k)\top}, c_j^\top, c_{j+1}^{(k-1)\top}, \ldots, c_m^{(k-1)\top})^\top$ for $1 \le j \le m$. The minimization (12) is easy to solve as it has closed form solution. Define $\mathcal{S}_j^k = \{i | d_{ij} \ne 0, 1 \le i \le n\}$ and $R^{j,k} = Y - \sum_{i<j} d_i^{(k)} c_i^{(k)} - \sum_{i>j} d_i^{(k)} c_i^{(k-1)}$. By direct calculation, the minimization (12) is equivalent to

$$c_j^{(k)} \in \arg\min_{c_j \in \mathcal{C}} \frac{\mu_j^k}{2}\|c_j - c_j^{(k-1)}\|_F^2 + \frac{1}{2}\sum_{i \in \mathcal{S}_j^k} \|r_i^{j,k} - d_{ij} c_j\|_F^2 + \lambda\|c_j\|_0, \qquad (13)$$

where $R^{j,k} = (r_1^{j,k\top}, \ldots, r_n^{j,k\top})^\top \in \mathbb{R}^{n \times p}$.

Proposition 1. *Suppose M is chosen such that $M > \sqrt{\frac{2\lambda}{r_j^k}}$, where $r_j^k = \sum_{i \in \mathcal{S}_j^k} d_{ij}^2 + \mu_j^k$, the minimization (13) has the closed form solution for all $1 \le j \le m$, given by*

$$c_j^{(k)} = \min(T_{\sqrt{2\lambda/r_j^k}}((\sum_{i \in \mathcal{S}_j^k} d_{ij} r_i^{j,k} + \mu_j^k c_j^{(k-1)})/r_j^k), M). \qquad (14)$$

Proof. By direct calculation, it can be seen that he minimization (13) is equivalent to the following minimization.

$$c_j^{(k)} \in \arg\min_{c_j \in \mathcal{C}} r_j^k \|c_j - (\sum_{i \in \mathcal{S}_j^k} d_{ij} r_i^{j,k} + \mu_j^k c_j^{(k-1)})/r_j^k\|_F^2 + 2\lambda \|c_j\|_0. \tag{15}$$

The variables in the minimization (15) above are separable. Thus, it is easy to see that the solution of (15) is exactly the one defined by (14).

Dictionary Update. Given the sparse code $c^{(k)}$, we update the dictionary $D^{(k+1)} = \{d_j\}_{j=1}^m$ atom by atom as follows:

$$d_j^{(k+1)} \in \text{Prox}_{\lambda_j^k}^{G(S_j^{(k)})}(d_j^{(k)} - \frac{1}{\lambda_j^k}\nabla_{d_j}Q(C^{(k)}, V_j^k)), \tag{16}$$

where

$$\begin{cases} S_j^k = (d_1^{(k+1)}, \dots, d_{j-1}^{(k+1)}, d_j, d_{j+1}^{(k)}, \dots, d_m^{(k)}), \\ V_j^k = (d_1^{(k+1)}, \dots, d_{j-1}^{(k+1)}, d_j^{(k)}, d_{j+1}^{(k)}, \dots, d_m^{(k)}). \end{cases}$$

Denote $d^{j,k} = d_j^{(k)} - \frac{1}{\lambda_j^k}\nabla_{d_j}Q(C^{(k)}, V_j^k)$, Then (16) can be reformulated as:

$$d_j^{(k+1)} \in \arg\min_{\|d_j\|_2=1} \|d_j - d^{j,k}\|_2^2, \tag{17}$$

From (17), it is easy to know $d_j^{(k+1)} = d^{j,k}/\|d^{j,k}\|_2$ for $1 \le j \le m$.

There are two step sizes, μ_j^k and λ_j^k needed to be set in the calculation. The step size μ_j^k can be set arbitrarily as long as there exists $a, b > 0$ such that $\mu_j^k \in (a, b)$, $\forall k = 1, 2, \dots, j = 1, \dots, m$. The step size λ_j^k can be chosen as $\lambda_j^k = \max(a, \rho L(d_j^{(k)}))$, where the λ_j^k can be chosen so as to

$$\|\nabla_{d_j}Q(C^{(k)}, \bar{D}_j^1) - \nabla_{d_j}Q(C^{(k)}, \bar{D}_j^2)\|_F \le L(d_j^k)\|d_j^1 - d_j^2\|_F,$$

for all $d_j^1, d_j^2 \in \mathbb{R}^n$ where $\bar{D}_j^i = (d_1^{(k+1)}, \dots, d_{j-1}^{(k+1)}, d_j^i, d_{j+1}^{(k)}, \dots, d_m^{(k)})$, $i = 1, 2$. Typically, we can choose $\mu_j^k = \mu_0$ and $L(d_j^k) = c_j^{(k)}c_j^{(k)^\top} + \alpha\|V_j^k\|_2$ for all $j = 1, 2, \dots, m$ and $k = 1, 2, \dots$. It can been seen that $L(d_j^k)$ is a bounded sequence since C is bounded in the model (5). See the Alg. 1 for the outline of the proposed incoherent dictionary learning method that solves (5).

3 Convergence Analysis of Algorithm 1

Before proving the convergence property of the Alg.1, we define the critical points for the non-convex and non-smooth functions [9].

Definition 1. *Given the non-convex function $f : \mathbb{R}^n \to \mathbb{R} \cup \{+\infty\}$ is a proper and lower semi-continuous function and $\text{dom} f = \{x \in \mathbb{R}^n : f(x) < +\infty\}$.*

Algorithm 1. Incoherent dictionary learning algorithm via solving (5).

1: **INPUT:** Training signals Y;
2: **OUTPUT:** Learned Incoherent Dictionary D;
3: **Main Procedure:**
  1. Set the initial dictionary $D^{(0)}$, $\rho > 1$, $a > 0$ and $K \in \mathbb{N}$.
  2. For $k = 0, 1, \ldots, K$,
  (a) Sparse Coding: for $j = 1, \ldots, m$, let $\mathcal{S}_j^k = \{i : d_{ij}^{(k)} \neq 0, 1 \leq i \leq n\}$,

$$r^{j,k} = Y - \sum_{i<j} d_i^{(k)} c_i^{(k)} - \sum_{i>j} d_i^{(k)} c_i^{(k-1)},$$

$$c^{j,k} = \sum_{i \in \mathcal{S}_j^k} d_{ij} r_i^{j,k} + \mu_j^k c_j^{(k-1)}, \quad r_j^k = \sum_{i \in \mathcal{S}_j^k} d_{ij}^2 + \mu_j^k, \tag{18}$$

$$c_j^{(k)} = \min(T_{\sqrt{2\lambda/r_j^k}}(c^{j,k}/r_j^k), M).$$

  (b) Update the step size: for $j = 1, \ldots, m$

$$V^{(k)} = C^{(k)} C^{(k)\top}, \quad L(d_j^{(k)}) = V_{j,j}^{(k)} + \alpha \|V^k\|_2.$$

  (c) Dictionary Update: let $\mu_j^k = \max\{\rho L(d_j^k), a\}$, for $k = 1, \ldots, m$,

$$d^{j,k} = d_j^{(k)} - \frac{1}{\mu_l^k} \nabla_{d_j} Q(C^{(k)}, V_j^k); \quad d_j^{(k+1)} = d^{j,k} / \|d^{j,k}\|_2. \tag{19}$$

- For $x \in \text{dom} f$, its Frechét subdifferential of f is defined as

$$\hat{\partial} f(x) = \{u : \liminf_{y \to x, y \neq x} (f(y) - f(x) - \langle u, y - x \rangle) / (\|y - x\|) \geq 0\}$$

and $\hat{\partial} f(x) = \emptyset$ if $x \notin \text{dom} f$.
- The Limiting Subdifferential of f at x is defined as

$$\partial f(x) = \{u \in \mathbb{R}^n : \exists x^k \to x, f(x^k) \to f(x) \text{ and } u^k \in \hat{\partial} f(x^k) \to u\}.$$

- The point x is a critical point of f if $0 \in \partial f(x)$.

Remark 3. (i) If x is a local minimizer of f then $0 \in \partial f(x)$. (ii) If f is the convex function, then $\partial f(x) = \hat{\partial} f(x) = \{u | f(y) \geq f(x) + \langle u, y - x \rangle, \forall y \in \text{dom} f\}$. In that case, $0 \in \partial f(x)$ is the first order optimal condition.

Theorem 1. *[Convergence Property] The sequence $\{(C^{(k)}, D^{(k)})\}$ generated by the algorithm 1, is a Cauchy sequence and converges to the critical point of (5).*

Proof. See Appendix A.

4   Experiments

We used the proposed incoherent dictionary learning method in sparse coding based recognition systems. The basic procedure is as follows. Firstly, the dictionary is learned from the training set using Alg. 1. Then, the sparse code C

for each sample in the training set, as well as the test set, is calculated using the proximal alternating algorithm [20]. At last, a linear classifier is trained and tested on the sparse codes. Two applications are considered in the experiments: face recognition and object classification. The experimental results showed that using the incoherent dictionary learned from the proposed method, the sparse coding based recognition systems may have some additional performance gain.

4.1 Experimental Setting

The performance is evaluated on two applications: face recognition on the Extended YaleB dataset [13] and the AR face dataset [19], and object classification on the Caltech-101 dataset [12]. Our approach is compared to two dictionary learning based methods:

- *K-SVD (Baseline)* [1] : The basic procedure is similar to ours, i.e., the dictionary is trained using K-SVD and the sparse codes are used to train a linear classifier. The dictionary learning process and the classifier training process are independent.
- *D-KSVD* [28] : This method is an extension of the above baseline method, which incorporates the classification error into the objective function of K-SVD dictionary learning. The dictionary and the linear classifier are trained simultaneously.

Note that both methods are built upon the K-SVD dictionary learning method [1] which does not impose dictionary incoherence, and all the tested methods are based on a simple linear classifier. The experimental setting is as follows:

- *Extended Yale B* : The extended YaleB database [13] contains 2,414 images of 38 human frontal faces under about 64 illumination conditions and expressions. There are about 64 images for each person. The original images were cropped to 192×168 pixels. Each face image is projected into a 504-dimensional feature vector using a random matrix of zero-mean normal distribution. The database is randomly split into two halves. One half was used for training the dictionary which contains 32 images for each person, and the other half was used for testing.
- *AR Face* : The AR face database [19] consists of over 4000 frontal images from 126 individuals. For each individual, 26 pictures were taken in two separate sessions. The main characteristic of the AR database is that it includes frontal views of faces with different facial expressions, lighting conditions and occlusion conditions. A subset of the database consisting of 2,600 images from 50 male subjects and 50 female subjects is used. For each person, twenty images are randomly picked up for training and the remaining images are for testing. Each face image is cropped to 165×120 and then projected onto a 540-dimensional feature vector.

- *Caltech101* : The Caltech101 dataset [12] contains 9,144 images from 102 classes (i.e., 101 object categories with 8677 images and one additional background category with 467 images) including vehicles, plants, animals, cartoon characters, and so on. The number of images in each category varies from 31 to 800. We use 20 samples per category for training the dictionary as well as the classifier and the rest for testing. The spatial pyramid feature presented in [28] is computed on each image as input.

To obtain reliable results, each experiment is repeated 30 times with different random splits of the training and testing images. The final classification accuracies are reported as the average of each run. Throughout the experiments, we fix the sparsity parameter λ to be 0.005 and the coherence parameter β to be 1. The iteration number K in Alg. 1 is fixed to be 10. The dictionary size is set 540 on the two face datasets and 3000 on the Caltech-101 dataset.

4.2   Experimental Results

The results and the conclusions are summarized as follows.

- **Convergence behavior.** The convergence behaviors of the K-SVD method and Alg. 1 on the YaleB face dataset are compared in Fig. 1, which plots the Frobenius norm of the increments of the sparse codes generated by two algorithms at each iteration. It can be seen that the code sequence generated by the K-SVD method does not converge to zero, which means that the K-SVD method has at most sub-sequence convergence. In contrast, the increments of the code sequence generated by Alg. 1 converges to zero which shows that the whole sequence converges.
- **Mutual coherence of dictionary.** The matrices of the mutual coherence of the dictionaries learned from the YaleB dataset are shown in Fig. 3, and its normalized histograms are shown in Fig. 2. It can be seen that mutual coherence of the dictionary from our approach can be significantly lower than that from the K-SVD method when the regularization parameter β on mutual coherence is set sufficiently large.
- **Classification performance.** The classification results are listed in Table 1. It can be seen that our approach performs slightly better than the compared methods.

Table 1. Classification accuracies (%) on two face datasets and one object dataset

Dataset	K-SVD	D-KSVD	Ours
Extended YaleB	93.10	94.10	95.72
AR Face	86.50	88.80	96.18
Caltech-101	68.70	68.60	72.29

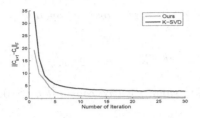

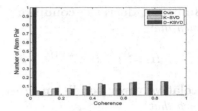

Fig. 1. The increments of the sequences generated by the methods

Fig. 2. The normalized histograms on the coherence matrices shown in Fig. 3

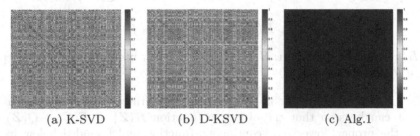

(a) K-SVD   (b) D-KSVD   (c) Alg.1

Fig. 3. The mutual coherence matrices of the dictionaries learned from the YaleB face dataset using the K-SVD method and Alg.1. The ith-column and jth-row element in each matrix represents the mutual coherence between the ith and j-th atom.

5   Summary and Conclusions

This paper aims at developing an alternating iteration scheme for learning an incoherent dictionary, which is the first available incoherent dictionary learning method with proved sequence convergence. The proposed work not only is of theoretical interest from the viewpoint of optimization, but also might be useful to practical sparse coding based applications.

Acknowledgment. The authors would like to thank the area chair and the reviewers for their helpful comments. The work of the authors was partially supported by Singapore MOE Research Grant R-146-000-165-112 and R-146-000-178-112.

Appendix A

In this appendix, we give a sketch of the proof of Theorem 1. The detailed proof is provided in the complementary material. The proof of Theorem 1 is built upon Theorem 2.9 in [4].

Theorem 2. *([4]) Assume $H(z)$ is a proper and lower semi-continuous function with $\inf H > -\infty$, the sequence $\{z^{(k)}\}_{k \in \mathbb{N}}$ is a Cauchy sequence and converges to the critical point of $H(z)$, if the following four conditions hold:*

(P1) **Sufficient decrease condition.** *There exists some positive constant ρ_1, such that*

$$H(z^{(k)}) - H(z^{(k+1)}) \geq \rho_1 \| z^{(k+1)} - z^{(k)} \|_F^2, \ \forall k = 1, 2, \ldots.$$

(P2) **Relative error condition.** *There exists some positive constant $\rho_2 > 0$, such that*

$$\| w^{(k+1)} \|_F \leq \rho_2 \| z^{(k+1)} - z^{(k)} \|_F, \ w^{(k)} \in \partial H(z^{(k)}), \ \forall k = 1, 2, \ldots.$$

(P3) **Continuity condition.** *There exists a subsequence $\{z^{(k_j)}\}_{j \in \mathbb{N}}$ and $\bar{z}$ such that*

$$z^{(k_j)} \to \bar{z}, \ H(z^{(k_j)}) \to H(\bar{z}), \quad as \ j \to +\infty.$$

(P4) $H(z)$ **is a KL function.** $H(z)$ *satisfies the* Kurdyka-Lojasiewicz *property in its effective domain.*

Let $\boldsymbol{Z}^{(k)} := (\boldsymbol{C}^{(k)}, \boldsymbol{D}^{(k)})$ denote the sequence generated by the algorithm 1. Firstly, it can be seen that the objective function $H(\boldsymbol{Z}) = F(\boldsymbol{C}) + Q(\boldsymbol{Z}) + G(\boldsymbol{D})$ is the proper, lower semi-continuous function and bounded below by 0 where F, Q, G are defined in (11). Secondly, the sequence $\{\boldsymbol{Z}^{(k)}\}_{k \in \mathbb{N}}$ generated by algorithm 1 is bounded since $\boldsymbol{D}^{(k)} \in \mathcal{D}$ and $\boldsymbol{C}^{(k)} \in \mathcal{C}$ for all $k = 1, 2, \ldots$. In the next, we show that the sequence $\{\boldsymbol{Z}^{(k)}\}$ satisfies the condition (P1)-(P4) using the following four lemmas. The proofs of these lemmas are presented in supplemental materials.

Lemma 1. *The sequence $\{\boldsymbol{Z}^{(k)}\}_{k \in \mathbb{N}}$ satisfies*

$$\begin{cases} H(\boldsymbol{T}_j^{(k+1)}, \boldsymbol{D}^{(k)}) \leq H(\boldsymbol{T}_{j-1}^{(k+1)}, \boldsymbol{D}^{(k)}) - \frac{\mu_j^k}{2} \| c_j^{(k+1)} - c_j^{(k)} \|_F^2, \\ H(\boldsymbol{C}^{(k+1)}, \boldsymbol{V}_j^{(k+1)}) \leq H(\boldsymbol{C}^{(k+1)}, \boldsymbol{V}_{j-1}^{(k+1)}) - \frac{\lambda_j^k - L(d_j^{(k)})}{2} \| d_j^{(k+1)} - d_j^{(k)} \|_F^2, \end{cases}$$

for $1 \leq j \leq m$, where

$$\begin{cases} \boldsymbol{T}_j^{(k)} = (c_1^{(k)\top}, \ldots, c_j^{(k)\top}, c_{j+1}^{(k-1)\top}, \ldots, c_m^{(k-1)\top})^\top, \ \boldsymbol{T}_0^{(k)} = \boldsymbol{C}^{(k-1)}, \\ \boldsymbol{V}_j^{(k)} = (d_1^{(k)}, \ldots, d_j^{(k)}, d_{j+1}^{(k-1)}, \ldots, d_m^{(k-1)}), \ \boldsymbol{V}_0^{(k)} = \boldsymbol{D}^{(k-1)}. \end{cases} \tag{20}$$

Sum up the above inequalities, we can obtain

$$H(\boldsymbol{C}^{(k)}, \boldsymbol{D}^{(k)}) - H(\boldsymbol{C}^{(k+1)}, \boldsymbol{D}^{(k+1)})$$

$$\geq \sum_{j=1}^m \left(\frac{\mu_j^k}{2} \| c_j^{(k+1)} - c_j^{(k)} \|_F^2 + \frac{\lambda_j^k - L(d_j^{(k)})}{2} \| d_j^{(k+1)} - d_j^{(k)} \|_F^2 \right). \tag{21}$$

Using the fact that there exist $a, b > 0$ such that $a < \mu_j^k, \lambda_j^k < b$ and $\lambda_j^k > L(d_j^{(k)})$, we can establish the sufficient decreasing property (P1) for $\{\boldsymbol{Z}^{(k)}\}_{k \in \mathbb{N}}$.

Lemma 2. *Let* $\boldsymbol{\omega}_C^{(k)} = (\boldsymbol{\omega}_C^{1\top}, \ldots, \boldsymbol{\omega}_C^{m\top})^\top$ *and* $\boldsymbol{\omega}_D^{(k)} = (\boldsymbol{\omega}_D^1, \ldots, \boldsymbol{\omega}_D^m)$ *where*

$$\begin{cases} \boldsymbol{\omega}_C^j = \nabla_{\boldsymbol{c}_j} Q(\boldsymbol{Z}^{(k)}) - \nabla_{\boldsymbol{c}_j} Q(\boldsymbol{T}_j^{(k)}, \boldsymbol{D}^{(k-1)}) - \mu_j^k(\boldsymbol{c}_j^{(k)} - \boldsymbol{c}_j^{(k-1)}), \\ \boldsymbol{\omega}_D^j = \nabla_{\boldsymbol{d}_j} Q(\boldsymbol{Z}^{(k)}) - \nabla_{\boldsymbol{d}_j} Q(\boldsymbol{C}^{(k)}, \boldsymbol{V}_j^{(k)}) - \lambda_j^k(\boldsymbol{d}_j^{(k)} - \boldsymbol{d}_j^{(k-1)}), \end{cases} \tag{22}$$

and $(\boldsymbol{T}_j^{(k)}, \boldsymbol{V}_j^{(k)})$ *is defined in* (20). *Then,* $\boldsymbol{\omega}^k := (\boldsymbol{\omega}_C^{(k)}, \boldsymbol{\omega}_D^{(k)}) \in \partial H(\boldsymbol{Z}^{(k)})$ *and there exists a constant* $\rho > 0$, *such that*

$$\|\boldsymbol{\omega}^k\|_F \le \rho \|\boldsymbol{Z}^{(k)} - \boldsymbol{Z}^{(k-1)}\|_F.$$

Lemma 3. *The sequence* $\{\boldsymbol{Z}^{(k)}\}_{k\in\mathbb{N}}$ *satisfies the Continuity condition (P3).*

For the property (P4), see [9] for the definition. An important class of functions that satisfies the Kurdyka-Lojasiewicz property is the so-called semi-algebraic functions [9].

Definition 2. *(Semi-algebraic sets and functions [9,3]) A subset* S *of* $\mathbb{R}^n$ *is called the semi-algebraic set if there exists a finite number of real polynomial functions* g_{ij}, h_{ij} *such that*

$$S = \bigcup_j \bigcap_i \{x \in \mathbb{R}^n : g_{ij}(x) = 0, h_{ij}(x) < 0\}.$$

A function f *is called the semi-algebraic function if its graph* $\{(x,t) \in \mathbb{R}^n \times \mathbb{R}, t = f(x)\}$ *is a semi-algebraic set.*

Theorem 3. *([9]) Let* f *is a proper and lower semicontinuous function. If* f *is semi-algebraic then it satisfies the K-L property at any point of* dom$f$.

Lemma 4. *All the function* $F(\boldsymbol{C})$, $Q(\boldsymbol{Z})$ *and* $G(\boldsymbol{D})$ *defined in* (11) *are semi-algebraic functions. Moreover,* $H(\boldsymbol{Z}) = F(\boldsymbol{C}) + Q(\boldsymbol{Z}) + G(\boldsymbol{D})$ *is the semi-algebraic function.*

References

1. Aharon, M., Elad, M., Bruckstein, A.: K-SVD: An algorithm for designing of overcomplete dictionaries for sparse representation. IEEE Trans. Signal Process. (2006)
2. Rakotomamonjy, A.: Direct optimization of the dictionary learning. IEEE Trans. Signal Process. (2013)
3. Attouch, H., Bolte, J., Redont, P., Soubeyran, A.: Proximal alternating minimization and projection methods for nonconvex problems: An approach based on the kurdyka-lojasiewicz inequality. Math. Oper. Res. 35(2), 438–457 (2010)
4. Attouch, H., Bolte, J., Svaiter, B.F.: Convergence of descent methods for semi-algebraic and tame problems: proximal algorithms, forward–backward splitting, and regularized gauss–seidel methods. Math. Program. Ser. A. 137(1-2), 91–129 (2013)
5. Bao, C., Cai, J., Ji, H.: Fast sparsity-based orthogonal dictionary learning for image restoration. In: ICCV (2013)

6. Bao, C., Ji, H., Quan, Y., Shen, Z.: ℓ_0 norm based dictioanry learning by proximal method with global convergence. In: CVPR (2014)
7. Barchiesi, D., Plumbley, M.D.: Learning incoherent dictionaries for sparse approximation using iterative projections and rotations. IEEE Trans. Signal Process. (2013)
8. Bobin, J., Starck, J.L., Fadili, J.M., Moudden, Y., Donoho, D.L.: Morphological component analysis: An adaptive thresholding strategy. IEEE Trans. Image Process. 16(11) (2007)
9. Bolte, J., Sabach, S., Teboulle, M.: Proximal alternating linearized minimization for nonconvex and nonsmooth problems. Math. Program. Ser. A., 1–36 (2013)
10. Chen, S., Donoho, D., Saunders, M.: Atomic decomposition by basis pursuit. SIAM J. Sci. Comput. (1999)
11. Dai, W., Xu, T., Wang, W.: Dictionary learning and update based on simultaneous code-word optimzation (simco). In: ICASSP. IEEE (2012)
12. Fei-Fei, L., Fergus, R., Perona, P.: Learning generative visual models from few training examples: An incremental bayesian approach tested on 101 object categories. In: CVPR Workshop of Generative Model Based Vision (WGMBV). IEEE (2004)
13. Georghiades, A.S., Belhumeur, P.N., Kriegman, D.J.: From few to many: Illumination cone models for face recognition under variable lighting and pose. IEEE Trans. Pattern Anal. Mach. Intell. (2001)
14. Jenatton, R., Mairal, J., Bach, F.R., Obozinski, G.R.: Proximal methods for sparse hierarchical dictionary learning. In: ICML (2010)
15. Jiang, Z., Lin, Z., Davis, L.: Learning a dicscriminative dictionary for sparse coding via label consistent K-SVD. In: CVPR (2011)
16. Mailhé, B., Barchiesi, D., Plumbley, M.D.: INK-SVD: Learning incoherent dictionaries for sparse representations. In: ICASSP (2012)
17. Mairal, J., Bach, F., Ponce, J., Sapiro, G.: Online learning for matrix factorization and sparse coding. JMLR (2010)
18. Mairal, J., Bach, F., Ponce, J., Sapiro, G., Zisserman, A.: Supervised dictionary learning. In: NIPS (2009)
19. Martínez, A., Benavente, R.: The ar face database. Tech. rep., Computer Vision Center (1998)
20. Parikh, N., Boyd, S.: Proximal algorithms. Found. Trends optim. 1(3), 123–231 (2013)
21. Ramirez, I., Sprechmann, P., Sapiro, G.: Classification and clustering via dictionary learning with structured incoherence and shared features. In: CVPR. IEEE (2010)
22. Rockafellar, R.T., Wets, R.J.B.: Variational analysis: grundlehren der mathematischen wissenschaften, vol. 317. Springer (1998)
23. Schnass, K., Vandergheynst, P.: Dictionary preconditioning for greedy algorithms. IEEE Trans. Signal Process. 56(5), 1994–2002 (2008)
24. Tosic, I., Frossard, P.: Dictionary learning. IEEE Signal Process. Mag. (2011)
25. Tropp, A.: Greed is good: algorithmic results for sparse approximation. IEEE Trans. Inf. Theory (2004)
26. Wright, J., Ma, Y., Mairal, J., Sapiro, G., Huang, T.S., Yan, S.: Sparse representation for computer vision and pattern recognition. Proc. IEEE 98(6), 1031–1044 (2010)
27. Xu, Y., Yin, W.: A fast patch-dictionary method for the whole image recovery. UCLA CAM report (2013)
28. Zhang, Q., Li, B.: Discriminative K-SVD for dictionary learning in face recognition. In: CVPR (2010)

Free-Shape Polygonal Object Localization[*]

Xiaolu Sun, C. Mario Christoudias, and Pascal Fua

CVLab, EPFL, Lausanne, Switzerland
{xiaolu.sun,mario.christoudias,pascal.fua}@epfl.ch

Abstract. Polygonal objects are prevalent in man-made scenes. Early approaches to detecting them relied mainly on geometry while subsequent ones also incorporated appearance-based cues. It has recently been shown that this could be done fast by searching for cycles in graphs of line-fragments, provided that the cycle scoring function can be expressed as additive terms attached to individual fragments. In this paper, we propose an approach that eliminates this restriction. Given a weighted line-fragment graph, we use its *cyclomatic number* to partition the graph into manageably-sized sub-graphs that preserve nodes and edges with a high weight and are most likely to contain object contours. Object contours are then detected as maximally scoring elementary circuits enumerated in each sub-graph. Our approach can be used with *any* cycle scoring function and multiple candidates that share line fragments can be found. This is unlike in other approaches that rely on a greedy approach to finding candidates. We demonstrate that our approach significantly outperforms the state-of-the-art for the detection of building rooftops in aerial images and polygonal object categories from ImageNet.

1 Introduction

Polygonal objects ranging from fields and rooftops in aerial images to signs, furniture, and facades in ground-level views are prevalent in man-made environments. They have received much attention since the very beginning of the Computer Vision field, starting with the Blocks World [35]. Many early approaches formulated the problem of finding them in terms of perceptual grouping of edges that exhibit the right geometry [21]. Over the years, it has become apparent that only looking at edges was insufficient and that, to distinguish valid polygonal regions from spurious ones, it was indispensable to also consider the pixels these edges enclose [5].

Many recent algorithms do this by treating image edges or line fragments as nodes of graphs whose cycles represent closed contours. Delineating polygonal regions is then accomplished by finding those cycles that minimize an appropriate objective function. Even though the number of potential cycles can grow very large even in moderately-sized graphs, this can be done efficiently when the objective function can be written as a sum of terms, one for each edge of the cycle [45,47]. However, this is limiting because using more complex non-linear

---

[*] This work was funded in part by the EU MyCopter project.

D. Fleet et al. (Eds.): ECCV 2014, Part VI, LNCS 8694, pp. 317–332, 2014.
© Springer International Publishing Switzerland 2014

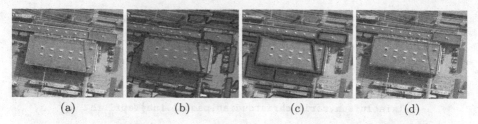

(a)   (b)   (c)   (d)

Fig. 1. Free-shape polygonal object detection: (a) Aerial image of a set of buildings and (b) detected image line fragments that define the nodes of our line fragment saliency graph and their associated image regions. (c) Graph node and edge weights are used to quickly prune the search space and focus on sub-regions likely to contain object contours. Thicker line fragments and darker red highlights reflect larger node and edge weights respectively, each line fragment highlighted by its maximum incident edge weight. (d) We detect polygonal objects as high scoring circuits in the partitioned line fragment graph. Detected rooftops are displayed in red. Best viewed in color.

objective functions, such as those based on kernel SVMs, is required in many real-world scenarios. Furthermore, when looking for multiple objects, these approaches tend to rely on finding the best candidate, removing the corresponding edges, and then finding the next one. This precludes finding shapes that share edges, which is important in densely packed environments.

In this paper, we overcome these limitations using a graph search algorithm that partitions the graph of line fragments into smaller ones using discriminative node and edge weighting functions that encode how likely a line fragment or line fragment pair is to belong to an object. We constrain the size of each sub-graph using its easy to compute *cyclomatic number* [14] to limit the number of its cycles. Object contours are then found as elementary circuits in each sub-graph. As we show, for typical image, line-fragment graphs, object contours can be found within relatively small-sized sub-graphs having only a few elementary circuits, that can be enumerated efficiently. Fig. 1 illustrates our approach. In contrast to previous methods, it lets us use generic shape and appearance cues to score each cycle that are not restricted to linearly additive measures and can easily generate multiple hypotheses that share some edges. As seen in our experiments, this yields significantly better accuracy at no increase in computational cost.

We evaluate our approach for the detection of building rooftops in aerial images and other polygonal object categories from ImageNet [12], and explore the use of Histogram of Oriented Gradients [11] and normalized color histogram representations as cycle scoring objective functions, each of which are non-additive. As seen in our experiments, our approach significantly outperforms recent polygonal and free-shape object detection methods [47,43].

2   Related Work

Early approaches detected shapes in images using perceptual saliency criteria to group image edgels [20,33,39]. An iterative optimization method to group image edgels based on local curvature and curvature variation was proposed in [39]. Similar ideas were explored in [20,33] that investigated measures such as co-curvilinearity and co-circularity for perceptual grouping. Spectral methods for grouping the elements of the resulting edgel graph [34,36,38] and probabilistic approaches useful for incorporating more global dependencies [10,13,16] and edgel detection uncertainty [9] have also been proposed. While useful for finding dominant shapes in images, these methods have largely focused on shape saliency and less on finding objects of a particular shape.

Voting methods based on the Hough Transform can be used to detect image contours of a specific shape [2,3,24,28]. With these approaches, each edgel votes for its shape parameters and shape instances are detected as peaks in the resulting hypothesis voting space. The Hough Transform has been demonstrated for the detection of simple shapes including lines, circles, and rectangles [24,28] and regular polygons whose edges inscribe a circle [3]. It has also been applied for the detection of arbitrary shapes [2], but becomes computationally prohibitive for complex shapes involving many parameters.

To overcome these limitations many methods have been proposed that leverage annotated images to learn models of object shape [4,8,7,19,25,32,40]. Statistical shape models define flexible and rich representations capable of efficiently modeling and detecing objects with a complex geometry. Initial approaches defined holistic or "top-down" models that incorpated global object shape statistics [4,8,7], a prevalent example being the Active Shape Model [8] that leverages dominant modes of object shape variation to define a deformable object template. More recent methods utilize local models of object geometry and learn a grammar of object parts that are individually detected in the image and then fused in a bottom-up fashion [19,25,32,40]. Although versatile, these methods have largely focused on modelling object shape and less on appearance.

Segmentation-driven detection methods comprise an alternative class of techniques that exploit image region or appearance cues to generate object hypothesis obtained from a bottom-up segmentation of the image [43,17,6,37,26]. [17,6] form object region hypothesis from multiple figure-ground image segmentations each obtained using either varying segmentation parameters or with different foreground seed locations. Similarly, [43] employs several hierarchical image segmentations computed across various image representations and grouping criteria. These methods largely focus on deriving category-independent region proposals, however, which although related is a different problem than what we address in this paper. Also, most of them do not account for region geometry.

Recent methods have focused on finding polygonal or *free-shape* objects using both object shape and appearance [44,46]. [46] extends the branch-and-bound method of [27] to find k-sided bounding polygons with a bag-of-words appearance model [41]. Similarly, [44] proposes a branch-and-cut algorithm to efficiently find the best scoring free-shape object region. While efficient, these methods rely on a linearly additive objective function. Yet many measures of interest involve non-additive scoring functions and therefore cannot be used in conjunction with these methods. In contrast, our approach can be employed for polygonal object detection with *any* scoring function.

Probably the closest approach to ours is the ratio-contour algorithm [45,47,48] and related approaches that formulate salient boundary detection as finding minimum cost cycles in a graph [5,15,29]. Finding the minimum cost cycle of a graph, however, can only be done efficiently when the scoring function can be written as a sum of terms, one for each edge of the cycle [45]. Furthermore, when searching for multiple objects, these approaches employ a *greedy* optimization. Each subsequent solution is found by removing the previous best solution from the search space, which precludes finding shapes with common nodes or edges. In contrast, our approach enables the use of generic shape and appearance measures beyond linearly additive ones and can easily generate multiple, overlapping hypotheses.

3   Polygonal Object Detection

Our goal is to find polygonal objects of arbitrary complexity. We start from line fragments and treat these fragments as nodes of a graph whose edges encode geometric relationships. Cycles in this graph define polygonal shapes that enclose an image region. Our problem then amounts to finding the best possible such cycles in terms of a suitable objective function. We are particularly interested in finding *elementary circuits*, i.e., connected cycles whose vertices have degree two, as these generally correspond to well defined object boundaries that are each comprised of a single simple cycle[1]. In general, this is difficult because, even in relatively small graphs, the number of potential cycles can be exceedingly large. For a fully connected graph with n nodes, the number of elementary circuits can grow faster than 2^n [23], which is computationally prohibitive for most real life applications. In this section, we first describe our graph construction approach in more detail. We then outline our graph-partitioning algorithm to efficiently search the potentially large space of all possible graph cycles.

3.1   Graph Construction

As discussed above, our first step is to extract line fragments and use them to build graphs such as the one of Fig. 2. As polygonal outlines should be evaluated not only according to their geometry but also to the color and texture of the area they enclose, we take our line fragments to be straight segments extracted using a hough-style algorithm from the boundaries of Maximally Stable Extremal Regions (MSERs) [30]. We find MSERs using a combined edge and intensity image whose edge scores are computed with the method of [1] as described in [42]. This results in a better over-segmentation of the image that more faithfully respects its underlying contours.

The detected image line fragments define the nodes of our graph. Each line fragment is oriented in a clockwise direction along the boundary of its associated

---

[1] Elementary circuits can contain self-intersections, however, this can be easily checked during their enumeration.

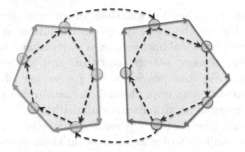

Fig. 2. Line fragment graph. Line segments are shown for two neighboring image regions colored according to their associated region that define the nodes of the graph. Each line fragment is oriented in a clockwise direction and we instantiate directed edges between nearby line fragments of compatible orientation, displayed as dashed, black arrows. Elementary circuits in the graph correspond to closed polygonal image contours whose image regions all lie within the same contour.

MSER region and we instantiate directed edges between nearby line fragments of compatible orientation, as illustrated in Figure 2. The distance between two directed lines is defined as the minimum distance between the *head* and *tail* endpoints of each line. In our implementation, we declare two lines as *nearby* if their distance is within 50 pixels of one another. A pair of lines are of a *compatible orientation* if they are nearby and their minimum head-tail distance is less than their head-head and tail-tail distances. Elementary circuits in the graph define closed polygonal outlines that enclose their respective MSERs. The large number of cycles in this graph is in general prohibitive making exact search difficult. In what follows, we outline an efficient search algorithm for addressing this hard optimization problem.

3.2   Graph-Partition Search Algorithm

More formally, let I be an image and $\{v_i\}_{i=1}^N$ the detected line fragments in I. To formulate our search problem we define a weighted, directed graph $G = \langle V, E \rangle$ whose nodes are the detected line fragments $v_i \in V$ and directed edges $e_{ij} \in E$ are defined between nearby line fragments. The node and edge weight functions, $u(v) : V \to \mathbb{R}$ and $w(e) : E \to \mathbb{R}$, encode how likely a line fragment or pair of line fragments is to belong to an object contour that are learned from labeled object contours as described in Section 3.4.

Each elementary circuit $c \in G$ defines a closed, polygonal outline. Let $f(c)$ be a scoring function that represents the likelihood that c truly is the outline of an object. We wish to find the image circuit or set of image circuits c^* that maximize f:

$$c^* = \text{argmax}_{c \in G} f(c). \tag{1}$$

In the special case of additive scoring functions defined over sums of the node and edge weights, u and w, this maximum can be computed in polynomial time

[45,47]. Yet, there are many scoring functions of interest that are non-additive. For such functions finding the globally optimal solution of Eq. 1 is difficult. Instead, we propose to find local optima over a partitioning of the line fragment graph to result in an efficient search algorithm and address this challenging optimization problem. We first provide a brief overview of cycle space graph theory that we use to obtain an upper bound on the number of cycles in a graph and then present our graph-partition search algorithm.

Consider a spanning tree T of G. For each non-tree edge $e \in G$ let c_e be the path connecting the endpoints of e in T. c_e is an elementary circuit of G, also referred to as a *fundamental circuit*. Together the c_e form a basis for the *cycle space* of G [14]. Let $c \in \{0, \pm 1\}^{|E|}$ define a cycle in G such that each entry of c is ± 1 if the corresponding directed edge in G belongs to it and is 0 otherwise[2]. Any cycle c can be expressed as a linear combination of the fundamental circuits c_e:

$$c = C_e \mathbf{x}, \tag{2}$$

where $C_e \in \{0, \pm 1\}^{|E|} \times \{0, \pm 1\}^m$, each column of C_e is a fundamental circuit c_e of G and $\mathbf{x} \in \{0, \pm 1\}^m$ are the coefficients of c. $m = |E| - |V| + 1$ is the *cyclomatic number* of G and is the dimension of its cycle space.

While any cycle can be expressed as a linear combination of cycle basis, for a directed graph not all linear combinations of cycle basis produce a valid graph cycle. Let $\mathcal{X} = \{\mathbf{x} \in \{0, \pm 1\}^m \mid C_e \mathbf{x} \text{ is a cycle in } G\}$ define the set of valid cycle coefficients. Our search problem can be re-expressed in terms of the cycle space of G as,

$$\mathbf{x}^* = \operatorname{argmax}_{\mathbf{x} \in \mathcal{X}} f(C_e \mathbf{x}). \tag{3}$$

Eq. 3 defines our problem in its most general form, in that it allows for the maximization of *any* scoring function f. Finding an exact solution, however, is difficult and would require time exponential in m. Moreover, although m can be used to obtain an upper bound on the number of cycles in a graph, a graph's cycle space can span generic cycles beyond elementary circuits. Instead, we propose an approximate solution based on a partitioning of the line fragment graph and restrict our search to elementary circuits that can be found efficiently for each sub-graph using [23].[3]

A key insight behind our approach is that object contours are typically contained within relatively small sized sub-graphs of the line fragment graph. Our goal is then to partition the graph into smaller sub-graphs that are most likely to contain object contours. Unlike other approximate search methods, most of which are based on a greedy merging of high scoring contour fragments [10,13,16], we prune weak edges so as to preserve the flexibility for the remaining fragments to re-form cycles according to more generic measures. This is accomplished by using the node and edge weight functions u and w to iteratively preserve nodes and edges with a high weight and discard those with a

---

[2] For ease of notation, we use c to denote both elementary circuits and generic graph cycles.

[3] When enumerating elementary circuits, we additionally constrain our search to ones that do not contain intersecting line fragments or graph edges.

low one. This results in an efficient search algorithm that operates on a set $G' = \{G_i = \langle V_i, E_i \rangle\}_{i=1}^{P}$, $V_i \subseteq V$ and $E_i \subseteq E$, of P small-sized sub-graphs obtained by a partitioning of G that retains nodes and edges with a large weight.

We can then re-express the original optimization of Eq. 1 with respect to this partitioning and enumerate the cycles of G as those of each of its sub-graphs,

$$c_{approx}^{*} = \operatorname{argmax}_{c \in G'} f(c). \tag{4}$$

The worst-case complexity of our algorithm is $O(2^{m_{\max}})$, where $m_{\max}$ is the cyclomatic number of the largest sized sub-graph. Although this already represents a significant savings for $m_{\max} \ll m$, the resulting algorithm can still be restrictive. Thankfully the number of elementary circuits in a typical line fragment sub-graph is significantly smaller than $2^{m_{\max}}$ and they can be enumerated rather efficiently[4].

Our graph search algorithm is summarized as Algorithm 1. The node weight function u is first used to prune low-scoring nodes from the graph whose weight is below a threshold μ. The edge weight function w is then recursively thresholded to divide G into P sub-graphs each having a cyclomatic number of at most $m_{\max}$, such that the lowest scoring edges are removed from the graph. Together μ and $m_{\max}$ define the parameters to our search algorithm that can be used to tradeoff computational cost with approximation quality. As evidenced in our experiments, our graph-partition based search algorithm results in empirically good solutions using generic weight measures while maintaining a relatively low computational cost.

3.3   Cycle Scoring Functions

The cycle scoring functions are used to model the global appearance and shape of an object and select the most promising cycles. We employ a Histogram of Oriented Gradients (HOG) representation in combination with a Support Vector Machine (SVM) classifier to define our cycle scoring function. Provided labeled object contours, we learn a HOG-SVM cycle scoring function for each object class as

$$f_{\mathrm{HOG}}(c) = \sum_i \alpha_i K(\Psi(c_i), \Psi(c)), \tag{5}$$

where c_i are circuit support vectors learned from training data and α_i their corresponding weights, and $K(\cdot)$ is a pre-specified kernel or similarity function. $\Psi(c)$ is a HOG appearance vector computed over its rectangular extent in the image, found by orienting c about its dominant orientation and normalizing it to a canonical scale.

The HOG-SVM scoring function cannot be decomposed over edge weights of G, particularly in the case of non-linear kernel functions. In fact, even for a linear kernel function, as it is scaled and oriented about each cycle, the HOG cycle

---

[4] In our experiments, setting $m_{\max} = 40$ resulted in approximately 3k elementary circuits per image on average.

Algorithm 1. Graph-Partition Search Algorithm

Input: An image I, line fragment graph $G = \langle V, E \rangle$, cycle score function $f(c) :$ $\{0,1\}^{|E|} \to \mathbb{R}$, and node and edge weight functions $u(v) : V \to \mathbb{R}$ and $w(e) : E \to \mathbb{R}$.

Parameters: Node weight threshold μ and sub-graph cyclomatic number threshold $m_{\max}$.

Output: Object contours c^*.

Initialize $C = \emptyset$.
if cyclomatic number of $G > m_{\max}$ **then**
    $\tau = \min_{e \in E} w(e)$.
    $V' = \{v \in V | u(v) \geq \mu\}$.
    $E' = \{e_{ij} \in E | (v_i, v_j \in V') \wedge (w(e_{ij}) > \tau)\}$.
    Define $G' = \langle V', E' \rangle$.
    for each connected component G_i of G' **do**
        $c_i = \text{GraphPartitionSearch}(G_i, f, u, w, \mu, m_{\max})$
        Add c_i to C.
    end for
else
    Enumerate elementary circuits C in G using [23].
end if

if initial call to GraphPartitionSearch **then**
    $c^* = \text{argmax}_{c \in C} f(c)$.
else
    $c^* = C$.
end if

Return: c^*.

---

feature is non-additive. The HOG representation has been widely applied for rectangular subwindow search [11,18]. In this work, we extend it for polygonal object detection. This can offer distinct advantages over the commonly used additive measures based on a bag-of-words [47], particularly for polygonal object classes whose shape is a discriminative cue.

In addition to HOG, we also consider a normalized color histogram feature, that for each RGB channel bins the color values within the cycle and normalizes each histogram to sum to one, and a bag-of-words representation as in [47] except with a Radial Basis Function (RBF) kernel. Similar to HOG, these define non-additive image measures that can be exploited by our approach.

3.4   Node and Edge Weight Functions

The node and edge weight functions encode how likely a line-fragment or line-fragment pair belong to an object that we use to guide the partitioning of the graph into meaningful sub-graphs. We use RBF-kernel SVMs to learn the node and edge weight functions from labeled line fragments and line fragment pairs based on their local geometry and appearance. A line fragment is labeled as

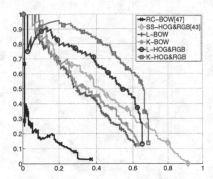

Fig. 3. *Precision-recall curves for building rooftop detection.* Results are displayed for the different settings of our approach and the baselines. The HOG and color RBF measure achieves the best performance, significantly outperforming the baselines and linear bag-of-words. Best viewed in color.

positive if it lies along the boundary of a ground-truth object instance and negative otherwise. Similarly, a pair of adjacent line fragments are labeled as positive if they both lie on the object boundary, and as negative if one lies on the boundary and the other does not.

We characterize the local appearance of a line fragment using a HOG descriptor computed over its scale and orientation normalized MSER region. We additionally use MSER color histogram features computed separately over both RGB and YCbCr channels and the MSER stability. For line pairs we compute a HOG descriptor over the scale and orientation normalized region defined by the combination of their MSERs and the absolute difference between their color histograms. Local geometry is then encoded using the angle and relative distance between adjacent lines as in [15]. The feature vector of a single line fragment or line fragment pair is then formed by concatenating its features into a single vector provided as input to the SVM.

4 Experiments

In this section, we demonstrate our approach for the purpose of detecting polygonal objects in man-made environments. We first consider the detection of building rooftops in aerial images. While there is an extensive literature on this topic (*e.g.*, for a survey see [31]), in this paper we focus on techniques that detect rooftops as cycles in line segment graphs [5,22] and compare to the state-of-the-art graph cycle detection method [47]. We then demonstrate our approach for more generic object detection using ImageNet [12]. In what follows, we first discuss our datasets, experimental setup and baselines, and then present our results.

Fig. 4. *Rooftop Detection.* Rooftop detections obtained by our approach and the baselines are displayed at a 50% recall rate. Correct detections are shown in green and false ones in red. Our approach significantly outperforms the baselines. Unlike bag-of-words, HOG not only encodes object appearance but also its global shape which can offer a better description of the polygonally shaped rooftops in these images and likely accounts for its better performance over ratio-contour. Additionally, false detections result in missed rooftops for ratio-contour, that do not degrade the recall of our approach even when using a bag-of-words scoring function. Best viewed in color.

4.1   Datasets

We use two datasets to evaluate our approach. The first consists of 65 aerial images of rural scenes containing several building rooftops many of which exhibit a fairly complex polygonal geometry. Each image is of size 1000×750 pixels. An example is shown in Figure 1. The second includes images from 10 different object categories from ImageNet [12]. They are sign, screen, remote control, cleaver, computer mouse, ipod, wine bottle, mug, beer bottle, and lampshade. We selected around 100 images per category, which were randomly split into equal-sized training and testing sets. We manually labeled the ground-truth contours of the objects in each image.

4.2   Experimental Setup and Baselines

We experiment with both additive and non-additive cycle scoring functions: a linear and RBF-kernel SVM using bag-of-words (BOW) features, which we refer to as **L-BOW** and **K-BOW** in our experiments and linear and RBF-kernel SVM with HOG and RGB color features referred to as **L-HOG&RGB** and **K-HOG&RGB**. Of these, **L-BOW** is the only additive one. For bag-of-words,

Table 1. Average precision on ImageNet. The average precision of each method is shown along with the mean average precision (mAP) across each category of ImageNet. Our approach results in a significant improvement over the baselines and linear bag-of-words.

Method/Category	sign	screen	remote	cleaver	mouse	ipod	wine	mug	beer	l-shade	mAP
RC-BOW [47]	0.37	0.43	0.42	0.06	0.10	0.27	0.08	0.16	0.15	0.05	0.21
SS-HOG&RGB [43]	0.35	0.43	0.46	0.30	0.37	0.38	0.47	**0.38**	**0.47**	0.34	0.39
L-BOW	0.42	0.25	0.60	0.32	0.26	0.38	0.29	0.15	0.17	0.17	0.30
K-BOW	0.47	0.30	0.54	0.34	0.33	0.40	0.36	0.19	0.27	0.32	0.35
L-HOG&RGB	0.49	0.49	0.63	0.42	0.50	0.32	0.47	0.20	0.34	0.49	0.44
K-HOG&RGB	**0.54**	**0.59**	**0.64**	**0.47**	**0.54**	**0.41**	**0.58**	0.27	0.40	**0.51**	**0.49**

we used SIFT keypoint descriptors and a dictionary containing 500 visual words computed with k-means. The cycle SVMs are trained from labeled samples found with our graph search algorithm. Cycles having an overlap greater than 60% with the ground-truth are labeled as positive and those with less than 50% overlap as negative. The *percent overlap* between two contours is computed as the area of their intersection divided by that of their union. For our graph search algorithm, we use a conservative node weight threshold of $\mu = -1$ and only disregard nodes that are highly unlikely to belong to an object and we cross-validate m_{max} with values $m_{max} = 10, 15, 20, 25, 30, 35, 40$ using 5-fold cross-validation on the training data.

We compare our approach with the state-of-the-art free shape object detection method–ratio-contour [47]. The ratio-contour algorithm is limited to additive measures, such as bag-of-words feature counts or area. We therefore evaluate it using a bag-of-words feature representation as described in [47] with the same MSER line fragments used by our approach, referred to as **RC-BOW** in our experiments. For multiple object detection, ratio-contour applies a greedy search that removes the optimal cycle from the graph and then is re-run to find the next one. In practice, we run it on each image until it cannot find anymore cycles. We also compare to the selective search algorithm of [43] as it is a representative approach that provides a similar or favorable performance to many of the recent segmentation-driven detection techniques [43], referred to as **SS** in our experiments. We use the code provided by the authors with the 'Fast' setting of their approach that resulted in a manageable number of object region hypothesis, on average 5.5k per image, and scored its regions using an K-HOG&RGB SVM classifier as this was our best performing scoring function.

We evaluate the baselines and each setting of our approach using precision-recall curves where detection accuracy is measured by the percentage overlap between the detected and ground-truth contours. As in previous work, a detection is considered to be correct if the detection accuracy is greater than 50%.

4.3   Results

Rooftop Dataset: Figure 3 displays the precision-recall curves for each method on this dataset. Our approach with the HOG and color RBF scoring function consistently yields the best performance. Unlike bag-of-words, HOG encodes both global shape and appearance which is important for detecting polygonal objects. Additionally color helps avoid false detections such as those belonging to grass or dark shadow regions. When only using bag-of-words, introducing a non-linear kernel function also results in a significant improvement. Ratio-contour, however, is limited to a linear bag-of-words classifier, and cannot take advantage of non-additive scoring functions.

Furthermore, even when using the same linear bag-of-words scoring function, our approach still outperforms ratio-contour. This is due to ratio-contour's greedy nature. False detections can result in missed detections. This is illustrated by Figure 4 that displays the detections obtained by our approach along with those of ratio-contour on a set of representative images. Compared with the combined HOG and color scoring function, linear bag-of-words results in many more false detections. These are often higher scoring than cycles corresponding to true object contours, which for ratio-contour results in deleted building rooftop hypotheses. By contrast, our approach is not affected by this problem.

Our approach also outperforms selective search both in detection accuracy and quality, for which example detections are also displayed in Figure 4. This is in part due to our use of geometry for forming region hypothesis resulting in cleaner polygonal outlines, but can also be attributed to our use of discriminative, category-specific node and edge weight functions that help to quickly reduce and focus region hypothesis to those likely to be an object and increase accuracy.

ImageNet Dataset: Table 1 shows the average precision obtained for each one of the 10 ImageNet categories we have worked with. The corresponding precision-recall curves are displayed in Figure 5. Our approach achieves the best performance using a HOG and color RBF classification function and yields a

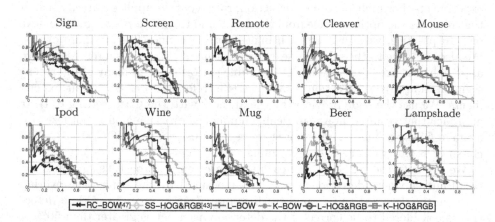

Fig. 5. *Precision-recall curves on Imagenet.* The results for the different settings of our approach and the baselines are shown for each category. Our approach obtains a significant improvement over the baselines and linear bag-of-words across all categories. Best viewed in color.

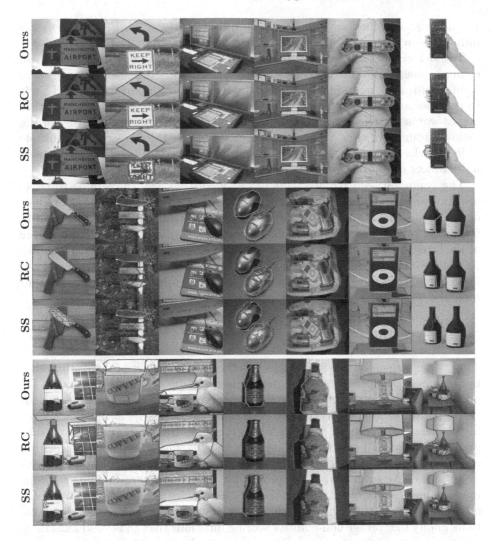

Fig. 6. *Polygonal object detection with ImageNet.* The detections obtained by our approach with the combined HOG and color RBF scoring function and the baselines are shown for example images from each category at 50% recall. Correct detections are shown in green and false ones in red. The baselines result in many false and missed detections that are significantly reduced with our approach. Best viewed in color.

significant improvement over the baselines, especially ratio-contour and linear bag-of-words, once again demonstrating the importance of non-additive measures like HOG. However, even for linear bag-of-words our approach exhibits a higher average precision than ratio-contour, which further illustrates the advantages of our graph search algorithm and suggests that it is a better way to prune the graph than relying on greedy search. We outperform selective search on 8 of the

10 datasets, with the exception of mug and beer bottle, as MSER detection was unreliable on these datasets, ratio-contour being similarly affected.

The detections returned by both our approach and the baselines on a set of example images from each category are shown in Figure 6. Ratio-contour suffers from significantly more false and missed detections than our approach. This is in part because for many of these categories, shape is an informative cue that bag-of-words does not capture and in part because of the greedy nature of the ratio-contour algorithm, which is not well suited to the detection of multiple objects. Selective search also results in more false detections and it often detects noisy object contours as it does take into account their geometry.

The computational requirements of our algorithm are comparable to those of ratio-contour. The rooftop dataset contains fairly large images that produce dense line-fragment graphs. For large graphs, ratio-contour is also costly and in fact takes longer than our approach. To process the rooftop dataset on one core of an Intel(R) Xeon(R) CPU @ 2.90 GHz, ratio-contour took 2 to 3 minutes per image on average, whereas our approach took about 1 minute. By contrast, for the ImageNet images of size 500×375, both our approach and ratio-contour took about 8 seconds per image on average.

5   Conclusion

This paper presented a graph-cycle based object localization algorithm that unlike previous approaches can exploit generic shape and appearance cues for polygonal object detection. We use the cyclomatic number to define an efficient graph-patition search algorithm and detect object boundaries as maximum scoring elementary circuits in a partitioned, image line fragment graph whose subgraphs preserve high-scoring node and edge weights. Our graph search algorithm can be used with *any* cycle scoring function to detect multiple polygonal objects in an image. We evaluated our approach for the detection of building rooftops in aerial images and other polygonal object categories from ImageNet. On these datasets, our approach achieved a significant improvement over the baselines due to its ability to leverage non-additive scoring functions that go beyond local measures of shape and appearance, and to consider multiple overlapping, hypotheses. Interesting avenues of future work include a broader exploration of cycle scoring functions and the use of alternative graph-cycle optimization strategies.

References

1. Arbelaez, P., Maire, M., Fowlkes, C., Malik, J.: Contour Detection and Hierarchical Image Segmentation. PAMI 33(5), 898–916 (2011)
2. Ballard, D.H.: Generalizing the Hough Transform to Detect Arbitrary Shapes. PR 13(2), 111–122 (1981)
3. Barnes, N., Loy, G., Shaw, D.: The Regular Polygon Detector. PR 43(3), 592–602 (2010)
4. Belongie, S., Malik, J., Puzicha, J.: Shape Matching and Object Recognition Using Shape Contexts. PAMI 24(24), 509–522 (2002)

5. Bignone, F., Henricsson, O., Fua, P., Stricker, M.: Automatic Extraction of Generic House Roofs from High Resolution Aerial Imagery. In: Buxton, B.F., Cipolla, R. (eds.) ECCV 1996. LNCS, vol. 1064, Springer, Heidelberg (1996)
6. Carreira, J., Sminchisescu, C.: Constrained Parametric Min-Cuts for Automatic Object Segmentation. In: CVPR 2010 (2010)
7. Chui, H., Rangarajan, A.: A New Point Matching Algorithm for Non-Rigid Registration. CVIU 89(2-3), 114–141 (2003)
8. Cootes, T., Taylor, C., Cooper, D., Graham, J.: Active Shape Models: Their Training and Application. CVIU 61(1), 38–59 (2005)
9. Cox, I.J., Rehg, J.M., Hingorani, S.L.: A Bayesian Multiple Hypothesis Approach to Contour Segmentation. IJCV 11, 5–24 (1993)
10. Crevier, D.: A Probabilistic Method for Extracting Chains of Collinear Segments. Image and Vision Computing (1999)
11. Dalal, N., Triggs, B.: Histograms of Oriented Gradients for Human Detection. In: CVPR 2005 (2005)
12. Deng, J., Dong, W., Socher, R., Li, L.J., Li, K., Fei-Fei, L.: Imagenet: A Large-Scale Hierarchical Image Database. In: CVPR 2009 (2009)
13. Dickson, W.: Feature Grouping in a Hierarchical Probabilistic Network. Image and Vision Computing (1991)
14. Diestel, R.: Graph Theory. Springer (2005)
15. Elder, J., Zucker, S.: Computing Contour Closure. In: Buxton, B.F., Cipolla, R. (eds.) ECCV 1996. LNCS, vol. 1064, Springer, Heidelberg (1996)
16. Elder, J.H., Krupnik, A., Johnston, L.A.: Contour Grouping with Prior Models. PAMI 25(25), 661–674 (2003)
17. Endres, I., Hoiem, D.: Category Independent Object Proposals. In: Daniilidis, K., Maragos, P., Paragios, N. (eds.) ECCV 2010, Part V. LNCS, vol. 6315, pp. 575–588. Springer, Heidelberg (2010)
18. Felzenszwalb, P., Mcallester, D., Ramanan, D.: A Discriminatively Trained, Multiscale, Deformable Part Model. In: CVPR 2008 (2008)
19. Ferrari, V., Jurie, F., Schmid, C.: From Images to Shape Models for Object Detection. IJCV 87, 284–303 (2010)
20. Guy, G., Medioni, G.: Inferring Global Perceptual Contours from Local Features. IJCV 20(1/2), 113–133 (1996)
21. Huertas, A., Cole, W., Nevatia, R.: Detecting Runways in Complex Airport Scenes. CVGIP 51(2) (1990)
22. Izadi, M., Saeedi, P.: Three-Dimensional Polygonal Building Model Estimation from Single Satellite Images. IEEE Trans. Geosci. Remote Sens. (2012)
23. Johnson, D.B.: Finding All the Elementary Circuits of a Directed Graph. SIAM 4(1) (1975)
24. Jung, C.R., Schramm, R.: Rectangle Detection Based on a Windowed Hough Transform. In: CGIP 2004 (2004)
25. Jurie, F., Schmid, C.: Scale-Invariant Shape Features for Recognition of Object Categories. In: CVPR 2004 (2004)
26. Kumar, M.P., Koller, D.: Efficiently Selecting Regions for Scene Understanding. In: CVPR 2010 (2010)
27. Lampert, C., Blaschko, M., Hofmann, T.: Beyond Sliding Windows: Object Localization by Efficient Subwindow Search. In: CVPR 2008 (2008)
28. Loy, G., Zelinsky, A.: Fast Radial Symmetry for Detecting Points of Interest. PAMI 25(8), 959–973 (2003)
29. Mahamud, S., Williams, L.R., Thornber, K.K., Xu, K.: Segmentation of Multiple Salient Closed Contours from Real Images. PAMI (2003)

30. Matas, J., Chum, O., Urban, M., Pajdla, T.: Robust Wide-Baseline Stereo from Maximally Stable Extremal Regions. IVC 22(10), 761–767 (2004)
31. Mayer, H.: Automatic Object Extraction from Aerial Imagery, a Survey Focusing on Buildings. CVIU 74(2), 138–149 (1999)
32. Opelt, A., Pinz, A., Zisserman, A.: A Boundary-Fragment-Model for Object Detection. In: Leonardis, A., Bischof, H., Pinz, A. (eds.) ECCV 2006. LNCS, vol. 3952, pp. 575–588. Springer, Heidelberg (2006)
33. Parent, P., Zucker, S.W.: Trace Inference, Curvature Consistency, and Curve Detection. PAMI 11(8) (1989)
34. Perona, P., Freeman, W.T.: A Factorization Approach to Grouping. In: Burkhardt, H.-J., Neumann, B. (eds.) ECCV 1998. LNCS, vol. 1406, pp. 655–670. Springer, Heidelberg (1998)
35. Roberts, L.: Machine Perception of Three-Dimensional Solids. Ph.D. thesis (1965)
36. Robles-Kelly, A., Hancock, E.R.: A Probabilistic Spectral Framework for Grouping and Segmentation. PR 37(7), 1387–1405 (2004)
37. Russakovsky, O., Ng, A.Y.: A Steiner Tree Approach to Object Detection. In: CVPR 2010 (2010)
38. Sarkar, S., Boyer, K.L.: Quantitative Measures of Change Based on Feature Organisation: Eigenvalues and Eigenvectors. CVIU 71(1), 110–136 (1998)
39. Shashua, A., Ullman, S.: Structural Saliency: the Detection of Globally Salient Structures Using a Locally Connected Network. In: ICCV 1988 (1988)
40. Shotton, J., Blake, A., Cipolla, R.: Contour-Based Learning for Object Detection. In: ICCV 2005 (2005)
41. Sivic, J., Russell, B., Efros, A., Zisserman, A., Freeman, W.: Discovering Objects and Their Location in Images. In: ICCV 2005 (2005)
42. Sun, X., Christoudias, M., Lepetit, V., Fua, P.: Real-Time Landing Place Assessment in Man-Made Environments. MVA (2013)
43. Uijlings, J.R.R., van de Sande, K.E.A., Gevers, T., Smeulders, A.W.M.: Selective Search for Object Recognition. IJCV 104(2), 154–171 (2013)
44. Vijayanarasimhan, S., Grauman, K.: Efficient Region Search for Object Detection. In: CVPR 2011 (2011)
45. Wang, S., Kubota, T., Siskind, J.M., Wang, J.: Salient Closed Boundary Extraction with Ratio Contour. PAMI 27(4) (2005)
46. Yeh, T., Lee, J., Darrell, T.: Fast Concurrent Object Localization and Recognition. In: CVPR 2009 (2009)
47. Zhang, Z., Cao, Y., Salvi, D., Oliver, K., Waggoner, J., Wang, S.: Free-Shape Subwindow Search for Object Localization. In: CVPR 2010 (2010)
48. Zhang, Z., Fidler, S., Waggoner, J., Dickinson, S., Siskind, J.M., Wang, S.: Supderedge Grouping for Object Localization by Combining Appearance and Shape Information. In: CVPR 2012 (2012)

Interactively Guiding Semi-Supervised Clustering via Attribute-Based Explanations

Shrenik Lad and Devi Parikh

Virginia Tech, Blacksburg, VA, USA

Abstract. Unsupervised image clustering is a challenging and often ill-posed problem. Existing image descriptors fail to capture the clustering criterion well, and more importantly, the criterion itself may depend on (unknown) user preferences. Semi-supervised approaches such as distance metric learning and constrained clustering thus leverage user-provided annotations indicating which pairs of images belong to the same cluster (must-link) and which ones do not (cannot-link). These approaches require many such constraints before achieving good clustering performance because each constraint only provides weak cues about the desired clustering. In this paper, we propose to use image attributes as a modality for the user to provide more informative cues. In particular, the clustering algorithm iteratively and actively queries a user with an image pair. Instead of the user simply providing a must-link/cannot-link constraint for the pair, the user also provides an attribute-based reasoning e.g. "these two images are similar because both are natural and have still water" or "these two people are dissimilar because one is way older than the other". Under the guidance of this explanation, and equipped with attribute predictors, many additional constraints are automatically generated. We demonstrate the effectiveness of our approach by incorporating the proposed attribute-based explanations in three standard semi-supervised clustering algorithms: Constrained K-Means, MPCK-Means, and Spectral Clustering, on three domains: scenes, shoes, and faces, using both binary and relative attributes.

1 Introduction

Image clustering is the problem of grouping images such that similar images fall in the same clusters and dissimilar images fall in different clusters. Image similarity as perceived by humans is difficult to capture by existing image descriptors. Moreover, the notion of similarity itself is often ill-defined. For instance, one user may want to cluster a group of faces such that people of the same gender, race and age fall in the same cluster, while a different user may want to cluster faces based on accessories such as glasses, makeup, etc. Clearly, without supervision, clustering is an ill-posed problem.

Semi-Supervised clustering approaches [1–8] leverage user-provided pairwise constraints either to learn an appropriate distance metric in the feature space (distance metric learning [5–8]) or to guide a clustering algorithm towards correct clusters (constrained clustering [1–4]). These pairwise constraints are either

D. Fleet et al. (Eds.): ECCV 2014, Part VI, LNCS 8694, pp. 333–349, 2014.

Fig. 1. An Illustration of our approach. The system interactively queries the user with a pair of images, and solicits "must-link" and "cannot-link" response along with an attribute-based explanation. Using attribute predictors, the system can automatically generate additional pairwise constraints.

must-link or cannot-link, indicating that the two images in the pair should belong to the same cluster or different clusters resp. These constraints allow the user to inject their domain knowledge or preferences in the clustering algorithm.

A fundamental problem with these approaches is that they require a large number of pairwise constraints in order to achieve decent performance. This is because the pairs of images to be annotated are typically randomly chosen, and are likely to be redundant. Active clustering approaches [9–11] reduce the number of required constraints by iteratively and actively selecting a pair to be annotated by a user in the loop. But each constraint still remains a weak low-level indication of the desired clustering. For instance, active PCK-Means [10] requires 5000 constraints to achieve 30% accuracy on a dataset of 500 face images as reported in [9].

We propose accessing the user's mental model of the desired clustering via a mid-level semantic representation i.e. visual attributes. Some attributes like *wearing glasses* or *having four legs* are binary in nature while others like *smiling* and *attractive* are relative [12–15]. Both binary and relative attributes have been shown to improve various computer vision tasks like image search [16, 17] and classification [13, 14, 18, 19]. In this paper, we show that attributes can be used for achieving more accurate clusterings when using semi-supervised clustering algorithms.

Specifically, for an actively selected image pair, the user provides a must-link or cannot-link constraint, along with an attribute-based explanation for that constraint. This explanation can be in terms of binary attributes e.g. "these two shoes are similar because both are *red* and *have high-heels*", or in terms of relative attributes e.g. "these two people are dissimilar because one is significantly *older* than the other". This form of an explanation is intuitive for a user. Equipped with pre-trained attribute predictors, the machine can infer a large number of constraints from just one user response. For instance, in the first example the machine can identify all shoes that are red and have high-heels and add must-link constraints between all possible pairs. In the second example the machine can identify pairs of images where the difference in age is even larger than the query pair, and add cannot-link constraints between these pairs. This results in significant gains in clustering accuracy. The scores of the attribute predictors can be used to assess the confidence of these automatically added constraints.

We demonstrate the effectiveness of our approach by incorporating binary and relative attribute-based explanations in three diverse semi-supervised clustering algorithms: Constrained K-Means [1], MPCK-Means [2] and Spectral Clustering [20] on three different domains: scenes (SUN [21]), faces (PubFig [13]) and consumer products (Shoes [22]) using real human studies. We also evaluate our system on user-specific or personalized clustering and show that our approach can be used to guide the system towards different clustering outputs.

2   Related Work

Semi-Supervised clustering approaches are either constraint-based [1–4] or metric-based [5–8]. Both these approaches use pairwise constraints (must-link and cannot-link) to guide a clustering algorithm towards correct clusters or to learn an appropriate distance metric for the given data. Basu et. al. [2] propose an integrated framework that incorporates constrained-clustering and distance metric learning. These approaches rely on large number of constraints in order to achieve satisfactory clustering performance even on small datasets with low-dimensional features.

Active clustering works like [9,11] reduce the number of constraints by querying a user on actively chosen pairs instead of completely random pairs. But these approaches are specific to the clustering algorithms they use. Biswas et. al. [9] present an active clustering algorithm that goes through all possible pairs and then re-clusters the data in order to identify the most informative pair. Hence, they use a simple Minimal Spanning Tree based clustering algorithm that can be run many times in a reasonable amount of time. Wauthier et al. [11] propose an active learning algorithm specifically for spectral clustering. Moreover, even though these approaches reduce the number of constraints, each constraint remains a weak indication of the desired clustering. Our attribute-based approach on the other hand allows the user to convey rich information which can be propagated to other unlabelled pairs in the dataset. It is also not specific to any clustering algorithm. We show that our approach can improve performance across different clustering algorithms including a mix of constraint- and metric-based approaches.

Attributes are mid-level concepts that have been extensively used for a variety of tasks in computer vision [13–19, 22–26]. The vocabulary of attributes can be pre-defined or it can be discovered [27, 28]. Recently, Attributes have been used as a mode of communication between humans and machines [16, 18, 19]. Donahue and Grauman [19] use spatial annotations and binary attributes to allow an annotator to provide an explanation for a particular class label. Whittle Search [16] uses relative attributes to allow a user to convey (potentially actively solicited [29]) feedback to a search engine to quickly find the desired target image. [15] uses attributes to avoid semantic drift in a bootstrapping approach by enforcing known relationships between categories (eg: "banquet halls are bigger than "bedrooms). An exhaustive set of such relationships are provided to the system as input (spirit to zero shot learning [14]). In our approach, we use attributes to propagate constraints to pairs of images in an interactive semi-supervised clustering setting. Parkash and Parikh [18] use relative attributes feedback (e.g. "this image is too open to be a forest") to identify additional negative examples from an unlabelled pool of images to train a classifier. Attributes have also been used for fine-grained classification with a human-in-the-loop who conveys domain knowledge by answering attribute-based questions at test time to aid the machine [25]. To the best of our knowledge, ours is the first work on interactive semantic explanation-based clustering of images. These explanations are used to propagate domain knowledge to other pairs of images in terms of both must-link and cannot-link constraints. The "domain knowledge" can easily be user-preferences, making our approach a natural fit to personalized clustering.

Crowd-in-the-loop clustering has been explored for dealing with a large collection of images. Crowdclustering [8,30] shows small subsets of images to MTurk workers and they are asked to annotate the images with keywords. Similarity of image pairs is then determined based on how many keywords they share. Tamuz et al. [31] learn a similarity measure for images in the form of a kernel matrix by posing triplet comparison queries to a crowd. Our approach can be used to make such crowd-in-the-loop efforts more cost effective by reducing human effort via attribute-based explanations.

The rest of this paper is organized as follows: Sec 3 briefly describes three semi-supervised clustering approaches that we augment using attribute-based explanations. Sec 4 describes the details of incorporating these explanations. Sec 5 presents our experimental results. We conclude the paper in Sec 6.

3   Semi-Supervised Clustering Approaches

Semi-Supervised clustering incorporates background knowledge in the form of pairwise constraints: must-link and cannot-link. Let M be the set of must-link constraints and C be the set of cannot-link constraints. The pairwise constraints lead to two types of transitive closure: 1) $(a, b) \in M$ and $(b, c) \in M \implies (a, c) \in M$. 2) $(a, b) \in M$ and $(b, c) \in C \implies (a, c) \in C$.

In the following subsections, we briefly describe the three semi-supervised clustering approaches that we augment using our attribute-based approach.

3.1   Constrained K-Means

Constrained K-Means or COP K-Means [1] is a modification of K-Means to incorporate pairwise constraints. Specifically, during the assignment step of K-Means, instead of assigning every datapoint to its nearest cluster, the datapoint is assigned to the nearest cluster which would not result in violating any constraints. The centroid estimation step remains the same. We use our own implementation of COP K-Means. During the assignment step, there are situations when a point cannot be assigned to any of the clusters because every assignment would result in violating some constraint. In such cases, we assign the point to the cluster with minimum violations.

3.2   MPCK-Means

Metric Pairwise Constrained K-Means or MPCK-Means [2] combines distance metric learning and constrained clustering in a unified framework. It minimizes the following objective function:

$$\sum_{\boldsymbol{x}_i} \left(\|\boldsymbol{x}_i - \boldsymbol{\mu}_{l_i}\|^2_{D_{l_i}} - \log\left(\det(D_{l_i})\right) \right) + \sum_{(\boldsymbol{x}_i, \boldsymbol{x}_j) \in M} w_{ij} \mathbb{1}[l_i \neq l_j] + \sum_{(\boldsymbol{x}_i, \boldsymbol{x}_j) \in C} w_{ij} \mathbb{1}[l_i = l_j]$$

$$(1)$$

Here, $\boldsymbol{x}_i$ denotes the ith datapoint, l_i is the cluster-id of $\boldsymbol{x}_i$, $\boldsymbol{\mu}_{l_i}$ is the corresponding centroid, D_{l_i} is the matrix that parameterizes the Mahalanobis distance metric for cluster l_i, w_{ij} is the weight (or importance) of the pairwise constraint $(\boldsymbol{x}_i, \boldsymbol{x}_j)$, and $\mathbb{1}$ denotes the indicator function. The objective function penalizes those assignments which violate many constraints (last two terms of objective) and also assignments where the datapoints are far from their respective centroids w.r.t. the learnt distance metric (first term of objective). The function is minimized by an Expectation Maximisation (EM) approach, where the E-step assigns points to the closest centroids according to the learnt distance metric, and the M-step estimates the centroids and learns the distance metric. We use the code provided by the authors. In our experiments, we enforce a common distance metric for all clusters. This was found to perform better [2].

3.3   Spectral Clustering

We use the spectral clustering algorithm from [20]. It consists of the following steps:

- Compute the $N \times N$ affinity matrix A for the N datapoints.
  $A_{ij} = \exp\left(\frac{-\|\boldsymbol{x}_i - \boldsymbol{x}_j\|^2}{2\sigma^2}\right)$ for $i \neq j$, $A_{ii} = 0$. The parameter σ controls how fast the affinity falls with increasing distances.
- Compute the Laplacian L of the affinity matrix and find its top K eigenvectors.
- Stack the eigenvectors as columns to form the $N \times K$ matrix E and normalize the rows of E to form a $N \times K$ matrix Y.

- Finally, cluster the N rows of matrix Y into K clusters using K-Means. The assignment of each row provides the cluster-id for each of the N datapoints.

Kamvar et al. [32], present a semi-supervised version of this spectral clustering algorithm. If $(\boldsymbol{x}_i, \boldsymbol{x}_j)$ is a must-link constraint, then $A(i, j)$ and $A(j, i)$ are set to 1 (zero distance) and if $(\boldsymbol{x}_i, \boldsymbol{x}_j)$ is a cannot-link constraint then $A(i, j)$ and $A(j, i)$ are set to 0 (∞ distance). In our experiments, we set the value of σ as the average pairwise distance between datapoints.

4   Approach

Let U denote the set of N images $\{\boldsymbol{x}_1, \boldsymbol{x}_2, \ldots, \boldsymbol{x}_N\}$ that we want to cluster into K groups. Let $\{a_1, a_2, \ldots, a_Q\}$ be the Q attributes in the predefined attributes vocabulary associated with the images. Recall that M and C are the set of must-link and cannot-link constraints respectively and we represent them by symmetric matrices M and C of dimensions $N \times N$, where $M(i, j)$ denotes whether image $\boldsymbol{x}_i$ and image $\boldsymbol{x}_j$ are must-linked and similarly $C(i, j)$ denotes whether image $\boldsymbol{x}_i$ and image $\boldsymbol{x}_j$ are cannot-linked. Initially M and C are empty, and will get filled up as we query the user on pairs of images at each iteration. Ideally, we would like to fill these matrices as accurately and in as few user iterations as possible. Our approach is as follows:

1. Cluster images into K clusters using unsupervised K-Means.
2. Identify the most uncertain pair (Sec 4.1) and present it to the user as query.
3. User provides a must-link or cannot-link label for the pair along with an attribute-based explanation (Sec 4.2). Perform transitive closure on all accumulated ground truth constraints.
4. Convert attribute explanation to additional (possibly noisy) constraints (Sec 4.3).
5. Cluster the images with the updated set of constraints using a semi-supervised clustering algorithm.
6. Repeat from step 2.

4.1   Active Selection of Pair

A pair of very similar images are likely to be must-links (ML), and images that are very different are likely to be cannot-links (CL). A must-link or cannot-link label on a pair of images that is neither too similar nor too dissimilar is likely be to be most informative for a semi-supervised clustering algorithm.

Let d_{ij} denote the distance between $\boldsymbol{x}_i$ and $\boldsymbol{x}_j$ in low-level feature space. Let *label* be a random variable that takes two states, ML (must-link) and CL (cannot-link). Let P_{ML}^{ij} and P_{CL}^{ij} be the probabilities of the pair (i, j) being a ML and CL respectively i.e.

$$P_{ML}^{ij} = P(label = ML \mid d_{ij}), \tag{2}$$

$$P_{CL}^{ij} = P(label = CL \mid d_{ij}) \tag{3}$$

Using Bayes rule

$$P(label = ML \mid d_{ij}) \propto P(d_{ij} \mid label = ML) * P(label = ML) \qquad (4)$$

$$P(label = CL \mid d_{ij}) \propto P(d_{ij} \mid label = CL) * P(label = CL) \qquad (5)$$

The distributions $P(d_{ij} \mid label = ML)$ and $P(d_{ij} \mid label = CL)$ are approximated as Gaussians. Their parameters are estimated from the pairwise distances of all pairs in same clusters and different clusters respectively, according to the current clustering. $P(label = ML)$ and $P(label = CL)$ are the proportion of pairs in same and different clusters. Similar in spirit to active learning for training classifiers [33], we select the pair with the highest entropy under the distribution $P(label \mid d_{ij})$ and present it to the user to solicit *label*.

4.2 Attribute-Based Explanation

We assume that the vocabulary of attributes is pre-defined and the attribute predictors have been trained offline. Presence of binary attributes can be predicted by standard classification tools [13, 14, 23]. Relative attribute models on the other hand predict the relative strength of attribute presence in images using ranking functions for each attribute in the vocabulary [12]. We use attributes (both binary and relative) to allow the user to convey to the machine the semantics that guide the similarity measure between images. This notion of similarity may be based on common sense knowledge, specific domain knowledge, or user's preferences.

In case of binary attributes, we allow attribute-based explanations of the following form: "These two faces are *similar* because both are *young* and *white*", "These two scenes are *dissimilar* because one is *natural* and other is not". In this way, the user can convey similarity along which visual properties suffices to make images similar, and discrepancies along which attributes are sufficient to make the images dissimilar. With relative attributes, the explanation for a must-link pair is of the form "These two shoes are *similar* because both are similarly *shiny* and *formal*" and "These two people are *dissimilar* because one is significantly *younger* than the other". In addition to relevance of attributes, this allows the user to indicate the required sensitivity (or the lack of it) to discrepancies along an attribute that the clustering algorithm should have to achieve the desirable clustering. This rich explanation allows the machine to infer much more than a single constraint from the user's response (as described in the next subsection).

One could argue that instead of actively querying the user, perhaps the user can describe the clustering criterion to the system in terms of attributes from the very beginning. There are two concerns with such an approach. First, if the attribute vocabulary is very large, indicating the relevance of each attribute would be cumbersome. This is especially the case if the user were to specify the desired sensitivity to differences in attribute strengths for each attribute (e.g. how similar does the age of two people need to be for them to fall in the same cluster? is a certain difference between two shoes in terms of heel height sufficient to put them in different clusters?). In our approach, the user can simply look at a pair of images and provide a response specific to those images. Second, the criterion for clustering a large number of images may not be crystal clear in the user's mind till they see specific pairs of images and are forced to think explicitly about the desired clustering output with respect to those images.

4.3   Incorporating Attribute-Based Explanation

Binary Attributes: Without loss of generality, lets assume that the cannot-link feedback on an image pair (x_i, x_j) is "These two images are *dissimilar* because one is a_q and the other is not". The dissimilar label in the feedback provides a ground truth constraint that (x_i, x_j) is cannot-linked and hence $C(i, j) = C(j, i) = 1$. The attribute-based explanation suggests that pairs of images where one has a_q and the other does not are likely to belong to different clusters. The machine can thus infer additional pairs $S_1 \times S_2$ as cannot-link constraints in the matrix C, where $S1$ is the set of images where a_q is predicted to be present using the pre-trained binary classifier for a_q, and S_2 is the set of images where a_q is predicted to be absent.

If the must-link feedback given by the user on the pair (x_i, x_j) is of the form "These two images are *similar* because both are $a_{q_1}, a_{q_2}, \ldots a_{q_T}$", it suggests that having attributes $a_{q_1}, a_{q_2}, \ldots a_{q_T}$ in common are sufficient to qualify two images as being similar. After adding the ground truth must-link constraint for the pair (x_i, x_j), the machine then uses the attribute classifiers of $a_{q_1}, a_{q_2}, \ldots a_{q_T}$ to find images that have all these attributes present in them. If the set of images is S, then all pairs in $S \times S$ are added as must-link constraints in the matrix M.

Relative Attributes: If the cannot-link feedback on image pair (x_i, x_j) is "These two images are *dissimilar* because x_i is way too a_q than x_j", the machine first adds a ground truth cannot-link constraint $C(i, j) = C(j, i) = 1$. It then creates the set S_G which consists of all images where degree of presence of a_q is predicted to be greater than x_i and the set S_L which consists of all images where degree of presence of a_q is predicted to be less than x_j. The pairs in $S_G \times S_L$ are added as cannot-link constraints in the matrix C, because all such pairs have a difference in relative strengths of a_q even larger than (x_i, x_j), which the user indicated is already too large for them to belong to the same cluster. For a must link feedback "These two images are *similar* because both are equally $a_{q_1}, a_{q_2}, \ldots a_{q_T}$", machine computes S_S, the set of images having the degree of presence of each attribute $a_{q_1}, a_{q_2}, \ldots a_{q_T}$ between the ranges specified by x_i and x_j. The pairs in $S_S \times S_S$ are added as must-link constraints in the matrix M along with the ground truth constraint $M(i, j) = M(j, i) = 1$.

Note that representing images in the attribute-space instead of a low-level feature-space is not likely to diminish the value of such attribute-based explanations. Information about which attributes are relevant to the clustering and which ones are not is still valuable. Moreover, we do not assume that the desired clustering is precisely defined by the available vocabulary of attributes. We only assume that some information about the clustering criterion can be explained in terms of some of the available attributes, and hypothesize that this information is significantly richer than the pairwise constraints alone. Both these hypotheses are empirically validated in our experiments (Sec 5.2).

Purity of Constraints: The constraints generated by the machine from attribute-based explanations are not expected to be 100% accurate because of various factors like error of attribute classifiers/rankers, discrepancy in perception of attributes between the machine and user, erroneous feedback on the part of the user, inconsistencies between the clustering criterion and attributes, etc. On average, we found the accuracy of our attribute-based constraints to be 86% for cannot-links and 60% for must-links. We solicit attribute explanations from the user only up to a certain point (100 iterations in our experiments). This is because the vocabulary of attributes is limited. After a point, attributes do not add too many new constraints (especially with binary attributes). For instance, we find that from 20th to 100th iterations, the number of newly added constraints is only 13% of what are added in the first 20 iterations. From that point onwards, the user provides only must-link and cannot-link labels for pairs and the number of impure constraints goes down with iterations. This gives the user an opportunity to fine tune the clustering after the broad brush strokes of attributes give them a head start.

Hard and Soft Constraints: The constraints created by the machine can be incorporated in two ways: hard and soft. In the hard setting, all the generated constraints are given confidence $= 1$ i.e. they are treated as being as important and reliable as ground truth constraints. On the other hand, in the soft setting, the machine-generated constraints are assigned confidences between 0 and 1 based on the confidence of attribute classifiers in predicting the attributes. This may provide robustness to incorrect attribute predictions. With binary attribute-based constraints, the confidence of a generated cannot-link constraint $(x_{i'}, x_{j'})$ is $c_{i'} * c_{j'}$, where $c_{i'}$ and $c_{j'}$ are the confidences of presence and absence of the attribute a_q in images $x_{i'}$ and $x_{j'}$ respectively. In case of a generated must-link constraint $(x_{i'}, x_{j'})$, $c_{i'}$ is the average confidence of presence of the q_T attributes in image $x_{i'}$, and $c_{j'}$ is the average confidence of presence of the q_T attributes in image $x_{j'}$. The final confidence assigned to the pair is $c_{i'} * c_{j'}$. When the cannot link feedback on pair (x_i, x_j) involves a relative attribute a_q, we first sort all the images according to the ranking function for attribute a_q. The confidence of a generated cannot-link constraint $(x_{i'}, x_{j'})$ is proportional to the total number of images that lie between $x_{i'}$ and x_i and between $x_{j'}$ and x_j in the sorted list. In case of a must-link feedback, the confidence of a generated must-link constraint $(x_{i'}, x_{j'})$ is proportional to how close $x_{i'}$ and $x_{j'}$ are in the sorted orderings on average across the q_T attributes. All the confidences are normalized to lie between 0 and 1. When multiple attribute explanations indicate the same pair to be cannot-linked or must-linked, we assign a confidence based on the explanation leading to the highest confidence.

Incorporation of Soft Constraints: MPCK-Means directly allows for soft-confidences in their formulation via the weights w_{ij} associated with each constraint in Equation 1. We set the weight w_{ij} to be the confidence computed for

Fig. 2. These are the 6 ground truth clusters in SUN600 dataset. They correspond to categories like transportation, industrial regions, sports/recreation etc.

(x_i, x_j) from user feedback. In spectral clustering, the affinity matrix A captures the similarity of datapoints. If the confidence of a cannot-link constraint (x_i, x_j) is c, we set $A(i, j) = 1 - c$, and if the confidence of a must-link constraint (x_i, x_j) is c, we set $A(i, j) = c$. COP K-Means does not allow handling of soft constraints and so we modify it slightly. During the assignment of a point to a cluster, instead of computing the number of violated constraints, we assign a datapoint to the cluster with the least sum of confidences of violated constraints.

5   Experiments and Results

5.1   Experimental Setup

Datasets: We demonstrate our approach on three domains. **Scenes:** We use the SUN Attributes dataset [34] that consists of indoor and outdoor scenes along with pre-trained attribute classifiers for 102 attributes like natural, open, enclosed, warm etc. Scene categories in the SUN dataset [21] are organized according to a hierarchy, where the first level has super-ordinate categories like indoor and outdoor scenes, the second level has basic-level categories like sports, transportation, desert, etc. and the third (last) level has more than 700 fine-grained categories. We choose six out of 16 categories from the second level of the hierarchy and create a dataset of 600 images called SUN600. The six categories cover scenes of various types like transportation, home/hotel indoor scenes, sports/recreation, etc. An illustration of the clusters can be seen in Fig 2. We use GIST [35] features for this dataset. **Faces:** We use the Public Figures Face Database [13] which consists of face images of 60 different public figures in their development set. Attribute predictions for 73 binary attributes like male, white, smiling, wearing glasses etc are available with the dataset. We use 570 images involving 38 people (Sec 5.3 has details regarding how the clusters are defined). The features used are pyramid HOG features [36]. **Shoes:** Berg et al. [22] provide a shoes dataset which is also used in [16]. Kovashka et al. [16] provide ranking predictors for 10 relative attributes like shiny, formal, open, sporty etc. We choose 1000 images belonging to four different categories namely, boots, flats, high-heels, and sneakers, and refer to this dataset as Shoes1000. We use the 960-d GIST features provided with the dataset. For SUN600 and Shoes1000 we assume that the categories are the desired clusters.

Human Studies: We collect attribute-based explanations for image pairs through real human studies on Amazon Mechanical Turk. For each dataset, we run unsupervised K-Means 300 times and choose the max-entropy pair each time according to our formulation (Sec 4.1). We present these pairs to users on MTurk and solicit attribute-based explanations. In our experiments, we pick a query at each iteration from this pool of pairs. This allows us to collect data offline and run exhaustive experiments on the collected data. Our MTurk interface shows the desired clustering on top by displaying 4 randomly chosen images from each cluster. These images are chosen offline for each dataset and are fixed across all HITs. Note that this is just to inform the workers of the desired clustering. In a real application, the users already have a clustering in mind. The clustering is not described to users in any other form. The users observe the clusters and visualize the similarity measure. They are presented with a pair and asked to indicate whether the two images belong to the same or different clusters. They are also asked to select attribute(s) from a list as explanation. In case of a cannot-link (CL) label, users are asked to select the main property (attribute) that makes the two images different. In the case of a must-link (ML) label, users are asked to select as many attributes as necessary to make the two images similar. Multiple attributes for CL can be easily incorporated, but a single attribute is least time consuming. Single attributes are often insufficient to establish similarity, hence users are free to select more for ML responses. One HIT had 5 image pairs and workers were paid 5 cents per HIT. To ensure good quality of responses, we took a majority vote over 3 different workers for the ML/CL response.

Baselines: We compare our approach with the following baselines

(a) K-Means: Unsupervised K-Means clustering without any pairwise constraints.
(b) Random: User provides a must-link or cannot-link constraint on a randomly chosen pair at each iteration. No attribute-based explanation is taken.
(c) Semi-Random: User provides constraint on a pair chosen randomly from outside the transitive closure of all previously labelled pairs. This is a stronger baseline than (b) which may solicit feedback on redundant pairs. No Attribute-based explanation is taken.
(d) Max-entropy: User provides constraints on the highest entropy pair as described in Sec 4.1. No attribute-based explanation is taken. A comparison to (c) semi-random baseline demonstrates the effect of our entropy formulation even when constraints are chosen from outside the transitive closure.
(e) Many-Random: The above baselines add only 1 constraint per iteration. To evaluate if our approach is benefiting from just more constraints as opposed to *meaningful* constraints, we compare with a baseline that expands the set of constraints every iteration by adding as many must-link and cannot-link constraints as our approach generates, but between random pairs of images. We experiment with both hard and soft constraints.
(f) Attributes-hard: User provides a constraint on the highest entropy pair along with an attribute-based explanation. Machine generates hard constraints.

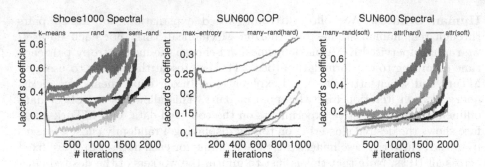

Fig. 3. Results of our approach on SUN600 and Shoes1000

(g) Attributes-soft: User provides a constraint on the highest entropy pair along with an attribute-based explanation. Machine generates soft constraints.

Evaluation Metric: We use the Jaccard's coefficient (JCC) to quantify the clustering accuracy. It is defined as follows:

$$\text{Jaccard's coefficient (JCC)} = \frac{SS}{SS+SD+DS}$$

where SS is the number of pairs which belong to the same clusters in the ground truth (GT) as well as the clustering output, SD is the number of pairs which belong to same clusters in GT but are incorrectly placed in different clusters by the clustering algorithm and DS is the number of pairs which belong to different clusters in GT but are placed in same clusters by the algorithm.

5.2   Results

The semi-supervised clustering algorithm can be any one of the 3 algorithms described in Sec 3. Results on Shoes1000 and SUN600 with some of the clustering algorithms are shown in Fig 3. The results for more clustering algorithms can be found in our supplementary material. Similar trends are observed when other metrics like F-Measure, Rand-Index, or NMI are used to measure performance. Results on PubFig will be presented when we show personalized clustering experiments (Sec 5.3). We observed that spectral clustering had lot of variance in performance between consecutive iterations, and so we averaged results across 6 random runs. We now discuss various aspects of our results in detail.

Active Selection of Pairs: In Fig 3 we see that for each of the non-attribute baselines, the initial region is nearly flat. This demonstrates that semi-supervised clustering algorithms do not gain much until a large number of pairs have been labelled [2,9]. The max-entropy baseline starts learning earliest followed by semi-random and pure-random. On average, we found that max-entropy picks pairs that the current clustering had classified incorrectly (placed in different clusters when they belong to the same cluster or vice versa) 40% of the times, while semi-random picks such pairs only 25% of the times. This shows that our active selection of image pairs is quite effective at picking informative pairs. Note that even when no information is gained through the constraint itself (60% of the times), the attribute-based explanation will still be informative.

Attribute Explanations: Our proposed approach in Fig 3 starts learning significantly earlier than non-attribute baselines, and outperforms these baselines across the board. Clustering accuracy increases by 15-20% in the first 100 iterations. This would have taken 20 times more constraints using the semi-supervised clustering algorithms without attribute explanations. The many-random baseline on the other hand performs even worse than the unsupervised version for many iterations. This shows that the additional constraints generated using the attribute explanations are important not just because of their quantity, but also because of their relevance to the desired clustering. Clustering in attribute space instead of low-level feature space does not diminish the effect of attribute-based explanations. For SUN600, unsupervised K-Means clustering in attribute space gives 20% accuracy (compared to 12% in low-level feature space). Attribute explanations in this case still lead to 15% performance gain after 100 iterations.

Timing Analysis: In interactive applications like these, it is important to consider the time spent by users in answering queries. In our approach, we observed that the time spent by MTurk workers per question (with attributes explanation) was around 17 secs on average as compared to 5 secs without attributes explanation. Moreover, as mentioned earlier, attribute explanations are taken only upto first 100 iterations. Using attributes, 70% accurate clusters can be obtained for Shoes1000 with just 40% of the user time as required by random approach. The algorithm can propagate the attribute explanations and identify the highest entropy pair in less than a second. The overall time per iteration is dominated by the underlying clustering algorithm (typically 5-20 secs).

Binary and Relative Attributes: We show clustering results using both relative attributes (Shoes1000) as well as binary attributes (SUN600). Both types of attributes are able to provide significant gains to the clustering algorithms as seen in Fig 3. We observed that the workers may use the same set of attributes in a future explanation. When binary attributes are used, the same attribute does not add any new information. This is because the constraints generated depend only on the attribute predictors, which do not change. For relative attributes on the other hand, repeated use of the same attributes can add new information because the constraints generated are relative to the image pairs on which the feedback was provided. Relative attributes allow the machine to be more specific while generating constraints. We found that the number of incorrect constraints are less (30% in Shoes1000) compared to for binary (40% in SUN600). Relative attributes also allow the user to provide more fine-grained feedback and are therefore more suitable for personalized clustering.

Hard vs. Soft Constraints: In Sec 4.3 we described two ways of incorporating the attribute explanations: hard and soft. The motivation behind soft constraints is to provide robustness to noisy attribute predictions. Comparing the soft and hard baselines in Fig 3, it can be observed that soft constraints usually perform

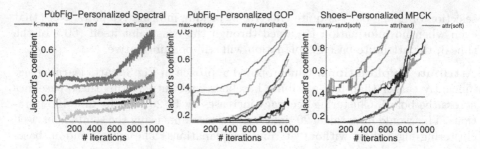

Fig. 4. Results of our approach on PubFig-Personalized and Shoes-Personalized

better than hard constraints for both our approach and the many-random baseline In case of spectral clustering with SUN600, soft baseline gives a significant gain over hard throughout the clustering process.

5.3   Personalized Clustering

Personalized Clustering: Apart from the usual common-sense or domain-knowledge based clustering, we also evaluated our system for user-specific or personalized clustering. The ideal way to do this is by showing the image dataset to an MTurk worker and asking them to visualize a clustering and guide our system iteratively using attribute-based explanations. The resulting clusters can then be evaluated by the same user. However, MTurk is not the right platform for such extensive long duration tasks. Having sufficient users come to our lab would limit the number of experiments we can conduct. Hence, we adopt the following strategy to simulate personalized clustering. We first create a ground truth (GT) clustering from a given set of images based on certain criteria (simulated preferences). We then solicit attribute-based explanations consistent with the desired clustering from MTurk workers using the same setup described in Sec 5.1. Since each worker sees the same clustering, responses from different workers can be thought of as coming from the same user.

We create the personalized GT clusters using two approaches: 1) By fixing the definition of each cluster in terms of attributes (PubFig) and 2) By merging several basic level categories to form clusters (Shoes). For PubFig, we create 4 clusters: {C1: white-male, C2: not-white-male, C3: female-lighthair, C4: female-darkhair}. We call this dataset PubFig-personalized. We used category level ground truth annotations to find the people that satisfy the various definitions. A total of 38 categories (people) satisfied atleast one of the cluster definitions. We used 15 images for each person resulting in 570 images total. For Shoes, the GT has the following configuration {C1: Athletic shoes-Sneakers, C2: Boots-Rainboots, C3: Clogs-Flats, C4: High Heels-Pumps-Stiletto}. We call this Shoes-personalized and it consists of 450 images covering 9 basic categories.

Results on Shoes-personalized and PubFig-personalized are shown in Fig 4. Our approach significantly outperforms all baselines in both the datasets. This shows the power of our approach in allowing users to more effectively inject their preferences in semi-supervised clustering algorithms as compared to existing approaches. Other trends like soft baseline performing better than hard, max-entropy better than random, etc. are observed in personalized clustering as well. Especially with PubFig-personalized, the results are exceptionally good. This may be because the clusters were created from attribute-based definitions. Note however that it is quite natural for humans to visualize groups or clusters based on certain attributes. Our approach can be used for organizing collections of personal photos or shopping products for efficient browsing and retrieval.

6   Conclusion

We presented an interactive approach for augmenting semi-supervised clustering approaches with attribute-based explanations. Using such a rich mode of communication, a user can convey his clustering criterion to the machine without having to annotate a large number of pairs of images. The clustering criterion can be domain knowledge which can be provided by a crowd, or it can be user preferences. We showed that by providing attribute-based explanations, the machine can get significant gains in clustering quality. We showed the generality of our approach by incorporating the attribute-based explanations in three diverse semi-supervised clustering algorithms, using both binary and relative attributes, in three different domains. Future work involves discovering a vocabulary of attributes simultaneously while clustering images and learning attribute models on-the-fly instead of using pre-trained attribute predictors.

Acknowledgements. This work was supported in part by a Google Faculty Research Award to DP.

References

1. Wagstaff, K., Cardie, C., Rogers, S., Schroedl, S.: Constrained k-means clustering with background knowledge. In: ICML, pp. 577–584. Morgan Kaufmann (2001)
2. Bilenko, M., Basu, S., Mooney, R.J.: Integrating constraints and metric learning in semi-supervised clustering. In: Proceedings of the Twenty-First International Conference on Machine Learning, ICML 2004. ACM, New York (2004)
3. Kulis, B., Basu, S., Dhillon, I., Mooney, R.: Semi-supervised graph clustering: a kernel approach. Machine Learning 74(1), 1–22 (2009)
4. Yi, J., Zhang, L., Jin, R., Qian, Q., Jain, A.: Semi-supervised clustering by input pattern assisted pairwise similarity matrix completion. In: Dasgupta, S., Mcallester, D. (eds.) Proceedings of the 30th International Conference on Machine Learning (ICML 2013), May 2013. JMLR Workshop and Conference Proceedings, vol. 28, pp. 1400–1408 (May 2013)
5. Xing, E.P., Ng, A.Y., Jordan, M.I., Russell, S.: Distance metric learning, with application to clustering with side-information. In: Advances in Neural Information Processing Systems, vol. 15, pp. 505–512. MIT Press (2003)
6. Davis, J.V., Kulis, B., Jain, P., Sra, S., Dhillon, I.S.: Information-theoretic metric learning. In: Proceedings of the 24th International Conference on Machine Learning, ICML 2007, pp. 209–216. ACM, New York (2007)

7. Weinberger, K.Q., Saul, L.K.: Distance metric learning for large margin nearest neighbor classification. J. Mach. Learn. Res. 10, 207–244 (2009)
8. Yi, J., Jin, R., Jain, A., Jain, S., Yang, T.: Semi-crowdsourced clustering: Generalizing crowd labeling by robust distance metric learning. In: Advances in Neural Information Processing Systems (NIPS), pp. 1781–1789 (2012)
9. Biswas, A., Jacobs, D.W.: Active image clustering: Seeking constraints from humans to complement algorithms. In: CVPR, pp. 2152–2159. IEEE (2012)
10. Basu, S., Banjeree, A., Mooney, E., Banerjee, A., Mooney, R.J.: Active semi-supervision for pairwise constrained clustering. In: Proceedings of the 2004 SIAM International Conference on Data Mining (SDM 2004), pp. 333–344 (2004)
11. Wauthier, F.L., Jojic, N., Jordan, M.I.: Active spectral clustering via iterative uncertainty reduction. In: Proceedings of the 18th ACM SIGKDD International Conference on Knowledge Discovery and Data Mining, KDD 2012, pp. 1339–1347. ACM, New York (2012)
12. Parikh, D., Grauman, K.: Relative attributes. In: ICCV (2011)
13. Kumar, N., Berg, A., Belhumeur, P., Nayar, S.: Attribute and simile classifiers for face verification. In: ICCV (2009)
14. Lampert, C., Nickisch, H., Harmeling, S.: Learning to detect unseen object classes by between-class attribute transfer. In: CVPR (2009)
15. Shrivastava, A., Singh, S., Gupta, A.: Constrained semi-supervised learning using attributes and comparative attributes. In: Fitzgibbon, A., Lazebnik, S., Perona, P., Sato, Y., Schmid, C. (eds.) ECCV 2012, Part III. LNCS, vol. 7574, pp. 369–383. Springer, Heidelberg (2012)
16. Kovashka, A., Parikh, D., Grauman, K.: Whittlesearch: Image search with attribute feedback. In: CVPR (2012)
17. Kumar, N., Belhumeur, P., Nayar, S.: FaceTracer: A search engine for large collections of images with faces. In: Forsyth, D., Torr, P., Zisserman, A. (eds.) ECCV 2008, Part IV. LNCS, vol. 5305, pp. 340–353. Springer, Heidelberg (2008)
18. Parkash, A., Parikh, D.: Attributes for classifier feedback. In: Fitzgibbon, A., Lazebnik, S., Perona, P., Sato, Y., Schmid, C. (eds.) ECCV 2012, Part III. LNCS, vol. 7574, pp. 354–368. Springer, Heidelberg (2012)
19. Donahue, J., Grauman, K.: Annotator rationales for visual recognition. In: ICCV (2011)
20. Ng, A.Y., Jordan, M.I., Weiss, Y.: On spectral clustering: Analysis and an algorithm. In: Advances in Neural Information Processing Systems, pp. 849–856. MIT Press (2001)
21. Xiao, J., Hays, J., Ehinger, K., Oliva, A., Torralba, A.: Sun database: Large-scale scene recognition from abbey to zoo. In: CVPR (2010)
22. Berg, T.L., Berg, A.C., Shih, J.: Automatic attribute discovery and characterization from noisy web data. In: Daniilidis, K., Maragos, P., Paragios, N. (eds.) ECCV 2010, Part I. LNCS, vol. 6311, pp. 663–676. Springer, Heidelberg (2010)
23. Farhadi, A., Endres, I., Hoiem, D., Forsyth, D.: Describing objects by their attributes. In: CVPR (2009)
24. Ferrari, V., Zisserman, A.: Learning visual attributes. In: NIPS (2007)
25. Branson, S., Wah, C., Schroff, F., Babenko, B., Welinder, P., Perona, P., Belongie, S.: Visual recognition with humans in the loop. In: Daniilidis, K., Maragos, P., Paragios, N. (eds.) ECCV 2010, Part IV. LNCS, vol. 6314, pp. 438–451. Springer, Heidelberg (2010)
26. Farhadi, A., Endres, I., Hoiem, D.: Attribute-centric recognition for cross-category generalization. In: CVPR (2010)

27. Rastegari, M., Farhadi, A., Forsyth, D.: Attribute discovery via predictable discriminative binary codes. In: Fitzgibbon, A., Lazebnik, S., Perona, P., Sato, Y., Schmid, C. (eds.) ECCV 2012, Part VI. LNCS, vol. 7577, pp. 876–889. Springer, Heidelberg (2012)
28. Parikh, D., Grauman, K.: Interactively building a discriminative vocabulary of nameable attributes. In: CVPR, pp. 1681–1688. IEEE (2011)
29. Parikh, D., Kovashka, A., Grauman, K.: Whittlesearch: Image search with relative attribute feedback. In: 2013 IEEE Conference on Computer Vision and Pattern Recognition, pp. 2973–2980 (2012)
30. Gomes, R.G., Welinder, P., Krause, A., Perona, P.: Crowdclustering. In: Shawe-Taylor, J., Zemel, R., Bartlett, P., Pereira, F., Weinberger, K. (eds.) Advances in Neural Information Processing Systems, vol. 24, pp. 558–566 (2011)
31. Tamuz, O., Liu, C., Belongie, S., Shamir, O., Kalai, A.T.: Adaptively learning the crowd kernel. CoRR abs/1105.1033 (2011)
32. Kamvar, S.D., Klein, D., Manning, C.D.: Spectral learning. In: IJCAI, pp. 561–566 (2003)
33. Joshi, A.J., Porikli, F., Papanikolopoulos, N.: Multi-class active learning for image classification. In: CVPR, pp. 2372–2379. IEEE (2009)
34. Patterson, G., Hays, J.: Sun attribute database: Discovering, annotating, and recognizing scene attributes. In: CVPR (2012)
35. Oliva, A., Torralba, A.: Modeling the shape of the scene: A holistic representation of the spatial envelope. IJCV (2001)
36. Bosch, A., Zisserman, A., Munoz, X.: Representing shape with a spatial pyramid kernel. In: Proceedings of the 6th ACM International Conference on Image and Video Retrieval, CIVR 2007, pp. 401–408. ACM, New York (2007)

Attributes Make Sense on Segmented Objects

Zhenyang Li, Efstratios Gavves, Thomas Mensink, and Cees G.M. Snoek

ISLA, Informatics Institute, University of Amsterdam, The Netherlands

Abstract. In this paper we aim for object classification *and* segmentation by attributes. Where existing work considers attributes either for the global image or for the parts of the object, we propose, as our first novelty, to learn and extract attributes on segments containing the entire object. Object-level attributes suffer less from accidental content around the object and accidental image conditions such as partial occlusions, scale changes and viewpoint changes. As our second novelty, we propose joint learning for simultaneous object classification and segment proposal ranking, solely on the basis of attributes. This naturally brings us to our third novelty: object-level attributes for zero-shot, where we use attribute descriptions of unseen classes for localizing their instances in new images and classifying them accordingly. Results on the Caltech UCSD Birds, Leeds Butterflies, and an a-Pascal subset demonstrate that *i)* extracting attributes on oracle object-level brings substantial benefits *ii)* our joint learning model leads to accurate attribute-based classification and segmentation, approaching the oracle results and *iii)* object-level attributes also allow for zero-shot classification and segmentation. We conclude that attributes make sense on segmented objects.

Keywords: attributes, segmentation, zero-shot classification.

1 Introduction

The goal of this paper is object classification *and* segmentation using attributes. Representing an image by attributes [17, 19, 25] like *big ear*, *trunk*, and *gray color* is appealing when examples are rare or non-existent, feature encodings are non-discriminative, or a semantic interpretation of the representation is desired. Consequently, attributes are a promising solution for fine-grained and zero-shot object classification [7], personalized object search [23], object description [17], and many other current challenges in computer vision. Different from existing work, which computes object attributes either on the entire image [1, 25, 28] or on parts of the object [6, 14, 19], we propose to predict the best possible segment that contains the entire object and compute all attributes on this segment.

One approach to object classification by attributes is to compute the attributes globally; see Fig. 1a. Lampert *et al.* [25] introduce a directed graphical attribute model for the recognition of animal categories, even in the absence of training examples, which is called zero-shot classification. Since their model optimizes attribute prediction, and not object classification, Akata *et al.* [1] adapt the model of [39] and propose attribute embedding learning for supervised

D. Fleet et al. (Eds.): ECCV 2014, Part VI, LNCS 8694, pp. 350–365, 2014.

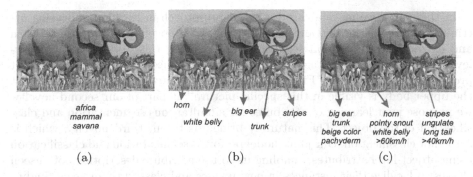

africa
mammal
savana

(a)

horn
white belly

big ear
trunk

stripes

(b)

big ear
trunk
beige color
pachyderm

horn
pointy snout
white belly
>60km/h

stripes
ungulate
long tail
>40km/h

(c)

Fig. 1. Attributes make sense on segmented objects. Illustration of different level of attributes, in a picture showing several animals: antelopes, an elephant, and a small zebra to the right of the elephant. (a) Considering the full image, one can only expect to describe generic attributes that apply to the whole scene. (b) When localizing attributes, one faces the problem that not all attributes can be localized. Partial occlusions, small scales, or uncommon viewpoints might reduce the visibility of a particular attribute. Moreover, several class-specific attributes are very hard to localize in practice. (c) We propose to constrain object-specific attributes on segmented objects, which allows for object-specific description and suppresses irrelevant background signal.

and zero-shot object classification. Inspired by Akata *et al.*, we also optimize attribute learning for object classification, including the challenging zero-shot setting. However, we observe that attributes most often reflect object level properties, *e.g.*, that an antelope has a *pointy snout*. Hence, considering the whole image as indicative of the attribute *pointy snout* is counter-intuitive.

The second approach to object classification by attributes focuses on localizing salient parts reflecting those attributes; see Fig. 1b. Ferrari and Zisserman [19] propose local attributes in superpixels and use them for attribute classification in novel images. Similarly, Bourdev *et al.* [6] localize attributes by employing part-based poselet responses, *e.g.*, cropped images of people *wearing hats*. These approaches assume that humans should provide the annotations for existing, pre-defined attributes. For this reason Duan *et al.* [14] propose to discover discriminative and localized attributes which have to be nameable and approved by humans. Jia *et al.* [13] and Wah *et al.* [36] also propose to build interactive systems to discover and localize attributes with humans in the loop. Generally speaking, pinpointing to certain image or object locations allows for finer definition of attributes. However, such methods appear to face certain limitations. For one, challenging image conditions, such as partial occlusion, small scales, or uncommon viewpoints make certain attribute locations visually unidentifiable. Second, certain object attributes simply cannot be localized. For example, localizing the attribute of an elephant being a *pachyderm* is impossible. Hence, an overly precise localization of attributes is often not needed, as attributes could be locally untraceable, either due to their nature or the imaging circumstances.

In this paper we make a case for a third approach in learning and using attributes. More specifically, and as part of our first novelty, we propose to learn and extract attributes from segmented objects. For this we assume category-level attributes, since it is the class and not the instance that pertains the object properties; for example in Fig. 1c. a zebra is a *quadruped* animal, even if just the upper body is visible in this specific picture. As part of our second novelty, we propose joint learning of attributes for simultaneous segmentation and classification of the object. This naturally brings us to our third novelty, which is zero-shot classification. Our joint model performs segmentation and classification using object-level attributes, enabling us to use attribute descriptions of unseen classes to localize their instances in new images and classify them accordingly.

The paper is organized as follows. We first discuss the related work in Section 2. In Section 3 we describe our model and how we efficiently infer the segment from which we extract object-level attributes. In Section 4 we validate our models using three publicly available datasets, Caltech UCSD Birds [37], Leeds Butterflies [38], and a-Pascal [17]. We show experimental results in both a fully supervised classification setting as well as in a zero-shot classification setting. We conclude our paper in Section 5.

2   Related Work

Classification and Segmentation. Embedding locality in image representation has become increasingly popular over the recent years. Several works have shown that localizing the object of interest is beneficial, not only for providing a spatial support for the object [2, 33], but also for classifying it more accurately [11, 20, 32]. Certainly, semantic segmentation and object detection have received most of their attention from attempts at using localities for classification.

Both the state-of-the-art methodologies, for semantic segmentation and object detection, adopt a similar two-step approach. In the first step, object location proposals are extracted. For object detection, bounding box proposals [2, 27, 32] are usually computed on the basis of local region coherence. Moreover, the authors of [4, 9, 15] showed that to obtain accurate object proposals for semantic segmentation, one needs to incorporate richer local properties, as well as strong machine learning techniques, like efficient graph cuts [22]. For fine-grained recognition, in [40], a joint object detection and segmentation framework is introduced to localize objects. In [12], Chai *et al.* make use of region-level cues for discriminative co-segmentation on multiple images. Here, we opt for segmentation object proposals, as they allow for a more precise delineation of the object, thus enabling a better learning of attribute representations.

Once having object proposals, we need to classify them against a pre-defined set of object classes. For object detection [32] and semantic segmentation [3, 8], employing non-linear kernel machines [9] and state-of-the-art feature encodings, such as second-order poolers [8], Fisher vectors [26, 29] or deep learning features [21] has shown to yield excellent results. In this work our goal is to be able to perform (zero-shot) object classification *and* segmentation. Therefore, we depart from the above works and proceed with the classification and segmentation of objects solely on the basis of attributes, as the use of low-level features [3, 8, 9, 21, 26] would prohibit us from detecting the unseen classes.

Label and Attribute Embedding. As attributes were originally designed for describing objects, the learned attributes are not necessarily optimal for classifying (novel) objects. For this reason Akata *et al.* [1] propose to embed class label in the space of attributes and use the WSABIE [39] learning criterion, adapted for attribute learning. This method optimizes the attribute learning directly for object classification instead of attribute prediction. Our major difference with [1] is that we look for the best possible segment, while predicting the label of an unseen image. The segments, which we search, are integrated as latent variables in our empirical risk function. From a theoretical standpoint, instead of considering a fixed margin equal to 1, we minimize our max-margin empirical risk over both the class label as well as the segmentation quality. This learning methodology allows for learning of high quality segments.

Efficient Region Computations. As semantic segmentation and object detection entail a great number of free variables, direct optimization of attribute models on a per segment basis results in a severe computational bottleneck. For this reason there have been several methodologies proposed in the literature for efficiently computing classification scores from multiple image regions. In [24] Lampert *et al.* employ a branch and bound optimization scheme for visiting several thousands of bounding box locations efficiently. Relaxing the constraints for a bounding box geometry, Vijayanarasimhan and Grauman [35] propose a similar optimization scheme for arbitrary, free form regions in an image. Yet, both these methods do not consider any efficient normalization of the representations, as that would render their methods highly inefficient. For this reasons Li *et al.* [26] propose codemaps, which allows for efficient, accurate and normalized region-level representations by reordering the encoding, pooling and classification steps over superpixels. In this work we make use of the codemaps framework.

Structured SVMs and Latent SVMs. In the current work the main focus is multi-class classification, while using the best object segment proposal for each class. Since the segment proposals are not explicitly evaluated, we treat them as latent variables of our model, a formulation that resembles latent SVM [18]. Moreover, we use margin rescaling of structured SVMs [31] to include a penalty for segment proposals with a low-overlap with the ground-truth segment. The penalty function is based on the intersection over union criterion, also used in structured output regression [5, 9].

Different from structured output regression our final objective is (zero-shot) multi-class classification, and not a structured output containing the best segment for each class label. Hence, our structured loss is built around mid-level attribute representations, which also need to be optimized for. For this reason we follow [1, 39] and employ an embedding function with a ranking objective instead of a multi-class SVM objective function. In this model the latent segment variables help to learn better attributes and attributes help to improve segmentation.

3   Object-Level Attributes

Given an image x, our classification function f is defined as follows:

$$f(x) = \arg\max_{y \in \mathcal{Y}} \max_{z \in Z(x)} F(z, y), \tag{1}$$

where z is a latent variable, $Z(x)$ indicates a set of segment proposals for image x, and $F(z, y)$ a compatibility function between segment z and label y. Intuitively, this function first finds the best scoring segment $z \in Z(x)$, for each class y. Then, the class $y \in \mathcal{Y}$ with the highest score is returned as a prediction. Note that we do not assume the object bounding box or object segmentation is known at prediction time. Instead the object segmentation is inferred as a latent variable given the image.

We describe attribute embedding in Section 3.1 and our learning objective in Section 3.2. In Section 3.3 we discuss how segment proposals are obtained and how Eq. 1 can be evaluated efficiently, using codemaps [26].

3.1   Attribute Embedding

We follow the label and attribute embedding approaches from [1,39], where each class label y is embedded in the m-dimensional space of attributes by $\phi(y) \in \mathbb{R}^m$. While [1, 39] embed the full image features, we embed the visual features of a segment z only. Let $\theta(z) \in \mathbb{R}^d$ be the embedding of segment z yielding a d-dimensional feature vector. In this work we use the state-of-the-art Fisher vector framework [29] for this visual embedding.

In our model, $F(z, y)$ measures the compatibility between segment z and the embedding of class y. This compatibility function is defined as:

$$F(z, y; W, \phi) = \theta(z)' W \phi(y), \tag{2}$$

where $W \in \mathbb{R}^{d \times m}$ is the model parameter matrix, which we need to learn.

We stack the attribute embeddings of each class $\phi(y)$ into an embedding matrix Φ for all classes. In the fully supervised setting, where visual examples for each class are provided, we also learn the class-to-attribute embedding Φ, similar to WSABIE [39]. In the case of zero-shot classification, we use the fixed attribute-to-class mapping $\Phi = \Phi^A$, which resembles ALE [1].

3.2 Learning

For training we assume a collection of images $\{(x_i, y_i, z_i)\}_{i=1}^N$, in which each image x_i has a ground truth label y_i and a ground truth object segment z_i. Furthermore, we assume that there exists a mapping from attributes to classes Φ^A, which defines the relevant attributes for each class. The goal is to learn the model parameters W and the mapping Φ to minimize the prediction errors, while selecting object segments of better quality. For learning we employ structured risk minimization, using a ranking objective built upon [1,5,39].

The loss function of a ground-truth image/label/segment triplet (x_i, y_i, z_i) for a prediction label y, is defined as:

$$\ell(y, z_i, y_i, x_i) = \max_{z \in Z(x_i)} \Delta(z, y, y_i, z_i) + F(z, y) - F(z_i, y_i). \tag{3}$$

The Δ function, which determines the margin, is defined as:

$$\Delta(z, y, z_i, y_i) = \begin{cases} 1 - O(z, z_i) & \text{if } y = y_i, \\ 1 & \text{otherwise,} \end{cases} \tag{4}$$

where $O(z, z_i)$ is the intersection over union between the selected segment z and the ground-truth segment z_i, similar to [5]. This margin re-scaling function enforces a margin of 1 if the label y and y_i do not match. When the labels do match, the margin is determined by the area of overlap between the segment z and the ground-truth segment z_i.

The following objective is used as the data term in the empirical risk:

$$R(W, \Phi) = \frac{1}{N} \sum_{i=1}^N \gamma(k_i) \sum_{y \in \mathcal{Y}} [\ell(y, z_i, y_i, x_i)]_+, \tag{5}$$

where k_i is an upper-bound on the rank of the correct label, γ transforms this rank into a weight, and where $[\cdot]_+ = \max(0, \cdot)$. The upper-bound on the rank is computed as the number of loss-generating labels:

$$k_i = \sum_{y \in \mathcal{Y}} [\![\ell(y, z_i, y_i, x_i) > 0]\!] \tag{6}$$

where, we use Iversons bracket notation to denote $[\![\cdot]\!] = 1$ if the condition is true, and 0 otherwise. Following [34], we define the rank to weight function as $\gamma(k) = \frac{1}{k} \sum_{j=1}^k \alpha_j$, using $\alpha_j = \frac{1}{j}$.

When applied on the entire image, i.e., when Eq. 3 is defined as $\ell(y, y_i, x_i) = \Delta(y, y_i) + F(x_i, y) - F(x_i, y_i)$, our objective function is identical to WSABIE/ALE.

Fully Supervised Learning. In the fully supervised case, where we have visual examples from all classes, we minimize the following regularized risk objective:

$$\min_{W, \Phi} \frac{\lambda}{2} ||W||^2 + \frac{\mu}{2} ||\Phi - \Phi^A||^2 + R(W, \Phi), \tag{7}$$

where λ and μ are trade-off parameters between the data term and the regularization, which we set using cross-validation. Regularizing towards the pre-defined class-to-attribute encoding $(\Phi - \Phi^A)$ allows us to exploit this high-level semantic prior. This could be particularly beneficial in the case when just a few examples per class are available.

Zero-Shot Classification. In the setting of zero-shot classification, visual training examples are given only for a subset of the classes, while evaluation is performed on a disjoint set of the classes. In this case the attribute embedding is fixed to the existing mapping $\Phi = \Phi^A$, and Eq. 7 reduces to:

$$\min_W \frac{\lambda}{2}||W||^2 + R(W, \Phi^A), \tag{8}$$

where λ is a trade-off parameter, which we set using cross-validation using a hold-out set of images from the known train classes.

3.3   Efficient Maximization

The main computational challenge of our method is efficiently solving Eq. 1 and Eq. 3 during training and evaluation. The number of possible segmentations in an image grows exponentially with the size of an image. To solve this problem efficiently we follow [26].

For each image, we start by extracting a set of superpixels S from an image, typically using $|S| \approx 500$. We then use a segment proposal algorithm, the off the shelve CPMC-algorithm [10], to obtain a set of approximately $1,000$ segments $Z(x)$. Even so, the maximization in Eq. 1 and Eq. 3 over such a large set of segments during training and evaluation remains expensive, especially for the high-dimensional visual embeddings we are using.

Since the visual embeddings are based on a sum-pooling operator of local image features, and since F (Eq. 2) is comprised of two linear components W and ϕ, we have:

$$\max_{z \in Z(x)} F(z, y) = \max_{z \in Z(x)} \sum_{s \in S(z)} F(s, y) = \max_{z \in Z(x)} \frac{1}{L_z} \sum_{s \in S(z)} \theta(s)'W\phi(y), \tag{9}$$

where $S(z)$ correspond to the set of superpixels in segment z and L_z is the ℓ_2-norm of the feature embedding of z. The decomposition over superpixels allows for on-the-fly calculations of the feature embeddings for all segments. For a given W and ϕ, the compatibility function $F(s, y)$ can be precomputed, and the maximization over segments boils down to just look-ups and summations.

At training time, the computational efficiency comes at the cost of higher memory requirements, as we need to maintain the feature embeddings for all superpixels per image. However, at test time both the computational and memory complexity are very low.

4 Experiments

4.1 Datasets and Experimental Setup

CUB-2011 Birds. We conduct our main experiments on the Caltech UCSD Birds 2011 dataset [37], as it fulfills three requirements. First, this dataset contains an extensive array of object categories that are visually difficult to distinguish. Second, the CUB-2011 dataset enjoys a detailed annotation of 312 human-understandable attributes, *e.g.,* whether a bird has a *striped wing* or a *curved beak.* Last, this dataset contains localization information in the form of segmentation masks. For the CUB-2011 dataset we use the standard training and test splits, without mirroring the training images. We use the provided segmentations only during training, unless stated otherwise. To obtain a mapping from attributes to classes we binarize the continuous attributes provided in the dataset; attributes are considered relevant for a class if their confidence is above the average confidence value of that attribute.

Butterflies. As a second dataset, we use a modification of the Leeds Butterfly Dataset [38]. This is a fine-grained multi-class dataset containing images and segmentation masks of ten butterfly species. We automatically transform the provided textual descriptions into a set of 20 attributes, mostly describing the color patterns of the butterflies, and automatically generate an attribute-to-class mapping. We also obtain the ground truth bounding boxes by automatically enclosing a bounding box around each segmentation mask. The dataset contains 620 images for training and 212 for testing.

a-Pascal++. As a third dataset, we use a modification of the a-Pascal [17] dataset, which we coin a-Pascal++. Our dataset combines the 64 attributes annotated for the a-Pascal dataset with the segmentation masks from the VOC Pascal Challenge [16]. Since the focus of our work is not segmentation inference, but segmentation-based classification, we select the images containing a single object. This makes a-Pascal++ a multi-class dataset with 20 classes, 64 attributes and segmentation masks, we use 1,429 images for training and 203 for testing. Note that the original a-Pascal dataset was used for describing attributes given objects [17], the bounding box object locations were available both during training and testing. In our work, we provide segmentation masks only at train time, at test time the object-level attributes are inferred.

Visual features. For the visual representation we follow the Fisher vector framework [29], computed on dense RGB-SIFT features [30] extracted every 2 pixels and at multiple scales, and projected to 80 dimensions using PCA. We experiment with different codebook sizes, and indicate the number of mixture components k used with each experiment. For the full image representation we use the Fisher vector with power-normalization and ℓ_2-normalization [29], while for the segment representation we use the ℓ_2-normalized Fisher codemaps [26]. For obtaining object segment proposals we use the off-the-shelf CPMC [10], which we approximate with the superpixels from [4].

Training. To train our models, we rely on stochastic gradient descent of the objective functions Eq. 7 and Eq. 8. We validate the regularization parameters and number of iterations on a subset of the train set, and re-train using these parameters on the whole train set. All experiments using the full image embedding are trained using the WSABIE/ALE objective, which equals to Eq. 7 and Eq. 8, when the full image is the only segment of an image.

Evaluation. We use three measures for evaluation. First, we use the *mean class accuracy* (MCA), where for each class the top-1 accuracy is computed and averaged over all classes. Second, we use the *mean class accuracy over correctly segmented objects* (MSO). MSO is computed similar to MCA, except that a prediction is considered correct only if both the label is correct and the overlap of the latent segment with the ground-truth segmentation meets the Pascal VOC criterion. This criterion requires that the intersection over the union (IoU) of the two segments is greater than 50%. In a similar vein, we use the *average overlap* (AO) to evaluate the quality of the inferred latent segments, disregarding the class label prediction.

4.2   Object-Level Attributes on Oracle Segments

In the first experiment we want to establish whether attributes on object segments are beneficial for object classification. To this end we design an oracle experiment, where we compare a full image feature embedding to using an embedding of visual features describing an oracle provided bounding box or segment. For all the three datasets, the oracle provides perfect object bounding boxes and segmentation masks, both during training and testing. The obtained accuracy on this experiment will not reflect reality, however it provides insight in the effectiveness of our proposed object-level attributes. We compare the Fisher vector embedding of the full image to the Fisher vector embedding of the oracle bounding box/segment, which we train with the ALE framework [1]. We present the aggregated results in Table 1.

As a preliminary, we note that our 40K Fisher vector (k=256) performs on par with the 64K Fisher vector used in [1], where 20.5% MCA is reported when evaluating ALE on the CUB-2011 Birds dataset. We observe that by using oracle object segments we obtain up to an absolute 31.5% accuracy increase. This improvement seems to be consistent over different datasets, each depicting different characteristics in the number of images, number of classes and visual relatedness among the classes. It is interesting to note that the improvement in accuracy is consistent across all categories (data not shown), and for various numbers of mixture components. Using oracle segments is also consistently better than using oracle bounding boxes, since bounding boxes inevitably include some background which may not depict the objects and thus the attributes. Having obtained evidence that extracting attributes on object-level helps, we proceed with the latent segments.

Table 1. Object-level attributes on oracle segments. We compare the performance of ALE [1] using full image embeddings with oracle bounding box/segment embeddings. By using oracle object-level attributes the classification accuracy increases substantially. Although these numbers are only theoretical, they serve as an upper bound of the classification accuracy that we may obtain.

Dataset	Codebook	Entire image MCA	Oracle bbox MCA	Oracle segment MCA
CUB-2011	$k = 16$	13.8	25.8	43.9
	$k = 256$	21.4	36.4	52.9
Butterflies	$k = 16$	83.8	96.9	99.1
a-Pascal++	$k = 256$	30.6	33.6	40.2

Table 2. Object-level attributes on latent segments. Object-level attributes optimized with our joint learning are up to around 4-21% more accurate than computing attributes on the full images. Note that for a larger number of mixture components accurate prediction also entails accurate segmentation.

Dataset	Codebook	Entire image MCA	Object-level attributes MCA	MSO	AO
CUB-2011	$k = 16$	13.8	35.2	29.9	60.5
	$k = 256$	21.4	39.2	35.5	66.3
Butterflies	$k = 16$	83.8	96.4	95.5	84.6
a-Pascal++	$k = 256$	30.6	35.0	24.7	48.2

4.3   Object-Level Attributes on Latent Segments

In the second experiment we evaluate the ability to infer the object segment as a latent variable in the model and to classify the segmented objects using attributes. During testing of a given image, our model is able to simultaneously predict the most likely label for the object and its respective segmentation mask.

We present the aggregated results in Table 2. We observe that our joint learning returns highly accurate results, as we improve over the full image results of [1] by around 4-21%. Note that the accuracy of the joint learning is reasonably close to the accuracy when using oracle segments, indicating that the returned segmentations are quite accurate. Moreover, we observe that for a larger codebook the discrepancy between accurate prediction and accurate prediction with accurate segmentation is smaller. Hence, a larger codebook is able to better suppress the background signal, thus returning simultaneously both accurate classifications and segmentations.

Fig. 2. Example classification and segmentation results using object-level attributes on latent segments. The segmentation masks are green-colored for correct label prediction and red-colored for wrong label prediction. The purple-colored ones indciate correct label predcition, but with low segmentation accuracy (IoU<0.5). It is noteworthy that even if the objects are labeled incorrectly, the selected segmentation masks are often very accurate.

In Fig. 2 we provide some illustrative examples of our classification and segmentation results. We make three observations. First, the predicted segments look in general of high quality. Second, even if the object segmentation does not meet the Pascal criterion, it often contains sufficient class specific information, for example the second column in Fig. 2. Third, even in the case when the predicted label is incorrect the segmentation is still focused on the object, see the third column in Fig. 2.

In Fig. 3a we present a comparison of the individual class accuracies between two methods. We observe that learning object-level attributes on latent segments brings a consistent improvement to almost all the classes. Last, we

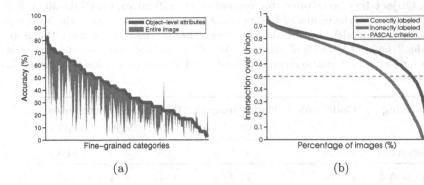

Fig. 3. Object-level attributes on latent segments. (a) Object-level attributes are consistently better than learning attributes on the entire image for almost all the classes. (b) The joint learning discovers segments that meet the PASCAL criterion for about 91% of the correctly labeled images and for about 75% of the incorrectly labeled images. Results computed on *CUB-2011* with $k=256$.

illustrate in Fig. 3b the quality of segmentations for both the correctly and incorrectly predicted objects. We observe that for the vast majority the quality of segmentations is quite high. We discover segments that meet the PASCAL criterion for about 91% of the correctly labelled images and for about 75% of the incorrectly labelled images. Therefore, our joint learning allows for a precise localization of objects.

Comparison with part-localized attributes. To compare our approach with a recent part-localized attribute model, we also conduct an experiment on a subset of CUB-2011: five categories consisting of different species of warblers. We follow the same experimental protocol as [14]. Our model of learning object-level attributes on latent segments scores 65.8% accuracy using a codebook of mixture components k=16, using full image embedding scores 42.2%, while the localized attribute model [14] reports ∼55%.

We conclude that the joint learning of object-level attributes with a segmentation model leads to accurate attribute-based classification.

4.4 Object-Level Attributes for Zero-Shot

In the third experiment we take advantage of the fact that our object-level attributes can be shared among classes. As a result, assuming that one is provided with an attribute-to-class mapping, one can perform zero-shot classification, which allows for simultaneous classification and segmentation of the object of interest. We experiment on the CUB-2011 dataset, using the same 150 train classes and 50 test classes as in [1].

We present the numerical results in Table 3. We observe that our approach improves the zero-shot classification accuracy, while returning the location of objects that belong to classes we have not seen before. For fair comparison with

Table 3. Object-level attributes for zero-shot classification on CUB-2011. For fair comparison with the results of the supervised experiment, we report the accuracy of the supervised model also for the 50 classes that we used for testing the zero-shot model. The joint learning of attributes is able to not only improve the zero-shot classification accuracy, but also return the location of objects that belong to previously unseen classes.

Setting	Codebook	Entire image	Object-level attributes		
		MCA	MCA	MSO	AO
Supervised	$k = 16$	27.1	51.5	43.0	61.8
Zero-shot	$k = 16$	11.3	15.7	12.4	56.3

White Eyed Vireo

Pred: White Eyed Vireo
Attri: has owl-like shape, brown eye, multi-colored tail, oil bill, rufous nape
IoU: 0.83

Northern Waterthrush

Pred: Northern Waterthrush
Attri: has orange eye, striped head, squared tail, spotted breast, buff throat
IoU: 0.68

Groove Billed Ani

Pred: Groove Billed Ani
Attri: has solid back, solid belly, upland-ground-like shape, rounded tail, black wing
IoU: 0.83

Western Gull

Pred: Western Gull
Attri: white back, white wing, white upperparts, duck-like shape, white under tail
IoU: 0.46

Belted Kingfisher

Pred: Acadian Flycatcher
Attri: has gray primary color, solid back, multi-colored breast, red leg, multi-colored belly
IoU: 0.56

Grasshopper Sparrow

Pred: Great Crested Flycatcher
Attri: has striped wing, striped back, solid belly, grey leg, striped head
IoU: 0.77

Fig. 4. Example results using object-level attributes for zero-shot classification and segmentation. Note that although we have not seen examples of these classes, the label predictions and the segmentations are reasonable.

the results of the supervised experiment, we report the accuracy of the supervised model also for the 50 classes that we used for evaluating the zero-shot model.

In Fig. 4 we present some visual examples of zero-shot classification and segmentation, together with the highest scoring attributes for the respective images, found after computing the contribution of each attribute to the final classification score of each respective image. Although at training time there were no examples of the classes on which we test, we are able to obtain satisfactory classifications and segmentations. Interestingly, the most important attributes seem relevant, even for the misclassified birds. For example, although a *Grasshopper Sparrow* was wrongly labeled as a *Great Crested Flycatcher*, the most important attributes fit to the image, namely the bird has a *striped wing*, a *striped back* and a *solid belly*.

We conclude that object-level attributes also make sense for zero-shot.

5   Conclusions

In this paper we revisit attribute-based representations, approaching them from the perspective of locality. To this end we have introduced object-level attributes, which are trained on segmented images with attribute descriptions. At test time, the object segmentation is treated as a latent variable, which is inferred. As part of our first contribution, we make the observation that attributes usually refer to visual properties of object classes not of an object instance, *e.g.,* whether a bird has a *curved beak* or an airplane has a *jet engine*. Using oracle object-level attributes we have experimentally shown on three different datasets that, indeed, localizing attributes leads to an impressive increase in accuracy. As a second contribution, we have proposed a joint learning framework, learning attribute embeddings while improving object segmentations using a max-margin ranking objective. The experimental results show that our learning framework yields classification accuracies which are two- to three-fold better in attribute-based classification, compared to using full image features. Moreover, we can also return high quality segmentations. Finally, we have applied object-level attributes to the task of zero-shot classification on the CUB-2011 bird dataset. In this setting, we infer class predictions and segmentation masks from bird classes for which no training data was available. The experimental results show that object-level attributes, also in the zero-shot setting, improve accuracy significantly. We therefore conclude that attributes make sense on segmented objects.

Acknowledgments. This research is supported by the STW STORY project and the Dutch national program COMMIT.

References

1. Akata, Z., Perronnin, F., Harchaoui, Z., Schmid, C.: Label-embedding for attribute-based classification. In: CVPR (2013)
2. Alexe, B., Deselaers, T., Ferrari, V.: Measuring the objectness of image windows. TPAMI (2012)
3. Arbelaez, P., Hariharan, B., Gu, C., Gupta, S., Bourdev, L., Malik, J.: Semantic segmentation using regions and parts. In: CVPR (2012)
4. Arbelaez, P., Maire, M., Fowlkes, C., Malik, J.: From contours to regions: An empirical evaluation. In: CVPR (2009)

5. Blaschko, M.B., Lampert, C.H.: Learning to localize objects with structured output regression. In: Forsyth, D., Torr, P., Zisserman, A. (eds.) ECCV 2008, Part I. LNCS, vol. 5302, pp. 2–15. Springer, Heidelberg (2008)
6. Bourdev, L., Maji, S., Malik, J.: Describing people: A poselet-based approach to attribute classification. In: ICCV (2011)
7. Branson, S., Wah, C., Schroff, F., Babenko, B., Welinder, P., Perona, P., Belongie, S.: Visual recognition with humans in the loop. In: Daniilidis, K., Maragos, P., Paragios, N. (eds.) ECCV 2010, Part IV. LNCS, vol. 6314, pp. 438–451. Springer, Heidelberg (2010)
8. Carreira, J., Caseiro, R., Batista, J., Sminchisescu, C.: Semantic segmentation with second-order pooling. In: Fitzgibbon, A., Lazebnik, S., Perona, P., Sato, Y., Schmid, C. (eds.) ECCV 2012, Part VII. LNCS, vol. 7578, pp. 430–443. Springer, Heidelberg (2012)
9. Carreira, J., Li, F., Sminchisescu, C.: Object recognition by sequential figure-ground ranking. IJCV (2012)
10. Carreira, J., Sminchisescu, C.: CPMC: Automatic object segmentation using constrained parametric min-cuts. TPAMI (2012)
11. Chai, Y., Lempitsky, V., Zisserman, A.: BiCoS: A bi-level co-segmentation method for image classification. In: ICCV (2011)
12. Chai, Y., Rahtu, E., Lempitsky, V., Van Gool, L., Zisserman, A.: TriCoS: A tri-level class-discriminative co-segmentation method for image classification. In: Fitzgibbon, A., Lazebnik, S., Perona, P., Sato, Y., Schmid, C. (eds.) ECCV 2012, Part I. LNCS, vol. 7572, pp. 794–807. Springer, Heidelberg (2012)
13. Deng, J., Krause, J., Fei-Fei, L.: Fine-grained crowdsourcing for fine-grained recognition. In: CVPR (2013)
14. Duan, K., Parikh, D., Crandall, D., Grauman, K.: Discovering localized attributes for fine-grained recognition. In: CVPR (2012)
15. Endres, I., Hoiem, D.: Category-independent object proposals with diverse ranking. TPAMI (2014)
16. Everingham, M., Van Gool, L., Williams, C.K.I., Winn, J., Zisserman, A.: The pascal visual object classes (voc) challenge. IJCV (2010)
17. Farhadi, A., Endres, I., Hoiem, D., Forsyth, D.: Describing objects by their attributes. In: CVPR (2009)
18. Felzenszwalb, P., Girshick, R., McAllester, D., Ramanan, D.: Object detection with discriminatively trained part based models. TPAMI (2010)
19. Ferrari, V., Zisserman, A.: Learning visual attributes. In: NIPS (2007)
20. Gavves, E., Fernando, B., Snoek, C., Smeulders, A., Tuytelaars, T.: Fine-grained categorization by alignments. In: ICCV (2013)
21. Girshick, R., Donahue, J., Darrell, T., Malik, J.: Rich feature hierarchies for accurate object detection and semantic segmentation. In: CVPR (2014)
22. Kolmogorov, V., Zabin, R.: What energy functions can be minimized via graph cuts? TPAMI (2004)
23. Kovashka, A., Grauman, K.: Attribute adaptation for personalized image search. In: ICCV (2013)
24. Lampert, C., Blaschko, M., Hofmann, T.: Efficient subwindow search: A branch and bound framework for object localization. TPAMI (2009)
25. Lampert, C., Nickisch, H., Harmeling, S.: Attribute-based transfer learning for object categorization with zero/one training example. TPAMI (2013)
26. Li, Z., Gavves, E., van de Sande, K., Snoek, C., Smeulders, A.: Codemaps segment, classify and search objects locally. In: ICCV (2013)

27. Manen, S., Guillaumin, M., Van Gool, L.: Prime object proposals with randomized prim's algorithm. In: ICCV (2013)
28. Parikh, D., Grauman, K.: Relative attributes. In: ICCV (2011)
29. Sánchez, J., Perronnin, F., Mensink, T., Verbeek, J.: Image classification with the fisher vector: Theory and practice. IJCV (2013)
30. van de Sande, K., Gevers, T., Snoek, C.: Evaluating color descriptors for object and scene recognition. TPAMI (2010)
31. Tsochantaridis, I., Joachims, T., Hofmann, T., Altun, Y.: Large margin methods for structured and interdependent output variables (2005)
32. Uijlings, J., van de Sande, K., Gevers, T., Smeulders, A.: Selective search for object recognition. IJCV (2013)
33. Uijlings, J., Smeulders, A., Scha, R.: The visual extent of an object. IJCV (2012)
34. Usunier, N., Buffoni, D., Gallinar, P.: Ranking with ordered weighted pairwise classification. In: ICML (2009)
35. Vijayanarasimhan, S., Grauman, K.: Efficient region search for object detection. In: CVPR (2011)
36. Wah, C., Branson, S., Perona, P., Belongie, S.: Multiclass recognition and part localization with humans in the loop. In: ICCV (2011)
37. Wah, C., Branson, S., Welinder, P., Perona, P., Belongie, S.: The Caltech-UCSD Birds-200-2011 Dataset. Tech. rep. (2011)
38. Wang, J., Markert, K., Everingham, M.: Learning models for object recognition from natural language descriptions. In: BMVC (2009)
39. Weston, J., Bengio, S., Usunier, N.: WSABIE: Scaling up to large vocabulary image annotation. In: IJCAI (2011)
40. Zhu, S., Angelova, A.: Efficient object detection and segmentation for fine-grained recognition. In: CVPR (2013)

Towards Transparent Systems: Semantic Characterization of Failure Modes

Aayush Bansal[1], Ali Farhadi[2], and Devi Parikh[3]

[1] Carnegie Mellon University, Pittsburgh, USA
[2] University of Washington, Seattle, USA
[3] Virginia Tech, Blacksburg, USA

Abstract. Today's computer vision systems are not perfect. They fail frequently. Even worse, they fail abruptly and seemingly inexplicably. We argue that making our systems more transparent via an explicit human understandable characterization of their failure modes is desirable. We propose characterizing the failure modes of a vision system using semantic attributes. For example, a face recognition system may say "If the test image is blurry, or the face is not frontal, or the person to be recognized is a young white woman with heavy make up, I am likely to fail." This information can be used at training time by researchers to design better features, models or collect more focused training data. It can also be used by a downstream machine or human user at test time to know when to ignore the output of the system, in turn making it more reliable. To generate such a "specification sheet", we discriminatively cluster incorrectly classified images in the semantic attribute space using L1-regularized weighted logistic regression. We show that our specification sheets can predict oncoming failures for face and animal species recognition better than several strong baselines. We also show that lay people can easily follow our specification sheets.

1 Introduction

"If you tell me precisely what it is a machine cannot do, then I can always make a machine which will do just that" - John von Neumann

State-of-the-art computer vision systems are complex. In spite of their complexity, they fail frequently. And in part *due to* their complexity, they fail in *seemingly* inexplicable ways. As sophisticated image features and statistical machine learning techniques become core tools in our computer vision systems, there is an increasing desire and critical need to make our systems transparent.

Every student is different. A good teacher adapts his teaching style and the amount of time he spends on each topic to the student's strengths and weaknesses. But without knowledge of the student's misconceptions, it would be difficult for the teacher to help the student make progress. Similarly, as researchers, we can design vision solutions more effectively if we systematically understand the failure modes of our systems. Identification of recurring failure modes via manual inspection of instances where the system fails is not feasible given the

D. Fleet et al. (Eds.): ECCV 2014, Part VI, LNCS 8694, pp. 366–381, 2014.

scale of the data involved in realistic applications[1]. Automatic means of summarizing failure modes are required. These characterizations need to be semantic so humans (researchers, end users) can understand them. Semantic characterizations of failure modes of vision systems as seen in Fig. 1 would be useful at both training and testing time.

At training time, researchers can bring to bear their intuitions and domain knowledge to design better features and develop more effective models. Classifiers and features can be specialized for individual failure modes (e.g. for white young women with makeup and bangs). Researchers can also collect more training data geared towards a subset of categories prone to failures. For instance, if a celebrity recognition system consistently fails to recognize old Asian actresses, one could collect more data for these subset of categories to re-train the system and potentially improve it.

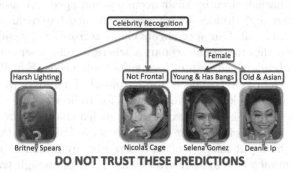

DO NOT TRUST THESE PREDICTIONS

Fig. 1. We advocate transparent computer vision systems. We characterize failure modes of a vision system using semantic attributes.

At test time, our characterization of failure modes can be used to automatically detect oncoming failure. Downstream applications that use the output of computer vision systems as input can benefit from such warnings. For example, an autonomous vehicle performing semantic segmentation in a video feed can skip frames that are predicted to be unreliable, and can make slightly delayed but more accurate decisions instead. An automatic prediction of the type of failure mode can be used to raise a flag and resort to a specialized classifier for that failure mode. A semantic characterization of failure modes can also be used to empower a human user of a vision system. Consider a lay person using a vision system to recognize celebrities. It would be useful if the system came with a "specification sheet" of sorts describing the possible failure modes. The one shown in Fig. 1 can guide the user to take better pictures that are well lit and have a frontal view of the face, making the system more reliable. For some failure modes (e.g. regarding demographics of categories that are difficult to recognize), there may be nothing the user can do to make the system more accurate. But at least he would know to not trust the system when recognizing celebrities with a certain appearance. This results in the system being more reliable when it is used and provides precaution in scenarios where it would have likely failed anyway. The resultant fewer unpleasant surprises improves the overall user experience. A

---

[1] In practice, this is often how researchers debug their systems, but it can not be done very systematically and does not scale well.

semantic characterization of the failure modes of a system can thus allow us to make today's vision systems more usable even with their existing imperfections.

Finally, a semantic characterization of failure modes makes vision systems more interpretable. This helps gain operator trust in applications involving semi-autonomous systems. Numerous technologies go unused in practice simply because of insufficient operator trust [1]. Vision systems today are typically characterized by their accuracy and speed. A user (individual, startup, federal agency) decides which system to use based on a desired accuracy and speed trade off. Our spec sheets characterize the system's performance in more depth by describing the scenarios where it fails. Users can make an informed decision about which system best suits their needs. E.g. If a user expects to be using a celebrity recognition app frequently for Indian movies, he may not pick an app that has known failure modes for Indians.

Why should we expect that such a characterization exists? It is because vision systems often suffer from *systematic* failure modes. For instance, the quality of the input image – often describable by semantic attributes – affects the performance of a system drastically. Lack of enough training data of certain groups of categories (e.g. old Asian actresses, Fig. 1) may lead to the inability of the system to recognize them well. Low inter-class variance among another set of categories (many young white actresses with heavy make up and bangs may look similar) may lead to a different (characterizable) systematic failure mode. Of course, similar to other sophisticated systems, vision systems also suffer from arbitrary non-systematic mistakes. These are not the focus of this paper.

In this paper, we propose an approach that automatically identifies patterns in failures, and summarizes them with a semantic characterization that humans can understand. For instance, a face recognition system may say "If the image has harsh lighting or the face is not frontal, I may give you an incorrect answer" or "If the person you are trying to recognize is a young female with bangs, this system may give you an incorrect answer" (Fig. 1). Attribute-based representations are a natural choice to generate this semantic characterization. Given a trained classification system and a labeled set of training images, we identify images that are correctly classified ("not-mistake images"), and those that are misclassified ("mistake images"). Both sets of images are annotated with a vocabulary of binary semantic attributes. The mistake images are discriminatively clustered using weighted L1-regularized (sparse) logistic regression in the space of annotated attributes. The "discriminative" part ensures that the (mistake) clusters have only a few attributes in common with the not-mistake images, the "weighted" part encourages the mistake images within each cluster to have many attributes in common, and the "sparse" part ensures that each cluster can be characterized via just a few attributes, leading to a compact representation of the failure modes. We evaluate our approach in two domains: face (celebrity) and animal species recognition. Our experiments demonstrate that (1) Our semantic specification sheets can capture failure modes of the system well (2) They outperform strong baselines in automatic prediction of oncoming failure, and (3) non-experts can follow our specification sheets well.

2   Related Work

Our work relates to existing bodies of work on estimating classifier confidence, on predicting failures of systems, and on the use of attributes, particularly for better communication between humans and machines.

Classifier Confidence Estimation: The confidence of a classifier in its decision is often correlated to the likelihood of it being correct. Reliably estimating the confidence of classifiers has received a lot of attention in the pattern recognition community [2–4]. Applications such as spam-filtering [5], natural language processing [6, 7], speech [8] and even computer vision [9] have leveraged these ideas. However, unlike our proposed specification sheets, these confidence estimation methods are not semantically interpretable.

Predicting Failure: Methods that predict overall performance of a system on a collection of test images by analyzing statistics of the test data or post-recognition scores [10–15] are not applicable to our goal of identifying specific failure modes of the system, and semantically characterizing them. Detecting errors has received a lot of attention in speech recognition [16, 17]. In computer vision, Jammalamadaka *et al.* [18] recently introduced evaluator algorithms for human pose estimators (HPE) that can detect if the HPE has succeeded. These techniques all use non-semantic features specific to their applications for predicting failure. Most related to our work is the recent work of Hoiem *et al.* [19]. They *analyzed* the impact of different object characteristics such as size, aspect ratio, occlusion, etc. on object detection performance. Our work discovers combinations of image attributes that correlate with failure. Our generated compact semantic specification sheets can *predict* when a mistake will be made, making our vision systems more usable. The attributes we consider are generic attributes and are not explicitly tied to the workings of these underlying system.

Attributes: Attributes have been used extensively, especially in the past few years, for a variety of applications [20–34]. Attributes have been used to learn and evaluate models of deeper scene understanding [20] that reason about properties of objects as opposed to just the object categories. They have also been used for alleviating annotation efforts via zero-shot learning [23, 21, 22] where a supervisor can teach a machine a novel concept simply by describing its properties (*e.g.* "a zebra is striped and has four legs" or "a zebra has a shorter neck than a giraffe"). Attributes have also been explored to improve object categorization [23], face verification [35] and scene recognition [36]. Attributes being both machine detectable and human understandable provide a mode of communication between the two. This has been exploited for improved image search by using attributes as keywords [25] or as interactive feedback [24]. Attributes have also been leveraged for more effective active learning by allowing the supervisor to provide attributes-based feedback to a classifier [26, 34]. Knowledge of a classifier's failure modes can help the supervisor provide more focused feedback. Attributes have also been used for generating automatic textual description of images [22, 37] that can potentially point out anomalies in objects [23]. Our work exploits attributes for the novel purpose of characterizing failure modes of a machine. Attributes have been used at test time with a human-in-the-loop answering relevant questions about a test image to help the machine classify an image more reliably [31]. Our specification sheets can be used by a user at test time, but for predicting the failures of a machine rather than aiding it. A combination of these two scenarios may be interesting to explore.

3   Approach

While our approach can be applied to any vision system, we use image classification as a case study in this paper. We are given a set of N images along with their corresponding class labels $\{(\boldsymbol{x}_i, y_i')\}, i \in \{1, \ldots, N\}, y' \in \{1, \ldots, C\}$, where C is the number of classes. We are also given a pre-trained classification system $H(\boldsymbol{x})$ whose failures we wish to characterize. Given an image $\boldsymbol{x}_i$, the system predicts a class label $\hat{y}_i'$ for the image i.e. $\hat{y}_i' = H(\boldsymbol{x}_i)$. We assign each image in our training set to a binary label $\{(\boldsymbol{x}_i, y_i)\}, y_i \in \{0, 1\}$, where $y_i = 0$ if $\hat{y}_i' = y'$ i.e. images $\boldsymbol{x}_i$ is correctly classified by H, otherwise $y_i = 1$. We annotate all images $\boldsymbol{x}_i$ using a vocabulary of M binary attributes $\{a_m\}, m \in \{1, \ldots, M\}$. Each image is thus represented with an M dimensional binary vector i.e. $\boldsymbol{x}_i \in \{-1, 1\}^M$ indicating whether attribute a_m is present in the image or not. We wish to discover a specification sheet, which we represent as a set of sparse lists of attributes – each list capturing a cluster of mistake images i.e. a failure mode.

3.1   Discriminative Clustering

We discriminatively cluster the mistake images in this ground truth attributes space. We initialize our clustering using k-means. This gives each of the mistake images a cluster index $c_i \in \{1, \ldots, K\}$. We denote all mistake images belonging to cluster k as $\{\boldsymbol{x}_i^k\}$. We train a discriminative function $h_k(\boldsymbol{x}_i)$ for each of the clusters that separates $\{\boldsymbol{x}_i^k\}$ from other "negative" images. Details of this function and the negative images follow in the next sub-section.

Let's say the score given by the discriminative function is $h_k(\boldsymbol{x}_i)$. We compute the score of all mistake images with respect to each of the K discriminative functions, and re-assign the image to the cluster whose function gives it the highest score. The updated cluster labels are

$$c_i^{(t+1)} = \operatorname*{argmax}_k h_k(\boldsymbol{x}_i) \tag{1}$$

where $t + 1$ denotes the next iteration. We re-train the discriminative functions using these updated cluster labels, and the process repeats. In our experiments, the process always converged, and took on average 3.6 iterations. We now describe the specifics of the discriminative function $h_k(\boldsymbol{x}_i)$.

3.2 L1-Regularized Logistic Regression

The discriminative function we train for each cluster is an L1-regularized logistic regression. It is trained to separate mistake images belonging to cluster k ($y_i^k = 1$) from all not-mistake images ($y_i^k = 0$). y_i^k is the label assigned to images for training the cluster-specific discriminative function. Notice that here y_i^k is not defined for images belonging to other mistake clusters $\boldsymbol{x}_i^l, l \in \{1, \ldots, K\}, l \neq k$, as they do not participate in training the discriminative function for cluster k. All discriminative functions share the same negative set i.e. the not-mistake images $\{\boldsymbol{x}_i^0\}$. We also experimented with using all other images in the training set (including mistake images assigned to other clusters) and using only mistake images assigned to the other clusters as negative set. We select between these three strategies via cross validation (Section 4.3).

When using logistic regression, the conditional probability that the label of an image is 1 is given by

$$p(y_i^k = 1 | \boldsymbol{x}_i, \boldsymbol{w}_k) = \frac{1}{1 + \exp(-\boldsymbol{w}_k^T \boldsymbol{x}_i)} \tag{2}$$

where $\boldsymbol{w}_k$ are the parameters to be learnt. These are learnt by

$$\underset{\boldsymbol{w}_k}{\mathrm{argmax}} \sum_i \log \left(p(y_i^k = 1 | \boldsymbol{x}_i, \boldsymbol{w}_k) \right) - \alpha \sum_{m=1}^{M} |w_{k,m}| \tag{3}$$

where $w_{k,m}$ is the mth entry in $\boldsymbol{w}_k$, $\sum_{m=1}^{M} |w_{k,m}|$ is the L1 regularization term, α is the parameter that trades off maximizing the likelihood of the data with minimizing the regularization term leading to a sparse $\boldsymbol{w}_k$. We use interior based method for this optimization [38].

Since the feature vectors representing the image are binary vectors indicating the presence or absence of semantic attributes in the image, reading off the non-zero weights in the learnt parameters $\boldsymbol{w}_k$, allows us to describe each cluster in a semantically meaningful way. See Fig. 2.

3.3 Weighted Logistic Regression

In addition to identifying attributes that separate mistake from not-mistake images, we also wish to ensure that images belonging to the same cluster share many attributes in common and more importantly, the attributes selected to characterize the clusters are present in most of the images assigned to that cluster. This will help make the specification sheet accurate and precise. To encourage this, rather than using a standard L1-regularized logistic regression as described above, we use a weighted logistic regression. At each iteration, we replace each binary attribute in the image representation with the proportion of

High Cheekbones
PointyNose
BigNose
Bangs
Brown Hair
Blonde Hair
Black Hair
White
Male

Not Male, Blonde Hair, Pointy Nose, High Cheekbones

Fig. 2. The learnt sparse discriminative function for each cluster (Section 3.2) can be directly converted to a compact semantic description of the cluster. For clarity, not all attributes are shown in this illustration.

images in the cluster that share the same (binary) attribute value. That is at the $(t+1)^{th}$ iteration, the mth feature value of x_i is

$$x_{i,m}^{(t+1)} = \begin{cases} \frac{1}{N^{k(t)}} \sum_{\{x_i^k\}^{(t)}} \delta_{x_{i,m},1}, & w_{k,m} > 0 \\ \frac{-1}{N^{k(t)}} \sum_{\{x_i^k\}^{(t)}} \delta_{x_{i,m},-1}, & w_{k,m} < 0 \\ x_{i,m}, & w_{k,m} = 0 \end{cases} \quad (4)$$

where δ_{ab}, the Kronecker delta, is 1 if $a = b$ and 0 otherwise, and $N^{k(t)}$ is the number of images assigned to the kth cluster at iteration t. Recall that $x_i \in \{-1, 1\}^M$. These are the ground truth attributes annotations of the image, and do not change with the clustering iterations. The summation counts the number of instances assigned to the kth cluster at iteration t that have the mth feature value agree with the sign of w for that feature. Hence, attributes that are present in most images in the cluster will have a higher weight, ensuring that it attracts even more images with that attribute to this cluster in the next cluster reassignment step. And same for the absent attributes. The weights will only impact those attributes for which w_k is non-zero.

As described above, correctly classified images form the negative set for our discriminative clustering approach. Hence, most images from reliable categories will be on the negative side, are unlikely to be captured in the characterization of failure modes. Our approach can be easily applied to individual or subsets of categories, which might also be insightful for researchers.

3.4   Hierarchical Clustering

The approach described above creates K scenarios, one for each cluster. Rather than having a list of scenarios to look through, a user may find a tree-structured specification sheet easier to navigate. To this end, we also experiment with performing the clustering described above in a hierarchical fashion. Specifically, given a branching factor B, we initialize the clustering using k-means with B clusters. We run the iterative discriminative clustering approach described above

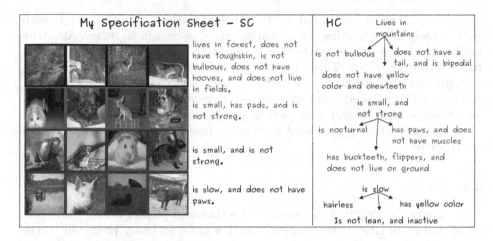

Fig. 3. Example specification sheets generated by our approach. Left: Simple clustering (SC): The failure modes are listed. For illustration, we show example images belonging to each cluster. Right: Hierarchical clustering (HC): Each path leading to a leaf is a failure mode *e.g.* "is slow and has yellow color" for the right most leaf of the bottom tree. Best viewed in color.

till convergence using weighted L1-regularized logistic regression. We then further cluster each of the B clusters into B clusters using the same iterative discriminative clustering, and so on, till the tree reaches a predetermined depth D. With this, we have now created a specification sheet. See Fig. 3 for an example.

4   Experiments

We now describe our experimental setup and the results we obtained.

4.1   Datasets

We experiment with two domains: face (celebrity) and animal species recognition. For faces, 2400 images from 60 categories (40 images per category) from the development set of the Public Figures Face Database (Pubfig) of Kumar *et al.* [35] are used. It contains 73 facial attributes such as race, gender, local features (e.g. pointy nose), hair color, etc. We annotated the categories with binary attribute annotations on Amazon Mechanical Turk. These will be made publicly available. For animals, 1887 images from 37 categories[2] (51 images per category) from the Animals with Attributes dataset (AwA) of Lampert *et al.* [21] containing 85 (annotated) attributes are used. 10 and 20 images per category from both

---

[2] We used the validation images from this dataset that were not used by the authors for training the attribute classifiers. Only 37 of the 50 categories had more than 50 such validation images.

datasets respectively were used to train their respective classifiers (SVM with RBF kernel) for recognizing the person or animal species in an image. Attribute predictors made available by the respective authors were used as image features to train these classifiers. This forms the pre-trained system provided as input to our approach, whose mistakes we wish to semantically characterize. For Pubfig / AwA, 10 / 12 images per category were used to generate our specification sheets, 10 / 8 images per category were used as a validation set and the remaining 10 / 11 images per category were used for testing. Results averaged across 10 splits are reported.

4.2   Metric

We evaluate the ability of our specification sheets to predict failure using precision and recall (PR), where we evaluate how often an image predicted by the specification sheet to be a failure truly is a failure (precision), and what percentage of the true failures are detected by the specification sheet (recall). Note that in the scenario where the user of a vision system uses our specification sheet to determine when to ignore the output of the system, another relevant dimension is the percentage of times the user would have to ignore the system. We define frequency-of-use for the user, FOU $= 1-$ proportion of test images classified to be failures. The lower the FOU, the worse the user experience. At low FOUs however, the vision system is likely to be highly accurate when it *is* used. Hence from a user perspective, the accuracy of system (ACC) vs. FOU trade-off might be more relevant than the precision-recall trade-off. The latter might be more relevant for researchers using these sheets to better understand their systems. A detailed discussion of the ACC vs. FOU metric and user-based evaluations of our specification sheets are contained in the supplementary material.

4.3   Selecting Specification Sheets

Our approach has the following parameters: (random) k-means initialization, the regularization weight α, number of clusters K for simple clustering or branching factor B and depth of tree D for hierarchical clustering and, the three choices of negative images to train the logistic regressors (Section 3.2). Different settings of these parameters can lead to specification sheets that tend to classify varying proportion of images as mistakes. We generate a pool of candidate specification sheets for 250 different k-means initializations, $\alpha \in \{5, 10, 20\}$ for hierarchical clustering and $\{10, 20, 30, 40, 50\}$ for simple clustering, $K \in [2, 20], B \in [2, 8], D \in [2, 4].$[3] In total this leads to about 20k specification sheets generated for hierarchical clustering and 71k for simple clustering. We measured the precision and recall for each specification sheet on held out validation data. Similar to methods of computing AP from precision-recall curves, we sample S (=21)

---

[3] We did not use all possible combinations of these. We avoid bringing together extreme values of parameters because that leads to extremely large and cumbersome specification sheets.

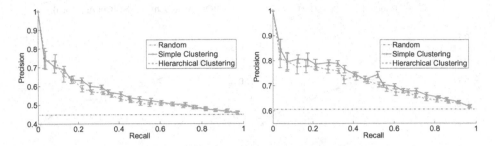

Fig. 4. Performance of our generated specification sheets capture failures. Left: Pubfig, Right: AwA.

Table 1. Area under the precision recall (PR) curve (left) and accuracy vs. frequency-of-use (ACC vs. FOU) curve (right) for different approaches. SC: simple clustering, HC: hierarchical clustering, all: using all attributes, sel: using a subset of attributes that are easy for lay people to understand.

	Random	SC - all	SC - sel	HC - all	HC - sel		Random	SC - all	SC - sel	HC - all	HC - sel
Pubfig	0.4473	0.5473	0.5421	0.5370	0.5291	Pubfig	0.5517	0.6181	0.6067	0.6157	0.5997
AwA	0.6061	0.7088	0.7079	0.6942	0.6963	AwA	0.3929	0.4777	0.4734	0.4636	0.4606

recall points $\in [0, 1]$ in increments of 0.05. Among all specification sheets with recall closest to each sampled point, we selected the sheet with the maximum precision on a held out validation set. Given a desired operating point at test time, we use the corresponding specification sheet. Selecting specification sheets from a large pool is a proxy for the continuous threshold one can vary to select arbitrary operating points on a precision recall curve.

4.4 Automatic Failure Prediction

At the core of it our approach is separating mistakes from not-mistakes, and hence has the potential to be used as a classifier confidence measure of sorts, to automatically predict oncoming failures. To this end, we use the following approach. We run an image through each of our S specification sheets, using *predicted* attributes instead of ground truth attributes. Recall that each specification sheet is formed by multiple logistic regressors – one for each cluster – each of which produces a probability of the image being a mistake. We build a feature vector for an image by concatenating these output probabilities along with the entropy of the main classifier whose mistakes we are characterizing. We train an SVM on this new representation to classify mistake images from not-mistake images. We have S such classifiers, one for each specification sheet. We average their responses on a test image to estimate the likelihood of that image being a mistake. Varying the threshold on this likelihood will result in different PR operating points.

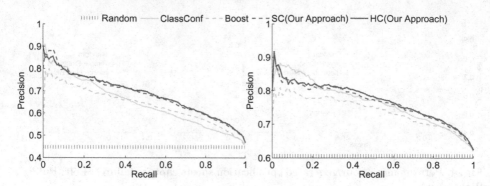

Fig. 5. Performance of our specification sheets *automatically* predicting oncoming failure. Left: Pubfig, Right: AwA.

Table 2. Area under the precision-recall (PR) curve. Comparison of various approaches to automatic failure prediction. CC: ClassConf, SC: simple (discriminative) clustering, HC: hierarchical (discriminative) clustering, GC: generative clustering.

	CC	Boost	SC	HC	CC+HC	Boost+CC	Boost+HC	HC+Boost+CC	GC	GC+CC	Rand
Pubfig	0.64	0.64	0.68	0.68	0.68	0.68	0.69	0.69	0.56	0.66	0.45
AwA	0.77	0.74	0.77	0.77	0.78	0.77	0.76	0.78	0.74	0.76	0.61

Table 3. Area under the ACC vs. FOU curve. Comparison of various approaches to automatic failure prediction. CC: ClassConf, SC: simple (discriminative) clustering, HC: hierarchical (discriminative) clustering, GC: generative clustering.

	CC	Boost	SC	HC	CC+HC	Boost+CC	Boost+HC	HC+Boost+CC	GC	GC+CC	Rand
Pubfig	0.7033	0.7130	0.7423	0.7316	0.7117	0.7390	0.7409	0.7387	0.6430	0.7293	0.5517
AwA	0.5594	0.5573	0.5752	0.5789	0.5640	0.5807	0.5821	0.5809	0.5297	0.5600	0.3929

4.5   Baselines

Our specification sheets are *fully* semantic, and thus should not be compared to non-semantic estimates of classifier confidence. We compare our automatic failure prediction approach to such non-semantic baselines. **ClassConf (CC):** The conventional approach to estimating the confidence of a classifier is computing the entropy of the probabilistic output of the classifier across the class labels (*e.g.* computed using Platts' method [39]) to a given test instance. This was one of the features used in our automatic failure prediction approach in Section 4.4. Placing a threshold on ClassConf to classify an image as being a likely mistake or not gives us a point on the PR curve. Varying this threshold gives us the entire curve. **Boost:** Our approach to automatic failure prediction employs multiple classifiers. This is related to boosting approaches [40]. We use Adaboost [41, 42] to learn the weights of 2000 decision trees[4], each with a maximum depth of 4 to differentiate between "mistake" and "not-mistake" images. We use the same image features as used by the classification system itself to train the weak learners.

---

[4] More trees did not further improve accuracy.

Perhaps using orthogonal features may lead to better failure prediction performance. **Rand:** We also compare to a baseline that assigns each image a random score between [0,1] as a likelihood of failure.

4.6   Results

Accuracies of the pre-trained classifiers on average were 55% and 40% for Pubfig and AwA respectively. Our goal is to semantically characterize the mistakes these classifiers tend to make. The results of oracle users[5] using our semantic specification sheets are shown in Fig. 4. Our specification sheets can predict oncoming failures with accuracy significantly better than chance.

Hierarchical vs. Simple Clustering: We compare the use of hierarchical clustering as opposed to simple clustering in Fig. 4. A hierarchical specification sheet is likely to be more convenient for a user to navigate through. But as we see for AwA (Fig. 4, right) it can perform slightly worse than simple clustering. See qualitative examples of specification sheets generated by our approach in Fig. 3. We also selected a subset of attributes that we thought were easier to understand by a lay person. We selected 45 attributes out of 73 for Pubfig and 58 out of 85 for AwA. Table 1 shows that performs stays fairly stable even with these fewer attributes.

Automatically Predicting Failures: The results of our specification sheet based *automatic* approach of predicting failures (Section 4.4) can be seen in Fig. 5 and Tables 2, 3. Our approach significantly outperforms the well accepted approach to estimating the confidence of a classifier. The boosting baseline is comparable to or worse than ClassConf. Adding our approach to ClassConf and Boost significantly improves performance. Combining all three generally leads to minor gains. Tables 2, 3 predict failure by combining predictions of multiple specification sheets (a total of 21 specification sheets; one for each sampled recall point) using an SVM. Hence, they shows improved performance over Table 1 which uses a single specification sheet.

Recall that the logistic regressors were trained on ground truth annotations of attributes. But for the automatic approach, at test time we use predicted attribute values for images. The performance may further improve if the logistic regressors were re-trained using the predicted attribute values for images at training time.

Note that Boost directly predicts failure from image features. We also learn a failure predictor, but on top of our specification sheet confidences. Our improved performance over Boost may be because attributes help transfer knowledge between categories and provide a semantic regularization of sorts. Other problems

---

[5] We assume that researchers can identify the presence/absence of attributes correctly, and hence will not make a mistake while following the specification sheet. Note that this does not result in a (even nearly) perfect failure prediction system. This is because the scenarios listed in the specification sheet are *learnt* summaries of the attributes incorrectly classified images tend to share in common.

(e.g. face verification [35]) have also shown that using attributes as an intermediate representation for classification outperforms direct classification from image features.

Additional Data: One might wonder: if the validation images used to train our specification sheets were instead used as additional training data to better train the underlying classification system, would its confidence measure be more accurate at failure prediction? To verify this, we retrained the base algorithm using train+val images. But performance of ClassConf did not improve (decreased little). This is not surprising. It is well known that strong classifiers can be overconfident.

Discriminative vs. Generative Clustering: We compare our discriminative clustering approach (Section 3.1) to generative clustering (GC). All mistake images are clustered using k-means clustering (which forms the initialization step for discriminative clustering) in the predicted attributes space.[6] Given a test image, its distance from the closest mistake cluster gives us an indication of its likelihood of being a mistake. Varying a threshold on this distance gives us a PR curve. We report the area under this curve in Table 2. We see that this generative approach performs significantly worse than our discriminative approach. To give it a further boost, we represent each image by its distance from all K clusters, and train a classifier on these K features and ClassConf to separate mistake images from not-mistake images. This (now partially discriminative approach: GC + ClassConf) results in better performance but still worse than our approach.

Human Studies: We conducted studies on Amazon Mechanical Turk to demonstrate that the semantic characterizations generated by our approach can be easily understood by non-computer vision experts also. Without any training about meaning of attributes, we showed subjects 24 failure modes each from celebrity face and animal species recognition by showing them the list of attributes that characterize the failure modes. The modes were selected by first randomy picking 50 failure modes (or clusters) from different specification sheets such that each was characterized by atleast 3 attributes. We then pruned out the ones that had attributes in common so as to ensure wide coverage of attributes. We had workers annotate 100 images as belonging to a failure mode or not (that is satisfying the attribute-based description or not). Each image was shown to 10 workers, and we took the majority vote. Workers were able to correctly identify whether an image belongs to a failure mode or not 85.37% and 73.96% of the time for Pubfig and AwA respectively (chance is 50%). Clearly, our specification sheets are truly human understandable. Note that our experimental evaluation covers the entire spectrum including 1. oracle users who can predict attributes reliably (Fig. 4) to evaluate the performance of our specification sheets in capturing failure modes; 2. real subjects on MTurk to see if they could easily understand these failure

---

[6] Performing the clustering in ground truth attributes space like our approach results in even worse performance because the test image is represented by predicted attributes and not ground truth for automatic prediction of failure. We use predicted attributes here to report a stronger baseline.

modes; and 3. without a user in the loop (Fig. 5) to demonstrate the effectiveness of our specification sheets for automatic (machine) failure prediction.

User Experience: For Pubfig, the simple clustering based specification sheets have 11 clusters on average. It involves the users having to check the values of about 7 attributes per cluster. Hierarchical clustering on the other hand has about 10 clusters but involves checking only about 4 attributes per cluster. For AwA, both simple and hierarchical clustering have 9 clusters on average, and involve checking on average about 7 and 4 attributes respectively per cluster.

5   Discussion

Like most machine learning systems, our approach can only predict what was seen during training. Existing vision systems suffer from plenty of systematic failure modes that are observed during validation. While capturing unseen failure modes is certainly desirable, capturing seen ones - even via predictive correlations (as opposed to causal relationships) - is a significant step towards making our systems transparent. The data, code, and specification sheets used in this work are available on the author's webpage.

Future Work: Discovering a vocabulary of application-specific attributes geared specifically towards predicting failures, and leveraging the sheets for the various applications discussed in the introduction is part of future work. Specification sheets can also help compare different vision systems designed to address similar tasks. This can explicitly reveal redundancies or complementary strengths among various approaches. This can be enlightening for the community, and can also be quite useful for a potential consumer of vision applications attempting to identify the system that is the best fit for the application at hand.

6   Conclusion

We proposed a discriminative clustering approach using L1-regularized weighted logistic regression to generate semantically understandable "specification sheets" that describe the failure modes of vision systems. We presented promising results for face and animal species recognition. We demonstrated that the specification sheets capture failure modes well, and can be leveraged to automatically predict oncoming failure better than a standard classifier confidence measure and a boosting baseline. By being better informed via our specification sheets, researchers can design better solutions to vision systems, and users can choose to not use the vision system in certain scenarios, increasing the performance of the system when it is used. Downstream applications can also benefit from our automatic failure prediction.

Acknowledgements. We thank Martial Hebert and anonymous reviewers for helpful insights and fruitful discussion. This work was supported in part by ARO YIP 65359NSYIP to D.P.

References

1. Stack, J.: Automation for underwater mine recognition: Current trends & future strategy. In: Proceedings of SPIE Defense & Security (2011)
2. Duin, R.P.W., Tax, D.M.J.: Classifier Conditional Posterior Probabilities. In: Amin, A., Pudil, P., Dori, D. (eds.) SPR 1998 and SSPR 1998. LNCS, vol. 1451, pp. 611–619. Springer, Heidelberg (1998)
3. Kukar, M.: Estimating confidence values of individual predictions by their typical-ness and reliability. In: ECAI (2004)
4. Muhlbaier, M., Topalis, A., Polikar, R.: Ensemble confidence estimates posterior probability. In: Oza, N.C., Polikar, R., Kittler, J., Roli, F. (eds.) MCS 2005. LNCS, vol. 3541, pp. 326–335. Springer, Heidelberg (2005)
5. Delany, S.J., Cunningham, P., Doyle, D., Zamolotskikh, A.: Generating estimates of classification confidence for a case-based spam filter. In: Muñoz-Ávila, H., Ricci, F. (eds.) ICCBR 2005. LNCS (LNAI), vol. 3620, pp. 177–190. Springer, Heidelberg (2005)
6. Dredze, M., Crammer, K.: Confidence-weighted linear classification. In: ICML (2008)
7. Bach, N., Huang, F., Al-Onaizan, Y.: Goodness: A method for measuring machine translation confidence. In: ACL (2011)
8. Jiang, H.: Confidence measures for speech recognition: A survey. Speech Commu-nication (2005)
9. Zhang, W., Yu, S.X., Teng, S.H.: Power svm: Generalization with exemplar clas-sification uncertainty. In: CVPR (2012)
10. Boshra, M., Bhanu, B.: Predicting performance of object recognition. PAMI (2000)
11. Wang, R., Bhanu, B.: Learning models for predicting recognition performance. In: ICCV (2005)
12. Scheirer, W.J., Rocha, A., Micheals, R.J., Boult, T.E.: Meta-recognition: The the-ory and practice of recognition score analysis. PAMI (2011)
13. Wang, P., Ji, Q., Wayman, J.L.: Modeling and predicting face recognition system performance based on analysis of similarity scores. PAMI (2007)
14. Scheirer, W., Kumar, N., Belhumeur, P., Boult, T.: Multi-attribute spaces: Cali-bration for attribute fusion and similarity search. In: CVPR (2012)
15. Scheirer, W., Rocha, A., Micheals, R., Boult, T.: Robust fusion: Extreme value theory for recognition score normalization. In: Daniilidis, K., Maragos, P., Paragios, N. (eds.) ECCV 2010, Part III. LNCS, vol. 6313, pp. 481–495. Springer, Heidelberg (2010)
16. Sarma, A., Palmer, D.D.: Context-based speech recognition error detection and correction. In: NAACL (Short papers) (2004)
17. Choularton, S.: Early stage detection of speech recognition errors (2009)
18. Jammalamadaka, N., Zisserman, A., Eichner, M., Ferrari, V., Jawahar, C.V.: Has my algorithm succeeded? An evaluator for human pose estimators. In: Fitzgibbon, A., Lazebnik, S., Perona, P., Sato, Y., Schmid, C. (eds.) ECCV 2012, Part III. LNCS, vol. 7574, pp. 114–128. Springer, Heidelberg (2012)
19. Hoiem, D., Chodpathumwan, Y., Dai, Q.: Diagnosing error in object detectors. In: Fitzgibbon, A., Lazebnik, S., Perona, P., Sato, Y., Schmid, C. (eds.) ECCV 2012, Part III. LNCS, vol. 7574, pp. 340–353. Springer, Heidelberg (2012)
20. Farhadi, A., Endres, I., Hoiem, D.: Attribute-centric recognition for cross-category generalization. In: CVPR (2010)

21. Lampert, C., Nickisch, H., Harmeling, S.: Learning to detect unseen object classes by between-class attribute transfer. In: CVPR (2009)
22. Parikh, D., Grauman, K.: Relative attributes. In: ICCV (2011)
23. Farhadi, A., Endres, I., Hoiem, D., Forsyth, D.: Describing objects by their attributes. In: CVPR (2009)
24. Kovashka, A., Parikh, D., Grauman, K.: Whittlesearch: Image search with relative attribute feedback. In: CVPR (2012)
25. Kumar, N., Belhumeur, P., Nayar, S.: FaceTracer: A search engine for large collections of images with faces. In: Forsyth, D., Torr, P., Zisserman, A. (eds.) ECCV 2008, Part IV. LNCS, vol. 5305, pp. 340–353. Springer, Heidelberg (2008)
26. Parkash, A., Parikh, D.: Attributes for classifier feedback. In: Fitzgibbon, A., Lazebnik, S., Perona, P., Sato, Y., Schmid, C. (eds.) ECCV 2012, Part III. LNCS, vol. 7574, pp. 354–368. Springer, Heidelberg (2012)
27. Berg, T.L., Berg, A.C., Shih, J.: Automatic attribute discovery and characterization from noisy web data. In: Daniilidis, K., Maragos, P., Paragios, N. (eds.) ECCV 2010, Part I. LNCS, vol. 6311, pp. 663–676. Springer, Heidelberg (2010)
28. Wang, J., Markert, K., Everingham, M.: Learning models for object recognition from natural language descriptions. In: BMVC (2009)
29. Wang, G., Forsyth, D.: Joint learning of visual attributes, object classes and visual saliency. In: ICCV (2009)
30. Ferrari, V., Zisserman, A.: Learning visual attributes. In: NIPS (2007)
31. Branson, S., Wah, C., Schroff, F., Babenko, B., Welinder, P., Perona, P., Belongie, S.: Visual recognition with humans in the loop. In: Daniilidis, K., Maragos, P., Paragios, N. (eds.) ECCV 2010, Part IV. LNCS, vol. 6314, pp. 438–451. Springer, Heidelberg (2010)
32. Wang, G., Forsyth, D., Hoiem, D.: Comparative object similarity for improved recognition with few or no examples. In: CVPR (2010)
33. Parikh, D., Grauman, K.: Interactively building a discriminative vocabulary of nameable attributes. In: CVPR (2011)
34. Biswas, A., Parikh, D.: Simultaneous active learning of classifiers & attributes via relative feedback. In: CVPR (2013)
35. Kumar, N., Berg, A., Belhumeur, P., Nayar, S.: Attribute and simile classifiers for face verification. In: ICCV (2009)
36. Patterson, G., Hays, J.: Sun attribute database: Discovering, annotating, and recognizing scene attributes. In: CVPR (2012)
37. Kulkarni, G., Premraj, V., Dhar, S., Li, S., Choi, Y., Berg, A.C., Berg, T.L.: Baby talk: Understanding and generating simple image descriptions. In: CVPR (2011)
38. Koh, K., Kim, S.J., Boyd, S.: An interior-point method for large-scale l1-regularized logistic regression. J. Mach. Learn. Res. (2007)
39. Platt, J.: Probabilistic outputs for support vector machines and comparison to regularized likelihood methods. In: Advances in Large Margin Classiers (2000)
40. Freund, Y., Schapire, R.E.: Experiments with a new boosting algorithm. In: Machine Learning International Workshop (1996)
41. Appel, R., Fuchs, T., Dollár, P., Perona, P.: Quickly boosting decision trees - pruning underachieving features early. In: ICML (2013)
42. Dollár, P.: Piotr's Image and Video Matlab Toolbox,
    http://vision.ucsd.edu/~pdollar/toolbox/doc/index.html

Orientation Covariant Aggregation of Local Descriptors with Embeddings

Giorgos Tolias, Teddy Furon, and Hervé Jégou

Inria, Rennes, France

Abstract. Image search systems based on local descriptors typically achieve orientation invariance by aligning the patches on their dominant orientations. Albeit successful, this choice introduces too much invariance because it does not guarantee that the patches are rotated consistently.

This paper introduces an aggregation strategy of local descriptors that achieves this covariance property by jointly encoding the angle in the aggregation stage in a continuous manner. It is combined with an efficient monomial embedding to provide a codebook-free method to aggregate local descriptors into a single vector representation.

Our strategy is also compatible and employed with several popular encoding methods, in particular bag-of-words, VLAD and the Fisher vector. Our geometric-aware aggregation strategy is effective for image search, as shown by experiments performed on standard benchmarks for image and particular object retrieval, namely Holidays and Oxford buildings.

1 Introduction

This paper considers the problem of particular image or particular object retrieval. This subject has received a sustained attention over the last decade. Many of the recent works employ local descriptors such as SIFT [1] or variants [2] for the low-level description of the images. In particular, approaches derived from the bag-of-visual-words framework [3] are especially successful to solve problems like recognizing buildings. They are typically combined with spatial verification [4] or other re-ranking strategies such as query expansion [5].

Our objective is to improve the quality of the first retrieval stage, before any re-ranking is performed. This is critical when considering large datasets, as re-ranking methods depend on the quality of the initial short-list, which typically consists of a few hundred images. The initial stage is improved by better matching rules, for instance with Hamming embedding [6], by learning a fine vocabulary [7], or weighting the distances [8,9]. In addition to the SIFT, it is useful to employ some geometrical information associated with the region of interest [6]. All these approaches rely on matching individual descriptors and therefore store some data on a per descriptor basis. Moreover, the quantization of the query's descriptors on a relatively large vocabulary causes delays.

Recently, very short yet effective representations have been proposed based on alternative encoding strategies, such as local linear coding [10], the Fisher

D. Fleet et al. (Eds.): ECCV 2014, Part VI, LNCS 8694, pp. 382–397, 2014.

vector [11] or VLAD [12]. Most of these representations have been proposed first for image classification, yet also offer very effective properties in the context of extremely large-scale image search. A feature of utmost importance is that they offer vector representations compatible with cosine similarity. The representation can then be effectively binarized [13] with cosine sketches, such as those proposed by Charikar [14] (*a.k.a.* LSH), or aggressively compressed with principal component dimensionality reduction (PCA) to very short vectors. Product quantization [15] is another example achieving a very compact representation of a few dozens to hundreds bytes and an efficient search because the comparison is done directly in the compressed domain.

This paper focuses on such short- and mid-sized vector representations of images. Our objective is to exploit some geometrical information associated with the regions of interest. A popular work in this context is the spatial pyramid kernel [16], which is widely adopted for image classification. However, it is ineffective for particular image and object retrieval as the grid is too rigid and the resulting representation is not invariant enough, as shown by Douze *et al.* [17].

Here, we aim at incorporating some relative angle information to ensure that the patches are consistently rotated. In other terms, we want to achieve a covariant property similar to that offered by Weak Geometry Consistency (WGC) [6], but directly implemented in the coding stage of image vector representations like Fisher, or VLAD. Some recent works in classification [18] and image search [19] consider a similar objective. They suffer from several shortcomings. In particular, they simply quantize the angle and use it as a pooling variable. Moreover the encoding of a rough approximation of the angles is not straightforwardly compatible with generic match kernels.

In contrast, we achieve the covariant property for any method provided that it can be written as a match kernel. This holds for the Fisher vector, LLC, bag-of-words and efficient match kernels listed in [20]. Our method is inspired by the kernel descriptor of Bo *et al.* [21], from which we borrow the idea of angle kernelization. Our method however departs from this work in several ways. First, we are interested in aggregating local descriptors to produce a vector image representation, whereas they construct new local descriptors. Second, we do not encode the gradient orientation but the dominant orientation of the region of interest jointly with the corresponding SIFT descriptor, in order to achieve the covariant property of the local patches. Finally, we rely on explicit feature maps [22] to encode the angle, which provides a much better approximation than efficient match kernel for a given number of components.

This paper is organized as follows. Section 2 introduces notation and discusses some important related works more in details. Our approach is presented in Section 3 and evaluated in Section 4 on several popular benchmarks for image search, namely Oxford5k [4], Oxford105k and Inria Holidays [23]. These experiments show that our approach gives a significant improvement over the state of the art on image search with vector representations. Importantly, we achieve competitive results by combining our approach with monomial embeddings, *i.e.*, with a *codebook-free* approach, as opposed to coding approaches like VLAD.

2   Preliminaries: Match Kernels and Monomial Embeddings

We consider the context of match kernels. An image is typically described by a set of local descriptors $\mathcal{X} = \{\mathbf{x}_1, \ldots, \mathbf{x}_i, \ldots\}$, $\mathbf{x}_i \in \mathbb{R}^d$, $\|\mathbf{x}_i\| = 1$. Similar to other works [24,20,6], two images described by $\mathcal{X}$ and $\mathcal{Y}$ are compared with a match kernel K of the form

$$K(\mathcal{X}, \mathcal{Y}) = \beta(\mathcal{X})\beta(\mathcal{Y}) \sum_{\mathbf{x} \in \mathcal{X}} \sum_{\mathbf{y} \in \mathcal{Y}} k(\mathbf{x}, \mathbf{y}), \tag{1}$$

where k is referred to as the local kernel and where the proportionality factor β ensures that $K(\mathcal{X}, \mathcal{X}) = K(\mathcal{Y}, \mathcal{Y}) = 1$. A typical way to obtain such a kernel is to map the vectors $\mathbf{x}$ to a higher-dimensional space with a function $\varphi : \mathbb{R}^d \to \mathbb{R}^D$, such that the inner product similarity evaluates the local kernel $k(\mathbf{x}, \mathbf{y}) = \langle \varphi(\mathbf{x}) | \varphi(\mathbf{y}) \rangle$. This approach then represents a set of local descriptors by a single vector

$$\mathbf{X} = \beta(\mathcal{X}) \sum_{\mathbf{x} \in \mathcal{X}} \varphi(\mathbf{x}_i), \qquad (\text{such that } \|\mathbf{X}\| = 1) \tag{2}$$

because the match kernel is computed with a simple inner product as

$$K(\mathcal{X}, \mathcal{Y}) = \beta(\mathcal{X})\beta(\mathcal{Y}) \sum_{\mathbf{x} \in \mathcal{X}} \sum_{\mathbf{y} \in \mathcal{Y}} \langle \varphi(\mathbf{x}) | \varphi(\mathbf{y}) \rangle = \langle \mathbf{X} | \mathbf{Y} \rangle. \tag{3}$$

This framework encompasses many approaches such as bag-of-words [3,25], LLC [10], Fisher vector [11], VLAD [12], or VLAT [26]. Note that some non-linear processing, such as power-law component-wise normalization [8,27], is often applied to the resulting vector. A desirable property of k is to have $k(\mathbf{x}, \mathbf{y}) \approx 0$ for unrelated features, so that they do not interfere with the measurements between the true matches. It is somehow satisfied with the classical inner product $k(\mathbf{x}, \mathbf{y}) = \langle \mathbf{x} | \mathbf{y} \rangle$. Several authors [24,26,9] propose to increase the contrast between related and unrelated features with a monomial match kernel of degree p of the form

$$K(\mathcal{X}, \mathcal{Y}) = \beta(\mathcal{X})\beta(\mathcal{Y}) \sum_{\mathbf{x} \in \mathcal{X}} \sum_{\mathbf{y} \in \mathcal{Y}} \langle \mathbf{x} | \mathbf{y} \rangle^p. \tag{4}$$

All monomial (and polynomial) embeddings admit exact finite-dimensional feature maps whose length rapidly increases with degree p (in $\mathcal{O}(d^p/p!)$). The order $p = 2$ has already demonstrated some benefit, for instance recently for semantic segmentation [28] or in image classification [26]. In this case, the kernel is equivalent to comparing the set of features based on their covariance matrix [26]. Equivalently, by observing that some components are identical, we can define the embedding $\varphi_2 : \mathbb{R}^d \to \mathbb{R}^{d(d+1)/2}$ mapping $\mathbf{x} = [x_1, \ldots, x_d]^\top$ to

$$\varphi_2(\mathbf{x}) = [x_1^2, \ldots, x_d^2, x_1 x_2 \sqrt{2}, \ldots, x_{d-1} x_d \sqrt{2}]^\top. \tag{5}$$

Similarly, the simplified exact monomial embedding associated with $p = 3$ is the function $\varphi_3 : \mathbb{R}^d \to \mathbb{R}^{(d^3 + 3d^2 + 2d)/6}$ defined as

$$\varphi_3(\mathbf{x}) = [x_1^3, \ldots, x_d^3, x_1^2 x_2 \sqrt{3}, \ldots, x_d^2 x_{d-1} \sqrt{3}, x_1 x_2 x_3 \sqrt{6}, \ldots, x_{d-2} x_{d-1} x_d \sqrt{6}]^\top. \tag{6}$$

Fig. 1. Similarities between regions of interest, based on SIFT kernel k (*left*), angle consistency kernel k_θ (*middle*) and both (*right*). For each local region, we visualize the values $k(\mathbf{x}, \mathbf{y})$, $k_\theta(\Delta\theta)$ and their product by the colors of the link (red=1).

3   Covariant Aggregation of Local Descriptors

The core idea of the proposed method is to exploit jointly the SIFT descriptors and the dominant orientation θ_x associated with a region of interest. For this purpose, we now assume that an image is represented by a set $\mathcal{X}^\star$ of tuples, each of the form $(\mathbf{x}, \theta_x)$, where $\mathbf{x}$ is a SIFT descriptor and $\theta_x \in [-\pi, \pi]$ is the dominant orientation. Our objective is to obtain an approximation of a match kernel of the form

$$K^\star(\mathcal{X}^\star, \mathcal{Y}^\star) = \beta(\mathcal{X}^\star)\beta(\mathcal{Y}^\star) \sum_{(\mathbf{x},\theta_x)\in\mathcal{X}^\star} \sum_{(\mathbf{y},\theta_y)\in\mathcal{Y}^\star} k(\mathbf{x}, \mathbf{y})\, k_\theta(\theta_x, \theta_y) \qquad (7)$$

$$= \langle \mathbf{X}^\star | \mathbf{Y}^\star \rangle, \qquad (8)$$

where k is a local kernel identical to that considered in Section 2 and k_θ reflects the similarity between angles. The interest of enriching this match kernel with orientation is illustrated by Figure 1, where we show that several incorrect matches are downweighted thanks to this information.

The kernel in (7) resembles that implemented in WGC [6] with a voting approach. In contrast, we intend to approximate this kernel with an inner product between two vectors as in (8), similar to the linear match kernel simplification in (3). Our work is inspired by the kernel descriptors [21] of Bo *et al.*, who also consider a kernel of a similar form, but at the patch level, to construct a local descriptor from pixel attributes, such as gradient and position.

In our case, we consider the coding/pooling stage and employ a better approximation technique, namely explicit feature maps [22], to encode $\mathcal{X}^\star$. This section first explains the feature map of the angle, then how it modulates the descriptors, and finally discusses the match kernel design and properties.

3.1   A Feature Map for the Angle

The first step is to find a mapping $\alpha : [-\pi, \pi] \to \mathbb{R}^M$ from an angle θ to a vector $\alpha(\theta)$ such that $\alpha(\theta_1)^\top \alpha(\theta_2) = k_\theta(\theta_1 - \theta_2)$. The function $k_\theta : \mathbb{R} \to [0, 1]$ is a shift invariant kernel which should be symmetric ($k_\theta(\Delta\theta) = k_\theta(-\Delta\theta)$), pseudo-periodic with period of 2π and monotonically decreasing over $[0, \pi]$. We consider in particular the following function:

$$k_{\mathsf{VM}}(\Delta\theta) = \frac{\exp(\kappa \cos(\Delta\theta)) - \exp(-\kappa)}{2\sinh(\kappa)}. \tag{9}$$

It is derived from Von Mises distribution $f(\Delta\theta; \kappa)$, which is often considered as the probability density distribution of the noise of the measure of an angle, and therefore regarded as the equivalent Gaussian distribution for angles. Although this is not explicitly stated in their paper, the regular Von Mises distribution is the kernel function implicitly used by Bo $et~al.$ [21] for kernelizing angles. Our function k_{VM} is a shifted and scaled variant of Von Mises, designed such that its range is $[0, 1]$, which ensures that $k_{\mathsf{VM}}(\pi) = 0$.

The periodic function k_{VM} can be expressed as a Fourier series whose coefficients are (see [29][Eq. (9.6.19)]):

$$k_{\mathsf{VM}}(\Delta\theta) = \left(I_0(\kappa) - e^{-\kappa} + 2\sum_{n=1}^{\infty} I_n(\kappa)\cos(n\Delta\theta) \right) \cdot \frac{1}{2\sinh(\kappa)}, \tag{10}$$

where $I_n(\kappa)$ is the modified Bessel function of the first kind of order n. We now consider the truncation $\bar{k}_{\mathsf{VM}}^N$ of the series to the first N terms:

$$\bar{k}_{\mathsf{VM}}^N(\Delta\theta) = \sum_{n=0}^{N} \gamma_n \cos(n\Delta\theta) \quad \text{with } \gamma_0 = \frac{(I_0(\kappa) - e^{-\kappa})}{2\sinh(\kappa)} \text{ and } \gamma_n = \frac{I_n(\kappa)}{\sinh(\kappa)} \text{ if } n > 0. \tag{11}$$

We design the feature map $\alpha(\theta)$ as follows:

$$\alpha(\theta) = (\sqrt{\gamma_0}, \sqrt{\gamma_1}\cos(\theta), \ldots, \sqrt{\gamma_N}\cos(N\theta), \sqrt{\gamma_1}\sin(\theta), \ldots, \sqrt{\gamma_N}\sin(N\theta))^\top. \tag{12}$$

This vector has $2N + 1$ components. Moreover

$$\alpha(\theta_1)^\top \alpha(\theta_2) = \gamma_0 + \sum_{n=1}^{N} \gamma_n(\cos(n\theta_1)\cos(n\theta_2) + \sin(n\theta_1)\sin(n\theta_2)) \tag{13}$$

$$= \sum_{n=0}^{N} \gamma_n \cos(n(\theta_1 - \theta_2)) \tag{14}$$

$$= \bar{k}_{\mathsf{VM}}^N(\theta_1 - \theta_2) \approx k_{\mathsf{VM}}(\theta_1 - \theta_2) \tag{15}$$

This process of designing a feature map is explained in full details by Vedaldi and Zisserman [22]. This feature map gives an approximation of the target function k_{VM}, which is more accurate as N is bigger.

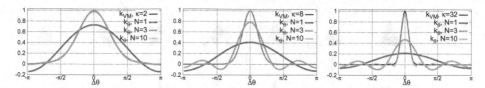

Fig. 2. Function k_{VM} for different values of κ and its approximation $\bar{k}_{VM}^N$ using 1, 3 and 10 frequencies, as implicitly defined by the corresponding mapping $\boldsymbol{\alpha} : [\pi, \pi] \to \mathbb{R}^{2N+1}$

Figure 2 illustrates the function k_{VM} for several values of the parameter κ and its approximation $\bar{k}_{VM}^N$ for different values of N. First note that $\bar{k}_{VM}^N$ may not fulfill the original requirements: its range might be wider than $[0, 1]$ and it might not be monotonically decreasing over $[0, \pi]$. Larger values of κ produce a more "selective" function of the angle, yet require more components (larger N) to obtain an accurate estimation. Importantly, the approximation stemming from this explicit angle mapping is better than that based on efficient match kernels [20], which converges slowly with the number of components. Efficient match kernels are more intended to approximate kernels on vectors than on scalar values. As a trade-off between selectivity and the number of components, we set $\kappa=8$ and $N=3$ (see Section 4). Accordingly, we use $\bar{k}_{VM}^3$ as k_θ in the sequel. The corresponding embedding $\boldsymbol{\alpha} : \mathbb{R} \to \mathbb{R}^7$ maps any angle to a 7-dimensional vector.

Remark: Instead of approximating a kernel on angles with finite Fourier series, one may rather consider directly designing a function satisfying our initial requirements (pseudo-period, symmetric, decreasing over $[0, \pi]$), such as

$$k_P(\Delta\theta) = \cos(\Delta\theta/2)^P \text{ with } P \text{ even.} \tag{16}$$

This function, thanks to power reduction trigonometric identities for even P, is re-written as

$$k_P(\Delta\theta) = \sum_{p=0}^{P/2} \gamma_p \cos(p\Delta\theta) \tag{17}$$

$$\text{with} \qquad \gamma_0 = \frac{1}{2^P}\binom{P}{P/2}, \gamma_p = \frac{1}{2^{P-1}}\binom{P}{P/2-p} \quad 0 < p \le P/2. \tag{18}$$

Applying (12) leads to a feature map $\boldsymbol{\alpha}(\theta)$ with $P+1$ components such that $\boldsymbol{\alpha}(\theta_1)^\top \boldsymbol{\alpha}(\theta_2) = k_P(\theta_1 - \theta_2)$. For this function, the interesting property is that the scalar product is exactly equal to the target kernel value $k_P(\theta_1 - \theta_2)$, and that the original requirements now hold. From our experiments, this function gives reasonable results, but requires more components than $\bar{k}_{VM}$ to achieve a shape narrow around $\Delta\theta = 0$ and close to 0 otherwise. The results for our image search application task using this function are slightly below our Von Mises variant for a given dimensionality. So, despite its theoretical interest we do not use it in our experiments. Ultimately, one would rather directly learn a Fourier embedding for the targeted task, in the spirit of recent works on Fourier kernel learning [30].

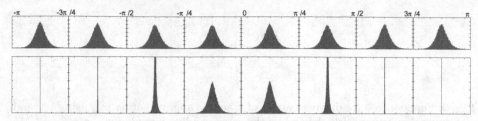

Fig. 3. Distribution of patch similarity for different values of orientation difference. In this figure, we split the angular space into 8 equally-sized bins and present the similarity distribution separately for each of these bins. Horizontal axis represents the similarity value between matching features. *Top*: distribution of similarities with kernel on SIFTs. *Bottom:* Distribution after modulation with α.

3.2 Modulation and Covariant Match Kernel

The vector α encoding the angle θ "modulates"[1] any vector $\mathbf{x}$ (or pre-mapped descriptor $\varphi(\mathbf{x})$) with a function $m : \mathbb{R}^{2N+1} \times \mathbb{R}^D \rightarrow \mathbb{R}^{(2N+1)D}$. Thanks to classical properties of the Kronecker product $\otimes$, we have

$$m(\mathbf{x}, \alpha(\theta)) = \mathbf{x} \otimes \alpha(\theta) = (x_1\alpha(\theta)^\top, x_2\alpha(\theta)^\top \dots, x_d\alpha(\theta)^\top)^\top. \quad (19)$$

We now consider two pairs of vectors and angle, $(\mathbf{x}, \theta_x)$ and $(\mathbf{y}, \theta_y)$, and their modulated descriptors $m(\mathbf{x}, \alpha(\theta_x))$ and $m(\mathbf{y}, \alpha(\theta_y))$. In the product space $\mathbb{R}^{(2N+1)D}$, the following holds:

$$
\begin{aligned}
m(\mathbf{x}, \alpha(\theta_x))^\top m(\mathbf{y}, \alpha(\theta_y)) &= (\mathbf{x} \otimes \alpha(\theta_x))^\top (\mathbf{y} \otimes \alpha(\theta_y)) \\
&= (\mathbf{x}^\top \otimes \alpha(\theta_x)^\top)(\mathbf{y} \otimes \alpha(\theta_y)) = (\mathbf{x}^\top \mathbf{y}) \otimes (\alpha(\theta_x)^\top \alpha(\theta_y)) \\
&= (\mathbf{x}^\top \mathbf{y})k_\theta(\theta_x - \theta_y). \quad (20)
\end{aligned}
$$

Figure 3 shows the distribution of the similarities between regions of interest before and after modulation, as a function of the difference of angles. Interestingly, there is no obvious correlation between the difference of angle and the SIFT: the similarity distribution based on SIFT is similar for all angles. This suggests that the modulation with angle provides complementary information.

Combination with coding/pooling techniques. Consider any coding method φ that can be written as match kernel (Fisher, LLC, Bag-of-words, VLAD, etc). The match kernel in (7), with our k_θ approximation, is re-written as

$$
\begin{aligned}
K^\star(\mathcal{X}^\star, \mathcal{Y}^\star) &= \beta(\mathcal{X}^\star)\beta(\mathcal{Y}^\star) \sum_{(\mathbf{x},\theta_x)\in\mathcal{X}^\star} \sum_{(\mathbf{y},\theta_y)\in\mathcal{Y}^\star} m(\varphi(\mathbf{x}), \alpha(\theta_x))^\top m(\varphi(\mathbf{y}), \alpha(\theta_y)), \\
&= \beta(\mathcal{X}^\star) \left(\sum_{(\mathbf{x},\theta_x)} m(\varphi(\mathbf{x}), \alpha(\theta_x)) \right)^\top \beta(\mathcal{Y}^\star) \left(\sum_{(\mathbf{y},\theta_y)} m(\varphi(\mathbf{y}), \alpha(\theta_y)) \right),
\end{aligned}
$$
$$(21)$$

---

[1] By analogy to communications, where modulation refers to the process of encoding information over periodic waveforms.

where we observe that the image can be represented as the summation $\mathbf{X}^\star$ of the embedded descriptors modulated by their corresponding dominant orientation, as

$$\mathbf{X}^\star = \beta(\mathcal{X}^\star) \sum_{(\mathbf{x},\theta_x)\in\mathcal{X}^\star} m(\varphi(\mathbf{x}),\boldsymbol{\alpha}(\theta_x)). \tag{22}$$

This representation encodes the relative angles and is already more discriminative than an aggregation that does not consider them. However, at this stage, the comparison assumes that the images have the same global orientation. This is the case on benchmarks like Oxford5k building, where all images are orientated upright, but this is not true in general for particular object recognition.

3.3   Rotation Invariance

We now describe how to produce a similarity score when the orientations of related images may be different. We represent the image vector $\mathbf{X}^\star$ as the concatenation of $2N + 1$ D-dimensional subvectors associated to one term of the finite Fourier series: $\mathbf{X}^\star = [\mathbf{X}_0^{\star\top}, \mathbf{X}_{1,c}^{\star\top}, \mathbf{X}_{1,s}^{\star\top}, \dots, \mathbf{X}_{N,c}^{\star\top}, \mathbf{X}_{N,s}^{\star\top}]^\top$. The vector $\mathbf{X}_0^\star$ is associated with the constant term in the Fourier expansion, $\mathbf{X}_{n,c}^\star$ and $\mathbf{X}_{n,s}^\star$, $1 \leq n \leq N$, correspond to the cosine and sine terms, respectively.

Imagine now that this image undergoes a global rotation of angle θ. Denote $\check{\mathcal{X}}$ the new set of pairs $(\mathbf{x}, \check{\theta}_x)$ with $\check{\theta}_x = \theta_x + \theta$, and $\check{\mathbf{X}}^\star$ is the new image vector derived from these local descriptors. It occurs that $\check{\mathbf{X}}_0^\star = \mathbf{X}_0^\star$ because this term does not depend on the angle, and that, for a given frequency bin n, elementary trigonometry identities lead to

$$\check{\mathbf{X}}_{n,c}^\star = \mathbf{X}_{n,c}^\star \cos n\theta + \mathbf{X}_{n,s}^\star \sin n\theta \tag{23}$$

$$\check{\mathbf{X}}_{n,s}^\star = -\mathbf{X}_{n,c}^\star \sin n\theta + \mathbf{X}_{n,s}^\star \cos n\theta. \tag{24}$$

This in turn shows that $\|\check{\mathbf{X}}^\star\| = \|\mathbf{X}^\star\|$. Therefore the rotation has no effect on the normalization factor $\beta(\mathcal{X}^\star)$.

When comparing two images with such vectors, the linearity of the inner product ensures that

$$\langle\check{\mathbf{X}}^\star|\mathbf{Y}^\star\rangle = \langle\mathbf{X}_0^\star|\mathbf{Y}_0^\star\rangle + \sum_{n=1}^{N} \cos n\theta \left(\langle\mathbf{X}_{n,c}^\star|\mathbf{Y}_{n,c}^\star\rangle + \langle\mathbf{X}_{n,s}^\star|\mathbf{Y}_{n,s}^\star\rangle\right) \tag{25}$$

$$+ \sum_{n=1}^{N} \sin n\theta \left(-\langle\mathbf{X}_{n,c}^\star|\mathbf{Y}_{n,s}^\star\rangle + \langle\mathbf{X}_{n,s}^\star|\mathbf{Y}_{n,c}^\star\rangle\right). \tag{26}$$

Here, we stress that the similarity between two images is a real trigonometric polynomial in θ (rotation angle) of degree N. Its $2N + 1$ components are fully determined by computing $\langle\mathbf{X}_0^\star|\mathbf{Y}_0^\star\rangle$ and the inner products between the subvectors associated with each frequency, i.e., $\langle\mathbf{X}_{n,c}^\star|\mathbf{Y}_{n,c}^\star\rangle$, $\langle\mathbf{X}_{n,s}^\star|\mathbf{Y}_{n,s}^\star\rangle$, $\langle\mathbf{X}_{n,c}^\star|\mathbf{Y}_{n,s}^\star\rangle$ and $\langle\mathbf{X}_{n,s}^\star|\mathbf{Y}_{n,c}^\star\rangle$. Finding the maximum of this polynomial amounts to finding the rotation maximizing the score between the two images.

Computing the coefficients of this polynomial requires a total of $D \times (1+4N)$ elementary operations for a vector representation of dimensionality $D \times (1+2N)$, that is, less than twice the cost of the inner product between $\mathbf{X}^\star$ and $\mathbf{Y}^\star$. Once these components are obtained, the cost of finding the maximum value achieved by this polynomial is negligible for large values of D, for instance by simply sampling a few values of θ. Therefore, if we want to offer the orientation invariant property, the complexity of similarity computation is typically twice the cost of that of a regular vector representation (whose complexity is equal to the number of dimensions).

Remark: This strategy for computing the scores for all possible orientations of the query is not directly compatible with non-linear post-processing of $\mathbf{X}^\star$ such as component-wise power-law normalization [27], except for the subvector $\mathbf{X}_0^\star$. We propose two possible options to overcome this problem.

1. The naive strategy is to compute the query for several hypothesis of angle rotation, typically 8. In theory, this multiplies the query complexity by the same factor 8. However, in practice, it is faster to perform the matrix-matrix multiplication, with the right matrix representing 8 queries, than computing separately the corresponding 8 matrix-vector multiplications. We use this simpler approach in the experimental section.
2. Alternately, the power-law normalization is adapted to become compatible with our strategy: we compute the modulus of the complex number represented by two components (sin and cos) associated with the same frequency n and the same original component in $\varphi(\mathbf{x})$. These two components are then divided by the square-root (or any power) of this modulus. Experimentally, this strategy is as effective as the naive option.

4   Experiments

We evaluate the performance of the proposed approaches and compare with state of the art methods on two publicly available datasets for image and particular object retrieval, namely Inria Holidays [23] and Oxford Buildings 5k [4]. We also combine the latter with 100k distractor images to measure the performance on a larger scale. The merged dataset is referred to as Oxford105k. The retrieval performance is measured with mean Average Precision (mAP) [4].

Our approach modulates any coding/pooling technique operating as a match kernel. Therefore, we evaluate the benefit of our approach combined with several coding techniques, namely

○ VLAD [12], which encodes a SIFT descriptor by considering the residual vector to the centroid.
○ The Fisher vector [11,27,31]. For image classification, Chatfield *et al.* [32] show that it outperforms concurrent coding techniques, in particular LLC [10]. We adopt the standard choice for image retrieval and use only the gradient with respect to the mean [12].

○ Monomomial embeddings of order 2 and 3 applied on local descriptors (See below for pre-processing), *i.e.*, the functions φ_2 in (5) and φ_3 in (6). For the sake of consistency, we also denote by φ_1 the function $\varphi_1 : x \to x$.

We refer to these methods combined with our approach with the symbol "$\otimes$": VLAD$\otimes$, Fisher$\otimes$, $\varphi_1\otimes$, $\varphi_2\otimes$ and $\varphi_3\otimes$, correspondingly. In addition, we compare against the most related work, namely the recent CVLAD [19] method, which also aims at producing an image vector representation integrating the dominant orientations of the patches. Whenever the prior work is not referenced, results are produced using our own (improved) implementations of VLAD, Fisher and CVLAD, so that the results are directly comparable with the same features.

4.1   Implementation Details

Local descriptors.   We use the Hessian-Affine detector [33] to extract the regions of interest, that are subsequently described by SIFT descriptors [1] post-processed with RootSIFT [34]. Then, following the pre-processing required for the Fisher vector [11,27,12], we apply PCA to reduce the vector to 80 components. An exception is done for VLAD and CVLAD with which we only use the PCA basis to center and rotate descriptors as suggested by Delhumeau [35], without dimensionality reduction. The resulting vector is subsequently ℓ_2-normalized.

The improved Hessian-Affine detector of Perdoch *et al.* [36] improves the retrieval performance. However, we do not use it, since it ignores rotations by making the gravity vector assumption. Instead, we use the original detector modified so that it has similar parameters (patch size equal to 41).

Codebook.   For all methods based on codebooks, we only consider distinct datasets for learning. More precisely and following common practice, the k-means and GMM (for VLAD and Fisher, respectively) are learned on Flickr60k for Inria Holidays and Paris6k [37] for Oxford buildings. We rely on the Yael library [38] for codebook construction and VLAD and Fisher encoding.

Post-processing.   The final image vector obtained by each method is power-law normalized [8,27,12]. This processing improves the performance by efficiently handling the burstiness phenomenon. Exploiting the dominant orientation in our covariant match kernel provides a complementary way to further handle the same problem. We mention that using the dominant orientation is shown effective in a recent work by Torii *et al.* [39]. With our angle modulation, this post-processing inherently captures and down weights patches with similar dominant orientation. The power-law exponent is set to 0.4 for Fisher and VLAD and to 0.2 for monomial embeddings. These values give best or close-to-best performance for the initial representations. The resulting vector is ℓ_2-normalized.

In addition to power-law normalization, we rotate the aggregated vector representation with a PCA rotation matrix [40,41]. This aims at capturing the co-occurrences to down-weight them either by whitening [40] or a second power-law normalization [41]. We adopt the latter choice (with exponent 0.5) to avoid

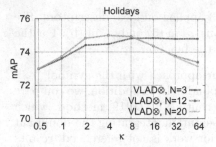
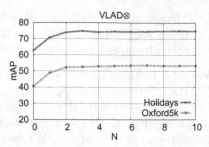

Fig. 4. Left: Performance on Holidays dataset of modulated VLAD for different values of κ and for different approximations. Right: Performance comparison of modulated VLAD for increasing number of components of the angle feature map. Zero corresponds to original VLAD (not modulated).

the sensitivity to eigenvalues (in whitening) when learning PCA with few input data. We refer to this Rotation and Normalization as RN in our experiments.

Optionally, to produce compact representations, we keep only the first few components (the most energetic ones) and ℓ_2-normalize the shortened vector.

Query rotation. In order to obtain rotation invariance jointly with power-law normalization and RN, we apply rotations of the query image and apply individual queries as described in Section 3 (option 1). We apply 8 query rotations on Holidays dataset. On Oxford5k, we rather adopt the common choice of not considering other possible orientations: Possible rotation of the query object is usually not considered since all the images are up-right.

4.2   Impact of the Parameters

The impact of the angle modulation is controlled by the function k_θ parametrized by κ and N. As shown in Figure 2, the value κ typically controls the "bandwitdh", *i.e.*, the range of $\Delta\theta$ values with non-zero response. The parameter N controls the quality of the approximation, and implicitly constrains the achievable bandwidth. It also determines the dimensionality of the output vector.

Figure 4 (left) shows the impact of these parameters on the performance. As to be expected, there is a trade-off between defining too narrow or too large. The optimal performance is achieved with κ in the range $[2, 8]$. Figure 4 (right) shows the performance for increasing number of frequencies, which rapidly converges to a fixed mAP. This is the mAP of the exact evaluation of (7). We set $N = 3$ as a compromise between dimensionality expansion and performance. Therefore the modulation multiplies the input dimensionality by 7.

4.3   Benefit of Our Approach

Table 1 shows the benefit of modulation when applied to the monomial embeddings φ_1, φ_2 and φ_3. The results are on par with the recent coding techniques like VLAD

Table 1. Impact of modulation on monomial embeddings of order 1, 2 and 3. The performance is reported for Holidays dataset. RN = Rotation and Normalization.

Method	φ_1	$\varphi_1\otimes$			φ_2		$\varphi_2\otimes$				φ_3	$\varphi_3\otimes$
RN						×			×	×		
N	–	1	3	6	–		1	3	1	3	–	1
#dim	80	240	560	1,040	3240	3,240	9,720	22,680	9,720	22,680	88,560	265,680
mAP	35.4	48.9	59.5	**63.2**	59.7	71.6	68.8	73.7	75.3	**79.9**	60.0	72.5

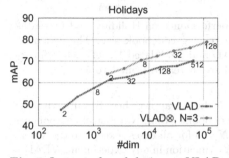
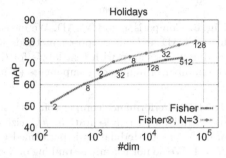

Fig. 5. Impact of modulation on VLAD and Fisher: Performance versus dimensionality of the final vector for VLAD (left) and Fisher (right) compared to their modulated counterparts. Codebook size is shown with text labels. Results for Holidays dataset.

or Fisher improved with modulation. We consider the obtained performance as one of our main achievements, because the representation is codebook-free and requires no learning. In addition, we further show the benefit of combining monomial embeddings with RN. This significantly boosts performance with the same vector dimensionality and negligible computational overhead.

We compare VLAD, Fisher and monomial embeddings to their modulated counterparts. Figure 5 shows that modulation significantly improves the performance for the same codebook size. However, given that the modulated vector is ×7 larger (with $N = 3$), the comparison focuses on the performance obtained with the same dimensionality. Even in this case, modulated VLAD⊗ and Fisher⊗ offer a significant improvement. We can conclude that it is better to increase the dimensionality by modulation than using a larger codebook.

4.4 Comparison to Other Methods

We compare our approach, in particular, to CVLAD, as this work also intends to integrate the dominant orientation into a vector representation. We consistently apply 8 query rotations for both CVLAD and our method on Holidays dataset. Figure 6 shows the respective performance measured for different codebooks. The proposed methods appear to consistently outperform CVLAD, both for the same codebook and for the same dimensionality. Noticeably, the modulated embedded monomial $\varphi_2\otimes$ is on par with or better than CVLAD.

We further conduct experiments using oriented dense [19] to compare VLAD⊗ to CVLAD. They achieve 87.2 and 86.5 respectively, on Holidays with codebook of size 512. This score is significantly higher than the one reported in [19].

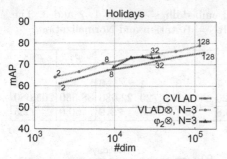 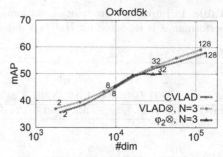

Fig. 6. Comparison to CVLAD. We measure performance on Holidays and Oxford5k for CVLAD and our proposed methods for increasing codebook size. The codebook cardinality is shown with text labels for CVLAD and modulated VLAD, while for φ_2 the number of frequency components (N) used are increased from 1 to 5.

Table 2. Performance comparison with state of the art approaches. Results with the use of full vector representation. #C: size of codebook. #dim: Number of components of each vector. Modulation is performed with $N = 3$ for all cases, except to φ_3, where $N = 1$. We do not use any re-ranking or spatial verification in any experiment. VLAD⊗ achieves **87.2** on Holidays and 80.5 on Oxford5k with #C=512 and oriented dense.

Method	#C	#dim	RN	Holidays	Oxford5k	Oxford105k
VLAD [12]	64	4,096		55.6	37.8	-
Fisher [12]	64	4,096		59.5	41.8	-
VLAD [12]	256	16,384		58.7	-	-
Fisher [12]	256	16,384		62.5	-	-
Arandjelovic [42]	256	32,536		65.3	**55.8**	-
Delhumeau [35]	64	8,192		65.8	51.7	45.6
Zhao [19]	32	32,768		**68.8**	42.7	-
VLAD⊗	32	28,672		74.8	52.5	46.3
VLAD⊗	32	28,672	×	81.0	61.8	**53.9**
Fisher⊗	32	17,920		76.0	51.0	44.9
Fisher⊗	32	17,920	×	81.2	60.7	52.2
Fisher⊗	64	35,840	×	**84.1**	**64.8**	-
φ_2⊗	n/a	22,680		73.7	50.1	44.3
φ_2⊗	n/a	22,680	×	79.9	60.5	51.9
φ_3⊗	n/a	265,680		72.5	53.5	-

Corresponding scores on Oxford5k are 50.5 and 50.7, respectively. However, note that it is very costly to densely extract patches aligned with dominant orientation.

We also compare to other prior works and present results in Table 2 for Holidays, Oxford5k and Oxford105k. We outperform by a large margin the state of the art with full vector representations. Further, our approach is arguably compatible with these concurrent approaches, which may bring further improvement. Note that RN also boosts performance for VLAD and Fisher. In particular with a codebook of size 32, they achieve 50.0 and 48.6 respectively on Oxford5k. Our scores on Holidays with Fisher⊗ and RN are also competitive to those reported by state-of-the-art methods based on large codebooks [9]. To our knowledge,

Table 3. Oxford105k: Performance comparison (mAP) after dimensionality reduction with PCA into 128 and 1024 components. The results with the full vector representation are with RN. Observe the consistent gain (in parentheses) brought by our approach for a *fixed* output dimensionality of 1,024 or 128 components.

Method	#dim	full dim	dim→1024	dim→128
VLAD	4,096	40.3	34.7	24.0
VLAD⊗	28,672	53.9	**40.7** (+7.0)	**27.5** (+3.5)
Fisher	2,560	39.3	37.3	25.2
Fisher⊗	17,920	52.2	39.9 (+2.6)	26.5 (+1.3)
φ_2	3,240	35.8	31.1	20.4
φ_2⊗	22,680	51.9	37.7 (+6.6)	24.0 (+3.6)

this is the first time that a vector representation compatible with inner product attains such image search performance.

On Oxford5k we do not evaluate multiple query rotations for our method. A simple way to enforce up-right objects for baseline methods is to use up-right features. Performance of VLAD with codebook of size 256 decreases from 51.3 to 49.4 by doing so, presumably because of small object rotations.

Finally, Table 3 reports the performance after dimensionality reduction to 128 or 1024 components. The same set of local features and codebooks are used for all methods. We observe a consistent improvement over the original encoding.

4.5 Timings

The image representation created by modulating the monomial embedding φ_2 using $N = 3$ takes on average 68 ms for a typical image with 3,000 SIFT descriptors. The resulting aggregated vector representation has 22,680 components. The average query time using cosine similarity on Oxford5k is 44 ms assuming no query rotation and 257 ms with the use of 8 possible fixed rotations (with the naive strategy discussed in Section 3.3). The corresponding timings for Oxford105k and vectors reduced to 128 dimensions are 55 ms and 134 ms, respectively. Note, these timings are better than those achieved by a bag-of-words representation with a large vocabulary, for which the quantization typically takes above 1 second with an approximate nearest neighbor search algorithm like FLANN [43].

5 Conclusion

Our modulation strategy integrates the dominant orientation directly in the coding stage. It is inspired by and builds upon recent works on explicit feature maps and kernel descriptors. Thanks to a generic formulation provided by match kernels, it is compatible with coding strategies such as Fisher vector or VLAD. Our experiments demonstrate that it gives a consistent gain compared to the original coding in all cases, even after dimensionality reduction. Interestingly, it is also very effective with a simple monomial kernel, offering competitive performance for image search with a coding stage not requiring any quantization.

Whatever the coding stage that we use with our approach, the resulting representation is compared with inner product, which suggests that it is compliant with linear classifiers such as those considered in image classification.

Acknowledgments. This work was supported by ERC grant VIAMASS no. 336054 and ANR project Fire-ID.

References

1. Lowe, D.: Distinctive image features from scale-invariant keypoints. IJCV 60(2), 91–110 (2004)
2. Bay, H., Ess, A., Tuytelaars, T., Gool, L.V.: SURF: Speeded up robust features. Computer Vision and Image Understanding 110(3), 346–359 (2008)
3. Sivic, J., Zisserman, A.: Video Google: A text retrieval approach to object matching in videos. In: ICCV (October 2003)
4. Philbin, J., Chum, O., Isard, M., Sivic, J., Zisserman, A.: Object retrieval with large vocabularies and fast spatial matching. In: CVPR (June 2007)
5. Chum, O., Philbin, J., Sivic, J., Isard, M., Zisserman, A.: Total recall: Automatic query expansion with a generative feature model for object retrieval. In: ICCV (October 2007)
6. Jégou, H., Douze, M., Schmid, C.: Improving bag-of-features for large scale image search. IJCV 87(3), 316–336 (2010)
7. Mikulík, A., Perdoch, M., Chum, O., Matas, J.: Learning a fine vocabulary. In: Daniilidis, K., Maragos, P., Paragios, N. (eds.) ECCV 2010, Part III. LNCS, vol. 6313, pp. 1–14. Springer, Heidelberg (2010)
8. Jégou, H., Douze, M., Schmid, C.: On the burstiness of visual elements. In: CVPR (June 2009)
9. Tolias, G., Avrithis, Y., Jégou, H.: To aggregate or not to aggregate: Selective match kernels for image search. In: ICCV (December 2013)
10. Wang, J., Yang, J., Yu, K., Huang, F.L., Gong, T., Locality-constrained, Y.: linear coding for image classification. In: CVPR (June 2010)
11. Perronnin, F., Dance, C.R.: Fisher kernels on visual vocabularies for image categorization. In: CVPR (June 2007)
12. Jégou, H., Perronnin, F., Douze, M., Sánchez, J., Pérez, P., Schmid, C.: Aggregating local descriptors into compact codes. Trans. PAMI (September 2012)
13. Perronnin, F., Liu, Y., Sanchez, J., Poirier, H.: Large-scale image retrieval with compressed Fisher vectors. In: CVPR (June 2010)
14. Charikar, M.: Similarity estimation techniques from rounding algorithms. In: STOC (May 2002)
15. Jégou, H., Douze, M., Schmid, C.: Product quantization for nearest neighbor search. Trans. PAMI 33(1), 117–128 (2011)
16. Lazebnik, S., Schmid, C., Ponce, J.: Beyond bags of features: spatial pyramid matching for recognizing natural scene categories. In: CVPR (June 2006)
17. Douze, M., Jégou, H., Singh, H., Amsaleg, L., Schmid, C.: Evaluation of GIST descriptors for web-scale image search. In: CIVR (July 2009)
18. Koniusz, P., Yan, F., Mikolajczyk, K.: Comparison of mid-level feature coding approaches and pooling strategies in visual concept detection. Computer Vision and Image Understanding 17(5), 479–492 (2013)
19. Zhao, W., Jégou, H., Gravier, G.: Oriented pooling for dense and non-dense rotation-invariant features. In: BMVC (September 2013)
20. Bo, L., Sminchisescu, C.: Efficient match kernel between sets of features for visual recognition. In: NIPS (December 2009)
21. Bo, L., Ren, X., Fox, D.: Kernel descriptors for visual recognition. In: NIPS (December 2010)
22. Vedaldi, A., Zisserman, A.: Efficient additive kernels via explicit feature maps. Trans. PAMI 34(3), 480–492 (2012)

23. Jegou, H., Douze, M., Schmid, C.: Hamming embedding and weak geometric consistency for large scale image search. In: Forsyth, D., Torr, P., Zisserman, A. (eds.) ECCV 2008, Part I. LNCS, vol. 5302, pp. 304–317. Springer, Heidelberg (2008)
24. Lyu, S.: Mercer kernels for object recognition with local features. In: CVPR (June 2005)
25. Csurka, G., Dance, C.R., Fan, L., Willamowski, J., Bray, C.: Visual categorization with bags of keypoints. In: ECCV Workshop Statistical Learning in Computer Vision (May 2004)
26. Picard, D., Gosselin, P.H.: Efficient image signatures and similarities using tensor products of local descriptors. Computer Vision and Image Understanding 117 (June 2013)
27. Perronnin, F., Sánchez, J., Mensink, T.: Improving the Fisher kernel for large-scale image classification. In: Daniilidis, K., Maragos, P., Paragios, N. (eds.) ECCV 2010, Part IV. LNCS, vol. 6314, pp. 143–156. Springer, Heidelberg (2010)
28. Carreira, J., Caseiro, R., Batista, J., Sminchisescu, C.: Semantic segmentation with second-order pooling. In: Fitzgibbon, A., Lazebnik, S., Perona, P., Sato, Y., Schmid, C. (eds.) ECCV 2012, Part VII. LNCS, vol. 7578, pp. 430–443. Springer, Heidelberg (2012)
29. Abramowitz, M., Stegun, I.A.: Handbook of mathematical functions with formulas, graphs, and mathematical tables. National Bureau of Standards Applied Mathematics Series, vol. 55. U.S. Government Printing Office (1964)
30. Băzăvan, E.G., Li, F., Sminchisescu, C.: Fourier kernel learning. In: Fitzgibbon, A., Lazebnik, S., Perona, P., Sato, Y., Schmid, C. (eds.) ECCV 2012, Part II. LNCS, vol. 7573, pp. 459–473. Springer, Heidelberg (2012)
31. Jaakkola, T., Haussler, D.: Exploiting generative models in discriminative classifiers. In: NIPS (December 1998)
32. Chatfield, K., Lempitsky, V., Vedaldi, A., Zisserman, A.: The devil is in the details: an evaluation of recent feature encoding methods. In: BMVC (September 2011)
33. Mikolajczyk, K., Tuytelaars, T., Schmid, C., Zisserman, A., Matas, J., Schaffalitzky, F., Kadir, T., Gool, L.V.: A comparison of affine region detectors. IJCV 65(1/2), 43–72 (2005)
34. Arandjelovic, R., Zisserman, A.: Three things everyone should know to improve object retrieval. In: CVPR (June 2012)
35. Delhumeau, J., Gosselin, P.H., Jégou, H., Pérez, P.: Revisiting the VLAD image representation. ACM Multimedia (October 2013)
36. Perdoch, M., Chum, O., Matas, J.: Efficient representation of local geometry for large scale object retrieval. In: CVPR (June 2009)
37. Philbin, J., Chum, O., Isard, M., Sivic, J., Zisserman, A.: Lost in quantization: Improving particular object retrieval in large scale image databases. In: CVPR (June 2008)
38. Douze, M., Jégou, H.: The Yael library. ACM Multimedia (November 2014)
39. Torii, A., Sivic, J., Pajdla, T., Okutomi, M.: Visual place recognition with repetitive structures. In: CVPR (June 2013)
40. Jégou, H., Chum, O.: Negative evidences and co-occurences in image retrieval: The benefit of PCA and whitening. In: Fitzgibbon, A., Lazebnik, S., Perona, P., Sato, Y., Schmid, C. (eds.) ECCV 2012, Part II. LNCS, vol. 7573, pp. 774–787. Springer, Heidelberg (2012)
41. Safadi, B., Quenot, G.: Descriptor optimization for multimedia indexing and retrieval. In: CBMI (June 2013)
42. Arandjelovic, R., Zisserman, A.: All about VLAD. In: CVPR (June 2013)
43. Muja, M., Lowe, D.G.: Fast approximate nearest neighbors with automatic algorithm configuration. In: VISAPP (February 2009)

Similarity-Invariant Sketch-Based Image Retrieval in Large Databases

Sarthak Parui and Anurag Mittal

Computer Vision Lab, Dept. of CSE
Indian Institue of Technology Madras, Chennai, India

Abstract. Proliferation of touch-based devices has made the idea of sketch-based image retrieval practical. While many methods exist for sketch-based image retrieval on small datasets, little work has been done on large (web)-scale image retrieval. In this paper, we present an efficient approach for image retrieval from millions of images based on user-drawn sketches. Unlike existing methods which are sensitive to even translation or scale variations, our method handles translation, scale, rotation (similarity) and small deformations. To make online retrieval fast, each database image is preprocessed to extract sequences of contour segments (chains) that capture sufficient shape information which are represented by succinct variable length descriptors. Chain similarities are computed by a fast Dynamic Programming-based *approximate substring* matching algorithm, which enables partial matching of chains. Finally, hierarchical k-medoids based indexing is used for very fast retrieval in a few seconds on databases with millions of images. Qualitative and quantitative results clearly demonstrate superiority of the approach over existing methods.

Keywords: Image Retrieval, Shape Representation and Matching.

1 Introduction

The explosive growth of digital images on the web has substantially increased the need of an accurate, efficient and user-friendly large scale image retrieval system. With the growing popularity of touch-based smart computing devices and the consequent ease and simplicity of querying images via hand-drawn sketches on touch screens [21], sketch-based image retrieval has emerged as an interesting problem. The standard mechanism of text-based querying could be imprecise due to wide demographic variations and it faces the issue of availability, authenticity and ambiguity in the tag and text information surrounding an image [35,37]. Sketch-based image retrieval, on the other hand, being a far more expressive way of image search, either alone or in conjunction with other retrieval mechanisms such as text, may yield better results. For instance, it may be possible to build a sketch in an on-line manner using the first few results of a text query system [3,20,24] and use this sketch for retrieving images that may not have any associated tag information. Image tag information may also be improved via an off-line process of sketch-based retrieval.

Several approaches have been proposed in the literature for sketch-based Object Detection and Retrieval. Ferrari *et al.* [15] describe a scale-invariant local shape feature

D. Fleet et al. (Eds.): ECCV 2014, Part VI, LNCS 8694, pp. 398–414, 2014.
© Springer International Publishing Switzerland 2014

that uses chains of k-connected Adjacent contour Segments (k-AS). To capture the global shape properties as well, Felzenszwalb *et al.* [14] use a *shape-tree* to form a hierarchical structure of contour segments and devise an efficient Dynamic Programming (DP)-based matching algorithm to match to the given sketch. Riemenschneider *et al.* [31] describe a set of highly-overlapping translation and rotation-invariant contour descriptors that measure the relative angles amongst a set of fixed number of sampled points along a contour. However, all of these methods and many other state-of-the-art methods for Object Detection and Retrieval [4,18,22,30,36,43] perform costly online matching operations based on complex shape features to enhance the detection performance on relatively small-sized datasets such as ETHZ [16] and MPEG-7 [19]. However, for a dataset with millions of images with a desired retrieval time of at most a few seconds, these methods are inapplicable/insufficient and efficient pre-processing and fast online retrieval are necessary features for large (web)-scale Image Retrieval.

Relatively fewer attempts have been made on the problem of sketch query-based image retrieval on large databases. Eitz *et al.* [13], Cao *et al.* [8] and Bozas and Izquierdo [6] measure the sketch-to-image similarity by comparing the edges and their directions at approximately the same location in the sketch and the image after scale normalization. For fast search, Cao *et al.* [8] build an inverted index structure based on the edge pixel locations and orientations of all the database images. However, all these approaches rely on a strong assumption that the user wants only spatially consistent images as the search result. Thus, they would miss images having the sketched object at a different translation, scale or rotation. Zhou *et al.* [44] determine the most "salient" object in the image and measure image similarity based on a descriptor built on the object. However, determining saliency is a very hard problem and the accuracy of even the state-of-the-art saliency methods is low. Riemenschneider *et al.* [32] extend their idea of [31] to large scale retrieval, where to make the processing fast, invariance to scale and rotation is compromised. Furthermore, due to using high-overlapping descriptors, the computational complexity is still very high for very large datasets.

In this paper, we propose a large scale sketch-based image retrieval approach that enables efficient similarity-invariant, deformation handling matching even for datasets with millions of images unlike any relevant existing work. First, the essential shape information of all the database images is represented in a similarity-invariant way in an offline process. This is accomplished by extracting long sequences of contour segments (chains) from each image and storing them succinctly using variable length descriptors in a similarity preserving way (Sec. 2). Second, an efficient DP-based *approximate substring* matching algorithm is proposed for fast matching of such chains between a sketch and an image or between two images. Note that, variability in the length of the descriptors makes the formulation unique and more challenging. Furthermore, partial matching is allowed to accommodate intra-class variations, small occlusions and the presence of non-object portions in the chains (Sec. 3). Third, a hierarchical indexing tree structure of the chain descriptors of the entire image database is built offline to facilitate fast online search by matching the chains along the tree (Sec. 4). Finally, a geometric verification scheme is devised for an on-the-fly elimination of false positives that may accidentally receive a high matching score due to partial shape similarity (Sec. 5). Qualitative and quantitative comparisons with the state-of-the-art on a dataset of 1.2 million images clearly indicate superior performance and advantages of our approach.

2   From Images to Contour Chains

In this section, we describe the offline preprocessing of database images with an objective of having a compact representation which can be used to efficiently match the images with a query sketch. Since a user typically draws object boundaries, an image representation based on contour information would be appropriate in this scenario.

2.1   Obtaining Salient Contours

At first, all the database images are normalized to a standard size taking the longest side size as 256 pixels. Then, the Berkeley Edge Detector [1] is used to generate a probabilistic edge-map of the image since it gives superior edges compared to traditional approaches such as Canny [7] by considering texture along with color and brightness in an image. Since such an edge map typically contains a lot of clutter edges (Fig. 1(b)), an intelligent grouping of edge pixels can yield better contours that have a higher chance of belonging to an object boundary. The method proposed by Zhu *et al.* [45] groups edge pixels by considering long connected edge sequences that have as little bends as possible, especially at the junction points. Contours that satisfy such a constraint are called *salient* contours in their work and this method is used to obtain a set of *salient* contours from each database image (Fig. 1(c)).

2.2   Creating Segments

The salient contours thus obtained may still contain some bends in them. Some articulation should be allowed at such bends since it has been observed that object shape perspective remains relatively unchanged under articulations at such bend points [5]. These bend points along the contour are determined as the local maxima of the curvature. The curvature of a point p_c is obtained using m points on either side of it as:

$$\kappa_{p_c} = \sum_{i=1}^{m} w_i \cdot \angle p_{c-i} p_c p_{c+i} \tag{1}$$

where w_i is the weight defined by a Gaussian function centered at p_c. This function robustly estimates the curvature at point p_c at a given scale m. The salient contours are split into different segments at such high curvature points and as a result, a set of straight line-like segments are obtained for an image (Fig. 1(d)).

2.3   Chaining the Segments

Given a set of straight line-like contour segments in an image, we design compact representation of an image by considering ordered sequences of segments that utilize the connectedness of the object boundary. The connectivity among the segments suggests an

Fig. 1. Creation of chains: (a) Original image, (b) Berkley edge-map [1], (c) Salient contours [45] extracted, (d) Extracted straight line-like segments, (e) Final chains obtained (black and blue)

underlying graph structure. Ferrari *et al.* [15] utilize this by constructing an unweighted *contour segment network* which links nearby edge segments, and then extracting $k(\leq 4)$ adjacent contour segments(k-AS) for a large number of image windows. They trace the object boundary by linking individual small k-AS at the multi-scale detection phase. Although such an approach performs well in clutter, it leads to a costly online matching operation, which motivates us to represent an object with much longer segment chains a priori for each image rather than with very small contour fragments.

It has been observed that long sequences of segments typically have a large intersection with important object boundaries. Therefore, in our approach, we try to extract the long sequences. To obtain such long sequences, in contrast to [15], a weighted (rather than an unweighted) graph is constructed where each end of a contour segment is considered as a vertex and the edge weight is equal to the length of the segment. Vertices from two different contour segments are also joined by an edge if they are spatially close. The weight of such an edge is taken as $\lambda_d \cdot \exp(-d/D)$, where d is the spatial distance between the two end points, D is the diagonal length of the normalized image and λ_d is a constant factor that provides a trade-off between the segment length and the inter-segment gap.

The weight of an edge in the graph represents the spatial extent of the segments and the connectedness between them. Therefore, a long path in the graph based on the edge weights relates to a long and closely connected sequence of contour segments which is what we desire in the image. As the graph may contain cycles, to get a unique long path, the maximum spanning tree[1] is constructed for each connected component using a standard minimum spanning tree algorithm [9] and the longest paths from such trees are determined using Depth First Search [9].

A long path thus obtained may deviate from the object boundary at the junction points. Ideally, to capture maximum shape information, all possible sequences through such junction points should be considered. However, this leads to an exponential blowup in the representation and is therefore impractical for a database of millions of images. Hence, as a trade-off between representative power and compactness, we follow a greedy approach by considering only edge-disjoint long sequences in the graph. These are determined by sequentially finding and removing the longest contour in the graph. Finally, an image is represented as a set of such non-overlapping long sequences of segments (Fig. 1(e)), and we call each of these sequences a *chain*. Fig. 2(a) shows the chains thus obtained in some common images.

---

[1] Maximum spanning tree of a graph can be computed by negating the edge weights and computing the minimum spanning tree.

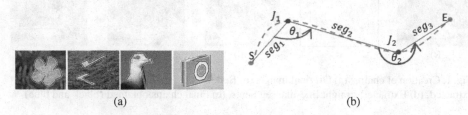

(a)   (b)

Fig. 2. Image Representation: (a) Chains extracted for some images. Different chains are represented using different colors. (b) The chain for the curve SE is composed of three line segments. The descriptor for this chain is $\Psi = \left\langle \gamma_i = \frac{l_{seg_i}}{l_{seg_{i+1}}}, \theta_i \mid i \in \{1,2\} \right\rangle$.

2.4   Creating Descriptors for Each Chain

In order to efficiently match two chains in a similarity-invariant way, we require a compact descriptor that captures the shape information of the extracted chains in a similarity-invariant way. Towards this goal, the local shape information is captured at the joints in a scale, in-plane rotation and position invariant way. For the ith joint of chain k (J_i^k), the segment length ratio $\gamma_i = \frac{l_{seg_i}}{l_{seg_{i+1}}}$ (l_{seg_i} denotes the length of the ith segment) and the anti-clockwise angle θ_i (range: $[0, 2\pi]$) between the corresponding pair of segments seg_i and seg_{i+1} are determined, as shown in Fig. 2(b). The descriptor Ψ^k for a chain k with N segments is then defined as an ordered sequence of such similarity-invariant quantities:

$$\Psi^k = \langle \gamma_i, \theta_i \mid i \in \{1 \ldots N-1\} \rangle \tag{2}$$

Note that, Riemenschneider *et al.* [31] also use joint information by measuring the relative angles among all pairs of sampled points along a contour. However, their representation is not scale invariant which leads to a costly online multi-scale matching phase. In contrast, the proposed descriptor is insensitive to similarities and succinct enough for efficiently representing and matching millions of images.

Having extracted chains from images and compactly representing them in a similarity-invariant way, we next describe an approach for efficiently matching such chains.

3   Matching Two Chains

Standard vectorial type of distance measures are not applicable for matching due to variability in the lengths of the chains. This constraint makes the task more challenging since most of the fast indexing mechanisms for large scale retrieval exploit a metric structure. Further, note that the object boundary is typically captured by only a portion of the chain in the database image. Therefore, a partial matching strategy of such chains needs to be devised which can be smoothly integrated with an indexing structure to efficiently determine object shape similarity.

Since image chains are typically noisy, a chain that captures an object boundary may have non-object contour segments on either side of the object boundary portion. Furthermore, we assume that the object boundary is captured by a more or less contiguous portion of the chain and is not split by large gaps. Although such large split-ups may occur in certain circumstances, allowing such matches leads to a lot of false matches of images due to too much relaxation of the matching criteria. This is illustrated in Fig. 3(a), where the split matches put together do not match with the intended shape structure. Thus, in our work, the similarity between two chains is measured by trying to determine the maximum (almost) contiguous matching portions of the sequences while leaving out the non-matching portions on either side from consideration (Fig. 3(b)). This is quite similar to the Longest Common Substring[2] problem [9] with some modifications. The matching strategy between two chains is formulated by first matching individual joints of two chains.

3.1 Joint Similarity

Since exact correspondence of the joints does not capture the deformation that an object may undergo, we provide a slack while matching and score the match between a pair of joints based on the deviation from exact correspondence. The score $S_{jnt}(x,y)$ for matching the xth joint of chain C_1 to the yth joint of chain C_2 is taken to be the product of three constituent scores:

$$S_{jnt}(x,y) = S_{lr}(x,y) \cdot S_{ang}(x,y) \cdot S_{sz}(x,y) \tag{3}$$

$S_{lr}(x,y)$ is the closeness in the segment length ratio at the xth and the yth joints of the two descriptors:

$$S_{lr}(x,y) = \exp\left(\lambda_{lr} \cdot \left(1 - \Omega\left(\gamma_x^{C_1}, \gamma_y^{C_2}\right)\right)\right) \tag{4}$$

where $\gamma_x = \frac{l_{seg_x}}{l_{seg_x+1}}$ as defined in Sec. 2.4, $\Omega(a,b) = \max(a/b, b/a), a, b \in \mathbb{R}_{>0}$ measures the relative similarity between two ratios ($\Omega(a,b) \in (0,1]$) and $\lambda_{lr}(= 0.5)$ is a constant. $S_{ang}(x,y)$ determines the closeness of the angles at the xth and y^{th} joints and is defined as:

$$S_{ang}(x,y) = \exp\left(-\lambda_{ang} \cdot \left|\theta_x^{C_1} - \theta_y^{C_2}\right|\right) \tag{5}$$

where, $\lambda_{ang}(= 2)$ is a constant. These two components measure the structure similarity between a pair of joints. Due to the insensitivity of the descriptor itself to scale, translation and rotation, these measures are invariant to such transformations. However, lengthy segments are more relevant to an object and should get a higher score. Thus, it is desirable to give a higher score to a pair of matched joints if the segment lengths corresponding to the joints are large. This is captured by S_{sz} and is defined as:

$$S_{sz}(x,y) = \min\left(\left(l_{seg_x}^{C_1} + l_{seg_x+1}^{C_1}\right), \left(l_{seg_y}^{C_2} + l_{seg_y+1}^{C_2}\right)\right) \tag{6}$$

where, seg_x and seg_{x+1} are the two segments on either side of a joint x. The information about individual segment lengths is also retained in the chain extraction stage for such a calculation.

---

[2] Substring, unlike subsequence, does not allow gap between successive tokens.

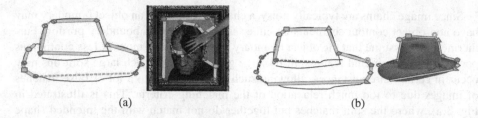

(a)   (b)

Fig. 3. (a) A match when fragmented skips are allowed. (b) A match when only almost-contiguous matches are allowed. Matched joints are shown with the same marker in the sketch and the image. Unmatched portions of the chains are indicated by dashed lines.

3.2 Chain Matching

Given the scoring mechanism between a pair of joints, the match score between two chains can be determined by calculating the cumulative joint matching score of contiguous portions in the two chains. Although exact matching of such portions can be considered, due to intra-class shape variations, small partial occlusion or noise, a few non-object joints may occur in the object boundary portion of the chain. To handle these non-object portions, some skips need to be allowed. Thus, the problem is formulated as one that finds *almost-contiguous* matches in the two descriptors that are to be matched. This is accomplished by applying a constant skip penalty α for the skips in the chain. To penalize lengthy skips more, the skip penalty is also weighted (ω_x) by the length of the segments on either side of a skipped joint x: $\omega_x = \left(l_{seg_x} + l_{seg_{x+1}}\right)$

Towards finding almost-contiguous matches, one can formulate the match score $M(p_1, q_1, p_2, q_2)$ for the portion of the chain between joints p_1 and q_1 in chain C_1 and joints p_2 and q_2 in chain C_2. Let the set J_1 and J_2 denote the set of joints of chains C_1 and C_2 respectively in this interval. Also let JM be a matching between J_1 and J_2 in this interval. We restrict JM to obey order constraint on the matches, i.e., if the joints a_1 and b_1 of the first chain are matched to the joints a_2 and b_2 respectively in the second chain, then a_1 occurring before b_1 implies that a_2 also occurs before b_2 and vice versa. Also let $X(\text{JM}) = \{x | (x, y) \in \text{JM}\}$ and $Y(\text{JM}) = \{y | (x, y) \in \text{JM}\}$ be the set of joints covered by JM. Then $M(p_1, q_1, p_2, q_2)$ is defined as:

$$M(p_1, q_1, p_2, q_2) = \max_{\substack{\text{JM} \in \text{ ordered} \\ \text{matchings in} \\ \text{interval}(p_1, q_1) \\ \text{and}(p_2, q_2)}} \left(\sum_{\substack{(x,y) \in \\ \text{JM}}} S_{jnt}(x, y) - \sum_{\substack{x \in \\ J_1 \setminus X(\text{JM})}} \omega_x^1 \alpha^1 - \sum_{\substack{y \in \\ J_2 \setminus Y(\text{JM})}} \omega_y^2 \alpha^2 \right)$$

(7)

Note that α^1 and α^2 may be different since while matching a sketch chain to an image chain, more penalty is given to a skip in the sketch chain ($\alpha = 0.07$) since it is considered cleaner and relatively more free from clutter compared to an image chain

($\alpha = 0.03$). Now, the maximum matching score ending at the joint q_1 of C_1 and q_2 of C_2 from any pair of starting joints, is defined as:

$$M(q_1, q_2) = \max_{p_1, p_2} M(p_1, q_1, p_2, q_2) \tag{8}$$

We take the matching score of a null set ($p_1 > q_1$ or $p_2 > q_2$) as zero which constrains $M(q_1, q_2)$ to take only non-negative values. Then, it is not difficult to prove that M can be rewritten using the following recurrence relation:

$$M(q_1, q_2) = \begin{cases} 0, & \text{if } q_1, q_2 = 0 \\ \max \begin{cases} M(q_1 - 1, q_2 - 1) + S_{jnt}(q_1, q_2) \\ M(q_1 - 1, q_2) - \omega_{q_1}^1 \alpha^1 \\ M(q_1, q_2 - 1) - \omega_{q_2}^2 \alpha^2 \\ 0 \end{cases}, & \text{otherwise} \end{cases} \tag{9}$$

This formulation immediately leads to an efficient Dynamic Programming solution that computes M for all possible values of q_1 and q_2 starting from the first joints to the last ones. A search for the largest value of $M(q_1, q_2)$ over all possible q_1 and q_2 will then give us the best almost-contiguous matched portions between two chains C_1 and C_2 that have the highest matching score. Furthermore, to handle an object flip, we match by flipping one of the chains as well and determine the best matching score as the one that gives the highest score between the two directions. We call the final score between two chains C_1 and C_2 as the Chain Score $CS(C_1, C_2)$. The entire operation of matching two chains takes $\mathcal{O}(n_{C_1} * n_{C_2})$ time, where n_{C_1} and n_{C_2} are the number of joints in chains C_1 and C_2 respectively. It has been observed that a chain typically consists of 12-17 joints leading to a running time of approximately 100-400 units of joint matching, which is not very high. Note that, this DP formulation is similar to the Smith-Waterman algorithm (SW) [39], which aligns two protein sequences based on a fixed alphabet-set and predefined matching costs. Meltzer and Soatto [25] use SW to perform matching between two images under wide-baseline viewpoint changes. Our method is slightly different from this since it performs matching based on a continuous-space formulation that measures the deviation from exact correspondence to handle deformation.

This chain-to-chain matching strategy is used to match two image chains during indexing and a sketch chain to an image chain during image retrieval. A brief description of Image Indexing is given next.

4 Image Indexing

Given a chain descriptor, matching it online with all chains obtained from millions of images will take considerable amount of time. Therefore, for fast retrieval of images from a large scale dataset, an indexing mechanism is required. Due to the variability in the length of the descriptors, it is difficult to use metric-based data structures, such as k-d tree [26] or Vantage-Point tree [42]. Therefore, in this work, an approach similar to hierarchical k-means [26,27] is used, in which a hierarchical structure is constructed by splitting the set of chains into k different clusters using the k-medoids [28,40] algorithm.

(Note that, because of the variable-length chain descriptors, *k-means* is inapplicable.) In our approach, k chains are chosen as the cluster centroids probabilistically using the initialization mechanism of *k-means++* [2] which increases both speed and accuracy. This operation is then recursively performed on the individual clusters to determine the clusters at different levels of the search tree. A leaf node of such a tree contains images in which at least one chain of each image matches to the medoid chain descriptor of that leaf node. Since an image has multiple chains, it can be present at multiple leaves.

5   Image Retrieval

A user typically draws the object boundary. From a touch-based device, the input order of the contour points of the object boundary is usually available. Therefore, sketch chains are trivially obtained and the corresponding descriptors are determined (Eq. 2). For each of these sketch chain descriptors, a search in the hierarchical k-medoids tree yields a small set of images in which at least one chain for each image matches with the query chain in the tree. Note that, for multiple sketch chains, we get multiple sets of images from the leaf nodes of the search tree, all of which are taken for the next step.

Given a set of retrieved images and corresponding matched chains, we devise a sketch-to-image matching strategy to rank the images. The matching score of an image for a given sketch is calculated based on the cumulative matching scores of individual matched chain pairs between the sketch and the image. Since the actual object boundary may be split across multiple chains, it is necessary to consider geometric consistency of the matched portions of multiple chains for correct retrievals. Although such geometric consistency has been studied previously in the literature [29,33,41], this is considered in a new context in this work.

5.1   Geometric Consistency between Matched Chains

The geometric consistency of the matched portions of a pair of chains $\mathbf{p} = (m(C_S), m(C_I))$ with respect to that of another chain pair $\mathbf{p}' = (m(C_S'), m(C_I'))$, where C_S and C_S' are the sketch chains and C_I, C_I' are the image chains, is measured based on two factors: i) *distance-consistency* $G_d(\mathbf{p}, \mathbf{p}')$ and ii) *angular-consistency* $G_a(\mathbf{p}, \mathbf{p}')$. Since only small skips are allowed while matching the object portion, the distance between the centroids of the matched chain portions remains relatively robust to the presence of noise. Therefore, $G_d(\mathbf{p}, \mathbf{p}')$ is defined in terms of the closeness of the distances between the chain centroids $d(m(C_S), m(C_S'))$ in the sketch and $d(m(C_I), m(C_I'))$ in the database image (Fig. 4). To achieve scale insensitivity, the distances are normalized by the total length of the matched portions of the corresponding chains.

$$G_d(\mathbf{p}, \mathbf{p}') = \exp\left(\lambda_c \cdot \left(1 - \Omega\left(\frac{d(m(C_S), m(C_S'))}{L_S}, \frac{d(m(C_I), m(C_I'))}{L_I}\right)\right)\right) \quad (10)$$

where, L_S=length $(m(C_S))$+ length$(m(C_S'))$, L_I=length $(m(C_I))$+ length $(m(C_I'))$ and $\lambda_c(=1)$ is a scalar constant and Ω is defined in Eq. 4. The next factor G_a measures *angular-consistency*. To achieve rotational invariance, the line joining the correspond-ing chain centers is considered as the reference axis and the angle difference at the ith

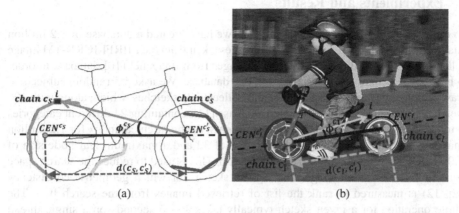

(a)   (b)

Fig. 4. Pairwise geometric consistency of the matched portions of a chain pair $\mathbf{p} = (C_S, C_I)$ with respect to $\mathbf{p}' = (C'_S, C'_I)$ uses (i) the distances $d(C_S, C'_S)$ and $d(C_I, C'_I)$ between their centroids (CEN) and (ii) the difference of angles $\left| \phi_i^{C_S} - \phi_i^{C_I} \right|$.

joint is determined (Fig. 4). $G_a(\mathbf{p}, \mathbf{p}')$ is defined using the average angle difference of all the individual matched joints in a chain:

$$G_a(\mathbf{p}, \mathbf{p}') = \exp\left(-\lambda_a \cdot \frac{1}{N^{J_\mathbf{P}}} \sum_{i=1}^{N^{J_\mathbf{P}}} \left| \phi_i^{C_S} - \phi_i^{C_I} \right| \right) \tag{11}$$

where, $N^{J_\mathbf{P}}$ is the number of matched joints between C_S and C_I and $\lambda_a(=2)$ is a scalar constant. Since, both G_d and G_a are should be high for consistent matching, we consider the pairwise geometric consistency $G(\mathbf{p}, \mathbf{p}')$ as a product of the constituent factors: $G(\mathbf{p}, \mathbf{p}') = G_d(\mathbf{p}, \mathbf{p}') \cdot G_a(\mathbf{p}, \mathbf{p}')$.

Erroneously matched chains are typically geometrically inconsistent with others and one may have both geometrically consistent and inconsistent pairs in a group of matched pairs between a sketch and an image. Therefore, the geometric consistency $GC(\mathbf{p})$ for a matched pair $\mathbf{p}$ is taken to be the maximum of $G(\mathbf{p}, \mathbf{p}')$ with respect to all other matched pairs $\mathbf{p}'$: $GC(\mathbf{p}) = \max_{\mathbf{p}'} G(\mathbf{p}, \mathbf{p}')$. This allows us to neglect the false matches while determining the consistent matched pairs. Finally, the similarity score of a database image I with respect to a sketch query S is determined as:

$$Score(I) = \sum_{\mathbf{p} \in P} GC(\mathbf{p}) \cdot CS(\mathbf{p}) \tag{12}$$

where $CS(\mathbf{p})$ is the *Chain Score* for the match of the chain pair $\mathbf{p}$ (Sec. 3.2) and P is the set of all matched pairs of chains between a sketch S and an image I. Since erroneously matched chains get very low score for consistency, effectively only the geometrically consistent chains are given weight for scoring an image. This score is used to determine the final matching of the database images, which can be used for ranked display of such images. Results of the experiments performed are presented next.

6   Experiments and Results

To evaluate the performance of our system, we have created a database of 1.2 million images, which contains 1 million Flickr images taken from the MIRFLICKR-1M image collection [17]. In addition, we included images from Imagenet [10] database in order to have some common object images in our database. We asked 5 random subjects to draw sketches on a touch-based tablet and collected 75 sketches, which, along with 100 sketches from a crowd-sourced sketch database [11], containing 24 different categories in total, are used for retrieval. In the experiments, the hierarchical index for 1.2 million images is generated with a branching factor of 32 and a maximum leaf node size of 100, which leads to a maximum tree depth of 6. This is used to reduce the search space to around 1500 similar images for a given sketch, for which geometric consistency (Eq. 12) is measured to rank the list of retrieved images from the search tree. The whole operation for a given sketch typically takes $1 - 5$ seconds on a single thread running on an Intel Core i7-3770 3.40GHz CPU, with the running time depending on the number of chains in the sketch and almost the whole processing time is consumed by the geometric verification phase. This time can be scaled down almost linearly with the number of cores as the geometric consistency check on each image can be done in parallel. The hierarchical index for our dataset required only around 150 MB of memory. We observed a memory footprint of approximately 6.5 GB while also storing the chain descriptors for all 1.2M images.

Visual results for 14 sketches of different categories of varying complexity are shown in Fig. 5. These clearly indicate insensitivity of our approach to similarity transforms (e.g 1st and 3rd retrieved image of the swan sketch). Furthermore, due to our partial matching scheme, an object is retrieved even under a viewpoint change if a portion of the distinguishing shape structure of the object is matched (e.g 8th image for swan). Global invariance to similarities as well as matching with flipped objects can be seen in the results for the bi-cycle sketch (7th and 10th retrieved image). False matches (e.g duck, parrot for the sketch of swan; face, wall-clock for lightbulb in Fig. 5) typically occur due to some shape similarity between the sketch and an object in the image, the probability of which is higher when the sketch is simple and/or contains only one chain (e.g lightbulb).

Quantitative measurement of the performance of a large scale retrieval system is not easy due to difficulty in obtaining the ground truth data, which is currently un-available for a web-scale dataset. Common metrics to measure retrieval performances (F-measure, Mean Average Precision [23] etc.) use recall which is impossible to compute without a full annotation of the dataset. Therefore, to evaluate the performance of our approach quantitatively, we use the Precision-at-K measure for different rank levels (K) for the retrieval results (Table 1). This is an acceptable measure since an end-user of a large scale Image Retrieval system typically cares only about the top results.

Unavailability of public implementation of any prior work makes it difficult to have a comparative study. Even though a Windows phone App (*Sketch Match*) [38] based on [8] is available, the database is not available to make a fair comparison to other algorithms. Hence, we re-implemented this algorithm [8] (EI) as well as another by Eitz *et al.* [12] (TENSOR) and tested their algorithms on our database for the purpose of comparison. Zhou *et al.* [44] did not provide complete implementation details in

Table 1. Precision (expressed as % of true positives) at different ranks for 175 retrieval tasks in 24 categories on a dataset of 1.2 million images. B: Best, W: Worst, A: Average performances are computed among sketches for each category and then averaged. CS+GC and CS indicate the performances with and without geometric verification respectively.

Method	Top 5			Top 10			Top 25			Top 50			Top 100			Top 250		
	B	W	A	B	W	A	B	W	A	B	W	A	B	W	A	B	W	A
TENSOR [12]	30.8	7.5	14.7	30	7.1	13.7	24.8	7	12.9	20.8	7	12.3	16.5	5.8	10.2	9.4	3	5.7
EI [8]	36.7	20.8	23.4	34.2	17.9	21.5	30	15.3	19.5	27	13.8	17.5	22.2	11.2	14.8	15.7	7.8	10.5
CS	50	11.7	26.1	42.1	10.8	22.9	33.5	7.8	18.5	27.8	5.7	15	23.1	5.1	12.9	18.3	4	9.7
CS+GC	80.8	42.5	60.8	72.5	38.3	53.6	54.7	29.3	39.5	40.3	20.7	28.5	31.8	16.3	22.2	23	12.5	16.5

their publication and it is not trivial to make [32] run efficiently on a very large database. Furthermore, [32] did not show any result on a large scale dataset and [44] shows results only for 3 sketches. Hence, these methods were not compared against.

Table 1 shows the best, worst and average retrieval scores (among multiple sketches of a given object category, averaged over all 24 categories). The significant deviation between the best and the worst retrieval performances indicate the diversity in the quality of the user sketches and the system response to it. It can be observed from Table 1 that our method significantly outperforms the other two methods on this large dataset. Both TENSOR [12] and EI [8] consider edge matchings approximately at the same location in an image as that of the sketch and therefore, the retrieved images from their system contain the sketched shape only at the same position, scale and orientation while images containing the sketched object at a different scale, orientation and/or position are missed leading to false retrievals (Fig. 6). Similar performance was observed by us on the *Sketch Match* app [38], a direct comparison with which is inappropriate since the databases are different. To evaluate the advantage of the geometry-based verification step, we also show the retrieval performance with and without this step and it can be observed that the geometric consistency check improves our results substantially. Note that, due to the unavailability of a fully annotated dataset of a million images, it is difficult to use an automated parameter learning algorithm. Hence, parameters are chosen emperically by trying out a few variations. Proper parameter learning/tuning could possibly improve the results further.

To provide easy comparisons on a standard dataset and compute the recall which is difficult for a large dataset, we tested our system on the ETHZ extended shape dataset [34] consisting of 385 images of 7 different categories with significant scale, translation and rotation variance. Out of 175 sketches used for evaluation in the large scale dataset, 63 sketches fall into different categories of ETHZ [34] and these are used for evaluation here. Although standard sketch-to-image matching algorithms for Object Detection that perform time consuming online processing would perform better than our approach on this small dataset, such comparison would be unfair since the objectives are different. Hence, we compare only against TENSOR [12] and EI [8]. In this dataset, we measure the percentage of positive retrievals in top 20 retrieved results which also gives an idea of recall of various approaches since the number of true positives is fixed. Table 2 shows the best, worst and average performance for the different sketches in a category (as for the previous dataset) while Fig 7 details the performance of our

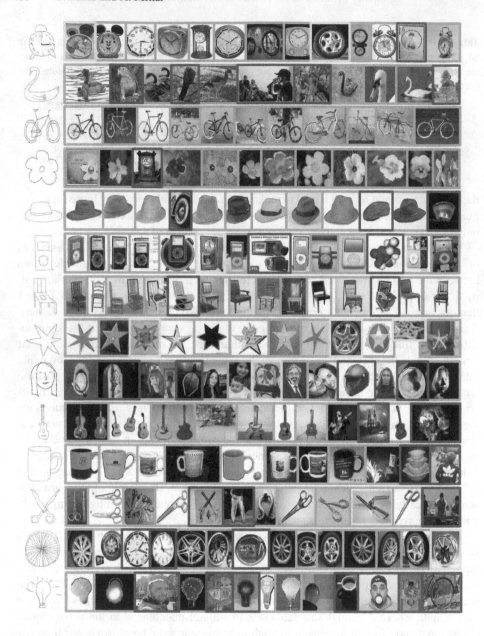

Fig. 5. Top retrieved images for 14 sketches from 1.2 million images. Retrieved images indicate similarity insensitivity and deformation handling of our approach. Chains are embedded on the retrieved images to illustrate the location of matchings. Multiple matched chains are shown using different colors. Correct, similar and false matches are illustrated by green, yellow and red boxes respectively (Best viewed in color).

approach for different categories (more results in the supplementary section). It can be seen that our method performs much better than other methods on this dataset as well. The performance on ETHZ models [16] is better than the average performance, which is expected since those sketches are computer generated and are therefore cleaner.

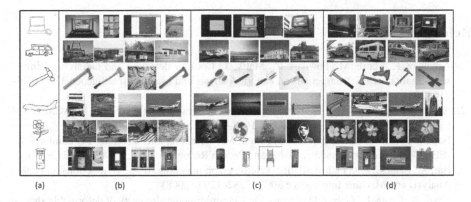

(a)   (b)   (c)   (d)

Fig. 6. Top 4 results by (b) Eitz *et al.* [12], (c) Cao *et al.* [8] and (d) our system on a 1.2 million image dataset for some sample sketches (a).

Table 2. Comparison of % of true positive retrievals in top 20 using our 63 sketches and ETHZ models [16] on ETHZ extended dataset [34]

Method	Our Sketches			ETHZ
	Best	Worst	Avg	Models [16]
TENSOR [12]	20	8.6	13.8	13.6
EI [8]	49.3	5	23.5	27.9
CS	51.4	14.3	35.3	33.6
CS+GC	**53.6**	**28.6**	**38.8**	**49.3**

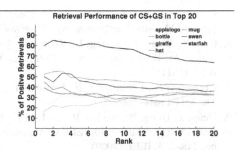

Retrieval Performance of CS+GS in Top 20

Fig. 7. Retrieval performance of the proposed algorithm (CS+GC) for different categories of the ETHZ extended shape dataset [34]

7 Conclusion

We have proposed a sketch-based fast image retrieval approach for large datasets that, unlike any prior work, handles similarity transformations and deformations of the object shape. This is achieved by preprocessing all the database images in which the essential shape information is extracted using multiple but a small number of variable length descriptors from contour chains. These descriptors are efficiently matched using a Dynamic Programming-based *approximate substring* matching algorithm that is used for chain indexing and then efficiently searching for matching image chains in a hierarchical k-medoids tree structure. Geometric verification on candidate images helps reducing the false positives. Extensive experiments performed on a 1.2 million Image Database indicate significant performance improvement over other existing methods. Our method, augmented by other techniques, could also be used for tagging images in an offline fashion or for improving online results.

References

1. Arbelaez, P., Maire, M., Fowlkes, C., Malik, J.: Contour detection and hierarchical image segmentation. IEEE Transactions on Pattern Analysis and Machine Intelligence 33(5), 898–916 (2011)
2. Arthur, D., Vassilvitskii, S.: k-means++: The advantages of careful seeding. In: ACM-SIAM Symposium on Discrete Algorithms, pp. 1027–1035 (2007)
3. Bagon, S., Brostovski, O., Galun, M., Irani, M.: Detecting and sketching the common. In: IEEE Conference on Computer Vision and Pattern Recognition, pp. 33–40. IEEE (2010)
4. Bai, X., Latecki, L.J.: Path similarity skeleton graph matching. IEEE Transactions on Pattern Analysis and Machine Intelligence 30(7), 1282–1292 (2008)
5. Basri, R., Costa, L., Geiger, D., Jacobs, D.: Determining the similarity of deformable shapes. Vision Research 38(15), 2365–2385 (1998)
6. Bozas, K., Izquierdo, E.: Large scale sketch based image retrieval using patch hashing. In: Bebis, G., et al. (eds.) ISVC 2012, Part I. LNCS, vol. 7431, pp. 210–219. Springer, Heidelberg (2012)
7. Canny, J.: A computational approach to edge detection. IEEE Transactions on Pattern Analysis and Machine Intelligence (6), 679–698 (1986)
8. Cao, Y., Wang, C., Zhang, L., Zhang, L.: Edgel index for large-scale sketch-based image search. In: IEEE Conference on Computer Vision and Pattern Recognition, pp. 761–768. IEEE (2011)
9. Cormen, T.H., Leiserson, C.E., Rivest, R.L., Stein, C.: Introduction to Algorithms, 3rd edn. The MIT Press (2009)
10. Deng, J., Dong, W., Socher, R., Li, L.J., Li, K., Fei-Fei, L.: Imagenet: A large-scale hierarchical image database. In: IEEE Conference on Computer Vision and Pattern Recognition, pp. 248–255. IEEE (2009)
11. Eitz, M., Hays, J., Alexa, M.: How do humans sketch objects? ACM Transactions on Graphics (Proc. SIGGRAPH) 31(4), 44 (2012)
12. Eitz, M., Hildebrand, K., Boubekeur, T., Alexa, M.: A descriptor for large scale image retrieval based on sketched feature lines. In: Eurographics Symposium on Sketch-Based Interfaces and Modeling, pp. 29–38 (2009)
13. Eitz, M., Hildebrand, K., Boubekeur, T., Alexa, M.: An evaluation of descriptors for large-scale image retrieval from sketched feature lines. Computers & Graphics 34(5), 482–498 (2010)
14. Felzenszwalb, P.F., Schwartz, J.D.: Hierarchical matching of deformable shapes. In: IEEE Conference on Computer Vision and Pattern Recognition, pp. 1–8. IEEE (2007)
15. Ferrari, V., Fevrier, L., Jurie, F., Schmid, C.: Groups of adjacent contour segments for object detection. IEEE Transactions on Pattern Analysis and Machine Intelligence 30(1), 36–51 (2008)
16. Ferrari, V., Tuytelaars, T., Van Gool, L.: Object detection by contour segment networks. In: Leonardis, A., Bischof, H., Pinz, A. (eds.) ECCV 2006. LNCS, vol. 3953, pp. 14–28. Springer, Heidelberg (2006)

17. Huiskes, M.J., Lew, M.S.: The MIR flickr retrieval evaluation. In: Proceedings of the 1st ACM International Conference on Multimedia Information Retrieval, pp. 39–43. ACM (2008)
18. Kokkinos, I., Yuille, A.: Inference and learning with hierarchical shape models. International Journal of Computer Vision 93(2), 201–225 (2011)
19. Latecki, L.J., Lakamper, R., Eckhardt, T.: Shape descriptors for non-rigid shapes with a single closed contour. In: IEEE Conference on Computer Vision and Pattern Recognition, pp. 424–429. IEEE (2000)
20. Lee, Y.J., Grauman, K.: Shape discovery from unlabeled image collections. In: IEEE Conference on Computer Vision and Pattern Recognition, pp. 2254–2261. IEEE (2009)
21. Lee, Y.J., Zitnick, C.L., Cohen, M.F.: Shadowdraw: real-time user guidance for freehand drawing. In: ACM Transactions on Graphics (Proc. SIGGRAPH), vol. 30, p. 27. ACM (2011)
22. Ma, T., Latecki, L.J.: From partial shape matching through local deformation to robust global shape similarity for object detection. In: IEEE Conference on Computer Vision and Pattern Recognition, pp. 1441–1448. IEEE (2011)
23. Manning, C.D., Raghavan, P., Schütze, H.: Introduction to information retrieval, vol. 1. Cambridge University Press (2008)
24. Marvaniya, S., Bhattacharjee, S., Manickavasagam, V., Mittal, A.: Drawing an automatic sketch of deformable objects using only a few images. In: Fusiello, A., Murino, V., Cucchiara, R. (eds.) ECCV 2012 Ws/Demos, Part I. LNCS, vol. 7583, pp. 63–72. Springer, Heidelberg (2012)
25. Meltzer, J., Soatto, S.: Edge descriptors for robust wide-baseline correspondence. In: IEEE Conference on Computer Vision and Pattern Recognition, pp. 1–8. IEEE (2008)
26. Muja, M., Lowe, D.G.: Fast Approximate Nearest Neighbors with Automatic Algorithm Configuration. In: International Conference on Computer Vision Theory and Application (VISSAPP), pp. 331–340. INSTICC Press (2009)
27. Nister, D., Stewenius, H.: Scalable recognition with a vocabulary tree. In: IEEE Conference on Computer Vision and Pattern Recognition, vol. 2, pp. 2161–2168. IEEE (2006)
28. Opelt, A., Pinz, A., Zisserman, A.: Learning an alphabet of shape and appearance for multi-class object detection. International Journal of Computer Vision 80(1), 16–44 (2008)
29. Philbin, J., Chum, O., Isard, M., Sivic, J., Zisserman, A.: Object retrieval with large vocabularies and fast spatial matching. In: IEEE Conference on Computer Vision and Pattern Recognition, pp. 1–8. IEEE (2007)
30. Ravishankar, S., Jain, A., Mittal, A.: Multi-stage contour based detection of deformable objects. In: Forsyth, D., Torr, P., Zisserman, A. (eds.) ECCV 2008, Part I. LNCS, vol. 5302, pp. 483–496. Springer, Heidelberg (2008)
31. Riemenschneider, H., Donoser, M., Bischof, H.: Using partial edge contour matches for efficient object category localization. In: Daniilidis, K., Maragos, P., Paragios, N. (eds.) ECCV 2010, Part V. LNCS, vol. 6315, pp. 29–42. Springer, Heidelberg (2010)
32. Riemenschneider, H., Donoser, M., Bischof, H.: Image retrieval by shape-focused sketching of objects. In: 16th Computer Vision Winter Workshop, p. 35 (2011)
33. Sattler, T., Leibe, B., Kobbelt, L.: SCRAMSAC: Improving RANSAC's efficiency with a spatial consistency filter. In: IEEE Conference on Computer Vision and Pattern Recognition, pp. 2090–2097. IEEE (2009)
34. Schindler, K., Suter, D.: Object detection by global contour shape. Pattern Recognition 41(12), 3736–3748 (2008)
35. Schroff, F., Criminisi, A., Zisserman, A.: Harvesting image databases from the web. IEEE Transactions on Pattern Analysis and Machine Intelligence 33(4), 754–766 (2011)
36. Scott, C., Nowak, R.: Robust contour matching via the order-preserving assignment problem. IEEE Transactions on Image Processing 15(7), 1831–1838 (2006)

37. Sigurbjörnsson, B., Van Zwol, R.: Flickr tag recommendation based on collective knowledge. In: Proceedings of the 17th International Conference on World Wide Web, pp. 327–336. ACM (2008)
38. SketchMatch, http://research.microsoft.com/en-us/projects/sketchmatch/
39. Smith, T.F., Waterman, M.S.: Identification of common molecular subsequences. Journal of Molecular Biology 147(1), 195–197 (1981)
40. Toyama, K., Blake, A.: Probabilistic tracking with exemplars in a metric space. International Journal of Computer Vision 48(1), 9–19 (2002)
41. Tsai, S.S., Chen, D., Takacs, G., Chandrasekhar, V., Vedantham, R., Grzeszczuk, R., Girod, B.: Fast geometric re-ranking for image-based retrieval. In: 17th IEEE International Conference on Image Processing, pp. 1029–1032. IEEE (2010)
42. Vlachos, M., Vagena, Z., Yu, P.S., Athitsos, V.: Rotation invariant indexing of shapes and line drawings. In: Proceedings of the 14th ACM International Conference on Information and Knowledge Management, pp. 131–138. ACM (2005)
43. Yarlagadda, P., Ommer, B.: From meaningful contours to discriminative object shape. In: Fitzgibbon, A., Lazebnik, S., Perona, P., Sato, Y., Schmid, C. (eds.) ECCV 2012, Part I. LNCS, vol. 7572, pp. 766–779. Springer, Heidelberg (2012)
44. Zhou, R., Chen, L., Zhang, L.: Sketch-based image retrieval on a large scale database. In: Proceedings of the 20th ACM International Conference on Multimedia, pp. 973–976. ACM (2012)
45. Zhu, Q., Song, G., Shi, J.: Untangling cycles for contour grouping. In: IEEE 11th International Conference on Computer Vision, pp. 1–8. IEEE (2007)

Discovering Object Classes from Activities

Abhilash Srikantha[1,2] and Juergen Gall[1]

[1] University of Bonn
[2] MPI for Intelligent Systems, Tuebingen
abhilash.srikantha@tue.mpg.de, gall@informatik.uni-bonn.de

Abstract. In order to avoid an expensive manual labelling process or to learn object classes autonomously without human intervention, object discovery techniques have been proposed that extract visually similar objects from weakly labelled videos. However, the problem of discovering small or medium sized objects is largely unexplored. We observe that videos with activities involving human-object interactions can serve as weakly labelled data for such cases. Since neither object appearance nor motion is distinct enough to discover objects in such videos, we propose a framework that samples from a space of algorithms and their parameters to extract sequences of object proposals. Furthermore, we model similarity of objects based on appearance and functionality, which is derived from human and object motion. We show that functionality is an important cue for discovering objects from activities and demonstrate the generality of the model on three challenging RGB-D and RGB datasets.

Keywords: Object Discovery, Human-Object Interaction, RGBD Videos.

1 Introduction

Approaches for object detection require a fair amount of annotated images in order to perform well [10]. Contemporary solutions such as crowdsourcing will be suboptimal in the long run due to high costs involved. As a result, there has been a recent shift of focus towards utilizing readily available weakly labelled data [2,6,26,36,40], particularly videos [27,33,34]. The fundamental assumption in all these approaches is that the object of interest is dominant and can be easily segmented. In other words, motion or appearance of the object are assumed to be distinct from the background. This is a valid constraint for large active objects such as moving vehicles or animals and is further aided by object- or action-centric nature of labelled videos on the Internet.

Moving away from commonly used categories such as airplanes, boats, cars, cats, horses etc., we propose to work on small and medium sized object categories such as pens and mugs that are used in daily routine. Weakly supervised learning in such areas is largely unexplored inspite of their obvious impact on applications in robotics, assisted living etc. One reason is the scarcity of data because such objects do not form popular subjects for generating and sharing videoclips. However, videos labelled with the context of human activity, like drinking or

D. Fleet et al. (Eds.): ECCV 2014, Part VI, LNCS 8694, pp. 415–430, 2014.

writing, are available in plenty. These videos, however, violate the fundamental assumption since the dominant subjects here are humans, their body parts and their immediate environment; thus forcing present day methods to failure as verified in our experiments. Another problem of existing methods for such videos is the assumption that similarity of objects is completely defined by their appearance features inspite of their frequent occlusion and low resolutions. Also, appearance and pose of objects change within a single video due to the human-object interaction involved. For these reasons, appearance-only approaches are limited for mining such objects as verified in our experiments.

We therefore propose an approach that addresses the problem of weakly supervised learning for medium or small sized objects from action videos where humans interact with them. Since existing methods fail for this task, we introduce a novel method consisting of two parts as illustrated in Figure 1. The first part addresses the problem that objects cannot be segmented by searching for dominant motion segments. Instead, we track randomly selected superpixels to generate many tubes per video as object candidates as illustrated in Figure 2. To this end, we do not rely on a single algorithm with a single parameter setting due to the variety in objects but sample from a space of algorithms and their parameters. We condition the sampling on human pose in order to make it more efficient. The second part addresses the problem that similarity of generated tubes is not well described by appearance features alone. We therefore propose a similarity measure that not only includes appearance and size but also encodes functionality of the object derived from relative human-object motion during the activity.

To demonstrate the generalization capabilities of our approach, we evaluate on three challenging datasets, namely two RGB-D datasets [16, 25] and one RGB dataset [35]. The datasets have been recorded with three different types of sensors: a time-of-flight camera [16], a structured light camera [25], and a color camera [35]. The quality of 3d or 2d pose information also differs greatly since it is automatically extracted with different methods. On all three datasets, we show that our approach is suitable to discover objects from videos of activities and investigate the importance of functionality in the current setup.

2 Related Work

Unsupervised object discovery in images [26, 39] or videos [37] aims at finding similar objects in a set of unlabelled visual data. In many cases, weak label information is available and can be used. For instance, images with an object class label can be collected thereby reducing the problem to identifying instances that co-occur in images and localizing them either through bounding boxes or segmentation masks [2, 6, 36, 40].

There are a few works that exploit weakly labelled videos for learning [27, 30, 33, 34]. The element these approaches have in common is that they strongly rely on motion in videos and often assume that deformation in objects is either rigid or articulated i.e. can be approximated by rigid parts. For instance, part-based models of animals are learned from videos and applied for detection in [34]. [30] uses a structure-from-motion approach to discover objects that share similar trajectories. Videos that are not necessarily related to an object class are used to learn features for object detection that are robust to temporal deformations in [27]. In [33] videos with object labels are utilized to generate training data for object detection. While the approach focuses on objects that can be relatively easily discovered and segmented in videos, our approach deals with medium and small sized objects that do not move at all or move only when they are used by a human. This makes it very difficult for them to be discovered in videos via conventional motion or appearance based methods. One can, however, exploit human motion as additional cue.

The idea of using human motion for scene understanding has recently gained attention [8, 15, 16, 18, 20, 21, 23, 25, 31, 32, 38] due to progress in human pose estimation and availability of commercial SDKs for depth data. In [31, 38], human trajectories in office environments or street scenes are extracted to segment image regions based on observed human behaviors. While the benefit of combining object detection and action recognition have been investigated in several works e.g. [13, 19, 29], the works [16, 23, 25, 32] focus on affordance cues that can be used for higher level video understanding e.g. action recognition. [23] learns relations between objects and their functionality to improve object detection or activity recognition. In [16], human motion is used to cluster objects of similar functionality in an unsupervised fashion. Further, descriptors learned for object functionality from hand-object interactions are applied to human activity recognition in [32]. The joint learning of activities and object affordances is addressed in [25]. Extracting object instances in egocentric videos using appearance-only cues and weak action-object labels using a framework that is made robust by incorporating motion information is dealt in [11].

Human models have also been used to hallucinate their interactions with given scenes. A detector for surfaces where humans can sit on is proposed in [18]. In this work, the sitting action is represented by a single human pose and its geometric relation to objects like chairs is learned. The approach is generalized in [21] where more relations between human poses and objects are used to label 3D scenes. In [20], a similar idea has been employed for static 2D images where the geometry of the scene is extracted. An exactly opposite approach is followed by [15] where human motion in a video is observed to extract scene geometry. Human motion has also been used for scene segmentation in [8].

3   Learning Object Models from Activities

An overview of the pipeline for discovering instances of a class in a set of RGB-D or RGB videos is illustrated in Figure 1. The input is a set of videos that is labelled with activities involving human-object interactions e.g. label *eating cereal* indicates the presence of a bowl.

To begin the pipeline, we assume that human pose either in 2d or 3d has already been extracted. This can easily be obtained from RGB-D videos using

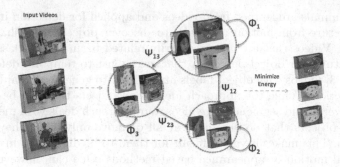

Fig. 1. Processing pipeline: Input is a set of action videos with human pose. Multiple sequences of object proposals (tubes) are generated from each video. By defining a model that encodes the similarity between tubes in terms of appearance and object functionality, instances of the common object class are discovered.

freely available SDKs, but is also straightforward for RGB videos due to the enormous progress in 2d pose estimation over the past years [35]. There are no other additional restrictions on the nature of input videos. In other words, videos may contain multiple activities, multiple persons and/or multiple objects e.g. *microwaving food, cleaning microwave* are different activities involving various objects, but they commonly feature a microwave.

In the next step, several object proposals are generated by selecting spatio-temporal regions called tubes from each video. This is modelled as a sampling process and is explained in Section 3.1. While most of these tubes will not contain the object of interest, the aim is to extract at least one tube that sufficiently overlaps with the object.

After having selected a set of tubes, we jointly select one tube per video that best describes the object. This is achieved by minimizing an energy functional built upon potentials that describe either the presence of an object in a tube or the similarity between tubes as explained in Section 3.2. As for these potentials, we employ similarity in appearance and functionality.

3.1   Generating Tubes

A straightforward way to generate tubes is to extract motion segments from videos as in [4, 33]. However, such methods do not generate meaningful tubes in the current scenario because motion is predominantly caused by entities like body parts. Instead, we extract frame based superixels in these videos and track them over time. We observed that the quality of tubes is sensitive to the method chosen and its parameters and that there is no single universal setting. We therefore consider a pool of trackers and randomly sample from it to extract tubes T_v from a video v. The probability that any tube of the video is selected therefore depends on the tracking algorithm τ and a superpixel S:

$$p(T_v) = \sum_S \sum_\tau p(T_v|\tau, S)p(\tau)p(S). \tag{1}$$

In our experiments, we use two trackers with uniform probability i.e. $p(\tau) = 0.5$. The first method uses the median optical flow [5] within the region of the superpixel to propagate it to the next or previous frame. The second method uses mean shift [7] where the RGB(D) histogram of the superpixel is used as template. While the method using dense optical flow works well for medium sized rigid objects, it easily gets distracted by fast or background motion for small objects.

Since long-term tracking is unreliable in either case, we limit the length of each tube to 300 frames or the shortest length of a video.

The superpixels S are generated using [12] which is modified to incorporate depth as feature. Similar to tracking, there is no single configuration optimal for all objects. While depth is helpful for many objects, it becomes unreliable for very small objects or reflective surfaces. We therefore compute superpixels in three different settings $\sigma \in \{RGB, D, RGBD\}$. The sampling of the superpixel also depends on the frame f in the video and a spatial prior $p(l|f)$ which depends on the frame:

$$p(S) = \sum_\sigma \sum_f \sum_l p(S|f, l, \sigma)p(l|f)p(f)p(\sigma). \tag{2}$$

For RGB videos, $p(\sigma = RGB) = 1$; otherwise $p(\sigma)$ is uniform. $p(f)$ is a prior on frames where the interaction is happening in the video. In our experiments, we use a uniform distribution i.e. we assume that the activity occurs anywhere in the video. For the spatial prior $p(l|f)$, we make use of the pose information since we are considering activities with human-object interactions. To this end, we compute the location variance of all joints within a temporal neighborhood of 15 frames and select the joint with highest variance. For RGB-D videos, we model $p(l|f)$ as a uniform distribution within the sphere centered at the joint location j at frame f and radius 400mm. Since RGB videos do not provide 3d information, we use the location of the parent joint j_p to compute the radius of the circle $\|\gamma(j - j_p)\|$ and its center $j + \gamma(j - j_p)$. In our experiments, we use $\gamma = 0.2$.

Sampling from (1) is straightforward and the tube generation process is illustrated in Figure 2. In our experiments, we sample 30 tubes T_v per video. It is important to note that we are only generating candidates at this point, the evaluation of the tubes is performed in the next step.

3.2   Joint Object Hypothesis Generation

Given a set of candidate tubes $\mathcal{T}_v$ in each video v, the goal is to select the tubes that contain the object class and are tight around the object. Similar to [9,33], this can be formulated as an energy minimization problem defined jointly over all videos N. Let $l_v \in \{1, ..., |\mathcal{T}_v|\}$ be a label that selects one tube out of a video, then the energy of all selected tubes $L = (l_1, \ldots, l_N)$ is defined as

Fig. 2. Illustrating the tube generation process. The top row from left to right: The first image shows joint trajectories. The most active joint is used to compute the spatial prior for selecting superpixels. The three images next to it show three superpixel representations computed using depth (D), color (RGB) and both (RGBD). Colored superpixels are within the specified distance of the most active joint. Second and third rows visualize tubes T_v sampled from the blue and green superpixel S respectively.

$$E\left(L\right) = \sum_v \Phi\left(l_v\right) + \sum_{v,w} \Psi\left(l_v, l_w\right). \tag{3}$$

The unary potentials Φ measure the likelihood of a single tube being a tight fit around an object. The binary potentials Ψ measure the homogeneity in object appearance and functionality of a pair of tubes. The energy is minimized by Tree-Reweighted Message Passing [24]. While the method does not find always the global optimum, it produces satisfying results as we show in our experiments. We now describe the various potentials involved.

3.3   Unary Potentials Φ

Unary terms measure the quality of tube l_v in video v. We identify four aspects that distinguish tubes tightly bound to objects that are manipulated from the rest.

Appearance Saliency has routinely been used for object discovery since the appearance of objects is often distinct from the background. We define saliency of the kth frame of a tube by the average χ^2 distance between the RGB-D or RGB distributions of the region inside each frame of the tube, I_k, and its surrounding region, S_k, which is of the same size.

$$\Phi^{app}(l_v) = \frac{1}{K} \sum_{k=1}^{K} \left(1 - \frac{1}{2} \sum_i \frac{(I_{k,i} - S_{k,i})^2}{I_{k,i} + S_{k,i}}\right) \tag{4}$$

The unary penalizes tubes that contain the object but are not tight, or tubes that cover only a part of the object. In both cases, the appearance inside and outside the tube is more similar than for a tight tube.

Pose-object Relation is useful to identify the object that is being manipulated. To this end, we measure the distance between the locally active end effector j_k and the center of the tube c_k for each frame of the tube. Depending on the data i.e. RGB or RGB-D videos, the distance is measured in 2d or 3d. Since the body does not need to be very close to the object over the entire length of the video e.g. for a microwave the contact might be very short, we perform $\alpha = 0.3$ trimmed mean filtering

$$\Phi^{Pose}(l_v) = \frac{1}{K} \sum_{k=\alpha \cdot K}^{(1-\alpha)\cdot K} \|c_{D(k)} - j_{D(k)}\| \tag{5}$$

where D is the sorted list of distances. The parameter α also makes the potential more robust to pose estimation errors.

Body part avoidance is necessary since they are dominant parts of input videos and satisfy the previous terms perfectly, hands in particular. To discourage trivial solutions such as these, we define a potential that penalizes the selection of body parts

$$\Phi^{body}(l_v) = \max \{\bar{p}_{skin}(I), \bar{p}_{upper}(I), \bar{p}_{lower}(I)\},$$

$$\text{with} \quad \bar{p}_x(I) = \frac{1}{K} \sum_k p_x(I_k) \tag{6}$$

where I_k is the color histogram of the tube at frame k. The probabilities for upper and lower body are modelled by 5-component Gaussian Mixture Models, which are learned from the video directly using the estimated pose. For skin, we use a generic model [22].

Size prior of an object is a cue that can be computed relative to human size independently of the dataset. Such priors are useful in scenarios where tubes are very small such that the other potentials become unreliable. To this end, we impose a Gaussian prior on the size of an object

$$\Phi^{size}(l_v) = \exp\left(\frac{(w_{l_v} - 2w_h)^2 + (h_{l_v} - 2h_h)^2}{2\sigma_h^2}\right) \tag{7}$$

where (w_h, h_h) and (w_{l_v}, h_{l_v}) are average width and height of the hand and tube respectively and σ_h is $0.75 \times (w_h + h_h)$.

Unary potential is formed by linearly combining the four terms as

$$\begin{aligned}\Phi(l_v) = &\lambda_1 \Phi^{app}(l_v) + \lambda_2 \Phi^{pose}(l_v) \\ &+ \lambda_3 \Phi^{body}(l_v) + \lambda_4 \Phi^{size}(l_v)\end{aligned} \tag{8}$$

where the weighting parameters λ_i are learned from a held out validation set as explained in Section 4.

3.4   Binary Potentials Ψ

The binary term measures similarity between two tubes l_v and l_w. We use two terms in this regard. While the first term measures similarity in appearance, the second measures similarity in human motion involved during the interaction.

Shape. As in [33], we use PHoG [3] to measure the similarity between two tubes. We describe the appearance of a tube by uniformly sampling 50 frames along its temporal extent and spatially binning each frame's gradients at different resolutions. Since objects can be transformed during object manipulation, we additionally align the sequences using dynamic time warping, where we use joint locations of the head, shoulders and hands as features. Since the alignment of two very different action sequences is meaningless, we apply the warping only if the average alignment error is below a certain threshold. The $\Psi^{shape}(l_v, l_w)$ is then defined as the median χ^2 distance between PHoG features from the corresponding frames k of l_v and l_w given as

$$\Psi^{shape}(l_v, l_w) = \underset{k}{\text{median}} \left\{ \frac{1}{2} \sum_i \frac{\left(P_{\omega_v(k),i} - P_{\omega_w(k),i}\right)^2}{P_{\omega_v(k),i} + P_{\omega_w(k),i}} \right\} \tag{9}$$

where ω_u is the dynamic time warping function for tube l_u and $P_{\omega_u(k),i}$ is i^{th} bin of the PHoG feature extracted from k^{th} frame of tube l_u after warping.

Functionality. Assuming that functionality the of an object correlates with its trajectory with respect to human motion, we measure the relative distance between the center of the tube and the human. After having tubes aligned as for the shape term, we sample 50 uniformly distributed corresponding frames of both tubes. To this end, we compute the distance between the center $c_{u(k)}$ of the tube l_u at frame k and the head position $h_{u(k)}$ and normalize it by the distance between the head and the locally active end effector $j_{u(k)}$:

$$d_{u(k)} = \frac{\|h_{u(k)} - c_{u(k)}\|}{\|h_{u(k)} - j_{u(k)}\|} \tag{10}$$

The normalization is important for 2d poses, but it also compensates in 3d for different body sizes. The potential $\Psi^{func}(l_v, l_w)$ is then the median of these differences after applying the dynamic time warping functions ω_u:

$$\Psi^{func}(l_v, l_w) = \underset{k}{\text{median}} \left\{ |d_{\omega_v(k)} - d_{\omega_w(k)}| \right\} \tag{11}$$

Binary potential is formed by linearly combining the two terms as

$$\Psi(l_v, l_w) = \lambda_5 \Psi^{shape}(l_v, l_w) + \lambda_6 \Psi^{func}(l_v, l_w) \tag{12}$$

where the weighting parameters λ_i are learned together with the weights of the unary potential (8) from a validation set.

4   Experiments

To evaluate the proposed approach and demonstrate its generalization capabilities for different types of input data, we perform experiments on two RGB-D and one RGB-dataset. We show that motion segmentation, e.g. as used in [33], fails drastically for discovering objects from videos with activities and evaluate the impact of various potentials in detail. We further compare our approach to an unsupervised approach [14] and a weakly supervised approach [33] that formulates an energy functional similar to (3). For any given tube, the unary potential is composed of the objectness measure [1], shape similarity calculated as PHoG consistency and appearance similarity calculated via SIFT Bag-of-Words. The binary potential quantifies similarity between a pair of tubes by evaluating PHoG based shape and SIFT-BoW based appearance congruity.

4.1   Datasets

We use three action datasets of varying modalities: ETHZ-activity [14], CAD-120 [25] and MPII-Cooking [35]. The ETHZ-activity is an RGB-D dataset captured by a color and a ToF camera with a resolution of 640×480 and 170×144, respectively. It contains 143 sequences of 12 high level activities performed by 6 different actors. Human pose extracted via a model based method consists of 13 3d joint locations from the upper body. Interactions are mostly restricted to a single object but with varying appearances. The 12 object classes vary from medium-size e.g. *teapot* and *mug* to small-size e.g. *marker* and *phone*. A typical frame illustrating the relative size of the objects is shown in Figure 3.

The CAD-120 is an RGB-D dataset recorded with a color camera and structured light for depth having VGA-resolutions for both modalities. It contains 120 sequences of 10 different high level activities performed by 4 different actors. Human pose consisting of 15 3d joint locations from the whole body is extracted using OpenNI SDK. The pose is noisy which is more pronounced for hands and legs. The activities involve interactions with various objects e.g. *making cereal* indicates the presence of instances of the object classes *box*, *milk* and *bowl*.

The MPII-Cooking is a high resolution (1624×1224) RGB dataset. It contains 65 sequences of 2 high-level activities performed by 12 different actors. The

Fig. 3. Sample images of human-object interaction from ETHZ-activity dataset, CAD-120 dataset and MPII cooking dataset in that order. Object of interest is bounded in red and pose overlayed in orange.

human pose is extracted by a part-based detection approach and consists of 8 2d joint locations for the upper body without head. For the binary potential $\Psi^{func}(l_v, l_w)$ (11), we take therefore the mean of both shoulders instead of the head as reference joint. Apart from involving multiple objects, the objects are often occluded or covered by food during the activity e.g. *plate* during the process of preparing a salad.

For evaluation, we labelled the objects in the three datasets by drawing tight bounding boxes around the objects for every 10th frame and interpolating intermediate bounding boxes. The annotations and evaluation scripts will be made publicly available.

4.2   Inference

The output of the system is a collection of tubes that best describe an object class common in all input videos. Discovered instances of object classes are shown in Figure 5. In order to evaluate the quality of these tubes, we study frame- and class-wise PASCAL IoU measures. A frame-IoU measure is defined as a ratio of areas of intersection over union of the ground truth and inferred bounding boxes. A tube-IoU is defined as the average of all frame-IoUs. Similarly, a class-IoU is defined as the average of all inferred tube-IoUs.

To learn the scalar weights λ of the energy model (3), (8), (12) and [33], we use ground-truth object annotations of one randomly chosen object class as validation in each dataset: *puncher* (ETHZ), *milkbox* (CAD) and *whisker* (MPII). In order to set these parameters, we perform a grid-search in $\{0.05, 0.25, 0.50, 0.75, 1.00\}$ and take the configuration that maximizes class-IoU for the validation class. We therefore exclude validation classes from all performance evaluations that follow.

4.3   Comparison

Firstly, we compare the proposed tube generation process with the object proposal technique [28] considering every 10th frame in the ETHZ-action dataset. While the recall of the proposal technique was (0.19, 0.58, 0.67) for (10^2, 10^3, 10^4) proposals per frame respectively, our approach as described in Section 3.1

Table 1. Average class-IoU of the proposed model (APP+SIZ+FUN) for the three datasets. All three types of potentials that model object appearance (APP), size prior (SIZ) and object functionality (FUN) are important for the final performance. Our proposed approach outperforms the method [33], which relies on motion segments and object appearance.

	prest-exact [33]	prest-modif	proposed	APP	APP+SIZ	FUN	APP+FUN	FUN+SIZ
ETHZ-Action	0.063	0.249	**0.447**	0.192	0.305	0.292	0.312	0.390
CAD-120	0.039	0.246	**0.410**	0.168	0.191	0.147	0.202	0.350
MPII-Cooking	0.023	0.221	**0.342**	0.079	0.149	0.229	0.235	0.288

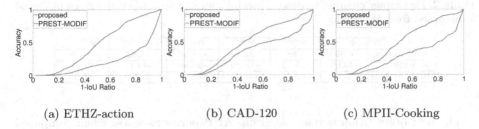

<table>
<tr><td>(a) ETHZ-action</td><td>(b) CAD-120</td><td>(c) MPII-Cooking</td></tr>
</table>

Fig. 4. Accuracy measured as fraction of bounding boxes with an IoU ratio greater equal than a given threshold. The x-axis plots 1-IoU i.e. the higher the value on the x-axis the more tolerant is the success threshold and the higher the accuracy. The accuracy is averaged over all classes.

achieves a recall of 0.65 for only 30 tubes per video. This verifies that the proposed tube generation module is well suited to the current scenario.

Further, we compare the proposed approach with a method for learning from weakly labelled videos [33] on all three datasets. The average class-IoU is presented in Table 1. The performance of the proposed approach supercedes that of [33] significantly. The reason for such poor performance of [33] is that the extracted motion segments do not correspond to objects in most cases and are therefore not suitable for the task at hand. We therefore modify the method by using the tube sampling approach introduced in Section 3.1 and the energy functional proposed in [33] to select tubes that most likely contain instances of the object class. We denote the modified approach as prest-modif in Table 1. In contrast to [33], prest-modif achieves improved results but is still inferior when compared to the energy functional used in the proposed approach.

To evaluate the quality of inferred tubes, we define class-accuracy as the fraction of bounding boxes with an IoU ratio greater equal than a given threshold. Figure 4 shows class-accuracy averaged over all classes for decreasing IoU ratios. For [33], the IoU ratio for nearly all bounding boxes is close to zero. We therefore plot the accuracy only for prest-modif. As can be seen, the average class-accuracy of the proposed method for different thresholds consistently outperforms that of prest-modif in all three datasets. The biggest difference in performance is for the ETHZ dataset at 1-IoU=0.8 where the performance of the proposed approach and prest-modif are 0.86 and 0.36 respectively. At IoU=0.5, the accuracies of the methods are (0.48, 0.16) for ETHZ, (0.56, 0.42) for CAD and (0.53, 0.29) for the MPII dataset respectively.

4.4   Impact of Potentials

In order to characterize the contribution of designed potentials, we group them into three categories: APP consisting of potentials that are intrinsic to object appearance $\{\Phi^{app}, \Psi^{shape}\}$, SIZ denotes the size prior $\{\Phi^{size}\}$ and FUN consisting of potentials derived from human-object interaction $\{\Phi^{pose}, \Phi^{body}, \Psi^{func}\}$. Performances of different group combinations are presented in Table 1.

Table 2. Percentage change in average class-IoU performance when any given potential is discarded from the model

	Φ^{app}	Φ^{pose}	Φ^{body}	Φ^{size}	Ψ^{shape}	Ψ^{func}
ETHZ-Action	0.35	1.88	-25.49	-13.50	-4.62	-8.86
CAD-120	-48.66	-15.73	-18.89	-20.80	-40.15	-9.19
MPII-Cooking	-15.85	0.06	-31.09	-10.70	0.058	-60.95

The first observation is that the group APP performs worse when compared to prest-modif for all datasets. This fall in performance is expected because APP uses only 2 potentials while the energy functional of prest-modif uses 6 terms to model the appearance of an object. The performance improves when the size prior is added (APP+SIZ). The functionality terms (FUN) outperform prest-modif and APP on the ETHZ and MPII datasets emphasizing the fact that human interaction is a valuable cue to discover objects, but not sufficient. Using the functionality and the appearance terms (FUN+APP), the performance is higher than using only one of them. Finally, the pair of (FUN+SIZ) performs best amongst all subset combinations, but only attains 80% of the accuracy attained by the full model. This indicates that object appearance, functionality and size prior are all important for maximal performance.

In addition, we present percentage change in class-IoU performance when each potential is discarded from the model in Table 2. It can be seen that performance drops upon eliminating any potential almost in all cases. For the CAD dataset, removing any potential has a negative effect. Appearance based features have minimal impact on the ETHZ dataset as they are not reliable for small objects and Ψ^{shape} has negligible impact on the MPII dataset owing to drastic variations in object appearances during interaction. The terms Φ^{body}, Φ^{size} and Ψ^{func} are required by all datasets as indicated by loss in performance when they are discarded.

Further, we study the robustness of pose-related potentials with respect to strong pose estimation noise on the CAD dataset. To this end, we add normally distributed noise with variance $100cm^2$, $200cm^2$ and $400cm^2$ to each 3d joint position. The average class-IoU then drops to 0.365, 0.342 and 0.323 respectively from the baseline of 0.410 (see Table 1). The performance, however, is still higher than without using these potentials (see APP+SIZ in Table 1).

4.5   Evaluating Object Models

As a final comparison, we study the quality of the inferred tubes for object detection. We split each dataset such that no actor occurs in both training and testing data. For training, we considered data from 5 out of 6 actors in ETHZ-action, 3 out of 4 actors in CAD-120 and 9 out of 12 actors in MPII-cooking datasets. The rest of the data was used for testing.

For object detection, we use a Hough forest [17] with 5 trees each trained with 50,000 positive and 50,000 negative patches (drawn uniformly from the background) and a maximal depth of 25. We do not make use of depth for

Table 3. Average precision (%) for different datasets comparing object models built from ground truth data (GTr.) and data inferred by the proposed method (Infer).

Class	GTr.	Infer	Class	GTr.	Infer	Class	GTr.	Infer	Class	GTr.	Infer
ETHZ-Action											
brush	45.1	33.6	calcul.	100.0	100.0	camera	83.5	73.0	remote	49.4	34.4
mug	38.0	39.5	headph.	69.8	69.8	marker	39.7	33.3	teapot	63.2	50.9
videog.	78.3	82.0	roller	99.6	69.0	phone	0.05	0.06	**Avg.**	60.6	53.2
CAD-120											
book	11.2	08.0	medbox.	58.3	40.4	bowl	24.5	25.0	mwave.	71.4	71.0
box	24.4	19.1	plate	16.2	14.1	cup	14.8	09.4	remote	14.1	17.6
			cloth	20.1	15.1	**Avg.**	29.4	24.4			
MPII-Cooking											
bowl	69.2	11.1	spiceh.	100.0	100.0	bread	25.5	06.2	squeez.	61.5	61.5
plate	43.4	43.4	tin	33.0	23.9	grater	02.2	01.2	**Avg.**	47.8	35.3

this experiment. For comparison, we use manually annotated bounding boxes of training images, i.e. every 10th frame of training sequences. This is denoted as 'GTr.' in Table 3. The 'Infer' training data is based on an equal number of frames from the automatically extracted tubes inferred by the proposed model.

The results show that optimal performance is achieved for categories like *calculator, mug* in ETHZ, *bowl, microwave* in CAD-120 and *spiceholder, squeezer* in MPII. A loss in performance is observed for many categories due to weaker supervision which is explained by the fact that the bounding boxes of extracted tubes are noisier than manually annotated training data. Nevertheless, performances of the object detectors trained on weakly supervised videos achieve 87.7% (ETHZ), 83.0% (CAD) and 74.4% (MPII) of that from full supervision.

We also compare with [14] which is an unsupervised approach that segments and clusters videos based on pose features. [14] generates 20 clusters for the ETHZ-action dataset without labels and only 3–21 object samples per cluster while our approach generates more than 300 samples per class. Although the resulting clusters cannot be directly compared with our approach, we manually labelled the clusters and trained object detectors for all 12 classes. The resulting average precision on ETHZ is 24.85% in comparison to 53.23% of our approach.

5 Conclusion

We have addressed the problem of discovering medium and small sized objects from videos with activities. Our experiments have shown that current approaches for learning from weakly labelled videos that rely on motion segmentation fail for this task. We have also shown that using object appearance alone is insufficient in such scenarios and that encoding functionality greatly improves performance. Interestingly, the results also revealed the complementary nature of appearance and functionality related potentials for object discovery. The generalization capabilities of our approach were demonstrated on three datasets that span a variety of different activities, modalities (RGB vs. RGB-D), and pose representations (2d vs. 3d). Finally, our weakly supervised approach outperformed an unsupervised approach and achieves between 74% and 88% of the performance of a fully supervised approach for object detection.

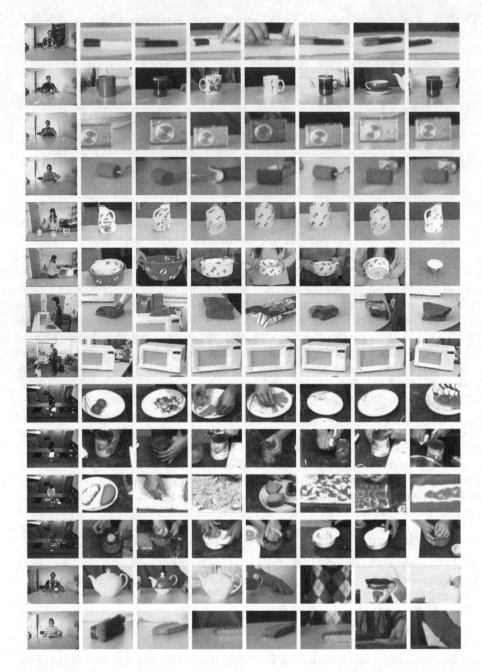

Fig. 5. Discovered instances of the object classes: *Marker, Mug, Camera, Roller, Milk-box, Bowl, Cloth, Microwave, Plate, Tin, Bread, Squeezer* and failure cases *Teapot, Brush*. The first image in each row shows relative object size by illustrating a typical action scene with overlayed pose and a bounding box around the object of interest. Since the objects are relatively small, images are best viewed by zooming in.

Acknowledgements. Authors acknowledge financial support from the DFG Emmy Noether program (GA 1927/1-1).

References

1. Alexe, B., Deselaers, T., Ferrari, V.: What is an object? In: CVPR, pp. 73–80 (2010)
2. Blaschko, M.B., Vedaldi, A., Zisserman, A.: Simultaneous object detection and ranking with weak supervision. In: NIPS, pp. 235–243 (2010)
3. Bosch, A., Zisserman, A., Munoz, X.: Representing shape with a spatial pyramid kernel. In: ACM Int. Conf. on Image and Video Retrieval, pp. 401–408 (2007)
4. Brox, T., Malik, J.: Object segmentation by long term analysis of point trajectories. In: Daniilidis, K., Maragos, P., Paragios, N. (eds.) ECCV 2010, Part V. LNCS, vol. 6315, pp. 282–295. Springer, Heidelberg (2010)
5. Brox, T., Malik, J.: Large displacement optical flow: descriptor matching in variational motion estimation. PAMI 33(3), 500–513 (2011)
6. Chum, O., Zisserman, A.: An exemplar model for learning object classes. In: CVPR, pp. 1–8 (2007)
7. Comaniciu, D., Meer, P.: Mean shift: a robust approach toward feature space analysis. PAMI 24(5), 603–619 (2002)
8. Delaitre, V., Fouhey, D.F., Laptev, I., Sivic, J., Gupta, A., Efros, A.A.: Scene semantics from long-term observation of people. In: Fitzgibbon, A., Lazebnik, S., Perona, P., Sato, Y., Schmid, C. (eds.) ECCV 2012, Part VI. LNCS, vol. 7577, pp. 284–298. Springer, Heidelberg (2012)
9. Deselaers, T., Alexe, B., Ferrari, V.: Localizing objects while learning their appearance. In: Daniilidis, K., Maragos, P., Paragios, N. (eds.) ECCV 2010, Part IV. LNCS, vol. 6314, pp. 452–466. Springer, Heidelberg (2010)
10. Everingham, M., Gool, L.V., Williams, C., Winn, J., Zisserman, A.: The pascal visual object classes (voc) challenge. IJCV 88, 303–338 (2010)
11. Fathi, A., Ren, X., Rehg, J.: Learning to recognize objects in egocentric activities. In: CVPR, pp. 3281–3288 (2011)
12. Felzenszwalb, P.F., Huttenlocher, D.P.: Efficient graph-based image segmentation. IJCV 59(2), 167–181 (2004)
13. Filipovych, R., Ribeiro, E.: Recognizing primitive interactions by exploring actor-object states. In: CVPR (2008)
14. Human Body Analysis. In: Fossati, A., Gall, J., Grabner, H., Ren, X., Konolige, K. (eds.) Consumer Depth Cameras for Computer Vision. Springer (2013)
15. Fouhey, D.F., Delaitre, V., Gupta, A., Efros, A.A., Laptev, I., Sivic, J.: People watching: Human actions as a cue for single view geometry. In: Fitzgibbon, A., Lazebnik, S., Perona, P., Sato, Y., Schmid, C. (eds.) ECCV 2012, Part V. LNCS, vol. 7576, pp. 732–745. Springer, Heidelberg (2012)
16. Gall, J., Fossati, A., van Gool, L.: Functional categorization of objects using real-time markerless motion capture. In: CVPR, pp. 1969–1976 (2011)
17. Gall, J., Yao, A., Razavi, N., Van Gool, L., Lempitsky, V.: Hough forests for object detection, tracking, and action recognition. PAMI 33(11), 2188–2202 (2011)
18. Grabner, H., Gall, J., Van Gool, L.: What makes a chair a chair? In: CVPR, pp. 1529–1536 (2011)
19. Gupta, A., Davis, L.: Objects in action: An approach for combining action understanding and object perception. In: CVPR, pp. 1–8 (2007)

20. Gupta, A., Satkin, S., Efros, A.A., Hebert, M.: From 3D scene geometry to human workspace. In: CVPR, pp. 1961–1968 (2011)
21. Jiang, Y., Koppula, H., Saxena, A.: Hallucinated humans as the hidden context for labeling 3D scenes. In: CVPR, pp. 2993–3000 (2013)
22. Jones, M., Rehg, J.: Statistical color models with application to skin detection. IJCV 46(1), 81–96 (2002)
23. Kjellström, H., Romero, J., Kragic, D.: Visual object-action recognition: Inferring object affordances from human demonstration. CVIU 115, 81–90 (2010)
24. Kolmogorov, V.: Convergent tree-reweighted message passing for energy minimization. PAMI 28(10), 1568–1583 (2006)
25. Koppula, H., Gupta, R., Saxena, A.: Learning human activities and object affordances from rgb-d videos. IJRR 32(8), 951–970 (2013)
26. Lee, Y.J., Grauman, K.: Learning the easy things first: Self-paced visual category discovery. In: CVPR, pp. 1721–1728 (2011)
27. Leistner, C., Godec, M., Schulter, S., Saffari, A., Werlberger, M., Bischof, H.: Improving classifiers with unlabeled weakly-related videos. In: CVPR, pp. 2753–2760 (2011)
28. Manen, S., Guillaumin, M., Van Gool, L.: Prime object proposals with randomized prim's algorithm. In: ICCV, pp. 2536–2543 (2013)
29. Moore, D., Essa, I., Hayes, M.: Exploiting human actions and object context for recognition tasks. In: ICCV, pp. 80–86 (1999)
30. Ommer, B., Mader, T., Buhmann, J.: Seeing the Objects Behind the Dots: Recognition in Videos from a Moving Camera. IJCV 83, 57–71 (2009)
31. Peursum, P., West, G., Venkatesh, S.: Combining image regions and human activity for indirect object recognition in indoor wide-angle views. In: ICCV, pp. 82–89 (2005)
32. Pieropan, A., Ek, C.H., Kjellstrom, H.: Functional object descriptors for human activity modeling. In: ICRA, pp. 1282–1289 (2013)
33. Prest, A., Leistner, C., Civera, J., Schmid, C., Ferrari, V.: Learning object class detectors from weakly annotated video. In: CVPR, pp. 3282–3289 (2012)
34. Ramanan, D., Forsyth, D.A., Barnard, K.: Building models of animals from video. PAMI 28(8), 1319–1334 (2006)
35. Rohrbach, M., Amin, S., Andriluka, M., Schiele, B.: A database for fine grained activity detection of cooking activities. In: CVPR, pp. 1194–1201 (2012)
36. Rubinstein, M., Joulin, A., Kopf, J., Liu, C.: Unsupervised joint object discovery and segmentation in internet images. In: CVPR, pp. 1939–1946 (2013)
37. Schulter, S., Leistner, C., Roth, P.M., Bischof, H.: Unsupervised object discovery and segmentation in videos. In: BMVC, pp. 391–404 (2013)
38. Turek, M.W., Hoogs, A., Collins, R.: Unsupervised learning of functional categories in video scenes. In: Daniilidis, K., Maragos, P., Paragios, N. (eds.) ECCV 2010, Part II. LNCS, vol. 6312, pp. 664–677. Springer, Heidelberg (2010)
39. Tuytelaars, T., Lampert, C.H., Blaschko, M.B., Buntine, W.: Unsupervised object discovery: A comparison. IJCV 88, 284–302 (2010)
40. Winn, J.M., Jojic, N.: Locus: Learning object classes with unsupervised segmentation. In: ICCV, pp. 756–763 (2005)

Weakly Supervised Object Localization with Latent Category Learning

Chong Wang, Weiqiang Ren*, Kaiqi Huang, and Tieniu Tan

National Laboratory of Pattern Recognition
Institute of Automation, Chinese Academy of Sciences

Abstract. Localizing objects in cluttered backgrounds is a challenging task in weakly supervised localization. Due to large object variations in cluttered images, objects have large ambiguity with backgrounds. However, backgrounds contain useful latent information, *e.g.*, the sky for aeroplanes. If we can learn this latent information, object-background ambiguity can be reduced to suppress the background. In this paper, we propose the latent category learning (LCL), which is an unsupervised learning problem given only image-level class labels. Firstly, inspired by the latent semantic discovery, we use the typical probabilistic Latent Semantic Analysis (pLSA) to learn the latent categories, which can represent objects, object parts or backgrounds. Secondly, to determine which category contains the target object, we propose a category selection method evaluating each category's discrimination. We evaluate the method on the PASCAL VOC 2007 database and ILSVRC 2013 detection challenge. On VOC 2007, the proposed method yields the annotation accuracy of 48%, which outperforms previous results by 10%. More importantly, we achieve the detection average precision of 30.9%, which improves previous results by 8% and can be competitive with the supervised deformable part model (DPM) 5.0 baseline 33.7%. On ILSVRC 2013 detection, the method yields the precision of 6.0%, which is also competitive with the DPM 5.0.

Keywords: weakly supervised learning, object localization, category learning, latent semantic analysis.

1 Introduction

Weakly supervised localization is challenging in cluttered conditions. Different from the supervised task, the annotation of object location is not given. Though it requires less labeling, it is challenging because of large object variations in cluttered backgrounds. In recent years, many studies in weakly supervised learning have been proposed. They adopt a similar framework, as shown in Fig.1(a). They first use region proposals to extract candidate regions [1, 32], then the object regions (correct localizations) are selected among the candidate regions by

---

* Chong Wang and Weiqiang Ren contributed equally to this work.

D. Fleet et al. (Eds.): ECCV 2014, Part VI, LNCS 8694, pp. 431–445, 2014.
© Springer International Publishing Switzerland 2014

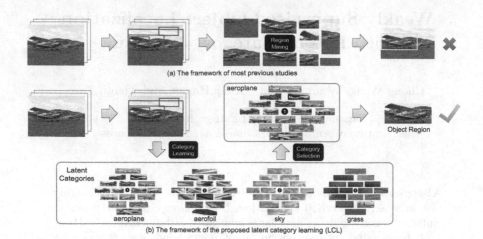

(a) The framework of most previous studies

aeroplane

Object Region

Category
Learning

Category
Selection

Latent
Categories

aeroplane   aerofoil   sky   grass

(b) The framework of the proposed latent category learning (LCL)

Fig. 1. The comparison of the framework of the proposed method and previous studies

region mining methods, *e.g.*, exhaustive search [20, 21], multiple instance learning [13, 28, 34], inter-intra-class modeling [5, 9, 23, 28, 29] and topic model [25, 30]. They have achieved promising results on object-centered conditions, in which objects occupy a large portion of an image [12]. However, on the cluttered condition such as the PASCAL VOC challenge [10], there still a long way to be competitive with the supervised approach [11].

In cluttered conditions, due to large object variations, objects usually have large ambiguity with backgrounds. Besides, in the weakly supervised task, only the image-level class labels are available, *e.g.*, the image has an aeroplane in Fig.1(a). However, a large number of candidate regions have a large background area, which makes it difficult to discover object regions in cluttered conditions, *e.g.*, the localization in Fig.1(a) contains too much background. However, backgrounds contain some latent information, *e.g.*, there is sky and grass in the image (Fig.1(a)). This latent information can be very useful because if it can be learned, the object-background ambiguity can be reduced to suppress the background, *e.g.*, the background area in Fig.1(b) is suppressed. Due to the unknown label of the candidate regions, learning these latent categories is an unsupervised learning problem. Many studies in unsupervised learning have attempted to discover the latent categories in object-centered conditions [4, 18, 19, 27, 30]. Inspired by them, we proposed to learn the latent categories in cluttered conditions.

In this paper, we propose the latent category learning (LCL) for weakly supervised localization. To learn the latent categories, we use the probabilistic Latent Semantic Analysis (pLSA) [16], which is a typical unsupervised learning method and achieves notable success in discovering latent semantics [30]. Fig.1(b) shows the framework of the proposed method. Compared to the previous studies in Fig.1(a), there are two main differences:

1) *Category Learning. Is it possible to learn meaningful latent categories in backgrounds?* We show that the typical unsupervised semantic analysis can

successfully learn the latent categories to represent objects, object parts and backgrounds, as shown in Fig.1(b).

2) *Category Selection.* After learning these categories, *which category contains the target object class?* We propose a category selection method by evaluating the discrimination of each category and select the most discriminative one. In this paper, we denote by "class" the given image-level object class and by "category" the latent category in an object class.

In the evaluation, we use the PASCAL VOC 2007 database [10] and ILSVRC 2013 detection challenge. For fair comparison with supervised methods, we use the complete dataset with only image-level class labels. On PASCAL VOC 2007, we obtain the annotation accuracy of 48%, which is 10% higher than the previous results [25, 28, 29]. More importantly, the LCL achieves the detection average precision of 30.9%, which outperforms previous results [23, 29] by 8% and can be competitive with the supervised deformable part model (DPM) 5.0 baseline 33.7% [15]. On ILSVRC 2013 detection challenge, we obtain the precision of 6.0% on the validation set, which is also competitive with the 8.8% by DPM.

2 Related Work

In recent years, many studies have been proposed in the weakly supervised localization, *e.g.*, exhaustive search [5,20,21,36], multiple instance learning [13,28,34], inter-intra-class modeling [9, 23, 29, 35] and topic model [25, 30]. Most of them adopt a similar framework, which has three main steps: (1) *Region Extraction*: region proposals extract candidate regions for each image; (2) *Region Representation*: feature representation is constructed for each region; (3) *Region Mining*: object regions (correct localizations) are discovered among the candidate regions. We review the main studies from these three parts.

Region Extraction. Nguyen *et al.* [20] and Pandy *et al.* [21] use dense regions in an initial bounding box as candidate regions, but the fixed size and shape make it difficult to generate enough object regions. To improve the quality of the candidate regions, various region proposals are used to extract regions based on object saliency. The one popularly used [9, 28, 29] is proposed by Alexe *et al.* [1], who present a generic objectness measure by combining multiple image cues in a Bayesian framework. Promising results have been obtained based on this proposal [1,9,28,29]. Recently, a segmentation based region proposal, named Selective Search [32], can generate regions with better objectness for its hierarchical segmentation and grouping strategies [6,14,32]. In this paper, we use the selective search for region extraction.

Region Representation. In [21], each candidate region is represented by the histogram of oriented gradients (HOG) descriptor [11]. With the additional viewpoint annotation, promising results are obtained on the subset of the PASCAL VOC 2007 challenge [10]. However, this gradient based low-level descriptor is sensitive to cluttered backgrounds. Many recent studies use the Bag-of-Words (BoW) feature for its mid-level object representation [3,9,23,28,29], and some researchers combine the low-level and mid-level features for better discrimination [9]. Recently, the deep networks have achieved great success in large-scale and challenging object recognition tasks for its semantic object representation, especially the Convolutional Neural Network (CNN) [14, 17]. In this paper, we use the CNN for region representation.

Region Mining. In [21] and [20], object regions are obtained based on exhaustive search in an initial bounding box, which is usually determined based on object saliency [5, 21]. However, the fixed size and shape make it difficult to collect enough object regions. To discover more objects, multiple instance learning considers inter-class relations by organizing the candidate regions as positive and negative bags [20, 22, 28, 34]. To improve the quality of the object regions, researchers further model intra-class relations to improve the similarity of the regions within the same object class [9, 23, 29, 35]. However, due to large object variations, localizations may have large background area. In fact, backgrounds contain useful latent categories, which can represent objects, object parts or backgrounds. They can be beneficial to reduce the object-background ambiguity and suppress the background area. Given only image-level class labels, learning these latent categories is an unsupervised learning problem. Some studies have attempted to learn them from large quantity of images in object-centered conditions [4, 18, 19, 27, 30]. Inspired by them, in this paper, we proposed to learn the latent categories in cluttered conditions.

3   Latent Category Learning

In this section, we present the latent category learning (LCL) for weakly supervised localization. We first introduce the extraction of the semantic candidate regions, then we elaborate how to learn the latent categories and discover the object regions among these categories. In this paper, we denote the object regions as correct localizations.

3.1   Region Extraction

Region proposal generates candidate regions for probable object locations. We use a segmentation based region proposal named Selective Search [32], which can generate regions with strong objectness [6, 14]. Compared to other region proposals [1], it is reported to have a higher overlap with ground truth bounding box but only with the comparable number of regions [32]. Fig.3(b) shows some examples on the training set of the PASCAL VOC 2007 database. Although objects vary a lot in size, illumination and occlusion, the selective search can extract object regions in most images.

After generating the candidate regions, the next step is to construct feature representation for them. In this paper, we use Convolutional Neural Network (CNN) to represent the regions. CNN has made a great breakthrough in many object recognition tasks [14, 17]. It can construct semantic object representation for its deep hierarchical structure. As demonstrated in [14], the classification results on ImageNet [8] can generalize well to the detection task in PASCAL VOC challenge. We train a CNN classification model on ILSVRC 2011 with the same setup to [14], which uses five convolutional layers and three fully-connected layers. We represent each candidate region by the *fc6* layer, which is the first fully-connected layer containing 4096 neurons. Therefore, the feature representation of each region has the dimension of 4096.

3.2   Category Learning

With the candidate regions extracted, in this part, we learn the latent categories from them. Due to the unknown object class label of these regions, learning the latent category is an unsupervised learning problem. In this paper, we use the typical pLSA for latent category learning.

We use positive images in an object class for category learning. Suppose we have N candidate regions in positive images, and the CNN representation of each region is d_j. In document analysis, the pLSA usually takes the histogram of occurrence frequency on visual words as input, while the CNN region representation satisfies this histogram input for two reasons. Firstly, due to the Rectified Linear Units [14], all the region representation is non-negative. Secondly, we consider each neuron in the *fc6* layer as a visual word, and the CNN representation is the occurrence confidence on these words. The larger confidence leads to the larger occurrence probability of a word (neuron). If a hard threshold function ($d_j >$T 1;else 0) is used on the CNN representation, it will turn into the 0,1 value, thus the representation is the same to the histogram of occurrence frequency; while if the threshold function is not used, the CNN representation is not the strict frequency but the soft version. Therefore, this CNN region representation can fit well in the framework of topic modeling.

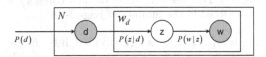

Fig. 2. The graphical model of the probabilistic Latent Semantic Analysis (pLSA) [30]

We denote each word (neuron) as w_i, thus the occurrence frequency of region d_j on w_i is the i-th dimension of d_j. In addition, there is a hidden topic variable z_k associated with all the visual words. We treat each topic z_k as a latent category in an object class. The pLSA optimizes the joint probability $P(w_i, d_j, z_k)$, which has the form of the graphical model shown in Fig.2 [30]. Marginalizing over the latent category z_k determines the conditional probability $P(w_i|d_j)$:

$$P(w_i|d_j) = \sum_{k=1}^{K} P(z_k|d_j) P(w_i|z_k), \tag{1}$$

where $P(z_k|d_j)$ is the probability of category z_k occurring in region d_j. Based on this term, each region has K probabilities for K latent categories. We consider that if region d_j has the maximum probability on category z_k, then d_j only

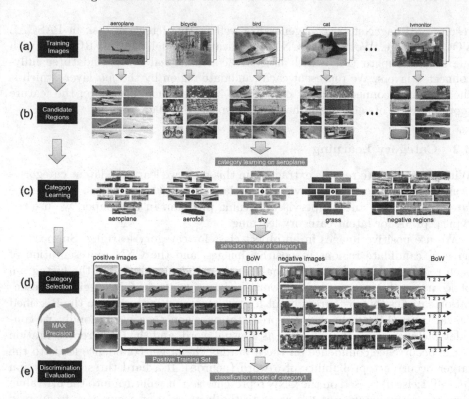

Fig. 3. The flowchart of the proposed latent category learning (LCL) for weakly supervised localization. (a) Original images on the PASCAL VOC 2007 training set. (b) Selective search and CNN extract semantic candidate regions. (c) Probabilistic Latent Semantic Analysis (pLSA) learns latent categories. (d) A selection model is trained for each latent category. (e) The discrimination of each category is evaluated by the classification model constructed in the manner of bag-of-words.

belongs to z_k. In this way, all regions are divided into K sets, each of which contains the regions with similar semantic meaning. Fig.3(c) shows some learned latent categories of the aeroplane class. These categories have strong semantic meanings, *e.g.*, category 1 represents the aeroplane, category 2 is the aerofoil, while others contain backgrounds such as sky and grass. The categories in each object class are learned separately to avoid a large memory cost.

3.3   Category Selection

After learning the latent categories, a problem is to decide *which one contains the object regions of the target object class?* In this part, we propose a category selection strategy to discover the object regions. The idea is based on the fact that the latent categories have different semantic meanings, thus they have different discrimination to the target object class. We exploit the different discrimination to find out the most discriminative category. To evaluate the discrimination, it is observed that in each latent category, the regions of positive and negative images have different occurrence frequencies on all the learned categories. For example, in category 1, regions of positive images have a high occurrence frequency on aeroplane but much lower frequency on others, while it is the opposite for the regions of negative images, as shown in Fig.3(d). Combined with image-level class labels, we select the category with the frequency which best differentiates the target object class and backgrounds.

Fig.3 is used for an illustration. To construct the frequency for each category, we first have to select the regions which can represent the category. We train a selection model to select them. For any target category (category 1), we consider the regions in it as positive regions, while the negative regions consist of two parts: the ones in other categories (category 2-4) and the ones from negative images (negative). Therefore, a selection model of the target category (category 1) can be trained. Secondly, we use the selection model to select the top T scored regions in each positive and negative image. We observe that the occurrence frequencies of the T selected regions is the BoW representation, as shown in Fig.3(d). Based on these regions, we construct the BoW image representation for each positive and negative image. Finally, with the BoW representation, a classification model of the target latent category (category 1) is trained on the training set with the image-level class label, and the discrimination of the model is evaluated by the classification precision on the validation set. By evaluating all categories, the one with the highest precision is considered as the most discriminative one, and its corresponding top T regions in positive images constitute the positive training set. Fig.3(d) shows the selection process and the positive training set on the aeroplane class.

In constructing the BoW representation, there are three steps: (1) *Codebook Generation*. We quantify each latent category by averaging the regions in it. Let $\mathbf{Z} = [\mathbf{z_1}, ..., \mathbf{z_K}]^T \in \Re^{M \times K}$ denote the codebook with K categories. We use the average to quantify the category for two reasons: one is that the regions in a category look very similar, and it is reasonable to use the center; another is that the regions in the correct category overlap heavily with the target object, thus averaging them is beneficial to suppress backgrounds. (2) *Feature Encoding*. In each image, suppose the T selected regions are denoted as $[\mathbf{d_1}, ..., \mathbf{d_T}]^T \in \Re^{M \times T}$, we encode each region by the Super Vector Coding [37]:

$$\left[\underbrace{0, ..., 0}_{(j-1)*M\ dim.} \ , \ \overbrace{\mathbf{d_i} - \mathbf{z_j}}^{M\ dim.} \ , \ \underbrace{0, ..., 0}_{(K-j)*M\ dim.} \right]. \tag{2}$$

$$s.t.\ \mathbf{z_j} = \arg\min_{\mathbf{z_k}} \|\mathbf{d_i} - \mathbf{z_k}\|_2$$

(3) *Feature Pooling*. After the encoding, average pooling [37] is used on the encoding of all the T regions to construct the BoW image representation, as shown in Fig.3(d).

4   Experimental Evaluation

In this section, we evaluate the proposed method on the PASCAL VOC 2007 dataset and ILSVRC 2013 detection challenge. We use the complete dataset with only image-level class labels for fair comparison with the supervised approach. The detailed setup is given as follows.

Region Extraction: In selective search, we use the source code released by Uijlings *et al.* [32]. We run the "fast" option to generate about 2000 candidate regions for an image. Then, to represent the regions, we train a convolutional neural network (CNN) on ILSVRC 2011 with five convolutional and three fully-connected layers, which has the same architecture to [14, 17]. We use the fc6 layer for representation with the dimensionality of 4096.

Category Learning and Selection: For each object class, all the regions from positive images are used for category learning. The number of the latent categories (K) is determined by the highest classification precision on different number, while K is around 30 for most classes. In training selection models in category selection, the number of the top selected regions (T) in each positive image is set up to be 10 to guarantee the quality of the predicted locations.

Training and Testing: In training the classification models and final object detectors, the stochastic dual coordinate ascent [24] in VLFeat [33] is adopted for high efficiency. In testing, we first select the regions with the score larger than -1, then the Non Maximum Suppression (NMS) [11] with the threshold of 0.5 is used to obtain final localizations.

4.1   Automated Annotation Results

Table 1 shows the annotation accuracy of the proposed LCL and the previous studies on the trainval set. The accuracy is measured by the percentage of training images in which an instance is correctly localized according to the PASCAL criterion, which requires the overlap of larger than 0.5 between the object region and the ground truth. We also use k-means in category learning as a baseline for comparison with pLSA. It is observed that LCL yields an annotation accuracy of 48.5%, which outperforms the previous best result by 10%. LCL improves most classes, and the improvement is quite promising on some difficult ones, *e.g.,* 18% on chair and 22% on plant. Besides, LCL-pLSA outperforms LCL-kmeans by a small margin, which shows that pLSA is slightly better in learning latent category, but it is much better than LCL-kmeans in the detection results, as shown below in Sec.4.2. Fig.4 shows some successful and failed difficult localizations by LCL on the trainval set. Although objects vary a lot in size, occlusion and illumination, LCL correctly localizes most difficult samples.

Though LCL shows promising improvements, it fails on some classes such as boat and table. Based on our observation, there are two main reasons for this: (1) Too much object variation. For example in boat, the size and appearance vary too much. Some images have small sailboats while some have large ships, which

Table 1. The comparison of annotation accuracy on PASCAL VOC 2007 trainval set

Method	plane	bike	bird	boat	bottle	bus	car	cat	chair	cow
Joint Learning [20]	30.7	16.5	23	14.9	4.9	29.6	26.5	35.3	7.2	23.4
MIL-SVM [2]	37.8	17.7	26.7	13.8	4.9	34.4	33.7	46.6	5.4	29.8
Drift Detect [29]	45.8	21.8	30.9	20.4	5.3	37.6	40.8	51.6	7	29.8
MIL-Negative [28]	42.4	46.5	18.2	8.8	2.9	40.9	73.2	44.8	5.4	29.8
Transfer Learning [26]	54.7	22.7	33.7	24.5	4.6	33.9	42.5	57	7.3	39.1
Beyasian Topic [25]	67.3	54.4	34.3	17.8	1.3	46.6	60.7	68.9	2.5	32.4
Multifold MIL [7]	56.6	58.3	28.4	20.7	6.8	54.9	69.1	20.8	9.2	50.5
LCL-kmeans	74.9	61.7	49.6	13.5	17.0	57.4	73.3	44.0	27.5	70.0
LCL-pLSA	80.1	63.9	51.5	14.9	21.0	55.7	74.2	43.5	26.2	53.4

Method	table	dog	horse	mbike	person	plant	sheep	sofa	train	tv	Accuracy
Joint Learning [20]	20.5	32.1	24.4	33.1	17.2	12.2	20.8	28.8	40.6	7	22.4
MIL-SVM [2]	14.5	32.8	34.8	41.6	19.9	11.4	25	23.6	45.2	8.6	25.4
Drift Detect [29]	27.5	41.3	41.8	47.3	24.1	12.2	28.1	32.8	48.7	9.4	30.2
MIL-Negative [28]	14.5	32.8	34.8	41.6	19.9	11.4	25	23.6	45.2	8.6	30.4
Transfer Learning [26]	24.1	43.3	41.3	51.5	25.3	13.3	28	29.5	54.6	11.8	32.1
Beyasian Topic [25]	16.2	58.9	51.5	64.6	18.2	3.1	20.9	34.7	63.4	5.9	36.2
Multifold MIL [7]	10.2	29.0	58.0	64.9	36.7	18.7	56.5	13.2	54.9	59.4	38.8
LCL-kmeans	16.3	56.3	55.3	69.5	13.6	40.0	60.3	46.2	45.5	61.9	**47.7**
LCL-pLSA	16.3	56.7	58.3	69.5	14.1	38.3	58.8	47.2	49.1	60.9	**48.5**

Fig. 4. Some successful and failed difficult localizations on the trainval set

makes it difficult to learn meaningful latent categories under the limited number of positive images. (2) Similar co-occurrent classes. For example the table, it always co-exists with chairs. They look very similar in most cases, *e.g.*, both the table and chair have a flat area with several legs, which makes it difficult to learn two different latent categories. Therefore, under the cases of too much variations and similar co-occurrent classes, it is challenging for LCL to generate good localizations.

4.2 Detection Results

Table 2 shows the detection mean average precision (mAP) of the proposed LCL, the previous studies and the supervised approaches on the PASCAL VOC 2007 test set. It is observed that LCL-pLSA yields a detection mAP of 30.9%, which improves the previous best result by 8% and improves most classes by a large margin, *e.g.*, 21% on aeroplane, 13% on cow, 10% on motorbike and 15% on sofa. We also make a breakthrough on the classes which are almost zero in previous results, *e.g.*, the improvement is about 11% on chair. More importantly, compared to the supervised approach, the 30.9% obtained by LCL-pLSA can be

Table 2. The comparison of the detection mAP on PASCAL VOC 2007 test set

Method	plane	bike	bird	boat	bottle	bus	car	cat	chair	cow
Drift-Detect [29]	13.4	44.0	3.1	3.1	0.0	31.2	43.9	7.1	0.1	9.3
Object-Centric [23]	-	-	-	-	-	-	-	-	-	-
Multifold MIL [7]	35.8	40.6	8.1	7.6	3.1	35.9	41.8	16.8	1.4	23.0
Latent SVM [31]	27.6	41.9	19.7	9.1	10.4	35.8	39.1	33.6	0.6	20.9
LCL-kmeans	41.5	29.7	24.9	12.0	10.7	30.3	40.9	31.8	10.5	21.8
LCL-pLSA	48.8	41.0	23.6	12.1	11.1	42.7	40.9	35.5	11.1	36.6
DPM 5.0 [11]	33.2	60.3	10.2	16.1	27.3	54.3	58.2	23.0	20.0	24.1
CNN Supervise [14]	68.1	72.8	56.8	43.0	36.8	66.3	74.2	67.6	34.4	63.5

Method	table	dog	horse	mbike	person	plant	sheep	sofa	train	tv	mAP
Drift-Detect [29]	9.9	1.5	29.4	38.3	4.6	0.1	0.4	3.8	34.2	0.0	13.9
Object-Centric [23]	-	-	-	-	-	-	-	-	-	-	15.0
Multifold MIL [7]	4.9	14.1	31.9	41.9	19.3	11.1	27.6	12.1	31.0	40.6	22.4
Latent SVM [31]	10.0	27.7	29.4	39.2	9.1	19.3	20.5	17.1	35.6	7.1	22.7
LCL-kmeans	15.4	29.4	24.3	37.8	19.1	14.7	33.1	24.1	36.2	43.0	**26.6**
LCL-pLSA	18.4	35.3	34.8	51.3	17.2	17.4	26.8	32.8	35.1	45.6	**30.9**
DPM 5.0 [11]	26.7	12.7	58.1	48.2	43.2	12.0	21.1	36.1	46.0	43.5	33.7
CNN Supervise [14]	54.5	61.2	69.1	68.6	58.7	33.4	62.9	51.1	62.5	64.8	58.5

Fig. 5. Some successful and failed difficult localizations on the test set

competitive with the deformable part model 5.0 released baseline 33.7%. The precision on most classes is comparable to DPM 5.0, and some classes show better precision, *e.g.,* the improvement is about 15% on aeroplane, 12% on bird, cat and cow, and 23% on dog. This result is very encouraging because without the tedious and ambiguous annotation of object locations, the weakly supervised localization yields the comparable detection precision to the supervised methods in cluttered image conditions. Some successful and failed difficult detections on the test set are shown in Fig.5, in which LCL correctly localizes most objects under large variations of size, occlusion and illumination.

Table 3 shows the detection mean average precision (mAP) of the proposed LCL and the DPM 5.0 baseline on the validation set of the ILSVRC 2013 detection challenge (200 object classes). For higher efficiency, we use the k-means in category learning instead of pLSA, and the number of latent categories (K) is fixed to be 30. It is observed that the proposed LCL yields the detection mAP of 6.0%, which can be competitive with DPM 5.0 baseline 8.8%. This result demonstrates that LCL can be effective in large-scale image conditions.

Table 3. The comparison of the detection mAP of the LCL-kmeans and DPM 5.0 baseline on the validation set of the ILSVRC 2013 detection challenge

ILSVRC 2013 detection challenge	mAP (Validation)
LCL-kmeans	6.0%
DPM 5.0 (without context)	8.8%

Table 4. The detection mAP of the proposed LCL by incorporating object structure and inter-class relation

Method	plane	bike	bird	boat	bottle	bus	car	cat	chair	cow
Drift-Detect [29]	13.4	44.0	3.1	3.1	0.0	31.2	43.9	7.1	0.1	9.3
LCL-pLSA	48.8	41.0	23.6	12.1	11.1	42.7	40.9	35.5	11.1	36.6
LCL+DPM	30.2	46.9	10.4	4.6	11.1	47.0	44.9	14.7	5.6	17.4
LCL+Context	48.9	42.3	26.1	11.3	11.9	41.3	40.9	34.7	10.8	34.7

Method	table	dog	horse	mbike	person	plant	sheep	sofa	train	tv	mAP
Drift-Detect [29]	9.9	1.5	29.4	38.3	4.6	0.1	0.4	3.8	34.2	0.0	13.9
LCL-pLSA	18.4	35.3	34.8	51.3	17.2	17.4	26.8	32.8	35.1	45.6	30.9
LCL+DPM	4.6	15.0	38.6	41.8	13.9	10.6	19.3	31.8	16.3	37.9	23.1
LCL+Context	18.8	34.4	35.4	52.7	19.1	17.4	35.9	33.3	34.8	46.5	**31.6**

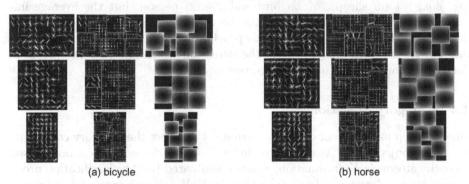

(a) bicycle   (b) horse

Fig. 6. The visualization of the detection model by using the LCL localizations as ground truth. Each detection model is trained with three components.

Though LCL has achieved comparable performance to DPM 5.0, the precision on some classes is relatively low, *e.g.*, bicycle, car, horse and person. We observe that for the classes which DPM beats LCL, most of them are the classes of rigid objects, *e.g.*, bicycle, boat, bottle, chair and table. Under this condition, object structures provide good representations because rigid objects do not change much. Combined with the HOG representation, the DPM achieves better results.

4.3   DPM and Context Embedding

To incorporate object structure and inter-class relations, we consider DPM and context in LCL for further enhancement. In DPM, we use the LCL annotations as ground truth, and the same setup to [11] is used, *i.e.*, 8 object parts and 3 object components. For the context, similar to the contextual operation in [11], we concatenate the region score, region location and the detection score of each class to the CNN region representation, thus the feature dimension of each candidate region is $4096 + 25 = 4121$.

Table.4 shows the detection mAP of LCL by incorporating DPM and context. LCL+DPM obtains a mAP of 23.1%, which is 9% higher than the Drift-Detect [29] which also trains DPM. However, compared to the LCL-pLSA, it decreases by 7% due to the inaccurate annotations of LCL, and the precision on most classes decreases a lot. But we see some promising improvements in detecting rigid objects, *e.g.,* the improvement over LCL-pLSA is about 6% in bicycle, 5% on bus and car, and 4% in horse. Fig.6 shows the detection model trained by LCL-pLSA with three components on the classes of bicycle and horse. The top two components describe the side views of the objects based on the different size, and the bottom component is more like the frontal or the rear view. These results show that incorporating object structures in latent category learning can be beneficial to detect rigid objects.

We see that by considering inter-class relations in LCL, performance can be further improved. LCL+Context achieves the mAP of 31.6%, which outperforms the LCL-pLSA baseline by 0.7%. The improvements on some classes are promising, *e.g.,* 9% on sheep, 3% on bird and 2% on person, but the average improvement is too small. The reason may be that the locations and scores of the detections are not accurate enough to provide meaningful co-occurrence information. As a result, this will hurt the detection precision, *e.g.,* the precision decreases about $1 \sim 2\%$ on boat, bus, cow and dog.

4.4   Category Selection

One key step in the latent category learning is to select the category containing the target object class. As elaborated in Sec.3.3, this category selection is based on each category's discrimination, which is evaluated by the classification precision on the validation set. In constructing the BoW image representation, we set the number of the top scored regions T to be 10. Fig.7 shows the Classification Mean Average Precision (Cls-mAP) of aeroplane and motorbike based on the number of latent categories of 20 and 30 respectively. The Maximum Average Best Overlap (MABO) [14] with ground truth is used to validate the correctness of the selection. It is observed that the highest Cls-mAP always corresponds to the highest MABO, *e.g.,* the 17*th* and 14*th* category in aeroplane and motorbike, which demonstrates the effectiveness of this selection strategy. However, we observe that the highest Cls-mAP does not have a large margin over the ones of other categories, *e.g.,* the 13*th* and 20*th* category of the aeroplane also has high precision. The reason is that the categories such as aerofoil and sky also contribute a lot to classify aeroplane. Although the margin is small, the most discriminative category can obtain the highest classification performance. In future, we will consider the more powerful Latent Dirichlet Allocation (LDA) to improve the discrimination.

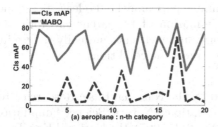

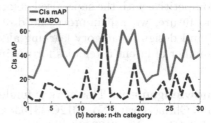

Fig. 7. The category selection on the classes of aeroplane and horse. The testing number of latent categories is set to be 20 and 30.

Another problem is how to set the number of latent categories for each object class. Due to the large variations of the number of positive images in different classes, using the appropriate number of latent categories is critical to learn meaningful ones. In our implementation, we initially set the number K to be 20 $\sim$ 60, then we use the above selection process to obtain the most discriminative category for each number. Finally, the number with the highest Cls-mAP is used. Table.5 shows the highest Cls-mAP and MABO of bicycle and cow under the different number of categories. We see the $K = 60$ is the best for both classes. If K is too small, the discriminative category contains many background regions; while if K is too large, object regions will be assigned to different latent categories which may not be discriminative to the target object class.

Table 5. The selection of the number of latent categories K on bicycle and cow

	Cls-mAP						MABO				
K	20	30	40	50	60	K	20	30	40	50	60
bicycle	66.7	67.6	65.2	68.4	**69.6**	bicycle	57.2	68.2	67.3	62.2	**70.0**
cow	45.6	47.1	48.5	44.1	**51.2**	cow	66.7	47.8	60.9	60.1	**68.8**

5   Conclusion

In this paper, we have proposed the latent category learning (LCL) for weakly supervised object localization. We first use a segmentation based region proposal to generate semantic candidate regions, each of which is represented by the Convolutional Neural Network (CNN) trained on ILSVRC 2011. Then, based on the large number of candidate regions, the probabilistic Latent Semantic Analysis (pLSA) is used to learn the latent categories, from which the category containing target object class is selected by evaluating each latent category's discrimination. Evaluation on the challenging PASCAL VOC 2007 dataset and the large-scale ILSVRC 2013 detection competition shows encouraging results achieved by LCL, with state-of-the-art annotation and detection performance among the weakly supervised localization methods. More importantly, the results are competitive with the supervised deformable part model 5.0 released baseline. In the future, we will improve the discrimination of the latent categories by LDA and design a category learning algorithm which automatically determine the number of latent categories for use in large-scale conditions.

Acknowledgement. This work is funded by the National Basic Research Program of China (Grant No. 2012CB316302), National Natural Science Foundation of China (Grant No. 61322209 and Grant No. 61175007), the National Key Technology R&D Program (Grant No. 2012BAH07B01).

References

1. Alexe, B., Deselaers, T., Ferrari, V.: What is an object? In: CVPR (2010)
2. Andrews, S., Tsochantaridis, I., Hofmann, T.: Support vector machines for multiple-instance learning. In: NIPS (2003)
3. Boureau, Y.L., Bach, F., LeCun, Y., Ponce, J.: Learning mid-level features for recognition. In: CVPR (2010)
4. Chen, X., Shrivastava, A., Gupta, A.: Neil: Extracting visual knowledge fromweb data. In: ICCV (2013)
5. Chum, O., Zisserman, A.: An exemplar model for learning object classes. In: CVPR (2007)
6. Cinbis, R.G., Verbeek, J., Schmid, C.: Segmentation driven object detection with fisher vectors. In: ICCV (2013)
7. Cinbis, R.G., Verbeek, J., Schmid, C.: Multi-fold mil training forweakly supervised object localization. In: CVPR (2014)
8. Deng, J., Dong, W., Socher, R., Li, L.J., Li, K., Fei-Fei, L.: Imagenet: A large-scale hierarchical image database. In: CVPR (2007)
9. Deselaers, T., Alexe, B., Ferrari, V.: Weakly supervised localization and learning with generic knowledge. IJCV 100(3) (2012)
10. Everingham, M., Gool, L.V., Williams, C.K.I., Winn, J., Zisserman, A.: The pascal visual object classes (voc) challenge. IJCV (2010)
11. Felzenszwalb, P.F., Girshick, R.B., McAllester, D., Ramanan, D.: Object detection with discriminatively trained part based models. TPAMI 32(9) (2010)
12. Fergus, R., Perona, P., Zisserman, A.: Object class recognition by unsupervised scale-invariant learning. In: CVPR (2003)
13. Galleguillos, C., Babenko, B., Rabinovich, A., Belongie, S.: Weakly supervised object localization with stable segmentations. In: Forsyth, D., Torr, P., Zisserman, A. (eds.) ECCV 2008, Part I. LNCS, vol. 5302, pp. 193–207. Springer, Heidelberg (2008)
14. Girshick, R., Donahue, J., Darrell, T., Malik, J.: Rich feature hierarchies for accurate object detection and semantic segmentation. In: CVPR (2014)
15. Girshick, R.B., Felzenszwalb, P.F., McAllester, D.A.: Discriminatively trained deformable part models, release 5,
    http://people.cs.uchicago.edu/~rbg/latent-release5/
16. Hofmann, T.: Probabilistic latent semantic indexing. In: SIGIR (1999)
17. Krizhevsky, A., Sutskever, I., Hinton, G.E.: Imagenet classification with deep convolutional neural networks. In: NIPS (2012)

18. Kumar, M.P., Packer, B., Koller, D.: Modeling latent variable uncertainty for loss-based learning. In: ICML (2012)
19. Li, Q., Wu, J., Tu, Z.: Harvesting mid-level visual concepts from large-scale internet images. In: CVPR (2013)
20. Nguyen, M.H., Torresani, L., de la Torre, F., Rother, C.: Weakly supervised discriminative localization and classification: a joint learning process. In: ICCV (2009)
21. Pandey, M., Lazebnik, S.: Scene recognition and weakly supervised object localization with deformable part-based models. In: ICCV (2011)
22. Ren, W., Wang, C., Huang, K., Tan, T.: On automatic and efficient localization of objects with weak supervision. In: ACCV (2014)
23. Russakovsky, O., Lin, Y., Yu, K., Fei-Fei, L.: Object-centric spatial pooling for image classification. In: Fitzgibbon, A., Lazebnik, S., Perona, P., Sato, Y., Schmid, C. (eds.) ECCV 2012, Part II. LNCS, vol. 7573, pp. 1–15. Springer, Heidelberg (2012)
24. Shalev-Shwartz, S., Zhang, T.: Stochastic dual coordinate ascent methods for regularized loss minimization. JMLR 14(1), 567–599 (2013)
25. Shi, Z., Hospedales, T.M., Xiang, T.: Bayesian joint topic modelling for weakly supervised object localisation. In: ICCV (2013)
26. Shi, Z., Siva, P., Xiang, T.: Transfer learning by ranking for weakly supervised object annotation. In: BMVC (2012)
27. Singh, S., Gupta, A., Efros, A.A.: Unsupervised discovery of mid-level discriminative patches. In: Fitzgibbon, A., Lazebnik, S., Perona, P., Sato, Y., Schmid, C. (eds.) ECCV 2012, Part II. LNCS, vol. 7573, pp. 73–86. Springer, Heidelberg (2012)
28. Siva, P., Russell, C., Xiang, T.: In defence of negative mining for annotating weakly labelled data. In: Fitzgibbon, A., Lazebnik, S., Perona, P., Sato, Y., Schmid, C. (eds.) ECCV 2012, Part III. LNCS, vol. 7574, pp. 594–608. Springer, Heidelberg (2012)
29. Siva, P., Xiang, T.: Weakly supervised object detector learning with model drift detection. In: ICCV (2011)
30. Sivic, J., Russell, B.C., Efros, A.A., Zisserman, A., Freeman, W.T.: Discovering objects and their location in images. In: ICCV (2005)
31. Song, H.O., Girshick, R., Jegelka, S., Mairal, J., Harchaoui, Z., Darrell, T.: On learning to localize objects with minimal supervision. arXiv:1403.1024 (2014)
32. Uijlings, J., van de Sande, K., Gevers, T., Smeulders, A.: Selective search for object recognition. IJCV (2013)
33. Vedaldi, A., Fulkerson, B.: VLFeat: An open and portable library of computer vision algorithms (2008), http://www.vlfeat.org/
34. Vijayanarasimhan, S., Grauman, K.: Keywords to visual categories: Multiple-instance learning for weakly supervised object categorization. In: CVPR (2008)
35. Wang, S., Joo, J., Wang, Y., Zhu, S.C.: Weakly supervised learning for attribute localization in outdoor scenes. In: CVPR (2013)
36. Zhang, Y., Chen, T.: Weakly supervised object recognition and localization with invariant high order features. In: BMVC (2010)
37. Zhou, X., Yu, K., Zhang, T., Huang, T.S.: Image classification using super-vector coding of local image descriptors. In: Daniilidis, K., Maragos, P., Paragios, N. (eds.) ECCV 2010, Part V. LNCS, vol. 6315, pp. 141–154. Springer, Heidelberg (2010)

Food-101 – Mining Discriminative Components with Random Forests

Lukas Bossard[1], Matthieu Guillaumin[1], and Luc Van Gool[1,2]

[1] Computer Vision Lab, ETH Zürich, Switzerland
lastname@vision.ee.ethz.ch
[2] ESAT, PSI-VISICS, K.U. Leuven, Belgium
vangool@esat.kuleuven.be

Abstract. In this paper we address the problem of automatically recognizing pictured dishes. To this end, we introduce a novel method to mine discriminative parts using Random Forests (RF), which allows us to mine for parts simultaneously for all classes and to share knowledge among them. To improve efficiency of mining and classification, we only consider patches that are aligned with image superpixels, which we call components. To measure the performance of our RF component mining for food recognition, we introduce a novel and challenging dataset of 101 food categories, with 101'000 images. With an average accuracy of 50.76%, our model outperforms alternative classification methods except for CNN, including SVM classification on Improved Fisher Vectors and existing discriminative part-mining algorithms by 11.88% and 8.13%, respectively. On the challenging MIT-Indoor dataset, our method compares nicely to other s-o-a component-based classification methods.

Keywords: Image classification, Discriminative part mining, Random Forest, Food recognition.

1 Introduction

Food is an important part of everyday life. This clearly ripples through into digital life, as illustrated by the abundance of food photography in social networks, dedicated photo sharing sites and mobile applications.[1] Automatic recognition of dishes would not only help users effortlessly organize their extensive photo collections but would also help online photo repositories make their content more accessible. Additionally, mobile food photography is now used to help patients estimate and track their daily calory intake, outside of any constraining clinical environment. However, current systems resort to nutrition experts [27] or Amazon Mechanical Turk [30] to label food items.

Despite these numerous applications, the problem of recognizing dishes and the composition of their ingredients has not been fully addressed by the computer vision community. This is not due to the lack of challenges. In contrast to scene classification or object detection, food typically does not exhibit any distinctive

---

[1] *E.g.*: foodspotting.com, sharedappetite.com, foodgawker.com, *etc.*

D. Fleet et al. (Eds.): ECCV 2014, Part VI, LNCS 8694, pp. 446–461, 2014.

Fig. 1. Typical examples of our dataset and corresponding mined components. From left to right: baby back ribs, chocolate cake, hot and sour soup, caesar salad, eggs benedict. [All our figures are best viewed in color]

spatial layout: while we can decompose an outdoor scene with a ground plane, a horizon and a sky region, or a human as a trunk with a head and limbs, we cannot find similar patterns relating ingredients of a mixed salad. The point of view, the lighting conditions, but also (and not least) the very realization of a recipe are among the sources of high intra-class variations. On the bright side, the nature of dishes is often defined by the different colors and textures of its different local components, such that humans can identify them reasonably well from a single image, regardless of the above variations. Hence, food recognition is a specific classification problem calling for models that can exploit local information.

As a consequence, we aim at identifying discriminative image regions which help distinguish each type of dish from the others. We refer to those as components and show a few examples in Fig. 1. To mine for such components, we introduce a weakly-supervised mining method which relies on Random Forests [14,4]. It is similar in spirit to previously proposed mid-level discriminative patch mining work [7,35,38,25,8,19,34,40]. Our Random Forest mining framework differs from all these works in the following points: First, it mines for discriminative components simultaneously for all classes, compared to independently. This speeds up the training process and allows to share knowledge between classes. Second, we restrict the search space for discriminative parts to patches aligned with superpixels, instead of sampling random image patches, in a spirit similar to what has been successfully proposed in the context of object detection [36,12]. As a consequence, not only do we manipulate regions that are consistent in color and texture, but we can afford extracting stronger visual features to improve classification. This also dramatically reduces the classification complexity on test images as the numbers of component classifiers/detectors can be fairly large (hundreds to several ten thousands): we typically use only a few dozens of superpixels per image, compared to tens of thousands of sliding windows.

The paper also introduces a new, publicly available dataset for real-world food recognition with 101'000 images. We coin this dataset *Food-101*, as it consists of 101 categories. To the best of our knowledge, this is the first public database of its kind. So far, research on food recognition has been either performed on closed, proprietary datasets [15] or on small-scale image sets taken in a controlled laboratory environment [5,39].

In summary, this paper makes the following contributions: (i) A novel discriminative part mining method based on Random Forests. (ii) A superpixel-based patch sampling strategy that prevents running many detectors on sliding windows. (iii) A novel, large scale and publicly available dataset for food recognition. (iv) Experiments showing that our approach outperforms the state-of-the-art Improved Fisher Vectors classifier [32] and the part-based mining approach of [34] on Food-101. On the MIT-Indoor dataset, our method compares nicely to very recent mining methods and is competitive with IFV.

We discuss related work in the next section. Our novel dataset is described in Section 3. In Section 4, we introduce our component mining and classification framework. Our method is evaluated in Section 5, and we conclude in Section 6.

2   Related Work

Image classification is a core problem for computer vision, with many recent advances coming from object recognition. Classical approaches exploit interest point descriptors, extracted locally or on a dense grid, then pooled into a vectorial representation to use SVM for classification. Recent advances highlight the importance of nonlinear feature encoding, e.g., Fisher Vectors [32] and spatial pooling [24]. A very recent and successful trend in classification is to try and identify discriminative object (or scene) parts (or patches) [7,35,38,25,8,19,34,40], drawing on the success of deformable part-based models (DPM) for object detection [9]. This can consist of (a) finding prototypes for regions of interest [31,40], (b) mining patches whose associated binary SVM obtains good classification accuracy on a validation set [34], (c) clustering patches with a multi-instance SVM (MI-SVM) [38] on a external dataset [25], (d) optimizing part detectors in a latent SVM framework [35], (e) evaluating many exemplar-SVMs [8,19] on sliding windows, exploiting discriminative decorrelation [13] to speed-up the process, or (f) identifying discriminative modes in the HOG feature space [7].

While this work represents a variant of discriminative part mining, it differs in various ways from previous work. In contrast to all other discriminative part mining methods, we efficiently and simultaneously mine for discriminative parts for all the categories in our dataset thanks to the multi-class nature of Random Forests. Secondly, while all other methods employ a computationally expensive (often multi scale) sliding window detection approach to produce the part score maps for the final classification step, our approach employs a simple yet effective window selection by exploiting image superpixels.

Concerning food recognition, most works follow a classical recognition pipeline, focusing on feature combination and on specialized datasets. [18] uses a private dataset of Japanese food, later augmented with more features and classes [20]. Similarly, [6] jointly classifies and estimates quantity of 50 Chinese food categories using private data. [28] uses DPM to locally pool features. Food images obtained in a controlled environment are also popular in the literature. The Pittsburgh food dataset [5] contains 101 classes, but with only 3 instances per class and 8 images per instance. Yang et al. [39] propose to learn spatial relationships between ingredients using pairwise features. This approach is bound to work only for standardized meals.

We resort to Random Forests (RF) [14,4] for mining discriminative regions in images. They are a well-established clustering and classification framework

Fig. 2. Here we show one example for 100 out of the 101 classes in our dataset. Note the high variance in food type, color, exposure and level of detail, but also visually and semantically similar food types.

and proved successful for many vision applications, including object recognition [3,29,33], object detection [11] and semantic segmentation [22,33]. Our use of RF is different compared to those works. Instead of directly using a RF for classification of patches [3] or learning specific locations of interest in images [40], we are using RF to discriminatively cluster superpixels into groups (leaves), and then use the leaf statistics to select the most promising groups (*i.e.*, mine for parts). For this key step, we have developed a *distinctiveness* measure for leaves, and ensure that distinctive but near-duplicate leaves are merged. Once parts are mined, the RF is entirely discarded and is not used at classification time (in contrast to [3,29,40]). Instead we model the mined components explicitly and directly using SVMs. At test time, only those SVM need to be evaluated on the image regions.

3   Dataset: Food-101

As noted above, to date, only the PFID dataset [5] is publicly available. However, it contains only standardized fast food images taken under laboratory conditions. Therefore, we have collected a novel real-world food dataset by downloading images from foodspotting.com. The site allows users to take images of what they are eating, annotate place and type of food and upload these information online. We chose the top 101 most popular and consistently named dishes and randomly sampled 750 training images. Additionally, 250 test images were collected for each class, and were manually cleaned. On purpose, the training images were not cleaned, and thus still contain some amount of noise. This comes mostly in the form of intense colors and sometimes wrong labels. We believe that real-world computer vision algorithms should be able to cope with such weakly labeled data if they are meant to scale well with the number of classes to recognise. All images were rescaled to have a maximum side length of 512 pixels and smaller ones were excluded from the whole process. This leaves us with a dataset of 101'000 real-world images in total, including very diverse but also visually and semantically similar food classes such as *Apple pie, Waffles, Escargots, Sashimi, Onion rings, Mussels, Edamame, Paella, Risotto, Omelette, Bibimbap, Lobster bisque, Eggs benedict, Macarons* to name a few. Examples are shown in Fig. 2. The dataset is available for download at http://www.vision.ee.ethz.ch/datasets/food-101/.

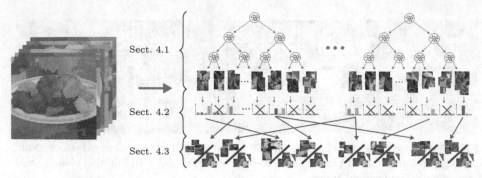

Fig. 3. Overview of our component mining. A Random Forest is used to hierarchically cluster superpixels of the training set. Then, discriminative clusters of superpixels in the leaves are selected and used to train the component models. After mining, the RF is not used anymore.

4   Random Forest Component Mining

In this section we show how we mine discriminative components using Random Forests [14,4] as visualized in Fig. 3. This has two benefits: In contrast to [7,35,38,25,34], components can be mined for all classes jointly because Random Forests are inherently multi-class learners. Compared to [7,8,19] which follow a bottom-up approach and thus need to evaluate all of the several thousands candidate component SVMs to assess how discriminant they are, Random Forest mining instead employs top-down clustering to generate a set of candidate components (Sect. 4.1). Thanks to the class-entropy criterion for choosing split functions, the generation of components is directly related to their discriminative power. We refine the selection of robust discriminative components in a second step (Sect. 4.2) by looking at consistent clusters across the trees of the forest and train robust component models afterwards (Sect. 4.3). The final classification step is then detailed in Sect. 4.4.

4.1   Candidate Component Generation

For generating candidate clusters, we train a weakly supervised Random Forest on superpixels associated with the class label of the image they stem from. By maximizing the information gain in each node, the forest will eventually separate discriminative superpixels from ambiguous ones that occur in several classes. Discriminative superpixels likely end up in the same leaf while non-discriminative ones are scattered.

Let a forest $\mathcal{F} = \{T_t\}$ be a set of trees T_t, each one trained on a random selection of samples (superpixels) $\mathcal{S} = \{s_i = (\mathbf{x}_i, y)\}$ where $\mathbf{x}_i \in \mathbb{R}^d$ is the feature vector of the sample s_i and y the class label of the corresponding image. For each node n we train a binary decision function $\phi_n : \mathbb{R}^d \to \{0, 1\}$ that sends each sample to either the left or right sub-tree and splits $\mathcal{S}$ into $\mathcal{S}_l$ and $\mathcal{S}_r$.

While training, at each node, the decision function ϕ is chosen out of a set of randomly generated decision functions $\{\phi_n\}$ so as to maximise the information gain criterion

$$\mathcal{I}(\mathcal{S}, \phi) = H(\mathcal{S}) - \left(\frac{|\mathcal{S}_l|}{|\mathcal{S}|} H(\mathcal{S}_l) + \frac{|\mathcal{S}_r|}{|\mathcal{S}|} H(\mathcal{S}_r) \right), \tag{1}$$

where $H(\cdot)$ is the class entropy of a set of samples. The training continues to split the samples until either a maximum depth is reached, or when too few samples, or samples of a single class are left. In this work we use linear classifiers [3] as decision functions, and more specifically resort to training binary SVMs:

$$\phi(\mathbf{x}) = 1_{[\mathbf{w}^\top \mathbf{x} + b > 0]}. \tag{2}$$

We generate different $\phi(\mathbf{x})$ by training them on randomly generated binary class partitions of the class labels in $\mathcal{S}$.

After training the forest, each tree T_t has a set of leaves $L_t = \{l\}$. In the sequel, we denote by $\mathcal{L} = \cup_t L_t$ the set of all leaves in the forest. They constitute the set of candidates for discriminative components. In the next section, we describe how we select the most discriminative ones.

4.2   Mining Components

After training the forest as described in Sect. 4.1, the input space has been partitioned into a set $\mathcal{L}$ of leaves. However, not all leaves have the same discriminative power and several leaves may carry similar information as they were trained independently. In this section, we propose a simple yet effective method to identify a diverse set of discriminative leaves for each class.

Based on the training data, each leaf l is associated with an empirical distribution of class labels $p(y|l)$. Using a validation set, we classify each sample s using the forest, and we define $\delta_{l,s} = 1$ if the sample has reached the leaf l, and 0 otherwise. For each sample, we can easily derive its class confidence score $p(y|s)$ from the statistics of the leaves it reached:

$$p(y|s) = \frac{1}{|\mathcal{F}|} \sum_{l \in \mathcal{L}} \delta_{l,s}\, p(y|l). \tag{3}$$

Note that $\sum_l \delta_{l,s}$ is equal to the number of trees in the forest, i.e., $|\mathcal{F}|$, as a sample reaches a single leaf in each tree.

A high class confidence score implies that most trees were able to separate the sample well from the other classes. To obtain components, we could use these discriminative samples directly in spirit of exemplar SVMs [26]. However, many discriminative samples are very similar. For efficiency, i.e., to reduce the number of component models, it makes sense to identify consistent clusters of discriminative samples instead and train a single model for each cluster.

This is readily possible by exploiting the leaves again. For a single class y, we can evaluate how many discriminative samples are located in each leaf l by considering the following measure:

$$\text{distinctiveness}(l|y) = \sum_s \delta_{l,s}\, p(y|s). \tag{4}$$

Leaves with high distinctiveness are those which collect many discriminative samples (*i.e.*, that have a high class confidence score), thus forming different clusters of discriminative samples. Note that discriminative clusters that are identified by different trees can be easily filtered out by a variation of non-maxima suppression: After sorting the leaves based on their distinctiveness, we ignore models that consist of more than half of the same superpixels as any better scoring leaf. This way, we increase the diversity of components while retaining the strongest ones. Although models with a very similar set of superpixels indicate a very strong component, diversity is more beneficial for classification as this provides richer input to the final classifier.

In Fig. 1 and 7, we show such examples of mined components and study the influence of the number of trees and their depth, but also the number N of discriminative components kept for each food category in Sect. 5.2.

4.3   Training Component Models

For each class, we then select the top N leaves and train for each one a linear binary SVM to act as a *component model*. For training, the most confident samples of class y of a selected leaf act as positive set while a large repository of samples act as negative. To speed-up this process, we perform iterative hard-negative mining. Note that nothing prevents a single leaf to be selected by several classes. This is not a problem at all, since only samples of a single class are used as positives for training a single model.

4.4   Recognition from Mined Components

For classifying an image, we only need to score all of its superpixels using the previously trained component models, instead of applying multi scale sliding window detectors [7,35,38,25,8,19,34,40]. This leaves us with a score vector of $K \times N$ component confidence scores for K classes and N components for each superpixel as illustrated in Fig. 4. In case of a sliding window detector, a standard approach is to max pool scores spatially and then use this representation to train an SVM. We use a spatial pyramid with 3 levels and adopt a slightly different approach for our superpixels: Each superpixel fully contributes to each spatial region it is part of. The scores are then averaged within each region. This loose spatial assignment has proved significantly beneficial for the task of food recognition compared to more elaborate aggregation methods like soft-assignment of superpixels to regions. For final classification, we train a structured-output multi-class SVM using the optimized cutting plane algorithm [17], namely using DLib's [21] implementation.

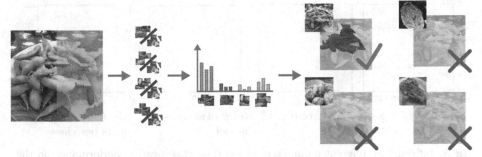

Fig. 4. At classification time, all superpixels of an input image are scored using the component models, afterwards a multi-class SVM with spatial pooling predicts the final class. In this visualisation, we show the confidence scores of edamame, french fries, beignets and bruschetta.

5 Experimental Evaluation

In the following, we refer to our approach as Random Forest Discriminant Components (RFDC) and evaluate it against various methods. For our novel Food-101 dataset (Sect. 3), 750 images of each class are used for training and the remaining 250 for testing. We measure performance with average accuracy, *i.e.* the fraction of test images that are correctly classified. We first give details of our implementation in Sect. 5.1 and analyze then the robustness of our approach with respect to its different parameters in Sect. 5.2. In Sect. 5.3, we compare to baselines and alternative state-of-the-art component-mining algorithms for classification. As our approach is generic and can be directly applied to other classification problems as well, we also evaluate on the MIT-Indoor dataset [31] in Sect. 5.4.

5.1 Implementation Details

We first describe the parameters that we held constant during the evaluation and which had empirically little influence on the overall classification performance.

Superpixels and Features. In this work, we have used the graph-based superpixels of [10]. In practice, setting $\sigma = 0.1$, $k = 300$ and a minimum superpixel size of 1% of the image area yields around 30 superpixels per image, and a total of about 2.4 million superpixels in the training set. Changes in those parameters had limited impact on the classification performance. For each superpixel, two feature types are extracted: Dense SURFs [2], which are transformed using signed square-rooting [1], and L*a*b color values. In our experiments it has proved beneficial to also extract features around the superpixels namely within its bounding box, to include more context. Both SURF and color values are encoded using Improved Fisher Vectors [32] as implemented in VlFeat [37] and a GMM with 64 modes. We perform PCA-whitening on both feature channels. In the end the two encoded feature vectors are concatenated, producing a dense vector with 8'576 values.

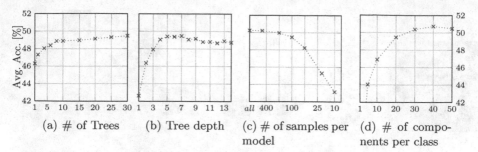

Fig. 5. Influence of different parameters of RFDC on classification performance on the Food-101 dataset

Component Mining. For component mining, we randomly sample 200'000 super-pixels from the 2.4 million to use as a validation set. Each tree is then grown on 200'000 randomly sampled superpixels from the remaining 2.2 million samples. At each node, we sample 100 binary partitions by assigning a random binary label to each present class. For each partition, a binary SVM is learnt, and the SVM that maximizes the criterion in Eq. 1 is kept. The training of SVMs is performed using at most 20'000 superpixels. And the splitting is stopped if a node contains less than 25 samples.

5.2   Influence of Parameters for Component Mining

To measure the influence of the parameters of RFDC, we proceed by fixing the values of the parameters and vary one dimension at the time. By default, we trained 30 trees and mined the parts at depth 7. We then used the top 20 scored component models per class and train each of them using their top 100 most confident samples as positive set.

Forest Parameters. Fig. 5 shows the influence of the number of trees, tree depth, number of samples per model and number of components per class on classification accuracy. RFDC is very robust with respect to those parameters. For instance, increasing the number of trees from 10 to 30 does not make a big difference in accuracy (see Fig. 5a), and tree depth has also little influence beyond 4 levels (Fig. 5b). Using more positive samples to train the component models (Sect. 4.3) improves classification performance of the system, but a plateau is reached beyond 200 samples (Fig. 5c). However, using only 200 positive samples results in significant speed-ups in training. Similar to other approaches [34], Fig. 5d shows that classification performance improves as the number of components per class grows. Also for this parameter the performance saturates. Moreover, the modest improvement in classification accuracy beyond 20 components per class comes with a dramatic increase in feature dimensionality (only worsen by spatial pooling): from 42'420 for 20 components, the dimensionality reaches 106'050 for 50 components and thus heavily impacts memory usage and speed. In conclusion, our RFDC method shows a very strong robustness with respect to its (hyper-)

Table 1. Classification performance for different feature types for RFDC. @K refers to the code book size.

Encoding & Features	Avg. Acc. [%]
- HOG	8.85
BOW SURF@1024	33.47
BOW SURF@1024 + Color@256	38.83
IFV SURF@64	44.79
IFV Color@64	14.24
IFV SURF@64 + Color@64	49.40

Table 2. Classification performance measured for the evaluated methods. All component mining approaches use 20 components per class.

Method	Avg. Acc. [%]
Global	
BOW [24]	28.51
IFV [32]	38.88
CNN [23]	56.40
Local	
RF [3]	32.72
RCF [29]	28.46
MLDS ($\approx$ [34])	42.63
RFDC (this paper)	50.76

parameters. Fine-tuning of these parameters is therefore not necessary in order to achieve good classification accuracy.

On Features. Using the standard settings as in the previous experiment, we compared different feature types for RFDC. For extracting HOG, we resize the superpixel patches to 64×64 pixels. For BOW and IFV encoding, we use the the dictionary sizes as shown in Tab. 1. Unsurprisingly, HOG is not well suited for describing food parts, as their patterns are rather specific. SURFs with BOW encoding yield significant improvement only superseded by IFV encoding.

5.3   Comparison on Food-101

To compare our RFDC approach to different methods, we use 30 trees with a max depth of 5. For mining, we keep 500 positive samples per component and 20 components per class. We compare against the following methods:

Bag-of-Words Histogram (BOW). As a baseline, we follow a classical classification approach using Bag-of-Word histograms of densely-sampled SURF features, combined with a spatial pyramid [24]. We use 1024 clusters learned with k-means as the visual vocabulary, and 3 levels of spatial pyramid. A structured-output multi-class SVM is then used for classification (see Sect. 4.4).

Improved Fisher Vectors (IFV). To compare against a state-of-the-art classification methods we apply Improved Fisher Vector encoding and spatial pyramids [32] to our problem. For this we employ the same parameters as in [19]. We also use a multi-class SVM for classification.

Random Forest Classification (RF). The Random Forest used for component mining (Sect. 4) can be used directly to predict the food categories, as it is a multi-class classifier. As in [3], we obtain the final classification by aggregating the class confidence score (Eq. 3) of each superpixel s_i and then classify an image $I = \{s_i\}$ using $y^* = \mathrm{argmax}_y \sum_{s_i \in I} p(y|s_i)$. This will highlight the benefit and importance of component mining (Sect. 4.2) and having another SVM for final classification.

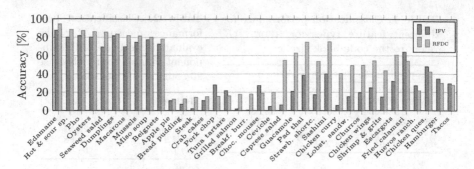

Fig. 6. Selected classification accuracies: The 10 best and 10 worst performing classes are shown as well as 11 classes with the highest improvement and the 8 additional classes for which performance was degraded compared to IFV. The improvements for single classes are visibly more pronounced than degradations.

Randomized Clustering Forests (RCF). The extremely randomized clustering forest approach of [29] can also be adapted to our problem. The trained RF for component mining can again be used to generate the feature vectors as in [29]. To obtain the final classification, a multi-class SVM is trained on top of these features. This comparison also will show the importance of dedicated component models.

Mid-Level Discriminative Superpixels (MLDS). We implemented the recent approach of [34] for comparison and replaced sliding HOG patches with superpixels. The negative set consists of 500'000 random superpixels and all the superpixels from one class (around 22'500) form the discovery set. We clustered the samples with k-means using a clusters/samples ratio of 1/3. For each class, we discovered discriminative superpixels by letting the algorithm iterate at most 10 times and train each SVM on the top 10 members. For selecting the 20 components per class, we used the discriminativeness measure as in [34] and Sect. 4.4 for classification. This comparison will demonstrate the benefit of RF component mining.

Convolutional Neural Networks (CNN). We also compare our approach with convolutional neural networks. To this end, we train a deep CNN on our dataset using the architecture of [23] as provided by the Caffe [16] library until it converged (450'000 iterations).

Quantitative Results. We report in Tab. 2 the classification accuracies obtained by the different methods discussed above on the Food-101 dataset. Among global classifiers, IFV significantly outperforms the standard BOW approach by 10%. Switching to local classification is clearly beneficial for the Food-101 dataset. The MLDS approach [34] using strong features on superpixels already gives an improvement of 3.75% with respect to IFV. Looking at the results of Random Forests, we first observe that using them directly for classification performs similar to BOW (about 33% accuracy). The bagging of the random trees is not able to recover from the potentially noisy leaves. Also Randomized Clustering Forests perform at a similar accuracy level. As the number of samples is very limited,

Fig. 7. Examples of discovered components. For each row, an example for the particular dish and examples of discovered components are shown. From top left to bottom right: cheese cake, spaghetti carbonara, strawberry shortcake, bibimbap, beef carpaccio, prime rib, sashimi, dumplings, fried rice and seaweed salad.

the intermediate binary representation is probably too sparse. When using the discriminative component mining together with multi-class SVM classification, we measure an accuracy of 50.76%, an improvement of 8.13% and 11.88% compared to MLDS and IFV, respectively. Also on this dataset, CNN set the state of the art and RFDC are outperformed by a margin of 5.64%. This is paid by a considerably longer training time of six days on a NVIDIA Tesla K20X.

Qualitative Results. In Figs. 1 and 7 we show a few examples of classes and their corresponding mined components. Note how the algorithm is able to find subtle visual components like the fruit compote for the cheese cake, single dumplings, or the strawberries of the strawberry short cake. For other classes, the discriminative visual components show more distinct textures like in the case of spaghetti carbonara, fried rice or meat texture. An interesting visualization is also possible thanks to superpixels. For each class, one can aggregate the component scores and therefore observe which regions in the images are responsible for the final classification. We illustrate such heat maps in Fig. 8. Again, we observe a great correlation between the most confident regions with the actual distinctive elements of each dish. Confusions are often because of visual similarity (onion rings vs. french fries, carrot cake vs. chocolate cake), clutter (prime rib vs. spring roll) or ambiguous examples (steak vs. risotto).

5.4 Results on MIT-Indoor

For running the experiments on the MIT-Indoor dataset, we use the same settings as for Food-101 except, that we sample 100'000 samples per bag. Additionally, we horizontally flip the images in the training set to generate a higher number of samples. For conducting the experiments, we follow the original protocol of [31] with approximately 80 training and 20 testing images per class (*restricted train set*). As this is a rather low number of training examples, we also report the

Fig. 8. Examples of the final output of our method. For each correctly classified image, we show the confidence heat map of the true and the second most confident class. For misclassified examples the confidence map of the wrongly predicted class and the true class are shown.

performance on the original test set, but with training on all available training images (*full train set*).

As summarized in Tab. 3, using 50 components per class our method yields 54.40% and 58.36% average accuracy for the restricted and full training set, respectively. While our approach does not match [7] on the restricted train set, the gap gets considerably smaller when training on the full train set. While [7] achieves their impressive results with 200 components per class, HOG features and multi scale sliding window detectors, our method evaluates only 50 components on typically 30 superpixels per image. For training, our full pipeline uses around 250 CPU hours (including vocabulary training, i/o *etc.*) with many parallelizable tasks (segmentation, feature extraction and encoding, training of single trees). Approximately 55% of the time is spent on training the forest, 15% for training the component models and 20% for the training of the final classifier.

Compared to other recent approaches, RFDC significantly outperforms [34] as well as all the other very recent sliding window methods of [19,25,38,35]. Note that some of them train their components on external data [25] or have a higher number of components ([35] uses 73 components per class). Clearly, one of the reasons for the achieved performance is the use of stronger features. On the other hand, stronger features can be used here only because our approach needs to evaluate only a small number of superpixels compared to thousands of sliding windows. Still, the full classification time (including feature extraction and Fisher encoding) of one image is around 0.8 seconds using 8 cores, where 70% of the time is spent on encoding and 25% for evaluating the part models.

Interestingly, most previously proposed part-based classification approaches based on sliding windows (or patches) and HOG features typically did not outperform IFV on other datasets until very recently [7]. Our Food-101 dataset (where RFDC outperforms IFV) therefore presents a bias significantly different from available sets, highlighting its interest as a novel benchmark.

Table 3. Recent results of discriminate part mining approaches and global approaches on the MIT-Indoor dataset

Method	Avg. Acc. [%]	Method	Avg. Acc. [%]
Part based		*Part based (this paper)*	
HOG Patches [34]	38.10	RFDC (restricted train set)	54.40
BOP [19]	46.10	RFDC (full training set)	58.36
MI-SVM [25]	46.40	*Global or mixed*	
MMDL [38]	50.15	IFV [19]	60.77
D-Parts [35]	51.40	IFV + BOP [19]	63.10
DMS [7]	64.03	IFV + DMS [7]	66.87

6 Conclusion

In this paper, we have introduced a novel large-scale benchmark dataset for recognition of food. We have also presented a novel method based on Random Forests to mine discriminative visual components and efficient classification. We have shown it to outperform state-of-the-art methods on food recognition except for CNN and obtaining competitive results compared to alternative recent part-based classification approaches on the challenging MIT-Indoor dataset.

Acknowledgments. We thank Matthias Dantone, Christian Leistner and Jürgen Gall for their helpful comments as well as the anonymous reviewers.

References

1. Arandjelović, R., Zisserman, A.: Three things everyone should know to improve object retrieval. In: CVPR (2012)
2. Bay, H., Tuytelaars, T., Van Gool, L.: SURF: Speeded Up Robust Features. In: ICCV (2006)
3. Bosch, A., Zisserman, A., Munoz, X.: Image Classification using Random Forests and Ferns. In: ICCV (2007)
4. Breiman, L.: Random forests. Machine Learning (2001)
5. Chen, M., Dhingra, K., Wu, W., Yang, L., Sukthankar, R., Yang, J.: PFID: Pittsburgh fast-food image dataset. In: ICIP (2009)
6. Chen, M.Y., Yang, Y.H., Ho, C.J., Wang, S.H., Liu, S.M., Chang, E., Yeh, C.H., Ouhyoung, M.: Automatic Chinese food identification and quantity estimation. In: SIGGRAPH Asia 2012 Technical Briefs (2012)
7. Doersch, C., Gupta, A., Efros, A.A.: Mid-level visual element discovery as discriminative mode seeking. In: NIPS (2013)
8. Endres, I., Shih, K., Jiaa, J., Hoiem, D.: Learning Collections of Part Models for Object Recognition. In: CVPR (2013)
9. Felzenszwalb, P.F., Girshick, R., McAllester, D., Ramanan, D.: Object detection with discriminatively trained part based models. PAMI (2010)
10. Felzenszwalb, P.F., Huttenlocher, D.P.: Efficient Graph-Based Image Segmentation. IJCV (2004)
11. Gall, J., Yao, A., Razavi, N., Van Gool, L., Lempitsky, V.: Hough forests for object detection, tracking, and action recognition. PAMI (2011)

12. Girshick, R., Donahue, J., Darrell, T., Malik, J.: Rich feature hierarchies for accurate object detection and semantic segmentation. In: CVPR (2014)
13. Hariharan, B., Malik, J., Ramanan, D.: Discriminative decorrelation for clustering and classification. In: Fitzgibbon, A., Lazebnik, S., Perona, P., Sato, Y., Schmid, C. (eds.) ECCV 2012, Part IV. LNCS, vol. 7575, pp. 459–472. Springer, Heidelberg (2012)
14. Ho, T.K.: Random decision forests. In: ICDAR (1995)
15. Hoashi, H., Joutou, T., Yanai, K.: Image Recognition of 85 Food Categories by Feature Fusion. In: ISM (2010)
16. Jia, Y.: Caffe: An open source convolutional architecture for fast feature embedding (2013), http://caffe.berkeleyvision.org/
17. Joachims, T., Finley, T., Yu, C.N.J.: Cutting-plane training of structural SVMs. Machine Learning (2009)
18. Joutou, T., Yanai, K.: A food image recognition system with Multiple Kernel Learning. In: ICIP (2009)
19. Juneja, M., Vedaldi, A., Jawahar, C., Zisserman, A.: Blocks That Shout: Distinctive Parts for Scene Classification. In: CVPR (2013)
20. Kawano, Y., Yanai, K.: Real-Time Mobile Food Recognition System. In: IEEE Conference on Computer Vision and Pattern Recognition Workshops (2013)
21. King, D.E.: Dlib-ml: A machine learning toolkit. JMLR (2009)
22. Kontschieder, P., Rota Bulò, S., Bischof, H., Pelillo, M.: Structured class-labels in random forests for semantic image labelling. In: ICCV (2011)
23. Krizhevsky, A., Sutskever, I., Hinton, G.E.: Imagenet classification with deep convolutional neural networks. In: NIPS (2012)
24. Lazebnik, S., Schmid, C., Ponce, J.: Beyond bags of features: Spatial pyramid matching for recognizing natural scene categories. In: CVPR (2006)
25. Li, Q., Wu, J., Tu, Z.: Harvesting mid-level visual concepts from large-scale internet images. In: CVPR (2013)
26. Malisiewicz, T., Gupta, A., Efros, A.A.: Ensemble of exemplar-svms for object detection and beyond. In: ICCV (2011)
27. Martin, C., Correa, J., Han, H., Allen, H., Rood, J., Champagne, C., Gunturk, B., Bray, G.: Validity of the remote food photography method (RFPM) for estimating energy and nutrient intake in near real-time. Obesity (2011)
28. Matsuda, Y., Hoashi, H., Yanai, K.: Multiple-Food Recognition Considering Co-occurrence Employing Manifold Ranking. In: ICPR (2012)
29. Moosmann, F., Nowak, E., Jurie, F.: Randomized clustering forests for image classification. PAMI (2008)
30. Noronha, J., Hysen, E., Zhang, H., Gajos, K.Z.: Platemate: crowdsourcing nutritional analysis from food photographs. In: ACM Symposium on UI Software and Technology (2011)
31. Quattoni, A., Torralba, A.: Recognizing indoor scenes. In: CVPR (2009)
32. Sánchez, J., Perronnin, F., Mensink, T., Verbeek, J.: Image Classification with the Fisher Vector: Theory and Practice. IJCV (2013)
33. Shotton, J., Johnson, M., Cipolla, R.: Semantic texton forests for image categorization and segmentation. In: CVPR (2008)
34. Singh, S., Gupta, A., Efros, A.A.: Unsupervised discovery of mid-level discriminative patches. In: Fitzgibbon, A., Lazebnik, S., Perona, P., Sato, Y., Schmid, C. (eds.) ECCV 2012, Part II. LNCS, vol. 7573, pp. 73–86. Springer, Heidelberg (2012)
35. Sun, J., Ponce, J.: Learning discriminative part detectors for image classification and cosegmentation. In: ICCV (2013)

36. Uijlings, J.R.R., van de Sande, K.E.A., Gevers, T., Smeulders, A.W.M.: Selective search for object recognition. IJCV (2013)
37. Vedaldi, A., Fulkerson, B.: VLFeat: An open and portable library of computer vision algorithms (2008), http://www.vlfeat.org/
38. Wang, X., Wang, B., Bai, X., Liu, W., Tu, Z.: Max-margin multiple-instance dictionary learning. In: NIPS (2013)
39. Yang, S.L., Chen, M., Pomerleau, D., Sukthankar, R.: Food recognition using statistics of pairwise local features. In: CVPR (2010)
40. Yao, B., Khosla, A., Fei-Fei, L.: Combining randomization and discrimination for fine-grained image categorization. In: CVPR (2011)

Latent-Class Hough Forests for 3D Object Detection and Pose Estimation

Alykhan Tejani, Danhang Tang, Rigas Kouskouridas, and Tae-Kyun Kim

Imperial Collge London
{alykhan.tejani06,d.tang11,r.kouskouridas,tk.kim}@imperial.ac.uk

Abstract. In this paper we propose a novel framework, *Latent-Class Hough Forests*, for 3D object detection and pose estimation in heavily cluttered and occluded scenes. Firstly, we adapt the state-of-the-art template matching feature, LINEMOD [14], into a scale-invariant patch descriptor and integrate it into a regression forest using a novel template-based split function. In training, rather than explicitly collecting representative negative samples, our method is trained on positive samples only and we treat the class distributions at the leaf nodes as latent variables. During the inference process we iteratively update these distributions, providing accurate estimation of background clutter and foreground occlusions and thus a better detection rate. Furthermore, as a by-product, the latent class distributions can provide accurate occlusion aware segmentation masks, even in the multi-instance scenario. In addition to an existing public dataset, which contains only single-instance sequences with large amounts of clutter, we have collected a new, more challenging, dataset for multiple-instance detection containing heavy 2D and 3D clutter as well as foreground occlusions. We evaluate the Latent-Class Hough Forest on both of these datasets where we outperform state-of-the art methods.

1 Introduction

Accurate localization and pose estimation of 3D objects is of great importance to many higher level tasks such as robotic manipulation, scene interpretation and augmented reality to name a few. The recent introduction of consumer-level depth sensors have allowed for substantial improvement over traditional 2D approaches as finer 3D geometrical features can be captured. However, there still remain several challenges to address including heavy 2D and 3D clutter, large scale and pose changes due to free-moving cameras as well as partial occlusions of the target object.

In the field of 2D object detection, part or patch-based methods, such as Hough Forests [10], have had much success. In addition to being robust against foreground occlusions, they remove detection disambiguation by clustering votes over many local regions into mutually consistent hypothesis. Furthermore, these methods typically separate foreground regions from background clutter/occluders by a discriminatively learnt model, additionally reducing the rate of false positives. However, for practical use, this requires the collection of a representative negative training set which is also able to generalize to unseen environments. At present there is a huge disparity in the number of RGB-D image datasets vs. 2D image datasets and furthermore, it is not clear how to

D. Fleet et al. (Eds.): ECCV 2014, Part VI, LNCS 8694, pp. 462–477, 2014.

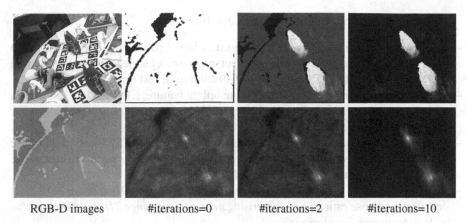

RGB-D images   #iterations=0   #iterations=2   #iterations=10

Fig. 1. An illustration of the algorithm used to update the latent class distributions. Columns 2-4 show intermediate results from different number of iterations of the algorithm, where row 1 shows the foreground confidence map, $\mathcal{Z}$, and row 2 shows the resulting Hough voting space. Note the contrast of the vote images have been enhanced for visualization.

select such a representative set in order to not create a unintentional bias to particular environments. In fact, many studies have shown that classifiers can show a significant drop in performance when evaluated on images outside of the training domain [35,6,27].

State-of-the-art approaches in 3D detection and pose estimation [7,16] avoid this issue by training just from 3D models of the target object. Whilst previously the requirement of 3D models may have been a disadvantage, with recent innovations in surface reconstruction techniques [24,36] these can now be obtained easily and efficiently using hand-held RGB-D cameras. Using these models, 3D features, either simple point-pair features [7] or holistic templates [16] are extracted from the model and matched to the scene at test time providing promising results, even for texture-less objects in heavily cluttered environments. While these results are encouraging, these methods have only been evaluated under little or no occlusion and under the assumption of only one instance present per image. However, as these methods have no knowledge of the background distribution in training, heavy background clutter can cause false regions to have significant responses. While this is a more prominent issue in the point-to-point methods, as planar regions of target objects are easily matched to background clutter, holistic template matching is by no means immune to this.

Motivated by these issues, we present the Latent-Class Hough Forest; a framework for 3D object detection and pose estimation. Unlike the traditional Hough Forest [10], which explicitly exploits classification labels during training, we train only from positive samples and use only the regression term. However, unlike a regression forest [8] we maintain class distributions at leaf nodes. During testing, these distributions are considered as latent variables that are iteratively updated, providing more accurate voting results. Furthermore, as a by-product, our method also produces accurate occlusion-aware figure-ground segmentation masks, which are useful for further post-processing procedures such as efficient occlusion-aware registration [38]. Fig. 1 illustrates this iterative procedure, the effect it has on the output voting results and the figure-ground segmentation masks.

Our main contributions can be summarized as follows:

- We propose the Latent-Class Hough Forest, a novel patch-based approach to 3D object detection and pose estimation; It performs one-class learning at the training stage, and iteratively infers latent class distributions at test time.
- We adapt the state-of-the-art 3D holistic template feature, LINEMOD [14], to be a scale invariant patch descriptor and integrate it into the random forest framework via a novel template-based splitting function.
- During the inference stage, we jointly estimate the objects 3D location and pose as well as a pixel wise visibility map, which can be used as an occlusion aware figure-ground segmentation for result refinement.
- We provide a new, more challenging public dataset for *multi-instance* 3D object detection and pose estimation, comprising *near and far range 2D and 3D clutter* as well as *foreground occlusions*

In the remainder of this paper we first discuss related work in Sec. 2 before introducing our method in Sec. 3. Following this, in Sec. 4, we provide a quantitative and qualitative analysis of our results as well as a comparison to current state-of-the art methods. Finally, in Sec. 5, we conclude with some final remarks and a discussion of future work.

2   Related Work

Throughout the years, several techniques for the detection and registration of objects have been proposed. From the literature, two main categories can be distinguished; nearest-neighbour approaches and learning based methods. Nearest neighbour methods can take a more local approach, such as feature matching, or a holistic approach such as template matching. Local approaches comprise of matching local 2D textural features or 3D geometrical features and transferring their spatial information to form a consistent object hypothesis [7,18,4,20]. On the other hand, template matching approaches [15,31,14,28] attempt to match global descriptors of the object to the scene; These templates can further be used to transfer contextual knowledge, such as 3D pose [16], to the detection. While, feature-point matching is inherently more robust to foreground occlusion, template matching has also been extended to incorporate occlusion reasoning, one notable work being [17]. However, these approaches makes strong assumptions about the occluder shape and location and may not generalize as well.

Learning based methods also comprise of local [10,25,9] and holistic [5,32] approaches. Learning based methods tend to quantize samples together and in turn often can generalize better to slight variations in translation, local shape and viewpoint. Furthermore, as an explicit background/foreground separation is learnt parametrically, these methods are geared to work in the presence of heavy background clutter, causing far less false positives than nearest neighbour approaches. However, the efficacy of this is heavily dependent on how representative the background training data is of the "real world", and this benefit does not always transfer across different domains. In fact, it has been shown that significant performance degradation can occur when the negative training set is not representative of target domain [35,6,27].

One-class classification is a branch of learning based methods focussed on learning only from positive samples. This branch of learning, first coined by by Moya *et al.*[23] and further developed by Tax [34] try to learn closed decision boundaries around the target class in the feature space. However, as observed by Tax, these methods suffer from the added issue of specifying the multi-dimensional margin of such a boundary to balance between false positives and negatives and incorrect assignment can significantly affect performance [34]. We refer the reader to [19] for an in-depth review of one-class classification techniques.

3   Proposed Method

Our goal is to achieve accurate 3D object detection and pose estimation via one-class training, whilst being robust to background clutter and foreground occlusions. To this end, we use only synthetic renderings of a 3D model for training. To leverage the inherent robustness to foreground occlusions, we adopt the state-of-the-art patch-based detector, Hough Forests [10], and for the patch representation we use the state-of-the-art 3D template descriptor, LINEMOD [14]. However, combining these components naively does not work for the following reasons: i) The absence of negative training data means that we cannot leverage the classification term of the Hough Forest, thus, relinquishing the ability to filter out false results caused by background clutter. ii) It is not clear how to integrate a template-based feature into the random forest framework; The main issue is that the synthetic training images have null space in the background whereas the testing patches will not. Thus, doing a naive holistic patch comparison, or the two-dimenson/ two-pixel tests (as used in [29,8,33]) can lead to test patches taking the incorrect route at split functions. iii) LINEMOD [14], in its current form, is not a scale-invariant descriptor; this gives rise to further issues, such as should we train detectors for multiple scales and how finely should we sample these scales in both the training and testing phases.

To address these issues, we propose the Latent-Class Hough Forest (LCHF); an adaptation of the conventional Hough Forest that performs one-class learning at the training stage, but uses a novel, iterative approach to infer latent class distributions at test time. In Sec. 3.1 we discuss how to build a LCHF, in particular we discuss how to adapt LINEMOD into a scale-invariant feature and how to integrate it into the random forest framework via a novel template-based split function. Following this, In Sec 3.2, we discuss how testing is performed with the LCHF and how we can iteratively update the latent class distributions and use them to refine our results.

3.1   Learning

Latent-Class Hough Forests are an ensemble of randomized binary decision trees trained using the general random forest framework [2]. During training, each tree is built using a random subset of the complete training data. Each intermediate node in the tree is assigned a split function and threshold to optimize a measure of information gain; this test is then used to route incoming samples either left or right. This process is repeated until some stopping criteria is met, where a leaf node containing application-specific contextual information is formed. Each stage in this learning process is highly application dependent and we will discuss each in turn below.

Training Data. In order to capture reasonable viewpoint coverage of the target object, we render synthetic RGB and depth images by placing a virtual camera at each vertex of a subdivided icosahedron of a fixed radius, as described in [13]. A tree is trained from a set of patches, $\{\mathcal{P}_i = (c_i, D_i, \mathcal{T}_i, \theta_i)\}$, sampled from the training images, where $c_i = (x_i, y_i)$ is the central pixel, D_i is the raw depth map of the patch, $\mathcal{T}_i$ is the template describing the patch and $\theta_i = (\theta_x, \theta_y, \theta_z, \theta_{ya}, \theta_{pi}, \theta_{ro})$ is the 3D offset from the patch center to the object center and the 3 Euler angles representing the object pose. The patch template is defined as $\mathcal{T}_i = (\{\mathcal{O}_i^m\}_{m \in \mathcal{M}}, \Delta_i)$, where $\mathcal{O}_i^m$ are the aligned reference patches for each modality, m, which are either the image gradient or normal vector orientations and $\Delta_i = \{(r, m)\}$, where $r = (\lambda \cdot x, \lambda \cdot y)$ is a discrete set of pairs made up of the 2D offsets (x, y) scaled by λ which is equal to the templates depth at the central pixel, and modalities, m, of the template features. The template features are evenly spread across the patch; features capturing the image gradients are taken only from the object contours and features capturing the surface normals are taken from the body of the object, the collection and representation of template features is the same as described in [14].

Split Function. Given a set of patches, $\mathcal{S}$, arriving at a node, a split function, h_i, is created by choosing a random patch, $\mathcal{P}_i$, and evaluating its similarity against all other patches, $\mathcal{P}_j \in \mathcal{S}$. Along with a randomly chosen threshold, τ_i, the incoming patches can be split into two distinct subsets $\mathcal{S}_l = \{\mathcal{P}_j | h_i(\mathcal{P}_j) \le \tau_i\}$ and $\mathcal{S}_r = \mathcal{S} \setminus \mathcal{S}_l$. The original similarity measure of [14], adapted to work over patches, is formulated as:

$$\varepsilon(\mathcal{P}_i, \mathcal{P}_j) = \sum_{(r,m)}^{\Delta_i} \left(\max_{t \in \mathcal{R}(c_j + r)} f_m \left(\mathcal{O}_i^m(c_i + r), \mathcal{O}_j^m(t) \right) \right) \tag{1}$$

where $\mathcal{R}(x)$ defines a small search window centred at location x and f_m $\left(\mathcal{O}_i^m(x), \mathcal{O}_j^m(y) \right)$ computes the dot product between quantized orientations at locations x and y for modality, m. Note, for clarity we keep the max operator and the explicit function, f_m in the formulation, however, we refer the reader to [14] for a discussion on how to compute these with constant time complexity using pre-processing techniques.

As neither the patch description, $\mathcal{P}_i$, nor the similarity measure, ε, account for scale, this similarity measure will only work if the patches, $\mathcal{P}_i$ and $\mathcal{P}_j$ are of the same scale. To remedy this, inspired by [29], we achieve scale-invariance by using the depth of the patch center to scale the offsets, r. More formally, we define a scale-invariant similarity measure, ε', as:

$$\begin{cases} \varepsilon'(\mathcal{P}_i, \mathcal{P}_j) &= \sum_{(r,m)}^{\Delta_i} \left(\max_{t \in \mathcal{R}(\varsigma_j(c_j + r))} f_m \left(\mathcal{O}_i^m(\varsigma_i(c_i + r)), \mathcal{O}_j^m(t) \right) \right), \\ \varsigma_x(c_x, r) &= c_x + \frac{r}{D_x(c_x)} \end{cases} \tag{2}$$

where $D_x(a)$ is the depth value at location a in patch $\mathcal{P}_x$.

This similarity measure is still not sufficient, as given two patches, both representing the same part of the target object, one synthetically generated and one from a testing image (containing background noise), the functions $f_m\left(\mathcal{O}_i^m\left(\varsigma_i\left(c_i+r\right)\right),\mathcal{O}_{train}^m\left(t\right)\right)$ and $f_m\left(\mathcal{O}_i^m\left(\varsigma_i\left(c_i+r\right)\right)\mathcal{O}_{test}^m\left(t\right)\right)$ will produce significantly different values if any template features, $(r,m)\in\Delta_i$, from the selected template falls in the null, background, space in the training patch or on to a foreground occluder in the testing patch. This can then cause the two patches to proceed down the tree in different directions, see Fig. 2 for an illustration of this issue. To this end, we alter the similarity function is as follows:

$$\begin{cases} \varepsilon''\left(\mathcal{P}_i,\mathcal{P}_j\right) & = \sum_{(r,m)}^{\Delta_i}\left(\max_{t\in\mathcal{R}\left(\varsigma_j\left(c_j+r\right)\right)}\iota\left(\mathcal{P}_i,\mathcal{P}_j,r\right)\cdot f_m\left(\mathcal{O}_i^m\left(\varsigma_i\left(c_i+r\right)\right),\mathcal{O}_j^m\left(t\right)\right)\right), \\ \iota\left(\mathcal{P}_i,\mathcal{P}_j,r\right) & = \delta\left(\left|\left|D_i\left(\varsigma_i\left(c_i+r\right)\right)-D_i\left(c_i\right)\right|-\left|D_j\left(\varsigma_j\left(c_j+r\right)\right)-D_j\left(c_j\right)\right|\right|<\epsilon\right) \end{cases} \quad (3)$$

where $\iota\left(\mathcal{P}_i,\mathcal{P}_j,r\right)$ is an indicator function that removes template features that are not spatially consistent with the patch's 3D surface from having an effect on the similarity score. The efficacy of this indicator function is illustrated in Fig 2. Finally, we can express the split function of a node as $h_i\left(\mathcal{P}_j\right)=\varepsilon''\left(\mathcal{P}_i,\mathcal{P}_j\right)$.

The effectiveness of a particular splitting function is evaluated by the information gain, however, as no negative data is present at training we cannot use the formulation of the Hough Forest [10]. Instead, we measure only the entropy of the offset and pose regression as done in the regression forest of Fanelli et al.[8]. This process is then repeated multiple times and the split, (h_i,τ_i), producing the highest information gain is selected as the nodes split function.

Constructing Leaf Nodes. The training data is recursively split by this process until the tree has reached a maximum depth or the number of samples arriving at a node fall below a threshold. When this criteria is met a leaf node is formed from the patches reaching it. The leaf node stores votes for both the center position of the object, $(\theta_x,\theta_y,\theta_z)$, and the pose, $(\theta_{ya},\theta_{pi},\theta_{ro})$. Following the approach of Girshick et al.[11] we only store the modes of the distribution which we find efficiently via the mean shift algorithm. Finally, similar to the Hough Forest [10], we create a class distribution at the leaf, however, as no background information reaches the leaves during training this distribution is initialized to $p_{fg}=1$ and $p_{bg}=0$ for the foreground and background probabilities respectively.

3.2 Inference

We want to estimate the probability of the random event, $E(\theta)$, that the target object exists in the scene under the 6 degrees of freedom pose $\theta=(\theta_x,\theta_y,\theta_z,\theta_{ya},\theta_{pi},\theta_{ro})$. We can calculate this by aggregating the conditional probabilities $P(E(\theta)|\mathcal{P})$ for each patch, $\mathcal{P}$. As we only model the effect that positive patches have on the pose estimation, the existence of an estimation at θ in the pose space assumes the vote originates from a foreground patch, that is $p_{fg}=1$, which is assumed for all patches initially. Thus, for a patch $\mathcal{P}$ evaluated on tree $\mathcal{T}$ and reaching leaf node l, we can formalise the conditional probability as:

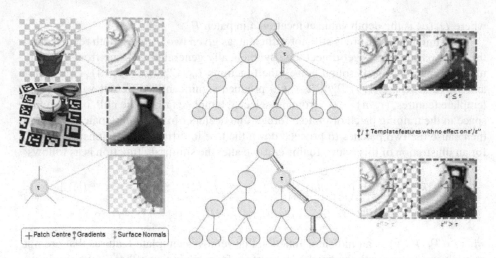

Fig. 2. A conceptual view of how our similarity measurement works. Left: rows 1 & 2 show two patches, one from training and one from testing; both are of different scale which is handled by Eq 2. Row 3 shows the learnt template, $\mathcal{T}$, at the highlighted node. Right: Shows how without the indicator function (Eq 3) the two patches can go down different paths in the tree, leading to wrong results.

$$p\left(E\left(\theta\right)|\mathcal{P}; \mathcal{T}\right) = p\left(E\left(\theta\right), p_{fg}^{l} = 1|\mathcal{P}\right)$$
$$= p\left(E\left(\theta\right)|p_{fg}^{l} = 1, \mathcal{P}\right) \cdot p\left(p_{fg}^{l} = 1|\mathcal{P}\right) \qquad (4)$$

where p_{fg}^{l} is the foreground probability at the leaf node, l. Finally, for a forest, $\mathcal{F}$, we simply average the probabilities over all trees:

$$p\left(E\left(\theta\right)|\mathcal{P}; \mathcal{F}\right) = \frac{1}{|\mathcal{F}|} \sum_{t}^{|\mathcal{F}|} p\left(E\left(\theta\right)|\mathcal{P}; \mathcal{T}_{t}\right) \qquad (5)$$

The first factor, $p\left(E\left(\theta\right)|p_{fg} = 1, \mathcal{P}\right)$, can be estimated by passing each patch down the forest and accumulating the votes stored at the leaf, in which votes from multiple trees can be combined in an additive manner, this gives us the same probabilities as in Eq. 5 up to a constant factor. The estimation is then deferred to the ability of locating local maxima in this aggregated space which, traditionally, has been done by either exhaustively searching the space combined with non-max suppression or by treating each vote as a point in the space and using mean shift to locate the modes. However, these approaches are usually applied to low dimensional (2D) spaces [10,26,21] or in cases where many of the data points (pixels) have already been removed via some pre-processing [8,33]. In our case, the pose voting space is 6 dimensional and in the case of evaluating all patches in a VGA image for several trees in the forest, the number of data points becomes very large and this solution is highly inefficient. To this end, we propose a three-stage localization technique; We initially aggregate all votes into a 2D voting space i.e. $p\left(E\left((\theta_x, \theta_y)\right)|\mathcal{P}\right)$ and use this space to locate the hypothesis with non-max suppression. We then further process the votes from patches within the bounding box of these hypothesis to locate modes in the 3D translation space, $(\theta_x, \theta_y, \theta_z)$, and finally use the patches to find the modes in the rotation space, $(\theta_{ya}, \theta_{pi}, \theta_{ro})$, given the estimated translation.

The second factor of Eq (4), $p\,(p_{fg} = 1|\mathcal{P})$, is traditionally estimated from the learnt class distribution at the leaf nodes. However, in the LCHF this is a latent distribution and all leaf nodes are in initially set to have $p_{fg} = 1$. Therefore, we propose a method similar to the co-training concept to iteratively update these distributions from the observable unlabelled data in the scene.

Co-training [1] is a technique, that has seen much success in many applications [22,3,37], where the main idea is to have two independent classifiers, in which each iteratively predicts labels for the unlabelled data and then uses these labels to update the other classifier. In the seminal work of Blum & Mitchell [1] it was stated that each classifier should be trained from different views/feature representations of the data, but it was later shown that using two classifiers trained originally on the same view will suffice [12], and this is the variant most similar to our method. Thus, to obtain classifiers, for each iteration of the co-training, we randomly partition the random forest, $\mathcal{F}$, into two forest subsets, $\mathcal{F}_1$ & $\mathcal{F}_2$, which can be seen as independent classifiers in their own right.

Following this, given a forest, $\mathcal{F}$, we select a random subset of the image patches and predict their labels by evaluating Eq (4) to obtain an initial object hypotheses set, $\Theta = \{\theta^i\}$. For the N most likely hypotheses, we backproject the contributing votes to their corresponding patches to obtain a consensus patch set, K_i as done in [20]. This patch set is then further reduced to a consensus pixel set, Π, as follows:

$$\begin{cases} \Pi & = \displaystyle\bigcup_{\theta^i \in \Theta} \left(\bigcup_{\mathcal{P}_j \in K_i} g\left(\mathcal{P}_j, \theta^i\right) \right), \\ g\left(\mathcal{P}_j, \theta^i\right) & = \{p_j \in \mathcal{P}_j | d\left(c_j, \theta_i\right) \le \alpha\varnothing \wedge d(p_j, c_j) \le \beta\varnothing\} \end{cases} \tag{6}$$

where p_j are pixels, d is the euclidean distance function, $\varnothing$ is the diameter of the target objects 3D model and α and β are scaling coefficients. The consensus pixel set contains the pixels from patches that vote for the selected hypotheses and are also spatially consistent with the hypothesis that they vote for.

All pixels in Π are then labelled as foreground pixels and all others as background, thus producing two labelled datasets from the patches extracted around those pixels, $\mathcal{P}^+$ and $\mathcal{P}^-$. These datasets are then passed as input to the second classifier, $\mathcal{F}_j$, where each leaf node, l, accumulates the patches that arrive at it, $\mathcal{P}_l$, and updates the leaf probability distribution as follows:

$$p_{fg}^l = \frac{|\{\mathcal{P}_i \mid \mathcal{P}_i \in (\mathcal{P}_l \cap \mathcal{P}^+)\}|}{|\mathcal{P}_l|} \tag{7}$$

This process is then repeated for a fixed number of iterations. Once finished, the final hypotheses set is produced by passing all patches down the complete forest, $\mathcal{F}$ and evaluating Eq (5) using the newly learnt p_{fg}^l. The overall principle of this co-training algorithm is depicted in Algorithm 1 and in Fig. 1.

Algorithm 1. Update Latent-Class Distributions

Require: An input image, $\mathcal{I}$; A Latent-Class Hough Forest, $\mathcal{F}$

1: **repeat**
2:     Randomly draw a subset of trees $\mathcal{F}_i$ from $\mathcal{F}$; $\mathcal{F}_j = \mathcal{F} \setminus \mathcal{F}_i$.
3:     Randomly sample a set of patches $\mathbb{P}$ from I.
4:     Propagate $\mathbb{P}$ down $\mathcal{F}_i$ collect hypotheses set Θ with Eq (5).
5:     Backproject top N hypotheses to obtain a consensus set Π (Eq. (6)).
6:     Partition $\mathcal{P} \in \mathbb{P}$ into positive and negative sets using the consensus set.

$$\mathcal{P}^+ = \{\mathcal{P}|\mathcal{P} \in \Pi\}$$
$$\mathcal{P}^- = \mathbb{P} \setminus \mathcal{P}^+$$

7:     Propagate $\mathcal{P}^+$ and $\mathcal{P}^-$ down $\mathcal{F}_j$ and update the leaf node distributions with Eq (7).
8: **until** Maximum iteration

Additionally, as a by-product of this process, we can produce a pixel-wise foreground confidence map, $\mathcal{Z}$, of the input image by labelling each pixel by the average p_{fg}^l (see Fig 1). Using the confidence map, $\mathcal{Z}$, and the final set of hypotheses, Θ, we can produce a final image segmentation mask, $\mathcal{M}$, by

$$\mathcal{M} = \bigcup_{\theta^i \in \Theta} \left(\mathbb{B}\left(\theta^i\right) \cap \mathcal{Z} \right) \tag{8}$$

where $\mathbb{B}(\theta)$ is a function that computes the bounding box from the hypothesis θ. This final segmentation, although not currently used, is useful for further refinement of the hypotheses, for example by using it as input for an occlusion-aware ICP alignment.

4   Experiments

We perform experiments on two 3D pose estimation datasets. The first is the publicly available dataset of of Hinterstoisser *et al.*[16], which contains 13 distinct objects each associated with an individual test sequence comprising of over 1,100 images with close and far range 2D and 3D clutter. Each test image is annotated with ground truth position and 3D pose.

For further experimentation, we propose a new dataset consisting of 6 additional 3D objects. We provide a dense 3D reconstruction of each object obtained via a commercially available 3D scanning tool [30]. For each object, similarly to [16], we provide an individual testing sequence containing over 700 images annotated with ground truth position and 3D pose. Testing sequences were obtained by a freely moving handheld RGB-D camera and ground truth was calculated using marker boards and verified manually. The testing images were sampled to produce sequences that are uniformly distributed in the pose space by $[0° - 360°]$, $[-80° - 80°]$ and $[-70° - 70°]$ in the yaw, roll and pitch angles respectively. Unlike the dataset of [16], our testing sequences contain *multiple object instances* and *foreground occlusions* in addition to near and far range 2D and 3D clutter, making it more challenging for the task of 3D object detection and pose estimation. Some example frames from this dataset can be seen in Fig 5.

In Sec. 4.1 we perform self comparison tests highlighting the benefits of adding scale-invariance to the template similarity measure (Eq. (2)) and using co-training to update the latent class distributions (Algorithm 1). Following this, in Sec. 4.2 we present a comparison of our method against the state of the art methods, namely LINEMOD [14] and the method of Drost *et al.*[7].

In all tests we use the metric defined in [16] to determine if an estimation is correct. More formally, for a 3D model $\mathcal{M}$, with ground truth rotation R and translation T, given an estimated rotation, $\hat{R}$ and translation, $\hat{T}$, the matching score is defined as

$$m = \operatorname*{avg}_{x \in \mathcal{M}} \|(Rx + T) - (\hat{R}x + \hat{T})\| \tag{9}$$

for non-symmetric objects and

$$m = \operatorname*{avg}_{x_1 \in \mathcal{M}} \operatorname*{min}_{x_2 \in \mathcal{M}} \|(Rx_1 + T) - (\hat{R}x_2 + \hat{T})\| \tag{10}$$

for symmetric objects. An estimation is deemed correct if $m \leq k_m d$, where k_m is a chosen coefficient and d is the diameter of $\mathcal{M}$.

Unlike [14], in which only the top N detections from each image are selected, we compute precision-recall curves and present the F1-Score which is the harmonic mean of precision and recall. We argue that this is a more accurate form of comparison, as directly comparing detections is inaccurate as some images may be harder than others, which is especially true in the case of occlussion and heavy clutter (as in our new dataset). Therefore, similarly to [28], we argue a more meaningful evaluation is to sort all detection scores across all images and calculate the general performance of the detector, given by the precision-recall curves.

In all experiments, unless otherwise stated, the parameters for our method are as follows. For each object class we train a Latent-Class Hough Forest comprising of 10 trees with a maximum depth of 25 trained from randomly selected set of training patches. Image patch templates centred at a pixel consist of 20 features in both the color gradient and normal channel. These features are selected anywhere in a search window centred at the central pixel with a maximum size of, but not further than, $\frac{1}{3}$ of the bounding box size in any direction and are chosen randomly in the same method as described in [14]. For the co-training stage we set the number of iterations empirically as 10 and the number of hypothesis to be backprojected per iteration as $N = 5$. We choose 5 as it is greater than the number of instances present in all datasets, however this number is not fixed and can be adapted based on application. Furthermore, in all experiments the coefficient k_m is set to the value of 0.15, the results with this coefficient are also found to be visually correct.

4.1 Self Comparisons

We perform two self comparisons on the dataset of Hinterstoisser *et al.*[16]. Firstly we compare the results of our method with and without updating the latent class distributions. As can be seen in Fig. 3 our approach with updating distributions improves the F1-Score by 2.8% on average and up to 8.2% on some objects. The biggest gains are seen in objects which have large amounts of indistinct planar regions, for which

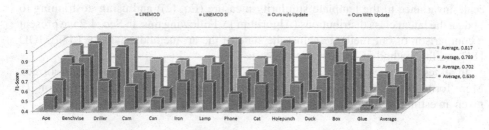

Fig. 3. F1-Scores for the 13 objects in the dataset of Hinterstoisser *et al.*[16]. We compare our approach with and without updating the latent class variables (Sec. 3.2). We additionally show results of the scale-invariant LINEMOD templates vs. the original LINEMOD templates [14].

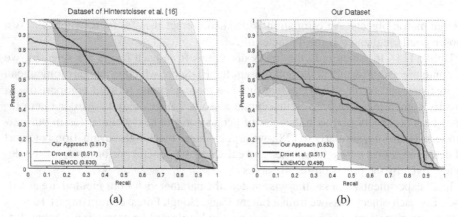

Fig. 4. Average Precision-Recall curve over all objects in the dataset of LINEMOD [16] (a) and our dataset (b). The shaded region represents one standard deviation above and below the precision value at a given recall value.

background clutter can easily be confused at the patch level. For example, the biggest improvements are seen in the Camera, Holepuncher and Phone objects which contain large planar regions. Furthermore, in Fig. 3 we also compare the results of LINEMOD [14] using holistic templates with the original similarity measure (Eq. (1)) and the scale-invariant similarity measure (Eq. (2)). As the scale-invariant version is trained using only one scale, the performance is increased 6-fold (623 templates as opposed to 3738). Furthermore, the performance is also increased by 7.2% on average, this is due to the fact that templates are able to be matched at scales not seen in the template learning stage of the original LINEMOD [14].

Table 1. F1-Scores for LINEMOD [14], the method of Drost *et al.*[7] and our approach for each object class for the dataset of Hinterstoisser *et al.*[16]

Approach	LINEMOD [14]	Drost *et al.*[7]	Our Approach
Sequence (# images)	F1-Score		
Ape(1235)	0.533	0.628	**0.855**
Bench Vise (1214)	0.846	0.237	**0.961**
Driller (1187)	0.691	0.597	**0.905**
Cam (1200)	0.640	0.513	**0.718**
Can (1195)	0.512	0.510	**0.709**
Iron (1151)	0.683	0.405	**0.735**
Lamp (1226)	0.675	0.776	**0.921**
Phone (1224)	0.563	0.471	**0.728**
Cat (1178)	0.656	0.566	**0.888**
Hole Punch (1236)	0.516	0.500	**0.875**
Duck (1253)	0.580	0.313	**0.907**
Box (1252)	**0.860**	0.826	0.740
Glue (1219)	0.438	0.382	**0.678**
Average (15770)	0.630	0.517	**0.817**

Table 2. F1-Scores for LINEMOD [14], the method of Drost *et al.*[7] and our approach for each object class for our new dataset [16]

Approach	LINEMOD [14]	Drost *et al.*[7]	Our Approach
Sequence (# images)	F1-Score		
Coffee Cup (708)	0.819	0.867	**0.877**
Shampoo (1058)	0.625	0.651	**0.759**
Joystick (1032)	0.454	0.277	**0.534**
Camera (708)	**0.422**	0.407	0.372
Juice Carton (859)	0.494	0.604	**0.870**
Milk (860)	0.176	0.259	**0.385**
Average (5229)	0.498	0.511	**0.633**

4.2 Comparison to State-of-the-Arts

We compare our method to two state-of-the-art methods, namely LINEMOD [14] and the method of Drost *et al.*[7]. For LINEMOD, we use our own implementation based on [14] and for the method of Drost *et al.*[7], we use a binary version kindly provided by the author and set the parameters to the recommended defaults. Furthermore, for the method of Drost *et al.*[7] we remove points further than 2000mm to reduce the effect of noise, as recommended by the authors. Note, this should not effect accuracy as all target objects are safely within this range.

In Fig. 4 we show the average precision-recall curves across all objects in both datasets respectively and in Tables 1 and 2 we show the F1-Score per object for each dataset. All methods show worse performance on the new dataset, which is to be

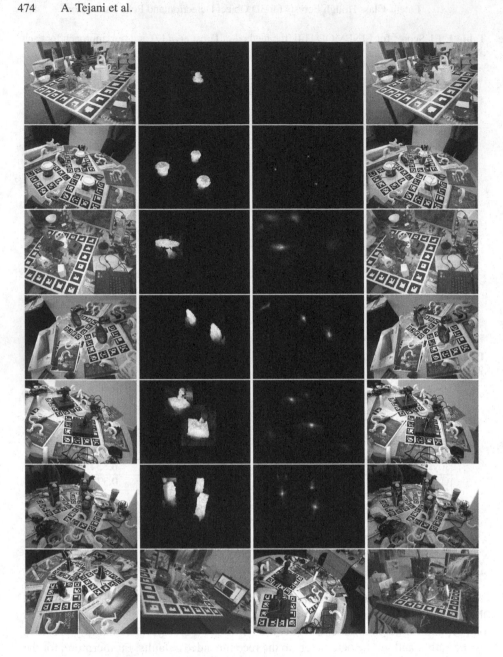

Fig. 5. Some qualitative results on both datasets. Rows 1-6 show, from left to right, the original RGB image, the final segmentation mask, the final Hough vote map and the augmented 3D axis of the estimated result. The final row shows some incorrect results.

suspected due to the introduction of occlusions as well as multiple object instances. As can be seen we outperform both state-of-the-arts in both datasets. However, a point to note is that by just picking the top detection from each image, as done in [16], the method of Drost *et al.*[7] and LINEMOD [14] are shown to be almost equal in accuracy (see [16] for this comparison), however, when considering the precision-recall curve, as we do, the method of Drost *et al.*has considerably lower precision values. This is due to the fact that this method does not take object boundaries into consideration, thus large planar regions of the target object can have a large surface overlap in the background clutter causing many false positives in addition to the true positives. Conversely, our method maintains high levels of precision at high recall which is due to the inferred latent class distributions simplifying the Hough space. In Fig. 5 we present some qualitative results on both datasets.

5 Conclusion

In this paper we have introduced a novel framework for accurate 3D detection and pose estimation of multiple object instances in cluttered and occluded scenes. We have demonstrated that these challenges can be efficiently met via the adoption of a state-of-the-art template matching feature into a patch-based regression forest. During training we employ a one-class learning scheme, i.e. training with positive samples only rather than involving negative examples. In turn, during inference, we engage the proposed Latent-Class Hough Forest that iteratively produces a more accurate estimation of the clutter/occluder distribution by considering class distribution as latent variables. As a result, apart from accurate detection results we can, further, obtain an highly representative occlusion-aware masks facilitating further tasks such as scene layout understanding, occlusion aware ICP or online domain adaption to name a few. Our method is evaluated using both the public dataset of Hinterstoisser *et al.* [16] and our new challenging one containing foreground occlusion and multiple object instances. Experimental evaluation provides evidence of our novel L-C Hough Forest outperforming all baselines highlighting the potential benefits of part-based strategies to address the issues of such a challenging problem.

Acknowledgement. This project was supported by the Omron Corporation.

References

1. Blum, A., Mitchell, T.: Combining labeled and unlabeled data with co-training. In: COLT. ACM (1998)
2. Breiman, L.: Random forests. Machine Learning (2001)
3. Chan, J., Koprinska, I., Poon, J.: Co-training with a single natural feature set applied to email classification. In: WIC (2004)
4. Choi, C., Christensen, H.I.: 3D pose estimation of daily objects using an rgb-d camera. In: IROS (2012)
5. Dalal, N., Triggs, B.: Histograms of oriented gradients for human detection. In: CVPR (2005)

6. Dollár, P., Wojek, C., Schiele, B., Perona, P.: Pedestrian detection: A benchmark. In: CVPR (2009)
7. Drost, B., Ulrich, M., Navab, N., Ilic, S.: Model globally, match locally: Efficient and robust 3D object recognition. In: CVPR (2010)
8. Fanelli, G., Gall, J., Van Gool, L.: Real time head pose estimation with random regression forests. In: CVPR (2011)
9. Felzenszwalb, P.F., Girshick, R.B., McAllester, D., Ramanan, D.: Object detection with discriminatively trained part based models. PAMI (2010)
10. Gall, J., Yao, A., Razavi, N., Van Gool, L., Lempitsky, V.: Hough forests for object detection, tracking, and action recognition. PAMI (2011)
11. Girshick, R., Shotton, J., Kohli, P., Criminisi, A., Fitzgibbon, A.: Efficient regression of general-activity human poses from depth images. In: 2011 IEEE International Conference on Computer Vision (ICCV), pp. 415–422. IEEE (2011)
12. Goldman, S., Zhou, Y.: Enhancing supervised learning with unlabeled data. In: ICML (2000)
13. Hinterstoisser, S., Benhimane, S., Lepetit, V., Navab, N.: Simultaneous recognition and homography extraction of local patches with a simple linear classifier (2008)
14. Hinterstoisser, S., Holzer, S., Cagniart, C., Ilic, S., Konolige, K., Navab, N., Lepetit, V.: Multimodal templates for real-time detection of texture-less objects in heavily cluttered scenes. In: ICCV (2011)
15. Hinterstoisser, S., Lepetit, V., Ilic, S., Fua, P., Navab, N.: Dominant orientation templates for real-time detection of texture-less objects. In: CVPR (2010)
16. Hinterstoisser, S., Lepetit, V., Ilic, S., Holzer, S., Bradski, G., Konolige, K., Navab, N.: Model based training, detection and pose estimation of texture-less 3D objects in heavily cluttered scenes. In: Lee, K.M., Matsushita, Y., Rehg, J.M., Hu, Z. (eds.) ACCV 2012, Part I. LNCS, vol. 7724, pp. 548–562. Springer, Heidelberg (2013)
17. Hsiao, E., Hebert, M.: Occlusion reasoning for object detection under arbitrary viewpoint. In: CVPR (2012)
18. Johnson, A.E., Hebert, M.: Using spin images for efficient object recognition in cluttered 3D scenes. PAMI (1999)
19. Khan, S.S., Madden, M.G.: One-class classification: Taxonomy of study and review of techniques. arXiv preprint arXiv:1312.0049 (2013)
20. Leibe, B., Leonardis, A., Schiele, B.: Combined object categorization and segmentation with an implicit shape model. In: ECCV (2004)
21. Leibe, B., Leonardis, A., Schiele, B.: Robust object detection with interleaved categorization and segmentation. IJCV (2008)
22. Liu, R., Cheng, J., Lu, H.: A robust boosting tracker with minimum error bound in a co-training framework. In: ICCV (2009)
23. Moya, M., Koch, M., Hostetler, L.: One-class classifier networks for target recognition applications. Tech. rep. (1993)
24. Newcombe, R.A., Davison, A.J., Izadi, S., Kohli, P., Hilliges, O., Shotton, J., Molyneaux, D., Hodges, S., Kim, D., Fitzgibbon, A.: Kinectfusion: Real-time dense surface mapping and tracking. In: 2011 10th IEEE International Symposium on Mixed and Augmented Reality (ISMAR), pp. 127–136. IEEE (2011)
25. Okada, R.: Discriminative generalized hough transform for object dectection. In: ICCV (2009)
26. Opelt, A., Pinz, A., Zisserman, A.: Learning an alphabet of shape and appearance for multi-class object detection. IJCV (2008)
27. Perronnin, F., Sánchez, J., Liu, Y.: Large-scale image categorization with explicit data embedding. In: CVPR (2010)
28. Rios-Cabrera, R., Tuytelaars, T.: Discriminatively trained templates for 3D object detection: A real time scalable approach. In: ICCV (2013)

29. Shotton, J., Sharp, T., Kipman, A., Fitzgibbon, A., Finocchio, M., Blake, A., Cook, M., Moore, R.: Real-time human pose recognition in parts from single depth images. ACM (2013)
30. Skanect (2014), http://skanect.manctl.com/
31. Steger, C.: Similarity measures for occlusion, clutter, and illumination invariant object recognition. In: Radig, B., Florczyk, S. (eds.) DAGM 2001. LNCS, vol. 2191, pp. 148–154. Springer, Heidelberg (2001)
32. Tang, D., Liu, Y., Kim, T.K.: Fast pedestrian detection by cascaded random forest with dominant orientation templates. In: BMVC (2012)
33. Tang, D., Yu, T.H., Kim, T.K.: Real-time articulated hand pose estimation using semi-supervised transductive regression forests. In: ICCV (2013)
34. Tax, D.M.: One-class classification (2001)
35. Torralba, A., Efros, A.A.: Unbiased look at dataset bias. In: CVPR (2011)
36. Weise, T., Wismer, T., Leibe, B., Van Gool, L.: In-hand scanning with online loop closure. In: 2009 IEEE 12th International Conference on Computer Vision Workshops (ICCV Workshops), pp. 1630–1637. IEEE (2009)
37. Yu, S., Krishnapuram, B., Rosales, R., Steck, H., Rao, R.B.: Bayesian co-training. In: NIPS (2007)
38. Zhang, Z.: Iterative point matching for registration of free-form curves and surfaces. International Journal of Computer Vision 13(2), 119–152 (1994)

FPM: Fine Pose Parts-Based Model with 3D CAD Models

Joseph J. Lim, Aditya Khosla, and Antonio Torralba

Massachusetts Institute of Technology
{lim,khosla,torralba}@csail.mit.edu

Abstract. We introduce a novel approach to the problem of localizing objects in an image and estimating their fine-pose. Given exact CAD models, and a few real training images with aligned models, we propose to leverage the geometric information from CAD models and appearance information from real images to learn a model that can accurately estimate fine pose in real images. Specifically, we propose FPM, a fine pose parts-based model, that combines geometric information in the form of shared 3D parts in deformable part based models, and appearance information in the form of objectness to achieve both fast and accurate fine pose estimation. Our method significantly outperforms current state-of-the-art algorithms in both accuracy and speed.

1 Introduction

Imagine an autonomous agent attempting to find a chair to sit on. Using a state-of-the-art object detection system, the agent finds a number of *correct* detections (as defined by the 0.5 intersection-over-union criterion) of chairs as shown in Figure 1(a). With the given set of *correct* detections, the agent could end up sitting anywhere from the bookshelf, to the floor! In order to better understand and interact with our environment, it is important to tackle the problem of fine pose estimation as shown in Figure 1(b).

Fig. 1. If an autonomous agent attempted to sit on a chair based on *correct* detections by an object detector (a), who knows where it might end up? Fine pose estimation, shown in (b), is one possible method to tackle this problem

(a) standard object detection (b) fine pose estimation

While fine pose estimation for simple 3D shapes has been studied since the early days of computer vision [28], estimating the fine pose of articulate 3D objects has received little attention. Given the recent success of the computer

D. Fleet et al. (Eds.): ECCV 2014, Part VI, LNCS 8694, pp. 478–493, 2014.

vision community in addressing object detection [8,13] and 3D scene understanding [12,24,4,33,16], fine pose estimation is becoming more and more approachable. In this work, we tackle the problem of instance-level fine pose estimation given only a single-view image. Specifically, we want to estimate the fine pose of objects in images, given a set of exact 3D models. We restrict our attention to instance-level detection as it provides several advantages over category-level detection. For example, we can get pixel-perfect alignment with per-instance exact 3D models. This would not be possible if we instead used a single generic model for a category, as categories contain large variation in shape across instances.

Recently, there has been an increasing interest in utilizing 3D models for object detection and pose estimation [39,27,10,19,34]. Despite this, using explicit 3D models for fine pose estimation presents various challenges. First, the space of possible poses of an object is extremely large. Even if we assume that the intrinsic parameters of the camera are known, we still have to estimate at least 6 parameters (translation and rotation) to determine the exact pose of the model. This is *three* more parameters than the typical 2D object detection problem (x, y, and *scale*), which already has a search space of millions of possible bounding boxes. Second, there is the issue of domain adaptation. While rendered images of 3D models look similar to real objects, there are some key differences that make it difficult to use the same set of features as we do for real images. For example, rendered images are often texture-less and do not contain occluding objects or surfaces.

In this paper, we propose an algorithm that combines appearance information from images with geometric information from 3D models for efficient fine pose estimation. Specifically, we introduce the notion of 3D part sharing that is enabled through the use of 3D models. As illustrated in Figure 2, 2D parts [8,9] are significantly affected by viewpoint, while 3D parts are shared across views. For each 3D part, we learn an *importance score* that measures the visibility and discriminative-ness of the given part. Our algorithm outperforms existing state-of-the-art methods in both speed and accuracy.

2   Related Work

Various recent works have tackled the problem of object-level pose estimation [37,21,11]. These studies make assumptions that a major structure is shared between objects, e.g. cuboid, and hence can use this set of relatively few models to infer the pose of objects. In this work, our goal is to differentiate fine details even within the same object category, e.g. our dataset contains at least 3 different types of bookcases. Using this fine differentiation, we can achieve finer pose estimation. There are a few recent papers [27,36,29] that have created a dataset for real images annotated with full 3D poses.

There have also been several works [15,18,23,22,32,38] addressing the problem of estimating the structure of a scene from a single image. The goal of these works is to recover a scene reconstruction, usually based on vanishing point estimations. These works are complementary to our work in that having reconstructed scene

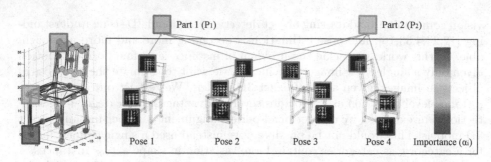

Fig. 2. Our goal is to learn a model that can estimate the fine pose of objects from a single image. Like deformable part models [8], we approach this problem by training root and part templates for a large number of views. While each part P_i has its own shape template w_i trained from rendered images, its importance weight α_i is trained with a small set of annotated real images. The goals of importance weight α_i for each part P_i are: (1) to be shared across different views in order to be able to train them only with a small set of real images, and (2) to learn the importance of each part. For example, some parts are occluded by other objects more often than others, and some parts are more discriminative than others. The importance weight α_i will encode this information.

information could benefit our algorithm to either prune the search space or to assign a prior, and vice versa.

The recent availability of affordable depth sensors has also led to an increase in the use of RGB-D data [21,11,3,30,26] to extract various types of 3D information from scenes such as depth, object pose, and intrinsic images. Our method can be easily modified to apply to this domain. For example, we can use depth as a cue to improve the quality of the local matching score.

In terms of the goal, our paper is most closely related to [27,2,20]. All these papers have a common theme of utilizing the synthetic 3D models for object detection and/or pose estimation. For example, all [27,2,20] and this paper infer part locations directly from the 3D models. [2] utilizes training part templates from lots of rendered images and applies to the object detection task. This paper also utilizes the rendered views for training part templates, but our work adds an explicit sharing part importance learned together with a small number of real images. Similar to this paper, the goal of [27] is to estimate the fine poses of objects using exact 3D models. However, unlike that work, we use a combination of modern object detection systems [8] and 3D part sharing to achieve a significant improvement in both detection accuracy and pose recall. Our algorithm is also more efficient ($\sim$ 5x speedup) despite searching over a larger space of potential poses.

In terms of the algorithm, our paper is most similar to [31,10]. They extend the deformable part model [8] to perform 3D pose detection. However, [10] requires the use of real images as training data, which can be extremely costly to collect for the task of fine pose estimation given the large number of views required ($\sim$ 324k/object). In contrast, our work only requires a small set of real images for finalizing our model. On the other hand, similar to our work, [31] uses 3D CAD models. However, unlike our work [31] uses rendered images without adapting to the statistics of real images.

3   FPM: Fine Pose Parts-Based Model

Given a set of CAD models, our goal is to accurately detect and pose-align them in RGB images if they contain instances of those objects. Let us formulate this problem in the standard object detection framework, say DPM [8]: we would (1) divide a single object into multiple mixture components - one corresponding to each 3D pose of the object we want to detect, (2) perform detection and (3) attempt to determine the exact mixture component that is responsible for the detected object so that we could identify the pose of the object. Let us do a simple thought experiment to determine the number of mixtures required: first, to parameterize the pose of an object, we require 6 values (3 rotation and 3 translation parameters). Then, we perform a rather coarse discretization of these parameters: say 5 x- and y-translations, 5 depths, 30 y-rotations, 5x- and z-rotations. This leads to 93750 mixture components[1] compared to the 2 or 3 usually used in DPM!

Now, let us assume that it were possible to do inference efficiently with 94k mixtures (each containing multiple parts!), but what about training these models? Even if we used a single example for training each mixture, we would need to take 94k images of a single object. This can be extremely difficult, if not impossible, to capture using physical objects.

In this work, we use CAD models to address the drawbacks above to efficiently and accurately detect and estimate the fine pose of objects using a small set of real images. We summarize the **advantages** of using CAD models below:

- CAD models allow us to render virtually an infinite set of views and discern between them relative to a given point of reference.
- Since we have exact CAD models of objects, we do not need to allow significant deformation between parts. Thus, given the pose, we can estimate the exact location of parts in the image.
- With a CAD model, parts are defined in 3D space allowing us to share information of each part across views. This allows us to use a limited set of training data to learn the importance of each part in 3D, which can then generalize to novel views.

While CAD models provide an appealing source of data, they have one major **disadvantage**: they can be difficult to combine with real images, as the statistics of rendered and real images are often significantly different. For example, as shown in Figure 3(b), occlusions by other objects do not usually occur in rendered images, and further, the appearance of the two domains is also significantly different e.g. the CAD model does not have well textured surfaces.

---

[1] In our implementation we actually have 324,000 components.

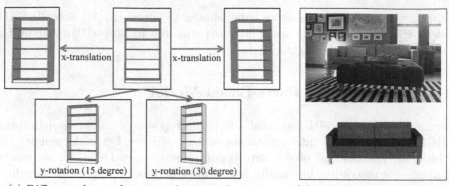

(a) Different shapes from translation and rotation   (b) Difference of modalities

Fig. 3. (a) This figure illustrates different shapes from various poses. It shows that fine poses cannot be covered by simply rotating objects at the center of the image. For example, y-rotation yields a different shape from x-translation. The line directions of the shelves do not match due to perspective projection. (b) Comparison between a real image and a rendered image. Rendered images do not have occlusion by other objects and lack other appearance details often seen in real images.

Thus, we need a model that combines the advantages of CAD models as described above, while addressing the difference in modality. To achieve this, we propose the Fine pose Parts-based Model (FPM) that combines the deformable part model (DPM)[8] trained on rendered images with objectness scores measured on real images. Specifically, we extend the DPM to have 3D shared parts that are trained using a large number of rendered images and a small number of real images. While the DPM with shared parts allows us to accurately estimate the pose of the object, the objectness scores allow us to leverage an unlabeled set of images to better estimate the location of the objects in the image. We describe our model in Section 3.1, the learning algorithm in Section 3.2 and finally the method of inference in Section 3.3.

3.1   Model

Here we define the problem more precisely: given a set of CAD models, and a small set of real images with the pose of the corresponding CAD models present in it, we want to train a model to perform fine pose estimation on new images containing the same set of objects, but with potentially different poses. Thus, we need a model that can robustly identify poses in test images that were not present in the training images.

In order to do this, we define a function $F_\Theta(x)$ that determines how well the pose, Θ, of a CAD model fits a rectangular image window, x:

$$F_\Theta(x) = \boldsymbol{\alpha}^\top \mathbf{S}_\Theta(x) + \boldsymbol{\beta}^\top \mathbf{O}_\Theta(x) + \boldsymbol{\gamma}^\top \mathbf{Q}_\Theta \tag{1}$$

where $\mathbf{S}_\Theta$, $\mathbf{O}_\Theta$ and $\mathbf{Q}_\Theta$ are the scores from the DPM with shared parts, objectness and model quality, respectively. Further, $\boldsymbol{\alpha}$, $\boldsymbol{\beta}$ and $\boldsymbol{\gamma}$ are the parameters defining the relative weight between the three terms learned using a max-margin framework as described in Section 3.2. Our goal is to maximize F_Θ for positive images/poses while minimizing it for negative images/poses. We describe the three terms, $\mathbf{S}_\Theta$, $\mathbf{O}_\Theta$ and $\mathbf{Q}_\Theta$ in detail below:

$\mathbf{S}_\Theta(x)$ - DPM with 3D Shared Parts: In this section, we describe how to extend the deformable parts based model (DPM) [8] to work in our scenario. This is a challenging problem because we do not have real images for all possible poses of the objects that we want to be able to identify, but have CAD models instead with a small set of pose-aligned images. Here, we extend the standard formulation of DPM to better exploit the extra information available through the use of CAD models, such as self-occlusion. Further, we show how to propagate information from a small set of pose-aligned images to detect novel poses in images through the use of 3D shared parts.

First, we begin by describing a simple parts-based model that can be trained using rendered images alone. For an image window x, and a pose Θ of a particular CAD model, the score, s_Θ, is given by:

$$s_\Theta(x) = \max_{P_i} \left[s_\Theta^r(x) + \sum_i s_\Theta^p(P_i, x) \right] \qquad (2)$$

where $s_\Theta^r(x) = \mathbf{w}_\Theta \cdot x_{HOG}$ is the score of the root template with pose Θ, and $s_\Theta^p(P_i, x) = \mathbf{w}_\Theta^{P_i} \cdot x_{HOG} - \phi \cdot d_i$ is the score of part template i with location P_i relative to the window x. x_{HOG} refers to the HOG [5] features extracted from the image window x, and ϕ refers to the deformation cost of part i being at a distance d_i from its expected location in the image. We can consider each discretized Θ as a traditional mixture (i.e. $324,000$ mixtures in our case). $\mathbf{w}_\Theta$ refers to the weight vector for the root template and $\mathbf{w}_\Theta^{P_i}$ refers to weight vector for part template i at pose Θ. Since exact 3D models are used here, we do not expect significant deformation of parts relative to the root template given a particular pose. Thus, we manually fix ϕ to a specific value.

Now, we describe the modifications made to the above model for our setting:

Obtaining Parts: Unlike [8], we do not treat parts as latent variables. Instead, we find parts in 3D space by identifying 'joints' in the 3D model as shown in Figure 4(a). Further, when adjacent joints connected via the mesh exceed a certain distance, an additional part is added in between. This results in about 10 to 30 parts per CAD model.

Learning Mixture Components: Given the large number of mixture components, it can be intractable to learn the weights $\mathbf{w}_\Theta$ using an SVM even when using rendered images because of computationally expensive steps such as hard-negative mining. As described in [17], we can use exemplar-LDA to efficiently learn the weights for the root and part templates. Thus, for a given CAD model, the weights, $\mathbf{w}_\Theta$, can be approximated as:

$$\hat{\mathbf{w}}_\Theta = \Sigma_{real}^{-1}(\mu_\Theta^+ - \mu_{real}^-) \qquad (3)$$

where μ_Θ^+ refers to the mean of the HOG features of images rendered at pose Θ, while Σ_{real} and μ_{real} are the covariance matrix and mean vector computed from *real* images. It is important to learn Σ_{real} and μ_{real} from real images in order to account for the difference in modalities. Note that we do not require annotated images to learn these matrices[2], and they can be efficiently modified for templates with different sizes as described in [17]. We follow a similar procedure to learn the weights for the parts.

Part Visibility: Since we use 3D CAD models, we can easily determine when a part becomes invisible due to self-occlusion. Thus, we multiply the s_Θ^p term in Eq. 2 with a binary variable $v_\Theta(P_i)$ for the visibility of each individual part P_i at pose Θ. It is set to 1 if a part is visible and 0 otherwise.

3D Shared Parts: As mentioned above, the train data contains a small set of real images with aligned poses - specifically, while we want to distinguish between $324,000$ unique poses, we only have at most 50 real images with aligned poses for training per CAD model in our dataset. How can we use this rather restricted amount of data to learn a model that generalizes to all poses?

Here, we propose to use parts shared in 3D space to propagate the information from the observed poses to the unobserved poses i.e., if we marginalize out the viewpoint, we only need to learn the importance of each 3D part of the model. This allows us to leverage information such as occlusion patterns, and the discriminativeness of different parts from real images. For example, in Figure 3(b), we would expect the sitting area of a sofa to be occluded by other objects (e.g. cushion) more often than the handles of the sofa. Further, some parts (e.g. corners) of a sofa could be more discriminative than others (e.g. lines). Thus, using 3D shared parts, we can propagate this information to all views.

Specifically, we define importance weights, α_i for each 3D shared part. Using 3D CAD models, obtaining part locations and correspondences between two views is trivial. Using the correspondence, we only have to enforce the same α_i for each P_i for all Θ. Figure 4(b) illustrates some of the learned α_i for two different models. We observe that parts that are typically occluded by other objects tend to have lower weights, while parts with more discriminative shapes tend to have higher weights. Similar to [2], α_i is used to rescale the part scores, but in this case we enforce α_i to be shared across views, and learn it directly from real images. Further, it is worth noting that learning α_i would be infeasible in our scenario without sharing.

Thus, the term $\mathbf{S}_\Theta(x)$ is given by:

$$\mathbf{S}_\Theta(x) = \begin{bmatrix} s_\Theta^r(x) & v_\Theta(P_1)s_\Theta^p(P_1, x) & \dots & v_\Theta(P_N)s_\Theta^p(P_N, x) \end{bmatrix}^\top \quad (4)$$

where N is the number of parts in our model, and thus $\boldsymbol{\alpha} \in \mathbb{R}^{N+1}$. Note that $\boldsymbol{\alpha}$ here is the same as that mentioned in Eq. 1. We learn its value jointly with β and γ in a max-margin framework, as described in Section 3.2.

---

[2] We use the covariance matrix and image mean provided by the authors of [17].

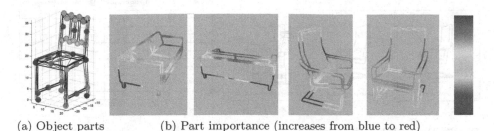

(a) Object parts   (b) Part importance (increases from blue to red)

Fig. 4. (a) Example of object parts for the given model (indicated by the different colored spheres) (b) Here, we visualize the importance weights, α_i, for each of the parts $i \in \{1 \ldots N\}$ as described in Section 3.1. Each part has its own shape template similar to other part-based methods [8]. However, our parts have additional (importance) weights which encode the importance of particular parts. The sharing of these weights enables us to train with rendered images using only a small number of annotated real images. The goal is to learn which part is frequently occluded by other objects or does not contain discriminative shapes from the real data, as this information cannot be derived from 3D CAD models alone. For example, the rear bottom parts of sofa and chair are often occluded by other objects and hence have very low weights.

$\mathbf{O_\Theta(x)}$ **- Objectness:** While the first term, $\mathbf{S_\Theta}$, in Eq. 1 largely deals with variation in geometry (and some appearance) across views, it suffers from the fact that rendered images are used for training, while real images are used for testing. While we have a limited set of pose-aligned images, we can use the generic concept of objectness [1] to identify whether an image window contains an object or not. We can simply obtain the objectness score for each image window, x, by using a typical objectness classifier [1]. However, in order to leverage the representational ability of the recent state-of-the-art deep learning features [25], we simply re-train the objectness classifier (Linear SVM) using selective search [35] and deep learning features extracted using Decaf [6] on the PASCAL VOC dataset [7]. For efficiency, we cache the objectness scores of all the selective search windows in both the train and test splits of our data.

Note that since we use selective search here, we cannot find the objectness scores for the exact windows used in our fine pose detection framework. Instead, given an arbitrary image window x, we find the selective search window that has the highest value of intersection over union and use its objectness score. In this way, we can find the value of function $\mathbf{O_\Theta(x)}$ for any image window x.

$\mathbf{Q_\Theta}$ **- Pose Quality:** When training with rendered images, the typical confident false-positives are from the views that are too *general* e.g., the back and side views of a bookcase are simply rectangles; they are not very discriminative and can easily match to a door, a whiteboard, or even a TV screen. We observe that the more near-empty cells a view of a model has, the more it suffers from false-positives. To address this, we use two terms that are suggestive of the *emptiness* of a given model view: (1) the norm of the root weight template at

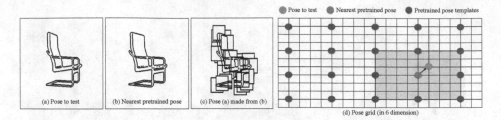

Fig. 5. Pose sliding window: During inference, when we match pose Θ (red dot) to the given image, we use the part templates from the nearest pre-trained pose Θ' (green dot). The only change from Θ' is the part location. Part locations are estimated based on the target pose Θ, and the part templates are trained based on Θ'. Blue dots indicate the poses that are pre-trained and hence have part templates, and yellow region indicates the area where the green dot could be covering.

pose Θ, $\|\hat{\mathbf{w}}_\Theta\|$, and (2) the number of visible mesh surfaces at pose Θ, n_Θ. Thus, $\mathbf{Q}_\Theta = [\|\hat{\mathbf{w}}_\Theta\|,\ n_\Theta]^\top$.

3.2   Learning

In this section, we describe how we learn the parameters $\boldsymbol{\alpha}$, $\boldsymbol{\beta}$ and $\boldsymbol{\gamma}$ of the model defined in Eq. 1. Note that all the functions $\mathbf{S}_\Theta$, $\mathbf{O}_\Theta$ and $\mathbf{Q}_\Theta$ as described in Section 3.1 are well defined i.e. they do not contain parameters that we need to learn here. Thus, Eq, 1 becomes a linear system that we can solve in a max-margin framework. Specifically, we learn $W = [\boldsymbol{\alpha}\ \boldsymbol{\beta}\ \boldsymbol{\gamma}]^\top$ using a linear SVM where the positive pose-aligned images are given in the training set, and we obtain negatives using random sampling of pose across different images. Further, we refine the weights using hard negative mining, similar to [8]. The SVM hyperparameter, C, is found using 5 fold cross-validation. We apply the same procedure to all CAD models independently.

3.3   Inference

During inference, we evaluate the function F as defined in Eq. 1 for each pose Θ. Given the difficulty of training separate classifiers for a continous pose space Θ, we instead discretize the pose into 9 x- and y-translations, 5 depths, 32 y-rotations, 5x- and z-rotations leading to 324,000 discretized poses $\{\Theta'_i\}$. Then, during inference, for each fine pose Θ, we find the nearest neighbor Θ'_i and borrow its trained weights for the root ($\hat{\mathbf{w}}_\Theta$) and part templates ($\hat{\mathbf{w}}_\Theta^{(i)}$). Figure 5 illustrates our approach. In essence, this is extremely similar to the sliding window approach, where each model from a discretized view is only run within the neighboring region of pose space where no discretized poses are present.

After all high scoring pose candidates are obtained, we also perform non-maximal suppression in pose space to obtain the final detection results. Further, to make the sliding window computation efficient, we use sparse coding on the weights of the root and part models as described in [14] allowing us to search this rather large space of fine poses in a reasonable amount of time.

4   Experiments

In this section, we evaluate the performance of our approach in detail, focusing on its ability to recover fine-pose. In particular, we evaluate both the average precision of pose estimation (Sec 4.1) and recall among top predictions (Sec 4.2). Further, we compare our method on a standard bounding box detection problem to other state-of-the-art methods (Sec 4.3).

Dataset: We use the dataset provided in [27] that contains pose-aligned 3D CAD models with real images. Specifically, we use the harder of the two datasets provided in [27]: the IKEA Room dataset. This dataset contains about 500 images where object poses are annotated for all available 3D CAD models.

4.1   Fine Pose Estimation

We compare the previous state-of-the-art method [27] and our method on various settings. We used average precision (AP) measure as suggested by [27] to evaluate our performance. Note that this AP measure takes pose into account, and not only the bounding box location. The normalized 3D space distance between the ground truth pose and the predicted pose is thresholded to determine true or false prediction. The results are summarized in Table 1.

We first evaluate our method at various settings: *only root, root+part without α, root+part with α,* and *all.* In case of *only root* and *root+part without α*, the detectors suffer from many false positives as compared to [27]. Many false positives occur by some poses having abnomarlly higher confidences than others. However, when we add sharing α and the full set of terms as proposed in Eq 1, our performance increases significantly as we leverage information learned from real images (part importance and objectness).

We further analyze how well our method performs at estimating pose when the bounding box localization is correct. For each ground truth object, we find its first estimated pose that has the highest confidence and has at least 0.7 intersection over union with the ground truth. Then, we compute the ratio of the number of correctly pose estimated objects to the total number of objects. Table 2 shows the result. The average performance of pose estimation given the ground truth bounding box is quite high, 0.84. This indicates that the pose alignment is reliable when the method can localize the target object.

Finally, we show qualitative results in Figure 6 and Figure 7. Figure 6 shows the top 4 false positive results with highest confidence from each class. There are interesting common behaviors. Many misalignments are due to shift in the global position but most of major parts are well-aligned. For example, most bookcase false positives are just one shelf unit shifted ground truth. This repetitive structure of bookcases is a common source of false positives and causes the major performance drop. Also, table and chair have most parts well-aligned to the ground truth, but are often assigned the wrong scale or produce flipped orientations. The major performance drop on the sofa class is due to the fact sofas undergo heavy occlusion, have no strong boundaries, and have complex textures compared to other classes. These differences make training with rendered images harder. Figure 7 shows some of the top correct detections. It is clear that when the correct pose is found, the alignment is reliable.

Table 1. Pose AP score: We compare our method against the previous state-of-the-art algorithm on IKEA room dataset for fine pose estimation. R, P and S refer to Root, Parts and Sharing respectively. When we use Root and/or Parts that are trained only on rendered images, the performance suffers. However, when combining with part sharing and objectness, our performance improves significantly and outperforms the previous state-of-the-art IKEA algorithm by Lim et al [27].

	bookcase *billy1*	chair *poang*	bookcase *expedit*	table *lack2*	sofa *karlstad*	bookcase *billy5*	chair *stefan*	sofa *ektorp*	mean
IKEA [27]	7.53	9.43	3.28	9.14	3.22	4.21	14.87	0.48	6.52
R	1.45	1.90	0.24	5.86	0.19	1.19	4.10	0.00	1.87
R+P	3.11	7.24	3.21	13.90	2.84	4.05	7.61	0.36	5.29
R+P+S	6.37	9.11	6.78	14.00	6.23	5.34	9.66	1.80	7.41
Full FPM	**10.52**	**14.02**	**9.30**	**15.32**	**7.15**	**6.10**	**16.00**	**5.66**	**10.51**

Table 2. Pose estimation given the oracle: Here we investigate how well our pose estimation method works when the object detection step was successful. For each ground truth object, we evaluate pose estimation only within the top detected bounding box that has at least 0.7 intersection over union with ground truth. The numbers indicate the proportion of pose estimates, within this set, that are correct. The average performance of pose estimation given the ground truth is quite high, 0.84.

bookcase *billy1*	chair *poang*	bookcase *expedit*	table *lack2*	sofa *karlstad*	bookcase *billy5*	chair *stefan*	sofa *ektorp*	mean
0.85	0.93	0.96	0.90	0.82	0.75	0.90	0.63	0.84

4.2   Pose Proposal

Recently, bounding box proposal algorithms have received a lot of attention [35,1,13]. The main motivation is to prune search windows by proposing a set of bounding boxes with a high recall on each image that can later be processed using an algorithm that is computationally more expensive. Following this motivation, we evaluate our algorithm for *pose proposal*. Instead of proposing a set of possible good bounding boxes, our algorithm can generate a set of pose candidates. The algorithm stays the same; however the emphasis of evaluation is now focused more on recall than precision, as compared to the AP measure. For example, with the AP measure, if the top 20% predictions are all correct without any further recall, one can still achieve 0.20 AP score; while this would not be able to serve the role of *pose proposal*.

1st false positive   2nd false positive   3rd false positive   4th false positive

Fig. 6. Top 4 false positives per class: (1) Many bookcase false positives are one shelf unit shifted from the ground truth. The repetitive structure of bookcase is a common source of false positives. (2) The major performance drop on the sofa class is due to the fact sofas undergo heavy occlusion, have no strong boundaries, and have complex textures compared to other classes. These difficulties make training with rendered images harder.

Fig. 7. Top correct detections: We show some of the top detections from each class.

Table 3. Pose Proposal: we measure the recall of our method among the top 2000 windows. It shows that our method can recover most of the poses for all objects within the top 2000 predictions. We also outperform [27].

	bookcase *billy1*	chair *poang*	bookcase *expedit*	table *lack2*	sofa *karlstad*	bookcase *billy5*	chair *stefan*	sofa *ektorp*	mean
[27]	0.83	0.86	0.89	0.83	0.37	0.88	0.77	0.56	0.75
FPM	**0.87**	**0.93**	**0.94**	**0.88**	**0.83**	**0.91**	**0.99**	**0.91**	**0.91**

Table 3 shows the result of recall for all methods. Because all methods will have a full recall in the limit, we limit the number of predictions to be under 2,000. Our method shows quite reliable recalls at all classes, while [27] fails severely to recall some classes. We believe this is because our model can handle flexible views without being limited to the preset variations of views. [27] depends on a bounded number of views and uses a RANSAC process that can fall into local minima. On the other hand, our method exhaustively examines all possible views. From this result, we can conclude that our method can effectively propose candidate poses for other post-processing algorithms (e.g. context modeling or segmentation).

4.3   Bounding Box Detection

While object bounding box detection is not our main target problem, our approach can nonetheless be used for this purpose. For pose estimation algorithms, we extract bounding boxes from predicted poses and apply non-max suppression from [8] before evaluation. We however train [8] with real images using the author-provided code. We evaluate the results at two different thresholds

Table 4. Bounding box AP measure: we compare our method against other state-of-the-art algorithms on the IKEA room dataset for bounding box detection. As we increase the threshold to 0.8, the performance of DPM drops significantly; while our method maintains the performance. It shows that our method is capable for fine detection. Our method also significantly outperforms the previous state-of-the-art algorithm [27] in both scenarios, obtaining higher AP for most of the object categories.

	bookcase *billy1*	chair *poang*	bookcase *expedit*	table *lack2*	sofa *karlstad*	bookcase *billy5*	chair *stefan*	sofa *ektorp*	mean
(a) Intersection over Union $\geq$ 0.5									
IKEA [27]	24.41	28.32	21.73	11.12	22.65	11.22	28.57	2.37	18.80
DPM [8]	**49.89**	**51.63**	**71.87**	**48.85**	34.01	**42.11**	**45.34**	**28.80**	**46.56**
FPM	23.51	29.83	37.26	38.16	**35.85**	33.00	30.52	27.13	31.91
(b) Intersection over Union $\geq$ 0.8									
IKEA [27]	**20.34**	14.43	15.74	9.14	15.32	7.73	20.45	1.58	13.09
DPM [8]	9.41	15.58	15.47	10.02	20.12	3.05	20.44	11.59	13.21
FPM	17.37	**22.36**	**22.89**	**29.88**	**22.26**	8.71	**24.31**	**12.64**	**20.05**

on bounding box intersection over union to examine an ability to capture fine details.

At a lower threshold of 0.5, DPM [8] performs strongly, and our method is relatively weak (in Table 4a). However, at a higher threshold of 0.8, our method outperforms [8] (in Table 4b). This result shows that [8] has a good coarse localization ability but fails capturing fine details. Because our method learns based on each fine pose, the result tends to have a better overlap with the ground truth than that of DPM. Note that DPM is fully trained with real images, and our method is trained based on rendered images and used real images to adapt. Further, we could improve our performance at the 0.5 detection threshold by incorporating scores from DPM into our model.

5   Conclusion

In this paper, we introduced a novel approach for fine-pose estimation that leverages geometric information from CAD models to address the problem of fine pose estimation. We show that our method is successfully able to combine the appearance information from relatively few real training images with rendered images from CAD models, outperforming existing approaches in various tasks. Notably, our algorithm significantly outperforms deformable part-based models [8] for high overlap detection, and significantly improves pose recall as compared to [27]. We believe that our work provides a platform to tackle higher level tasks such as contextual reasoning in scenes using the fine poses of objects.

Acknowledgements. We thank Hamed Pirsiavash for inspiring discussions, and Phillip Isola, Andrew Owens, and Carl Vondrick for many helpful comments.

References

1. Alexe, B., Deselaers, T., Ferrari, V.: What is an object? In: IEEE Conference on Computer Vision and Pattern Recognition, pp. 73–80 (2010)
2. Aubry, M., Maturana, D., Efros, A., Russell, B., Sivic, J.: Seeing 3d chairs: exemplar part-based 2D-3D alignment using a large dataset of cad models. In: IEEE Conference on Computer Vision and Pattern Recognition (2014)
3. Barron, J.T., Malik, J.: Intrinsic scene properties from a single RGB-D image. In: IEEE Conference on Computer Vision and Pattern Recognition (2013)
4. Choi, W., Chao, Y.W., Pantofaru, C., Savarese, S.: Understanding indoor scenes using 3D geometric phrases. In: IEEE Conference on Computer Vision and Pattern Recognition (2013)
5. Dalal, N., Triggs, B.: Histograms of oriented gradients for human detection. In: IEEE Conference on Computer Vision and Pattern Recognition (2005)
6. Donahue, J., Jia, Y., Vinyals, O., Hoffman, J., Zhang, N., Tzeng, E., Darrell, T.: Decaf: A deep convolutional activation feature for generic visual recognition. arXiv preprint arXiv:1310.1531 (2013)
7. Everingham, M., Van Gool, L., Williams, C.K.I., Winn, J., Zisserman, A.: The PASCAL Visual Object Classes Challenge 2007 (VOC 2007) Results (2007)
8. Felzenszwalb, P.F., Girshick, R.B., McAllester, D.: Discriminatively trained deformable part models (2009)
9. Felzenszwalb, P.F., Huttenlocher, D.P.: Pictorial structures for object recognition. International Journal of Computer Vision 61(1), 55–79 (2005)
10. Fidler, S., Dickinson, S.J., Urtasun, R.: 3D object detection and viewpoint estimation with a deformable 3D cuboid model. In: Advances in Neural Information Processing Systems (2012)
11. Fisher, M., Hanrahan, P.: Context-based search for 3D models. ACM Trans. Graph. 29(6) (December 2010)
12. Fouhey, D.F., Delaitre, V., Gupta, A., Efros, A.A., Laptev, I., Sivic, J.: People watching: Human actions as a cue for single view geometry. In: Fitzgibbon, A., Lazebnik, S., Perona, P., Sato, Y., Schmid, C. (eds.) ECCV 2012, Part V. LNCS, vol. 7576, pp. 732–745. Springer, Heidelberg (2012)
13. Girshick, R., Donahue, J., Darrell, T., Malik, J.: Rich feature hierarchies for accurate object detection and semantic segmentation. In: IEEE Conference on Computer Vision and Pattern Recognition (2014)
14. Girshick, R., Song, H.O., Darrell, T.: Discriminatively activated sparselets. In: International Conference on Machine Learning (2013)
15. Gupta, A., Satkin, S., Efros, A.A., Hebert, M.: From 3D scene geometry to human workspace. In: IEEE Conference on Computer Vision and Pattern Recognition (2011)
16. Gupta, S., Arbelaez, P., Malik, J.: Perceptual organization and recognition of indoor scenes from RGB-D images. In: IEEE Conference on Computer Vision and Pattern Recognition (2013)
17. Hariharan, B., Malik, J., Ramanan, D.: Discriminative decorrelation for clustering and classification. In: Fitzgibbon, A., Lazebnik, S., Perona, P., Sato, Y., Schmid, C. (eds.) ECCV 2012, Part IV. LNCS, vol. 7575, pp. 459–472. Springer, Heidelberg (2012)
18. Hedau, V., Hoiem, D., Forsyth, D.: Thinking inside the box: Using appearance models and context based on room geometry. In: Daniilidis, K., Maragos, P., Paragios, N. (eds.) ECCV 2010, Part VI. LNCS, vol. 6316, pp. 224–237. Springer, Heidelberg (2010)
19. Hejrati, M., Ramanan, D.: Analyzing 3D objects in cluttered images. In: Advances in Neural Information Processing Systems (2012)

20. Hejrati, M., Ramanan, D.: Analysis by synthesis: 3D object recognition by object reconstruction. In: IEEE Conference on Computer Vision and Pattern Recognition (2014)
21. Henry, P., Krainin, M., Herbst, E., Ren, X., Fox, D.: Rgbd mapping: Using depth cameras for dense 3D modeling of indoor environments. In: RGB-D: Advanced Reasoning with Depth Cameras Workshop in Conjunction with RSS (2010)
22. Hoiem, D., Efros, A.A., Hebert, M.: Geometric context from a single image. In: IEEE International Conference on Computer Vision (2005)
23. Hoiem, D., Hedau, V., Forsyth, D.: Recovering free space of indoor scenes from a single image. In: IEEE Conference on Computer Vision and Pattern Recognition (2012)
24. Jia, Z., Gallagher, A., Saxena, A., Chen, T.: 3D-based reasoning with blocks, support, and stability. In: IEEE Conference on Computer Vision and Pattern Recognition (2013)
25. Krizhevsky, A., Sutskever, I., Hinton, G.E.: Imagenet classification with deep convolutional neural networks. In: Advances in Neural Information Processing Systems (2012)
26. Lai, K., Bo, L., Ren, X., Fox, D.: Detection-based object labeling in 3D scenes. In: IEEE International Conference on on Robotics and Automation (2012)
27. Lim, J.J., Pirsiavash, H., Torralba, A.: Parsing ikea objects: Fine pose estimation. In: IEEE International Conference on Computer Vision (2013)
28. Lowe, D.: Fitting parameterized three-dimensional models to images. IEEE Transactions on Pattern Analysis and Machine intelligence (1991)
29. Matzen, K., Snavely, N.: Nyc3dcars: A dataset of 3D vehicles in geographic context. In: Proc. Int. Conf. on Computer Vision (2013)
30. Silberman, N., Hoiem, D., Kohli, P., Fergus, R.: Indoor segmentation and support inference from RGBD images. In: Fitzgibbon, A., Lazebnik, S., Perona, P., Sato, Y., Schmid, C. (eds.) ECCV 2012, Part V. LNCS, vol. 7576, pp. 746–760. Springer, Heidelberg (2012)
31. Pepik, B., Gehler, P., Stark, M., Schiele, B.: 3d2pm - 3D deformable part models. In: Fitzgibbon, A., Lazebnik, S., Perona, P., Sato, Y., Schmid, C. (eds.) ECCV 2012, Part VI. LNCS, vol. 7577, pp. 356–370. Springer, Heidelberg (2012)
32. Satkin, S., Lin, J., Hebert, M.: Data-driven scene understanding from 3D models. In: British Machine Vision Conference (2012)
33. Schwing, A.G., Fidler, S., Pollefeys, M., Urtasun, R.: Box In the Box: Joint 3D Layout and Object Reasoning from Single Images. In: Proc. ICCV (2013)
34. Sun, M., Su, H., Savarese, S., Fei-Fei, L.: A multi-view probabilistic model for 3D object classes. In: IEEE Conference on Computer Vision and Pattern Recognition (2009)
35. Uijlings, J., van de Sande, K., Gevers, T., Smeulders, A.: Selective search for object recognition. International Journal of Computer Vision (2013)
36. Xiang, Y., Mottaghi, R., Savarese, S.: Beyond pascal: A benchmark for 3D object detection in the wild. In: IEEE Winter Conference on Applications of Computer Vision (2014)
37. Xiao, J., Russell, B., Torralba, A.: Localizing 3D cuboids in single-view images. In: Advances in Neural Information Processing Systems (2012)
38. Zhao, Y., Zhu, S.C.: Scene parsing by integrating function, geometry and appearance models. In: IEEE Conference on Computer Vision and Pattern Recognition (2013)
39. Zia, M., Stark, M., Schindler, K.: Explicit occlusion modeling for 3D object class representations. In: IEEE Conference on Computer Vision and Pattern Recognition (2013)

Learning High-Level Judgments
of Urban Perception

Vicente Ordonez and Tamara L. Berg

University of North Carolina at Chapel Hill, Chapel Hill, NC 27599, USA
{vicente,tlberg}@cs.unc.edu

Abstract. Human observers make a variety of perceptual inferences
about pictures of places based on prior knowledge and experience. In
this paper we apply computational vision techniques to the task of predicting the perceptual characteristics of places by leveraging recent work
on visual features along with a geo-tagged dataset of images associated
with crowd-sourced urban perception judgments for wealth, uniqueness,
and safety. We perform extensive evaluations of our models, training and
testing on images of the same city as well as training and testing on images of different cities to demonstrate generalizability. In addition, we
collect a new densely sampled dataset of streetview images for 4 cities
and explore joint models to collectively predict perceptual judgments
at city scale. Finally, we show that our predictions correlate well with
ground truth statistics of wealth and crime.

1 Introduction

Sense of place is a feeling or perception held by people about a location. It is
often used to refer to those characteristics that make a place unique or foster a
sense of belonging, but may also refer to characteristics that are not inherently
positive such as fear [31].

In this paper we apply computer vision techniques to predict human perceptions of place. In particular we show that – perhaps surprisingly – it is possible to predict human judgments of safety, uniqueness, and wealth of locations
with remarkable accuracy. We also find that predictors learned for one place
are applicable to predicting perceptions of other unseen locations, indicating the
generalizability of our models. Additionally, we explore models to jointly predict
perceptions coherently across an entire city. Finally, we also find good correlations with ground truth statistics of crime and wealth when predicting on a more
densely sampled set of images.

The world, or even a single city, is a large continuous evolving space that
can not be experienced at once. The seminal work of Lynch, *The Image of the
City* [19] was influential in urban design and the approach of social scientists
to urban studies. Of course, collecting human judgments is a time consuming
and costly process. With accurate computational prediction tools, we could extend human labeled data of a place to nearby locations or potentially the entire
world, thus enabling social scientists to better understand and analyze public

D. Fleet et al. (Eds.): ECCV 2014, Part VI, LNCS 8694, pp. 494–510, 2014.

Fig. 1. Our goal is to learn the human perception of safety, wealth, and uniqueness for street level images. Human judgments agree that the image shown on the left is safer than the image shown on the right.

perceptions of places. Additionally, there are many potential applications of our method such as answering important questions that people might have about a place. For example, what areas should I avoid on my visit to NYC? In what neighborhoods in Chicago might I like to buy a house? Which blocks of Boston are the most unique?

Most computer vision algorithms related to places have focused on tasks like scene classification, (e.g. [16,26,33,29,18]) or parsing scene images into constituent objects and background elements (e.g. [30,10,15,32]). But, places are about much more than semantics. People perceive different qualities about a place, e.g. whether it is a safe place, an interesting place, or a beautiful place.

These notions are related to recent work on attributes, especially on predicting attributes of scenes [24]. Attributes such as scary, soothing, and stressful in the SUN Attribute dataset [24] are related to perceptual characteristics of safety, but are collected for a very different type of data. Our goal is somewhat different; while the SUN Attribute dataset consists of general internet images collected from Flickr, we look at streetview photos sampled densely across multiple cities (see Fig 2 for a comparison). In addition, past work on scene attribute recognition predicts attributes of images independently for each image. We take an approach that predicts attributes of all images within a location jointly using a graph based framework. Since images taken in nearby locations usually have similar perceptual characteristics this improves perceptual characteristic prediction performance. Finally, we also look at predicting perceptions at a much larger scale, e.g. on image sets spanning entire cities.

Our approach learns from a large data set collected by the *Place Pulse* project [28]. This dataset consists of 2920 streetview images of NYC and Boston. Ratings are collected from people regarding their perceptions of safety, uniqueness, and wealth. We train models for both classification (Sec 4.2, predicting e.g. which parts of a city are most or least safe), and regression (Sec 4.3, directly predicting perceptual ratings). Our quantitative evaluations demonstrate reliable performance for both tasks when training and testing on images from the same city. In addition, we experiment with training on images collected from one city and testing on images of another city and show good generalizability. Qualitative results also show that our learned models can predict which neighborhoods are most safe within a city. In addition to the original dataset, we

Place Pulse v1.0: Unsafe   SUN Attributes: Scary

Fig. 2. Left: Sample images of *unsafe* street images. **Right:** Sample *scary* images from the SUN Attributes dataset [24]. Note, the distinct differences in types of image content between the collections.

collect additional photos for prediction (Sec 3.2) by densely sampling streetview images of NYC (8863 photos), and Boston (9596 photos), and 2 locations not in the original dataset – Chicago (12502 photos) and Baltimore (11772 photos). Finally, we show that our predictions of safety correlate well with statistics about crime and wealth in the 2 new cities, Chicago and Baltimore (Sec 6).

The main contributions of our paper are:

- Classification and regression models to predict human perceptions of the safety, uniqueness, and wealth depicted in images of places.
- Models to jointly predict perceptual characteristics of entire cities.
- Experiments demonstrating that perceptual characteristics of places can be predicted effectively when training and testing on the same city and when training and testing on different cities.
- Maps visualizing perceptual characteristics densely predicted over cities.
- Experimental evidence showing correlation between perceptual predictions and crime and wealth statistics.

2   Related Work

We discuss here several lines of research related to this work. We would also like to acknowledge a few concurrent efforts in perceptual prediction using urban data, most notably Naik *et.al.* [21], Arietta *et. al.* [2], Quercia *et.al.* [27] and Khosla *et. al* [14].

Scene Recognition & Reconstruction: There has been a lot of progress in scene recognition in recent years [16,26,33,24]. However, this research has mainly focused on scene categorization [16,26,33]. and recently on recognizing attributes of scenes [24]. Our task is somewhat different, trying to estimate human perceptions of place both of individual photos and in a coherent manner across larger extents, such as across an entire city. Additionally, rather than looking at all scene images, we focus on outdoor street level images of cities. For this task, there seem to be strong visual cues related to our high level knowledge and experience with places. Content cues that may be related to perception of place include paintings on the walls (certain types of graffiti), presence or absence of green areas, presence of metallic fences and other objects, or amount and type of clutter. Another area of research related to place looks at reconstructing 3d models of scenes [1][9]. Recent methods operate at city scale. Our work could help put a semantic layer on top of these efforts by adding perceptual information to geometric models of places.

Geo-Locating Images. One previous related computer vision application is that of automatic image localization [11,34]. The work of Hays and Efros [11] uses a data-driven approach to predict image location (latitude and longitude) based on a collection of millions of geo-tagged images from Flickr. Later work from Zamir *et.al* [34] uses Google Street View images for this purpose. While these methods attempt to guess where a picture was taken, we try to predict aspects of the picture itself. In Hays and Efros [11] the authors also demonstrate that other meta-information such as population and elevation can be estimated based on geo-location predictions. Our work is similar in spirit in that we want to predict meta-information about images, but computes the prediction directly from the image content rather than using outside information such as elevation or population maps.

Perceptual Tasks: There has been recent interest in the vision community on predicting perceptual characteristics of images. Related tasks include predicting the aesthetic quality of images [6][20][12], discovering mid-level representations that are distinctive to a city [7] or to a style of object [17], and efforts to predict the memorability of images [12]. The most relevant to our work is the aesthetics task since it mimics the positive and negative nature of photos also present in predicting the safety of a location. For aesthetics, various approaches have been tried, including attribute based methods which train aesthetics classifiers based on the outputs of individual high level attribute detectors [6]. Though attribute based methods are intuitive, later work from Marchesotti *et.al* [20] found that generic image descriptors in combination with appropriate encoding methods can also produce state-of-the-art results. We use this insight to build our feature representations using recent state of the art image descriptors, in particular fisher vector (FV) encodings [25] and DeCAF convolution network based features [8].

3   Data

We use two main data sources in our work: a) the *Place Pulse 1.0* dataset collected by Salesses *et.al* [28] and labeled using crowdsourcing (Sec 3.1), and b) a larger street view dataset we collected for this work (Sec 3.2).

3.1   Place Pulse 1.0

We use the publicly available images from the *Place Pulse 1.0* dataset [28]. This dataset contains 1689 streetview images sampled across New York City and

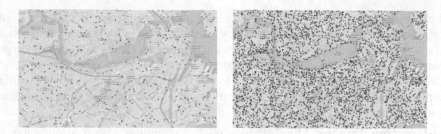

Fig. 3. The left image shows the sampling locations for the Place Pulse v1.0 dataset and the right image show the sampling locations of our unlabeled dataset for a zoomed-in section of the Boston/Cambridge area

1231 images of Boston. For each image in the dataset the authors provide meta-information related to location – geo-tags of latitude longitude – and camera rotation information. Each image i also comes with aggregated human judgment scores of perceived safety ($q_{i,s} \in Q_s$), uniqueness ($q_{i,u} \in Q_u$) and wealth/class ($q_{i,w} \in Q_w$). The locations in the dataset were randomly sampled across each city, with the exception of some locations for which there are multiple different views.

Perception scores for the 3 measures were collected via crowdsourcing using a website created for this purpose. On this website, a user is presented with two images side-by-side and asked to answer a relative perceptual judgment question, e.g. "Which place looks safer?". The user could select either the left or right image or tie. The goal of this project was to compute 3 scores for each image in the dataset $Q_s = \{q_{i,s}\}$, $Q_u = \{q_{i,u}\}$, $Q_w = \{q_{i,w}\}$ corresponding to safety, uniqueness, and wealth respectively. Due to practical considerations (limited numbers of users), not all possible pairs of images for a given city could be directly compared. Instead, the authors merged the pairwise rankings into an overall ranking by taking into account the relative judgments of the images against which each image was compared. This problem is a direct analog to the notion of "strength of schedule" [23] in sport matches.

Perceptual scores $q_{i,k}$ for perception type $k \in \{s, u, w\}$ for image i are:

$$q_{i,k} = \frac{10}{3}\left(W_{i,k} + \frac{1}{w_{i,k}}\sum_{j_1=1}^{w_{i,k}} W_{j_1,k} - \frac{1}{l_{i,k}}\sum_{j_2=1}^{l_{i,k}} L_{j_2,k} + 1\right) \tag{1}$$

$$W_{i,k} = \frac{w_{i,k}}{w_{i,k} + l_{i,k} + t_{i,k}} \quad , \quad L_{i,k} = \frac{l_{i,k}}{w_{i,k} + l_{i,k} + t_{i,k}} \tag{2}$$

Where the counts $w_{i,k}, l_{i,k}, t_{i,k}$ denote the number of times the image i won, lost, or tied compared to other images for perception metric k. The constant ($\frac{10}{3}$) was selected so that the output scores fall in the range $0 - 10$.

3.2   External Dataset

We additionally collect a much larger dataset of geo-tagged images for New York (8863 images) and Boston (9596 images), as well as for two new cities, Baltimore

(11772 images) and Chicago (12502 images). To collect this dataset, we use the Google Street View API to sample images from random locations within the boundaries of each city. To provide a better idea of the scale and coverage of our extended dataset, in Figure 3 we show side by side sampled locations for a zoomed-in area of Boston from the *Place Pulse 1.0* dataset (left) and our more densely sampled dataset (right). This denser sampling will allow us to generate urban perception maps and analysis at more detailed resolutions.

4   Predicting Urban Perceptions

We model and evaluate prediction of urban perceptions in two tasks, as a classification problem (Section 4.2), and as a regression problem (Section 4.3). First we describe the image representations used in these tasks (Section 4.1).

4.1   Image Representation

Since the seminal work of Oliva and Torralba on modeling the spatial envelope of the image [22], there have been several proposals for scene representations that leverage spatial information. The recent work of Juneja *et. al.* [13] presents a benchmark of several scene representations, including both low-level feature representations and mid-level representations. They find that using low-level features with rich encoding methods like Fisher vectors [25] can produce state-of-the-art results on challenging scene recognition problems.

For our work we evaluate three feature representations: Gist [22], SIFT + Fisher Vectors [25], and the most recent generic deep convolutional activation features (DeCAF) of Donahue *et. al.* [8]. For SIFT-FV we compute the SIFT features densely across five image resolutions, then perform spatial pooling by computing the FV representations on a 2x2 grid over the image and for the whole image. We build a visual dictionary with 128 components using Gaussian Mixture Models. Additionally, we use the rootSIFT variant and adopt other recommendations from Chatfield *et. al.* [4]. For the DeCAF features we use the output of the sixth convolutional layer in the neural network.

4.2   Classification

We set up the classification problem protocol in a similar manner to that used in image aesthetics tasks [20,5,6], where one tries to discriminate between images with high perceptual scores from images with low perceptual scores (commonly used in perceptual tasks since the scores of images middling perception values may not be stable across people). For classification, we define the binary labels $y_{i,k} \in \{1, -1\}$ for both training and testing as:

$$y_{i,k} = \begin{cases} 1 & \text{if } rank(q_{i,k}) \text{ in the top } \delta\% \\ -1 & \text{if } rank(q_{i,k}) \text{ in the bottom } \delta\% \end{cases} \tag{3}$$

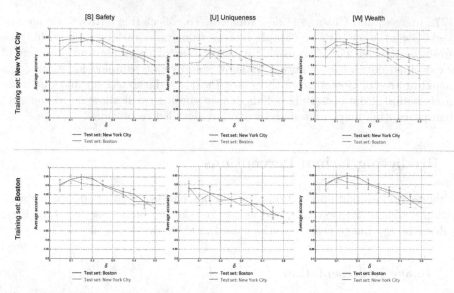

Fig. 4. Each figure shows the mean accuracy of the classification for different values of the δ parameter. The blue line represents performance reported on images from the same city as the training data. The red line represents the performance reported on images from a different city than those used for training.

We parameterize the classification problem by a variable δ and calculate performance as we adjust δ. As we move the value of our parameter δ the problem becomes more difficult since the visual appearance of the positive and negative images starts to become less evident up to the point when $\delta = 0.5$. At the same time when δ has smaller values the positive and negative images are easier to classify but we have access to less data.

We learn models to predict $y_{i,k}$ from input image representations x_i using an ℓ_2-regularized with a squared hinge-loss function linear SVM classifier:

$$\hat{y}_{i,k} = sgn(w_k^\mathsf{T} x_i) \tag{4}$$

$$w_k = \underset{\overset{*}{w}_k}{\arg\min} \frac{1}{2} \overset{*}{w}_k^\mathsf{T} \overset{*}{w}_k + c \sum_{i=1}^{n} (max(0, 1 - \breve{y}_{i,k} \overset{*}{w}_k^\mathsf{T} \breve{x}_i))^2 \tag{5}$$

Where we set the regularization parameter c using held-out data and learn w_k using training data $\{\breve{x}_i, \breve{y}_{i,k}\}$.

We examine two scenarios: a) training and testing perceptual prediction models on images from the same city, and b) training models on images from one city and testing on images from another city. We show some qualitative results of perceptual image classification in Figure 5.

We report classification performance on the Place Pulse dataset [28] in Figure 4 as mean average AUC, with error bars computed over 10 random splits for the SIFT + FV features. We performed the same analysis using Gist and DeCAF features and found them to be nearly on par for this task. Classification

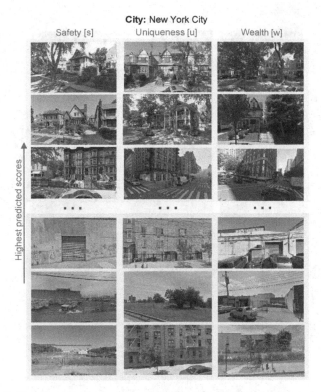

Fig. 5. Classification predictions on a our large densely sampled external dataset of street images of New York City. We show the images predicted as high and low – safety, uniqueness, wealthiness – at the top and the bottom respectively.

is evaluated for several values of δ, ranging from $\delta = 0.05$ to $\delta = 0.5$. The blue line in each plot represents accuracies for the scenario where we train and test on images from the same city. The red line in each plot represents accuracies for the scenario in which we train on one city and test on another city. For instance, the blue line in the top left plot in Figure 4 shows results for classifying images of New York City as {highly safe vs highly unsafe} using images of New York City as training data. The red line in the same plot corresponds to results of classifying images of Boston as {highly safe vs highly unsafe} using images of New York City as training data. The performance for training on one city and testing on another is slightly lower than training and testing on the same city, but reaches nearly the same performance for larger values of δ.

Several conclusions can be drawn from these plots. The first is that we can reliably predict the perceptual characteristics of safety, uniqueness, and wealth for streetview images. The second is that that uniqueness [U] seems to be the most difficult task to infer using our feature representations. This might be due to the more subjective definition of uniqueness.

We also find that we can train perceptual models on one city and then use them to reliably predict perceptions for another city, indicating the

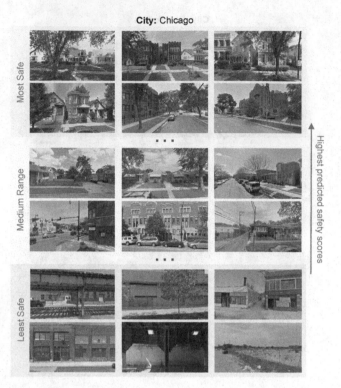

Fig. 6. Regression predictions of safety for a previously unseen city. Here models are trained on images from Boston and New York City from the *Place Pulse v1.0* dataset and predictions are performed on a large newly collected streetview dataset of Chicago.

generalizability of our models to new places. This is important since our ultimate goal is to apply these methods to cities across the globe and collecting training data for every city in the world would be infeasible.

4.3 Regression

We also study perceptual characteristic prediction as a regression problem, where we want to predict aggregated human scores, defined in Eq. (1), using linear regression. Here, our ground truth labels are $y_{i,k} = q_{i,k}$ for image i and perceptual measure k. Therefore, we make predictions $\hat{y}_{i,k}$ as follows:

$$\hat{y}_{i,k} = w_k^\mathsf{T} x_i \tag{6}$$

$$w_k = \arg\min_{\overset{*}{w_k}} \frac{1}{2} \overset{*}{w}_k^\mathsf{T} \overset{*}{w}_k + c \sum_{i=1}^{n} (max(0, |\breve{y}_{i,k} - \overset{*}{w}_k^\mathsf{T} \breve{x}_i| - \epsilon))^2 \tag{7}$$

Where we optimize the squared loss error on the predictions subject to an ℓ_2 regularization on the parameters. We optimize for the regularization parameter c on held-out data and learn w_k using training data $\{\breve{x}_i, \breve{y}_{i,k}\}$.

Table 1. Results on the original Google Street View images from from the PlacePulse dataset (2011). We report the *Pearson product-moment correlation coefficient r* for the predicted regression values as compared to human perceptual scores for several training and testing data scenarios.

Training data	Metric	Test on New York			Test on Boston		
		Gist	FV	DeCaf	Gist	FV	DeCaf
New York	Safety	0.6365	**0.6869**	0.6808	0.6412	0.6566	**0.7008**
	Uniqueness	0.5265	0.5168	**0.5453**	0.4978	0.4358	**0.5186**
	Wealth	0.6149	0.6468	**0.6478**	0.5715	0.6001	**0.6608**
Boston	Safety	0.5972	0.6202	**0.6362**	0.6710	0.6740	**0.7180**
	Uniqueness	0.4474	0.3767	**0.4596**	0.5203	0.4941	**0.5471**
	Wealth	0.5640	0.5555	**0.6015**	0.5916	0.6419	**0.6782**

Table 2. Generalization of the PlacePulse annotations on updated Google StreetView images (2013). We report the *Pearson product-moment correlation coefficient r* for the predicted regression values as compared to human perceptual scores for several training and testing data scenarios.

Training data	Metric	Test on New York			Test on Boston		
		Gist	FV	DeCaf	Gist	FV	DeCaf
New York	Safety	0.5436	**0.5890**	0.5603	0.5165	0.5275	**0.5578**
	Uniqueness	0.4388	**0.4510**	0.4449	0.4072	0.3598	**0.4363**
	Wealth	0.5328	**0.5659**	0.5518	0.4698	0.4949	**0.5631**
Boston	Safety	0.5062	0.4895	**0.5211**	0.5531	**0.5839**	0.5757
	Uniqueness	0.4023	0.3479	**0.4158**	0.4208	0.3712	**0.4527**
	Wealth	0.4972	0.4801	**0.5173**	0.5238	0.5367	**0.5863**

Regression results for predicting safety, uniqueness, and wealth are presented in Table 1, computed over 10 folds of the data for Gist, SIFT-FV and DeCAF image descriptors. As in our classification experiments, we examine two scenarios: training and testing on the same city, and training on one city and testing on a different city. We find that our models are able to predict perceptual scores well, with r-correlation coefficients ranging from 0.4 to 0.7. Again we find uniqueness to be the most challenging perceptual characteristic for prediction. Here DeCAF features provided the highest generalization performance when testing on data from a different city. We show some qualitative results across the spectrum of predicted scores for the city of Chicago in Figure 6 (Note we did not have images of Chicago available for training). We additionally show prediction scores for several metrics on a map in Figure 8.

Generalization across Time: The original PlacePulse dataset annotations were collected in 2011 with the available Google Street View images at that time.

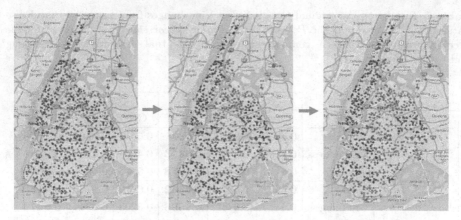

Fig. 7. The input map on the left are isolated predictions of perceptual safety for New York City. The next two images are joint predictions of safety/unsafety using our collective model with different smoothing parameters.

We additionally downloaded updated images for the same locations and views, most of which were taken in 2013. We run the same regression experiments on this set of images using the original perceptual scores as labels and show results in Table 2. We find that even though performance drops somewhat we are still able to learn representative and reasonably accurate models for each concept.

5   Collective Urban Perception

In the previous models, prediction for classification and regression was performed independently for each image. However, images of a place are not independent. The safety of one city block is tightly correlated with the safety of the next block down the street. In this section, we explore models for collective inference of perceptual characteristics within a city. In particular, we model a city as a graph where each node $n_i \in N$ is represented by a set of variables $\{p_i = (lat_i, lon_i), x_i\}$ where p_i is a latitude-longitude coordinate and x_i is the feature representation for the image. We connect the nodes in the graph to define the edge set E by associating each node n_i with its closest K neighbors based on the euclidean distance between pairs of node coordinates (p_i, p_j). For our experiments we use a connectivity factor of $K = 10$.

Now, let's say our goal is to label every node in the graph as unsafe or not. We first define unsafe as any point in our training data that has an image with a perceptual score $q_{i,s}$ in the bottom 25% of the training set. We set our goal to predict a joint labeling $\hat{Y} = \{y_i\}$ that maximizes:

$$\hat{Y} = \arg\max_Y \prod_i \Phi_1(y_i|x_i, w_s) \prod_{i,j \in E} \Phi_2(y_i, y_j|x_i, x_j, p_i, p_j, \alpha_1, \alpha_2) \qquad (8)$$

$$-\ln \Phi_1 = y_i w_s^\mathsf{T} x_i \qquad (9)$$

$$-\ln \Phi_2 = \left(\frac{\alpha_1}{\|x_i - x_j\|} + \frac{\alpha_2}{\|p_i - p_j\|} \right) \cdot 1[y_i = y_j] \qquad (10)$$

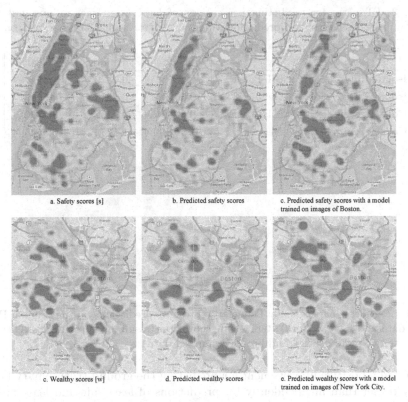

a. Safety scores [s]   b. Predicted safety scores   c. Predicted safety scores with a model
                                                               trained on images of Boston.

c. Wealthy scores [w]   d. Predicted wealthy scores   e. Predicted wealthy scores with a model
                                                               trained on images of New York City.

Fig. 8. Regression results scaled and shown as a heatmap for all the point locations in the Place Pulse Dataset. Left column shows ground truth scores, middle column shows predictions from the regression model, and right column shows predictions of the regression model when trained on a different city.

Where the unary potentials parameter w_s is based on our regression model (Section 4.3). The pairwise potentials for smoothing are based on two criteria: Visually similar images should be encouraged to take the same label, and images that are spatially close to each each other should be encouraged to take the same label. This global optimization is in general difficult, but because we are using submodular potentials we can optimize this in polynomial time using Graphcuts [3].

We use this model to jointly predict perceptual scores for least safe, unique, and wealthy images coherently across all images in New York City. Results for average f1-scores computed over 10 folds (with line search to tune parameters α_1 and α_2) are shown in Table 3 for both the SIFT-FV and DeCAF features. To reduce correlations between images used in training and testing we select train-test splits of the data by clustering the data points using k-means on image coordinates ($k = 10$). Each cluster is used as the test data for one fold and the rest of the images are used for training.

Table 3. F1-scores for predicting perceptions of least safe, least unique and least wealthy places using isolated predictions and our collective unsafety prediction model

		¬Safe	¬Unique	¬Wealth
Isolated prediction	[SIFT + FV]	0.6077	0.4420	**0.5755**
Isolated prediction	[DeCAF]	0.5929	0.4652	0.5613
Collective prediction	[SIFT + FV]	0.6069	0.4457	0.5700
Collective prediction	[DeCAF]	**0.6089**	**0.4777**	0.5545

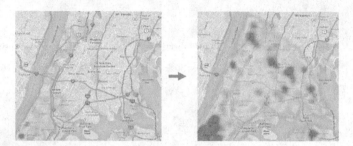

Fig. 9. Large scale experiments: Left map represents predictions on the original Place Pulse dataset for New York, Right map shows the result of applying classification models to our more densely and broadly sampled data

We find a positive improvement for predicting the ground-truth binary labels jointly rather than independently for predictions of least safe and least unique places. For predicting which images are not wealthy we don't find any improvement, perhaps indicating that wealthiness is more localized.

On the qualitative side we now have, akin to foreground-background segmentation, a model that can produce arbitrarily dense or sparse region representations of safe/unsafe areas depending on the parameter choice of the pairwise potentials. We show some results to this effect in Figure 7. From these maps, we can see a birds eye view of which parts of New York City are most safe or unsafe. If we use less smoothing we can see more fine-grained predictions of safety at the neighborhood level. Notably the blue area includes Manhattan and certain neighborhoods in Brooklyn and Queens like Park Slope and Forest Hills which are known to be particularly safe areas of these boroughs.

6   Additional Experiments and Results

Large Scale Experiments on Unlabeled Data: So far, we have been evaluating our models on the *Place Pulse v1.0* dataset, but we have also collected a much larger, densely sampled dataset of the original two cities (New York City and Boston) and two new cities (Baltimore and Chicago). Therefore, we run our models on these datasets as well. In Figure 9 we show predictions on our New York City dataset compared to the original samples from Place Pulse. Our dataset contains not only denser sampling, but also areas that were not present

a. The map on the left shows household income statistics, the map on the right shows our predicted scores.

b. The map on the left shows homicide statistics, the map on the right shows our predicted safety scores.

Fig. 10. The pair of maps on the left showcase the positive correlation between household income statistics and our predicted perceptual scores of wealthiness. The pair of maps on the right showcase the negative correlation between homicide statistics and our predicted perceptual scores of safety.

in the original study. For instance we include samples from extended areas like the Bronx. Figure 9 shows qualitative results for perceptions of wealth for the Bronx using our predicted scores. The results seem to confirm anecdotal evidence of affluence of certain areas in the Bronx such as Riverdale or Country Club, both upper middle class neighborhoods[1].

Correlation of Our Models with Crime Statistics: The authors of the Place Pulse dataset found that human perception judgments are informative about crime statistics of homicides for New York City. We go further, predicting safety, wealth, and uniqueness on two cities for which we have no ground truth perceptual judgments. We compute correlations between our predictions and reported statistics of homicides and household income per county[2]. We aggregate our predictions over counties and compare to reported statistics in Figure 10. We find a moderate positive Pearson-correlation coefficient of 0.51 between Baltimore household income and our predictions of wealth. In Figure 10a we observe good predictions for the two wealthiest counties in Baltimore, but miss a third cluster in South Baltimore. We also find a moderate negative Pearson-correlation coefficient of -0.36 between homicide statistics and our predictions of safety (Figure 10b). If we restrict our analysis to counties for which we have a larger number of sample images n then we obtain stronger correlations: $[0.53$ $(n > 200)$, 0.61 $(n > 300)$ for income/wealth predictions and $[-0.41$ $(n > 200)$,-0.47 $(n > 300)]$ for crime/safety predictions (by even denser sampling we could potentially extend this to all locations). For Chicago we find weaker correlation coefficients of 0.32 for wealth and -0.21 for safety when compared to similar statistics.

---

[1] http://en.wikipedia.org/wiki/Riverdale,_Bronx and
http://en.wikipedia.org/wiki/Country_Club,_Bronx

[2] Data obtained from the Baltimore City Health Department 2011 report and from http://www.robparal.com/ for Chicago.

7   Conclusions

In this paper we have shown that visual models can predict human perceptions of place. In particular, we demonstrated experimental evaluations for classification and regression predictions of safety, uniqueness, and wealth. We also produced models for joint prediction of perceptual characteristics. Finally, we demonstrated uses of our model for predicting perceptual characteristics at city scale and confirmed our findings for novel cities through correlations with crime statistics. These findings take us one step toward understanding sense of place.

Acknowledgments. This work was funded in part by NSF Awards 1445409 and 1444234.

References

1. Agarwal, S., Furukawa, Y., Snavely, N., Simon, I., Curless, B., Seitz, S.M., Szeliski, R.: Building rome in a day. Communications of the ACM 54(10), 105–112 (2011)
2. Arietta, S., Efros, A., Ramamoorthi, R., Agrawala, M.: City forensics: Using visual elements to predict non-visual city attributes. IEEE Transactions on Visualization and Computer Graphics (2014)
3. Boykov, Y., Kolmogorov, V.: An experimental comparison of min-cut/max-flow algorithms for energy minimization in vision. IEEE Transactions on Pattern Analysis and Machine Intelligence 26(9), 1124–1137 (2004)
4. Chatfield, K., Lempitsky, V., Vedaldi, A., Zisserman, A.: The devil is in the details: an evaluation of recent feature encoding methods. In: BMVC 2011 (2011)
5. Datta, R., Joshi, D., Li, J., Wang, J.Z.: Studying aesthetics in photographic images using a computational approach. In: Leonardis, A., Bischof, H., Pinz, A. (eds.) ECCV 2006. LNCS, vol. 3953, pp. 288–301. Springer, Heidelberg (2006)
6. Dhar, S., Ordonez, V., Berg, T.L.: High level describable attributes for predicting aesthetics and interestingness. In: 2011 IEEE Conference on Computer Vision and Pattern Recognition (CVPR), pp. 1657–1664. IEEE (2011)
7. Doersch, C., Singh, S., Gupta, A., Sivic, J., Efros, A.A.: What makes paris look like paris? ACM Transactions on Graphics (SIGGRAPH) 31(4) (2012)
8. Donahue, J., Jia, Y., Vinyals, O., Hoffman, J., Zhang, N., Tzeng, E., Darrell, T.: DeCAF: A Deep Convolutional Activation Feature for Generic Visual Recognition. ArXiv e-prints (October 2013)
9. Frahm, J.-M., et al.: Building rome on a cloudless day. In: Daniilidis, K., Maragos, P., Paragios, N. (eds.) ECCV 2010, Part IV. LNCS, vol. 6314, pp. 368–381. Springer, Heidelberg (2010)
10. Gould, S., Fulton, R., Koller, D.: Decomposing a scene into geometric and semantically consistent regions. In: ICCV (2009)
11. Hays, J., Efros, A.A.: Im2gps: estimating geographic information from a single image. In: IEEE Conference on Computer Vision and Pattern Recognition, CVPR 2008, pp. 1–8. IEEE (2008)
12. Isola, P., Parikh, D., Torralba, A., Oliva, A.: Understanding the intrinsic memorability of images. In: NIPS, pp. 2429–2437 (2011)

13. Juneja, M., Vedaldi, A., Jawahar, C.V., Zisserman, A.: Blocks that shout: Distinctive parts for scene classification. In: IEEE Conference on Computer Vision and Pattern Recognition (2013)
14. Khosla, A., An, B., Lim, J.J., Torralba, A.: Looking beyond the visible scene. In: IEEE Conference on Computer Vision and Pattern Recognition (CVPR), Ohio, USA (June 2014)
15. Ladicky, L., Russell, C., Kohli, P., Torr, P.H.: Associative hierarchical crfs for object class image segmentation. In: 2009 IEEE 12th International Conference on Computer Vision, pp. 739–746. IEEE (2009)
16. Lazebnik, S., Schmid, C., Ponce, J.: Beyond bags of features: Spatial pyramid matching for recognizing natural scene categories. In: 2006 IEEE Computer Society Conference on Computer Vision and Pattern Recognition, vol. 2, pp. 2169–2178. IEEE (2006)
17. Lee, Y.J., Efros, A.A., Hebert, M.: Style-aware mid-level representation for discovering visual connections in space and time. In: 2011 IEEE International Conference on Computer Vision (ICCV) (2013)
18. Li, L.-J., Su, H., Lim, Y., Fei-Fei, L.: Objects as attributes for scene classification. In: Kutulakos, K.N. (ed.) ECCV 2010 Workshops, Part I. LNCS, vol. 6553, pp. 57–69. Springer, Heidelberg (2012)
19. Lynch, K.: The image of the city, vol. 11. MIT Press (1960)
20. Marchesotti, L., Perronnin, F., Larlus, D., Csurka, G.: Assessing the aesthetic quality of photographs using generic image descriptors. In: 2011 IEEE International Conference on Computer Vision (ICCV), pp. 1784–1791. IEEE (2011)
21. Naik, N., Philipoom, J., Raskar, R., Hidalgo, C.: Streetscore-predicting the perceived safety of one million streetscapes. In: Proceedings of the IEEE Conference on Computer Vision and Pattern Recognition Workshops, pp. 779–785 (2014)
22. Oliva, A., Torralba, A.: Modeling the shape of the scene: A holistic representation of the spatial envelope. International Journal of Computer Vision 42(3), 145–175 (2001)
23. Park, J., Newman, M.E.: A network-based ranking system for us college football. Journal of Statistical Mechanics: Theory and Experiment 2005(10), P10014 (2005)
24. Patterson, G., Hays, J.: Sun attribute database: Discovering, annotating, and recognizing scene attributes. In: 2012 IEEE Conference on Computer Vision and Pattern Recognition (CVPR), pp. 2751–2758. IEEE (2012)
25. Perronnin, F., Sánchez, J., Mensink, T.: Improving the fisher kernel for large-scale image classification. In: Daniilidis, K., Maragos, P., Paragios, N. (eds.) ECCV 2010, Part IV. LNCS, vol. 6314, pp. 143–156. Springer, Heidelberg (2010)
26. Quattoni, A., Torralba, A.: Recognizing indoor scenes. In: IEEE Conference on Computer Vision and Pattern Recognition, CVPR 2009, pp. 413–420. IEEE (2009)
27. Quercia, D., O'Hare, N.K., Cramer, H.: Aesthetic capital: What makes london look beautiful, quiet, and happy? In: Proceedings of the 17th ACM Conference on Computer Supported Cooperative Work & Social Computing, CSCW 2014, pp. 945–955. ACM, New York (2014),
    http://doi.acm.org/10.1145/2531602.2531613
28. Salesses, P., Schechtner, K., Hidalgo, C.A.: The collaborative image of the city: mapping the inequality of urban perception. PloS One 8(7), e68400 (2013)
29. Sudderth, E., Torralba, A., Freeman, W., Willsky, A.: Learning hierarchical models of scenes, objects, and parts. In: ICCV (October 2005)
30. Tighe, J., Lazebnik, S.: Finding things: Image parsing with regions and per-exemplar detectors. In: CVPR (2013)

31. Tuan, Y.F.: Landscapes of fear. Basil Blackwell, Oxford (1980)
32. Wang, H., Gould, S., Koller, D.: Discriminative learning with latent variables for cluttered indoor scene understanding. Communications of the ACM, Research Highlights 56, 92–99 (2013)
33. Xiao, J., Hays, J., Ehinger, K.A., Oliva, A., Torralba, A.: Sun database: Large-scale scene recognition from abbey to zoo. In: 2010 IEEE Conference on Computer Vision and Pattern Recognition (CVPR), pp. 3485–3492. IEEE (2010)
34. Zamir, A.R., Shah, M.: Accurate image localization based on google maps street view. In: Daniilidis, K., Maragos, P., Paragios, N. (eds.) ECCV 2010, Part IV. LNCS, vol. 6314, pp. 255–268. Springer, Heidelberg (2010)

CollageParsing: Nonparametric Scene Parsing by Adaptive Overlapping Windows

Frederick Tung and James J. Little

Department of Computer Science, University of British Columbia, Vancouver, Canada
{ftung,little}@cs.ubc.ca

Abstract. Scene parsing is the problem of assigning a semantic label to every pixel in an image. Though an ambitious task, impressive advances have been made in recent years, in particular in scalable nonparametric techniques suitable for open-universe databases. This paper presents the CollageParsing algorithm for scalable nonparametric scene parsing. In contrast to common practice in recent nonparametric approaches, CollageParsing reasons about mid-level windows that are designed to capture entire objects, instead of low-level superpixels that tend to fragment objects. On a standard benchmark consisting of outdoor scenes from the LabelMe database, CollageParsing achieves state-of-the-art nonparametric scene parsing results with 7 to 11% higher average per-class accuracy than recent nonparametric approaches.

Keywords: image parsing, semantic segmentation, scene understanding.

1 Introduction

Computer vision enables us to understand scenes at many different levels of abstraction. At the most abstract, we may be concerned with determining the general semantic category of a scene [19], [26], [32], [36], such as *forest* or *urban*. Alternatively, instead of assigning an abstract category label to the scene, we may be interested in describing the scene by its semantic attributes [10], [27], [28], such as *rugged*. This paper is concerned with understanding scenes at the pixel level. Scene parsing is the challenging problem of assigning a semantic label to every pixel in the image. Semantic labels can span both amorphous background categories such as *grass* or *sea* (sometimes referred to "stuff" in the literature [16]), as well as localized object categories such as *person* or *car* (sometimes referred to as "things").

In recent years, the growth of online image collections and the adoption of crowdsourcing methods for annotating datasets have led to an interest in developing scalable methods that are suitable for open-universe datasets [34]. An open-universe dataset is one that is continually changing as users contribute new images and annotations, such as LabelMe [29]. Nonparametric methods are particularly well suited to open-universe datasets since they are data driven and require no training. As the dataset expands, there is no need to continually retrain the category models. This paper describes the CollageParsing algorithm for scalable nonparametric scene parsing.

D. Fleet et al. (Eds.): ECCV 2014, Part VI, LNCS 8694, pp. 511–525, 2014.
© Springer International Publishing Switzerland 2014

Current state-of-the-art nonparametric algorithms for scene parsing match superpixels in the query image with superpixels in contextually similar database images. An advantage of superpixel based parsing is the ability to label large, cohesive groups of pixels at once. However, while superpixel based techniques tend to effectively label large regions of background ("stuff") categories, they fare less well on object ("thing") categories. There are at least two reasons for this gap. First, superpixel features are not very discriminative for objects. State-of-the-art object recognition algorithms employ more discriminative HOG or SIFT based features. There is no widely accepted feature descriptor for superpixels; various low-level features are often combined heuristically. Second, superpixels tend to fragment objects. Conceptually, superpixel based techniques reason about pieces of objects and apply auxiliary techniques on top to combine these pieces in a principled way. For instance, semantic label co-occurrence probabilities are commonly incorporated via a Markov random field model [8], [21], [34].

CollageParsing addresses both of these issues through its use of mid-level, "content-adaptive" windows instead of low-level superpixels. Window selection is content-adaptive in the sense that it is designed to capture entire objects and not only fragments of objects (Section 3.2). Surrounding contextual information is also partially captured by the windows. To describe the content-adaptive windows, CollageParsing employs HOG features, which have been demonstrated to be effective for object recognition [6], [7], [12]. Figure 3, explained in more detail in Section 3.3, shows the intuition behind CollageParsing's window-based label transfer.

Parametric scene parsing methods have a small advantage in accuracy over nonparametric methods, however as a tradeoff they require large amounts of model training (for example, training just the per-exemplar detector component of the extended SuperParsing algorithm [33] on a dataset of 45,000 images requires four days on a 512-node cluster), making them less practical for open-universe datasets. As we show in the experiments, CollageParsing achieves state-of-the-art results among nonparametric scene parsing methods, and comparable performance with state-of-the-art parametric methods while not requiring expensive model training.

2   Related Work

Analyzing a scene at the level of labelling individual pixels with their semantic category is an ambitious task, but recent years have seen impressive progress in this direction.

Heitz and Koller [16] developed a graphical model to improve the detection of objects ("things") by making use of local context. In this work, local context refers to "stuff" classes such as *road* or *sky*. The "Things and Stuff" graphical model comprises candidate detection windows, region (superpixel) features, and their spatial relationships. Approximate inference is performed using Gibbs sampling.

Liu et al. [21] proposed the nonparametric label transfer technique for scene parsing. Liu et al.'s approach takes as input a database of scenes annotated with semantic labels. Given a query image to be segmented and labelled, the algorithm finds the image's nearest neighbors in the database, warps the neighbors to the query image using SIFT Flow [22], and "transfers" the annotations from the neighbors to the query image using a Markov random field model to integrate multiple cues.

Tighe and Lazebnik's SuperParsing algorithm [34] for scene parsing takes a similar nonparametric approach but operates on the level of superpixels. The query image's superpixels are labelled using a Markov random field model, based on similar superpixels in the query's nearest neighbor images in the database. The nonparametric semantic class labelling is combined with additional parametric geometry classification (sky, vertical, horizontal) to improve labelling consistency. Eigen and Fergus [8] proposed two extensions to SuperParsing. First, weights are learned for each descriptor in the database in a supervised manner to reduce the influence of distractor superpixels. Second, to improve the labelling of rare classes, the retrieved set of neighbor superpixels is augmented with superpixels from rare classes with similar local context. Myeong et al. [25] applied link prediction techniques to superpixels extracted from the query image and its nearest neighbors to learn the pairwise potentials for Markov random field based superpixel labeling, similar to SuperParsing. Singh and Košecká [31] proposed a nonparametric superpixel based method in which a locally adaptive nearest neighbor technique is used to obtain neighboring superpixels. The authors also proposed refining the retrieval set of query image neighbors by comparing spatial pyramids of predicted labels.

Instead of computing the set of nearest neighbor images at query time, the PatchMatchGraph method of Gould and Zhang [14] builds offline a graph of patch correspondences across all database images. Patch correspondences are found using an extended version of the PatchMatch algorithm [2] with additional "move" types for directing the local search for correspondences.

Farabet et al. [9] developed a parametric scene parsing algorithm combining several deep learning techniques. Dense multi-scale features are computed at each pixel and input to a trained neural network to obtain feature maps. Feature maps are aggregated over regions in a hierarchical segmentation tree. Regions are classified using a second neural network and pixels are finally labelled by the ancestor region with the highest purity score.

Tighe and Lazebnik [33] recently extended the SuperParsing algorithm with per-exemplar detectors (Exemplar-SVMs [23]). The data term based on superpixel matching is the same as in the SuperParsing algorithm. A detector based data term is obtained by running the per-exemplar detectors of class instances found in the retrieval set and accumulating a weighted sum of the detection masks. The two data terms are input to another trained SVM to obtain the class score for a pixel, and the final smooth class prediction is determined using a Markov random field.

Isola and Liu [18] proposed a "scene collage" model and explored applications in image editing, random scene synthesis, and image-to-anaglyph. In contrast to CollageParsing, the scene collage is an image representation: it represents an image by layers of warped segments from a dictionary.

3   Algorithm Description

Figure 1 shows a high-level overview of the CollageParsing pipeline. Given a database of images and a query image, the algorithm first finds the query image's nearest neighbors in the database according to a global image similarity measure (Section 3.1). The resulting short list of database images is referred to as the retrieval set. Content-adaptive windows are then extracted from the query image (Section 3.2). The query image's windows are matched with the content-adaptive windows in the retrieval set to compute a unary potential (or energy) for labelling each pixel with each semantic category (Section 3.3). The unary potential is combined with a pairwise potential in a Markov random field to obtain an initial labelling, which is refined by aligning the labelling to the query image's superpixels (Section 3.4). Finally, the previous steps are repeated with a *semantic* retrieval set consisting of similarly labelled images (Section 3.5).

3.1   Forming the Retrieval Set

The retrieval set aims to find a subset of database images that are contextually similar to the query image, and is a typical component of nonparametric scene analysis methods [15], [21], [34]. In addition to filtering out semantically irrelevant database images that are likely to be unhelpful, a small retrieval set makes nearest neighbor based label transfer practical on large datasets. To form the retrieval set, CollageParsing compares the query image to the database images using Gist [26] and HOG visual words [21], [37]. Specifically, the database images are sorted by similarity to the query image with respect to these two features, and the K best average ranks are selected as the retrieval set.

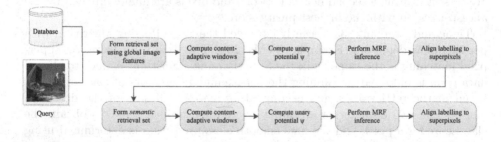

Fig. 1. High-level overview of the CollageParsing pipeline. A query image is labelled in two iterations of the pipeline. The first iteration computes a retrieval set from global image features (Gist and HOG visual words) and outputs an initial image labelling that is then used to produce a semantic retrieval set for the second iteration.

3.2   Computing Content-Adaptive Windows

To implement content-adaptive windows, the current implementation of CollageParsing adopts the "objectness" algorithm of Alexe et al. [1].

Alexe et al. [1] defined the "objectness" of an image window as the likelihood that the window contains a foreground object of any kind instead of background texture such as grass, sky, or road. The authors observed that objects often have a closed boundary, a contrasting appearance from surroundings, and/or are unique in the image. Several cues are proposed to capture these generic properties: multiscale saliency, colour contrast, edge density, and superpixels straddling. The multiscale saliency cue is a multiscale adaptation of Hou and Zhang's visual saliency algorithm [17]. The color contrast cue measures the difference between the color histograms of the window and its surrounding rectangular ring. The edge density cue measures the proportion of pixels in the window's inner rectangular ring that are classified as edgels. The superpixels straddling cue measures the extent to which superpixels straddle the window (contain pixels both inside and outside the window). Windows that tightly bound an object are likely to have low straddling. Cues are combined in a Naive Bayes model. Our implementation of CollageParsing uses Alexe et al.'s publicly available implementation of objectness[1] with the default parameter values. Figure 2 shows a few examples of content-adaptive windows extracted using the objectness algorithm.

Fig. 2. Examples of image windows with high "objectness" [1]. In each image, windows with the top five objectness scores are shown. Images are from the SIFT Flow dataset [21].

Other algorithms for generating class-generic object window predictions, such as van de Sande's hierarchical segmentation based windows [30], can also be used in place of objectness at this stage in the pipeline.

Conceptually, CollageParsing performs nonparametric label transfer by matching content-adaptive windows in the query image with content-adaptive windows in the retrieval set. Each content-adaptive window is described using HOG features. The HOG features are dimension and scale adaptive: the algorithm sets a target of six HOG cells along the longer dimension and allows the number of HOG cells along the shorter dimension to vary according to the window dimensions. When matching windows in the query image to windows in the retrieval set, only windows with the same HOG feature dimensions are compared. Each HOG feature vector is augmented with the scaled, normalized spatial coordinates of the window centroid, following the common practice of spatial coding

---

[1] v1.5, available at http://groups.inf.ed.ac.uk/calvin/objectness/

in object recognition methods [3], [24], [35]. Spatial coding encourages matches to come from spatially similar regions in the respective images.

3.3 Computing Unary Potentials

Figure 3 shows a high-level visualization of the computation of the unary potential. Conceptually, the unary potential is computed by transferring the category labels from the most similar content-adaptive windows in the retrieval set, in a collage-like manner.

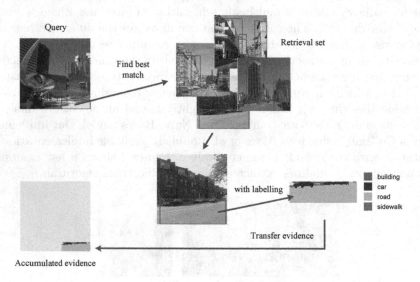

Fig. 3. Visualization of the computation of the unary potential ψ. The contribution of one window in the query image is depicted.

More formally, let $\psi(c, p)$ denote the unary potential or energy associated with assigning a semantic label of category c to pixel p:

$$\psi(c, p) = - \sum_{w \in W_q} \delta[L(\tilde{w}', p - \text{offset}(w)) = c]\phi_{\text{sim}}(w, w')\phi_{\text{idf}}(c) \qquad (1)$$

$$w' = \arg\min_{u \in W_{\text{rs}}} ||f(w) - f(u)||_2$$

$\tilde{w}'$ is w' resized to the dimensions of w

where w is a window in the set of content-adaptive windows in the query image, denoted W_q; $f(\cdot)$ is the HOG-based feature descriptor as described in Section 3.2; w' is the nearest neighbor window of w in the set of content-adaptive windows in the retrieval set, denoted W_{rs}; $\tilde{w}'$ is a resized version of w' such that it matches the dimensions of w; and $L(\cdot, \cdot)$ maps a window and an offset to a category label, or null if the offset is outside the window bounds. The term $p - \text{offset}(w)$

gives the window-centric coordinates of the pixel p in window w. Therefore, $L(\tilde{w}', p - \text{offset}(w))$ gives the category label of the projection or image of p in the matched window w'.

The term $\phi_{\text{sim}}(w, w')$ is a weight that is proportional to the similarity between w and w'. Intuitively, higher quality matches should have greater influence in the labelling. We define

$$\phi_{\text{sim}}(w, w') = s_f(w, w')s_l(w, w') \tag{2}$$

where $s_f(w, w')$ is the similarity between the two HOG-based feature descriptors, and to include color information $s_l(w, w')$ is the similarity between the windows' RGB color histograms. The feature descriptor distance is already computed in Eq. 1 and we convert it to a similarity score by

$$s_f(w, w') = \exp(-\alpha||f(w) - f(u)||_2) \tag{3}$$

where α controls the exponential falloff. For the similarity between the windows' color histograms we take the histogram intersection.

The term $\phi_{\text{idf}}(c)$ is a weight that is inversely proportional to the frequency of category c in the retrieval set:

$$\phi_{\text{idf}}(c) = \frac{1}{N(c)^\gamma} \tag{4}$$

where $N(c)$ denotes the number of pixels of category c in the retrieval set. Eq. 4 performs a softened IDF-style weighting to account for differences in the frequency of categories. The constant γ controls the strength of the penalty given to high frequency categories, and as we show later in the experiments, influences the tradeoff between overall per-pixel and average per-class accuracy.

After computing $\psi(c, p)$ for all categories c and pixels p in the query image, all values are rescaled to be between -1 and 0.

Figure 4 visualizes the unary potential for an example query image from the SIFT Flow dataset [21].

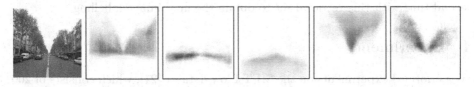

Fig. 4. Visualization of the unary potential for a sample query image (see also bottom row of Fig. 7). From left to right: building, car, road, sky, and tree categories.

3.4   Performing MRF Inference

The unary potential ψ is combined with a pairwise potential θ defined over pairs of adjacent pixels. For θ we adopt the same pairwise potential term as in SuperParsing, which is based on the co-occurrences of category labels [34]:

$$\theta(c_p, c_q) = -\log[(P(c_p|c_q) + P(c_q|c_p))/2]\delta[c_p \neq c_q] \qquad (5)$$

where c_p and c_p are the category labels assigned to pixels p and q, which are adjacent. Intuitively, the pairwise term biases the labelling towards category transitions that are more frequently observed.

The global MRF energy function over the field of category labels $\mathbf{c} = \{c_p\}_{p \in I}$ is given by

$$E(\mathbf{c}) = \sum_{p \in I} \psi(c_p, p) + \lambda \sum_{(p,q) \in \varepsilon} \theta(c_p, c_q) \qquad (6)$$

where ε is the set of pixel pairs (adjacent pixels) and λ is the MRF smoothing constant. The MRF energy is minimized using α/β-swap, a standard graph cuts technique [4], [5], [20].

To improve the alignment of the labelling with the query image structure, the labelling is then refined so that superpixels in the query image share the same label. All pixels within a superpixel are assigned the most common (mode) label in the superpixel. Superpixels are extracted using the graph-based method of Felzenszwalb and Huttenlocher [11], following Tighe and Lazebnik [34].

3.5   Retrieving Semantic Neighbors

Recall that the original retrieval set consisted of database images with similar Gist and HOG visual words to the query image (Section 3.1). Ideally, a retrieval set should consist of *semantically* similar database images. A retrieval set constructed from global image features provides a good first approximation. As a second approximation, the query image labelling is used to retrieve similarly labelled database images. Specifically, the database images are ranked by the pixel-by-pixel labelling correspondence with the query image labelling (in practice, the label fields may need to be resized). The K top ranked database images form the semantic retrieval set, and the CollageParsing pipeline is executed a second time with this retrieval set to obtain the final image labelling.

4   Experiments

We performed experiments on the SIFT Flow dataset [21], which consists of 200 query images and 2,488 database images from LabelMe. Images span a range of outdoor scene types, from natural to urban. Pixels are labelled with one of 33 semantic categories. The label frequencies are shown in Figure 5.

Table 1 shows the experimental results and a comparison with the state-of-the-art nonparametric and parametric approaches on this dataset. We set the

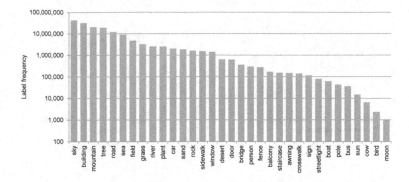

Fig. 5. Frequency counts of the semantic categories in the SIFT Flow dataset

Table 1. Per-pixel and per-class labelling accuracy on the SIFT Flow dataset [21]

	Per-pixel	Per-class
State-of-the-art nonparametric		
Liu et al. [21]	76.7	-
Gould and Zhang [14]	65.2	14.9
Tighe and Lazebnik [34]	77.0	30.1
Myeong et al. [25]	77.1	32.3
Eigen and Fergus [8]	77.1	32.5
Singh and Košecká [31]	79.2	33.8
CollageParsing	77.1	41.1
State-of-the-art parametric		
Farabet et al. [9], "natural"	78.5	29.6
Farabet et al. [9], "balanced"	74.2	46.0
Tighe and Lazebnik [33]	78.6	39.2

retrieval set size $K = 400$, $\alpha = 0.1$, $\gamma = 0.38$, and the MRF smoothing parameter λ to 0.01. We investigate the effect of these parameters on the algorithm performance later in this section. Both the overall per-pixel accuracy and the average per-class accuracy are reported. Average per-class accuracy is a more reliable measure of how well the algorithm performs across different categories, not just on the most commonly occurring ones.

CollageParsing obtains higher per-class accuracy than all state-of-the-art nonparametric alternatives, by a wide margin, demonstrating its effectiveness across different categories and not only common "stuff" categories such as sky or grass. In particular, gains of 7 to 11% in per-class accuracy are obtained over state-of-the-art superpixel based approaches [8], [25], [31], [34], confirming our intuition described earlier that reasoning about mid-level, content-adaptive windows can be more productive than reasoning about low-level fragments.

CollageParsing's performance is also comparable to state-of-the-art parametric approaches. Compared with Tighe and Lazebnik's extended SuperParsing

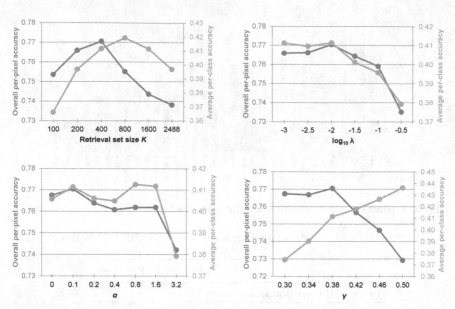

Fig. 6. Effects of varying the retrieval set size K, the MRF smoothing parameter λ, α, and γ on overall per-pixel accuracy and average per-class accuracy

algorithm with per-exemplar detectors and a combination SVM [33], CollagePars-ing obtains 1.9% higher per-class accuracy and 1.5% lower per-pixel accuracy. Compared with Farabet et al.'s system [9] with "natural" training, at a tradeoff of 1.4% lower per-pixel accuracy an 11.5% per-class improvement is obtained. Farabet et al.'s system with "balanced" training achieves higher per-class accuracy, however at this setting the per-pixel accuracy falls below almost all nonparametric approaches in Table 1.

In contrast to state-of-the-art parametric approaches, as a nonparametric approach CollageParsing does not require expensive model training. As discussed in Section 1, this characteristic makes CollageParsing (and other nonparametric approaches) particularly well suited for open-universe datasets since no model re-training is required as the dataset expands. On a dataset of 45,000 images with 232 semantic labels, just the per-exemplar detector component of Tighe and Lazebnik [33] requires four days on a 512-node cluster to train. On a dataset of 715 images with eight semantic labels [13], Farabet et al. [9] requires "48h on a regular server" to train. At query time, our current implementation of CollageParsing requires approximately two minutes on a desktop to label an image through two passes of the pipeline (Figure 1). Our current implementation contains Matlab components that are not yet optimized for speed, and further improvements in the labelling time may be possible in future. Labelling time can also be reduced by stopping after a single pass of the pipeline, skipping the second pass with a semantic retrieval set. A modest cost in labelling accuracy is incurred. On the SIFT Flow dataset, the second pass with a semantic retrieval set improves per-pixel accuracy by 2.0% and per-class accuracy by 1.4%.

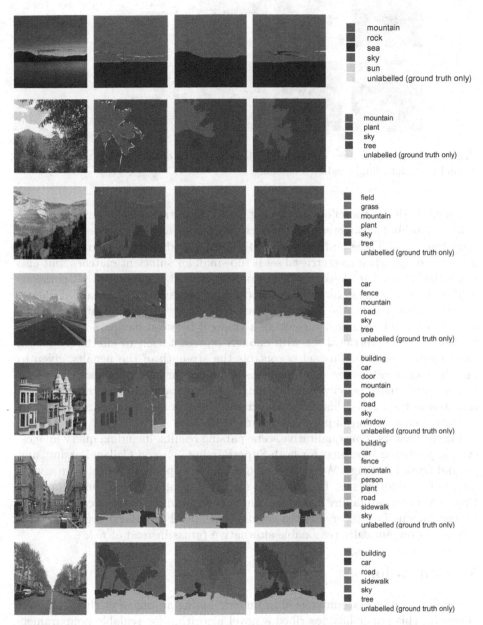

Fig. 7. Examples of scene parsing results on the SIFT Flow dataset. From left to right: query image, ground truth labelling, SuperParsing [34] predicted labelling, CollageParsing predicted labelling.

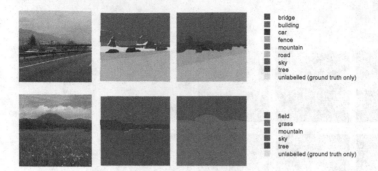

Fig. 8. Examples of failures on the SIFT Flow dataset. From left to right: query image, ground truth labelling, predicted labelling.

Figure 6 shows the effect of varying α, γ, the retrieval set size K, and the MRF smoothing parameter λ on the overall per-pixel and average per-class accuracy. Similar to Tighe and Lazebnik [34], we observed that the overall per-pixel accuracy drops when the retrieval set is too small for sufficient matches, but also when the retrieval set becomes large, confirming that the retrieval set performs a filtering role in matching query windows to semantically relevant database images. Interestingly, the average per-class accuracy drops off later than the overall per-pixel accuracy, suggesting a tradeoff between having a compact retrieval set and a retrieval set with enough representation to effectively match rarer categories. The constant γ controls the strength of the penalty given to high frequency categories. As γ increases, evidence for high frequency categories is discounted more heavily, and labelling is biased towards rarer categories. As reflected in the figure, this tends to increase the average per-class accuracy but at the expense of overall per-pixel accuracy.

Figure 7 shows some qualitative scene parsing results, including query images, system predicted labellings for both SuperParsing [34] and CollageParsing, and ground truth labellings. We found CollageParsing to perform robustly on a wide range of outdoor scenes, from natural (top) to urban (bottom) environments. Figure 8 shows two failure examples. The second example shows a case in which CollageParsing fails to predict the ground truth label for a large region but still provides a semantically reasonable alternative (*grass* instead of *field*).

5   Conclusion

In scene parsing we are interested in understanding an image at the pixel level of detail. This paper has described a novel algorithm for scalable nonparametric scene parsing that reasons about mid-level, content-adaptive windows, in contrast to recent state-of-the-art methods that focus on lower level superpixels. The CollageParsing pipeline consists of forming a retrieval set of similar database images, computing content-adaptive windows using the objectness technique [1], matching content-adaptive windows to accumulate a unary potential or energy for labelling each pixel with each semantic category label, and combining the unary potential with a co-occurrence based pairwise potential in a Markov random field framework. The initial labelling from Markov random field inference is refined by aligning the labelling with the query image superpixels. Finally, a second pass through the pipeline is taken with a semantic retrieval set of similarly labelled database images. Experiments on the SIFT Flow benchmark [21] demonstrate the viability of CollageParsing, which obtains 7 to 11% higher average per-class accuracy than state-of-the-art nonparametric methods [8], [25], [31], [34], and comparable accuracy with state-of-the-art parametric methods [9], [33] while not requiring expensive model training.

As future work we plan to investigate whether other relevant image inference can be incorporated into the CollageParsing pipeline to further improve performance, such as the geometric inference that complements the semantic labelling in SuperParsing [34]. We would also like to assess the feasibility of using approximate nearest neighbor search methods to speed up window matching at query time.

Acknowledgements. This work was funded in part by the Natural Sciences and Engineering Research Council of Canada.

References

1. Alexe, B., Deselaers, T., Ferrari, V.: Measuring the objectness of image windows. IEEE Transactions on Pattern Analysis and Machine Intelligence 34(11), 2189–2202 (2012)
2. Barnes, C., Shechtman, E., Finkelstein, A., Goldman, D.B.: PatchMatch: a randomized correspondence algorithm for structural image editing. In: Proc. ACM SIGGRAPH (2009)
3. Boiman, O., Shechtman, E., Irani, M.: In defense of nearest-neighbor based image classification. In: Proc. IEEE Conference on Computer Vision and Pattern Recognition (2008)
4. Boykov, Y., Kolmogorov, V.: An experimental comparison of min-cut/max-flow algorithms for energy minimization in vision. IEEE Transactions on Pattern Analysis and Machine Intelligence 26(9), 1124–1137 (2004)
5. Boykov, Y., Veksler, O., Zabih, R.: Efficient approximate energy minimization via graph cuts. IEEE Transactions on Pattern Analysis and Machine Intelligence 20(12), 1222–1239 (2001)
6. Chen, X., Shrivastava, A., Gupta, A.: NEIL: extracting visual knowledge from web data. In: Proc. IEEE International Conference on Computer Vision (2013)
7. Dalal, N., Triggs, B.: Histograms of oriented gradients for human detection. In: Proc. IEEE Conf. Computer Vision and Pattern Recognition, vol. 1, pp. 886–893 (2005)
8. Eigen, D., Fergus, R.: Nonparametric image parsing using adaptive neighbor sets. In: Proc. IEEE Conference on Computer Vision and Pattern Recognition, pp. 2799–2806 (2012)
9. Farabet, C., Couprie, C., Najman, L., LeCun, Y.: Scene parsing with multiscale feature learning, purity trees, and optimal covers. In: Proc. International Conference on Machine Learning (2012)

10. Farhadi, A., Endres, I., Hoiem, D., Forsyth, D.: Describing objects by their attributes. In: Proc. IEEE Conference on Computer Vision and Pattern Recognition, pp. 1778–1785 (2009)
11. Felzenszwalb, P.F., Huttenlocher, D.P.: Efficient graph-based image segmentation. International Journal of Computer Vision 59(2), 167–181 (2004)
12. Felzenszwalb, P., Girshick, R., McAllester, D., Ramanan, D.: Object detection with discriminatively trained part-based models. IEEE Transactions on Pattern Analysis and Machine Intelligence 32(9), 1627–1645 (2010)
13. Gould, S., Fulton, R., Koller, D.: Decomposing a scene into geometric and semantically consistent regions. In: Proc. IEEE International Conference on Computer Vision (2009)
14. Gould, S., Zhang, Y.: PATCHMATCHGRAPH: Building a graph of dense patch correspondences for label transfer. In: Fitzgibbon, A., Lazebnik, S., Perona, P., Sato, Y., Schmid, C. (eds.) ECCV 2012, Part V. LNCS, vol. 7576, pp. 439–452. Springer, Heidelberg (2012)
15. Hays, J., Efros, A.A.: Scene completion using millions of photographs. In: Proc. ACM SIGGRAPH (2007)
16. Heitz, G., Koller, D.: Learning spatial context: Using stuff to find things. In: Forsyth, D., Torr, P., Zisserman, A. (eds.) ECCV 2008, Part I. LNCS, vol. 5302, pp. 30–43. Springer, Heidelberg (2008)
17. Hou, X., Zhang, L.: Saliency detection: a spectral residual approach. In: Proc. IEEE Conference on Computer Vision and Pattern Recognition (2007)
18. Isola, P., Liu, C.: Scene collaging: analysis and synthesis of natural images with semantic layers. In: Proc. IEEE International Conference on Computer Vision (2013)
19. Juneja, M., Vedaldi, A., Jawahar, C.V., Zisserman, A.: Blocks that shout: distinctive parts for scene classification. In: Proc. IEEE Conference on Computer Vision and Pattern Recognition (2013)
20. Kolmogorov, V., Zabih, R.: What energy functions can be minimized via graph cuts? IEEE Transactions on Pattern Analysis and Machine Intelligence 26(2), 147–159 (2004)
21. Liu, C., Yuen, J., Torralba, A.: Nonparametric scene parsing via label transfer. IEEE Transactions on Pattern Analysis and Machine Intelligence 33(12), 2368–2382 (2011)
22. Liu, C., Yuen, J., Torralba, A.: SIFT Flow: dense correspondence across scenes and its applications. IEEE Transactions on Pattern Analysis and Machine Intelligence 33(5), 978–994 (2011)
23. Malisiewicz, T., Gupta, A., Efros, A.A.: Ensemble of Exemplar-SVMs for object detection and beyond. In: Proc. IEEE International Conference on Computer Vision, pp. 89–96 (2011)
24. McCann, S., Lowe, D.G.: Spatially local coding for object recognition. In: Lee, K.M., Matsushita, Y., Rehg, J.M., Hu, Z. (eds.) ACCV 2012, Part I. LNCS, vol. 7724, pp. 204–217. Springer, Heidelberg (2013)
25. Myeong, H., Chang, J.Y., Lee, K.M.: Learning object relationships via graph-based context model. In: Proc. IEEE Conference on Computer Vision and Pattern Recognition, pp. 2727–2734 (2012)
26. Oliva, A., Torralba, A.: Modeling the shape of the scene: a holistic representation of the spatial envelope. International Journal of Computer Vision 42(3), 145–175 (2001)
27. Parikh, D., Grauman, K.: Relative attributes. In: Proc. IEEE International Conference on Computer Vision, pp. 503–510 (2011)

28. Patterson, G., Hays, J.: SUN Attribute database: discovering, annotating, and recognizing scene attributes. In: Proc. IEEE Conference on Computer Vision and Pattern Recognition, pp. 2751–2758 (2012)

29. Russell, B.C., Torralba, A., Murphy, K., Freeman, W.T.: LabelMe: a database and web-based tool for image annotation. International Journal of Computer Vision 77(1-3), 157–173 (2008)

30. van de Sande, K.E.A., Uijlings, J.R.R., Gevers, T., Smeulders, A.W.M.: Segmentation as selective search for object recognition. In: Proc. IEEE International Conference on Computer Vision, pp. 1879–1886 (2011)

31. Singh, G., Košecká, J.: Nonparametric scene parsing with adaptive feature relevance and semantic context. In: Proc. IEEE Conference on Computer Vision and Pattern Recognition, pp. 3151–3157 (2013)

32. Singh, S., Gupta, A., Efros, A.A.: Unsupervised discovery of mid-level discriminative patches. In: Fitzgibbon, A., Lazebnik, S., Perona, P., Sato, Y., Schmid, C. (eds.) ECCV 2012, Part II. LNCS, vol. 7573, pp. 73–86. Springer, Heidelberg (2012)

33. Tighe, J., Lazebnik, S.: Finding things: image parsing with regions and per-exemplar detectors. In: Proc. IEEE Conference on Computer Vision and Pattern Recognition, pp. 3001–3008 (2013)

34. Tighe, J., Lazebnik, S.: Superparsing: scalable nonparametric image parsing with superpixels. International Journal of Computer Vision 101(2), 329–349 (2013)

35. Tuytelaars, T., Fritz, M., Saenko, K., Darrell, T.: The NBNN kernel. In: Proc. IEEE International Conference on Computer Vision, pp. 1824–1831 (2011)

36. Wu, J., Rehg, J.M.: CENTRIST: a visual descriptor for scene categorization. IEEE Transactions on Pattern Analysis and Machine Intelligence 33(8), 1489–1501 (2011)

37. Xiao, J., Hays, J., Ehinger, K., Oliva, A., Torralba, A.: SUN database: large-scale scene recognition from abbey to zoo. In: Proc. IEEE Conference on Computer Vision and Pattern Recognition, pp. 3485–3492 (2010)

Discovering Video Clusters from Visual Features and Noisy Tags

Arash Vahdat, Guang-Tong Zhou, and Greg Mori

School of Computing Science, Simon Fraser University, Canada
{avahdat,gza11,mori}@cs.sfu.ca

Abstract. We present an algorithm for automatically clustering tagged videos. Collections of tagged videos are commonplace, however, it is not trivial to discover video clusters therein. Direct methods that operate on visual features ignore the regularly available, valuable source of tag information. Solely clustering videos on these tags is error-prone since the tags are typically noisy. To address these problems, we develop a structured model that considers the interaction between visual features, video tags and video clusters. We model tags from visual features, and correct noisy tags by checking visual appearance consistency. In the end, videos are clustered from the refined tags as well as the visual features. We learn the clustering through a max-margin framework, and demonstrate empirically that this algorithm can produce more accurate clustering results than baseline methods based on tags or visual features, or both. Further, qualitative results verify that the clustering results can discover sub-categories and more specific instances of a given video category.

1 Introduction

We have witnessed substantial progress in the acquisition and storage of videos. For example, there are 100 hours of videos uploaded to YouTube every single minute [1]. With this rapid increase in the scale of video collection, effective and efficient video analysis techniques are increasingly in demand and crucial for organization of this content.

Automatic clustering of videos is an essential means of video analysis. Clustering has important uses – it can provide users with browsing capability, enabling exploration of the content of a video dataset. It can also provide sub-categories, that can for instance be used to train specific detectors for different sub-categories or otherwise provide a more detailed understanding of a topic.

To cluster videos, a straight-forward approach is to extract visual features (e.g. HOG3D [2]) from video appearance, and then apply a standard clustering algorithm. For instance, Wang et al. [3] cluster images strictly based on appearance, and Niebles et al. [4] develop topic models based on video bag-of-words approaches. However, these methods are generally limited in performance due to the lack of semantics in low-level visual appearance.

To bridge the semantic gap, other approaches turn to semantic cues associated with a video. Video tags are often considered for this purpose due to their easy

D. Fleet et al. (Eds.): ECCV 2014, Part VI, LNCS 8694, pp. 526–539, 2014.
© Springer International Publishing Switzerland 2014

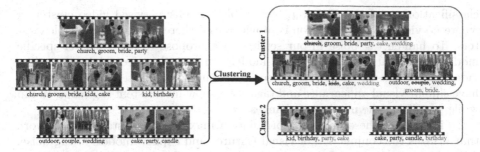

Fig. 1. Video tags provide rich information that can be used for discovering clusters from unconstrained web videos. An algorithm for automatically clustering videos with noisy tags is proposed that explicitly models tag label noise. The proposed approach can be used to remove noisy tags or to add missing tags to a video while finding clusters.

accessibility. These tags range from user-generated content to video captions to semantically meaningful attributes automatically produced by vision algorithms. Different from the low-level visual cues extracted from video appearance, tags provide a complementary view of high-level video semantics. There has been much work in recent years clustering tagged videos. For example, Zeng et al. [5] utilize a learned model over text-based tags to cluster search results. Schroff et al. [6] cluster videos by location based tags. Hsu et al. [7] build hierarchical clustering using tags extracted from user-contributed comments.

Note that visual features and tags are two heterogeneous cues. It is intuitive and beneficial to combine them into a single clustering framework. However, implementing the "combination" is non-trivial. As revealed in our experiments, simply concatenating the two features does not work well since it disregards the hierarchical nature in between low-level visual features and high-level tag semantics. Even a "hierarchical" model – for example, Zhou et al. [8] build tag models from visual features and then use the resultant tag models to assist in clustering – leads to sub-optimal performance. It is because this type of methods learn tag models and clustering in two disjoint processes, and there is no interaction among them. To address the problem, we develop a structured model that jointly considers the interaction between visual features, video tags and video clusters – tags are modeled beyond visual features, and video clusters are determined by jointly examining the tags and visual features.

Another serious problem related to tagged video clustering is that tags are always noisy – obtaining perfect, accurate tags is unlikely in any realistic setting. Consider the examples of tagged videos in Fig. 1. Some tags relevant to the video content are mentioned, while others are "false positives", either irrelevant to the content or not visually discernible. Further, tags are not mentioned with perfect recall – if a tag is not present it does not mean the corresponding concept is not in a video. See the tags highlighted in red in Figure 1 for an example. A recent solution by Vahdat and Mori [9] suggests to "flip" a tag label by revealing the inconsistency of video appearance with other videos (from the same class) that share the same tag. Note that this solution is tailored to supervised binary classification problems. However, our problem is unsupervised video clustering where no video-level supervision is provided and there are always multiple clusters. To handle tag noise in our settings, we propose to learn cluster-specific models in a joint framework. Each model can actively select high-responding videos as its cluster members. Videos from the same cluster are expected to have similar visual appearance and tags – we allow inconsistent tag labels to flip while penalizing the number of changes.

To implement these ideas, we formulate a max-margin clustering framework that utilizes the conjunction of visual features and explicit models of tag noise. An alternating descent algorithm is developed to effectively solve the resultant non-convex optimization problem. We show empirically that our method aids in clustering, and outperforms approaches that are based strictly on text-based tags or prediction of tags from visual data. Quantitative results show that the method recovers more accurate clusters, and qualitative results further demonstrate the ability to discover sub-categories among videos of a given type.

2   Previous Work

There exists a rich literature on video analysis. In this work, we focus on "unconstrained" videos that are collected by users in a variety of acquisition environments. Specifically, we work on the TRECVID MED collection [10] which provides a standard benchmark for unconstrained web video analysis.

Video analysis mainly includes the tasks of video clustering, video retrieval and video recognition. We have reviewed various video clustering methods above, so we omit their description here for brevity. For video retrieval, significant research effort has been devoted in the form of event detection applied to the TRECVID MED collection. We refer the readers to an excellent state-of-the-art work of Natarajan et al. [11] for more details. Video recognition has been an active research area in computer vision. For example, Izadinia and Shah [12] recognized complex video events (e.g. "parade", "landing fish") from low-level event tags (e.g. "people marching", "person reeling"). A recent work by Vahdat and Mori [9] developed a method for modeling tag label noise for improving video classification. We build on this line of work, instead focusing on the problem of unsupervised video clustering. Furthermore, beyond single event-level labeling for videos, other research has focused on labeling videos with a set of tags. A representative work in this area by Qi et al. [13] predicted multiple correlative tags in a structural SVM framework. The obtained tags can aid in video clustering, retrieval and recognition tasks.

The framework we develop for clustering is based on the max-margin clustering (MMC) approach of Xu et al. [14], which searches for clusterings of input instances that have a large margin between different clusters. As compared to other standard clustering methods (such as K-means and Spectral Clustering), MMC jointly optimizes cluster-specific models and instance-specific labeling assignments, and often generates better clusters [14–17]. A recent work by Zhou et al. [8] applied a variant of MMC to cluster videos with latent tags. We extend this framework by two aspects: i) we explicitly model tag noise, and show that incorporating noisy labels can produce more accurate clustering; and ii) (as mentioned before) we use a structured model to capture interaction between visual features, tags and video clusters, instead of using two disjoint processes for learning tag models and clustering [8].

Sub-categories have been studied in the context of fine-grained recognition of a given class or topic. The most popular technique for sub-categorization uses latent variable models: it first utilizes clustering strategies to initialize sub-categories, and then encode sub-category information as latent variables for learning sub-category models. Yang and Toderici [18] use co-watch data to learn sub-categories on YouTube videos. Hoai and Zisserman [19] develop a discriminative approach to sub-category discovery. We show that our clustering algorithm can be used to discover sub-categories within a video category, and different from previous approaches we utilize a structured noisy tag model for this clustering.

3   Tag-Based Video Clustering

Consider the problem of discovering clusters of similar videos in unconstrained web videos, similar to YouTube-type videos generated by amateur users. In the most naive way, one can extract visual features from videos and cluster them in visual feature space using off-the-shelf techniques like K-means. The main drawback of this technique is that the formed clusters tend to lack semantic meaning. The problem arises from the underlying visual features used in the clustering. Low level features often fail to represent higher level semantics. Therefore, the resultant clusters are created according to the distance of input samples in the visual feature space which may not match to the conceptual difference that humans associate to the samples.

In contrast, one can explore other sources of information for video clustering rather than pure visual features. Often there are other data available, such as user-provided tags which are common among internet video sharing websites. Tags may refer to objects, actions, scenes or other semantically meaningful entities in a video. Clusters formed on tags are more likely to be semantically meaningful clusters than those created using visual features solely, as the clusters are created in semantically meaningful tag space where similar videos are more likely to share the same tags.

However, tags available on video sharing websites are typically very noisy. The source of noise may vary in different cases, but mainly it can be due to the ambiguity of the process. Tagging is a very subjective task and users may not agree on the tags that should be assigned to the same video. Users can fail to identify some tags relevant to their content; sometimes they introduce spam tags to increase their chance in the retrieval process by misleading the system with tags that are not actually present in their video. In this case, clusters created from tags will be prone to this noise, and may represent a group of irrelevant videos. On the other hand, obtaining high-quality and noise-free tags can be a very expensive annotation process.

In this paper, we are aiming at an alternative approach to video clustering that works with noisy tags. To implement the idea, we develop a structured model that considers the interaction between video visual features, video tags and video clusters. This structured model enables us to detect tags in a video that are correlated with clusters. In contrast to previous tag-based clustering approaches (e.g. [8]), our model will be equipped with a tag model that recognizes tags on a video using visual features. The tag model will help us detect noise by revealing the inconsistency of a video's visual features with the other samples that share the same tag.

First, we introduce the details of the visual feature-tag-clustering model used for detecting tags and clustering videos. Next, in Sec. 3.2 we present structured max-margin clustering approach followed by our flip max-margin clustering approach that clusters videos using noisy tags in Sec. 3.3. Finally, the details of the optimization are described in Sec. 3.4.

3.1   Cluster Model for Visual Features and Tags

In this work, a structured model is defined for representing the relationship between visual features and tags in a video cluster. The model is designed such that both video clustering and tagging can be performed jointly. For this purpose, we incorporate a tag model to detect tags present in a video, and a tag-cluster interaction model to represent the correlated tags and clusters.

Let us represent a video by x and a set of T binary tags using $\mathbf{t} = \{t_i\}$ for $i = 1, 2, \ldots, T$ where $t_i \in \{-1, 1\}$ represents the presence and absence of i-th tag respectively by 1 and -1. The scoring function $w^\top \phi(x, \mathbf{t}, y)$, which measures the compatibility score between cluster y and tag labeling $\mathbf{t}$ for the video x is defined as:

$$w^\top \phi(x, \mathbf{t}, y) = \sum_{i=1}^{T} t_i \alpha_i^\top \theta(x) + \sum_{i=1}^{T} \beta_{i,y}^\top \varphi(t_i) \tag{1}$$

Here, $\theta(x)$ is a global feature extracted from video x, α_i is the appearance parameter for the i-th label and the term $t_i \alpha_i^\top \theta(x)$ measures the compatibility of the global feature with the i-th tag label. $\varphi(t_i)$ is a vector of size two that indicates whether -1 or 1 has been taken by t_i using $[1, 0]$ or $[0, 1]$, and, $\beta_{i,y}^\top \varphi(t_i)$ measures the compatibility between the i-th tag and the cluster y. Specifically, $\beta_{i,y}$ is a two-dimensional weight vector that represents how likely each case of the tag t_i (e.g. presence as $t_i = 1$ or absence as $t_i = -1$) is associated with the cluster y. Naturally, a large value of $\beta_{i,y}$ on the presence case means that videos in the cluster y tend to have the tag t_i, and a large value of $\beta_{i,y}$ on the absence case means that videos in the cluster y tend to not have the tag t_i. $\{\alpha_i\}_{i=1}^{i=T}$ and $\{\beta_{i,y}\}_{i=1,y=1}^{i=T,y=K}$ are the parameters of our model that are represented altogether by w. Next, the training criterion for learning w is discussed.

3.2 Structured Max-Margin Clustering

The goal of video clustering is to group videos into clusters such that videos in the same cluster are similar. A variety of clustering methods exists in the literature, using different video features and different clustering criteria.

First of all, the features used in clustering have crucial impact on the quality of clusters. Video clustering may be performed over low-level visual features, or semantically meaningful tags, or both.

Apart from the features, the clustering criterion constitutes another dimension of flexibility. Among the widely used approaches, K-means assigns samples to clusters such that intra-cluster variation is minimum, or Spectral Clustering [20] uses eigenvalues of the affinity matrix of the data to map data to an embedding space before clustering. Max-margin clustering (MMC) [14] instead finds a labeling so that the margin between clusters will be maximal.

Here, we extend the MMC approach to the case that there is a structured labeling of tags for each input video available for training. We present a new clustering framework that learns the parameters of the model such that both tag prediction and video clustering can be performed jointly. Given N training videos, $\{x_n, \mathbf{t}_n\}_{n=1}^{n=N}$ to be clustered into K clusters, the goal of structured max-margin clustering (Structured MMC) is to find the labeling $y_n \in \{1, 2, \ldots, K\}$ using the following optimization problem:

$$\min_{w, \xi_n, y_n} \frac{\lambda}{2} ||w||_2^2 + \sum_{n=1}^{N} \xi_n \tag{2}$$

$$\text{s.t.} \quad w^\top \phi(x_n, \mathbf{t}_n, y_n) \geq w^\top \phi(x_n, \mathbf{t}, y) + \Delta_{\mathbf{t}, \mathbf{t}_n}^{y, y_n} - \xi_n \quad \forall \mathbf{t}, \forall y$$

$$L \leq \sum_{n=1}^{N} \mathbb{1}_{(y_n = k)} \leq U \qquad \forall k \in \{1, 2, \ldots, K\}$$

which minimizes the norm of parameters $||w||_2^2$ while assigning training examples to clusters as well as tagging them with a minimum structured error measured by the slack variables ξ_n. λ is a hyper parameter that controls the balance between the norm of model parameters and constraint violation. The first constraint enforces that the compatibility score of video x_n, its tag label $\mathbf{t}_n$ and assigned cluster y_n is greater than any other hypothesized labeling. Here, the margin is re-scaled based on how different the hypothesized labeling is from the annotation using the loss function $\Delta_{\mathbf{t}, \mathbf{t}_n}^{y, y_n}$. Note that the loss function is a function of both cluster assignments and video tags. Therefore, the Structured MMC defined in Eq. 2 not only maximizes the margin between clusters, but also learns parameters such that the annotated tags have higher scores than hypothesized tag labels.

The second constraint in Eq. 2 enforces balanced clusters where L and U are the lower and upper bounds controlling the size of each cluster. The same constraint is used in [8] to prevent the algorithm from finding the trivial clustering that assigns all the videos to one cluster.

Note that the optimization problem in Eq. 2 differs from previous clustering techniques in that both the structured prediction of tags and clustering are formulated in a unified framework. This is an essential capability as after learning model parameters, w, using training videos, the model can potentially be used to jointly tag and cluster unseen videos.

3.3 Flip Max-Margin Clustering

The Structured MMC algorithm described above relies on the tags given in the training phase. However, in the case of noisy tags the quality of clusters can be poor since they are formed based on unreliable tags. Further, tags that are missing on training videos can have a significant effect on the clustering results, since the model will unduly penalize their absence on a particular video.

Instead of treating the tags provided on training videos as fixed, we explicitly model the possibility of incorrect tags on input videos. Motivated by the idea of Flip SVM [9], we propose flip max-margin clustering (Flip MMC) that is allowed to change tags in the course of training. In this approach, the training algorithm may correct some tag label noise by considering their inconsistency in visual feature space with respect to the videos sharing the same tag. But at the same time, the algorithm is penalized for label changes to prevent the situation where all the tags are set to the same category.

In order to operationalize this idea, we modify the optimization problem for Structured MMC in Eq. 2. We change this optimization problem to include uncertainty in tags, allowing a certain number of tags to "flip" or change. This will let the clustering algorithm adaptively correct tags on a training video believed to be erroneous, adding missing tags to a video and/or deleting spurious ones.

Let us define the refined tag labels for the n-th training example by $\mathbf{t}'_n = \{t'_{ni}\}^{i=T}_{i=1}$. Intuitively, the refined tag label should be similar to annotated (noisy) tag label, $\mathbf{t}_n$, except a few tags *flipped* based on inconsistency with other videos in the same cluster. Here, the label change cost function $\Delta'_{\mathbf{t}_n, \mathbf{t}'_n}$ is defined to penalize training algorithm from making refined tag label very different from the annotated tags, $\mathbf{t}_n$. In this case, the optimization problem of Flip MMC is formulated as:

$$\min_{w, \xi_n, \xi'_n, y_n, \mathbf{t}'_n} \frac{\lambda}{2}||w||^2_2 + \sum_{n=1}^{N} \xi_n + \gamma \sum_{n=1}^{N} \xi'_n \tag{3}$$

$$\text{s.t.} \quad \xi'_n \geq \Delta'_{\mathbf{t}_n, \mathbf{t}'_n}$$

$$w^\top \phi(x_n, \mathbf{t}'_n, y_n) \geq w^\top \phi(x_n, \mathbf{t}, y) + \Delta^{y, y_n}_{\mathbf{t}, \mathbf{t}'_n} - \xi_n \quad \forall \mathbf{t}, \forall y$$

$$L \leq \sum_{n=1}^{N} \mathbb{1}_{(y_n = k)} \leq U \qquad \forall k \in \{1, 2, \dots, K\}$$

which minimizes the norm of parameters $||w||^2_2$ while assigning training examples to clusters as well as recognizing refined tag labels, $\mathbf{t}'_n$ constrained to be similar to annotated tags, $\mathbf{t}'_n$. λ and γ are hyper parameters that controls the balance between the norm of model parameters, constraint violation for refined tag label, ξ_n and the tag label change cost ξ'_n. The second constraint enforces that the compatibility score of video x_n, its refined tag label t'_n and assigned cluster y_n is greater than any other hypothesized labeling where the margin is rescaled using Δ^{y,y_n}_{t,t'_n} similar to Structured MMC. In this work, both Δ'_{t_n,t'_n} and Δ^{y,y_n}_{t,t'_n} are assumed to be a decomposable loss function that can be decomposed to a sum of losses measured on individual tag/cluster annotation. Here, simple hamming loss functions are used for both functions. Note that γ controls the amount of annotated label change allowed in training. By setting it to ∞ Flip MMC becomes Structured MMC.

We emphasize that our framework is general, and can handle video datasets with more or less noisy tags. For example, in a case with less noise, the trade off parameter γ can be set to a large value to prevent too many flips. Or, the label change cost function Δ'_{t_n,t'_n} can be renormalized to penalize flipping erroneous tags less, especially if there is some prior information available regarding the amount of noise for each tag.

3.4 Optimization

The Flip MMC framework proposed in the previous section jointly optimizes the model parameters that describe each cluster, finds the best assignment of videos to clusters, and refines the tag labeling to reduce the noise in tag annotation. Similar to MMC, the Flip MMC optimization is a challenging non-convex optimization problem due to the discrete optimization that assigns videos to clusters and refines tag labels.

Here this non-convex optimization problem is rewritten in unconstrained format as:

$$\min_w \frac{\lambda}{2}||w||_2^2 + R_w \tag{4}$$

where R_w is the the risk function defined in the form of an assignment problem:

$$R_w = \min_{y_n} \sum_{n=1}^N R'_w(y_n) \tag{5}$$

$$\text{s.t.}\quad L \le \sum_{n=1}^N \mathbb{1}_{(y_n=k)} \le U$$

where $R'_w(y_n)$ computes the "mis-clustering" cost of assigning the n-th video to the cluster y_n using:

$$R'_w(y_n) = \min_{t'_n} \max_{y,t} \left(w^\top \phi(x_n, t, y) + \Delta^{y,y_n}_{t,t'_n} - w^\top \phi(x_n, t'_n, y_n) + \gamma \Delta'_{t'_n,t_n} \right). \tag{6}$$

In Eq. 6 annotated tags change to t'_n such that the error of assigning the video x_n to y_n is minimal while number of changes are being penalized by $\Delta'_{t'_n,t_n}$.

In order to address the unconstrained optimization problem in Eq. 4, we develop a coordinate descent-style algorithm shown in the supplementary material. This algorithm alternates between finding the parameters of each cluster (w) and finding an assignment of videos to clusters. The algorithm mainly consists of three steps performed iteratively. First, "mis-clustering" cost is computed in Eq. 6, and then it is used for computing risk function by solving the assignment problem in Eq. 5. Finally, the model parameters are updated given the risk values using the NRBM approach of Do and Artières [21], which is a non-convex extension of the cutting plane algorithm. The details of the training algorithm can be found in the supplementary material.

4   Experiments

In this section, the proposed video clustering technique is examined for two different tasks. First, the method is evaluated for the general video clustering task based on tags, and later it is used for discovering sub-categories of complex video events.

Dataset: For the experiments, we use our model to cluster web videos in the TRECVID MED 2011 dataset [10]. We use the Event Kit video collection that includes 2379 videos from 15 event categories: "board trick", "feeding animal", "landing fish", "wedding ceremony", and "woodworking project", "birthday party", "changing a tire", "flash mob", "getting a vehicle unstuck", "grooming animal", "making sandwich", "parade", "parkour", "repairing appliance", and "sewing project". Each category contains about 150 videos.

Visual Feature: For all experiments HOG3D features [2], k-means quantized into a 1000-word codebook are used. For all techniques that require visual features, the approximated Histogram Intersection Kernel via feature extension [22] is used to provide higher quality results.

Tags: The noisy tags generated in Vahdat and Mori [9] TRECVID MED 2011 dataset are used in the experiments. [9] uses text analysis tools to extract binary tags based on one-sentence long textual description of videos provided with the dataset in the "judgment files." As tags are generated from arbitrary sentences, there is a large amount of noise inherited in tag annotation. The 114 tags that have more than 10 occurrences in the dataset are used here.

4.1   Video Clustering

In this section, the proposed clustering approach is used to cluster the web videos in the TRECVID MED 2011 dataset. Following previous work [8, 14–17], the videos are grouped into the number of event categories in the dataset ($K = 15$). The Flip MMC and Structured MMC approach are compared with four sets of baselines:

Visual Features: The first set are based on approaches that work directly on the visual features without considering any tag annotation. Here a video is represented by a global bag-of-words feature vector. We have examined three conventional approaches including the K-means algorithm, Spectral Clustering [20], and the MMC approach implemented in [8]. Furthermore, to mitigate the effect of randomness, K-means and Spectral Clustering are run 10 times with different initial seeds and the average results are recorded in the experiments.

Binary Tags: The second set of baselines is the same baselines where visual features are replaced with binary tag annotations. Here a video is represented by a vector of binary variables indicating the annotated presence/absence of tags , and the same K-means algorithm, Spectral Clustering [20], and the MMC approach [8] are used for clustering videos.

Binary Tags and Visual Features: The third set of baselines are created by representing each video using the concatenation of their visual features as well as binary tag labels. The baseline shows the case where information from heterogeneous sources are combined in a naive way.

Detection Scores: The fourth set of baselines trains SVM tag detectors from visual features, and represents each video by a vector of tag detection scores. Note that these baselines consider tag detection and clustering as two separated steps. In contrast, our approach models tags and clusters in a joint framework, while correcting noisy tags. As above, we have conducted K-means, Spectral Clustering and MMC on this data. We have also compared the latent max-margin clustering (Latent MMC) approach proposed in [8], which clusters videos based on the latent presence/absence of video tags. Note that Latent MMC originally builds tag detectors on a different dataset other than the one for clustering. As we assume tag annotation on the clustering dataset, a fair comparison is made by training tag detectors on the same clustering data for all the compared methods.

Parameters: MMC, Latent MMC, Structured MMC and Flip MMC require setting the lower bound (L) and upper bound (U) values in cluster balance constraint. For all these methods we set L and U to $0.9\frac{N}{K}$ and $1.1\frac{N}{K}$ respectively. For all the methods, the trade off parameter, λ is chosen as the best from the range $\{0.1, 1, 10\}$, and the other trade-off parameter of Flip MMC γ, is set to 0.1. All MMC based clustering we used the same initialization of clusters resulted from Spectral Clustering. The same optimization package is used for all the MMC-like methods for a fair comparison.

We use Hamming loss for both Structured MMC and Flip MMC. $\Delta'_{t',t}$, the label change cost function is also defined as Hamming loss which basically counts the number of label changes. For flip part, we defined cost function such that it prevents label flips from a positive tag to a negative tag. The rational behind this type of loss function is the fact that in the TRECVID MED dataset, sentences used for generating tag annotation are entered by expert annotators. It is assumed that the annotators have not entered spam sentences. So, the extracted tags are actually present in the video, and there is no need to remove them. However, it is natural to assume that sentences does not contain all the potential tags annotated (mentioned) in the sentence.

Performance Measures: Four standard measurements are used to evaluate the quality of the clusters: purity [14] measures the accuracy of the dominating class in each cluster, normalized mutual information (Normalized MI) [23] is from the

Table 1. Quantitative comparison of clusters generated by different approaches. *Visual Features* represents the set of baselines that perform on visual features, *Binary Tags* are the baselines that work with binary tags directly, *Binary tags and Visual Features* are those that use both visual features and binary tags, and *Detection Scores* denotes the set of baselines that use tag detection scores. *Our model* refers to the models of Structured MMC (defined in Sec. 3.1) and Flip MMC (defined in Sec. 3.3).

	Purity	Normalized MI	Rand index	F-measure
Visual Features:				
K-means	0.26	0.19	0.88	0.14
Spectral Clustering	0.25	0.20	0.88	0.15
MMC	0.25	0.19	0.88	0.14
Binary Tags:				
K-means	0.51	0.52	0.86	0.30
Spectral Clustering	0.71	0.73	0.93	0.56
MMC	0.76	0.72	0.95	0.64
Binary Tags and Visual Features:				
K-means	0.51	0.49	0.90	0.34
Spectral Clustering	0.76	0.74	0.94	0.62
MMC	0.79	0.72	0.95	0.66
Detection Scores:				
K-means	0.63	0.60	0.93	0.50
Spectral Clustering	0.82	0.76	0.96	0.69
MMC	0.83	0.78	0.96	0.73
Latent MMC	0.86	0.82	0.97	0.79
Our model:				
Structured MMC	0.87	0.84	0.97	0.79
Flip MMC	**0.90**	**0.88**	**0.98**	**0.84**

information-theoretic perspective and calculates the mutual dependence of the predicted clustering and the ground-truth partitions, Rand index [24] evaluates true positives within clusters and true negatives between clusters and balanced F-measure considers both precision and recall.

Results: The quantitative comparison of the proposed clustering approach with baselines is presented in Table 1. On the TRECVID MED 2011 dataset, Flip MMC achieves the highest performance in terms of all the measurements. The comparison between Structured MMC and Flip MMC shows the efficiency of label flip in getting better clusters. Surprisingly, the performance of K-means, Spectral Clustering and MMC gain a significant boost when discrete tag labels were replaced with the detection scores of an SVM classifier that is trained on the training dataset. This may be due to the fact that SVM maps binary tag labels to a continuous domain where the magnitude of scores are correlated with the strength of the presence of the tag. The comparison between *Visual Features* and *Binary Tags* baseline sets confirms the fact that in general clustering videos based on tags can actually result in semantically meaningful clusters, and finally

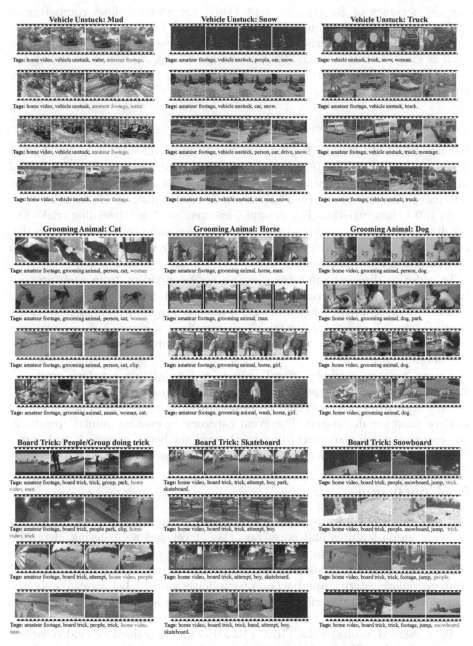

Fig. 2. Qualitative visualization of sub-categories discovered from event categories in TRECVID MED 2011 dataset. Each row represents three sub-categories of an event category. For each sub-category four highest-scored videos are visualized. The tags associated for each video is also reported along with red tags added by Flip MMC. In most cases the formed clusters represent a semantically meaningful sub-category. The semantic content of each cluster can be extracted by manually checking common detected tags, and is reported on top.

the low accuracy of *Binary Tags and Visual Features* baselines comparing to our approach shows that naive approaches such as feature concatenation may improve the accuracy of techniques that rely on individual sources of information such as visual features or tags, but, in contrast our approach can wisely use the information in visual features to refine annotated tag labels that result in better clusters.

4.2   Sub-categorization

In this section, the proposed approach is used to discover sub-categories of event categories in TRECVID MED 2011. Due to the complex nature of events defined in the TRECVID MED dataset, the amount of intra-class variation is very large. Sub-categorization of events can be potentially used to discover clusters that have lower intra-class variation. For example, an event such as "boarding trick" can involve snowboards, skateboards, or other devices; can occur in scenes ranging from urban streets to watery environs; and has other variations, much of which is captured in relevant tags.

In order to discover sub-categories, we consider videos from each ground-truth event category in turn. Videos of each event category are clustered into six clusters. Representative samples of the results for "grooming animal", "getting a vehicle unstuck", and "boarding trick" are visualized in Figure 2. As we are using tags for clustering videos, the discovered clusters are in general semantically meaningful.

Figure 2 shows examples of sub-categories for "getting a vehicle unstuck" that correspond to the type of vehicle, or the environment in which the vehicle has been stuck. Clusters that correspond to getting a vehicle unstuck from mud or snow are discovered. The event category "grooming animal" results in sub-categories that vary according to the animal being groomed, and snowboard/skateboard variants are discovered in the "boarding trick" event category.

5   Conclusion

We have presented a method for automatically obtaining clusters of videos by utilizing visual features and noisy tags. We developed a clustering algorithm based on max-margin clustering that finds groups of videos by optimizing a max-margin criterion separating each cluster from competing ones. Different from previous clustering approaches, we explicitly model label noise. We showed empirically that this was effective, resulting in more accurate clustering than a set of baseline methods.

We presented results on the TRECVID MED unconstrained web video dataset that verified the efficacy of the proposed method. In particular, one could discover either high-level event categories or semantically meaningful sub-categories of events by utilizing noisy tag data in conjunction with visual features. Noisy tag data are commonplace, and methods for effectively using them for clustering could facilitate more efficient methods for exploring and understanding web video collections.

References

1. YouTube: Statistics - youtube (2014) (accessed February 27, 2014)
2. Kläser, A., Marszalek, M., Schmid, C.: A spatio-temporal descriptor based on 3D-gradients. In: BMVC (2008)
3. Wang, Y., Jiang, H., Drew, M.S., Li, Z.N., Mori, G.: Unsupervised discovery of action classes. In: CVPR (2006)
4. Niebles, J.C., Wang, H., Fei-Fei, L.: Unsupervised learning of human action categories using spatial-temporal words. In: BMVC (2006)
5. Zeng, H.J., He, Q.C., Chen, Z., Ma, W.Y.: Learning to cluster search results. In: SIGIR (2004)
6. Schroff, F., Zitnick, C.L., Baker, S.: Clustering videos by location. In: BMVC (2009)
7. Hsu, C.F., Caverlee, J., Khabiri, E.: Hierarchical comments-based clustering. In: SAC (2011)
8. Zhou, G.T., Lan, T., Vahdat, A., Mori, G.: Latent maximum margin clustering. In: NIPS (2013)
9. Vahdat, A., Mori, G.: Handling uncertain tags in visual recognition. In: ICCV (2013)
10. Over, P., Awad, G., Michel, M., Fiscus, J., Kraaij, W., Smeaton, A.F., Quenot, G.: TRECVID 2011 — an overview of the goals, tasks, data, evaluation mechansims and metrics. In: TRECVID (2011)
11. Natarajan, P., Wu, S., Vitaladevuni, S.N.P., Zhuang, X., Tsakalidis, S., Park, U., Prasad, R., Natarajan, P.: Multimodal feature fusion for robust event detection in web videos. In: CVPR (2012)
12. Izadinia, H., Shah, M.: Recognizing complex events using large margin joint low-level event model. In: Fitzgibbon, A., Lazebnik, S., Perona, P., Sato, Y., Schmid, C. (eds.) ECCV 2012, Part IV. LNCS, vol. 7575, pp. 430–444. Springer, Heidelberg (2012)
13. Qi, G.J., Hua, X.S., Rui, Y., Tang, J., Mei, T., Zhang, H.J.: Correlative multi-label video annotation. In: ACM MM (2007)
14. Xu, L., Neufeld, J., Larson, B., Schuurmans, D.: Maximum margin clustering. In: NIPS (2004)
15. Valizadegan, H., Jin, R.: Generalized maximum margin clustering and unsupervised kernel learning. In: NIPS (2006)
16. Zhang, K., Tsang, I.W., Kwok, J.T.: Maximum margin clustering made practical. In: ICML (2007)
17. Zhao, B., Wang, F., Zhang, C.: Efficient multiclass maximum margin clustering. In: ICML (2008)
18. Yang, W., Toderici, G.: Discriminative tag learning on youtube videos with latent sub-tags. In: CVPR (2011)
19. Hoai, M., Zisserman, A.: Discriminative sub-categorization. In: CVPR (2013)
20. Ng, A.Y., Jordan, M.I., Weiss, Y.: On spectral clustering: Analysis and an algorithm. In: NIPS (2001)
21. Do, T.M.T., Artières, T.: Large margin training for hidden markov models with partially observed states. In: ICML (2009)
22. Vedaldi, A., Zisserman, A.: Efficient additive kernels via explicit feature maps. IEEE Trans. on Pattern Analysis and Machine Intelligence 34(3), 480–492 (2012)
23. Kvalseth, T.O.: Entropy and correlation: Some comments. IEEE Transactions on Systems, Man and Cybernetics 17(3), 517–519 (1987)
24. Rand, W.M.: Objective criteria for the evaluation of clustering methods. Journal of the American Statistical Association 66(336), 846–850 (1971)

Category-Specific Video Summarization

Danila Potapov, Matthijs Douze, Zaid Harchaoui, and Cordelia Schmid

Inria*

Abstract. In large video collections with clusters of typical categories, such as "birthday party" or "flash-mob", category-specific video summarization can produce higher quality video summaries than unsupervised approaches that are blind to the video category.

Given a video from a known category, our approach first efficiently performs a temporal segmentation into semantically-consistent segments, delimited not only by shot boundaries but also general change points. Then, equipped with an SVM classifier, our approach assigns importance scores to each segment. The resulting video assembles the sequence of segments with the highest scores. The obtained video summary is therefore both short and highly informative. Experimental results on videos from the multimedia event detection (MED) dataset of TRECVID'11 show that our approach produces video summaries with higher relevance than the state of the art.

Keywords: video summarization, temporal segmentation, video classification.

1   Introduction

Most videos from YouTube or DailyMotion consist of long-running, poorly-filmed and unedited content. Users would like to browse, i.e., to *skim through* the video to quickly get a hint on the semantic content. Video summarization addresses this problem by providing a short video summary of a full-length video. An ideal video summary would include all the important video segments and remain short in length. The problem is extremely challenging in general and has been subject of recent research [1,2,3,4,5,6].

Large collections of videos contain clusters of videos belonging to specific categories with typical visual content and repeating patterns in the temporal structure. Consider a video of a "birthday party" (see Figure 1). It is unclear how an unsupervised approach for video summarization would single out the short segments corresponding to "blow the candles", "applause", etc.

In this paper, we propose a category-specific summarization approach. A first distinctive feature of our approach is the temporal segmentation algorithm. While most previous works relate segment boundaries to shot boundaries, our temporal segmentation algorithm detects general change points. This includes

---

* LEAR team, Inria Grenoble Rhône-Alpes, Laboratoire Jean Kuntzmann, CNRS, Univ. Grenoble Alpes, France.

D. Fleet et al. (Eds.): ECCV 2014, Part VI, LNCS 8694, pp. 540–555, 2014.

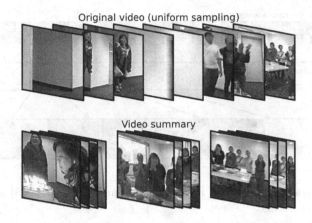

Original video (uniform sampling)

Video summary

Fig. 1. Original video, and its video summary for the category "birthday party"

shot boundaries, but also sub-shot boundaries where the transitions between sub-shots is gradual. A second feature is the category-specific supervised importance-scoring algorithm, which scores the *relative importance* of segments within each category, in contrast to video-specific importance [1,2,7].

Our approach works as follows (see Figure 2). First, we perform an automatic kernel-based temporal segmentation based on state-of-the-art video features that automatically selects the number of segments. Then, equipped with an SVM classifier for importance scoring that was trained on videos for the category at hand, we score each segment in terms of importance. Finally, the approach outputs a video summary composed of the segments with the highest predicted importance scores. Thus, our contributions are three-fold:

- we propose a novel approach, **KVS**, for supervised video summarization of realistic videos, that uses state-of-the-art image and video features
- we introduce a new dataset, **MED-Summaries**[1], along with a clear annotation protocol, to evaluate video summarization
- we obtain excellent experimental results on MED-Summaries, showing that KVS delivers video summaries with higher overall importance, as measured by two performance metrics.

2   Related Work

Video Summarization. Truong & Venkatesh [7] present a comprehensive overview and classification of video summarization methods. The task is difficult to define and many methods are domain-specific (sports, news, rushes, documentary, etc.). However, to our knowledge, there are no publicly available

---

[1] The annotations and the evaluation codes are available at
http://lear.inrialpes.fr/people/potapov/med_summaries.php

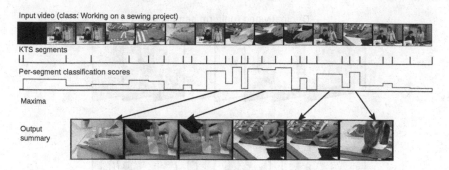

Fig. 2. Overall scheme of our Kernel Video Summarization (KVS) approach

implementations or datasets, for eg. sports videos summarization, that could be used for comparison with more recent approaches. Summaries may focus on dominant concepts [8], relate to the video's story [6], the user's preferences, the query context [4], or user attention [9]. A video is either summed up as a sequence of keyframes [3,5,2] or by video excerpts [6].

Video summarization received much attention when NIST was running the Trecvid Rushes summarization task (2006-2008). The evaluation was conducted on a dataset of significant size, with an expensive manual annotation of the ground-truth [8]. However, the methods were mostly specific to the domain, i.e. they focused on detecting redundant shots of a scene, and clapperboards.

For professional and low-dynamic TV broadcast videos (e.g. from [8,4] or Open Video Archive), shot boundaries naturally split a video into "visual sentences". Early summarization methods [7] extract one or more keyframes to represent a shot, often independently from the other shots. Recent works, including this one, focus on user-generated data [3,5,6,10], which typically do not contain shot boundaries.

Without supervision, summarization methods must rely on low-level indices to determine the relevance of parts of a video [9,11,12]. When the video domain is known, summarization can be strongly supervised. For example, soccer games [13,14] or feature films [15] have standard phases that can be manually identified. A few previous works [3,6,5] produced summaries using features crafted for specific visual categories. In contrast to these works, our approach builds short yet highly informative category specific video summaries, using generic state-of-the-art visual features.

In [16,17], the main task is to remove redundant video footage, which is detected as easy to reconstruct based on sparse coding from the rest of the video. A recent work [10] also segments a video at a finer level than shots and relies on supervised mutual information to identify the important segments. The main difference with our work is the use of state-of-the-art video features and the quantitative evaluation of the approach. Leveraging crawled internet photos is another recent trend for video summarization [18,5].

There are several ways of evaluating video summarization methods [7]. Most works [3,6,5,11] conduct *user studies* to compare different summaries of the same video. The *concept coverage* metric evaluates the number of important objects or actions included in the summary [3,8]. Although it requires time-consuming manual annotation of videos, the annotations can be reused to evaluate multiple approaches. When the goal is to simplify video navigation, the time it takes a user to perform some data exploration task can be used as a quality metric [8]. *Automatic comparison to reference summaries* comes from text summarization literature [19]. It relies on a user-generated summary of a video and a metric to compare it to the algorithm's summary [5,2,18]. The protocol used in this paper combines concept coverage with a comparison to multiple reference summaries.

Temporal Video Segmentation. Computer vision methods often utilize spatial or temporal segmentation to raise the abstraction level of the problem and reduce its dimensionality. Segmentation can help to solve image classification, scene reconstruction [20] and can serve as a basis for semantic segmentation [21]. Similarly, video segmentation usually implies dividing a video into spatio-temporal volumes [22,23]. Temporal video segmentation often means detecting shot or scene boundaries, that are either introduced by the "director" through editing or simply correspond to filming stops.

The proliferation of user-generated videos created a new challenge for semantic temporal segmentation of videos. Lee et al. [3] used clustering of frame color histograms to segment temporal events. In [6] a video is split in sub-shots depending on the activity of the wearer of a head-mounted camera: "static", "moving the head" or "in transit". Similar to these works we focus on the content of the segment rather than its boundaries.

Most shot boundary detection methods focus on differences between consecutive frames [24], relying on image descriptors (pixel color histograms, local or global motion [7], or bag-of-features descriptors [25]). Our temporal segmentation approach takes into account the differences between *all pairs of frames*. Therefore, the approach allows to single-out not only shot boundaries but also *change points* in general that correspond to non-abrupt boundaries between two consecutive segments with different semantic content.

3 Kernel Video Summarization

We start by giving definitions of the main concepts and building blocks of our approach.

Video Summary. A video is partitioned in segments. A *segment* is a part of the video enclosed between two timestamps. A *video summary* is a video composed of a subset of the temporal segments of the original video.

A *summary* is a condensed synopsis of the whole video. It conveys the most *important* details of the original video. A segment can be non-informative due to signal-level reasons like abrupt camera shake and dark underexposed segments commonly present in egocentric videos [3,6].

A segment can be considered *important* due to multiple reasons, depending on the video category and application goals: highlights of sport matches, culmination points of movies [7], influential moments of egocentric videos [6].

We make the assumption that the notion of importance can be learned from a set of videos belonging to the video category. This point of view stems from the Multimedia Event Recounting task at Trecvid: selecting segments containing evidence that the video belongs to a certain event category. Similarly, we define importance as a *measure of relevance to the type of event*. Fig. 3 shows an example video together with the importance of its segments.

Our definition of importance spans an ordinal scale, ranging from 0 "no evidence" to 3 "the segment alone could classify the video into the category". More details are given in Sec. 4.1.

Fig. 3. Our definition of importance on the "Changing a vehicle tire" category. These frames come from a 1-minute video where a support car follows a cyclist during a cycle race. The main event — changing a bicycle tire — takes less than one third of the video. The figure shows central frames of user-annotated segments together with their importance score.

The proposed method, **KVS**, decomposes into three steps: i) kernel temporal segmentation; ii) importance-scoring of segments; iii) summary building. Figure 2 summarizes our approach.

3.1   Kernel Temporal Segmentation

Our Kernel Temporal Segmentation (KTS) method splits the video into a set of non-intersecting temporal segments. The method is fast and accurate when combined with high-dimensional descriptors.

Our temporal segmentation approach is a kernel-based change point detection algorithm. In contrast to shot boundary detection, change point detection is a more general statistical framework [26]. Change point detection usually focuses on piecewise constant one dimensional signals corrupted by noise, and the goal is to detect the jumps in the signal. It is able to statistically discriminate between jumps due to noise and jumps due to the underlying signal. Change-point detection has been subject of intense theoretical and methodological study in statistics and signal processing; see [26,27] and references therein. Such methods enjoy strong theoretical guarantees, in contrast to shot boundary techniques that are mostly heuristic and tuned to the types of video transitions at hand (cut, fade in/out, etc.). We propose here a retrospective multiple change-point detection approach, based on [28], that considers the whole signal at once.

Given the matrix of frame-to-frame similarities defined through a positive-definite kernel, the algorithm outputs a set of optimal "change points" that correspond to the boundaries of temporal segments. More precisely, let the video be a sequence of descriptors $x_i \in X$, $i = 0, \ldots, n - 1$. Let $K : X \times X \to \mathbb{R}$ be a kernel function between descriptors. Let $\mathcal{H}$ be the feature space of the kernel $K(\cdot, \cdot)$. Denote $\phi : X \to \mathcal{H}$ the associated feature map, and $\|\cdot\|_{\mathcal{H}}$ the norm in the feature space $\mathcal{H}$. We minimize the following objective

$$\underset{m; \, t_0, \ldots, t_{m-1}}{\text{Minimize}} \quad J_{m,n} := L_{m,n} + Cg(m, n) \tag{1}$$

where m is the number of change points and $g(m, n)$ a penalty term (see below). $L_{m,n}$ is defined from the within-segment kernel variances $v_{t_i, t_{i+1}}$:

$$L_{m,n} = \sum_{i=0}^{m} v_{t_{i-1}, t_i}, \quad v_{t_i, t_{i+1}} = \sum_{t=t_i}^{t_{i+1}-1} \|\phi(x_t) - \mu_i\|_{\mathcal{H}}^2, \quad \mu_i = \frac{\sum_{t=t_i}^{t_{i+1}-1} \phi(x_t)}{t_{i+1} - t_i} \tag{2}$$

Automatic Calibration. The number of segments could be set proportional to the video duration, but this would be too loose. Therefore, the objective of Equation (1) decomposes into two terms: $L_{m,n}$ which measures the overall within-segment variance, and $g(m, n)$ that penalizes segmentations with too many segments. We consider a BIC-type penalty [29] with the parameterized form $g(m, n) = m(\log(n/m) + 1)$ [30]. Increasing the number of segments decreases $L_{m,n}$ (2), but increases the model complexity. This objective yields a trade-off between under- and over-segmentation. We propose to cross-validate the C parameter using a validation set of annotated videos. Hence we get kernel-based temporal segmentation algorithm where the number of segments is set automatically from data.

Algorithm. The proposed algorithm is described in Algo. 1. First, the kernel is computed for each pair of descriptors in the sequence. Then the segment variances are computed for each possible starting point t and segment duration d. It can be done efficiently by precomputing the cumulative sums of the matrix [31]. Then the dynamic programming algorithm is used to minimize the objective (2). It iteratively computes the best objective value for the first j descriptors and i change points. Finally, the optimal segmentation is reconstructed by backtracking. The total runtime cost of the algorithm is in $O(m_{\max} n^2)$. The penalization introduces a minimal computational overhead because the dynamic programming algorithm already computes $L_{i,n}$ for all possible segment counts.

3.2 Learning to Predict Importance Scores

For each category, we train a linear SVM classifier from a set of videos with video-level labels, assuming that a classifier originally trained to classify the full

Algorithm 1. Kernel temporal segmentation

Input: temporal sequence of descriptors $\mathbf{x}_0, \mathbf{x}_1, \ldots, \mathbf{x}_{n-1}$	Cost
1. Compute the Gram matrix A : $a_{i,j} = K(\mathbf{x}_i, \mathbf{x}_j)$	$dn^2/2$
2. Compute cumulative sums of A	n^2
3. Compute unnormalized variances	$2n^2$

$$v_{t,t+d} = \sum_{i=t}^{t+d-1} a_{i,i} - \frac{1}{d} \sum_{i,j=t}^{t+d-1} a_{i,j}$$

$$t = 0, \ldots, n-1, \quad d = 1, \ldots, n-t$$

4. Do the forward pass of the dynamic programming algorithm	$2m_{\max}n^2$

$$L_{i,j} = \min_{t=i,\ldots,j-1}\left(L_{i-1,t} + v_{t,j}\right), \quad L_{0,j} = v_{0,j}$$

$$i = 1, \ldots, m_{\max}, \quad j = 1, \ldots, n$$

5. Select the optimal number of change points	$2m_{\max}$

$$m^\star = \arg\min_{m=0,\ldots,m_{\max}} L_{m,n} + Cg(m,n)$$

6. Find change-point positions by backtracking	$2m^\star$

$$t_{m^\star} = n, \quad t_{i-1} = \arg\min_t\left(L_{i-1,t} + v_{t,t_i}\right)$$

$$i = m^\star, \ldots, 1$$

Output: Change-point positions $t_0, \ldots, t_{m^\star-1}$

videos can be used to score importance of small segments. This assumption is reasonable for videos where a significant proportion of segments have high scores. The opposite case, when a very small number of segments allow to classify the video ("needle in a haystack"), is outside the scope of the paper.

At training time, we aggregate frame descriptors of a video as if the whole video was a single segment. In this way a video descriptor has the same dimensionality as a segment descriptor. For each category we use videos of the category as positive examples and the videos from the other categories as negatives. We train one binary SVM classifier per category.

At test time, we segment the video using the KTS algorithm and aggregate Fisher descriptors for each segment. The relevant classifier is then applied to the segment descriptors, producing the *importance map* of the video.

In order to evaluate the summarization separately from the classification, we assume that the category of the video is known in advance. While recent methods specifically targeted at video classification [32,33] are rather mature, depending on them for our evaluation would introduce additional noise.

3.3   Summary Building with KVS

Finally, a summary is constructed by concatenating the most important segments of the video. We assume that the duration of the summary is set a priori. Segments are included in the summary by the order of their importance until the duration limit is achieved (we crop the last segment to satisfy the constraint).

4   MED-Summaries Dataset

Most existing works evaluate summaries based on user studies, which are time-consuming, costly and hard to reproduce.

We introduce a new dataset, called **MED-summaries**. The proposed benchmark simplifies the evaluation by introducing a clear and automatic evaluation procedure, that is tailored to category-specific summarization. Every part of the video is annotated with a category-specific importance value. For example, for the category "birthday party", a segment that contains a scene where someone is blowing the candles is assigned a high importance, whereas a segment just showing children around a table is assigned a lower importance.

We use the training set of the Trecvid 2011 MED dataset (12, 249 videos) to train the classifier for importance scoring. Furthermore, we annotate 60 videos from this training set as a validation set. To test our approach we annotate 100 videos from the official test set (10 per class), where most test videos have a duration from 1 to 5 minutes. Annotators mark the temporal segments and their importance; the annotation protocol is described in section 4.1. To take into account the variability due to different annotators, annotations were made by several people. In the experimental section we evaluate our results with respect to the different annotations and average the results. The different metrics for evaluation are described in section 4.2. See the dataset's website for details.

4.1   Annotation Protocol

Segment Annotation. The annotation interface shows one test video at a time, which can be advanced by steps of 5 frames. First, we ask a user to annotate temporal segments. Temporal segments should be *semantically consistent*, i.e. long enough for a user to grasp what is going on, but it must be possible to describe it in a short sentence. For example it can be "a group of people marching in the street" for a video of the class "Parade", or "putting one slice of bread onto another" for the class "Making a sandwich".

Some actions are repetitive or homogeneous, e.g. running, sewing, etc. In that case we ask to specify the "period" — minimum duration of a sub-segment that fully represents the whole segment. For example, watching 2-3 seconds of a running person is sufficient to describe the segment as "a person is running".

We require all shot boundaries to be annotated as change points, but change points do not necessarily correspond to shot boundaries. Often a shot contains a single action, but the main part is shorter than the whole segment. In this case we ask to localize precisely the main part.

Importance Annotation. For each semantic segment we ask a user *"Does the segment contain evidence of the given event category?"*. The possible answers are:

0: No evidence
1: Some hints suggest that the whole video could belong to the category
2: The segment contains significant evidence of the category
3: The segment alone classifies the video to the category

While audio can be used during annotation, we specify that if something is only mentioned in onscreen text or speech, then it should not be labeled as important.

In preliminary experiments we found that annotators tend to give too high importance to very short segments, that often have ambiguous segmentation and importance score. Therefore, we preprocess the ground-truth before the evaluation — we decrease the annotated importance for segments smaller than 4 seconds proportionally to the segment duration.

4.2 Evaluation Metrics

We represent the manually annotated ground-truth segments $\mathbf{S} = \{S_1, \ldots, S_n\}$ of a video by:

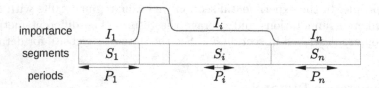

An automatic temporal segmentation is represented by the sequence of segments $\mathbf{S}' = \{S'_1, \ldots, S'_m\}$.

To evaluate **segmentation** we define a symmetric f-score metric as:

$$f(\mathbf{S}, \mathbf{S}') = \frac{2 \cdot p(\mathbf{S}, \mathbf{S}') \cdot p(\mathbf{S}', \mathbf{S})}{p(\mathbf{S}, \mathbf{S}') + p(\mathbf{S}', \mathbf{S})}, \tag{3}$$

where the similarity of two segmentations $\mathbf{A}$ and $\mathbf{B}$ is

$$p(\mathbf{A}, \mathbf{B}) = \frac{1}{|\mathbf{A}|} |\{A \in \mathbf{A} \text{ st. } \exists B \in \mathbf{B} \text{ matching } A\}| \tag{4}$$

where $|\mathbf{A}|$ is the number of segments in $\mathbf{A}$. We consider segments A and B are matching if the temporal overlap over the union ratio is larger than 0.75, and when a segment has an annotated period, it is reduced to a sub-segment no shorter than the period, that maximizes the overlap over the union.

To evaluate **summarization** we define two metrics: the importance ratio and the meaningful summary duration.

A computed summary is a subset of the segments $\widetilde{\mathbf{S}} = \{\widetilde{S}_1, \cdots, \widetilde{S}_{\tilde{m}}\} \subset \mathbf{S}'$. We say a ground truth segment S_i is *covered* by a detected segment $\widetilde{S}_j$ if

$$\text{duration}\big(S_i \cap \widetilde{S}_j\big) > \alpha P_i \tag{5}$$

When the period equals the segment duration this means that a fraction α of the ground truth segment is covered by the detected segment. We use $\alpha = 80\%$ to enforce visually coherent summaries, which was validated using the ground-truth. Note that this definition allows covering several ground truth segments by a single detected segment, as in the following example:

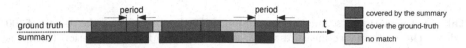

Let $C(\widetilde{\mathbf{S}}) \subset \mathbf{S}$ be the subset of ground truth segments covered by the summary $\widetilde{\mathbf{S}}$. Given the duration of the summary $\mathcal{T}(\widetilde{\mathbf{S}}) = \sum_{j=1}^{\tilde{m}} \text{duration}(\widetilde{S}_j)$ and its total importance $\mathcal{I}(\widetilde{\mathbf{S}}) = \sum_{i \in C(\widetilde{\mathbf{S}})} I_i$, we define the *importance ratio* as

$$\mathcal{I}^*(\widetilde{\mathbf{S}}) = \frac{\mathcal{I}(\widetilde{\mathbf{S}})}{\mathcal{I}^{\max}(\mathcal{T}(\widetilde{\mathbf{S}}))}, \quad \text{with} \quad \mathcal{I}^{\max}(T) = \max_{\substack{\mathbf{A} \subset \mathbf{S} \ \text{s.t.} \\ \mathcal{T}(\mathbf{A}) \leq T}} \mathcal{I}(\mathbf{A}) \tag{6}$$

We use the *maximum possible summary importance* $\mathcal{I}^{\max}(T)$ as a normalization factor. This normalization takes into account the duration and the redundancy of the video and ensures that $\mathcal{I}^*(\widetilde{\mathbf{S}}) \in [0,1]$.

It turns out that maximizing the summary importance given the ground-truth segmentation and importance is NP-hard, as it is a form of knapsack problem. Therefore we use a greedy approximate summarization: we reduce each segment to its period, sort the segments by decreasing importance (resolving ties by favoring shorter segments), and constructing the optimal summary from the top-ranked segments that fit in the duration constraint.

A second measure is the *meaningful summary duration*, **MSD**. A meaningful summary is obtained as follows. We build it by adding segments by order of classification scores until it covers a segment of importance 3, as defined by the ground-truth annotation. This guarantees that the gist of the input video is represented at this length and measures how relevant the importance scoring is. Summaries assembling a large number of low-importance segments first are mediocre summaries and get a low MSD score. Summaries assembling high-importance segments first get a high MSD score. In our experiments we report the median MSD score over all test videos as a performance measure.

5   Results

5.1   Baselines

As the videos are annotated by several users, we can evaluate their annotations with respect to each other in a leave-one-out manner (**Users**). This quantifies the task's ambiguity and gives an upper bound on the expected performance.

For segmentation we use a shot detector (**SD**) of Massoudi et al. [24] as a baseline. *For classification* we use two baselines: one with the shot detector, where shots are classified with an SVM (**SD+SVM**) and one where the segments are selected by clustering instead of SVM scores (**KTS+Cluster**).

The SD+SVM baseline is close to an event detection setup, where a temporal window slides over the video, and an SVM score is computed for every position of the window [32,34]. However, we pre-select promising windows with the SD segmentation.

Table 1. Evaluation of segmentation and summarization methods on the test set of 100 videos. The performance measures are average f-measure for segmentation (higher is better) and median Meaningful Summary Duration for summarization (lower is better).

Method	Segmentation Avg. f-score	Summarization MSD (s)
Users	49.1	10.6
SD + SVM	30.9	16.7
KTS + Cluster	**41.0**	13.8
KVS	**41.0**	**12.5**

Clustering descriptors produces a representative set of images or segments of the video, where long static shots are given the same importance as short shots [5]. We use a simple k-means clustering, as the Fisher Vectors representing segments (see next section) can be compared with the L2 distance [35]. The summary is built by adding one segment from each cluster in turn. First we add segments nearest to each centroid, ordered by increasing duration, then second nearest, etc.

Our KVS method combines the KTS segmentation with a SVM classifier.

5.2 Implementation Details

Video Descriptors & Classifier. We process every 5-th frame of the video. We extract SIFT descriptors on a dense grid at multiple scales. The local descriptors are reduced to 64 dimensions with PCA. Then a video frame is encoded with a Fisher Vector [35] based on a GMM of 128 Gaussians, producing a $d=16512$ dimension vector.

For segmentation we normalize frame descriptors as follows. Each dimension is standardized within a video to have zero mean and unit variance. Then we apply signed square-rooting and L_2 normalization. We use dot products to compare Fisher vectors and produce the kernel matrix.

For classification, the frame descriptors from a segment are whitened under the diagonal covariance assumption as in [35]. Then we apply signed square-rooting and L_2-normalization. The segment descriptor is the average of the frame descriptors. This was shown to be the best pooling method for frame descriptors [32,33].

The linear SVM classifier for each class is built from about 150 positive and 12000 negative training videos from the MED 2011 training dataset. The C parameter of the classifier is optimized using cross-validation.

We use grid-search on the 60-video validation set to optimize the parameters of the different methods. The shot detector (**SD**) has a single threshold T. Our **KVS** method relies on a single parameter C that controls the number of segments (equation 1). For the clustering method, the optimal ratio of the number of clusters over the number of segments was found to be $1/5^{th}$.

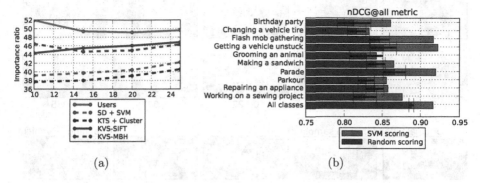

(a)   (b)

Fig. 4. Summarization of the 100-video test dataset. (a) Importance ration of Equation (6) for different durations of the summary. (b) Correlation of SVM scores and scores assigned by users.

On average, the annotated segments are 3.5 s long, and so are **SD** segments. The **KTS** method produces segments of 4.5 s on average.

5.3 Segmentation

Table 1 shows the segmentation quality of users and algorithms. For algorithms we average the f-scores of Equation (3) over segmentations from different users. For users we report the average f-score of the leave-one-out evaluation, i.e. we assume each user in turn to be the ground truth. The proposed approach KTS outperforms the competing method SD in terms of temporal segmentation performance. Surely, human segmentations are better than the algorithms', which means that the annotation protocol is consistent. Yet, the average f-score of users is not close to 100%, which suggests that the segment annotation task is somewhat subjective.

5.4 Summarization

The MSD metric in Table 1 shows that the temporal segmentation output by KTS has a significant impact on the summary's quality. Indeed, the SD+SVM method generally produces longer summaries than KTS+Cluster.

Fig. 4a shows the summarization quality for different summary durations. The user curve gives an upper bound on what can be achieved, by evaluating the consensus between annotators, following the leave-one-out procedure as before. The proposed approach, KVS, is the closest to the user curve. Again, KVS clearly outperforms the competing methods KTS+Cluster and SD+SVM. We also run an experiment where the SIFT low-level descriptor is replaced by the MBH motion descriptor [36]. We get 2% improvement for 10 sec. and 1% drop for longer summaries compared to SIFT. A recent work [32] also reports little difference between SIFT and MBH on the MED 2011 dataset.

Fig. 5. Illustrations of summaries constructed with our method. We show the central frame in each segment with the SVM score below.

We also investigate how well SVM scores correlate with user importance, irrespective of the segmentation mismatches. We score ground truth segments from all videos of a class with SVM, and order the segments by descending score. Ideally segments with importance 3 should be in the top of the list, and non-relevant segments at the bottom. Since ground truth scores are discrete (from 0 to 3), we use the nDCG ranking metric [37], $nDCG = Z_p^{-1} \sum_{i=1}^{p} I^{(i)} (\log_2 i)^{-1}$, where $I^{(i)}$ is the annotated importance score of the ith segment in the ranked list; p is the total number of segments over all videos of the class; Z_p is the normalization factor such that a perfect ranking's nDCG is 1.

Fig. 4b shows that, for 9 out of 10 classes, the SVM ranking is stronger than the random ranking.

Note that our approach does not require a ground-truth segmentation nor importance annotation for the training set. Therefore there can be some information loss due to unrelated clutter. To quantify this loss, we run an experiment by cross-validation on the test set where we use as positives during training the segments with the highest-importance scores, and observe an increase of 3 points in performance with respect to learning from full videos. Thus, a multiple instance learning (MIL) approach might give some improvement and is a possible extension of our approach.

Figure 5 illustrates our approach.

6   Conclusion

We proposed a novel approach to video summarization, called KVS, that delivers short and highly-informative summaries, that assemble the most important segments for a given video category.

KVS requires a set of training videos for a given category so that the method can be trained in a supervised fashion, but does not rely on segment annotations in the training set. We also introduced a new dataset for category-specific video summarization, MED-Summaries, that is publicly available, along with the annotations and the evaluation code that computes the performance metrics introduced in this paper.

Acknowledgements. This work was supported by the European integrated project AXES, the MSR/INRIA joint project, the LabEx PERSYVAL-Lab (ANR-11-LABX-0025), and the ERC advanced grant ALLEGRO. We thank the LEAR team members and Hyun Oh Song who helped with the annotation.

References

1. Liu, Y., Zhou, F., Liu, W., De la Torre, F., Liu, Y.: Unsupervised summarization of rushes videos. In: ACM Multimedia (2010)
2. de Avila, S., Lopes, A., et al.: VSUMM: A mechanism designed to produce static video summaries and a novel evaluation method. Pattern Recognition Letters 32(1), 56–68 (2011)

3. Lee, Y.J., Ghosh, J., Grauman, K.: Discovering important people and objects for egocentric video summarization. In: CVPR (2012)
4. Wang, M., Hong, R., Li, G., Zha, Z.J., Yan, S., Chua, T.S.: Event driven web video summarization by tag localization and key-shot identification. Transactions on Multimedia 14(4), 975–985 (2012)
5. Khosla, A., Hamid, R., Lin, C.J., Sundaresan, N.: Large-scale video summarization using web-image priors. In: CVPR (2013)
6. Lu, Z., Grauman, K.: Story-driven summarization for egocentric video. In: CVPR (2013)
7. Truong, B.T., Venkatesh, S.: Video abstraction: A systematic review and classification. ACM Transactions on Multimedia Computing, Communications, and Applications 3(1), 3 (2007)
8. Over, P., Smeaton, A.F., Awad, G.: The Trecvid 2008 BBC rushes summarization evaluation. In: 2nd ACM TRECVID Video Summarization Workshop (2008)
9. Ma, Y.F., Hua, X.S., Lu, L., Zhang, H.J.: A generic framework of user attention model and its application in video summarization. Transactions on Multimedia (2005)
10. Li, K., Oh, S., Perera, A.G.A., Fu, Y.: A videography analysis framework for video retrieval and summarization. In: BMVC (2012)
11. Ngo, C.W., Ma, Y.F., Zhang, H.J.: Video summarization and scene detection by graph modeling. Circuits and Systems for Video Technology 15(2) (2005)
12. Divakaran, A., Peker, K., Radhakrishnan, R., Xiong, Z., Cabasson, R.: Video summarization using Mpeg-7 motion activity and audio descriptors. In: Video Mining, vol. 6. Springer (2003)
13. Xie, L., Xu, P., Chang, S.F., Divakaran, A., Sun, H.: Structure analysis of soccer video with domain knowledge and hidden markov models. Pattern Recognition Letters 25(7) (2004)
14. Rui, Y., Gupta, A., Acero, A.: Automatically extracting highlights for TV baseball programs. In: ACM Multimedia (2000)
15. Sundaram, H., Xie, L., Chang, S.F.: A utility framework for the automatic generation of audio-visual skims. In: ACM Multimedia (2002)
16. Zhao, B., Xing, E.P.: Quasi real-time summarization for consumer videos. In: CVPR (2014)
17. Cong, Y., Yuan, J., Luo, J.: Towards scalable summarization of consumer videos via sparse dictionary selection. Transactions on Multimedia (2012)
18. Kim, G., Sigal, L., Xing, E.P.: Joint summarization of large-scale collections of web images and videos for storyline reconstruction. In: CVPR (2014)
19. Lin, C.Y.: Rouge: A package for automatic evaluation of summaries. In: ACL Workshop on Text Summarization Branches, pp. 74–81 (2004)
20. Hoiem, D., Efros, A.A., Hebert, M.: Automatic photo pop-up. ACM Transactions on Graphics 24(3), 577–584 (2005)
21. Tighe, J., Lazebnik, S.: SuperParsing: Scalable nonparametric image parsing with superpixels. In: Daniilidis, K., Maragos, P., Paragios, N. (eds.) ECCV 2010, Part V. LNCS, vol. 6315, pp. 352–365. Springer, Heidelberg (2010)
22. Lezama, J., Alahari, K., Sivic, J., Laptev, I.: Track to the future: Spatio-temporal video segmentation with long-range motion cues. In: CVPR (2011)
23. Grundmann, M., Kwatra, V., Han, M., Essa, I.: Efficient hierarchical graph-based video segmentation. In: CVPR (2010)
24. Massoudi, A., Lefebvre, F., Demarty, C.H., Oisel, L., Chupeau, B.: A video fingerprint based on visual digest and local fingerprints. In: ICIP (2006)

25. Chasanis, V., Kalogeratos, A., Likas, A.: Movie segmentation into scenes and chapters using locally weighted bag of visual words. In: CIVR (2009)
26. Kay, S.M.: Fundamentals of Statistical signal processing, vol. 2: Detection theory. Prentice Hall PTR (1998)
27. Harchaoui, Z., Bach, F., Moulines, E.: Kernel change-point analysis. In: NIPS (2008)
28. Harchaoui, Z., Cappé, O.: Retrospective mutiple change-point estimation with kernels. In: IEEE Workshop on Statistical Signal Processing, pp. 768–772 (2007)
29. Hastie, T., Tibshirani, R., Friedman, J.: The elements of statistical learning: data mining, inference and prediction, 2nd edn. Springer (2009)
30. Arlot, S., Celisse, A., Harchaoui, Z.: Kernel change-point detection. arXiv:1202.3878 (2012)
31. Crow, F.C.: Summed-area tables for texture mapping. ACM SIGGRAPH Computer Graphics 18, 207–212 (1984)
32. Oneata, D., Verbeek, J., Schmid, C.: Action and Event Recognition with Fisher Vectors on a Compact Feature Set. In: ICCV (2013)
33. Cao, L., Mu, Y., Natsev, A., Chang, S.-F., Hua, G., Smith, J.R.: Scene aligned pooling for complex video recognition. In: Fitzgibbon, A., Lazebnik, S., Perona, P., Sato, Y., Schmid, C. (eds.) ECCV 2012, Part II. LNCS, vol. 7573, pp. 688–701. Springer, Heidelberg (2012)
34. Gaidon, A., Harchaoui, Z., Schmid, C.: Temporal localization with actoms. PAMI (2013)
35. Perronnin, F., Sánchez, J., Mensink, T.: Improving the fisher kernel for large-scale image classification. In: Daniilidis, K., Maragos, P., Paragios, N. (eds.) ECCV 2010, Part IV. LNCS, vol. 6314, pp. 143–156. Springer, Heidelberg (2010)
36. Wang, H., Kläser, A., Schmid, C., Liu, C.L.: Dense trajectories and motion boundary descriptors for action recognition. IJCV (2013)
37. Manning, C.D., Raghavan, P., Schütze, H.: Introduction to information retrieval, Cambridge, vol. 1 (2008)

Assessing the Quality of Actions

Hamed Pirsiavash, Carl Vondrick, and Antonio Torralba

Massachusetts Institute of Technology
{hpirsiav,vondrick,torralba}@mit.edu

Abstract. While recent advances in computer vision have provided reliable methods to recognize actions in both images and videos, the problem of assessing how well people perform actions has been largely unexplored in computer vision. Since methods for assessing action quality have many real-world applications in healthcare, sports, and video retrieval, we believe the computer vision community should begin to tackle this challenging problem. To spur progress, we introduce a learning-based framework that takes steps towards assessing how well people perform actions in videos. Our approach works by training a regression model from spatiotemporal pose features to scores obtained from expert judges. Moreover, our approach can provide interpretable feedback on how people can improve their action. We evaluate our method on a new Olympic sports dataset, and our experiments suggest our framework is able to rank the athletes more accurately than a non-expert human. While promising, our method is still a long way to rivaling the performance of expert judges, indicating that there is significant opportunity in computer vision research to improve on this difficult yet important task.

1 Introduction

Recent advances in computer vision have provided reliable methods for recognizing actions in videos and images. However, the problem of automatically quantifying *how well* people perform actions has been largely unexplored.

We believe the computer vision community should begin to tackle the challenging problem of assessing the quality of people's actions because there are many important, real-world applications. For example, in health care, patients are often monitored and evaluated after hospitalization as they perform daily tasks, which is expensive undertaking without an automatic assessment method.

Fig. 1. We introduce a learning framework for assessing the quality of human actions from videos. Since we estimate a model for what constitutes a high quality action, our method can also provide feedback on how people can improve their actions, visualized with the red arrows.

D. Fleet et al. (Eds.): ECCV 2014, Part VI, LNCS 8694, pp. 556–571, 2014.

In sports, action quality assessments would allow an athlete to practice in front of a camera and receive quality scores in real-time, providing the athlete with rapid feedback and an opportunity to improve their action. In retrieval, a video search engine may want to sort results based on the quality of the action performed instead of only the relevance.

However, automatically assessing the quality of actions is not an easy computer vision problem. Human experts for a particular domain, such as coaches or doctors, have typically been trained over many years to develop complex underlying rules to assess action quality. If machines are to assess action quality, then they must discover similar rules as well.

In this paper, we propose a data-driven method to *learn* how to assess the quality of actions in videos. To our knowledge, we are the first to propose a general framework for learning to assess the quality of human-based actions from videos. Our method works by extracting the spatio-temporal pose features of people, and with minimal annotation, estimating a regression model that predicts the scores of actions. Fig.1 shows an example output of our system.

In order to quantify the performance of our methods, we introduce a new dataset for action quality assessment comprised of Olympic sports footage. Although the methods in this paper are general, sports broadcast footage has the advantage that it is freely available, and comes already rigorously "annotated" by the Olympic judges. We evaluate our quality assessments on both diving and figure skating competitions. Our results are promising, and suggest that our method is significantly better at ranking people's actions by their quality than non-expert humans. However, our method is still a long way from rivaling the performance of expert judges, indicating that there is significant opportunity in computer vision research to improve on this difficult yet important task.

Moreover, since our method leverages high level pose features to learn a model for action quality, we can use this model to help machines understand people in videos as well. Firstly, we can provide interpretable feedback to performers on how to improve the quality of their action. The red vectors in Fig.1 are output from our system that instructs the Olympic diver to stretch his hands and lower his feet. Our feedback system works by calculating the gradient for each body joint against the learned model that would have maximized people's scores. Secondly, we can create highlights of videos by finding which segments contributed the most to the action quality, complementing work in video summarization. We hypothesize that further progress in building better quality assessment models can improve both feedback systems and video highlights.

The three principal contributions of this paper revolve around automatically assessing the quality of people's actions in videos. Firstly, we introduce a general learning-based framework for the quality assessment of human actions using spatiotemporal pose features. Secondly, we then describe a system to generate feedback for performers in order to improve their score. Finally, we release a new dataset for action quality assessment in the hopes of facilitating future research on this task. The remainder of this paper describes these contributions in detail.

2   Related Work

This paper builds upon several areas of computer vision. We briefly review related work:

Action Assessment: The problem of action quality assessment has been relatively unexplored in the computer vision community. There have been a few promising efforts to judge how well people perform actions [1–3], however, these previous works have so far been hand-crafted for specific actions. The motivation for assessing peoples actions in healthcare applications has also been discussed before [4], but the technical method is limited to recognizing actions. In this paper, we propose a generic learning-based framework with state-of-the-art features for action quality assessment that can be applied to most types of human actions. To demonstrate this generality, we evaluate on two distinct types of actions (diving and figure skating). Furthermore, our system is able to generate interpretable feedback on how performers can improve their action.

Photograph Assessment: There are several works that assess photographs, such as their quality [5], interestingness [6] and aesthetics [7, 8]. In this work, we instead focus on assessing the quality of human actions, and not the quality of the video capture or its artistic aspects.

Action Recognition: There is a large body of work studying how to recognize actions in both images [9–13] and videos [14–18], and we refer readers to excellent surveys [19, 20] for a full review. While this paper also studies actions, we are interested in *assessing* their quality rather than *recognizing* them.

Features: There are many features for action recognition using spatiotemporal bag-of-words [21, 22], interest points [23], feature learning [24], and human pose based [25]. However, so far these features have primarily been shown to work for recognition. We found that some of these features, notably [24] and [25] with minor adjustments, can be used for the quality assessment of actions too.

Video Summarization: This paper complements work in video summarization [26–31]. Rather than relying on saliency features or priors, we instead can summarize videos by discarding segments that did not impact the quality score of an action, thereby creating a "highlights reel" for the video.

3   Assessing Action Quality

We now present our system for assessing the quality of an action from videos. On a high level, our model learns a regression model from spatio-temporal features. After presenting our model, we then show how our model can be used to provide feedback to the people in videos to improve their actions. We finally describe how our model can highlight segments of the video that contribute the most to the quality score.

3.1 Features

To learn a regression model to the action quality, we extract spatio-temporal features from videos. We consider two sets of features: low-level features that capture gradients and velocities directly from pixels, and high-level features based off the trajectory of human pose.

Low Level Features: Since there has been significant progress in developing features for *recognizing* actions, we tried using them for *assessing* actions too. We use a hierarchical feature [24] that obtains state-of-the-art performance in action recognition by learning a filter bank with independent subspace analysis. The learned filter bank consists of spatio-temporal Gabor-like filters that capture edges and velocities. In our experiments, we use the implementation by [24] with the network pre-trained on the Hollywood2 dataset [32].

High Level Pose Features: Since most low-level features capture statistics from pixels directly, they are often difficult to interpret. As we wish to provide feedback on how a performer can improve their actions, we want the feedback to be interpretable. Inspired by actionlets [25], we now present high level features based off human pose that are interpretable.

Given a video, we assume that we know the pose of the human performer in every frame, obtained either through ground truth or automatic pose estimation. Let $p^{(j)}(t)$ be the x component of the jth joint in the tth frame of the video. Since we want our features to be translation-invariant, we normalize the joint positions relative to the head position:

$$q^{(j)}(t) = p^{(j)}(t) - p^{(0)}(t)$$

where we have assumed that $p^{(0)}(t)$ refers to the head. Note that $q^{(j)}$ is a function of time, so we can represent it in the frequency domain by the discrete cosine transform (DCT): $Q^{(j)} = Aq^{(j)}$ where A is the discrete cosine transformation matrix. We then use the k lowest frequency components to create the feature vector $\phi_j = \left| Q^{(j)}_{1:k} \right|$ where $A_{1:k}$ selects the first k rows of A. We found that only using the low frequencies helps remove high frequency noise due to pose estimation errors. We use the absolute value of the frequency coefficients Q_i.

We compute ϕ_j for every joint for both the x- and y-components, and concatenate them to create the final feature vector ϕ. We note that if the video is long, we break it up into segments and concatenate the features to produce one feature vector for the entire video. This inreases the temporal resolution of our features for long videos.

Actionlets [25] uses a similar method with Discrete Fourier Transform (DFT) instead. Although there is a close relationship between DFT and DCT, we see better results using DCT. We believe this is the case since DCT provides a more compact representation. Additionally, DCT coefficients are real numbers instead of complex, so less information is lost in the absolute value operation.

Successes   Failures

Fig. 2. Pose Estimation Challenges: Some results for human pose estimation on our action quality dataset. Since the performers contort their body in unusual configurations, pose estimation is very challenging on our dataset.

In order to estimate the joints of the performer throughout the video $p^{(j)}(t)$, we run a pose estimation algorithm to find the position of the joints in every frame. We estimate the pose using a Flexible Parts Model [33] for each frame independently. Since [33] finds the best pose for a single frame using dynamic programming and we want the best pose across the entire video, we find the N-best pose solutions per frame using [34]. Then we associate the poses using a dynamic programming algorithm to find the best track in the whole video. The association looks for the single best smooth track covering the whole temporal span of the video. Fig.2 shows some successes and failures of this pose estimation.

3.2 Learning

We then pose quality assessment as a supervised regression problem. Let $\Phi_i \in \mathbb{R}^{k \times n}$ be the pose features for video i in matrix form where n is the number of joints and k is the number of low frequency components. We write $y_i \in \mathbb{R}$ to denote the ground-truth quality score of the action in video i, obtained by an expert human judge. We then train a linear support vector regression (L-SVR) [35] to predict y_i given features Φ_i over a training set. In our experiments, we use libsvm [36]. Optimization is fast, and takes less than a second on typical sized problems. We perform cross validation to estimate hyperparameters.

Domain Knowledge: We note that a comprehensive model for quality assessment might use domain experts to annotate fine-tuned knowledge on the action's quality (e.g., "the leg must be straight"). However, relying on domain experts is expensive and difficult to scale to a large number of actions. By posing quality assessment as a machine learning problem with minimal interaction from an expert, we can scale more efficiently. In our system, we only require a single real number per video corresponding to the score of the quality.

Prototypical Example: Moreover, a fairly simple method to assess quality is to check the observed video against a ground truth video with perfect execution, and then determine the difference. However, in practice, many actions can have multiple ideal executions (e.g., a perfect overhand serve might be just as good as a perfect underhand serve). Instead, our model can handle multi-modal score distributions.

3.3 Feedback Proposals

As a performer executes an action, in addition to assessing the quality, we also wish to provide feedback on how the performer can improve his action. Since our regression model operates over pose-based features, we can determine how the performer should move to maximize the score.

We accomplish this by differentiating the scoring function with respect to joint location. We calculate the gradient of the score with respect to the location of each joint $\frac{\partial S}{\partial p^{(j)}(t)}$ where S is the scoring function. By calculating the maximum gradient, we can find the joint and the direction that the performer must move to achieve the largest improvement in the score.

We are able to analytically calculate the gradient. Recall that L-SVR learns a weight vector $W \in \mathbb{R}^{k \times n}$ such that W predicts the score of the action quality by the dot-product:

$$S = \sum_{f=1}^{k} \sum_{j=1}^{n} W_{fj} \Phi_{fj}$$

where Φ_{fj} is the fth frequency componenet for the jth joint. After basic algebra, we can compute the gradient of the score S with respect to the location of each joint $p^{(j)}(t)$:

$$\frac{\partial S}{\partial p^{(j)}(t)} = \sum_{f=1}^{k} A_{ft} W_{fj} \cdot \text{sign} \left(\sum_{t'=1}^{T} \left(A_{ft'} (p^{(j)}(t') - p^{(0)}(t')) \right) \right)$$

By computing $\max_{p^{(j)}(t)} \frac{\partial S}{\partial p^{(j)}(t)}$, we can find the joint and the direction the performer must move to most improve the score.[1]

3.4 Video Highlights

In addition to finding the joint that will result in the largest score improvement, we also wish to measure the *impact* a segment of the video has on the quality score. Such a measure could be useful in summarizing the segments of actions that contribute to high or low scores.

We define a segment's impact as how much the quality score would change if the segment were removed. In order to remove a segment, we compute the most likely feature vector had we not observed the missing segment. The key observation is that since we only use the low frequency components in our feature vector, there are more equations than unknowns when estimating the DCT coefficients. Consequently, removing a segment corresponds to simply removing some equations.

---

[1] We do not differentiate with respect to the head location because it is used for normalization.

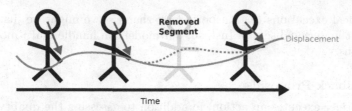

Fig. 3. Interpolating Segments: This schematic shows how the displacement vector changes when a segment of the video is removed in order to compute impact. The dashed curve is the original displacement, and the solid curve is the most likely displacement given observations with a missing segment.

Let $B = A^+$ be the inverse cosine transform where A^+ is the psuedo-inverse of A. Then, the DCT equation can be written as $Q^{(j)} = B^+ q^{(j)}$. If the data from frames u through v is missing, then the inferred DCT coefficients are $\hat{Q}^{(j)} = (B_{\overline{u:v}})^+ q^{(j)}$ where $B_{\overline{u:v}}$ is the sub-matrix of B that excludes rows u through v. The frequency components $\hat{Q}^{(j)}$ are the same dimensionality as $Q^{(j)}$, but they have inferred the missing segment with the most likely joint trajectory. Fig.3 visualizes how the features change with this transformation.

We use $\hat{Q}^{(j)}$ to create the feature vector for the video with the missing segment. Finally, we determine the impact of the missing segment by calculating the difference in scores between the original feature vector and the feature vector with the missing segment.

4   Experiments

In this section, we evaluate both our quality assessment method and feedback system for quality improvement with quantitative experiments. Since quality assessment has not yet been extensively studied in the computer vision community, we first introduce a new video dataset for action quality assessment.

4.1   Action Quality Dataset

There are two primary hurdles in building a large dataset for action quality assessment. Firstly, the score annotations are subjective, and require an expert. Unfortunately, hiring an expert to annotate hundreds of videos is expensive. Secondly, in some applications such as health care, there are privacy and legal issues involved in collecting videos from patients. In order to establish a baseline dataset for further research, we desire freely available videos.

We introduce an Olympics video dataset for action quality assessment. Sports footage has the advantage that it can be obtained freely, and the expert judge's scores are frequently released publicly. We collected videos from YouTube for two categories of sports, diving and figure skating, from recent Olympics and other worldwide championships. The videos are long with multiple instances of actions performed by multiple people. We annotated the videos with the start

Fig. 4. Diving Dataset: Some of the best dives from our diving dataset. Each column corresponds to one video. There is a large variation in the top-scoring actions. Hence, providing feedback is not as easy as pushing the action towards a canonical "good" performance.

Fig. 5. Figure Skating Dataset: Sample frames from our figure skating dataset. Notice the large variations of routines that the performers attempt. This makes automatic pose estimation challenging.

and end frame for each instance, and we extracted the judge's score. The dataset will be publicly available.

Diving: Fig.4 shows a few examples of our diving dataset. Our diving dataset consists of 159 videos. The videos are slow-motion from television broadcasting channels, so the effective frame rate is 60 frames per second. Each video is about 150 frames, and the entire dataset consists of 25,000 frames. The ground truth judge scores varies between 20 (worst) and 100 (best). In our experiments, we use 100 instances for training and the rest for testing. We repeated every experiment 200 times with different random splits and averaged the results. In addition to the Olympic judge's score, we also consulted with the MIT varsity diving coach who annotated which joints a diver should adjust to improve each dive. We use this data to evaluate our feedback system for the quality improvement algorithm.

Figure Skating: Fig.5 shows some frames from our figure skating dataset. This dataset contains 150 videos captured at 24 frames per second. Each video is almost 4,200 frames, and the entire dataset is 630,000 frames. The judge's score ranges between 0 (worst) and 100 (best). We use 100 instances for training and the rest for testing. As before, we repeated every experiment 200 times with different random splits and averaged the results. We note that our figure skating

Table 1. Diving Evaluation: We show mean rank correlation on our diving dataset. Higher is better. The pose-based features provide the best performance.

Method	STIP	Hierarchical	Pose+DFT	Pose+DCT
SVR	0.07	0.19	0.27	**0.41**
Ridge Reg	0.10	0.16	0.19	0.27

Table 2. Figure Skating Evaluation: We calculate mean rank correlation on our figure skating dataset. Higher is better. The hierarchical network features provide the best results. Although pose based features are not superior, they still enable high level analysis by providing feedback for quality improvement. We believe pose based features can benefit from using a better pose estimation.

Method	STIP	Hierarchical	Pose+DFT	Pose+DCT
SVR	0.21	**0.45**	0.31	0.35
Ridge Reg	0.20	**0.44**	0.19	0.25

tends to be more challenging for pose estimation since it is at a lower frame rate, and has more variation in the human pose and clothing (e.g., wearing skirt).

4.2   Quality Assessment

We evaluate our quality assessment on both the figure skating and diving dataset. In order to compare our results against the ground truth, we use the rank correlation of the scores we predict against the scores the Olympic judges awarded. Tab.1 and Tab.2 show the mean performance over random train/test splits of our datasets. Our results suggest that pose-based features are competitive, and even obtain the best performance on the diving dataset. In addition, our results indicate that features learned to recognize actions can be used to assess the quality of actions too. We show some of the best and worst videos as predicted by our model in Fig.6.

We compare our quality assessment against several baselines. Firstly, we compare to both space-time interest points (STIP) and pose-based features with Discrete Fourier Transform (DFT) instead of DCT (similar to [24]). Both of these features performed worse. Secondly, we also compare to ridge regression with all feature sets. Our results show that support vector regression often obtains significantly better performance.

We also asked non-expert human annotators to predict the quality of each diver in the diving dataset. Interestingly, after we instructed the subjects to read the Wikipedia page on diving, non-expert annotators were only able to achieve a rank correlation of 19%, which is half the performance of support vector regression with pose features. We believe this difference is evidence that our algorithm is starting to learn which human poses constitute good dives. We note, however, that our method is far from matching Olympic judges since they

| Gold Medal | Silver Medal | 2nd to last place | Last place |

Our Score: 98.68   Our Score: 83.25   Our Score: 56.10   Our Score: 39.60
Judge Score: 96.35   Judge Score: 93.13   Judge Score: 43.72   Judge Score: 37.30

High Action Quality   Low Action Quality

Fig. 6. Examples of Diving Scores: We show the two best and worst videos sorted by the predicted score. Each column is one video with ground truth and predicted score written below. Notice that in the last place video, the diver lacked straight legs in the beginning and did not have a tight folding pose. These two pitfalls are part of common diving advice given by coaches, and our model has learned this independently.

are able to predict the median judge's score with a rank correlation of 96%, suggesting that there is still significant room for improvement.[2]

4.3   Limitations

While our system is able to predict the quality of actions with some success, it has many limitations. One of the major bottlenecks is the pose estimation. Fig.2 shows a few examples of the successes and failures of the pose estimation. Pose estimation in our datasets is very challenging since the performers contort their body in many unusual configurations with significant variation in appearance. The frequent occlusion by clothing for figure skating noticeably harms the pose estimation performance. When the pose estimation is poor, the quality score is strongly affected, suggesting that advances in pose estimation or using depth sensors for pose can improve our system. Future work in action quality can be made robust against these types of failures as well by accounting for the uncertainty in the pose estimation.

---

[2] Olympic diving competitions have two scores: the technical difficulty and the score. The final quality of the action is then the product of these two quantities. Judges are told the technical difficulty apriori, which gives them a slight competitive edge over our algorithms. We did not model the technical difficulty in the interest of building a general system.

Fig. 7. Diving Feedback Proposals: We show feedback for some of the divers. The red vectors are instructing the divers to move their body in the direction of the arrow. In general, the feedback instructs divers to tuck their legs more and straighten their body before entering the pool.

Our system is designed to work for one human performer only, and does not model coordination between multiple people, which is often important for many types of sports and activities. We believe that future work in explicitly modeling team activities and interactions can significantly advance action quality assessment. Moreover, we do not model objects used during actions (such as sports balls or tools), and we do not consider physical outcomes (such as splashes in diving), which may be important features for some activities. Finally, while our representation captures the movements of human joint locations, we do not explicitly model their synchronization (e.g., keeping legs together) or repetitions (e.g., waving hands back and forth). We suspect a stronger quality assessment model will factor in these visual elements.

4.4   Feedback for Improvement

In addition to quality assessment, we evaluate the feedback vectors that our method provides. Fig.7 and Fig.8 show qualitatively a sample of the feedback that our algorithm suggests. In general, the feedback is reasonable, often making modifications to the extremities of the performer.

In order to quantitatively evaluate our feedback method, we needed to acquire ground truth annotations. We consulted with the MIT diving team coach who watched a subset of the videos in our dataset (27 in total) and provided suggestions on how to improve the dive. The diving coach gave us specific feedback (such as "move left foot down") as well as high-level feedback (e.g., "legs should be straight here" or "tuck arms more"). We translated each feedback from the coach into one of three classes, referring to whether the diver should adjust his upper body, his lower body, or maintain the same pose on each frame. Due to the subjective nature of the task, the diving coach was not able to provide more

Fig. 8. Figure Skating Feedback Proposals: We show feedback for some of the figure skaters where the red vectors are instructions for the figure skaters.

Fig. 9. Feedback Limitations: The feedback we generate is not perfect. If the figure skater or diver were to rely completely on the feedback above, they may fall over. Our model does not factor in physical laws, motivating work in support inference [37, 38].

detailed feedback annotations. Hence, the feedback is coarsely mapped into these three classes.

We then evaluate our feedback as a detection problem. We consider a feedback proposal from our algorithm as correct if it suggests to move a body part within a one second range of the coach making the same suggestion. We use the magnitude of the feedback gradient as the importance of the feedback proposal. We use a leave-one-out approach where we predict feedback on a video heldout from training. Our feedback proposals obtain 53.18% AP overall for diving, compared to 27% AP chance level. We compute chance by randomly generating feedback that uniformly chooses between the upper body and lower body.

Since our action quality assessment model is not aware of physical laws, the feedback suggestions can be physically implausible. Fig.9 shows a few cases where if the performer listened to our feedback, they might fall over. Our method's lack of physical models motivates work in support inference [37, 38].

Interestingly, by averaging the feedback across all divers in our dataset, we can find the most common feedback produced by our model. Fig.10 shows the magnitude of feedback for each frame and each joint averaged over all divers. For visualization proposes, we warp all videos to have the same length. Most of the feedback suggests correcting the feet and hands, and the most important frames

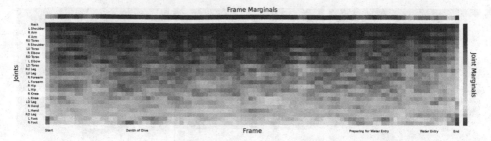

Fig. 10. Visualizing Common Feedback: We visualize the average feedback magnitude across the entire diving dataset for each joint and frame. Red means high feedback and blue means low feedback. The top and right edges show marginals over frames and joints respectively. R and L stand for right and left respectively, and U and D stand for upper and lower body, respectively. Feet are the most common area for feedback on Olympic divers, and that the beginning and end of the dive are the most important time points.

turn out to be the initial jump off the diving board, the zenith of the dive, and the moment right before the diver enters the water.

4.5   Highlighting Impact

We qualitatively analyze the video highlights produced by finding the segments that contributed the most to the final quality score. We believe that this measure can be useful for video summarization since it reveals, out of a long video, which clips are the most important for the action quality. We computed impact on a routine from the figure skating dataset in Fig.11. Notice when the impact is near zero, the figure skater is in a standard, up-right position, or in-between maneuvers. The points of maximum impact correspond to jumps and twists of the figure skater, which contributes positively to the score if the skater performs it correctly, and negatively otherwise.

4.6   Discussion

If quality assessment is a subjective task, is it reasonable for a machine to still obtain reasonable results? Remarkably, the independent Olympic judges agree with each other 96% of the time, which suggests that there is some underlying structure in the data. One hypothesis to explain this correlation is that the judges are following a complex system of rules to gauge the score. If so, then the job of a machine quality assessment system is to extract these rules. While the approach in this paper attempts to learn these rules, we are still a long way from high performance on this task.

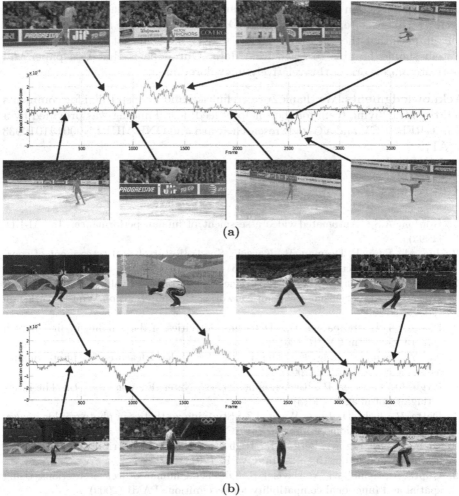

Fig. 11. Video Highlights: By calculating the impact each frame has on the score of the video, we can summarize long videos with the segments that have the largest impact on the quality score. Notice how, above, when the impact is close to zero, the skater is usually in an upright standard position, and when the impact is large, the skater is performing a maneuver.

5 Conclusions

Assessing the quality of actions is an important problem with many real-world applications in health care, sports and search. To enable these applications, we have introduced a general learning-based framework to automatically assess an action's quality from videos as well as to provide feedback for how the performer can improve. We evaluated our system on a dataset of Olympic divers and figure skaters, and we show that our approach is significantly better at assessing an action's quality than a non-expert human. Although the quality of an action is a subjective measure, the independent Olympic judges have a large correlation. This implies that there is a well defined underlying rule that a computer vision system should be able to learn from data. Our hope is that this paper will motivate more work in this relatively unexplored area.

Acknowledgments. We thank Zoya Bylinkskii and Sudeep Pillai for comments and the MIT diving team for their helpful feedback. Funding was provided by a NSF GRFP to CV and a Google research award and ONR MURI N000141010933 to AT.

References

1. Gordon, A.S.: Automated video assessment of human performance. In: AI-ED. (1995)
2. Jug, M., Perš, J., Dežman, B., Kovačič, S.: Trajectory based assessment of coordinated human activity. Springer (2003)
3. Perše, M., Kristan, M., Perš, J., Kovacic, S.: Automatic Evaluation of Organized Basketball Activity using Bayesian Networks. Computer Vision Winter Workshop (2007)
4. Pirsiavash, H., Ramanan, D.: Detecting activities of daily living in first-person camera views. In: CVPR. (2012)
5. Ke, Y., Tang, X., Jing, F.: The design of high-level features for photo quality assessment. In: CVPR. (2006)
6. Gygli, M., Grabner, H., Riemenschneider, H., Nater, F., Van Gool, L.: The interestingness of images. (2013)
7. Datta, R., Joshi, D., Li, J., Wang, J.Z.: Studying aesthetics in photographic images using a computational approach. In: ECCV. (2006)
8. Dhar, S., Ordonez, V., Berg, T.L.: High level describable attributes for predicting aesthetics and interestingness. In: CVPR. (2011)
9. Gupta, A., Kembhavi, A., Davis, L.S.: Observing human-object interactions: Using spatial and functional compatibility for recognition. PAMI (2009)
10. Yao, B., Fei-Fei, L.: Action recognition with exemplar based 2.5d graph matching. In: ECCV. (2012)
11. Yang, W., Wang, Y., Mori, G.: Recognizing human actions from still images with latent poses. In: CVPR. (2010)
12. Maji, S., Bourdev, L., Malik, J.: Action recognition from a distributed representation of pose and appearance. In: CVPR. (2011)
13. Delaitre, V., Sivic, J., Laptev, I., et al.: Learning person-object interactions for action recognition in still images. In: NIPS. (2011)
14. Laptev, I., Perez, P.: Retrieving actions in movies. In: ICCV. (2007)
15. Sadanand, S., Corso, J.J.: Action bank: A high-level representation of activity in video. In: CVPR. (2012)
16. Rodriguez, M., Ahmed, J., Shah, M.: Action mach a spatio-temporal maximum average correlation height filter for action recognition. In: CVPR. (2008) 1–8
17. Efros, A., Berg, A., Mori, G., Malik, J.: Recognizing action at a distance. In: CVPR. (2003)
18. Shechtman, E., Irani, M.: Space-time behavior based correlation. In: PAMI. (2007)

19. Poppe, R.: A survey on vision-based human action recognition. Image and Vision Computing **28**(6) (2010) 976–990
20. Aggarwal, J.K., Ryoo, M.S.: Human activity analysis: A review. ACM Comput. Surv. 16
21. Wang, H., Ullah, M.M., Klaser, A., Laptev, I., Schmid, C.: Evaluation of local spatio-temporal features for action recognition. In: BMVC. (2009)
22. Niebles, J., Chen, C., Fei-Fei, L.: Modeling temporal structure of decomposable motion segments for activity classification. ECCV (2010)
23. Laptev, I.: On space-time interest points. ICCV (2005)
24. Le, Q.V., Zou, W.Y., Yeung, S.Y., Ng, A.Y.: Learning hierarchical invariant spatio-temporal features for action recognition with independent subspace analysis. In: CVPR. (2011)
25. Wang, J., Liu, Z., Wu, Y., Yuan, J.: Mining actionlet ensemble for action recognition with depth cameras. In: CVPR. (2012)
26. Ekin, A., Tekalp, A.M., Mehrotra, R.: Automatic soccer video analysis and summarization. Transactions on Image Processing (2003)
27. Khosla, A., Hamid, R., Lin, C.J., Sundaresan, N.: Large-scale video summarization using web-image priors. In: CVPR. (2013)
28. Gong, Y., Liu, X.: Video summarization using singular value decomposition. In: CVPR. (2000)
29. Rav-Acha, A., Pritch, Y., Peleg, S.: Making a long video short: Dynamic video synopsis. In: CVPR. (2006)
30. Ngo, C.W., Ma, Y.F., Zhang, H.J.: Video summarization and scene detection by graph modeling. Circuits and Systems for Video Technology (2005)
31. Jiang, R.M., Sadka, A.H., Crookes, D.: Hierarchical video summarization in reference subspace. Consumer Electronics, IEEE Transactions on (2009)
32. Marszalek, M., Laptev, I., Schmid, C.: Actions in context. In: CVPR. (2009)
33. Yang, Y., Ramanan, D.: Articulated pose estimation with flexible mixtures-of-parts. In: CVPR. (2011)
34. Park, D., Ramanan, D.: N-best maximal decoders for part models. In: ICCV. (2011)
35. Drucker, H., Burges, C.J., Kaufman, L., Smola, A., Vapnik, V.: Support vector regression machines. NIPS (1997)
36. Chang, C.C., Lin, C.J.: Libsvm: a library for support vector machines. ACM Transactions on Intelligent Systems and Technology (TIST) (2011)
37. Silberman, N., Hoiem, D., Kohli, P., Fergus, R.: Indoor segmentation and support inference from rgbd images. In: ECCV. (2012)
38. Zheng, B., Zhao, Y., Yu, J.C., Ikeuchi, K., Zhu, S.C.: Detecting potential falling objects by inferring human action and natural disturbance. In: IEEE Int. Conf. on Robotics and Automation (ICRA). (2014)

HiRF: Hierarchical Random Field
for Collective Activity Recognition in Videos

Mohamed Rabie Amer, Peng Lei, and Sinisa Todorovic

Oregon State University
School of Electrical Engineering and Computer Science, Corvallis, OR, USA
{amerm,leip,todorovics}@onid.orst.edu

Abstract. This paper addresses the problem of recognizing and localizing coherent activities of a group of people, called collective activities, in video. Related work has argued the benefits of capturing long-range and higher-order dependencies among video features for robust recognition. To this end, we formulate a new deep model, called Hierarchical Random Field (HiRF). HiRF models only hierarchical dependencies between model variables. This effectively amounts to modeling higher-order temporal dependencies of video features. We specify an efficient inference of HiRF that iterates in each step linear programming for estimating latent variables. Learning of HiRF parameters is specified within the max-margin framework. Our evaluation on the benchmark New Collective Activity and Collective Activity datasets, demonstrates that HiRF yields superior recognition and localization as compared to the state of the art.

Keywords: Activity recognition, hierarchical graphical models.

1 Introduction

This paper presents a new deep model for representing and recognizing collective activities in videos. A collective activity is characterized by coherent behavior of a group of people both in time and space. Coherence, for example, can be a result of all individuals in the group simultaneously performing the same action (e.g., joint jogging), or coordinated space-time interactions among people in the group (e.g., people assembling by approaching one another, or standing and periodically moving in a line). In addition to localizing time intervals where collective activities occur, we are also interested in localizing individuals that participate in the activities. While prior work has addressed recognition of collective activities, their localization has received scant attention.

Localizing collective activities in videos is challenging. It requires reasoning across a wide range of spatiotemporal scales about individual actions and trajectories, along with people interactions within various groupings. Moreover, as a group of people typically occupy a relatively large percentage of the field of view, capturing their collective activity often requires the camera to move, so recognition and localization have to be performed under camera motion.

Initial work focused on designing a heuristic descriptor of the entire video aimed at capturing coherence of a group's behavior over relatively large spatiotemporal extents [7,8,20]. Recent work specified a variety of graphical models for modeling collective activities. For example, Hierarchical Conditional Random Field (HCRF) used

D. Fleet et al. (Eds.): ECCV 2014, Part VI, LNCS 8694, pp. 572–585, 2014.

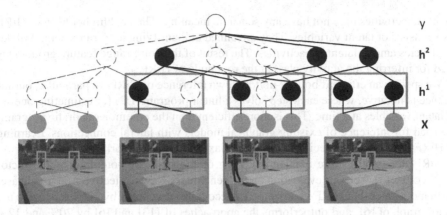

Fig. 1. Hierarchical Random Field (HiRF) for detecting and localizing collective activities. (Top) HiRF encodes the following variables: activity label y; latent temporal-connectivity variables h^2; latent frame-wise connectivity variables h^1; and observable video features x, namely, noisy person detections. (Bottom) Our results on the New Collective Activity Dataset [6] for the activity "Talking". HiRF identifies relevant actors per frame (green), and groups person detections into temporal segments (blue) relevant for recognizing "Talking". Detections estimated as background are marked gray, and latent groupings of background video parts are marked with dashed lines.

in [17] is capable of encoding only short-term dependencies of video features, and thus may poorly discriminate between distinct activities with similar short-term but different long-range properties (e.g., group assembling vs. group walking). More advanced approaches seek to integrate people tracking with reasoning about people actions using hierarchical models [22], AND-OR graphs [2], factor graphs [6,13], or flow models [14]. However, as the complexity of these models increases, finding efficient and sufficiently accurate approximations of their intractable inference becomes more challenging.

In this paper, we advance existing work by specifying a new graphical model of collective activities, called Hierarchical Random Field (HiRF). HiRF is aimed at efficiently capturing long-range and higher-order spatiotemporal dependencies of video features, which have been shown by prior work as critical for characterizing collective activities. HiRF aggregates input features into mid-level video representations, which in turn enable robust recognition and localization. This is because the multiscale aggregation identifies groupings of foreground features, and discards features estimated as belonging to background clutter. In this way, HiRF localizes foreground in the video.

Similar to models used by recent work [2,6,13,14], HiRF also seeks to capture long-range temporal dependencies of visual cues. However, the key difference is that HiRF avoids the standard strategy to establish lateral temporal connections between model variables. Instead, HiRF encodes temporal dependencies among video features through strictly hierarchical ("vertical") connections via two hierarchical levels of latent variables, as illustrated in Fig. 1. At the leaf level, HiRF is grounded onto video features, extracted by applying a person detector in each frame. The next level of HiRF consists of latent variables, which serve to spatially group foreground video features into subactivities relevant for recognition. Since this feature grouping is latent, the identified latent subactivities may not have any semantic meaning. The next higher level of HiRF also consists of latent variables. They are aimed at identifying long-range temporal dependencies among latent subactivities. The result of this long-range feature grouping is used for inferring the activity class at the root node of HiRF.

We specify an efficient bottom-up/top-down inference of HiRF. In particular, our inference is iterative, where each step solves a linear program (LP) for estimating one set of latent variables at a time. This is more efficient than the common quadratic programming used for inference of existing graphical models with lateral connections. Learning of HiRF parameters is specified within the max-margin framework.

HiRF does not require explicit encoding of higher-order potentials as the factor graphs of [6,13]. Yet, our evaluation on the benchmark New Collective Activity dataset [6] demonstrates that HiRF yields superior recognition accuracy by 4.3% relative to the factor graph of [6], and outperforms the approaches of [13] and [6] by 20% and 12% on the Collective Activity dataset [7]. To the best of our knowledge, we present the first evaluation of localizing people that participate in collective activities on the New Collective Activity dataset.

In the following, Sec. 2 reviews related work; Sec. 3 formulates HiRF; Sec. 4 specifies inference; Sec. 5 explains learning; and Sec. 6 presents our results.

2   Related Work

There is a large volume of literature on capturing spatiotemporal dependencies among visual cues for activity recognition [1,25,5]. Representative models include Dynamic Bayesian Networks [28,27], Hidden Conditional Random Fields (HCRFs) [24,17], hierarchical graphical models[17,16,15,22], AND-OR graphs [21,2], and Logic Networks [19,4]. In these models, higher-order dependencies are typically captured by latent variables. This generally leads to NP-hard inference. Intractable inference is usually addressed in a heuristic manner by, for example, restricting the connectivity of variables in the model to a tree [24]. Our HiRF is not restricted to have a tree structure, while its strictly hierarchical connectivity enables efficient inference and learning.

HiRF is also related to Shape Boltzmann Machines [10] used for object segmentation in images. They locally constrain the allowed extent of dependencies between their model variables so as to respect image segmentation. We also locally constrain the connectivity between our latent variables over certain temporal windows along the video, in order to identify latent subactivities relevant for recognition of the collective activity. HiRF is also related to Conditional Random Fields of [18,12] which encode higher-order potentials of image features using Restricted Boltzmann Machines. Similarly, HiRF uses a hierarchy of latent variables to identify latent groupings of video features, which amounts to encoding their higher-order dependencies in time and space.

3   The Model

This section, first, introduces some notation and definitions which will be used for specifying our HiRF model, then reviews closely related models used for representing collective activities, and finally defines HiRF.

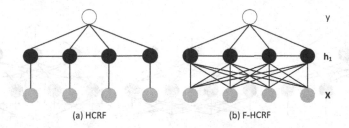

Fig. 2. Closely related existing models: (a) HCRF [23,24] contains a hidden layer h^1 that is temporally connected with lateral edges, while every hidden node h_i^1 is connected to only one observable node x_i. (b) F-HCRF [17] extends HCRF such that every hidden node h_i^1 is connected to many observable nodes x, capturing long-range temporal dependencies.

HiRF is a graphical model defined over a graph, $\mathcal{G} = (\mathcal{V}, \mathcal{E})$. Nodes $\mathcal{V}$ represent: observable video features $x = \{x_i : x_i \in \mathbb{R}^d\}$, integer latent variables $h = \{h_i : h_i \in \mathcal{H}\}$, and a class label $y \in \mathcal{Y}$. Edges $\mathcal{E}$ encode dependencies between the nodes in $\mathcal{V}$. HiRF is characterized by a posterior distribution, $P(y, h|x; w)$, where w are model parameters. The posterior distribution has the Gibbs form: $P(\cdot) = \exp(-E(\cdot))/Z$, where $E(\cdot)$ is the energy, and Z is the partition function.

In the following, we explain our novelty by defining $E(\cdot)$ for a progression of closely related models, shown in Fig. 2.

3.1   Review of Hidden Conditional Random Field

HCRF [23,24] extends the expressiveness of standard CRF by introducing a *single* layer of hidden variables h^1 between x and y, where each h_i is connected to a single x_i. Each h_i may take a value from a set of integers, called "topics". In this way, video features can be grouped into latent "topics", and thus capture their dependencies. The energy of HCRF is defined as

$$E_{\text{HCRF}}(y, h|x) = -\left[\sum_i w^0 \cdot \phi^0(y, h_i^1) + \sum_i w^1 \cdot \phi^1(h_i^1, x_i) + \sum_{i,j} w^2 \cdot \phi^2(y, h_i^1, h_j^1) \right],$$

(1)

where "$\cdot$" denotes scalar multiplication of two vectors; $\phi(y, h, x) = (\phi^0, \phi^1, \phi^2)$ are feature vectors with all elements equal to zero except for a single segment of non-zero elements indexed by the states of latent variables; and $w = (w^0, w^1, w^2)$ are model parameters.

The one-to-one connectivity between h^1 and x in HCRF, however, poorly captures long-range dependancies. To overcome this issue, HCRF has been extended to the feature-level HCRF (F-HCRF) [17] by establishing a full connectivity between the hidden nodes and observable nodes. The energy of F-HCRF is defined as

$$E_{\text{F-HCRF}}(y, h|x) = -\left[\sum_i w^0 \cdot \phi^0(y, h_i^1) + \sum_{i,j} w^1 \cdot \phi^1(h_i^1, x_j) + \sum_{i,j} w^2 \cdot \phi^2(y, h_i^1, h_j^1) \right].$$

(2)

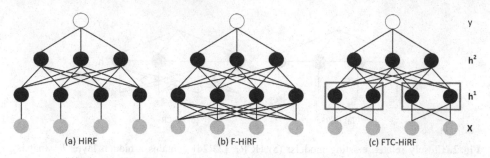

Fig. 3. Variants of HiRF. (a) HiRF introduces an additional hidden layer h^2 to HCRF and removes all lateral connections between the hidden nodes; (b) F-HiRF extends HiRF by establishing the full connectivity between nodes of the hidden layer h^1 and the leaf nodes x; and (c) FTC-HiRF extends F-HiRF by introducing temporal constraints on the connectivity of hidden nodes h^1 to the leaf nodes for reasoning about subactivities of the collective activity.

3.2 Formulation of HiRF

In this section, we formulate HiRF by: (1) Adding another layer of hidden variables to HCRF and F-HCRF reviewed in Sec. 3.1; (2) Removing the lateral temporal connections between all hidden variables; and (3) Enforcing local constraints on temporal connections between the hidden variables. The extensions (1) and (2) are aimed at more efficiently capturing higher-order and long-range temporal dependencies of video features. The extension (3) is aimed at automatically capturing domain knowledge that complex collective activities are typically temporally structured into subactivities, which bound the extent of long-range temporal dependencies of video features. Since these subactivities may not have a particular semantic meaning, but may be relevant for recognition, we use (3) to model subactivities as latent groupings of the first layer of hidden variables h^1, as further explained below.

We first define two variants of our model — namely, HiRF which extends HCRF, and F-HiRF which extends F-HCRF by introducing a new layer of hidden variables, h^2, between h^1 and y, as illustrated in Fig. 3. Their energy functions are defined as

$$E_{\text{HiRF}}(y, \boldsymbol{h}|\boldsymbol{x}) = -\left[\sum_i \boldsymbol{w}^0 \cdot \boldsymbol{\phi}^0(y, h_i^2) + \sum_i \boldsymbol{w}^1 \cdot \boldsymbol{\phi}^1(h_i^1, \boldsymbol{x}_i) + \sum_{i,j} \boldsymbol{w}^2 \cdot \boldsymbol{\phi}^2(h_i^1, h_j^2)\right],$$

$$E_{\text{F-HiRF}}(y, \boldsymbol{h}|\boldsymbol{x}) = -\left[\sum_i \boldsymbol{w}^0 \cdot \boldsymbol{\phi}^0(y, h_i^2) + \sum_{i,j} \boldsymbol{w}^1 \cdot \boldsymbol{\phi}^1(h_i^1, \boldsymbol{x}_j) + \sum_{i,j} \boldsymbol{w}^2 \cdot \boldsymbol{\phi}^2(h_i^1, h_j^2)\right],$$

$$(3)$$

where we use the same notation for feature vectors, $\boldsymbol{\phi}(y, \boldsymbol{h}, \boldsymbol{x}) = (\boldsymbol{\phi}^0, \boldsymbol{\phi}^1, \boldsymbol{\phi}^2)$, and model parameters, $\boldsymbol{w} = (\boldsymbol{w}^0, \boldsymbol{w}^1, \boldsymbol{w}^2)$, as defined for (1) and (2).

In (3), y encodes the activity class label, and latent integer variables h^2 and h^2 are aimed at identifying and grouping foreground video features relevant for recognizing the activity. Specifically, every node h_i^2 may take binary values, $h_i^2 \in \{0, 1\}$, indicating figure-ground assignment of video features. Every node h_i^1 may take integer values, $h_i^1 \in \mathcal{H} = \{0, \ldots, |\mathcal{H}|\}$, indicating latent groupings of video features into "topics".

As shown in Fig. 3, both HiRF and F-HiRF have only hierarchical edges between variables. The newly introduced hidden layer h^2 serves to replace the lateral connections of HCRF and F-HCRF. At the same time, h^2 enables long-range temporal connectivity between the hidden nodes without introducing higher order potentials. From (3), the key difference between HiRF and F-HiRF is that we allow only one-to-one connectivity between the hidden layer h^1 and observable nodes x in HiRF, whereas this connectivity is extended to be full in F-HiRF. In this way, our F-HiRF is expected to have the same advantages of F-HCRF over HCRF, mentioned in Sec. 3.1.

We next extend F-HiRF to Temporally Constrained F-HiRF, called FTC-HiRF. FTC-HiRF enforces local constraints on temporal dependencies of the hidden variables. Similar to Shape Boltzmann Machines [10], we partition the first hidden layer h^1 such that every partition has access only to a particular temporal segment of the video. While the partitions of h^1 cannot directly connect to all video segments, their long-range dependencies are captured through connections to the second hidden layer h^2.

Specifically, in FTC-HiRF, the first hidden layer h^1 is divided into subsets, $h^1 = \{h_t^1 : t = 1, \ldots, T\}$, where each h_t^1 can be connected only to the corresponding temporal window of video features x_t. The energy of FTC-HiRF is defined as

$$E_{\text{FTC-HiRF}}(y, h|x) = - \Big[\sum_i w^0 \cdot \phi^0(y, h_i^2) + \sum_t \sum_{(i,j) \in t} w^1 \cdot \phi^1(h_{it}^1, x_{jt}) + \sum_{i,j} w^2 \cdot \phi^1(h_i^2, h_j^1) \Big], \tag{4}$$

where the third term includes all the hidden variables h^1 from all temporal partitions.

3.3   Definitions of the Potential Functions

The section defines the three types of potential functions of HiRF, specified in (3).

The potential $[w^0 \cdot \phi^0(y, h_i^2)]$ models compatibility between the class label $y \in \mathcal{Y} = \{a : a = 1, 2, \ldots\}$, and the particular figure-ground indicator $h_i^2 \in \{b : b = 0, 1\}$. The parameters $w^0 = [w_{ab}^0]$ are indexed by the activity class labels of y, and binary states of h_i^2. We define this potential as

$$w^0 \cdot \phi^0(y, h_i^2) = \sum_{a \in \mathcal{Y}} \sum_{b \in \{0,1\}} w_{ab}^0 \mathbb{1}(y = a)\mathbb{1}(h_i^2 = b). \tag{5}$$

The potential $[w^1 \cdot \phi^1(h_i^1, x_j)]$ models compatibility between the "topic" assigned to $h_i^1 \in \mathcal{H} = \{c : c = 1, \ldots, |\mathcal{H}|\}$, and the d-dimensional video feature vector x_j, when nodes x_j and h_i^1 are connected in the graphical model. The parameters $w^1 = [w_c^1]$ are indexed by the "topics" of h_i^1. We define this potential as

$$w^1 \cdot \phi^1(h_i^1, x_j) = \sum_{c \in \mathcal{H}} w_c^1 \cdot x_j \mathbb{1}(h_i^1 = c). \tag{6}$$

The potential $[w^2 \cdot \phi^2(h_i^1, h_j^2)]$ models compatibility between the figure-ground assignment of $h_j^2 \in \{b : b = 0, 1\}$, and the "topic" assigned to $h_i^1 \in \mathcal{H} = \{c : c = 1, \ldots, |\mathcal{H}|\}$ when nodes h_j^2 and h_i^1 are connected in the graphical model. The parameters $w^2 = [w_{bc}^2]$ are indexed by the binary states of h_j^2 and the "topics" of h_i^1. We define this potential as

$$w^2 \cdot \phi^2(h_i^1, h_j^2) = \sum_{b \in \{0,1\}} \sum_{c \in \mathcal{H}} w_{bc}^2 \mathbb{1}(h_j^2 = b)\mathbb{1}(h_i^1 = c). \tag{7}$$

4   Bottom-up/Top-down Inference Using Linear Programming

Given a video x and model parameters w, the goal of inference is to predict y and h as

$$\{\hat{y}, \hat{h}\} = \arg\max_{y,h} w \cdot \phi(y, h, x). \tag{8}$$

We solve this inference problem by iterating the following bottom-up and top-down computational steps.

Bottom-up pass. In the bottom-up pass of iteration τ, we first use the observable variables x and $\hat{h}^2(\tau-1)$ to estimate $\hat{h}^1(\tau)$, then, from $\hat{h}^1(\tau)$ and $\hat{y}(\tau-1)$ we compute $\hat{h}^2(\tau)$, and finally, we use $\hat{h}^2(\tau)$ to estimate $\hat{y}(\tau)$. To this end, we reformulate the potentials, given by (5)–(7), as linear functions of the corresponding unknown variables, using auxiliary binary vectors $z_i^1 \in \{0,1\}^{|\mathcal{H}|}$, $z_i^2 \in \{0,1\}^2$, and $z^y \in \{0,1\}^{|\mathcal{Y}|}$, where $z_{i,c}^1 = 1$ if $h_i^1 = c \in \mathcal{H}$, and $z_{i,b}^2 = 1$ if $h_i^2 = b \in \{0,1\}$, and $z_a^y = 1$ if $y = a \in \mathcal{Y}$. Thus, from (3), (6), and (7), we derive the following LPs for each node i of our model:

$$z_i^1(\tau) = \arg\max_{z_i^1} z_i^1 \cdot \left[\sum_j w^1 \cdot x_j + \sum_j w^2 \cdot z_j^2(\tau-1) \right], \text{ s.t. } \sum_{c \in \mathcal{H}} z_{i,c}^1 = 1, \tag{9}$$

$$z_i^2(\tau) = \arg\max_{z_i^2} z_i^2 \cdot \left[\sum_j w^2 \cdot z_j^{1(\tau)} + w^0 \cdot z^y(\tau-1) \right], \text{ s.t. } \sum_{b \in \{0,1\}} z_{i,b}^2 = 1, \tag{10}$$

$$z^y(\tau) = \arg\max_{z^y} z^y \cdot \left[\sum_i w^0 \cdot z_i^2(\tau-1) \right], \text{ s.t. } \sum_{a \in \mathcal{Y}} z_a^y = 1 \tag{11}$$

Top-down pass. In the top-down pass, we solve the above LPs in the reverse order.

In our experiments, we observed convergence for $\tau_{\max} = 10$. After $\tau_{\max}$ iterations, the LP solutions $z_i^1(\tau_{\max})$, $z_i^2(\tau_{\max})$, and $z^y(\tau_{\max})$ uniquely identify $\hat{h}$ and $\hat{y}$. Due to the LP formulations in (9)–(11), our inference is more efficient than the quadratic-optimization based inference algorithms of recent approaches presented in [17,6,13].

5   Max-Margin Learning

We use the max-margin framework for learning HiRF parameters, as was done in [24] for learning HCRF parameters. In particular, we use the latent-SVM to learn w on labeled training examples $\mathcal{D} = \{(x^{(l)}, y^{(l)}) : l = 1, 2, \dots\}$, by solving the following optimization problem:

$$\min_w \underbrace{\left[\frac{C}{2} \|w\|^2 + \sum_l w \cdot \phi(\hat{y}^{(l)}, \hat{h}^{(l)}, x^{(l)}) + \Delta(\hat{y}, y^{(l)}) \right]}_{f(w)} - \underbrace{\left[\sum_l w \cdot \phi(y^{(l)}, h^{*(l)}, x^{(l)}) \right]}_{g(w)} \tag{12}$$

where $\Delta(\hat{y}, y^{(l)})$ is the 0-1 loss, $w \cdot \phi(\hat{y}^{(l)}, \hat{h}^{(l)}, x^{(l)}) = \max_{y,h} w \cdot \phi(y, h, x^{(l)})$, and $w \cdot \phi(y^{(l)}, h^{*(l)}, x^{(l)}) = \max_h w \cdot \phi(y^{(l)}, h, x^{(l)})$. The presence of hidden variables h in (12) make the overall optimization problem non-convex. The problem in (12) can be expressed as a difference of two convex terms $f(w)$ and $g(w)$, and thus can be solved using the CCCP algorithm [26]. Our learning iterates two steps: (i) Given w, each $\hat{y}^{(l)}$, $\hat{h}^{(l)}$, and $h^{*(l)}$ can be efficiently estimated using our bottom-up/top-down inference explained in Sec. 4; (ii) Given the 0-1 loss $\Delta(\hat{y}, y^{(l)})$ and all features $\phi(\hat{y}^{(l)}, \hat{h}^{(l)}, x^{(l)})$ and $\phi(y^{(l)}, h^{*(l)}, x^{(l)})$, w can be estimated by the CCCP algorithm.

6 Results

This section specifies our evaluation datasets, implementation details, evaluation metrics, baselines and comparisons with the state of the art.

We evaluate our approach on the Collective Activity Dataset (CAD) [7], and New Collective Activity Dataset (New-CAD) [6]. CAD consists of 44 videos showing 5 collective activities: crossing, waiting, queuing, walking, and talking. For training and testing, we use the standard split of $3/4$ and $1/4$ of the videos from each class. In every 10th frame, CAD provides annotations of bounding boxes around people performing the activity, their pose, and activity class. We follow the same experimental setup as described in [17]. New-CAD consists of 32 videos showing 6 collective activities – namely, gathering, talking, dismissal, walking together, chasing, queuing – and 9 interactions – specifically, approaching, walking-in-opposite-direction, facing-each-other, standing-in-a-row, walking-side-by-side, walking-one-after-the-other, running-side-by-side, running-one-after-the-other, and no-interaction – and 3 individual actions called walking, standing still, and running. The annotations include 8 poses. As in [6], we divide New-CAD into 3 subsets, and run 3-fold training and testing.

Implementation Details. We first run the person detector of [11] that uses HOG features [9]. The detector is learned to yield high recall. On CAD and New-CAD, we get the average false positive rates of 15.6% and 18.1%, respectively. Each person detection corresponds to one leaf node in HiRF, and is assigned an action descriptor, x_i, similar to the descriptor used in [17]. We compute the action descriptor by concatenating a person descriptor that captures the person's pose and action, and another contextual descriptor that captures the poses and actions of nearby persons. The person descriptor is a $|\mathcal{Y}| \cdot 8$-dimensional vector that consists of confidences of two classifiers which use HOG features of the person's detection bounding box – namely, confidences of SVM over $|\mathcal{Y}|$ action classes, and confidences of the 8-way pose detector presented in [7]. The contextual descriptor is a $|\mathcal{Y}| \cdot 8$-dimensional vector that computes the maximum confidences over all person descriptors associated with the neighboring person detections. We use 10 nodes at the h^1 level, and 20 nodes at the h^2 level, empirically estimated as providing an optimal trade-off between accuracy and model complexity. We establish the fully connectivity between all nodes of levels h^1 and h^2. To enforce temporal constraints in FTC-HiRF, we split the video into T time intervals, and allow connections between h_{it}^1 nodes and leaf nodes x_{jt} only within their respective intervals $t = 1, \ldots, T$. The optimal $T = 10$ is empirically evaluated. Training takes about 6 hours, on a 3.40GHz PC with 8GB RAM.

Baselines. Our baselines include HCRF and F-HCRF specified in Sec. 3.1 and illustrated in Fig. 2. The comparison between our HiRF and HCRF evaluates the effect of replacing the temporal lateral connections in the HCRF with strictly hierarchical connections in HiRF. F-HiRF and FTC-HiRF are variants of HiRF. F-HiRF fully connects all nodes of the hidden layer h^1 with all observable variables x. FTC-HiRF splits the observable nodes into T disjoint sets x_t, $t = 1, \ldots, T$, corresponding to T time intervals in the video, and connects each node of the hidden layer h^1 only with the corresponding set of observable nodes x_t. The comparison between F-HiRF and FTC-HiRF evaluates the effect of temporally constraining the video domain modeled by each node of the hidden layer h^1. In the following, we will assume that our default model is FTC-HiRF.

Comparison. We compare FTC-HiRF with the state-of-the-art temporal approaches of [2,6,13]. These approaches apply a people tracker, and thus additionally use tracking information for inferring their Factor Graphs (FG) [6,13] and spatiotemporal And-Or graphs [2]. FTC-HiRF *does not* use any tracking information. For a fair comparison with non-temporal approaches of [3,17,7] that conduct per-frame reasoning about activities using SVM [7], F-HCRF [17], and spatial And-Or graph [3], we define a special variant of our model, called HiRFnt. HiRFnt has the same formulation as HiRF except that it uses observables (i.e., person detections) only from a single frame. Thus, inference of HiRFnt is performed for every individual video frame. Also, note that for evaluation on New-CAD all prior work uses a higher level of supervision for training their hidden variables – namely, the available interaction labels – whereas, we do not use these labels in our training.

Fig. 4. Person detections using the detector of [11] set to give high recall, and our results using FTC-HiRF on: (top) the New-CAD dataset, and (bottom) the CAD dataset, for the activity "talking". The estimated foreground and background are marked green and red, respectively. The blue frames indicate our localization of the activity's temporal extent. Note that more than one detection falling on the same person may be estimated as foreground.

Evaluation Metrics. We evaluate classification accuracy in (%), and precision and recall of localizing foreground video parts. A true positive is declared if the intersection of the estimated foreground and ground truth is larger than 50% of their union.

Experiments. We first evaluate individual components of our model by comparing the performance of our model variants. Then, we compare FTC-HiRF against the state of the art. Fig. 4 shows our example results on CAD and New-CAD. As can be seen, in these examples, FTC-HiRF successfully detected the activity and localized foreground associated with the recognized activity. In general, FTC-HiRF successfully estimates foreground-background separation, as long as the background activities do not have similar spatiotemporal layout and people poses as the foreground activity.

Fig. 5 shows the sensitivity of FTC-HiRF to the input parameters on the CAD and New-CAD datasets. As can be seen, our model is relatively insensitive to a range of parameter values, but starts overfitting for higher values.

Tab. 1 and Tab. 2 show the comparison of FTC-HiRF and other variants of our approach with the baselines on CAD and New-CAD. As can be seen, in comparison with HCRF, HiRF reduces the running time of inference, and achieves a higher average classification accuracy. These results demonstrate the advantages of using strictly hierarchical connections in our approach. F-HiRF slightly improves the results of HiRF, but has a longer running time. The longer running time is due to the full connectivity between the h^1 level and the leaf level. Finally, FTC-HiRF improves the classification accuracy of F-HiRF, and at the same time runs faster than F-HiRF. The training and test times of FTC-HiRF are smaller than those of F-HiRF, since convergence in inference is achieved faster due to a more constrained graph connectivity in FTC-HiRF.

Tab. 3, and Tab. 4 show the comparison of FTC-HiRF with the state of the art on CAD and New-CAD. As can be seen, we are able to achieve higher classification accuracy, under faster running times. Our non-temporal variant HiRFnt outperforms HCRF [17] by 6.2% and spatiotemporal And-Or graph [2] by 3% on both datasets.

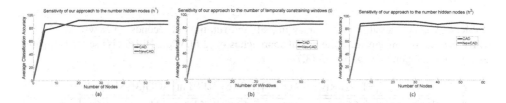

Fig. 5. Sensitivity of FTC-HiRF to the input parameters on the CAD (blue) and New-CAD (red) datasets. Average classification accuracy when using different numbers of: (a) Nodes at the h^1 level; (b) Temporal intervals T; (c) Nodes at the h^2 level.

Table 1. CAD: Average classification accuracy in [%], and run time in seconds

Class	HCRF [24]	F-HCRF [17]	FTC-HCRF [17]	HiRF	F-HiRF	FTC-HiRF
Walk	83.3	83.9	87.6	84.1	86.2	89.7
Cross	71.2	71.7	78.7	76.8	78.1	86.5
Queue	79.2	80.5	82.2	81.1	83.4	98.2
Wait	71.8	73.6	75.8	74.3	75.1	85.9
Talk	99.1	99.3	99.4	99.3	99.4	99.6
Avg	80.9	81.8	84.7	83.1	84.4	92.0
Time	400	440	300	100	150	120

Table 2. New-CAD: Average accuracy in [%], and run time in seconds

Class	HCRF [24]	F-HCRF [17]	FTC-HCRF [17]	HiRF	F-HiRF	FTC-HiRF
Gathering	45.3	47.1	52.3	49.2	52.1	54.9
Talking	84.1	84.5	83.9	84.7	86.2	89.3
Dismissal	78.2	79.6	80.6	78.1	82.8	87.6
Walking	89.3	89.1	89.0	89.4	91.2	94.3
Chasing	93.5	93.5	93.7	94.1	96.4	98.2
Queuing	93.0	93.1	94.3	93.8	95.6	99.2
Avg	80.6	81.1	82.3	81.5	84.0	87.2
Time	400	440	300	100	150	120

Table 3. Average classification accuracy in [%], and run time in seconds on CAD. FTC-HiRF is used to compare against temporal approaches of [2,6,13], while HiRFnt is used to compare against non-temporal approaches of [3,17,7].

Class	FTC-HiRF	ST-AOG [2]	FG [6]	FG [13]	HiRFnt	AOG [3]	HCRF [17]	SVM [7]
Walk	89.7	83.4	65.1	61.5	77.3	74.7	80	58.6
Cross	86.5	81.1	61.3	67.2	81.2	77.2	68	59.4
Queue	98.2	97.5	95.4	81.1	96.2	95.4	76	80.6
Wait	85.9	83.9	82.9	56.8	78.4	78.3	69	81.9
Talk	99.6	98.8	94.9	93.3	99.6	98.4	99	86.0
Avg	92.0	88.9	80.0	72.0	86.6	84.8	78.4	72.5
Time	120	180	N/A	N/A	80	160	N/A	N/A

Table 4. Average classification accuracy in [%], and run time in seconds on New-CAD. FTC-HiRF is used to compare against temporal approaches of [2,6], while HiRFnt is used to compare against non-temporal approaches of [3,7].

Class	FTC-HiRF	ST-AOG[2]	FG [6]	HiRFnt	AOG[3]	SVM [7]
Gathering	54.9	48.9	43.5	51.2	44.2	50.0
Talking	89.3	86.5	82.2	83.1	76.9	72.2
Dismissal	87.6	84.1	77.0	79.2	50.1	49.2
Walking	94.3	92.5	87.4	88.1	84.3	83.2
Chasing	98.2	96.5	91.9	92.6	91.2	95.2
Queuing	99.2	97.2	93.4	92.1	92.2	95.9
Avg	87.3	84.2	83.0	81.0	74.8	77.4
Time	120	180	N/A	80	160	N/A

Tab. 5 shows our precision and false positive rates for localizing the activities on CAD. As can be seen, HiRFnt successfully localizes foreground, and outperforms the spatial And-Or graph of [3] by 3.7% in precision.

Tab. 6 shows our precision and false positive rates for localizing the activities on New-CAD. To the best of our knowledge, we are the first to report localization results on New-CAD.

Table 5. Average precision and false positive rates in (%) on CAD

Class	FTC-HiRF Precision	FTC-HiRF FP	HiRFnt Precision	HiRFnt FP	S-AOG [3] Precision	S-AOG [3] FP
Walk	70.0	7.6	68.1	8.0	65.3	8.2
Cross	78.3	8.1	75.0	8.4	69.6	8.7
Queue	79.1	5.0	78.7	5.1	76.2	5.2
Wait	76.7	7.0	74.1	7.4	68.3	7.7
Talk	87.9	5.7	84.4	6.0	82.1	6.2
Avg	78.4	6.7	76.0	7.0	72.3	7.2

Table 6. Average precision and false positive rates in (%) on New-CAD

Class	FTC-HiRF Precision	FTC-HiRF FP	HiRFnt Precision	HiRFnt FP
Gathering	77.8	15.6	77.5	18.5
Talking	85.1	6.4	80.9	6.5
Dismissal	72.2	11.1	68.2	14.1
Walking	74.5	3.1	72.2	3.5
Chasing	68.0	7.7	65.2	10.5
Queuing	92.7	6.5	88.1	7.2
Avg	77.7	8.4	75.2	10.0

7 Conclusion

We have presented a new deep model, called Hierarchical Random Field (HiRF), for modeling, recognizing and localizing collective activities in videos. HiRF extends recent work that models activities with HCRF by: 1) Adding another layer of hidden variables to HCRF, 2) Removing the lateral temporal connections between all hidden variables, and 3) Enforcing local constraints on temporal connections between the hidden variables for capturing latent subactivities. We have also specified new inference of HiRF. Our inference iterates bottom-up/top-down computational steps until convergence, where each step efficiently estimates the latent variables using a linear program. Efficiency comes from our formulation of the potentials of HiRF as linear functions in each set of the hidden variables, given current estimates of other variables. This advances prior work which requires more complex quadratic programing in inference. Our empirical evaluation on the benchmark Collective Activity Dataset [7] and New Collective Activity Dataset [6] demonstrates the advantages of using strictly hierarchical connections in our approach. Our model is relatively insensitive to a range of input parameter values, but starts overfitting for higher values. In comparison with HCRF, HiRF reduces the running time of inference, and achieves a higher average classification accuracy. Also, HiRF outperforms the state-of-the-art approaches, including Factor Graphs [6,13] and spatiotemporal And-Or graphs [2], in terms of classification accuracy, precision, and recall.

Acknowledgment. This work was supported in part by grant NSF RI 1302700 and DARPA MSEE FA 8650-11-1-7149.

References

1. Aggarwal, J., Ryoo, M.: Human activity analysis: A review. ACM Comput. Surv. 43, 16:1–16:43 (2011)
2. Amer, M., Todorovic, S., Fern, A., Zhu, S.: Monte carlo tree search for scheduling activity recognition. In: ICCV (2013)
3. Amer, M.R., Xie, D., Zhao, M., Todorovic, S., Zhu, S.-C.: Cost-sensitive top-down/Bottom-up inference for multiscale activity recognition. In: Fitzgibbon, A., Lazebnik, S., Perona, P., Sato, Y., Schmid, C. (eds.) ECCV 2012, Part IV. LNCS, vol. 7575, pp. 187–200. Springer, Heidelberg (2012)
4. Brendel, W., Fern, A., Todorovic, S.: Probabilistic event logic for interval-based event recognition. In: CVPR (2011)
5. Chaquet, J.M., Carmona, E.J., Fernández-Caballero, A.: A survey of video datasets for human action and activity recognition. CVIU 117(6), 633–659 (2013)
6. Choi, W., Savarese, S.: A unified framework for multi-target tracking and collective activity recognition. In: Fitzgibbon, A., Lazebnik, S., Perona, P., Sato, Y., Schmid, C. (eds.) ECCV 2012, Part IV. LNCS, vol. 7575, pp. 215–230. Springer, Heidelberg (2012)
7. Choi, W., Shahid, K., Savarese, S.: What are they doing?: Collective activity classification using spatio-temporal relationship among people. In: ICCV (2009)
8. Choi, W., Shahid, K., Savarese, S.: Learning context for collective activity recognition. In: CVPR (2011)
9. Dalal, N., Triggs, B.: Histograms of oriented gradients for human detection. In: CVPR (2005)
10. Eslami, S.M.A., Heess, N., Williams, C.K.I., Winn, J.: The shape boltzmann machine: a strong model of object shape. IJCV (2013)
11. Felzenszwalb, P., McAllester, D., Ramanan, D.: A discriminatively trained, multiscale, deformable part model. In: CVPR (2008)
12. Kae, A., Sohn, K., Lee, H., Learned-Miller, E.: Augmenting crfs with boltzmann machine shape priors for image labeling. In: CVPR (2013)
13. Khamis, S., Morariu, V.I., Davis, L.S.: Combining per-frame and per-track cues for multi-person action recognition. In: Fitzgibbon, A., Lazebnik, S., Perona, P., Sato, Y., Schmid, C. (eds.) ECCV 2012, Part I. LNCS, vol. 7572, pp. 116–129. Springer, Heidelberg (2012)
14. Khamis, S., Morariu, V., Davis, L.: A flow model for joint action recognition and identity maintenance. In: CVPR (2012)
15. Lan, T., Sigal, L., Mori, G.: Social roles in hierarchical models for human activity recognition. In: CVPR (2012)
16. Lan, T., Wang, Y., Mori, G.: Discriminative figure-centric models for joint action localization and recognition. In: ICCV (2011)
17. Lan, T., Wang, Y., Yang, W., Robinovitch, S.N., Mori, G.: Discriminative latent models for recognizing contextual group activities. TPAMI (2012)
18. Li, Y., Tarlow, D., Zemel, R.: Exploring complositional high order pattern potentials for structured output learning. In: CVPR (2013)
19. Morariu, V.I., Davis, L.S.: Multi-agent event recognition in structured scenarios. In: Computer Vision and Pattern Recognition (CVPR) (2011)
20. Odashima, S., Shimosaka, M., Kaneko, T., Fukui, R., Sato, T.: Collective activity localization with contextual spatial pyramid. In: Fusiello, A., Murino, V., Cucchiara, R. (eds.) ECCV 2012 Ws/Demos, Part III. LNCS, vol. 7585, pp. 243–252. Springer, Heidelberg (2012)

21. Pei, M., Jia, Y., Zhu, S.C.: Parsing video events with goal inference and intent prediction. In: ICCV (2011)
22. Ryoo, M.S., Aggarwal, J.K.: Stochastic Representation and Recognition of High-level Group Activities. IJCV (2011)
23. Wang, S.B., Quattoni, A., Morency, L.P., Demirdjian, D., Darrell, T.: Hidden conditional random fields for gesture recognition. In: CVPR (2006)
24. Wang, Y., Mori, G.: Hidden part models for human action recognition: Probabilistic versus max margin. TPAMI (2011)
25. Weinland, D., Ronfard, R., Boyer, E.: A survey of vision-based methods for action representation, segmentation and recognition. CVIU 115, 224–241 (2011)
26. Yuille, A.L., Rangarajan, A.: The concave-convex procedure. Neural Comput. 15(4), 915–936 (2003)
27. Zeng, Z., Ji, Q.: Knowledge based activity recognition with Dynamic Bayesian Network. In: Daniilidis, K., Maragos, P., Paragios, N. (eds.) ECCV 2010, Part VI. LNCS, vol. 6316, pp. 532–546. Springer, Heidelberg (2010)
28. Zhu, Y., Nayak, N.M., Roy-Chowdhury, A.K.: Context-aware modeling and recognition of activities in video. In: CVPR (2013)

Part Bricolage: Flow-Assisted Part-Based Graphs for Detecting Activities in Videos

Sukrit Shankar, Vijay Badrinarayanan, and Roberto Cipolla

Machine Intelligence Lab, Division of Information Processing,
University of Cambridge, UK

Abstract. Space-time detection of human activities in videos can significantly enhance visual search. To handle such tasks, while solely using low-level features has been found somewhat insufficient for complex datasets; mid-level features (like body parts) that are normally considered, are not robustly accounted for their inaccuracy. Moreover, the activity detection mechanisms do not constructively utilize the importance and trustworthiness of the features.

This paper addresses these problems and introduces a unified formulation for robustly detecting activities in videos. Our *first contribution* is the formulation of the detection task as an undirected node- and edge-weighted graphical structure called *Part Bricolage (PB)*, where the node weights represent the type of features along with their importance, and edge weights incorporate the probability of the features belonging to a known activity class, while also accounting for the trustworthiness of the features connecting the edge. Prize-Collecting-Steiner-Tree (PCST) problem [19] is solved for such a graph that gives the best connected subgraph comprising the activity of interest. Our *second contribution* is a novel technique for robust body part estimation, which uses two types of state-of-the-art pose detectors, and resolves the plausible detection ambiguities with pre-trained classifiers that predict the trustworthiness of the pose detectors. Our *third contribution* is the proposal of fusing the low-level descriptors with the mid-level ones, while maintaining the spatial structure between the features.

For a quantitative evaluation of the detection power of *PB*, we run *PB* on Hollywood and MSR-Actions datasets and outperform the state-of-the-art by a significant margin for various detection paradigms.

Keywords: Activity Understanding, Pose Estimation, Graph Structures.

1 Introduction

Recognition/classification of human activities in videos attempts to understand the movements of the human body using computer vision and machine learning techniques, and classify them in an already seen activity category/class. The evaluation of recognition procedures is generally done on the datasets where the videos are spatio-temporally cropped to the volume of activity. On the other hand, the activity detection task requires the correct classification of an activity along with its spatio-temporal localization. For practical applications, the detection task is more viable, and most activity detection techniques have employed an exhaustive sliding-window search methodology for this

D. Fleet et al. (Eds.): ECCV 2014, Part VI, LNCS 8694, pp. 586–601, 2014.

purpose. However, the sliding-window search based detection procedures are computationally very expensive. The recent work of [5] introduced a graph-based detection procedure which is computationally efficient, and can be made to incorporate various types of recognition procedures.

To handle recognition tasks, standalone low-level features like Histogram of Oriented Gradients (HoG) [7], Histogram of Optical Flows (HoF) [17] etc., although conventionally quite successful, have been lately found somewhat insufficient for complex datasets like Hollywood2 [23]. To improve performance, researchers have tried to build mid-level representations from these low-level features. With mid-level features, the recognition is based on the assumption that the pose detection/body part estimation is quite accurate, which limits the final accuracy. In cases where some flow information is used to do better estimation of poses, the possible conflicts owing to multiple and confusing body part detections are not resolved, resulting in the recognition of very limited types of activities. Similar problems have also proved to be an impediment to the accuracy of the state-of-the-art detection procedures.

Inspired by the work of [5], we formulate the activity detection as a graph problem, but introduce more generality in what the graph can represent. To show its significance, we propose novel techniques for extracting mid-level features in videos and fusing them with low-level descriptors. These techniques solve some of the major shortcomings of the state-of-the-art activity classification methods, and thus can also be used for the same under an appropriate binding framework.

1.1 Related Work and Problems

This subsection discusses the activity recognition/classification and detection approaches that have been adopted in recent times in the literature, highlighting their positive aspects along with the associated shortcomings. We delineate the low-level and mid-level feature representation based methods for activity classification, and also mention the major fallacies in the generality of the state-of-the-art activity detection frameworks[1]. Finally, we highlight our major contributions.

Low-Level Descriptors for Activity Classification: The most studied approaches thus far for activity recognition are based on the usage of low-level features with bag-of-words models. Introduced by [16], sparse space-time interest points and subsequent methods, such as local ternary patterns [41], joint sparse representations [12], dense interest points [37,30], better motion cues [14] and discriminative class-specific features [15], typically compute a bag-of-words representation out of local features and use them for classification. The work of [35] uses densely rather than sparsely sampled trajectories for better performance, and [36] builds upon this work to incorporate more types of low-level features while also accounting for camera motion. Fusing many low-level features with flow information can be looked upon as extracting abstract mid-level representations. [13] forms a mid-level representation using spatio-temporal patches

---

[1] Although this paper does not target the activity classification problem in isolation from the detection problem, we review the activity classification methods in order to convince the reader with the novelty of our proposed techniques of extracting mid-level features in videos with pre-trained classifiers that predict the trustworthiness of the part detectors, and fusing the low-level descriptors with the mid-level ones while maintaining the spatial structure between them.

consisting of object detections and low-level features. Their method is targeted more towards context based representation and less towards robustly modelling complex human movements. Some authors [26] have tried to somewhat extend the bag-of-words concept to form a high-level descriptor from a large number of small action detectors. The work of [44] follows a two-layered structured approach for activity classification, where the first layer encodes low-level features, and the second layer extracts mid-level representations called *Actons* from the first layer. Authors in [20] use a top-down approach where the top layer consists of coarse body parts, and the lower layers contain hierarchically segmented body portions. Their method however, uses low-level features for body-part estimation and hierarchical segmentation, and thus lacks robustness which limits their use for complex datasets.

Most of these methods are predominantly global recognition methods and are not well-suited for use in the recognition of complex activities; however, methods like [12,30,36,44] that have performed relatively well on complex datasets have indirectly built coarse mid-level representations from low-level features.

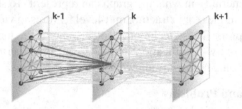

Fig. 1. This is the graphical structure of our Part Bricolage (PB) model discussed in Section 2.1. The figure shows all the possible connections between the nodes of three consecutive frames $k-1$, k, $k+1$ of a video. The *green* connections are highlighted to emphasize how a node is connected to its neighbours in the same frame; while the *yellow* connections indicate the connections of a node in frame k to the nodes in the next frame. The *red* lines show the connections to the node in frame k from nodes in frame $k-1$. The solution to the PCST problem over this graph finds an optimal subgraph that consist nodes and connections, representing the activity of interest. *Best Viewed in Color.*

Poses for Activity Classification: The work of [24] was one of the first to do recognition of basic activities by body part estimation. Many state-of-the-art pose estimation systems use action-specific priors to simplify the pose estimation problem [6,18,32]; while others use pose information for classifying actions [21,28,33,38]. Approaches using pose information for labelling activities mostly consider image datasets and depend on key-pose matching, while the methods using action specific priors for pose refinement typically require additional action labels. The key-pose matching techniques generally prove robust for very discriminative sequences and fail for complex datasets Apart from the requirement of additional training data, the technique of pose refinement from action labels suffers from the inability to account for occlusions. The work of [40] has tried to couple the two approaches, but the coupling is targeted more towards better 3D pose estimation for basic activities using flow information. The method does not tend to consider the ambiguities/conflicts that occur in real movie videos. The work of

[43] has proposed a 3D kinematics descriptor called the *Moving Pose*, but their method requires depth information for training and inference.

Some recent works for pose-based activity recognition have tried to use flow information with state-of-the-art pose detectors like poselets [2], flexible mixture of parts (FMP) [39] and stretchable models [27]. The work of [25] attempts to find key frames based on poselet detections for activity recognition. However, they do not consider the fact that poselets for complex videos can be conflicting and it is generally difficult to know the correct poselet based only on the probability scores[2]. As a result, they show very marginal improvements, even for datasets with basic interactive activities. Also, they expect the entire video dataset to be manually annotated with poselet bounding boxes, which is a serious limitation for video sequences. The work of [11] interleaves flow and pose information to cater to the inherent inaccuracy of the body part detectors. However, they do so only for lower arms, and their work is targeted more towards background-foreground segmentation in videos. Researchers in [34] estimate the body parts on a spatial and temporal basis using pose and flow information. However, their method tries to refine joints-based pose representations using motion fields, which is only robust for very simple actions like gestures, where joints can be estimated to a reasonable accuracy. Consequently, the method does not generalize to complex actions.

Activity Detection Methods: Template-based activity recognition methods attempt to do recognition by detection and therefore, can also be considered as activity detectors. The methods of [26,9,31,22] are the popular methods in this class. However, such methods do not form generic activity detection frameworks, since they are strictly tied to the underlying recognition procedures, and do not aim to do precise detection.

The work of [5] is the most recent approach that shows state-of-the-art results explicitly for activity detection. It considers the problem of precisely segmenting the spatio-temporal volumes of the desired activity by a max-weighted connected subgraph search (MWCS) methodology. Their approach is computationally efficient as compared to sliding-window search methods. However, they formulate the problem as a node-only-weighted graph, which limits the incorporation of the importance and trustworthiness of features, thereby lacking global generality.

We present a unified approach for activity detection, which addresses some of the key issues mentioned above. Our major contributions are as follows:

1. We formulate the task of detecting activities in unconstrained videos as an undirected node- and edge-weighted graphical structure called *Part Bricolage (PB)*, where the node weights represent the type of features along with their importance, and edge weights incorporate the probability of the features belonging to a known activity class, while also accounting for the trustworthiness of the features connecting the edge. Prize-Collecting-Steiner-Tree (PCST) problem [19] is solved for such a graph that gives the best connected subgraph comprising the activity of interest. Fig 1 provides an intuition of the graphical formulation.

---

[2] In the pose estimation systems such as poselets [2] and flexible mixture of parts (FMP) [39], although the probabilities of detections are also estimated alongside, they can only be trusted when the probabilities are high enough (say greater than 0.5). For lower probabilities (say less than 0.5), simply sorting them does not help to rank detections according to their degree of correctness. For complex videos, generally, a lot of detections are with low probabilities and thus, ambiguity resolving procedures demand an exploration.

2. We propose a novel technique for robust body part estimation, which uses two types of state-of-the-art pose detectors, and resolves the plausible detection ambiguities with pre-trained classifiers that predict the trustworthiness of the pose detectors.

3. We propose the fusion of low-level descriptors with the mid-level ones, while maintaining the spatial structure between them. This helps to better model the motion relationships in a video, specially when the detected mid-level features are sparse.

2   Approach

This section describes our *Part Bricolage (PB)* model, giving the necessary details and highlighting its various advantages. We first explain the complete formulation of our graphical structure, while also mentioning our technique of fusing mid-level features with the low-level ones (without compromising the spatial structure between them) for better motion representation. We then present our novel technique of robustly estimating the human body parts.

2.1   The Graphical Structure

Let us consider a video with K frames with each frame indexed as k ($k = 1, \ldots, K$). Let each frame in the video have N_k points (pixels to which features are associated) regularly spaced over the entire spatial region. As we shall later describe in the subsequent subsections, these points provide necessary information about the video. For consistency across frames , we make $N_k = N$, i.e. the number of points in each frame as same[3]. For such a video, we form a undirected graphical structure $G = (V, E, c, d)$ with node values $d : V \rightarrow \mathbb{R}^{\geq 0}$, edge costs $c : E \rightarrow \mathbb{R}^{\geq 0}$ and connections such that each node in a frame k is connected to its eight neighbouring points in frame k and nine neighbouring points in frame $k + 1$ (Fig 1). A node can possibly consist of multiple points; however, under a generic formulation, we consider each point as a node. Considering multiple points in a node reduces the granularity for doing detection.

We intend that for such a graph, the weights of the nodes should reflect the types of features that the nodes contain along with their importance, and the edge connections should contain the weights that indicate the cost of transiting from one node to another. If such a graph has to yield an activity of interest, then the edge costs should be more between the nodes that do not form a part of the targeted activity, and also between the nodes that represent the presence of features (related to human motion) with lower confidence levels. Where the two nodes which are connected together represent features relevant to the activity of interest and also with high confidence levels, the cost of transition between them should be less, indicating that the optimal subgraph that we wish to find out should contain such connected nodes.

Graph Optimization: We first describe the graph optimization problem that we intend to solve for localizing the activity of interest. Specifically, we find the solution

---

[3] For all our experiments, we take N equal to one-tenth the number of pixels in a frame. This choice is mostly empirical, and suffices when the activity of interest occupies most of the spatial region. For cases where the spatial occupation of the activities is less, N can be increased.

of a Prize-Collecting-Steiner-Tree (PCST) problem, which for an undirected, connected, node- and edge-weighted graph, finds the optimal subgraph maximizing the node weights and minimizing the edge costs. Given the way we define the node weights and the edge costs (as intuitively explained at the start of this subsection), solution to the PCST problem suffices for the activity detection task.

DEFINITION 1: (Max-Weighted-Connected-Subgraph (MWCS) Problem) - Given a connected, undirected, node-only-weighted graph $Z = (V_Z, E_Z, w)$ with weights $w : V_Z \rightarrow \mathbb{R}$, find a connected subgraph $T = (V_T, E_T)$ of $Z, V_T \subseteq V_Z, E_T \subseteq E_Z$, that maximizes the score $w(T) = \sum_{v \in V_T} w(v)$.

DEFINITION 2: (Prize-Collecting-Steiner-Tree (PCST) Problem) - Given a connected, undirected, node- and edge-weighted graph $G = (V_G, E_G, c, d)$ with node values $d : V_G \rightarrow \mathbb{R}^{\geq 0}$, edge costs $c : E_G \rightarrow \mathbb{R}^{\geq 0}$, the (PCST) Problem [19] attempts to find a connected subgraph $T = (V_T, E_T)$ of G, $V_T \subseteq V_G, E_T \subseteq E_G$, that maximizes

$$q(T) = \sum_{v \in V_T} d(v) - \sum_{e \in E_T} c(e) \qquad (1)$$

We use the light-weight Heinz library provided by the authors of [8], which solves a Max-Weighted-Connected-Subgraph (MWCS) problem. Given a PCST problem over graph G, we first convert it to a MWCS problem over an augmented graph Z, and then solve that using the Heinz library. We now show that such a conversion is theoretically feasible, and causes no alteration in the final solution.

PROCESS 1 - (Converting $G = (V_G, E_G, c, d)$ to $Z = (V_Z, E_Z, w)$) - For every edge $e \in E_G$ connecting nodes $u, v \in V_G$ with edge cost $c(e)$ and node profits $d(u)$ and $d(v)$, form two edges (u, a) and (a, v) in E_Z by using an auxiliary node $a \in V_Z$, where u and v contain the same profits as in G ($w(u) = d(u), w(v) = d(v)$), and $w(a) = -c(e)$.

The equivalence of G and Z easily follows from Definitions 1 & 2. Now, with the augmented graph Z, one must make sure that the optimal subgraph found by solving the MWCS problem over Z always contains the nodes u, v for an auxiliary node a, since the initial graph G never contained any a nodes. We thus state the following theorem:

THEOREM 1 - Given $G = (V_G, E_G, c, d)$ with node values $d : V_G \rightarrow \mathbb{R}^{\geq 0}$, edge costs $c : E_G \rightarrow \mathbb{R}^{\geq 0}$, the vertex-weighted graph Z obtained by Process 1, when solved for the MWCS problem (Definition 1) can never contain a single-connected auxiliary node $a \in V_Z$.

PROOF - For the graph $Z = (V_Z, E_Z, w)$ with weights $w : V_Z \rightarrow \mathbb{R}$, let the optimal Max-Weighted-Connected-Subgraph be $T = (V_T, E_T)$ of $Z, V_T \subseteq V_Z, E_T \subseteq E_Z$. Let $S \subseteq V_Z$ be a set of vertices, such that $\forall\, s \in S$, s is directly connected to $h \in V_T$. Let $S_{k'}; k' = 1, \ldots, K'$ represent all possible subsets of S. Then, since T is the optimal subgraph, $\forall\, k' = 1, \ldots, K'$

$$\sum_{h \in V_T} w(h) > \sum_{h \in V_T} w(h) + \sum_{s \in S_{k'}} w(s) \tag{2}$$

$$\Rightarrow w(s) < w(h) \tag{3}$$

Since, $w(a)$ is negative (Process 1), and weights of vertices u, v connected to a are positive (Definition 2),

$$w(a) < w(u), \quad w(a) < w(v) \tag{4}$$

Thus, if $a \in V_T$, neither of u or v can belong to $S_{k'}$ for any k', since that would contradict Equ (3) with Equ (4). But, if $a \in V_T$ is singly connected, atleast one of $S_{k'}$ should have either u or v. Hence, $a \in V_T$ cannot be singly connected. **This proves Theorem 1.** Note that in the above proof, we avoid the equality sign, assuming that the weights on vertices and edges of G are never zero. This is a valid assumption, since zero-weighted nodes and edges can always be deleted from the graph without affecting the cost of the optimal subgraph. It is important to note that for finding a solution to a PCST problem, all the node and the edge weights should be non-negative, i.e. $d : V \rightarrow \mathbb{R}^{\geq 0}$ and $c : E \rightarrow \mathbb{R}^{\geq 0}$.

From the above mathematical analysis, it is easy to see that one can convert the graph $Z = (V_Z, E_Z, w)$ to $G = (V_G, E_G, c, d)$ by assigning the negative of the minimum of the node weights of Z as the cost to all the edges in G, and adding the same to all the node weights of Z and assigning to G; provided that there is at least one node in Z with a negative weight. Then, solving PCST problem over G will be equivalent to solving the MWCS problem over Z. Thus, the two problems are related. However, if one formulates the activity detection task as a solution to the MWCS problem, it limits the design since all edge weights are same. In contrast, formulation of the detection task as a solution to the PCST problem offers flexible design choices.

Defining Node Weights: As stated earlier, we intend to represent mid-level (such as body parts) as well as low-level features (like optical flow [1]) by the nodes in the graph. We consider six body parts in a human - torso, head, two legs and two hands. Let b_1 refer to the *bounding box* of a head, b_2 that of a torso, b_3 and b_4 of two legs, and b_5 and b_6 of two legs. For a video frame, given human body-part detections, each point (node) on the frame can belong to one of $b_i; i = 1, \ldots, 6$ or can be seen as not belonging to any of b_i (for nodes outside the human body parts). We define the weight of a node $v \in V$ of the graph G as follows:

$$d(v) = \big\{ 0.20i \ \forall \ v \subset b_i, i = 1, 2 \ ; \ 0.60 \ \forall \ v \subset b_i, i = 3, 4 \ ; \ 0.80 \ \forall \ v \subset b_i, i = 5, 6 \big\} \tag{5}$$

If a point indicates a reasonable amount of flow field, but does not belong to any b_i, it is assigned a weight of 0.5, else the point gets a weight of 0.01, indicating that it is not associated to any features under consideration. The node weights considered here define the importance of the features being considered. Note that for the nodes lying inside the bounding boxes of human body parts, we assign different weights based on the type of the body part that they represent. Since the human motions are more prominent due to legs and hands as compared to the head and torso, the nodes representing legs and hands are assigned higher weights. Since mid-level representations like poses are more robust than mere flow information, the nodes representing only the flow information are assigned the middle weight, indicating that such information is less important than the detection of the limbs, but more than the detection of torsos and heads. In case a node happens to lie inside the bounding boxes of two features (due to partially overlapping bounding boxes), the node is made to represent the body part that would assign it a higher weight. For each node in the graph, let the probability of its occurrence be denoted by $p(v)$. For nodes not containing any of the body parts or the flow field, $p(v) = 0.01$. For the nodes containing the flow field, $p(v) = 1$, and for the nodes belonging to the body parts, $p(v)$ is assigned according to the trustworthiness of their detection as outlined in section 2.2.

Note above that we provide the flexibility of the body parts being represented in conjunction with the flow field. This maintains the spatial structure between the body parts and the flow information. Such a fusion offers us an advantage when the detections of the body parts are sparse. For instance, consider a case where the legs could not be detected within a frame, but the torsos and the head were detected. For a walking activity, the nodes representing the legs in the frame will be associated with a motion field, which when represented in a graphical structure naturally encodes motion relationships.

Before we discuss how the edge costs in our graphical structure are defined, we explain the training procedure. For videos in the training set, once the node weights are defined, we form a histogram over the entire video, one for each feature type (6 body parts and flow information). For each feature type, the bins represent the 6 body parts and 10 orientations of the flow descriptor, and the frequency of each bin indicates how many times the feature has occurred around a 50-frame temporal span of a node. Given the training videos and the associated activity class labels, binary linear-SVM classifiers using [4] are learnt for each each feature type. Thus, given a feature in the test set, once can predict whether the feature belongs to a known activity class or not, along with the degree of its presence. Note that during training, the probabilities of occurrences of the features and the edge costs are not considered. This is because, training is done on clean datasets with a pre-specified activity volume, and hence there lies no need to run a graph optimization problem. For test videos, the edge costs need to be incorporated according to the statistics of the training set and also the trustworthiness of the detected features.

Defining Edge Costs: The edge cost in the graph needs to be defined such that the cost is high if one is transiting to a node that represents a feature with lesser importance or lesser confidence level or the one which does not belong to an activity of interest. For an edge connecting any two nodes v_1 and v_2, if either of the nodes represent a feature that does not belong to any known activity class, the edge cost is assigned the maximum value of 1. In all other cases, the edge cost is defined as follows:

$$c(e_{(v_1, v_2)}) = \min(0.01, (|p(v_1) - p(v_2)|) \times (j(v_1) + j(v_2))/2) \qquad (6)$$

where $p(v_1), p(v_2)$ are the probabilities of occurrences of the features at nodes v_1 and v_2 respectively, and $j(v_1), j(v_2)$ indicate the degrees to which the features at nodes v_1 and v_2 belong to a known activity class. A higher value of $j(v)$ indicates lesser presence of the feature in an activity class. All values are normalized so that the edge cost is always between 0 and 1. This is to prevent biasing in the graph.

Given a test video, once the node weights and the edge costs are assigned over the graph, we also store the activity class to which each node belongs. In case, the feature at a node does not belong to any known activity class, no information is stored. The PCST solution is computed over the graph, and the optimal subgraph is found representing the spatio-temporal localization of the activity. A histogram is computed over all nodes of this optimal subgraph, which indicates the number of nodes belonging to each known activity class. The class that exhibits the maximum frequency in the histogram is assigned to the test video.

2.2   Estimation of Human Body Parts

For a video with K frames, we start by running two state-of-the-art body part detectors, viz. poselets [2] and the flexible mixture of parts (FMP) [39], for frames separated by 0.25 sec in time duration. This is because, normally within this duration, poses in an activity do not change significantly enough that they cannot be tracked with the flow information. This condition mostly suffices for sports videos as well. Choosing a sparse set of frames for pose detection not only reduces the computational complexity, but also relaxes the requirement of a highly accurate pose detector. Let there be $m = 1, \ldots, M; M < K$ frames for which we run body part detectors.

Learning Classifiers: The FMP and poselet detections are not accurate for all types of poses. Although, they both return a probability score that indicates the accuracy of the detection, we observe that for lower probability scores, the detections cannot be ranked according to the degree of their accuracy by simply sorting these scores. We therefore, try to learn classifiers for both the poselets and FMP, which can indicate the trust in the detection scores. For this, we form an image dataset consisting of images from PASCAL VOC 2007 [10] and INRIA and Buffy image datasets considered in [39]. This dataset consists of around 1100 images with full body poses, partial body poses, multiple and overlapping poses, and null poses.

For FMP annotation, we run FMPs on each of the images of our image dataset, note the returned probability scores and the body-part detections, and manually annotate whether (a) the detection was fully accurate (all 6 body parts were correct) - *category* C_1, (b) the detection was correct for head and torso, but was erroneous for some/all limbs - *category* C_2 and (c) the detection was not acceptable (no more than 1 out of 6 body parts were correct) - *category* C_3. We have thus three categories and the associated probability scores. Using this, we learn linear-SVM classifiers [3] using the LIBSVM library [4], which given a probability score categorizes the FMP detection. Note that for detections with FMP, we utilize the code provided by the authors of [39], and use their pre-trained model. The accuracy of the classifiers of these classes is evaluated by doing 50 random initializations of training and test data set (with a 50% train/test split). We always achieved the classification accuracy of around 90% for the test dataset. This shows that the classifiers that we have learnt from manual annotation can be trusted[4].

---

[4] Note that we learn classifiers by annotating a dataset of images, and not the video datasets under consideration. These classifiers are learnt once and need not be changed depending on the video dataset used for evaluation.

Fig. 2. First Row - *(Left Column)* The figure shows the torso and human body detections using our adaptive threshold with the poselets, without which no parts were detected. *(Right Column)* The figure shows some accurate FMP detections (belonging to the class C_1). **Second Row -** *(Left Column)* The figure shows FMP detections for the class C_2 where the head and torsos can be trusted, but not the limbs. *(Right Column)* The figure shows some FMP detections belonging to the class C_3. In such a case, the FMP detections cannot be trusted at all. As a result, our algorithm then depends solely on the torso and head detections from the poselets. **Third Row -** The figure shows the torso and human body detections using poselets, where the FMP detections belonged to the class C_3. **Fourth Row -** The figures show multiple torso and head detections using poselets. Using the approach specified in Algorithm 1, the correct torso detections were found out. *Best Viewed in Color.*

Poselets have a major advantage of predicting the viewpoints of body parts as compared to FMPs. However, since we do not model viewpoints in our framework, and the number of masks associated with the limbs in the poselets are comparatively much lesser than those of torso and head; we use poselet estimations only for the torso and full human body detection. For poselets, we perform detections using the code provided by [2]. We observe that the detection threshold (the probability score above which the torso detections and human detections are considered valid) set in the code of [2] many a times misses some key torso/poselet detections. Thus, we make the detection threshold for poselets adaptive in nature, i.e. we consider all poselet firings until *atleast* two torsos are detected in an image. The threshold can also be adapted so as to make more than a minimum of two torso detections, but we choose only two, since we do not have collective activities in our video datasets. We then note the returned probability scores for various torso and human body firings with poselets, note their regions of

---

Algorithm 1: Choosing Appropriate Body Parts

---

foreach *frame m* *discover the best part detections using learnt classifiers for FMP* **do**

    (a) Initialize all nodes v with weights $d(v) = 0.01$ (from Eqn (5)) and probability of occurrence $p(v) = 0.01$. Initially none of the nodes belong to any body part.

    (b) Run FMP and identify the category C of detection.

    if $(C == C_1)$ *correct detection* **then**

        (c) Include the FMP detected parts for the frame.

        (d) Assign the probability of 1 to the nodes contained inside each detected part. **else if**

    $(C == C_2)$ *limbs may be missing but torso and head can be trusted* **then**

        (e) Include the detected torso and the head for the frame.

        (f) Assign probability of 1 to the respective nodes.

        (g) Include the detected limbs for the frame.

        (h) Assign probability of 0.5 to the respective nodes. **else**

    $C = C_3$ & *FMP detection cannot be trusted*

        (i) Discard the FMP detections.

end

foreach *frame m* *detect torsos and human bodies using poselets* **do**

    (j) Run Poselets and note the torso and human body detections

    if *multiple torsos are contained inside a human body box* **then**

    | (k) Associate the human body box to the torso having the highest detection score.

    end

    if *a single torso is contained inside multiple human body boxes* **then**

    | (l) Associate the torso to the human body box to which it is most symmetrical.

    end

    One now establishes one-to-one mapping between a torso and a human body detection

    foreach *torso-human body pair* **do**

    | (m) Estimate the head part of the body.

    end

    foreach *torso-head pair* **do**

        (n) Check if the torso and head have a significant overlap with any of FMP detections

        if *significant overlap occurs* **then**

          (o) Discard the torso and head detections and continue with the FMP ones. **else**

        (p) Consider the torso and the head detection.

        (q) Assign probability of 1 to the respective nodes.

    end

end

Apply Algorithm 2

---

detections, and manually annotate the images into the following two categories: *category C_4* - where torso detections (with poselets) are not correct, and *category C_5* - where torso detections (with poselets) are correct. We observe that segregating the torso and human body detections with poselets based on such probability scores in not feasible, since there are generally many good detections even with very low probabilities. Thus, no classifiers are learnt for the same. However, a higher probability score generally indicates a more confident detection. Also, a torso that is more symmetrically placed within the human body generally indicates a better detection.

After running the poselets and FMPs on a given video, we get many part detections along with their probabilities of occurrences for each of the M frames. We select the most appropriate parts amongst them using Algorithm 1, for which we reuse the learnt classifiers (mentioned above). For predicting the spatial position of the body parts between m^{th} and $(m+1)^{th}$ frames, we utilize the flow information (see Algorithm 2). We reiterate that for any frame where part detections are included according to Algorithm 1, the overlapping of the bounding boxes of the parts is not a problem, since a node is always assigned to the bounding box of the part that gives it the maximum weight (as discussed in Section 2.1 - *Defining Node Weights*). See Fig 2 for getting a pictorial representation of ideas presented in this sub-section and Algorithms 1 and 2.

Algorithm 2: Estimate body parts for the frames between m and $m+1$

---

m and $m+1$ do not represent adjacent frames, but those for which detection is done one after the other

foreach *frames $(m, m+1)$* **do**

    foreach *bounding box of the body part detected in m* **do**

        Track the body part of frame m in $m+1$

        (T1) For the bounding box of a body part in m, $b_m \in b_i$, find the flow field using optical flow [1] between frames m and $m+1$. Let $Y(b_m)$ refer to the type of body part that b_m contains (torso, hands, etc.). Use flow field to estimate the bounding box of that body part in frame $m+1$ as b_{m+1}. Let p_{b_m} refer to the probability of occurrence of $Y(b_m)$, and $p_{b_{m+1}}$ to that of $Y(b_{m+1})$. Initialize $p_{b_{m+1}} = p_{b_m}$.

        (T2) If frame $m+1$ contains body parts of type $Y(b_m)$, find the spatial locations of all such parts. If any such body part with bounding box b_p and probability of occurrence p_p is in a close neighbourhood (typically one-tenth of the size of the frame) of b_{m+1}, then $b_{m+1} = b_p$ and $p_{b_{m+1}} = p_p$. In case of multiple parts near the neighbourhood of b_{m+1}, the closest one is considered.

        (T3) Let H_1 be the color histogram of the part in b_m and H_2 for that in $b_m + 1$. Compute the mass in the difference between H_1 and H_2 and divide it by the the mass in H_1, to give r_{c_H}. This value gives the change in appearance of the part.

        Estimate the position and probability of the occurrence of that part for the frames in between

        (T4) Penalize $p_{b_{m+1}}$ for the difference in appearance. So, $p_{b_{m+1}} := p_{b_{m+1}}(1 - r_{c_H})$

        (T5) For a frame n in between m and $m+1$, b_n is found by linearly interpolating b_m and b_{m+1}. Similarly, p_{b_n} is found by linearly interpolating p_{b_m} and $p_{b_{m+1}}$.

    end

end

---

3 Results and Discussion

This section presents the results obtained with our *Part Bricolage* model for the task of activity detection. Note that for activity detection, the task is to predict the spatio-temporal bound of an activity along with the class label.

Table 1. Activity Detection Results with Part Bricolage (PB): Mean Overlap Accuracy for temporal detection on Hollywood (AP = AnswerPhone, GC = GetOutCar, HS = HandShake) dataset; and temporal and spatio-temporal detection (using full-person ground truth) on MSR-Actions dataset. It can be seen that the full *PB* outperforms the state-of-the-art procedures by a significant margin for all detection paradigms. The results deteriorate significantly for the Hollywood dataset if we do not use poselet detections. This is because the Hollywood dataset contains many partial body poses, where FMPs do not work well. Also, when the flow information is not fused with the mid-level body part detections, the accuracy gets affected, thereby justifying our design choice. *Best Viewed in Color.*

	Hollywood (Temporal)								MSR (Temporal)			MSR (Spatio-Temporal)		
	AP	GC	HS	Hug	Kiss	SitDown	SitUp	StandUp	Box	Clap	Wave	Box	Clap	Wave
ST-SubVol [42]	0.29	0.22	0.33	0.44	0.42	0.28	0.20	0.30	0.07	0.06	0.26	0.045	0.017	0.101
MWCS [5]	0.39	0.29	0.41	0.52	0.49	0.37	0.38	0.37	0.09	0.17	0.29	0.047	0.063	0.112
PB (Ours) - Poselets	0.21	0.18	0.31	0.29	0.29	0.27	0.24	0.31	0.19	0.25	0.39	0.131	0.114	0.201
PB (Ours) - Flow	0.35	0.29	0.41	0.42	0.39	0.35	0.32	0.36	0.11	0.18	0.31	0.066	0.078	0.165
PB (Ours) Full	**0.45**	**0.36**	**0.49**	**0.56**	**0.50**	**0.46**	**0.41**	**0.46**	**0.21**	**0.26**	**0.43**	**0.147**	**0.127**	**0.235**

We use the uncropped Hollywood [17][5] and the MSR-Actions [42] datasets for the evaluation of our *PB* model for activity detection purposes. The Hollywood dataset can be considered as a subset of Hollywood2 dataset, and contains around 470 videos having 8 action classes, viz. *AnswerPhone, GetOutCar, HandShake, HugPerson, Kiss, SitDown, SitUp, StandUp*. For detection on Hollywood dataset, we train with the cropped clips, and test with the uncropped videos. The train/test split is around 50% and the videos are chosen as specified in [17]. The MSR-Actions dataset is quite different from the Hollywood dataset, since the test sequences normally contain multiple actions with people frequently crossing each other and changing their position over time. Thus, MSR-Actions dataset presents a very good validation benchmark for the activities with dynamic occlusions. The dataset contains 16 videos having 3 action classes, viz. *Boxing, Hand Clapping, Hand Waving*. Since the KTH dataset [29] also contains these three action classes, we train using the KTH videos and test on all the sequences of the MSR-Actions dataset. This is a standard norm for activity detection as recommended by [42,5].

Our *Part Bricolage* model is specifically targeted for activity detection. Although the idea of robust body part estimations, and fusing of low-level and mid-level features in a graph can be utilized for activity classification as well, a seemingly different binding framework may be more suited. The graphical structure based binding framework that we have adopted in this paper is best suited for the problem of activity detection. To evaluate *PB* for detection, we thus choose datasets which contain some real movie activities (like in Hollywood) or simple activities with a lot of dynamic occlusions (like in MSR-Actions dataset), where detection task is challenging. Also, the state-of-the-art activity classification procedures cannot be directly incorporated in either of our PCST-type framework or MWCS-framework [5], since those procedures neither possess an inherent quantization of their descriptors, nor any notion of trustworthiness of features.

---

[5] Hollywood dataset contains both the noisy *uncropped* versions of the video sequences which contain about 40% extraneous frames, as well as the *clean* or cropped versions of the sequences, which have been trimmed temporally to the action of interest.

We present temporal detection results on the Hollywood dataset, and the temporal and spatio-temporal detection results on the MSR-Actions dataset. Note that since the activities in Hollywood dataset are spatially trimmed, only temporal detection is required. Table 1 presents all the detection results. We use the mean overlap accuracy as the evaluation metric, following [42,5]. For both temporal or full spatio-temporal detection, this metric computes the intersection of the predicted detection region with the ground truth, divided by the union.

Table 1 presents the detection results with our *PB* model, while also showing some intermediate results in order to justify our design choices. It is clear that *PB* model outperforms the state-of-the-art procedures by a significant margin on both the datasets, for the temporal as well as the spatio-temporal detection paradigm. It can be seen that results without the incorporation of the part detections from poselets deteriorate significantly for the Hollywood dataset, unlike the MSR-Actions dataset. This is understandable since the MSR-Actions dataset generally contains full body poses for which FMP part detections are quite accurate. This is not the case for the Hollywood dataset, where one finds lesser number of full body poses, and FMP part detections mostly fail. It can also be seen that the results without the incorporation of any flow information (low-level feature) shows deterioration for both the datasets. This clearly establishes the advantage of our proposal of fusing the mid-level features like body parts with the low-level features like optical flow within the graph structure. The lack of flow information affects the detection accuracy for the videos, where the mid-level representations are sparse, or complete body poses cannot be estimated with acceptable trustworthiness and the missing part show some movement. Also, in the cases where there are a lot of dynamic occlusions, flow information helps to separate the activity of interest.

It is noteworthy that comparisons in Table 1 are made after making the temporal and spatial granularity of our *PB* model to 5 frames (instead of one frame) as done in [5]. We consider a block of 25 points (5 points per frame for 5 frames) as a node here. This is consistent with our discussion in Section 2.1 where we mentioned that a node can possibly contain many points to decrease the granularity.

4 Conclusions and Future Work

We have introduced a unified formulation for robustly detecting activities in videos. Central to our formulation is an undirected node- and edge-weighted graphical structure called *Part Bricolage (PB)*, where the node weights represent the type of features along with their importance, and edge weights incorporate the probability of the features belonging to a known activity class, while also accounting for the trustworthiness of the features connecting the edge. Prize-Collecting-Steiner-Tree (PCST) problem [19] is solved for such a graph that gives the best connected subgraph comprising the activity of interest. We have introduced a novel technique for robust body part estimation, which uses two types of state-of-the-art pose detectors, and resolves the plausible detection ambiguities with pre-trained classifiers that predict the trustworthiness of the pose detectors. We have also proposed the fusion of low-level descriptors with the mid-level ones, while maintaining the spatial structure between them. Quantitative results establish the advantages of our various design choices, and show that our *PB* model outperforms the state-of-the-art detection procedures by a significant margin.

PB model can be extended to have a human-detector-initiated graph partitioning which can cater to simultaneous activities. Also, the distinction between left and right limbs can be made explicit. Better parametric models can also be incorporated, and node and edge weights of the graph can be associated with probabilistic graphical frameworks to detect collective, highly contextual as well as subtle human motions.

Acknowledgements. We thank Dr. Gunnar W. Klau and Mohammed El-Kebir of CWI (Centrum Wiskunde & Informatica) Life Sciences Group at Amsterdam, Netherlands for providing us the Heinz library, and for giving us the directions to solve the PCST problem using it.

References

1. Black, M.J., Anandan, P.: A framework for the robust estimation of optical flow. In: Proceedings of the Fourth International Conference on Computer Vision, pp. 231–236. IEEE (1993)
2. Bourdev, L., Malik, J.: Poselets: Body part detectors trained using 3d human pose annotations. In: ICCV (2009)
3. Burges, C.J.: A tutorial on support vector machines for pattern recognition. Data Mining and Knowledge Discovery 2(2), 121–167 (1998)
4. Chang, C.C., Lin, C.J.: LIBSVM: A library for support vector machines. ACM Transactions on Intelligent Systems and Technology 2, 27:1–27:27 (2011), software available at http://www.csie.ntu.edu.tw/~cjlin/libsvm
5. Chen, C.Y., Grauman, K.: Efficient activity detection with max-subgraph search. In: CVPR (2012)
6. Chen, J., Kim, M., Wang, Y., Ji, Q.: Switching gaussian process dynamic models for simultaneous composite motion tracking and recognition. In: CVPR (2009)
7. Dalal, N., Triggs, B.: Histograms of oriented gradients for human detection. In: CVPR (2005)
8. Dittrich, M.T., Klau, G.W., Rosenwald, A., Dandekar, T., Müller, T.: Identifying functional modules in protein–protein interaction networks: an integrated exact approach. Bioinformatics 24(13), i223–i231 (2008)
9. Efros, A.A., Berg, A.C., Mori, G., Malik, J.: Recognizing action at a distance. In: CVPR (2003)
10. Everingham, M., Van Gool, L., Williams, C.K.I., Winn, J., Zisserman, A.: The PASCAL Visual Object Classes Challenge 2007 (VOC 2007) Results (2007), http://www.pascal-network.org/challenges/VOC/voc2007/workshop/index.html
11. Fragkiadaki, K., Hu, H., Shi, J.: Pose from flow and flow from pose. In: CVPR (2013)
12. Gopalan, R.: Joint sparsity-based representation and analysis of unconstrained activities. In: CVPR (2013)
13. Jain, A., Gupta, A., Rodriguez, M., Davis, L.S.: Representing videos using mid-level discriminative patches. In: CVPR (2013)
14. Jain, M., Jégou, H., Bouthemy, P., et al.: Better exploiting motion for better action recognition. In: CVPR (2013)
15. Kovashka, A., Grauman, K.: Learning a hierarchy of discriminative space-time neighborhood features for human action recognition. In: CVPR (2010)
16. Laptev, I.: On space-time interest points. IJCV 64(2-3), 107–123 (2005)
17. Laptev, I., Marszalek, M., Schmid, C., Rozenfeld, B.: Learning realistic human actions from movies. In: CVPR (2008)

18. Lee, C.S., Elgammal, A.: Coupled visual and kinematic manifold models for tracking. IJCV 87(1-2), 118–139 (2010)
19. Ljubić, I., Weiskircher, R., Pferschy, U., Klau, G.W., Mutzel, P., Fischetti, M.: An algorithmic framework for the exact solution of the prize-collecting steiner tree problem. Mathematical Programming 105(2-3), 427–449 (2006)
20. Ma, S., Zhang, J., Ikizler-Cinbis, N., Sclaroff, S.: Action recognition and localization by hierarchical space-time segments. In: ICCV (2013)
21. Maji, S., Bourdev, L., Malik, J.: Action recognition from a distributed representation of pose and appearance. In: CVPR (2011)
22. Malgireddy, M., Inwogu, I., Govindaraju, V.: A temporal bayesian model for classifying, detecting and localizing activities in video sequences. In: CVPR (2012)
23. Marszalek, M., Laptev, I., Schmid, C.: Actions in context. In: CVPR (2009)
24. Ramanan, D., Forsyth, D.A.: Automatic annotation of everyday movements. In: NIPS (2003)
25. Raptis, M., Sigal, L.: Poselet key-framing: A model for human activity recognition. In: CVPR (2013)
26. Sadanand, S., Corso, J.J.: Action bank: A high-level representation of activity in video. In: CVPR (2012)
27. Sapp, B., Weiss, D., Taskar, B.: Parsing human motion with stretchable models. In: CVPR (2011)
28. Schindler, K., Van Gool, L.: Action snippets: How many frames does human action recognition require? In: CVPR (2008)
29. Schuldt, C., Laptev, I., Caputo, B.: Recognizing human actions: a local svm approach. In: ICPR (2004)
30. Shi, F., Petriu, E., Laganiere, R.: Sampling strategies for real-time action recognition. In: CVPR (2013)
31. Sullivan, M., Shah, M.: Action mach: Maximum average correlation height filter for action recognition. In: CVPR (2008)
32. Taylor, G.W., Sigal, L., Fleet, D.J., Hinton, G.E.: Dynamical binary latent variable models for 3d human pose tracking. In: CVPR (2010)
33. Thurau, C., Hlaváč, V.: Pose primitive based human action recognition in videos or still images. In: CVPR (2008)
34. Wang, C., Wang, Y., Yuille, A.L.: An approach to pose-based action recognition. In: CVPR (2013)
35. Wang, H., Klaser, A., Schmid, C., Liu, C.L.: Action recognition by dense trajectories. In: CVPR (2011)
36. Wang, H., Schmid, C., et al.: Action recognition with improved trajectories. In: ICCV (2013)
37. Wang, H., Ullah, M.M., Klaser, A., Laptev, I., Schmid, C., et al.: Evaluation of local spatio-temporal features for action recognition. In: BMVC (2009)
38. Yang, W., Wang, Y., Mori, G.: Recognizing human actions from still images with latent poses. In: CVPR (2010)
39. Yang, Y., Ramanan, D.: Articulated pose estimation with flexible mixtures-of-parts. In: CVPR (2011)
40. Yao, A., Gall, J., Van Gool, L.: Coupled action recognition and pose estimation from multiple views. IJCV 100(1), 16–37 (2012)
41. Yeffet, L., Wolf, L.: Local trinary patterns for human action recognition. In: ICCV (2009)
42. Yuan, J., Liu, Z., Wu, Y.: Discriminative subvolume search for efficient action detection. In: CVPR (2009)
43. Zanfir, M., Leordeanu, M., Sminchisescu, C.: The moving pose: An efficient 3D kinematics descriptor for low-latency action recognition and detection. In: ICCV (2013)
44. Zhu, J., Wang, B., Yang, X., Zhang, W., Tu, Z.: Action recognition with actons. In: ICCV (2013)

GIS-Assisted Object Detection and Geospatial Localization

Shervin Ardeshir, Amir Roshan Zamir, Alejandro Torroella, and Mubarak Shah

Center for Research in Computer Vision at the University of Central Florida
http://crcv.ucf.edu/projects/GIS-Object/

Abstract. Geographical Information System (GIS) databases contain information about many objects, such as traffic signals, road signs, fire hydrants, etc. in urban areas. This wealth of information can be utilized for assisting various computer vision tasks. In this paper, we propose a method for improving object detection using a set of priors acquired from GIS databases. Given a database of object locations from GIS and a query image with metadata, we compute the expected spatial location of the visible objects in the image. We also perform object detection in the query image (e.g., using DPM) and obtain a set of candidate bounding boxes for the objects. Then, we fuse the GIS priors with the potential detections to find the final object bounding boxes. To cope with various inaccuracies and practical complications, such as noisy metadata, occlusion, inaccuracies in GIS, and poor candidate detections, we formulate our fusion as a higher-order graph matching problem which we robustly solve using RANSAC. We demonstrate that this approach outperforms well established object detectors, such as DPM, with a large margin.

Furthermore, we propose that the GIS objects can be used as cues for discovering the location where an image was taken. Our hypothesis is based on the idea that the objects visible in one image, along with their relative spatial location, provide distinctive cues for the geo-location. In order to estimate the geo-location based on the generic objects, we perform a search on a dense grid of locations over the covered area. We assign a score to each location based on the similarity of its GIS objects and the imperfect object detections in the image. We demonstrate that over a broad urban area of >10 square kilometers, this semantic approach can significantly narrow down the localization search space, and occasionally, even find the correct location.

1 Introduction

Currently, the accurate locations of many static objects in urban areas, e.g., bus stops, road signs, fire hydrants, ATMs, subway stations, building outlines, and even trees, are documented in databases, commonly known as GIS. Such databases provide valuable semantically meaningful information, and their coverage and accuracy is constantly increasing. Therefore, it is natural to develop computer vision systems which can effectively leverage this information.

D. Fleet et al. (Eds.): ECCV 2014, Part VI, LNCS 8694, pp. 602–617, 2014.
© Springer International Publishing Switzerland 2014

In this context, we propose a method for improving object detection in images of outdoor urban scenes using GIS. The metadata of images are commonly available with the image in Exif tags. Using the GIS databases and the metadata, we project the GIS objects onto the image and use them as priors for object detection. However, a slight inaccuracy in the metadata or the GIS database, which is quite common, leads to completely misplaced projections which makes fusing them with the image content challenging. We resolve this issue by formulating our object detection problem as a higher-order graph matching instance which we solve using robust estimation techniques.

Furthermore, in the same context, we extend the use of GIS to even the cases with unknown camera locations and show that the objects in the image and their relative spatial relationship can be used for finding the GPS location where an image was taken. As an example, assume a traffic signal, a bus stop, and a trash can are visible in an image. At a city scale, this information would narrow down the feasible geo-locations for this image to some extent if the geo-locations of all traffic signals, bus stops, trash cans are known. Now assume it is known that the trash can is towards the north of the traffic signal, and the bus stop is on their east. One would imagine that there will not exist many locations in the city consistent with this arrangement, even though the objects are generic and common. We will show that, interestingly, the geometric relationship between these generic objects in fact provides distinctive cues for discovering the location of an image. However, the inaccuracies in GIS and the imperfect performance of state-of-the-art-object detectors are some of the critical issue which we address in our framework by employing a robust matching method.

GIS has been used for various applications in computer vision [21,22], in particular registration of aerial images based on semantic segments. As another example, Matzen et al. [14] use geographic and geometric information for detecting vehicles using a set of viewpoint-aware detectors. However, the majority of existing image geo-localization techniques do not leverage any type of semantic information, e.g., semantic objects. They are often based on establishing low-level feature correspondences, e.g., SIFT [13] or BoVW histograms, between the query image and a reference dataset of images. Several methods which adopt this approach for Street view[24,18,9,25], satellite or Birdseye view [1,12], or crowdsourced images [17,16,11,23] have been developed to date. Several other methods for identifying landmarks in images, e.g., [3], have been proposed which to some extent leverage the location-level semantic information (i.e., the landmarks). Recently, Shafique et al. [15] developed a system for coarse geographical information estimation from an image based on the annotations provided by the user. Lee et al. [10] proposed a method for discovering a set of "visual styles" which can be linked to historical and geographical information. Bioret et al. [2] localized images based on matching them to building outlines. Even though some of the aforementioned methods leverage high-level information to some extent, in general, very little work towards rigorous integration of semantic information in the geo-localization process has been reported to date.

In the context of object detection, several techniques for assisting the process of detection using various type of prior context have been proposed [4,19,20]. For instance, Hoiem et al. [8] proposed a method for utilizing a set of general spatial priors for improving object detection (unlike our approach which uses location-specific priors and a graph matching formulation). However, the use of large scale and detailed GIS databases available for urban area has not been explored to date. This paper provides the first method for unifying *wide area* image localization and object detection in one robust framework which is centered around semantically tangible information.

2   GIS-Assisted Object Detection

Given the metadata, we gather a set of priors about the objects that are potentially in the field of view of the camera. Since some of them might be occluded by buildings or other objects, we perform occlusion handling to find a set of objects which are expected to be visible in the image. In addition, we perform object detection in the image to have some candidate bounding boxes using the content of the image. Then we fuse these two utilizing graph matching in order to find the final object detections.

2.1   Obtaining Priors from GIS

We want to extract a set of priors about the spatial locations of the objects in the image. We extract the metadata (e.g., the camera location, focal length, camera model (yielding the sensor size), and possibly compass direction) from the Exif tag of the images and use it for forming the camera matrix, C, which maps the 3D world coordinates to the 2D image coordinates. Camera matrix has the standard form of $P = C[R \mid T]$, where R, T, and C are the rotation, translation, and calibration matrices, respectively. Using the information in the Exif tag, C can be obtained using the following equation:

$$C = \begin{bmatrix} f \times s_x & l_y/2 & 0 \\ 0 & 1 & 0 \\ 0 & l_x/2 & f \times s_y \end{bmatrix}, \tag{1}$$

where f is the focal length of the camera, s_x and s_y are the sensor size and l_x and l_y are the number of pixels is x and y coordinates of the image. We assume a fixed height for the camera (1.7m) and also zero roll and pitch as they are not recorded in the Exif tag (we will later see that graph matching will handle the shift caused by this approximation), but yaw is recorded by the compass. Therefore, R and T can be formed employing these approximations and the geo-location and compass information recorded in the Exif tag. The following equation yields the homogeneous coordinates of the projections of GIS objects in the image:

$$\begin{bmatrix} x_i \\ 1 \end{bmatrix} = P X_i, \tag{2}$$

where X_i denotes the 3D GPS coordinates[1] of the ith object in the GIS database which is in the field of view of the camera, and x_i represents an estimation of the two dimensional spatial location of the ith object in the image plane.

In GIS, each object is represented by a single GPS location. However, the typical height of the objects, such as fire hydrants or bus stops, are known and often fixed. Thus, We assume fixed heights for the objects (e.g., 5.5m for traffic signal) and compute two projections points for each GIS object, one for its bottom and another one for its top. This process is shown in figure 1. Figure (a) shows the position and the view of the camera, in addition to the GIS objects[2]. Figure 1 (b) shows the projections, i.e., x_i. However, many of the GIS objects will be occluded by buildings or other GIS objects, so we need an occlusion handling mechanism to eliminate the occluded GIS objects from our projections which is described next.

Fig. 1. The process of acquiring GIS projections for two sample images. Part (a) illustrates the camera view (yellow lines) shown in the overhead view with the occlusion segments (red) and GIS objects. Part (b) shows the projections prior to occlusion handling. Part (c) shows the final projections after occlusion handling along with their corresponding objects.

2.2   Occlusion Handling

Two main resources of the occlusions are buildings and other GIS objects. GIS database includes very accurate data about the outline of buildings. Therefore, we define an occlusion set as the union of the GIS projections and the projections of the building outlines. We perform the occlusion handling by enforcing that

---

[1] All GPS positions are converted to East-North-Up metric Cartesian coordinates system for the sake of simplicity.

[2] In the entire paper, street lights, trash cans, traffic signal, fire hydrants, bus stops, and traffic signs are shown with green, purple, red, yellow, cyan and blue markers, respectively.

the ray connecting the GIS object to the camera is not blocked by any member of the occlusion set.[3]

The non-occluded objects are shown for two samples in figure 1 (c). As apparent in the figure, many GIS projections are found to be occluded which indeed matches the content of the image.

2.3   Graph Matching

In practice, the GIS projections are rarely at the correct object positions in the image. That is because even a slight inaccuracy in the metadata or the employed approximations about the camera rotation parameters (roll and pitch) may considerably shift the projections from their correct position. This is can be clearly observed in figure 1 (c). However, the *relative geometric relationships* of the objects are yet preserved.

In order to compute a set of potential bounding boxes for the objects in the image, we perform a content-based detection (in our experiments using DPM [7,6]). These detections are usually far from perfect and contain a significant number of false positives due to the complexity of the scene and the nontrivial appearance of our objects. However, a subset of these DPM detections is expected to match the projections acquired from GIS. We formulate the problem of identifying this subset as graph matching.

In graph matching (assume a bipartite graph for the sake of simplicity), two sets of nodes and a number of edges between the two node sets are given; the goal is to exclusively assign the nodes of the first set to the nodes of the second set in a way that an objective function is minimized. Our aim is to assign each GIS projection to one of the DPM detections in a way that the overall geometry of the scene is preserved, even though the projections are not necessarily in the correct locations and the DPM detections include a lot of incorrect bounding boxes. Thus, we define our problem as a graph matching instance in which the first set of nodes represents the GIS projections that survived occlusion handling and the other set represents the DPM detections. Each DPM detection or GIS projection is represented by one node which is connected to all of the nodes of the *same class* in the other set through edges. In other words, each edge denotes one potential correspondence between a GIS projection and a DPM detection. Graph matching selects a subset of the edges in a way that the correspondences they induce best fit a *global affine model*. This process is illustrated in figure 2.

We assume the geometric model between the projections and the correct subset of detections can be approximated using an affine transformation. Since the inaccuracies in the metadata lead to a global transformation in the image, the projections are often translated, rotated, and scaled. Also, the GIS objects are often on the ground plane and the images in the urban area usually show a relatively wide view. Therefore, the affine model, even though not perfect, is

---

[3] Since the GIS projections include more than one pixel, this process is performed for all of the pixels on the projection, and an object is assumed to be occluded if more than 50% of its pixels are occluded.

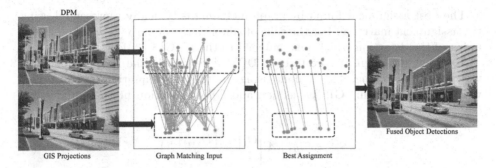

Fig. 2. An example of the graph matching process. The DPM detections and GIS projections are used to form a bipartite graph encoding the feasible assignment of objects. Solving the higher-order graph matching problem yields the best assignment which has the least cost for fitting an affine transformation. The corresponding object detection results are shown in the rightmost figure.

a reasonable approximation. In addition, the degree of freedom of affine is less than its alternatives which is desirable especially for the locations where few GIS objects are found to be visible in the image.

We solve this graph matching instance using a method based on RANSAC. The main difference between regular affine fitting and our problem is that, the preliminary correspondences in regular affine fitting are typically one-to-one, while in our problem, one GIS projection is preliminarily matched to *any* of the detections of the same class and vice versa; however, only one of these correspondences can be included in the final matching. To solve this problem using RANSAC, we randomly select three correspondences *which do not involve assigning one node to multiple nodes*, and find their corresponding affine model. Then the number of correspondences which fit this affine transformation are counted and interpreted as the score of the estimated model; however, if one node is involved in two inlier correspondences, only one of them is be counted. This process is repeated until a termination condition (convergence or maximum number of iterations) is met.

Our graph matching formulation is in fact a higher-order graph matching problem and not a linear assignment problem, such as bipartite matching. That is because our objective function, i.e., affine error, can be approximated using at least three correspondences and not one (unlike linear assignment problems which assumes a cost/weight is assigned to each correspondence). As an alternative to RANSAC for solving our graph matching problem, the recent tensor-based hypergraph matching techniques [5,26] can sufficiently approximate the solution in a fraction of a second. However, they allow for local deformations in the affine model, while employing RANSAC would enforce a *global* affine model on the matching correspondences; a global model is favorable for our problem as we know that the reason behind the misalignment is mainly the imperfect camera parameters (which typically lead to global shifts) and not local deformations in the objects or scene elements.

The best assignment found by graph matching is typically represented using the assignment matrix χ. For the sake of simplicity, assume $\chi(i)$ determines the index of the detection which was matched to the ith GIS projection.

We want to assign a score to each DPM detection in the image which survived graph matching. This is done using the following equation based on how well the corresponding GIS projection and DPM detection fit the found affine transformation:[4]

$$S_i^G = Sig\left(\left\|A\begin{bmatrix}O_i\\1\end{bmatrix} - \begin{bmatrix}D_{\chi(i)}\\1\end{bmatrix}\right\|\right), \tag{3}$$

where A is the best found affine matrix, $\|.\|$ denotes Euclidean distance, and O_i represents the spatial location of the center of the ith GIS projection. Similarly, D represents the spatial locations of the (center of) detections by DPM. Therefore, $D_{\chi(i)}$ is the spatial location of the DPM detection matched to the ith GIS projection. sig is a sigmoid function of the form $sig(x) = 2\frac{1}{1+e^{-\sigma x}}$ with $\sigma = -0.05$, which transforms the affine error to a score ranging from 0 to 1. Besides the geometry of the arrangement of objects, we wish to incorporate the content-based confidence of the detection returned by DPM. This is done using a linear mixture of the score based on the geometry and the one based on the content (represented by S^I) which is the actual score returned by DPM normalized to range from 0 to 1:

$$S_i = \alpha S_i^G + (1-\alpha)S^I{}_{\chi(i)}, \tag{4}$$

where α is a linear mixture constant. Therefore, S_i denotes an updated score for object i based on the image content and its geometric consistency with the GIS. In the experiments section, we will see that the precision-recall curves of the object detection obtained using this method significantly outperforms DPM and the other baselines.

3   Geo-localization Using Generic Objects

As discussed earlier, the objects which are visible in the image as well as their geometric relationship form a discriminative cue for finding the location that the image was taken at. We propose a method for finding the geo-location of an image based on the semantic objects therein and their relative geometry. However, two issues make this process challenging: First, as discussed before, the object detections found in the image are far from perfect. Second, the GIS projections are often off the right spatial location. Our method, which is in fact based on the object detection process described in section 2, is capable of handling these issues.

---

[4] This could be also applied to all DPM detections, and not only the ones which are selected by graph matching, by allowing multiple DPM detections to match to one GIS projection after finding the best affine model using graph matching, or assuming the geometric score of zero, $S^G = 0$, for the detections which were not selected by graph matching.

To find the location of the query image, we perform a search on a dense grid of geo-locations ($20m$ apart) for the covered area. On each location, we search over different compass orientations as well ($20°$ apart). This dense grid is shown for a sample covered area in figure 3 (b). We perform the object detection method described in section 2 on the query image using each of these feasible location-orientation pairs (i.e., assuming these are the correct location and orientation of the camera) and obtain the following score for the location-orientation pair:

$$ L = \beta \sum_{i=1}^{|O|} S(i) + (1 - \beta) \sum^{c} \frac{\min(|\ O^c\ |, |\ D^c\ |)}{\max(|\ O^c\ |, |\ D^c\ |)}, \tag{5} $$

where $|.|$ denotes the size of a set. The parameter β is the the linear mixture constant, and c represent the object classes $c \in \{\text{Traffic Signal, Trash Can,...}\}$ (e.g., $D^{\text{Traffic Signal}}$ and $O^{\text{Traffic Signal}}$ are the DPM detection and GIS projections of Traffic Signals for a particular location-orientation). The first term captures how well the matching subset of DPM detections fits the GIS data of that particular location (including the spatial geometry of the objects). The second term has an intersection-over-union form and quantifies the difference between the presence and absence of the objects in the image compared to the GIS database (no geometry). If for each GIS projection an inlier detection was found by the graph matching, the left term yields a high score. On the contrary, if most of the GIS objects were found to be matching to unreliable detections, this term will give a lower score. The linear mixture of these two terms is the overall geo-localization score for a particular location and orientation. We perform this search for all the grid points with different orientations and rank different location-orientation pairs based on the score.

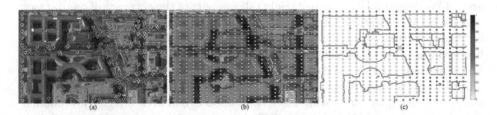

Fig. 3. The process of geo-localizing a query image based on the GIS objects in a sample region. Figure (a) shows the GIS objects in the region. Figure (b) illustrates the grid geo-locations along with the building outlines. Figure (c) shows the score of each grid geo-location obtained from equation 5. The ground truth location is marked with the yellow cross; notice that the grid points near the ground truth obtained a high score. The points which fall on buildings gain the score of zero.

This method is merely based on semantic objects and can significantly narrow down the search space for the location of the query image. We will show that the combination of the presence/absence of the objects and their geometric arrangement (i.e., the right and left terms of equation 5) is a distinctive cue for finding the right geo-location. That means even though the objects are generic and can be found in many locations in the city, their geometric relationship contains distinctive cues about the location.

This process is illustrated in figure 3. The GIS objects and grid geo-locations are shown for a subregion covered by our GIS database. The score each location achieves is shown in figure 3 (c). As apparent in the figure, the ground truth location marked with the yellow cross obtains a higher score compared to the majority of other locations.

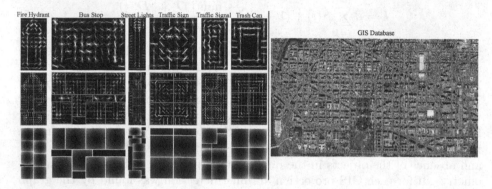

Fig. 4. Left: the learned DPM models for our six GIS objects. **Right**: part of the coverage of our dataset for Washington, DC. The GIS object are overlaid on the map.

4   Experiments

We performed our evaluations using a GIS database of over 10 square kilometers area of Washington DC. Figure 4 (right) shows part of the coverage of our dataset along with the locations of GIS objects. Our GIS database includes accurate locations of street lights, bus stops, traffic signals, traffic signs, trash cans, and fire hydrants as well as the building outlines (the color-coding of all markers and bounding boxes of the objects is specified in the footnote 2). We trained our DPM detectors (using the code of authors [7,6]) for each object, illustrated in figure 4 (left), by annotating more than 6000 urban area images downloaded from Panpramio and Flickr including 420 instances of bus stops, 921 street lights, 1056 traffic signals, 1264 traffic signs, 625 fire hydrants, and 646 trash cans.[5] Our test set includes 223 consumer images downloaded from Panoramio and Flickr. We set the linear mixure constants, β and α, to 0.5 in our experiments.

4.1   Object Detection Results

Figure 5 illustrates the results of different steps of our framework for the task of object detection. The first column shows the output of DPM on the images. It can be observed that there are a notable number of false positives and mis-detections

---

[5] For the GIS datab, training images, annotations, DPM models, and further information, please visit http://crcv.ucf.edu/projects/GIS-Object/

Fig. 5. Sample object detection results. For each sample, the detections found by DPM and our method, along with the GIS projections and the ground truth are shown. Our method significantly improved the results in these challenging urban-area images.

Table 1. Quantitative comparison of the proposed object detection method vs. the baselines

	DPM	GIS Proj.	Top DPM	Ours
Traffic Sign	0.087	0.002	0.095	**0.190**
Traffic Signal	0.543	0.027	0.561	**0.760**
Trash Can	0.043	0.000	0.041	**0.125**
Fire Hydrant	0.010	0.000	0.012	**0.090**
Street Light	0.123	0.001	0.129	**0.270**
mAP	0.1612	0.006	0.1676	**0.287**

due to the small size of the objects, poor lighting conditions and partial occlusions in the objects. The second column shows the projections extracted from the GIS data. As apparent in the figure, the locations of the projections on the image are not that accurate, while their relative geometry is consistent with the image content. The output of our method is illustrated in the third column. Comparing it with the last column (ground truth), the significant improvement of our method over the DPM and GIS projection results can be observed.

The precision-recall curves of the object detection can be seen in figure 6, in which the blue curve corresponds to the output of our method. The black curve shows the accuracy for the projections if we consider them as the detections. The red curve shows the performance of DPM, and the green curve illustrates the results of a naive fusion method in which the top k detections of the DPM model were maintained and the rest were eliminated from the detections (k is the

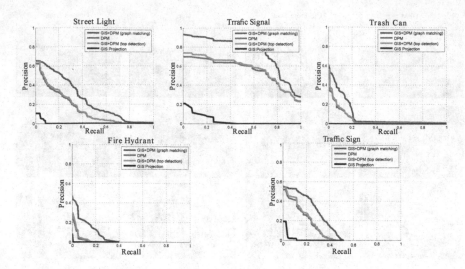

Fig. 6. The PR curves of our object detection method and the baselines. The DPM detector of bus stops yields very poor detection results because of the vast diversity and complexity of their appearance. Thus, we exclude it from the rest of our experiments.

number of projections of one class which are visible in the image). Table 1 provides the quantitative comparison of our method vs. DPM and GIS projections in terms of mAP which shows the significant improvement by our method.

Impact of the Number of Object Classes: since our method is leveraging the geometric relationship among different classes of objects, the more number of object classes we have, the higher overall accuracy we expect to obtain. Table 2 shows the effect of the number of object classes on the overall accuracy of our method. "n objects" means we ran our method using all feasible n-class combinations of object classes (i.e., $\binom{5}{n}$) and averaged their mAP. It can be observed that an increase in the number of object classes leads to notable improvement in the overall results.

Table 2. Effect of the number of object categories

	All Objects	Four Obj.	Three Obj.	Two Obj.	One Obj.
mAP	0.28	0.26	0.17	0.12	0.08

Significance of Each Class: the goal of this experiment is to evaluate the contribution of each object class in the overall accuracy. For this purpose, the object detection performance of our method was calculated by excluding one of the object classes from the process. Table 3 shows how the accuracy would be affected after neglecting each object. As an example, not incorporating GIS information about the traffic signals makes the overall object detection accuracy drop significantly, thus traffic signals have a notable contribution in the overall accuracy. That is primarily because they are rarely occluded (similar to street lights and unlike trash cans and fire hydrants) and have a discriminative shape which can be detected easily. On the other hand, some objects, such as trash cans and fire hydrants, have a negative effect on the accuracy due to being frequently occluded and having a less distinctive appearance.

Table 3. The contribution of each object to the overall object detection results. Some of the more robust classes, e.g., Traffic signal, have a positive contribution, whereas the less reliable classes, e.g., trash can, have a negative contribution.

	All Objects	Street Light	Traffic Sign	Trash Can	Traffic Signal	Fire Hydrant
mAP	0.28	0.26	0.26	0.33	0.17	0.29

4.2 Geo-localization Results

For the task of geo-localization, a grid of > 25000 candidate points ($20m$ apart) was overlaid on the map. However, many of these points were placed on buildings, so only 4134 candidate points needed to be searched over. Each grid point was evaluated with 18 different orientations ($20°$ apart), and the highest score among them was then assigned to that particular location.

Figure 8 shows four different localization examples. We use the GPS-tag of the query image in the Exif tag (after manual verification of the correctness) as the ground truth. The first column shows the query image and the objects present in it. The second column shows the objects detected by the DPM, and the last 5 columns show the top 5 location candidates for the image. The ground truth location, marked with the red boundary, obtains a high score due to the good matching between the content of the image and the GIS data of the location. The reason some arbitrary locations may get a high score is the poor object detection

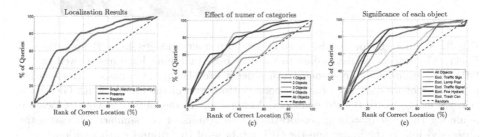

Fig. 7. Quantitative geo-localization results. Figure (a) shows the overall results (blue) along with the results obtained using only the presence/absence of objects (i.e., the left term in equation 5). Figure (b) illustrates the impact of the number of incorporated object classes. Figure (c) details the contribution of each object class.

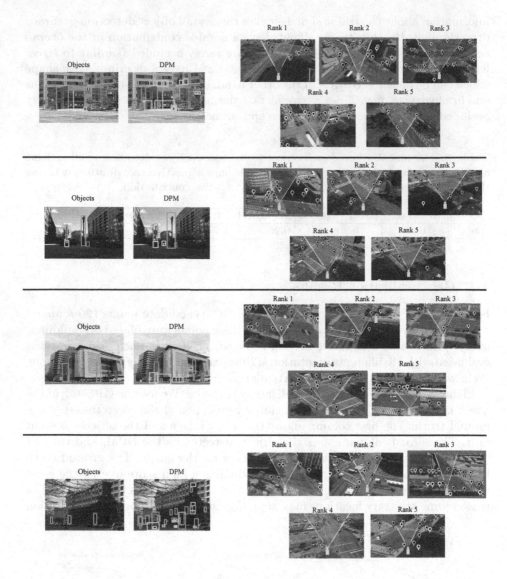

Fig. 8. Sample geo-localization results for four query images from Panoramio and Flickr. The images corresponding to the five best matching locations as well as the DPM detections and the ground truth objects are shown. The image corresponding to the correct location (i.e., the grid point within $20m$ of the ground truth GPS location.) is marked with the red boundary. As apparent in the figure, the correct location is among the best matching geo-locations as a results of the similarity between the objects visible in the image and the GIS database of the ground truth location.

results by DPM. That is because too many missed objects or false positives may form a random geometric arrangement in the image which matches the GIS objects of an arbitrary location.

Figure 7 (a) shows the quantitative localization accuracy of our method. We adopt the popular performance metric in image geo-localization literature [12,25] which employs a plot with the horizontal axis representing the rank of the ground truth location in the geo-localization results, and the vertical axis showing the percentage of test images with the ground truth location within a particular rank. The red curve in figure 7 (a) was computed by using only the information about the presence/absence of the objects in the image (i.e., the right term in equation 5). It can be observed that leveraging the geometric relationship leads to higher accuracy shown using the red curves.

Impact of Number of Object Classes: Similar to the experiments for object detection, we evaluated the localization results using fewer number of objects. Figure 7 (b) shows that, generally, utilizing more object classes leads to more accurate localization, as a results of incorporating more information.

Significance of Different Classes: similar to the experiment for object detection, we evaluated the importance of each object class in geo-localization. Figure 7 (c) shows localization results by excluding one of the object classes from the process; the amount of drop in the overall accuracy is indicative of the positive contribution of that particular class in the geo-localization results). Again, as shown in table 3, reliable objects, such as traffic signals, are confirmed to have a larger positive contribution in the localization results.

Failure Analysis: the root of the majority of the failure cases of our framework, for both object detection and geo-localization, is not being able to find the correct corresponding object bounding box among the DPM detections. In general, there are 3 main reasons for that: having no DPM detection for an object, misalignment by graph matching, and the inaccuracies of the GIS data (missing or misplaced objects). An experiment on a subset of our data showed the aforementioned reasons caused 25%, 41.6% and 33.4% of failures cases, respectively.

5   Conclusion

We proposed a method for improving object detection using a set of priors acquired from GIS databases. Given a database of object locations and a query image with metadata, we projected the GIS objects onto the image and fused them with candidate object detections acquired from DPM. In order to handle various inaccuracies and practical difficulties, we formulate our fusion as a higher-order graph matching problem which we robustly solved using RANSAC.

Furthermore, we proposed that the GIS objects can be used for discovering the GPS location from where an image was taken at. For this purpose, we performed a search on a dense grid of locations over the covered area and assigned a score to each geo-location quantifying the similarity between its GIS information and the image content based on the objects visible therein. We showed that this intuitive and semantic approach can significantly narrow down the search space, and sometimes, even find the correct GPS location.

References

1. Bansal, M., Sawhney, H.S., Cheng, H., Daniilidis, K.: Geo-localization of street views with aerial image databases. In: Proceedings of the 19th ACM International Conference on Multimedia, pp. 1125–1128. ACM (2011)
2. Bioret, N., Moreau, G., Servieres, M.: Towards outdoor localization from gis data and 3D content extracted from videos. In: IEEE International Symposium on Industrial Electronics (ISIE), pp. 3613–3618. IEEE (2010)
3. Crandall, D., Backstrom, L., Huttenlocher, D., Kleinberg, J.: Mapping the world's photos. In: International World Wide Web Conference (2009)
4. Dasiopoulou, S., Mezaris, V., Kompatsiaris, I., Papastathis, V.K., Strintzis, M.: Knowledge-assisted semantic video object detection. IEEE Transactions on Circuits and Systems for Video Technology 15(10), 1210–1224 (2005)
5. Duchenne, O., Bach, F., Kweon, I.S., Ponce, J.: A tensor-based algorithm for high-order graph matching. Pattern Analysis and Machine Intelligence (PAMI) 33(12), 2383–2395 (2011)
6. Felzenszwalb, P.F., Girshick, R.B., McAllester, D., Ramanan, D.: Object detection with discriminatively trained part based models. Pattern Analysis and Machine Intelligence (PAMI) 32(9), 1627–1645 (2010)
7. Girshick, R.B., Felzenszwalb, P.F., McAllester, D.: Discriminatively trained deformable part models, release 5,
   http://people.cs.uchicago.edu/~rbg/latent-release5/
8. Hoiem, D., Efros, A.A., Hebert, M.: Putting objects in perspective. In: International Conference on Computer Vision (ICCV) (2008)
9. Knopp, J., Sivic, J., Pajdla, T.: Avoiding confusing features in place recognition. In: Daniilidis, K., Maragos, P., Paragios, N. (eds.) ECCV 2010, Part I. LNCS, vol. 6311, pp. 748–761. Springer, Heidelberg (2010)
10. Lee, Y.J., Efros, A.A., Hebert, M.: Style-aware mid-level representation for discovering visual connections in space and time. In: International Conference on Computer Vision (ICCV) (2013)
11. Li, Y., Snavely, N., Huttenlocher, D., Fua, P.: Worldwide pose estimation using 3D point clouds. In: Fitzgibbon, A., Lazebnik, S., Perona, P., Sato, Y., Schmid, C. (eds.) ECCV 2012, Part I. LNCS, vol. 7572, pp. 15–29. Springer, Heidelberg (2012)
12. Lin, T.Y., Belongie, S., Hays, J.: Cross-view image geolocalization. In: Computer Vision and Pattern Recognition (CVPR) (2013)
13. Lowe, D.G.: Distinctive image features from scale-invariant keypoints. In: International Journal of Computer Vision (IJCV) (2004)
14. Matzen, K., Snavely, N.: Nyc3dcars: A dataset of 3D vehicles in geographic context. In: International Conference on Computer Vision (ICCV) (2013)
15. Park, M., Chen, Y., Shafique, K.: Tag configuration matcher for geo-tagging. In: Proceedings of the 21st ACM SIGSPATIAL International Conference on Advances in Geographic Information Systems, pp. 374–377. ACM (2013)

16. Sattler, T., Leibe, B., Kobbelt, L.: Fast image-based localization using direct 2d-to-3D matching. In: International Conference on Computer Vision (ICCV) (2010)
17. Sattler, T., Leibe, B., Kobbelt, L.: Improving image-based localization by active correspondence search. In: Fitzgibbon, A., Lazebnik, S., Perona, P., Sato, Y., Schmid, C. (eds.) ECCV 2012, Part I. LNCS, vol. 7572, pp. 752–765. Springer, Heidelberg (2012)
18. Schindler, G., Brown, M., Szeliski, R.: City-scale location recognition. In: Computer Vision and Pattern Recognition (CVPR) (2007)
19. Torralba, A.: Contextual priming for object detection. International Journal of Computer Vision (IJCV) 53(2), 169–191 (2003)
20. Torralba, A., Murphy, K.P., Freeman, W.T., Rubin, M.A.: Context-based vision system for place and object recognition. In: International Conference on Computer Vision (ICCV), pp. 273–280. IEEE (2003)
21. Uchiyama, H., Saito, H., Servieres, M., Moreau, G., Ecole Centrale de Nantes - CERMA IRSTV: AR GIS on a physical map based on map image retrieval using llah tracking. In: Machine Vision and Application (MVA), pp. 382–385 (2009)
22. Wang, L., Neumann, U.: A robust approach for automatic registration of aerial images with untextured aerial lidar data. In: Computer Vision and Pattern Recognition (CVPR), pp. 2623–2630 (June 2009)
23. Zamir, A.R., Ardeshir, S., Shah, M.: GPS-Tag renement using random walks with an adaptive damping factor. In: Computer Vision and Pattern Recognition (CVPR) (2014)
24. Zamir, A.R., Shah, M.: Accurate image localization based on google maps street view. In: Daniilidis, K., Maragos, P., Paragios, N. (eds.) ECCV 2010, Part IV. LNCS, vol. 6314, pp. 255–268. Springer, Heidelberg (2010)
25. Zamir, A.R., Shah, M.: Image geo-localization based on multiple nearest neighbor feature matching using generalized graphs. IEEE Transactions on Pattern Analysis and Machine Intelligence (T-PAMI) (2014)
26. Zass, R., Shashua, A.: Probabilistic graph and hypergraph matching. In: Computer Vision and Pattern Recognition (CVPR), pp. 1–8 (June 2008)

Context-Based Pedestrian Path Prediction*

Julian Francisco Pieter Kooij[1,2], Nicolas Schneider[1,2],
Fabian Flohr[1,2], and Dariu M. Gavrila[1,2]

[1] Environment Perception, Daimler R&D, Ulm, Germany
{nicolas.schneider,fabian.flohr}@daimler.com
[2] Intelligent Systems Laboratory, Univ. of Amsterdam, The Netherlands
{J.F.P.Kooij,D.M.Gavrila}@uva.nl

Abstract. We present a novel Dynamic Bayesian Network for pedestrian path prediction in the intelligent vehicle domain. The model incorporates the pedestrian situational awareness, situation criticality and spatial layout of the environment as latent states on top of a Switching Linear Dynamical System (SLDS) to anticipate changes in the pedestrian dynamics. Using computer vision, situational awareness is assessed by the pedestrian head orientation, situation criticality by the distance between vehicle and pedestrian at the expected point of closest approach, and spatial layout by the distance of the pedestrian to the curbside. Our particular scenario is that of a crossing pedestrian, who might stop or continue walking at the curb. In experiments using stereo vision data obtained from a vehicle, we demonstrate that the proposed approach results in more accurate path prediction than only SLDS, at the relevant short time horizon ($1\,s$), and slightly outperforms a computationally more demanding state-of-the-art method.

Keywords: intelligent vehicles, path prediction, situational awareness, visual focus of attention, Dynamic Bayesian Network, Linear Dynamical System.

1 Introduction

The past decade has seen a significant progress on video-based pedestrian detection. In the intelligent vehicle domain, this has recently culminated in the market introduction of active pedestrian systems that can perform automatic braking in case of dangerous traffic situations. An area that holds major potential for further improvement is situation assessment. Current active pedestrian systems are designed conservatively in their warning and control strategy, emphasizing the current pedestrian state (i.e. position) rather than prediction, in order to avoid false system activations. Indeed, pedestrian path prediction is a challenging problem, due to the highly dynamic nature of pedestrian motion, and systems need to react with limited computation time. Small deviations of, say, $30\,cm$ in the estimated lateral position of the pedestrian can make all the difference, as this might place the pedestrian just inside or outside the driving corridor.

---

* Electronic supplementary material -Supplementary material is available in the online version of this chapter at http://dx.doi.org/10.1007/978-3-319-10599-4_40
Videos can also be accessed at http://www.springerimages.com/videos/978-3-319-10598-7

D. Fleet et al. (Eds.): ECCV 2014, Part VI, LNCS 8694, pp. 618–633, 2014.
© Springer International Publishing Switzerland 2014

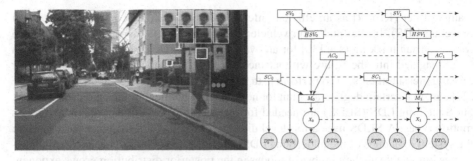

Fig. 1. Left: Pedestrian path prediction from an approaching vehicle, using situation criticality, pedestrian awareness thereof, and positioning vs. curbside. Right: DBN as directed graph, unrolled for two time slices. Discrete/continuous/observed nodes are rectangular/circular/shaded.

This paper focuses on the accurate path prediction of pedestrians intending to laterally cross the street, as observed by a stereo camera on-board an approaching vehicle (accident analysis shows that this scenario accounts for a majority of all pedestrian fatalities in traffic [23]). We argue that the pedestrian's decision to stop is for a large degree influenced by three factors: the existence of an approaching vehicle on collision course, the pedestrian's awareness thereof, and the spatial layout of the environment. We therefore propose a Dynamic Bayesian Network (DBN), which captures these factors as latent states on top of a Switching Linear Dynamical System (SLDS), thus controlling changes in the pedestrian dynamics. We estimate situation criticality by the distance between vehicle and pedestrian at the expected point of closest approach. Situational awareness assesses whether the pedestrian has seen the vehicle at some point up to now (whether the pedestrian currently sees the vehicle is estimated by means of the head orientation). Spatial layout is captured by the distance of the pedestrian to the road curbside. See Fig. 1 for an illustration of the scenario. The observables (shaded nodes in the graphical model), i.e. distance at closest approach, pedestrian location, head orientation, curbside location, are provided by external, state-of-the-art system components, for which we do not make novelty claims.

All DBN parameters are estimated from annotated training data. In the experiments, we collected data of pedestrians crossing in a supervised setting in traffic situations, where the vehicle has an implicit right-of-way. It would be straightforward to apply the approach to traffic situations where traffic lights or pedestrian crossings change the right-of-way, by adding an (observed) context variable to the DBN. Our approach can also be extended to additional motion types (e.g. pedestrian crossing the road in a curved path) or, more generally, to robot navigation in human-inhabited environments.

2   Previous Work

In this section, we focus on techniques for pedestrian state estimation and path prediction. For vision-based pedestrian detection, see recent surveys e.g. [10,12]. For pedestrian head/body orientation estimation, see e.g. [5,13,14].

State estimation in dynamical systems often involves the assumption that the underlying model is linear and that the noise is Gaussian, mainly due to the availability of the

Kalman filter (KF) [7] as an efficient inference algorithm for such Linear Dynamical Systems (LDS). In the intelligent vehicle domain, the KF is the most popular choice for pedestrian tracking (see [30] for an overview). The state distribution of a LDS can be propagated into the future without incorporating new observations to account for missing measurements, or to perform path prediction. The Extended and Unscented KF [24] can, to a certain degree, account for non-linear dynamical or measurement models, but Switching LDS (SLDS) are needed for maneuvering targets that alternate various motion types. A SLDS uses a top-level discrete Markov chain to select per time step the system dynamics of the underlying LDS. However, exact inference and learning becomes intractable as the number of modes in the posterior distribution grows exponential over time in the number of the switching states [27]. One solution is to approximate the posterior by samples using some Markov Chain Monte Carlo method [26,29]. Sampling can also be used when extending the SLDS hierarchy, e.g. to impose distributions on persistent state durations [26], or learn an SLDS mixture to cluster trajectories which exhibit similar switching behavior [21]. However, sampling is impractical for online real-time inference as convergence can be slow. Another solution is Assumed Density Filtering (ADF) [6,25], which approximates the posterior at every time step with a simpler distribution. ADF can be applied to discrete state DBNs, known as Boyen-Koller inference [8], and more generally to mixed discrete-continuous state spaces with conditional Gaussian posterior [22]. Interacting Multiple Model KF [7] is related to ADF for SLDS, as it mixes the states of several KF filters running in parallel, and has been applied for path prediction in the intelligent vehicle domain [18,30].

Whereas SLDSs can account for changes in dynamics, a switch in dynamics will only be detected after sufficient observations contradict the currently predominant dynamic model. If we wish to anticipate instead of react to changes in dynamics, a model should include possible causes for change. These influences on pedestrian behavior can be captured on an individual level using agent models, which have been used to reason about pedestrian intent [4,19] (i.e. where does observed agent want to go), account for preferences to move around certain regions of a static scene [19], and avoid collision with other agents, as is done in social force models [2,16]. [32] enhanced social force towards group behavior by introducing sub-goals such as "following a person". The related Linear Trajectory Avoidance model [28] for short-term path prediction uses the expected point of closest approach to foreshadow and avoid possible collisions.

These agent-based models assume that pedestrians are fully aware of their environment [19,28]. However, this assumption does not hold when dealing with inattentive pedestrians in the intelligent vehicle context. [15] presented a study on head turning behaviors at pedestrian crosswalks regarding the best point of warning for inattentive pedestrians. They used gyro sensors to record head turning and let pedestrians press a button when they recognize an approaching vehicle. Apart from this sole study of Visual Focus of Attention (VFOA) in intelligent vehicle context we are aware of, VFOA has been investigated in other application contexts. For example, [5] used a HOG-based head detector to determine pedestrian attention for automated surveillance, and [3] combined contextual cues in a DBN to model influence of group interaction on VFOA.

Within the class of non-parametric methods for path prediction and action classification, [18] recently proposed two non-linear, higher order Markov models to estimate whether a crossing pedestrian will stop at the curbside, one using Gaussian Process Dynamical Models (GPDM), and one using Probabilistic Hierarchical Trajectory Matching (PHTM). Both models use dense optical flow features in the pedestrian bounding box, in addition to the positional information. The first approach learns a GPDM of the dense flow for walking and stopping motion to predict future flow fields (and thereby lateral velocity). PHTM matches feature vectors of flow and position to a hierarchically organized tracklet database to extrapolate motion. Both approaches were shown to perform similar, and outperform the first-order Markov LDS and SLDS models, albeit at a large computational cost ([18] reports GPDM/PHTM is three/two orders of magnitude slower than KF). [20] considered the complementary case, whether a standing pedestrian will start to walk at the curbside. This only involved action classification and no path prediction, and an infrastructure-based sensor setup (no on-board vehicle sensing).

3   Proposed Approach

We are interested in modeling the motion dynamics of a pedestrian from the viewpoint of an approaching vehicle, in order to perform accurate path prediction. We consider that non-maneuvering pedestrian movement is well captured by a LDS with a basic motion model (e.g. constant position, constant velocity, constant turn rate) [7], and that maneuvering pedestrian movement can be suitably represented by means of an SLDS. Thus, the switching state indicates which basic motion model to use at any moment.

In this paper, we propose to condition the transition matrix of the SLDS switching state on latent factors that are likely going to influence the pedestrian's motion type. In a scenario of a lateral crossing pedestrian, we argue that the pedestrian's decision to continue walking or to stop is largely influenced by the existence of an approaching vehicle on collision course, the pedestrian's awareness thereof, and the position of the pedestrian with respect to the curbside.

Hence, we consider our main paper contribution a DBN which captures these three factors as latent states on top of an SLDS (see current section). The proposed approach goes beyond the state-of-the-art on pedestrian path prediction in vehicle context, which has considered the pedestrian in isolation, i.e. context free [18,20,30], and agent models that ignore a pedestrian's perception and resulting situational awareness [4,19,28].

3.1   Graphical Model

The proposed DBN is shown in Fig. 1. We distinguish two sets of variables: those relating to a SLDS (consisting of switching state M, latent position state X and associated observation Y) and those related to the scene context, i.e. spatial layout, situation criticality and the pedestrian's awareness (consisting of discrete latent variables $Z = \{SV, HSV, SC, AC\}$) that influence the SLDS switching state, and associated observables $E = \{HO, D^{min}, DTC\}$. These variables are now discussed in turn. Details on parameter estimation and computation of observables are given in Sec. 4.2.

SLDS. A SLDS contains a discrete switching state M_t, a continuous hidden state X_t, and a linear observation of the state Y_t with noise $\mathcal{N}(0, R)$ added. In our application, we consider that any moment can exhibit one of two motion types, *walking* ($M_t = m_w$) and *standing* ($M_t = m_s$). While the velocity of any standing person is zero, different people can have different walking velocities, i.e. some people move faster than others. Let x_t denote a person's lateral position at time t (after vehicle ego-motion compensation) and v_t the corresponding velocity. Furthermore, v^{m_w} is the personal walking velocity of the pedestrian. The motion dynamics over a period Δt can then be described as,

$$x_t = x_{t-\Delta t} + v_t \Delta t + \epsilon_t \Delta t \qquad\qquad v_t = \begin{cases} 0 & \text{iff } M_t = m_s \\ v^{m_w} & \text{iff } M_t = m_w \end{cases} \qquad (1)$$

Here $\epsilon_t \sim \mathcal{N}(0, Q)$ is zero-mean process noise that allows for deviations of the fixed velocity assumption. We will assume fixed time-intervals, and from here on set $\Delta t = 1$.

We include the velocity v^{m_w} in the state of an SLDS, together with the position x_t, such that we can filter both as we obtain observations over time, i.e. $X_t = [x_t, v_t^{m_w}]^\top$,

$$X_t = A^{(M_t)} X_{t-1} + \begin{bmatrix} \epsilon_t \\ 0 \end{bmatrix} \qquad\qquad \epsilon_t \sim \mathcal{N}(0, Q) \qquad (2)$$

$$Y_t = C X_t + \eta_t \qquad\qquad \eta_t \sim \mathcal{N}(0, R) \qquad (3)$$

where the switching state M_t selects the appropriate linear state transformation $A^{(m)}$,

$$A^{(m_s)} = \begin{bmatrix} 1 & 0 \\ 0 & 1 \end{bmatrix} \qquad A^{(m_w)} = \begin{bmatrix} 1 & 1 \\ 0 & 1 \end{bmatrix}. \qquad (4)$$

$Y_t \in \mathbb{R}$ is the observed lateral position with observation matrix $C = [1\ 0]$. The initial distribution on the state X_0 expresses our prior beliefs about a pedestrian's position and walking speed, as learned from the training data (see Sec. 4.2). From the definition of the SLDS, we obtain the following conditional probability distributions for the graphical model, $P(X_t|X_{t-1}, M_t) = \mathcal{N}(X_t|A^{(M_t)}X_{t-1}, Q)$ and $P(Y_t|X_t) = \mathcal{N}(Y_t|CX_t, R)$.

Context. The transition probability of the SLDS switching state is conditioned on the Boolean latent context variables Z. Although all these variables are discrete, during inference the uncertainty propagates from the observables to these variables (and over time), resulting in posterior distributions that contain values between 0 and 1. Each contextual configuration $Z_t = z$ is associated with a motion model transition probability $\mathcal{P}_z$, where $\mathcal{P}(\cdot)$ indicates that the distribution is represented by a probability table, and the subscript here denotes a table for each value z, such that

$$P(M_t|M_{t-1}, Z_t = z) = \mathcal{P}_z(M_t|M_{t-1}). \qquad (5)$$

The temporal transition of the context in Z is factorized by the probability tables

$$P(Z_t|Z_{t-1}) = \mathcal{P}(HSV_t|HSV_{t-1}, SV_t) \times \mathcal{P}(SV_t|SV_{t-1}) \\ \times \mathcal{P}(SC_t|SC_{t-1}) \times \mathcal{P}(AC_t|AC_{t-1}). \qquad (6)$$

The latent *Sees-Vehicle* (SV) variable indicates whether the pedestrian is currently seeing the vehicle. *Has-Seen-Vehicle* (HSV) indicates whether the pedestrian is aware of the vehicle, i.e. whether $SV_{t'}$ = true for some $t' \leq t$. The transition probability of HSV_t encodes simply a logical OR between the Boolean HSV_{t-1} and SV_t nodes:

$$P(HSV_t|HSV_{t-1}, SV_t) = \begin{cases} 1 & \text{iff } HSV_t = (HSV_{t-1} \vee SV_t) \\ 0 & \text{otherwise.} \end{cases} \tag{7}$$

The latent variable *Situation-Critical* (SC) indicates whether a situation is critical when both, pedestrian and vehicle, continue with their current velocities. *At-Curb* (AC) indicates if the pedestrian is currently at the distance from the curbside (as found in the training data) where a person would stop if they choose to wait and postpone crossing the road. The SV, SC and AC nodes furthermore depend on their value in the preceding time step, which improves the temporal consistency of these latent variables.

Next we discuss observations E_t which provide evidence for the latent context Z_t,

$$P(E_t|Z_t) = P(HO_t|SV_t) \times P(D_t^{min}|SC_t) \times P(DTC|AC_t). \tag{8}$$

The *Head-Orientation* observable HO_t serves as evidence for the *Sees-Vehicle* (SV_t) variable. We apply multiple classifiers to the head image region, each trained to detect the head in a particular looking direction (for details, see Section 4.1), and HO_t is then a vector with the classifier responses. The values in this vector form different unnormalized distributions over the classes, depending on whether the pedestrian is looking at the vehicle or not. However, if the head is not clearly observed (e.g. it is too far, or in the shadow), all values are typically low, and the observed class distribution provides little evidence of the true head orientation. We therefore model HO_t as a sample from a Multinomial distribution conditioned on SV_t, with parameter vector p_{sv},

$$P(HO_t|SV_t = sv) = \text{Mult}(HO_t|p_{sv}). \tag{9}$$

As such, higher classifier outputs count as stronger evidence for the presence of that class in the observation. In the other limit of all zero outputs, HO_t will have equal likelihood for any value of SV_t.

For *Situation-Critical* (SC), we consider the minimum distance D^{min} between the pedestrian and vehicle, if their paths would be extrapolated in time with fixed velocity [28]. While this indicator makes naive assumptions about the vehicle and pedestrian motion, it is still informative as a measure of how critical the situation is, and thereby, as part of our model, will lead to more accurate pedestrian path prediction. We define a Gamma distribution over D^{min} given SC, parametrized by shape a and scale b,

$$P(D_t^{min}|SC_t = sc) = \Gamma(D_t^{min}|a_{sc}, b_{sc}). \tag{10}$$

To obtain evidence for *At-Curb* (AC_t), we detect the curb ridge in the image, and measure its lateral position near the pedestrian. These noisy measurements are filtered with a constant position Kalman filter with zero process noise, such that we obtain an accurate estimate of the expected curb position, x_t^{curb}. *Distance-To-Curb*, DTC_t, is then calculated as the difference between the expected filtered position of the pedestrian, $\mathbf{E}[x_t]$, and of the curb, x_t^{curb}. Note that for path prediction we can estimate DTC even at future time steps, using predicted pedestrian positions, and accordingly predict AC too. The distribution over DTC_t given AC is modeled as a Normal distribution,

$$P(DTC_t|AC_t = ac) = \mathcal{N}(DTC_t|\mu_{ac}, \sigma_{ac}). \tag{11}$$

3.2   Inference

The DBN is used in a forward filtering procedure to incorporate all available observations of new time instances directly when they are received. We have a mixed discrete-continuous DBN where the exact posterior includes a mixture of $|M|^T$ Normal modes after T time steps, hence exact inference is intractable. We therefore resort to Assumed Density Filtering [22,25] for approximate inference, where after each time step the found posterior is approximated by a simpler distribution. The procedure consists of executing the following three steps for each time instance: predict, update, and collapse.

We will let $\overline{P}_t(\cdot) \equiv P(\cdot|O_{1:t-1})$ denote a prediction for time t (i.e. before receiving the observation O_t), and $\widehat{P}_t(\cdot) \equiv P(\cdot|O_{1:t})$ denote an updated estimate for time t (i.e. after observing O_t). Finally, $\widetilde{P}_t(\cdot)$ is the collapsed or approximated updated distribution that will be carried over to the predict step of the next time instance $t + 1$.

Predict. To predict time t we use the posterior distribution of $t - 1$, which is factorized into the joint distribution over the latent discrete nodes $\widetilde{P}_{t-1}(M_{t-1}, Z_{t-1})$ and the conditional Normal distribution $\widetilde{P}_{t-1}(X_{t-1}|M_{t-1}) = \mathcal{N}(X_{t-1}|\widetilde{\mu}_{t-1}^{(M_{t-1})}, \widetilde{\Sigma}_{t-1}^{(M_{t-1})})$.

First, the joint probability of the discrete nodes in the previous and current time steps is computed using the factorized transition tables of Eq. (5) and (6),

$$\overline{P}_t(M_t, M_{t-1}, Z_t, Z_{t-1}) = P(M_t|M_{t-1}, Z_t)P(Z_t|Z_{t-1})\widetilde{P}_{t-1}(M_{t-1}, Z_{t-1}). \quad (12)$$

Then for the continuous latent state X_t we predict the effect of the linear dynamics of all possible models M_t on the conditional Normal distribution of each M_{t-1},

$$\overline{P}_t(X_t|M_t, M_{t-1}) = \int P(X_t|X_{t-1}, M_t) \times \widetilde{P}_{t-1}(X_{t-1}|M_{t-1}) \, dX_{t-1}. \quad (13)$$

Applying Eq. (2), we find that the parametric form of (13) is the Kalman prediction step

$$\mathcal{N}(X_t|\overline{\mu}_t^{(M_t, M_{t-1})}, \overline{\Sigma}_t^{(M_t, M_{t-1})}) =$$
$$\int \mathcal{N}(X_t|A^{(M_t)}X_{t-1}, Q) \times \mathcal{N}(X_{t-1}|\widehat{\mu}_{t-1}^{(M_{t-1})}, \widehat{\Sigma}_{t-1}^{(M_{t-1})}) \, dX_{t-1}. \quad (14)$$

Update. The update step incorporates the observations of the current time step to obtain the joint posterior. For each joint assignment (M_t, M_{t-1}), the LDS likelihood term is

$$P(Y_t|M_t, M_{t-1}) = \int P(Y_t|X_t) \times \overline{P}_t(X_t|M_t, M_{t-1}) \, dX_t$$
$$= \mathcal{N}(Y_t|C\overline{\mu}_t^{(M_t, M_{t-1})}, \overline{\Sigma}_t^{(M_t, M_{t-1})} + R), \quad (15)$$

where we make use of Eq. (3). Combining this with the prediction (Eq. (12)) and contextual likelihood (Eq. (8)), we obtain the posterior as one joint probability table

$$\widehat{P}_t(M_t, M_{t-1}, Z_t, Z_{t-1}) \propto P(Y_t|M_t, M_{t-1})P(E_t|Z_t)\overline{P}_t(M_t, M_{t-1}, Z_t, Z_{t-1}) \quad (16)$$

where we normalize the r.h.s. over all possible $(M_t, Z_t, M_{t-1}Z_{t-1})$ combinations to obtain the distribution on the l.h.s. The posterior distribution over the continuous state,

$$\widehat{P}_t(X_t|M_t, M_{t-1}) \propto P(Y_t|X_t) \times \overline{P}_t(X_t|M_t, M_{t-1})$$
$$= \mathcal{N}(X_t|\widehat{\mu}_t^{(M_t, M_{t-1})}, \widehat{\Sigma}_t^{(M_t, M_{t-1})}) \tag{17}$$

has parameters $\left(\widehat{\mu}_t^{(M_t, M_{t-1})}, \widehat{\Sigma}_t^{(M_t, M_{t-1})}\right)$ for the $|M|^2$ possible transition conditions, which are obtained using the standard Kalman update equations.

Collapse. In the third step, the state of the previous time step is marginalized out from the joint posterior distribution, such that we only keep the joint distribution of variables of the current time instance, which will be used in the predict step of the next iteration.

$$\widetilde{P}_t(M_t, Z_t) = \sum_{M_{t-1}} \sum_{Z_{t-1}} \widehat{P}_t(M_t, M_{t-1}, Z_t, Z_{t-1}) \tag{18}$$

Likewise, we approximate the $|M|^2$ Normal distributions by just $|M|$ distributions,

$$\widetilde{P}_t(X_t|M_t) = \sum_{M_{t-1}} \widehat{P}_t(X_t|M_t, M_{t-1}) \times P(M_{t-1}|M_t) = \mathcal{N}(X_t|\widetilde{\mu}_t^{(M_t)}, \widetilde{\Sigma}_t^{(M_t)}) \tag{19}$$

Here, the parameters $\left(\widetilde{\mu}_t^{(M_t)}, \widetilde{\Sigma}_t^{(M_t)}\right)$ are found by Gaussian moment matching [22,25], and $P(M_{t-1}|M_t)$ through marginalizing and normalizing $\widehat{P}_t(M_t, M_{t-1}, Z_t, Z_{t-1})$.

4   Experiments

4.1   Dataset and Observations

Our dataset consists of 58 sequences recorded using a stereo camera (baseline $22\, cm$, $16\, fps$, 1176×640 pixels) mounted behind the windshield of a vehicle[1]. All sequences involve single pedestrians with the intention to cross the street, but feature different situation criticalities (critical[2] vs. non-critical), pedestrian situational awareness (vehicle seen vs. vehicle not seen) and pedestrian behavior (stopping at the curbside vs. crossing). Due to the focus on potentially dangerous situations, both driver and pedestrian were instructed during recording sessions. The dataset contains four different male pedestrians and eight different locations. Each sequence lasts several seconds (min / max / mean: $2.53\, s$ / $13.27\, s$ / $7.15\, s$), and pedestrians are generally unoccluded, though brief occlusions by poles or trees occur in three sequences.

Positional ground truth (GT) is obtained by manual labeling of the pedestrian bounding boxes and computing the median disparity over the upper pedestrian body area using dense stereo [17]. Analysis of crossing trajectories shows an mean gait cycle of

---

[1] The dataset, including annotations, will be made available for non-commercial, research purposes within a year after publication. Please contact the last author.

[2] N.B. None of the experiments exposed pedestrians to danger; "critical situation" refers to a theoretic outcome where both the approaching vehicle and pedestrian would not stop.

17.3 frames ($1.0\,s$) with 1.6 frames ($0.1\,s$) standard deviation. GT for contextual observations is obtained by labeling head orientation (16 discrete clock-wise increasing orientation angles). Sequences where potentially dangerous situations occur, i.e. when either pedestrian or vehicle should stop to avoid a collision, have been labeled as critical. Sequences are further labeled with event tags and time-to-event (TTE, in frames) values. For stopping pedestrians, TTE = 0 is when the last foot is placed on the ground at the curbside, and for crossing pedestrians at the closest point to the curbside (before entering the roadway). Frames before/after an event have negative/positive TTE values.

A HOG/linSVM pedestrian detector [9] provides measurements, given region-of-interests supplied by an obstacle detection component using dense stereo data. The resulting bounding boxes are used to calculate a median disparity over the upper pedestrian body area. The vehicle ego-motion compensated lateral position in world coordinates is then used as positional observation Y_t.

For the observed head orientation HO_t, the angular domain of $[0°, 360°)$ is split into eight discrete orientation classes of $0°, 45°, \cdots, 315°$. We trained a detector for each class [13], i.e. $f_0, \cdots, f_{315}$, such that the detector response $f_o(I_t)$ is the strength for the evidence that the observed image region I_t contains the head in orientation class o. For each detector we used neural networks with local receptive fields [33] trained in a one vs. rest manner. We used a separate training set with 9300 manually contour labeled head samples from 6389 gray-value images with a min./max./mean pedestrian height of 69/344/122 pixels (c.f. [14]). For additional training data, head samples were mirrored and shifted, and 22109 non-head samples were generated in areas around heads and from false positive pedestrian detections. For detection, we generate candidate head regions in the upper pedestrian detection bounding box from disparity based image segmentation. The most likely head image region I^* is selected from all candidates based on disparity information and detector responses. Before classification, head image patches are rescaled to $16 \times 16\,px$. The head observation $HO_t = [f_0(I_t^*), \cdots, f_{315}(I_t^*)]$ contains the confidences of the selected region.

The expected minimum distance D^{min} between pedestrian and vehicle is calculated as in [28] for each time step based on current position and velocity. Vehicle speed is provided by on-board sensors, for pedestrians the first order derivative is used and averaged over the last 10 frames. For DTC, the curbside is detected with a basic Hough transform [11]. The image region of interest is determined by the specified accuracy of a state-of-the-art vehicle localization approach (GPS+INS) using map data [31]. Y_t^{curb} is then the mean lateral position of the detected line back-projected to world coordinates.

4.2   Parameter Estimation

All distribution parameters are estimated from annotated training data. For stopping sequences, the GT switching state is defined as $M_t = m_s$ at moments with TTE $>= 0$, and as $M_t = m_w$ at all other moments, crossing sequences always have $M_t = m_w$. From the GT at time $t = 0$ we estimate the position and walking speed prior for X_0. Process noise Q is estimated from the differences of the estimated mean walking speed and a pedestrian's true walking speeds, and observation noise $\mathcal{N}(0, R)$ is estimated by the difference between GT and measured positions.

Considering head observation HO, we assume pedestrians recognize an approaching vehicle (GT label SV_t = true) when the GT head direction is in a range of $\pm 45°$ around angle $0°$ (head is pointing towards the camera), and do not see the vehicle (SV_t = false) for angles outside this range (future human studies could allow a more precise threshold, or provide an angle distribution, the study in [15] only reported the frequency of head turning). For each ground truth label sv, we estimate the orientation class distributions p_{sv} by averaging the class weights in the corresponding head measurements. For the observation D^{min}, we define per trajectory one value for all SC_t labels ($\forall_t SC_t$ = true for trajectories with critical situations, $\forall_t SC_t$ = false otherwise), and estimate the distributions $\Gamma(D^{min}|a_{sc}, b_{sc})$. The distributions $\mathcal{N}(DTC_t|\mu_{ac}, \sigma_{ac})$ are estimated from GT curb positions and *At-Curb* labels, which are set to AC_t = true only at time instances where $-1 \leq$ TTE ≤ 1 when crossing, and TTE ≥ -1 when stopping. Finally, it is straightforward to estimate prior and transition probability tables for the discrete contextual quantities SV, AC from their GT labels. The same applies to the dynamic switching state M, conditioned on HSV, SC and AC. The transition probability for HSV is a logical OR, as described in 3.1. Since we only set SC labels once per sequence, we fix the SC transition probability to $1/100$ for changing state.

4.3   Evaluation

The dataset is divided into five sub-scenarios, listed in Table 1. Four sub-scenarios represent "normal" pedestrian behaviors (e.g. the pedestrian stops if he is aware of a critical situation and crosses otherwise). The fifth sub-scenario is anomalous, since the pedestrian crosses even though he is aware of the critical situation. We compare our proposed DBN with full context, referred to as *SC+HSV+AC*, to model variations with less context, and to a fixed velocity Kalman Filter with acceleration noise (see caption Table 1).

Leave-one-out cross-validation is used to separate training and test sequences, though sequences from the anomalous sub-scenario are excluded from the training data. For each time t with state X_t, we create a predictive distribution for X_{t+t_p} at t_p time steps in the future by iteratively applying the *Predict* and *Collapse* steps (see Sec. 3.2), and only *Update* with the DTC likelihood (Eq. (11)) using the predicted positions,

$$\overline{P}_{t_p|t}(X_{t+t_p}) \equiv \overline{P}(X_{t+t_p}|Y_{1:t}). \tag{20}$$

We define two performance metrics for a sequence, namely the Euclidean distance between lateral predicted expected position x_{t+t_p} and lateral GT position G_{t+t_p}, and the log likelihood of G under the predictive distribution:

$$error(t_p|t) = |\mathbb{E}\left[\overline{P}_{t_p|t}(x_{t+t_p})\right] - G_{t+t_p}| \tag{21}$$

$$predll(t_p|t) = \log\left[\overline{P}_{t_p|t}(G_{t+t_p})\right] \tag{22}$$

Note that the predictive log likelihood of [1] corresponds to $predll(0|t)$.

Comparison of Model Variations. The results in Table 1 show the predictive log likelihood $predll$ for $t_p = 16$ time steps ($\sim 1\,s$) in the future, averaged over the second up to TTE = 0 when the pedestrian reaches the curb. In the first three normal sub-scenarios,

Table 1. Prediction log likelihood of the GT pedestrian position for $t_p = 16$ frames ($\sim 1\ s$) ahead, for different sub-scenarios (rows) and models (columns), for TTE $\in [-15, 0]$. The first four sub-scenarios contain "normal" pedestrian behavior. The fifth case is anomalous (*lower* likelihood is better). Model variations (best SLDS variant marked in bold): full context (SC+HSV+AC), no curb (SC+HSV), only head (HSV), only criticality (SC), no context (SLDS), KF (LDS).

Sub-scenario	SC+HSV+AC	SC+HSV	HSV	SC	SLDS	LDS
non-critical, vehicle not seen, crossing	-0.61	-0.53	**-0.52**	-0.59	-0.59	-1.90
non-critical, vehicle seen, crossing	-0.53	**-0.45**	-0.46	-0.47	-0.49	-1.93
critical, vehicle not seen, crossing	-0.48	-0.34	**-0.17**	-0.59	-0.33	-1.88
critical, vehicle seen, stopping	**-0.33**	-0.70	-1.13	-0.80	-1.26	-1.88
critical, vehicle seen, crossing	**-0.90**	-0.27	-0.15	-0.25	-0.13	-1.88

all five SLDS-based models perform similarly, clearly outperforming the LDS (which has similar low likelihoods across the board, i.e. it is unspecific for any sub-scenario). However, in the fourth sub-scenario (pedestrian sees the vehicle in a critical situation and stops), the simpler DBNs have low predictive likelihoods, except for our proposed model. Without the full context, the other models are not capable to predict *if*, *where* and *when* the pedestrian will stop. For the anomalous fifth sub-scenario, only the proposed model results in *lower* likelihood than for normal behavior, which is a useful property for anomaly detection. A future driver warning strategy could benefit from the more accurate path prediction of our SC+HSV+AC model in high likelihood situations, whereas falling back to simpler models/strategies when anomalies are detected.

Fig. 2 illustrates a sequence from the stopping sub-scenario (fourth row in Table 1), with a snapshot just *before* (TTE $= -20$) and *after* (TTE $= -9$) the pedestrian becomes aware of the critical situation. At TTE $= -20$, the predicted distributions of all models are close together and indicate that the pedestrian continues walking (the LDS does so with high uncertainty). At TTE $= -9$, the mean position predictions of the LDS are furthest away from the GT (still within one std.dev. because of high uncertainty). The SLDS-only prediction shows a comparatively low uncertainty, but the predicted means have a high distance to the GT (not within one std.dev.). Predictions of the SC+HSV model are closer to the true positions, since it captures the situational awareness of the pedestrian and therefore assigns a higher probability, compared to SLDS, to switch to the standing model m_s. The SC+HSV+AC model makes the best predictions as it also anticipates where the pedestrian will stop, namely at the curbside.

In the context of action classification, Fig. 3 shows for various model variations, (left) the standing probability $\tilde{P}_t(M_t = m_s)$, and (right) the $error(t_p|t)$ for predictions made $t_p = 16$ frames ahead, plotted against the TTE. In the first sub-scenario (top row), the pedestrian crosses in a critical situation without seeing the approaching vehicle. All models have a very low stopping probability, but since a few sequences have ambiguous head observations, our proposed model does not exclude the possibility that the vehicle has been seen. This translates to a higher stopping probability near the curb, and to a higher error of the average prediction for a short while. Still, the model recuperates as the pedestrian approaches the curb and shows no sign of slowing down, which informs the model that the pedestrian did not see the vehicle (i.e. joint inference also means that observed motion dynamics can disambiguate low-level head orientation estimation). In

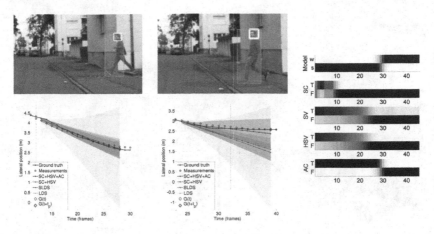

Fig. 2. Example of a pedestrian that will stop at the curb after becoming aware of a critical situation. Predictions are made $t_p = 16$ ($\sim 1\,s$) time steps ahead from different times t. Top left: Pedestrian with head detection bounding box (white), tracking bounding box (green), collapsed predicted distribution of the SC+HSV+AC model (blue ellipses show one and two std.dev.) and curb detection (blue line) made at time $t = 12$ (TTE $= -20$). Top center: The pedestrian became aware of the critical situation, shown is time step $t = 23$ (TTE $= -9$). Bottom left: Predictions (mean and std.dev.(shaded)) made at $t = 12$ (dashed green line and diamond) for the lateral position at time $t + t_p$ (red diamond indicates the GT at $t + t_p$) . Vertical black line denotes the event. Black dots indicate position measurements, the black line the GT positions. Colored lines are predicted positions by different models. Bottom center: Predictions of the lateral position at $t + t_p$ made from $t = 23$. Right: Inferred marginal distributions for the latent binary variables in the SC+HSV+AC model, using gray scale coded probability from 0 (black) to 1 (white). Horizontal axis is time. Variable labels are True and False, and walking and standing.

the second sub-scenario (bottom row), the pedestrian is aware of the critical situation and stops at the curb. Now, all models show an increasing stopping probability towards the event point. In a few scenarios, the SLDS switches too early to the standing state, reacting to perceived de-acceleration (noise) of the pedestrian walking, hence the high std. dev. of the SLDS over all sequences early on. However, on average the SLDS assigns a higher probability to standing (> 0.5) than walking after the pedestrian has already reached the curb (TTE > 0). It can only react to changing dynamics, but not anticipate it. Our proposed model, on the other hand, gives the best action classification (highest stopping probability at TTE $= 0$). It anticipates the change in motion dynamics a few frames earlier as the SLDS, benefiting from the combined knowledge about situation criticality and spatial layout. Further, the knowledge about the spatial layout helps to keep the standing probability low while the pedestrian is still far away from the curb. The model with limited context information ends up in between proposed model and SLDS. Accordingly, our proposed model has the lowest prediction error (bottom right plot). Averaged over the sequences, it outperforms the baseline SLDS model by up to $0.39\,m$ (at TTE $= 1$) and the SC+HSV model with up to $0.16\,m$ (at TTE $= -10$).

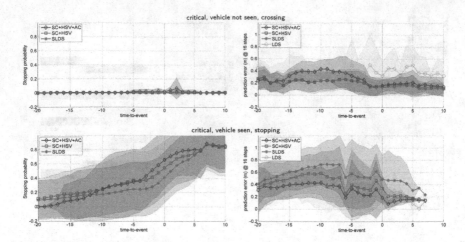

Fig. 3. Stopping probability (left) and lateral prediction error (right) when predicting 16 time steps ($\sim 1\,s$) ahead in the two critical sub-scenarios. Top: Pedestrian is not aware of the critical situation and crosses. Bottom: Pedestrian is aware of the critical situation and stops. Shown are mean and standard deviation (shaded) of each measure over all corresponding sequences, for our proposed model (SC+HSV+AC), an intermediate model without spatial layout information (SC+HSV), the baseline SLDS model without contextual cues, and a LDS.

Idealized Vision Measurements. To investigate how the vision components affect performance, we train and test using GT as idealized measurements for pedestrian location, curb location, and head orientation. We find that the lateral pedestrian and curb measurements are sufficiently accurate: GT does not notably change the results. Ideal head measurements alter the five sub-scenario scores of the SC+HSV+AC model w.r.t. Table 1 to -0.57, -1.08, -0.32, -0.12 ("normal" cases), and to -3.67 (anomalous case). Note that predictions became more accurate for critical sub-scenarios, less accurate in the second sub-scenario (non-critical, vehicle seen, crossing) at moments that are deemed critical since seeing the vehicle implies stopping, and that the likelihood of the anomalous fifth sub-scenario is still the lower than all other sub-scenarios, as expected.

Comparison with PHTM. Fig. 4 shows a comparison of the mean prediction error of our proposed model with the state-of-the-art PHTM model [18] which uses optical flow features and an exemplar database, on the four "normal" sub-scenarios. On two of these sub-scenarios (upper right and lower left plots) the proposed model outperforms PHTM slightly, both in terms of mean and variance, in particular on the arguably most important sub-scenario for a pedestrian safety application: critical, vehicle not seen, crossing. On the last sub-scenario (lower right plot) PHTM performs slightly better.

Computational Costs. The computational costs of the various approaches were assessed on standard PC hardware (Intel Core i7 X990 CPU at 3.47 GHz), see Table 2. We differentiate between the computational cost for obtaining the observables and that for

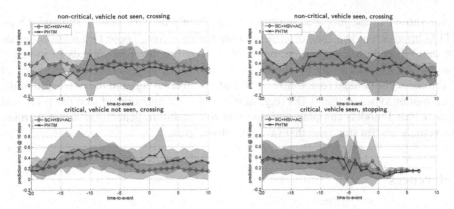

Fig. 4. The plots show the lateral prediction error of our proposed model and the PHTM model in various sub-scenarios. The lines show the avg. error over all sequences in a sub-scenario, after aligning the results by their TTE values, and the shaded region shows the std. dev. of the error.

Table 2. Computational costs for the different models per frame (avg. per frame, in ms)

Approach	Observables	State est. & pred.	Total
SC+HSV+AC	160	40	200
SLDS	60	10	70
LDS	60	0.4	60
PHTM	70	600	670

performing state estimation and prediction. In terms of observables, all approaches used positional information derived from a dense stereo-based pedestrian detector (about $60\,ms$). The additional observables used in our proposed SC+HSV+AC model (e.g. head orientation and curb detection) cost an extra $100\,ms$ to compute. PHTM on the other hand requires computing dense optical flow within the pedestrian bounding box (about $10\,ms$). But, as seen in Table 2, the proposed model is *one order* of magnitude more efficient than PHTM when considering only the state estimation and prediction component (this even though PHTM implements its trajectory matching by an efficient hierarchical technique [18]), and it is three times more efficient in total.

5   Conclusions

We presented a novel model for pedestrian path prediction in the intelligent vehicle domain. The model, a DBN, incorporated the pedestrian situational awareness, situation criticality and spatial layout of the environment (curbside) as latent states on top of an SLDS, thus controlling changes in the pedestrian dynamics. The proposed model overall outperformed simpler models with or without partial contextual cues by predicting GT pedestrian positions more accurate (up to $0.39\,m$ compared to the SLDS when predicting $\sim 1\,s$ ahead) and with *higher* likelihood in situations similar to those in the training set. In atypical situations, it predicted GT pedestrian position with a *lower* likelihood, a desirable property for anomaly detection.

We show that the proposed approach even slightly outperformed a state-of-the-art PHTM approach at less than *a third* of computational cost. These two approaches do not stand directly in competition, however, as they use different sources of information that could conceivably be combined. Further work involves the incorporation of additional scene context (e.g. traffic light, pedestrian crossing) and the extension of the basic motion types of the SLDS (e.g. turning). We are encouraged that the presented context-based models can play an important role in future generation driver warning and vehicle control strategies that save pedestrian lives.

References

1. Abbeel, P., Coates, A., Montemerlo, M., Ng, A.Y., Thrun, S.: Discriminative training of Kalman filters. In: Robotics: Science and Systems, pp. 289–296 (2005)
2. Antonini, G., Martinez, S.V., Bierlaire, M., Thiran, J.P.: Behavioral priors for detection and tracking of pedestrians in video sequences. IJCV 69(2), 159–180 (2006)
3. Ba, S., Odobez, J.: Multiperson visual focus of attention from head pose and meeting contextual cues. IEEE PAMI 33(1), 101–116 (2011)
4. Bandyopadhyay, T., Won, K., Frazzoli, E., Hsu, D., Lee, W., Rus, D.: Intention-aware motion planning. In: Algorithmic Foundations of Robotics X, pp. 475–491. Springer (2013)
5. Benfold, B., Reid, I.: Guiding visual surveillance by tracking human attention. In: Proc. BMVC (2009)
6. Bishop, C.M.: Pattern Recognition and Machine Learning, vol. 1. Springer (2006)
7. Blackman, S., Popoli, R.: Design and Analysis of Modern Tracking Systems. Artech House Norwood (1999)
8. Boyen, X., Koller, D.: Tractable inference for complex stochastic processes. In: Proc. of UAI, pp. 33–42. Morgan Kaufmann Publishers Inc. (1998)
9. Dalal, N., Triggs, B.: Histograms of oriented gradients for human detection. In: Proc. CVPR, pp. 886–893. IEEE (2005)
10. Dollár, P., Wojek, C., Schiele, B., Perona, P.: Pedestrian detection: An evaluation of the state of the art. IEEE PAMI 34(4), 743–761 (2012)
11. Duda, R.O., Hart, P.E.: Use of the Hough transformation to detect lines and curves in pictures. Commun. ACM 15(1), 11–15 (1972)
12. Enzweiler, M., Gavrila, D.M.: Monocular pedestrian detection: Survey and experiments. IEEE PAMI 31(12), 2179–2195 (2009)
13. Enzweiler, M., Gavrila, D.M.: Integrated pedestrian classification and orientation estimation. In: Proc. CVPR, pp. 982–989. IEEE (2010)
14. Flohr, F., Dumitru-Guzu, M., Kooij, J.F.P., Gavrila, D.M.: Joint probabilistic pedestrian head and body orientation estimation. In: IEEE Intell. Veh. (2014)
15. Hamaoka, H., Hagiwara, T., Tada, M., Munehiro, K.: A study on the behavior of pedestrians when confirming approach of right/left-turning vehicle while crossing a crosswalk. In: IEEE Intell. Veh., pp. 106–110 (2013)
16. Helbing, D., Molnár, P.: Social force model for pedestrian dynamics. Phys. Rev. E 51(5), 4282 (1995)
17. Hirschmüller, H.: Stereo processing by semiglobal matching and mutual information. IEEE PAMI 30(2), 328–341 (2008)
18. Keller, C.G., Gavrila, D.M.: Will the pedestrian cross? A study on pedestrian path prediction. IEEE Trans. ITS 15(2), 494–506 (2014)

19. Kitani, K.M., Ziebart, B.D., Bagnell, J.A., Hebert, M.: Activity forecasting. In: Fitzgibbon, A., Lazebnik, S., Perona, P., Sato, Y., Schmid, C. (eds.) ECCV 2012, Part IV. LNCS, vol. 7575, pp. 201–214. Springer, Heidelberg (2012)
20. Köhler, S., Schreiner, B., Ronalter, S., Doll, K., Brunsmann, U., Zindler, K.: Autonomous evasive maneuvers triggered by infrastructure-based detection of pedestrian intentions. In: IEEE Intell. Veh., pp. 519–526 (2013)
21. Kooij, J.F.P., Englebienne, G., Gavrila, D.M.: A non-parametric hierarchical model to discover behavior dynamics from tracks. In: Fitzgibbon, A., Lazebnik, S., Perona, P., Sato, Y., Schmid, C. (eds.) ECCV 2012, Part VI. LNCS, vol. 7577, pp. 270–283. Springer, Heidelberg (2012)
22. Lauritzen, S.L.: Propagation of probabilities, means, and variances in mixed graphical association models. Journal of the American Statistical Association 87(420), 1098–1108 (1992)
23. Meinecke, M.M., Obojski, M., Gavrila, D.M., Marc, E., Morris, R., Töns, M., Lettelier, L.: Strategies in terms of vulnerable road user protection. In: EU Project SAVE-U, Deliverable D6 (2003)
24. Meuter, M., Iurgel, U., Park, S.B., Kummert, A.: Unscented Kalman filter for pedestrian tracking from a moving host. In: IEEE Intell. Veh., pp. 37–42 (2008)
25. Minka, T.P.: Expectation propagation for approximate Bayesian inference. In: Proc. of UAI, pp. 362–369. Morgan Kaufmann Publishers Inc. (2001)
26. Oh, S.M., Rehg, J.M., Balch, T., Dellaert, F.: Learning and inferring motion patterns using parametric segmental switching linear dynamic systems. IJCV 77(1-3), 103–124 (2008)
27. Pavlovic, V., Rehg, J.M., MacCormick, J.: Learning switching linear models of human motion. In: Advances in NIPS, pp. 981–987 (2000)
28. Pellegrini, S., Ess, A., Schindler, K., Van Gool, L.: You'll never walk alone: Modeling social behavior for multi-target tracking. In: Proc. ICCV, pp. 261–268 (2009)
29. Rosti, A.V.I., Gales, M.J.F.: Rao-Blackwellised Gibbs sampling for switching linear dynamical systems. In: Proc. of the IEEE ICASSP, vol. 1, pp. 809–812 (2004)
30. Schneider, N., Gavrila, D.M.: Pedestrian path prediction with recursive Bayesian filters: A comparative study. In: Weickert, J., Hein, M., Schiele, B. (eds.) GCPR 2013. LNCS, vol. 8142, pp. 174–183. Springer, Heidelberg (2013)
31. Schreiber, M., Knöppel, C., Franke, U.: LaneLoc: Lane marking based localization using highly accurate maps. In: IEEE Intell. Veh., pp. 449–454 (2013)
32. Tamura, Y., Le, P.D., Hitomi, K., Chandrasiri, N., Bando, T., Yamashita, A., Asama, H.: Development of pedestrian behavior model taking account of intention. In: IEEE IROS, pp. 382–387 (2012)
33. Wöhler, C., Anlauf, J.K.: A time delay neural network algorithm for estimating image-pattern shape and motion. IVC 17(3-4), 281–294 (1999)

Sliding Shapes for 3D Object Detection in Depth Images

Shuran Song and Jianxiong Xiao

Princeton University
http://slidingshapes.cs.princeton.edu

Abstract. The depth information of RGB-D sensors has greatly simplified some common challenges in computer vision and enabled breakthroughs for several tasks. In this paper, we propose to use depth maps for object detection and design a 3D detector to overcome the major difficulties for recognition, namely the variations of texture, illumination, shape, viewpoint, clutter, occlusion, self-occlusion and sensor noises. We take a collection of 3D CAD models and render each CAD model from hundreds of viewpoints to obtain synthetic depth maps. For each depth rendering, we extract features from the 3D point cloud and train an Exemplar-SVM classifier. During testing and hard-negative mining, we slide a 3D detection window in 3D space. Experiment results show that our 3D detector significantly outperforms the state-of-the-art algorithms for both RGB and RGB-D images, and achieves about ×1.7 improvement on average precision compared to DPM and R-CNN. All source code and data are available online.

1 Introduction

Template matching with the image pattern is inadequate for three-dimensional scene analysis for many reasons, such as occlusion, changes in viewing angle, and articulation of parts. The patterns at image level are not invariant.

– Nevatia and Binford, 1977 [1].

Despite rapid progress on image patch classification [2–6], object detection remains an open research challenge. Meanwhile, the availability of inexpensive RGB-D sensors, such as Microsoft Kinect, Apple PrimeSense, Intel RealSense, and Google Project Tango, has greatly simplified some common challenges in vision and enabled breakthroughs for several tasks, such as body pose estimation [7, 8], intrinsic image [9], segmentation [10, 11] and 3D modeling [12]. In this paper, we propose an algorithm to use depth images for generic object detection and we achieve significantly performance improvement compared to the state-of-the-art results on RGB images [2].

The **main idea** is to exploit the depth information in a data-driven fashion to overcome the major difficulties in object detection, namely the variations of texture, illumination, shape, viewpoint, self occlusion, clutter and occlusion. For a given object category (e.g. chair), we use Computer Graphics (CG) CAD models from the Internet. We render each CG model from hundreds of viewpoints to obtain synthetic depth maps, as if they are viewed by a typical RGB-D sensor. As shown in Fig. 1, for each rendering, a feature vector is extracted from the 3D point cloud corresponding to the rendered depth map to train an exemplar Support Vector Machine (SVM) [3], using negative data

D. Fleet et al. (Eds.): ECCV 2014, Part VI, LNCS 8694, pp. 634–651, 2014.

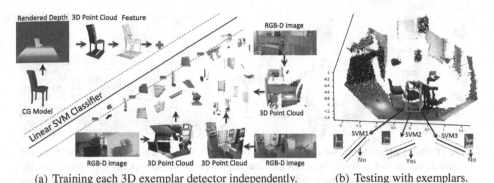

(a) Training each 3D exemplar detector independently.   (b) Testing with exemplars.

Fig. 1. Sliding Shapes: We extract 3D features of point cloud from depth rendering of CG model to train a 3D classifier. And during testing time, we slide a window in 3D to evaluate the score for each window using an ensemble of Exemplar-SVMs.

from a RGB-D dataset [10]. During testing and hard-negative mining, we slide a 3D detection window in the 3D space to match the exemplar shape and each window. Finally, we use depth map segmentation to further improve the performance.

The success of our design is based on several **key insights**: To handle *texture* and *illumination* variance, we use depth maps instead of RGB images. To handle *shape* variance, we use a data-driven approach to leverage a collection of CG models that cover the space of shape variance in real world. We also add a small variance on the size of CG model to improve the robustness. Furthermore, in contrast to direct mesh alignment [13], learning the SVM using both positive and negative data also increases the generality of the detector. To handle *viewpoint* variance, we can densely render different viewpoints of an object to cover all typical viewing angles. To handle *depth-sensor error and noise*, we use CG models to obtain perfect rendering and use it as positive training data (experiments in Table. 2 shows that it helps a lot). To bridge the *domain gap* between CG training data and RGB-D testing data, we render the depth map (but not color) as if the CG model is viewed from a typical RGB-D sensor. To handle *clutter* (e.g. a chair with its seat under a table), we use 3D sliding window with a mask to indicate which parts should be considered during classification. To handle *inter-object occlusion*, we make use of the depth map to reason about the source of occlusion and regard the occluded area as missing data. To make use of *self-occlusion*, we render the CG model and compute the Truncated Signed Distance Function (TSDF) [14] as a feature.

Since our *generic* object detector does not reply on any assumption about the background or requires a dominant supporting plane [15, 16], and its *single-view* nature doesn't require a (semi-)complete scan of an object [17], it can be used as a basic building block for general scene understanding tasks. To improve the testing *speed* during 3D convolution, we generalize integral image [18] to 3D to skip empty windows.

In the following section, we will describe our algorithm in greater details. In Section 3, we will talk about the evaluation metric and experiments to evaluate the algorithm. In Section 4, we will discuss the relation of our proposed method with existing ones.

Fig. 2. Training procedure: We use a collection of CG models to train a 3D detector. For each CG model, we render it from hundreds of view angles to generate a pool of positive training data. For each rendering, we train an Exemplar-SVM model. And we ensemble all SVMs from renderings of CG chair models to build a 3D chair detector.

2   The Sliding Shapes Detector

During training (Sec. 2.1), we learn an ensemble of linear Exemplar-SVM classifiers, each of which is trained with a rendered depth map from CG model as the single positive and many negatives from labeled depth maps. During testing (Sec. 2.2), we take a depth image with the gravity direction as input. The learned SVMs are used to classify a sliding window in 3D and output 3D bounding boxes with detection scores. We design four types of 3D features (Sec. 2.3) and propose several methods to handle clutter, occlusion and missing depth (Sec. 2.4).

2.1   Training

Fig. 2 shows the the training process of our Sliding Shapes detector, where we treat each viewpoint rendering as an exemplar and train a separate classifier for it.

Rendering Depth Maps. For each object category, a set of CG models with typical shapes is collected from the Internet to cover the intra-category shape variance. Because most objects in real environment have some support surfaces (e.g. chairs are typically on the floor), we also synthesize a support surface when rendering the graphic model to emulate such condition. For each CG model, we render it from different view angles and locations in the 3D space. Specifically, we render the CG models varying the following parameters: orientation, scale, 3D location, and camera tilt angle. Some assumptions are made based on dataset statistics and observation to reduce the sample space. We assume most objects are aligned on gravity direction so there is only rotation around gravity axis. We also obtained the statistics of object sizes and 3D locations of each category from the training set, and sample viewpoint parameters based on this prior. Apart from sampling the above parameters, we also slightly scaling the meshes to improve the robustness. Finally, we render the depth map as if the CG model is viewed from a typical RGB-D sensor, by using the same camera intrinsic parameters, and resolution to virtual camera.

Training Exemplar-SVMs. As shown in shown in Fig. 1, after converting each depth rendering of CG model to a 3D point cloud, we extract a feature vector and use it as positive to train a linear Exemplar-SVM [3]. The initial negatives are randomly picked point cloud from annotated Kinect images (RMRC dataset [10, 19]) that do not overlap with ground truth positives. We perform hard negative mining by searching hard negatives over the entire training set.

No Calibration. Although we train each Exemplar-SVM separately, we do not calibrate our detectors as [3], mainly because of the limited size of RMRC dataset [10, 19]. Calibration requires the training (or validation) set to have a similar positive distribution as the testing set. Especially, most of the exemplar should fire at least once in order to adjust their scores accordingly. In our case, we have an Exemplar-SVM for each viewpoint in each CG model. The total number of exemplar models largely exceeds the total number of positive object instances in RMRC dataset, and some detectors will never fire in the training set, which makes calibration not possible.

2.2 Testing

During testing, we exhaustively classify each possible bounding box in the 3D space using all Exemplar-SVMs, each of which evaluates whether the corresponding shape exists inside the bounding box, and output a detection score. Then we perform non-maximum suppression on all detection boxes in 3D.

3D Local Search. Given an Exemplar-SVM trained on a CG model rendered at a specific 3D location relative to the virtual camera, we perform 3D convolution only at the nearby region. Such restriction on search space improves the speed as well as detection accuracy, because objects far away from the training location are of different point density, and presents different self-occlusion condition due to their difference in view angles. The SVM and 3D feature may not be robust enough to model this difference. Therefore, we take a more conservative search with restriction to only nearby locations.

Jumping Window. In 2D sliding window scheme, it is not a trivial task to efficiently filter out unnecessary window positions (e.g. [5]). However in 3D, there is a lot of empty space which can be safely skipped. To identify the empty boxes and skip them during convolution, a 3D integral image is computed for each testing image, where each cell stores the sum of point count of all cells that on the front-left-up side of the cell. During convolution, given a model's window size and its current cell location, the total number of points inside this window can be quickly calculated from the 3D integral image in constant time. If the total number of points inside this window is smaller than 50, our detector skips this window without performing the dot product.

Bounding Box Adjustment. The initial resulting bounding boxes form convolution are aligned with the defined feature axes, which is not optimal for most objects. Therefore, after we obtain the axis-aligned bounding box, we replace it with a tighter bounding boxes aligned with objects' principle axes, which are imported from the CG models.

2.3 View-Dependent 3D Features

To support sliding a window in 3D, the 3D space is divided into cubic cells of size 0.1 meter, and several features are extracted from each cell. To capture properties of 3D objects such as their geometrical shape, orientation and distance to camera, we design the following features and combine all of them, forming a discriminative descriptor.

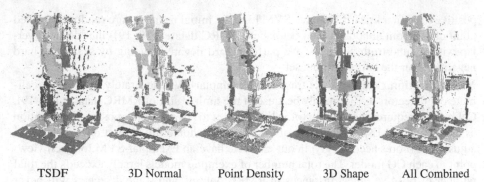

TSDF   3D Normal   Point Density   3D Shape   All Combined

Fig. 3. Visualization of "inverse" features using nearest neighbor (refer to the footnote). We reduce the feature dimension into three and map them into RGB color space. Therefore, similar colors between two cells indicate that they are similar in the high-dimensional feature space.

Point Density Feature. To describe point density distribution inside a cell, we divide each cell into $6 \times 6 \times 6$ voxels, and build a histogram of the number of points in each voxel. A 3D Gaussian kernel is used to weight each point, canceling the bias of the voxel discretization. After obtaining the histogram inside the cell, which is a 216 dimensional vector, we randomly pick 1000 pairs of entries and compute the difference within each pair (inspired by the stick feature in [7]). The stick feature is then concatenated with the original count histogram. Such descriptor captures both the first order (point count) and second order (count difference) statistics of the point cloud.

3D Shape Feature. Apart from point distribution across voxels, their distribution within voxels are also important clue, which we use local 3D shape feature to encode. We divide each cell into $3 \times 3 \times 3$ voxels, and represent the internal point cloud distribution of a voxel by their scatter-ness (λ_1), linear-ness ($\lambda_1 - \lambda_2$) and surface-ness ($\lambda_2 - \lambda_3$), obtained from the principal components of the point cloud (assume the eigenvalues of the covariance matrix of the points are $\lambda_1 > \lambda_2 > \lambda_3$).

3D Normal Feature. Surface normal is critical to describe the orientation of an object. To compute 3D normals, we pick 25 nearest neighbor for each point, and estimate the surface normal at that point as the direction of the first principal component. We divided the orientation half-sphere into 24 bins uniformly, and for each cell, we build a histogram of the normal orientation across these bins as normal feature.

TSDF Feature. Self-occlusion is a useful cue for view-based shape matching. We adopt Truncated Signed Distance Function (TSDF) [14] as one of the features. Different from other features that only describe local information within a single cell, TSDF feature is a volumetric measure of the global shape. For each cell divided into $6 \times 6 \times 6$ voxels, TSDF value of each voxel is defined as the signed distance between the voxel center and the nearest object point on the line of sight from the camera. The distance is clipped to be between -1 and 1 and the sign here indicates whether cell in front of or behind the surface. After computing the TSDF value for each voxel, we use the same random-stick as in point density feature to calculate difference within pairs and concatenate it with the original TSDF vector.

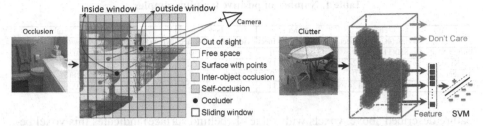

(a) Occlusion reasoning using the occluder's location.   (b) Occupation mask to slide a shape.

Fig. 4. Beyond sliding windows. Depth and 3D mesh are used to handle occlusion and clutter.

Feature Coding and Combining. We perform dictionary coding on top each of them [20]. Specifically, we use k-means to obtain 50 cluster centers for each type of the features as our codebook. Every feature vector $\mathbf{x}$ is then coded as a 50-dimensional vector $\mathbf{f}$ containing its distance to each of the 50 centers: $\mathbf{f}(i) = \exp(-(\|\mathbf{x} - \mathbf{c}_i\|^2))/\sigma_i^2$, where σ_i^2 is the standard deviation of i-th cluster. After feature coding we concatenate all coded feature vectors to from the final combined feature vector.

Feature Visualization. In order to visualize our features, we use a nearest neighbor approach similar as [21] to "inverse" our feature[1]. Fig. 3 shows an example to illustrate what property each type of feature captures. The inverse TSDF feature has very distinctive color for cells in front of and behind surfaces, indicating its ability to describe the relation between cells and surfaces. The 3D normal feature captures surface orientation but not the shape inside the cell. The point destiny feature doesn't capture the right shape on the leg of the chair, although the point cloud used for feature reconstruction has similar point density with the original cell. For the shape feature, because the covariance matrix of point coordinates cannot be calculate for cells has points smaller than 3, therefore it is unable to distinguish empty cell with cells have 1 to 3 points. The combined feature achieves the best reconstruction result, suggesting that it has a better ability to describes the model than each single feature alone.

2.4   Beyond Sliding Window

Different from standard sliding window approach, we improve robustness of our model by adjusting features according to occlusion, missing value and clutter.

Occlusion Modeling. A difficult problem in 2D object detection is occlusion. Occluders usually lower the detection scores considerably, since they replace part of the target objects with themselves in the 2D image, which usually violates learned rules describing the target objects. Ideally, one would exclude the occluded region and mark them as "don't care", but robustly recognizing such region is just as challenging. However, because we have depth as input, such occlusion can be easily identified. In the TSDF

---

[1] Firstly, a large pool of feature vector (for one single cell) and their corresponding point cloud are collected. Then given a new feature vector, we reconstruct the point cloud by searching for its nearest neighbor among all collected feature vectors, and replace the original cell with point cloud from the nearest neighbor found.

Table 1. Number of positive training samples

	chair		toilet		bed		sofa		table	
	#view(#CG)	#Kinect	# view(#CG)	#Kinect	#view(#CG)	#Kinect	#view(#CG)	#Kinect	#view(#CG)	#Kinect
Sliding Shapes	880(11)	0	473(2)	0	95(11)	0	547(5)	0	202(5)	0
Kinect	0(0)	124	0(0)	11	0(0)	52	0(0)	92	0(0)	70
Kinect align	97(9)	0	5(1)	0	26(9)	0	29(6)	0	18(5)	0
kinect+CG	880(11)	124	473(2)	11	95(11)	52	547(5)	92	202(5)	70

feature described above, voxels with value -1 (behind surface) indicates this voxel being occluded. We want to exclude only the real inter-object occlusion region and use the self-occlusion ones as an useful cue. We identify the occlusion type by checking depth value of the occlusion source, and compare it with the depth of current sliding window (Fig. 4(a)). If the occlusion source is outside the sliding window, it is an inter-object occlusion. For voxels under inter-object occlusion, we set their feature vectors (after feature coding) to zeros, so that they make no contribution to the final detection score in the linear SVM. After setting their feature to zeros, we also append an extra bit flagging to the end of the feature vector, giving SVM a way to weight the special condition. To avoid false positives on those heavily occluded location, we count the total number of occluded cells, and if it is above threshold, we will keep the feature unchanged, which naturally penalizes the detection scores.

Missing Depth and Boundary. Similarly, objects with vast missing depth or partially outside the field of view are likely to get missed if not handled explicitly, since some part of the objects would have the same feature as empty cells and thus considerably lower the detection score. Therefore, we identify those cells and set their features to zeros. Similar as occlusion, for the cells with missing depth or out of sight, we also append an extra bit flagging to the end of the feature vector.

Clutter. In general, a 3D bounding box is not a tight representation for objects, leaving a large portion of empty space that produces redundant and sometimes misleading feature. Especially, our training positives are clean CG models which implicitly assume empty cell inside the bounding box apart from the object of interest. But during testing, the object are often surrounded by clutter. Therefore, we construct an occupation mask for each training CG model to select the cells inside or close to its mesh surface (Fig. 4(b)), and only use the features inside the occupation mask to train classifiers.

Post-processing Using Segmentation. We observe that the top false positives of our algorithm detect an object as a part of a big object (e.g. the first row of Fig. 10), because of the local nature of sliding windows. To prune this kind of false positives, we use plane fitting on 3D point cloud to obtain a segmentation. For each detection result B, we pick the largest segment S_i inside its bounding box and compute the overlap ratio $R = \frac{\text{area}(S_i \cap B)}{\text{area}(S_i)}$. If R is larger than a certain threshold (learned from training set), it means that the current hypothesis is a part of a larger object, and we reduce its score by 1. This post-processing step is more helpful for toilet and sofa, while less helpful to bed and table (see Table 2).

3   Evaluation

The 3D CG models that we used for training are collected from Trimble 3D Warehouse. The total number of CG models and the rendering view point are shown in Table 1.

Fig. 5. Detection results. Here we show multiple detections in one image.

We evaluate our Sliding Shapes detector on RMRC dataset (a subset of NYU Depth v2 [10] with 3D box annotation derived from [19]). We choose five common indoor objects: chair, toilet, bed, sofa, and table, and manually go through the annotation to make sure that they are correctly labelled. We split RMRC dataset into 500 depth images for training and 574 depth images for testing. We split the dataset in a way that the images from same video are grouped together and appear only in training or testing set, and try to balance the instance number in training and testing set for each category.

Our algorithm takes a depth image from RGB-D sensor with the gravity direction as input. Aligning the point cloud and CG model with the gravity direction enables the axis-aligned sliding window for detection. Note that the gravity direction can be obtained via several ways. For example, if a RGB-D camera is mounted on a robot, we know the robot's configuration and its camera tilt angle. For the cameras on the mobile devices, we can use the accelerometer to obtain the gravity direction and camera's relative tilt angle. For this paper, the gravity direction for the RMRC dataset is provided as ground truth. For datasets without ground truth gravity direction, it is also easy to compute by fitting planes to the floor and walls [22].

Without local search and jumping window, our time complexity is exactly the same with Exemplar-SVMs [3]. On average, there are 25,058 3D detection windows per image. Local search reduces it to 19%. Jumping window reduces it to 44%. Using both, it reduces to 8%. For testing, it takes about 2 second per detector to test on a depth image in Matlab. The computation is naturally parallelizable except the non-maximal suppression at the end of detection. For training, it takes 4 to 8 hours to train a single detector with single thread in Matlab, which is also naturally parallelizable.

3.1 Evaluation Metric

We adopt the standard 2D object detection evaluation scheme as in PASCAL VOC [23], with the following modifications. PASCAL VOC evaluation criteria uses 2D bounding box overlapping ratio (intersection over union), assuming they are aligned with images axis. For 3D, we calculate the 3D bounding box overlapping ratio, we assume the boxes

Table 2. Comparision. The numbers are the average precisions for various algorithms, categories and evaluation metrics. 3D and 2D are evaluation using normal ground truth boxes; 2D+ and 3D+ are evaluation using all ground truth boxes including difficult cases. The best preforming 2D and 3D algorithms are in **bold**. * indicates the result is evaluated using different training-testing splits.

		chair				toilet				bed				sofa				table			
		3D+	3D	2D+	2D	3D+	3D	2D+	2D	3D+	3D	2D+	2D	3D+	3D	2D+	2D	3D+	3D	2D+	2D
RGB-D or 3D	Sliding Shapes	**0.316**	**0.765**	**0.331**	**0.749**	**0.643**	**0.736**	**0.644**	**0.736**	**0.381**	**0.741**	**0.412**	**0.751**	**0.315**	**0.403**	0.339	**0.418**	**0.289**	**0.474**	**0.314**	**0.478**
	without seg	0.312	0.752	0.326	0.741	0.588	0.681	0.588	0.681	0.381	0.740	0.411	0.750	0.303	0.384	0.324	0.390	0.289	0.474	0.313	0.478
	Kinect	0.09	0.18	0.144	0.211	0.180	0.268	0.183	0.269	0.147	0.243	0.187	0.254	0.050	0.040	0.074	0.049	0.012	0.008	0.035	0.015
	Kinect align	0.251	0.607	0.251	0.566	0.440	0.528	0.444	0.531	0.369	0.693	0.403	0.696	0.20	0.235	0.190	0.202	0.265	0.405	0.278	0.372
	Kinect+CG	0.129	0.286	0.185	0.327	0.449	0.538	0.456	0.544	0.164	0.280	0.208	0.296	0.052	0.043	0.075	0.053	0.012	0.008	0.035	0.015
	[24]	-	-	0.147*	-	-	-	-	-	-	-	0.32*	-	-	-	0.155*	-	-	-	-	-
	gDPM [25]	-	-	0.133*	-	-	-	-	-	-	-	0.33*	-	-	-	0.110*	-	-	-	0.045*	-
RGB	DPM-VOC[2]	-	-	0.176	**0.446**	-	-	-	-	-	-	-	-	-	-	0.163	**0.213**	-	-	0.127	0.175
	DPM-SUN[2]	-	-	0.131	0.345	-	-	0.309	**0.532**	-	-	0.279	**0.503**	-	-	0.109	0.132	-	-	0.120	0.157
	DPM-RMRC[2]	-	-	0.115	0.269	-	-	**0.344**	0.419	-	-	**0.318**	0.427	-	-	0.099	0.137	-	-	0.045	0.048
	RCNN-VOC[6]	-	-	**0.182**	0.342	-	-	-	-	-	-	-	-	-	-	**0.200**	0.203	-	-	**0.213**	**0.237**

are aligned with gravity direction, but make no assumption on the other two axes. To compare with 2D detection, the evaluation on 2D is done by projecting both ground truth and detection boxes into 2D and compute their 2D overlapping ratio. For 2D, a predicted box is considered to be correct if the overlapping ratio is more than 0.5. To let the same result produce similar precision-recall curve for 2D and 3D evaluation empirically, we set the threshold to be 0.25 for 3D. Similar as PASCAL VOC, we also add a difficult flag to indicate whether the ground truth is difficult to detect. The difficult cases include heavy occlusion, missing depth and out of sight. We evaluate on normal ground truth boxes (denoted as 3D and 2D), as well as on all ground truth boxes including difficult cases (denoted as 3D+ and 2D+) respectively.

3.2   Experiments

Fig. 5 shows example results of our Sliding Shapes detector, and Fig. 10 and 11 show some failure cases. Our detector not only recognizes the object, but also identifies its orientation and type of 3D style, which is imported from the corresponding model proposing the detection. Fig. 8 demonstrates the power of our design. Row 1 and 2 are cases where our detector successfully handles occlusion. Row 3 shows that the occupation masks can filter out the clutter, where a dining table is partially inside the proposed box, yet it does not affect the chair detector since it is not in the occupation mask. Row 4 shows the case with severe missing depth. Even with the whole back of the chair missing, our detector is able to detect it, although the corresponding CG model is not identical to the object.

Comparison. We compare our Sliding Shapes detector quantitatively with 2D and 3D detector. In the 2D case, we compare with standard DPM [2] and the state-of-the-art deep learning algorithm RCNN [6]. We show the result of DPM trained on PASCAL VOC 2010[23], SUN2012[26], and RMRC dataset. In RGBD/3D case we compare with [24] which use 2D HOG on RGBD image with 2D sliding window, and gDPM [25] which trains a geometry driven deformable part model. Table 2 shows the average precision. Our approach achieves about ×1.7 improvement on average precision compared to the best of all RGB algorithms, and also outperforms other RGB-D or 3D detectors.

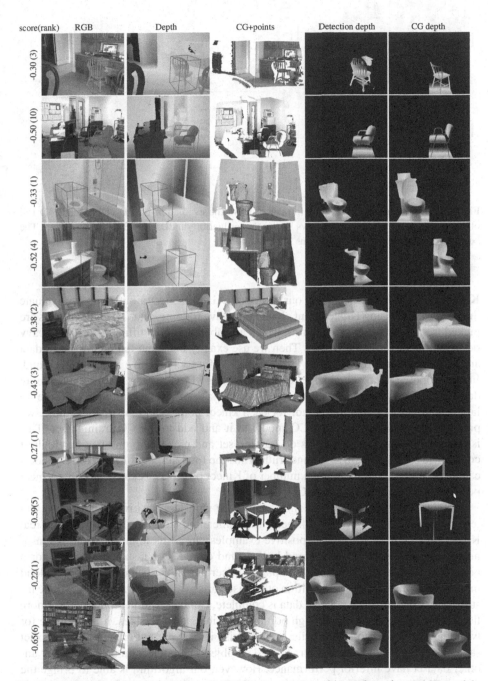

Fig. 6. True positives. Besides labels, our detector also predicts object orientation and 3D model.

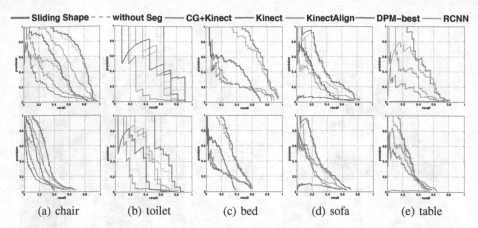

Fig. 7. Precision-recall curve. The top rows shows the evaluation on 2D (DPM) and 3D (all others) ground truth, The bottom rows shows the evaluation on 2D+ and 3D+ ground truth. The best preforming 2D and 3D algorithms are in bold.

Kinect vs. CG Model. To justify our choice of CG models as training data, we evaluate the performance using Kinect point cloud as positive training data. The point clouds are picked from training set ground truth which are labeled as non difficult (to avoid heavy occlusion or vast missing depth). Then we use exactly the same feature, negative data and training procedure to train an Exemplar-SVM for each positive Kinect point cloud. In our proposed approach, a large number of rendered CG models are used as training data. To achieve a fair comparison, we limit the size of the CG training set to be no larger than the Kinect point cloud: for each kinect point cloud positive example, we pick the most similar rendered CG model to it and add to the CG training set. This is done by testing all CG models on training set and picked top one that has highest confidence for each positive ground truth. Thus the total number of picked CG models can only be smaller than the total number of Kinect positives, because multiple Kinect positives may correspond to one CG model.

In Table 2 [Kinect align], we shows that even with less positive training data, detectors trained on CG models still peform siginficanly better. We believe that the real Kinect depth data is inferior as positive examples due to its high variation in sensor noise, missing depth, occlusion and background clutter. For instance, in order for a point cloud to match well to an exemplar with certain parts occluded, the point cloud must have similar occlusion condition otherwise parts available for matching will be insufficient, whereas if the positive data is complete, candidate point clouds can be more flexible as long as there are enough portion of visible parts. Besides, it is very rare for two object instances to have similar sensor noise if they are not captured under exact same condition. Usually, classifiers trained on objects isolated from background or another dataset have inferior performance. However, our algorithm is able to bridge the domain gap between CG training data and RGB-D testing data, and achieve a significant improvement. We also tested the combination using both CG models and Kinetic point clouds as positive to train the detector. Table 2 [Kinect+CG] shows that it is does

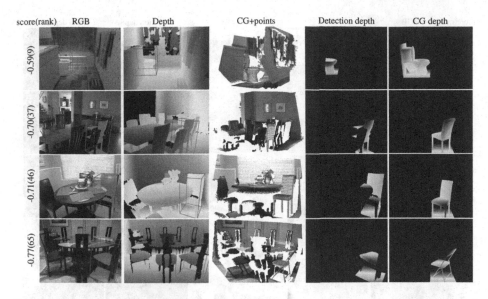

Fig. 8. Challenging cases. The difficulties are mainly come from occlusion, missing value and clutter. Green in RGB image highlights the points in box. In CG + points the point cloud in detection box is replaced by the exemplar CG model. Black in depth indicates missing value.

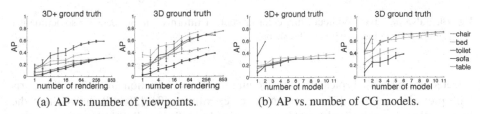

(a) AP vs. number of viewpoints.   (b) AP vs. number of CG models.

Fig. 9. Average Precision (AP) vs. number of positive data

not yield a better performance than just using CG models alone, which suggests that the information is redudant and the point cloud quality of Kinect model are bad.

Number of Exemplars. We experiment on how the size of positive training data (number of GC models and number of viewpoint rendering) affect the performance. Given number of training view points / model, we randomly pick 5 possible cases to evaluate the average precision. Fig. 9 shows how the average precision changes, when the number of rendering viewpoints and number of CG models changes.

4   Related Works and Discussions

Our work has been inspired by research in object recognition of images, range scans, depth maps, RGB-D and CAD models, but we only refer to the most relevant ones here.

Image-Based Detection: Popular detectors typically train a classifier on image area within a window, and test using the classifier via a sliding window [2, 3, 27] or on

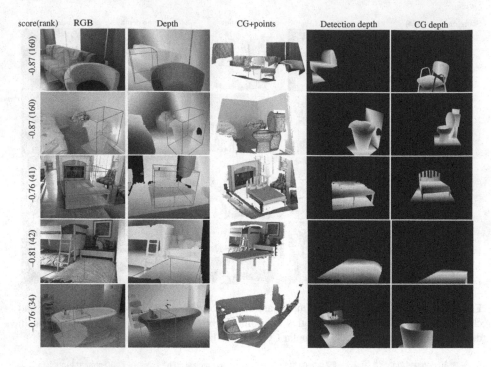

Fig. 10. False positives. Without using color or context information, our detector sometime get confused between objects with similar shape.

selected areas [4–6]. Typical ways to account for object variation are deformable parts with pictorial structure [2] and ensemble of exemplars [3]. [28–30] showed that the latter option is much simpler and has the generalizability to all object categories. Our model can be understood as a novel way to extend this framework to 3D. There are also works on using CAD models for training [31–36], but they are not for depth images.

Semantic Segmentation: A popular way of formulating object recognition in 3D is to predict the semantic label for each region of a depth map or 3D mesh [37, 38, 11, 10, 39–44]. Because of the bottom-up nature, these algorithms can only see a part of object but not the whole object. One advantage of a sliding window based approach is to enable the classifier to use the information for the whole object to make a decision.

Voting: There are many works focus on how to integrate local information via voting [20, 45–49], such as Hough voting or Implicit Shape Model. This type of models can consider multiple local regions at the same time for object recognition, but it is difficult to formulate them in a data-driven machine-learning framework to weight the relative importance and correlation among objects parts (especially negative correlation).

Keypoint Matching: Just as SIFT keypoints for image matching [50], a popular type of algorithms [51–60] is to detect keypoints on a 3D point cloud or a mesh, generate descriptors for the keypoints (e.g. spin image and 3D shape context), and use the matching to align with models in the training data. Same as voting-based approach, the

Fig. 11. Misses. Note that in many cases there are considerable missing value in depth data, object out of sight, or ground truth being poorly localized. We also miss object instances very different from training data, such as folded chairs.

non-learning nature of this type of algorithms make it very difficult to discriminatively learn from a data to weight the importance of different keypoints.

Model Fitting: Similar to keypoint matching, model fitting algorithms align an input with the training models [61], but without using descriptors. There are robust algorithms that fit 3D shapes to the scene [62–64]. But again, because of the non-data-driven nature, these approachs have the same problem that it cannot learn from data.

3D Classification: Classification-based approaches [65–68, 51, 69–79] typically consider the whole object at the same time by extracting a holistic feature for the whole object and classifying the feature vector via a classifier. But the typical setting is to have the segmented object as the input (or even a solo 3D model with complete mesh), and classify an object into one of the fixed categories, which is a much easier task than object detection that needs to localize the object and tell a non-object window apart.

2.5D Detector: There are several seminal works that try to extend standard 2D image-based object detector to use depth maps [24, 80, 81, 25, 82]. The main difference is that our algorithm operates fully in 3D, using 3D sliding windows and 3D features, which can handle occlusion and other problems naturally.

RGB-D Scene Understanding: Besides the RGB-D segmentation and detection works mentioned above, [83, 19, 84] proposed to estimate the room layout, support surfaces, and scene understanding for the whole room including objects. Our 3D detector can be used as a basic building block of object detection for all these higher level tasks.

5   Conclusion

We propose an algorithm for generic 3D object detection for RGB-D images. Our detector can exploit the depth information in a data-driven fashion to overcome the major limitations in object detection, namely the variations of texture, illumination, shape, viewpoint, self occlusion, clutter, occlusion and sensor noises. One of the major limitation now is the lack of a good RGB-D testing set for evaluation that contains more images, more instances, and more reliable annotation. Currently, we are capturing a large-scale RGB-D dataset using the new Microsoft Kinect V2 time-of-flight sensor. As future work, we plan to investigate how to combine with RGB-based detection, and learn the 3D features automatically from data [85], as well as exploring context information in 3D [86].

References

1. Nevatia, R., Binford, T.O.: Description and recognition of curved objects. Artificial Intelligence (1977)
2. Felzenszwalb, P.F., Girshick, R.B., McAllester, D., Ramanan, D.: Object detection with discriminatively trained part based models. PAMI (2010)
3. Malisiewicz, T., Gupta, A., Efros, A.A.: Ensemble of exemplar-svms for object detection and beyond. In: ICCV (2011)
4. Wang, X., Yang, M., Zhu, S., Lin, Y.: Regionlets for generic object detection. In: ICCV (2013)
5. Uijlings, J.R.R., van de Sande, K.E.A., Gevers, T., Smeulders, A.W.M.: Selective search for object recognition (2013)
6. Girshick, R., Donahue, J., Darrell, T., Malik, J.: Rich feature hierarchies for accurate object detection and semantic segmentation. In: CVPR (2014)
7. Shotton, J., Girshick, R., Fitzgibbon, A., Sharp, T., Cook, M., Finocchio, M., Moore, R., Kohli, P., Criminisi, A., Kipman, A., et al.: Efficient human pose estimation from single depth images. PAMI (2013)
8. Shotton, J., Sharp, T., Kipman, A., Fitzgibbon, A., Finocchio, M., Blake, A., Cook, M., Moore, R.: Real-time human pose recognition in parts from single depth images. Communications of the ACM (2013)
9. Barron, J.T., Malik, J.: Intrinsic scene properties from a single rgb-d image. In: CVPR (2013)
10. Silberman, N., Hoiem, D., Kohli, P., Fergus, R.: Indoor Segmentation and Support Inference from RGBD Images. In: Fitzgibbon, A., Lazebnik, S., Perona, P., Sato, Y., Schmid, C. (eds.) ECCV 2012, Part V. LNCS, vol. 7576, pp. 746–760. Springer, Heidelberg (2012)
11. Gupta, S., Arbelaez, P., Malik, J.: Perceptual organization and recognition of indoor scenes from RGB-D images. In: CVPR (2013)
12. Izadi, S., Kim, D., Hilliges, O., Molyneaux, D., Newcombe, R., Kohli, P., Shotton, J., Hodges, S., Freeman, D., Davison, A., Fitzgibbon, A.: Kinectfusion: Real-time 3D reconstruction and interaction using a moving depth camera. In: UIST (2011)
13. Johnson, A.E., Hebert, M.: Using spin images for efficient object recognition in cluttered 3d scenes. PAMI (1999)
14. Newcombe, R.A., Davison, A.J., Izadi, S., Kohli, P., Hilliges, O., Shotton, J., Molyneaux, D., Hodges, S., Kim, D., Fitzgibbon, A.: Kinectfusion: Real-time dense surface mapping and tracking. In: ISMAR (2011)
15. Tang, J., Miller, S., Singh, A., Abbeel, P.: A textured object recognition pipeline for color and depth image data. In: ICRA (2012)
16. Kim, Y.M., Mitra, N.J., Yan, D.M., Guibas, L.: Acquiring 3D indoor environments with variability and repetition. TOG (2012)
17. Nan, L., Xie, K., Sharf, A.: A search-classify approach for cluttered indoor scene understanding. TOG (2012)
18. Crow, F.C.: Summed-area tables for texture mapping. TOG (1984)
19. Guo, R., Hoiem, D.: Support surface prediction in indoor scenes. In: ICCV (2013)
20. Knopp, J., Prasad, M., Willems, G., Timofte, R., Van Gool, L.: Hough transform and 3D SURF for robust three dimensional classification. In: Daniilidis, K., Maragos, P., Paragios, N. (eds.) ECCV 2010, Part VI. LNCS, vol. 6316, pp. 589–602. Springer, Heidelberg (2010)
21. Vondrick, C., Khosla, A., Malisiewicz, T., Torralba, A.: HOGgles: Visualizing Object Detection Features. In: ICCV (2013)
22. Xiao, J., Owens, A., Torralba, A.: SUN3D: A database of big spaces reconstructed using sfm and object labels. In: ICCV (2013)

23. Everingham, M., Van Gool, L., Williams, C.K.I., Winn, J., Zisserman, A.: The pascal visual object classes (voc) challenge (2010)
24. Ye, E.S.: Object detection in rgb-d indoor scenes. Master's thesis, UC Berkeley (2013)
25. Shrivastava, A., Gupta, A.: Building part-based object detectors via 3D geometry. In: ICCV (2013)
26. Xiao, J., Hays, J., Ehinger, K.A., Oliva, A., Torralba, A.: SUN database: Large-scale scene recognition from abbey to zoo. In: CVPR (2010)
27. Dalal, N., Triggs, B.: Histograms of oriented gradients for human detection. In: CVPR (2005)
28. Hoiem, D., Chodpathumwan, Y., Dai, Q.: Diagnosing error in object detectors. In: Fitzgibbon, A., Lazebnik, S., Perona, P., Sato, Y., Schmid, C. (eds.) ECCV 2012, Part III. LNCS, vol. 7574, pp. 340–353. Springer, Heidelberg (2012)
29. Divvala, S.K., Efros, A.A., Hebert, M.: How important are "Deformable parts" in the deformable parts model? In: Fusiello, A., Murino, V., Cucchiara, R. (eds.) ECCV 2012 Ws/Demos, Part III. LNCS, vol. 7585, pp. 31–40. Springer, Heidelberg (2012)
30. Zhu, X., Vondrick, C., Ramanan, D., Fowlkes, C.: Do we need more training data or better models for object detection? In: BMVC (2012)
31. Zia, M.Z., Stark, M., Schiele, B., Schindler, K.: Detailed 3D representations for object recognition and modeling. PAMI (2013)
32. Lim, J.J., Pirsiavash, H., Torralba, A.: Parsing ikea objects: Fine pose estimation. In: ICCV (2013)
33. Satkin, S., Hebert, M.: 3dnn: Viewpoint invariant 3D geometry matching for scene understanding. In: ICCV (2013)
34. Krause, J., Stark, M., Deng, J., Fei-Fei, L.: 3D object representations for fine-grained categorization. In: 3dRR 2013 (2013)
35. Liebelt, J., Schmid, C.: Multi-view object class detection with a 3D geometric model. In: CVPR (2010)
36. Aubry, M., Maturana, D., Efros, A.A., Russell, B.C., Sivic, J.: Seeing 3D chairs: exemplar part-based 2D-3D alignment using a large dataset of cad models. In: CVPR (2014)
37. Ren, X., Bo, L., Fox, D.: Rgb-(d) scene labeling: Features and algorithms. In: CVPR (2012)
38. Koppula, H.S., Anand, A., Joachims, T., Saxena, A.: Semantic labeling of 3d point clouds for indoor scenes. In: NIPS (2011)
39. Zheng, B., Zhao, Y., Yu, J.C., Ikeuchi, K., Zhu, S.C.: Beyond point clouds: Scene understanding by reasoning geometry and physics. In: CVPR (2013)
40. Kim, B., Kohli, P., Savarese, S.: 3D scene understanding by Voxel-CRF. In: ICCV (2013)
41. Hernández-López, J.J., Quintanilla-Olvera, A.L., López-Ramírez, J.L., Rangel-Butanda, F.J., Ibarra-Manzano, M.A., Almanza-Ojeda, D.L.: Detecting objects using color and depth segmentation with kinect sensor. Procedia Technology (2012)
42. Anguelov, D., Taskarf, B., Chatalbashev, V., Koller, D., Gupta, D., Heitz, G., Ng, A.: Discriminative learning of markov random fields for segmentation of 3D scan data. In: CVPR (2005)
43. Knopp, J., Prasad, M., Gool, L.V.: Scene cut: Class-specific object detection and segmentation in 3D scenes. In: 3DIMPVT (2011)
44. Lin, H., Gao, J., Zhou, Y., Lu, G., Ye, M., Zhang, C., Liu, L., Yang, R.: Semantic decomposition and reconstruction of residential scenes from lidar data. TOG (2013)
45. Salas-Moreno, R.F., Newcombe, R.A., Strasdat, H., Kelly, P.H., Davison, A.J.: Slam++: Simultaneous localisation and mapping at the level of objects. In: CVPR (2013)
46. Drost, B., Ulrich, M., Navab, N., Ilic, S.: Model globally, match locally: Efficient and robust 3D object recognition. In: CVPR (2010)
47. Park, I.K., Germann, M., Breitenstein, M.D., Pfister, H.: Fast and automatic object pose estimation for range images on the gpu. Machine Vision and Applications (2010)

48. Woodford, O.J., Pham, M.T., Maki, A., Perbet, F., Stenger, B.: Demisting the hough transform for 3D shape recognition and registration (2014)
49. Velizhev, A., Shapovalov, R., Schindler, K.: Implicit shape models for object detection in 3D point clouds. In: International Society of Photogrammetry and Remote Sensing Congress (2012)
50. Zhang, J., Marszałek, M., Lazebnik, S., Schmid, C.: Local features and kernels for classification of texture and object categories: A comprehensive study (2007)
51. Blum, M., Springenberg, J.T., Wulfing, J., Riedmiller, M.: A learned feature descriptor for object recognition in rgb-d data. In: ICRA (2012)
52. Johnson, A.: Spin-Images: A Representation for 3-D Surface Matching. PhD thesis, Robotics Institute, Carnegie Mellon University (1997)
53. Tombari, F., Salti, S., Di Stefano, L.: Unique signatures of histograms for local surface description. In: Daniilidis, K., Maragos, P., Paragios, N. (eds.) ECCV 2010, Part III. LNCS, vol. 6313, pp. 356–369. Springer, Heidelberg (2010)
54. Zaharescu, A., Boyer, E., Varanasi, K., Horaud, R.: Surface feature detection and description with applications to mesh matching. In: CVPR (2009)
55. Frome, A., Huber, D., Kolluri, R., Bülow, T., Malik, J.: Recognizing objects in range data using regional point descriptors. In: Pajdla, T., Matas, J(G.) (eds.) ECCV 2004. LNCS, vol. 3023, pp. 224–237. Springer, Heidelberg (2004)
56. Alexandre, L.A.: 3D descriptors for object and category recognition: a comparative evaluation. In: Workshop on Color-Depth Camera Fusion in Robotics at the IROS (2012)
57. Fouhey, D.F., Collet, A., Hebert, M., Srinivasa, S.: Object recognition robust to imperfect depth data. In: Fusiello, A., Murino, V., Cucchiara, R. (eds.) ECCV 2012 Ws/Demos, Part II. LNCS, vol. 7584, pp. 83–92. Springer, Heidelberg (2012)
58. Glover, J., Popovic, S.: Bingham procrustean alignment for object detection in clutter (2013)
59. Körtgen, M., Park, G.J., Novotni, M., Klein, R.: 3D shape matching with 3D shape contexts. In: The 7th Central European Seminar on Computer Graphics (2003)
60. Chen, H., Bhanu, B.: 3D free-form object recognition in range images using local surface patches. Pattern Recognition Letters (2007)
61. Besl, P.J., Mckay, H.D.: A method for registration of 3-D shapes. PAMI (1992)
62. Jiang, H., Xiao, J.: A linear approach to matching cuboids in RGBD images. In: CVPR (2013)
63. Jia, Z., Gallagher, A., Saxena, A., Chen, T.: 3D-based reasoning with blocks, support, and stability. In: CVPR (2013)
64. Wu, K., Levine, M.D.: Recovering parametric geons from multiview range data. In: CVPR (1994)
65. Bo, L., Lai, K., Ren, X., Fox, D.: Object recognition with hierarchical kernel descriptors. In: CVPR (2011)
66. Bo, L., Ren, X., Fox, D.: Unsupervised feature learning for rgb-d based object recognition. In: Experimental Robotics (2013)
67. Bo, L., Ren, X., Fox, D.: Depth kernel descriptors for object recognition (2011)
68. Socher, R., Huval, B., Bhat, B., Manning, C.D., Ng, A.Y.: Convolutional-recursive deep learning for 3D object classification. In: NIPS (2012)
69. Lai, K., Bo, L., Ren, X., Fox, D.: Sparse distance learning for object recognition combining RGB and depth information. In: ICRA (2011)
70. Lai, K., Bo, L., Ren, X., Fox, D.: A scalable tree-based approach for joint object and pose recognition. In: AAAI (2011)
71. El-Gaaly, T., Torki, M.: Rgbd object pose recognition using local-global multi-kernel regression. In: ICPR (2012)
72. Zhang, H., El-Gaaly, T., Elgammal, A., Jiang, Z.: Joint object and pose recognition using homeomorphic manifold analysis. In: AAAI (2013)

73. Karpathy, A., Miller, S., Fei-Fei, L.: Object discovery in 3D scenes via shape analysis. In: ICRA (2013)
74. Shao, T., Xu, W., Zhou, K., Wang, J., Li, D., Guo, B.: An interactive approach to semantic modeling of indoor scenes with an rgbd camera. TOG (2012)
75. Hetzel, G., Leibe, B., Levi, P., Schiele, B.: 3D object recognition from range images using local feature histograms. In: CVPR (2001)
76. Golovinskiy, A., Kim, V.G., Funkhouser, T.: Shape-based recognition of 3D point clouds in urban environments. In: ICCV (2009)
77. Xiong, X., Munoz, D., Bagnell, J.A.D., Hebert, M.: 3-D scene analysis via sequenced predictions over points and regions. In: ICRA (2011)
78. Zhu, X., Zhao, H., Liu, Y., Zhao, Y., Zha, H.: Segmentation and classification of range image from an intelligent vehicle in urban environment (2010)
79. Wohlkinger, W., Vincze, M.: Ensemble of shape functions for 3D object classification. In: ROBIO (2011)
80. Lai, K., Bo, L., Ren, X., Fox, D.: Detection-based object labeling in 3D scenes. In: ICRA (2012)
81. Zhu, M., Derpanis, K.G., Yang, Y., Brahmbhatt, S., Zhang, M., Phillips, C., Lecce, M., Daniilidis, K.: Single image 3D object detection and pose estimation for grasping (2014)
82. Kim, B., Xu, S., Savarese, S.: Accurate localization of 3D objects from rgb-d data using segmentation hypotheses. In: CVPR (2013)
83. Zhang, J., Kan, C., Schwing, A.G., Urtasun, R.: Estimating the 3D layout of indoor scenes and its clutter from depth sensors. In: ICCV (2013)
84. Lin, D., Fidler, S., Urtasun, R.: Holistic scene understanding for 3D object detection with RGBD cameras. In: ICCV (2013)
85. Wu, Z., Song, S., Khosla, A., Tang, X., Xiao, J.: 3D ShapeNets for 2.5D object recognition and Next-Best-View prediction. ArXiv e-prints (2014)
86. Zhang, Y., Song, S., Tan, P., Xiao, J.: PanoContext: A whole-room 3D context model for panoramic scene understanding. In: Fleet, D., Pajdla, T., Schiele, B., Tuytelaars, T. (eds.) ECCV 2014. LNCS, vol. 8694, pp. 681–698. Springer, Heidelberg (2014)

Integrating Context and Occlusion for Car Detection by Hierarchical And-Or Model

Bo Li[1,2], Tianfu Wu[2,*], and Song-Chun Zhu[2]

[1] Beijing Lab of Intelligent Information Technology, Beijing Institute of Technology
[2] Department of Statistics, University of California, Los Angeles
boli86@bit.edu.cn, {tfwu,sczhu}@stat.ucla.edu

Abstract. This paper presents a method of learning reconfigurable hierarchical And-Or models to integrate context and occlusion for car detection. The And-Or model represents the regularities of car-to-car context and occlusion patterns at three levels: (i) layouts of spatially-coupled N cars, (ii) single cars with different viewpoint-occlusion configurations, and (iii) a small number of parts. The learning process consists of two stages. We first learn the structure of the And-Or model with three components: (a) mining N-car contextual patterns based on layouts of annotated single car bounding boxes, (b) mining the occlusion configurations based on the overlapping statistics between single cars, and (c) learning visible parts based on car 3D CAD simulation or heuristically mining latent car parts. The And-Or model is organized into a directed and acyclic graph which leads to the Dynamic Programming algorithm in inference. In the second stage, we jointly train the model parameters (for appearance, deformation and bias) using Weak-Label Structural SVM. In experiments, we test our model on four car datasets: the KITTI dataset [11], the street parking dataset [19], the PASCAL VOC2007 car dataset [7], and a self-collected parking lot dataset. We compare with state-of-the-art variants of deformable part-based models and other methods. Our model obtains significant improvement consistently on the four datasets.

Keywords: Car Detection, Context, Occlusion, And-Or Graph.

1 Introduction

The recent literature of object detection has been focused on three aspects to improve accuracy performance: using hierarchical models such as discriminatively trained deformable part-based models (DPM) [8] and And-Or tree models [27], modeling occlusion implicitly or explicitly [19,26,28,23,25], and exploiting contextual information [30,6,17,29,4]. In this paper, we present a method of learning reconfigurable hierarchical And-Or models to integrate context and occlusion for car detection in the wild, e.g., car detection in the recently proposed challenging KITTI dataset [11] and the Street-Parking dataset [19].

---

* Corresponding author.

D. Fleet et al. (Eds.): ECCV 2014, Part VI, LNCS 8694, pp. 652–667, 2014.
© Springer International Publishing Switzerland 2014

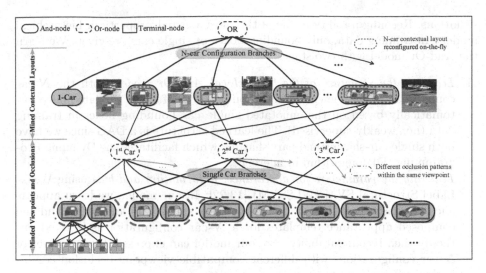

Fig. 1. Illustration of our reconfigurable hierarchical And-Or model for car detection. It represents contextual layouts and viewpoint-occlusion patterns jointly by modeling strong spatially-coupled N-car (e.g., $N = 1, 2, 3$) together and composing visible parts explicitly for single cars. See text for details. (Best viewed in color)

Fig. 1 illustrates the And-Or model learned for car detection. It is organized into a directed and acyclic graph (DAG) and embeds object detection grammar [32,9]. It consists of three types of nodes: And-nodes representing decompositions, Or-nodes representing structural variations and Terminal-nodes grounding symbols (i.e., objects and parts) to image data.

i) The root Or-node represents different N-car configurations which capture both car viewpoints (when $N \geq 1$) and car-to-car contextual information (when $N > 1$). Each configuration is then represented by an And-node (e.g., car pairs and car triples shown in the figure). The contextual information reflects the layout regularities of N cars in real scenarios (such as cars in a parking lot and street-parking cars).

ii) A specific N-car configuration is represented by an And-node which is decomposed into N single cars. Each single car is represented by an Or-node (e.g., the 1st car and the 2nd car), since we have different combinations of viewpoints and occlusion patterns (e.g., the car in the back of a car-pair can have different occluding situations due to the layouts).

iii) Each viewpoint-occlusion pattern is represented by an And-node which is further decomposed into parts. Parts are learned using car 3D CAD simulation as done in [19] or the heuristic method as done in DPM [8]. The green dashed bounding boxes show some examples corresponding to different occlusion patterns (i.e., visible parts) within the same viewpoint.

The proposed And-Or model is flexible and reconfigurable to account for the large variations of car-to-car layouts and viewpoint-occlusion patterns in complex situations. Reconfigurability is one of the most desired property in hierarchical models. In training data, only bounding boxes of single cars are given. We learn the And-Or model with two stages:

i) *Learning the structure of the hierarchical And-Or model.* Both the N-car configurations and viewpoint-occlusion patterns of single cars are mined automatically based on the annotated single car bounding boxes in training data (i.e., weakly-supervised). The learned structure is a DAG since we have both single-car-sharing and part-sharing, which facilitates the Dynamic Programming (DP) algorithm in inference.

ii) *Learning the parameters for appearance, deformation and bias* using Weak-Label Structural SVM (WLSSVM) [13,22]. In our model, we learn appearance templates and deformation models for single cars and parts, and the composed appearance templates for a N-car configuration is inferred on-the-fly (i.e., reconfigurability). So, our model can express a large number of N-car configurations with different compatible viewpoint-occlusion combinations of single cars.

In experiments, we test our model on four car datasets: the KITTI dataset [11], the Street-Parking dataset [19], the PASCAL VOC2007 car dataset [7] and a self-collected Parking Lot dataset (to be released with this paper). Experimental results show that the proposed hierarchical And-Or model is capable of modeling context and occlusion effectively. Our model outperforms different state-of-the-art variants of DPM [8] (including the latest implementation [14]) on all the four datasets, as well as other state-of-the-art models [2,12,25,19] on the KITTI and the Street-Parking datasets. The code and data will be available on the author's homepage[1].

The remaining of this paper is organized as follows. Sec.2 overviews the related work and summarizes our contributions. Sec.3 presents the And-Or model and defines its scoring functions. Sec.4 presents the method of mining contextual N-car configurations and the occlusion patterns of single cars in weakly-labeled training data. Sec.5 discusses the learning of model parameters using WLSSVM, as well as details of the DP inference algorithm. Sec.6 presents the experimental results and comparisons of the proposed model on the four car datasets. Sec.7 concludes this paper with discussions.

2   Related Work and Our Contributions

Single Object Models and Occlusion Modeling. Hierarchical models are widely used in recent literature of object detection and most existing works are devoted to learning a single object model. Many work share the similar spirit to the deformable part-based model [8] (which is a two-layer structure) by exploring deeper hierarchy and global part configurations [27,31,13], with strong manually-annotated parts [1] or available 3D CAD models [24], or by keeping

---

[1] http://www.stat.ucla.edu/~tfwu/project/OcclusionModeling.htm

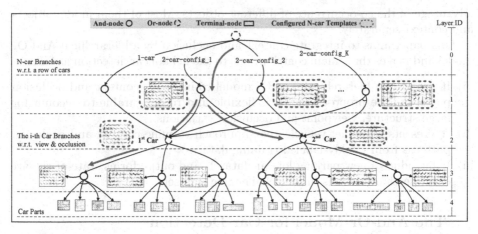

Fig. 2. The learned And-Or model for car detection (only a portion of the whole model is shown here for clarity). The node in layer 0 is the root Or-node, which has a set of child And-nodes representing different N-car configurations in layer 1 ($N \leq 2$ is considered). The nodes in layer 2 represent single car Or-nodes, each of which has a set of child And-nodes representing single cars with different viewpoints and occlusion patterns. We learn appearance templates for single cars and their parts (nodes in layer 3 and 4), and the composite templates for a N-car is reconfigured on-the-fly in inference (as illustrated by the green solid arrows). (Best viewed in color)

human in-the-loop [3]. To address the occlusion problem, methods of regularizing part visibilities are used in learning [15,19]. Those models do not represent contextual information, and usually learn another separate context model using the detection scores as input features. Recently, an And-Or quantization method is proposed to learn And-Or tree models [27] for generic object detection in PASCAL VOC [7] and learn car 3D And-Or models [18] respectively, which could be useful in occlusion modeling.

Object-Pair and Visual Phrase Models. To account for the strong co-occurrence, object-pair [20,28,23,25] and visual phrase [26] methods implicitly model occlusions and interactions using a X-to-X or X-to-Y composite template that spans both one object (i.e., "X" such as a person or a car) and another interacting object (i.e., "X" or "Y" such as the other car in a car-pair in parking lots or a bicycle on which a person is riding). Although these models can handle occlusion better than single object models in occluded situations, the object-pair or visual phrase are often manually designed and fixed (i.e., not reconfigurable in inference), and as investigated in the KITTI dataset [25], their performance are worse than original DPM in complex scenarios.

Context Models. Many context models have been exploited in object detection showing performance improvement [30,6,17,29,4]. In [29], Tu and Bai integrate the detector responses with background pixels to determine the foreground pixels. In [4], Chen, et. al. propose a multi-order context representation to take advantage of the co-occurrence of different objects. Most of them model objects and context separately.

This paper aims to integrate context and occlusion by a hierarchical And-Or model and makes three main contributions to the field of car detection as follows.

i) It proposes a hierarchical And-Or model to integrate context and occlusion patterns. The proposed model is flexible and reconfigurable to account for large structure, viewpoint and occlusion variations.

ii) It presents a simple, yet effective, approach to mine context and occlusion patterns from weakly-labeled training data.

iii) It introduce a new parking lot car dataset, and outperforms state-of-the-art car detection methods in four challenging datasets.

3   The And-Or Model for Car Detection

3.1   The And-Or Model and Scoring Functions

Our And-Or model follows the image grammar framework proposed by Zhu and Mumford [32] which has shown expressive power to represent a large number of configurations using a small dictionary. In this section, we first introduce the notations to define the And-Or model and its scoring function. Fig. 2 shows the learned car And-Or model which has 5 layers.

The And-Or model is defined by a 3-tuple $\mathcal{G} = (\mathcal{V}, E, \Theta)$, where $\mathcal{V} = \mathcal{V}_{\text{And}} \cup \mathcal{V}_{\text{Or}} \cup \mathcal{V}_T$ represents the set of nodes consisting of three subsets of And-nodes, Or-nodes and Terminal-nodes respectively, E the set of edges organizing all the nodes into a DAG, and $\Theta = (\Theta^{app}, \Theta^{def}, \Theta^{bias})$ the set of parameters (for appearance, deformation and bias respectively, to be defined later). Denote by $ch(v)$ the set of child nodes of a node $v \in \mathcal{V}_{\text{And}} \cup \mathcal{V}_{\text{Or}}$.

Appearance Features. We adopt the Histogram of Oriented Gradients (HOG) feature [5,8] to describe car appearance. Let I be an image defined on a lattice. Denote by $\mathcal{H}$ the HOG feature pyramid computed for I using λ levels per octave, and by Λ the lattice of the whole pyramid. Let $p = (l, x, y) \in \Lambda$ specify a position (x, y) in the l-th level of the pyramid $\mathcal{H}$.

Deformation Features. We allow local deformation when composing the child nodes into a parent node (e.g., composing car parts into a single car or composing two single cars into a car-pair). In our model, car parts are placed at twice the spatial resolution w.r.t. single cars, while single cars and composite N-cars are placed at the same spatial resolution. We penalize the displacements between the anchor locations of child nodes (w.r.t. the placed parent node) and their actual deformed locations. Denote by $\delta = [dx, dy]$ the displacement. The deformation feature is defined by $\Phi^{def}(\delta) = [dx^2, dx, dy^2, dy]'$.

A **Terminal-node** $t \in \mathcal{V}_T$ grounds a symbol (i.e., a single car or a car part) to image data (see Layer 3 and 4 in Fig.2). Given a parent node A, the model for t is defined by a 4-tuple $(\theta_t^{app}, s_t, a_{t|A}, \theta_{t|A}^{def})$ where $\theta_t^{app} \subset \Theta^{app}$ is the appearance template, $s_t \in \{0, 1\}$ the scale factor for placing node t w.r.t. its parent node, $a_{t|A}$

a two-dimensional vector specifying an anchor position relative to the position of parent node A, and $\theta^{def}_{t|A} \subset \Theta^{def}$ the deformation parameters. Given the position $p_A = (l_A, x_A, y_A)$ of parent node A, the scoring function of node t is defined by,

$$score(t|A, p_A) = \max_{\delta \in \Delta}(< \theta^{app}_t, \Phi^{app}(\mathcal{H}, p_t) > - < \theta^{def}_{t|A}, \Phi^{def}(\delta) >), \quad (1)$$

where Δ is the space of deformation (i.e., the lattice of the corresponding level in the feature pyramid), $p_t = (l_t, x_t, y_t)$ with $l_t = l_A - s_t\lambda$ and $(x_t, y_t) = 2^{s_t}(x_A, y_A) + a_{t|A} + \delta$, and $\Phi^{app}(\mathcal{H}, p_t)$ the extracted HOG features. $< \cdot, \cdot >$ denotes the inner product.

An **And-node** $A \in \mathcal{V}_{\text{And}}$ represents a decomposition of a large entity (e.g., a N-car layout at Layer 1 or a single car at Layer 3 in Fig.2) into its constituents (e.g., N single cars or a small number of car parts). The scoring function of node A is defined by,

$$score(A, p_A) = \sum_{v \in ch(A)} score(v|A, p_A) + b_A \quad (2)$$

where $b_A \in \Theta^{bias}$ is the bias term. Each single car And-node (at Layer 3) can be treated as the And-Or Structure proposed in [19] or the DPM [8]. So, our model is very flexible to incorporate state-of-the-art single object models. For N-car layout And-nodes (at Layer 1), their child nodes are Or-nodes and the scoring function $score(v|A, p_A)$ is defined below.

An **Or-node** $O \in \mathcal{V}_{\text{Or}}$ represents different structure variations (e.g., the root node at Layer 0 and the i-th car node at Layer 2 in Fig.2). For the root Or-node O, when placing at the position $p \in \Lambda$, the scoring function is defined by,

$$score(O, p) = \max_{v \in ch(O)} score(v, p). \quad (3)$$

where $ch(O) \subset \mathcal{V}_{\text{And}}$. For the i-th car Or-node O, given a parent N-car And-node A placed at p_A, the scoring function is then defined by,

$$score(O|A, p_A) = \max_{v \in ch(O)} \max_{\delta \in \Delta}(score(v, p_v) - < \theta^{def}_{O|A}, \Phi^{def}(\delta) >), \quad (4)$$

where $p_v = (l_v, x_v, y_v)$ with $l_v = l_A$ and $(x_v, y_v) = (x_A, y_A) + \delta$.

3.2   The DP Algorithm in Detection

In detection, we place the And-Or model at all positions $p \in \Lambda$ and retrieve the parse trees for all positions at which the scores are greater than the detection threshold. A *parse tree* is an instantiation of the And-Or model by selecting the best child of each encountering Or-node as illustrated by the green arrows in Fig.2. Thank to the DAG structure of our And-Or model, we can utilize the efficient DP algorithm in detection which consists of two stages:

- Following the depth-first-search (DFS) order of nodes in the And-Or model, the bottom-up pass computes appearance score maps and deformed score maps for the whole feature pyramid $\mathcal{H}$ for all Terminal-nodes, And-nodes and Or-nodes. The deformed score maps can be computed efficiently by the generalized distance transform [10] algorithm as done in [8].
- In the top-down pass, we first find all the positions $\mathbb{P}$ for the root Or-node O with score $score(O,p) \geq \tau, p \in \mathbb{P} \subset \Lambda$. Then, following the breadth-first-search (BFS) order of nodes, we can retrieve the parse tree at each p.

Post-processing. To generate the final detection results of single cars for evaluation, we apply N-car guided non-maximum suppression (NMS), since we deal with occlusion: (i) Overlapped N-car detection candidates might report multiple predictions for the same single car. For example, if a car is shared by two neighboring 2-car detection candidates, it will be reported twice; (ii) Some of the cars in a N-car detection candidate are highly overlapped due to occlusion, and if we directly use conventional NMS we will miss the detection of the occluded cars. In our N-car guided NMS, we enforce that all the N single car bounding boxes in a N-car prediction will not be suppressed by each other. The similar idea is also used in [28].

4   Learning the Model Structure by Mining Context and Viewpoint-Occlusion Patterns

In this section, we present the methods of learning the structure of our And-Or model by mining context and viewpoint-occlusion patterns in the positive training dataset. Denote by $D^+ = \{(I_1, \mathbb{B}_1), \cdots, (I_n, \mathbb{B}_n)\}$ the positive training dataset where $\mathbb{B}_i = \{B_i^j = (x_i^j, y_i^j, w_i^j, h_i^j)\}_{j=1}^{k_i}$ is the set of k_i annotated single car bound boxes in image I_i (where (x, y) is the left-top corner and (w, h) the width and height).

Generating the N-car positive samples from D^+. Denote the set of N-car positive samples by,

$$D_{N-car}^+ = \{(I_i, B_i^J); k_i \geq N, J \subseteq [1,k_i], |J|=N, B_i^J \subseteq \mathbb{B}_i, i \in [1,n]\}, \tag{5}$$

we have,

- D_{1-car}^+ consists of all the single car bounding boxes which do not overlap the other ones in the same image. For $N \geq 2$, D_{N-car}^+ is generated iteratively.
- To generate D_{2-car}^+, for each positive image $(I_i, \mathbb{B}_i) \in D^+$ with $k_i \geq 2$, we enumerate all valid 2-car configurations starting from $B_i^1 \in \mathbb{B}_i$: (i) select the current B_i^j as the first car ($1 \leq j \leq k_i$), (ii) obtain all the surrounding car bounding boxes $\mathcal{N}_{B_i^j}$ which overlap B_i^j, and (iii) select the second car $B_i^k \in \mathcal{N}_{B_i^j}$ which has the largest overlap if $\mathcal{N}_{B_i^j} \neq \emptyset$ and $(I_i, B_i^J) \notin D_{2-car}^+$ (where $J = \{j, k\}$).

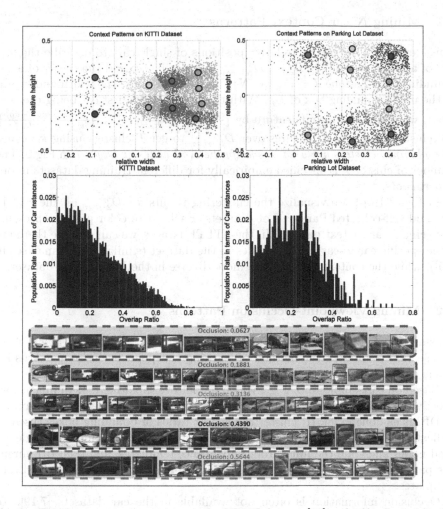

Fig. 3. *Top*: 2-car context patterns on the KITTI dataset [11] and self-collected Parking Lot dataset. Each context pattern is represented by a specific color set, and each circle stands for the center of each cluster. *Middle*: Overlap ratio histograms of the KITTI dataset and the Parking Lot dataset (we show the occluded cases only). *Bottom*: some cropped examples with different occlusions. The 2 bounding boxes in a car pair are shown in red and blue respectively. (Best viewed in color).

– To generate D^+_{N-car} ($N > 2$), for each positive image with $k_i \geq N$ and $\exists (I_i, B^K_i) \in D^+_{(N-1)-car}$, (i) select the current B^K_i as the seed, (ii) obtain the neighbors $\mathcal{N}_{B^K_i}$ each of which overlap at least one bounding box in B^K_i, (iii) select the bounding box $B^j_i \in \mathcal{N}_{B^K_i}$ which has the largest overlap and add (I_i, B^J_i) to D^+_{N-car} (where $J = K \cup \{j\}$) if valid.

4.1   Mining N-car Context Patterns

Consider $N \geq 2$, we use the relative positions of single cars to describe the layout of a N-car sample $(I_i, B_i^J) \in D_{N-car}^+$. Denote by (cx, cy) the center of a car bounding box. Assume $J = \{1, \cdots, N\}$. Let w_J and h_J be the width and height of the union bounding box of B_i^J. With the center of the first car being the centroid, we define the layout feature by $[\frac{cx_i^2 - cx_i^1}{w_J}, \frac{cy_i^2 - cy_i^1}{h_J}, \cdots, \frac{cx_i^N - cx_i^1}{w_J}, \frac{cy_i^N - cy_i^1}{h_J}]$. We cluster these layout features over D_{N-car}^+ to get T clusters using k-means. *The obtained clusters are used to specify the And-nodes at Layer 1 in Fig.2.* The number of cluster T is specified empirically for different training datasets in our experiments.

In Fig. 3 (top), we visualize the clustering results for D_{2-car}^+ on the KITTI [11] and self-collected Parking Lot datasets. Each set of color points represents a specific 2-car context pattern. In the KITTI dataset, we can observe there are some specific car-to-car "peak" modes in the dataset (similar to the analyses in [25]), while the context patterns are more diverse in the Parking Lot dataset.

4.2   Mining Viewpoint-Occlusion Patterns

As stated above, we present the method of specifying Layer $0-2$ in Fig.2. In this section we present the method of learning viewpoint-occlusion patterns for single cars (i.e., Layer 3 and 4 in Fig.2).

Based on car samples in D_{1-car}^+ which do not overlap other cars in images, we specify the single car And-nodes and part Terminal-nodes by learning a mixture of DPMs as done in [8]: (i) cluster the aspect ratios of bounding boxes (used to indicate the latent viewpoints) over D_{1-car}^+ to obtain a small number of single car And-nodes and train the initial root appearance templates, and then (ii) pursue the part Terminal-nodes for each single car And-node based on the trained root templates.

Occlusion information is often not available in the car datasets [7,19]. To obtain occlusion information of single cars, we focus on D_{2-car}^+ and use overlap ratios between single cars to mine occlusion patterns. In Fig.3 (Middle), we show the two histograms of overlap ratios over D_{2-car}^+ plotted on the KITTI [11] and self-collected Parking Lot datasets respectively. In Fig. 3 (Bottom), we show some cropped training positives in the two datasets from which we can observe that overlap ratios roughly reflects the degree of occlusion. Based on the histograms, we mine the viewpoint-occlusion patterns by two methods:

– We adopt the occlusion modeling method proposed in [19] which utilizes car 3D CAD simulation. In addition to the histograms of overlap ratios, we also use the histograms of sizes and aspect ratios of single car bounding boxes to guide the process of synthesizing the occlusion layouts using car 3D CAD models. Then we can learn the And-Or structure for single cars which consists of a small set of consistently visible parts and a number of optional part clusters. Details are referred to [19].

– We cluster the overlap ratios into a small number clusters and each cluster represents an occlusion pattern. The training samples in each cluster are used to train the single car templates and the parts similar to [21,25]. Based on the learned unoccluded single car templates and the estimated threshold using D^+_{1-car}, a car in a car pair is initialized as occluded one if the score is less than the threshold. If the scores of both cars are greater than the threshold, we select the car with lower score as the occluded one. The "unoccluded" car in a car pair is added to D^+_{1-car} if had. Then, we use the same learning method as for D^+_{1-car} except that we only pursue part Terminal-nodes in the "visible" portion of the bounding box of the occluded cars.

5   Learning the Parameters by WLSSVM

In the training data, we only have annotated bounding boxes for single cars. The parse tree pt for each N-car positive sample is hidden. The parameters $\Theta = (\Theta^{app}, \Theta^{def}, \Theta^{bias})$ are learned iteratively. We initialize the parse tree for each N-car positive sample as stated in Sec.4. Then, during learning, we run the DP inference to assign the optimal parse trees for them. We adopt the WLSSVM method [13] in learning. The objective function to be minimized is defined by,

$$\mathcal{E}(\Theta) = \frac{1}{2}\|\Theta\|^2 + C\sum_{i=1}^{M} L'(\Theta, x_i, y_i) \tag{6}$$

where $x_i \in D^+_{N-car}$ represents a training sample ($N \geq 1$) and y_i is the N bounding box(es). $L'(\Theta, x, y)$ is the surrogate loss function,

$$L'(\Theta, x, y) = \max_{pt\in\Omega_{\mathcal{G}}} [score(x, pt; \Theta) + L_{margin}(y, box(pt))] -$$
$$\max_{pt\in\Omega_{\mathcal{G}}} [score(x, pt; \Theta) - L_{output}(y, box(pt))] \tag{7}$$

where $\Omega_{\mathcal{G}}$ is the space of all parse trees derived from the And-Or model $\mathcal{G}$, $score(x, pt; \Theta)$ computes the score of a parse tree as stated in Sec.3, and $box(pt)$ the predicted bounding box(es) base on the parse tree. As pointed out in [13], the loss $L_{margin}(y, box(pt))$ encourages high-loss outputs to "pop out of the first term in the RHS, so that their scores get pushed down. The loss $L_{output}(y, box(pt))$ suppresses high-loss outputs in the second term in the RHS, so the score of a low-loss prediction gets pulled up. More details are referred to [13,22]. The loss function is defined by,

$$L_{\ell,\tau}(y, box(pt)) = \begin{cases} \ell & \text{if } y = \perp \text{ and } pt \neq \perp \\ 0 & \text{if } y = \perp \text{ and } pt = \perp \\ \ell & \text{if } y \neq \perp \text{ and } \exists\, B \in y \text{ with } ov(B, B') < \tau, \forall B' \in box(pt) \\ 0 & \text{if } y \neq \perp \text{ and } ov(B, B') \geq \tau, \forall\, B \in y \text{ and } \exists B' \in box(pt) \end{cases} \tag{8}$$

where $\perp$ represents background output and $ov(\cdot, \cdot)$ is the intersection-union ratio of two bounding boxes. Following the PASCAL VOC protocol we have $L_{margin} = L_{1,0.5}$ and $L_{output} = L_{\infty,0.7}$. In practice, we modify the implementation in [14] for our loss formulation.

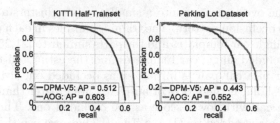

Fig. 4. Precision-recall curves on the test subset splitted from th KITTI trainset (Left) and the Parking Lot dataset (Right)

6   Experiments

6.1   Detection Results on the KITTI Dataset

The KITTI dataset [11] is a recently proposed challenging dataset which provides a large number of cars with different occlusion scenarios. It contains 7481 training images and 7518 testing images, which are captured from an autonomous driving platform. We follow the provided benchmark protocol for evaluation. Since the authors of [11] have not released the test annotations, we test our model in the following two settings.

Training and Testing by Splitting the Trainset. We randomly split the KITTI trainset into the training and testing subsets equally.

Baseline Methods. Since DPM [8] is a very competitive model with source code publicly available, we compare our model with the latest version of DPM (i.e., voc-release5 [14]). The number of components are set to 16 as the baseline methods trained in [11], other parameters are set as default.

Parameter Settings. We consider N-car with $N = 1, 2$. We set the number of context patterns and viewpoint-occlusion patterns to be 10 and 16 respectively in Sec.4. As a result, the learned hierarchical And-Or model has 10 2-car configurations in layer 1, and 16 single car branches in layer 3 (see Fig. 2).

Detection Results. The left figure of Fig. 4 shows the precision-recall curves of DPM and our model. Our model outperforms DPM by 9.1% in terms of average precision (AP). The performance gain comes from both precision and recall, which shows the importance of context and occlusion modeling.

Testing on the KITTI Benchmark. We test the trained models above (i.e., using half training set) on the KITTI testset. The detection results and performance comparison are shown in Table 1. This benchmark has three subsets (*Easy, Moderate, Hard*) w.r.t the difficulty of object size, occlusion and truncation. Our model outperforms all the other methods tested on this benchmark. Specifically, our model outperforms OC-DPM [25] on all the three subsets by 5.32%, 1.08%, and 1.74%. We also compare with the baseline DPM trained by ourselves using the voc-release5 code [14], the performance gain of our model

Table 1. Performance comparision (in AP) with baselines on KITTI benchmark [11]

Methods	Easy	Moderate	Hard
mBow [2]	36.02%	23.76%	18.44%
LSVM-MDPM-us [8]	66.53%	55.42%	41.04%
LSVM-MDPM-sv [8,12]	68.02%	56.48%	44.18%
MDPM-un-BB [8]	71.19%	62.16%	48.43%
OC-DPM [25]	74.94%	65.95%	53.86%
DPM (trained by ourselves using [14])	77.24%	56.02%	43.14%
AOG	**80.26%**	**67.03%**	**55.60%**

mainly comes from the *Moderate and Hard* car subsets, with 11.01% and 12.46% in terms of AP respectively. For other DPM based methods trained by the benchmark authors, our model outperforms the best one - MDPM-un-BB by 9.07%, 4.87% and 7.17% respectively.

Note that our model is trained using half of the KITTI trainset, while other methods in the benchmark use more training data (e.g., 1/6 cross validation). The performance improvement by our model is significant. As mentioned by [25], because of the large number of cars in KITTI dataset, even a small amount (1.6%) of AP increasing is still considered significant.

The first 3 rows of Fig. 5 show the qualitative results of our model. The red bounding boxes show the successful detection, the blue ones the missing detection, and the green ones the false alarms. We can see our model is robust to detect cars with severe car-to-car occlusion and clutter. The failure cases are mainly due to too severe occlusion, too small car size, car deformation and/or inaccurate (or multiple) bounding box localization.

6.2   Detection Results on the Parking Lot Dataset

Although the KITTI dataset [11] is very challenging, the camera viewpoints are relatively restricted due to the camera platform (e.g., no birdeye's view), and there is a less number of cars in each image than the ones in parking lot images. Our self-collected parking lot dataset provides more features on these two aspects. As shown in Fig. 5, this dataset has more diversity in terms of viewpoints and occlusions. It contains 65 training images and 63 testing images. Although the number of images is small, the number of cars is noticeably large, with 3346 cars (including left-right mirrored ones) for training and 2015 cars for testing.

Evaluation Protocol. We follow the PASCAL VOC evaluation protocol [7] with the overlap of intersection over union being greater than or equal to 60% (instead of original 50%). In practice, we set this threshold to make a compromise between localization accuracy and detection difficulty. The detected cars with bounding box height smaller than 25 pixels do not count as false positives as done in [11]. We compare with the latest version of DPM implementation [14] and set the number of context patterns and viewpoint-occlusion patterns to be 10 and 18 respectively.

Fig. 5. Examples of successful and failure cases by our model on the KITTI dataset (first 3 rows), the Parking Lot dataset (the 4-th and 5-th rows) and the Street Parking dataset (the last two rows). Best viewed in color and magnification.

Detection Results. In the right of Fig. 4 we compare the performance of our model with DPM. Our model obtains 55.2% in AP, which outperforms the latest version of DPM by 10.9%. The fourth and fifth rows of Fig. 5 show the qualitative results of our model. Our model is capable of detecting cars with different occlusion and viewpoints.

6.3 Detection Results on the Street Parking Dataset

The Street Parking dataset [19] is a recently proposed car dataset with emphases on occlusion modeling of cars in street scenes. We test our model on this dataset to verify the ability of occlusion modeling of our And-Or model. We use two versions of our model for comparison: (i) A hierarchical And-Or model with greedy latent parts, denoting as $AOG^\dagger$, and (ii) A hierarchical And-Or model with visible parts learned based on car 3D CAD simulation, denoting as $AOG^\ddagger$. $AOG^\dagger$ and $AOG^\ddagger$ have the same number of context patterns and occlusion patterns, 8 and 16 respectively. To compare with the benchmark methods, we follow the evaluation protocol provided in [19].

Results of our model and other benchmark methods are shown in Table 2, we can see our $AOG^\dagger$ outperforms DPM [14] and And-Or Structure [19] by 10.1% and 4.3% respectively. We believe this is because our model takes both context and occlusion into account, and the flexible structure provides more representability of occlusion. Our $AOG^\ddagger$ further improves the performance of $AOG^\dagger$

Table 2. Performance comparision (in AP) on the Street Parking dataset [19]

	DPM [14]	And-Or Structure [19]	our AOG†	our AOG‡
AP	52.0%	57.8%	62.1%	**65.3%**

Fig. 6. Visualization of part layouts output by our AOG† (Top) and AOG‡ (Bottom). Best viewed in color and magnification.

by 3.2%, which show the advantage of modeling occlusion using visible parts. The last two rows in Fig. 5 show some qualitative examples. Our AOG is capable of detecting occluded street-parking cars, meanwhile it also has a few inaccurate detection results and misses some cars that are too small or uncommon in the trainset. Fig. 6 shows the inferred part bounding boxes by AOG† and AOG‡. We can observe that the semantic parts in AOG‡ are meaningful, although they may be not accurate enough in some examples.

6.4   Detection Results on the PASCAL VOC2007 Car Dataset

As analyzed by Hoiem, et. al. in [16], cars in PASCAL VOC dataset do not have much occlusion and car-to-car context. We test our And-Or model on the PASCAL VOC2007 car dataset and show that our model is comparable to other single object models. We compare with the latest version of DPM [14]. The APs are 60.6% (our model) and 58.2% (DPM) respectively. We will submit more results in VOC in the future work.

7   Conclusion

In this paper, we propose a reconfigurable hierarchical And-Or model to integrate context and occlusion for car detection in the wild. The model structure is learned by mining context and viewpoint-occlusion patterns at three levels: a) N-car layouts, b) single car and c) car parts. Our model is a DAG where DP algorithm can be used in inference. The model parameters are learned by WLSSVM[13]. Experimental results show that our model is effective in modeling context and occlusion information in complex situations, and obtains better performance over state-of-the-art car detection methods. In our on-going work, we apply the proposed method to other object categories and study different ways of mining the context and occlusion patterns (e.g., integrating with the And-Or quantization methods [27,18]).

Acknowledgement. B. Li is supported by China 973 Program under Grant no. 2012CB316300 and the National Key Technology Research and Development Program of the Ministry of Science and Technology of China under Grant No. 2014BAK14B03. T.F. Wu and S.C. Zhu are supported by DARPA MSEE project FA 8650-11-1-7149, MURI grant ONR N00014-10-1-0933, and NSF IIS1018751. We thank Dr. Wenze Hu for helpful discussion.

References

1. Azizpour, H., Laptev, I.: Object detection using strongly-supervised deformable part models. In: Fitzgibbon, A., Lazebnik, S., Perona, P., Sato, Y., Schmid, C. (eds.) ECCV 2012, Part I. LNCS, vol. 7572, pp. 836–849. Springer, Heidelberg (2012)
2. Behley, J., Steinhage, V., Cremers, A.: Laser-based Segment Classification Using a Mixture of Bag-of-Words. In: IROS (2013)
3. Branson, S., Perona, P., Belongie, S.: Strong supervision from weak annotation: Interactive training of deformable part models. In: ICCV (2011)
4. Chen, G., Ding, Y., Xiao, J., Han, T.X.: Detection evolution with multi-order contextual co-occurrence. In: CVPR (2013)
5. Dalal, N., Triggs, B.: Histograms of oriented gradients for human detection. In: CVPR (2005)
6. Desai, C., Ramanan, D., Fowlkes, C.: Discriminative models for multi-class object layout. IJCV 95(1), 1–12 (2011)
7. Everingham, M., Van Gool, L., Williams, C., Winn, J., Zisserman, A.: The pascal visual object classes (voc) challenge. IJCV (2010)
8. Felzenszwalb, P., Girshick, R., McAllester, D., Ramanan, D.: Object detection with discriminatively trained part-based models. TPAMI (2010)
9. Felzenszwalb, P., McAllester, D.: Object detection grammars. Tech. rep., University of Chicago, Computer Science TR-2010-02 (2010)
10. Felzenszwalb, P., Huttenlocher, D.: Distance transforms of sampled functions. Theory of Computing (2012)
11. Geiger, A., Lenz, P., Urtasun, R.: Are we ready for autonomous driving? the kitti vision benchmark suite. In: CVPR (2012)
12. Geiger, A., Wojek, C., Urtasun, R.: Joint 3D estimation of objects and scene layout. In: NIPS (2011)
13. Girshick, R., Felzenszwalb, P., McAllester, D.: Object detection with grammar models. In: NIPS (2011)
14. Girshick, R.B., Felzenszwalb, P.F., McAllester, D.: Discriminatively trained deformable part models, release 5,
   http://people.cs.uchicago.edu/~rbg/latent-release5/
15. Hejrati, M., Ramanan, D.: Analyzing 3D objects in cluttered images. In: NIPS (2012)
16. Hoiem, D., Chodpathumwan, Y., Dai, Q.: Diagnosing error in object detectors. In: Fitzgibbon, A., Lazebnik, S., Perona, P., Sato, Y., Schmid, C. (eds.) ECCV 2012, Part III. LNCS, vol. 7574, pp. 340–353. Springer, Heidelberg (2012)

17. Hoiem, D., Efros, A., Hebert, M.: Putting objects in perspective. IJCV 80(1), 3–15 (2008)
18. Hu, W., Zhu, S.C.: Learning 3D object templates by quantizing geometry and appearance spaces. TPAMI (to appear, 2014)
19. Li, B., Hu, W., Wu, T.F., Zhu, S.C.: Modeling occlusion by discriminative and-or structures. In: ICCV (2013)
20. Li, B., Song, X., Wu, T.F., Hu, W., Pei, M.: Coupling-and-decoupling: A hierarchical model for occlusion-free object detection. PR 47, 3254–3264 (2014)
21. Mathias, M., Benenson, R., Timofte, R., Van Gool, L.: Handling occlusions with franken-classifiers. In: ICCV (2013)
22. McAllester, D., Keshet, J.: Generalization bounds and consistency for latent structural probit and ramp loss. In: NIPS (2011)
23. Ouyang, W., Wang, X.: Single-pedestrian detection aided by multi-pedestrian detection. In: CVPR (2013)
24. Pepik, B., Stark, M., Gehler, P., Schiele, B.: Teaching 3d geometry to deformable part models. In: CVPR (2012)
25. Pepik, B., Stark, M., Gehler, P., Schiele, B.: Occlusion patterns for object class detection. In: CVPR (2013)
26. Sadeghi, M., Farhadi, A.: Recognition using visual phrases. In: CVPR (2011)
27. Song, X., Wu, T.F., Jia, Y., Zhu, S.C.: Discriminatively trained and-or tree models for object detection. In: CVPR (2013)
28. Tang, S., Andriluka, M., Schiele, B.: Detection and tracking of occluded people. In: BMVC (2012)
29. Tu, Z., Bai, X.: Auto-context and its application to high-level vision tasks and 3D brain image segmentation. TPAMI (2010)
30. Yang, Y., Baker, S., Kannan, A., Ramanan, D.: Recognizing proxemics in personal photos. In: CVPR (2012)
31. Zhu, L., Chen, Y., Yuille, A., Freeman, W.: Latent hierarchical structural learning for object detection. In: CVPR (2010)
32. Zhu, S.C., Mumford, D.: A stochastic grammar of images. Found. Trends. Comput. Graph. Vis. (2006)

PanoContext: A Whole-Room 3D Context Model for Panoramic Scene Understanding

Yinda Zhang[1], Shuran Song[1], Ping Tan[2], and Jianxiong Xiao[1]

[1] Princeton University
[2] Simon Fraser University
http://panocontext.cs.princeton.edu

Abstract. The field-of-view of standard cameras is very small, which is one of the main reasons that contextual information is not as useful as it should be for object detection. To overcome this limitation, we advocate the use of 360° full-view panoramas in scene understanding, and propose a whole-room context model in 3D. For an input panorama, our method outputs 3D bounding boxes of the room and all major objects inside, together with their semantic categories. Our method generates 3D hypotheses based on contextual constraints and ranks the hypotheses holistically, combining both bottom-up and top-down context information. To train our model, we construct an annotated panorama dataset and reconstruct the 3D model from single-view using manual annotation. Experiments show that solely based on 3D context without any image region category classifier, we can achieve a comparable performance with the state-of-the-art object detector. This demonstrates that when the FOV is large, context is as powerful as object appearance. All data and source code are available online.

1 Introduction

Recognizing 3D objects from an image has been a central research topic since the computer vision field was established [1]. While the past decade witnesses rapid progress on bottom-up object detection methods [2–6], the improvement brought by the top-down context cue is rather limited, as demonstrated in standard benchmarks (e.g. PASCAL VOC[3]). In contrast, there are strong psychophysical evidences that context plays a crucial role in scene understanding for humans [7, 8].

We believe that one of the main reasons for this gap is because the field of view (FOV) for a typical camera is only about 15% of that of the human vision system[1]. This problem is exemplified in Fig. 1. The narrow FOV hinders the context information in several ways. Firstly, a limited FOV sees only a small fraction of all scene objects, and therefore, observes little interplay among them. For example, on average, there is only 1.5 object classes and 2.7 object instances per image in PASCAL VOC. Secondly,

---

[1] The approximate FOV of a single human eye is about 95°. Two eyes give us almost 180° FOV. Considering the movement of eyeballs (head rotation excluded, peripheral vision included), the horizontal FOV of the human vision system is as high as 270°. However, the FOV of a typical camera is much smaller. For example, on standard full-frame cameras, the horizontal FOV is only 39.6° (or 54.4°) with a standard 50mm lens (or with a 35mm wide-angle lens).

D. Fleet et al. (Eds.): ECCV 2014, Part VI, LNCS 8694, pp. 668–686, 2014.
© Springer International Publishing Switzerland 2014

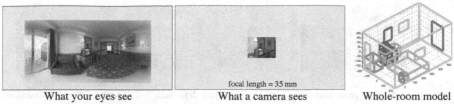

What your eyes see   What a camera sees   Whole-room model

focal length = 35 mm

Fig. 1. Comparison of field-of-view. A camera with narrow FOV might not see a bed in a bedroom which complicates the context model.

the occurrence of an object becomes unpredictable with a small FOV. For example, a typically bedroom should have at least one bed, which can serve as a strong context cue. But in a bedroom picture of small FOV (Fig. 1), there might or might not be a bed, depending on the direction the camera looks at. Given a much limited FOV, it is unfair to ask computer vision algorithms to match the performance of human vision. Therefore, we advocate the use of panoramic images in scene understanding, which nowadays can be easily obtained by camera arrays (e.g. Google Streetview), special lenses (e.g. 0-360.com), smartphones (e.g. cycloramic.com) or automatic image stitching algorithms (e.g. [9–11]).

We present a whole-room 3D context model to address the indoor scene understanding problem from a single panorama (Fig. 2). In a panorama, characteristic scene objects such as beds and sofas are usually visible despite occlusion, so that we can jointly optimize the room layout and object detection to exploit the contextual information in its full strength. Our output is a 3D room layout with recognized scene objects represented by their 3D bounding boxes. We use context to decide number of instances, to assign object semantics, to sample objects, to valid whole-room hypotheses, to extract room model feature, to reconstruct 3D and to adjust final result. An example of input and output are provided in Fig. 2.

Our method consists of two steps: bottom-up hypotheses generation and holistic hypotheses ranking. It starts by generating hypotheses for the room layout and object bounding boxes in a bottom-up fashion using a variety of image evidences, e.g. edge, segmentation, orientation map and geometric context. 3D scene hypotheses are formed from these hypothesized room layouts and object bounding boxes. A trained Support Vector Machine (SVM) [12] ranks these 3D scene hypotheses and chooses the best one. Finally, we locally refine good hypotheses to further maximize their SVM scores. The SVM is trained utilizing both image information and room structure constrains from our training data, which consists of high-resolution panorama images with detail object annotations and 3D ground truth reconstructed using the 2D annotations.

The whole-room contextual information is critical in many key steps of our system. During *hypothesis generation*, the object categories are predicted based on its relative location in the room. We sample the number of object instances according to the typical distribution of each object category, guided by the pairwise position relationship among objects. During *hypothesis ranking*, we firstly align each hypothesis with the 3D rooms from the training set to tell if it is valid. This non-parametric room alignment captures high order relationship among all objects, which cannot be represented well by pairwise constraints. Secondly, we also build a room model for each hypothesis. This room

Input: a single-view panorama   Output: object detection   Output: 3D reconstruction

Fig. 2. Input and output. Taken a full-view panorama as input, our algorithm detects all the objects inside the panorama and represents them as bounding boxes in 3D, which also enables 3D reconstruction from a single-view.

model includes color and texture statistics for the foreground and background. Since we know all the objects and room layout in 3D, we can calculate these statistics easily from image regions unoccluded by objects.We use this model to judge how well a hypothesis explains the image evidences. Thirdly, because we map each hypothesis to 3D space by reconstructing the objects and room layouts, a wrong room layout hypothesis is typically ranked low by the SVM, since it often produces unreasonable 3D bounding boxes of objects. This implicit 3D interaction between objects and room layout enables us to identify many bad hypotheses. During *final adjustment*, we also use the object number distribution and pairwise context model to guide the search.

As demonstrated in our experiments, we can recognize objects using only 3D contextual information (without a classifier to discriminate object categories based on image feature), and still achieve a comparable performance with the state-of-the-art object detector [2], which learns a mapping from image region feature to object category. This shows that context is as powerful as object appearance and much more useful than we previously thought. The root of context model being under-utilized is partly because the regular FOVs are too small.

In the following section, we will describe our algorithm in greater details. We will also talk about the construction of a 3D panorama data set and present experiments to evaluate the algorithm in Sec. 3. In Sec. 5, we will discuss the relation of our proposed method with existing ones.

2   PanoContext: A Whole-Room 3D Context Model

As shown in Fig. 2, our input is a panorama covering 360° horizontal and 180° vertical FOV represented in equirectangular projection. Our output is a 3D box representation of the sceneWe adopt the Manhattan world assumption, assuming that the scene consists of 3D cuboids aligned with three principle directions[2].

Our method first generates whole-room hypotheses and then ranks them holistically. The challenge for hypotheses generation is to maintain high recall using a managable number of hypotheses, while the challenge for holistic ranking is to have high precision. To generate hypotheses, we first estimate vanishing points by Hough Transform based

---

[2] We focus on indoor scenes only, although our algorithm may be generalized to outdoor scenes as well. We assume an object can either stand on the ground, sit on another object, or hang on a wall (i.e. no object floats in space). We also assume that the height of camera center is 1.6 meters away from the floor to obtain a metric 3D reconstruction.

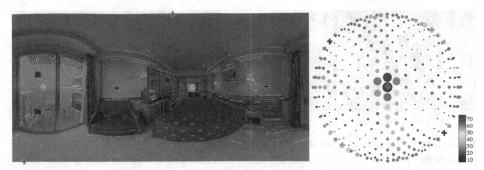

Fig. 3. Hough transform for vanishing point detection. The **left** image shows the detected edges and vanishing points. The colors indicate the edge directions. The **right** image shows the votes on each bin of the half sphere. The sizes and colors both indicate the number of votes.

on the detected line segments (Sec. 2.1). We then generate 3D room layout hypotheses from line detections and verify them with the computed geometric context and orientation map on the panorama (Sec. 2.2). For objects, we generate 3D cuboid hypotheses using rectangle detection and image segmentation (Sec. 2.3). Next, we use sampling to generate full scene hypotheses, each of which has a 3D room and multiple 3D objects inside (Sec. 2.4). To choose the best hypothesis that is supported by the image evidence and structurally meaningful (i.e. satisfying all context constraints), we extract various features and train a SVM to rank these hypotheses holistically (Sec. 2.5). Finally, we locally adjust the top hypothesis and search for a solution that maximizes the SVM score by adding, deleting and swapping an object.

2.1 Vanishing Point Estimation for Panoramas

We detect line segments on the panorama and use them to vote for the vanishing directions (Fig. 3). To take full advantage of previous line segment detection works on standard photo,we convert a panorama image to a set of perspective images, and run the state-of-the-art Line Segment Detection (LSD) algorithm [13] in each perspective image, and warp all detected line segments back to the panorama.

A line segment in 3D space corresponds to a section of a great circle on a sphere, and displays as a curve in panorama. For each line l, we use n to denote the normal of the plane where its great circle lies in. The vanishing direction v associated with the line l should be perpendicular to n. We use a hough transform [14] to find all vanishing directions. We uniformly divide the unit sphere into bins by recursively dividing triangles of a icosahedron. A line segments l will vote for a bin whose center n_b satisfies $n_b \cdot n = 0$. We then find three mutually orthogonal bins with maximal sum of votes as three vanishing directions. After that, we snap all line segments to align with their vanishing directions.

2.2 Room Layout Hypothesis Generation

Because the room layout is essential to generate good object cuboid hypotheses in 3D, we first obtain some good room layouts to reduce the burden of 3D object detection

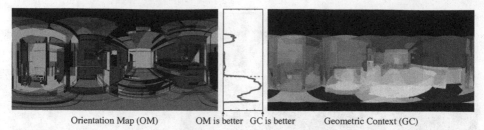

Orientation Map (OM)   OM is better GC is better   Geometric Context (GC)

Fig. 4. OM vs. GC. Here shows the OM and GC for the panorama image in Fig. 1. The curve at the center shows the accuracy comparison between OM and GC as the vertical view angle changes (data is from all training images). We can clearly see that OM is better at the upper part while GC is better at the lower part, and there is a clear threshold to combine them.

in the next step. We randomly generate many room layout hypotheses and keep those consistent with a pixel-wise surface normal direction map estimated on panorama.

A 3D room layout can be generated by sampling line segments as room corners [15]. Geometrically, five lines determine a cuboid in 3D space except some degenerative cases. We classify each line segment with two labels from top/bottom, front/back, and right/left according to its association to the vanishing directions, and randomly sample five non-degenerative lines to form a room layout hypothesis. To reduce the number of hypotheses while keeping the good ones, we use the surface normal consistency with a pixel-wise surface direction estimation from panorama to rank these hypotheses and choose the top 50 (since the recall starts to saturate around 50 in Fig. 11).

Orientation Map (OM) [16] and Geometric Context (GC) [15] provide pixel-wise surface normal estimation for ordinary perspective images. We convert a panorama into several overlapping perspective images, and apply OM and GC on these images respectively and project results back to the panorama. From our training data with manually marked ground truth wall orientations, we observe that GC provides better normal estimation at the bottom (probably because the model was trained using images looking slightly downwards), and OM works better at the top half of an image (probably less cluttered.), as shown in Fig. 4. Therefore, we combine the top part of OM and the bottom part of GC to evaluate the room layout. As can be seen from Fig. 11(left), the recall rate is significantly improved by combining OM and GC. Fig. 7 shows some good room layout hypotheses, which are generally very close to the ground truth.

2.3   3D Object Hypotheses Generation

After generating a set of good 3D room layout hypotheses, the next step is to generate 3D cuboid hypotheses for major objects in the room. To obtain high recall for hypotheses generation, we use two complementary approaches: a detection-based method to apply a 2D rectangle detector to the projections of a panorama along the three principle directions, and a segmentation-based method to segment the image and fit a 3D cuboid to each segment by sampling its boundaries.

Detection-Based Cuboid Generation: We project the input panorama orthographically to six axis-aligned views, and run a rectangle detector in each projection respectively (Fig. 5(top)). Our rectangle detector is similar as Deformable Part Model [2] but

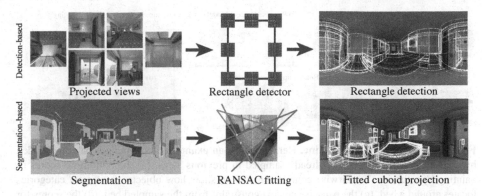

Fig. 5. Two ways to generate object hypotheses: detection and segmentation.

without spring-like constraints. We define a part at each corner and the middle of each edge of the rectangle. We use the SUN primitive dataset [17] containing 382 annotated cuboid images, and transform each cuboid surface to an axis aligned rectangle to train each part detector independently. During testing, we first compute the response maps of all part detectors, and sum up them according to the models. We set a low threshold to ensure high recall.We then generate cuboid hypotheses from the 3D rectangles.

Segmentation-Based Cuboid Generation: Some scene objects, such beds and sofas, do not have strong edges, and cannot be reliably detected by the rectangle detection. Therefore, we generate additional cuboid hypotheses from image segmentation (Fig. 5(bottom)) by selective search [4]. Specifically, for each segment, we evaluate how well its shape can be explained by the projection of a cuboid. We create many cuboids by randomly sampling 6 rays at the segment boundary passing through the three vanishing points. Among these cuboids, we choose the best one whose projection has the largest intersection over union score with the segment.

2.4 Whole-Room Scene Hypotheses Generation

After obtain a hypothesis pool for room layout and objects, we generate a pool of whole-room hypotheses, each consisting of a room layout with several cuboid objects inside. To achieve high recall with a manageble number of hypotheses, we classify the semantic meaning of each cuboid and use pairwise context constraints to guide our sampling.

Semantic Label: Intuitively, the semantic object type is strongly correlated with the cuboid shape and its 3D locations in the room. We train a random forest classifier to estimate the semantic type of a cuboid according to its size, aspect ratio and relative position in the room. And we achieve the multiple-label classification accuracy at around 70% This shows that the context between room and objects is very strong.

Pairwise Constraint: There are strong pairwise context constraints between scene objects. For instance, nightstands are usually nearby a bed, and a TV set often faces a bed. For two object types, we collect all instances of the pair $\{\langle \mathbf{p}_1, \mathbf{p}_2 \rangle\}$ from our training database. We register all these instances by a rotation in the ground plane to ensure the closest wall to $\mathbf{p}_1$ is on its left. We then take the displacement vector $\mathbf{p}_1 - \mathbf{p}_2$

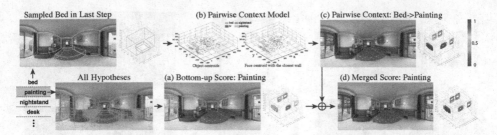

Fig. 6. Example sampling pipeline. Here we show an example of sampling a painting guided by context, given that a bed is already sampled in previous steps. (a) the bottom-up scores of painting hypotheses, (b) pairwise context statistics to show how objects of different categories locates around a bed, (c) the pairwise context constraint from the sampled bed, (d) the scores for merging bottom-up scores and pairwise context.

as a sample, and capture the pairwise location constraint by all collected samples. Such a set of samples are plotted in Fig. 6(a). When testing the validity of a pair of objects, we compute their displacement vector and search for the K nearest neighbors in the sample set. The mean distance to the K nearest neighbors will be transferred to a probability by a sigmoid function.

Whole-Room Sampling: We generate a complete scene hypothesis as following,

1. Randomly select a room layout according to their scores evaluated by GC and OM (higher score with a higher probability).
2. Decide the number of instances for each object type and the sampling order for different object types according to statistic prior. Fig. 6 shows an example of order list on left side.
3. Start from the first object. Search for cuboids of the selected object type, and randomly choose a cuboid according to bottom up score, e.g. rectangle detection score, semantic classifier score. Hypothesis with higher score would be sampled with higher probability.
4. Go to the next object, we combine the bottom-up scores and the pairwise context constraint with all the previously selected objects. A new object will be randomly selected according to merged scores. For example, the unary bottom-up score is effective in pruning invalid hypotheses (Fig. 6(a)), and pairwise score can further enhance it (Fig. 6(c)). As shown in Fig. 6(d), the rectangles on head of the bed are further highlighted, and those on windows are depressed. We can see the hypotheses around the true painting are all with high score and thus we have a higher chance to get a correct object.
5. Given all the sampled object so far, repeat the previous step until all the instances have been sampled.

Comparing with completely random sampling, our method can avoid obviously unreasonable scene hypotheses, and thus ensure high recall with a managable number of samples. Fig. 7 shows some sampling results.

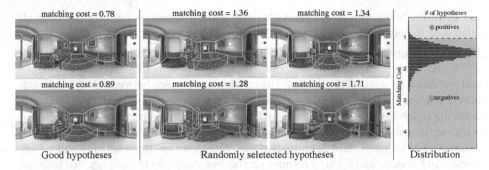

matching cost = 0.78 | matching cost = 1.36 | matching cost = 1.34 | # of hypotheses

⊕ positives

matching cost = 0.89 | matching cost = 1.28 | matching cost = 1.71 | ⊖ negatives

Good hypotheses | Randomly seletected hypotheses | Distribution

Fig. 7. Whole-room hypotheses. On the left we show some good hypotheses selected based on matching cost. At the center we show some random hypotheses to visualize the hypothesis space.

2.5 Data-Driven Holistic Ranking

After generating a large list of whole-room hypotheses, we train a SVM model to rank them and choose the best hypothesis, holistically for the whole-room.

Linear SVM: Our goal is to learn a mapping from a panorama $\mathbf{x}$ to a scene parsing result $\mathbf{y}$. Because $\mathbf{y}$ is a structural output, we formulate the problem as a 0-1 loss structural SVM [18], i.e. a binary linear SVM[3]. We define a feature vector $\mathbf{f}(\mathbf{x}, \mathbf{y})$ for a panorama $\mathbf{x}$ and its hypothesis $\mathbf{y}$. The binary label l indicates whether $\mathbf{y}$ is close enough to the manually annotated ground truth $\mathbf{y}^*$, i.e. $l = [\Delta(\mathbf{y}, \mathbf{y}^*) < \epsilon]$. During training, for each panorama $\mathbf{x}_n$, we sample M hypotheses $\{\mathbf{y}_n^m\}^{m=1,\cdots,M}$. We use all N panoramic images from our training set to train the binary SVM by MN pairs of $\{\langle \mathbf{f}(\mathbf{x}_n, \mathbf{y}_n^m), l_n^m \rangle\}_{n=1,\cdots,N}^{m=1,\cdots,M}$. Since we typically have hundreds of panoramas and thousands of hypotheses, there are about a million training data for the SVM[4]. During testing, the SVM score is used to choose the best hypothesis with maximal SVM score.

Matching Cost: $\Delta(\mathbf{y}, \mathbf{y}^*)$ measures the difference between a whole-room hypothesis $\mathbf{y}$ and its ground truth $\mathbf{y}^*$. We first register the two scenes by matching their vanishing directions and room centers. We compute the the average 3D distance between corresponding vertices between pairs of cuboids of the same semantic type, one from each scene. We search for bipartite matching minimal distance for each semantic label. $\Delta(\mathbf{y}, \mathbf{y}^*)$ is the sum of all bipartite matching distances plus the constant penalty for unmatched cuboids in both scenes. We use this score to decide the labels for the data to train the SVM. Because it is hard to find a good threshold, we choose two conservative

---

[3] We use a 0-1 loss structural SVM because the ranking among the bad hypotheses is unimportant, and we only want to find the best one. Our experiment also shows that it is very slow to train a general structural SVM using the standard cutting plane algorithm, and the general structural SVM is very sensitive to the loss function. A 0-1 loss structure SVM is basically a binary linear SVM that can be trained efficiently and is robust to the loss-function.

[4] To learn the SVM efficiently with less restriction on computation memory, we use all the positive data and randomly choose a subset of negative data to train an initial version of the SVM. We then repeatedly test the SVM on the remaining negative samples, and add the false positives into the SVM training, until there are no hard negatives (similar to hard negative mining in object detection [2]).

thresholds to make sure all positives are good and all negatives are bad. We drop all other data in between as we cannot tell their quality reliably.

Holistic Features: The feature vector $f(x, y)$ is a concatenation of object level feature f^{object} and room level feature f^{room}. Thus, it encodes both bottom-up image evidence and top-down contextual constraints. The relative importance between all the information is learned by the SVM in a data-driven way using the training data. f^{object} measures the reliability of each single object. On each object hypothesis, rectangle detector score, segmentation consistency score, sum/mean/std on each channel of OM and GC, entropy of color name, and 2D projected size (area on panorama sphere) will be extracted and concatenated into a column vector. For each object category, we take the sum/mean/max/min features of all instances in the category to form the feature vector. For categories with no object, we set the features zeros. We concatenate the features for all object categories to a single vector as f^{object} to form the holistic feature. Since the number of categories is fixed, the total dimension is also fixed.

Non-parametric Room Alignment: The room level feature f^{room} checks whether the hypothesized structure, i.e. the room layout and the arrangement of all objects, can be found in reality. We propose a non-parametric data-driven brute-force context model by aligning a hypothesis with the 3D rooms from the training set. Specifically, for a hypothesis y, we would match it with all manual annotations $\{y_1^*, y_2^*, \cdots, y_N^*\}$ in the training set. After registering two scenes, we can efficiently compute the distances between all pairs of cuboids in the two scenes. The distance is defined as a combination of center distance, volume intersection over union, and semantic type consistency. Since our training data has limited size, we apply various transformations T on the ground truth rooms to increase the database diversity. Specifically, we increase/decrease the size of the room, while keep the relative positions of all objects in room unchanged, or keep their absolute distance to a wall fixed. We further allow a universal scaling on the whole scene. The room level feature f^{room} is defined as the 10 smallest matching costs $\Delta(y, T(y_n^*))$ between a hypothsis y and these transformed rooms from the ground truth $\{T(y_n^*)\}$, and the accumulated sums and products of these 10 numbers.

Room-Only Color Model: To consider all the objects together, we divide image region to foreground (pixels covered by objects) and background (other pixels). In each regions, we extract the same feature defined in f^{object}. This provides context information integrating both bottom-up and top-down information, and it is part of f^{room}.

Local Adjustment: The top hypothesis returned by the SVM could be limited by the size of our hypothesis pool. So we apply a local refinement to the SVM returned hypothesis for a result with higher SVM score. Specifically, we can delete, add, or swap an object using the pairwise context constraints, or completely re-sample an object. If this generates a result with higher SVM score, we will accept the new result and perform local refinement again nearby the new result.

3   Experiments

3.1   Annotated 3D Panorama Dataset

We collected 700 full-view panoramas for home environments from SUN360 database [19], including 418 bedrooms and 282 living rooms. We split our dataset into two halves

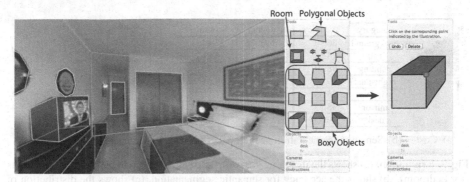

Fig. 8. Panoramic annotation tool. To annotate a 3D cuboid, the user picks a viewpoint from [Tools], and clicks on the key points of the 3D bounding boxes on the panorama. The screen displays an indication about what is the next corner to click on, as shown on the right.

for training and testing respectively.The data is manually annotated in house by five persons. After that, an author went through each image to correct mistakes and ensure consistency among the annotation.

To annotate panorama, we designed a WebGL annotation tool in browser, which renders a 360° panorama as a texture wrapped inside a sphere with the camera located at the center (Fig. 8). To annotate an object, the user first chooses one of the nine predefined viewpoints of a cuboid (shown in the black box in Fig. 8), because a different viewpoint requires a different set of vertices to be specified. When the user is marking these vertices, the interface will highlight the corresponding vertex on a 3D cuboid on the right. We ask the annotator to mark the 3D bounding box as tight as possible and align it with major orientations of the object. A key novelty of our tool is to first let the user to choose one of the nine predefined viewpoints for each cuboid object, and click each visible vertices guided by the instruction. We found that this interface is much easier to use than [17], where the viewpoint is implicit. For rectangular objects (e.g. painting), we annotate its four corners using a polygon tool. To label the room layout, we design a specialized primitive to ask the user to click the eight corners of the room.

We further convert 2D annotations to 3D scene models. Assuming each object is a perfect cuboid and can only rotate horizontally around a vertical axis. The task of generating 3D scene models amounts to find the parameters for each scene object to minimize the reprojection error between the 3D cuboid and annotations. Furthermore, we enforce each object can only be at one of the following positions, standing on the ground, sitting on another object, or attaching to a wall. We formulate all these constraints to a single non-linear optimization to minimize reprojection errors from all objects.

3.2 Evaluation

Some results for both bedroom and living rooms are shown in Fig. 10, where we can see that the algorithm performs reasonably.

Matching Cost to the Ground Truth: The most straightforward way for evaluation is to compare the prediction with the ground truth, using the matching cost that we

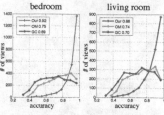

category	accuracy	category	accuracy
background	86.90	wardrobe	27.44
bed	78.58	tv	34.81
painting	38.70	door	19.40
nightstand	39.66	chair	9.61
window	35.58	sofa	11.10
mirror	38.15	cabinet	5.46
desk	29.55	average	35.00

(a) Cost   (b) Semantic segmentation accuracy (bedroom)   (c) Compare with regular FOV.

Fig. 9. Evaluation. (a) shows the matching cost distribution for the top hypotheses of our results (for bedroom). (b) shows the accuracy for semantic segmentation. (c) shows the distribution of views across different surface orientation prediction accuracy (see the supp. material for more).

defined to choose label for the SVM training in Sec. 2.5. The average matching cost is 1.23, which is much better than the pure bottom-up hypotheses generation (average cost is 1.55). We show the histogram for the distributions of the matching cost in Fig. 9(a).

Semantic Image Segmentation: We also covert the 3D understanding results into a semantic segmentation mask on the panorama images and compare the results with the ground truth as in PASCAL VOC segmentation challenge [3]. During conversion, we use the 3D bounding boxes of the objects to create a mask with occlusion testing. To avoid the artifact of panorama projection, instead of comparing panorama segmentation results, we uniformly sample rays of different orientation on the sphere and compare the label of the prediction and ground truth. Fig. 9(b) shows the accuracy.

4   How Important Is Larger FOV and Context?

To justify the importance of FOV for context model, we conduct five types of comparison. First, we show that a larger FOV provides stronger context to recover room layout.Second, we show that full-room context provides stronger cue for recognizing objects than an object detector, which classifies an image patch (i.e. small FOV). Third, we decompose our system and disable some key usages of global context information, to see the importance of context during sampling and ranking. Fourth, we vary the effective range of FOV in the context model to demonstrate the larger FOV enables stronger context. Finally, we combine our context model with standard object detectors, to demonstrate the complementary natural of context and local object appearance.

Is Larger FOV Helpful for Room Layout Estimation? To demonstrate the importance of panorama, we compare our algorithm with [16] and [15] on regular field-of-view images. We warp the panorama images into perspective images using 54.4° FOV, run [16] and [15] on these images to obtain surface orientation estimation for regular FOV images. We warp our result and the ground truth to these perspective views for comparison. From the comparison shown in Fig. 9(c), we can see that by using panorama, our algorithm significantly outperforms these results on regular FOV images.

room █ bed █ window █ door █ nightstand █ desk █ sofa █ chair █ coffee table
painting █ mirror █ cabinet █ wardrobe █ dining table █ tv stand █ end table █ tv

Fig. 10. Example results. The first column is the input panorama and the output object detection results. The second column contains intermediate steps for generating cuboid hypotheses from bottom-up sampling as well as the combination of OM and GC. The third column is the results visualized in 3D. (Best view in color. More results are available in the supplementary material.)

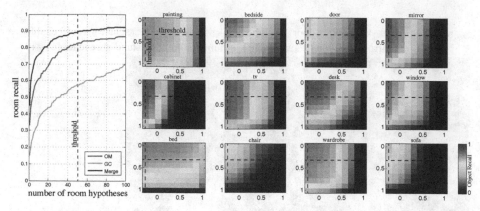

Fig. 11. Recall. Left: The room recall verse the number of top room hypotheses ranked by the OM, GC and our combination of OM and GC, which shows that merging OM and GC significantly improves the result and justifies that 50 is a good threshold. Right: The object recall w.r.t. the rectangle detection score (horizontal axes) and random forest score (vertical axes).

Is Context as Powerful as Local Image Appearance for Object Detection? Using only our top 1 prediction for each panorama images, we can compute the precision and recall for each object category. Therefore, we compare with the state-of-the-art object detector. We train DPM [2] using the SUN database [20]. To test it on panorama images, we warp a panorama into many regular perspective images and run the trained DPM on it. Fig. 12(a) shows the result of the comparison. We can see that our model performs better than DPM at many object categories. This demonstrates that by using only 3D contextual information without any image feature for categorization, we can still achieve a comparable performance with object detectors using image features.

Is Context Important in Sampling and Ranking? We disable the pairwise context model for sampling and the room alignment matching cost for ranking respectively and together to show the power of each one. In Fig. 12(a), the detection performances for nightstand and tv keep on decreasing when disabling more context model. These objects are usually in a common size and shape, and thus cannot be discriminated easily with bottom up image evidence. Context information can be especially useful under this situation. However, for painting and door, the performance does not change much. It could be that these objects usually have strong relations with the walls, and we didn't turn off the wall-object context, so the pairwise or high level context doesn't matter much. Such strong context between wall and objects further shows the advantage of using panorama, in which all the wall, floor, and ceiling are visible.

Is Larger FOV Better for Context? We narrow down the FOV that is allowed to for pairwise context model. Pair of cuboids far in term of FOV cannot affect each other by pairwise context model during the whole-room hypothesis sampling. Fig. 12(b) shows the F-score ($\sqrt{\text{precision} \times \text{recall}}$) of object detection w.r.t. different FOVs. We can see that the F-score curves are all in a decreasing tendency when the FOV is getting smaller. It shows that the big FOV is essential in providing more context information.

Is Context Complementary with Local Object Appearance? We combine to our model with object detector to answer this question. We run DPM on each object

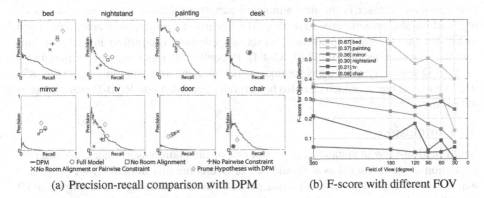

(a) Precision-recall comparison with DPM   (b) F-score with different FOV

Fig. 12. Object detection. (a) the performance of our system by partially disable some key usage of context, and the comparison with DPM. (b) F-score of our system with decreasing field of view. The performance becomes worse when the FOV is getting smaller.

hypothesis, and prune those with low score during the scene hypothesis sampling. The result is shown in Fig. 12(a). We can see that for categories on which both DPM and context perform well, merging them will achieve higher performance, like bed, tv, painting. It proves that the context information is complementary to image evidence. For categories that DPM does not work well, the improvement benefit from merging is very limited as expected, like mirror, desk. For the objects without much context, e.g. chair, though the performance is improved, it is still not comparable with DPM. Maybe this shows that context can hurt the detection performance for objects with flexible locations. Note that this is just a simple test to show the effect of merging DPM with our system, there are actually many parts in our model which can be improved by a strong image feature based detector. The confidence score from detector can be used as a power bottom up feature of object hypotheses during the sampling and holistic ranking.

5   Related Works

There are many exceptional works that inspired the design of our algorithm. The surface orientation and depth estimation from a single image is studied in [21–28]. The state-of-the-art of single view room layout estimation can be found in [15, 16, 29–51]. Our work extends them to full-view panorama to fully exploit the contextual information. There are also many great works that model context and object relations [52–63] and parse a scene [30, 64, 65] in a unified way. Although they have some success on reasoning about 3D, their main focus is still on 2D, while our context model is fully in 3D. For scene parsing grammar, several approaches such as And-Or graph, stochastic grammar, or probabilistic languages have been proposed [66–73]. Our data-driven sampling and discriminative training provides a simple but powerful way to combine the bottom-up image evidence and top-down context information. Same with our assumptions, 3D cuboids are also a popular representation for scene understanding [15, 17, 34, 47, 48, 74–76]. For object recognition datasets, there are several mainstream datasets that contain object annotation in regular pictures [3, 19, 20, 77–81].

Our panorama dataset is the first annotated panorama dataset for scene understanding, and we also provide ground truth in 3D. For using panoramas in computer vision tasks, there are several projects focus on scene viewpoint recognition, localization, image extrapolation and warping [19, 82–84]. Recently, the rapid increase of popularity of RGB-D sensors enables many seminar works on scene understanding in 3D [74, 85–94]. We expect our approach can also be naturally extended into RGB-D panoramas or 3D rooms [95].

6   Conclusion

Small field-of-view in standard cameras is one of the main reasons that contextual information is not as useful as it should be. To overcome this limitation, we propose a whole-room 3D context model that takes a 360° panorama as input and outputs a 3D bounding box of the room and detects all major objects inside. Experiments show that our model can recognize objects using only 3D contextual information without any image feature for categorization, and still achieves a comparable performance with the state-of-the-art object detector using image features for categorization. We showcase that the root of context model being under-utilized is partly because regular FOVs are too small, and that context is more powerful than we thought. We believe that this is a useful message, because our community is not fully aware that we make recognition more difficult than it should be.

References

1. Roberts, L.G.: Machine perception of 3-D solids. PhD thesis, Massachusetts Institute of Technology (1963)
2. Felzenszwalb, P.F., Girshick, R.B., McAllester, D., Ramanan, D.: Object detection with discriminatively trained part-based models. PAMI (2010)
3. Everingham, M., Van Gool, L., Williams, C.K., Winn, J., Zisserman, A.: The PASCAL visual object classes (voc) challenge. IJCV (2010)
4. Uijlings, J.R.R., van de Sande, K.E.A., Gevers, T., Smeulders, A.W.M.: Selective search for object recognition. IJCV (2013)
5. Wang, X., Yang, M., Zhu, S., Lin, Y.: Regionlets for generic object detection. In: ICCV (2013)
6. Girshick, R., Donahue, J., Darrell, T., Malik, J.: Rich feature hierarchies for accurate object detection and semantic segmentation. arXiv preprint arXiv:1311.2524 (2013)
7. Biederman, I.: On the semantics of a glance at a scene (1981)
8. Torralba, A.: Contextual influences on saliency (2004)
9. Lowe, D.G.: Distinctive image features from scale-invariant keypoints. IJCV (2004)
10. Brown, M., Lowe, D.G.: Recognising panoramas. In: ICCV (2003)
11. Brown, M., Lowe, D.G.: Automatic panoramic image stitching using invariant features. IJCV (2007)
12. Fan, R.E., Chang, K.W., Hsieh, C.J., Wang, X.R., Lin, C.J.: Liblinear: A library for large linear classification. JMLR (2008)
13. von Gioi, R.G., Jakubowicz, J., Morel, J.M., Randall, G.: LSD: a Line Segment Detector. Image Processing On Line (2012)
14. Hough, P.V.: Machine analysis of bubble chamber pictures. In: International Conference on High Energy Accelerators and Instrumentation, vol. 73 (1959)

15. Hedau, V., Hoiem, D., Forsyth, D.: Recovering the spatial layout of cluttered rooms. In: ICCV (2009)
16. Lee, D.C., Hebert, M., Kanade., T.: Geometric reasoning for single image structure recovery. In: CVPR (2009)
17. Xiao, J., Russell, B.C., Torralba, A.: Localizing 3D cuboids in single-view images. In: NIPS (2012)
18. Joachims, T., Finley, T., Yu, C.N.J.: Cutting-plane training of structural svms. In: Machine Learning (2009)
19. Xiao, J., Ehinger, K.A., Oliva, A., Torralba, A.: Recognizing scene viewpoint using panoramic place representation. In: CVPR (2012)
20. Xiao, J., Hays, J., Ehinger, K.A., Oliva, A., Torralba, A.: SUN database: Large-scale scene recognition from abbey to zoo. In: CVPR (2010)
21. Delage, E., Lee, H., Ng, A.Y.: Automatic single-image 3D reconstructions of indoor man-hattan world scenes. In: ISRR (2005)
22. Coughlan, J.M., Yuille, A.: Manhattan world: Compass direction from a single image by bayesian inference. In: ICCV (1999)
23. Hoiem, D.: Seeing the world behind the image: spatial layout for 3D scene understanding. PhD thesis, Carnegie Mellon University (2007)
24. Saxena, A., Sun, M., Ng, A.: Make3D: Learning 3D scene structure from a single still image. PAMI (2009)
25. Hoiem, D., Efros, A.A., Hebert, M.: Automatic photo pop-up. TOG (2005)
26. Hoiem, D., Efros, A.A., Hebert, M.: Putting objects in perspective. IJCV (2008)
27. Hoiem, D., Efros, A.A., Hebert, M.: Closing the loop in scene interpretation. In: CVPR (2008)
28. Hoiem, D., Efros, A.A., Hebert, M.: Geometric context from a single image. In: ICCV (2005)
29. Gupta, A., Satkin, S., Efros, A.A., Hebert, M.: From scene geometry to human workspace. In: CVPR (2011)
30. Han, F., Zhu, S.C.: Bottom-up/top-down image parsing by attribute graph grammar. In: ICCV (2005)
31. Zhao, Y.: chun Zhu, S.: Image parsing with stochastic scene grammar. In: NIPS (2011)
32. Wang, H., Gould, S., Koller, D.: Discriminative learning with latent variables for cluttered indoor scene understanding. In: Daniilidis, K., Maragos, P., Paragios, N. (eds.) ECCV 2010, Part II. LNCS, vol. 6312, pp. 435–449. Springer, Heidelberg (2010)
33. Yu, S., Zhang, H., Malik, J.: Inferring spatial layout from a single image via depth-ordered grouping. In: IEEE Workshop on Perceptual Organization in Computer Vision (2008)
34. Hedau, V., Hoiem, D., Forsyth, D.: Thinking inside the box: Using appearance models and context based on room geometry. In: Daniilidis, K., Maragos, P., Paragios, N. (eds.) ECCV 2010, Part VI. LNCS, vol. 6316, pp. 224–237. Springer, Heidelberg (2010)
35. Lee, D.C., Gupta, A., Hebert, M., Kanade, T.: Estimating spatial layout of rooms using vol-umetric reasoning about objects and surfaces. In: NIPS (2010)
36. Pero, L.D., Guan, J., Brau, E., Schlecht, J., Barnard, K.: Sampling bedrooms. In: CVPR (2011)
37. Yu, L.F., Yeung, S.K., Tang, C.K., Terzopoulos, D., Chan, T.F., Osher, S.: Make it home: automatic optimization of furniture arrangement. TOG (2011)
38. Pero, L.D., Bowdish, J.C., Fried, D., Kermgard, B.D., Hartley, E.L., Barnard, K.: Bayesian geometric modelling of indoor scenes. In: CVPR (2012)
39. Hedau, V., Hoiem, D., Forsyth, D.: Recovering free space of indoor scenes from a single image. In: CVPR (2012)
40. Schwing, A.G., Hazan, T., Pollefeys, M., Urtasun, R.: Efficient structured prediction for 3D indoor scene understanding. In: CVPR (2012)

41. Xiao, J., Hays, J., Russell, B.C., Patterson, G., Ehinger, K., Torralba, A., Oliva, A.: Basic level scene understanding: Categories, attributes and structures. Frontiers in Psychology (2013)

42. Guo, R., Hoiem, D.: Beyond the line of sight: Labeling the underlying surfaces. In: Fitzgibbon, A., Lazebnik, S., Perona, P., Sato, Y., Schmid, C. (eds.) ECCV 2012, Part V. LNCS, vol. 7576, pp. 761–774. Springer, Heidelberg (2012)

43. Satkin, S., Hebert, M.: 3DNN: Viewpoint invariant 3D geometry matching for scene understanding. In: ICCV (2013)

44. Satkin, S., Lin, J., Hebert, M.: Data-driven scene understanding from 3D models. In: BMVC (2012)

45. Choi, W., Chao, Y.W., Pantofaru, C., Savarese, S.: Understanding indoor scenes using 3D geometric phrases. In: CVPR (2013)

46. Del Pero, L., Bowdish, J., Kermgard, B., Hartley, E., Barnard, K.: Understanding bayesian rooms using composite 3D object models. In: CVPR (2013)

47. Zhao, Y., Zhu, S.C.: Scene parsing by integrating function, geometry and appearance models. In: CVPR (2013)

48. Schwing, A.G., Fidler, S., Pollefeys, M., Urtasun, R.: Box in the box: Joint 3D layout and object reasoning from single images (2013)

49. Schwing, A.G., Urtasun, R.: Efficient exact inference for 3D indoor scene understanding. In: Fitzgibbon, A., Lazebnik, S., Perona, P., Sato, Y., Schmid, C. (eds.) ECCV 2012, Part VI. LNCS, vol. 7577, pp. 299–313. Springer, Heidelberg (2012)

50. Chao, Y.-W., Choi, W., Pantofaru, C., Savarese, S.: Layout estimation of highly cluttered indoor scenes using geometric and semantic cues. In: Petrosino, A. (ed.) ICIAP 2013, Part II. LNCS, vol. 8157, pp. 489–499. Springer, Heidelberg (2013)

51. Furlan, A., Miller, D., Sorrenti, D.G., Fei-Fei, L., Savarese, S.: Free your camera: 3D indoor scene understanding from arbitrary camera motion. In: BMVC (2013)

52. Rabinovich, A., Vedaldi, A., Galleguillos, C., Wiewiora, E., Belongie, S.: Objects in context. In: ICCV (2007)

53. Tu, Z.: Auto-context and its application to high-level vision tasks. In: CVPR (2008)

54. Choi, M.J., Torralba, A., Willsky, A.S.: A tree-based context model for object recognition. PAMI (2012)

55. Choi, M.J., Torralba, A., Willsky, A.S.: Context models and out-of-context objects. Pattern Recognition Letters (2012)

56. Choi, M.J., Lim, J.J., Torralba, A., Willsky, A.S.: Exploiting hierarchical context on a large database of object categories. In: CVPR (2010)

57. Desai, C., Ramanan, D., Fowlkes, C.C.: Discriminative models for multi-class object layout. IJCV (2011)

58. Ladicky, L., Russell, C., Kohli, P., Torr, P.H.S.: Graph cut based inference with co-occurrence statistics. In: Daniilidis, K., Maragos, P., Paragios, N. (eds.) ECCV 2010, Part V. LNCS, vol. 6315, pp. 239–253. Springer, Heidelberg (2010)

59. Sudderth, E.B., Torralba, A., Freeman, W.T., Willsky, A.S.: Describing visual scenes using transformed objects and parts. IJCV (2008)

60. Sudderth, E.B., Torralba, A., Freeman, W.T., Willsky, A.S.: Depth from familiar objects: A hierarchical model for 3D scenes. In: CVPR (2006)

61. Sudderth, E., Torralba, A., Freeman, W., Willsky, A.: Describing visual scenes using transformed dirichlet processes. In: NIPS (2005)

62. Sudderth, E.B., Torralba, A., Freeman, W.T., Willsky, A.S.: Learning hierarchical models of scenes, objects, and parts. In: ICCV (2005)

63. Sudderth, E.B., Jordan, M.I.: Shared segmentation of natural scenes using dependent pitman-yor processes. In: NIPS (2008)

64. Li, C., Kowdle, A., Saxena, A., Chen, T.: Towards holistic scene understanding: Feedback enabled cascaded classification models. PAMI (2012)
65. Heitz, G., Gould, S., Saxena, A., Koller, D.: Cascaded classification models: Combining models for holistic scene understanding. In: NIPS (2008)
66. Wu, T., Zhu, S.C.: A numerical study of the bottom-up and top-down inference processes in and-or graphs. IJCV (2011)
67. Battaglia, P.W., Hamrick, J.B., Tenenbaum, J.B.: Simulation as an engine of physical scene understanding. Proceedings of the National Academy of Sciences (2013)
68. Tenenbaum, J.B., Kemp, C., Griffiths, T.L., Goodman, N.D.: How to grow a mind: Statistics, structure, and abstraction. Science (2011)
69. Mansinghka, V.K., Kulkarni, T.D., Perov, Y.N., Tenenbaum, J.B.: Approximate bayesian image interpretation using generative probabilistic graphics programs. In: NIPS (2013)
70. Han, F., Zhu, S.C.: Bottom-up/top-down image parsing with attribute grammar. PAMI (2009)
71. Tu, Z., Chen, X., Yuille, A.L., Zhu, S.C.: Image parsing: Unifying segmentation, detection, and recognition. IJCV (2005)
72. Li, L.J., Socher, R., Fei-Fei, L.: Towards total scene understanding: Classification, annotation and segmentation in an automatic framework. In: CVPR (2009)
73. Li, L.J., Su, H., Xing, E.P., Li, F.F.: Object bank: A high-level image representation for scene classification & semantic feature sparsification. In: NIPS (2010)
74. Lin, D., Fidler, S., Urtasun, R.: Holistic scene understanding for 3D object detection with rgbd cameras. In: ICCV (2013)
75. Fidler, S., Dickinson, S.J., Urtasun, R.: 3D object detection and viewpoint estimation with a deformable 3d cuboid model. In: NIPS (2012)
76. Xiao, J., Furukawa, Y.: Reconstructing the world's museums. IJCV (2014)
77. Russell, B.C., Torralba, A., Murphy, K.P., Freeman, W.T.: LabelMe: a database and web-based tool for image annotation. IJCV (2008)
78. Bell, S., Upchurch, P., Snavely, N., Bala, K.: OpenSurfaces: a richly annotated catalog of surface appearance. TOG (2013)
79. Deng, J., Dong, W., Socher, R., Li, L.J., Li, K., Fei-Fei, L.: Imagenet: A large-scale hierarchical image database. In: CVPR (2009)
80. Shotton, J., Winn, J., Rother, C., Criminisi, A.: TextonBoost for image understanding: Multiclass object recognition and segmentation by jointly modeling texture, layout, and context. IJCV (2009)
81. Russell, B.C., Torralba, A.: Building a database of 3D scenes from user annotations. In: CVPR (2009)
82. Ni, K., Kannan, A., Criminisi, A., Winn, J.: Epitomic location recognition. In: CVPR (2008)
83. Zhang, Y., Xiao, J., Hays, J., Tan, P.: Framebreak: Dramatic image extrapolation by guided shift-maps. In: CVPR (2013)
84. He, K., Chang, H., Sun, J.: Rectangling panoramic images via warping. TOG (2013)
85. Song, S., Xiao, J.: Sliding shapes for 3D object detection in depth images. In: Fleet, D., Pajdla, T., Schiele, B., Tuytelaars, T. (eds.) ECCV 2014. LNCS, vol. 8694, pp. 647–664. Springer, Heidelberg (2014)
86. Wu, Z., Song, S., Khosla, A., Tang, X., Xiao, J.: 3D ShapeNets for 2.5D object recognition and Next-Best-View prediction. ArXiv e-prints (2014)
87. Guo, R., Hoiem, D.: Support surface prediction in indoor scenes (2013)
88. Gupta, S., Arbelaez, P., Malik, J.: Perceptual organization and recognition of indoor scenes from rgb-d images. In: CVPR (2013)
89. Silberman, N., Hoiem, D., Kohli, P., Fergus, R.: Indoor segmentation and support inference from RGBD images. In: Fitzgibbon, A., Lazebnik, S., Perona, P., Sato, Y., Schmid, C. (eds.) ECCV 2012, Part V. LNCS, vol. 7576, pp. 746–760. Springer, Heidelberg (2012)

90. Jiang, H., Xiao, J.: A linear approach to matching cuboids in RGBD images. In: CVPR (2013)
91. Kim, B., Kohli, P., Savarese, S.: 3D scene understanding by Voxel-CRF. In: ICCV (2013)
92. Zhang, J., Kan, C., Schwing, A.G., Urtasun, R.: Estimating the 3D layout of indoor scenes and its clutter from depth sensors. In: ICCV (2013)
93. Jia, Z., Gallagher, A., Saxena, A., Chen, T.: 3D-based reasoning with blocks, support, and stability. In: CVPR (2013)
94. Zheng, B., Zhao, Y., Yu, J.C., Ikeuchi, K., Zhu, S.C.: Beyond point clouds: Scene understanding by reasoning geometry and physics. In: CVPR (2013)
95. Xiao, J., Owens, A., Torralba, A.: SUN3D: A database of big spaces reconstructed using sfm and object labels. In: ICCV (2013)

Unfolding an Indoor Origami World

David Ford Fouhey, Abhinav Gupta, and Martial Hebert

The Robotics Institute, Carnegie Mellon University

Abstract. In this work, we present a method for single-view reasoning about 3D surfaces and their relationships. We propose the use of mid-level constraints for 3D scene understanding in the form of convex and concave edges and introduce a generic framework capable of incorporating these and other constraints. Our method takes a variety of cues and uses them to infer a consistent interpretation of the scene. We demonstrate improvements over the state-of-the art and produce interpretations of the scene that link large planar surfaces.

1 Introduction

Over the last few years, advances in single-image 3D scene understanding have been driven by two threads of research. The first thread asks the basic representation question: What are the right primitives to extract local likelihoods of surface orientation? From geometric context [12] to recent papers on data-driven 3D primitives [6], most approaches in this thread have focused on using large amounts of labeled data to train appearance-based models for orientation likelihoods. While there have been enormous performance gains, these approaches are fundamentally limited by their local nature. The second thread that has pushed the envelope of 3D understanding focuses on reasoning. These approaches stitch together local likelihoods to create a global understanding of the scene. Some include conditional random field (CRF)-based smoothness reasoning [26], cuboidal room layout [10] and volumetric representation of objects [8,22], 3D objects [35], and groups of objects [1,40,41].

Most efforts in reasoning have used either local domain-agnostic constraints or global domain-specific constraints. For instance, CRF-based approaches include the constraint that regions with similar appearance should have similar orientation. These end up, however, enforcing little more than smoothness. This has led to high-level top-down constraints given by domain-specific knowledge. For example, most indoor approaches assume a Manhattan world in which the surface normals lie on three principal directions [3]. Second only to the Manhattan-world constraint is the cuboidal room constraint, in which the camera is assumed to be inside a cube and inference becomes predicting the cube's extent [10]. While this has been enormously influential, the camera-inside-a-box representation leaves the interior and most interesting parts of the scene, for instance furniture, uninterpreted. Recent work has aimed at overcoming this by finding volumetric primitives inside scenes, conventionally cuboids [8,22,36,31], and in simple scenes

D. Fleet et al. (Eds.): ECCV 2014, Part VI, LNCS 8694, pp. 687–702, 2014.

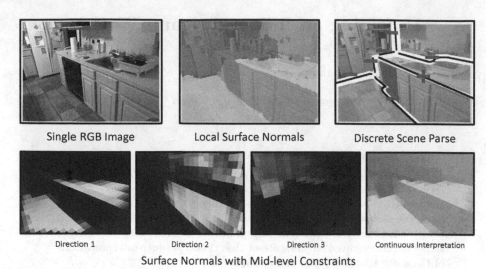

Single RGB Image   Local Surface Normals   Discrete Scene Parse

Direction 1   Direction 2   Direction 3   Continuous Interpretation

Surface Normals with Mid-level Constraints

Fig. 1. We propose the use of mid-level constraints from the line-labeling era and a parametrization of indoor layout to "unfold" a 3D interpretation of the scene in the form of large planar surfaces and the edges that join them. In contrast to local per-pixel normals, we return a discrete parse of the scene in terms of surfaces and the edges between them in the style of Kanade's Origami World as well updated continuous evidence integrating these constraints. **Normal legend: blue → X;** green → Y; red → Z. **Edge Legend: convex +; concave −. Figures best viewed in color.**

such as the UIUC dataset of [10], cuboid representations have increased the robustness of 3D scene understanding. Nonetheless, cuboid-based object reasoning is fundamentally limited by its input, local likelihoods, and it is not clear that it generalizes well to highly cluttered scenes.

In this paper, we propose an alternate idea: while there have been great efforts and progress in both low and high-level reasoning, one missing piece is mid-level constraints. Reasoning is not a one-shot process, and it requires constraints at different levels of granularity. For cluttered and realistic scenes, before we can go to cuboids, we need to a way to piece together local evidence into large planar surfaces and join them with edges. This work aims to address this problem.

These mid-level constraints linking together planes via convex and concave edges have been extensively studied in the past. There is a vast line-labeling literature (e.g., classic works [2,14,34]); among these works, we are principally inspired by Kanade's landmark Origami World paper [18], which reasoned directly about surfaces as first-class objects and the edges between them. As systems, line-labeling efforts failed due to weak low-level cues and a lack of probabilistic reasoning techniques; however, they hold a great deal of valuable insight.

Inspired by these pioneering efforts, we introduce mid-level constraints based on convex and concave edges and show how these edges help link multiple surfaces in a scene. Our contributions include: (a) a generic framework and novel

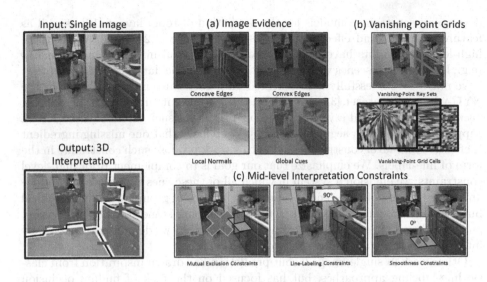

Input: Single Image   (a) Image Evidence   (b) Vanishing Point Grids

Concave Edges   Convex Edges   Vanishing-Point Ray Sets

Output: 3D Interpretation   Local Normals   Global Cues   Vanishing-Point Grid Cells

(c) Mid-level Interpretation Constraints

90°

0°

Mutual Exclusion Constraints   Line-Labeling Constraints   Smoothness Constraints

Fig. 2. Overview of the proposed approach. (Left) We take a single image of an indoor scene and produce a 3D interpretation in terms of surfaces and the edges that join them. (Right) We accumulate evidence from inferred surface normal discontinuities in the scene (convex blue, concave green), local surface normals, and room layout. (b) We formulate the problem as assembling a coherent interpretation from a collection of vanishing-point aligned grids. (c) This interpretation must respect observed edges joining segments as well as constraints such as mutual exclusion and smoothness.

parametrization of superpixels that helps to incorporate likelihoods and constraints at all levels of reasoning; (b) the introduction of mid-level constraints for 3D scene understanding as well as methods for finding evidence for them; (c) a richer mid-level interpretation of scenes compared to local normal likelihoods that can act as a stepping-stone for subsequent high-level volumetric reasoning.

2   Related Work

Determining the 3D layout of a scene has been a core computer vision problem since its inception, beginning with Robert's ambitious 1965 "Blocks World" thesis [28]. Early work such as [2,14] often assumed a simple model in which the perceptual grouping problem was solved and there were no nuisance factors. Thus, the 3D layout problem could be posed as constraint satisfaction over the visible lines. These methods, however, failed to pan out in natural images because the actual image formation process is much more noisy than was assumed.

After many decades without success, general 3D layout inference in relatively unconstrained images began making remarkable progress [5,11,12,29] in the mid-2000s, powered by the availability of training data. This sparked a renaissance during which progress started being made on a variety of long-standing 3D understanding problems. In the indoor world, a great deal of effort went into developing constrained models for the prediction of room layout [10] as well as features [6,23,27] and effective methods for inference [4,22,31,32]. While these high-level constraints have been enormously successful in constrained domains (e.g., less cluttered scenes with visible floors such as the datasets of [10,38]), they have not been successfully demonstrated on highly cluttered scenes such as the NYU v2 Depth Dataset [33]. Indeed, on these scenes, it turns out to be difficult *even with depth* to find a variety of simple primitives such as cuboids [16,17,39], support surfaces [7], or segmentations [9]. We believe that one missing ingredient is effective mid-level constraints, and in this work propose such constraints in the form of line-labels. We emphasize that our goal is to complement prior high-level constraints: we envision a system in which all of these cues cooperate to produce an understanding of the scene at a number of levels of grouping in a hierarchical but feedback manner. This work acts as a stepping stone towards this vision, and introduces a framework for layout estimation that we demonstrate can easily integrate constraints from a variety of levels.

Other work in single-image layout prediction has drawn inspiration from classic line-labeling approaches, but has focused on the task of finding occlusion boundaries [13,15,24]. While important, occlusion boundaries only provide a 2.1D sketch (e.g., like [25]) and provide no information in a single image about the surface orientation without their complementary normal discontinuity labels. In this work, we focus on this other class of labels, namely convex and concave edges. These have been applied in the context of stereo [37], but have largely been ignored in the single-image layout community, apart from work on shape recovery using hand-marked folds [19].

3   Overview

In this work, our goal is: given a single image, group pixels into planes, and infer the orientations of these planes and the convex/concave nature of edges. Similar to previous indoor scene understanding approaches, we assume a Manhattan world, which restricts the orientation of planes to three principal directions. Generally, this constraint is implicitly encoded by first grouping pixels into regions via appearance and then solving the surface normal problem as a 3-way classification problem. Our key idea is to reformulate the problem and solve the grouping and classification problem jointly by using top-down superpixels. Given the estimated vanishing points, we determine three possible grids of superpixels aligned with these vanishing points and the problem of classification becomes finding the "active" grid cell at every pixel.

Inferring the active grid cells using image evidence is a severely underconstrained problem, like most single image 3D tasks. Therefore, we include a variety of constraints based on (a) mutual exclusion; (b) appearance and smoothness; (c) convex/concave edge likelihoods; and (d) global room layout. Some are enforced as a unary, while others, such as (c), are binary in nature. Our objective is therefore a quadratic with mutual exclusion constraints. Additionally, the superpixel variables must be integer if one wants a single interpretation of each pixel

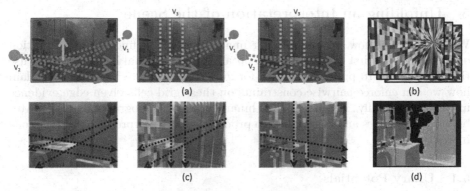

Fig. 3. Parametrization of the method. (a) We sweep rays (dotted lines) from each vanishing point, defining a pencil of lines. The intersection of two pencils of lines defines a superpixel with normal (solid line) perpendicular to the normals of the generating vanishing points. (b) We represent layout by activations of these superpixel grids. (c) We show the likelihoods on each grid cell for the ground truth surface normals (d).

(1 corresponding to active, 0 to non-active). The resulting problem is thus NP-hard in general. We propose to optimize both the integral and relaxed problems: integral solutions are themselves rich inferences about the scene, but we believe the relaxed solutions can act as inputs to higher-level reasoning processes.

We formalize our parametrization of the problem in Section 4 and discuss how we combine all the available evidence into one model in Section 5. Finally, we introduce an approach to finding surface normal discontinuities in Section 6.

4   Parametrization

The first step in our approach is estimating the vanishing points and creating grid cells in 3 principal directions. These act as superpixels defined by geometry rather than appearance. These grids are generated by sweeping rays from pairs of vanishing points, as shown in Fig. 3. The orientation of cells in the grids is defined by the normal orthogonal to the two generating vanishing points. Thus, a cell not only defines a grouping but also an orientation. Therefore any interpretation of the scene in terms of Manhattan-world surface normals that respects this grid can be represented as a binary vector $\mathbf{x}$ encoding which grid cells are active. To illustrate this, we show the likelihoods for the ground truth over grid cells in Fig. 3 (c). This formulation generalizes many previous parametrization of the 3D layout problem, for instance the parametrization proposed in [10,31]. As we demonstrate with our potentials, our parametrization enables the easy arbitration between beliefs about layout encoded at every pixel such as [6,20] and beliefs encoded parametrically, such as room layouts or cuboids [10,22,31]. Note that our grids overlap, but only one grid cell can be active at each pixel location; we enforce this with a mutual exclusion constraint.

5   Unfolding an Interpretation of the Scene

We now present how we combine our image evidence to find an interpretation of the scene. We first explain how we obtain surface normal likelihoods and use them as unaries to provide evidence for grid cells in Sec. 5.1. We then explain how we can enforce pairwise constraints on these grid cells given edge evidence in Sec. 5.2. Finally, we introduce a binary quadratic program that arbitrates between these cues and constraints to produce a final interpretation of the scene in Sec. 5.3.

5.1   Unary Potentials

The first kind of cue for finding whether grid cell i is active ($x_i = 1$) or not ($x_i = 0$) is local evidence at the grid cell location. In this work, we use two complementary cues based on techniques for inferring evidence of surface normals and transform them into potentials that capture how much we should prefer x_i to take the value 1. Recall that every grid cell represents not only a grouping but also an orientation, and therefore one can easily convert between likelihoods for orientation at a location and likelihoods of each grid cell being activated.

Local evidence: A wide variety of approaches have been proposed for estimating local surface normal likelihoods from image evidence. We adopt the top-performing approach for doing this, Data-driven 3D Primitives [6] (3DP), which builds a bank of detectors that are associated with local surface configurations. At test time, the method convolves the bank with the image at multiple scales and transfers the associated local surface configuration to the test image wherever each detector has a high response. We soft-assign each pixel to each grid, producing a probability map of each orientation over the image. The local evidence potential of a grid cell i $\phi_{\text{local}}(i)$ is the probability of its orientation averaged over its support.

Global room-fitting evidence: Global room fitting constraints have been important and successful in the single image 3D understanding community. These seek to model the room as a vanishing-point-aligned box. We run the room-fitting method of Hedau et al. [10], which produces a ranked collection of 3D cuboid room hypotheses, where each wall corresponds to one of our grids' directions. At every pixel, we build a histogram of each direction, weighted by the inverse of the rank of the room and suppressing pixels predicted as clutter. The room-fitting evidence potential of a grid cell i $\phi_{\text{room}}(i)$ is the frequency of its orientation averaged over its support.

5.2   Binary Potentials

The second kind of cue for whether a cell i is active or not comes from considering it in conjunction with its neighbors. We use binary potentials characterizing preferences for pairs of grid cells. These operate within the same grid (i.e., on cells of the same orientation) and across grids (i.e., on cells with different orientations). These allow us to probabilistically integrate mid-level constraints via

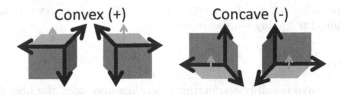

Fig. 4. A subset of valid arrangements in the image plane of surfaces (colors) and convex and concave edges (black) in our scene interpretation method with a gray surface normal arrow for disambiguation

convex and concave edges. In this section, we describe our potential for achieving this as well as a standard appearance smoothness potential.

Line-labeling: The presence of a convex or concave edge tells us not only that a discontinuity may exist, but also what sorts of labels can occur on either side. For instance, in Manhattan-world scenes, a convex edge at the top of a counter tells us there is a horizontal surface above and a vertical surface below. Because this edge constrains the labels of adjoining surfaces, it is more powerful than a simple smoothness term, which would only permit a labeling change at the edge.

We therefore include a potential that combines inferred convex and concave edges with a dictionary of surface configurations to reward interpretations of the scene in terms of grid cell activations that match our assumptions and available image evidence. We present a basic method for obtaining evidence of convexity and concavity in Section 6, but our potential is agnostic to the source of evidence.

We build an explicit enumeration of arrangements in the image plane that satisfy observing a scene formed by continuous Manhattan-world aligned polyhedra, e.g., a concave edge joining two vertical surfaces with the rightwards facing surface on the left. One half of the preferred arrangements is displayed in Fig. 4; the other half is an analogous y-inverted set. Some scenes may not satisfy our assumptions about the world and our image evidence may be wrong, and we therefore do not make hard decisions as in past line-labeling work [2,14,18], but instead form a potential encouraging interpretations that agree with our beliefs. Specifically, given two grid cells with different orientations, we can determine what edge we expect to see in our dictionary, and reward the mutual activation of the two grid cells if we see that edge. We use the potential $\psi_{\text{line}}(i, j) = \exp(-\beta_{line}e_{i,j}^2)$ where $e_{i,j}$ is the inferred probability of that edge from image evidence (i.e., mean image evidence over the edge joining two superpixels). We compute this potential over adjacent pairs of grid cells (i.e., sharing a vanishing point ray) but with different orientations. We compute this separately for convex and concave edges, letting the learning procedure decide their weight.

Smoothness: Adjacent and similar looking parts of the scene should generally have similar labels. As is common in the segmentation literature, we use a Potts-like model: we compute color histograms over LAB space (10 bins per dimension) for grid cells i and j, yielding histograms h_i and h_j; the potential is $\psi_{\text{smooth}}(i, j) = \exp(-d(h_i, h_j)^2)$, where d is the χ^2 distance. We compute the potential over adjacent grid cells with the same orientation, rewarding similarly colored regions for having similar orientation.

5.3   Inference

We need to resolve possibly conflicting potentials and infer the best interpretation of the scene given the available evidence. Mathematically, we formulate this as an optimization over a vector $\mathbf{x} \in \{0,1\}^n$, where each x_i represents whether grid cell i is active and where $\mathbf{x}$ contains the grid cells from all grids.

Our unary potentials $\{\mathbf{u}_i\}$ and binary potentials $\{\mathbf{B}_j\}$ are collated as a vector $\mathbf{c} = \sum_k \lambda_k \mathbf{u}_k$ and matrix $\mathbf{H} = \sum_l \alpha_l \mathbf{B}_l$ respectively, where c_i and $H_{i,j}$ respectively represent the costs of turning grid cell i on and the cost of turning both grid cell i and j on. Since two active overlapping cells imply that their pixels have two interpretations, we add a mutual-exclusion constraint. This is enforced on cells i and j that are on different grids and have sufficient overlap ($|\cap|/|\cup| \geq 0.2$ in all experiments). This can be formulated as a linear constraint $x_i + x_j \leq 1$. Finally, since our output is in the image plane and our cells are not all the same size, we weight the unary potentials by their support size and binaries by the minimum size of the cells involved.

Our final optimization is a binary quadratic program,

$$\underset{\mathbf{x} \in \{0,1\}^n}{\arg\max} \, \mathbf{c}^T \mathbf{x} + \mathbf{x}^T \mathbf{H} \mathbf{x} \quad \text{s.t.} \quad \mathbf{C}\mathbf{x} \leq \mathbf{1}, \tag{1}$$

where $\mathbf{C}$ stacks the mutual-exclusion linear constraints. Inference of this class of problems is NP-hard; we obtain a solution with the Gurobi solver, which first solves a continuous relaxation of Eqn. 1 and then performs a branch-and-bound search to produce an integral solution. The relaxed solution also acts as an updated belief about the scene, and may serve as a cue for the next layer of scene reasoning. We learn trade-off parameters $\{\lambda_k\}$, $\{\alpha_l\}$ by grid-search for each of the five potentials on a reduced set of images in the training set.

6   Finding Convex and Concave Edges

Our method needs a source of convex and concave edges in a scene. In this section, we describe a simple method for obtaining them. We produce surface normal discontinuity maps from depth data and adapt the 3D Primitives approach [6] to transfer oriented surface normal discontinuities.

We begin by generating surface normal discontinuity labels for our method. We sweep a half-disc at 8 orientations at 7 scales over the image to get cross-disc normal angles at every pixel and orientation. These are noisy at each scale, but the stable ones (i.e., low variance over all scales), tend to be high quality. Example normal discontinuity labels are shown in Fig. 5.

Given this data, we use a simple transfer method to infer labels for a new scene with a bank of 3D primitive detectors from [6]. Each detector is associated with a set of bounding boxes corresponding to the locations on which the detector was

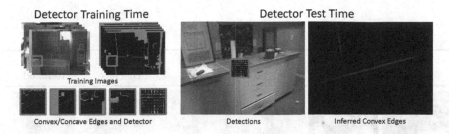

Fig. 5. An illustration of our approach for finding surface normal discontinuities. At training time, we automatically compute surface normal discontinuity maps (convex blue, concave green, missing data gray). At test time, we run a bank of 3D primitive detectors in the image; these detectors are trained to recognize a set of patches. We transfer the convex and concave edge patches associated with each detector.

trained. In the original approach, the surface normals in these boxes were transferred to new images. Instead of transferring surface normals, we transfer the normal discontinuity label, separating by type (convex/concave) and orientation (8 orientations). Thus edge probabilities only accumulate if the detections agree on both type and orientation. At every pixel, the empirical frequency of normal discontinuity labels gives a probability of each edge type at each orientation. This is complementary to the local evidence unary: at the corner of a room, for instance, while a set of detectors may not agree on the specific surface normal configuration, they might agree that there is a concave edge.

7   Experiments

Our output space is a richer interpretation of images compared to per-pixel prediction of surface normals. Evaluating this output in terms of line labelings or linkages of planes is not possible since there are no baseline approaches, ground-truth labels, or established evaluation methodologies. We therefore evaluate one of the outputs of our approach, surface normals, for which there exist approaches and methodologies. We adopt the setup used by the state-of-the-art on this task [6], and evaluate on the challenging and highly cluttered NYU v2 dataset [33].

7.1   Experimental Setup

Training and Testing: Past work on single image 3D using NYU v2 [6,21] has reported results on a variety of train/test splits, complicating inter-method comparisons. To avoid this, we report results on the training and testing splits used by Silberman et al. [33] in their support prediction problem.

Quantitative Metrics: We quantitatively evaluate the surface normal aspect of our approach. However, we strongly believe that the existing per-pixel quantitative metrics for this task are sometimes misleading. For instance, in Fig. 6,

Input Image	Ground Truth	3DP non-MW	3DP MW	Proposed Discrete	Proposed Relaxed

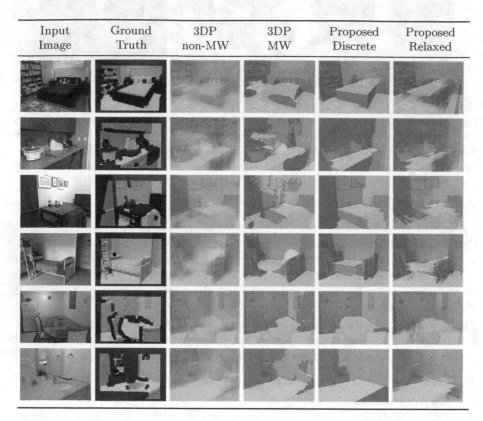

Fig. 6. Selected results on the NYU Dataset comparing our approach to the state-of-the-art, 3D Primitives. To help visualize alignment, we blend the predicted normals with the image.

Fig. 7. Surface connection graphs of scenes automatically obtained from a single image. Our method infers a parse of the scene in terms of large vanishing-point-aligned regions and the edges between them (convex: +, concave: −).

Table 1. Results on NYU v2 for per-pixel surface normal prediction. Our approach improves over Manhattan-world methods in every evaluation metric.

	Summary Stats. (Lower Better)			% Good Pixels (Higher Better)		
	Mean	Median	RMSE	11.25°	22.5°	30°
Manhattan-world Techniques						
Proposed	**35.1**	**19.2**	**48.7**	**37.6**	**53.3**	**58.9**
Fouhey et al. [6]	36.0	20.5	49.4	35.9	52.0	57.8
Hedau et al. [10]	40.0	23.5	44.1	34.2	49.3	54.4
Lee et al. [23]	43.3	36.3	54.6	25.1	40.4	46.1
non-Manhattan-world Techniques						
Fouhey et al. [6]	**34.2**	**30.0**	**41.4**	**18.6**	**38.6**	**49.9**
Karsch et al. [20]	40.7	37.8	46.9	8.1	25.9	38.2
Hoiem et al. [12]	36.0	33.4	41.7	11.4	31.3	44.5
Saxena et al. [30]	48.0	43.1	57.0	10.7	27.0	36.3

row 1, our method does worse than [6] on mean and median error, even though it conveys the cuboidal nature of the bed more precisely and segments it into three faces. However, in the absence of other metrics, we still evaluate performance on the metrics introduced in [6]: summary statistics (mean, median, root mean square error) and percent-good-pixels metrics (the fraction of pixels with error less than a threshold t). Note that each metric characterizes a different aspect of performance, not all of which are equally desirable.

Baselines: Our primary point of comparison is 3DP [6], which is the state-of-the-art and outperforms a diverse set of approaches. In particular, the informative comparison to make is with the Manhattan-world version of 3DP: Manhattan-world methods generally produce results that are nearly correct (correct vanishing point) or off by 90° (incorrect one), which is implicitly rewarded by some metrics (% Good Pixels) and penalized by others (mean, RMSE). This makes comparisons with methods not making the assumption difficult to interpret. Nonetheless, to give context, we also report results for the baseline approaches of [6], including but separately presenting non-Manhattan-world ones.

Implementation Details: *Vanishing points:* We use the vanishing point detector introduced in [10]. *Grid cells:* The grids used in this work are formed by 32 and 64 rays from exterior and interior vanishing points. *Implausible Grid Cells:* Some grid cells near vanishing points represent implausible surfaces (e.g., an enormous plane at just the right angle); we softly suppress these. *Holes in gridding:* the grid cells will not all line up, leaving a small fraction of the scene uninterpreted. We fill these with nearest-neighbor inpainting. *Training our potentials:* Most potentials are learned from data, but we must use their test-time behavior on the train set to learn our potential trade-offs. For the room-fitting potential, we use 2× cross-validated output; for 3DP-based potentials, we suppress detections on the few images on which the detector was trained.

$\longrightarrow$ Decreasing Performance (Median Error (°), % Pixels < 30°) $\longrightarrow$					
Perf.	7.8° 70.7%	11.2° 61.3%	13.4° 57.7%	21.5° 52.0%	24.6° 45.7%	44.5° 38.2%

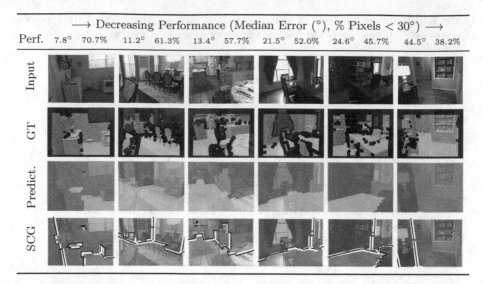

Fig. 8. Results automatically sampled across the method's performance range. Performance reported as median error and % Pixels < 30°. Results were sorted by mean rank over all criteria and six results were automatically picked to evenly divide the list.

Input Image	Ground Truth	Local Evidence	+ Room Fitting	+Potts Smoothing	+Line Labeling

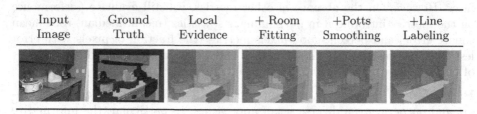

Fig. 9. Qualitative analysis of the method components. Right-to-left: We start with local, then global unaries, followed by smoothness then line-labeling binaries.

7.2   Results

Predicting Surface Normals: We show selected qualitative results in Fig. 6 that illustrate the contributions of our method, as well as an automatically selected performance range in Fig. 8. Consider Fig. 6: our method can often accurately capture object boundaries, especially in comparison with the normal-snapping approach described in [6], which produces noticeable spotting or bending artifacts. Our top-down parametrization mitigates this issue by constraining the space of interpretations, resulting in more plausible explanations. Our mid-level constraints help with the recovery of hard-to-see surfaces, such as surfaces on top of counters or beds (rows 1, 4) or sides of cabinets (row 6). These small surfaces are frequently smoothed away by the Potts model, but are recovered when our line labeling potentials are used.

We report quantitative results in Table 1. Our method outperforms the state-of-the-art for Manhattan-world prediction in every metric. This is important

Table 2. Component-wise analysis on NYU v2 [33]: we report results with parts of the full system removed to analyze the contributions of each method to overall performance.

	Mean	Median	RMSE	11.25°	22.5°	30°
Unaries Only	36.0	19.9	49.6	36.8	52.4	58.0
Smoothness Only	35.4	19.7	48.9	37.4	53.0	58.5
Full Method	**35.1**	**19.2**	**48.7**	**37.6**	**53.3**	**58.9**

since each metric captures a different aspect of performance. It also does better than the non-Manhattan-world methods in all metrics except the ones that heavily penalize Manhattan-world techniques, mean and RMSE; nonetheless, even on mean error, it is second place overall. Although our system outperforms the state-of-the-art, we stress that per-pixel metrics must be considered carefully.

Qualitative Scene Parses: Our approach produces surface connection graphs in the style of Kanade's Origami World [18]. We decode plane relationships in an interpretation via our edge dictionary illustrated in Fig. 4: given two adjoining surfaces and their orientations, we decode their relation according to our scene formation assumptions (contiguous Manhattan-world polyhedra). We then automatically render qualitative parses of the scene as shown in Fig. 7. As this work does not handle occlusion, failures in decoding relationships occur at configurations that are impossible without occlusion (e.g., vertical-atop-other-vertical).

Ablative Analysis: We now describe experiments done to assess the contributions of each component. We show an example in Fig. 9 that characterizes qualitatively how each part tends to change the solution: an initial shape is captured by the local evidence potential and is improved by the room fitting potential. Smoothness potentials remove noise, but also remove small surfaces like counters. The line-labeling potentials, however, can enable the better recovery of the counter. We show quantitative results in Table 2: each step contributes; our line-labeling potentials reduce the median error the most.

Confidence of Predictions: Accurately predicting scene layout in every single pixel of every single image is, for now, not possible. Therefore, a crucial question is: can a method identify when it is correct? This is important, for instance, as a cue for subsequent reasoning or for human-in-the-loop systems.

We compute performance-vs-coverage curves across the dataset by sweeping a threshold over per-pixel confidence for our approach and [6] in Fig. 10. Our method's confidence at a pixel is the normalized maximum value of overlapping superpixel variables in the relaxed solution. Our method ranks its predictions well: when going from 100% to 25% coverage, the median error drops by 7.3° and % Pixels < 11.25° increases by 11.7%. Thus the framework is capable of identifying which of its predictions are most likely to be correct. Additionally, the method out-performs [6] on all metrics, averaging along the curve and at all operating points except the ultra-sparse regime.

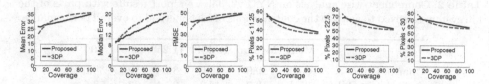

Fig. 10. Performance vs. coverage curves for the system and the next-best method, 3DP. Each plot quantifies accuracy in a metric against fraction of pixels predicted.

Input Image	Ground Truth	Convex Edges	Concave Edges	3DP Evidence	Discrete Interpretation

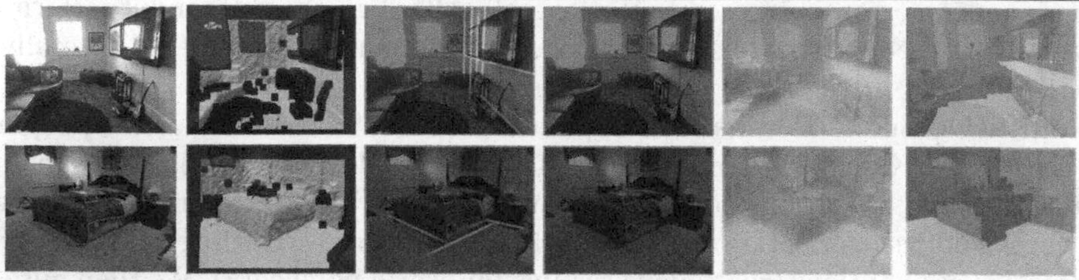

Fig. 11. Failure modes and limitations: (Top) Local evidence can be misleading. An edge is seen below the TV, and our method "folds" its interpretation accordingly. (Bottom) We model only unary and binary relationships between cells; higher order reasoning may allow the recognition of the top of the bed from its sides.

Failure Modes and Limitations: We report some failure modes and limitations in Fig. 11. Our primary failure mode is noisy evidence from inputs. These tend to correspond to mistaken but confident interpretations (e.g., the fold preferred by our model in the first row). Sometimes layouts inferred by our system violate high-level constraints: in the second row, for instance, our interpretation is unlikely globally although it makes sense locally. By reasoning about the proposed pieces, we can reject it without the surface on top necessary to make it plausible. This is consistent with our vision of the 3D inference process: this paper has argued that mid-level constraints are valuable, not that they are the end of the scene interpretation story. Rather than solve all problems at once, we must pass updated evidence to subsequent reasoning.

Acknowledgments. This work was supported by an NDSEG Fellowship to DF, NSF IIS-1320083, ONR MURI N000141010934, and a gift from Bosch Research & Technology Center.

References

1. Choi, W., Chao, Y.W., Pantofaru, C., Savarese, S.: Understanding indoor scenes using 3D geometric phrases. In: CVPR (2013)
2. Clowes, M.: On seeing things. Artificial Intelligence 2, 79–116 (1971)
3. Coughlan, J., Yuille, A.: The Manhattan world assumption: Regularities in scene statistics which enable Bayesian inference. In: NIPS (2000)
4. Del Pero, L., Bowdish, J., Fried, D., Kermgard, B., Hartley, E.L., Barnard, K.: Bayesian geometric modeling of indoor scenes. In: CVPR (2012)
5. Delage, E., Lee, H., Ng, A.Y.: A dynamic Bayesian network model for autonomous 3D reconstruction from a single indoor image. In: CVPR (2006)
6. Fouhey, D.F., Gupta, A., Hebert, M.: Data-driven 3D primitives for single image understanding. In: ICCV (2013)
7. Guo, R., Hoiem, D.: Support surface prediction in indoor scenes. In: ICCV (2013)
8. Gupta, A., Efros, A.A., Hebert, M.: Blocks world revisited: Image understanding using qualitative geometry and mechanics. In: Daniilidis, K., Maragos, P., Paragios, N. (eds.) ECCV 2010, Part IV. LNCS, vol. 6314, pp. 482–496. Springer, Heidelberg (2010)
9. Gupta, S., Arbelaez, P., Malik, J.: Perceptual organization and recognition of indoor scenes from RGB-D images. In: CVPR (2013)
10. Hedau, V., Hoiem, D., Forsyth, D.: Recovering the spatial layout of cluttered rooms. In: ICCV (2009)
11. Hoiem, D., Efros, A., Hebert, M.: Automatic photo pop-up. In: SIGGRAPH (2005)
12. Hoiem, D., Efros, A., Hebert, M.: Geometric context from a single image. In: ICCV (2005)
13. Hoiem, D., Efros, A.A., Hebert, M.: Recovering occlusion boundaries from an image. IJCV 91(3), 328–346 (2011)
14. Huffman, D.: Impossible objects as nonsense sentences. Machine Intelligence 8, 475–492 (1971)
15. Jia, Z., Gallagher, A., Chang, Y.J., Chen, T.: A learning based framework for depth ordering. In: CVPR (2012)
16. Jia, Z., Gallagher, A., Saxena, A., Chen, T.: 3D-based reasoning with blocks, support, and stability. In: CVPR (2013)
17. Jiang, H., Xiao, J.: A linear approach to matching cuboids in RGBD images. In: CVPR (2013)
18. Kanade, T.: A theory of origami world. Artificial Intelligence 13(3) (1980)
19. Karsch, K., Liao, Z., Rock, J., Barron, J.T., Hoiem, D.: Boundary cues for 3D object shape recovery. In: CVPR (2013)
20. Karsch, K., Liu, C., Kang, S.B.: Depth extraction from video using non-parametric sampling. In: Fitzgibbon, A., Lazebnik, S., Perona, P., Sato, Y., Schmid, C. (eds.) ECCV 2012, Part V. LNCS, vol. 7576, pp. 775–788. Springer, Heidelberg (2012)
21. Ladický, L., Shi, J., Pollefeys, M.: Pulling things out of perspective. In: CVPR (2014)
22. Lee, D.C., Gupta, A., Hebert, M., Kanade, T.: Estimating spatial layout of rooms using volumetric reasoning about objects and surfaces. In: NIPS (2010)
23. Lee, D.C., Hebert, M., Kanade, T.: Geometric reasoning for single image structure recovery. In: CVPR (2009)
24. Liu, M., Salzmann, M., He, X.: Discrete-continuous depth estimation from a single image. In: CVPR (2014)
25. Nitzberg, M., Mumford, D.: The 2.1D sketch. In: ICCV (1990)

26. Ramalingam, S., Kohli, P., Alahari, K., Torr, P.: Exact inference in multi-label CRFs with higher order cliques. In: CVPR (2008)
27. Ramalingam, S., Pillai, J., Jain, A., Taguchi, Y.: Manhattan junction catalogue for spatial reasoning of indoor scenes. In: CVPR (2013)
28. Roberts, L.: Machine perception of 3D solids. PhD Thesis (1965)
29. Saxena, A., Chung, S.H., Ng, A.Y.: Learning depth from single monocular images. In: NIPS (2005)
30. Saxena, A., Sun, M., Ng, A.Y.: Make3D: Learning 3D scene structure from a single still image. TPAMI 30(5), 824–840 (2008)
31. Schwing, A.G., Fidler, S., Pollefeys, M., Urtasun, R.: Box In the Box: Joint 3D Layout and Object Reasoning from Single Images. In: ICCV (2013)
32. Schwing, A.G., Urtasun, R.: Efficient Exact Inference for 3D Indoor Scene Understanding. In: Fitzgibbon, A., Lazebnik, S., Perona, P., Sato, Y., Schmid, C. (eds.) ECCV 2012, Part VI. LNCS, vol. 7577, pp. 299–313. Springer, Heidelberg (2012)
33. Silberman, N., Hoiem, D., Kohli, P., Fergus, R.: Indoor segmentation and support inference from RGBD images. In: Fitzgibbon, A., Lazebnik, S., Perona, P., Sato, Y., Schmid, C. (eds.) ECCV 2012, Part V. LNCS, vol. 7576, pp. 746–760. Springer, Heidelberg (2012)
34. Sugihara, K.: Machine Interpretation of Line Drawings. MIT Press (1986)
35. Xiang, Y., Savarese, S.: Estimating the aspect layout of object categories. In: CVPR (2012)
36. Xiao, J., Russell, B., Torralba, A.: Localizing 3D cuboids in single-view images. In: NIPS (2012)
37. Yamaguchi, K., Hazan, T., McAllester, D., Urtasun, R.: Continuous markov random fields for robust stereo estimation. In: Fitzgibbon, A., Lazebnik, S., Perona, P., Sato, Y., Schmid, C. (eds.) ECCV 2012, Part V. LNCS, vol. 7576, pp. 45–58. Springer, Heidelberg (2012)
38. Yu, S.X., Zhang, H., Malik, J.: Inferring spatial layout from a single image via depth-ordered grouping. In: Workshop on Perceptual Organization (2008)
39. Zhang, J., Chen, K., Schwing, A.G., Urtasun, R.: Estimaing the 3D Layout of Indoor Scenes and its Clutter from Depth Sensors. In: ICCV (2013)
40. Zhao, Y., Zhu, S.: Image parsing via stochastic scene grammar. In: NIPS (2011)
41. Zhao, Y., Zhu, S.: Scene parsing by integrating function, geometry and appearance models. In: CVPR (2013)

Joint Semantic Segmentation and 3D Reconstruction from Monocular Video

Abhijit Kundu, Yin Li, Frank Dellaert, Fuxin Li, and James M. Rehg

Georgia Institute of Technology, Atlanta, USA

Abstract. We present an approach for joint inference of 3D scene structure and semantic labeling for monocular video. Starting with monocular image stream, our framework produces a 3D volumetric semantic + occupancy map, which is much more useful than a series of 2D semantic label images or a sparse point cloud produced by traditional semantic segmentation and Structure from Motion(SfM) pipelines respectively. We derive a Conditional Random Field (CRF) model defined in the 3D space, that jointly infers the semantic category and occupancy for each voxel. Such a joint inference in the 3D CRF paves the way for more informed priors and constraints, which is otherwise not possible if solved separately in their traditional frameworks. We make use of class specific semantic cues that constrain the 3D structure in areas, where multiview constraints are weak. Our model comprises of higher order factors, which helps when the depth is unobservable. We also make use of class specific semantic cues to reduce either the degree of such higher order factors, or to approximately model them with unaries if possible. We demonstrate improved 3D structure and temporally consistent semantic segmentation for difficult, large scale, forward moving monocular image sequences.

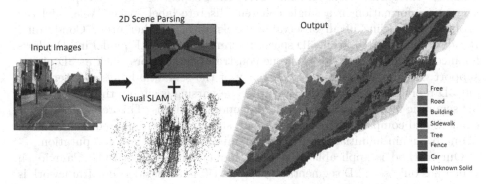

Fig. 1. Overview of our system. From monocular image sequence, we first obtain 2D semantic segmentation, sparse 3D reconstruction and camera poses. We then build a volumetric 3D map which depicts both 3D structure and semantic labels.

1 Introduction

To successfully navigate and perceive the 3D world, a robot needs to infer both its own position and information of the 3D environment. Vision-based Simultaneous

D. Fleet et al. (Eds.): ECCV 2014, Part VI, LNCS 8694, pp. 703–718, 2014.

Localization and Mapping (SLAM) estimates the location of the robot while incrementally building a map of the environment. However, SLAM only reveals the structural information of the scene and the result is limited to a sparse 3D point cloud. Scene parsing, on the other hand, labels each pixel in an image or video with object categories (e.g. *Tree*, *Road*), thus providing semantic only information of the scene. But in many applications such as autonomous driving, it is important to understand both the structural and semantic information of the surroundings. In this paper, we propose a joint 3D reconstruction and scene parsing system from a fast forward-moving monocular camera.

Autonomous driving applications often involve fast forward-moving cameras. In these cases, multi-view stereo could fail due to textureless surfaces and/or low parallax, and the visual SLAM pipeline for a monocular camera only provides a very sparse set of 3D measurements. Previous work on joint reconstruction and scene parsing [9,26] require dense depth measurements and cannot accommodate to this problem.

Lifting the requirement of dense depth measurements, our input contains only sparse 3D point cloud but dense semantic labels on each pixel of each frame, the latter can be obtained through evaluating a scene parsing engine (e.g. [20]) on all the frames. We use category-specific sensor models to enhance the depth estimates, especially when no direct depth information is available. On the other hand, the knowledge of unoccupied space from successive camera positions help to reduce a lot of 3D structural ambiguities, as well as to improve structural estimates along weakly supported surfaces [12], where only vague structural information is available.

The 3D scene is represented in the form of 3D cubic subvolumes (voxel) along with per-voxel semantic labels (see Fig.1). The voxel labels include both solid semantic categories (e.g. *Car*) and *Free*, thus capturing both occupancy and semantic information in a single coherent discrete label space. We model the problem of labeling of all observable voxels with a higher order Conditional Random Field (CRF) in the 3D space. Inference of the CRF model in 3D allows for incorporating more realistic scene constraints and priors, such as 3D object support. Besides, full temporal coherency of the semantic labels is inherent to our 3D representation, because our 2D scene parsing is simply the projection of 3D semantic reconstruction to different camera positions. This representation is efficient and compact with an Octree data structure where unused voxels in the 3D map remain uninitialized and require minimal storage and computation.

Our method is applicable to popular monocular sequences like Camvid [4] which has only seen 2D segmentation results till now. Besides, our framework is flexible and can be easily extended to other sensors like laser or stereo cameras. It is quite efficient compared to standard multi-view stereo pipelines and still properly deals with noisy measurements and uncertainty. Thus, our method could find immediate use in many applications like autonomous robot navigation.

3D geometric information plays an important role in 2D semantic segmentation [2,27,19,6]. For example, Brostow et al. [2] incorporate sparse SfM features with 2D appearance features for each frame, and demonstrated its advantage over 2D appearance features alone. Ladicky et al. [19] propose a joint optimization of dense stereo and semantic segmentation for every frame. However, temporal consistency of the segmentation is not considered in their methods. Several recent attempts [6,24,31] have addressed temporal continuity, either by pre-processing with supervoxel-based video segmentation [31], or by additional higher order potentials that enforce label consistency among projections of the same 3D point [6]. Still, most of these methods run in the 2D image space only. Our volumetric representation performs inference in 3D and achieve full temporal coherency without additional cost.

Semantic segmentation can be used to estimate 3D information [22,10,25]. For example, Liu et al. [22] guide the 3D reconstruction from a single image using semantic segmentation. Depth from semantics, though not as reliable as the SfM or multi-view stereo, has its own strengths: (1) it is complementary to the traditional geometric approaches; (2) it offers a potential denser depth measurement than SfM; (3) it is applicable for a larger range of sceneries than multi-view stereo. For a fast forward-moving monocular camera, the SfM gives very sparse point cloud and the multi-view stereo fails due to low parallax, whereas we can still rely on segmentation results.

The most relevant work are [9,26] who have independently proposed methods for simultaneous semantic segmentation and 3D reconstruction. However, both of these methods require dense depth measurements. Dense depth maps allow them to make relatively restrictive assumptions, e.g. Haene et al. [9] consider every pixel with missing depth as *Sky*. These assumptions do not hold in case of fast forward-moving monocular camera, where we only have a very sparse point cloud from SfM. Unlike [26], we propose a joint optimization scheme of both semantic segmentation and 3D reconstruction. And unlike [9], we use semantic category specific sensor models to estimate the depth as much as possible, instead of simply inserting *Free* labels for voxels with missing depth.

We explicitly model *Free* space. For applications like autonomous driving, *Free* space information is directly used in higher level tasks like path planning. Also, *Free* space provides cues to improve 3D reconstruction, especially along weakly supported surfaces [12] which is very common with forward moving cameras in urban scenes. In our framework, the *Free* space information from other cameras helps to reduce ambiguities in 3D structure.

This paper makes the following contributions:

- From a fast forward-moving monocular camera, we introduce a novel higher order CRF model for joint inference of 3D structure and semantics in a 3D volumetric model. The framework does not require dense depth measurements and efficiently utilize semantic cues and 3D priors to enhance both depth estimation and scene parsing.
- We present a data-driven category-specific process for dynamically instantiating potentials in the CRF. Our method performs tractable joint inference of 3D structure and semantic segmentation in large outdoor environments.

– We present results on challenging forward-moving monocular sequences such as CamVid and Leuven which demonstrate the value of our approach. The results have shown improved temporal continuity in scene parsing as well as improved 3D structure.

2 Problem Formulation and Notation

We are interested in the 3D map $\mathcal{M}$ comprising of several sub-volumes $m_i \in \mathcal{M}$. Where each m_i is a categorical random variable corresponding to voxel i, that can be either *Free* or one of the **solid** semantic objects like *Road, Building, Tree*, etc. For example in the Camvid [4] dataset, we used a 9 dimensional label space $\mathcal{L}_{\mathcal{M}} = \{Free, Road, Building, Sidewalk, Tree, Fence, Person, Car, UnknownSolid\}$. Note that this joint label space, $\mathcal{L}_{\mathcal{M}}$ is mutually exhaustive and is different from the label space $\mathcal{L}_{\mathcal{I}}$ of 2D image level semantic categories. For example there is no *Sky* in $\mathcal{L}_{\mathcal{M}}$, a common state used in 2D image scene parsing. Choosing this label space $\mathcal{L}_{\mathcal{M}}$ allows us to do the joint inference of both semantic category and and 3D structure of the scene with a single random variable per voxel.

Each pixel location $x \in \Omega$ in the images is a source of potential measurement, where $\Omega = \{1..h\} \times \{1..w\}$, with $w, h \in \mathbb{Z}^+$ being image size. We have two kinds of measurements : *with-depth* measurements denoted by z^r and *semantic-only* measurements denoted as z^s. Each measurement has an associated semantic label $l \in \mathcal{L}_{\mathcal{I}}$, obtained from the 2D semantic classifier output (§ 6.2) at that pixel. Each *with-depth* measurement has an additional depth $d \in \mathbb{R}$ information, which in our case is obtained from visual SLAM (§ 6.1).

The observed data is composed of all the measurements and camera poses i.e. $\mathcal{D} = \{\mathbf{z}^r_{1:P}, \mathbf{z}^s_{1:Q}, \mathbf{g}_{1:T}\}$, where $\mathbf{z}^r_{1:P}$, $\mathbf{z}^s_{1:Q}$ and $\mathbf{g}_{1:T}$ respectively denotes the set of *with-depth* measurements, *semantic-only* measurements and camera trajectory up-to time T, which in our case is simply equivalent to number of images processed. Each $g_t \in \mathrm{SE}(3)$ is a single camera pose from the camera trajectory. Since we have multiple number of *with-depth* and *semantic-only* measurements per frame, we index them using p and q respectively, where $1 \le p \le P$ and $1 \le q \le Q$. Also we only have very sparse depth measurements, so $P \ll Q$.

We use subscript notation to denote associated camera pose, pixel semantic label, co-ordinate and depth (if available) for a particular measurement. Thus for a *semantic-only* measurement z^s_q, $l_q \in \mathcal{L}_{\mathcal{I}}$ denotes 2D image semantic label at pixel coordinate x_q with camera pose g_q. Similarly for p-th *with-depth* measurement z^r_p, d_p encodes the depth of the associated 3D point X_p, measured along the ray emanating from pixel location x_p with semantic label l_p and taken from camera pose g_p. We will sometime drop the superscript in z, when the type of measurement z^r (*with-depth*) or z^s (*semantic-only*) does not matter.

A single measurement z_k only affects a subset of voxels $\mathbf{m}_k \in \mathcal{M}$. For our camera sensor, these voxels are a subset of the voxels lying along the ray emanating from camera center through the corresponding image pixel coordinate of the measurement, denoted as $R_k = \mathrm{Ray}(x_k, g_k)$. Thus the set of voxels affected by a particular measurement z^r_p (or z^s_q) is represented by $\mathbf{m}_p \in R_p$ ($\mathbf{m}_q \in R_q$).

3 Probabilistic Model

We utilize a discriminative CRF model on $P(\mathcal{M}|\mathcal{D})$ to avoid directly modeling the complex dependencies [21,28] among correlated sources of *with-depth* and *semantic-only* measurements. Unlike traditional occupancy grid mapping [30] we do not assume each m_i as independent from each other. Instead, we make use of the standard *static world* conditional independence assumptions of each measurement z_k given the map $\mathcal{M}$, and independence of the map $\mathcal{M}$ w.r.t.the camera trajectory $\mathbf{g}_{1:T}$. Given these assumptions, we can factorize the posterior over map $\mathcal{M}$ given all the observation data

$$P(\mathcal{M}|\mathcal{D}) \propto P(\mathcal{M}|\mathbf{g}_{1:T})P(\mathbf{z}_{1:P}^r, \mathbf{z}_{1:Q}^s|\mathcal{M}, \mathbf{g}_{1:T})$$

$$= P(\mathcal{M}) \prod_{p=1}^{P} P(z_p^r|\mathcal{M}, g_p) \prod_{q=1}^{Q} P(z_q^s|\mathcal{M}, g_q) \tag{1}$$

$$= \underbrace{P(\mathcal{M})}_{\text{prior}} \prod_{p=1}^{P} \underbrace{P(z_p^r|\mathbf{m}_p, g_p)}_{\substack{\text{forward } \textit{with-depth} \\ \text{measurement model}}} \prod_{q=1}^{Q} \underbrace{P(z_q^s|\mathbf{m}_q, g_q)}_{\substack{\text{forward } \textit{semantic-only} \\ \text{measurement model}}} \tag{2}$$

where the conditional independence assumptions were applied to obtain (1), and since each measurement is only dependent on a subset of voxels in $\mathcal{M}$, we can further reduce (1) to get (2). (2) uses forward sensor measurement model [30] (measurement likelihood). However, if we adopt this factorization, we would need to learn a complicated sensor model in order to parametrize the forward sensor likelihoods $P(z_k|\mathbf{m_k}, g_k)$. Reapplying Bayes rule on (2), we get the inverse sensor model version as

$$P(\mathcal{M}|\mathcal{D}) \propto \underbrace{P(\mathcal{M})}_{\text{prior}} \prod_{p=1}^{P} \underbrace{\frac{P(\mathbf{m}_p|z_p^r, g_p)}{P(\mathbf{m}_p)}}_{\substack{\text{inverse } \textit{with-depth} \\ \text{measurement model}}} \prod_{q=1}^{Q} \underbrace{\frac{P(\mathbf{m}_q|z_q^s, g_q)}{P(\mathbf{m}_q)}}_{\substack{\text{inverse } \textit{semantic-only} \\ \text{measurement model}}} \tag{3}$$

which provides the hints that our factors should be similar to posterior probabilities. We can rewrite both (2) and (3) in terms of factors [16]:

$$P(\mathcal{M}|\mathcal{D}) = \frac{1}{Z(\mathcal{D})} \underbrace{\psi_\pi(\mathcal{M})}_{\text{prior factor}} \prod_{p=1}^{P} \underbrace{\psi_r^p(\mathbf{m}_p; z_p^r, g_p)}_{\substack{\text{with-depth} \\ \text{measurement factors}}} \prod_{q=1}^{Q} \underbrace{\psi_s^q(\mathbf{m}_q; z_q^s, g_q)}_{\substack{\text{semantic-only} \\ \text{measurement factors}}} \tag{4}$$

where $Z(\mathcal{D})$ is the partition function over the observed data. We now discuss the prior factor and the measurement factors.

Priors: In the above $P(\mathcal{M})$ or the prior factor ψ_π encodes the prior distribution over the huge set of all possible $\mathcal{L}_m^{|\mathcal{M}|}$ maps. However most of these maps are highly implausible and we can enforce some constraints in form of priors to improve our solution. We enforce the following priors over the map:

- **Spatial smoothness:** Our 3D world is not completely random and exhibits some sort of spatial smoothness.
- **Label compatibility:** Certain pair of classes are more/less likely to occur adjacent to one another. For example a *Car* voxel is unlikely to be adjacent to a *Building* voxel.
- **3D Support:** For most solid semantic categories (with the exception of *Tree*), an occupied voxel increases the chance of the voxels below it to belong to the same occupied category.
- **Free space Support:** *Free* space provides cues to improve 3D reconstruction along weakly supported surfaces [12]. Highly-supported free space boundaries are more likely to occupied.

We model spatial smoothness and label compatibility using pairwise potentials (§ 4.4). 3D and Free space support constraints are implemented with unary potentials (§ 4.1). Therefore, our $\psi_\pi(\mathcal{M})$ factorizes into pairwise and unary factors.

Measurement Factors: Measurement factors $\psi_r^p(\mathbf{m}_p; z_p^r, g_p)$ and $\psi_s^q(\mathbf{m}_q; z_q^s, g_q)$ encode the constraints imposed by a particular *with-depth* and *semantic-only* measurement respectively. In general, this forms a higher order clique involving multiple voxels $\mathbf{m}_k \subset \mathcal{M}$. However for certain kind of measurements, e.g. *with-depth* measurements or *semantic-only* measurements with *Sky* label, the factor $\psi(\mathbf{m}_k | z_k, g_k)$ can be approximated by a product of unaries on each voxel in $\mathbf{m}_k$. For example when we have a *with-depth* measurement, all voxels along the ray from camera center till the observed depth are more likely to *Free*. And the voxel corresponding to the observed 3D point is likely to belong to a solid semantic category. We use category-specific measurement models (described in § 4.2 and § 4.3) which can be either unary factors or higher order factors.

CRF Model: As discussed in the above two paragraphs we model the prior factor and the measurement factors in (4) with unary, pairwise and higher order potentials. Thus, rearranging the factors in (4) in terms of their arity, we get

$$P(\mathcal{M}|\mathcal{D}) = \frac{1}{Z(\mathcal{D})} \prod_i \psi_u^i(m_i) \prod_{i,j \in \mathcal{N}} \psi_p(m_i, m_j) \prod_{R \in \mathcal{R}} \psi_h(\mathbf{m}_R) \qquad (5)$$

Here $\psi_u^i(m_i)$ is the unary potential defined over each m_i, and encodes local evidence. The pairwise potential, $\psi_p(m_i, m_j)$ over two neighboring voxels falling into a neighborhood $\mathcal{N}$ enforces spatial smoothness and label compatibility among them. Higher order cliques $\psi_h(\mathbf{m}_R)$ are defined over set of voxels $\mathbf{m}_R$ along some ray emanating from a 2D image projection and helps with missing depth information. Fig.2(a) shows the corresponding factor graph $\mathcal{H}$ of the model.

A single *semantic-only* measurement z_q^s for certain classes is ill-posed for updating states of the affected voxels $\mathbf{m}_q$ since we do not know which voxel reflects back the measurement. Häne et al.[9] simply updates all $\mathbf{m}_q$ with *Free* unaries for measurements missing depth, which is clearly an improper model. In

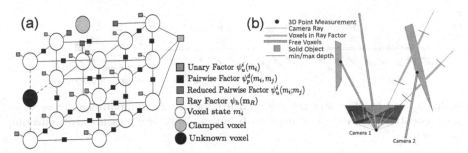

Fig. 2. (a) Factor Graph $\mathcal{H}$ of our framework. (b) Illustration of sensor models and higher order Ray factors. See text for more details.

our approach, we handle such measurements without range/depth, by forming higher order factor connecting voxels along a ray. However a naive approach will lead to forming huge higher order cliques and since every pixel in every image is an potential measurement, and inference in the graphical model can become intractable very soon. To circumvent this issue, whenever applicable, we make use of semantic cues to model them with unaries or at least reduce the scope of such higher order factors.

4 Potentials

4.1 Basic Unary Potentials

We have different types of measurements, and they affect m_i differently. For example 3D depth measurement alone do not contain any semantic label information and influence all semantic label probabilities equally. Also each category of semantic observation affects the belief state of a voxel m_i, differently than others. We define the following two basic forms of unary measurement factors:

$$\psi_{\text{MISS}}(m_i) = \begin{cases} 0.6 & \text{if } m_i = \textit{Free} \\ \frac{0.4}{|\mathcal{L}_{\mathcal{M}}|-1} & \text{if } m_i \neq \textit{Free} \end{cases} \quad \text{and} \quad \psi^l_{\text{HIT}}(m_i) = \begin{cases} 0.3 & \text{if } m_i = \textit{Free} \\ 0.55 & \text{if } m_i \equiv l \\ \frac{0.15}{|\mathcal{L}_{\mathcal{M}}|-2} & \text{if } m_i \notin \{l, \textit{Free}\} \end{cases} \quad (6)$$

Fig.3 illustrates the measurement factors ψ_{MISS} and ψ^{Road}_{HIT}. Note that, we have made use use of inverse sensor model $P(m|z,g)$ for these factors. This is motivated by the fact that, it is much more easier [30] to elicit model parameters for $P(m|z,g)$ compared to the forward sensor likelihoods $P(z|m,g)$, and can be done without resorting to complicated sensor model learning. We kept the parameters same as that of laser based occupancy sensor model used in [11].

The unary potential $\psi^i_u(m_i)$ combines all the unary measurement factors that affect m_i. Thus the final unary potential over a voxel is factor product of a certain number of ψ_{MISS} and ψ^l_{HIT} factors only.

$$\psi^i_u(m_i) = [\psi_{\text{MISS}}(m_i)]^{N_M} \prod_{l \in \mathcal{L}_{\mathcal{I}} \backslash Sky} [\psi^l_{\text{HIT}}(m_i)]^{N_{Hl}} \quad (7)$$

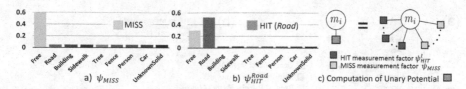

Fig. 3. a) and b) illustrates the MISS and HIT factors. c) Computation of per voxel unary potential as a product of unary contributions of several measurements affecting that voxel.

where N_M is the total number of MISS unary factors over m_i and N_{Hl} being the number of HIT factors over m_i for semantic category l. Fig.3(c) depicts the factor graph view of this potential.

As new measurements are obtained, we keep on inserting new factors into the affected voxels. The set of voxels affected, and the kind of unary factors that gets inserted depends on the measurement type (discussed in next two subsections).

4.2 Measurements with Depth

We use a projective camera sensor model, wherein the basic assumption is that each measurement is formed by reflection from a occupied voxel at some particular depth, and all voxels from the camera center to that depth are *Free*. So for all voxels from camera center till the observed depth, we insert a MISS factor which increases the probability for these voxels being *Free*. And for the voxel corresponding to the observed 3D point X_p, we insert a HIT factor which makes the probability of belonging to a particular solid semantic state high. Our framework is not limited to monocular only system, the same approach can also be extended to a Laser+Vision system, where measurements from lasers affect all solid semantic category probabilities equally.

4.3 Semantic Only Measurement

With sparse reconstruction most points in the image do not have direct depth measurements. However certain classes of measurements still provide a good estimation of depth. Observing *Sky* tells us that all voxels along the observed ray are more likely to be *Free*. Fig.4 LEFT shows average depth for some semantic categories across different parts of the image. We computed these statistics on the sequence seq05VD of Camvid. We first form a uniform 2D grid over the image, and then for each such grid in the image, we accumulate the depths from visual SLAM point clouds whose projection on the image lie on that grid. This gives us information about how good a *semantic-only* measurement z_q^s is in estimating the 3D depth. For each semantic class, all measurements with 2D projection x lying on the same grid gets same statistics. Two kind of statistics are computed for each such possible $(l_q, x_q) \in \mathcal{L}_\mathcal{I} \times \Omega$ measurement. The *min* depth and *max* depth for each (l_q, x_q) tells us the minimum and maximum possible depth along pixel co-ordinate x_q for 2D semantic category l_q. We then also estimate inverse sensor model $P(\mathbf{m}_p|z_q^s, g_q)$. Fig.4 shows the plots of inverse sensor model along with min/max depth for two specific *semantic-only* measurements, ($l_q =$ *Road*, $x_q = [400, 700]$) and ($l_q =$ *Building*, $x_q = [100, 300]$). When the statistics shows a small min-to-max bound e.g. *Road* and the inverse sensor model has a high peak, we insert unary factors according to this inverse sensor model.

However for certain classes like *Building*, depth uncertainty is too high to make it effective, since they can occur at different depths. Using unaries for these measurements introduces a lot of artifacts. So for these class of *semantic-only* measurements we construct a higher order factor involving all the voxels along the ray that lie between *min* depth and *max* depth computed for that semantic measurement. Solid *semantic-only* measurements like *Building, tree*, even though does not say much about the depth, confirms the fact that there is at least one occupied voxel along the ray induced by that observation. Our **Higher order Ray Potential** simply encodes this fact and can attain only two possible values:

$$\psi_h(\mathbf{m}_R) = \begin{cases} \alpha & \text{if atleast one of } \mathbf{m}_R \text{ is } \neg Free \\ \beta & \text{if all of } \mathbf{m}_R \text{ is } Free \end{cases} \tag{8}$$

where $\mathbf{m}_R$ is set of voxels along a particular ray involved in the factor and $\alpha > \beta$. We make use of the class specific prior knowledge of the minimum depth and maximum depth of the reflecting voxel along a particular 2D back-projection. So for a ray factor $\psi_h(\mathbf{m}_R)$ caused by a measurement z_q^s, $\mathbf{m}_R = \{m_i : m_i \in R_q, min(l_q, x_q) \leq \text{depth}(m_i, g_q) \leq max(l_q, x_q)\}$. This reduces the number of voxels $|\mathbf{m}_R|$ involved in $\psi_h(\mathbf{m}_R)$, which could otherwise be very large (see Fig.2(b) for illustration). A further reduction is facilitated by strong free space measurements (see § 5.3). In contrast, the higher order factors used in [23] involve all the voxels starting from the camera. Another contrast to [23] is that our ray factor captures single view constraints which is orthogonal to multiview higher-order factors of [23] requiring costly photoconsistency computations across multiple views. Note that the higher order factor (8) is a sparse one and its of the same form as $\mathcal{P}^n$ Potts model [15] (a special case of Pattern potentials[17]) which allows us to do tractable inference (§ 6.3).

4.4   Spatial Smoothness and Label Compatibility

The pairwise factor $\psi_p^d(m_i, m_j)$ enforces spatial smoothness and label compatibility between pairs of neighboring voxels defined by 3D neighborhood $\mathcal{N}$. Thus each voxel can have a maximum of 26 pairwise factors. The pairwise factors ψ_p^d are also dependent on relative direction d (horizontal or vertical) between the voxels. This allows us to capture properties like *Road* or *Sidewalk* voxels are more likely to be adjacent to each other in horizontal direction. So our pairwise potential is like Potts model, except that we set different weights for certain specific pairs of labels. To prevent *Free* voxels encroach other solid voxels, we set a lower cost for a $\psi_p^d(m_i = Free, m_j \neq Free)$ than other pairs in $\mathcal{L}_\mathcal{M} \times \mathcal{L}_\mathcal{M}$.

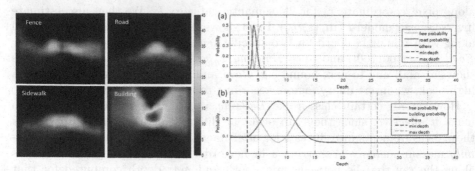

Fig. 4. LEFT: Average per category depthmap of Camvid [4] (subsequence # seq05VD) for *Fence, Road, Sidewalk* and *Building*. RIGHT: shows the inverse sensor model $P(m_i|z_q^s, g_q)$ for voxels i along the ray emanating from 2D point x_q as function of depth from camera center. (a) shows the inverse sensor model for a *Road* point measurement at 2D point co-ordinate, $x_q = [400, 700]$. (b) row shows the inverse sensor model for a *Building* observation at point $[100, 300]$. The plots also shows the min and max depth for these measurements.

5   Data-Driven Graphical Model Construction

The final graphical model is dynamically constructed and fully specified once all unary potentials has been computed.

5.1   Data Structure for Scene Representation

We use an octree based volumetric data structure which provides a compact storage of the scene. In the octree representation, when a certain subvolume observes some measurement, the corresponding node in the octree is initialized. Any *uninitialized* node in the octree represents *Unknown* areas. *Unknown* voxels are not included in the space over which we construct the graphical model and run our inference algorithm. This is different than other common approaches [23,9] of inferring over all voxels within a bounding box.

Of all factors used in our model, only the unary factor ψ_u^i is of different values for every m_i. All other factors like pairwise factors ψ_p or higher order ray factors ψ_h even though has different scopes, are fixed functions and we need to just store only **one instance** of them. Each node of the octree stores the local belief $bel(m_i)$ (as *log* probabilities) which is equal to the prior probability at time zero, and is incrementally updated to yield the final unary factor $\psi_u^i(m_i)$. Thus unlike a naive approach, we do not need to explicitly store all measurements, which is huge even for a short video sequence. Also note that all other factors apart from ψ_u^i are either precomputed, can be computed directly from voxel co-ordinates or from ψ_u^i itself without needing access to the raw measurement data.

5.2   Clamping

Even for nodes which have been initialized, if the local belief $bel(m_i)$ for a particular state $\in \mathcal{L}_\mathcal{M}$ has reached a very high probability (we used 0.98), we fix m_i to that state and treat it like evidence. This clamping of voxels which are already very confident about its label, reduces the total number of variables involved in the inference and also the scope of pairwise/higher-order factors attached to them. A pairwise factor between m_i and m_j gets *reduced* to unary factor $\psi_u^i(m_i) = \psi_p(m_i, m_j = Free)$, when m_j gets clamped to *Free* label. In Fig.2(a), the shaded node ● represents such a clamped voxel and ■ denotes the reduced pairwise factors. Clamping of confident voxels and conservative generation of set of voxels over which we do the final inference, allows us to scale to longer sequences and not just scenes with a small fixed bounding box.

5.3   Scope Reduction of Higher Order Ray Potentials

Since the final graphical model structure $\mathcal{H}$ is computed only after all the unary potentials have been computed, it allows for further reduction of number of voxels $|\mathbf{m}_R|$ involved in higher order ray factors (8). We illustrate this with help of Fig.2(b). Suppose Camera1 receives a *semantic-only* measurement, which results in a higher order ray factor involving voxels lying between min and max depth for that measurement. But strong free space measurements coming from other cameras (e.g. Camera2 in Fig.2(b)) helps us in further reducing the number of voxels $|\mathbf{m}_R|$ in the scope of that ray factor.

5.4   3D Support and Free Space Support

Most solid semantic categories (with exceptions e.g. *Tree*) have a 3D support, as in an occupied voxel increases the chance of the voxels below it to belong to the same occupied category. So for voxels which have been clamped to semantic categories like *Building, Fence, Pole*, we insert a extra HIT unary factor corresponding to the same semantic category for all voxels lying directly below.

As shown by [12], highly-supported free space boundaries are more likely to be occupied. This is important for driving sequences, since most surfaces like road are very weakly supported by measurements. For voxels for which have been clamped to *Free*, we first check if there are *Unknown* voxels directly adjacent to it. If upon back-projecting these *Unknown* voxel coordinates to the images, we get a strong consensus in a solid semantic label: we initialize that voxel node and insert a single HIT unary factor corresponding to that label.

6   System Pipeline

With input monocular images, we first perform visual SLAM and an intial 2D scene parsing using standard semantic segmentation methods [20,18]. We then do a data-driven graphical model construction (§ 5.1) based on these measurements, followed by a final inference step.

6.1   Visual SLAM

Visual SLAM estimates the camera trajectory $g_{1:t}$ and sparse 3D point cloud $\{X\}$ where $g_t \in SE(3)$ and $X \in \mathbb{R}^3$. We do frame-to-frame matching of sparse 2D feature points, followed by RANSAC based relative pose estimation to obtain an initial estimate of the camera poses. A further improvement in feature tracking is obtained by rejecting matches across a image pair if the matched points lie on areas labeled as different semantic categories by the 2D semantic classifier. Finally we use bundle adjustment [13,1], which iteratively refines the camera poses and the sparse point cloud by minimizing a sum of all re-projection errors. Once bundle adjustment has converged, we obtain a set of sparse 3D points and corresponding camera poses from which each of these points have been observed.

6.2   Initial 2D Scene Parsing

We use the unary potentials used by Ladicky et al. [20] consisting of color, histogram of oriented gradients (HOG), pixel location features and several filter banks. We then use the dense CRF implementation of [18] to get the baseline 2D scene parsing. Since we directly work from per pixel semantic labels, any other scene parsing method can be used instead.

6.3   Inference Algorithm

For doing inference over the graphical model, we use the maximum a-posteriori (MAP) estimate $\mathcal{M}^* = \arg\max_{\mathcal{M}} P(\mathcal{M}|\mathcal{D})$ to assign a label to to each m_i. The rationale behind MAP is the big progress [14] of efficient approximate MAP inference in recent years. We use a modified message passing implementation of [14]. We use tree-reweighted (TRW) [32] messaging schedules. For computing messages to and from the higher order factors (8) we use the approach of [29]. Since our higher order factors (8) are sparse, all n outgoing messages from these higher order factors can be computed in $O(n)$ ($O(1)$ amortized) time.

7   Experiments and Evaluation

Since we are jointly estimating both 3D structure and semantic segmentation, it is expected that we improve upon both of them. In this section we define the evaluation criteria for measuring the above and show results to verify our claim. We demonstrate results of our method on Camvid [4] and Leuven [5,19] datasets. Both these datasets involve difficult fast forward moving cameras and has been standard dataset for semantic segmentation papers [3,19,31,24,6]. Leuven dataset contains stereo image pairs, but we demonstrate results only using monocular (left) images. To the best of our knowledge, we are not aware of any other work which has demonstrated joint 3D reconstruction and semantic segmentation on these standard monocular datasets. We additionally provide results on small subsequence of KITTI [8], again using monocular (left) images. Additional results and videos are available at the project website[1] and in supplementary material.

---

[1] http://www.cc.gatech.edu/~akundu7/projects/JointSegRec

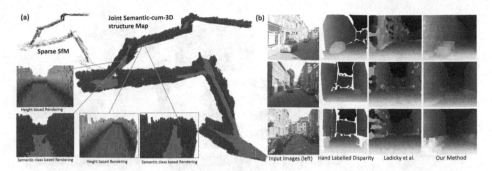

Fig. 5. Leuven [19] Results. (a): the output semantic reconstruction of the Leuven sequence, using only left (monocular) images. *Free* voxels are not shown for clarity. Note the improvement compared to initial SfM pointcloud. (b) Comparisons with the stereo method of Ladicky et al. [19], by using monocular (*left*) images *only*. We obtain 2D depth maps by back-projecting our 3D map onto the cameras. Notice the significant improvement over the depth maps of [19] when compared to the hand labeled disparity image provided by [19].

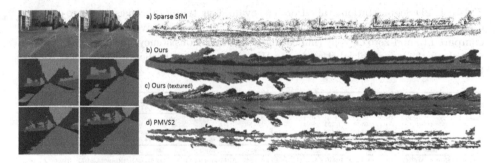

Fig. 6. CamVid [4] Results. LEFT: Top row shows two consecutive input images, middle row shows baseline 2D segmentation and bottom row shows 2D segmentation obtained by back-projecting our 3D semantic map. Note the temporal inconsistency in baseline 2D segmentation (middle row). RIGHT: a) 3D reconstruction and camera trajectory from Visual SLAM. b) Our 3D semantic + occupancy map using the same legend as in Fig.1. *Free* voxels are not shown for clarity. c) shows the same map, but textured. d)Reconstruction result by PMVS2 [7]. Note the improvement in our map (b,c) compared to sparse SfM(a)and PMVS2(d).

7.1   3D Structure Quality

We vastly improve upon the baseline 3D structure estimated through traditional SfM approach. Fig.6 shows some of our 3D reconstructions of a part of Camvid [4]. Note the improvement obtained over state of the art multi-view stereo [7] and sparse SfM in Fig.6. In the Leuven sequence, shown in Fig.5, we compare against the stereo based 2.5D method of Ladicky et al. [19] for joint segmentation and stereo. We back-project our 3D semantic map onto the cameras to obtain per frame depth/disparity image. Fig.5 qualitatively demonstrates the better quality of our 3D structure estimate, both in comparison to the stereo

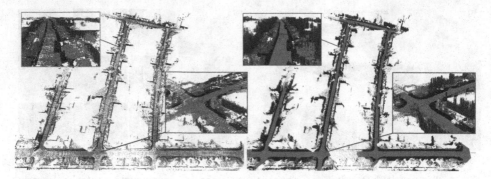

Fig. 7. KITTI [8] Results (seq 05). LEFT: We use LIDAR measurements available in KITTI using only the unary potentials described in this paper. RIGHT: Results with monocular (left) images and our full CRF model. As can be seen in the figure, even with just monocular images, we are able to achieve more complete reconstruction. For fair comparison, we only used those laser rays from the 360° LIDAR that can be seen by the left camera.

Table 1. 2D Segmentation evaluation. For evaluating temporal consistency, we give average Entropy H of SfM feature tracks (See § 7.2). Our results gives perfect zero entropy compared to non-zero entropy (indicating temporal inconsistency) for [24,19,31,20]. We also show the per pixel label accuracy. We again obtain the best results. Best scores has been highlighted.

CAMVID seq05VD	Building		Road		Car		Sidewalk		Sky		Tree		Fence		All	
	H(bits)	Acc(%)	H(bits)	Acc(%)	H(bits)	Acc(%)	H(bits)	Acc(%)	H(bits)	Acc(%)	H(bits)	Acc(%)	H(bits)	Acc(%)	H(bits)	Acc(%)
Ours	0.0	98.30	0.0	97.77	0.0	95.75	0.0	98.33	NA	99.27	0.0	83.63	0.0	73.74	0.0	95.51
[20]	0.114	98.52	0.024	95.99	0.231	89.41	0.177	96.53	NA	99.81	0.168	83.02	0.299	75.59	0.095	94.58
[24]	0.114	94.78	0.016	98.85	0.106	99.69	0.184	94.11	NA	99.21	0.173	80.34	0.249	39.06	0.084	92.41
[31]	0.025	95.01	0.004	98.97	0.046	99.87	0.062	73.17	NA	99.26	0.037	74.08	0.107	4.38	0.019	87.88

LEUVEN	Building		Road		Car		Sidewalk		Sky		Bike		Pedestrian		All	
	H(bits)	Acc(%)	H(bits)	Acc(%)	H(bits)	Acc(%)	H(bits)	Acc(%)	H(bits)	Acc(%)	H(bits)	Acc(%)	H(bits)	Acc(%)	H(bits)	Acc(%)
Ours	0.0	96.51	0.0	99.40	0.0	91.78	0.0	66.97	NA	95.30	0.0	83.82	0.0	NA	0.0	95.74
[19]	0.046	95.84	0.116	98.75	0.150	91.42	0.429	74.89	NA	93.29	0.264	84.68	0.686	61.76	0.094	95.24

KITTI seq05	Building		Road		Car		Sidewalk		Sky		Tree		Fence		All	
	H(bits)	Acc(%)	H(bits)	Acc(%)	H(bits)	Acc(%)	H(bits)	Acc(%)	H(bits)	Acc(%)	H(bits)	Acc(%)	H(bits)	Acc(%)	H(bits)	Acc(%)
Ours	0.0	98.90	0.0	98.72	0.0	96.95	0.0	98.35	NA	99.37	0.0	96.45	0.0	96.34	0.0	97.20
[20]	0.165	97.47	0.113	87.85	0.203	98.14	0.158	96.00	NA	99.75	0.129	97.47	0.220	91.55	0.163	95.15

disparity maps and to baseline sparse SfM, even though only monocular(left) images were used compared to stereo method of [19]. In Fig.7, we compare against unary-only results with LIDAR sensor in KITTI [8].

7.2 Segmentation Quality

From our 3D joint semantic map, we can obtain 2D segmentation result by simply back-projecting it to each camera views. We evaluate segmentation quality in terms of both per pixel segmentation label accuracy and also temporal consistency of the segmentation in videos. We achieve significant improvement in both the measures over state of the art. To evaluate temporal consistency, we first select a set of confident SfM feature tracks which has very low re-projection errors after bundle adjustment. So these static 3D points should ideally be having same label from all the images it is visible from. So lower entropy (less changes in labels) for these SfM feature tracks is an indication of better temporal consistency. Table 1 shows the entropy scores for several state of art methods [24,19,31,20] where a higher entropy (in *bits*) indicates more temporal inconsistency. As a consequence of our model and 3D representation we achieve *perfect* consistency. We also evaluate per-pixel label accuracy and as shown in Table 1, our method achieves a noticeable gain over state of the art. The supplementary material has more discussion on these results.

8 Conclusion

We presented a method for joint inference of both semantic segmentation and 3D reconstruction, and thus provides a more holistic 3D understanding of the scene. Our framework offers several advantages : (a) Joint optimization of semantic segmentation and 3D reconstruction allows us to exploit more constraints and apply more informed regularization achieving improvement in both the tasks; (b) The 3D graphical model allows to incorporate more powerful 3D geometric cues compared to standard 2D image based spatial smoothness constraints; (c) It works for difficult forward moving monocular cameras, where sparse SfM is the only robust reconstruction method, and obtaining dense depth maps (required by [9,26]) is difficult; (d) We obtain full temporally consistent segmentations, without ad hoc constraints as in other 2D video segmentation methods [6,24,31]; (e) The output is in the form of a 3D volumetric semantic + occupancy map, which is much more useful than a series of 2D semantic label images or sparse pointcloud and it thus finds several applications like autonomous car navigation.

Acknowledgment. This work was supported by ARO-MURI award W911NF-11-1-0046.

References

1. Agarwal, S., Mierle, K.: Others: Ceres solver (2012),
   https://code.google.com/p/ceres-solver/
2. Brostow, G.J., Shotton, J., Fauqueur, J., Cipolla, R.: Segmentation and recognition using structure from motion point clouds. In: Forsyth, D., Torr, P., Zisserman, A. (eds.) ECCV 2008, Part I. LNCS, vol. 5302, pp. 44–57. Springer, Heidelberg (2008)
3. Brostow, G.J., Shotton, J., Fauqueur, J., Cipolla, R.: Segmentation and recognition using structure from motion point clouds. In: Forsyth, D., Torr, P., Zisserman, A. (eds.) ECCV 2008, Part I. LNCS, vol. 5302, pp. 44–57. Springer, Heidelberg (2008)
4. Brostow, G., Fauqueur, J., Cipolla, R.: Semantic object classes in video: A high-definition ground truth database. PRL 30(2), 88–97 (2009)
5. Cornelis, N., Leibe, B., Cornelis, K., Van Gool, L.: 3D urban scene modeling integrating recognition and reconstruction. IJCV 78(2-3), 121–141 (2008)
6. Floros, G., Leibe, B.: Joint 2D-3D temporally consistent segmentation of street scenes. In: CVPR (2012)
7. Furukawa, Y., Ponce, J.: Accurate, dense, and robust multiview stereopsis. PAMI 32(8), 1362–1376 (2010)
8. Geiger, A., Lenz, P., Urtasun, R.: Are we ready for autonomous driving? the kitti vision benchmark suite. In: CVPR (2012)

9. Häne, C., Zach, C., Cohen, A., Angst, R., Pollefeys, M.: Joint 3D scene reconstruction and class segmentation. In: CVPR (2013)
10. Hoiem, D., Efros, A., Hebert, M.: Recovering surface layout from an image. IJCV 75(1), 151–172 (2007)
11. Hornung, A., Wurm, K.M., Bennewitz, M., Stachniss, C., Burgard, W.: OctoMap: An efficient probabilistic 3D mapping framework based on octrees. Autonomous Robots (2013)
12. Jancosek, M., Pajdla, T.: Multi-view reconstruction preserving weakly-supported surfaces. In: CVPR (2011)
13. Kaess, M., Johannsson, H., Roberts, R., Ila, V., Leonard, J., Dellaert, F.: iSAM2: Incremental smoothing and mapping using the Bayes tree. IJRR 31, 217–236 (2012)
14. Kappes, J.H., Speth, M., Reinelt, G., Schnorr, C.: Towards efficient and exact map-inference for large scale discrete computer vision problems via combinatorial optimization. In: CVPR (2013)
15. Kohli, P., Ladick, L., Torr, P.: Robust higher order potentials for enforcing label consistency. IJCV 82(3), 302–324 (2009)
16. Koller, D., Friedman, N.: Probabilistic Graphical Models: Principles and Techniques. The MIT Press (2009)
17. Komodakis, N., Paragios, N.: Beyond pairwise energies: Efficient optimization for higher-order mrfs. In: CVPR (2009)
18. Krahenbuhl, P., Koltun, V.: Efficient inference in fully connected crfs with gaussian edge potentials. In: NIPS (2011)
19. Ladicky, L., Sturgess, P., Russell, C., Sengupta, S., Bastanlar, Y., Clocksin, W., Torr, P.H.: Joint optimisation for object class segmentation and dense stereo reconstruction. In: BMVC (2010)
20. Ladicky, L., Russell, C., Kohli, P., Torr, P.: Associative hierarchical crfs for object class image segmentation. In: ICCV (2009)
21. Lafferty, J.D., McCallum, A., Pereira, F.C.N.: Conditional random fields: Probabilistic models for segmenting and labeling sequence data. In: ICML (2001)
22. Liu, B., Gould, S., Koller, D.: Single image depth estimation from predicted semantic labels. In: CVPR (2010)
23. Liu, S., Cooper, D.B.: Ray markov random fields for image-based 3D modeling: model and efficient inference. In: CVPR (2010)
24. Miksik, O., Munoz, D., Bagnell, J.A., Hebert, M.: Efficient temporal consistency for streaming video scene analysis. In: ICRA (2013)
25. Saxena, A., Chung, S., Ng, A.: 3-D Depth Reconstruction from a Single Still image. IJCV 76(1), 53–69 (2008)
26. Sengupta, S., Greveson, E., Shahrokni, A., Torr, P.H.S.: Urban 3D semantic modelling using stereo vision. In: ICRA (2013)
27. Sturgess, P., Alahari, K., Ladicky, L., Torr, P.H.S.: Combining appearance and structure from motion features for road scene understanding. In: BMVC (2009)
28. Sutton, C., McCallum, A.: An introduction to conditional random fields. PAMI 4(4), 267–373 (2012)
29. Tarlow, D., Givoni, I.E., Zemel, R.S.: Hop-map: Efficient message passing with high order potentials. In: AISTATS (2010)
30. Thrun, S., Burgard, W., Fox, D.: Probabilistic robotics. MIT Press (2005)
31. Tighe, J., Lazebnik, S.: Superparsing: Scalable nonparametric image parsing with superpixels. International Journal of Computer Vision (2012)
32. Wainwright, M.J., Jordan, M.I.: Graphical models, exponential families, and variational inference. Foundations and Trends® in Machine Learning 1(1-2), 1–305 (2008)

A New Variational Framework
for Multiview Surface Reconstruction

Ben Semerjian

Urban Robotics, Inc., Portland, Oregon, USA

Abstract. The creation of surfaces from overlapping images taken from
different vantages is a hard and important problem in computer vision.
Recent developments fall primarily into two categories: the use of dense
matching to produce point clouds from which surfaces are built, and the
construction of surfaces from images directly. This paper presents a new
method for surface reconstruction falling in the second category. First,
a strongly motivated variational framework is built from the ground up
based on a limiting case of photo-consistency. The framework includes a
powerful new edge preserving smoothness term and exploits the input images exhaustively, directly yielding high quality surfaces instead of dealing with issues (such as noise or misalignment) after the fact. Numeric
solution is accomplished with a combination of Gauss-Newton descent
and the finite element method, yielding deep convergence in few iterates.
The method is fast, robust, very insensitive to view/scene configurations,
and produces state-of-the-art results in the Middlebury evaluation.

Keywords: Surface reconstruction, surface fairing, multiview stereo,
Gauss-Newton, finite element method.

1 Introduction

One of the grandest problems in structure from motion concerns the creation of
surfaces from images given known view extrinsics and intrinsics. This problem is
important because it yields a dense and useful geometric representation of that
which was photographed. The problem's complexity stems from many reasons:
nonlinear relation between surface and pixel, discontinuities and folds in the
scene, image noise, ambiguity in textureless regions, scaling and implementation
difficulties, illumination changes, and scene changes, to name a few.

There has been much work done on the topic, boosted in part by advance-
ments in computing power. One way to approach surface reconstruction is to
first perform dense matching on pairs of images (*e.g.* [12][18]), then create a
point cloud from the matches via triangulation (*e.g.* [15][31]), and finally create a surface from the point cloud (*e.g.* [19][29]). This methodology is popular
for several reasons, including the availability of very fast and accurate dense
matching algorithms, the fact that a point cloud is sometimes desired instead
of a surface, processing speed, and relatively simple implementation due to the
clear separation between steps. There are disadvantages too, most significant is

D. Fleet et al. (Eds.): ECCV 2014, Part VI, LNCS 8694, pp. 719–734, 2014.
© Springer International Publishing Switzerland 2014

that the output surfaces might lack accuracy and have excess noise; this is partly because these methods are based on pixel matching instead of surface generation (for example, planar correspondences do not imply planar surfaces).

The main other class of methods basically create surfaces directly from the images, a technique often called "multiview stereo", examples of which include [17][24]. Since these focus on building surfaces instead of matching pixels, they have the potential for higher quality output. Furthermore, they inherently handle multiview relations, which enables higher accuracy.

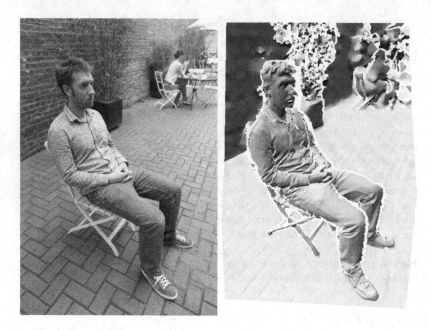

Fig. 1. Example of the proposed surface reconstruction in action: one of three handheld images (left) and surface output (right) rendered with Oren-Nayar shading [27]

The primary contribution of this work is a new method for surface reconstruction belonging to the second class described above, a sample application of which is shown in Figure 1. New ideas are combined with established concepts from multiview stereo, optical flow, and surface fairing. Perhaps unusual for a computer vision topic, numeric solution uses the finite element method with inspiration from continuum mechanics. The resulting surfaces are computed quickly and in an arbitrarily scalable manner, and since the formulation is continuous the range of depth (or disparity) has no effect on computation speed or memory. The resulting surfaces not only are accurate in an absolute sense, they also have smooth, accurate normals. A method of selecting high quality surfaces is also presented (enabled by the high accuracy of normals), yielding a means to avoid surface fusion and limits on the scale of output.

1.1 Related Work

The use of variational formulations to approach image matching problems (*e.g.* surface reconstruction, dense correspondence, or optical flow) is nothing new, and some of the strongest works on these topics go that route. In [5], a problem is built using the combination of data and smoothness to provide high accuracy optical flow. There, the data term penalizes for differences both in image intensity and in image gradient. This is extended in [4] to the case of "large displacement", extending the same data term with bias toward sparse features. Though indeed accurate and valid for large displacement, this will not work in the case of significant affine changes (such as rotation) since such will transform the image gradient, preventing it from being matched.

To deal with affine changes, [21] and [17] exploit surface normals to define local coordinate transforms, and use cross correlation oriented with those local transforms (potentially with normalization [23]) for the data term. This makes for not only a more flexible problem, but also a stronger one because the data term introduces a coupling over the surface due to its dependence on normal, forcing a higher level of consistency in the output (otherwise, the role of coupling rests entirely with the smoothness term). An issue with this approach is the need for selection of correlation window size: too small results in hampered robustness, too large smears things together. Despite many gains, the pointwise nature of [4] lending to simplicity and high accuracy is lost.

Regarding smoothing (or regularization), which is necessary to deal with image noise and textureless regions, [17] adds bending energy in the style of [20] to the minimization. This is fast, simple, and smooths effectively without biasing the solution toward minimum surface area, as a mean curvature approach would do. There are disadvantages though, as pointed out in [6][25], including poor numerical qualities and mesh-dependent behavior. They suggest principal curvature based smoothing with an elaborate curvature calculation, which works better and also does not induce surface area bias.

One issue common in these and other works is the fact that they rely on the computation of curvatures (or other second order quantities) on triangular meshes, which not only is fragile (individual mesh faces have no curvature) but as shown in [35] is guaranteed to suffer from at least one pathology no matter how elaborate. To make matters worse, these complicated quantities are typically minimized with gradient descent (*e.g.* [17][16][9]), which is sensible for simplicity but gives only linear convergence.

In this work, a notion of "infinitesimal patch" is introduced, giving pointwise illumination invariant error measurements as in [5] with the affine invariance and coupling of [17]. A scale invariant curvature-like smoothness term is used, whose magnitude is minimized (instead of its square) for edge and discontinuity preservation in the way second order total generalized variation [2] works. Discretization is accomplished using a second order finite element method [3], which represents the solution as a continuously differentiable function, implying continuous surface normals. The Gauss-Newton method [36] is used for numeric minimization, giving near second order convergence in few iterates.

2   Design of the Framework

Consider N overlapping images, whose greyscale content is notated as $B_i(\mathbf{u}_i)$ where $\mathbf{u}_i = (u_i, v_i)$ is a pixel coordinate on image i. Each image point $\mathbf{u}_i$ is the projection [14] of a 3D point $\mathbf{X}$ according to

$$w_i \mathbf{u}_i = K_i R_i (\mathbf{X} - \mathbf{c}_i) \tag{1}$$

where K_i, R_i, and $\mathbf{c}_i$ are respectively the intrinsics, rotation, and position of view i, and w_i is a quantity known as *depth*.

In this work, surface reconstruction will be posed as the problem of finding depth on one of these images, arbitrarily the first, as a function of pixel coordinate. That is, the goal is to find $w_0(\mathbf{u}_0)$. Such effectively defines 3D points as a function of image point as well, using the projection formula above.

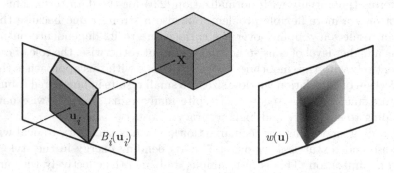

Fig. 2. A cube imaged by two views. Left frame: projected as a grey image onto view i, right frame: projected as depth image onto view 0.

This of course implies that only that which is viewable by the first view can be reconstructed; however one can create a depth image for every image available and reconstruct an arbitrarily large scene that way. As will be shown later, the fact that disparate surfaces are created with this strategy is not problematic (though they can be fused if desired, *e.g.* [29]), and the amount of focused effort the algorithm can put into the creation of a single depth image has benefit.

2.1   The Minimization Problem

Since the depth of image 0 will be the individual focus here, to simplify notation subscripts will be dropped for quantities referring to view 0. In other words, $B = B_0$, $w = w_0$, and $\mathbf{u} = \mathbf{u}_0$. The problem of finding the depth function $w(\mathbf{u})$ will then be posed as the minimization of the functional

$$\sum_{i>j\geq 0}^{N-1} \iint_{O_i \cap O_j} d\big(B_i, B_j, \mathbf{u}_i(w(\mathbf{u})), \mathbf{u}_j(w(\mathbf{u}))\big) + \alpha |\nabla B(\mathbf{u})| S\big(w(\mathbf{u})\big) \, du dv \tag{2}$$

where d is a photo-consistency measure between images i and j, S is a smoothness function, α is a smoothness factor, and O_i is the subset of all points on image 0 which are viewed by image i (that is, the *overlap* between 0 and i).

Note that the summation, which appears outside of the integral, covers every combination of i and j once. This sets up interactions between every possible combination of views, and these interactions occur over the intersections of the overlap domains O_i and O_j. The smoothness term is also under the summation though it does not involve i or j, this is done so that the number of smoothness contributions equals the number of data combinations.

2.2   Photo-Consistency

Photo-consistency is the data of the minimization; it measures correspondence fitness based on image content. The function $d(B_i, B_j, \mathbf{u}_i, \mathbf{u}_j)$ therefore penalizes for mismatch between the given images at the given coordinates. Note that in (2) there is one term for every possible combination of overlapping images.

Two views. To ease the derivation of this function, two views (0 and i) will be considered first without any notion of 3D. A correspondence from image 0 to image i may then be represented generally by a piecewise smooth function $\mathbf{u}_i(\mathbf{u})$. Put into words, this functional representation takes as input a coordinate on image 0 and gives a coordinate on image i.

To build the photo-consistency function, consider a 3×3 patch of pixels centered around an arbitrary point $\mathbf{u}$ on image 0. The correspondence function $\mathbf{u}_i(\mathbf{u})$ defines not only the location of the corresponding patch on i, but also the local coordinate system which describes the shape of the patch. This is illustrated in Figure 3.

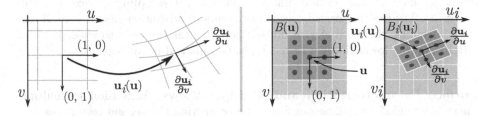

Fig. 3. Left: relation between coordinates on 0 and i at some arbitrary point, right: a patch on image 0 and a corresponding contorted patch on image i

Elaborating on "local coordinate system", the Jacobian of $\mathbf{u}_i(\mathbf{u})$ is:

$$J_i(\mathbf{u}) = \begin{bmatrix} \frac{\partial \mathbf{u}_i}{\partial u} & \frac{\partial \mathbf{u}_i}{\partial v} \end{bmatrix} = \begin{bmatrix} \frac{\partial u_i}{\partial u} & \frac{\partial u_i}{\partial v} \\ \frac{\partial v_i}{\partial u} & \frac{\partial v_i}{\partial v} \end{bmatrix} \tag{3}$$

where the columns may be seen as basis vectors on image i corresponding to the standard basis on image 0. These vectors define the shape of the patch.

Based on all this, a data term may be easily written as the magnitude of the (nine element) difference between the patches, with averages subtracted for brightness invariance. We can do much better though: by scaling the patch sizes by some factor Δs, dividing the patch differences by Δs, and taking the limit $\Delta s \to 0$, the data term simplifies to:

$$d(B_i, B_0, \mathbf{u}_i, \mathbf{u}_0) = |J_i^\mathsf{T} \nabla_i B_i - \nabla B| \quad ; \quad \nabla_i = \begin{pmatrix} \frac{\partial}{\partial u_i} \\ \frac{\partial}{\partial v_i} \end{pmatrix} \tag{4}$$

where the gradient operators are applied on the images in their own individual coordinates as shown. Note that the magnitude of the residual is used instead of the square; this makes numeric solution a little more complicated but ultimately yields better results.

This data term is in essence a difference in image gradients, but with the gradient of B_i contorted into the coordinates of view 0 using the Jacobian. In fact, the above could be derived more readily by writing the differences in gradients of 0 and i in the coordinates of 0, and then using the chain rule to change derivatives. The above derivation is interesting though, as it reveals that this sort of gradient matching is like patch matching, but with "infinitesimal patches". This strongly suggests that, under this formulation at least, another term penalizing for differences in raw color as in [4] is unnecessary.

This result gives the promised qualities: simple pointwise nature as in [4], illumination invariance, local affine invariance, and "built in" coupling between pixels due to the use of the Jacobian. One way to visualize the benefit of that last item is that a single mismatched point will unfavorably affect its neighbors due to distruption of the Jacobian.

Note that while this measure is pointwise on paper, in practice finite differences are used to differentiate images and a 3×3 sampling of pixels is still necessary. The limiting case derived above remains advantageous for several reasons, including the fixed size of finite differences (as opposed to chosen size of patch) and the lower number of residuals: two instead of (at least) nine.

Surface Parameterization and Multiple Views. Extension to multiple views is straightforward, accomplished by contorting the second term:

$$d(B_i, B_j, \mathbf{u}_i, \mathbf{u}_j) = |J_i^\mathsf{T} \nabla_i B_i - J_j^\mathsf{T} \nabla_j B_j| \tag{5}$$

where $J_0 = I$ is implied.

In order for this to make sense for surface reconstruction, the fact that the N abstract correspondence functions $\mathbf{u}_i(\mathbf{u})$ can be replaced with functions dependent on depth w instead is used. Writing projection equations (1) for views 0 and i separately and eliminating the 3D point yields this parameterization:

$$\mathbf{u}_i(w(\mathbf{u})) = \frac{1}{wr_i + t_{z,i}} \begin{pmatrix} wp_i + t_{x,i} \\ wq_i + t_{y,i} \end{pmatrix} \tag{6}$$

where the quantity in the denominator is the depth on view i, and the following definitions are made for compactness:

$$M_i = K_i R_i R_0^T K_0^{-1} \ , \quad \mathbf{t}_i = K_i R_i (\mathbf{c}_0 - \mathbf{c}_i) \ , \quad \begin{pmatrix} p_i \\ q_i \\ r_i \end{pmatrix} = M_i \mathbf{u} \ . \tag{7}$$

To emphasize, (5) was derived using pixel correspondences but for surface reconstruction is completely parameterized by the surface as represented by the depth function $w(\mathbf{u})$ via the relation (6). This implies that the Jacobian J_i must be written in terms of depth as well, which is possible by differentiating (6), involving the gradient of the depth function. This is in contrast with other approaches (*e.g.* [17]) that rely on the surface normal, a more complicated quantity, and one that is more difficult to involve in an optimization.

One potential weakness here is that since all of the gradients are in essence projected onto view 0, there will be some form of asymmetry in the photo-consistency measure. One possible means of alleviating this, still without introducing surface normal, is to project onto i and j separately:

$$d_{\mathrm{Sym}}(B_i, B_j, \mathbf{u}_i, \mathbf{u}_j) = |\nabla_i B_i - J_i^{-\mathsf{T}} J_j^{\mathsf{T}} \nabla_j B_j| + |J_j^{-\mathsf{T}} J_i^{\mathsf{T}} \nabla_i B_i - \nabla_j B_j| \ . \tag{8}$$

In practice this does not alter the surfaces significantly while adding significant complexity, it is therefore not considered.

2.3 Smoothness Function

As is well established in the study of differential geometry, quantities derived from curvature are high performing (though complicated) measures of surface quality, fairness, and noise [25][22].

It would seem natural then to add a curvature-derived quantity to the minimization here in order to keep the output of surface reconstruction fair and high-quality. Unfortunately, smoothness penalties derived from raw curvature are unsuitable because they will involve the scale of the 3D output. This is highly undesirable because scale is ambiguous in structure from motion problems [33].

To remedy this, [17] multiplies curvature with depth (canceling scale), however such is ad-hoc and not certain to work universally. In this work, the fact that curvature can be measured from spatial changes in surface normal is exploited.

For example, one of many definitions for the mean curvature of a surface is the divergence (with respect to 3D space) of the normal [13]. Following this, the smoothness term used here is based on the first derivatives of the normal, not against 3D space, but against image coordinates:

$$S(\mathbf{u}) = |\nabla \hat{\mathbf{n}}(\mathbf{u})| \ . \tag{9}$$

To emphasize, the unit normal is a dimensionless function of shape, and since differentiation is against pixel coordinate this quantity is free from physical scale. This fairness measure may be thought of as the curvature of the surface as *seen* by view 0.

Note that in (2) the magnitude of the gradient of B appears as a factor on S. This results in a texture/contrast invariant balance between data and smoothness; one might imagine that omitting such for more smoothness in areas with less contrast would make sense, however experiment shows that full contrast invariance works better. Furthermore, if the smoothness factor α is understood to have pixel coordinate units, the data and smoothness terms in (2) will both have the same units. This suggests a well-formed problem which will have very consistent behavior at multiple scales (the meaning of scale explained in the section on numeric solution), which is demonstrated in Figure 4.

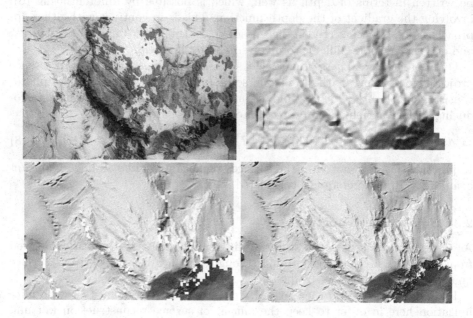

Fig. 4. From top left: a 2400 × 1596 aerial image of the peak and northeastern upper reaches of Mt. Hood taken with a nadir-looking wide angle lens; depth images at scales 64, 16, and 4, rendered with Oren-Nayar shading [27]. Sixteen other images were used to reconstruct these surfaces with $\alpha = 0.6$. Note that the coarse scale captures the overall shape of the terrain, while the fine scale sharply reveals every crevasse without sacrificing smoothness. These images feature a variety of reconstruction difficulties: high/low texture transitions, shadow noise, highly oblique surfaces, and sharp edges.

3   Numeric Solution

With the raw variational problem fully defined, numeric solution now will be described. It consists of three basic ingredients: a discretization reducing $w(\mathbf{u})$ to an interpolation on a regular 2D grid, a means of minimizing (2) at fixed scale and domain, and a coarse to fine domain management scheme.

3.1 Discretization

The finite element method is used to discretize the problem. This method is extremely popular in the study of continuum mechanics and other fields [28], but unfortunately has made few appearances in computer vision.

To briefly summarize, the method as applied here defines the unknown depth function $w(\mathbf{u})$ as a set of bicubic patches on a square grid of spacing σ. The grid intersection points are called *nodes*, and each node carries the value, gradient, and mixed second derivative of depth at that point, giving rise to a solution surface that is continuously differentiable by definition (*i.e.* without differencing).

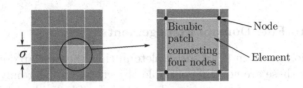

Fig. 5. Illustration of the finite element method discretization used

This representation is substituted into (2) and the integrals are evaluated with the midpoint method; all of the nodal values therefore form the discrete unknowns of the problem. Advantages of this approach include a clear and natural discretization of (2); more importantly, the smoothness of the solution implies continuous Jacobians in (5) and continuous normals in (9). A simpler discretization would require finite differences for these quantities, leading to messy implementations and much less effective smoothing.

3.2 Minimization

At some fixed spacing σ and set of domains O_i, the minimization of (2) is carried out using the Gauss-Newton method. That is, steps are taken by solving for a Newton step $\mathbf{p}$ to be applied to all nodes from the linear system

$$H\mathbf{p} = -\mathbf{g} \quad ; \quad H \approx J^\mathsf{T} J, \quad \mathbf{g} = J^\mathsf{T}\mathbf{r} \tag{10}$$

using a Hessian matrix H approximated as shown. Often, this is done by storing the Jacobian J and residuals $\mathbf{r}$ for the whole problem (this is different from the Jacobians of (5)), however in this case the residuals are too many and it is more practical to directly store the gradient $\mathbf{g}$ and approximate Hessian H.

The solution of one step is carried out using the conjugate gradient method [36], explicitly preconditioned with a Cholesky factorization [36] of the 4×4 diagonal blocks of H. This normally is not regarded as a very powerful preconditioner, however it is adequate for this problem because H tends to be relatively well-conditioned, because the blocks are moderate-sized, and also because the solution happens over multiple scales as in [8].

Unregulated steps work quite well (perhaps surprisingly), and step control (*e.g.* trust region, line search) is unnecessary. The minimization is allowed to run till the steps change the reprojections in amounts significantly smaller than one pixel.

The fact that both data (5) and smoothness (9) involve the magnitudes of vectors (as opposed to squares) makes the optimization potentially difficult; iterative re-weighting is used here to keep it simple. That is, squares of d and S are used for the computation of H and g, weighted by the reciprocals of their magnitudes. This is relatively simple to implement, and is surprisingly effective for data + smoothness type problems, for example the algorithm in [7] yields excellent results in just one iteration.

3.3   Coarse to Fine Domain Management

The minimization problem (2) is incomplete in that the overlap domains O_i are unknown. Since these are not differentiable objects and appear only fixed in (2), a set of heuristics are used to manage them outside of individual minimizations. This is done over multiple scales, coarse to fine, gradually refining both the solution $w(\mathbf{u})$ and the domains.

Initially, the spacing σ is set to a power of two larger than typical sparse point spacing but smaller than image dimensions, *e.g.* $\sigma = 128$. The input images are Gaussian blurred with standard deviation $0.12\sigma + 0.2$. The initial domain is fitted to sparse points at this spacing.

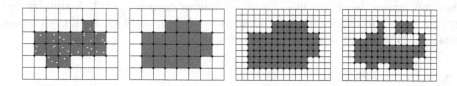

Fig. 6. Various domain operations. Left to right: initial domain with sparse points, expanded domain, domain at halved spacing, cleaned domain with topology change.

The solution process proceeds as follows: with scale and domains fixed, minimize (2) as described in the previous section, expand the domains by extrapolating, clean them to remove occlusions and non-converged points, and repeat a number of times, leading to convergence of both domain and depth. The spacing is then halved and the process repeated. Completion happens when (2) is minimized at $\sigma = 2$, or at some a coarser terminal spacing if lower resolution is considered adequate. Going below $\sigma = 2$ will add no benefit, since that is the point where the total number of degrees of freedom will equal the number of pixels. Behavior with decreasing scale is shown in Figure 4.

The expansion operation is an extrapolation of all of the boundary nodes using thin plates [1], the purpose of which is to enlarge the domains. The more complicated cleaning operation removes non-converged nodes (those tend to be mismatches), elements covering adequately textured pixels with a normalized cross correlation [23] less than zero, spots on individual domains violating the visibility constraint [32], and elements that are suspected of lying on an occlusion boundary. The test for occlusion is similar to that in [11]: a small singular value of the Jacobian at a node is indicative.

4   Practical Usage

The methodology outlined here yields one surface for one image. Though potent, this is restrictive since one cannot expect that which is viewed by one image to cover all that is interesting in an arbitrary set of images. The obvious remedy is to separately output surfaces from different groups of overlapping images. Though this could mean redundant work, there is the significant benefit of scalability: an arbitrary number of surfaces can be processed, provided the number of overlapping images is controlled (in practice, approximately ten images per surface works well). Furthermore, the work is trivial to parallelize – individual processing units work on individual surfaces.

Fig. 7. Ama Dablam in the Himalayas; 639 depth images have been separately computed and outputted as meshes, taking less than an hour on 24 cores. Top: raw surfaces, bottom: after cutting (10 minute computation), with some permitted overlap. Helicopter photography by David Breashears, December 2010, www.glacierworks.com.

Such collections of surfaces can be fused into single surfaces [29][19]. Though this specific task is not arbitrarily scalable, it is very effective for the creation of mensurable, high quality surfaces.

For visual applications there is another option: the outputted surfaces can be "cut" so that surface points are kept only if best viewed by the view that generated them, and deleted otherwise. These cut surfaces can then be optimally meshed in two dimensions [10] (since they are individually represented as 2D functions $w(\mathbf{u})$), and then either "zippered" [34] or simply presented together without any fusion. An example of this is shown in Figure 7.

The criteria for surface cutting is based on the *surface resolving power* (derivation may be found in supplemental material):

$$\frac{dQ}{dA} = -\hat{\mathbf{n}} \cdot \left(\nabla_{\mathbf{X}} u \times \nabla_{\mathbf{X}} v \right) \tag{11}$$

where A is a physical area, Q is a projected pixel area, and $\mathbf{u}$ is the projection (1) of the 3D point $\mathbf{X}$ being evaluated. This may be interpreted as a "pixels per surface area" measure taking obliqueness into account, and the image which views a point best will score highest in surface resolving power. That point is deleted from all other images.

5   Results

Figure 8 shows the output of this work compared to ground truth and two other high performers in the Middlebury multiview stereo evaluation [30]. For this, a maximum of 15 views were used to output every individual depth image, and $\alpha = 0.2$. Generation of all 363 depth images took just under an hour on a 12 core machine; these were then fused together using Poisson reconstruction [19], taking an additional 10 minutes on one core.

In addition to being accurate, the result of this work clearly rivals others in terms of smoothness, sharpness, and visual quality; for example, the mouth of the stegosaurus is resolved, its scales are sharp, its toes are distinct, and there is

Fig. 8. Left to right: surface reconstructions of Furukawa2 [9], Shroers [29], this work, and ground truth for Middlebury's Dino dataset

Fig. 9. Left to right: one of five 2746×1832 images of a ceramic bull figurine taken with a telephoto lens, reconstruction from stereo correspondences using elas [12], reconstruction at $\alpha = 4$ and scale 4 using this work. Rendered with mean curvature colorization, best viewed in color.

nearly no noise to be found. Its specular characteristics (which reveal curvature and surface quality [26]) also match the ground truth most closely.

In Figure 9, comparison is made against elas, a high ranking stereo correspondence method [12]. Every surface point is triangulated from five densely matched points via reprojection error minimization [14]. While the surface is accurate in an absolute sense, the normals are almost random and curvature is not controlled; a surface such as this could not be cut using (11) due to inaccuracy of normal. It should be noted though that elas took less than 9 seconds, while the result of this work took 150 seconds.

Figure 7 demonstrates capability on a large physical scale. This shows what can be done with high accuracy surfaces foregoing fusion. The mountain in the center of the model is well resolved due to proximity with the camera; in contrast, the far content (up to 20 km away) serves as backdrop material, lacking fidelity without being noisy, much as it is in the source imagery.

Methods relying on fusion such as [19] or [29] would be unable to neatly mix far and near in a single reconstruction because these generally scale poorly with physical scale; methods such as [12] or [18] would also suffer because of the large disparities (a consequence of large depth ranges).

Figure 10 shows in detail and higher resolution one reconstruction from the image set in Figure 7. The seven images used were taken with a forward looking wide angle lens; all of the epipoles are in the image as shown in the figure. Though there is no stereo at an epipole and less than a pixel of parallax near Mt. Everest, the reconstruction is successful in making the most of what is available. Of particular note is the very consistent action of smoothing: the perceived curvatures are very even across all depth scales, and there is no increase in noise due to contrast changes, the epipoles, or distance from camera.

Fig. 10. Surface reconstruction of Ama Dablam (foreground peak) in the Himalayas using seven images and $\alpha = 0.3$, with Mt Everest 15 km away in the background. Helicopter photography by David Breashears, December 2010, www.glacierworks.com.

6 Conclusion

In this paper, a novel surface reconstruction method was built from scratch. With only a single tunable parameter controlling smoothness, it has been shown to output accurate, smooth, sharp, natural-looking surfaces. It is arbitrarily scalable and performs uniformly across many different kinds of images. A method for discarding surfaces that are better seen by other views was also given, reducing the need for fusion and allowing models of arbitrary size to be reconstructed.

Another notable aspect of this work is the use of the finite element method, which has unfortunately made few appearances in computer vision. Its application resulted in solutions with built-in differentiability, necessary for the smoothness term to work properly.

The highly effective smoothness function (9) could be used in other vision problems, such as shape from shading. Other possibilities for future work include the incorporation of sparse features as in [4], dense initialization with stereo correspondences, stronger occlusion handling, and refinement of view parameters alongside surfaces for very high accuracy output.

References

1. Bookstein, F.L.: Principal warps: Thin-plate splines and the decomposition of deformations. IEEE Transactions on Pattern Analysis and Machine Intelligence 11(6), 567–585 (1989)

2. Bredies, K., Kunisch, K., Pock, T.: Total generalized variation. SIAM Journal on Imaging Sciences 3(3), 492–526 (2010)
3. Brenner, S.C., Scott, R.: The mathematical theory of finite element methods, vol. 15. Springer (2008)
4. Brox, T., Bregler, C., Malik, J.: Large displacement optical flow. In: IEEE Conference on Computer Vision and Pattern Recognition, CVPR 2009, pp. 41–48. IEEE (2009)
5. Brox, T., Bruhn, A., Papenberg, N., Weickert, J.: High accuracy optical flow estimation based on a theory for warping. In: Pajdla, T., Matas, J(G.) (eds.) ECCV 2004. LNCS, vol. 3024, pp. 25–36. Springer, Heidelberg (2004)
6. Desbrun, M., Meyer, M., Schröder, P., Barr, A.H.: Implicit fairing of irregular meshes using diffusion and curvature flow. In: Proceedings of the 26th Annual Conference on Computer Graphics and Interactive Techniques, pp. 317–324. ACM Press/Addison-Wesley Publishing Co. (1999)
7. Farbman, Z., Fattal, R., Lischinski, D., Szeliski, R.: Edge-preserving decompositions for multi-scale tone and detail manipulation. In: ACM Transactions on Graphics (TOG), vol. 27, p. 67. ACM (2008)
8. Fattal, R., Lischinski, D., Werman, M.: Gradient domain high dynamic range compression. In: ACM Transactions on Graphics (TOG), vol. 21, pp. 249–256. ACM (2002)
9. Furukawa, Y., Ponce, J.: Accurate, dense, and robust multiview stereopsis. IEEE Transactions on Pattern Analysis and Machine Intelligence 32(8), 1362–1376 (2010)
10. Garland, M., Heckbert, P.S.: Fast polygonal approximation of terrains and height fields. School of Computer Science, Carnegie Mellon University (1995)
11. Gay-Bellile, V., Bartoli, A., Sayd, P.: Direct estimation of nonrigid registrations with image-based self-occlusion reasoning. IEEE Transactions on Pattern Analysis and Machine Intelligence 32(1), 87–104 (2010)
12. Geiger, A., Roser, M., Urtasun, R.: Efficient large-scale stereo matching. In: Kimmel, R., Klette, R., Sugimoto, A. (eds.) ACCV 2010, Part I. LNCS, vol. 6492, pp. 25–38. Springer, Heidelberg (2011)
13. Goldman, R.: Curvature formulas for implicit curves and surfaces. Computer Aided Geometric Design 22(7), 632–658 (2005)
14. Hartley, R., Zisserman, A.: Multiple view geometry in computer vision. Cambridge University Press (2003)
15. Hartley, R.I., Sturm, P.: Triangulation. Computer vision and image understanding 68(2), 146–157 (1997)
16. Hernández, C., Vogiatzis, G., Cipolla, R.: Multiview photometric stereo. IEEE Transactions on Pattern Analysis and Machine Intelligence 30(3), 548–554 (2008)
17. Hiep, V.H., Keriven, R., Labatut, P., Pons, J.P.: Towards high-resolution large-scale multi-view stereo. In: IEEE Conference on Computer Vision and Pattern Recognition, CVPR 2009, pp. 1430–1437. IEEE (2009)
18. Hirschmuller, H.: Accurate and efficient stereo processing by semi-global matching and mutual information. In: IEEE Computer Society Conference on Computer Vision and Pattern Recognition, CVPR 2005, vol. 2, pp. 807–814. IEEE (2005)
19. Kazhdan, M., Bolitho, M., Hoppe, H.: Poisson surface reconstruction. In: Proceedings of the Fourth Eurographics Symposium on Geometry Processing (2006)
20. Kobbelt, L., Campagna, S., Vorsatz, J., Seidel, H.P.: Interactive multi-resolution modeling on arbitrary meshes. In: Proceedings of the 25th Annual Conference on Computer Graphics and Interactive Techniques, pp. 105–114. ACM (1998)

21. Kolev, K., Klodt, M., Brox, T., Cremers, D.: Continuous global optimization in multiview 3D reconstruction. International Journal of Computer Vision 84(1), 80–96 (2009)
22. Lee, C.H., Varshney, A., Jacobs, D.W.: Mesh saliency. ACM Transactions on Graphics (TOG) 24, 659–666 (2005)
23. Lewis, J.: Fast normalized cross-correlation. Vision Interface 10, 120–123 (1995)
24. Liu, Y., Cao, X., Dai, Q., Xu, W.: Continuous depth estimation for multi-view stereo. In: IEEE Conference on Computer Vision and Pattern Recognition, CVPR 2009, pp. 2121–2128. IEEE (2009)
25. Meyer, M., Desbrun, M., Schröder, P., Barr, A.H.: Discrete differential-geometry operators for triangulated 2-manifolds. In: Visualization and Mathematics III, pp. 35–57. Springer (2003)
26. Nordström, M., Järvstråt, N.: An appearance-based measure of surface defects. International Journal of Material Forming 2(2), 83–91 (2009)
27. Oren, M., Nayar, S.K.: Generalization of lambert's reflectance model. In: Proceedings of the 21st Annual Conference on Computer Graphics and Interactive Techniques, pp. 239–246. ACM (1994)
28. Reddy, J.N., Gartling, D.K.: The finite element method in heat transfer and fluid dynamics. CRC Press (2010)
29. Schroers, C., Zimmer, H., Valgaerts, L., Bruhn, A., Demetz, O., Weickert, J.: Anisotropic range image integration. In: Pinz, A., Pock, T., Bischof, H., Leberl, F. (eds.) DAGM/OAGM 2012. LNCS, vol. 7476, pp. 73–82. Springer, Heidelberg (2012)
30. Seitz, S.M., Curless, B., Diebel, J., Scharstein, D., Szeliski, R.: A comparison and evaluation of multi-view stereo reconstruction algorithms. In: 2006 IEEE Computer Society Conference on Computer Vision and Pattern Recognition, vol. 1, pp. 519–528. IEEE (2006)
31. Stewenius, H., Schaffalitzky, F., Nister, D.: How hard is 3-view triangulation really? In: Tenth IEEE International Conference on Computer Vision, ICCV 2005, vol. 1, pp. 686–693. IEEE (2005)
32. Sun, J., Li, Y., Kang, S.B., Shum, H.Y.: Symmetric stereo matching for occlusion handling. In: IEEE Computer Society Conference on Computer Vision and Pattern Recognition, CVPR 2005, vol. 2, pp. 399–406. IEEE (2005)
33. Szeliski, R., Kang, S.B.: Shape ambiguities in structure from motion. IEEE Transactions on Pattern Analysis and Machine Intelligence 19(5), 506–512 (1997)
34. Turk, G., Levoy, M.: Zippered polygon meshes from range images. In: Proceedings of the 21st Annual Conference on Computer Graphics and Interactive Techniques, pp. 311–318. ACM (1994)
35. Wardetzky, M., Mathur, S., Kälberer, F., Grinspun, E.: Discrete laplace operators: no free lunch. In: Symposium on Geometry Processing, pp. 33–37 (2007)
36. Wright, S., Nocedal, J.: Numerical optimization, vol. 2. Springer, New York (1999)

Multi-body Depth-Map Fusion
with Non-intersection Constraints

Bastien Jacquet[1], Christian Häne[1], Roland Angst[2], and Marc Pollefeys[1]

[1] ETH Zürich, Switzerland
[2] Stanford, USA

Abstract. Depthmap fusion is the problem of computing dense 3D reconstructions from a set of depthmaps. Whereas this problem has received a lot of attention for purely rigid scenes, there is remarkably little prior work for dense reconstructions of scenes consisting of several moving rigid bodies or parts. This paper therefore explores this multi-body depthmap fusion problem. A first observation in the multi-body setting is that when treated naively, ghosting artifacts will emerge, ie. the same part will be reconstructed multiple times at different positions. We therefore introduce non-intersection constraints which resolve these issues: at any point in time, a point in space can only be occupied by at most one part. Interestingly enough, these constraints can be expressed as linear inequalities and as such define a convex set. We therefore propose to phrase the multi-body depthmap fusion problem in a convex voxel labeling framework. Experimental evaluation shows that our approach succeeds in computing artifact-free dense reconstructions of the individual parts with a minimal overhead due to the non-intersection constraints.

Keywords: Multi-view stereo, multi-body structure-from-motion, depthmap fusion, convex optimization, Dynamic Scene Dense 3D Reconstruction.

1 Introduction

While there exists a large body of work for *rigid* multi-view stereo and depth-map fusion methods, there is remarkably little prior work for dense, entirely image-based 3D reconstructions of multi-body scenes where multiple rigid parts move with different transformations between two frames. However, this is a highly relevant setting since many man-made scenes or objects actually contain multiple moving rigid parts, for example pieces of furniture, adjustable screens, doors, etc. A dense 3D reconstruction together with a dense segmentation of the scene into functional parts is interesting for applications where a user can interact with the reconstructed objects, eg. by opening a door or by pulling out a drawer. This paper therefore addresses this multi-body depth-map fusion problem, and as a byproduct also provides a dense segmentation into differently moving parts. We note that sparse multi-body structure-from-motion (SfM) has received some attention in previous work, see eg. [1]. Since our paper clearly focuses on the

D. Fleet et al. (Eds.): ECCV 2014, Part VI, LNCS 8694, pp. 735–750, 2014.

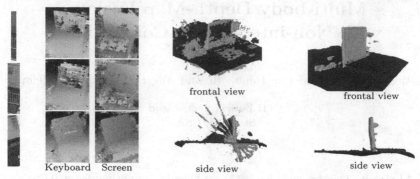

Input images   Depth maps   Independent reconstructions   Proposed approach with non-intersection constraints

Fig. 1. In multi-body depth-map fusion, we are trying to compute a dense reconstruction from a set of input depth-maps of a scene containing multiple moving rigid objects or parts (in the visualized example, the screen rotates w.r.t. the keyboard). A straight-forward approach which treats the reconstruction of each rigid part independently leads to severe artifacts, like a part being reconstructed multiple times at slightly different poses (especially visible in the side view where features of the desk, keyboard, and screen get reconstructed multiple times). The approach proposed in this paper introduces non-intersection constraints which enable complex interactions between the individual reconstruction problems thereby eliminating almost all those artifacts.

dense reconstruction, which requires known camera poses, we assume that those camera poses are provided by such a sparse multi-body SfM component. For the sake of completeness, we will nonetheless highlight several particular issues with the sparse multi-body setting in Sec. 4. Our multi-body depth-map fusion algorithm only requires depth-maps and camera poses registered to a common references frame. Recent depth-cameras could therefore be used as well, even though in this paper we only consider depth-maps computed from RGB images. As described in detail in Sec. 5, we are building on top of a convex voxel labeling framework for dense rigid reconstructions. In a nutshell, those frameworks label a voxel as either 'occupied' or 'freespace' based on a spatial regularization term together with a data fidelity term derived from depth-maps. Those methods provide accurate results for rigid scenes. As multi-body or articulated scenes are assembled from multiple rigid parts, an intuitive idea is to instantiate a separate voxel grid for each part and solve multiple labeling problems independently.

However, this leads to severe ghosting artifacts in the reconstructions: described in more detail in Sec. 3, the same part will be reconstructed multiple times, maybe even in a voxel grid associated to another part (see Fig. 1). In order to prevent this from happening, the grids must be allowed to interact with each other. Indeed, if we consider whether the reconstructions of all the parts are intersection free, we see that ghosting artifacts actually lead to intersections with other parts. Hence, our physically-motivated method is based on a remarkably simple, yet powerful idea: a moving rigid part can not occupy a point in space which is already occupied by another rigid part. These *non-intersection constraints* can be formulated as linear inequality constraints which link the previously independent labeling problems together. This results in complex interactions of regularization and data terms between different grids and will resolve the ghosting artifacts. It is important to note that despite rather weak data terms due to noisy depth maps, the non-intersection constraints result in a strong mutual exclusion principle which provides a clear part-based 3D segmentation. Interestingly, those non-intersection constraint also enable to 'carve out' regions which have never been directly observed in the input images. For example, observing how a drawer moves in and out of the drawer casing together with the non-intersection constraints immediately lead to the conclusion that the drawer casing must be hollow, a fact which is reproduced by our algorithm.

In contrast to previous convex depth-map fusion formulations for rigid scenes, our formulation contains two entirely different types of constraints: the non-intersection constraints and the standard variational formulation of the total variation regularizer. In order to efficiently handle this large optimization problem, we propose to use a preconditioned primal-dual proximal method [2]. Moreover, the set of non-intersection constraints can be quite large. Fortunately, only a small fraction of those constraints will be active at the globally optimal solution, lending itself to an efficient constraint generation procedure. An experimental evaluation shows that our algorithm achieves its goals of a dense multi-body reconstruction. In summary, the contributions of this paper are:

i) Introduction of the problem of dense consistent multi-body depth-map fusion and presentation of a solution based on convex non-intersection constraints which not only prevents ghosting artifacts but also carves out voxels in unseen regions which are occupied by another part.

ii) Description of a convex voxel labeling algorithm which is solved with a preconditioned primal-dual proximal method and with an efficient constraint generation procedure.

2   Related Work

Image based 3D reconstruction methods have made large progress in recent years. Structure-from-motion (SfM) [3] is nowadays a well-established technique to accurately compute camera poses and sparse 3D point clouds. While originally assuming an entirely rigid scene, sparse 3D reconstruction methods have been extended to deal with multiple rigid bodies [1] or with articulated objects [4,5], and even to more general non-rigidly deforming objects [6,7]. Each of those classes of objects or scenes comes with its own challenges. For example, finding a globally consistent scale for all the objects in a multi-body rigid scene is a non-trivial task, for which no solution exists in the most general case of entirely independently moving rigid objects [8]. Notably, parts of an articulated rigid objects are not allowed to move freely, a fact which manifests itself for example in a rank-constraint for a feature trajectory matrix which can be used to infer joint locations and a global scale [9]. In order to constrain the solution space, reconstruction methods for deformable objects require a prior for regularization, such as local rigidity [10], physically-inspired models [11], or a low-dimensional subspace model [12]. Even though non-rigidly deformable objects certainly represent an important class of objects, in this paper we focus on reconstructing multi-body rigid and articulated scenes, mainly because these scenes can be broken down into multiple moving rigid parts, whose interaction with each other can be captured in a mathematically exact way, as will be described later.

For multi-body rigid scenes, recent efforts in multi-body structure-from-motion led to the simultaneous computation of motion, segmentation and depth-maps from images [13,14]. These approaches estimate the different incremental motions from video with an iterative alternating scheme, and output a single [14] or a sequence [13] of depth-maps, with a segmentation mask and the associated motion for each object. One could feed those into a separate per-object depth-map fusion. However, deferring a reasoning in 3D can lead to ghosting artifacts where parts intersect or get reconstructed multiple times. This happens when a part remains photoconsistent w.r.t. another part, eg. for object shadows on the ground plane, as can be seen in [13,14]'s results. Our goal differs from theirs as we aim at volumetric, non-intersecting and time-consistent 3D models from unordered depth-maps. [13,14] can therefore be used to generate input depth-maps for our method.

In the Computer Graphics community, Chang and Zwicker's work [15] also addresses the problem of registering data from an articulated object in different configurations, mainly in order to infer the articulation chain and the assignment of points to parts. However, their focus differs from ours: while we are interested in a dense volumetric reconstruction from image data, their approach requires high-quality outlier-free point clouds as input so that no optimization over the 3D locations of the points is required. Unfortunately, image based methods require a SfM stage and point clouds acquired by SfM techniques tend to be very noisy and contaminated with many outliers, the same being true for RGBD-sensors. Those outliers are not handled by their method. Moreover, non-intersection constraints are not considered at all in [15].

Once camera poses are known from a sparse reconstruction method, dense reconstruction algorithms can be used to compute and extract 3D surfaces. Also known as multi-view stereo, this field contains a large amount of previous work. We refer the reader to [16] and its excellent accompanying website for further related work in this area. Carving out regions in 3D which project to non-occupied areas in the images have lead to the well-understood concept of the visual-hull [17]. Phrasing the multi-view stereo problem as a binary labeling problem of a 3D voxel grid with labels 'occupied' or 'freespace' and adding regularization, [18] has used graph-cuts to optimize the resulting energy minimization problem. Shortly after that, this discrete graph-cut formulation has been rephrased in the continuous setting as a convex optimization problem [19], where an efficient, highly parallelizable algorithm has been introduced. More generally, convex relaxations of binary or multi-label problems can be used to combine data evidence from images with a regularization term, usually a total-variation term, in an efficient,

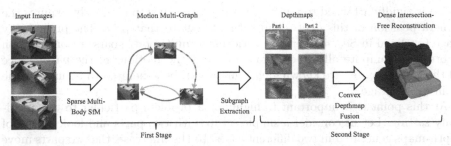

Fig. 2. The overall dense reconstruction pipeline takes an unordered set of images as input. As a preliminary stage, a sparse multi-body SfM component extracts a motion multigraph: a node represents an image and each edge represents a relative rigid transformation (of the camera or a rigid part) between two images. After selecting the appropriate subgraph for each part, depthmaps can be computed for that part. In the main stage, those depthmaps are fused in a volumetric convex voxel labeling framework where each part is reconstructed in a separate voxel grid. However, non-intersection constraints between the parts enable a complex interaction between all those grids, thereby carving out voxels in unseen areas which are occupied by another part and avoiding reconstruction artifacts such as 'ghost parts'.

highly parallelizable framework [20]. Our multi-body depth-map fusion approach builds on top of such convex relaxations. Recent approaches with RGBD cameras [21] only consider the unary data term and ignore any pairwise or higher-order regularization term, thereby sacrificing accuracy in favour of speed. Such a fusion approach has recently been extended for articulated model-based tracking [22]. Analogously to our approach, the model is represented by instantiating a separate voxel grid for each rigid part. An iterative-closest point algorithm between a new RGBD frame and the model is used to update the camera position, and given this camera position the new data evidence is fused into the grids. Hence in direct comparison to our approach, [22] is much faster but also less accurate, ignores the physical non-intersection constraints, and requires a RGB-D camera together with a continuous stream of images for incremental computation.

3   Problem Description and System Overview

The input to our algorithm consists of a set of depth-maps taken from a scene with multiple moving rigid objects or parts. Furthermore, the camera is also allowed to move. The number of parts G is assumed to be known.

Our reconstruction pipeline contains a preliminary depth-map generation stage, and a main fusion stage, see Fig. 2. The depth-map fusion stage is based on a volumetric fusion of depth-maps in a voxel grid. In contrast to previous approaches which consider a single rigid object and thus only a single voxel grid, we propose to use a separate voxel grid for each part in order to tackle the dense multi-body depth-map fusion problem. This second stage will be described in detail in Sec. 5. As we will see, in order to define a data term for a certain image and part, the depth-maps must be registered to those voxel grids, each of which is rigidly attached to a part. This registration step obviously requires the camera position of this depth-map with respect to that part. The preliminary stage (outlined in Sec. 4) therefore performs a multi-body sparse reconstruction in order to compute all the camera poses and the motions of the parts. Once all the camera poses are known, depth-maps can be generated to be used in the main fusion stage.

At this point it is important to highlight a problem particular to the multi-body setting. Let us consider a simple setup with two parts and look at sets of depth-maps generated in two different cases. In the first case, the two parts move with respect to each other between any two images. The resulting depth-maps for each part will contain highly confident measurements in regions where that part is visible and contain random measurements with low confidence in regions of the other part because the motions of the two parts are different and thus inconsistent for computing a single depth-map. In the second case however, only the camera moves and the two parts stay rigid with respect to each other. The depth-maps for those images will be the same for both parts and contain highly confident measurements for *both* parts. Fusing all those depth-maps from the first and second case for each part independently will lead to *ghost parts*: the highly confident measurements of the second case provide consistent evidence for both parts in each one of the two voxel grids, whereas the inconsistent regions with low confidence in depth-maps of the first case would be simply treated as outlying measurements for example due to occlusions. In summary, the two parts would get reconstructed in both voxel grids leading to ghost parts which would occupy the same points in space once a voxel in one grid is mapped to the other grid.

Therefore, our proposed fusion process allows the grids to interact with each other in a complex way so that parts are guaranteed to not intersect with each other at any point in time. This does not only avoid ghost parts, it also allows to carve out regions in space which have never been observed directly in any of the images.

4   Sparse Multi-body Structure-from-Motion

As mentioned in the introduction, the main contribution of this paper is the dense depth-map fusion formulation with non-intersection constraints. To compute the required camera poses, iterative approaches similar to those used in [13,14] could be used. We preferred a non-iterative one that we quickly outline in this section explain, for the sake of completeness. This first stage mostly uses existing building blocks for sparse multi-body SfM.

4.1   Extracting Relative Transformations

Since each part is allowed to move with respect to other parts and the camera, we initially treat the reconstruction of each part as a separate rigid SfM problem. Sparse feature point correspondences are therefore fed into a sequential

RANSAC which extracts all the essential matrices with sufficient inlier support. While being a fairly simple and straight-forward approach, sequential RANSAC has proven to be sufficient for our purposes. As two-view epipolar geometry might lead to many spurious inliers (eg. due to repetitive structure), a three-view verification is performed to eliminate inaccurately detected essential matrices. An additional benefit of three-view verification is that the scale for relative transformations within a three-view verified cluster of images is fixed (two-view relations only provide the translation up to scale) and a consisten reference coordinate frame can be chosen for this cluster. It is important to note that such a cluster can nonetheless contain relative transformations from multiple different parts: Whenever two parts do not move with respect to each other between two images (as visualized by the dashed arrow in Fig. 2), their three-view verified relative transformations which link to those two images will be assigned to the same cluster thereby fixing a consistent scale between the two parts. If a part is never static with respect to another part, additional heuristics such as a common ground plane or motion constraints can be used [8,23]. For simplicity, we decided to take two pictures with a moving camera where no part is moving. This provides a common reference frame and scale for all the relative transformations. Conceptually, at this point, a multigraph with a node for each image and an oriented edge for each extracted relative rigid transformation captures the geometric relations between the images.

4.2   Motion Segmentation

In order to get the rigid motion of part g, the correct subset of edges needs to be selected from the multigraph. Note that an edge can be selected multiple times: this happens if two or more parts do not move with respect to each other between two images. This is a special instance of the motion segmentation problem for which a fair amount of previous work exists [1,24,5,8,13,14]. If a feature point on a certain part can be tracked throughout all the images, the motion segmentation becomes trivial for that part. If this is not the case, heuristics based on color similarity, spatial proximity, etc. can be used to 'stitch' partial feature trajectories together and read off the correct segmentation from the result. Since motion segmentation is not the focus of our work, we ask for user input to manually correct erroneously stitched trajectories.

Interestingly, the dense reconstruction framework can handle some potential errors in the motion segmentation. This robustness is mainly due to the following observations. (i) Each subgraph is built from robust, three-view verified relations because the original multigraph is built that way as well. The motion subgraph for part g is further refined by running a rigid bundle adjustment on that subgraph. This further eliminates wrongly included or inaccuratly estimated relative transformations. (ii) Remaining inaccurately registered views in a subgraph will be handled by two components in our framework: Firstly, inaccurate views lead to depthmaps with low confidence scores and hence they will contribute less to the data term. Secondly, the depth map fusion algorithm uses a robust data cost and a regularization term which inhibit outlying measurements to some extent.

4.3   Generating Cost Volumes

Once the subgraph and thus relative transformations for each part is known, depthmaps for that part can be generated for each node (ie. camera view) in the subgraph. We are currently using a CUDA-implemented plane-sweep algorithm similar to [25] for the computation of the depth maps. The depth maps of a specific part g are all registered into a separate cost volume for that part. Specifically, given the positions of the grid g and camera, each depth map is converted into a truncated signed distance field and these values are aggregated in a voxel grid $\mathbf{d}_g$. The contribution to the signed distance field of a depth measurement at a certain pixel in a depthmap is weighted with a pixel confidence score based on the disparity matching cost for that pixel. These voxel grids are then used as data evidence in the dense reconstruction step. The orientation and extents of the voxel grid for a part are given by a well-aligned and tightly fitted bounding box around the sparse point cloud associated to that part. This bounding box is robustly estimated by considering the distributions of the projection of this point cloud onto normal directions of dominant scene planes contained in that point cloud. Note that in this way, the grids are best aligned with respect to each part and are not axis-aligned to each other.

5   Dense Multi-body Depth-Map Fusion

5.1   Preconditioned Primal-Dual Proximal Method

Continuous Formulation. Motivated by widely-used convex formulations for binary segmentation problems [19,20], our formulation is based on a separate 'occupancy indicator function' $x_g : V_g \rightarrow [0,1]$ for each grid $g \in \{1,\ldots,G\}$. V_g denotes a spatial volume around part g and a value of $x_g(v) = 1$ denotes that this point $v \in V_g$ is occupied by part g whereas $x_g(v) = 0$ denotes unoccupied freespace. The local data evidence $d_g(x_g)$ from the depth maps is combined with a regularization term $r_g(x_g)$ in a continuous energy function. Specifically, we follow a convex fusion framework with the widely-used total-variation regularization $r_g(x_g) = \int_{V_g} \|\nabla x_g(v)\| dv$ and a unary data term $\langle d_g, x_g \rangle = \int_{V_g} d_g(v) x_g(v) dv$ [19]. Hence, the continuous energy functional looks like

$$E(x) = \sum_g r_g(x_g) + \mu \langle d_g, x_g \rangle, \tag{1}$$

where $x = \{x_1, \ldots, x_G\}$ denotes the set of occupancy densities and $\mu \in \mathbb{R}$ is a parameter balancing data fidelity with the regularization. For later reference, we note the variational representation of the total-variation $\int_{V_g} \|\nabla x_g(v)\| dv = \max_{p_g:\|p_g(v)\|\leq 1} \int_{V_g} \langle p_g(v), \nabla x_g(v)\rangle dv$, which makes use of a dual vector-valued function $p_g : V_g \rightarrow \mathbb{R}^3$.

Since each rigid part g is allowed to move in the scene, the volumes V_g actually move rigidly with respect to each other and thus also with respect to a fixed global coordinate system. The non-intersection constraints impose that at any point in time, no point in space can be occupied by more than one part. Formally, let $T_{t,g_0 \to g}$ denote the rigid transformation which maps a point $v \in V_{g_0}$ from grid g_0 at time t to the local coordinates of grid g. The transformations $T_{t,g_0 \to g}$ are computed as described in Sec. 4. Hence, we have access to transformations at points in time t for which we have image observations. The non-intersection constraints then become

$$\forall v \in V_{g_0} : \sum_{g \in \{1,\dots,G\}} x_g(T_{t,g_0 \to g}(v)) \le 1. \tag{2}$$

Note that for known $T_{t,g_0 \to g}$, the non-intersection constraints are linear inequality constraints with respect to the unknown functions x_g. This observation is important since this allows us to include those non-intersection constraints in a convex optimization framework.

Discretization. In the discrete setting, the volumes V_g are represented by appropriately sized and aligned voxel grids around each part. The set of indices for voxels in grid g is also denoted by V_g, and the number of voxels in grid g equals $n_g = |V_g|$. $\mathbf{x}_{v_g} \in [0,1]$ denotes the occupancy indicator of a voxel $v_g \in V_g$, whereas $\mathbf{x}_g = \left(\Downarrow_{v_g \in V_g} \mathbf{x}_{v_g} \right) \in [0,1]^{n_g}$ is the vertical concatenation of labels for voxel grid g. Similarly, the complete vector of occupancy indicator variables is given by $\mathbf{x} = \left(\Downarrow_{g \in G} \mathbf{x}_g \right) \in [0,1]^{\Sigma_g n_g}$. An analogous notation is used for dual variables $\mathbf{p}_v$ and the unary data costs $\mathbf{d}_g$. Using the variational form of the total variation, the discrete version of Eq. (1) is

$$E(\mathbf{x}) = \sum_g \sum_{v_g \in V_g} \max_{\mathbf{p}_{v_g}} \langle \mathbf{p}_{v_g}, \nabla \mathbf{x}_{v_g} \rangle - i(\mathbf{p}_{v_g} \le 1) + \mu \mathbf{d}_{v_g} \mathbf{x}_{v_g} + i(\mathbf{x}_{v_g} \in [0,1]), \tag{3}$$

where i denotes the indicator function (0 if condition is met, ∞ if not) and $\nabla \mathbf{x}_{v_g}$ is computed with finite forward differences. As we will see in Sec. 5.2, the non-intersection constraints can be represented as a linear inequality $\mathbf{Ax} \le \mathbf{b}$. After introducing Lagrange multipliers $\mathbf{z}$ in order to handle this linear constraint set, the primal-dual formulation of the resulting optimization problem looks like

$$\min_{\mathbf{x}} \max_{\mathbf{p},\mathbf{z}} \left\langle \begin{pmatrix} \mathbf{z} \\ \mathbf{p} \end{pmatrix}, \mathbf{Kx} \right\rangle - F^*(\mathbf{p},\mathbf{z}) + G(\mathbf{x}), \tag{4}$$

$$\text{where } F^*(\mathbf{p},\mathbf{z}) = i(\mathbf{p} \le 1) + \langle \mathbf{z}, \mathbf{b} \rangle + i(\mathbf{z} \ge \mathbf{0}) \tag{5}$$

$$G(\mathbf{x}) = \mu \langle \mathbf{d}, \mathbf{x} \rangle + i(\mathbf{x} \in [0,1]) \tag{6}$$

$$\mathbf{K} = \left[\mathbf{A}^T, \nabla^T \right]^T. \tag{7}$$

The function F^* (convex conjugate of F) acts on the dual variables and G on the primal variables and the linear operator $\mathbf{K}$ connects these two sets of variables. Here, the sparse matrix $\nabla \in \mathbb{R}^{3 \Sigma_g n_g \times \Sigma_g n_g}$ contains the finit forward difference coefficients for gradients $\nabla \mathbf{x}_{v_g}$.

Optimization. This is a large-scale convex optimization problem and we need to carefully select a suitable algorithm. We decided to use a first order primal-dual proximal algorithm [20,26], mainly because the individual update steps in this algorithm decouple and can be parallelized easily. Experimentally, we have confirmed that a preconditioned proximal algorithm [2] converges much faster than its non-preconditioned counterpart. This is due to the fact that our linear operator $\mathbf{K}$ captures two different type of constraints, namely the non-intersection constraints and the constraints due to the variational form of the total variation. Not only contain the matrices $\mathbf{A}$ and ∇ a different number of rows, these rows also contain an entirely different pattern of non-zero entries with values on a different order of magnitude. Using a single step-length for all the dual variables as done in a non-preconditioned proximal method can therefore lead to slow convergence. However, as Chambolle and Pock have shown in [2], a preconditioned primal-dual proximal algorithm with a diagonal preconditioner can choose an adaptive step length per variable. For the sake of completeness and since the derivations need some attention, the required prox-steps of F^* and G for the preconditioned version will be derived in the following. The preconditioned prox-step replaces the standard L2-norm $\|.\|_2$ with a Mahalanobis distance $\|.\|_\Sigma$, in our case Σ is a diagonal positive-definite matrix. Even though F^* decouples into separate prox-steps for $\mathbf{p}$ and $\mathbf{z}$, the prox-step for the latter involves a sum between a linear term $\langle \mathbf{z}, \mathbf{b} \rangle$ and the indicator function $i(\mathbf{z} \geq \mathbf{0})$ leading to the following derivation

$$\text{prox}_{\langle \cdot, \mathbf{b} \rangle + i(\cdot \geq 0), \Sigma}(\tilde{\mathbf{z}}) = \arg\min_{\mathbf{z}} \left(\langle \mathbf{z}, \mathbf{b} \rangle + i(\mathbf{z} \geq \mathbf{0}) + \|\mathbf{z} - \tilde{\mathbf{z}}\|_\Sigma^2 \right) \tag{8}$$

$$= \Sigma^{\frac{1}{2}} \arg\min_{\mathbf{z}' = \Sigma^{-\frac{1}{2}}\mathbf{z}} \left(\langle \Sigma^{\frac{1}{2}}\mathbf{z}', \mathbf{b} \rangle + i(\Sigma^{\frac{1}{2}}\mathbf{z}' \geq \mathbf{0}) + \left\|\mathbf{z}' - \Sigma^{-\frac{1}{2}}\tilde{\mathbf{z}}\right\|_\mathbf{I}^2 \right)$$

$$= \Sigma^{\frac{1}{2}} \arg\min_{\mathbf{z}'} \left(\langle \mathbf{z}', \Sigma^{T\frac{1}{2}}\mathbf{b} \rangle + i(\mathbf{z}' \geq \mathbf{0}) + \left\|\mathbf{z}' - \Sigma^{-\frac{1}{2}}\tilde{\mathbf{z}}\right\|_\mathbf{I}^2 \right)$$

$$= \Sigma^{\frac{1}{2}} \text{prox}_{i(\cdot \geq 0), \mathbf{I}}(\Sigma^{-\frac{1}{2}}\tilde{\mathbf{z}} - \Sigma^{T\frac{1}{2}}\mathbf{b}) = \begin{cases} \tilde{\mathbf{z}} - \Sigma\mathbf{b} & \text{if } \tilde{\mathbf{z}} - \Sigma\mathbf{b} > 0 \\ 0 & \text{if } \tilde{\mathbf{z}} - \Sigma\mathbf{b} \leq 0 \end{cases}.$$

In the second last step, we have used the property that a non-preconditioned prox-step involving a linear term $\langle \mathbf{z}', \Sigma^{T\frac{1}{2}}\mathbf{b} \rangle$ is equivalent to applying the prox-step to the difference $\Sigma^{-\frac{1}{2}}\tilde{\mathbf{z}} - \Sigma^{T\frac{1}{2}}\mathbf{b}$ (see also Table 1 iv in [26]). Since Σ is chosen diagonal, the prox-steps for $\mathbf{z}$ still decouple. The derivation for the prox-step of the primal variable follows exactly the same steps and gives

$$\text{prox}_{\mu\langle \mathbf{d}, \cdot \rangle + i(\cdot \in [0,1]), \mathbf{T}}(\tilde{\mathbf{x}}) = \max(0, \min(1, \tilde{\mathbf{x}} + \mu\mathbf{Tf})). \tag{9}$$

A similar derivation for the dual variable $\mathbf{p}_{v_g}$ with $\Sigma_{\mathbf{p}_{v_g}} = \sigma_{v_g}^2 \mathbf{I}_3$ provides

$$\text{prox}_{i(\|\cdot\| \leq 1), \Sigma_{v_g}}(\tilde{\mathbf{p}}) = \begin{cases} \tilde{\mathbf{p}} & \text{if } \|\tilde{\mathbf{p}}\|_2 \leq 1 \\ \dfrac{\tilde{\mathbf{p}}}{\|\tilde{\mathbf{p}}\|_2} & \text{if } \|\tilde{\mathbf{p}}\|_2 > 1 \end{cases}, \tag{10}$$

Algorithm 1: First-Order Primal-Dual Algorithm

---

parameters: Time step sizes

$$\tau_j = \frac{1}{\sum\limits_{i=1}^{m} |\mathbf{K}_{i,j}|^{2-\alpha}}, \mathbf{T} = \mathrm{diag}\,(\tau_j), \; \sigma_i = \frac{1}{\sum\limits_{j=1}^{n} |\mathbf{K}_{i,j}|^{\alpha}}, \mathbf{\Sigma} = \mathrm{diag}\,(\sigma_i),$$

primal-dual step trade-off $\alpha \in [0,2]$

output   : Minimizer $\mathbf{x}$ for the multi-body depth-map fusion problem.

1 **while** *not converged* **do**
2 | // Primal Variable Update:
3 | $\tilde{\mathbf{x}} = \mathbf{x}^t - \mathbf{T}\mathbf{K}^T \begin{pmatrix} \mathbf{z}^t \\ \mathbf{p}^t \end{pmatrix}$;
4 | // Primal Variable Prox-Step:
5 | $\mathbf{x}^{t+1} = \mathrm{prox}_{\mu\langle \mathbf{d},\cdot \rangle + i(\cdot \in [0,1]),\mathbf{T}}(\tilde{\mathbf{x}})$;
6 | // Reflection step:
7 | $\hat{\mathbf{x}} = 2\mathbf{x}^{t+1} - \mathbf{x}^t$;
8 | // Dual Variable Update:
9 | $\begin{pmatrix} \tilde{\mathbf{z}} \\ \tilde{\mathbf{p}} \end{pmatrix} = \begin{pmatrix} \mathbf{z}^t \\ \mathbf{p}^t \end{pmatrix} + \mathbf{\Sigma}\mathbf{K}\hat{\mathbf{x}}$;
10 | $\mathbf{z}^{t+1} = \mathrm{prox}_{i(\cdot \geqslant 0),}(\tilde{\mathbf{z}} - \mathbf{\Sigma}_{\mathbf{z}}\mathbf{b})$;
11 | $\mathbf{p}^{t+1} = \mathrm{prox}_{i(\|\cdot\| \leqslant 1),\mathbf{\Sigma}_{\mathbf{p}}}(\tilde{\mathbf{p}})$;
12 | $t = t+1$;

---

ie. the preconditioning does not affect this prox-step. In summary, a first-order primal-dual preconditioned proximal algorithm for our non-intersection constrained multi-body depth-map fusion problem looks like outlined in Alg. 1[1]. Note again that all the prox-steps decompose into elementwise prox-steps which can be solved analytically and in parallel.

5.2   Non-intersection Constraints as Linear Inequalities

This section derives the discretized linear inequality constraints which enforce the non-intersection constraints. We recall that $T_{t,g \to g'}$ denotes the rigid transformation from grid (or rigid part) g to g' at frame t. Let $w_{t,v_g \cap v_{g'}}$ denote the intersection volume between voxels v_g and $v_{g'}$ at time t. This is computed by applying the rigid transformation $T_{t,g \to g'}$ to the voxel cube $v_g \in V_g$ which yields the corresponding translated and rotated cube at time t expressed in coordinates of grid g'. Even though there exist efficient and fast algorithms for exact voxel cube intersections [27], we opted for a simple estimation procedure of the intersection volume between two voxels. Inspired by Monte Carlo integration and efficient collision detection procedures from computer graphics, a voxel v_g is subdivided into n regularly spaced sample points. Each sample point is transformed into the other grid and a counter $n_{v_{g'}}$ is increased for the voxel $v_{g'}$ which

---

[1] The primal-dual trade-off was fixed to $\alpha = 1$ for all our experiments.

contains the transformed point. The final intersection volume is then estimated as $w_{t,v_g \cap v_{g'}} \approx \frac{n_{v_{g'}}}{n}$. In practice, we used $n = 16^3$ sampling points. With this notation in place, the discrete version of the non-intersection constraint in Eq. (2) reads like the following: For each frame t and each voxel $v \in V_{g_0}$ in the grid g_0, it must hold that

$$\sum_g \sum_{v_g \in V_g} w_{t,v \cap v_g} x_{v_g} \leq 1. \tag{11}$$

Those constraints can be concisely captured in a linear matrix inequality $\mathbf{A}x \leq 1$, where the entries of the matrix $\mathbf{A}$ are equal to the weights $w_{t,v \cap v_g}$. Obviously, some of those constraints are redundant (due to symmetry reasons) and therefore not required. Notably, most of the voxels are not intersecting, hence, most of the weights $w_{t,v \cap v_g}$ will be zero resulting in a highly sparse matrix. In practice, there are roughly 6.5 non-zero entries per grid in each row of the matrix $\mathbf{A}$. Nevertheless, the overall number of intersection constraints and thus rows in $\mathbf{A}$ can be very large. Fortunately, only a very small fraction of those constraints will be active at the globally optimal solution. Therefore, we follow a constraint generation approach in our implementation: after a certain number of iterations, we search for violated constraints and those constraints which are close to becoming violated and add those as additional rows to the constraint matrix. Note that when adding new rows to matrix $\mathbf{A}$, σ_i and τ_j need to be updated.

The constraint generation procedure can be formulated with a complexity of $O(n_t n_{g_0} G)$ where n_t denotes the number of images where parts have moved w.r.t. each other. The outermost loop iterates over all time instances $t \in \{1, \ldots, n_t\}$. The next loop iterates over all voxels $v \in V_{g_0}$ in a reference grid g_0[2]. Again motivated by collision detection procedures in computer graphics, a sequence of increasingly more complex conservative checks are employed in order to determine early on whether constraint $[t, v]$ is not violated and can be skipped. For those checks, potentially intersecting voxels in other grids $g \neq g_0$ are efficiently computed with integer index arithmetic as neighbor of $T_{t,g_0 \to g}(v)$. This constraint generation procedure incurs only a small overhead to the primal-dual method.

6   Results

We present an experimental evaluation on the following datasets and we also refer to the supplemental material for further results:

- **Laptop:** This data set contains 18 images of a laptop where the screen is rotating around its fixed axis w.r.t. the keyboard. The screen is not moving w.r.t. the keyboard in all the frames, ie. in some frames only the camera moved and the scene was perceived as being entirely rigid during those

---

[2] Here, we implicitly assume that grid g_0 is sufficiently large so that by iterating over its voxels, all the non-intersection constraints are considered. A better approach would be to use a hierarchical space partitioning scheme to efficiently compute the regions in which voxel grids intersect. However, we leave that for future work.

Background and casing

Drawer

Input images   Sample depth maps   Intersection-free reconstruction

Fig. 3. When a drawer moves in and out of the casing, the intersection-constraints automatically carve out a tight hole in the casing in order to avoid any intersections between the drawer and the casing. Moreover, the drawer is reconstructed only once, ie. no ghosting artifacts are present. The visualized depth maps correspond to the input image on the top left. Note that this example only uses 6 input images from one side of the drawer and hence, due to absence of data evidence, the reconstruction on other sides can be inaccurate.

frames. For this example, we have used a best-K ($K = 6$) depthmap matching cost which is robust to occlusions and, more importantly for our setting, also to changes in the rigid configuration of the two parts. This choice results in depthmaps which are fairly consistent for both parts at the same time. Some of those depthmaps are shown in Fig. 1. We can clearly see that the regions of the screen and keyboard in those depthmaps will both provide consistent data evidence in the keyboard and screen voxel grid. Without any non-intersection constraints, the screen should therefore also be reconstructed in the keyboard grid (and the other way around for the keyboard in the screen grid). As the results show, the screen will indeed be reconstructed multiple times, in our case 6 times since we observed 6 different configurations between the keyboard and the screen. However, with activated non-intersection constraints, those ghosting artifacts vanish and the screen and keyboard will be reconstructed exactly once, each in its own grid.

– **Drawer:** The drawer dataset consists of 6 images. 4 different non-rigid configurations have been observed while pushing the drawer into the drawer casing. Hence, in three images, the scene was again perceived as entirely rigid. In contrast to the laptop example where we have used a best-K depthmap matching, all the views contribute to a depthmap estimate this time. Fig. 3 shows an example of the resulting depthmaps for one specific point of view. Note that even though there is a bias towards either the casing or the drawer, there is a fair amount of noise present in those depthmaps. Nevertheless, our algorithm provides an artifact free reconstruction and thus segmentation into the two parts. Moreover, the non-intersection constraints prevent intersections even in unseen or weakly observed areas, resulting in a tight hole in the casing of the drawer such that the drawer can slide in.

The non-intersection constraints obviously increase the time and memory requirements slightly compared to entirely independent reconstructions. It is difficult to exactly quantify the time overhead due to those constraints, since the additional complexity for the constraint generation largely depends on how many occupied and intersecting voxels there are in a per-part independent reconstruction (and hence on the proximity between the parts). In our experiments, the overall time overhead for the primal-dual algorithm was usually within 25 – 50%. We observed a similar overhead for the memory requirements. We currently do not remove constraints which were added to the constraint matrix at some point and got satisfied later on. Such a step could certainly be added if required.

7   Conclusion and Future Work

In this paper, we have introduced the multi-body depth-map fusion problem. In order to prevent ghosting artifacts, we have considered the non-intersection constraints which can be formalized as linear inequalities. These inequalities have been integrated in a convex voxel labeling framework, leading to complex interactions between separate voxel grids for each rigid part. As the experimental evaluation shows, this approach eliminates ghosting artifacts. Moreover, regions which have never been observed in the images, like the interior of a drawer case, will be carved out if an intersection with another part would result otherwise. Intuitively, a part can be used to carve out unseen regions in other parts. From an optimization point of view, we verified that a preconditioned primal-dual proximal method converges must faster than its non-preconditioned counterpart. This can be attributed to the fact that our optimization problem contains two entirely different types of dual variables, a setting in which preconditioning is known to be beneficial. Since only a small fraction of the intersection constraints will be active at the globally optimal solution, a constraint generation approach has been introduced to handle the large set of non-intersection constraints without incurring a large overhead to the primal-dual method.

Acknowledgments. This work has been supported by the Max Planck Center for Visual Computing and Communication, by the 4DVideo ERC Starting Grant Nr. 210806 and by the Swiss National Science Foundation under Project Nr. 143422.

References

1. Costeira, J.P., Kanade, T.: A multi-body factorization method for motion analysis. In: ICCV, pp. 1071–1076. IEEE Computer Society, Washington, DC (1995)
2. Pock, T., Chambolle, A.: Diagonal preconditioning for first order primal-dual algorithms in convex optimization. In: ICCV, pp. 1762–1769. IEEE Computer Society, Washington, DC (2011)

3. Hartley, R., Zisserman, A.: Multiple view geometry in computer vision, 2nd edn. Cambridge University Press (2004)
4. Ross, D.A., Tarlow, D., Zemel, R.S.: Learning articulated structure and motion. IJCV 88(2), 214–237 (2010)
5. Katz, D., Brock, O.: Interactive segmentation of articulated objects in 3D. In: Workshop on Mobile Manipulation at ICRA 2011 (2011)
6. Brand, M.: A direct method for 3d factorization of nonrigid motion observed in 2D. In: CVPR, pp. 122–128. IEEE Computer Society, Washington, DC (2005)
7. Torresani, L., Hertzmann, A., Bregler, C.: Nonrigid structure-from-motion: Estimating shape and motion with hierarchical priors. In: IEEE TPAMI, pp. 878–892
8. Ozden, K., Schindler, K., Van Gool, L.: Multibody structure-from-motion in practice. In: IEEE TPAMI, pp. 1134–1141
9. Yan, J., Pollefeys, M.: A factorization-based approach for articulated nonrigid shape, motion and kinematic chain recovery from video. In: IEEE TPAMI, pp. 865–877
10. Taylor, J., Jepson, A.D., Kutulakos, K.N.: Non-rigid structure from locally-rigid motion. In: CVPR Computer Society, pp. 2761–2768. IEEE Computer Society, Washington, DC (2010)
11. Agudo, A., Calvo, B., Montiel, J.M.M.: 3D reconstruction of non-rigid surfaces in real-time using wedge elements. In: Fusiello, A., Murino, V., Cucchiara, R. (eds.) ECCV 2012 Ws/Demos, Part I. LNCS, vol. 7583, pp. 113–122. Springer, Heidelberg (2012)
12. Garg, R., Roussos, A., de Agapito, L.: Dense variational reconstruction of non-rigid surfaces from monocular video. In: CVPR, pp. 1272–1279. IEEE Computer Society (2013)
13. Zhang, G., Jia, J., Bao, H.: Simultaneous multi-body stereo and segmentation. In: 2011 IEEE International Conference on Computer Vision (ICCV), pp. 826–833 (November 2011)
14. Roussos, A., Russell, C., Garg, R., Agapito, L.: Dense multibody motion estimation and reconstruction from a handheld camera. In: 2012 IEEE International Symposium on Mixed and Augmented Reality (ISMAR), pp. 31–40 (November 2012)
15. Chang, W., Zwicker, M.: Global registration of dynamic range scans for articulated model reconstruction. ACM Transactions on Graphics 30(3), 26:1–26:15 (2011)
16. Seitz, S.M., Curless, B., Diebel, J., Scharstein, D., Szeliski, R.: A comparison and evaluation of multi-view stereo reconstruction algorithms. In: CVPR, pp. 519–528. IEEE Computer Society (2006)
17. Laurentini, A.: The visual hull concept for silhouette-based image understanding. In: IEEE TPAMI, pp. 150–162
18. Lempitsky, V.S., Boykov, Y.: Global optimization for shape fitting. In: IEEE Conference on Computer Vision and Pattern Recognition, CVPR 2007, Minneapolis, Minnesota, USA, June 18-23, pp. 1–8. IEEE Computer Society, Washington, DC (2007)
19. Zach, C.: Fast and high quality fusion of depth maps. In: 3DPVT 2008, Atlanta, GA, USA, June 18-20 (2008)
20. Chambolle, A., Pock, T.: A first-order primal-dual algorithm for convex problems with applications to imaging. Journal of Mathematical Imaging and Vision 40(1), 120–145 (2011)
21. Newcombe, R.A., Davison, A.J., Izadi, S., Kohli, P., Hilliges, O., Shotton, J., Molyneaux, D., Hodges, S., Kim, D., Fitzgibbon, A.: Kinectfusion: Real-time dense surface mapping and tracking. In: IEEE Symposium on Mixed and augmented reality (ISMAR 2011), pp. 127–136. IEEE (2011)

22. Malleson, C., Klaudiny, M., Hilton, A., Guillemaut, J.Y.: Single-view rgbd-based reconstruction of dynamic human geometry. In: The IEEE International Conference on Computer Vision (ICCV) Workshops (June 2013)
23. Jacquet, B., Angst, R., Pollefeys, M.: Articulated and restricted motion subspaces and their signatures. In: 2013 IEEE Conference on Computer Vision and Pattern Recognition (CVPR), pp. 1506–1513. IEEE (2013)
24. Tron, R., Vidal, R.: A benchmark for the comparison of 3-D motion segmentation algorithms. In: IEEE Conference on Computer Vision and Pattern Recognition, CVPR 2007, Minneapolis, Minnesota, USA, June 18-23. IEEE Computer Society, Washington, DC (2007)
25. Yang, R., Pollefeys, M.: Multi-resolution real-time stereo on commodity graphics hardware. In: Proceedings of the 2003 IEEE Computer Society Conference on Computer Vision and Pattern Recognition, vol. 1, pp. I-211–I-217 (June 2003)
26. Combettes, P.L., Pesquet, J.C.: Proximal Splitting Methods in Signal Processing. ArXiv e-prints (December 2009)
27. Reveillès, J.P.: The geometry of the intersection of voxel spaces. Electronic Notes in Theoretical Computer Science 46, 285–308 (2001)

Shape from Light Field Meets Robust PCA[*]

Stefan Heber[1] and Thomas Pock[1,2]

[1] Institute for Computer Graphics and Vision
Graz University of Technology
[2] Safety & Security Department
AIT Austrian Institute of Technology

Abstract. In this paper we propose a new type of matching term for multi-view stereo reconstruction. Our model is based on the assumption, that if one warps the images of the various views to a common warping center and considers each warped image as one row in a matrix, then this matrix will have low rank. This also implies, that we assume a certain amount of overlap between the views after the warping has been performed. Such an assumption is obviously met in the case of light field data, which motivated us to demonstrate the proposed model for this type of data. Our final model is a large scale convex optimization problem, where the low rank minimization is relaxed via the nuclear norm. We present qualitative and quantitative experiments, where the proposed model achieves excellent results.

Keywords: light field, nuclear norm, low rank.

1 Introduction

One of the most studied problems in Computer Vision (CV) is stereo. Given two or more images, taken from a static scene, but from different viewpoints, stereo algorithms try to find points in the different images, that correspond to the same scene point. Therefore the problem is also denoted as the correspondence problem. One distinguishes between local (*cf.* [30]) and global methods (*e.g.* [4]). In both cases one has to define a matching term, that measures the similarity between two image positions. In the case of two-frame stereo this matching term measures how well positions in the reference view match certain positions in the warped view. In the general case of multi-view stereo [25,12,31], proposed methods usually only match the different warped views with a predefined reference view. By increasing the number of matchings, *i.e.* also among the warped views, one could increase the robustness to various problems, which disturb the matching. Such problems can depend on the scene itself, like *e.g.* due to depth discontinuities, specularity, reflections, *etc.*, but could also represent problems of the used image capturing device *e.g.* pixel errors, sensor noise, *etc.*. In order

[*] This research was supported by the FWF-START project *Bilevel optimization for Computer Vision*, No. Y729 and the Vision+ project *Integrating visual information with independent knowledge*, No. 836630.

D. Fleet et al. (Eds.): ECCV 2014, Part VI, LNCS 8694, pp. 751–767, 2014.

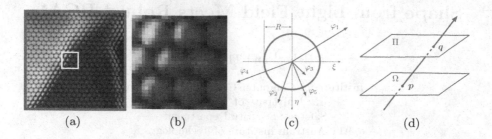

Fig. 1. (a) and (b) show two closeup views of the raw image data captured with a *plenoptic 1.0* camera. One can clearly see the effect of the micro-lens array, where each micro-lens splits incoming light into rays of different directions. Each of those light rays then hits the behind placed sensor at a slightly different location. (c) shows a sketch of the parametrization used in the RPCA light field model (*cf.* (10)). (d) is a visualization of the so-called two plane parametrization of the light field.

to fully exploit the potential of increasing the stability and the accuracy of the reconstruction an algorithm must be able to perform an all vs. all matching. Inspired by low rank models like robust Principal Component Analysis (RPCA) [7], the proposed method tackles this problem by introducing a novel matching term, which globally measures how well the different views can we warped to a common warping center. Hence, this global matching term defines a measure on the complete set of warped images, and we will see that this can also be interpreted as an all vs. all matching between the involved views. To the best of our knowledge such a stereo-model with a global matching term has not been proposed before.

One extreme case of a multi-view system is light field imaging, where a large amount of highly overlapping views are available. One way to capture a light field is by using a so-called plenoptic camera, where the different views are noise and highly aliased. We will show in the experiment section that the proposed method performs especially well for this type of data.

In what follows, we will first give a brief introduction to light field imaging in Section 1.1, followed by a short overview of RPCA [7] in Section 1.2.

1.1   Light Fields

Computer Vision traditionally focuses about extracting information out of images captured with traditional cameras. Nowadays there exist a variation of unconventional cameras, that do not capture traditional images. Among those devices are for instance cameras with coded apertures [20,35], multi-view systems [40], or plenoptic cameras [1,24,23]. All of those cameras have in common, that each point at the sensor sums over a set of light rays, where the optic defines the mapping between light rays and the sensor position. Hence, one can distinguish between different image capturing devices by analyzing the combination of light rays, that hit certain points at the sensor. The so-called light field [21] is a representation of all light rays, that hit the sensor plane from different directions. Thus, the light field can be seen as a common denominator across different types of cameras. In a pinhole camera for instance each sensor records one light ray. The sensor in a conventional camera records the integral of light rays over the lens aperture. A plenoptic camera seeks to capture the complete light field, *i.e.* it tries to record all light rays hitting certain points at the sensor separately. An image captured with a plenoptic camera can be considered as not static, *i.e.* that the image can be modified after is has been taken, w.r.t. viewpoint, focus and depth of field. Capturing the different light rays per sensor position is achieved by placing a microlens-array in front of the sensor of a traditional camera (*cf.* Figure 1(a) and 1(b)). Note, that a plenoptic camera can not capture the complete light field, it can only capture a light field with a certain directional and spatial resolution. The directional resolution depends on the number of pixels which capture the image of one microlens, and the spatial resolution depends on the overall size of the sensor. The basic concept of a plenoptic camera was first proposed by Lippmann [22] in 1908 and has then been developed and improved [11,13,15], but plenoptic cameras became feasible not until recent years [24,23,28]. The reason is simple due to the fact, that adequate high quality microlens arrays, and high resolution sensors, were not available till recent years.

Mathematically, a light field $\hat{L}$ is a 4D function, which is usually parametrized via the so called two plane parametrization (*cf.* Figure 1(d))

$$\hat{L} : \Omega \times \Pi \to \mathbb{R}, \qquad (\boldsymbol{p}, \boldsymbol{q}) \mapsto \hat{L}(\boldsymbol{p}, \boldsymbol{q}) \tag{1}$$

where $\boldsymbol{p} := (x, y)^{\mathrm{T}}$ denotes a point in the image plane $\Omega \subset \mathbb{R}^2$ and $\boldsymbol{q} := (\xi, \eta)^{\mathrm{T}}$ denotes a points in the lens plane $\Pi \subset \mathbb{R}^2$. There are different ways to visualize the 4D light field. One way is to fix two coordinates and vary over the remaining two. The most useful representations are epipolar and sub-aperture images. An epipolar image is obtained by fixing one spatial coordinate of $\boldsymbol{p}$ and one directional coordinat of $\boldsymbol{q}$. A sub-aperture image is an images where the directional component $\boldsymbol{q}$ is kept constant, and one varies over all spatial positions $\boldsymbol{p}$. Sub-aperture images can also be seen as images extracted out of the light field with slightly different viewpoints, but parallel to a common image plane. Such images clearly show the connection between light fields and multi-view stereo systems, and thus this representation will be used in the proposed model.

Light fields have been used for various image processing applications, such as digital refocusing [18,23], extending the depth of field [23], image super-resolution [3,37], and depth estimation [36,16,32]. In the case of depth estimation, the method proposed by Wanner *et al.* [36] makes use of the epipolar representation of the light field, where they additionally enforce global visibility constraints. Heber *et al.* [16] proposed a method, which uses the sub-aperture representation of the light field, where all views are matched against the center view. Finally, Tao *et al.* [32] suggested a method, that combines the defocus and correspondence depth cues.

1.2   Robust Principal Component Analysis

In many practical situation it is well justified to assume that the given data lies approximately on a low dimensional linear subspace [14,10,2,33]. This means, if data points are stacked as column or row vectors of a matrix M, then M should have low rank. This leads to the following model

$$M = L_0 + E_0,\tag{2}$$

where L_0 is assumed to have low rank and E_0 is a perturbation matrix representing the noise. This property has been exploited by classical Principal Component Analysis (PCA) [14,17,19], which solves the following minimization problem

$$\begin{array}{cl} \underset{L,E}{\text{minimize}} & \|E\|_F \\ \text{subject to} & \text{rank}(L) \leqslant r \\ & M = L + E \end{array}\tag{3}$$

where $\|.\|_F$ denotes the Frobenius norm. In problem (3) it is assumed that the entries in E are independent and identically distributed (iid) according to an isotropic Gaussian distribution. In this case PCA provides an optimal estimate to L_0. Also note, that problem (3) can be solved exactly using the singular value decomposition (SVD) of M.

PCA is used extensively for data analysis and dimension reduction, but it may fail in general if the assumptions about the perturbation matrix E are not met, *i.e.* that a few corrupted entries in M, which significantly deviate from the true solution, can lead to an estimate L, that is far away from L_0. Thus, PCA is only effective against small Gaussian noise, but it is highly sensitive to even sparse errors of high magnitude. Such errors are quite common in many applications due to corrupted data, sensor failures, *etc.* Also note, that the rank r of M needs to be known a priori, which is usually not the case in real-world applications.

An algorithm that efficiently extract the principal components of such data even in the presence of large errors was proposed by Candès *et al.* [7]. They assume the rank of L to be unknown, and hence formulate a matrix rank minimization problem, where they want to find the lowest rank that generates M when added with unknown sparse outliers. More specifically, they consider the following combinatorial optimization problem

$$\underset{L,E}{\text{minimize}} \quad \text{rank}(L) + \mu\|E\|_0 \quad \text{subject to} \quad M = L + E,\tag{4}$$

where $\|.\|_0$ denotes the number of non zero entries (ℓ^0 norm). Problem (4) is NP hard, and hence can not be solved efficiently. Thus they relax the problem by using the nuclear norm and the ℓ^1 norm to encourage low rankness and sparsity, respectively. Note, that the ℓ^1 norm is the largest convex function below $\|.\|_0$, and the nuclear norm, denoted as $\|.\|_*$, is the largest convex function below the rank function. The nuclear norm of a matrix $X \in \mathbb{R}^{n_1 \times n_2}$ is defined as

$$\|X\|_* = \sum_{i=1}^{n} \sigma_i(X) \quad \text{with} \quad n := \min\{n_1, n_2\},\tag{5}$$

where $\sigma_1(X) \geqslant \sigma_2(X) \geqslant \ldots \geqslant \sigma_n(X) \geqslant 0$ are the singular values of X. By considering the definition of the nuclear norm one sees, that this norm can be interpreted as the ℓ^1 norm of the vector of singular values of X *i.e.* the ℓ^1 norm of the spectrum. This also shows the close relation to compressed sensing.

By using these relaxations, the problem of separating the low rank component from a sparse component can be cast into a convex problem, denoted as Principal Component Pursuit (PCP) problem

$$\underset{L,E}{\text{minimize}} \quad \|L\|_* + \mu\|E\|_1 \quad \text{subject to} \quad M = L + E. \tag{6}$$

Also note, that problem (6) can be recast as a semidefinite program (SDP). The method termed Robust Principal Component Analysis (RPCA) performs well in practice and provides the low rank solution, even if up to a third of the observations are grossly corrupted.

Inspired by the RPCA [7], we formulate a holistic matching term for a multi-view stereo model, where we warp images in a way to minimize the rank of the set of warped images. The proposed model assumes that the different images provide a certain amount of overlap, which is particularly true for light field data. Thus, we will demonstrate it on this type of data, but the proposed model is not limited to the light field setting.

It is worth mentioning, that similar ideas have been used by Yigang Peng *et al.* [26] to calculate misalignments of a set of images. However, their method is limited to one global domain transformation, *i.e.* the misalignments between images are modeled as transformations from a finite dimensional group, that has a parametric representation (*e.g.* the similarity group $SE(2) \times \mathbb{R}_+$, the 2D affine group $Aff(2)$, or the planar homography group $GL(3)$).

Contribution

The contribution of this paper is threefold. First, we propose a novel variational multi-view stereo model based on low rank minimization, where the main contribution relies in the theoretical novelty of the RPCA matching term, which can be interpreted as an all vs. all matching term. Second, we present an extension of the proposed model to simultaneous image super-resolution on all low rank components. Third, we show how to apply the model to the light field setting, yielding the RPCA light field model. We then provide a simple optimization scheme, which is describe in detail in Section 3. Final we also present qualitative and quantitative experiments on synthetic and real-world data in Section 4.

2   RPCA Matching

In this section we describe the proposed model, which includes the novel RPCA matching term. The main idea of the model is to globally measure how well a set of warped images is aligned, *i.e.* our model warps images of different viewpoints to a predefined warping center in a way, such that the set of warped images can be split up into a low rank component and into an sparse component. In mathematical terms the combinatorial problem, which we want to solve can be formulated as follows

$$\underset{L,S,u}{\text{minimize}} \quad \mu \operatorname{rank}(L) + \lambda \|S\|_0 + \mathcal{R}(u) \tag{7}$$

$$\text{subject to} \quad I(u) = L + S$$

where λ, $\mu > 0$ are modeling parameters, and $\mathcal{R}(u)$ denotes a convex regularization term on the disparity variables u. Moreover, $I(u) \in \mathbb{R}^{M \times mn}$ denotes the set of M warped images of size $m \times n$, where each row of $I(u)$ represents one image. The main idea of the proposed model is to estimate a piecewise smooth disparity map, that allows to warp the input images in such a way, that the set of warped images $I(u)$ can be split up into a low rank component L and into a sparse outlier component S. Unfortunately, with the ℓ^0 minimization on S and on the spectrum of L the problem is NP-hard. Note, that the rank of L equals the ℓ^0 norm of the spectrum of L.

Now we follow RPCA [7] and consider a convex relaxation of the above problem, *i.e.* we will relax the sparsity assumption of S with the ℓ^1 norm, and we will model the low rank constraint of L with the nuclear norm. This leads to the following problem

$$\underset{u,L,S}{\text{minimize}} \quad \mu \|L\|_* + \lambda \|S\|_1 + \mathcal{R}(u) \tag{8}$$

$$\text{subject to} \quad I(u) = L + S$$

By eliminating the constraint we then obtain

$$\underset{u,L}{\text{minimize}} \quad \mu \|L\|_* + \lambda \|L - I(u)\|_1 + \mathcal{R}(u). \tag{9}$$

Compared to models with a pointwise or local data fidelity term, this model now globally measures how well the warped images match with each other, *i.e.* all views are considered equivalently important, or in other words this can be seen as an all vs. all matching. Moreover it adjusts the warped views to cope with sparse outliers which are present due to *e.g.* occlusion, specularity, or pixel errors. Also note that we do not define the matching between different views explicitly. The proposed model uses an implicit all vs. all matching via the nuclear norm. Problem (9) can also be interpreted as stereo reconstruction with simultaneously denoising the warped images. So it can be seen as solving jointly the stereo and denoising problem. In order to obtain a convex model we will use first order Taylor approximations to linearize the warped images in a final step.

2.1   Application to Light Field Imaging

In the case of light field data, we will warp so-called sub-aperture images to a predefined warping center, *e.g.* the center view of the light field. Assuming an ideal *plenoptic 1.0 camera* and using a similar notation as in [16], the sub-aperture images are defined as follows (*cf.* Figure 1(c))

$$\tilde{I}_i(\tilde{u}) := \left(\hat{L} \left(\boldsymbol{p} - \tilde{u}(\boldsymbol{p}) \frac{\varphi_i}{R}, \varphi_i \right) \right)_{\boldsymbol{p} \in \hat{\Omega}}, \quad \text{with} \quad 1 \leqslant i \leqslant M, \tag{10}$$

where M denotes the number of different sub-aperture images, φ_i is the directional offset of the ith sub-aperture image, $\hat{\Omega} := \{(x,y)^{\mathrm{T}} \in \mathbb{N}_0^2 \,|\, x < n,\, y < m\}$ is the discrete image grid, and $\tilde{u} : \hat{\Omega} \to \mathbb{R}$ is the disparity between the warping center and images with a predefined directional offset distance R. By reshaping the images $\tilde{I}_i(\tilde{u})$ as row vectors, one can define the matrix $I(u) \in \mathbb{R}^{M \times mn}$, where each row represents one sup-aperture image as defined in (10). For this purpose we define a vectorization operator vec(.), which transforms an image in matrix representation to a column vector in row major representation, *i.e.* that the ith row of $I(u)$ in problem (9) is now equivalent to $\mathrm{vec}(\tilde{I}_i(\tilde{u}))^{\mathrm{T}}$.

In order to obtain a convex model we have to linearize the warped images. Therefore, we use a first order Taylor approximation for each sub-aperture image at the position $\tilde{u}_0$

$$\hat{L} \left(\boldsymbol{p} - \tilde{u}_0(\boldsymbol{p}) \frac{\varphi_i}{R}, \varphi_i \right) + (\tilde{u}(\boldsymbol{p}) - \tilde{u}_0(\boldsymbol{p})) \frac{\|\varphi_i\|}{R} \nabla_{-\frac{\varphi_i}{\|\varphi_i\|}} \hat{L} \left(\boldsymbol{p} - \tilde{u}_0(\boldsymbol{p}) \frac{\varphi_i}{R}, \varphi_i \right), \tag{11}$$

where $\nabla_{\boldsymbol{v}}$ denotes the directional derivatives with direction $[\boldsymbol{v}, \boldsymbol{0}]$. To simplify notation we define $\tilde{A}_i$ and $\tilde{B}_i \in \mathbb{R}^{m \times n}$ similar as in [16]

$$\tilde{A}_i := \left(\frac{\|\varphi_i\|}{R} \nabla_{-\frac{\varphi_i}{\|\varphi_i\|}} L \left(\boldsymbol{p} - \tilde{u}_0(\boldsymbol{p}) \frac{\varphi_i}{R}, \varphi_i \right) \right)_{\boldsymbol{p} \in \hat{\Omega}}, \tag{12}$$

$$\tilde{B}_i := \left(L \left(\boldsymbol{p} - \tilde{u}_0(\boldsymbol{p}) \frac{\varphi_i}{R}, \varphi_i \right) \right)_{\boldsymbol{p} \in \hat{\Omega}}. \tag{13}$$

Now we set $b_i = \mathrm{vec}(\tilde{B}_i)$ and $A_i = \mathrm{diag}(\mathrm{vec}(\tilde{A}_i))$, which allows to rewrite problem (9) as the following convex optimization problem

$$\underset{u,L}{\text{minimize}} \quad \mu \|L\|_* + \lambda \sum_{i=1}^{M} \|l_i^{\mathrm{T}} - b_i - A_i(u - u_0)\|_1 + \mathcal{R}(u), \tag{14}$$

where l_i denotes the ith row of L, $u = \mathrm{vec}(\tilde{u})$ and $u_0 = \mathrm{vec}(\tilde{u}_0)$. To obtain a reliable solution we use the well justified assumption, that the disparity map u should be piecewise smooth. We model this assumption by defining $\mathcal{R}(u)$ to be the Total Generalized Variation (TGV) [5], which is a generalization of the well known Total Variation (TV). To be more specific, TGV of second order (TGV^2) will be our choice for the regularization term. Note, that TGV^2 favors piecewise linear solutions, whereas *e.g.* TV favors piecewise constant solutions. This means that the regularization term can be defined as follows

$$\mathcal{R}(u) := \min_w \alpha_1 \|\nabla u - w\|_{\mathcal{M}} + \alpha_0 \|\nabla w\|_{\mathcal{M}}, \tag{15}$$

where $\|.\|_{\mathcal{M}}$ denotes a Radon norm for vector-valued and matrix-valued Radon measures, and $\alpha_0, \alpha_1 > 0$ are weighting parameters. Also note, that ∇ and ∇

Algorithm 1. Primal-Dual Algorithm for the RPCA Light Field Depth Model

Require: Choose $\sigma > 0$ and $\tau > 0$, s.t. $\tau\sigma = 1$. Set $\Sigma_{p_u}^{-1}$, $\Sigma_{p_w}^{-1}$, T_u^{-1}, and T_w^{-1} as explained in the text, $n = 0$, and the rest arbitrary.

while $n < iter$ **do**

// Dual step
$$p_u^{n+1} \leftarrow \mathcal{P}_{\{\|\cdot\|_\infty \leqslant 1\}} \left(p_u^n + \sigma \Sigma_{p_u}^{-1} \alpha_1 \left(\nabla \bar{u}^n - \bar{w}^n\right)\right)$$
$$p_w^{n+1} \leftarrow \mathcal{P}_{\{\|\cdot\|_\infty \leqslant 1\}} \left(p_w^n + \sigma \Sigma_{p_w}^{-1} \alpha_0 \left(\nabla \bar{w}^n\right)\right)$$
for $1 \leqslant i \leqslant M$ **do**
$$p_i^{n+1} \leftarrow \mathcal{P}_{\{\|\cdot\|_\infty \leqslant 1\}} \left(p_i^n + \frac{\sigma}{2}\lambda \left(\boldsymbol{DB}(\bar{l}_i^n)^\mathrm{T} - b_i - A_i(\bar{u}^n - u_0)\right)\right)$$
end for

// Primal step
$$u^{n+1} \leftarrow u^n - \tau\, T_u^{-1} \left(\alpha_1 \nabla^\mathrm{T} p_u^{n+1} - \lambda \sum_i A_i p_i^{n+1}\right)$$
$$w^{n+1} \leftarrow w^n - \tau\, T_w^{-1} \left(\alpha_0 \boldsymbol{\nabla}^\mathrm{T} p_w^{n+1} - \alpha_1 p_u^{n+1}\right)$$
for $1 \leqslant i \leqslant M$ **do**
$$l_i^{n+1} \leftarrow l_i^n - \frac{\tau}{\lambda^2}\lambda \boldsymbol{B}^\mathrm{T}\boldsymbol{D}^\mathrm{T} p_i^{n+1}$$
end for
$$L^{n+1} \leftarrow (\mathrm{id} + \tfrac{\tau\mu}{\lambda^2}\partial G)^{-1} \left(L^{n+1}\right)$$

$$\bar{u}^{n+1} \leftarrow 2\,u^{n+1} - u^n$$
$$\bar{w}^{n+1} \leftarrow 2\,w^{n+1} - w^n$$
$$\bar{L}^{n+1} \leftarrow 2\,L^{n+1} - L^n$$

// Iterate
$n \leftarrow n + 1$

end while

---

denote finite difference operators, where the first one calculates the finite differences in x and y direction, and the second one is defined as $\boldsymbol{\nabla} := \mathrm{diag}(\nabla, \nabla)$.

We further extend problem (14) to simultaneous super-resolution on all low rank sub-aperture images l_i^T. Following the work by Unger *et al.* [34] we introduce linear operators for downsampling and blurring, denoted as $\boldsymbol{D}$ and $\boldsymbol{B}$, respectively.

$$\underset{u,L}{\text{minimize}} \quad \mu\|L\|_* + \lambda \sum_{i=1}^M \|\boldsymbol{DB}l_i^\mathrm{T} - b_i - A_i(u - u_0)\|_1 + \mathcal{R}(u), \quad (16)$$

where the low rank component L is now computed at a higher resolution.

3   Optimization

In this section we describe how to optimize the proposed RPCA light field model (16). We start with reformulating the problem into a saddle-point formulation. Therefore we introduce the dual variables p_u, p_w, and p_i ($1 \leqslant i \leqslant M$) and obtain the following formulation

$$\min_{\substack{u,w,L}} \max_{\substack{\|p_u\|_\infty \leqslant 1 \\ \|p_w\|_\infty \leqslant 1 \\ \|p_i\|_\infty \leqslant 1}} \left\{ \mu \|L\|_* + \lambda \sum_{i=1}^M \langle DBl_i^T - b_i - A_i(u - u_0), p_i \rangle + \right. \tag{17}$$

$$\left. \alpha_1 \langle \nabla u - w, p_u \rangle + \alpha_0 \langle \nabla w, p_w \rangle \right\},$$

where $\langle .,. \rangle$ denotes the standard inner product. This problem can be further rewritten into the following standard form

$$\min_{\hat{x} \in X} \max_{\hat{y} \in Y} \quad \langle K\hat{x}, \hat{y} \rangle + G(\hat{x}) - F^*(\hat{y}), \tag{18}$$

with

$$K = \begin{bmatrix} \alpha_1 \nabla & -\alpha_1 \,\mathrm{id} & 0 & \dots & 0 \\ 0 & \alpha_0 \nabla & 0 & \dots & 0 \\ -\lambda A_1 & 0 & \lambda DB & \dots & 0 \\ \vdots & \vdots & & \ddots & \\ -\lambda A_M & 0 & 0 & & \lambda DB \end{bmatrix}, \quad \hat{x} = \begin{bmatrix} u \\ w \\ l_1^T \\ \vdots \\ l_M^T \end{bmatrix}, \quad \hat{y} = \begin{bmatrix} p_u \\ p_w \\ p_1 \\ \vdots \\ p_M \end{bmatrix}, \tag{19}$$

where id denotes the identity operator. Furthermore, $G(\hat{x}) = \mu\|L\|_*$ and $F^*(\hat{y})$ contains the remaining terms in (17). Also note that $G(\hat{x})$ only operates on the variable L, thus we will redefine it to consider only those variables, *i.e.* $G(L) = \|L\|_*$. A problem of the form (18) can then be solved using the first-order primal dual algorithm proposed by Chambolle *et al.* [9]. Furthermore, we also use positive-definite preconditioning matrices Σ and T to improve the convergence speed of the algorithm as proposed by Pock *et al.* [29]. Here T represents a diagonal matrix of the same size as K, where each diagonal element represents the squared ℓ^2 norm of the corresponding column of K. Σ is calculated in a similar way, but now each diagonal element represents the ℓ^0 norm of the corresponding row in K. The final update scheme is shown in Algorithm 1, where Σ_{p_u} and Σ_{p_w} represent blockdiagonal matrices of Σ that correspond to the dual variables p_u and p_w, respectively. Likewise T_u and T_w represent the according blockdiagonal matrices of T for u and w, respectively. Further, $\mathcal{P}_{\{\|.\|_\infty \leqslant 1\}}$ denotes the reprojection operator, w.r.t. the ℓ^∞ norm denoted as $\|.\|_\infty$, and $(\mathrm{id} + \tau \partial G)^{-1}(L)$ is the proximity operator of the function $G(L)$, which can be calculated by minimizing the following problem.

$$(\mathrm{id} + \tau \partial G)^{-1}(L) = \operatorname*{argmin}_X \left(\|X\|_* + \frac{1}{2\tau}\|X - L\|_F^2 \right) \tag{20}$$

Problem (20) can be solved using spectral soft thresholding. In order to do so we first calculate the singular value decomposition (SVD) of L, *i.e.*

$$L = U\tilde{\Sigma}V^T, \quad \text{with} \quad \tilde{\Sigma} = \mathrm{diag}\left(\sigma_1(L), \dots, \sigma_{\mathrm{rank}(L)}(L)\right), \tag{21}$$

and then apply the soft thresholding operation on each singular value, which yields

$$(\mathrm{id} + \tau \partial G)^{-1}(L) = U \operatorname{diag}\left(\left(\sigma_1(L) - \tau\right)_+, \ldots, \left(\sigma_{\mathrm{rank}(L)}(L) - \tau\right)_+ \right) V^{\mathrm{T}}, \quad (22)$$

where $(x)_+ := \max\{0, x\}$.

This concludes the optimization scheme, which solves problem (14). In a final step, we embed Algorithm 1 into a coarse to fine warping scheme [6], which is necessary because of the linearization involved in (11). Moreover, it is also worth to mention, that one can use a structure texture decomposition [39] on the input images to cope with illumination changes.

4   Experimental Results

In this section we will evaluate the proposed algorithm on synthetic and real world scenes. For the synthetic evaluation we use the Light Field Benchmark Dataset (LFBD) [38]. This dataset contains synthetically generated light fields, where each light field is represented by 81 sub-aperture images arranged on a regular 9×9 grid. The light fields are rendered using Blender[1], and the dataset additionally provides a ground truth depth for each sub-aperture image.

We also present a qualitative real world evaluation for light fields from the Stanford Light Field Archive. The light fields in this dataset are captured using a multi-camera array [40] and contain 289 views on a 17×17 grid. Moreover, we also present some qualitative real-world results for light fields captured with the consumer Lytro camera[2]. The Lytro camera captures light fields with a spatial resolution of 380×330 microlenses and a directional resolution of 10×10 pixels per microlens.

4.1   Synthetic Evaluation

We start with the synthetic evaluation. Here we compare our approach to the work by Heber et al. [16]. They proposed a variational model with a pointwise ℓ^1 data term combined with an image driven TGV regularization term (ITGV), i.e. the prior is connected with the image content via an anisotropic diffusion tensor. Moreover, their model selects a predefined reference view (in this case this is the center view) and matches all the other views against the reference view. Thus, contrary to the proposed model, it only uses a subset of all possible matching combinations between the different views, and the views are also not equal important, i.e. the model encodes basically a one vs. all matching.

For the experiments we define the warping center to be the center view of the light field and we extract sub-aperture images with a predefined baseline to the warping center. More precisely, we set $\varphi_1 = \mathbf{0}$ (center view), and define the vectors φ_i for $2 \leqslant i \leqslant 9$ in (10) such that they all have the same length R,

---

[1] http://www.blender.org/
[2] https://www.lytro.com/

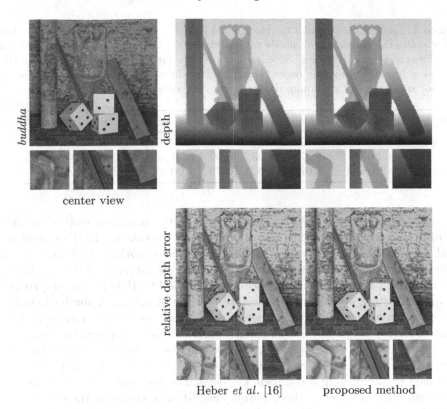

Fig. 2. Qualitative and quantitative results for the *buddha* scene of the Light Field Benchmark Dataset (LFBD). The figure shows the center view of the light field, followed by the color coded depth maps and error maps for the method proposed by Heber *et al.* [16] as well as for the proposed method. The error maps show in green (red) the pixels with a relative depth error of less (more) than 0.2%. Note that the proposed method is much more accurate, especially at occlusion boundaries, due to the robust all vs. all matching term.

and such that their directions are evenly distributed. Also note, that we use the same baseline R as in [16], which results in the same experimental setting as in [16], and thus allows to draw a comparison. Also note, that we do not use the extension for super-resoluation in this case, *i.e.* $D = B =$ id.

Figure 2 shows an example depth map result for the method proposed in [16] and for the proposed RPCA light field model. By considering the closeup views of the depth map results, one sees that the proposed method achieves a higher accuracy, especially at occlusion boundaries. Figure 2 also presents a comparisons in terms of the relative depth error. We highlighted the regions with a relative depth error larger (smaller) than 0.2% in red (green). Note, that an evaluation based on a smaller relative depth error than 0.2% is not meaningful on this daterset, due to the fact that the depth discretization of the provided

Table 1. Quantitative results for the Light Field Benchmark Dataset (LFBD). The table shows the percentage of pixels with a relative depth error of more than 0.2% for the different synthetic scenes. Note, that the results for the method proposed in [16] are taken from the according paper. The results for the method proposed by Wanner *et al.* [36] are obtained by running the accompanying source-code.

	buddha	*buddha2*	*mona*	*papillon*	*stillLife*	*horses*	*medieval*
Wanner *et al.* [36]	7.28	26.55	15.08	16.64	4.50	16.44	24.33
Heber *et al.* [16]	8.37	15.05	12.90	8.79	6.33	16.83	11.09
proposed model	**5.03**	**11.52**	**12.75**	**8.00**	**4.20**	**11.78**	**11.09**

ground truth is too low. We again observe that the proposed method is more robust to certain outliers, *e.g.* due to occlusion or specularity. In the case of the buddha scene shown in Figure 2 the proposed model provides a solution, where only 5.03% of the pixels have a relative depth error larger than 0.2%, whereas the one vs. all data-fidelity term used in the method by Heber *et al.* [16] creates a solution with a significantly larger error region of 8.37%. A similar behavior can be observed for the other scenes in the dataset, as can be seen in Table 1. Furthermore, Table 1 also shows results for the method proposed by Wanner *et al.* [36], which calculates a globally consistent depth labeling. Note that this comparison might not be very fair, because the results by Wanner *et al.* are obtained by performing a complete grid-search to find the best parameter settings, whereas the other methods are only hand-tuned. However, the results show that the method proposed in [16] already outperforms the method by Wanner *et al.* [36] on several scenes by quite a bit. Finally, the proposed model outperforms both competitors on the complete dataset, but the better performance comes at the price of a higher computational time of several minutes. It is also worth to mention, that the method proposed by Tao *et al.* [32] fails on this dataset completely, as also reported in their paper.

Super-resolution

Next we present super-resolution results for the extended RPCA light field model (16). We define the downsampling operator D and the blurring operator B as proposed by Unger *et al.* [34]. Figure 3 shows closeup views of the obtained upsampling results for two scenes of the LFBD. Here we used 21 sub-aperture images for the reconstruction, where the low rank components of the warped sub-aperture images have been magnified by a factor of three. By considering the super-resolved results shown in Figure 3 one recognizes a clear increase in sharpness.

4.2   Real World Experiments

Now we continue with the real-world evaluation. Figure 4 present a qualitative comparison to the method proposed by Wanner *et al.* [36]. Here we use a light

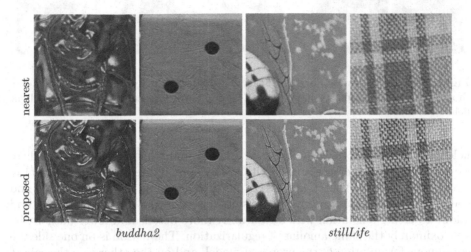

Fig. 3. Qualitative results of the extended version of the RPCA light field model (*cf.* (16)) for the *buddha2* and *stillLife* scene of the Light Field Benchmark Dataset (LFBD). The figure shows closeup views of the nearest neighbor interpolated center view, as well as closeup views of one super-resolved low rank component, where the super-resolved results provide increased sharpness.

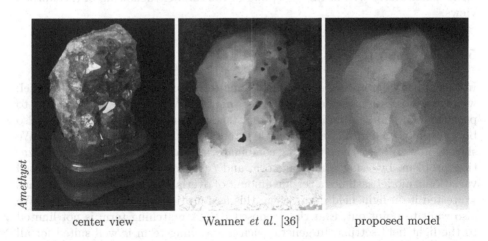

Fig. 4. Qualitative comparison for a light field from the Stanford Light Field Archive. The figure shows from left to right, the center view of the light field, the results for the method proposed by Wanner *et al.* [36] (image is taken from their paper) and the result for the proposed RPCA light field model.

Fig. 5. Qualitative results, for light fields captured with a Lytro camera. The figure shows color coded disparity maps as well as the according center views of the light field.

field from the Stanford Light Field Archive as input for our algorithm, where we extract 17 sub-aperture images with evenly spread directional offsets φ_i ($1 \leqslant i \leqslant 17$). Also note, that the scene is quite challenging, due to reflective and specular surface. By comparing the results one sees that the proposed method allows to create a solution with significantly more details and fewer outliers, by approximately the same amount of regularization. The reason is on one side the continuous formulation of the proposed model, and on the other side the robust implicit all vs. all matching term.

In Figure 5 we also present results for light fields captured with the Lytro camera. Therefore, we extract 17 sub-aperture images from the raw images captured with such a camera. Note, that these sub-aperture images have a quite low resolution of 380×330, and include a significant amount of noise and outliers. Nevertheless, the proposed method is capable to create piecewise smooth depth maps, with clear depth discontinuities. Also note, that the proposed method performs particularly well in this case, due to the implicit denoising of the warped views.

5   Conclusion

In this paper we proposed a global matching term for a multi-view stereo model, which has not been considered before for this task. We formulated our model to perform a low rank minimization on the stack of warped images, which can also be interpreted as an all vs. all matching between the images in the stack. We showed how to relax the according combinatorial problem to a convex optimization problem, by using a nuclear norm and ℓ^1 norm relaxation. The proposed variational model assumes a certain amount of overlap in the warped views. Thus we tested it on light field data, where this assumption is obviously fulfilled. We also want to point out, that the proposed RPCA matching term is not limited to the light field setting. In general such a matching term is well suited for all kind of problems with highly redundant input data.

Finally we want to mention, that the proposed model can still be further refined by performing additionally iterative ℓ^1 reweighting. Such a refinement procedure can be applied on the ℓ^1 term in problem (14) [8], as well as on the nuclear norm [27], to further increase the accuracy especially at depth discontinuities. Implementing and evaluating such a refinement is left as future work.

References

1. Adelson, E.H., Wang, J.Y.A.: Single lens stereo with a plenoptic camera. IEEE Transactions on Pattern Analysis and Machine Intelligence 14(2), 99–106 (1992)
2. Belkin, M., Niyogi, P.: Laplacian eigenmaps for dimensionality reduction and data representation. Neural Computation 15, 1373–1396 (2002)
3. Bishop, T.E., Favaro, P.: The light field camera: Extended depth of field, aliasing, and superresolution. IEEE Transactions on Pattern Analysis and Machine Intelligence 34(5), 972–986 (2012)
4. Boykov, Y., Veksler, O., Zabih, R.: Fast approximate energy minimization via graph cuts. IEEE Trans. Pattern Anal. Mach. Intell. 23(11), 1222–1239 (2001)
5. Bredies, K., Kunisch, K., Pock, T.: Total generalized variation. SIAM Journal on Imaging Sciences 3(3), 492–526 (2010)
6. Brox, T., Bruhn, A., Papenberg, N., Weickert, J.: High accuracy optical flow estimation based on a theory for warping. In: Pajdla, T., Matas, J(G.) (eds.) ECCV 2004. LNCS, vol. 3024, pp. 25–36. Springer, Heidelberg (2004)
7. Candès, E.J., Li, X., Ma, Y., Wright, J.: Robust principal component analysis? J. ACM 58(3), 1–37 (2011)
8. Candès, E.J., Wakin, M.B., Boyd, S.P.: Enhancing sparsity by reweighted ℓ_1 minimization (2007)
9. Chambolle, A., Pock, T.: A first-order primal-dual algorithm for convex problems with applications to imaging. Journal of Mathematical Imaging and Vision 40, 120–145 (2011)
10. Chen, S.S., Donoho, D.L., Saunders, M.A.: Atomic decomposition by basis pursuit. SIAM Journal on Scientific Computing 20, 33–61 (1998)
11. Coffey, D.F.W.: Apparatus for making a composite stereograph (December 1936)
12. Collins, R.T., Collins, R.T.: A space-sweep approach to true multi-image matching (1996)
13. Dudnikov, Y.A.: Autostereoscopy and integral photography. Optical Technology 37(3), 422–426 (1970)
14. Eckart, C., Young, G.: The approximation of one matrix by another of lower rank. Psychometrika 1, 211–218 (1936)
15. Fife, K., Gamal, A.E., Philip Wong, H.S.: A 3mpixel multi-aperture image sensor with 0.7m pixels in 0.11m cmos (February 2008)
16. Heber, S., Ranftl, R., Pock, T.: Variational Shape from Light Field. In: International Conference on Energy Minimization Methods in Computer Vision and Pattern Recognition (2013)
17. Hotelling, H.: Analysis of a complex of statistical variables into principal components. J. Educ. Psych. 24 (1933)
18. Isaksen, A., McMillan, L., Gortler, S.J.: Dynamically reparameterized light fields. In: SIGGRAPH, pp. 297–306 (2000)
19. Jolliffe, I.T.: Principal Component Analysis. Springer, Berlin (1986)

20. Levin, A., Fergus, R., Durand, F., Freeman, W.T.: Image and depth from a conventional camera with a coded aperture. ACM Trans. Graph. 26(3) (July 2007)
21. Levoy, M., Hanrahan, P.: Light field rendering. In: Proceedings of the 23rd Annual Conference on Computer Graphics and Interactive Techniques, SIGGRAPH 1996, pp. 31–42. ACM, New York (1996)
22. Lippmann, R.: La photographie intégrale. Comptes-Rendus, Académie des Sciences 146, 446–551 (1908)
23. Ng, R.: Digital Light Field Photography. Phd thesis, Stanford University (2006), http://www.lytro.com/renng-thesis.pdf
24. Ng, R., Levoy, M., Brédif, M., Duval, G., Horowitz, M., Hanrahan, P.: Light field photography with a hand-held plenoptic camera. Tech. rep., Stanford University (2005)
25. Okutomi, M., Kanade, T.: A multiple-baseline stereo. IEEE Trans. Pattern Anal. Mach. Intell. 15(4), 353–363 (1993)
26. Peng, Y., Ganesh, A., Wright, J., Xu, W., Ma, Y.: Rasl: Robust alignment by sparse and low-rank decomposition for linearly correlated images. IEEE Transactions on Pattern Analysis and Machine Intelligence 34(11), 2233–2246 (2012)
27. Peng, Y., Suo, J., Dai, Q., Xu, W., Lu, S.: Robust image restoration via reweighted low-rank matrix recovery. In: Gurrin, C., Hopfgartner, F., Hurst, W., Johansen, H., Lee, H., O'Connor, N. (eds.) MMM 2014, Part I. LNCS, vol. 8325, pp. 315–326. Springer, Heidelberg (2014)
28. Perwass, C., Wietzke, L.: Single lens 3d-camera with extended depth-of-field (2012)
29. Pock, T., Chambolle, A.: Diagonal preconditioning for first order primal-dual algorithms in convex optimization. In: International Conference on Computer Vision (ICCV), pp. 1762–1769. IEEE (2011)
30. Scharstein, D., Szeliski, R.: A taxonomy and evaluation of dense two-frame stereo correspondence algorithms. Int. J. Comput. Vision 47(1-3), 7–42 (2002)
31. Stühmer, J., Gumhold, S., Cremers, D.: Real-time dense geometry from a handheld camera. In: Goesele, M., Roth, S., Kuijper, A., Schiele, B., Schindler, K. (eds.) Pattern Recognition. LNCS, vol. 6376, pp. 11–20. Springer, Heidelberg (2010)
32. Tao, M.W., Hadap, S., Malik, J., Ramamoorthi, R.: Depth from combining defocus and correspondence using light-field cameras (December 2013)
33. Tenenbaum, J.B., de Silva, V., Langford, J.C.: A Global Geometric Framework for Nonlinear Dimensionality Reduction. Science 290(5500), 2319–2323 (2000)
34. Unger, M., Pock, T., Werlberger, M., Bischof, H.: A convex approach for variational super-resolution. In: Goesele, M., Roth, S., Kuijper, A., Schiele, B., Schindler, K. (eds.) Pattern Recognition. LNCS, vol. 6376, pp. 313–322. Springer, Heidelberg (2010)
35. Veeraraghavan, A., Raskar, R., Agrawal, A., Mohan, A., Tumblin, J.: Dappled photography: Mask enhanced cameras for heterodyned light fields and coded aperture refocusing. ACM Trans. Graph. 26(3) (July 2007)
36. Wanner, S., Goldluecke, B.: Globally consistent depth labeling of 4D lightfields. In: IEEE Conference on Computer Vision and Pattern Recognition (CVPR) (2012)
37. Wanner, S., Goldluecke, B.: Spatial and angular variational super-resolution of 4D light fields. In: Fitzgibbon, A., Lazebnik, S., Perona, P., Sato, Y., Schmid, C. (eds.) ECCV 2012, Part V. LNCS, vol. 7576, pp. 608–621. Springer, Heidelberg (2012)
38. Wanner, S., Meister, S., Goldluecke, B.: Datasets and benchmarks for densely sampled 4D light fields. In: Vision, Modelling and Visualization (VMV) (2013)

39. Wedel, A., Pock, T., Zach, C., Bischof, H., Cremers, D.: An Improved Algorithm for TV-L^1 Optical Flow. In: Cremers, D., Rosenhahn, B., Yuille, A.L., Schmidt, F.R. (eds.) Statistical and Geometrical Approaches to Visual Motion Analysis. LNCS, vol. 5604, pp. 23–45. Springer, Heidelberg (2009)
40. Wilburn, B., Joshi, N., Vaish, V., Talvala, E.V., Antunez, E., Barth, A., Adams, A., Horowitz, M., Levoy, M.: High performance imaging using large camera arrays. ACM Trans. Graph. 24(3), 765–776 (2005)

Cross-Age Reference Coding for Age-Invariant Face Recognition and Retrieval

Bor-Chun Chen[1], Chu-Song Chen[1], and Winston H. Hsu[2]

[1] Institute of Information Science, Academia Sinica, Taipei, Taiwan
[2] National Taiwan University, Taipei, Taiwan

Abstract. Recently, promising results have been shown on face recognition researches. However, face recognition and retrieval across age is still challenging. Unlike prior methods using complex models with strong parametric assumptions to model the aging process, we use a data-driven method to address this problem. We propose a novel coding framework called Cross-Age Reference Coding (CARC). By leveraging a large-scale image dataset freely available on the Internet as a reference set, CARC is able to encode the low-level feature of a face image with an age-invariant reference space. In the testing phase, the proposed method only requires a linear projection to encode the feature and therefore it is highly scalable. To thoroughly evaluate our work, we introduce a new large-scale dataset for face recognition and retrieval across age called Cross-Age Celebrity Dataset (CACD). The dataset contains more than 160,000 images of 2,000 celebrities with age ranging from 16 to 62. To the best of our knowledge, it is by far the largest publicly available cross-age face dataset. Experimental results show that the proposed method can achieve state-of-the-art performance on both our dataset as well as the other widely used dataset for face recognition across age, MORPH dataset.

Keywords: Face Recognition, Aging.

1 Introduction

Face related problems (e.g., face detection, face recognition) are important but challenging, and they have drawn many computer vision researchers' attention for decades. For matching faces, there are four key factors that compromise the accuracy: pose, illumination, expression, and aging [12]. Many researches had been dedicated to solve the face recognition problem with the existence of one or more types of these variations. Recently, due to the improvement of the face and facial landmark detection accuracy as well as the increase of the computational power, researches [4,27,2] show that we can achieve near-human performance on face verification benchmark taken in the unconstrained environments such as Labeled Faces in the Wild dataset (LFW) [11]. However, as LFW dataset contains large variations in pose, illumination, and expression, it contains little variation in aging. As can be seen in Figure 3 that faces across age can be very different, therefore, face matching with age variation is still very challenging.

D. Fleet et al. (Eds.): ECCV 2014, Part VI, LNCS 8694, pp. 768–783, 2014.

Face recognition and retrieval across age has a wide range of applications. For example, finding missing persons and child trafficking in forensic applications, and automatic photo annotation in personal media. However, as most age-related works on face image analysis focus on age estimation and simulation, works focusing on face recognition and retrieval across age are limited.

By taking advantage of widely available celebrity images on the Internet, we propose a new approach to address this problem with a different angle from prior works. Instead of modeling the aging process with strong parametric assumptions, we adopt a data driven approach and introduce a novel coding method called Cross-Age Reference Coding (CARC). Our basic assumption is that if two people look alike when they are young, they might also look similar when they both grow older. Based on this assumption, CARC leverages a set of reference images available freely from the Internet to encode the low-level features of a face image with an averaged representation in reference space. As shown in Figure 1, two images of the same person will have similar representations using CARC because they both look similar to certain reference people (with different ages), and experimental results with CARC shown in section 5 support this assumption. Since images downloaded from Internet could be noisy, CARC is designed to be robust against such noise. Note that although the idea of using a reference set for face recognition was proposed in other literatures such as [13,39], they did not consider the age variation. The proposed method is essentially different because we incorporate the age information of the reference set into the coding framework.

We notice that benchmarks for evaluating age-invariant face recognition and retrieval are limited because it is hard to collect images of the same person with different ages. In order to thoroughly evaluate our work, we introduce a new cross-age face dataset called Cross-Age Celebrity Dataset (CACD) by collecting celebrity images on the Internet[1]. Because many celebrities are active for a long period, we can easily obtain images of them with different ages. CACD contains more than 160,000 face images of 2,000 celebrities across ten years with age ranging from 16 to 62. To our best knowledge, this is the largest publicly available cross-age face dataset. Examples of the dataset can be found in Figure 3. By conducting extensive experiments, we show that the proposed method can outperform state-of-the-art methods on both MORPH [26] and CACD.

To sum up, contributions of this paper include:

- We propose a new coding framework called CARC that leverages a reference image set (available from Internet) for age-invariant face recognition and retrieval.
- We introduce a new large-scale face dataset, CACD, for evaluating face recognition and retrieval across age. The dataset contains more than 160,000 images with 2,000 people and is made publicly available[2].

---

[1] Note that although celebrity images were used in other benchmarks such as LFW [11] or Pubfig [13], none of them focus on collecting celebrity images across age.

[2] Available at http://bcsiriuschen.github.io/CARC/

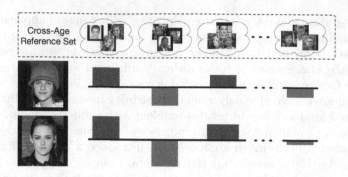

Fig. 1. Each cluster on the top represents the images of one reference person. We use images of n different people as our reference set, and encode each local feature of testing image as an n dimensional feature. Because the reference set contains images with different ages, we can convert each local feature into age-invariant representation using the proposed method. Two images of the same person with different ages will have similar features in the new reference space and therefore we can achieve high accuracy for face recognition and retrieval across age.

– We conduct extensive experiments on MORPH and CACD and show that CARC can outperform state-of-the-art methods on both datasets.

The rest of the paper is organized as follow: section 2 discusses the related work. Section 3 describes the proposed coding framework, Cross-Age Reference Coding. Section 4 introduces our dataset, Cross-Age Celebrity Dataset. Section 5 gives the experimental results, and section 6 concludes this paper.

2   Related Work

2.1   Face Recognition and Retrieval

Face recognition has been investigated for decades by many researchers. Turk and Pentland introduce the idea of eigenface [31] in 1991, which is one of earliest successes in the face recognition research; Ahonen et al. [1] successfully apply texture descriptor, local binary pattern (LBP), on the face recognition problem. Wright et al. [35] propose to use sparse representation derived from training images for face recognition. The method is proved to be robust against occlusions for face recognition. Recently, Chen et al. [4] use a high dimensional version of LBP and achieve near-human performance on the LFW dataset.

Some researches also use a reference set to improve the accuracy of face recognition and retrieval. Kumar et al. [13] propose to use attribute and simile classifier, SVM classifier trained on reference set, for face verification. Berg et al. [3] further improve the method by using "Tom-vs-Pete" classifier. Yin et al. [39] propose an associate-predict model using 200 identities in Multi-PIE dataset [9] as a reference set. Wu et al. [36] propose an identity-based quantization using a dictionary constructed by 270 identities for large-scale face image retrieval.

Although these methods achieve salient performance on face recognition, they do not work well when the age variation exists because they do not consider the age information in the reference set.

2.2   Age-Invariant Face Recognition

Most existing age-related works for face image analysis focus on age estimation [14,15,40,25,34,7,38,6,10,22,21] and age simulation [16,30,28,29,24]. In recent years, researchers have started to focus on face recognition across age. One of the approaches is to construct 2D or 3D aging models [16,7,24] to reduce the age variation in face matching. Such models usually rely on strong parametric assumptions, accurate age estimation, as well as clean training data, and therefore they do not work well in unconstrainted environments. Some other works focus on discriminative approaches. Ling et al. [19] use gradient orientation pyramid with support vector machine for face verification across age progression. Li et al. [17] use multi-feature discriminant analysis for close-set face identification. Gong et al. [8] propose to separate the feature into identity and age components using hidden factor analysis. Different from the above methods, we propose to adopt a data-driven approach to address this problem. By taking advantage of a cross-age reference set freely available on the Internet, and using a novel coding framework called CARC, we are able to achieve high accuracy for face recognition and retrieval with age variation.

2.3   Face Dataset

There are many face datasets available for researches in face recognition. Among all the datasets, LFW [11] is one of the most popular dataset for face verification task in unconstrainted environments, and it contains 13,233 images of 5,749 people extracted from the news program. Pubfig [13] is another dataset collected in the unconstrainted environments. It aims to improve the LFW dataset by providing more images for each individual, and it contains 58,797 images with 200 people. For age estimation and face recognition across age, FG-NET [20] and MORPH [26] are the two most widely used datasets. FG-NET contains 1,002 images of 82 people with age range from 0 to 69. MORPH contains 55,134 images of 13,618 people with age range from 16 to 77. Information and comparison of these datasets can be found in Table 1 and Figure 5. Compared to existing datasets, our dataset contains a larger number of images of different people in different ages.

3   Cross-Age Reference Coding (CARC)

3.1   System Overview

Figure 2 shows the system overview of the proposed method. For every image in the database, we first apply a face detection algorithm to find the locations of the

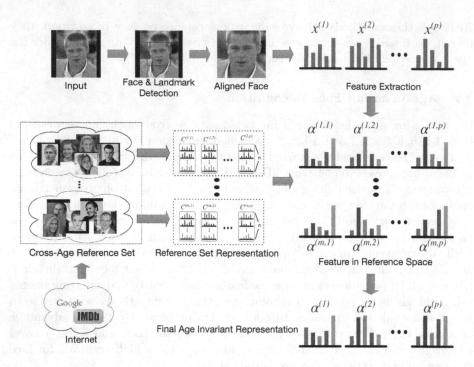

Fig. 2. System overview of the proposed method. For each image, we first apply face and facial landmarks detection. We then extract local feature (high-dimensional LBP) from each landmark, and use CARC to encode the local features into the age-invariant representation with three steps. First, by using a cross-age reference set collected from Internet, we compute the reference set representations. Second, we map the local feature extracted from the images into reference space in each of the m years. Finally, we aggregate the m features from different years into a final age-invariant representation for the input image. The final representation is $n \times p$ dimensions where n is the number of reference people and p is the number of facial landmarks. Details of CARC are described in section 3.

faces in the image. We adopt the widely used Viola-Jones face detector [32] for the task. For each face, we then locate sixteen different facial landmarks using face alignment algorithm. Xiong et al. [37] recently propose a supervised decent method for face alignment. Their method uses supervised learning to replace the expensive computation in second order optimization schemes and can efficiently locate the landmarks with high accuracy; therefore we adopt their method to locate the facial landmarks. After landmarks finding, the face is aligned using similarity transform to make the eyes located at the same horizontal positions for all images.

After the face is aligned, we extract local features from each landmark. Among all kinds of different local features, high-dimensional local binary pattern [4] has shown promising results in face verification task. Therefore, we adopt a similar pipeline to extract local features from face images. Around each of these sixteen landmarks, we crop a fixed-size patch with 5 different scales. Each patch is then divided into 4×4 cells, and we extract a 59-dimensional uniform local binary pattern [23] from each cell. Features extracted from the same landmarks are then concatenated together as a descriptor for the landmark. The feature dimension for each landmark is 4,720. We use principal component analysis (PCA) to reduce the dimension to 500 for each landmark for further processing.

We then apply CARC to encode the local features into age-invariant representation. CARC contains three main steps: (1) computing reference set representations for different reference people in different years using age-varying reference images obtained from the Internet (cf. section 4), (2) encoding local features into reference space using the reference set representations, and (3) aggregating the features found in step 2 to yield a final age-invariant representation. The following sections will describe each step in detail.

3.2   Reference Set Representations

Using the local features extracted from images of the reference people, we can compute the reference set representations using the follow equation:

$$C_i^{(j,k)} = \frac{1}{N_{ij}} \sum_{\substack{identity(x^{(k)})=i \\ year(x^{(k)})=j}} x^{(k)},$$

$$\forall i = 1, \ldots, n \ \ j = 1, \ldots, m, \ \ k = 1, \ldots, p \qquad (1)$$

where $C_i^{(j,k)} \in R^d$ is the reference representation of the person i in year j at landmark k and n is the number of reference people, m is the number of years, p is the number of landmarks. It is computed by averaging over all the features $(x^{(k)})$ from the same reference person in the same years, N_{ij} is the total number of such images. Because the reference set is directly obtained from the Internet, it might contain noise. Taking average is helpful to compute a representation more robust to such noisy data.

3.3   Encoding Feature into the Reference Space

Given a set of n reference person representation $C^{(j,k)} = [C_1^{(j,k)}, C_2^{(j,k)}, \ldots C_n^{(j,k)}]$ and a new feature $x^{(k)}$ extracted at landmark k, we want to use the reference representation to encode the new feature. To achieve this goal, we first define a vector $\alpha^{(j,k)} \in R^{n \times 1}$, which represents the relationship to n reference people (as shown in Figure 1) in year j for the feature extracted at landmark k. We know that $\alpha_i^{(j,k)}$ should be big if the testing feature $x^{(k)}$ is close to the i_{th} reference person, and small otherwise. Here we consider finding such representation by solving a least squared problem with Tikhonov regularization:

$$\underset{\alpha^{(j,k)}}{minimize} \left\| x^{(k)} - C^{(j,k)} \alpha^{(j,k)} \right\|^2 + \lambda \left\| \alpha^{(j,k)} \right\|^2, \ \ \forall j, k, \qquad (2)$$

However, it does not consider the temporal relationship between representations across different years, whereas one person is similar to a reference person at year j, he/she is most likely similar to the same reference person at adjacent years $j-1$ and $j+1$. Therefore, we add a temporal constraint to reflect this issue in our coding scheme. We first define a tridiagonal matrix L as follow:

$$L = \begin{bmatrix} 1 & -2 & 1 & 0 & \dots & 0 & 0 & 0 \\ 0 & 1 & -2 & 1 & \dots & 0 & 0 & 0 \\ \vdots & \vdots & \vdots & \vdots & \vdots & \vdots & \vdots & \vdots \\ 0 & 0 & 0 & 0 & \dots & 1 & -2 & 1 \end{bmatrix} \in R^{(m-2)\times m}. \tag{3}$$

L is a smoothness operator for the temporal constraint to make $\alpha_i^{(j,k)}$ similar to $\alpha_i^{(j+1,k)}$ and $\alpha_i^{(j-1,k)}$ by minimizing their difference. Let:

$$A^{(k)} = [\alpha^{(1,k)}, \alpha^{(2,k)}, \dots, \alpha^{(m,k)}] \in R^{n\times m}, \quad \forall k. \tag{4}$$

The testing features $x^{(k)}$ can now be cast to the new reference space by minimizing the following objective function with Tikhonov regularization and temporal smoothing:

$$\underset{A^{(k)}}{minimize} \sum_{j=1}^{m} \left(\left\| x^{(k)} - C^{(j,k)}\alpha^{(j,k)} \right\|^2 + \lambda_1 \left\| \alpha^{(j,k)} \right\|^2 \right) + \lambda_2 \left\| LA^{(k)T} \right\|^2, \quad \forall k. \tag{5}$$

The first term in the above equation is to make sure the reconstruction error in reference space is small, and the second term is to let the coefficients of the same reference person across adjacent years become similar.

Solving Equation 5 is simple because it is a $l2$-regularized least-squared problem. We first define new matrices $\hat{C}^{(k)}$ and $\hat{L}$ as follows:

$$\hat{C}^{(k)} = \begin{bmatrix} C^{(1,k)} & 0 & \dots & 0 \\ 0 & C^{(2,k)} & \dots & 0 \\ \vdots & \vdots & \vdots & \vdots \\ 0 & 0 & \dots & C^{(m,k)} \end{bmatrix} \in R^{md\times mn}, \quad \forall k \tag{6}$$

$$\hat{L} = \begin{bmatrix} I & -2I & I & 0 & \dots & 0 & 0 & 0 \\ 0 & I & -2I & I & \dots & 0 & 0 & 0 \\ \vdots & \vdots & \vdots & \vdots & \vdots & \vdots & \vdots & \vdots \\ 0 & 0 & 0 & 0 & \dots & I & -2I & I \end{bmatrix} \in R^{(m-2)n\times mn}, \tag{7}$$

and we define the vector $\hat{\alpha}^{(k)} = [\alpha^{(1,k)T}, \alpha^{(2,k)T}, \dots, \alpha^{(m,k)T}]^T \in R^{mn}$ and $\hat{x}^{(k)} = [x^{(k)T}, \dots, x^{(k)T}] \in R^{md}$. We can now rewrite Equation 5 as:

$$\underset{\hat{\alpha}^{(k)}}{minimize} \left\| \hat{x}^{(k)} - \hat{C}^{(k)}\hat{\alpha}^{(k)} \right\|^2 + \hat{\lambda}_1 \left\| \hat{\alpha}^{(k)} \right\|^2 + \hat{\lambda}_2 \left\| \hat{L}\hat{\alpha}^{(k)} \right\|^2, \quad \forall k \tag{8}$$

which is a standard regularized least square problem with a closed-form solution:

$$\hat{\alpha}^{(k)} = \left(\hat{C}^{(k)T}\hat{C}^{(k)} + \hat{\lambda}_1 I + \hat{\lambda}_2 \hat{L}^T \hat{L}\right)^{-1}\hat{C}^{(k)T}\hat{x}^{(k)}, \quad \forall k. \tag{9}$$

Let $\hat{P}^{(k)} = \left(\hat{C}^{(k)T}\hat{C}^{(k)} + \hat{\lambda}_1 I + \hat{\lambda}_2 \hat{L}^T \hat{L}\right)^{-1}\hat{C}^{(k)T}$, we can precompute $\hat{P}^{(k)}$ as a projection matrix so that when a query image comes, we can efficiently map it to the reference set space via a linear projection.

3.4   Aggregating Representation across Different Years

We want to aggregate the representations in reference space across different years. Here we propose to use max pooling to achieve the goal:

$$\alpha_i^{(k)} = \max\left(\alpha_i^{(1,k)}, \alpha_i^{(2,k)}, \ldots, \alpha_i^{(m,k)}\right), \quad \forall i, k. \tag{10}$$

By using max pooling, the final representation will have a high response to one reference person as long as it has a high response to the person in any year. So when there are two images of the same person at different ages, the younger image might have a high response at a certain reference celebrity in an early year, while the older image might have a high response at the same celebrity but in a later year. The final representations for these two images will both have high response at that specific reference person because of the max pooling aggregation. Therefore, we can achieve age-invariant face recognition and retrieval. Note that [18] provides a theoretical support for the use of max pooling with reference images.

After we obtain the final representation, we use cosine similarity to compute the matching scores between images for face recognition and retrieval.

4   Cross-Age Celebrity Dataset (CACD)

4.1   Celebrity Name Collection

We first form a list of celebrity names that we want to include in the dataset. In order to create a large-scale dataset with diversity in ages, we identify two important criteria to decide whose name should be on the list: (1) the people on the list should have different ages, and (2) these people must have many images available on the Internet for us to collect. We select our names from an online celebrity database, IMDb.com[3], and the former criterion is satisfied by collecting names with different birth years; while the later one is satisfied by collecting names of popular celebrities. In detail, we collect names of celebrities whose birth date is from 1951 to 1990. In this 40 years period, we collect the names of top 50 popular celebrities from each birth year with 2,000 names in total. Similar approach is adopted in [33] to collect celebrity names.

---

[3] IMDb.com is one of the largest online movie database, and it contains profiles of millions of movies and celebrities.

Fig. 3. Examples of images collected. Numbers on the top are the birth years of the celebrities, and numbers on the left indicate the years in which the images were taken. Images in the same column are of the same celebrity.

4.2 Image Collection

We use Google Image Search to collect images. In order to collect celebrities images across different ages, we use a combination of celebrity name and year as keywords. For example, we use "Emma Watson 2004" as keywords to retrieve Emma Watson's images taken in 2004. These might include photos taken in an event held in 2004 or images from a 2004 movie such as "Harry Potter and the Prisoner of Azkaban." For each celebrity, we collect images across ten years from 2004 to 2013. Since we already know the birth years of the celebrities, we can calculate the ages of celebrities in the images by simply subtract the birth year from the year of which the photo was taken. Examples of images collected can be found in Figure 3. Note that the dataset might contain noise because we could accidentally collect images of other celebrities in the same event or movie, and some of the celebrities might retire from the public during some periods between 2004 to 2013 and have little photos available at that time, which could make year few labels incorrect. Nevertheless, the proposed coding method is robust to such noise and proved to have good performance in our experiments (cf. section 5).

4.3 Dataset Statistics

After applying face detection [32] to all images, there are more than 200,000 images containing faces for all 2,000 celebrities. However, some of the images are duplicated. We use a simple duplicate detection algorithm based on low-level features to remove such images. After removing duplicate images, we have around 160,000 face images left. For a subset of 200 celebrities, we manually check

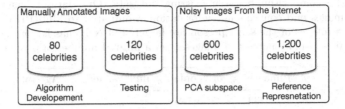

Fig. 4. CACD contains images of 2,000 celebrities. 200 of them are manually annotated. We randomly separate these 200 celebrities into two subset: 80 of them are used for algorithm development and parameter selection, and the other 120 are used for testing. 600 out of 1,800 celebrities without annotation are used for computing the PCA subspace. Another 1,200 is used as reference set.

the images and remove the noisy images in the dataset[4]. These 200 celebrities are used for algorithm development and evaluation. More specifically, we further separate images of these 200 celebrities into two subsets. One of them contains 80 celebrities and should be used for algorithm development and parameter selection; the other 120 celebrities are for testing. The protocol for using the dataset in our experiments are shown in Figure 4. The dataset contains 163,446 images of 2,000 celebrities after removing the noisy images, which is the largest publicly available cross-age dataset to the best of our knowledge. Table 1 shows the statistics of the dataset and comparison to other existing face datasets. From this table, our dataset has the largest amount of images and contains age information. Compared to MORPH dataset, age gaps for CACD between images of the same person are larger. FG-NET has larger age gaps but it only contains few images from a limited number of people. Figure 5 shows the distribution of the datasets with different ages. Both MORPH and our dataset do not contain images with age of 10 or younger, while FG-NET has more images of younger ages. However, our dataset has more images for all other ages.

5   Experiments

5.1   Experiment on Cross-Age Celebrity Dataset

In Cross-Age Celebrity Dataset, there are images of a total of 2,000 celebrities. We separate the dataset into four parts as shown in Figure 4: images of 200 celebrities with manual annotations are used for evaluating the algorithms: (1) 80 out of these 200 celebrities are used for parameters selection and (2) the other 120 are used for reporting testing results; (3) images of another 600 celebrities are used for computing the PCA subspace; (4) the final images of 1,200 celebrities are used for reference representations.

---

[4] Note that we manually removed noisy images from these 200 celebrities by checking the image content. However, since some of the images are hard to identify even for humans, the subset might contain noises. Also, we only employ simple duplicate detection method, thus the dataset might still have near-duplicate images.

Table 1. The comparison between existing datasets. Our dataset has the largest amount of images and contains age information. Compared to MORPH dataset, age gaps between images of the same person are larger. FG-NET has larger age gaps but it only contains a small amount of images from a limited number of people.

Dataset	# of images	# of people	# images/person	Age info.	Age gap
LFW [11]	13,233	5,749	2.3	No	-
Pubfig [13]	58,797	200	293.9	No	-
FGNet [20]	1,002	82	12.2	Yes	0-45
MORPH [26]	55,134	13,618	4.1	Yes	0-5
Ours (CACD)	163,446	2,000	81.7	Yes	0-10

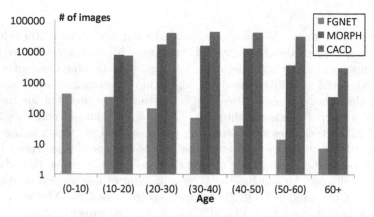

Fig. 5. The distribution of the dataset with different ages. Both MORPH and our dataset do not contain images with age of 10 or younger, while FG-NET has more images of younger ages. However, our dataset has more images in all other ages.

Parameters Selection. For selecting the parameters in our algorithm, we use images taken in 2013 as query images and images taken in other years (2004-2012) as database images. Mean average precision (MAP) is used as our evaluation metrics. For the retrieval results of each query image, precision at every recall level is computed and averaged to get average precision (AP). MAP is then computed by averaging AP from all query images. There are few parameters in the proposed method we need to decide: the PCA feature dimensions d, regularization parameters in the coding framework $\hat{\lambda}_1$, $\hat{\lambda}_2$, and number of reference celebrities used n.

For PCA feature dimensions d, we run experiments from 100 to 1,000 and find that the performance stops to improve after 500, so we fix our feature dimension d to 500 in the further experiments. For regularization parameters and number of celebrities, we first randomly select half reference celebrities and adjust $\hat{\lambda}_1$ and $\hat{\lambda}_2$ from 10^0 to 10^4. The results are shown in Figure 6 (a). We can see that adding temporal constraint in our coding framework can help the performance

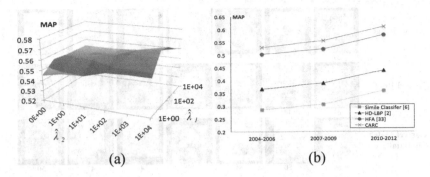

Fig. 6. (a) Validation results of Cross-Age Reference Coding on our CACD using different parameters. The results show using temporal constraint can improve the performance. The parameters are set to $(\hat{\lambda}_1, \hat{\lambda}_2) = (10^1, 10^4)$. (b) The retrieval results on CACD compare to other state-of-the-art methods. The proposed method consistently shows the best performance across different years.

Table 2. Rank-1 identification results on MORPH dataset. The proposed method achieves the highest recognition rate compared to other state-of-the-art methods.

Method	Recognition rate
Park et al. (2010) [24]	79.8%
Li et al. (2011) [17]	83.9%
Gong et al. (2013) [8]	91.1%
Ours	**92.8%**

as it increases with $\hat{\lambda}_2$. We set $(\hat{\lambda}_1, \hat{\lambda}_2) = (10^1, 10^4)$ where they achieve the best performance in the validation set for testing. For the number of celebrities n, we then randomly select reference celebrities from 40 to 1,200 and find that the performance stops to improve after 600. Therefore we fix the number of celebrities to 600 for testing.

Compare to State-of-the-Art Methods. We compare CARC to several different state-of-the-art methods, including: (1) high-dimensional local binary pattern [4] (HD-LBP), the local feature used for cross-age celebrity coding. We also use PCA to reduce the dimension to 500 for features from each landmark. (2) Simile Classifier [13]: we train a linear-SVM for each reference celebrity and use the sign distance to the decision boundary as feature. We use LIBLINEAR package [5] to carry out the computation and the number of the reference celebrities is also set as 600. (3) Hidden Factor Analysis [8] (HFA), a state-of-the-art method for age-invariant face recognition. We use high-dimensional local binary pattern as input feature and the parameters are tuned to the best setting according to their paper. We use the images of 120 celebrities for testing. We conduct experiments with three different subsets. In all three subsets, images taken in 2013 are

Fig. 7. Some cases where the proposed method fails. The first row contains the probe images, the second row shows the rank-1 result using the proposed method, and the third row shows the correct match in the gallery. The number on the bottom shows the age of the image.

used as query images. The database contains images taken in 2004-2006, 2007-2009, 2010-2012 for each of the three subsets respectively. For all methods, we use cosine similarity as the similarity measure. The performance of all methods in terms of MAP is shown in Figure 6(b). We can see that the proposed method outperforms other methods in all three different subsets. Simile Classifier has the worst performance. It is because SVM classifier is not robust to noise and age variation in the training data. The performance drops on all methods when the age gap is larger, which reveals the difficulty of face retrieval with age variation. Nevertheless, both HFA and the proposed method can achieve higher performance on the subset with large age gap compared to baseline features on the subset with small age gap. It shows the effectiveness of the age-invariant methods. CARC achieves higher performance than HFA, which shows that CARC can better utilize the noisy reference set and is more robust to age variation.

5.2   Experiment on MORPH Dataset

To show the generalizability of the proposed method, we also conduct face recognition experiment on MORPH dataset. For this dataset, we follow the experimental setting in [17] for close set face identification. We randomly select 10,000 subjects in the MORPH dataset and use the youngest images of these 10,000 subjects to construct the gallery set, and the oldest images of the subjects are used as the probe set. Both gallery and probe consist of 10,000 images from 10,000 different subjects. We then randomly select another 600 subjects from the dataset as reference set for our algorithm. Images of subjects other than these 10,600 subjects are then used to compute PCA and LDA subspaces as in [8], and we reduce the dimension to 1,000 for features from each landmark.

We compare our algorithm to several state-of-the-art methods including, (1) a generative aging model [24], (2) a discriminative model for age-invariant face recognition [17], and (3) hidden factor analysis, currently the best result on the dataset [8]. The results in terms of rank-1 recognition rate of our algorithm compared to other methods are shown in Table 2. We can see that the proposed method can achieve better performance compared to other state-of-the-art methods. Some examples of incorrect matching are shown in Figure 7. Although our system can achieve an accuracy higher than 92%, it can still fail in some cases, especially when the probe and gallery are significantly different. Some of these cases are really hard even for human to recognize. For some applications, we do not need to have perfect rank-1 accuracy, and we only need to find the correct match in the top-k results. Our system can achieve more than 98% accuracy in top-20 results and 94.5% mean average precision in the MORPH dataset.

6 Conclusions

In this paper, we propose a new approach for age-invariant face recognition and retrieval called Cross-Age Reference Coding. Using the proposed method, we can map low-level feature into an age-invariant reference space. Experimental results show that the proposed method can outperform state-of-the-art methods on both MORPH and CACD datasets and achieve high accuracy in face recognition across age. We also introduce a large-scale face dataset, Cross-Age Celebrity Dataset, for the purpose of face recognition with age variation. To the best of our knowledge, the dataset is the largest publicly available cross-age face dataset, and we hope the dataset can help researchers to improve the result of face recognition. In the future, we want to investigate how to effectively choose a subset from the reference people and further improve the performance of age-invariant face recognition and retrieval.

References

1. Ahonen, T., Hadid, A., Pietikainen, M.: Face description with local binary patterns: Application to face recognition. IEEE Transactions on Pattern Analysis and Machine Intelligence 28(12), 2037–2041 (2006)
2. Barkan, O., Weill, J., Wolf, L., Aronowitz, H.: Fast high dimensional vector multiplication face recognition. In: Proc. IEEE Int'l Conf. Computer Vision (2013)
3. Berg, T., Belhumeur, P.N.: Tom-vs-pete classifiers and identity-preserving alignment for face verification. In: BMVC, vol. 1, p. 5 (2012)
4. Chen, D., Cao, X., Wen, F., Sun, J.: Blessing of dimensionality: High-dimensional feature and its efficient compression for face verification. In: 2013 IEEE Conference on Computer Vision and Pattern Recognition (CVPR), pp. 3025–3032. IEEE (2013)
5. Fan, R.E., Chang, K.W., Hsieh, C.J., Wang, X.R., Lin, C.J.: Liblinear: A library for large linear classification. The Journal of Machine Learning Research 9, 1871–1874 (2008)
6. Fu, Y., Huang, T.S.: Human age estimation with regression on discriminative aging manifold. IEEE Transactions on Multimedia 10(4), 578–584 (2008)
7. Geng, X., Zhou, Z.H., Smith-Miles, K.: Automatic age estimation based on facial aging patterns. IEEE Transactions on Pattern Analysis and Machine Intelligence 29(12), 2234–2240 (2007)

8. Gong, D., Li, Z., Lin, D., Liu, J., Tang, X.: Hidden factor analysis for age invariant face recognition. In: 2013 IEEE 14th International Conference on Computer Vision. IEEE (2013)
9. Gross, R., Matthews, I., Cohn, J., Kanade, T., Baker, S.: Multi-pie. Image and Vision Computing 28(5), 807–813 (2010)
10. Guo, G., Fu, Y., Dyer, C.R., Huang, T.S.: Image-based human age estimation by manifold learning and locally adjusted robust regression. IEEE Transactions on Image Processing 17(7), 1178–1188 (2008)
11. Huang, G.B., Ramesh, M., Berg, T., Learned-Miller, E.: Labeled faces in the wild: A database for studying face recognition in unconstrained environments. Tech. Rep. 07-49, University of Massachusetts, Amherst (October 2007)
12. Jain, A.K., Klare, B., Park, U.: Face matching and retrieval in forensics applications. IEEE MultiMedia 19(1), 20 (2012)
13. Kumar, N., Berg, A.C., Belhumeur, P.N., Nayar, S.K.: Attribute and simile classifiers for face verification. In: 2009 IEEE 12th International Conference on Computer Vision, pp. 365–372. IEEE (2009)
14. Kwon, Y.H., da Vitoria Lobo, N.: Age classification from facial images. In: Proceedings of the 1994 IEEE Computer Society Conference on Computer Vision and Pattern Recognition, CVPR 1994, pp. 762–767. IEEE (1994)
15. Lanitis, A., Draganova, C., Christodoulou, C.: Comparing different classifiers for automatic age estimation. IEEE Transactions on Systems, Man, and Cybernetics, Part B: Cybernetics 34(1), 621–628 (2004)
16. Lanitis, A., Taylor, C.J., Cootes, T.F.: Toward automatic simulation of aging effects on face images. IEEE Transactions on Pattern Analysis and Machine Intelligence 24(4), 442–455 (2002)
17. Li, Z., Park, U., Jain, A.K.: A discriminative model for age invariant face recognition. IEEE Transactions on Information Forensics and Security 6(3), 1028–1037 (2011)
18. Liao, Q., Leibo, J.Z., Mroueh, Y., Poggio, T.: Can a biologically-plausible hierarchy effectively replace face detection, alignment, and recognition pipelines? CoRR abs/1311.4082 (2013)
19. Ling, H., Soatto, S., Ramanathan, N., Jacobs, D.W.: Face verification across age progression using discriminative methods. IEEE Transactions on Information Forensics and Security 5(1), 82–91 (2010)
20. Face and Gesture Recognition Working group: FG-NET Aging Database (2000)
21. Montillo, A., Ling, H.: Age regression from faces using random forests. In: 2009 16th IEEE International Conference on Image Processing (ICIP), pp. 2465–2468. IEEE (2009)
22. Mu, G., Guo, G., Fu, Y., Huang, T.S.: Human age estimation using bio-inspired features. In: IEEE Conference on Computer Vision and Pattern Recognition, CVPR 2009, pp. 112–119. IEEE (2009)
23. Ojala, T., Pietikainen, M., Maenpaa, T.: Multiresolution gray-scale and rotation invariant texture classification with local binary patterns. IEEE Transactions on Pattern Analysis and Machine Intelligence 24(7), 971–987 (2002)
24. Park, U., Tong, Y., Jain, A.K.: Age-invariant face recognition. IEEE Transactions on Pattern Analysis and Machine Intelligence 32(5), 947–954 (2010)
25. Ramanathan, N., Chellappa, R.: Face verification across age progression. IEEE Transactions on Image Processing 15(11), 3349–3361 (2006)
26. Ricanek, K., Tesafaye, T.: Morph: A longitudinal image database of normal adult age-progression. In: 7th International Conference on Automatic Face and Gesture Recognition, FGR 2006, pp. 341–345. IEEE (2006)

27. Simonyan, K., Parkhi, O.M., Vedaldi, A., Zisserman, A.: Fisher vector faces in the wild. In: Proc. BMVC, vol. 1, p. 7 (2013)

28. Suo, J., Chen, X., Shan, S., Gao, W.: Learning long term face aging patterns from partially dense aging databases. In: 2009 IEEE 12th International Conference on Computer Vision, pp. 622–629. IEEE (2009)

29. Suo, J., Zhu, S.C., Shan, S., Chen, X.: A compositional and dynamic model for face aging. IEEE Transactions on Pattern Analysis and Machine Intelligence 32(3), 385–401 (2010)

30. Tsumura, N., Ojima, N., Sato, K., Shiraishi, M., Shimizu, H., Nabeshima, H., Akazaki, S., Hori, K., Miyake, Y.: Image-based skin color and texture analysis/synthesis by extracting hemoglobin and melanin information in the skin. ACM Transactions on Graphics (TOG) 22, 770–779 (2003)

31. Turk, M.A., Pentland, A.P.: Face recognition using eigenfaces. In: Proceedings of the IEEE Computer Society Conference on Computer Vision and Pattern Recognition, CVPR 1991, pp. 586–591. IEEE (1991)

32. Viola, P., Jones, M.J.: Robust real-time face detection. International Journal of Computer Vision 57(2), 137–154 (2004)

33. Wang, D., Hoi, S.C., He, Y., Zhu, J.: Retrieval-based face annotation by weak label regularized local coordinate coding. In: Proceedings of the 19th ACM International Conference on Multimedia, pp. 353–362. ACM (2011)

34. Wang, J., Shang, Y., Su, G., Lin, X.: Age simulation for face recognition. In: 18th International Conference on Pattern Recognition, ICPR 2006, vol. 3, pp. 913–916. IEEE (2006)

35. Wright, J., Yang, A.Y., Ganesh, A., Sastry, S.S., Ma, Y.: Robust face recognition via sparse representation. IEEE Transactions on Pattern Analysis and Machine Intelligence 31(2), 210–227 (2009)

36. Wu, Z., Ke, Q., Sun, J., Shum, H.Y.: Scalable face image retrieval with identity-based quantization and multireference reranking. IEEE Transactions on Pattern Analysis and Machine Intelligence 33(10), 1991–2001 (2011)

37. Xiong, X., De la Torre, F.: Supervised descent method and its applications to face alignment. In: 2013 IEEE Conference on Computer Vision and Pattern Recognition (CVPR), pp. 532–539. IEEE (2013)

38. Yan, S., Wang, H., Tang, X., Huang, T.S.: Learning auto-structured regressor from uncertain nonnegative labels. In: IEEE 11th International Conference on Computer Vision, ICCV 2007, pp. 1–8. IEEE (2007)

39. Yin, Q., Tang, X., Sun, J.: An associate-predict model for face recognition. In: 2011 IEEE Conference on Computer Vision and Pattern Recognition (CVPR), pp. 497–504. IEEE (2011)

40. Zhou, S.K., Georgescu, B., Zhou, X.S., Comaniciu, D.: Image based regression using boosting method. In: Tenth IEEE International Conference on Computer Vision, ICCV 2005, vol. 1, pp. 541–548. IEEE (2005)

Reverse Training: An Efficient Approach for Image Set Classification

Munawar Hayat, Mohammed Bennamoun, and Senjian An

School of Computer Science and Software Enginnering,
The University of Western Australia, 35 Stirling Highway,
Crawley, WA 6009 Australia

Abstract. This paper introduces a new approach, called *reverse training*, to efficiently extend binary classifiers for the task of multi-class image set classification. Unlike existing binary to multi-class extension strategies, which require multiple binary classifiers, the proposed approach is very efficient since it trains a single binary classifier to optimally discriminate the class of the query image set from all others. For this purpose, the classifier is trained with the images of the query set (labelled positive) and a randomly sampled subset of the training data (labelled negative). The trained classifier is then evaluated on rest of the training images. The class of these images with their largest percentage classified as positive is predicted as the class of the query image set. The confidence level of the prediction is also computed and integrated into the proposed approach to further enhance its robustness and accuracy. Extensive experiments and comparisons with existing methods show that the proposed approach achieves state of the art performance for face and object recognition on a number of datasets.

Keywords: Image Set Classification, Face and Object Recognition.

1 Introduction

Face or object recognition is traditionally treated as a single image based classification problem, that is, given a single query image, we are required to find its best match in a gallery of images. However, in many real-world applications (e.g. recognition from surveillance videos, multi-view camera networks and personal albums), multiple images of a person or an object are readily available. Recognition from these multiple images is studied under the framework of image set classification. Classification from image sets (as opposed to single image based classification) is more promising as it aims to effectively handle a wide range of appearance variations, which are commonly present within images of the same object in an image set. These variations can be caused by changing lighting conditions, different view points, non-rigid deformations and occlusions [5, 12, 17]. For these reasons, image set classification has attained significant research attention in recent years [3, 8, 9, 11, 14, 20, 25–27, 29, 30].

Although image set classification provides a plentitude of data of the same object under different variations, it simultaneously poses many challenges to

D. Fleet et al. (Eds.): ECCV 2014, Part VI, LNCS 8694, pp. 784–799, 2014.

make effective use of this data. The major focus of the existing image set classification methods has therefore been to find a suitable representation which can effectively model the appearance variations within images of an image set. For example, the methods in [10, 14, 19, 25, 27, 28] use subspaces to model image sets, and set representative exemplars (generated from affine hull/convex hull) are used in [3, 11] for image set representations. The mean of the set images is used for set representation in [11, 18, 20] and image sets are represented as a point on a manifold geometry in [8, 26]. The main motivation behind a single entity representation of image sets (e.g. subspace, exemplar image, mean, a point on the manifold) is to achieve compactness and computational efficiency. However, these representations do not necessarily encode all of the information contained in the images of the image set. In this paper, we take a different approach and avoid representing an image set by a single entity. We retain the images of the image set in their original form and instead design an efficient classification framework to effectively deal with the plentitude of the data involved.

The proposed image set classification framework is built on well-developed learning algorithms. Although, these algorithms are originally designed for classification from single images, they can be adapted for image set classification by first individually classifying images of a query set and then devising an appropriate voting strategy (see Sec 4.2). However, due to the plentitude of data involved in the case of image set classification, a straight forward extension of these algorithms from single image based to image set classification would be computationally burdensome. Specifically, since most of the popular learning algorithms (e.g. Support Vector Machines, AdaBoost, regression, logistic regression and decision tree algorithms) are inherently binary classifiers, their extension to a multi-class classification problem (such as image set classification) requires training of multiple binary classifiers. One-vs-one and one-vs-rest are the two most commonly adapted strategies for this purpose. For a k-class classification problem, $\frac{k(k-1)}{2}$ and k binary classifiers are respectively trained for one-vs-one and one-vs-rest. Although, one-vs-rest trains comparatively fewer classifiers, it requires images from all classes to train each binary classifier. Adapting either of the well-known one-vs-one or one-vs-rest strategies for image set classification would therefore require a lot of computational effort, since either the number of images involved is quite large or a fairly large number of binary classifiers has to be trained.

The framework proposed in this paper trains a very few number of binary classifiers (mostly one or a maximum of five) on a very small fraction of images for the task of multi-class image set classification. The framework (see block diagram in Fig 1) first splits training images from all classes into two sets $\mathcal{D}_1$ and $\mathcal{D}_2$. The division is done such that $\mathcal{D}_1$ contains uniformly randomly sampled images from all classes with the total number of images in $\mathcal{D}_1$ being equal to the number of images of the query image set. Next, a linear binary classifier is trained to optimally separate images of the query set from $\mathcal{D}_1$. Note that $\mathcal{D}_1$ has some images which belong to the class of the query set. However, since these images are very few in number, the classifier treats them as outliers. The trained classifier therefore learns to discriminate the class of the query set from all other

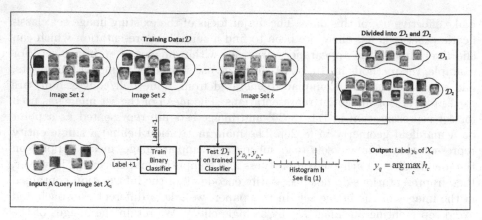

Fig. 1. Block diagram of the proposed method. Training data is divided into two sets $\mathcal{D}_1$ and $\mathcal{D}_2$. $\mathcal{D}_1$ contains uniformly randomly sampled images from all classes such that the size of $\mathcal{D}_1$ is the same as the size of the query image set $\mathcal{X}_q$. A binary classifier is trained, with images of $\mathcal{X}_q$ (labeled +1) and $\mathcal{D}_1$ (labeled −1). The classifier is then tested on the images of $\mathcal{D}_2$. Knowing the class labels of images of $\mathcal{D}_2$ which are classified +1, we formulate a histogram (see Eq. 1), which is then used to decide about the class of $\mathcal{X}_q$. See a toy example in Fig 2 for illustration.

classes. Next, the learned classifier is evaluated on the images of $\mathcal{D}_2$ ($\mathcal{D}_2$ contains all training images except the ones in $\mathcal{D}_1$). The images of $\mathcal{D}_2$ which are classified to belong to the images of the query set are of our interest. Knowing the original class labels of these training images, we formulate a histogram which is then used to decide about the class of the query set. A complete detailed description of the proposed framework is presented in Sec 3 along with an illustration using a toy example in Fig. 2.

The main strengths and contributions of this paper are as follows. 1) A new concept is introduced to extend any binary classifier for multi-class image set classification. Compared with the existing binary to multi-class strategies (e.g. one-vs-one, one-vs-rest), the proposed approach is computationally very efficient. It only requires training of a fixed number of binary classifiers (1 to 5 compared with k or $\frac{k(k-1)}{2}$) using a small number of images. 2) Along with the predicted class label of the query image set, the proposed method gives a confidence level of its prediction. This information is very useful and can be used as an indication of potential miss-classification. Knowing pre-hand about a query image set being miss-classified makes it possible to use another binary classifier. The proposed method can therefore accommodate the fusion of information from different types of binary classifiers before declaring the final class label of the query image set. 3) The proposed method is easily scalable to new classes. Unlike many existing image set classification methods, the computational complexity of the proposed method is not affected much with the addition of new classes in the gallery (see Sec. 4.2). Many of the existing methods would require retraining on the complete dataset (when new classes are enrolled), whereas, the proposed method requires no additional training and can efficiently discriminate the query class from other classes using a fixed number of binary classifiers.

2   Related Work

The major challenge addressed by the existing research on image set classification has been to find a representation which can effectively model the appearance variations within images of an image set. Two different approaches have been adopted for this purpose. The **first** approach models the variations within images of a set by a statistical distribution and uses a measure such as KL-divergence to compare two sets. Methods based on this approach are called parametric model based methods [2,22]. One major limitation of these methods is their reliance on a very strong assumption about the existence of a statistical correlation between image sets. The **second** approach for image set representation avoids such assumptions. The methods based on this approach are called non-parametric model based methods [3,8,9,11,14,20,23,25–27,29,30] and have shown to give a superior performance compared with the parametric model based methods. A brief overview of the non-parametric model based methods is given below.

Subspaces have been very commonly used by the non-parametric methods to represent image sets. Examples include image sets represented by linear subspaces [14,28], orthogonal subspaces [19] and a combination of linear subspaces [25,27]. Principal angles are then used to compare subspaces. A drawback of these methods is that they represent image sets of different sizes by a subspace of the same dimensions. These methods cannot therefore uniformly capture the critical information from image sets with different set lengths. Specifically, for sets with a larger number of images and diverse appearance variations, the subspace-based methods cannot accommodate all the information contained in the images. Image sets can also be represented by their geometric structures i.e. affine hull or convex hull models. For example, Affine Hull Image Set Distance (AHISD) [3] and Sparse Approximated Nearest Points (SANP) [11] use affine hull, whereas Convex Hull Image Set Distance (CHISD) [3] uses the convex hull of the images to model an image set. The set-to-set distance is then determined in terms of the Euclidean distance between the set representative exemplars which are generated from the corresponding geometric structures. Although these methods have shown to produce a promising performance, they are prone to outliers and are computationally expensive (since they require a direct one-one comparison of the query set with all sets in the gallery). Some of the non-parametric model based methods represent an image set as a point on a certain manifold geometry e.g. Grassmannian manifold [8,25] and Lie group of Riemannian manifold [26]. The mean of the set images is also used for image set representation in [11,18,20].

In this paper, we argue that a single entity (e.g. a mean image, a subspace, a point on a manifold, an exemplar generated from a geometric structure) for image set representation can be sub-optimal, insufficient and could result in the loss of information from the images of the set. For example, for image sets represented by a subspace, the amount of the retained information depends on the selected dimensions of the subspace. In the case of image sets represented by their mean images, the mean image could be visually very different from the rest of the images in the set. For illustration purposes, consider taking the mean of two face images from the right and left profile views. The mean image would be blurred and contain two superimposed faces. Similarly, generating representative exemplars from geometric structures could result in exemplars which are practically non-existent and are very different from the original images of the set. We therefore take an altogether different approach which does not require any image set representation. Instead the images are retained in their original form and a novel classification concept is proposed which incorporates well-developed learning algorithms to optimally discriminate the class of the query image set from all other classes. A detailed description of the proposed framework is presented next.

3   Proposed Framework

Problem Description: For k classes of a training data, we are given k image sets $\mathcal{X}_1, \mathcal{X}_2, \cdots \mathcal{X}_k$ and their corresponding class labels $y_c \in [1, 2, \cdots k]$. An image set $\mathcal{X}_c = \{\mathbf{x}^{(t)} | y^{(t)} = c; t = 1, 2, \cdots N_c\}$ contains all N_c training images $\mathbf{x}^{(t)}$ belonging to class c. Note that for training data with multiple image sets per class, we combine images from all sets into a single set. During classification, we are given a query image set $\mathcal{X}_q = \{\mathbf{x}^{(t)}\}_{t=1}^{N_q}$, and the task is to find the class label y_q of $\mathcal{X}_q$.

3.1   Image Set Classification Algorithm

The proposed image set classification algorithm is summarized in Alg 1. The details are presented below.

1. Images from all training sets are gathered into a single set $\mathcal{D} = \{\mathcal{X}_1, \mathcal{X}_2, \cdots \mathcal{X}_k\}$. Next, $\mathcal{D}$ is divided into two sets: $\mathcal{D}_1$ and $\mathcal{D}_2$. Let $\mathcal{D}_{1c}$ be a randomly sampled subset of $\mathcal{X}_c$ with a set size $N_{\mathcal{D}_{1c}}$, where $N_{\mathcal{D}_{1c}} = \frac{N_q}{k}$ rounded to the nearest integer, then the set $\mathcal{D}_1$ is formed by the union $\bigcup_c \mathcal{D}_{1c}$, $c = 1, 2, \cdots k$. $\mathcal{D}_2$ is achieved by $\mathcal{D}_2 = \mathcal{D} \setminus \mathcal{D}_1$. The class label information of images in $\mathcal{D}_1$ and $\mathcal{D}_2$ is stored in sets $\mathbf{y}_{\mathcal{D}_1} = \{y^{(t)} \in [1, 2, \cdots k], t = 1, 2, \cdots N_{\mathcal{D}_1}\}$ and $\mathbf{y}_{\mathcal{D}_2} = \{y^{(t)} \in [1, 2, \cdots k], t = 1, 2, \cdots N_{\mathcal{D}_2}\}$ respectively.

2. Next, we train a binary classifier C_1. Training is done on the images of $\mathcal{X}_q$ and $\mathcal{D}_1$. All images in $\mathcal{X}_q$ are labeled +1 while the images in $\mathcal{D}_1$ are labeled −1. Since images from all classes are present in $\mathcal{D}_1$, the classifier learns to separate images of $\mathcal{X}_q$ from the images of other classes. Note that $\mathcal{D}_1$ does have a small number of images from the same class as of $\mathcal{X}_q$. However, since these images are very few, the selected binary classifier (see Sec 3.2) treats them as outliers and learns to discriminate the class of the query image set from all other classes.

3. The trained classifier C_1 is then tested on the images of $\mathcal{D}_2$. The images in $\mathcal{D}_2$ classified as $+1$ (same as images of $\mathcal{X}_q$) are of interest. Let $\mathbf{y}_{\mathcal{D}_2^+} \subset \mathbf{y}_{\mathcal{D}_2}$ contain the class labels of images of $\mathcal{D}_2$ classified $+1$ by the classifier C_1.

4. A normalized frequency histogram $\mathbf{h}$ of class labels in $\mathbf{y}_{\mathcal{D}_2^+}$ is computed. The cth value of the histogram, $\mathbf{h}_c$, is given by the percentage of the images of class c in $\mathcal{D}_2$ which are classified $+1$. Formally, $\mathbf{h}_c$ is given by the ratio of *the number of images of $\mathcal{D}_2$ belonging to class c and classified as $+1$* **to** *the total number of images of $\mathcal{D}_2$ belonging to class c.* This is given by,

$$\mathbf{h}_c = \frac{\sum\limits_{y^{(t)} \in \mathbf{y}_{\mathcal{D}_2^+}} \delta_c(y^{(t)})}{\sum\limits_{y^{(t)} \in \mathbf{y}_{\mathcal{D}_2}} \delta_c(y^{(t)})} \quad , \text{where} \tag{1}$$

$$\delta_c(y^{(t)}) = \begin{cases} 1, & y^{(t)} = c \\ 0, & \text{otherwise.} \end{cases}$$

5. A class in $\mathcal{D}_2$ with most of its images classified as $+1$ can be predicted as the class of $\mathcal{X}_q$. The class label y_q of $\mathcal{X}_q$ is therefore given by,

$$y_q = \arg\max_c \mathbf{h}_c \tag{2}$$

We can also get a confidence level d of our prediction of y_q. This is defined in terms of the difference between the maximum and the second maximum values of the histogram $\mathbf{h}$,

$$d = \max_{c \in \{1 \cdots k\}} \mathbf{h}_c - \max_{c \in \{1 \cdots k\} \setminus y_q} \mathbf{h}_c. \tag{3}$$

We are more confident about our prediction if the predicted class is a 'clear winner'. In the case of closely competing classes, the confidence level of the prediction will be low.

6. We declare the class label of $\mathcal{X}_q$ (as in Eq. 2) provided the confidence d is greater than a certain threshold. The value of the threshold is determined empirically by performing experiments on a cross validation set. Otherwise, if the confidence level d is less than the threshold, steps 1-5 are repeated, for different random samplings of images into $\mathcal{D}_1$ and $\mathcal{D}_2$. After every iteration, a mean histogram $\bar{\mathbf{h}}$ is computed using the histogram of that iteration and the previous iterations. The confidence level d is also computed after every iteration using,

$$d = \max_{c \in \{1 \cdots k\}} \bar{\mathbf{h}}_c - \max_{c \in \{1 \cdots k\} \setminus y_q} \bar{\mathbf{h}}_c. \tag{4}$$

Iterations are stopped if the confidence level d becomes greater than the threshold or if a maximum of five iterations have already been done. Doing more iterations enhances the robustness of the method (since different images are selected into $\mathcal{D}_1$ and $\mathcal{D}_2$ for every iteration) but at the cost of increased computational effort. Our experiments revealed that a maximum of five iterations is a good trade-off between the robustness and the computational efficiency.

Algorithm 1. The proposed Image Set Classification algorithm

Input: Training image sets $\mathcal{X}_1, \mathcal{X}_2, \cdots \mathcal{X}_k$; Query image set $\mathcal{X}_q$; *threshold*

1: $\mathcal{D} \leftarrow \{\mathcal{X}_1, \mathcal{X}_2, \cdots \mathcal{X}_k\}$ ▷ $\mathcal{D}$: All training images

2: $\mathcal{D}_1 \leftarrow \bigcup_c \mathcal{D}_{1c}$ where $\mathcal{D}_{1c}$ is a random subset of $\mathcal{X}_c$

3: $\mathcal{D}_2 \leftarrow \mathcal{D} \setminus \mathcal{D}_1$ ▷ $\mathcal{D}$ divided into $\mathcal{D}_1$ and $\mathcal{D}_2$

4: $C_1 \leftarrow train(\mathcal{D}_1, \mathcal{X}_q)$ ▷ $\mathcal{X}_q$ labeled $+1$ and $\mathcal{D}_1$ labeled -1

5: $l_{\mathcal{D}_2} \leftarrow test(C_1, \mathcal{D}_2)$ ▷ Test $\mathcal{D}_2$ on classifier C_1

6: $y_{\mathcal{D}_2^+} \leftarrow l_{\mathcal{D}_2}, y_{\mathcal{D}_2}$ ▷ labels of images of $\mathcal{D}_2$ classified $+1$

7: $\mathbf{h} \leftarrow y_{\mathcal{D}_2^+}, y_{\mathcal{D}_2}$ ▷ Normalized histogram, see Eq 1

8: $d \leftarrow \mathbf{h}$ ▷ Confidence level, see Eq. 3

9: **if** $d > threshold$ **then**

10:      $y_q \leftarrow \arg\max_c \mathbf{h}_c$

11: **else**

12:      **repeat**   ▷ Repeat for different random selections in $\mathcal{D}_1$ and $\mathcal{D}_2$

13:          $d, \bar{\mathbf{h}} \leftarrow$ Repeat Steps 2-8

14:      **until** $d \geq threshold$ or repeated 5 times

15:      **if** $d > th$ **then**

16:          $y_q \leftarrow \arg\max_c \bar{\mathbf{h}}_c$

17:      **else**

18:          $y_q \leftarrow$ Repeat for another binary classifier C_2

19:      **end if**

20: **end if**

Output: Label y_q of $\mathcal{X}_q$

---

7. If the confidence level d (see Eq 4) is greater than the threshold, we declare the class label of $\mathcal{X}_q$ as $y_q = \arg\max_c \bar{\mathbf{h}}_c$. Otherwise, if the confidence level is lower than the threshold, declaring the class label would highly likely result in miss-classification. We therefore seek the opinion of another binary classifier C_2. The procedure is repeated for a different binary classifier C_2. The decision about y_q is then made based on the confidence levels of C_1 and C_2. The prediction of the more confident classifier is considered as the final decision. The description about the choice of the binary classifiers C_1 and C_2 is given next.

3.2 The Choice of the Binary Classifiers

The proposed framework requires a binary classifier to distinguish between images of $\mathcal{X}_q$ and $\mathcal{D}_1$. The choice of the binary classifier should be such that it should generalize well to unseen data while testing. Moreover, since the binary classifier is being trained on images of $\mathcal{X}_q$ and $\mathcal{D}_1$ and some images in $\mathcal{D}_1$ have the same class as of $\mathcal{X}_q$, the binary classifier should treat these images as outliers. For these reasons, Support Vector Machine (SVM) with a linear Kernel is deemed to be an appropriate choice. It is known to show excellent generalization to unknown test data and can effectively handle outliers.

Two classifiers (C_1 and C_2) are used by the proposed framework. C_1 is the linear SVM with **L2** regularization and **L2** loss function, while C_2 is the linear

SVM with **L1** regularization and **L2** loss function [4]. Specifically, given a set of training example-label pairs $\left(\mathbf{x}^{(t)}, y^{(t)}\right)$, $y^{(t)} \in \{+1, -1\}$, C_1 solves the following optimization problem,

$$\min_{\mathbf{w}} \frac{1}{2} \mathbf{w}^T \mathbf{w} + C \sum_t \left(\max \left(0, 1 - y^{(t)} \mathbf{w}^T \mathbf{x}^{(t)} \right) \right)^2, \tag{5}$$

while, C_2 solves the following optimization problem,

$$\min_{\mathbf{w}} |\mathbf{w}|_1 + C \sum_t \left(\max \left(0, 1 - y^{(t)} \mathbf{w}^T \mathbf{x}^{(t)} \right) \right)^2. \tag{6}$$

Here $\mathbf{w}$ is the coefficient vector to be learned and $C > 0$ is the penalty parameter used for regularization. After learning the SVM parameter $\mathbf{w}$, classification is performed based on the value of $\mathbf{w}^T \mathbf{x}^{(t)}$. Note that the coefficient vector $\mathbf{w}$ learned by the classifier C_2 (trained for challenging examples) is sparse. Learning a sparse $\mathbf{w}$ for C_2 further enhances the generalization for the challenging cases.

3.3   Illustration with a Toy Example

The proposed image set classification algorithm is illustrated with the help of a toy example in Fig 2. Let us consider a three class set classification problem in which we are given three training sets $\mathcal{X}_1$, $\mathcal{X}_2$, $\mathcal{X}_3$ and a query set $\mathcal{X}_q$. The data points of the training sets and the query set are shown in Fig 2 (a). First, we form $\mathcal{D}_1$ by randomly sampling points from $\mathcal{X}_1$, $\mathcal{X}_2$ and $\mathcal{X}_3$. Fig 2 (b) shows the datapoints of $\mathcal{D}_1$ and $\mathcal{X}_q$. Next, a linear SVM is trained by labeling the datapoints of $\mathcal{X}_q$ as +1 and $\mathcal{D}_1$ as −1. Note that SVM (Fig 2 (c)) ignores the miss-labeled points (the points of $\mathcal{X}_3$ in $\mathcal{D}_1$) and treats them as outliers. Finally, we classify the data points of $\mathcal{D}_2$ from the learned SVM boundary. Fig 2 (d) shows that the SVM labels the points of $\mathcal{X}_3$ in $\mathcal{D}_2$ as +1. The proposed algorithm therefore declares the class of $\mathcal{X}_3$ to be the class of $\mathcal{X}_q$.

4   Experiments

We evaluate the performance of the proposed method for the task of image set classification with applications to face and object recognition. For face recognition, we perform experiments on three video datasets (Honda/UCSD [15], CMU Mobo [7], YouTube Celebrities [13]) and an RGB-D Kinect dataset (obtained by combining three Kinect datasets). For object recognition, we use ETH-80 dataset [16]. Below, we first give a brief description of each of these datasets followed by the adopted experimental configurations. We then present a performance comparison of the proposed method with the baseline multi-class classification strategies (Sec. 4.2). Finally, in Sec. 4.3, we compare our method with the existing state of the art image set classification methods.

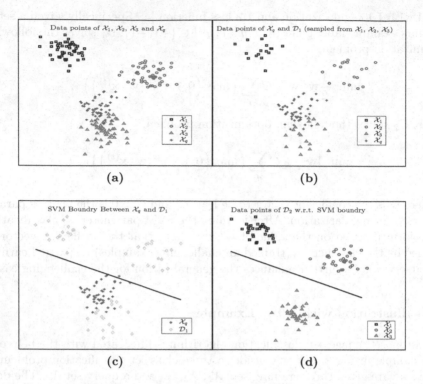

Fig. 2. Toy example to illustrate the proposed method. Consider a training data with three classes and the task is to find the class of $\mathcal{X}_q$ **(a)**. Data points from three training image sets $\mathcal{X}_1$, $\mathcal{X}_2$, $\mathcal{X}_3$ and a query image set $\mathcal{X}_q$ are shown. **(b)** Data points from $\mathcal{X}_q$ and $\mathcal{D}_1$ (uniformly randomly sampled from $\mathcal{X}_1$, $\mathcal{X}_2$ and $\mathcal{X}_3$) are shown. **(c)** The learnt SVM boundary between $\mathcal{X}_q$ (labeled $+1$) and $\mathcal{D}_1$ (labeled -1). **(d)** The data points of $\mathcal{D}_2$ w.r.t. the learnt SVM boundary. Since the points of $\mathcal{X}_3$ in $\mathcal{D}_2$ lie on the same side of the boundary as the points of $\mathcal{X}_q$, the proposed method declares $\mathcal{X}_q$ to be from $\mathcal{X}_3$. Figure best seen in colour.

4.1   Evaluated Datasets and Experimental Settings

The Honda/UCSD Dataset [15] contains 59 video sequences (with 12 to 645 frames in each video) of 20 subjects. We use Viola and Jones face detection [24] algorithm to extract faces from video frames. The extracted faces are then resized to 20×20. For our experiments, we consider each video sequence as an image set and follow the standard evaluation configuration provided in [15]. Specifically, 20 video sequences are used for training and the remaining 39 sequences are used for testing. Three separate experiments are performed by considering all frames of a video as an image set and limiting the total number of frames in an image set to 50 and 100 (to evaluate the robustness for fewer images in a set). Each Experiment is repeated 10 times for different random selections of training and testing image sets.

The CMU Mobo (Motion of Body) dataset [7] contains a total of 96 video sequences of 24 subjects walking on a treadmill. The faces from the videos are extracted using [24] and resized to 40×40. Similar to [11, 26], we consider each video as an image set and use one set per subject for training and the remaining sets for testing. To achieve a consistency, experiments are repeated ten times for different training and testing sets.

YouTube Celebrities [13] dataset contains 1910 videos of 47 celebrities. The dataset is collected from YouTube and the videos are acquired under real-life scenarios. The faces in the dataset therefore exhibit a wide range of diversity and appearance variations in the form of changing illumination conditions, different head pose rotations and expression variations. Since the resolution of the face images is very low, face detection by [24] fails for a significant number of frames for this dataset. We therefore use tracking [21] to extract faces. Specifically, knowing the location of the face window in the first frame (provided with the dataset), we use the method of Ross *et al.* [21] to track the face region in the subsequent frames. The extracted face region is then resized to 30×30. In order to perform experiments, we treat the faces acquired from each video as an image set and follow the five fold cross validation experimental setup similar to [11, 25–27]. The complete dataset is divided into five equal folds with minimal overlap. Each fold has nine image sets per subject, three of which are used for training and the remaining six are used for testing.

Composite Kinect Dataset is achieved by combining three distinct Kinect datasets: CurtinFaces [17], Biwi Kinect [5] and an in-house dataset acquired in our laboratory. The number of subjects in each of these datasets is 52 (5000 RGB-D images), 20 (15,000 RGB-D images) and 48 (15000 RGB-D images) respectively. The random forrest regression based classifier of [6] is used to detect faces from the Kinect acquired images. The images in the composite dataset have a large range of variations in the form of changing illumination conditions, head pose rotations, expression deformations, sunglass disguise, and occlusions by hand. For performance evaluation, we randomly divide RGB-D images of each subject into five uniform folds. Considering each fold as an image set, we select one set for training and the remaining sets for testing. The experiments are repeated five times for different selections of training and testing sets.

ETH-80 Object Dataset contains images of eight object categories. These include cars, cows, apples, dogs, cups, horses, pears and tomatoes. Each object category is further divided into ten subcategories such as different brands of cars or different breeds of dogs. Each subcategory contains images under 41 orientations. For our experiments, we use the 128×128 cropped images [1] and resize them to 32×32. We follow an experimental setup similar to [14, 25, 26]. Images of an object in a subcategory are considered as an image set. For each object, five subcategories are randomly selected for training and the remaining five are used for testing. 10 runs of experiments are performed for different random selections of the training and testing sets.

Table 1. Performance Comparison with the baseline methods

Methods	Honda	Mobo	YouTube	Kinect	ETH
one-vs-one	92.1 ± 2.2	94.7 ± 2.0	67.7 ± 4.0	94.3 ± 3.5	96.2 ± 2.9
one-vs-rest	94.6 ± 1.9	96.7 ± 1.6	68.4 ± 4.2	94.6 ± 3.3	97.6 ± 1.5
This Paper	$\mathbf{100.0 \pm 0.0}$	$\mathbf{97.8 \pm 0.7}$	$\mathbf{74.1 \pm 3.5}$	$\mathbf{98.1 \pm 1.9}$	95.5 ± 2.0

Average identification rates of our method and two well-known multi-class classification strategies. The proposed method achieves good performance on all five datasets. See Table 2 for a comparison of the computational complexity.

4.2 Comparison with the Baseline Methods

Linear SVM based one-vs-one and one-vs-rest multi-class classification strategies are used as baseline methods for comparison. Note that these baseline methods are suitable for classification from single images. For image set classification, we first individually classify every image of the query image set and then use majority voting to decide about the class of the query image set. Experimental results in terms of average identification rates and standard deviations on all datasets are presented in Table 1. The results presented for Honda/UCSD dataset are only for full-lengths of videos considered as image sets. The results show that, amongst the compared baseline multi-class classification strategies, one-vs-rest performs slightly better than one-vs-one.

Table 2. Complexity Analysis

Method	Total binary classifiers	Images to train each classifier
One-vs-one	$\frac{k(k-1)}{2}$ {1081}	$2N_c$ {600}
One-vs-rest	k {47}	$\sum_{c=1}^{k} N_c$ {14000}
This Paper	$1 - 5$	$2N_q$ {200}

The proposed method trains just few binary classifiers and the number of images used for training is very small. The typical parameters values for YouTube Celebrities dataset are given in brackets.

Table 2 presents a comparison of the computational complexity in terms of the required number of binary classifiers and the number of images used to train each of these classifiers. One-vs-one trains $\frac{k(k-1)}{2}$ binary classifiers and uses images from two classes to train each classifier. Although the number of classifiers trained for one-vs-rest are comparatively less (k compared with $\frac{k(k-1)}{2}$), the number of images used to train each binary classifier is quite large (all images of the dataset are used). In comparison, our proposed method trains a few binary classifier (a maximum of five for the challenging cases) and the number of images used for training is also small.

Table 3. Performance Comparison on Honda/UCSD dataset

	MSM	DCC	MMD	MDA	AHISD	CHISD
All	88.2 ± 3.8	92.5 ± 2.2	92.0 ± 2.2	94.3 ± 3.3	91.2 ± 1.7	93.6 ± 1.6
100	85.6 ± 4.3	89.2 ± 2.4	85.5 ± 2.1	91.7 ± 1.6	90.7 ± 3.2	91.0 ± 1.7
50	83.0 ± 1.7	82.0 ± 3.3	83.1 ± 4.4	85.6 ± 5.8	89.8 ± 2.1	90.5 ± 2.0

	SANP	CDL	MSSRC	SSDML	RNP	**This Paper**
All	95.1 ± 3.0	98.9 ± 1.3	97.9 ± 2.6	86.4 ± 3.6	95.9 ± 2.1	$\mathbf{100.0 \pm 0.0}$
100	94.1 ± 3.2	96.2 ± 1.2	96.9 ± 1.3	84.3 ± 2.2	92.3 ± 3.2	$\mathbf{99.7 \pm 0.8}$
50	91.9 ± 2.7	93.9 ± 2.2	94.3 ± 1.4	83.4 ± 1.7	90.2 ± 3.2	$\mathbf{99.4 \pm 1.1}$

Average identification rates and standard deviations of different methods on Honda/UCSD dataset. The experiments are performed by considering all frames of the video as an image set as well as limiting the set length to 100 and 50 frames. The results show that the proposed method not only achieves the best performance but also maintains a consistency in its performance for reduced set lengths.

4.3 Comparison with Existing Image Set Classification Methods

We present a comparison of our method with a number of recently proposed state of the art image set classification methods. The compared methods include Mutual Subspace Method [28], Discriminant Canonical Correlation Analysis (DCC) [14], Manifold-to-Manifold Distance (MMD) [27], Manifold Discriminant Analysis (MDA) [25], the Linear version of the Affine Hull-based Image Set Distance (AHISD) [3], the Convex Hull-based Image Set Distance (CHISD) [3], Sparse Approximated Nearest Points (SANP) [11], Covariance Discriminative Learning (CDL) [26], Mean Sequence Sparse Representation Classification (MSSRC) [20], Set to Set Distance Metric Learning (SSDML) [30] and Regularized Nearest Points (RNP) [29]. We use the implementations provided by the respective authors for all methods except CDL. We carefully implemented CDL since it is not publicly available. The parameters for all methods are optimized for best performance.

The experimental results in terms of the average identification rates along with standard deviations of different methods on Honda/UCSD dataset are presented in Table 3. The proposed method achieves perfect classification for all frames of the video sequence considered as an image set. Once the total number of images in the set is reduced to 100 and 50, the average identification rates archived by the method are 99.7% and 99.4% respectively. This suggests the robustness of the method w.r.t. the number of images in the set and its suitability for real-life scenarios with a limited availability of images in the set.

The average identification rates and standard deviations for different methods on CMU/Mobo, YouTube Celebrities, Kinect and ETH datasets are summarized in Table 4. The results suggest that the proposed method outperforms most of

Table 4. Performance on CMU/Mobo, YouTube, Kinect and ETH-80 datasets

Methods	Mobo	YouTube	Kinect	ETH
MSM FG'98 [28]	96.8 ± 2.0	50.2 ± 3.6	89.3 ± 4.1	75.5 ± 4.8
DCC TPAMI'07 [14]	88.8 ± 2.4	51.4 ± 5.0	92.5 ± 2.0	91.7 ± 3.7
MMD CVPR'08 [27]	92.5 ± 2.9	54.0 ± 3.7	93.9 ± 2.2	77.5 ± 5.0
MDA CVPR'09 [25]	80.9 ± 12.3	55.1 ± 4.5	93.4 ± 3.6	77.2 ± 5.5
AHISD CVPR'10 [3]	92.9 ± 2.1	61.5 ± 5.6	91.6 ± 2.2	78.7 ± 5.3
CHISD CVPR'10 [3]	96.5 ± 1.2	60.4 ± 5.9	92.7 ± 1.9	79.5 ± 5.3
SANP TPAMI'12 [11]	97.6 ± 0.9	65.6 ± 5.6	93.8 ± 3.1	77.7 ± 7.3
CDL CVPR'12 [26]	90.0 ± 4.4	56.4 ± 5.3	94.5 ± 1.0	77.7 ± 4.2
RNP FG'13 [29]	96.1 ± 1.4	65.8 ± 5.4	96.2 ± 2.5	81.0 ± 3.2
MSSRC CVPR'13 [20]	97.5 ± 0.9	59.4 ± 5.7	95.5 ± 2.3	90.5 ± 3.1
SSDML ICCV'13 [30]	95.1 ± 2.2	66.2 ± 5.2	86.9 ± 3.4	81.0 ± 6.6
This Paper	$\mathbf{97.8 \pm 0.7}$	$\mathbf{74.1 \pm 3.5}$	$\mathbf{98.1 \pm 1.9}$	$\mathbf{95.5 \pm 2.0}$

Experimental performance of different methods in terms of average identification rates and standard deviations on CMU/Mobo, YouTube Celebrities, Kinect and ETH-80 datasets. The proposed method achieves the best performance on all four datasets. Especially, the performance improvement is more significant for YouTube and ETH-80 datasets.

Table 5. Timing Comparison on YouTube Celebrities dataset

Method	MSM	DCC	MMD	MDA	AHISD	CHISD	SANP	CDL	MSSRC	SSDML	RNP	Ours
Train	N/A	27.9	N/A	7.2	N/A	N/A	N/A	549.6	N/A	389.3	N/A	N/A
Test	1.1	0.2	68.1	0.1	3.1	5.3	22.4	7.2	54.2	18.5	0.5	6.5

Time in seconds required for offline training and online testing of one image set on YouTube Celebrities dataset. 'N/A' means that the method does not perform any offline training.

the existing methods on all datasets. The difference in the performance is more significant for YouTube Celebrities dataset which is the most challenging dataset since the videos have been acquired in real-life scenarios and the resolution of the face images is very low due to the high compression.

Timing Comparison: Table 5 lists the times (in seconds) for different methods using the respective Matlab implementations on a core i7 machine. Specifically, the time required for offline training and the time needed to test one image set on YouTube Celebrities dataset are provided. The reported time for our method is for five iterations of steps 1-5 of our algorithm (see Sec. 3.1). It should be noted that many of the existing methods [3, 11, 20, 28, 29] as well as our method are online. Online methods do not perform any offline training and can easily adapt to newly added and previously unseen training data. However, one major limitation of our method and the existing online methods is that all the computation is done at run-time and comparatively more memory storage is required.

4.4 Analysis and Discussions

The state of the art performance of the proposed method is attributed to the fact that unlike existing methods, it does not resort to a single entity representation (such as a subspace, the mean of set images or an exemplar image) for all images of the set. Any potential loss of information is therefore avoided by retaining the images of the set in their original form. Moreover, well-developed classification algorithms are efficiently incorporated within the proposed framework to optimally discriminate the class of the query image set from the remaining classes. Furthermore, since the proposed method provides a confidence level for its prediction, classification decisions from multiple classifiers can be fused to enhance the overall performance of the method.

A visual inspection of the challenging YouTube Celebrities dataset revealed that many of the miss-classified query image sets had face images with a head pose (such as profile views) which is otherwise not very commonly present in the training images of the dataset. For such cases, only those images in $\mathcal{D}_2$ which have the same pose as that of images of $\mathcal{X}_q$ (irrespective of their classes) are classified as $+1$. In our future work, we plan to develop a method to estimate the pose of the face images. The pose information will then be used to sample images into $\mathcal{D}_1$ and $\mathcal{D}_2$. For example, if most of the images of $\mathcal{X}_q$ are in right profile views, our sampling of the training images into $\mathcal{D}_1$ and $\mathcal{D}_2$ will be such that only the images with the right profile views will be considered. This will help to overcome the bias in the classification due to head pose.

5 Conclusion

This paper introduced a new concept which is embedded in a framework to extend the well known binary classifiers for multi-class image set classification. Compared with the popular one-vs-one and one-vs-rest binary to multi-class strategies, the proposed approach is very efficient as it trains a fixed number of binary classifiers (one to five) and uses very few images for training. The proposed method has been evaluated for the task of video based face recognition on Honda/UCSD, CMU/Mobo & YouTube Celebrities datasets, RGB-D face recognition from a Kinect dataset and object recognition from ETH-80 dataset. The experimental results and a comparison with the existing methods show that the proposed method consistently achieves the state of the art performance.

Acknowledgements. This work is supported by SIRF scholarship from The University of Western Australia (UWA) and Australian Research Council (ARC) grant DP110102166.

References

1. Eth80, http://www.d2.mpi-inf.mpg.de/Datasets/ETH80 (accessed: July 05, 2014)
2. Arandjelovic, O., Shakhnarovich, G., Fisher, J., Cipolla, R., Darrell, T.: Face recognition with image sets using manifold density divergence. In: 2005 IEEE Conference on Computer Vision and Pattern Recognition (CVPR), pp. 581–588. IEEE (2005)
3. Cevikalp, H., Triggs, B.: Face recognition based on image sets. In: IEEE Conference on Computer Vision and Pattern Recognition, CVPR 2010, pp. 2567–2573. IEEE (2010)
4. Fan, R.E., Chang, K.W., Hsieh, C.J., Wang, X.R., Lin, C.J.: LIBLINEAR: A library for large linear classification. Journal of Machine Learning Research 9, 1871–1874 (2008)
5. Fanelli, G., Gall, J., Van Gool, L.: Real time head pose estimation with random regression forests. In: 2011 IEEE Conference on Computer Vision and Pattern Recognition (CVPR), pp. 617–624. IEEE (2011)
6. Fanelli, G., Weise, T., Gall, J., Van Gool, L.: Real time head pose estimation from consumer depth cameras. In: Mester, R., Felsberg, M. (eds.) DAGM 2011. LNCS, vol. 6835, pp. 101–110. Springer, Heidelberg (2011)
7. Gross, R., Shi, J.: The cmu motion of body (mobo) database. Tech. rep. (2001)
8. Harandi, M.T., Sanderson, C., Shirazi, S., Lovell, B.C.: Graph embedding discriminant analysis on grassmannian manifolds for improved image set matching. In: 2011 IEEE Conference on Computer Vision and Pattern Recognition (CVPR), pp. 2705–2712. IEEE (2011)
9. Hayat, M., Bennamoun, M., An, S.: Learning non-linear reconstruction models for image set classification. In: 2014 IEEE Conference on Computer Vision and Pattern Recognition, CVPR (2014)
10. Hayat, M., Bennamoun, M., El-Sallam, A.A.: Clustering of video-patches on grassmannian manifold for facial expression recognition from 3d videos. In: 2013 IEEE Workshop on Applications of Computer Vision, WACV (2013)
11. Hu, Y., Mian, A.S., Owens, R.: Face recognition using sparse approximated nearest points between image sets. IEEE Transactions on Pattern Analysis and Machine Intelligence 34(10), 1992–2004 (2012)
12. Khan, S.H., Bennamoun, M., Sohel, F., Togneri, R.: Automatic feature learning for robust shadow detection. In: 2014 IEEE Conference on Computer Vision and Pattern Recognition, CVPR (2014)
13. Kim, M., Kumar, S., Pavlovic, V., Rowley, H.: Face tracking and recognition with visual constraints in real-world videos. In: 2008 IEEE Conference on Computer Vision and Pattern Recognition (CVPR), pp. 1–8. IEEE (2008)
14. Kim, T.K., Kittler, J., Cipolla, R.: Discriminative learning and recognition of image set classes using canonical correlations. IEEE Transactions on Pattern Analysis and Machine Intelligence 29(6), 1005–1018 (2007)
15. Lee, K.C., Ho, J., Yang, M.H., Kriegman, D.: Video-based face recognition using probabilistic appearance manifolds. In: 2003 IEEE Conference on Computer Vision and Pattern Recognition (CVPR), vol. 1, p. I–313. IEEE (2003)
16. Leibe, B., Schiele, B.: Analyzing appearance and contour based methods for object categorization. In: 2003 IEEE Conference on Computer Vision and Pattern Recognition (CVPR), vol. 2, p. II–409. IEEE (2003)
17. Li, B.Y., Mian, A.S., Liu, W., Krishna, A.: Using kinect for face recognition under varying poses, expressions, illumination and disguise. In: 2013 IEEE Workshop on Applications of Computer Vision (WACV), pp. 186–192. IEEE (2013)

18. Lu, J., Wang, G., Moulin, P.: Image set classification using holistic multiple order statistics features and localized multi-kernel metric learning. In: 2013 IEEE Conference on International Conference on Computer Vision, ICCV (2013)
19. Oja, E.: Subspace methods of pattern recognition, vol. 4. Research Studies Press, England (1983)
20. Ortiz, E., Wright, A., Shah, M.: Face recognition in movie trailers via mean sequence sparse representation-based classification. In: 2013 IEEE Conference on Computer Vision and Pattern Recognition (CVPR), pp. 3531–3538 (2013)
21. Ross, D.A., Lim, J., Lin, R.S., Yang, M.H.: Incremental learning for robust visual tracking. International Journal of Computer Vision 77(1-3), 125–141 (2008)
22. Shakhnarovich, G., Fisher, J.W., Darrell, T.: Face recognition from long-term observations. In: Heyden, A., Sparr, G., Nielsen, M., Johansen, P. (eds.) ECCV 2002, Part III. LNCS, vol. 2352, pp. 851–865. Springer, Heidelberg (2002)
23. Uzair, M., Mahmood, A., Mian, A., McDonald, C.: A compact discriminative representation for efficient image-set classification with application to biometric recognition. In: 2013 International Conference on Biometrics (ICB). IEEE (2013)
24. Viola, P., Jones, M.J.: Robust real-time face detection. International Journal of Computer Vision 57(2), 137–154 (2004)
25. Wang, R., Chen, X.: Manifold discriminant analysis. In: IEEE Conference on Computer Vision and Pattern Recognition, CVPR 2009, pp. 429–436. IEEE (2009)
26. Wang, R., Guo, H., Davis, L.S., Dai, Q.: Covariance discriminative learning: A natural and efficient approach to image set classification. In: 2012 IEEE Conference on Computer Vision and Pattern Recognition (CVPR), pp. 2496–2503. IEEE (2012)
27. Wang, R., Shan, S., Chen, X., Gao, W.: Manifold-manifold distance with application to face recognition based on image set. In: IEEE Conference on Computer Vision and Pattern Recognition, CVPR 2008, pp. 1–8. IEEE (2008)
28. Yamaguchi, O., Fukui, K., Maeda, K.I.: Face recognition using temporal image sequence. In: 1998 IEEE International Conference on Automatic Face and Gesture Recognition (FG), pp. 318–323. IEEE (1998)
29. Yang, M., Zhu, P., Gool, L.V., Zhang, L.: Face recognition based on regularized nearest points between image sets, pp. 1–7 (2013)
30. Zhu, P., Zhang, L., Zuo, W., Zhang, D.: From point to set: Extend the learning of distance metrics. In: 2013 IEEE Conference on International Conference on Computer Vision (ICCV). IEEE (2013)

Real-Time Exemplar-Based Face Sketch Synthesis

Yibing Song[1], Linchao Bao[1], Qingxiong Yang[1,*], and Ming-Hsuan Yang[2]

[1] Department of Computer Science
Multimedia Software Engineering Research Centre (MERC)
City University of Hong Kong, Hong Kong, China
MERC-Shenzhen, Guangdong, Hong Kong, China
[2] Department of Electrical Engineering and Computer Science
University of California at Merced, Merced, California, USA

Abstract. This paper proposes a simple yet effective face sketch synthesis method. Similar to existing exemplar-based methods, a training dataset containing photo-sketch pairs is required, and a K-NN photo patch search is performed between a test photo and every training exemplar for sketch patch selection. Instead of using the Markov Random Field to optimize global sketch patch selection, this paper formulates face sketch synthesis as an image denoising problem which can be solved efficiently using the proposed method. Real-time performance can be obtained on a state-of-the-art GPU. Meanwhile quantitative evaluations on face sketch recognition and user study demonstrate the effectiveness of the proposed method. In addition, the proposed method can be directly extended to the temporal domain for consistent video sketch synthesis, which is of great importance in digital entertainment.

Keywords: Face Hallucination, Texture Synthesis.

1 Introduction

Face sketch synthesis has a wide range of applications ranging from digital entertainment to law enforcement. Regarding general sketch synthesis, there are basically two types of methods: the image-based method and the exemplar-based method. Image-based sketch synthesis methods typically produce strokes and shadings according to edges in the input image while exemplar-based methods reconstruct new sketches from existing sketches. Although image-based methods can produce meaningful stylistic effects in some sense, their results are usually more like the input images, rather than artistic work from artists (since strokes only co-exist with strong edges in the image). Especially when it comes to face sketch, image-based methods will commonly fail to capture important facial details (see Fig. 1). On the other hand, exemplar-based methods can usually produce higher-quality sketches, but are computationally too intensive due to the matching process to a large amount of existing data.

The state-of-the-art exemplar-based face sketch synthesis methods are based on the Markov Random Field (MRF) models [19,22,24]. Generally, face photos and sketches

---

* Corresponding author. Complete experimental results (including the source code) are provided on the authors' webpage.

D. Fleet et al. (Eds.): ECCV 2014, Part VI, LNCS 8694, pp. 800–813, 2014.
© Springer International Publishing Switzerland 2014

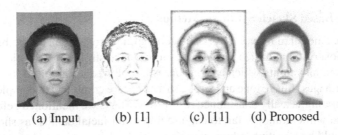

(a) Input   (b) [1]   (c) [11]   (d) Proposed

Fig. 1. Image-based and exemplar-based face sketch synthesis. (b) and (c) are sketches generated from image-based methods [1,11] and (d) is obtained from the proposed exemplar-based method. Image-based methods can handle general images well where image features can mainly be described through edges. For face photos where features can not be explicitly described as edges, these methods are less stylistic and cannot expressively present facial details compared with exemplar-based methods.

in training dataset are divided into patches, and the "best" sketch patch for representing a test photo patch will be selected via solving a MRF. These MRF-based methods can generally produce high-quality face sketches, but are computationally too intensive to become real-time applications. For example, the runtime of the most efficient exemplar-based method [24] for producing a 250×200 face sketch is over 40 seconds on a PC with Intel Core i7 3.4 GHz CPU.

In this work, we propose a face sketch synthesis method that can effectively produce face sketches in real-time speed. A K-NN search [3] is performed between a test photo and training photos to find the matched K patches at each pixel location and displacement vectors[1] are generated. Then the linear combination method [13] can be used at each pixel location to compute a corresponding sketch estimation. However, the resulting face sketch using this approach is noisy. An example is presented in Fig. 3(b).

The next step is to denoise the baseline performance which is the main contribution of this paper. The K displacement vectors from each neighboring pixel around one center pixel are used to compute single sketch estimation using [13]. As a result, a simple averaging of these sketch estimations can greatly reduce noise and can be used as the final denoised sketch value (Fig. 3(f)).

The advantages of this work are summarized as follows:

- The proposed method is more efficient than the state-of-the-art in the literature. Real-time performance can be obtained on an NVIDIA Geforce GTX 780 GPU.
- Quantitative evaluation on face sketch recognition and user study demonstrate that the proposed method is more effective.
- The proposed method can be easily extended to temporal domain for consistent video sketch synthesis.

2   Related Work

A literature survey of image-based and exemplar-based sketch synthesis methods is presented in the following:

---

[1] The displacement vectors contain relative positions between test and training photo patches.

2.1 Image-Based Sketch Synthesis Methods

There is huge amount of research work and commercial products on image-based sketch synthesis. Most of them utilize image edges to produce strokes or stylistic effects. For instance, bilateral weights which are responses to color edges are used in [11] to produce sketch images. Image tone and stroke structures are combined to complement each other in generating visually constrained results in [14]. As we mentioned before, image-based method will commonly fail to capture important facial details (as shown in Fig. 1), which would be sensitive to human beings.

2.2 Exemplar-Based Sketch Synthesis Methods

Research on exemplar-based methods derives from the supervised style transformation framework [12]. As illustrated in [10], exemplar-based methods outperform traditional parametric (image-based) methods because they can handle styles which are difficult to describe parametrically. Meanwhile their repertoire can be easily extended by the user at any time. Currently exemplar-based face sketch synthesis can be mainly categorized as profile sketch synthesis [7,21,5] and shading sketch synthesis [16,19,24]. Compared with profile sketches, shading sketches are more expressive in representing facial structures and thus more popular.

In [16] a global eigen-transformation is computed for synthesizing face sketches from face photos. A locally linear combination method is proposed in [13] to solve the non-linearity problems. A dense execution of [13] will lead to noise. The methods based on MRF models [19,22,24] alleviate noise when synthesizing sketches. The use of MRF encodes smoothness constraints on neighboring sketch patches during the global optimization process, thus artifacts between different sketch patches can be reduced. To bridge the modality difference between input images and output sketches, several algorithms [23,18] consider the inter modality between photos and sketches by projecting facial features onto the same space.

3   Face Sketch Synthesis

We give a brief overview of the baseline algorithm in Sec. 3.1 and propose an image denoising method for face sketch synthesis in Sec. 3.2.

3.1 Motivation

The baseline approach of exemplar-based face sketch synthesis method [13] is illustrated in Fig. 2, which includes K-NN search and linear combination of patches specified in the following. If linear patch combination [13] is conducted densely, the synthesized sketch (Fig. 3(b)) contains significant amount of noise due to the modality gap between photo and sketch.

A potential solution is using existing image denoising algorithms to eliminate the sketch noise. However, a direct use of the state-of-the art denoising algorithms, e.g., NLM [6] and BM3D [8] shows little improvement as can be seen in Fig. 3(c) and (e). A simple extension is using the test photo in Fig. 3(a) as the guidance image for NLM. The denoised sketch, however, looks similar to photo rather than sketch (Fig. 3(d)). We thus aim at developing a denoising algorithm that is suitable for face sketch synthesis.

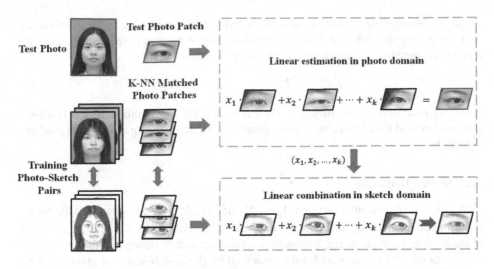

Fig. 2. Illustration of the baseline approach [13]. For each patch in the test photo, K-NN search and linear estimation are performed in the photo domain to obtain the matched training photo patches and linear weights $(x_1, x_2, \cdots, x_k)$. The weights are used in the sketch domain to map the corresponding training sketch patches into output patch.

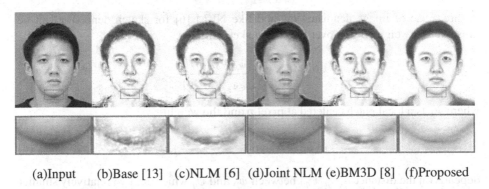

(a)Input   (b)Base [13]   (c)NLM [6]   (d)Joint NLM (e)BM3D [8]   (f)Proposed

Fig. 3. Baseline synthesized results and improvements. (a) is an input test photo and (b) is the sketch obtained from the baseline approach [13]. (c) to (e) are denoised sketches obtained from NLM [6], a simple extension of NLM with (a) as the guidance, and BM3D [8], respectively. (f) is the sketch obtained from proposed sketch denoising algorithm.

K-NN Search and Linear Estimation. For the patch centered at each pixel in a test photo, we search for the most similar patch on each training photo and the top K similar patches are selected. When performing K-NN search we generate a cost volume by continuously shift training photos to compute a difference image slice with respect to test photo. Then box filer [17] is applied to the cost volume for filtering (the filtered cost is the patch matched cost). Let $\mathbf{T}_p$ denote a vector containing the pixel values of the patch centered at pixel p in the tested photo, and $\mathbf{I}_p^1$ to $\mathbf{I}_p^K$ denote vectors containing the pixel values of the K corresponding matched patches, respectively. The coefficients of a linear mapping function that maps the K matched patches to the testing patch $\mathbf{T}_p$ can be obtained by solving the following linear system

$$x_p^1 \mathbf{I}_p^1 + x_p^2 \mathbf{I}_p^2 + \cdots + x_p^K \mathbf{I}_p^K = \mathbf{T}_p, \tag{1}$$

where x_p^1 to x_p^K are the coefficients. When K is low ($K = 5$ in this paper), it is a low-rank system and the coefficients can be computed efficiently using a conjugate gradient solver [15].

3.2   Sketch Denoising

In Sec. 3.1, K displacement vectors $\Delta_p = [\Delta_p^1, \Delta_p^2, \cdots, \Delta_p^K]$ are computed and the corresponding linear mapping functions are represented by coefficients $X_p = \{x_p^1, x_p^2, \cdots, x_p^K\}$ at each pixel location p. Let S denote the training sketch images so that $S_{p+\Delta_p^1}$ to $S_{p+\Delta_p^K}$ correspond to the sketch values selected by the K-NN search at pixel p in Sec. 3.1. A coarse sketch estimation at each pixel p can be obtained to form a coarse sketch image as follows:

$$E_p = \sum_{k=1}^{K} x_p^k S_{p+\Delta_p^k}. \tag{2}$$

A direct use of image denoising method like NLM [6] for sketch denoising can be presented as weighted sum over the coarse sketch image:

$$S_p^{NLM} = \frac{\sum_{q \in \Psi_p} w(p, q) E_q}{\sum_{q \in \Psi_p} w(p, q)}, \tag{3}$$

where Ψ_p is a local patch centered at pixel p and the weight

$$w(p, q) = \exp(-\frac{d(\psi_p, \psi_q)}{2\sigma^2}), \tag{4}$$

depends on the distance $d(\psi_p, \psi_q)$ between ψ_p and ψ_q which are two relatively smaller sketch patches centered at pixel p and q, respectively. This type of direct application of image denoising techniques is not suitable for noisy sketch image as shown in Fig. 3(c) and (e). A simple extension is to adjust the weight by extracting the two local patches ψ_p and ψ_q from the noise-free photos to eliminate the errors due to sketch noise. That is, we use the noise-free photo as a guidance to compute the weight at each pixel location. However, the improvement is not nontrivial as shown in Fig. 3(d).

The reason that traditional image denoising methods and their simple extensions fail lies in the use of incorrect weights. The coarse sketch image is not natural, and the traditional assumption that two image pixels are similar if the two corresponding patches are similar is invalid for a coarse sketch image.

Instead of determining a better representation of the weight $w(p, q)$ to represent the similarity between any two sketch image pixels, we focus on grouping sketch estimates that are believed to be similar. This idea is motivated by the BM3D [8] method which groups correlated patches in the image domain to create multiple estimations.

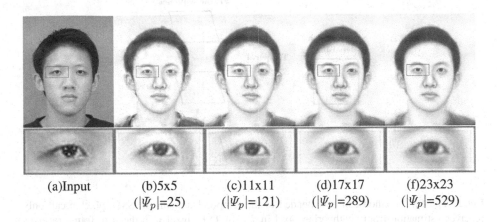

(a)Input	(b)5x5	(c)11x11	(d)17x17	(f)23x23
	$(|\Psi_p|=25)$	$(|\Psi_p|=121)$	$(|\Psi_p|=289)$	$(|\Psi_p|=529)$

Fig. 4. Performance with respect to the size of patch Ψ_p. The proposed SSD method appears to be fairly robust against different values of $|\Psi_p|$ when it is sufficient large, e.g., 100) to eliminate the sketch noise. It well preserves facial details like the tiny eye reflections.

The grouping scheme used in this paper is based on linear local model. Under this assumption the linear mapping function computed at a pixel q from K-NN can be used together with the displacement vectors to compute not only the sketch estimate at pixel q but also the sketch estimates for all pixel p inside a local neighbor of pixel q. Let E_p^q denote the sketch estimate at pixel p that are computed based on the linear mapping function and displacement vectors obtained using K-NN at pixel q, we have

$$E_p^q = \sum_{k=1}^{K} x_q^k S_{p+\Delta_q^k},\tag{5}$$

where $E_p^p = E_p$ in Eq. 2. The sketch estimate E_p^q is guaranteed to be similar to E_p according to the linear local model, as long as pixel p and q are close. The denoising process is thus straightforward. Let S^{SSD} denote the denoised sketch image, the denoised sketch value at a pixel location p is

$$S_p^{\mathrm{SSD}} = \frac{\sum_{q\in\Psi_p} 1 \cdot E_p^q}{\sum_{q\in\Psi_p} 1} = \frac{1}{|\Psi_p|}\sum_{q\in\Psi_p} E_p^q,\tag{6}$$

where $|\Psi_p|$ is the number of pixels in patch Ψ_p. We refer to this sketch denoising method as Spatial Sketch Denoising (**SSD**) and extend it to the time domain in the following. The size of patch $|\Psi_p|$ is the only parameter used in the proposed SSD algorithm. However, the performance of SSD is robust to this parameter as demonstrated in Fig. 4. Specifically the proposed SSD method can well preserve facial details like the tiny eye reflections in the closeups.

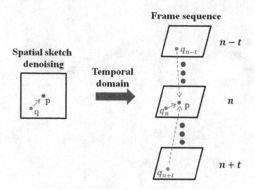

Fig. 5. The SSD method can be extended to the temporal domain. In SSD, pixel p can only receives estimation from neighboring pixel in Ψ_p. In TSD, pixel p in the n-th frame receives estimation from neighboring pixel in Ψ_p in a number of frames within a time window.

Temporal Sketch Denoising (TSD). The proposed SSD method can be extended to the temporal domain for video sketch synthesis. Temporal incoherence of synthesized results lead to noticeable artifacts in videos. As shown in Fig. 5, pixels on the synthesized sketch can be considered as the averaging result of multiple estimations created from neighboring pixels from both spatial and temporal domains. Let t denote temporal radius in the time window, the denoised sketch value at pixel p for the n-th frame is

$$S_p^{\text{TSD}} = \frac{1}{(2t+1)|\Psi_p|} \sum_{i=n-t}^{n+t} \sum_{q_i \in \Psi_p} E_p^{q_i}, \tag{7}$$

where $E_p^{q_i}$ is the sketch estimation computed for pixel p based on the linear mapping function and displacement vectors from pixel q_i in the i-th frame.

4   Experiments

In all the experiments, we set the search radius of displacement vector to 5 pixels in the K-NN search process (i.e., $|\Delta| = 121$). The number of candidate correspondences K is set to 5. The size of the Ψ is 17×17 pixels. We conduct quantitative and qualitative evaluations in two aspects. First, we evaluate the proposed algorithm against state-of-the-art methods on benchmark datasets in terms of effectiveness and run time performance. Second, we evaluate algorithms on generating user preferred sketches with human subject studies.

4.1   Evaluations on Benchmark Datasets

We carry out quantitative and qualitative experiments on the CUHK student dataset [19] and the AR dataset [2]. The CUHK student dataset [19] consists of 188 photo-sketch pairs where 88 pairs are used for training and the rest are for testing. In the AR dataset [2]

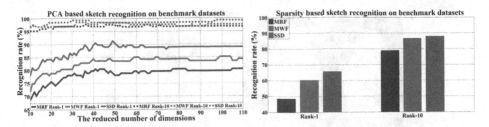

Fig. 6. Quantitative evaluations on benchmark datasets. The proposed SSD method performs favorably against the MRF and MWF methods under PCA based [9] and sparsity based [20] sketch recognition rates.

which consists of 123 photo-sketch pairs, we use the leave-one-out strategy as conducted in the MRF and MWF methods. The proposed SSD method takes about 4 seconds to process one test photo on the CUHK student dataset using 3.4GHz i7 machine and C++ programming language. In addition, the proposed method can be executed in 20 FPS on an Nvidia GeForce GTX 780 GPU, which is 80× faster than CPU implementation. Moreover, the proposed algorithm does not need any off-line training whereas the other methods [19,22,24,23,18] entail such procedures.

Quantitative evaluation of face sketch synthesis methods can be conducted through face sketch recognition as suggested in [22]. That is, for each photo in the training set, the synthesized sketch should be matched to the corresponding sketch drawn by an artist. If an algorithm achieves higher sketch recognition rates, it suggests that this method is more effective to synthesize sketches.

We perform sketch recognition evaluation on the whole 223 synthesized sketches from the CUHK [19] and AR [2] datasets. The proposed SSD method is evaluated with the state-of-the-art MRF and MWF methods using two metrics: PCA based recognition rate [9] and sparsity based recognition rate [20]. The rank-1 and rank-10 sketch recognition rates are also used for evaluation.

Sketch recognition results of different methods are shown in Fig. 6. The PCA based and sparsity based sketch recognition rates indicate the proposed SSD method achieves higher recognition rates than those with the MRF and MWF methods under the rank-1 metric. Using the rank-10 metric, the proposed SSD method performs well against the state-of-the-art methods in both PCA and sparsity based recognition rates. Fig. 6 demonstrates the proposed SSD method performs favorably against the MRF and MWF methods in effectiveness to synthesize sketches on average.

Qualitative evaluation results of the SSD, MRF and MWF methods are shown in Fig. 7. The holistic results show that the MRF method does not synthesize dominant facial structures (i.e., eyes or hair) well. Without linear estimation the MRF method is not effective in synthesizing a suitable patch from training data for some test patches with facial features significantly different from those of the training set. On the other hand, the results from the MWF method contain significant amount of noise on some facial components (i.e., noses and mouths). Details of some dominant facial regions are also blurred (i.e., hair and mouths). With the linear estimation process and sketch denoising, the proposed SSD method is able to synthesize distinct features and reduce noise. More qualitative evaluations can be found in the complete experimental results.

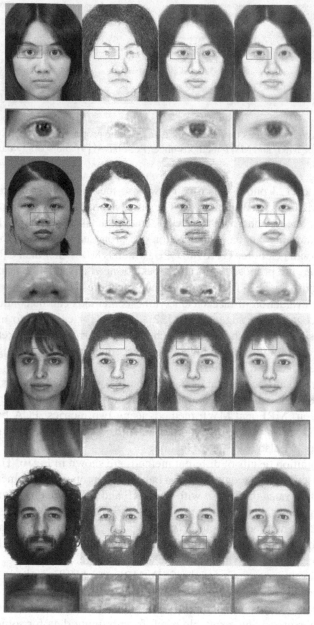

(a) Test photo (b) MRF [19] (c) MWF [24]   (d) SSD

Fig. 7. Qualitative evaluation on benchmark datasets. (a) test photos. (b) sketches generated by the MRF method. (c) sketches generated by the MWF method. (d) sketches generated by the proposed SSD method. The results show that the proposed SSD method performs favorably against the MRF and MWF methods in preserving details and removing noise.

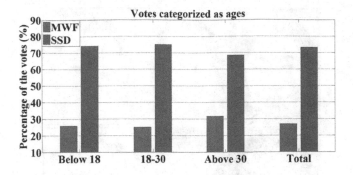

Fig. 8. Quantitative evaluation of user study on the real-world photos. There were 153 subjects participating. Among them 31 people are under age 18, 84 people age from 18 to 30, and 38 people are above age 30. Their sketches are synthesized by using the CUHK student dataset. The proposed SSD method performs favorably against the MWF method across all demographics.

4.2 Evaluations on Real-World Datasets

In this section, we conduct evaluations on real-world photos and videos. In Sec. 4.1 the MRF method is shown not effective to synthesize facial structures. Thus the focus is put on the evaluation of the proposed SSD, TSD and MWF methods.

Evaluations on Real-World Photos. For the face photos captured in the real-world scenes we first rectify them to fit the benchmark dataset condition. We then perform a user study to find which kind of sketches is user preferred. The criteria of sketch evaluation is subjective and in some cases they are the opposite (e.g., some prefer sketches to be similar to photos for realism while others opt for stylistic sketches). Thus, user preference is achieved by letting subjects evaluate synthesized sketches of their own photos.

There are 153 participants in the user study. For each test, we synthesize two sketches of one subject by using the proposed SSD and MWF methods. Then the subject is asked to identify the preferred one according to his (her) own preference. The answer of each subject is considered as one vote of each method. Fig. 8 shows the final votes of each method where the proposed SSD method performs favorably against the MWF method across all demographics.

Fig. 9 shows some results from the user study. On each row, the sketches marked in red are the user preferred sketches. On the top two rows there is significant noise which deteriorates the facial details (e.g., eyes and noses) shown in (b) while this noise is greatly reduced in (c). It indicates when the facial structures of sketches can not be synthesized effectively the majority of subjects do not prefer. On the bottom two rows the facial details are effectively synthesized in both (b) and (c). Thus, user preference is random and there is almost no difference between the votes of these two methods in this case. As in the real-world datasets significant noise often occurs and deteriorates the facial details of the sketches synthesized by the MWF method while noise is greatly

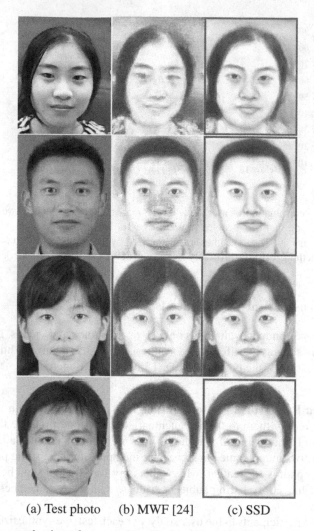

(a) Test photo   (b) MWF [24]   (c) SSD

Fig. 9. Qualitative evaluation of user study on real-world photos. (a) test photos. (b) sketches generated by MWF. (c) sketches generated by SSD. The sketches marked in red indicate user preference. In the top two rows significant noise deteriorates the facial details of sketches (e.g., eyes and noses) shown in (b). So the majority of subjects do not prefer. In the bottom two rows the facial details of sketches are effectively synthesized in both (b) and (c). User preference is random.

reduced on the ones synthesized by the SSD method, the proposed SSD method performs favorably against the MWF method on average across all demographics. Fig. 9 demonstrate that the proposed SSD method is more effective in reducing noise and thus synthesizing user preferred sketches.

Evaluations on the Real-World Videos. For video sketch synthesis we evaluate the proposed TSD method with the SSD and MWF methods. For the TSD method we set

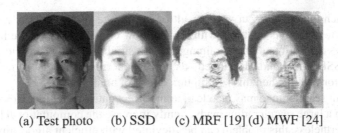

(a) Test photo   (b) SSD   (c) MRF [19] (d) MWF [24]

Fig. 10. Limitations of sketch synthesis methods. (a) test photo captured with cast shadow on the right. (b)-(d) are synthesized results by the proposed SSD, MRF and MWF methods, respectively. Incorrect patch matching occurs in all the methods. For (c) and (d), significant noise is generated on the facial parts where the lighting conditions are different from those in the training dataset. In (b) blurry artifacts occur on those facial parts.

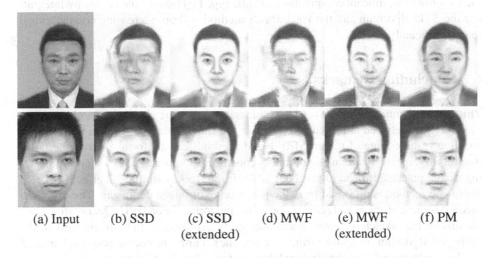

(a) Input   (b) SSD   (c) SSD   (d) MWF   (e) MWF   (f) PM
                           (extended)   (extended)

Fig. 11. Integration of PatchMatch [4]. (a) input photo with varying pose. (b) sketch generated by the SSD method using original search range. (c) sketch generated by the SSD method using large search range. (d) sketches generated by the MWF method original search range. (e) sketch generated by the MWF method using large search range. (f) sketch generated by the integration of PatchMatch and SSD method, which takes constant time cost regardless of search range.

the number of temporal coherent frames as 5. As the temporal coherence can not be displayed clearly on the paper, a video is included in the complete experimental results to demonstrate the temporal consistency of the proposed TSD method.

5   Limitations and Discussion

While the proposed algorithm performs well in synthesizing face sketches, the performance hinges on whether good patches can be matched from the training set to a test photo. When lighting conditions are significantly different from those in the dataset, incorrect patch matching occurs as a result of inaccurate K-NN search. As shown in Fig. 10(a), a test photo is captured with cast shadow on the right. For the face regions where patches can be found in the training set with similar lighting conditions (e.g., left cheek), the SSD, MRF and MWF methods perform normally. However, none of these methods perform well when this assumption does not hold.

Insufficient search range may also lead to incorrect patch matching. However, patch match within a large search radius inadvertently increase the computational load significantly. Nevertheless, this problem can be alleviated with efficient algorithms to search for patches such as the PatchMatch (PM) [4] method. Fig. 11 shows some experiments with photos of varying poses. The synthesized results in Fig. 11(b) and (d) are generated from the SSD and MWF methods using the same search range adopted on the benchmark datasets. When patches can be correctly matched across different poses by increasing the search range, better sketches can be generated as shown in (c) and (e) at the expense of significant computational loads. Fig. 11(f) shows the results by integrating the SSD algorithm and the PatchMatch method without increasing computational load significantly.

6   Concluding Remarks

This paper formulates face sketch synthesis as an image denoising problem. The modality gap between photos and sketches in the training dataset leads to noise on the baseline results. State-of-the-art MRF based methods can be formulated as the baseline improvements by adding smoothness constraints to reduce noise when synthesizing sketch patches. Instead of involving MRF framework, a simple yet effective sketch denoising method is proposed from the perspective of image denoising. The proposed method is more efficient and achieves real-time performance on GPU. Quantitative evaluations on face sketch recognition and user study demonstrate the effectiveness of the proposed algorithm for synthesizing face sketches. Furthermore, the proposed method can be easily extended to the temporal domain for video sketch synthesis.

Acknowledgement. This work was supported in part by a GRF grant from the Research Grants Council of Hong Kong (RGC Reference: CityU 122212), the NSF CAREER Grant #1149783 and NSF IIS Grant #1152576. The authors would like to thank Hao Zhou for providing his code for [24].

References

1. Adobe: Adobe photoshop cs6
2. Aleix, M., Robert, B.: The ar face database. Tech. Rep. CVC Technical Report 24, Purdue University (1998)
3. Altman, N.S.: An introduction to kernel and nearest-neighbor nonparametric regression. The American Statistician (1992)
4. Barnes, C., Shechtman, E., Finkelstein, A., Goldman, D.: Patchmatch: a randomized correspondence algorithm for structural image editing. In: SIGGRAPH (2009)

 5. Berger, I., Shamir, A., Mahler, M., Carter, E., Hodgins, J.: Style and abstraction in portrait sketching. In: SIGGRAPH (2013)
 6. Buades, A., Coll, B., Morel, J.M.: A non-local algorithm for image denoising. In: CVPR (2005)
 7. Chen, H., Xu, Y.Q., Shum, H.Y., Zhu, S.C., Zheng, N.N.: Example-based facial sketch generation with non-parametric sampling. In: ICCV (2001)
 8. Dabov, K., Foi, A., Katkovnik, V., Egiazarian, K.: Image denoising by sparse 3-d transform-domain collaborative filtering. TIP (2007)
 9. Delac, K., Grgic, M., Grgic, S.: Independent comparative study of pca, ica, and lda on the feret data set. IJIST (2005)
10. Freeman, W.T., Tenenbaum, J.B., Pasztor, E.: An example-based approach to style translation for line drawings. MERL Technical Report (1999)
11. Gastal, E.S., Oliveira, M.M.: Domain transform for edge-aware image and video processing. In: SIGGRAPH (2011)
12. Hertzmann, A., Jacobs, C.E., Oliver, N., Curless, B., Salesin, D.H.: Image analogies. In: SIGGRAPH (2001)
13. Liu, Q., Tang, X., Jin, H., Lu, H., Ma, S.: A nonlinear approach for face sketch synthesis and recognition. In: CVPR (2005)
14. Lu, C., Xu, L., Jia, J.: Combining sketch and tone for pencil drawing production. In: NPAR (2012)
15. Paige, C.C., Saunders, M.A.: Lsqr: An algorithm for sparse linear equations and sparse least squares. ACM Transactions on Mathematical Software (1982)
16. Tang, X., Wang, X.: Face sketch synthesis and recognition. In: CVPR (2003)
17. Viola, P., Jones, M.: Rapid object detection using a boosted cascade of simple features. In: CVPR (2001)
18. Wang, S., Zhang, L.: Y., L., Pan, Q.: Semi-coupled dictionary learning with applications in image super-resolution and photo-sketch synthesis. In: CVPR (2012)
19. Wang, X., Tang, X.: Face photo-sketch synthesis and recognition. PAMI (2009)
20. Wright, J., Yang, A.Y., Ganesh, A., Sastry, S.S., Ma, Y.: Robust face recognition via sparse representation. PAMI (2009)
21. Xu, Z., Chen, H., Zhu, S.C., Luo, J.: A hierarchical compositional model for face representation and sketching. PAMI (2008)
22. Zhang, W., Wang, X., Tang, X.: Lighting and pose robust face sketch synthesis. In: Daniilidis, K., Maragos, P., Paragios, N. (eds.) ECCV 2010, Part VI. LNCS, vol. 6316, pp. 420–433. Springer, Heidelberg (2010)
23. Zhang, W., Wang, X., Tang, X.: Coupled information-theoretic encoding for face photo-sketch recognition. In: CVPR (2011)
24. Zhou, H., Kuang, Z., Wong, K.: Markov weight fields for face sketch synthesis. In: CVPR (2012)

Domain-Adaptive Discriminative One-Shot Learning of Gestures

Tomas Pfister[1], James Charles[2], and Andrew Zisserman[1]

[1]Visual Geometry Group, Department of Engineering Science, University of Oxford
[2]Computer Vision Group, School of Computing, University of Leeds

Abstract. The objective of this paper is to recognize gestures in videos – both localizing the gesture and classifying it into one of multiple classes.

We show that the performance of a gesture classifier learnt from a single (strongly supervised) training example can be boosted significantly using a 'reservoir' of weakly supervised gesture examples (and that the performance exceeds learning from the one-shot example or reservoir alone). The one-shot example and weakly supervised reservoir are from different 'domains' (different people, different videos, continuous or non-continuous gesturing, *etc.*), and we propose a domain adaptation method for human pose and hand shape that enables gesture learning methods to generalise between them. We also show the benefits of using the recently introduced Global Alignment Kernel [12], instead of the standard Dynamic Time Warping that is generally used for time alignment.

The domain adaptation and learning methods are evaluated on two large scale challenging gesture datasets: one for sign language, and the other for Italian hand gestures. In both cases performance exceeds the previous published results, including the best skeleton-classification-only entry in the 2013 ChaLearn challenge.

1 Introduction

Gesture recognition has recently received an increasing amount of attention due to the advent of Kinect and socially important applications, *e.g.* sign language to speech translation [8], becoming more tractable. However, the majority of approaches to gesture (and action) recognition rely on strongly supervised learning, which requires ground truthing large quantities of training data. This is inherently expensive and does not scale to large, evolving gesture languages with high levels of variation. As a result, several recent works have attempted to learn gestures at the other extreme – from single training examples using one-shot learning [16,17,19,20,22,24,33]. However, given the vast variability in how gestures are performed, and the variation in people and camera viewpoints, learning accurate, generalizable models with so little supervision is somewhat challenging, to say the least. Another avenue of work has explored learning gestures from practically infinite sources of data with weak supervision [7,11,23,26,28], *e.g.* TV broadcasts with aligned subtitles (or similarly actions from movies with aligned transcripts [1,3,14]). While these works have also shown promise, they

D. Fleet et al. (Eds.): ECCV 2014, Part VI, LNCS 8694, pp. 814–829, 2014.
© Springer International Publishing Switzerland 2014

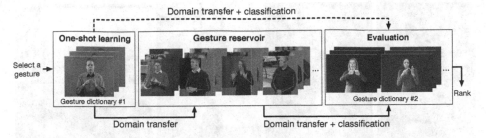

Fig. 1. Domain-adaptive discriminative one-shot gesture learning. Domain-adapted one-shot learning is used to obtain additional training data from a huge weakly supervised gesture repository of another domain. These new samples are used to 'boost' the one-shot learner with additional discriminative power. Evaluations are carried out under further domain adaptation on another one-shot learning dataset. Dashed line shows the **baseline** and the solid lines show the **proposed method**.

have also demonstrated the limitations of the weak supervision available for gestures today: it is so weak and noisy that it is very difficult to learn from it alone [7,11,28].

In this paper we show the benefit of combining these two gesture recognition approaches, one-shot learning and weakly supervised learning. The key idea is that, given suitable domain adaptations, one-shot learning can gain an enormous performance boost from utilising weakly supervised data from different domains.

Consider a common gesture recognition scenario as depicted in Fig. 1. Here we have one or more videos (one-shot learning examples; gesture 'dictionaries') showing an example of each gesture, and a huge dataset of weakly labelled videos from another domain (the 'gesture reservoir') containing some instances of the same gestures. This scenario arises naturally in gesture languages, such as sign language, which have many video dictionaries (online and on DVDs) with examples of signs, and a plentiful supply of signed data (*e.g.* sign language-translated TV broadcasts, shown in Fig. 2 (right); or linguistic research datasets). In the case of TV broadcasts the weak supervision is provided by aligned subtitles (that specify a temporal interval where the word *may* occur), though the supervision is also noisy as the subtitle word may not be signed. In the case of linguistic research datasets (and some gesture datasets [19]) the supervision is often at the video clip level, rather than a tighter temporal interval.

Our aim is to boost the performance of one-shot learning by using this large 'reservoir' of weakly supervised gestures. In the one-shot case there is strong supervision (but only one example). In the reservoir there are many examples exhibiting variations in people, expression, speed, but only weak supervision – the temporal interval is not tight. The goal is to obtain a weak classifier from one-shot learning and use it to select further examples from the reservoir. A stronger classifier can then be trained from the gesture variations and large variation of people in the reservoir. This is a form of semi-supervised learning, but here the affinity function requires domain adaptation in going between the one-shot and gesture reservoir videos.

Fig. 2. Sample frames from the four datasets with upper body pose estimates overlaid. From left to right: BSL dictionary 1, BSL dictionary 2, ChaLearn and BSL-TV.

This is a very challenging task since the video dictionaries and gesture reservoir can be of wildly differing video domains (see Fig. 2): different size and resolutions; different people; and with gestures performed at significantly different prosody and speed. Furthermore, one domain may contain continuous gestures (*e.g.* most weakly supervised datasets) while another (*e.g.* most one-shot learning datasets) only contains gestures performed with clear breaks in-between.

In the remainder of this paper we show that not only can a weakly supervised gesture reservoir be used to significantly boost performance in gesture recognition, but also that the availability of multiple one-shot learning datasets enables evaluation of gesture recognition methods for problems where test data was previously absent. Our contributions are: (i) a method for learning gestures accurately and discriminatively from a single positive training example (in the spirit of one-shot learning and exemplar SVMs/LDAs [21, 25]); (ii) a domain adaptation method for human pose and hand shape that enables generalisation to new domains; and (iii) a learning framework for gestures that employs the recently introduced Global Alignment Kernel [12].

In the evaluations we show that our method achieves a significant performance boost on two large gesture datasets. We also release pose estimates for two gesture dictionaries[1].

2   Domain-Adaptive Discriminative One-Shot Learning

In this section we first overview the learning framework, and then describe the details of the visual features (hand trajectory and hand shape) and their domain transfer which involves space and time transformations.

---

[1] http://www.robots.ox.ac.uk/~vgg/research/sign_language

Figure 1 shows an overview of the learning framework. There are three domains: two gesture one-shot 'dictionaries' and one large weakly supervised 'gesture reservoir'. One dictionary is used for training, the other for testing.

The method proceeds in four steps: (1) train a discriminative one-shot gesture detector from the first dictionary, separately for each gesture; (2) that detector is then used to discover new samples of the same gesture in the weakly supervised gesture reservoir – the search for the sample is restricted to a temporal interval provided by the weak supervision; (3) these new samples are used to train what is effectively a stronger version of the original one-shot gesture classifier; and (4) this strong classifier is evaluated on a second one-shot dictionary.

2.1 Discriminative One-Shot Gesture Learning Framework

Given the two video dictionaries (one for training, the other for evaluation) and a weakly labelled gesture reservoir, let δ^1, δ^2 and ν denote their respective features (here the hand trajectories). For example, $\delta^1 = \{\delta^1_1, \ldots, \delta^1_q, \ldots\}$ where δ^1_q is a variable-length vector (depending on the length of the gesture video) of hand positions over all frames in the qth gesture video of dictionary 1.

Imagine we are learning a gesture for 'snow' in BSL (shown in Fig. 3). We first train a discriminative one-shot gesture detector for 'snow' on the features of the first dictionary (δ^1). To do this, we use a time-and-space-aligned gesture kernel ψ (defined in Sect. 2.2) in a dual SVM to learn weights α from

$$\max_{\alpha_i \geq 0} \sum_i \alpha_i - \frac{1}{2} \sum_{jk} \alpha_j \alpha_k y_j y_k \psi(\mathbf{x}_j, \mathbf{x}_k) \quad \forall i \; 0 \leq \alpha_i \leq C \quad \sum_i \alpha_i y_i = 0 \quad (1)$$

where we set the learning feature to $\mathbf{x} = \delta^1$ (hand trajectories of the videos in dataset δ^1), y_i are binary video labels (1 for the 'snow' dictionary video, -1 for others), and $\psi(,)$ is the kernel. This is the one-shot learning – as an exemplar SVM [25].

In the second step, we use this model to discover new samples of 'snow' in the weakly supervised gesture reservoir (restricted to the temporal intervals provided by the weak supervision). A very large number of samples in the reservoir are scored to find gestures that are most similar to 'snow' (and dissimilar to the other gestures) in the first dictionary. This yields a vector of scores s

$$s(\nu) = \sum_i \alpha_i y_i \psi(\mathbf{x}_i, \nu) + b \quad (2)$$

where ν are the features for reservoir subsequences with a weakly supervised label 'snow'. Here, $s(\nu)$ is a vector of scores of length $|\nu|$ (the number of samples in the weakly supervised sequences of the gesture reservoir). The top scored samples represent gestures in the reservoir that are most similar to 'snow' in the the first dictionary, but with high variability in space, time and appearance (thanks to the time and space adaptations).

In the third step, the top samples of $s(\nu)$ (by score), along with a set of negative samples from the gesture reservoir, are used to train a stronger version

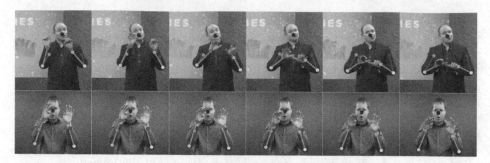

Fig. 3. Frames showing variation in gesture speed and prosody across two domains (top and bottom). The example gesture shown here is 'snow' in BSL, which mimics snow falling down. Although the frame rate is the same, the speed at which the gestures are produced are considerably different.

of the original one-shot gesture classifier for 'snow' (training details are given in Sect. 2.4). We do this by retraining (1) with this new training set $\mathbf{x} = \nu_{\text{retrain}}$ (of cardinality around 2,000 samples). Due to only selecting the top samples of the gesture reservoir for training, we develop resilience to noisy supervision.

In the fourth and final step, this stronger model is evaluated on the second dictionary by ranking all gesture videos using the score $s(\delta^2)$ of the stronger classifier. This provides a measure of the strength of the classifier without requiring any expensive manual annotation.

2.2   Domain Adaptations

A major challenge in gesture recognition is that not only are the gestures performed by different people with different body shapes, but the same gestures are performed at very different speeds and prosody across domains and people (see Fig. 3). We tackle this problem by measuring distance under domain adaptations in both space and time. We next discuss the domain adaptations used to define this kernel ψ.

Time Alignment. Dynamic Time Warping (DTW) [30,31] is a popular method for obtaining the time alignment between two time series and measuring their similarity. However, there have been problems incorporating it into a discriminative framework (*e.g.* into kernels [2, 18, 32, 35]) due to the DTW 'distance' not satisfying the triangle inequality. As a result, it cannot be used to define a positive definite kernel. Furthermore, it is unlikely to be robust as a similarity measure as it only uses the cost of the minimum alignment.

In this work we use a recently proposed positive definite kernel, the Global Alignment (GA) kernel [12,13]. In addition to being positive definite, it has the interesting property of considering *all* possible alignment distances instead of only the minimum (as in DTW). The kernel computes a soft-minimum of all alignment distances, generating a more robust result that reflects the costs of all paths:

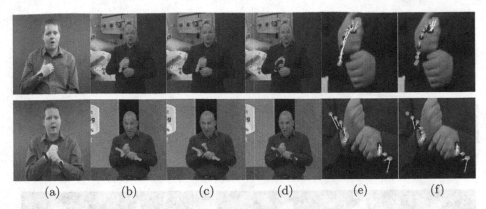

(a)   (b)   (c)   (d)   (e)   (f)

Fig. 4. Human pose transformation across domains. (top) BSL for 'heart' with overlaid wrist trajectory; (bottom) BSL for 'gram'. (a) wrist trajectory for domain 1, (b) trajectory for domain 2, (c) trajectory of domain 1 mapped onto domain 2 with a spatial transformation, (d) transformation with minimisation of the local position 'slack', (e) zoomed-in similarity without temporal alignment (white lines represent wrist point correspondences across the two domains), and (f) similarity with temporal alignment. As shown, the distance (proportional to the sum of the lengths of the white point correspondence lines) is significantly lower under alignment. Best seen in colour.

$$k_{\mathrm{GA}}(\mathbf{x}, \mathbf{y}) = \sum_{\pi \in \mathcal{A}(n,m)} e^{-D_{\mathbf{x},\mathbf{y}}(\pi)} \qquad (3)$$

where $D_{\mathbf{x},\mathbf{y}}(\pi) = \sum_{i=1}^{|\pi|} \|x_{\pi(i)} - y_{\pi(i)}\|$ denotes the Euclidean distance between two time series $\mathbf{x}, \mathbf{y}$ under alignment π, and $\mathcal{A}(n, m)$ denotes all possible alignments between two time series of length n and m. In our case $\mathbf{x}, \mathbf{y}$ are two time series of spatially aligned human joint positions, *i.e.* the joint 'trajectories' of two gestures that are being compared. By incorporating all costs into the kernel we improve classification results compared to only considering the minimal cost.

Spatial Alignment. Since the hands play an important role in gestures, knowing where the wrists are is valuable to any gesture recognition method. However, an issue with human joint positions is that they are not directly comparable across domains due to differences in both position, scale and human body shape. We use two simple yet effective affine transformations, one global and another local in time, that allow for translation and anisotropic scaling. This encodes a typical setup in gesture datasets, where, for a particular gesture, the persons stay at roughly the same distance from the camera (global transform), but may move slightly left or right (local transform). The global transformation learns the anisotropic scaling and translation, and the local transformation estimates an x translation, mapping into a canonical frame in which poses from different domains can be directly compared.

The global transform is computed from the median positions of the shoulders and elbows (selected since they are comparable across videos) over the whole

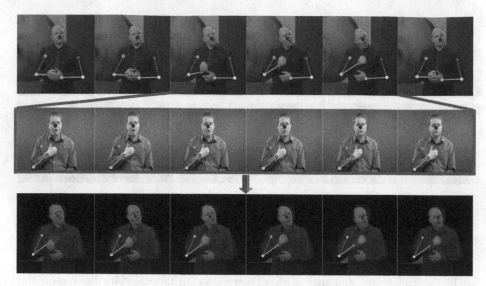

Fig. 5. Domain adaptation in space and time. Top: video sequence from the gesture reservoir; **Middle:** automatic time alignments to another sequence from a one-shot learning domain; **Bottom:** domain-adapted (space and time aligned) sequences, with the middle sequence overlaid on the top one. For ease of visualisation the example only uses a dominant hand, so only the dominant hand is matched (this is determined from the one-shot learning dictionary). In most cases, the transformation involves both hands.

video. The x translation is estimated locally from the median head and shoulder positions over a small temporal window (50 frames). Fig. 5 shows a visualisation of the transformation.

Even after spatial transformations, the absolute position for the gesture (relative to the torso) generally differs slightly. We solve that by adding some 'slack' to allow for slight absolute position differences. We do this by minimising the l_2 distance between wrist trajectories (of the two videos that are compared) over a small local square patch of width $u = $ (dist. between shoulders)/10. Fig. 4(c-d) shows an example of the original and corrected positions.

The composition of the global and local transformations define the spatial transformation ϕ, *i.e.* $\phi(x)$ is the mapping from the trajectory in the video to the spatial canonical frame.

Final Kernel. The final kernel is a composition of the the time alignment k_{GA} and spatial transformations ϕ, yielding the kernel $\psi(\mathbf{x}, \mathbf{y}) = k_{\mathrm{GA}}(\phi(\mathbf{x}), \phi(\mathbf{y}))$.

2.3   Hand Shape Filter

As Fig. 2 demonstrates, hand shape carries much of the discriminative information in gestures, particularly in complex gesture languages such as sign language, and needs to be included in order to successfully learn gestures. We use a hand

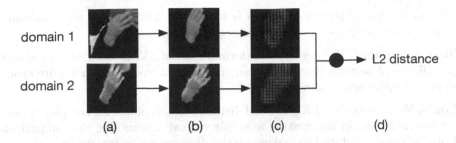

Fig. 6. Hand shape descriptor. (a) Badly segmented hands (due to overlap with skin) in two domains, (b) hands assigned to their hand cluster exemplars, (c) HOG of size-normalised exemplars, and (d) hands are compared across domains in terms of l_2 distance between the HOGs of the hand exemplars.

shape descriptor to discard false positives of reservoir samples where the wrist trajectories of the one-shot learning domain and the gesture reservoir match, but the hand shape is different (the similarity score is below a threshold).

Comparing hand shapes across domains is not straightforward since the domains may be of different resolution, contain different persons, lighting *etc.* Moreover, our pose estimator only provides wrist positions (not hand centres). We next describe a domain-independent, somewhat lighting-invariant hand shape descriptor that addresses these challenges.

We follow the method of Buehler *et al.* [7] where hands are first segmented, and then assigned to a cluster index. The clusters are used both to provide a distance between hand shapes and also to aid in the segmentation. To compare two hands in different domains, we assign them to their respective local domain hand cluster exemplars and measure their similarity as the distance between the HOGs of their cluster exemplars (shown in Fig. 6).

In detail, GraphCut [5,29] is used for an initial segmentation (with skin colour posteriors obtained from a face detector), and the segmented hands are represented using HOG features (of dimensionality $15 \times 15 \times 31$). The segmentation is performed within a box defined by an estimate of hand centre position (based on the elbow-wrist vector). Hand exemplars are then formed by clustering HOG vectors for examples that are *far away* from the face using k-means ($K = 1000$). These are effectively 'clean' hand clusters, without face regions in the foreground segmentation. For an input image, HOG vectors are matched to their nearest hand cluster, resulting in a 'cleaned' segmentation of the hand.

2.4   Implementation Details

Learning Framework. For each word, the positive training samples are obtained from the top ranked positive samples of each reservoir video. If there are w_c occurrences of the word in the subtitles of a reservoir video, then the top $5w_c$ positive samples are used – note, no non-maximum suppression is used when sliding the classifier window so there are multiple responses for each occurrence. The number of positives is capped at 1,000, and 1,000 randomly sampled reservoir gestures are used as negatives.

Time Alignment. We use the dual formulation of SVMs since our space and time alignment method provides the alignments as kernels, not in feature space (so primal optimisation is not suitable).

Hands. We precompute a $K \times K$ hand distance matrix offline for any pair of one-shot learning domain and gesture reservoir videos. At runtime, the comparison of two gestures is reduced to looking up the distance in the matrix for each pair of time-aligned frames, and summing up the distances.

Computation Time. The computation times for the preprocessing steps are: pose estimation 0.4s/frame; hand segmentation 0.1s/frame. Time alignment is approx 0.001s per gesture pair, or 1,000s for a 1000×1000 kernel matrix. Other costs (*e.g.* spatial alignments, SVM training and testing, subtitle preprocessing *etc.*) are negligible in comparison (a few seconds per gesture/video).

3 Datasets

Four datasets are employed in this work: a sign language dataset extracted from TV broadcasts; two sign language dictionaries; and a dataset of Italian hand gestures. Samples from each gesture dataset are shown in Figure 2.

3.1 BSL-TV Sign Language Dataset

This contains 155 hours of continuous British Sign Language (BSL), performed by 45 signers, with over 1,000 different continuous signs per 1hr video (and an estimated over 4,000 different signs in total). This dataset is particularly challenging to use as the supervision (in the form of subtitles) is both weak and noisy. It is weak as the subtitles are not temporally aligned with the signs – a sign (typically 8–15 frames long) could be anywhere in the overlapping subtitle video sequences (typically 400 frames). Furthermore, it is noisy as the occurrence of a word in the subtitle does not always imply that the word is signed (typically the word is signed only in 20–60% of the subtitle sequences). Furthermore, the gestures are continuous (no breaks between signs) and contain considerable variation (in terms of gesturing speed, signers, and regional gesturing differences).

Data Preprocessing. Given a word, the subtitles define a set of subtitle sequences in which the word occurs (8–40 sequences depending on how many times the word occurs), each around 15s long. As in [28], we slide a window along each subtitle sequence (fixed to 13 frames since that captures the majority of the gestures; gestures shorter than 13 frames are 'cropped' by the time alignment). This produces in total roughly 400 temporal windows per subtitle sequence, which are reduced to 100 candidate temporal windows per subtitle sequence using the method of [28], where only windows in which the signer also mouths the sign are considered. Upper body joint tracks are obtained automatically using the Random Forest regressor of Charles *et al.* [9,10,27].

3.2 Two BSL Dictionary Datasets

The video dictionaries are: 'Signstation' (BSL dictionary 1) [6] and 'Standard BSL dictionary' (BSL dictionary 2) [4]. The first contains 3,970 videos (total 2.5 hours), one for each word; and the second contains 3,409 videos (total 3 hours), and covers 1,771 words (the majority of words signed in one or more regional variation). BSL dictionary 1 contains a single signer, whereas BSL dictionary 2 contains multiple signers and multiple regional variations. There is no overlap of signers between the two dictionaries. The two datasets contain different sets of gestures, and intersect (*i.e.* have common words) only for a subset of these.

Data Preprocessing. Upper body joint tracks are obtained automatically using the method of Charles *et al.* [9]. In order to effectively use this data (as one-shot training and testing material), it is first necessary to find the pairs of gestures (across the dictionaries) that are the same. This is made difficult by the fact that the dictionaries contain different regional variations of the same gestures (*i.e.*, we cannot simply assume gestures with the same English word label are the same). We therefore need to look for visual similarity as well as the same English word label. We automatically find a subset of words pairs of the same gesture performed the same way by computing a time-and-space aligned distance (see Sect. 2.2) from upper body joint positions for all gesture pairs of the same word, selecting pairs with distance below a threshold (set from a small manually labelled set of pairs). This list of pairs is manually verified and any false matches (mainly due to incorrect pose estimates) are filtered away. This results in 500 signs in common between the two dictionaries.

3.3 ChaLearn Gesture Dataset

The fourth dataset is the ChaLearn 2013 Multi-modal gesture dataset [15], which contains 23 hours of Kinect data of 27 persons performing 20 Italian gestures. The data includes RGB, depth, foreground segmentations and Kinect skeletons. The data is split into train, validation and test sets, with in total 955 videos each lasting 1–2min and containing 8–20 non-continuous gestures. In comparison, each 15s subtitle sequence in BSL-TV contains 30–40 gestures (in which the gesture may or may not occur), and are continuous, so they cannot be easily segmented.

4 Evaluation

Experiments are conducted on the four datasets introduced in Sect. 3. See our website for example videos showing qualitative results.

4.1 One-Shot Detection of Gestures in the Gesture Reservoir

Here we evaluate the first main component of our method, *i.e.* how well can we spot gestures in the gesture reservoir given a one-shot learning example? We compare it to previous work [28] that took a different approach (based on

Multiple Instance Learning, MIL) to extracting gestures from weakly supervised gesture datasets. We show that we vastly outperform previous work on the same data with our conceptually much simpler one-shot learning approach.

Manual Ground Truth. The test dataset, a six hour subset of BSL-TV, is annotated for six gestures (bear, gram, heart, reindeer, snow and winter), with on average 18 occurrences for each gesture, and frame-level manual ground truth from Pfister *et al.* [28] (where we spent a week to label 41 words frame-by-frame). A benefit of the domain adaptation method is that it renders this expensive manual labelling unnecessary, since the training and test sets no longer need to be of the same domain. This enables the use of supervised datasets from other domains for testing (as done in the next experiment with a dictionary).

Task. The task for each of the six gestures is, given one of the 15s temporal windows of continuous gestures, to find which windows contain the target gesture and provide a ranked list of best estimates. Only about 0.5s out of 15s actually contain an instance of the gesture; the remainder contain other gestures. A gesture is deemed 'correct' if it overlaps at least 50% with ground truth.

Results. Precision-recall curves for the gestures are given in Fig. 8(left). As shown, thanks to our domain-adapted one-shot learning method, we vastly outperform the approach of Pfister *et al.* which uses MIL to pick temporal windows that occur frequently where subtitles say they should occur (and infrequently elsewhere). In contrast, [28] do not use any direct supervision (which our domain-adapted one-shot learner provides). This shows very clearly the high value of one-shot learning for extracting additional gesture training data. In fact, our method can complement Pfister *et al.*'s by using it for gestures that exist in our one-shot learning domains, and using [28] for other gestures.

4.2 Domain-Adapted Discriminative One-Shot Gesture Learner

In this key experiment we evaluate our discriminative one-shot learning method trained on the 155 hour BSL-TV gesture reservoir. The method is evaluated on a second one-shot learning domain ('BSL dictionary 2') on the same gestures as in the first one-shot learning domain ('BSL dictionary 1'), but in a different domain, signed at different speeds by different people. The second dictionary is used as the testing set to reduce annotation effort (the BSL-TV reservoir does not come with frame-level labels). Sect. 3 explains how these cross-dictionary gesture 'pairs' that contain the same sign signed the same way are found.

Baseline One-Shot Learner. We compare our method to an enhanced one-shot learning method trained on one one-shot learning domain ('BSL dictionary 1') and tested on the other ('BSL dictionary 2'), without any weakly supervised additional training data from the gesture reservoir (as shown at the top of Fig. 1). The method uses the time and space domain adaptations.

Training and Testing Set. The cross-dictionary gesture 'pairs' that contain the same sign signed the same way (found as explained in Sect. 3) define an 'in-common' set of 500 signs. The training set consists of the 150 gestures from BSL

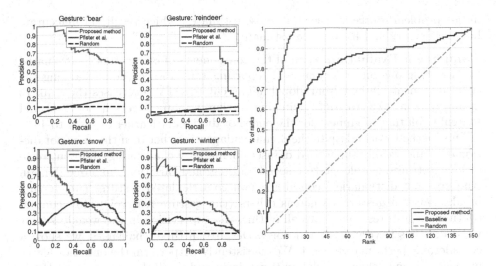

Fig. 8. Left: Gesture spotting accuracy on the gesture reservoir for BSL-TV, with a comparison to Pfister *et al.* [28]. PR curves are for four gestures with ground truth (see website for curves for remaining gestures). **Right:** Gesture classifier accuracy evaluated on gesture dictionary 'BSL dictionary 2'. The graph shows the cumulative distribution function of the ranks for the baseline and our proposed method. For example, 87% of gestures are ranked within the top 15.

dictionary 1 from the in-common set for which a sufficient number of examples exist in the BSL-TV gesture reservoir (set to at least 16 subtitle occurrences). The testing set consists of the same set of 150 gestures from BSL dictionary 2.

Test Task and Evaluation Measure. Each of the 150 training gestures is evaluated independently. For each gesture, the gesture classifier is applied to all 150 test gestures, one of which contains the correct gesture. The output of this step is, for each gesture classifier, a ranked list of 150 gestures (with scores). The task is to get the correct gesture first. Each gesture classifier is assigned the rank of the position in the 150-length list in which the correct gesture appears.

Results. Fig. 8(right) shows a cumulative distribution function of the ranks for the baseline and our proposed method using the gesture reservoir. We clearly see that, although the baseline ranks 66% of the gestures within the first top 60, learning from the reservoir beats it, with all gestures ranked within the first 25, 13% as rank 1, 41% within the first 5, and 70% within the first 10. We believe this is due to the high training data variability that the additional supervision from the gesture reservoir provides (from multiple persons, with gestures performed with many different speeds *etc.*).

There are two principal failure modes: first, the majority of gestures with ranks above 15 are due to several gestures out of the test gestures having very similar hand trajectories and hand shapes. With an already challenging discrimination problem, this causes confusions when the gesture in the evaluation set is performed very differently from any gesture in the training reservoir. The other major problem source is inaccurate pose estimates, which results in inaccurate hand trajectory and hand shape estimates.

Component Evaluation. Each of the components of our method is evaluated by switching one off at a time, and reporting rank-15 accuracy. Changing the time alignment method from global alignment to DTW decreases the rank-15 accuracy from 87% to 51%; switching off hand shape lowers it to 72%; and switching off time alignment for the one-shot dictionary learner drops it to 46%.

Our method works despite the domain adaptations between the one-shot dictionaries and weakly supervised datasets being very challenging: different resolutions, settings, people, gesture speed and regional variations; and one domain (the one-shot dictionaries) containing non co-articulated gestures (*i.e.* having breaks between gestures) whereas others (the gesture reservoir) only contain continuous gestures. To add to all of this, the supervision in the weakly supervised datasets is very weak and noisy. Despite all these challenges, we show a considerable performance boost. We consistently outperform the one-shot learning method, and achieve much higher precision and recall than previous methods in selecting similar gestures from the gesture reservoir using weak supervision.

4.3   Comparison on ChaLearn Multi-modal Dataset

On the ChaLearn dataset we define the one-shot learning domain as the training data for one person, and keep the remaining training data (of the 26 other persons) as the unlabelled 'gesture reservoir'. Only Kinect skeletons are kept for the reservoir. We compare this setup to using all the ground truth for training.

Task. The task here is, given a test video (also containing distractors), to spot gestures and label them into one out of 20 gesture categories.

Audio for Gesture Segmentation. Gestures only appear in a small subset of the dataset frames, so it makes sense to spot candidate windows first. To this end we use the same method as the top entries in the ChaLearn competition: segment gestures using voice activity detection (the persons pronounce the word they gesture). However, we do not use audio for classification since our purpose is to evaluate our vision-based classifier. We therefore compare only to methods that do not use audio for classification but only use it for segmentation (including the winner's method without audio classification).

Baseline, Our Method and Upper Bound. The baseline is domain-adapted one-shot learning (where training data comes from a single person from the 27 person training dataset; we report an average and standard deviation over each possible choice). This is compared to our method that uses the one-shot learner to extract additional training data from the unlabelled 'gesture reservoir'. The upper bound method uses all training data with manual ground truth.

Experiment Overview. In Experiment 1 we compare in detail to the competition winner [34] with the same segmentation method (audio), using only skeleton features for classification, and evaluating in terms of precision and recall on the validation set. In Experiment 2 we compare to competition entrants using the standard competition evaluation measure on test data, the Levenshtein distance $L(R,T)$, where R and T are ordered lists (predicted and ground truth) corresponding to the indices of the recognized gestures (1–20); distances are summed over all test videos and divided by the total number of gestures in ground truth.

Results for Experiment 1. Our method achieves very respectable performance using a fraction of the manually labelled data that the other competition entrants use. The competition winner's method gets Precision $P = 0.5991$ and Recall $R = 0.5929$ (higher is better) using skeleton features for classification [34]. Using this exact same setup and test data, our baseline one-shot learner achieves $P = 0.4012$ (std 0.015) and $R = 0.4162$ (std 0.011) – notably by only using a single training example, whereas the winner used the whole training set containing more than 400 training examples per class. Our results are improved further to $P = 0.5835$ (std 0.021), $R = 0.5754$ (std 0.015) by using gestures extracted from the gesture reservoir, still only using one manually labelled training example per gesture. Using the whole training set yields $P = 0.6124$, $R = 0.6237$.

Results for Experiment 2. In terms of Levenshtein distance, our method improves from the baseline 0.5138 (std 0.012) to 0.3762 (std 0.015) (lower is better). With only a single training example (two orders of magnitude less manually labelled training data than other competition entries) we achieve similar performance to the best method using skeleton for classification ('SUMO', score 0.3165 [15]), and using the full training set we outperform them at 0.3015.

5   Conclusion

We have presented a method that utilises weakly supervised training data containing multiple instances of a gesture to significantly improve the performance of a gesture classifier. Another benefit of our framework with two dictionary datasets is that it lets us avoid a very expensive laborious task that has been a big issue for weakly supervised gesture recognition: large-scale evaluation. Our approach is applicable to gesture recognition in general – where the upper body and hands are mostly visible, and the person is communicating with gestures.

Acknowledgements: We are grateful to Patrick Buehler and Sophia Pfister for help and discussions. Financial support was provided by EPSRC grant EP/I012001/1.

References

1. Ali, S., Shah, M.: Human action recognition in videos using kinematic features and multiple instance learning. IEEE PAMI 32(2), 288–303 (2010)
2. Baisero, A., Pokorny, F.T., Kragic, D., Ek, C.: The path kernel. In: ICPRAM (2013)
3. Bojanowski, P., Bach, F., Laptev, I., Ponce, J., Schmid, C., Sivic, J.: Finding actors and actions in movies. In: Proc. ICCV (2013)

4. Books, M.: The standard dictionary of the British sign language. DVD (2005)
5. Boykov, Y., Jolly, M.P.: Interactive graph cuts for optimal boundary and region segmentation of objects in N-D images. In: Proc. ICCV (2001)
6. Bristol Centre for Deaf Studies: Signstation, http://www.signstation.org (accessed March 1, 2014)
7. Buehler, P., Everingham, M., Zisserman, A.: Learning sign language by watching TV (using weakly aligned subtitles). In: Proc. CVPR (2009)
8. Chai, X., Li, G., Lin, Y., Xu, Z., Tang, Y., Chen, X., Zhou, M.: Sign language recognition and translation with Kinect. In: Proc. Int. Conf. Autom. Face and Gesture Recog. (2013)
9. Charles, J., Pfister, T., Everingham, M., Zisserman, A.: Automatic and efficient human pose estimation for sign language videos. IJCV (2013)
10. Charles, J., Pfister, T., Magee, D., Hogg, D., Zisserman, A.: Domain adaptation for upper body pose tracking in signed TV broadcasts. In: Proc. BMVC (2013)
11. Cooper, H., Bowden, R.: Learning signs from subtitles: A weakly supervised approach to sign language recognition. In: Proc. CVPR (2009)
12. Cuturi, M.: Fast global alignment kernels. In: ICML (2011)
13. Cuturi, M., Vert, J., Birkenes, Ø., Matsui, T.: A kernel for time series based on global alignments. In: ICASSP (2007)
14. Duchenne, O., Laptev, I., Sivic, J., Bach, F., Ponce, J.: Automatic annotation of human actions in video. In: Proc. CVPR (2009)
15. Escalera, S., Gonzàlez, J., Baró, X., Reyes, M., Guyon, I., Athitsos, V., Escalante, H., Sigal, L., Argyros, A., Sminchisescu, C.: Chalearn multi-modal gesture recognition 2013: grand challenge and workshop summary. In: ACM MM (2013)
16. Fanello, S., Gori, I., Metta, G., Odone, F.: Keep it simple and sparse: real-time action recognition. J. Machine Learning Research 14(1), 2617–2640 (2013)
17. Farhadi, A., Forsyth, D., White, R.: Transfer learning in sign language. In: Proc. CVPR (2007)
18. Gaidon, A., Harchaoui, Z., Schmid, C.: A time series kernel for action recognition. In: Proc. BMVC (2011)
19. Guyon, I., Athitsos, V., Jangyodsuk, P., Escalante, H., Hamner, B.: Results and analysis of the ChaLearn gesture challenge 2012. In: Proc. ICPR (2013)
20. Guyon, I., Athitsos, V., Jangyodsuk, P., Hamner, B., Escalante, H.: ChaLearn gesture challenge: Design and first results. In: CVPR Workshops (2012)
21. Hariharan, B., Malik, J., Ramanan, D.: Discriminative decorrelation for clustering and classification. In: Fitzgibbon, A., Lazebnik, S., Perona, P., Sato, Y., Schmid, C. (eds.) ECCV 2012, Part IV. LNCS, vol. 7575, pp. 459–472. Springer, Heidelberg (2012)
22. Ke, Y., Sukthankar, R., Hebert, M.: Event detection in crowded videos. In: Proc. ICCV (2007)
23. Kelly, D., McDonald, J., Markham, C.: Weakly supervised training of a sign language recognition system using multiple instance learning density matrices. Trans. Systems, Man, and Cybernetics 41(2), 526–541 (2011)
24. Krishnan, R., Sarkar, S.: Similarity measure between two gestures using triplets. In: CVPR Workshops (2013)
25. Malisiewicz, T., Gupta, A., Efros, A.A.: Ensemble of exemplar-SVMs for object detection and beyond. In: Proc. ICCV (2011)
26. Nayak, S., Duncan, K., Sarkar, S., Loeding, B.: Finding recurrent patterns from continuous sign language sentences for automated extraction of signs. J. Machine Learning Research 13(1), 2589–2615 (2012)

27. Pfister, T., Charles, J., Everingham, M., Zisserman, A.: Automatic and efficient long term arm and hand tracking for continuous sign language TV broadcasts. In: Proc. BMVC (2012)
28. Pfister, T., Charles, J., Zisserman, A.: Large-scale learning of sign language by watching TV (using co-occurrences). In: Proc. BMVC (2013)
29. Rother, C., Kolmogorov, V., Blake, A.: Grabcut: interactive foreground extraction using iterated graph cuts. In: Proc. ACM SIGGRAPH (2004)
30. Sakoe, H.: Dynamic programming algorithm optimization for spoken word recognition. IEEE Transactions on Acoustics, Speech, and Signal Processing (1978)
31. Sakoe, H., Chiba, S.: A similarity evaluation of speech patterns by dynamic programming. In: Nat. Meeting of Institute of Electronic Communications Engineers of Japan (1970)
32. Shimodaira, H., Noma, K., Nakai, M., Sagayama, S.: Dynamic time-alignment kernel in support vector machine. In: NIPS (2001)
33. Wan, J., Ruan, Q., Li, W., Deng, S.: One-shot learning gesture recognition from RGB-D data using bag of features. J. Machine Learning Research 14(1), 2549–2582 (2013)
34. Wu, J., Cheng, J., Zhao, C., Lu, H.: Fusing multi-modal features for gesture recognition. In: ICMI (2013)
35. Zhou, F., De la Torre, F.: Generalized time warping for multi-modal alignment of human motion. In: Proc. CVPR (2012)

Author Index

Printed in the United States
By Bookmasters

e) Genauere Untersuchung der optischen Verhältnisse, namentlich beim Parabolspiegel.

Die Gleichungen (14) und (15) genügen für den praktischen Entwurf noch nicht, da sie nur zur Errechnung einer *mittleren* Lichtstärke im Bündel führen. Das wäre für die Praxis nur dann ausreichend, wenn tatsächlich die Lichtstärke im gesamten Bündel konstant und damit gleich dem Mittelwert der Lichtstärke I_B wäre. In Wirklichkeit ist aber die Lichtstärke innerhalb des Bündels sehr ungleichmäßig verteilt und hängt bei Verwendung von Parabolspiegeln stark von der Größe und Gestalt der Lichtquelle, bei Verwendung anderer Spiegelformen auch noch von der gewählten Gestalt der Meridiankurve des Spiegels ab. Im folgenden werden nur die Verhältnisse beim Parabolspiegel betrachtet, da dieser für Scheinwerfer ausschließlich, für Anstrahler immer dann Verwendung findet, wenn kleine Ausstrahlungswinkel verlangt werden. Spiegel für größere Ausstrahlungswinkel sind in ihrer Konstruktion und ihren Eigenschaften in E 3 behandelt.

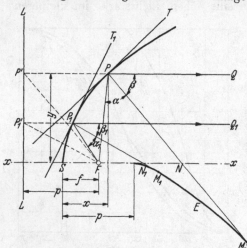

Abb. 618. Eigenschaften der Parabel.

Eine kurze Betrachtung der Parabel als Erzeugende des ein Umdrehungsparaboloid darstellenden Parabolspiegels werde vorangeschickt, da für die folgenden das Gebiet der Optik berührenden Zusammenhänge die aufgeführten mathematischen Beziehungen an der Parabel von Bedeutung sind. In Abb. 618 ist ein Parabelast als *Meridianschnitt des Parabolspiegels* dargestellt. Die Bezeichnungen in dieser Abbildung haben folgende Bedeutung:

$x — x$ Achse der Parabel = Umdrehungsachse des Parabolspiegels,
L = Leitlinie,
$2p$ = Parameter,
$f = p/2$ = Brennweite,
F = Brennpunkt,
S = Scheitelpunkt = Koordinatenanfangspunkt,
x = Abszisse des Parabelpunktes P (x_1 entsprechend für P_1),
y = Ordinate des Parabelpunktes P (y_1 entsprechend für P_1),
T = Tangente an die Parabel im Punkt P (T_1 entsprechend für P_1),
N = Normale der Parabel im Punkt P (N_1 entsprechend für P_1),
E = Evolute der Parabel.

Die Berechnung der Parabel für eine gegebene Brennweite f erfolgt mittels der Scheitelgleichung:

$$y^2 = 2px = 4fx, \tag{16}$$

oder der Polargleichung mit dem Pol F:

$$r = \frac{p}{2 \cdot \cos^2 \frac{\varphi}{2}}. \tag{17}$$

Aus Gleichung (16) erhält man für jeden im Abstand x vom Scheitel S senkrecht zur Achse geführten Schnitt den *Krümmungsradius des Spiegels* in diesem Schnitt:

$$R = y = 2\sqrt{f \cdot x}, \tag{18}$$

bzw. den *Durchmesser der Spiegelöffnung*:

$$D = 2y = 4\sqrt{f \cdot x}. \tag{19}$$